Mind Readings
AN ANTHOLOGY FOR WRITERS

Gary Colombo

Los Angeles City College

Bedford / St. Martin's

Boston ◆ New York

For Bedford/St. Martin's

Developmental Editor: John E. Sullivan III
Production Editor: Stasia Zomkowski
Senior Production Supervisor: Maria Gonzalez
Marketing Manager: Brian Wheel
Editorial Assistant: Caroline Thompson
Copyeditor: Alison Greene
Text Design: Claire Seng-Niemoeller
Cover Design: Laura Shaw Design
Cover Art: "Catching Thoughts." digital © Dave Cutler
Composition: Pine Tree Composition
Printing and Binding: Haddon Craftsmen/RRD

President: Charles H. Christensen
Editorial Director: Joan E. Feinberg
Editor in Chief: Karen S. Henry
Director of Marketing: Karen Melton
Director of Editing, Design, and Production: Marcia Cohen
Managing Editor: Elizabeth M. Schaaf

Library of Congress Control Number: 2001095038

Manufactured in the United States of America.

6   5   4   3   2   1
f   e   d   c   b   a

For information, write: Bedford/St. Martin's, 75 Arlington Street, Boston, MA 02116
617-399-4000

ISBN: 0-312-39082-3

Acknowledgments

Diane Ackerman, "Taste: The Social Sense" from *A Natural History of the Senses* by Diane Ackerman. Copyright © 1990 by Diane Ackerman. Used by permission of Random House, Inc.

James Baldwin, "Sonny's Blues." Originally published in *The Partisan Review*, later collected in *Going to Meet the Man* by James Baldwin, published by Vintage Books. Copyright © 1957 and renewed © 1985 by James Baldwin. Reprinted by permission of the James Baldwin Estate.

Mary Catherine Bateson, "A Mutable Self." Submitted excerpt from *Peripheral Visions* by Mary Catherine Bateson. Copyright © 1994 by Mary Catherine Bateson. Reprinted by permission of HarperCollins Publishers, Inc.

Roy F. Baumeister, "The Self and Society: Changes, Problems, and Opportunities" from *Self and Society*, edited by Richard D. Ashmore and Lee Jussim. Copyright © by Roy F. Baumeister. Reprinted by permission of author.

John Berger, "Why Look at Animals?" from *About Looking* by John Berger. Copyright © 1980 by John Berger. Used by permission of Pantheon Books, a division of Random House, Inc.

Acknowledgments and copyrights are continued at the back of the book on pages 778–779, which constitute an extension of the copyright page. It is a violation of the law to reproduce these selections by any means whatsoever without the written permission of the copyright holder.

Preface for Instructors

Something New

Mind Readings offers a fresh approach for composition classrooms. Designed for use in first-year college writing courses, *Mind Readings* brings together 53 selections that invite students to become critical thinkers by reflecting on the process of thinking itself. Over the past few decades some of the world's most celebrated scholars and writers have devoted their energies to the task of explaining the mystery of how the mind works. Philosophers, physicists, linguists, biologists, and researchers in human, animal, and artificial intelligence have joined forces to map the mind and to explore the ways in which we experience the world around us. *Mind Readings* exploits this historic convergence of academic disciplines by addressing crucial personal and social issues emerging from the field of cognitive science.

Among the selections in *Mind Readings,* students will encounter some of the best popular science writing done in the last ten years as they take up issues that are sure to dominate twenty-first-century classrooms — issues such as the changing shape of selfhood, the ethics of human cloning, the nature of violence, and the relationships among human, animal, and machine minds. *Mind Readings* challenges students to think critically about how we perceive and interpret the world. It encourages them to explore the mystery of human memory and to probe the secrets of "other" minds. It appeals to contemporary college students by recognizing the impact of technology on their daily lives — and by raising questions about the way that modern science is transforming what it means to be human in an increasingly technological age.

Features

A Refreshing and Versatile New Theme — As the first composition anthology inspired by research on cognition, consciousness, and personal identity, *Mind Readings* provides students with a wealth of materials that they will find both engaging and timely. The concept of mind has made a comeback in scientific and humanist studies during the past few decades. For the greater part of the twentieth century, it was difficult to talk meaningfully in academic circles about things like feelings, memories, perceptions, imagination, and intentions. Under the sway of scientific behaviorism, the "black box" of the mind was deemed off limits. Even in the humanities, generations of students were warned against indulging in the "intentional fallacy" and urged not to worry about what authors meant or intended when they wrote. But over the last thirty years the "theory of mind" has retaken center stage in the on-going debate about what it means to be human.

Each chapter in *Mind Readings* approaches the theme of the mind from a perspective that invites personal connection and touches on broader social and cultural issues. In all, the book approaches the challenge of reading minds from the following six perspectives:

Chapter 1: Reading the Senses

Chapter 2: Reading Memory

Chapter 3: Reading the Self

Chapter 4: Reading Other Minds

Chapter 5: Reading Animal Minds

Chapter 6: Reading Cyberminds

As students work through *Mind Readings,* they'll engage in some of the most important intellectual and social debates of the day—debates that spring from changing conceptions about the functions of the senses, the fragmented nature of memory, the evolution of selfhood, and the challenges involved in interpreting "other" forms of intelligence. They'll learn about language as they explore the difficulty of translating life experience into words. They'll learn about the writing process as they investigate the roles of imagination and history in the "constructive" process of recollection. They'll become more effective critical thinkers as they learn to "read" and respond to the expectations, values, and biases that lay hidden in every text and mind they encounter. Ultimately, *Mind Readings* helps students to become better readers and writers by asking them to explore how theory of mind and the art of interpretation shape every aspect of their lives.

New Issues for Composition and Critical Thinking—The themes addressed in *Mind Readings* connect naturally with issues that are bound to spark student interest, issues such as

• the politics of memory

• the ethics of human cloning

• the issues of animal intelligence and animal rights

• the differences between male and female minds

• the interpretive problems involved in "hate-crime" legislation

• the meaning of selfhood across cultures

• the challenge of reading "other" minds

• the origin of violent minds

• the impact of electronic technology on human identity and relationships

• the gendered nature of computer technology

- the mythic significance of cyberspace

- the ethical and social implications of artificial intelligence

As we enter the twenty-first century, issues of human identity and the boundaries between human, natural, and artificial forms of intelligence are moving to the fore in discussions that cut across all the traditional academic, social, political, and ethical divides. *Mind Readings* gives students the chance to debate some of the most challenging social and ethical questions of a new technological age.

Direct Connections with Composition—The theme of mind reading also offers a perfect complement to the goals of the composition classroom. The development of critical thinking, reading, and writing depends, in great part, on the ability to anticipate the expectations, values, and intentions of others, just as it depends on our ability to read, evaluate, and interpret our own values and intentions. Because mind reading plays such a central role in the development of writing, you'll find direct connections here between the theme of each chapter and essential aspects of your writing curriculum. In fact, each of the book's six chapter introductions makes these connections explicit in the following special sections:

Chapter 1: "Making Sense"—Addresses the use of concrete details, images, and figures of speech as techniques for conveying the sensory experience in words.

Chapter 2: "Writing as Remembering: The Writing Process"—Introduces the multistage writing process as a means of stimulating recall while "cooking" ideas.

Chapter 3: "Style and Voice: The Writer's Self"—Discusses the creation of a linguistic sense of self through the development of voice.

Chapter 4: "Readers as 'Others' "—Reviews the role of audience analysis in the structuring of essay introductions and body paragraphs.

Chapter 5: "Arguing Animals: Mind Reading and Reasoning"—Explores the role of reader analysis in the development of sound arguments.

Chapter 6: "Hypertext and Web Search"—Introduces the notion of cyberwriting and problems involved with Internet research.

Readings that Bridge the Sciences & Humanities—Because the study of the mind represents one of the most ambitious interdisciplinary undertakings in modern times, you'll find contributions in these pages representing a broad variety of academic fields, voices, and styles. As they explore *Mind Readings*, students will encounter selections by leading thinkers and writers in scientific fields like biology, animal ethology, zoology, genetics, neurology, psychology, computer science, and artificial intelligence. They'll read theories of memory and identity by outstanding neuroscientists like Daniel L. Schacter and Robert Sapolsky. They'll encounter the decidedly "anti-anthrocentric" views of primatologists, zoologists, and paleontologists, like Frans de Waal, Francine Patterson, and Richard Leakey. They'll even have the chance to meet some of the world's leading thinkers in the field of computer science, theorists like Northwestern University's Roger C. Schank, Indiana University's Douglas Hofstadter, and Hans Moravec, founder of the Center for Mobile Robotics at Carnegie Mellon University.

These science-oriented readings are balanced by a broad selection of contributions from the social sciences and humanities. About half the selections in *Mind Readings* were penned by naturalists, philosophers, anthropologists, sociologists, historians, and scholars in English and gender studies. In these pages, students will read anthropologist Mary Catherine Bateson's analysis of the variable meaning of the self in different cultural contexts and political theorist Jean Bethke Elshtain's impassioned argument against research in human cloning. They'll be invited to listen in on University of Chicago historian Martha C. Nussbaum as she speculates about the role of literature in the development of empathy and civic culture, and to match wits with Princeton University's famed "practical ethicist" Peter Singer as he argues the case for animal rights.

Of course, *Mind Readings* also includes a number of powerful personal essays and classic works of short fiction. You'll find selections here by Diane Ackerman, James Baldwin, John Berger, Loren Eiseley, Ian Frazier, William Gibson, Guillermo Gómez-Peña, Patricia Hampl, bell hooks, Maxine Hong Kingston, John (Fire) Lame Deer, Barry Lopez, Rubén Martínez, Bill McKibben, Faith McNulty, Scott Russell Sanders, Andrew Sullivan, Ellen Ullman, and Alice Walker. These more intimate and imaginative selections complement the book's analytical pieces. They encourage students to make personal connections with the theoretical concepts they'll find here and may also be used as points of departure for discussions and speculative writings about the nature of the mind.

An Emphasis on Popular Media and Visual Literacy—Throughout *Mind Readings* you'll discover assignments linking readings and paper assignments to popular films, television shows, and other forms of popular culture. Diane Ackerman's exploration of the social and biological functions of taste, for example, connects beautifully with a number of classic movies—films such as *Tampopo*, *Babette's Feast*, and *Big Night*. *Mind Readings* invites students to explore the relation between personal and historical memory in Akira Kurosawa's *Rashomon*, to analyze changing views of the self in films like *Magnolia* and *American Beauty*, to probe representations of violence in works like *Taxi Driver* and *Pulp Fiction*, and to compare attitudes toward artificial intelligence and cyberspace in films like *Metropolis*, *Blade Runner*, *The Matrix*, and *A.I.: Artificial Intelligence*. Readings by media critics Bill McKibben, Walker Percy, John Berger, Mark Slouka, Charles Siebert, and Claudia Springer address the issues of mass media's impact on the senses, the creation of artificial "wildness" in television nature programming, the "Disneyfication" of animals, and the gender politics of android heroes. In addition, *Mind Readings* includes a number of selections that foster the development of visual literacy — readings associated with blindness and the appreciation of art by Georgina Kleege, the interpretation of paintings by neurologist Daniel Schacter, and the role of advertising in the development of personal identity by psychologist Mihaly Csikszentmihalyi.

Editorial Apparatus

The extensive editorial apparatus that accompanies *Mind Readings* provides you with a wealth of materials designed to help students learn and make your course a success. These include the following:

Comprehensive Introduction for Students — The book offers students a detailed introductory essay that presents the concept of "theory of mind," explains its connections with reading, writing, and critical thinking, and offers an overview of the text's structure and editorial features. This essay also introduces the concept of active reading and discusses strategies for taking notes and using reader-response journals.

Detailed Chapter Introductions — Each of the book's six chapters includes a comprehensive introductory essay that engages student interest in the chapter topic and provides the historical and cultural context required to enhance student understanding. Each introduction also offers students a comprehensive overview of chapter contents and a special subsection exploring connections between the chapter topic and critical issues in writing instruction.

Headnotes and Prereading Activities — Carefully researched headnotes, contextualizing topics and offering background information on authors, introduce each of the selections in *Mind Readings*. Prereading activities can be used as the basis of brief collaborative in-class projects or as topics for "free writes" or journal entries.

Questions for Discussion and Critical Thinking — Every selection in *Mind Readings* is followed by two sets of questions designed to help students engage the ideas they encounter, to sharpen their critical responses, and to encourage the habit of making productive intertextual connections. *Exploring the Text* questions focus on the content of the selection and ask students to assess authorial assumptions, values, and rhetorical choices. *Further Explorations* questions challenge students to take the next step in critical analysis — to discover relationships between the ideas they encounter in readings throughout the book and to apply these ideas to situations, social issues, and cultural phenomena outside the classroom.

Essay Options — A detailed set of *Essay Options* accompanies every selection in *Mind Readings*. Overall, you'll find more than 125 suggestions for paper assignments throughout the book's six chapters. Running the gamut from personal responses to full-blown research papers, these assignments are designed to help move students seamlessly from reading to writing and to challenge them to engage the ideas they encounter in *Mind Readings* at the highest intellectual and academic level. Although you'll find a healthy mix of personal and academic writing topics in every chapter, the book's thematic structure reflects the progression of assignments commonly associated with first-year writing courses.

Extensive Instructor's Manual — Resources for Teaching Mind Readings provides hands-on guidance about how to get the most from reading selections, discussion questions, and essay options. It offers overviews for approaching individual reading selections as well as suggestions for assignment pairings and sequences. Additional hints and suggestions for adapting the materials in *Mind Readings* to your classroom are also included.

Online Resources — The TopLinks Web site for *Mind Readings* contains annotated research links. For more information, visit <www.bedfordstmartins .com/mindreadings> to explore this site and other helpful electronic resources for both students and instructors.

Acknowledgments

The logical place to begin with acknowledgments at Bedford/St. Martin's is always with Chuck Christensen, who can conjure up more clearheaded vision and offer more encouragement over a cup of coffee than your average mortal publisher. I also want to thank Joan Feinberg for supporting this project at Bedford/St. Martin's and John Sullivan, whose wise counsel, cool head, and gift for guiding harried authors make him quite possibly the perfect editor. A number of other collaborators at Bedford/St. Martin's also deserve recognition, including Steve Scipione, whose sagacity behind the scenes helped at many points along the way; Karen Melton and Brian Wheel, for their marketing expertise; Caroline Thompson, who attended to innumerable details with grace and care; Eva Pettersson, for securing permissions under tight deadlines; Elizabeth Schaaf and Stasia Zomkowski, for their careful attention while steering the book through production. I am grateful to them all.

I would also like to thank the following instructors who gave helpful, detailed feedback: Lynn Z. Bloom, University of Connecticut; Hugh English, City University of New York; Paul Heilker, Virginia Polytechnic Institute and State University; Sonia Maasik, University of California, Los Angeles; Kate Manski, University of Illinois at Chicago; and Kenneth Smith, Indiana University, South Bend.

Finally, I want to thank Elena, Gabe, and Mia — three minds that always keep me perched on the edge of my seat and hoping to read more.

Contents

CHAPTER 2

Reading Memory: Rebuilding the Past   135

CHAPTER 3

Reading the Self: Ghosts in the Machine?   247

CHAPTER 4

Reading Other Minds: Inside the Black Box   367

saying to us. If we have heard the same story or a similar story before we can also understand more easily what we are being told."

CHAPTER 6
Reading Cyberminds:
The Internet to Artificial Intelligence   640

Mind Reading and College Writing

The Brain—is wider than the Sky—
For—put them side by side—
The one the other will contain
With ease—and You beside—
         —EMILY DICKINSON

"Open your mind! We move together, our
minds sharing the same thoughts. . . ."
         —MR. SPOCK

Why Read Minds?

Mr. Spock was ahead of his time. Resident alien genius of the starship *Enterprise,* the elf-eared Mr. Spock was a new kind of hero in 1966. While the rest of the *Star Trek* crew relied on the power of technology to dominate the universe, Spock relied on the power of his own overdeveloped mind. When *Enterprise* computers went down and the ship faced certain disaster, Spock's remarkable brain would intervene to do the math. When Captain Kirk broke down under the stress of weekly Klingon raids, Spock's cool intelligence would save the day. When faced with an uncooperative alien spy, Mr. Spock would deploy the most formidable weapon in his mental arsenal—the Vulcan "mind meld." Going forehead to forehead with his other-worldly foe, Spock would risk his exquisite consciousness by merging it directly with the twisted thoughts of his enemy. Having ransacked his opponent's brain and discovered the secret plan meant to doom the Federation, he would collapse, spent by his heroic mental efforts.

Spock was ahead of his time because he knew that the mind—not space—was the real "final frontier." Along with Emily Dickinson, he understood that the brain is literally "wider than the Sky." Just about the time that the first *Star Trek* episode aired back in the 1960s, a revolution was beginning in university laboratories and classrooms across the country. For decades, psychologists and biologists had restricted their research to only those aspects of human and animal behavior that could be observed directly. From the perspective of "behaviorism," living creatures were pretty much like machines: people and animals were thought to have parts, like clocks, that could be disassembled and analyzed, parts that came together to carry out functions — like eating, learning, and mating. Seen within this framework, the mind was irrelevant: creatures possessed brains that could be dissected and probed, but the phenomena of mind was deemed just too slippery for science to grasp. The mind was seen as a sentimental fiction — a throwback to anti-quated religious concepts like the soul or the spirit.

All this changed during the "cognitive revolution." Perhaps the most important intellectual development of the last fifty years, the field of cognitive science united thinkers from disciplines across the university in pursuit of the secrets of the mind. Biologists, zoologists, and primatologists embraced the new science of mind because they wouldn't settle for explanations of animal behavior that reduced the creative play of their subjects to the level of uncon-scious mechanical reflexes. Linguists, neurologists, and philosophers returned to the mind as a way of accounting for the complexities of human conscious-ness. Researchers in the fields of computer science and artificial intelligence spurred the movement on as they attempted to imitate, in silicon, the flexibil-ity and power of human thought. The cognitive revolution changed the way we think about what it means to be human. It has challenged our deepest as-sumptions about ourselves and our relation to the other intelligent creatures with whom we share the natural world. It has united some of the finest minds in the sciences and humanities in the quest for an answer to what is perhaps the most challenging puzzle we as a species have ever encountered — the puzzle of the mind itself.

Mind Readings invites you to take part in this revolution as you develop the intellectual habits you'll need to become an accomplished reader and writer of college-level academic prose. After all, what better topic could there be for honing your own mental abilities than the mind? As you read selections about how we interpret our experiences through the senses, about the creative nature of human memory, or about how we construct a self, you'll have the chance to put the ideas you encounter to immediate use in your own papers and essays. The insights you garner about what it takes to read "other" minds — human, animal, and mechanical — will help you become an effective reader of the intentions and motives that lurk in the structure and style of every piece of writing. And because *Mind Readings* focuses on issues and themes related to the cognitive revolution, it offers you a range of topics and readings that span the academic disciplines. You'll encounter plenty of ex-amples of powerful personal writing in these pages, but you'll also find as many or more selections by well-known philosophers and scientists. *Mind*

Readings challenges you to think critically about some of the thorniest issues raised by the technological advances of the past century—issues like the nature of the self, the legality of cloning, the rights of animals, and the possibility of machine intelligence.

Of course, the idea of reading minds might be something you're more likely to associate with carnival sideshows or second-rate night club acts. You know the routine: a guy in a tux with a turban on his head holds sealed notes from the audience against his forehead and "reads" their messages through the power of ESP. Actually, the kind of mind reading you'll practice here is easier and more powerful than this kind of trumped-up clairvoyance. All of us read minds every day; we just don't wear turbans or go forehead to forehead like Mr. Spock when we do it. Because we humans are intensely social animals, our minds develop in harmony with the other minds around us. Children read the moods, desires, and intentions of their parents from their tone of voice, words, and gestures. Students read the attitudes and values of their teachers in their choice of subject, classroom style, and sense of humor. From moment to moment, we monitor the other people around us, creatively reconstructing in our own minds a model of their mental states—a miniature "theory of mind" that tells us what they believe, what they want, and what they are likely to do to get it.

Here's a quick example of this theory of mind at work, cited by linguist Stephen Pinker in *The Language Instinct*[1]:

Woman: I'm leaving you.
Man: Who is he?

As Pinker indicates, we can understand these two lines of dialogue because we grasp the assumptions that the man makes about the woman's motives and intentions. Our theory of mind for the typical male tells us that he's likely to assume she's leaving because she's fallen in love with another man—and not, heaven forbid, because she's fed up with him or with men in general. The ability to engage in this kind of on-the-spot interpretation is what makes the difference between having a brain and having a mind. Babies are born with brains, but their minds take time to develop. It's not until sometime between the first and second years of life that the average child develops a functional theory of mind and can thus begin to grasp and even play with sophisticated ideas like deliberate deception and make-believe. Equipped with a fully functional theory of mind, we can begin to empathize with others. We can put ourselves into another person's shoes, predict the motives and intentions that underlie another's actions, and predict how our own actions and intentions will make others feel. Theory of mind is what makes it possible for us to live together in the vast social network of assumptions that we call "culture". It is what makes us who and what we are. It, perhaps more than any other mental attribute, is what makes us human.

What's Here

Mind Readings challenges you to think critically about the mind and the process of thinking itself as you sharpen the skills you'll need to become an effective reader and writer of academic texts. Each of the six chapters you'll find here focuses on a different aspect of the mind and a different set of social or ethical issues related to mind reading. The first three chapters look inward, approaching the mind from what might be seen as a "user's" perspective. In "Reading the Senses: From Sight to Insight," you'll explore the nature and the meaning of sensory perception. You'll be challenged to think about why human beings "taste" things, how we "construct" the visual world around us, and how our views of the senses have changed over the past two hundred years. You'll also have the opportunity to consider some of the challenges involved in translating your lived sense experience into the relatively abstract medium of language. The book's second chapter, "Reading Memory: Rebuilding the Past," extends this exploration of the mind by taking up a topic close to every writer's heart. Learning how to conjure the muse of memory—how to encourage yourself to remember what you have to say in the first place—is the secret to writing successfully on any topic. In this chapter, you'll consider how the mind shapes memories for specific purposes and explore the complex relationship between memory, creativity, and the truth. You'll also encounter readings that ask you to think critically about the politics of personal and impersonal memories, and the role that memory plays in the creation of our sense of who we are. The book's third chapter, "Reading the Self: Ghosts in the Machine?" focuses exclusively on questions relating to personal identity. Here you'll find readings that challenge you to analyze the materials human beings use to spin a sense of self—materials that range from the clothes you wear to the cultures you identify with and even the stories you've chosen to tell about your life. This chapter also raises important questions about the future of the self—questions about the self in relation to the ethics of cloning and about whether the very concept of selfhood is becoming dysfunctional in today's self-indulgent capitalist culture.

The second half of *Mind Readings* looks outward by addressing issues related to the existence of "other" minds. In "Reading Other Minds: Inside the Black Box," we'll take up some of the difficulties that arise whenever we use our theories of mind to interpret the intentions of those around us. Readings in this chapter address the problem of how we can transcend the limitations of our own assumptions about other minds—assumptions conditioned by factors like age, gender, culture, education, and personal experience. They also invite you to explore how we read the motives and intentions of the most dangerous "others" in our midst, the minds of the violent. Next, we leave the realm of human experience behind as we venture into the world of animal intelligence. In "Reading Animal Minds: Objects or Equals?" you'll have the chance to consider how human attitudes are changing about animal thinking and about human/animal relationships. Selections in this chapter ask you to think about the meaning of zoos, the impact of television programming on our views of the animal world, and the case for the "personhood" of primates. You'll also find readings that challenge you to take a stand on important social questions related to the human use of animals for food, entertainment, and laboratory research. The final chapter of *Mind Readings* carries this exploration of other minds to its logical extreme. In "Reading Cyberminds: The Internet to Artificial Intelligence," you'll explore the world of artificial intelligence and consider how the electronic revolution is changing what it means to be human in the twenty-first century. Taking up topics like the impact of the Internet, the culture of cyberspace, and the gender politics of information technology, this chapter challenges you to evaluate how computing is reshaping our collective consciousness. It also raises questions about how machines think, about how we could possibly know if they do, and how machine minds may, in fact, render "meat" minds obsolete sometime within the next century.

Because thinkers from so many different fields have participated in the cognitive revolution, the selections you'll encounter in this book are remarkably varied in style, tone, and content. *Mind Readings* introduces you to writers representing a broad range of scientific disciplines, including fields like biology, animal ethology, zoology, genetics, neurology, psychology, anthropology, computer science, and artificial intelligence. Of course, you'll also discover a number of thought-provoking selections here by humanists, naturalists, philosophers, sociologists, and historians to balance your picture of the mind and its interaction with broader social and cultural concerns. Finally, *Mind Readings* augments these academic selections with a number of powerful personal essays and works of short fiction. These more imaginative forms of writing illustrate the theoretical perspectives you'll encounter in the book's analytical companion pieces and offer points of departure for your own speculative writings about the nature of the mind.

A Note on Active (Mind) Reading

Whether or not you realize it, your ability to understand and respond to written texts is inextricably bound up with your ability to engage in effective mind reading. Most of the time, we think of reading as a kind of mechanical activity: when you read, you run your eyes over the page, take in the words that are there in front of you, and decode them into meanings. Seen from this relatively simplistic perspective, reading amounts to little more than mental word processing—just keep your eyes moving left to right and your brain automatically translates the little black markings you see into concepts and ideas. Of course, this view doesn't explain why some folks read more easily than others or why some come away from reading with a richer understanding of what they've read. It also doesn't help to explain how to improve your reading skills: if it's all just a matter of mechanical scanning and automatic word processing, then there's really nothing you can do except read faster or try to focus your mental "decoder" more intently on the words that appear before you, an approach that results in frustration more often than it does in reading improvement.

Most accomplished readers intuitively know that meanings just don't leap off the page. In fact, most understand that overly focusing on the meaning of words has little to do with the development of real reading proficiency. To become an accomplished reader, you have to begin by staying focused not on the words but on the mind that lurks behind them. Good readers don't simply ask what the words mean; they ask more probing questions about the author who wrote them and about the intellectual context within which a particular piece of writing is situated. From the outset, experienced readers want to know who the author is. They wonder about her background and the motives that brought her to her topic. Most importantly, they ask themselves questions about the writer's intention or position. Does she approve or disapprove of her subject? Does she want to convince us to adopt a particular view of it or to take action to achieve a particular result? What, overall, is she trying to say or communicate about her topic through this particular piece of writing? Good readers keep such "global" questions in the forefront of their minds as they pick their way through the uncharted territory of an essay or article. They focus not on the words per se, but on the intentions that underlie them — the ideas, values, and beliefs that existed in the mind of the writer at the moment of composing.

Keeping the mind of the writer in focus by asking yourself probing questions is what spells the difference between active and passive reading. Active readers engage the text in an interactive dialogue. As they read — in fact, even before they begin reading — they pepper the text with questions that help them develop a mental picture of the writer and the message she wants to convey. Of course, good readers have their own bag of tricks to help them ferret out authorial intentions. The most common of these reading strategies has to do with keeping an eye out for the "hot spots" commonly found in most forms of expository writing. These are the places where writers typically make their intentions most explicit. You're probably already familiar with these zones of authorial intentionality — the title, headings, graphs, and visual images that an author uses to help clarify her position; the thesis statement or main idea that typically appears someplace in the first few paragraphs; the main or supporting ideas of each paragraph that are commonly found within a few lines of each paragraph's beginning or end; the restatement of authorial position that often accompanies a conclusion. All of these areas in an essay or article are likely to offer clues to the writer's position. The trick is to constantly keep yourself focused on the mind and intentions of the writer as you wend your way through the ideas, illustrations, and anecdotes she weaves into her presentation.

Here's a rough list of the kinds of questions you, as an active reader, might want to ask yourself as you begin to work your way through the expository selections in this book:

- What do the title, headings, and subheadings divulge about the general topic and the author's position or intentions?

- Where do the introduction, body, and conclusion of the article begin and end?

- What strategy does the writer use in the introduction to gain the reader's interest and to provide context for the topic?

- What larger social or intellectual controversies or debates are involved with this topic?

- What parties or interest groups are aligned with these debates or controversies?

- Where and what is the writer's thesis or main idea?

- What is the author's purpose in writing?

- What are the main points of each body paragraph or section?

- How do these supporting points relate to the author's thesis or overall intention?

- What kinds of support in terms of evidence, illustrations, examples, statistical data, etc., does the author offer to back up her claims or clarify her thinking?

- What image does the reader get from the style and tone of the essay about the writer as a person? What can you tell about her values, attitudes, background, political views, etc.?

- How does the author expect the reader to respond to her ideas? What does she expect the reader to do, if anything, as a result of understanding this essay?

Just remember that there's no sure-fire formula for success when it comes to active reading. No single list of questions will help you unearth the motives and intentions of a writer—particularly if you begin to answer them mechanically without really focusing on the mind behind the text. The moment you forget that writing involves you in a critical interaction with another living intelligence, you're doomed to slide into the pointless frustrations of passive reading. Although it may seem odd, reading always implicates you in a relationship. Even if you're reading an essay by an author who lived centuries before your time and in lands far away, you've got to enter into a living dialogue with her and do your share to make your relationship with this distant "other" mind work.

Taking Notes

Note taking offers another technique for the support of active reading. Experienced readers know that keeping a pencil in hand is the best way to keep your mind sharp as you work your way through a complicated text. There are three basic approaches for taking effective notes: highlighting, glossing, and dialoguing. All three promote deeper reading comprehension by helping you stay focused on the broader task of interpretation. The most common of these note-making strategies, highlighting, involves little more than underlining or coloring over passages that strike you as important in terms of the author's intentions or argument. Of course, the trick to effective highlighting is knowing when to start and stop. Inexperienced readers often highlight either too little or too much: highlight too little and you're left without a record of what's important. Highlight too much and you end up with a sea of underlining or a fluorescent page that glows banana yellow in the dark and is just as useless. Effective readers aim at highlighting passages that convey information about the author's intentions and arguments; they don't waste time by underlining every idea and fact they encounter as they read. Glossing involves writing brief notes in the margins of your book that label the main points of each paragraph or body section. Think of glossing as providing a handy index to the content of the essay—an indispensable tool for students who will eventually have to write text-based papers in response to the materials they cover in class. Dialoguing is a variant of glossing. In this form of graphically aided active reading, you jot down your questions, comments, and reactions to the ideas you read as they occur to you. Just cram them into the margins of your text along with your glosses. This running marginal commentary not only provides you with a record of your moment-to-moment experience of the text, it also helps you stay connected with the active dialogue of ideas that the author hopes to establish with her audience.

Here's an example of all three note-making strategies at work, based on the first page of Mark Slouka's challenging personal essay "Listening for Silence":

Listening for (Silence) — The topic? (Why do we need to "listen" for it?)

MUSIC, Claude Debussy once famously remarked, is the
stuff between the notes, an observation that resonates,
pardon the pun, from the flawless spacing of a Billie   *Links silence to*
Holiday tune to the deletions—whether generous or   *light & love!*
cruel—in our daily lives. Essentially neuter, neither
balm nor curse, (silence) like (light) or (love) requires a
medium to give it meaning, takes on the color of its
host, adapts easily to our fears and needs. Quite apart

from whether we seek or shun it, silence orchestrates the music of our days.

I'm well aware, of course, that one man's music is another man's noise, that the primary differences between a cork-lined room and solitary confinement are the lock on the door and the sensibility of the inmate. I wish not to define silence but to inquire about its absence, and I ask the question not to restate the obvious—that silence, in its way, is fundamental to life, the emotional equivalent of carbon—but because everywhere I turn I see a culture willing to deny that essential truth. In my idle moments I picture a god from my son's book of myths (with an Olympian straw and sucked-in cheeks) drawing the silence out of the land, and if the conceit is fanciful, the effect, sadly, is not: as silence disappears, the world draws tighter, borders collapse, the public and the private bleed and intermix. Victim to the centripetal pull, the imagination crackles with the static of outside frequencies, while somewhere in the soul—listen!—a cell phone is chirping. Answer it quickly, before someone else does.

Huh?

Thesis
Contemp. culture destroys silence?

Is he suggesting that electronic tech. has destroyed silence?

Although Slouka's meditation on the demise of silence in contemporary society doesn't fit the predictable pattern of the traditional academic essay, effective note taking can help the dedicated reader grasp his intentions as a writer. In the example above, key lines, like those containing Slouka's thesis, are highlighted to help them stand out for future reference. Since glossing is a "body" strategy and the illustration comes from Slouka's introduction, only two obvious glosses are offered—the note that refers to silence as the heart of music in the opening paragraph and the label that identifies the essay's thesis. The remainder of the notes fall into the category of dialogue, even the casual "Huh?" that documents the reader's response to Slouka's reference to a cork-lined room and solitary confinement. Sometimes responding to passages that confuse you can lead to future insights. So don't hesitate to dialogue with your author, even if you're not certain about the point she's trying to make.

Keeping a Reading-Response Journal

Yet another approach to active reading and note taking involves keeping a reading-response journal. Reading-response journals offer you a place to experiment with pre- and postreading responses to the selections you'll be assigned in your class. You may, for example, want to freewrite in your journal in response to the prewriting assignments and exercises that are associated with each of the selections you'll find in *Mind Readings*. You may also want to use your journal as a place to freewrite your immediate reactions to the essays, stories, and articles you read or as a place to record your responses to the discussion and study questions that follow each selection. You might find that the journal is a particularly good forum for airing your personal responses to reading selections or for acting out imaginary dialogues between yourself and the author. Some students find it particularly effective to *draw* their responses in their journals: visually oriented students often find it helpful to use pictorial imagery to engage the ideas they encounter in their readings. In fact, students have even been known to "storyboard" their reactions to reading selections in order to strengthen their comprehension. The secret to keeping an effective reading-response journal lies in recognizing that your journal exists for you alone. There's no tried and true formula for success. You have to discover the tricks and techniques that work best for you — the approaches that help you engage as personally and directly as possible with the texts you read. No approach is too radical or outrageous, as long as it helps you stay in touch with the author's main and supporting ideas.

Here's an example of a personal freewrite in response to Slouka's "Listening for Silence":

> I hate the way this thing gets going. The yadda-yadda Claude Debussy (whoever that is) famous remark is almost enough to make me choke. And it's too bad Slouka didn't like silence enough to spare us the pun in line two. But he might be right tho about what's happening to silence in today's society. I see — or hear — it everywhere I go — taking the bus down Vermont to school at 8 in the morning or at night when the LAPD helicopters circle for hours overhead. Silence is dead in this city. (But I still can't stand the way this guy talks — "in my idle moments" — "if the conceit is fanciful" — "a cell phone is chirping" — [ever hear a cell phone chirp?]. . . .

You may have a totally different reaction to Slouka's essay and to his style as a writer. A reading-response journal isn't a place where you should be worried about "correctness" — whether it's the correctness of your grammar or the correctness of your interpretation. It's a place for you to experiment with techniques meant to help you bridge the chasm of time and space that separates you from the mind of the author whose ideas you're reading. A reading-response journal represents a kind of "neutral" terrain where your mind can meet the mind of an author on the reciprocal terms established by the art of active reading.

Note

Stephen Pinker, *The Language Instinct: How the Mind Creates Language.* New York: William Morrow & Co., 1994, p. 227.

1

Reading the Senses
From Sight to Insight

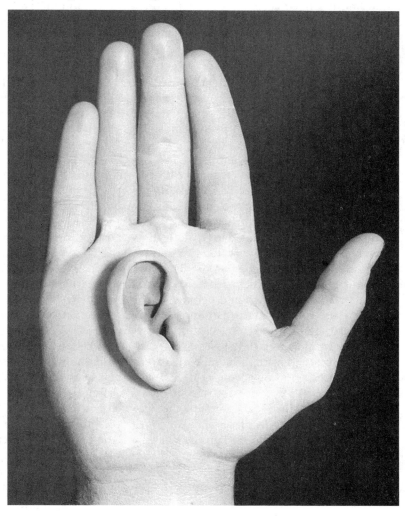

The Doors of Perception

In 1972, psychologist John Lilly initiated a series of now-famous and highly controversial experiments in sensory deprivation. Lilly suspended volunteer subjects in "womb tanks"—water-filled enclosures specially designed to eliminate all forms of sensory stimulation. Floating for days in body-temperature water and deprived of all sensory input, Lilly's subjects lost touch with time and drifted in and out of consciousness. Eventually, they lost their ability to discriminate between reality and dream and became prey to disconcertingly vivid and sometimes even violent hallucinations. Some of Lilly's subjects, for example, reported being pursued by fantastic, threatening creatures that had mysteriously gained access to the tank. Others entered into dreamlike scenarios and carried on hallucinatory conversations with people they believed to be present. In a number of cases, Lilly's subjects experienced such a complete breakdown of their sense of self that he was forced to terminate the experiment for their own safety.

Lilly's womb tank experiments underscore the important role that sight, hearing, taste, touch, and smell play in relation to the human mind. The senses are the mind's outposts; they mediate between the realm of our inner experience and the outer world of people and things. They are literally, as Aldous Huxley termed them, the "doors of perception"—the physical portals through which our bodies admit bits and pieces of the world for analysis. Photons of light energy reflected by a tree stream into the vision-producing apparatus of the eye; molecules of a sizzling steak ricochet into the olfactory sensors that line our noses; the concluding chord of a Bach fugue sets off a series of vibrations in our inner ear. Our senses bind us to the material world. They warn us of impending danger, inform us of our own physical needs, and provide us with the information we need to satisfy them. But, as Lilly's provocative experiments suggest, the senses also do much more. The five senses define the boundary between self and other. They trace the difference between the real and the imaginary and help us discriminate between mind and madness. The senses lie at the root of human consciousness: together, they collaborate to provide us with the most important sense of all—our sense of self.

That's why reading the senses is a good way to begin our exploration of the mind. The senses are the source of everything that we think and feel. They are the foundation of our "common sense" and the basis of all of our knowledge of the universe. Since the age of Aristotle, philosophers have affirmed that "There is nothing in the intellect that was not first in sensation." Reading the senses is also a good place to begin your development as a college writer and critical thinker. Reflecting on the senses and the process of perception offers you the chance to write from the authority of direct, personal experience. It also challenges you to see that even your most intensely personal experience is, in fact, a kind of "text"—a sensory document shaped by broader cultural values, attitudes, and expectations—a text that, like all texts, is open to interpretation and revision.

Today, we live in a world that celebrates the senses. From mega-screen TV to Surround Sound audio and worldwide Internet access, the story of contemporary society is the story of the triumph of sensory stimulation. But the senses haven't always been held in such high repute. During the millennia leading up to the electronic age, nearly every major organized religion condemned sensual excess and viewed sense experience with either suspicion or contempt. For centuries, Christian theologians have warned against indulging the "pleasures of the flesh" and threatened those who succumbed to their sensual appetites with the prospect of eternal punishment in the fire and brimstone of hell. The senses, from the traditional Christian perspective, belong to the "fallen world" of Adam and Eve and thus link us to the "lower," more bestial orders of creation—the animals rather than the angels. Christian fundamentalists, like the Puritans who ventured west to the "New World" in 1620, restricted all forms of sensual gratification, including the enjoyment of secular music, plays, and painted images. The Pilgrims even banished sensory stimulation from their style of dress, preferring simple dark coats and capes—fashion's forerunners of the sober, American business suit. In Eastern religions, the senses have similarly been considered a source of error and illusion. In Hinduism, for example, sense experience is believed to underlie the false appearances of the material world—the "veils of Maya" that obscure "Brahman" or spiritual enlightenment. To achieve a state of grace, one must learn to meditate—to close one's eyes and mind to the chaos of sensory experience and to transcend to a higher mental and spiritual plane. East or West, spiritual hygiene has long been associated with rituals aimed at cleansing the senses, either through abstinence or regimens of spiritual exercise that limit or discipline sensory stimulation.

Secular philosophers haven't exactly championed the senses either. Legend has it that the pre-Socratic Greek philosopher Democritus held the senses in such disdain that he put out his eyes so that he would be able to think more effectively. The father of the theory of "atomism," Democritus believed that all physical objects are composed of tiny uniform particles and that objects appear solid only because of the faultiness of our perceptions. The senses, and the "bastard" picture of reality that they offer, were, from his perspective, the source of all human error. Later, Plato also found the senses wanting, but for a subtly different reason. In a famous passage from the *Phaedrus,* he has Socrates explain that knowledge of the truth emerges only from direct intuition of the eternal "ideas" or "forms" that are imperfectly shadowed forth through the phenomena we perceive with our senses. Living in the world of the senses for Plato is like living among the deceptive shadows of a dimly lit cave, shadows that can be dispelled only by means of careful reasoning and vigilant skepticism.

Influenced by Greek philosophy, modern science continued to view sensory experience with suspicion. The seventeenth-century French philosopher René Descartes literally banished the senses from the realm of objective truth when he formulated his famous dictum: "I think, therefore I am." For

Descartes, and the four centuries of scientists who have been influenced by his thinking, direct sensory experience can be made reliable only if it is translated into mathematical form and subjected to rigorous intellectual scrutiny. Since the days of Copernicus and Galileo, thinking like a scientist has meant doubting the direct evidence of the senses: your eyes tell you that the sun rises daily in the east and that the earth is the center of the universe, but mathematical analysis says otherwise. Your nose may tell you that epidemic diseases are caused by poverty, but only a microscope — the mind's improvement upon the eye — can reveal the existence of bacteria. For the past four centuries, science has been based on the assumption that the senses can be misleading and that the true "facts" of nature are discernible only through rigorous mathematical modeling and controlled experimentation.

Writing and the Senses

It shouldn't be surprising, then, that language subtly reflects an antisensory bias. The English language is a wonderfully flexible instrument for communicating ideas and describing events, but, in general, English, like most languages, struggles with the direct communication of sense experience. You may not have any trouble explaining the layout of your hometown or analyzing the class or racial composition of your city, but putting your personal experience of how it *feels* to live in your particular neighborhood into words can be a daunting task. That's because language offers literally thousands of names for things, creatures, and the actions that relate them, but relatively few words or expressions dedicated to conveying subjective sensory experience. To convey the "touch" of things we have a few general terms like *rough* and *smooth;* for taste we have the obvious gastronomic spectrum of *bitter, sweet,* and *sour;* for smell there are a few additional descriptors like *acrid* and *rotten.* Even the vocabulary of visual experience — clearly our dominant sense — is limited: we can say a great deal about the *things* we perceive, but relatively few words or expressions are devoted to describing *how* we see the world around us. Our vistas may be *bright, dim,* or *shadowy,* but beyond a handful of adjectives dedicated to illumination, language is relatively mute when it comes to conveying the felt experience of sight.

The notable exception — so notable that it proves the rule — is the sense of hearing. Perhaps because language is itself a creature of the ear, we have plenty of words dedicated to describing what we hear. English offers hundreds of strong active verbs that evoke specific aural experiences — words like *buzz, crack, thunder, rumble, crunch, groan, creak, swish, thud, warble, trill,* and *bark.* Indeed, language seems to delight in mimicking the sounds we hear. This verbal phenomenon, known technically as onomatopoeia, gives the writer a palette of sounds that can be used to convey the aural dimension of sensory experience in considerable detail. But ultimately, even these words may fall short of conveying the texture of a particular experience of sound. After all, the ring of the school bell that summoned you to class on your first day of kindergarten still probably resounds in your memory with a more exciting— or a more ominous—tone than do the thousands of school bells you have heard ever since.

Fortunately, the mind is equipped with resources that allow us to cope with the relative poverty of language in relation to sense experience. Good writers know that readers will intuit or empathize with their mental state if they have enough concrete sensory detail to work with. That's why effective writers include as much specific detail in descriptive passages as possible. It's one thing to tell the reader that "I love the taste of hot food" and quite another to say "I loved the eye-watering heat of habanero chilies mixed with the fire-roasted sweetness of coal-black achos that my grandmother ladled onto my plate when I was a boy." Concrete sensory details layered densely like this create the illusion of sensory experience: they provide readers with the cues they need to reconstruct the experience in their own imagination. Listen for a moment as nature writer Bill McKibben uses sensory detail to convey the experience of an early morning swim in a mountain lake:

> . . . I ease myself down from the rocks into the chilly water, feeling the mud between my toes. I stand for a minute, aware of the line on my calves between the cold water and the warmth of the sun, and then dive in a taut stretch. I can feel the water rushing past my head, smoothing back my hair. As I stroke out to the middle, I'm conscious of the strength and pull of my shoulder blades. I haul myself out onto a rock in the middle of the pond, and sit there dripping. A breeze comes up, and lifts the hairs on my back, each one giving a nearly imperceptible tug at my skin. Under hand and thigh I can feel the roughness and the hardness of the rock. (188–189)

McKibben could simply have said that his early morning swim was "refreshing" or that it had "awakened" all his senses, and he would have captured the general import of this experience. But in doing so he would have missed its "feel." The sensual details McKibben provides in his description—the tensing of a muscle, the contrast of temperatures on his calves, the prickling of individual hairs on his back when a cool breeze comes up—invite the reader to recall similar sense experiences in memory and to join him, imaginatively at least, as he swims alone across an icy mountain lake.

Good writers also recognize that the senses rarely exist in isolation. We, along with Aristotle, may commonly divide sense impressions into five tidy categories, but in the reality of lived experience the world presents itself as a rich mixture of sights, sounds, textures, smells, and tastes. Here's an example from an essay by Louise Erdrich, in which she describes how, as a teen growing up in South Dakota, she shared her sleeping bag with a skunk during a night spent on her high school football field:

Inside the bag, I felt as if I might smother. Carefully, making only the slightest of rustles, I drew the bag away from my face and took a deep breath of the night air, enriched with skunk, but clear and watery and cold. It wasn't so bad, and the skunk didn't stir at all, so I watched the moon — caught that night in an envelope of silk, a mist — pass over my sleeping field of guts and glory. The grass in spring that has lain beneath the snow harbors a sere dust both old and fresh. I smelled that newness beneath the rank tone of my bag-mate — the stiff fragrance of damp earth and the thick pungency of newly manured fields a mile or two away — along with my sleeping bag's smell, slightly mildewed, forever smoky. The skunk settled closer and began to breathe rapidly; its feet jerked a little like a dog's. I sank against the earth, and fell asleep too. (110–111)

Erdrich isn't content to tell us that she's cold and smells something "skunky." Instead, she paints a picture that blends several different visual, tactile, auditory, and olfactory impressions into a complex sensory experience. We hear — and feel — the rustling of her sleeping bag. We taste the chill of the night air, thick and refreshing like a gulp of cold water. We smell — and touch — the "stiff fragrance" of the wet ground she sleeps on, as well as the "thick" odor of newly manured fields nearby. Erdrich relies on powerful sensory images to convey the feeling of this experience to her readers, but what really ignites the imagination and allows us to join her and her malodorous friend in their shared sleep is the density of the sense experience she describes. Skillful writer that she is, Erdrich knows how to layer sense impressions in this passage, weaving one into and through another, to produce a total sensory experience that surrounds the reader and invites imaginative identification.

Accomplished writers also use indirect description to capture and convey the feeling of their sense experiences. The moon Erdrich sees floating above the football field isn't literally suspended in an "envelope of silk"; it just strikes her that way as she watches it move in and out of the surrounding mist. One of the oldest tricks in the writer's toolbox is to convey the texture of subjective experiences indirectly by means of well-crafted analogies, similes, and metaphors — figures of speech that describe one thing or experience in terms of another. Here's an example of this doubling of sense experience from Henry David Thoreau's *Walden*:

On the 29th of April, as I was fishing from the bank of the river near the Nine-Acre-Corner bridge, standing on the quaking grass and willow roots, where the muskrats lurk, I heard a singular rattling sound, somewhat like that of the sticks which boys play with their fingers, when, looking up, I observed a very slight and graceful hawk, like a night-hawk, alternately soaring like a ripple and tumbling a rod or two over and over, showing the underside of its wings, which gleamed like a satin ribbon in the sun, or like the pearly inside of a shell. . . . It was the most ethereal flight I had ever witnessed. It did not simply flutter like a butterfly, nor soar like the larger hawks, but it sported with proud reliance in the fields of air; mounting again and again with its strange chuckle, it repeated its free and beautiful fall, turning over and over like a kite, and then recovering from its lofty tumbling, as if it had never set its foot on terra firma. (364)

Thoreau compares the "look" of this hawk in flight to a ripple of water on a lake, the tumbling of a kite, and—negatively—to the flutter of butterfly wings. He hears the hawk's cry as the rattle produced by boys playing with sticks and a "strange chuckle." The underside of the bird's wings aren't simply "white" or "shining"; they remind Thoreau of "satin ribbon" or "the pearly inside of a shell." Analogies, similes, and metaphors double the descriptive power of language: they allow us to capture the impact of one sense experience by refracting it through the memory of another.

Chapter Overview

The selections included in this chapter are meant to guide you as you explore the complex interrelationships of self, sense, and language. We begin with an example of sensuous writing at its best: in "Take the F," Ian Frazier documents the sights, smells, and sounds he encounters during his daily commute through Brooklyn, New York. Frazier's multisensory celebration of urban life illustrates how language can convey the "feel" of a place—and offers a model for your own attempt at capturing in words the flavor of daily life in your hometown. This introductory essay is followed by a quartet of readings addressing four of the primary senses. In "A Passage of the Hands," renowned naturalist Barry Lopez reflects on the "education" of his sense of touch and on the way that touching has shaped his sense of self. Next, Diane Ackerman investigates the many functions of taste in an essay from her acclaimed *Natural History of the Senses*. This wide-ranging exploration of the phenomenon of taste invites you to consider not only how the aesthetics of food differ from culture to culture, but also how taste itself connects us to issues of life and death. Mark Slouka follows Ackerman with an elegant reflection on the status of silence in an era of mass communication. Slouka's meditation on the meaning and uses of silence raises questions about the impact of capitalism on the senses and on the self. This section concludes with "The Olfactory Revolution," an introduction to the cultural history of smell that demonstrates how our senses have evolved over time and that invites you to reflect on the changing cultural significance of sensory experience.

The next pair of readings focuses more narrowly on the topic of vision. In "Seeing Things," K. C. Cole explores what it means for a scientist to "see" subatomic particles. Cole's thoughtful examination of the relation between vision and scientific knowledge reminds us that every act of seeing involves interpretation, whether facilitated by our eyes or by sophisticated scientific apparatus. In "The Mind's Eye," Georgina Kleege develops this theme from a different point of view. Legally blind since the age of 11, Kleege describes what the process of seeing is like for her and raises questions about how the sighted view blindness and the vision impaired. The chapter concludes with two selections that challenge our assumptions about the quality and authority of sense experience. In

"Television and the Twilight of the Senses," Bill McKibben considers how our addiction to television insulates us from full sensuous appreciation of the natural world. Walker Percy's "The Loss of Creature" approaches the same idea from a slightly different perspective. In this philosophic reflection on the relation of history, mind, and personal experience, Percy argues that life in a technologically advanced culture makes it almost impossible for us to "see" anything, no matter how hard or carefully we use our sense of sight.

Sources

Ackerman, Diane. *A Natural History of the Senses.* New York: Random, 1991.
Erdrich, Louise. "Skunk Dreams." *The Best American Essays, 1994.* Ed. Tracy Kidder. Boston: Houghton, 1994.
Giannetti, Eduardo. *Lies We Live By: The Art of Self-Deception.* Trans. John Gledson. New York: Bloomsbury, 2000.
Humphrey, Nicholas. *A History of the Mind: Evolution and the Birth of Consciousness.* New York: HarperCollins, 1993.
McKibben, Bill. *The Age of Missing Information.* New York: Penguin, 1992.
Ree, Jonathan. *I See a Voice: Deafness, Language, and the Senses—A Philosophical History.* New York: Holt, 1999.
Thoreau, Henry David. *Walden.* New York: Penguin, 1983.

Take the F

IAN FRAZIER

How exciting is your morning commute? Most of us learn to ignore the sights and sounds we encounter as we shuttle back and forth between home, school, and work. We tune out our cross-town trips and reserve awareness for more important matters — the one-of-a-kind experiences or "peak moments" that rarely happen on the bus. But as Ian Frazier suggests in this award-winning essay, the workaday world of our home neighborhoods offers a kaleidoscope of sensory experience to the finely attuned eye and ear. Frazier's celebration of the sights, sounds, smells, and rhythms of life in Brooklyn, New York, demonstrates how sensuous detail can bring even the most commonplace subject alive. It also offers you a good model for writing an essay of your own about what it's like to live in your hometown, city, or neighborhood. After graduating from Harvard University in 1977, Frazier (b. 1951) joined the staff of the *New Yorker* magazine. His publications include *Great Plains* (1989), *Family* (1994), and the novel *Coyote vs. Acme* (1996). His most recent book, *On the Rez* (2000), explores life among the Oglala Sioux Indians of the Pine Ridge Indian Reservation.

BEFORE READING

Working in small groups or independently in your journal, brainstorm a list of "sense impressions" commonly associated with life in a typical, heavily industrialized American city.

What sights, sounds, smells, tastes, and textures do you think of when you think of cities like Brooklyn, Philadelphia, Chicago, Detroit, or Los Angeles? How closely do these impressions agree with those of your classmates? Overall, how would you describe the dominant impression of life in a major American urban center?

Brooklyn, New York, has the undefined, hard-to-remember shape of a stain. I never know what to tell people when they ask me where in it I live. It sits at the western tip of Long Island at a diagonal that does not conform neatly to the points of the compass. People in Brooklyn do not describe where they live in terms of north or west or south. They refer instead to their neighborhoods, and to the nearest subway lines. I live on the edge of Park Slope, a neighborhood by the crest of a low ridge that runs through the borough. Prospect Park is across the street. Airplanes in the landing pattern for La Guardia Airport sometimes fly right over my building; every few minutes, on certain sunny days, perfectly detailed airplane shadows slide down my building and up the building opposite in a blink. You can see my building from the plane — it's on the left-hand side of Prospect Park, the longer patch of green you cross after the expanse of Green-Wood Cemetery.

We moved to a co-op apartment in a four-story building a week before our daughter was born. She is now six. I grew up in the country and would not have expected ever to live in Brooklyn. My daughter is a city kid, with less sympathy for certain other parts of the country. When we visited Montana, she was disappointed by the scarcity of pizza places. I overheard her explaining — she was three or four then — to a Montana kid about Brooklyn. She said, "In Brooklyn, there is a lot of broken glass, so you have to wear shoes. And, there is good pizza." She is stern in her judgment of pizza. At the very low end of the pizza-ranking scale is some pizza she once had in New Hampshire, a category now called New Hampshire pizza. In the middle is some OK pizza she once had at the Bronx Zoo, which she calls zoo pizza. At the very top is the pizza at the pizza place where the big kids go, about two blocks from our house.

Our subway is the F train. It runs under our building and shakes the floor. The F is generally a reliable train, but one spring as I walked in the park I saw emergency vehicles gathered by a concrete-sheathed hole in the lawn. Firemen lifted a metal lid from the hole and descended into it. After a while, they reappeared, followed by a few people, then dozens of people, then a whole lot of people — passengers from a disabled F train, climbing one at a time out an exit shaft. On the F, I sometimes see large women in straw hats reading a newspaper called the *Caribbean Sunrise,* and Orthodox Jews bent over Talmudic texts in which the footnotes have footnotes, and groups of teenagers wearing identical red bandannas with identical red plastic baby pacifiers in the corners of their mouths, and female couples in porkpie hats, and young men with the silhouettes of the Manhattan skyline razored into their short side hair from one temple around to the other, and Russian-speaking men with thick wrists and big wristwatches, and a hefty, tall woman with long, straight blond hair who hums and closes her eyes and absently practices cello fingerings on the metal subway pole. As I watched the F-train passengers emerge among the grass and trees of Prospect Park, the faces were as varied as usual, but the expressions of indignant surprise were all about the same.

Just past my stop, Seventh Avenue, Manhattan-bound F trains rise from underground to cross the Gowanus Canal. The train sounds different—lighter, quieter—in the open air. From the elevated tracks, you can see the roofs of many houses stretching back up the hill to Park Slope, and a bumper crop of rooftop graffiti, and neon signs for Eagle Clothes and Kentile Floors, and flat expanses of factory roofs where seagulls stand on one leg around puddles in the sagging spots. There are fuel-storage tanks surrounded by earthen barriers, and slag piles, and conveyor belts leading down to the oil-slicked waters of the canal. On certain days, the sludge at the bottom of the canal causes it to bubble. Two men fleeing the police jumped in the canal a while ago; one made it across, the other quickly died. When the subway doors open at the Smith–Ninth Street stop, you can see the bay, and sometimes smell the ocean breeze. This stretch of elevated is the highest point of the New York subway system. To the south you can see the Verrazano-Narrows Bridge, to the north the World Trade towers. For just a few moments, the Statue of Liberty appears between passing buildings. Pieces of a neighborhood—laundry on clotheslines, a standup swimming pool, a plaster saint, a satellite dish, a rectangle of lawn—slide by like quickly dealt cards. Then the train descends again; growing over the wall just before the tunnel is a wisteria bush, which blooms pale blue every May.

I have spent days, weeks on the F train. The trip from Seventh Avenue to   5
midtown Manhattan is long enough so that every ride can produce its own minisociety of riders, its own forty-minute Ship of Fools.° Once a woman an arm's length from me on a crowded train pulled a knife on a man who threatened her. I remember the argument and the principals, but mostly I remember the knife—its flat, curved wood-grain handle inlaid with brass fittings at each end, its long, tapered blade. Once a man sang the words of the Lord's Pray to a mournful, syncopated tune, and he fitted the mood of the morning so exactly that when he asked for money at the end the riders reached for their wallets and purses as if he'd pulled a gun. Once a big white kid with some friends was teasing a small old Hispanic lady, and when he got off the train I looked at him through the window and he slugged it hard next to my face. Once a thin woman and a fat woman sitting side by side had a long and loud conversation about someone they intended to slap silly: "Her butt be in the *hospital!*" Bring out the ar-*tillery!*" The terminus of the F in Brooklyn is at Coney Island, not far from the beach. At an off hour, I boarded the train and found two or three passengers and, walking around on the floor, a crab. The

Ship of Fools: Refers to the medieval custom of isolating people with mental illnesses on boats traveling from city to city; hence, any gathering of unusually colorful or odd types of people.

passengers were looking at the crab. Its legs clicked on the floor like varnished fingernails. It moved in this direction, then that, trying to get comfortable. It backed itself under a seat, against the wall. Then it scooted out just after some new passengers had sat down there, and they really screamed. Passengers at the next stop saw it and laughed. When a boy lifted his foot as if to stomp it, everybody cried, "Noooh!" By the time we reached Jay Street–Borough Hall, there were maybe a dozen of us in the car, all absorbed in watching the crab. The car doors opened and a heavyset woman with good posture entered. She looked at the crab; then, sternly, at all of us. She let a moment pass. Then she demanded, "*Whose* is *that?*" A few stops later, a short man with a mustache took a manila envelope, bent down, scooped the crab into it, closed it, and put it in his coat pocket.

The smells in Brooklyn: coffee, fingernail polish, eucalyptus, the breath from laundry rooms, pot roast, Tater Tots. A woman I know who grew up here says she moved away because she could not stand the smell of cooking food in the hallway of her parents' building. I feel just the opposite. I used to live in a converted factory above an army-navy store, and I like being in a place that smells like people live there. In the mornings, I sometimes wake to the smell of toast, and I still don't know exactly whose toast it is. And I prefer living in a borough of two and a half million inhabitants, the most of any borough in the city. I think of all the rural places, the pine-timbered canyons and within-commuting-distance farmland, that we are preserving by not living there. I like the immensities of the borough, the unrolling miles of Eastern Parkway and Ocean Parkway and Linden Boulevard, and the disheveled outlying parks strewn with tree limbs and with shards of glass held together by liquor-bottle labels, and the tough bridges—the Williamsburg and the Manhattan—and the gentle Brooklyn Bridge. And I like the way the people talk; some really do have Brooklyn accents, really do say "dese" and "dose." A week or two ago, a group of neighbors stood on a street corner watching a peregrine falcon on a building cornice contentedly eating a pigeon it had caught, and the sunlight came through its tail feathers, and a woman said to a man, "Look at the tail, it's so ah-range," and the man replied, "Yeah, I soar it." Like many Americans, I fear living in a no-where, in a place that is no-place; in Brooklyn, that doesn't trouble me at all.

Everybody, it seems, is here. At Grand Army Plaza, I have seen traffic tie-ups caused by Haitians and others rallying in support of President Aristide,° and by St. Patrick's Day parades, and by Jews of the Lubavitcher sect° celebrating the birthday of their Grand Rebbe° with a slow procession of ninety-three motor homes—one for each year of his life. Local taxis have bumper stickers that say "Allah Is Great"; one of the men who made the bomb that

President Aristide: President of Haiti (b. 1953).
of the Lubavitcher sect: A sect of Orthodox Judaism.
Grand Rebbe: The spiritual leader of the Lubavitcher sect.

blew up the World Trade Center used an apartment just a few blocks from me. When an election is held in Russia, crowds line up to cast ballots at a Russian polling place in Brighton Beach. A while ago, I volunteer-taught reading at a public elementary school across the park. One of my students, a girl, was part Puerto Rican, part Greek, and part Welsh. Her looks were a lively combination, set off by sea-green eyes. I went to a map store in Manhattan and bought maps of Puerto Rico, Greece, and Wales to read with her, but they didn't interest her. A teacher at the school was directing a group of students to set up chairs for a program in the auditorium, and she said to me, "We have a problem here—each of these kids speaks a different language." She asked the kids to tell me where they were from. One was from Korea, one from Brazil, one from Poland, one from Guyana, one from Taiwan. In the program that followed, a chorus of fourth and fifth graders sang "God Bless America," "You're a Grand Old Flag," and "I'm a Yankee-Doodle Dandy."

People in my neighborhood are mostly white, and middle class or above. People in neighborhoods nearby are mostly not white, and mostly middle class or below. Everybody uses Prospect Park. On summer days, the park teems with sound—the high note is kids screaming in the water sprinklers at the playground, the mid-range is radios and tape players, and the bass is idling or speeding cars. People bring lawn furniture and badminton nets and coolers, and then they barbecue. Charcoal smoke drifts into the neighborhood. Last year, local residents upset about the noise and litter and smoke began a campaign to outlaw barbecuing in the park. There was much unfavorable comment about "the barbecuers." Since most of the barbecuers, as it happens, are black or Hispanic, the phrase "Barbecuers Go Home," which someone spray-painted on the asphalt at the Ninth Street entrance to the park, took on a pointed, unkind meaning. But then park officials set up special areas for barbecuing, and the barbecuers complied, and the controversy died down.

Right nearby is a shelter for homeless people. Sometimes people sleep on the benches along the park, sometimes they sleep in the foyer of our building. Once I went downstairs, my heart pounding, to evict a homeless person who I had been told was there. The immediate, unquestioning way she left made me feel bad; later I always said "Hi" to her and gave her a dollar when I ran into her. One night, late, I saw her on the street, and I asked her her last name (by then I already knew her first name) and for a moment she couldn't recall it. At this, she shook her head in mild disbelief.

There's a guy I see on a bench along Prospect Park West all the time. Once   10
I walked by carrying my year-old son, and the man said, "Someday he be carrying you." At the local copy shop one afternoon, a crowd was waiting for copies and faxes when a man in a houndstooth fedora came in seeking signatures for a petition to have the homeless shelter shut down. To my surprise, and his, the people in the copy shop instantly turned on him. "I suppose because they're poor they shouldn't even have a place to sleep at night," a woman said as he backed out the door. On the park wall across the street from my building, someone has written in black marker:

COPS PROTECT CITIZENS
WHO PROTECT US FROM COPS.

Sometimes I walk from my building downhill and north, along the Brooklyn waterfront, where cargo ships with scuffed sides and prognathous bows lean overhead. Sometimes I walk by the Brooklyn Navy Yard, its docks now too dormant to attract saboteurs, its long expanses of chain-link fence tangled here and there with the branches of ailanthus trees growing through. Sometimes I head southwest, keeping more or less to the high ground — Bay Ridge — along Fifth Avenue, through Hispanic neighborhoods that stretch in either direction as far as you can see, and then through block after block of Irish. I follow the ridge to its steep descent to the water at the Verrazano-Narrows; Fort Hamilton, an army post dating from 1814, is there, and a small Episcopal church called the Church of the Generals. Robert E. Lee once served as a vestryman of this church, and Stonewall Jackson was baptized here. Today the church is in the shade of a forest of high concrete columns supporting an access ramp to the Verrazano-Narrows Bridge.

Sometimes I walk due south, all the way out Coney Island Avenue. In that direction, as you approach the ocean, the sky gets bigger and brighter, and the buildings seem to flatten beneath it. Dry cleaners advertise "Tallis Cleaned Free with Every Purchase Over Fifteen Dollars." Then you start to see occasional lines of graffiti written in Cyrillic.° Just past a Cropsey Avenue billboard welcoming visitors to Coney Island is a bridge over a creek filled nearly to the surface with metal shopping carts that people have tossed there over the years. A little farther on, the streets open onto the beach. On a winter afternoon, bundled-up women sit on the boardwalk on folding chairs around a portable record player outside a restaurant called Gastronom Moscow. The acres of trash-dotted sand are almost empty. A bottle of Peter the Great vodka lies on its side, drops of water from its mouth making a small depression in the sand. A man with trousers rolled up to his shins moves along the beach, chopping at driftwood with an ax. Another passerby says, "He's vorking hard, that guy!" The sunset unrolls light along the storefronts like tape. From the far distance, little holes in the sand at the water's edge mark the approach of a short man wearing hip boots and earphones and carrying a long-handled metal detector. Treasure hunters dream of the jewelry that people must have lost here over the years. Some say that this is the richest treasure beach in the Northeast. The man stops, runs the metal detector again over a spot, digs with a clamming shovel, lifts some sand, brushes through it with a gloved thumb, discards it. He goes on, leaving a trail of holes behind him.

I like to find things myself, and I always try to keep one eye on the ground as I walk. So far I have found seven dollars (a five and two ones), an earring in the shape of a strawberry, several personal notes, a matchbook with a 900 number to call to hear "prison sex fantasies," and two spent .25-caliber shells.

Cyrillic: The alphabet used in Slavic languages.

Once on Carroll Street, I saw a page of text on the sidewalk, and I bent over to read it. It was page 191 from a copy of *Anna Karenina*.° I read the whole page. It described Vronsky° leaving a gathering and riding off in a carriage. In a great book, the least fragment is great. I looked up and saw a woman regarding me closely from a few feet away. "You're reading," she said wonderingly. "From a distance, I t'ought you were watchin' ants."

My favorite place to walk is the Brooklyn Botanic Garden, not more than fifteen minutes away. It's the first place I take out-of-towners, who may not associate Brooklyn with flowers. In the winter, the garden is drab as pocket lint, and you can practically see all the way through from Flatbush Avenue to Washington Avenue. But then in February or March a few flowerings begin, the snowdrops and the crocuses, and then the yellow of the daffodils climbs Daffodil Hill, and then the magnolias — star magnolias, umbrella magnolias, saucer magnolias — go off all at once, and walking among them is like flying through cumulus clouds. Then the cherry trees blossom, some a soft and glossy red like makeup, others pink as a dessert, and crowds fill the paths on weekends and stand in front of the blossoms in their best clothes and have their pictures taken. Security guards tell people, "No eating, no sitting on the grass — this is a garden, not a park." There are traffic jams of strollers, and kids running loose. One security guard jokes into his radio, "There's a pterodactyl on the overlook!" In the pond in the Japanese Garden, ducks lobby for pieces of bread. A duck quacks, in Brooklynese, "Yeah, yeah, yeah," having heard it all before.

Then the cherry blossoms fall, they turn some paths completely pink next to the grass's green, and the petals dry, and people tread them into a fine pink powder. Kids visit on end-of-school-year field trips, and teachers yell "Shawon, get back on line!" and boys with long T-shirts printed from neck to knee with an image of Martin Luther King's face run by laughing and swatting at one another. The yellow boxes that photographic film comes in fall on the ground, and here and there an empty bag of Crazy Calypso potato chips. The lilacs bloom, each bush with a scent slightly different from the next, and yellow tulips fill big round planters with color so bright it ascends in a column, like a searchlight beam. The roses open on the trellises in the Rose Garden and attract a lively air traffic of bees, and June wedding parties, brides and grooms and their subsidiaries, adjust themselves minutely for photographers there. A rose called the Royal Gold smells like a new bathing suit, and is as yellow.

In our building of nine apartments, two people have died and six have 15
been born since we moved in. I like our neighbors — a guy who works for Off-Track Betting, a guy who works for the Department of Correction, a woman who works for Dean Witter, an in-flight steward, a salesperson of subsidiary rights at a publishing house, a restaurant manager, two lawyers, a retired

Anna Karenina: Novel (1877) by Russian author Leo Nikolayevich Tolstoy (1828–1910).
Vronsky: Hero of *Anna Karenina*.

machinist, a Lebanese-born woman of ninety-five—as well as any I've ever had. We keep track of the bigger events in the building with the help of Chris, our downstairs neighbor. Chris lives on the ground floor and often has conversations in the hall while her foot props her door open. When our kids are sick, she brings them her kids' videos to watch, and when it rains she gives us rides to school. One year, Chris became pregnant and had to take a blood-thinning medicine and was in and out of the hospital. Finally, she had a healthy baby and came home, but then began to bleed and didn't stop. Her husband brought the baby to us about midnight and took Chris to the nearest emergency room. Early the next morning, the grandmother came and took the baby. Then for two days nobody heard anything. When we knocked on Chris's door we got no answer, and when we called we got an answering machine. The whole building was expectant, spooky, quiet. The next morning I left the house and there in the foyer was Chris. She held her husband's arm, and she looked pale, but she was returning from the hospital under her own steam. I hugged her at the door, and it was the whole building hugging her. I walked to the garden seeing glory everywhere. I went to the Rose Garden and took a big Betsy McCall rose to my face and breathed into it as if it were an oxygen mask.

EXPLORING THE TEXT

1. What is Frazier saying about life in Brooklyn? Why does he feel this way toward the city? How does his view of Brooklyn compare with common or stereotypical views of life in large American metropolitan areas like New York, Chicago, Detroit, or Philadelphia?

2. Reread Frazier's essay, making note of specific passages that convey sense impressions of life in Brooklyn. Which passages strike you as particularly visual in orientation? Which convey impressions of the sounds, smells, tastes—and even the "feel"—of life in Frazier's neighborhood? What particular descriptive techniques or strategies does Frazier employ to convey the experience of Brooklyn in all of its sensuous diversity?

3. How many brief illustrative stories or anecdotes can you identify in Frazier's description of Brooklyn? What do these stories add to his essay? Which of these vignettes strike you as being particularly effective? Why?

4. Comment on the way Frazier ends the essay. Why do you think he chose to conclude with the story of Chris and her trip to the hospital? What does this final scene add to the meaning of "Take the F"?

FURTHER EXPLORATIONS

1. Make a collage of images from current popular magazines or newspapers that expresses what it is like to live in a major modern American city. How do the images you collect compare with the image of the city presented in Frazier's essay? How might you account for any differences that you find?

2. Write a journal entry in which you try to capture in words the sense impressions you gather during a walk across campus or through the place where you currently live. Try your hand using sense images, analogies, and anecdotes to convey the feeling or mood of the area. Share these in small groups to see if your classmates recognize the locations you have chosen.

3. Compare Frazier's use of illustrative anecdotes to the role that stories play in Barry Lopez's "A Passage of the Hands" (p. 27). When do each of these authors turn to storytelling in their essays? What kinds of information do their stories convey to the reader? Which stories in these selections strike you as being the most effective? Why? How would your response to these essays change if the stories they contain were replaced by general statements?

4. How does Frazier's sensuous appreciation of daily life in the city compare with Bill McKibben's experience of swimming alone on Crow Mountain (p. 109)? To what extent does Frazier's experience of the New York subway system challenge or confirm McKibben's notion that pleasure always involves contrasting sensations and is never the same as mere comfort?

5. Contrast Frazier's experience of his neighborhood and his commute on the F train to the notion of "sovereign" experience presented by Walker Percy in "The Loss of the Creature" (p. 118). What role does familiarity play in the way that Frazier and Percy view the process of perception? In general, do you think that familiarity dulls or enriches your ability to appreciate day-to-day experiences? Explain.

ESSAY OPTIONS

1. Write an essay in imitation of "Take the F" based on your cross-town commute or focusing on a particular neighborhood in the city or town where you live. Try to convey to your reader all of the sense impressions associated with this journey or part of town — including, if you can, auditory, olfactory, and tactile impressions as well as visual details. Feel free to combine sense images, similes, metaphors, and brief personal anecdotes to express your experience of this commonplace part of your daily life.

2. Write an essay comparing the techniques that Frazier uses to convey the sensuous experience of life in New York with those used by Barry Lopez to capture the sensuous experience of touch in "A Passage of the Hands" (p. 27). To what extent do these authors use naming, concrete detail, simile, and metaphor to express subjective mental states? What role does storytelling play in their writing? Which essay seems more objective? Which more personal? Why?

A Passage of the Hands

BARRY LOPEZ

Touch has been described as the most primitive and the most personal of the five senses. Our ability to touch links us to the petri dish universe of the amoeba, where tactile sense receptors signal the location of potential predators, mates, or morsels of food. Touch also links us to the human beings we love most—our parents, siblings, friends, and lovers. As Harvard-based psychologist Ashley Montigue notes in his famous study of the subject, touch plays a central role in the emotional and physical development of every human being: deprive children of caresses during their first few months of life and they will tend to weigh less, be more susceptible to disease, and show slower rates of mental development than their better-cared-for counterparts. We turn to touch to verify what's real and to validate the evidence of our other, less immediate senses. When you see something looming before you in the darkness, you reach out to touch it to determine if it's a solid object or just a play of shadows; when you're reunited with friends after a long separation, you touch them to assure yourself that they are really there beside you "in the flesh."

Touch is so central to our sense of self, it seems odd that the vocabulary of touching is so poor. Once a writer has exhausted a short list of general words like *rough, smooth, coarse,* and *silky,* there's little else to say without recourse to simile or metaphor—a fact that seems especially ironic since writers use the organ of touch—the hand—as the tool of their art. In this selection, Barry Lopez (b. 1945) offers one solution to the problem of capturing the meaning of touch in words. In this essay from *About This Life: Journeys on the Threshold of Memory* (1997), Lopez recounts the education of his sense of touch by exploring the role that his hands have played in shaping his sense of self. Lopez's essay also offers a good example of how verbal imagery can be used to evoke the whole spectrum of tactile experience, from the subtle to the searing. A prolific writer and recipient of the National Book Award, Lopez has authored five books of fiction and six of nonfiction. His work has also been published regularly in leading magazines such as the *Atlantic Monthly* and *Harper's,* where he serves as contributing editor. His most recent book is *Light Action in the Caribbean: Stories* (2000).

BEFORE READING

Write a brief journal entry about a powerful early childhood memory you have of touching something remarkable. What was it? What did it feel like? Why do you think this sense impression has remained alive in your memory all these years? Compare your tactile recollections in groups to see if you can discover any similarities in these early experiences.

My hands were born breech in the winter of 1945, two hours before sunrise. Sitting with them today, two thousand miles and more from that spot, turning each one slowly in bright sunshine, watching the incisive light raise short, pale lines from old cuts, and seeing the odd cant of the left ring finger, I know they have a history, though I cannot remember where it starts. As they began, they gripped whatever might hold me upright, surely caressed and kneaded my mother's breasts, yanked at the restrictions of pajamas. And then they learned to work buttons, to tie shoelaces and lift the milk glass, to work together.

The pressure and friction of a pencil as I labored down the spelling of words right-handed raised the oldest permanent mark, a callus on the third joint of the middle finger. I remember no trying accident to either hand in these early years, though there must have been glass cuts, thorn punctures, spider bites, nails torn to the cuticle, scrapes from bicycle falls, pin blisters from kitchen grease, splinters, nails blackened from door pinches, pain lingering from having all four fingers forced backward at once, an the first true weariness, coming from work with lumber and stones, with tools made for larger hands.

It is from these first years, five and six and seven, that I am able to remember so well, or perhaps the hands themselves remember, a great range of texture—the subtle corrugation of cardboard boxes, the slickness of the oilcloth on the kitchen table, the shuddering bend of a horse's short-haired belly, the even give in warm wax, the raised oak grain in my school-desk top, the fuzziness of dead bumblebees, the coarseness of sheaves immediate to the polished silk of unhusked corn, the burnish of rake handles and bucket bails, the rigidness of the bony crest rising beneath the skin of a dog's head, the tackiness of flypaper, the sharpness of saws and ice picks.

It is impossible to determine where in any such specific memory, of course, texture gives way to heft, to shape, to temperature. The coolness of a camellia petal seems inseparable from that texture, warmth from the velvet rub of a horse's nose, heft from a brick's dry burr. And what can be said, as the hand recalls the earliest touch and exploration, of how texture changes with depth? Not alone the press of the palm on a dog's head or fingers boring to the roots of wool on a sheep's flank, but of, say, what happens with an orange: the hands work in concert to disassemble the fruit, running a thumb over the beaded surface of the skin, plying the soft white flay of the interior, the string net of fiber clinging to the translucent skin cases, dividing the yielding grain of the flesh beneath, with its hard, wrinkled seeds. And, further, how is one to separate these textures from a memory of the burst of fragrance as the skin is torn, or from the sound of the sections being parted—to say nothing of the taste, juice dripping from the chin, or the urge to devour, then, even the astringent skin, all initiated by the curiosity of the hands?

Looking back, it's easy to see that the education of the hands (and so the person) begins like a language: a gathering of simple words, the assembly of simple sentences, all this leading eventually to the forging of instructive metaphors. Afterward nothing can truly be separated, to stand alone in the hands' tactile memory. Taking the lay of the dog's fur, the slow petting of the loved dog is the increasingly complicated heart speaking with the hand.

Still, because of an occasional, surprising flair of the hands, the insistence of their scarred surfaces, it is possible for me to sustain the illusion that they have a history independent of the mind's perception, the heart's passion; a history of gathering what appeals, of expressing exasperation with their own stupidity, of faith in the accrual of brute work. If my hands began to explore complex knowledge by seeking and sorting texture — I am compelled to believe this — then the first names my memory truly embraced came from the hands' differentiating among fruits and woven fabrics.

Growing on farms and in orchards and truck gardens around our home in rural California was a chaos of fruit: navel and Valencia oranges, tangerines, red and yellow grapefruit, pomegranates, lemons, pomelos, greengage and damson plums, freestone and cling peaches, apricots, figs, tangelos, Concord and muscadine grapes. Nectarines, Crenshaw, casaba, and honeydew melons, watermelons, and cantaloupes. My boyish hands knew the planting, the pruning, the picking, and the packing of some of these fruits, the force and the touch required. I sought them all out for the resilience of their ripeness and knew the different sensation of each — pips, radius, cleavage. I ate even tart pomegranates with ardor, from melons I dug gobs of succulent meat with mouth and fingers. Slicing open a cantaloupe or a melon with a knife, I would hesitate always at the sight of the cleft fistula of seeds. It unsettled me, as if it were the fruit's knowing brain.

The fabrics were my mother's. They were stacked in bolts catawampus on open shelves and in a closet in a room in our small house where she both slept and sewed, where she laid out skirts, suits, and dresses for her customers. Lawn, organdy, batiste, and other fine cottons; cambric and gingham; silks — moiré, crepe de chine, taffeta; handkerchief and other weights of linen; light wools like gabardine; silk and cotton damasks; silk and rayon satins; cotton and wool twills; velvet; netted cloths like tulle. These fabrics differed not only in their texture and weave, in the fineness of their threads, but in the way they passed or reflected light, in their drape, and, most obviously from a distance, in their color and pattern.

I handled these fabrics as though they were animal skins, opening out bolts on the couch when Mother was working, holding them against the window light, raking them with my nails, crumpling them in my fist, then furling them as neatly as I could. Decades later, reading "samite of Ethnise" and "uncut rolls of brocade of Tabronit" in a paperback translation of Wolfram von Eschenbach's *Parzival*,° I watched my free hand rise up to welcome the touch of these cloths.

It embarrassed and confounded me that other boys knew so little of cloth, 10 and mocked the knowledge; but growing up with orchards and groves and vine fields, we shared a conventional, peculiar intimacy with fruit. We pelted one another with rotten plums and the green husks of walnuts. We flipped

Parzival: French medieval epic poem.

gourds and rolled melons into the paths of oncoming, unsuspecting cars. This prank of the hand—throwing, rolling, flipping—meant nothing without the close companionship of the eye. The eye measured the distance, the crossing or closing speed of the object, and then the hand—the wrist snapping, the fingers' tips guiding to the last—decided upon a single trajectory, measured force, and then a rotten plum hit someone square in the back or sailed wide, or the melon exploded beneath a tire or rolled cleanly to the far side of the road. And we clapped in glee and wiped our hands on our pants.

In these early years—eight and nine and ten—the hands became attuned to each other. They began to slide the hafts of pitchforks and pry bars smoothly, to be more aware of each other's placement for leverage and of the slight difference in strength. It would be three or four more years before, playing the infield in baseball, I would sense the spatial and temporal depth of awareness my hands had of each other, would feel, short-hopping a sharp grounder blind in front of third base, flicking the ball from gloved-left to bare-right hand, making the cross-body throw, the balletic poise of the still fingers after the release, would sense how mindless the beauty of it was.

I do not remember the ascendancy of the right hand. It was the one I was forced to write with, though by that time the right hand could already have asserted itself, reaching always first for a hammer or a peach. As I began to be judged according to the performance of my right hand alone—how well it imitated the Palmer cursive,° how legibly it totaled mathematical figures—perhaps here is where the hands first realized how complicated their relationship would become. I remember a furious nun grabbing my six-year-old hands in prayer and wrenching the right thumb from under the left. Right over left, she insisted. *Right over left.* Right over left in praying to God.

In these early years my hands were frequently folded in prayer. They, too, collected chickens' eggs, contended with the neat assembly of plastic fighter planes, picked knots from bale twine, clapped chalkboard erasers, took trout off baited hooks, and trenched flower beds. They harbored and applauded homing pigeons. When I was eleven, my mother married again and we moved east to New York. The same hands took on new city tasks, struggled more often with coins and with tying the full Windsor knot.° Also, now, they pursued a more diligent and precise combing of my hair. And were in anxious anticipation of touching a girl. And that caress having been given, one hand confirmed the memory later with the other in exuberant disbelief. They overhauled and pulled at each other like puppies.

I remember from these years—fourteen and fifteen and sixteen—marveling at the dexterity of my hands. In games of catch, one hand tipped the falling ball to the other, to be seized firmly in the same instant the body crashed to the ground. Or the hands changed effortlessly on the dribble at the start of a fast break in basketball. I remember disassembling, cleaning, and

Palmer cursive: A style of handwriting.

the full Windsor knot: A complicated knot used for men's ties.

reassembling a two-barrel carburetor, knowing the memory of where all the parts fit was within my hands. I can recall the baton reversal of a pencil as I wrote then erased, wrote then erased, composing sentences on a sheet of paper. And I remember how the hands, so clever with a ball, so deft with a pair of needle-nose pliers, fumbled attaching a cymbidium orchid so close to a girl's body, so near the mysterious breast.

By now, sixteen or so, my hands were as accustomed to books, to maga-   15
zines, newspapers, and typing paper, as they were to mechanic's tools and baseballs. A blade in my pocketknife was a shape my fingers had experienced years earlier as an oleander leaf. The shape of my fountain pen I knew first as a eucalyptus twig, drawing make-believe roads in wet ground. As my hands had once strained to bring small bluegills to shore, now they reeled striped bass from the Atlantic's surf. As they had once entwined horses' manes, now they twirled girls' ponytails. I had stripped them in those years of manure, paint, axle grease, animal gore, plaster, soap suds, and machine oil; I had cleaned them of sap and tar and putty, of pond scum and potting soil, of fish scales and grass stains. The gashes and cuts had healed smoothly. They were lithe, strenuous. The unimpeded reach of the fingers away from one another in three planes, their extreme effective span, was a subtle source of confidence and wonder. They showed succinctly the physical intelligence of the body. They expressed so unmistakably the vulnerability in sexual desire. They drew so deliberately the curtains of my privacy.

One July afternoon I stood at an ocean breakwater with a friend, firing stones one after another in long, beautiful arcs a hundred feet to the edge of the water. We threw for accuracy, aiming to hit small breaking waves with cutting *thwips*. My friend tired of the game and lay down on his towel. A few moments later I turned and threw in a single motion just as he leaped to his feet. The stone caught him full in the side of the head. He was in the hospital a month with a fractured skull, unable to speak clearly until he was operated on. The following summer we were playing baseball together again, but I could not throw hard or accurately for months after the accident, and I shied away completely from a growing desire to be a pitcher.

My hands lost innocence or gained humanity that day, as they had another day when I was pulled off my first dog, screaming, my hands grasping feebly in the air, after he'd been run over and killed in the road. Lying awake at night I sometimes remember throwing the near deadly stone, or punching a neighbor's horse with my adolescent fist, or heedlessly swinging a 16-gauge shotgun, leading quail—if I hadn't forgotten to switch off the trigger safety, I would have shot an uncle in the head. My hands lay silent at my sides those nights. No memory of their grace or benediction could change their melancholy stillness.

While I was in college I worked two summers at a ranch in Wyoming. My hands got the feel of new tools—foot nips, frog pick, fence pliers, skiving knife. I began to see that the invention, dexterity, and quickness of the hands could take many directions in a man's life; and that a man should be attentive to what his hands loved to do, and so learn not only what he might be good at for a long time but what would make him happy. It pleased me to smooth every wrinkle from a saddle blanket before I settled a saddle squarely on a horse's back. And I liked, too, to turn the thin pages of a Latin edition of the *Aeneid*° as I slowly accomplished them that first summer, feeling the impression of the type. It was strengthening to work with my hands, with ropes and bridles and hay bales, with double-bitted axes and bow saws, currying horses, scooping grain, adding my hands' oil to wooden door latches in the barn, calming horses at the foot of a loading ramp, adjusting my hat against the sun, buckling my chaps on a frosty morning. I'd watch the same hand lay a book lovingly on a night table and reach for the lamp's pull cord.

I had never learned to type, but by that second summer, at nineteen, I was writing out the first few stories longhand in pencil. I liked the sound and the sight of the writing going on, the back pressure through my hand. When I had erased and crossed out and rewritten a story all the way through, I would type it out slowly with two or sometimes four fingers, my right thumb on the space bar, as I do to this day. Certain keys and a spot on the space bar are worn through to metal on my typewriters from the oblique angles at which my fingernails strike them.

Had I been able to grasp it during those summers in Wyoming, I might have   20
seen that I couldn't get far from writing stories and physical work, either activity, and remain happy. It proved true that in these two movements my hands found their chief joy, aside from the touching of other human beings. But I could not see it then. My hands only sought out and gave in to the pleasures.

I began to travel extensively while I was in college. Eventually I visited many places, staying with different sorts of people. Most worked some substantial part of the day with their hands. I gravitated toward the company of cowboys and farmers both, to the work of loggers and orchardists, but mostly toward the company of field biologists, college-educated men and women who worked long days open to the weather, studying the lives of wild animals. In their presence, sometimes for weeks at a time, occasionally in stupefying cold or under significant physical strain, I helped wherever I could and wrote in my journal what had happened and, sometimes, what I thought of what had happened. In this way my hands came to know the prick and compression of syringes, the wiring and soldering of radio collars, the arming of anesthetizing guns, the setting of traps and snares, the deployment of otter trawls and plankton tows, the operation of calipers and tripod scales, and the manipulation of various kinds of sieves and packages used to sort and store parts of dead animals, parts created with the use of skinning and butchering knives, with bone saws, teasing needles, tweezers, poultry shears, and hemostatic clamps. My hands were in a dozen kinds of blood, including my own.

Aeneid: Latin epic poem by Virgil (70–19 B.C.) featuring the adventures of Aeneas, legendary founder of Rome.

Everywhere I journeyed I marveled at the hands of other creatures, at how their palms and digits revealed history, at how well they performed tasks, at the elegant and incontrovertible beauty of their design. I cradled the paws of wolves and polar bears, the hooves of caribou, the forefeet of marine iguanas, the fore-flippers of ringed seals and sperm whales, the hands of wallabies, of deer mice. Palpating the tendons, muscles, and bones beneath the skin or fur, I gained a rough understanding of the range of ability, of expression. I could feel where a broken bone had healed and see from superficial scars something of what a life must have been like. Deeper down, with mammals during a necropsy, I could see how blood vessels and layers of fat in a paw or in a flipper were arranged to either rid the creature of its metabolic heat or hoard it. I could see the evidence of arthritis in its phalanges, how that could come to me.

I have never touched a dead human, nor do I wish to. The living hands of another person, however, draw me, as strongly as the eyes. What is their history? What are their emotions? What longing is there? I can follow a cabinet-maker's hands for hours as they verify and detect, shave, fit, and rub; or a chef's hands adroitly dicing vegetables or shaping pastry. And who has not known faintness at the sight of a lover's hand? What man has not wished to take up the hands of the woman he loves and pore over them with reverence and curiosity? Who has not in reverie wished to love the lover's hands?

Years after my mother died I visited her oldest living friend. We were doing dishes together and she said, "You have your mother's hands." Was that like-ness a shade of love? And if now I say out of respect for my hands I would buy only the finest tools, is that, too, not love?

The hands evolve, of course. The creases deepen and the fingers begin to 25 move two or three together at a time. If the hands of a man are put to hard use, the fingers grow blunt. They lose dexterity and the skin calluses over like hide. Hardly a pair of man's hands known to me comes to mind without a bro-ken or dislocated finger, a lost fingertip, a permanently crushed nail. Most women my age carry scars from kitchen and housework, drawer pinches, scalds, knife and glass cuts. We hardly notice them. Sunlight, wind, and weather obscure many of these scars, but I believe the memory of their occurrence never leaves the hands. When I awaken in the night and sense my hands cupped together under the pillow, or when I sit somewhere on a porch, idly watching wind crossing a ripening field, and look down to see my hands nested in my lap as if asleep like two old dogs, it is not hard for me to believe they know. They remember all they have done, all that has happened to them, the ways in which they have been surprised or worked themselves free of des-perate trouble, or lost their grip and so caused harm. It's not hard to believe they remember the heads patted, the hands shaken, the apples peeled, the hair braided, the wood split, the gears shifted, the flesh gripped and stroked, and that they convey their feelings to each other.

In recent years my hands have sometimes been very cold for long stretches. It takes little cold now to entirely numb thumbs and forefingers. They cease to speak what they know. When I was thirty-one, I accidentally cut the base of my left thumb, severing nerves, leaving the thumb confused about what was cold, what was hot, and whether or not it was touching something or only thought so. When I was thirty-six, I was helping a friend butcher a whale. We'd been up for many hours under twenty-four-hour arctic daylight and were tired. He glanced away and without thinking drove the knife into my wrist. It was a clean wound, easy to close, but with it I lost the nerves to the right thumb. Over the years each thumb has regained some sensitivity, and I believe the hands are more sympathetic to each other because of their similar wounds. The only obvious difference lies with the left hand. A broken metacarpal forced a rerouting of tendons to the middle and ring fingers as it healed and raised a boss of carpal bone tissue on the back of the hand.

At the base of the right thumb is a scar from a climbing accident. On the other thumb, a scar the same length from the jagged edge of a fuel-barrel pump. In strong sunlight, when there is a certain tension in the skin, as I have said, I can stare at my hands for a while, turning them slowly, and remember with them the days, the weather, the people present when some things happened that left scars behind. It brings forth affection for my hands. I recall how, long ago, they learned to differentiate between cotton and raw silk, between husks of the casaba and the honeydew melon, and how they thrilled to the wire bristle of a hog's back, how they clipped the water's surface in swimming-pool fights, how they painstakingly arranged bouquets, how they swung and lifted children. I have begun to wish they would speak to me, tell me stories I have forgotten.

I sit in a chair and look at the scars, the uneven cut of the nails, and reminisce. With them before me I grin as though we held something secret, remembering bad times that left no trace. I cut firewood for my parents once, winter in Alabama, swamping out dry, leafless vines to do so. Not until the next day did I realize the vines were poison ivy. The blisters grew so close and tight my hands straightened like paddles. I had to have them lanced to continue a cross-country trip, to dress and feed myself. And there have been days when my hands stiffened with cold so that I had to quit the work being done, sit it out and whimper with pain as they came slowly back to life. But these moments are inconsequential. I have looked at the pale, wrinkled hands of a drowned boy, and I have seen handless wrists.

If there were a way to speak directly to the hands, to allow them a language of their own, what I would most wish to hear is what they recall of human touch, of the first exploration of the body of another, the caresses, the cradling of breast, of head, of buttock. Does it seem to them as to me that we keep learning, even when the caressed body has been known for years? How do daydreams of an idealized body, one's own or another's, affect the hands' first tentative inquiry? Is the hand purely empirical? Does it apply an imagination? Does it retain a man's shyness, a boy's clumsiness? Do the hands anguish if there is no one to touch?

Tomorrow I shall pull blackberry vines and load a trailer with rotten 30
timber. I will call on my hands to help me dress, to turn the spigot for water for coffee, to pull the newspaper from its tube. I will put my hands in the river

and lift water where the sunlight is brightest, a playing with fractured light I never tire of. I will turn the pages of a book about the history of fire in Australia. I will sit at the typewriter, working through a story about a trip to Matagorda Island in Texas. I will ask my hands to undress me. Before I turn out the light, I will fold and set my reading glasses aside. Then I will cup my hands, the left in the right, and slide them under the pillow beneath my head, where they will speculate, as will I, about what we shall handle the next day, and dream, a spooling of their time we might later remember together and I, so slightly separated from them, might recognize.

EXPLORING THE TEXT

1. What does Lopez mean when he says that his hands have had their own education? What are the formative experiences of Lopez's hands? What do these tactile experiences tell us about him as a person?

2. How does Lopez convey the feeling of specific tactile experiences? Find two or three descriptive passages and explore the techniques he employs to express the sensation of touch.

3. Note Lopez's use of storytelling in this selection. Where does he pause in the description of his hands' education to introduce an anecdote? What purpose do stories serve in this essay?

4. At one point in the selection, Lopez says that "a man should be attentive to what his hands loved to do, and so learn not only what he might be good at for a long time but what would make him happy" (para. 18). To what extent does Lopez's depiction of the experience of touch reflect a particularly male perspective? How might "A Passage of the Hands" be different if it had been written by a woman?

FURTHER EXPLORATIONS

1. Examine the role that touch plays in Ian Frazier's "Take the F" (p. 18). How would you account for the relative lack of tactile imagery in Frazier's description of life in New York? Using Lopez's essay as a model, how might tactile experience be introduced to Frazier's essay?

2. Compare the education of Barry Lopez's hands with the education that Scott Russell Sanders receives through the tools he inherits from his father and grandfather (p. 142). What lessons do these men learn about life through their hands? What values, attitudes, and beliefs do they gain through their experiences of physical labor? To what extent do they experience and convey intimacy through touch?

3. How can the concepts of "remembering" and "remembered" selves as discussed by Susan Engel in "Then and Now: Creating a Self Through the Past" (p. 192) be applied to Lopez's reflection on the history of his hands? What "persona" does Lopez project of himself through this exercise in sense memory? What motives might underlie his decision to depict himself in this way?

4. Using Arnold M. Ludwig's discussion on the role that storytelling plays in the "composition" of individual identity (p. 292), discuss the various "roles," "plots,"

or "scripts" that Lopez employs to shape his self-image in this selection. What "models" might Lopez be emulating, consciously or unconsciously, in the way he presents himself?

ESSAY OPTIONS

1. Using Lopez's "A Passage of the Hands" as a model, write the history of your own hands, describing their education, development, and your relationship to them. Begin by brainstorming a list of memorable past experiences involving your hands or sense of touch. Freewrite about these initial memories, and let them suggest other recollections and stories. Think about the lessons you've learned about life through your hands and your sense of touch, and about the skills, values, attitudes and beliefs you've acquired through their use. Think about how your hands have shaped your sense of who you are today.

2. In "Taste: The Social Sense" (p. 36), Diane Ackerman explores how the sense of taste functions from what might be termed a "species perspective," rather than from the perspective of the individual. Using Lopez's reflection on the education of his hands as a point of departure, write an essay in which you compare the species functions of taste, as noted by Ackerman, with the functions of touch. To what extent are taste and touch similar as senses? What do they help us, as a species, do? What do they tell us about the nature of human relationships? About what it means to be a human being? About how we, as a species, relate to the natural world?

Taste: The Social Sense

DIANE ACKERMAN

Ever crave a mouthwatering slice of *fugu?* You might if you were born in Japan. *Fugu* is the flesh of the toxic puffer fish, an extraordinary delicacy that requires preparation by a specially trained sushi chef. Every year a number of diners who eat poorly prepared *fugu* slip into a coma before completing their meal, and yet, according to Diane Ackerman, people still line up to experience this potentially lethal gastronomic treat.

Human beings, it seems, are obsessed with the sense of taste. Each year the publishing industry cranks out hundreds of cookbooks celebrating the latest gastronomic fads. Bookstore news racks are lined with "gourmet" magazines offering mouthwatering descriptions of culinary achievements from exotic locales all over the globe. Newspapers carry weekly food sections and restaurant reviews so we'll know where the seafood tastes best and who sells the juiciest steaks in town. Taste is universal and local: every culture has its own culinary biases, but all cultures celebrate taste. As Diane Ackerman observes in this selection from her classic treatment of the human senses, taste is the "social sense." Perhaps more than vision, hearing, smell, and even touch, our sense of taste is born and educated in the context of the cultures we belong to, and taste is the one sense experience we habitually cultivate in company and compare with others. For Ackerman, however, taste is more than a simple marker of cultural boundaries: the existence of taste suggests something deeper—something unsettling—about the kind of creatures we human beings are. Ackerman (b. 1948) is a poet and the author of nine works of nonfiction, including *A Natural History of the Senses* (1991), the source of this essay. Her latest book is *The Senses of Animals: Poems* (2001).

BEFORE READING

In your journal, freewrite about the flavors you associate with your home culture. What tastes connect you with your family and your neighborhood? As an alternative, write about the most exotic experience of taste you've encountered in a cross-cultural situation. What was it? What was the situation? How did you handle it?

The other senses may be enjoyed in all their beauty when one is alone, but taste is largely social. Humans rarely choose to dine in solitude, and food has a powerful social component. The Bantu feel that exchanging food makes a contract between two people who then have a "clanship of porridge." We usually eat with our families, so it's easy to see how "breaking bread" together would symbolically link an outsider to a family group. Throughout the world, the stratagems of business take place over meals; weddings end with a feast; friends reunite at celebratory dinners; children herald their birthdays with ice cream and cake; religious ceremonies offer food in fear, homage, and sacrifice; wayfarers are welcomed with a meal. As Brillat-Savarin° says, "every . . . sociability . . . can be found assembled around the same table: love, friendship, business, speculation, power, importunity, patronage, ambition, intrigue . . ." If an event is meant to matter emotionally, symbolically, or mystically, food will be close at hand to sanctify and bind it. Every culture uses food as a sign of approval or commemoration, and some foods are even credited with supernatural powers, others eaten symbolically, still others eaten ritualistically, with ill fortune befalling dullards or skeptics who forget the recipe or get the order of events wrong. Jews attending a Seder° eat a horseradish dish to symbolize the tears shed by their ancestors when they were slaves in Egypt. Malays celebrate important events with rice, the inspirational center of their lives. Catholics and Anglicans take a communion of wine and wafer. The ancient Egyptians thought onions symbolized the many-layered universe, and swore oaths on an onion as we might on a Bible. Most cultures embellish eating with fancy plates and glasses, accompany it with parties, music, dinner theater, open-air barbecues, or other forms of revelry. Taste is an intimate sense. We can't taste things at a distance. And how we taste things, as well as the exact makeup of our saliva, may be as individual as our fingerprints.

Brillat-Savarin: Jean-Anthelme Brillat-Savarin (1755–1826) one of the first people to write seriously about food.

Seder: Feast commemorating the exodus of the Jews from Egypt, observed in Jewish households on the eve of the first day of Passover.

Food gods have ruled the hearts and lives of many peoples. Hopi Indians, who revere corn, eat blue corn for strength, but all Americans might be worshipping corn if they know how much of their daily lives depended on it. Margaret Visser, in *Much Depends on Dinner,* gives us a fine history of corn and its uses: livestock and poultry eat corn; the liquid in canned foods contains corn; corn is used in most paper products, plastics, and adhesives; candy, ice cream, and other goodies contain corn syrup; dehydrated and instant foods contain cornstarch; many familiar objects are made from corn products, brooms and corncob pipes to name only two. For the Hopis, eating corn is itself a form of reverence. I'm holding in my hand a beautifully carved Hopi corn kachina doll made from cottonwood; it represents one of the many spiritual essences of their world. Its cob-shaped body is painted ocher, yellow, black, and white, with dozens of squares drawn in a cross-section-of-a-kernel design, and abstract green leaves spearing up from below. The face has a long, black, rootlike nose, rectangular black eyes, a black ruff made of rabbit fur, white string corn-silk-like ears, brown bird-feather bangs, and two green, yellow, and ocher striped horns topped by rawhide tassels. A fine, soulful kachina, the ancient god Maïs stares back at me, tastefully imagined.

Throughout history, and in many cultures, *taste* has always had a double meaning. The word comes from the Middle English *tastern,* to examine by touch, test, or sample, and continues back to the Latin *taxare,* to touch sharply. So a taste was always a trial or test. People who have taste are those who have appraised life in an intensely personal way and found some of it sublime, the rest of it lacking. Something in bad taste tends to be obscene or vulgar. And we defer to professional critics of wine, food, art, and so forth, whom we trust to taste things for us because we think their taste more refined or educated than ours. A companion is "one who eats bread with another," and people sharing food as a gesture of peace or hospitality like to sit around and chew the fat.

The first thing we taste is milk from our mother's breast,[1] accompanied by love and affection, stroking, a sense of security, warmth, and well-being, our first intense feelings of pleasure. Later on she will feed us solid food from her hands, or even chew food first and press it into our mouths, partially digested. Such powerful associations do not fade easily, if at all. We say "food" as if it were a simple thing, an absolute like rock or rain to take for granted. But it is a big source of pleasure in most lives, a complex realm of satisfaction both physiological and emotional, much of which involves memories of childhood. Food must taste good, must reward us, or we would not stoke the furnace in each of our cells. We must eat to live, as we must breathe. But breathing is involuntary, finding food is not; it takes energy and planning, so it must tantalize us out of our natural torpor. It must decoy us out of bed in the morning and prompt us to put on constricting clothes, go to work, and perform tasks we may not enjoy for eight hours a day, five days a week, just to "earn our daily bread," or be "worth our salt," if you like, where the word *salary* comes from. And, because we are omnivores, many tastes must appeal to us, so that we'll try new foods. As children grow, they meet regularly throughout the day—at mealtimes—to hear grown-up talk, ask questions, learn about customs, language, and the world. If language didn't arise at mealtimes, it certainly evolved and became more fluent there, as it did during group hunts.

We tend to see our distant past through a reverse telescope that compresses it: a short time as hunter-gatherers, a long time as "civilized" people. But civilization is a recent stage of human life, and, for all we know, it may not be any great achievement. It may not even be the final stage. We have been alive on this planet as recognizable humans for about two million years, and for all but the last two or three thousand we've been hunter-gatherers. We may sing in choirs and park our rages behind a desk, but we patrol the world with many of a hunter-gatherer's drives, motives, and skills. These aren't knowable truths. Should an alien civilization ever contact us, the greatest gift they could give us would be a set of home movies: films of our species at each stage in our evolution. Consciousness, the great poem of matter, seems so unlikely, so impossible, and yet here we are with our loneliness and our giant dreams. Speaking into the perforations of a telephone receiver as if through the screen of a confessional, we do sometimes share our emotions with a friend, but usually this is too disembodied, too much like yelling into the wind. We prefer to talk *in person,* as if we could temporarily slide into their feelings. Our friend first offers us food, drink. It is a symbolic act, a gesture that says: *This food will nourish your body as I will nourish your soul.* In hard times, or in the wild, it also says *I will endanger my own life by parting with some of what I must consume to survive.* Those desperate times may be ancient history, but the part of us forged in such trials accepts the token drink and piece of cheese and is grateful.

Food and Sex

What would the flutterings of courtship be without a meal? As the deliciously sensuous and ribald tavern scene in Fielding's *Tom Jones*° reminds us, a meal can be the perfect arena for foreplay. Why is food so sexy? Why does a woman refer to a handsome man as a real dish? Or a French girl call her lover *mon petit chou* (my little cabbage)? Or an American man call his girlfriend cookie? Or a British man describe a sexy woman as a bit of crumpet (a flat, toasted griddlecake well lubricated with butter)? Or a tart? Sexual hunger and physical hunger have always been allies. Rapacious needs, they have coaxed and driven us through famine and war, to bloodshed and serenity, since our earliest days.

Looked at in the right light, any food might be thought aphrodisiac. Phallic-shaped foods such as carrots, leeks, cucumbers, pickles, sea cucumbers (which become tumescent when soaked), eels, bananas, and asparagus all have been prized as aphrodisiacs at one time or another, as were oysters and figs because they reminded people of female genitalia; caviar because it was a female's eggs; rinoceros horn, hyena eyes, hippopotamus snout, alligator tail,

---

Fielding's *Tom Jones:* Eighteenth-century English novel by Henry Fielding (1707–1754), containing a celebrated seduction scene over dinner.

camel hump, swan genitals, dove brains, and goose tongues, on the principle that anything so rare and exotic must have magical powers; prunes (which were offered free in Elizabethan brothels); peaches (because of their callipygous rumps?); tomatoes, called "love apples," and thought to be Eve's temptation in the Garden of Eden; onions and potatoes, which look testicular, as well as "prairie oysters," the cooked testicles of a bull; and mandrake root, which looks like a man's thighs and penis. Spanish fly, the preferred aphrodisiac of the Marquis de Sade,° with which he laced the bonbons he fed prostitutes and friends, is made by crushing a southern European beetle. It contains a gastrointestinal irritant and also produces a better blood flow, the combination of which brings on a powerful erection of either the penis or the clitoris, but also damages the kidneys; it can even be fatal. Musk, chocolate, and truffles also have been considered aphrodisiac and, for all we know, they might well be. But, as sages have long said, the sexiest part of the body and the best aphrodisiac in the world is the imagination.

Primitive peoples saw creation as a process both personal and universal, the earth's yielding food, humans (often molded from clay or dust) burgeoning with children. Rain falls from the sky and impregnates the ground, which brings forth fruit and grain from the tawny flesh of the earth—an earth whose mountains look like reclining women, and whose springs spurt like healthy men. Fertility rituals, if elaborate and frenzied enough, could encourage Nature's bounty. Cooks baked meats and breads in the shape of genitals, especially penises, and male and female statues with their sexual organs exaggerated presided over orgiastic festivities where sacred couples copulated in public. A mythic Gaia° poured milk from her breasts and they became the galaxies. The ancient Venus figures° with global breasts, swollen bellies, and huge buttocks and thighs symbolized the female life-force, mother to crops and humans. The earth itself was a goddess, curvy and ripe, radiant with fertility, aspill with riches. People have thought the Venus figures imaginative exaggerations, but women of that time may indeed have resembled them, all breasts, belly, and rump. When pregnant, they would have bulged into quite an array of shapes.

Food is created by the sex of plants or of animals; and we find it sexy. When we eat an apple or peach, we are eating the fruit's placenta. But, even if that weren't so, and we didn't subconsciously associate food with sex, we would still find it sexy for strictly physical reasons. We use the mouth for many things—to talk and kiss, as well as to eat. The lips, tongue, and genitals all have the same neural receptors, called Krause's end bulbs, which make them ultrasensitive, highly charged. There's a similarity of response.

Marquis de Sade: Count Donatien de Sade (1740–1814), infamous for his writings about sexual aberrations.

Gaia: The earth mother goddess in Greek mythology.

Venus figures: Sculptured female figures from the Neolithic era associated with fertility cults.

A man and woman sit across from one another in a dimly lit restaurant.   10
A small bouquet of red-and-white spider lilies sweetens the air with a cinna-
monlike tingle. A waiter passes with a plate of rabbit sausage in molé sauce.
At the next table, a blueberry soufflé oozes scent. Oysters on the half shell,
arranged on a large platter of shaved ice, one by one polish the woman's
tongue with silken saltiness. A fennel-scented steam rises from thick crabcakes
on the man's plate. Small loaves of fresh bread breathe sweetly. Their hands
brush as they both reach for the bread. He stares into her eyes, as if filling
them with molten lead. They both know where this delicious prelude will lead.
"I'm so hungry," she whispers.

The Omnivore's Picnic

You have been invited to dinner at the home of extraterrestrials, and asked to
bring friends. Being considerate hosts, they first inquire if you have any dietary
allergies or prohibitions, and then what sort of food would taste good to you.
What do humans eat? they ask. Images cascade through your mind, a cornu-
copia of plants, animals, minerals, liquids, and solids, in a vast array of
cuisines. The Masai enjoy drinking cow's blood. Orientals eat stir-fried puppy.
Germans eat rancid cabbage (sauerkraut), Americans eat decaying cucumbers
(pickles), Italians eat whole deep-fried songbirds, Vietnamese eat fermented
fish dosed with chili peppers, Japanese and others eat fungus (mushrooms),
French eat garlic-soaked snails. Upper-class Aztecs ate roasted dog (a hairless
variety named *xquintli,* which is still bred in Mexico). Chinese of the Chou
dynasty liked rats, which they called "household deer,"[2] and many people still
do eat rodents, as well as grasshoppers, snakes, flightless birds, kangaroos, lobsters, snails, and bats. Unlike most other animals, which fill a small yet ample
niche in the large web of life on earth, humans are omnivorous. The Earth
offers perhaps 20,000 edible plants alone. A poor season for eucalpytus will
wipe out a population of koala bears, which have no other food source. But
human beings are Nature's great ad libbers and revisers. Diversity is our delight. In time of drought, we can ankle off to a new locale, or break open a cactus, or dig a well. When plagues of locusts destroy our crops, we can forage on
wild plants and roots. If our herds die, we find protein in insects, beans, and
nuts. Not that being an omnivore is easy. A koala bear doesn't have to worry
about whether or not its next mouthful will be toxic. In fact, eucalyptus is
highly poisonous, but a koala has an elaborately protective gut, so it just eats
eucalyptus, exactly as its parents did. Cows graze without fear on grass and
grain. But omnivores are anxious eaters. They must continually test new foods
to see if they're palatable and nutritious, running the risk of inadvertently poisoning themselves. They must take chances on new flavors, and, doing so, they
frequently acquire a taste for something offbeat that, though nutritious, isn't
the sort of thing that might normally appeal to them — chili peppers (which
Columbus introduced to Europe), tobacco, alcohol, coffee, artichokes, or
mustard, for instance. When we were hunter-gatherers, we ate a great variety

of foods. Some of us still do, but more often we add spices to what we know, or find at hand, *for variety,* as we like to say. Monotony isn't our code. It's safe, in some ways, but in others it's more dangerous. Most of us prefer our foods cooked to the steaminess of freshly killed prey. We don't have ultrasharp carnivore's teeth, but we don't need them. We've created sharp tools. We do have incisor teeth for slicing fruits, and molars for crushing seeds and nuts, as well as canines for ripping flesh. At times, we eat nasturtiums and pea pods and even the effluvia from the mammary glands of cows, churned until it curdles, or frozen into a solid and attached to pieces of wood.

Our hosts propose a picnic, since their backyard is a meadow lit by two suns, and they welcome us and our friends. Our Japanese friend chooses the appetizer: sushi, including shrimp still alive and wriggling. Our French friend suggests a baguette, or better still croissants, which have an unlikely history, which he insists on telling everyone: to celebrate Austria's victory against the invading Ottoman Turks, bakers created pastry in the shape of the crescent on the Turkish flag, so that the Viennese could devour their enemies at table as they had on the battlefield. Croissants soon spread to France and, during the 1920s, traveled with other French ways to the United States. Our Amazonian friend chooses the main course—nuptial kings and queens of leaf-cutter ants, which taste like walnut butter, followed by roasted turtle and sweet-fleshed piranha. Our German friend insists that we include some spaetzle and a loaf of darkest pumpernickel bread, which gets its name from the verb *pumpern,* "to break wind," and *Nickel,* "the devil," because it was thought to be so hard to digest that even the devil would fart if he ate it. Our Tasaday friend wants some natek, a starchy paste his people make from the insides of caryota palm trees. The English cousin asks for a small platter of potted ox tongues, very aged blue cheese, and, for dessert, trifle—whipped cream and slivered almonds on top of a jam-and-custard pudding thick with sherry-soaked lady-fingers.

To finish our picnic lunch, our Turkish friend proposes coffee in the Turkish style—using a mortar and pestle to break up the beans, rather than milling them. To be helpful, he prepares it for us all, pouring boiling water over coffee grounds through a silver sieve into a pot. He brings this to a light boil, pours it through the sieve again, and offers us some of the clearest, brightest coffee we've ever tasted. According to legend, he explains, coffee was discovered by a ninth-century shepherd, who one day realized that his goats were becoming agitated whenever they browsed on the berries of certain bushes. For four hundred years, people thought only to chew the berries. Raw coffee doesn't brew into anything special, but in the thirteenth century someone decided to roast the berries, which releases a pungent oil and the mossy-bitter aroma now so familiar to us. Our Indian friend passes round cubes of sugar, which we are instructed to let melt on the tongue as we sip our coffee, and our minds roam back to the first recorded instance of sugar, in the Atharvaveda, a sacred Hindu text from 800 B.C., which describes a royal crown made of glittering sugar crystals. Then he circulates a small dish of coriander seeds, and we pinch a few in our fingers, set them on our tongues, and feel our mouths freshen from the aromatic tang. A perfect picnic. We thank our hosts for laying on such a splendid feast, and invite them to our house for dinner next. "What do jujubarians eat?" we ask. . . .

The Heart of Craving

It's not to my taste, we say, by which we mean a hankering or preference, and it's amazing how individual taste can be — but only if survival is not at stake. When I worked on a cattle ranch in New Mexico, I used to eat in the cookhouse with the rest of the cowhands, most of whom were Mexican-Americans with little schooling and absolutely no education in nutrition. Their workdays were so arduous that their bodies took over for them, dictating what they needed to survive the physical labor and blinding heat of the day. Each morning, they would eat pure protein — as many as six eggs at once, with two glasses of whole milk, and bacon — for breakfast. Although they drank a lot of water and lemonade, they spurned coffee, tea, or other drinks with caffeine. They ate almost no desserts and very little sugar, but each meal included the hottest of hot peppers. Often they would spread them on bread to make a scalding jalapeño-pepper sandwich. At night they ate lightly, and the meal consisted mainly of carbohydrates. If asked, they would say simply that they ate what tasted good, what they liked to eat, but their taste in food had clearly evolved to fuel the rigors of their life.

This self-protective yen is also true on a larger scale: whole countries prefer cuisines that help them keep cool (in the Middle East), or sedated (in the tropics), or protect them against regional illnesses — as Pete Farb and George Armelagos say in their book which, like Pullars', is entitled *Consuming Passions*, "Ethiopian *chow*, consisting primarily of chili but containing up to fifteen other spices, has been shown to inhibit almost completely staphylococcus, salmonella, and other microorganisms." Hot peppers contain high amounts of beta carotene (converted by the body into vitamin A), which has antioxidant cancer-fighting properties, as well as capsaicin, which makes one sweat, lowering the body temperature. Consider the age-old English habit of drinking tea with milk: tea contains a lot of tannin, which is toxic and can cause cancer, but milk protein reacts with the tannin in a protective way, preventing the body from absorbing it. Esophagal cancer is much higher in countries like Japan, where tea is drunk unadulterated, than it is in England, where people add a milk buffer to it. Farb and Armelagos describe some interesting additional national cravings:

> Peasants in Mexico prepare maize for making tortillas by soaking it in water in which they have previously dissolved particles of limestone, a practice which we certainly consider unusual. But . . . this preparation multiplies the calcium content to at least twenty times that in the original maize while possibly increasing the availability of certain amino acids — important because the peasants inhabit

15

an environment where animal foods are scarce. . . . In places in Africa people eat fish wrapped in a banana leaf whose acidity dissolves the fish bones and thereby makes the calcium in them available; the French practice of cooking fish with sorrel has the same effect. Putrefied food . . . eaten in numerous societies . . . enhances the nutritive value . . . since the bacteria that cause putrefaction manufacture such vitamins as B[1]. . . .

There's no question that, at least for certain nutrients, if a person is in true need, some gustatory yen or body wisdom takes over. Patients with Addison's disease become ill because of a deficiency of the adrenal hormones. They've been known to crave salt with a vengeance, subconsciously medicating themselves. One way they do this is by eating large amounts of licorice, which contains glasorisic acid, a substance that causes sodium retention, and while doctors certainly don't prescribe it, they find that Addison's sufferers feel better if they eat a lot of licorice.

Some Quechua Indians of Peru subsist largely on potatoes, but because the growing season is so short, they're often forced to eat only partially ripened ones. Potatoes contain solanine, a bitter toxic alkaloid, but the Quechuas find that if they smear kaolin clay on the potatoes, it masks the bitterness and they don't get upset stomachs. The kaolin also detoxifies the alkaloids in the potatoes, making them simultaneously tastier and more nutritious.

It's odd to think of people eating dirt. Salt is the only rock we really seem to enjoy, but that's because we are small marine environments on the move, with salt in our blood, our urine, our flesh, our tears. However, you can still find clay for sale in some of the open-air markets in the southern United States. Pregnant women buy it. In Africa, pregnant women occasionally eat termite mounds. It's thought that they're after calcium and certain other minerals missing from their diet. In Ghana, some villages support themselves by selling egg-shaped balls of clay, which are rich in potassium, magnesium, zinc, copper, calcium, iron, and other minerals. A pregnant woman's craving for dairy products makes good nutritional sense, because if the fetus doesn't get enough calcium, it will take it from the mother's bones and teeth. Most cultures have taboos for pregnant women, certain fish or fungi or spices they must not eat, but these are not the same as a woman's craving certain foods. The increased blood volume of a pregnant woman lowers her sodium level, and as a result she doesn't taste saltiness as easily as she did when she wasn't pregnant; she may crave really salty foods, like the legendary pickle. Among the many explanations for why pregnant women crave ice cream and other sweets, one of the most interesting modern theories is that they crave foods which produce the neurotransmitter serotonin, which they'll need to help withstand the pain of childbirth.

Some foods may stimulate endorphins—morphinelike painkillers produced by the brain—and give us a sense of comfort and calm. This is why, even though we know that salty foods, greasy foods, and candy and other sweets aren't good for us, we have a taste for them anyway. Neurobiologists suspect that endorphins and other neurochemicals control our hunger for certain kinds of foods. According to this thinking, when we eat sweets we flood our bodies with endorphins and feel tranquil. When people are under stress, and their need for endorphins goes up, they may crave a box of cookies. Since our hunger for fats, proteins, and carbohydrates is controlled by specific neurotransmitters, which can easily get out of balance, we need only binge to knock the neurotransmitters out of whack, which leads to further binging, further imbalances, and so on. In one experiment, depriving rats of their breakfast threw off their neurotransmitters and they gorged later in the day. . . .

Et Fugu, Bruté?° Food as Thrill-Seeking

A nation of sensation-addicts might dine as chic urbanites do, on rhubarb and   20
raspberry tortes, smoked lobster, and hisbiscus-wrapped monkfish, wiped with raspberry butter, baked in a clay oven, and then elevated briefly in mesquite smoke. When I was in college, I didn't eat goldfish or cram into Volkswagens, or chug whole bottles of vodka, but others did, in a neo–Roaring Twenties ennui. Shocking the bourgeoisie has always been the unstated encyclical° of college students and artists, and sometimes that includes grossing out society in a display of bizarre eating habits. One of the classic *Monty Python's Flying Circus*° sketches shows a chocolate manufacturer being cross-examined by policemen for selling chocolate-covered baby frogs, bones and all ("without the bones, they wouldn't be crunchy!" he whines), as well as insects, and other taboo animals sure to appal western taste buds. I've met field scientists of many persuasions who have eaten native foods like grasshoppers, leeches, or bats stewed in coconut milk, in part to be mannerly, in part out of curiosity, and I think in part to provide a good anecdote when they returned to the States. However, these are just nutritious foods that fall beyond our usual sphere of habit and custom.

We don't always eat foods for their taste, but sometimes for their feel. I once ate a popular duck dish in Amazonian Brazil, *pato no tucupi* (Portuguese for *pato*, "duck" + *no*, "within" + *tucupi*, "extracted juice of manioc") whose main attraction is that it's anesthetic: it makes your mouth as tingly numb as Benzedrine. The numbing ingredient is *jambu* (in Latin, *Spilanthes*), a yellow daisy that grows throughout Brazil and is sometimes used as a cold remedy. The effect was startling—it was as if my lips and whole mouth were vibrating. But many cultures have physically startling foods. I adore hot peppers and other spicy foods, ones that sandblast the mouth. We say "taste," when we

Et Fugu, Bruté?: A play on Caesar's question *"Et tu, Brute?"* (You too, Brutus?) at the moment of his assassination in William Shakespeare's *Julius Caesar.*

encyclical: In Roman Catholicism, a general letter sent by the Pope on church matters; hence, any official policy.

Monty Python's Flying Circus: A popular English television comedy series that aired from 1969 to 1974.

describe such a food to someone else, but what we're really talking about is a combination of touch, taste, and the absence of discomfort when the deadening or sandblasting finally stops. The thinnest line divides Szechwan hot-pepper sauce from being thrilling (causing your lips to tingle even after the meal is over), and being sulfurically hot enough to cause a gag response as you eat it.[3] A less extreme example is our liking for crunchy or crisp foods, like carrots, which have little taste but lots of noise and mouth action. One of the most successful foods on earth is Coca-Cola, a combination of intense sweetness, caffeine, and a prickly feeling against the nose that we find refreshing. It was first marketed as a mouthwash in 1888, and at that time contained cocaine, a serious refresher—an ingredient that was dropped in 1903. It is still flavored with extract of coca leaves, but minus the cocaine. Coffee, tea, tobacco, and other stimulants all came into use in the western world in the sixteenth and seventeenth centuries, and quickly percolated around Europe. Fashionable and addictive, they offered diners a real nervous-system jolt, either of narcotic calm or caffeine rush, and, unlike normal foods, they could be taken in doses, depending on how high one wished to get or how addicted one already was.

In Japan, specially licensed chefs prepare the rarest sashimi delicacy: the white flesh of the puffer fish, served raw and arranged in elaborate floral patterns on a platter. Diners pay large sums of money for the carefully prepared dish, which has a light, faintly sweet taste, like raw pompano. It had better be carefully prepared, because, unlike pompano, puffer fish is ferociously poisonous. You wouldn't think a puffer fish would need such chemical armor, since its main form of defense is to swallow great gulps of water and become so bloated it is too large for most predators to swallow. And yet its skin, ovaries, liver, and intestines contain tetrodotoxin, one of the most poisonous chemicals in the world, hundreds of times more lethal than strychnine or cyanide. A shred small enough to fit under one's fingernail could kill an entire family. Unless the poison is completely removed by a deft, experienced chef, the diner will die mid-meal. That's the appeal of the dish: eating the possibility of death, a fright your lips spell out as you dine. Yet preparing it is a traditional art form in Japan, with widespread aficionados. The most highly respected *fugu* chefs are the ones who manage to leave in the barest touch of the poison, just enough for the diner's lips to tingle from his brush with mortality but not enough to actually kill him. Of course, a certain number of diners do die every year from eating *fugu*, but that doesn't stop intrepid *fugu*-fanciers. The ultimate *fugu* connoisseur orders *chiri*, puffer flesh lightly cooked in a broth made of the poisonous livers and intestines. It's not that diners don't understand the bizarre danger of puffer-fish toxin. Ancient Egyptian, Chinese, Japanese, and other cultures all describe *fugu* poisoning in excruciating detail: it first produces dizziness, numbness of the mouth and lips, breathing trouble, cramps, blue lips, a desperate itchiness as of insects crawling all over one's body, vomiting, dilated pupils, and then a zombielike sleep, really a kind of neurological paralysis during which the victims are often aware of what's going on around them, and from which they die. But sometimes they wake. If a Japanese man or woman dies of *fugu* poison, the family waits a few days before burying them, just in case they wake up. Every now and then someone poisoned by *fugu* is nearly buried alive, coming to at the last moment to describe in horrifying detail their own funeral and burial, during which, although they desperately tried to cry out or signal that they were still alive, they simply couldn't move.

Though it has a certain Russian-roulette quality to it, eating *fugu* is considered a highly aesthetic experience. That makes one wonder about the condition that we, in chauvinistic shorthand, refer to as "human." Creatures who will one day vanish from the earth in that ultimate subtraction of sensuality that we call death, we spend our lives courting death, fomenting wars, watching sickening horror movies in which maniacs slash and torture their victims, hurrying our own deaths in fast cars, cigarette smoking, suicide. Death obsesses us, as well it might, but our response to it is so strange. Faced with tornadoes chewing up homes, with dust storms ruining crops, with floods and earthquakes swallowing up whole cities, with ghostly diseases that gnaw at one's bone marrow, cripple, or craze—rampant miseries that need no special bidding, but come freely, giving their horror like alms—you'd think human beings would hold out against the forces of Nature, combine their efforts and become allies, not create devastations of their own, not add to one another's miseries. Death does such fine work without us. How strange that people, whole countries sometimes, wish to be its willing accomplices.

Our horror films say so much about us and our food obsessions. I don't mean the ones in which maniacal men carting chain saws and razors punish single women for living alone or taking jobs—although those are certainly alarming. I don't mean ghost stories, in which we exhale loudly as order falls from chaos in the closing scenes. And I don't mean scary whodunits, at the end of which the universe seems temporarily less random, violent, and inexplicable. Our real passion, by far, is for the juiciest of horror films in which vile, loathsome beasts, gifted with ferocious strength and cunning, stalk human beings and eat them. It doesn't matter much if the beast is a fast-living "Killer Shrew" or a sullen "Cat People" or an abstract "Wolfen" or a nameless, acid-drooling "Alien." The pattern is always the same. They dominate the genre. We are greedy for their brand of terror.

The plain truth is that we don't seem to have gotten used to being at the top of our food chain. It must bother us a great deal, or we wouldn't keep making movies, generation after generation, with exactly the same scare tactics: the tables are turned and we become fodder. All right, so we may be comfortable at the top of the chain as we walk around Manhattan, but suppose—oh, ultimate horror!—that on other planets *we're* at the bottom of *their* food chain? Then you have the diabolically scary "Aliens,"° who capture human beings, use them as hosts for their maggotlike young, and actually hang them up on slime gallows in a pantry.

Aliens: Extraterrestial creatures featured in the 1979 film *Alien* and its sequels.

We rush obsessively to movie theaters, sit in the cavelike dark, and confront the horror. We make contact with the beasts and live through it. The next week, or the next summer, we'll do it all over again. And, on the way home, we keep listening for the sound of claws on the pavement, a supernatural panting, a vampiric flutter. We spent our formative years as a technologyless species scared with good reason about lions and bears and snakes and sharks and wolves that could, and frequently did, pursue us. You'd think we'd have gotten over that by now. One look at the cozy slabs of cow in a supermarket case, neatly cut, inked, and wrapped, should tell us to relax. But civilization is a more recent phenomenon than we like to think. Are horror films our version of the magic drawings on cave walls that our ancestors confronted? Are we still confronting them?

Fugu might not seem to have much to do with nuclear disarmament or world peace, but it's a small indicator of our psyches. We find the threat of death arousing. Not all of us, and not all the time. But enough do often enough to keep the rest of us peace-loving sorts on our toes when we'd rather be sitting down calmly to a sumptuous meal with friends.

Beauty and the Beasts

In Jean Cocteau's° extraordinary film version of the classic fairy tale "Beauty and the Beast," a sensitive beast lives in a magical castle, the walls and furnishings of which are all psychosensitive. On the back of the Beast's chair, in Latin, runs the motto: *All men are beasts when they don't have love.* Every evening, the literate, humane beast must go out hunting for his dinner, chase down a deer and feed on its steaming flesh, or die of starvation. Afterward, he suffers the most bitter anguish, and his whole body involuntarily begins to smoke. The unstated horror of our species reveals itself in that moment. Like the sensitive Beast, we must kill other forms of life in order to live. We must steal their lives, sometimes causing them great pain. Every one of us performs or tacitly approves of small transactions with torture, death, and butchery each day. The cave paintings reflected the reverence and the love the hunter felt for his prey. In our hearts, we know that life loves life. Yet we feast on some of the other life-forms with which we share our planet; we kill to live. Taste is what carries us across that rocky moral terrain, what makes the horror palatable, and the paradox we could not defend by reason melts into a jungle of sweet temptations.

Notes

1. This special milk, called "colostrum," is rich in antibodies, the record of the mother's epidemiologic experience.

Jean Cocteau's: Jean Cocteau (1889–1963), French writer, artist, and filmmaker.

2. It was the food-obsessed Chinese who started the first serious restaurants during the time of the T'ang dynasty (A.D. 618–907). By the time the Sung dynasty replaced the T'ang, there were all-purpose buildings, with many private dining rooms, where one went for food, sex, and barroom gab.

3. Water won't work as an antidote because it doesn't mix with oil, the binding in Chinese food; plain rice is the best remedy.

EXPLORING THE TEXT

1. According to Ackerman, what functions are associated with food and eating in human societies? What other functions might you be able to add to this list?

2. Why does Ackerman call taste the "social" sense? How can taste be both social and highly intimate or individual? Does taste play such an intensely social role in the ethnic and cultural groups with which you're familiar?

3. What is Ackerman's attitude toward food? Toward taste? How does her perspective on her topic and her attitude toward it change during the course of the reading? Overall, what is she saying about the sense of taste? To what extent would you agree with her?

4. How would you describe Ackerman's strategy as a writer in this selection? Does she approach her topic with a clear and consistent thesis? What seems to be her purpose? What kind of reaction does she want from her readers?

5. Ackerman relies on dramatic vignettes (like the "dinner for two" scenario in para. 10) and on masses of historical detail in her exploration of taste. What does each of these strategies do for the reader? What effect does each have? Which do you find most effective? Why?

FURTHER EXPLORATIONS

1. To what extent does Barry Lopez's account of the education of his sense of touch in "A Passage of the Hands" (p. 27) challenge Ackerman's assertion that taste is "*The* Social Sense"? What aspects of touch in Lopez's essay strike you as being distinctly social? Which sense, touch or taste, seems more "intimate"? Why?

2. Drawing on the ideas presented by Ackerman and K. C. Cole (p. 75), discuss the similarities between visual perception and taste. What roles do socialization and familiarity play in the way we see and taste things? To what extent are both sight and taste learned or acquired skills? What role does interpretation play in visual perception and taste?

3. View *Like Water for Chocolate, Babette's Feast, Tampopo, Big Night,* or any other film depicting the role of food, dining, and the sense of taste in a specific cultural context. How do characters in the film view food and its meanings? What social function does food play in the film? To what extent does the film's portrayal of food and taste reflect Ackerman's complex view of this "social" sense?

4. To what extent do films like *Silence of the Lambs* or *Hannibal* illustrate Ackerman's contention that food and eating play a crucial role in the creation of cinematic horror? How does the figure of Hannibal Lechter embody our cultural ambivalence about the function of taste?

ESSAY OPTIONS

1. Write an essay about the tastes that distinguish your home culture. What specific dishes do you associate with your cultural background? What flavors, textures, and specific ingredients give these foods their special character? What "meanings" or memories do these foods evoke? What foods within your home culture are associated with special holidays or rituals? What might these foods symbolize? What "supernatural powers" might they possess? Overall, how would you describe the role that food plays in the context of your home culture?

2. Write an essay in which you describe the "education" of your sense of taste, beginning with your earliest gustatory memories and noting what you would consider to be the most important lessons you've learned as an "omnivore." How important is taste in your home culture? How great a role does it play in defining your sense of self?

3. Using the alternative *Before Reading* assignment on page 37 as a point of departure, write an essay about your first or most memorable cross-cultural experience of taste. What was the situation? What did this experience mean for you? What did you learn from it?

Listening for Silence

MARK SLOUKA

Hearing has been described as the least intentional of the senses. We don't often *choose* what we hear: the roar of traffic on a nearby freeway, the rumble of thunder from an approaching storm, the wail of a distant ambulance, or the bits of conversation on a city street all pass in and out of consciousness without our aid or effort. You don't have to aim your ears in a particular direction to hear the screech of tires that signals danger somewhere outside your house. You don't even have to be awake to hear a baby's cry or an unexpected creak in the floorboards in the middle of the night. More than any of the other senses, hearing stands on the outposts of the self, ready day or night to detect the faintest sign of danger.

That's why hearing places us in such danger today. As Mark Slouka suggests in this elegantly composed reflection on silence, we live in a world that has capitulated to an onslaught of sound. Radios, televisions, cars, trains, jets, cell phones, sirens, and urban crowds flood our ears with the din of nonstop sensation—an aural deluge that threatens to deafen us to the soaring beauties and darker intonations of existence. Slouka's exploration of the meaning of silence raises questions about the purpose of hearing in a technologically advanced culture. It also challenges us to consider the risks of living in a world where sense itself has become a commodity. A contributing editor to *Harper's Magazine,* the source of this selection, Slouka (b. 1958) is the author of *Lost Lake* (1998), a collection of stories, and *War of the Worlds* (1995) a critique of the electronic revolution. He lives in New York where he teaches at Columbia University.

BEFORE READING

Freewrite in your journal about the last time you can recall clearly hearing silence. Where were you? What were the circumstances? What was this experience like? Compare your observations with those of your classmates, and discuss whether or not you think silence is becoming an "endangered" experience.

M usic, Claude Debussy° once famously remarked, is the stuff between the notes, an observation that resonates, pardon the pun, from the flawless spacing of a Billie Holiday° tune to the deletions—whether generous or cruel—in our daily lives. Essentially neuter, neither balm nor curse, silence, like light or love, requires a medium to give it meaning, takes on the color of its host, adapts easily to our fears and needs. Quite apart from whether we seek or shun it, silence orchestrates the music of our days.

I'm well aware, of course, that one man's music is another man's noise, that the primary differences between a cork-lined room° and solitary confinement are the lock on the door and the sensibility of the inmate. I wish not to define silence but to inquire about its absence, and I ask the question not to restate the obvious—that silence, in its way, is fundamental to life, the emotional equivalent of carbon—but because everywhere I turn I see a culture willing to deny that essential truth. In my idle moments I picture a god from my son's book of myths (with an Olympian straw and sucked-in cheeks) drawing the silence out of the land, and if the conceit is fanciful, the effect, sadly, is not: as silence disappears, the world draws tighter, borders collapse, the public and the private bleed and intermix. Victim to the centripetal pull, the imagination crackles with the static of outside frequencies, while somewhere in the soul—listen!—a cell phone is chirping. Answer it quickly, before someone else does.

*

At the close of the millennium, a new Tower of Babel,° monolingual (despite the superficial mixture of tongues), homogeneous (because almost invariably pitched in the vernacular of the marketplace), casts its shadow over the land. Ubiquitous, damn near inescapable, it is rearranging the way we live, forcing crucial adjustments in our behavior, straining our capacity for adaptation. If it continues to grow, as I believe it will, future generations may one day distinguish our age not for its discovery of Elsewhere, as

---

Claude Debussy: French composer (1862–1918).

Billie Holiday: American blues singer (1915–1959).

cork-lined room: Refers to the acoustically insulated bedroom of nineteenth-century French novelist Marcel Proust (1871–1922).

Tower of Babel: In Genesis 11:1–9, God creates many languages to confound the understanding of the descendents of Noah who, because they originally shared a single language, were able to build a tower that challenged heaven; hence, any confusion of languages.

E. B. White° called the world beyond the television screen, but for its colonization of silence.

Ensnared in webs of sound, those of us living in the industrialized West today must pick our way through a discordant, infinite-channeled auditory landscape. Like a radio stuck on permanent scan, the culture lashes us with skittering bits and bytes, each dragging its piece of historical or emotional context: a commercial overheard in traffic, a falsely urgent weather report, a burst of canned laughter, half a refrain. The pager interrupts lectures, sermons, second acts, and funerals. Everywhere a new song begins before the last one ends, as though to guard us against even the potential of silence. Each place we turn, a new world—synthetic, fragmented, often as not jacked into the increasingly complex grid that makes up the global communications network—encroaches on the old world of direct experience, of authentic, unadorned events with their particular, unadorned sounds.

Although a great deal has been said about our increasingly visual age, the   5 changes to our aural landscape have gone relatively unremarked. The image has grown so voracious that any child asked to sum up the century will instantly visualize Einstein's hair and Hitler's mustache, mushroom clouds and moon landings; this despite the fact that each of these visual moments has its aural correlative, from the blast over Hiroshima to the high-pitched staccato ravings of the Führer, to Neil Armstrong's static-ridden "giant leap for mankind."

But make no mistake: sound will have its dominion. The aural universe, though subtler than the one that imprints itself on our retina, is more invasive, less easily blocked. It mocks our sanctuaries as light never can. If my neighbor decides to wash his car in front of my study window, as he does often, I can block out the uninspiring sight of his pimpled posterior by drawing the shades; to block out his stereo, I must kill noise with noise. We hear in our sleep. There is no aural equivalent for the eyelid. In our day, when the phone can ring, quite literally, anywhere on the planet, this is not necessarily good news.

I have nothing against my aural canal. I adore music (though I make it badly). I have nothing against a good party, the roar of the crowd. But I make a distinction between nourishment and gluttony: the first is a necessity, even a pleasure; the second, a symptom. Of what? In a word, fear. One of the unanticipated side effects of connectedness. Perhaps because it's never enough, or because, having immersed ourselves in the age of mediation (as Bill Gates refers to it), accustomed ourselves to its ways and means, we sense our dependency. Or because, finally, like isolated apartment dwellers running the TV for company, we sense a deeper isolation beneath the babble of voices, the poverty of our communications. So, adaptable to a fault, we embrace this brave new cacophony, attuned, like apprentice ornithologists, to the distinguishing calls of a mechanical phylum. Capable of differentiating between the cheeps and chimes of the cell phones, portable phones, baby monitors, pagers, scanners, personal digital assistants, laptop computers, car alarms, and so on that fill our lives, we've grown adept, at the same time, at blocking them out with sounds of our own, at forcing a privacy where none exists.

E. B. White: Elwyn Brooks White (1899–1985), American journalist and essayist.

At the supermarket, a middle-aged man in a well-cut suit is calling some-one a bitch on the phone. Unable to get to the ricotta cheese, I wait, vaguely uncomfortable, feeling as though I'm eavesdropping. At the gym, the beeps of computerized treadmills clash with the phones at the front desk, the an-nouncements of upcoming discounts, the disco version of Gordon Lightfoot's "If You Could Read My Mind." A number of individuals in Walkman ear-phones, unaware that they've begun to sing, bellow and moan like the deaf.

"I love a wide margin to my life," Thoreau° remarked, quaintly, referring to the space — the silence — requisite for contemplation, or, more quaintly, the forming of a self. A century and a half later, aural text covers the psychic page, spills over; the margin is gone. Walking to work, we pass over rumbling pipes and humming cables, beneath airplane flight corridors and satellite broad-casts, through radio and television transmissions whose sounds, reconstituted from binary code, mix and mingle, overlap and clash, and everywhere drifts the aural refuse of our age.

Thus may the stuff between the discordant notes of our lives require — and   10
I'm not unaware of the irony here — a few words in its defense. Begin any-where. The cottage in which I spend my summers is silent yet full of sound: the rainy hush of wind in the oaks, the scrabble of a hickory nut rolling down the roof, the slurp of the dog in the next room, interminably licking him-self . . . I've never known perfect silence. I hope to avoid making its acquain-tance for some time to come, yet I court it daily.

My ambivalence toward silence is natural enough: the grave, the scythe, the frozen clock, all the piled symbols of death, reinforce an essential truth, a primal fear: beneath the sloping hood, death is voiceless. Silence spits us out and engulfs us again, one and all, and all the noisemakers on Bourbon Street,° all the clattering figurines in Cuernavaca,° can't undo the unpleasant fact that *el día,* properly understood, always ends in *la muerte,* that quiet, like a pair of great parentheses around a dependent clause, closes off our days. Sorry.

But if it's true that all symphonies end in silence, it's equally true that they begin there as well. Silence, after all, both buries and births us, and just as life without the counterweight of mortality would mean nothing, so silence alone, by offering itself as the eternal Other, makes our music possible. The image of Beethoven composing against the growing void, like all clichés, illuminates a common truth: fear forces our hand, inspires us, makes visible the things we love.

But wait. Does this mean that all is well? That the pendulum swings, the chorus turns in stately strophe and antistrophe,° the buds of May routinely answer winter's dark aphelion?° Not quite. We are right to be afraid of silence,

Thoreau: Henry David Thoreau (1817–1862), American writer.

Bourbon Street: Mardi Gras parade route in New Orleans.

Cuernavaca: Resort town outside Mexico City famed for its celebration of "El Dia de Los Muertos," the Day of the Dead.

strophe and antistrophe: The circling and countercircling dance of the chorus in Greek tragedy.

aphelion: The point in the orbit of a planet when it is farthest from the sun.

to resist that sucking vacuum—however much we depend on it—to claw and scratch against oblivion. The battle is in deadly earnest. And therein lies the joke. Resistance is one thing, victory another.

Left partially deaf by a childhood inflammation of the mastoid bones, Thomas Edison throughout his life embraced the world of silence, reveled in its space, allowed it to empower him; as much as any man, perhaps, he recognized silence as the territory of inspiration and cultivated its gifts. Deafness, his biographers agree, acted like an auditory veil, separating him from the world's distractions, allowing him to attend to what he called his business: thinking.

I mention these facts, however, not for the small and obvious irony—that a man so indebted to silence should do more than any other to fill the world with noise—but to set the context for a scene I find strangely compelling. In June 1911, hard at work on what would eventually become a disk phonograph, Edison hired a pianist to play for him (as loudly as possible) the world's entire repertoire of waltzes. And there, in the salon at Glenmont, either out of frustration at not being able to hear the music to his satisfaction or, as I'd like to believe, out of sudden desperate love for the thing he'd missed (as charged as any of love's first fumblings), the sixty-four-year-old Edison got on his hands and knees and bit into the piano's wood, the better to hear its vibrations. Will Edison's fate be our own? Afloat in the river of sound loosed upon the world by Edison's inventions, having drunk from it until our ears ring, we now risk a similar thirst.

Tacked to the wall above my desk, staring out from a page torn from the back of the *New York Times Magazine*, are the faces of seventeen men and women whose portraits were taken by KGB° photographers more than half a century ago, then filed, along with hundreds of thousands like them, in the top-secret dossiers of Stalin's secret police. Over the years, I've come to know the faces in these photographs nearly as well as I know those of the living. I study them often—the woman at the left whose graying hair has begun to loosen, the beautiful young man at the right, the fading lieutenant at the bottom corner whose cheeks, I suspect, had the same roughness and warmth as my father's—because each and every one of them, within hours of having his or her picture taken, was driven to a forest south of Moscow and executed; because all, or nearly all, knew their fate at the time their pictures were taken; and because, finally, having inherited a good dose of Slavic morbidity (and sentimentalism), I couldn't bear to compound the silence of all of those lives unlived by returning them—mothers and fathers, sons and lovers—to the oblivion of yet another archive, the purgatory of microfiche. On my wall, in some small measure, they are not forgotten; they have a voice.

KGB: (Russian) *Komitét gosudárstvennoĭ bezopásnosti;* the Soviet State Security Committee, the Soviet counterpart of the U.S. Central Intelligence Agency.

Today, as the panopticon° reveals to us as never before the agony of our species, the lesson is repeated daily. We read it in the skulls of Srebrenica,° growing out of the soil, in the open mouths of the dead from Guatemala to the Thai-Cambodian border, whose characteristic posture—head back, neck arched—seems almost a universal language: the harvest of dictatorship, properly understood, is not death, but silence. Mr. Pinochet's° *los desaparecidos*° (like Slobodan Milosevic's° or Heinrich Himmler's° are really *los callados* (the silenced), the snuffing of their voices only the last, most brutal expression of a system dependent on silence as a tool of repression. The enforced quiet of censorship and propaganda, of burning pages and jammed frequencies, is different from the gun to the temple only in degree, not in kind.

And yet who could deny that silence, though both the means and the end of totalitarian repression, is also its natural enemy? That silence, the habitat of the imagination, not only allows us to grow the spore of identity but, multiplied a millionfold, creates the rich loam in which a genuine democracy thrives? In the silence of our own minds, in the quiet margins of the text, we are made different from one another as well as able to understand others' differences from us.

In the famous John Cage° composition *4'33"*, the pianist walks onstage, bows, flips the tail of his tuxedo, and seats himself at the piano. Taking a stopwatch out of his vest pocket, he presses the start button, then stares at the keys for precisely four minutes and thirty-three seconds. When the time is up, he closes the piano and leaves the stage.

Nearly half a century after it was first performed, *4'33"* rightly strikes us   20
as hackneyed and worn, a postmodern cliché intent on blurring a line (between art and non-art, order and disorder, formal structure and random influence) that has long since been erased. As simple theater, however, it still has power. Cage's portrait of the artist frozen before his medium, intensely aware of his allotted time, unable to draw a shape out of the universe of possibilities, carries a certain allegorical charge, because we recognize in its symbolism—

panopticon: A surveillance system devised by English jurist and philosopher Jeremy Bentham (1748–1832) that made it possible for a single guard to visually inspect large numbers of prison or asylum inmates; hence, the culture of surveillance associated with modern electronic communications and mass media.

Srebrenica: Site of reported atrocities during the Balkan war [1941–1995].

Mr. Pinochet: Augusto Pinochet (b. 1915), former dictator of Argentina.

los desaparecidos: (Spanish) "The disappeared."

Slobodan Milosevic's: Slobodan Milosevic (b. 1941), former president of Yugoslavia, indicted by the United Nations for war crimes in 1999.

Heinrich Himmler's: Heinrich Himmler (1900–1945), World War II Nazi leader officially responsible for the program of genocide carried out against European Jews.

John Cage: John Milton Cage (1912–1992), American composer.

so apparently childlike, so starkly Manichaean°—a lesson worthy of Euripedes:° art, whatever its medium, attempts to force a wedge beneath the closed lid of the world, and fails; the artist, in his or her minutes and seconds, attempts to say—to paint, to carve; in sum, to communicate—what ultimately cannot be communicated. In the end, the wedge breaks; the lid stays shut. The artist looks at his watch and leaves the stage, his "success" measurable only by the relative depth of his failure. Too bad. There are worse things.

But if silence is the enemy of art, it is also its motivation and medium: the greatest works not only draw on silence for inspiration but use it, flirt with it, turn it, for a time, against itself. To succeed at all, in other words, art must partake of its opposite, suggest is own dissolution. Examples are legion: once attuned to the music of absence, the eloquence of omission or restraint, one hears it everywhere—in the sudden vertiginous stop of an Elizabeth Bishop° poem; in the space between souls in an Edward Hopper° painting; in Satchmo's° mastery of the wide margins when singing "I'm Just a Lucky So and So." In the final paragraph of Frank O'Connor's° small masterpiece "Guests of the Nation," an Irish soldier recalls looking over a patch of bog containing the graves of two British soldiers he's just been forced to execute and observes simply, "And anything that happened to me afterwards, I never felt the same about again." Such a black hole of a line, dense with rejected possibilities, merciless in its willingness to sacrifice everything for a quick stab at truth. . . .

If one of the characteristics of capitalism is that it tends to shut down options, narrow the margins, then perhaps what we are seeing these days is one of the side effects of the so-called free market: most of the noises we hear are the noises of buying and selling. Even the communication between individuals has been harnessed to the technologies that make them possible: to be deprived of the fax machine, the cell phone, the TV, the pager, etc., is to be relegated to silence. Communication, having been narrowed into whatever can be squeezed into binary code, has been redefined by the marketplace into a commodity itself.

Yet capitalism, we know, always tries to feed the hungers it creates, to confect its own antidotes—so long as the price is right. As the vast silences of the republic are paved over by designer outlets and shopping malls, a kind of island ecosystem remains, self-conscious in its fragility, barely viable. The proof is detectable in any upscale travel magazine: there you will find exclusive spas

Manichaean: Refers to a religion originated by Manes, a third-century Persian religious prophet, based on the idea that two opposing forces, good/light and evil/darkness, underlie all creation; hence, any thinking marked by a dualistic contrast.

Euripedes: (ca 484–406 B.C.), Greek dramatist.

Elizabeth Bishop: (1911–1979), American poet.

Edward Hopper: (1882–1967), American painter.

Satchmo's: Louis "Satchmo" Armstrong (1901–1971), American jazz musician.

Frank O'Connor's: Frank O'Connor, pseudonym of Michael John O'Donovan (1903–1966), Irish author.

advertising the promise of silence—no pagers, no cell phones, just the sounds of lakewater lapping—as though silence were a rare Chardonnay or an exclusive bit of scenery, which, of course, is precisely what it now is.

That silence, like solitude, is now a commodity should not surprise us. Money buys space, and space buys silence; decibels and dollars are inversely proportional. Lacking money, I've lived with noise—with the sounds of fucking and feuding in the airshaft, MTV and Maury Povich° coming through the walls, in apartments with ceilings so thin I could hear the click of a clothes hanger placed on a rod or the lusty stream of an upstairs neighbor urinating after a long night out. I've accepted this, if not gracefully, at least with a measure of resignation. The great advantage that money confers, I now realize, is not silence per se but the *option* of silence, the privilege of choosing one's own music, of shutting out the seventeen-year-old whose boombox nightly rattles my panes.

But if the ability to engineer one's own silence has been one of the age- 25
old prerogatives of wealth, it's also true that the rapidly changing aural landscape of the late twentieth century has raised the status (and value) of silence enormously. As the world of the made, to recall e. e. cummings,° replaces the world of the born, as the small sounds of fields at dusk or babies crying in the next apartment are erased by the noise of traffic and Oprah, as even our few remaining bits of wilderness are pressed thin and flat beneath satellite transmissions, Forest Service bulldozers, and airplane flight corridors, we grow sentimental for what little has escaped us and automatically reach for our wallets. Like a telltale lesion that appears only on those who are desperately ill, value—even outrageous value—often blossoms on things just before they leave us, and if the analogy is an ugly one, it is also appropriate; the sudden spasm of love for the thing we're killing, after all, is as obscene as it is human. As we continue to pave the world with sound, we will continue to crave what little silence escapes us, an emptiness made audible by its disappearance.

Maury Povich: (b. 1939), American television talk-show host.
e. e. cummings: Edward Estlin Cummings (1894–1962), American poet.

EXPLORING THE TEXT

1. What has happened to silence, according to Slouka, in contemporary society? To what extent would you agree that we live in a "new Tower of Babel"—an age that has seen the "colonization of silence"? To what extent does your personal experience confirm or challenge this claim?

2. What value does Slouka see in silence? What does silence do for us? What does it make possible? What negative associations does silence hold for Slouka? How does he reconcile these two aspects of his topic?

3. What is the point of the story Slouka tells about the KGB photo that hangs above his desk? What, according to Slouka, is the complex relationship between silence and totalitarianism? Between silence and art? What connection, if any, can you discern between Slouka's comments on silence, death, and oppression, and the social function of art?

4. Why have we immersed ourselves in sound, in Slouka's view? What personal, social, and economic motives have prompted us to banish silence? What evidence do you see to support the claim that silence has been commodified in contemporary capitalist society?

FURTHER EXPLORATIONS

1. Compare the status of hearing in contemporary Western culture, as described by Slouka, with that of the sense of smell, as described by the authors of "The Olfactory Revolution" (p. 59). Why has hearing eclipsed smell in terms of its importance as a source of information? What broader historical, technological, and cultural changes does this shift in sensory dominance reflect?

2. How might the theory of perception presented by K. C. Cole in "Seeing Things" (p. 75) help explain the destructive impact that Slouka believes sound has had on individuals in contemporary society? To what extent do you think our sense of sight has been "colonized" by the forces of capitalist technology, as has been, in Slouka's view, our sense of hearing?

3. Compare the role played by illustrative anecdotes in Slouka's analysis of sound and silence, Ian Frazier's "Take the F" (p. 18), and Barry Lopez's "A Passage of the Hands" (p. 27). When and why do these authors insert stories into their essays? How do their uses of storytelling differ?

4. Locate and examine a reproduction of Edward Hopper's "Nighthawks"; a copy of Henri Matisse's "Three Dancers," as discussed by Georgina Kleege in "The Mind's Eye" (p. 93); and René Magritte's "The Menaced Assassin," mentioned in Daniel L. Schacter's "Building Memories" (p. 157). In what sense do these paintings make silence or sound visible? How would you describe the experience of silence conveyed by each of these paintings? What other great visual works of art can you think of that materialize silence in this way?

ESSAY OPTIONS

1. Return to the personal essay you wrote in response to Ian Frazier's "Take the F" (p. 18) and rewrite it, after doing additional preparation and brainstorming, relying only on your sense of hearing. What sounds do you encounter on your daily commute? What sounds convey the feeling and texture of life in your neighborhood? What is lost or gained by expressing this experience solely through the sounds you hear?

2. Drawing on the ideas presented by Slouka, Constance Classen et al. (p. 58), Bill McKibben (p. 109), and Walker Percy (p. 118), write an essay in which you explore the notion that our sensuous appreciation of the world is being undermined by life in contemporary technological society. To what extent does your personal experience support the idea that our direct, sensuous relationship to reality is being subverted by technological progress?

3. Drawing on the ideas and experiences presented by Slouka in this selection, K. C. Cole in "Seeing Things" (p. 75), Georgia Kleege in "The Mind's Eye" (p. 93), Bill McKibben in "Television and the Twilight of the Senses" (p. 109), and/or Walker

Percy in "The Loss of the Creature" (p. 118), write an essay exploring the relationship between sensory deprivation and original thinking. Why might sensory isolation or an unusual sensory perspective lead to new insights and discoveries?

The Olfactory Revolution

CONSTANCE CLASSEN, DAVID HOWES, AND ANTHONY SYNNOTT

Most of us have a one-size-fits-all attitude toward the senses. Barring disability, we tend to assume that one person's view of the world is like another's, just as we commonly think that a tone that sounds "flat" to one person probably sounds "flat" to someone else. We also tend to assume that the senses have stayed pretty much the same over time. After all, did the ancient Greeks hear things differently than we do today? Or, for that matter, when our australopithecine ancestors gazed up at the night sky from Olduvai Gorge in East Africa two million years ago, did they see the world with radically different eyes?

It may be hard to imagine evolutionary changes in the way we sense the world around us, but as the authors of this selection argue, changes in the way we react to odors are matters of verifiable fact. According to these well-respected researchers, the Western world has undergone an "olfactory revolution" since the era of the Enlightenment and the rise of modern science, a revolution that has transformed our relationship to the realm of scent. The sensory evolution that Classen, Howes, and Synnott trace suggests not only that modern noses are more intolerant than noses in the past, but that this new sensitivity reflects a revolution in the way we view men, women, and the mind in relation to the natural world. Constance Classen (b. 1957) is the author of *Inca Cosmology and the Human Body* (1993) and *Worlds of the Senses* (1993). David Howe (b. 1957) is the editor of *The Varieties of Sensory Experience* (1991). Anthony Synnott (b. 1940) is the author of *The Body Social* (1993). All three teach at Concordia University in Canada. This selection originally appeared in *Aroma: The Cultural History of Smell* (1994).

BEFORE READING

Close your eyes and imagine that you are walking down a boulevard in eighteenth-century Paris. What odors, fragrances, and aromas might you be likely to encounter as you stroll through the streets of this important center of the European Enlightenment? As an alternative assignment, write about a place in memory that you associate with a particular fragrance or aroma. What memories do you connect with the recollection of this smell?

The Perfumed Body

When considering the odors of yesteryear it is important to keep in mind that standards of personal cleanliness were quite different in the pre-modern West from what they are today. Prior to the eighteenth century bathing tended to be considered more as a sensual pastime, and therefore somewhat decadent, than as a means of cleaning oneself. Thus St. Francis of Assisi,° for example, included dirt as an insignia of holiness. Furthermore, it was thought that water not only morally corrupted the body, but physically corrupted it as well by rendering it moist and soft—feminine—and vulnerable to unhealthy air and disease.

The dangers believed to be inherent in bathing can be seen by the precautions which were observed when the rare bath *was* taken. Francis Bacon,° for instance, gave the following prescription for a bath which seems more like an elaborate perfuming than a wash with water.

> First, before bathing, rub and anoint the Body with Oyle, and Salves, that the Bath's moistening heate and virtue may penetrate into the Body, and not the liquor's watery part: then sit 2 houres in the Bath; after Bathing wrap the Body in a seare-cloth made of Masticke, Myrrh, Pomander and Saffron, for staying the perspiration or breathing of the pores, until the softening of the Body, having layne thus in seare-cloth 24 hours, bee growne solid and hard. Lastly, with an ointment of Oyle, Salt and Saffron, the seare-cloth being taken off, anoint the Body.[1]

When Henri IV of France, on requiring the presence of one of his ministers, learned that the man was taking a bath, he insisted on putting off the meeting until the next day: "He orders you to expect him tomorrow in your nightshirt, your leggings, your slippers and your night-cap, so that you come to no harm as a result of your recent bath."[2]

There were some people who took baths fairly often in spite of their reputed dangers. Elizabeth I of England, for example, reportedly took a bath once a month "whether she need it or no."[3] For most, however, washing was restricted to the hands and perhaps face. The gentry used scented water for this purpose, as described by Shakespeare in *The Taming of the Shrew:*

> Let one attend him with a silver basin
> Full of rose water, and bestrew'd with flowers.[4]

Such toilet waters were preferred to soap, which, being made of tallow or whale oil and potash, was often too coarse and foul-smelling to be used on the skin. The body might be cleansed by being rubbed with a scented cloth. "To

St. Francis of Assisi: (1182–1226), Italian founder of the Franciscan order.

Francis Bacon: Baron Verulam, Viscount St. Albans (1561–1626), English philosopher, essayist, scientist, and statesman.

cure the goat-like stench of armpits," writes a sixteenth-century French hygienist, "it is useful to press and rub the skin with a compound of roses."[5] In fact, clothes themselves were regarded as cleansing the body of dirt. Washing one's clothes, therefore, served the same purpose as washing one's body, and with much greater safety. Hair, in turn, was cleaned by being rubbed with scented powders. The breath was freshened by chewing herbs such as aniseed, rinsing the mouth with cinnamon or myrrh water, or sucking on perfumed candies — "kissing comfits."

The importance of perfuming oneself lay in the fact that perfumes were not just thought to mask unpleasant odors, but to actually dispel them. Furthermore, fragrance was held to be therapeutic, serving to strengthen and stimulate mind and body. Aside from these practical considerations, however, Europeans took immense pleasure in perfume. This pleasure reached a height of expression in the sixteenth and seventeenth centuries when, among the wealthy, everything from letters to lapdogs was scented.

Apart from the customary floral fragrances and the imported spices,   5 scents of animal origin — musk, civet and ambergris — were very popular during the Renaissance. Musk was extracted from a scent gland of the musk deer, native to India and China, and civet from that of the civet cat of Ethiopia and Indonesia. Ambergris is an excretory product of the sperm whale found floating on the ocean or washed up on shore and used primarily as a fixative for other scents. Its source remained a mystery until the start of the whaling industry in the eighteenth century, when whalers found lumps of it inside the whales they were cutting up.

For Westerners, these exotic substances were invested with legendary qualities. Much as the gathering of cinnamon was once thought to be fraught with risk, for example, stories were now told of the extraordinary cunning and skill required by the hunter of the musk deer. (In fact, musk deer have been hunted almost to extinction for their precious pods of musk.) Furthermore, due to their animal origin, musk and civet were believed to radiate a potent natural vitality. This led to their use as olfactory aphrodisiacs by amorous ladies and gentlemen. Thus, when a character in *Much Ado About Nothing* rubs himself with civet, it's "as much as to say, the sweet youth's in love."[6]

Fragrances were used singly or blended together to form compound perfumes. Rose and musk was one common combination, and a favorite of both Henry VIII of England and his daughter Elizabeth. Not only the body would be perfumed, however, but virtually everything worn on the body as well. Clothes were washed with lavender and dusted with aromatic powders. Gloves and shoes were made of perfumed leather and chosen as much for their scent as for their appearance. Ornate pomanders containing musk and spices, and pouncet boxes full of perfumed powders or snuff, were carried in the hand or worn around the waist or neck. Bracelets and necklaces were made out of beads of hardened perfume. Rings concealed grains of scent in tiny, perforated boxes. Even gemstones might be odorized with perfume. (In fact, this practice may have been thought of as simply bringing out the gem's innate essence, for one theory had it that stones were originally made of water condensed by odor.)[7] Taking into account all these different ways in which perfumes were worn on the person, in addition to natural body odors, the gentry of this period must have been odoriferous indeed.

Perfume, however, was not considered simply something to be passively bought and worn, but a means of diversion. Ladies, and sometimes gentlemen, of the court enjoyed making floral waters at their own stills and creating personal blends of fragrance. As in the days of ancient Rome, perfumes often formed part of the entertainment on social occasions. One elaborate seventeenth-century plan for a banquet, for example, had the guests throwing eggshells filled with rose-water at each other. At a banquet given in Naples in 1476, a miniature fountain spraying orange-flower water adorned the table. On an occasion when Queen Elizabeth entertained a delegation of French ambassadors, "two cannons were shot off, the one with sweet powder, and the other with sweet water, verie odoriferous and pleasant."[8]

This olfactory largesse was continued among the aristocracy of the eighteenth century. At the Versailles court of Louis XV, known as "la Cour parfumée," fashion dictated that a different perfume be worn each day of the week. In order to ensure that she would never be left without a scent, the king's lover, the Marquise de Pompadour, reportedly spent a million francs creating a perfume bank.

One perfume which was catching on in the seventeen hundreds was Eau de Cologne. Created by Italian perfumers living in Cologne and composed of rosemary and citrus essences dissolved in grape spirit, Eau de Cologne had originally been a plague preventive. By the nineteenth century it was enormously popular as a perfume all over Europe. Napoleon was said to be so fond of this scent that he would splash a vial of it over his head every morning.[9]

Nonetheless, there were many during these centuries of extensive perfume use who disapproved of perfume. Chief among these were Protestant reformers, such as the Puritans. Their views on perfume were those of the early Christians: it encouraged personal vanity and licentiousness. Moreover, perfume disguised humanity's innate state of corruption with its artificial sweetness. Bodies which are now "so perfumed and bathed in odoriferous waters," warned a seventeenth-century pamphlet, "must one day be throwne (like stinking carrion) into a rank & rotten grave."[10] These views did not immediately stem the outpouring of scent, but they did have an effect on popular attitudes towards perfume in the centuries to come.

In any case, as we shall see below, fragrance trends were changing. By the late eighteenth century musk and civet were no longer in favor as perfumes. They were too strong, too animalistic, their "excremental" odors repulsed, rather than attracted, persons with a refined sense of smell. The new perfume ideal was that of delicate floral and herbal scents: lavender, rosemary, violet, thyme, rose. There were exceptions to this rule — the Empress Josephine, for example, adored musk as much as her husband did Eau de Cologne — but on the whole the new floral ideal would dictate perfume fashion until the twentieth century.[11]

The Olfactory Revolution

In the late eighteenth and early nineteenth centuries movements for sanitary reform began to grow in the cities of Europe. With the multiplication of factories and the rise in urban populations, the problem of waste and garbage disposal had become truly monumental. The need for reform of this sort was made more pressing by the cholera and typhus epidemics of the nineteenth century which were suspected of being spread by the odors of waste products.

Earnest reformers applied themselves to the task of recording in vivid detail the filth and stench of their cities in the hope that their writings would help bring about change. The British physician John Hogg, for example, decried the existence of slaughter-houses "reeking with gore" in London and the attendant driving of huge herds of animals through the city:

> Whole trains of coaches, omnibuses, and wagons are stopped by bullocks and sheep . . . often do the poor animals, overheated, and faint with thirst, rush towards a gutter of liquid filth, and drain it of its black and putrid contents, often do they drop and die in the streets from ill-usage and exhaustion, and frequently are they crushed and destroyed by the wheels of heavy-laden vehicles, and so the butcher's knife is cheated of its victim![12]

Apart from the herds of animals driven to be slaughtered, thousands of cows were kept in the city by dairies. Hogg writes that these establishments could be smelled from several streets away, and that "it is not the ambrosial breath of the cow that is experienced . . . but it is the filth that is accumulated in the sheds where the cows are so closely packed."[13]

Another British physician, Hector Gavin, wrote a report on an olfactory tour he had made of a London suburb in which each street seemed more foul than the last, the only alleviation being an occasional flower garden. "I could not remain to make notes of this place, so overpowering was the stench," he writes of one stop on his tour, and of another, "the stench was perfectly unendurable."[14] Worst of all was the yard of a manure manufactory:

> To my right in this yard, was a large accumulation of dung, &c.; but, to the left, there was an extensive layer of a compost of blood, ashes, and nitric acid, which gave out the most horrid, offensive, and disgusting concentration of putrescent odors it has ever been my lot to fall victim of.[15]

Such manure manufactories underline the fact that there was a profit to be made out of refuse. Dung, of course, had value as a fertilizer. It was also employed by tanneries to soften leather. Sugar refineries, in turn, made use of vast amounts of animal blood and parts in their processing. In *Les Misérables* Victor Hugo decries the "loss of the hundred millions which France annually throws away," by letting potentially valuable manure be carried away to the sea.[16]

> Those heaps of garbage at the corners of the stone blocks, these tumbrils of
> mire jolting through the streets at night, these horrid scavengers' carts, these
> fetid streams of subterranean slime which the pavement hides from you, do you
> know what all this is? It is the flowering meadow . . . it is perfumed hay, it is
> golden corn, it is bread on your table, it is warm blood in your veins, it is health,
> it is joy, it is life.[17]

This, of course, was the traditional farmer's perspective whereby the odors of
excrement were tolerable, and even desirable, because they turned into the
scents of harvest. In the ever-expanding cities of Europe, however, there were
no nearby fields to fertilize, and so streets and rivers continued to float with
sewage.

It was not only waste and its malodors which were considered dangerous
by the sanitary reformers, however, but also the exhalations of living beings.
Scientists, after observing animals writhe to death inside the vacuum of bell
jars, had concluded that the circulation of air was essential to life. Without
fresh air, therefore, the poor, crammed in their suffocating dwellings, would
die of their own exhalations like animals in bell jars. Thus Gavin writes, for
example:

> The air which is breathed within the dwellings of the poor is often most insuffer-
> ably offensive to strangers. It is loaded with the most unhealthy emanations from
> the lungs and persons of the occupants — from the fecal remains which are com-
> monly retained in the rooms — and from the accumulations of decomposing
> refuse which nearly universally abound. . . . In numerous instances, I found the
> air in the rooms of the poor . . . so saturated with putrescent exhalations, that to
> breathe it was to inhale a dangerous, perhaps fatal, poison.[18]

Once the problem was described, the difficulty lay in trying to rectify it. One
major objection to keeping filth off the streets was that a great number of
poor — street sweepers, scavengers, manure sellers, and so on — depended on
it for their livelihood.[19] Indeed, in Paris in 1832, when attempts were made to
improve the removal of rubbish, the poor rioted.[20] It was a question of
environment versus employment, and when faced with this choice, many
nineteenth-century officials, businessmen and workers came down on the side
of employment, as they often do over similar issues today. Clean streets were
a luxury, they argued, jobs were a necessity.

With regard to human waste, networks of drains existed in the larger
towns, but these were poorly made and inadequate. Again, there were reasons
for delaying improvements. Individuals and communities were resistant to
change and unwilling to spend money on expensive sewage systems. There
was also the matter of all the door-to-door waste collectors who would be put
out of work. In London, a legal issue was even made out of who had property
rights over human waste — those who produced it, those who owned the property in which it was produced, or the state? Then again, waste being a very in-

delicate matter, there were many persons in that prim age who were unwilling to discuss it at all or even admit its existence.[21]

In the end, it took the increasing numbers of deaths from cholera epidemics to convince reluctant governments to institute measures of sanitary reform—house inspections, flush toilets, sewage systems, and so on. There was an olfactory impetus as well. Hot summers intensified urban stench until it became unbearable even for hardened city dwellers.[22] In London, for example, the summer of 1858 was so foul that it was suggested that Parliament be moved out of the city.[23] Instead, the great work of urban waste disposal began.

In the late nineteenth century the discovery was made that it was not smells that spread disease, but germs. However, since the germs which communicated diseases such as typhus and cholera could be found in waste products, the safe disposal of waste remained as important as before. As the network of drains and sewers spread, the olfactory ambience of European towns and cities slowly lost its excremental flair. With waste odors out of the way, the populace grew less tolerant of industrial stenches, and these too became subject to government control.[24] Foul odors were no longer considered an unpleasant but inevitable part of life; they were now an unacceptable affront to public sensibility, if not to public health, which could and should be eradicated.

This revolution in civic cleanliness was accompanied by a revolution in personal cleanliness. Baths, for instance, had reappeared in Europe in the eighteenth century. One important turn-about which made bathing acceptable and even desirable was that, whereas previously bathing had been thought to endanger one's health, it was now thought to be good for health. Body dirt, it was claimed, prevented perspiration and oil from being released by the skin, thus causing illness. As one late eighteenth-century French report put it: "Major diseases . . . most often occur when evacuations of the skin do not take place, nothing presenting a greater obstacle to this than body dirt and filth."[25]

Hence, while before it had been thought necessary to leave one's skin unwashed so as to prevent it from being invaded by external effluvia, it now was argued that it was necessary to wash one's skin so as to allow it to release corrupt internal fluids. Scientific support was lent to these new beliefs by grotesque experiments in which it was observed that animals would slowly asphyxiate when their skin, coated with tar, was unable to breathe.[26] In the sixteenth century Francis Bacon had prescribed a bath routine which would carefully limit the "breathing of the pores"; the emphasis now was on bathing in order to let one's skin breathe.

As the upper and middle classes, at first reluctantly, began to purify their bodies, their homes and their streets of dirt, they grew more conscious of the malodors of the working classes which did not. Among many in this latter group, the old standards and methods of personal cleanliness held good until the end of the nineteenth century. An English study on hygiene conducted in

1842, for instance, reports a laborer replying, when asked how often he washed, that: "I never wash my body; I let my shirt rub the dirt off, my shirt will show that; I wash my neck and ears and face, of course."[27]

Furthermore, the poor did not (and could not) separate the functions and odors of their households into discrete compartments—bedroom, bathroom, kitchen, dining room—as the moneyed classes did. Odors thus mingled indiscriminately in the crowded homes of the poor, increasing the revulsion felt towards them by the sensitized bourgeoisie, who had come to associate olfactory promiscuity with moral promiscuity. A Victorian perfumer writes, for example:

> Among the lower orders, bad smells are little heeded; in fact, "noses have they, but they smell not"; and the result is, a continuance to live in an atmosphere laden with poisonous odors, whereas anyone with the least power of smelling retained shuns such odors, as they would anything else that is vile or pernicious.[28]

The olfactory reform of the poor was thus intimately linked with their moral reform. The new doctrine of cleanliness did eventually penetrate the working classes, due to the teaching of hygienic practices in the expanding school system, the amelioration of the living conditions of workers and the construction of public baths.[29] Even then, bathing was not necessarily, as we tend to think today, a purifying experience. George Orwell,° for instance, recalled from the baths of his schooldays in the 1910s, "the slimy water of the plunge bath," "the always-damp towels with their cheesy smell," and "the sweaty smell of the changing room." He noted in conclusion: "It is not easy for me to think of my schooldays without seeming to breathe in a whiff of something cold and evil-smelling."[30] While the foul scents of Orwell's schoolboy baths are reminiscent of the bad-odored old days, however, his hypersensitivity to them is characteristic of the new, sanitized, olfactory order.

Interestingly, this rise in personal cleanliness was accompanied by a decline in the use of perfumes. The most apparent reason for this would seem to be that, once bathing was an established practice, perfumes were no longer needed to mask unpleasant body odors. Nevertheless, there were a number of other factors influencing this shift as well. At the same time as washing with water was increasingly being judged healthy, perfumes were being stigmatized as unhealthy. No longer attributed any protective qualities by the medical profession, perfumes were instead deemed to clog the pores, or to enfeeble through their heavy vapors.[31] Indeed, for some, perfumes were almost as unhealthy as stenches. The great nineteenth-century sanitary reformer Edward Chadwick, for instance, was of the opinion that "all smell is disease."[32]

Perfumes were therefore taken out of the pharmacy and relegated to the cosmetics counter, and their role was changing there as well. In the late eighteenth century, styles in clothes and cosmetics became more subdued, and the

25

George Orwell: Pseudonym of Eric Blair (1903–1950), English author and social critic.

use of perfumes was likewise toned down. The French Revolution, with its revolt against aristocratic excess, furthered this trend towards sobriety. While the imagined corruption of the poor was associated with filth and stench, that of the aristocracy had its olfactory sign in heavy perfumes. The rising middle classes, in contrast, would find their niche in the safe middle ground of olfactory neutrality.

One important factor which linked perfume in particular to extravagance, was its ephemeral nature. Money that was spent on perfume literally evaporated, a process that represented the antithesis of bourgeois values of converting money into solid assets. Buying perfume was like scattering your money to the wind. Perfumes, consequently, no longer considered essential, entered the category of wasteful frivolity.

Scents served not only to mark differences of class during this period, but also of gender. Up until the end of the eighteenth century, perfumes had been extensively used by men and women alike. At that time, as has been noted, the use of perfumes declined. Whereas many men left off wearing scents altogether, however, women merely changed to lighter, floral fragrances.

Furthermore, traditionally the same perfumes had been used by both men and women. It is related of George IV of England (who reigned from 1820 to 1830), for example, that he first encountered what was to be his favorite scent for his own person worn by a princess at a ball.[33] By the late nineteenth century, however, certain scents — in particular, sweet floral blends — were deemed exclusively feminine, while other, sharper, scents were characterized as masculine. The burgeoning perfume industry capitalized on these trends by creating and promoting perfumes specifically for women, and, to a much lesser extent, others, marketed as aftershaves or colognes, for men.

What were the reasons for this olfactory divide of the sexes? The typing of perfumes as frivolous, for one, made them suitable only for "frivolous creatures," and in nineteenth-century society that meant women. Sweet, floral fragrances were considered feminine by nature because, according to the gender standards of the day, "sweetness" and "floweriness" were quintessentially feminine characteristics. If the flower garden was classified as a female domain, however, the woods were typed as a male one, making "woodsy" scents, such as pine and cedar, an acceptable alternative for men. Properly, nonetheless, men were expected to disdain all such olfactory artifice and smell only of clean male skin and tobacco. This emphasis on the olfactory difference between men and women was part of a general cultural insistence at the time that the sexes appear in all ways to be different.[34]

It was not just perfume which became feminized in the nineteenth century, however, but the whole sense of smell. Beginning with the Enlightenment,° smell had been increasingly devalued as a means of conveying or

30

---

the Enlightenment: An intellectual movement of eighteenth century Europe marked by the rejection of social, political, and philosophical ideas based on faith in favor of those based on reason.

acquiring essential truths. The odor of sanctity° was no longer an influential concept, nor were smells thought to have therapeutic powers. Sight, instead, had become the pre-eminent means and metaphor for discovery and knowledge, the sense *par excellence* of science. Sight, therefore, increasingly became associated with men, who—as explorers, scientists, politicians or industrialists—were perceived as discovering and dominating the world through their keen gaze. Smell, in turn, was not considered the sense of intuition and sentiment, of homemaking and seduction, all of which were associated with women. It was maps, microscopes and money on the one hand, and potpourris, pabulum° and perfume on the other. Significantly, however, smell was also the sense of "savages" and animals, two categories of beings who, like women, were deprecated and exploited by contemporary Western culture.[35]

The upheaval of the First World War further altered the perception of smell by causing many of the qualities which had come to be associated with it—sentimentality, intuition, nostalgia—to be considered obsolete and even ridiculous in the fast-paced and hard-nosed modern world. Potpourris had no place in the functional twentieth-century home. Flower shows could not compete with the cinema. It was at this time that the modern olfactory era began in the West, an era characterized by the widespread deodorization of public and private space; the restriction of perfumes to personal use, often on special occasions only and primarily by women; and a general devaluation of, and inattention to, olfactory power and meaning.[36] . . .

Smell and Science

The interest in smell shown by writers of the nineteenth century was also manifested by scientists. Whereas literature tended to glorify smell, however, science tended to depreciate it. Already in the sixteenth century, René Descartes° had made it clear that the sense of science was to be sight and this position was strengthened in the following centuries. Smells, so hard to measure, name or recreate, were undoubtedly among the least accessible sensory stimuli to the methods of science.

Nonetheless, during the eighteenth and nineteenth centuries, when science was avidly exploring the former domains of religion, folklore and alchemy, odors were for a time an important subject of scientific investigation and discourse. Human odors, for example, were enthusiastically, if not very reliably, classified by sex, race, age, diet and even hair color (brunettes were said to smell pungent and blondes musky) by the scientists of the period.[37]

It was the odors of putridity, however, which captured most of the scientific interest directed towards smell, as Alain Corbin has amply documented in his

the odor of sanctity: A mystical fragrance believed by medieval church leaders to signify the presence of the Holy Spirit.

pabulum: Baby food.

René Descartes: (1596–1650), French philosopher.

book on the perception of smell in eighteenth- and nineteenth-century France. This was due to the general belief in stench as a major source of disease. Certain scholars thus devoted themselves to studying the odors of street filth; others investigated the scents exhaled by prison or hospital walls; still others, the odors produced by the decomposition of corpses or excrement. Dedicated physicians and chemists, surveying the stenches of polluted rivers, produced descriptions of fetidity which rival the olfactory poetics of Ben Jonson's° "The Famous Voyage," but within the context of a scientific enquiry.[38]

All this came to an end in the late eighteen hundreds. Aromatics had already been dismissed by science as serving only to mask, not transform, foul odors. Now, Pasteur's° discovery that most familiar diseases are caused by germs led scientists to conclude that foul odors themselves were not agents of illness, but merely rather unimportant byproducts. The medical community left smells behind and moved on to microbes. In the scientific paradigm of the universe, odors had become inessential.[39]   35

Paralleling and informing the scientific discourse on smell, was the philosophical discourse. According to the dominant philosophic trends of the Enlightenment, smell offered neither a significant means of acquiring knowledge nor of aesthetic enjoyment. Condillac° in his *Treatise on the Sensations,* for example, remarked that "of all the senses [smell] is the one that seems to contribute the least to the operations of the human mind."[40] His contemporary Kant° agreed, relegating smell to the dustheap of the senses:

> To which organic sense do we owe the least and which seems to be the most dispensible? The sense of smell. It does not pay us to cultivate it or to refine it in order to gain enjoyment; this sense can pick up more objects of aversion than of pleasure (especially in crowded places) and, besides, the pleasure coming from the sense of smell cannot be other than fleeting and transitory.[41]

Such an all-out condemnation of smell reeks of a major sensory repression. Yet, as the scientists and psychologists of the nineteenth and early twentieth centuries would argue, the suppression of the sense of smell was one of the defining characteristics of "civilized man." Darwin° had postulated that humans lost their acuity of smell in the process of evolving from animals.[42] The marginalization of smell in human society, therefore, appeared necessary for evolutionary and cultural progress, while any attempt to cultivate smell would signify a regression to an earlier, more primitive state. Freud° and previously

Ben Jonsons: Benjamin Jonson (1572–1637), English dramatist.

Pasteurs: Louis Pasteur (1822–1895), French chemist and microbiologist.

Condillac: Etienne Bonnot de Condillac (1715–1780), French philosopher.

Kant: Immanuel Kant (1724–1804), German philosopher.

Darwin: Charles Robert Darwin (1809–1882), English naturalist and author of *The Origin of Species* (1859), which first presented the theory of evolution through natural selection.

Freud: Sigmund Freud (1856–1939), Austrian neurologist credited as the founder of modern psychoanalysis.

Herder° held that smell had given way to sight when the human species began to walk upright, removing the nose from the proximity of scent trails and increasing the visual field. Since, according to Freud, individuals repeat the process of evolution in their psychological development, as a person matures, the reveling in odor of the infant should likewise give way to visual pleasures. Adults who continue to emphasize the olfactory are hence arrested in their psychological development.[43]

At the turn of the twentieth century, Havelock Ellis° wrote extensively on the psychology of smell. He concluded, as had others in his field, that:

> The perfume exhaled by many holy men and women . . . was doubtless due . . . to abnormal nervous conditions, for it is well known that such conditions affect the odor, and in insanity, for instance, the presence is noted of bodily odors which have sometimes even been considered of diagnostic importance.[44]

The "odor of sanctity" occurring after death, in turn, was attributed by Ellis to a confusion with the *odor mortis*. As for the reputed olfactory sensitivity of many saints, he noted that "smell and taste hallucinations appear to be specially frequent in forms of religious insanity."[45] Not only could insanity be productive of abnormal odors and olfactory delusions, odors could also be productive of insanity. Ellis notes that "dealers in musk are said to be specially liable to precocious dementia."[46]

The olfactory imagery in the works of many nineteenth-century writers was also explained by Ellis in terms of a psychological disorder:

> It is certain also that a great many neurasthenic° people . . . are peculiarly susceptible to olfactory influences. A number of eminent poets and novelists — especially, it would appear, in France — seem to be in this case.[47]

The German writer Max Nordau stated this position more strongly in his book *Degeneration*. In this work he condemns Zola,° for example, for presenting characters in his novels not as "normal individuals, viz., in the first instance as optical and acoustic phenomena, but as olfactory perceptions."[48] Sight and hearing are thus established as the acceptable media for the perception of others, while smell becomes abnormal. Nordau rhetorically asks: "Why should the sense of smell be neglected in poetry? Has it not the same rights as all the other senses?"[49] He responds by saying that individuals cannot set themselves against "the march of organic evolution":

Herder: Johann Gottfried von Herder (1744–1803), German philosopher and writer.
Havelock Ellis: Henry Havelock Ellis (1859–1939), English psychologist and writer.
neurasthenic: A person suffering from neurasthenia, a psychological disorder characterized by fatigue, lack of motivation, and depression.
Zola: Emile Zola (1840–1902), French novelist.

The underdeveloped or insufficiently developed senses help the brain little or not at all, to know and understand the world. . . . Smellers among degenerates represent an atavism° going back, not only to the primeval period of man, but infinitely more remote still, to an epoch anterior to man.[50]

Not all contemporary scientists agreed with this position, however. In fact, there were some who went to the other extreme and elaborated theories of smell almost as mystical as the olfactory revelations of the saints. One such, August Galopin, in a book entitled *Le parfum de la femme*, asserted that

[t]he purest marriage that can be contracted between a man and a woman, is that engendered by olfaction and sanctioned by a common assimilation in the brain of the animated molecules due to the secretion and evaporation of two bodies in contact and sympathy.[51]

Such aromaphiles were blowing against the wind, however, and it is not their work, but that of Freud and Ellis which survived to influence posterity.

The late nineteenth- and early twentieth-century scholars of olfaction were aware of the continuing presence of traditional olfactory beliefs in many rural European communities. These they tended to dismiss, however, as curious but archaic customs. Similarly, there was significant interest among anthropologists in describing the olfactory practices of non-Western cultures; but this was not with the purpose of elevating the sense of smell, but rather of devaluing the peoples who so elaborated it. A higher olfactory consciousness in non-European cultures was taken as one more proof of their lower status on the evolutionary scale of civilization.[52]

Such comparative studies of olfactory and other sensory practices lost   40 favor after the Second World War. The odors and flavors of other cultures, it was thought, were mere "picturesque" details that belonged more in travelogues than in serious anthropological literature. Furthermore, studying the role of smell among Third World peoples seemed to smack too much of the unsavory racist theories of the nineteenth century which associated smell with savagery. Just as the anthropologists of that time had sought to denigrate non-Europeans by bringing out their reliance on the "lower" sense of smell, modern anthropologists sought to render them as "civilized" as Europeans, by deodorizing their cultures.

By the mid-twentieth century, anthropologists, with a few exceptions,[53] would stop even noticing cultural differences of smell. There was now no apparent alternative to the olfactory illiteracy of the modern West. Whatever (marginal) role smell played in the West was (and is) assumed to be the same the world over. . . .

atavism: A recurrence of or a reversion to a past style, form, manner, outlook, or approach; hence, a throwback.

Notes

1. Cited in F. Muir, *An Irreverent and Almost Complete Social History of the Bathroom*, New York, Stein & Day, 1983, p. 35.

2. Cited in Vigarello, *Concepts of Cleanliness: Changing Attitudes in France Since the Middle Ages*, J. Birrell (trans.), Cambridge, Cambridge University Press, 1988, p. 12.

3. Wright, *Clean and Decent: The Fascinating History of the Bathroom and the Water Closet*, Toronto, University of Toronto Press, 1960, p. 75.

4. Rowse (ed.), *The Annotated Shakespeare*, New York, Clarkson N. Potter, 1978, vol. 1, *The Taming of the Shrew*, induction 1, scene 1, p. 124.

5. H. de Monteux, *Conservation de santé et prolongation de la vie*, Paris, 1572, p. 265, cited in Vigarello, *Concepts of Cleanliness*, p. 17.

6. Rowse (ed.), *The Annotated Shakespeare*, vol. 1, *Much Ado About Nothing*, act 3, scene 2, p. 418.

7. L. Thorndike, *A History of Magic and Experimental Science*, vol. 7, New York, Columbia University Press, 1958, pp. 235, 264.

8. J. Nichols, *The Progresses of Queen Elizabeth*, London, John Nichols & Son, 1823, p. 319.

9. C. J. S. Thompson, *Mystery and Lure of Perfume*, London, John Lane The Bodley Head, 1929, pp. 143–6, 164–6; Corbin, *The Foul and the Fragrant: Odor and the French Social Imagination*, M. Kochan, R. Porter, and C. Prendergast (trans.), Cambridge Mass., Harvard University Press, 1986, p. 115.

10. F. P. Wilson (ed.), *The Plague Pamphlets of Thomas Dekker*, Oxford, Clarendon Press, 1925, p. 29.

11. Corbin, *The Foul and the Fragrant*, pp. 66–75.

12. J. Hogg, *London As It Is*, London, John Maccone, 1837, p. 220.

13. Ibid., p. 225.

14. H. Gavin, *Sanitary Ramblings*, London, John Churchill, 1848, pp. 9, 20.

15. Ibid., p. 27.

16. V. Hugo, *Les Misérables*, C. Wilbour (trans.), New York, Modern Library, n.d., p. 1056.

17. Ibid., p. 1054.

18. Gavin, *Sanitary Ramblings*, p. 69.

19. R. Reynolds, *Cleanliness and Godliness*, London, George Allen & Unwin, 1943, p. 91.

20. Corbin, *The Foul and the Fragrant*, p. 213.

21. Ibid., pp. 79–104; McLaughlin, *Coprophilia*, p. 151.

22. Corbin, *The Foul and the Fragrant*, p. 22.

23. McLaughlin, *Coprophilia or A Peck of Dirt*, London, Cassell, 1971, p. 148.

24. See, for example, Corbin, *The Foul and the Fragrant*, pp. 227–8.

25. G. Daignan, *Ordre de service des hôpitaux militaires*, Paris, 1785, p. 173, cited in Vigarello, *Concepts of Cleanliness*, p. 150.

26. Vigarello, *Concepts of Cleanliness*, p. 171.

27. Cited in McLaughlin, *Coprophilia*, p. 136.

28. C. H. Piesse (ed.), *Piesse's Art of Perfumery*, London, Piesse & Ludin, 1891, p. 32.

29. Vigarello, *Concepts of Cleanliness*, pp. 194–201.

30. Cited in Muir, *Social History of the Bathroom*, p. 25.

31. Vigarello, *Concepts of Cleanliness*, pp. 137–41.

32. Cited in P. Stalybrass and A. White, *The Politics and Poetics of Transgression,* Ithaca, N.Y., Cornell University Press, 1986, p. 139.

33. Thompson, *Mystery and Lure of Perfume,* p. 166.

34. See Classen, *Worlds of Sense: Exploring the Senses in History and Across Cultures,* London, Routlege, 1993, pp. 87–93.

35. Ibid., p. 31.

36. Ibid., pp. 34–5.

37. Corbin, *The Foul and the Fragrant,* pp. 35–48; H. Ellis, *Studies in the Psychology of Sex,* vol. 1, New York, Random House, 1942, [1899], part 3, pp. 48–81.

38. Corbin, *The Foul and the Fragrant,* pp. 1–61.

39. Ibid., pp. 67–70, 223–4.

40. E. B. de Condillac, *Treatise on the Sensations,* G. Carr (trans.), Los Angeles, University of Southern California Press, 1930, p. xxxi.

41. I. Kant, *Anthropology from a Pragmatic Point of View,* V. L. Dowdell (trans.), Carbondale and Edwardsville, Southern Illinois University Press, 1978 [1798], 22, p. 46. Annick Le Guérer discusses attitudes towards olfaction in Western philosophy in *Scent: The Mysterious and Essential Powers of Smell,* R. Miller (trans.), New York, Turtle Bay Books, 1992, pp. 141–203.

42. C. Darwin, *The Descent of Man and Selection in Relation to Sex,* New York, D. Appleton, 1898, pp. 17–18.

43. S. Freud, *Civilization and its Discontents,* J. Strachey (trans.), New York, W. W. Norton, 1961, p. 46.

44. Ellis, *Psychology of Sex,* vol. 1, p. 62.

45. Ibid., p. 72.

46. Ibid., p. 107.

47. Ibid., pp. 72–3.

48. M. Nordau, *Degeneration,* New York, D. Appleton, 1902, p. 502.

49. Ibid.

50. Ibid., pp. 502–3.

51. A. Galopin, *Le parfum de la femme,* 1886, cited in Ellis, *Psychology of Sex,* p. 78.

52. In *The Descent of Man,* Darwin stated that "the sense of smell is of extremely slight service, if any, even to the dark coloured races of men, in whom it is more highly developed than in the white and civilized races" (pp. 17–18).

53. Notably Claude Lévi-Strauss. See, for example, his book *The Raw and the Cooked: Introduction to a Science of Mythology,* vol. 1, J. and D. Weightman (trans.), New York, Harper & Row, 1969.

EXPLORING THE TEXT

1. How, according to the authors, did pre-eighteenth-century Europeans feel about odors and personal hygiene? How well does this image compare with your pre-conceptions about life in pre-Enlightenment Europe or with depictions of pre-Enlightenment Europe that you have encountered in popular movies like *Shakespeare in Love, Elizabeth,* or other more recent period films?

2. According to the authors, what role did religion, science, and the rise of the middle class play in the "olfactory revolution" that occurred in the eighteenth century? How were changes in attitudes toward odor linked to the issue of "moral

reform"? To what extent would it be fair to say that odor continues to have moral implications in contemporary American society?

3. How and why did scents become gendered in the West? Are certain scents still associated with masculinity and others with femininity today? What does this suggest about modern views of male and female gender roles?

4. How, according to the authors, has the status of the sense smell as a source of knowledge changed since the advent of modern science? Why have these changes occurred and what do they suggest about European views of what it means to be civilized? To what extent would you agree?

FURTHER EXPLORATIONS

1. Working in groups, discuss current American attitudes toward smell and scent. Is there any evidence to suggest that American attitudes toward the sense of smell are changing? Is smell making a comeback, or are we as a culture still devoted to the project of "deodorization" that began during the olfactory revolution?

2. Drawing on "The Olfactory Revolution" and Diane Ackerman's "Taste" (p. 36), compare the role that culture plays in relation to the development of our senses of taste and smell. To what extent would you agree that odor is a culturally determined quality? Do aromas and scents play a more significant role in some cultures than they do in others? On what evidence do you base your conclusion?

3. Return to Ian Frazier's "Take the F" (p. 18), and examine how the senses of taste and smell are involved in his description of his daily commute. How does Frazier convey his olfactory and gustatory experience of life in New York? To what extent do vision and hearing dominate the verbal picture he presents?

4. How might Bill McKibben's (p. 109) analysis of television's impact on the senses support the idea that the West has been undergoing an "olfactory revolution" over the past century? Would McKibben be likely to agree that technology favors the "intellectual" senses of sight and hearing over the more "primitive" senses of taste, touch, and smell?

ESSAY OPTIONS

1. Although the sense of smell is rarely if ever deliberately "educated" in today's post-Enlightenment school systems, school itself is an experience that is often closely associated with a variety of strong olfactory memories. Write an essay describing the olfactory impressions of your own experience of schooling—from the smells of kindergarten through the scents and aromas that accompanied you through middle school to graduation.

2. Write an essay in which you map out the "olfactory geography" of your city, college campus, or some other area you are well acquainted with. What specific places, neighborhoods, or buildings can be identified by odor? What information do these smells communicate, and what feelings or moods do they evoke in relation to the places they are associated with?

Seeing Things

K. C. COLE

As every secondary school student knows, the scientific method revolves around the concepts of close observation and experimentation. But as science pushes the boundaries of knowledge farther and farther beyond the scale of day-to-day experience, it becomes increasingly hard to say exactly what scientists are seeing when they observe natural phenomena. What, for instance, does the physicist "see" when tracking the paths of quarks, gluons, and other subatomic particles as they course through an accelerator? What does the astronomer "see" when poring over heaps of numerical data generated by a radio telescope? As K. C. Cole suggests in this selection, contemporary scientists have mastered the art of indirect perception, relying on high-tech apparatus to extend the reach of their senses far beyond normal biological limits. Indeed, the history of modern science from Galileo to Niels Bohr can be seen as the technological extension of the human sensory system into distinctly inhuman realms of experience. Yet, as Cole indicates in this engaging meditation on the relation of mind and vision, the way we see things in our daily lives is equally indirect and, in a sense, artificial. Human vision may appear to be effortless, but as Cole reminds us, our ability to see the world around us always involves sophisticated acts of interpretation and a rich background of culturally conditioned assumptions. A graduate of Columbia University, Cole is the science writer for the *Los Angeles Times* and author of *The Universe and the Teacup: The Mathematics of Truth and Beauty* (1998), which won the American Institute of Physics Award for Best Science Writing in 1995. She is also the author of *First You Build a Cloud and Other Reflections on Physics as a Way of Life* (1999), the source of this selection, and most recently, *The Hole in the Universe: How Scientists Peered Over the Edge of Emptiness and Found Everything* (2001).

BEFORE READING

Freewrite in your journal about what you see when you look up at the night sky. What, do you imagine, might an astronomer see? A filmmaker? A meteorologist? An astrologer? A philosopher? A theologian? Why might these people each view the night sky differently?

We're pretty good at picking out things in what looks like noise.

> — University of Florida astronomer ROBERT PEÑA,
> while observing on the Keck Telescope on Mauna Kea,
> Hawaii, with UCLA astronomer Andrea Ghez

And sometimes we're pretty imaginative.

> — ANDREA GHEZ

Many years ago, when I first began delving into the curious Alice in Wonderland world of particle physics — that subatomic never-never land inhabited by quarks and gluons, entities strange and charmed — I asked my friend the physicist how anyone could believe in such seemingly ephemeral objects, things that no one could ever really see. And he answered, "It all depends on what you mean by seeing."

Like many people, I always feel somewhat skeptical when I hear physicists confidently claiming to have "seen" particles effervescing into existence for a mere billionth of a second, or massive quasars teetering 10 billion light-years away at the very brink of space and time.[1] I know for a fact that they have seen no such thing. Quarks and quasars are invisible to the naked eye. At best, the physicist has seen a bump on a curve plotting the ratio of various kinds of particles produced in a subatomic collision or the faint fingerprints left by 10 billion-year-old photons on silicon detectors; more often, such a "sighting" is in truth a conclusion laboriously drawn from long hours of computer calculation and long chains of inferences and assumptions. Hardly the sort of thing to inspire an exultant "Eureka!" (Or even "Land ho!") Sometimes the things that scientists say they see are so removed from actual quarks or quasars that one wonders if they (or we) should believe their eyes.

Physicists "see" exotic particles by bombarding them with other particles and analyzing the patterns created as the particles bounce back into their electronic detectors. The first person to "see" the atomic nucleus used much the same method, except that the electronic detector used was the human eye. During World War I, Ernest Rutherford aimed a beam of particles streaming from a radioactive rock toward a thin sheet of gold foil. Most of the particles passed right through. But some—surprisingly—were scattered through very large angles and a few were even reflected *backward*. "It was about as

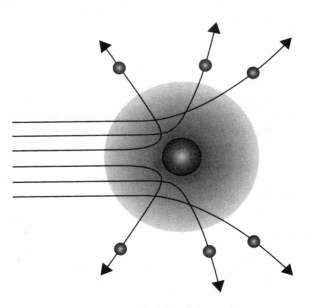

FIGURE 1.1   How Rutherford "saw" the nucleus.

credible," said Rutherford, "as if you had fired a fifteen-inch shell at a piece of tissue paper and it came back and hit you." From this Rutherford concluded that the atom was not a uniform mass, as previously thought, but something rather more like a miniature solar system, with almost all of the mass concentrated in a small, central nuclear "sun." Most of the particles passed right through because there was very little inside the gold atoms for them to hit; if a particle did chance to hit the nucleus, however, it could be reflected backward like a ball hitting a brick wall.

Today, physicists similarly "see" all kinds of particles by bombarding all kinds of targets with all kinds of other particles, and they use sophisticated electronic equipment to analyze their results. But in truth, seeing inside an atom is not so different from seeing a friend or a building. It only *seems* unreal and abstract, because the details of the process are slightly less familiar: The way we go about seeing things in everyday life is scarcely what you'd call "direct."

I see this page, for example, because rapidly vibrating atoms in the filament of the lightbulb overhead and in the sun outside my window some 93 million miles away are sending out streams of light particles called photons, some of which are showering down right now on the paper's black-and-white surface. A few of these photons collide (as in an atom smasher) with the molecules in the ink, and are absorbed; others hit the pigment in the paper and are redirected back in the direction of my eyes. If they penetrate the pupil, they will be focused by a lens onto a light-sensitive screen (the retina), a sophisticated electronic detector that passes along information about the photons' energies, trajectories, and frequencies to my brain in the form of digital bits. On the basis of laborious calculations and long chains of inferences and assumptions, my brain concludes that the light patterns represent printed words, conveying some rough translation of the writer's passing thoughts. 10

Of course, my eyes, like particle detectors and telescopes, are tuned in only to the narrowest band of information coming from the outside world. The pupil is but a tiny porthole in a sea of radiation. In a universe alight with images, we are mostly in the dark. Human eyes respond only to those electromagnetic vibrations that make waves between .00007 and .00004 of a centimeter long. Yet, as I type, I am bombarded by other kinds of electromagnetic waves as small as atoms and as large as mountains, coming from the far reaches of space, from the inside of my own body, from the radio transmitter twenty miles away. I know that these signals are there, in the room with me, because if I flip on the radio or television I will suddenly be able to see or hear them, in the same way that visions suddenly "appear" before me the minute I open my eyes. If I had still other kinds of detectors (I can sense some of the infrared radiation on the surface of my skin as heat), I could pick up still other kinds of signals. Yet we walk through this dense web of radiant information every day without being the least aware of its existence.

Radiation is only one kind of information to which we are mostly blind. We are deaf to most of the sound around us. Our chemical senses (taste and smell) are extremely limited compared to those of a plant, or a cell, or a dog.

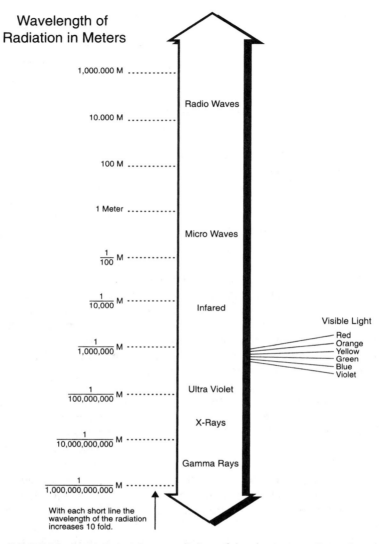

Wavelength of Radiation in Meters

1,000.000 M

Radio Waves

10.000 M

100 M

1 Meter

Micro Waves

$\frac{1}{100}$ M

$\frac{1}{10,000}$ M   Infared

Visible Light

$\frac{1}{1,000,000}$ M

Red
Orange
Yellow
Green
Blue
Violet

$\frac{1}{100,000,000}$ M   Ultra Violet

X-Rays

$\frac{1}{10,000,000,000}$ M

Gamma Rays

$\frac{1}{1,000,000,000,000}$ M

With each short line the wavelength of the radiation increases 10 fold.

FIGURE 1.2   Visible light is but a small sliver of the electromagnetic spectrum.

We can barely perceive the difference between hot and cold: a blindfolded person can't tell whether she has been burned by a hot iron or dry ice. Even our perception of forces is curtailed by our size. While we can easily sense the pull of gravity, we are almost completely insensitive to the pulls and pushes of air resistance and surface tension that are major forces in the lives of cells and flies. We don't have to push the air out of the way to walk through it, as the gnat does; on the other hand, the electrical force of cohesion is relatively so much stronger for a small creature that the fly can crawl up the wall, completely ignoring gravity. To say that we are narrow-minded (or at least "narrow-sensed") is the least of it.

Naturalist Loren Eiseley writes of coming upon a spiderweb in a forest. The spider is confined to its own two-dimensional universe, totally oblivious to the plants or people around it, even to the pencil Eiseley uses to reach out and pluck it: "Spider thoughts in a spider universe—sensitive to raindrop and moth flutter, nothing beyond, nothing allowed for the unexpected, the inserted pencil from the outside world."

We live in a spiderweb, too—a three-dimensional spiderweb spun in the unseen context of our four-dimensional space—and we are only beginning to become aware of the vast universe outside. Our perceptions of time and space are largely limited to things in our own experience, of our own relative size. We find it almost impossibly difficult to comprehend numbers much larger than those we can count on our own fingers and toes, or spans of time much longer than our lifetimes. Looking outside our spiderweb takes an enormous leap of the imagination.

From our spider point of view, the world is clearly flat. It is also obviously   10
motionless. It was probably Galileo who first proposed the idea that we cannot tell by experiment alone whether we are moving or not. Put yourself inside the closed cabin of a steadily moving ship, he said. Allow small winged creatures like gnats to fly around, watch fish swimming in a bowl, toss objects back and forth, notice how things fall to the ground. No matter how many experiments you perform, "you shall not be able to discern the least alteration in all the forenamed effects, nor can you gather by any of them whether the ship moves or stands still."

What you perceive as "standing still" at the equator is in reality a rapid spin around the earth's axis at the dizzying rate of 1,000 miles per hour. In addition, the entire spinning earth is whizzing around the sun with a speed of almost 20 miles per second. The solar system itself is moving with respect to the center of our galaxy at 120 miles per second, and our galaxy, the Milky Way, is rushing toward the neighboring Andromeda Galaxy (from its point of view) at 50 miles per second. And that's not all: if you looked at the earth from a far-off quasar, you might see us speeding away at 165,000 miles per second, close to the speed of light.

What Galileo stumbled upon in stepping out of his spiderweb was what Einstein would later refine into the theory of relativity. Einstein saw that there were other things we couldn't perceive, like the elastic nature of space and time. We were being deceived by our senses into thinking that our own Euclidean three-dimensional geometry was the geometry of the universe. Einstein was out of his senses. He saw that it didn't matter whether or not our own crude perceptual instruments could pick up the tiny increases in the mass of objects as they moved faster. It was a limitation of our instruments. Today's particle accelerators routinely push particles to speeds almost as fast as the speed of light, and see them gain forty thousand times their initial weight in the process!

In addition to all the things that we *can't* see are the things that we *don't* see because we choose to ignore them. Right now, I am choosing to ignore the sounds of my own breathing, the feel of the ring on my finger, the sight of the glasses that are right in front of my nose—and even the nose on my face. Shutters and pupils are meant not to let information in but to shut it out. As anyone knows who has ever held a camera, too much information is easily as blinding as too little. If you played all nine Beethoven symphonies at once, you would hear nothing but noise.

But deciding what to turn on and off and when is a dangerous business—especially since we are mostly unaware of it. Recently, four people sat in my living room directly underneath a loud antique clock. At 3:05 I asked whether the clock had struck three. Two people insisted it had and two insisted it hadn't.

Our eyes automatically erase the oversize feet and out-of-focus images   15 that are clear to the more objective camera's eye. Distractions erase reams of information, which is one reason there is a difference between "listening" and "hearing." It is a physical fact that you cannot listen to even two conversations at once, or see in sharp focus more than the narrowest sliver of a visual field.

Sorting information from "noise" is one of the most important processes in all of perception. Yet it is also obviously a minefield of potential mistakes. There is a simple and striking illusion in which two facing profiles suddenly appear as a vase, which just as suddenly can fade again into two facing profiles. You cannot see both vase and faces at once, because you cannot see something as background and foreground (or information and "noise") at once. Whatever is in the background becomes as invisible as if it weren't there, even though you may be looking right at it.

Mostly what disappears are the sights we get used to—like our noses and eyeglasses, but also our sunsets and even the sounds of our children. Steady signals fatigue our senses, numbing our powers of response. Dogs will sleep through all kinds of everyday noises only to snap into alertness at the soft step of an intruder; parents have been known to snore through sirens and garbage trucks only to awake alert at the merest whimper from their newborn baby.

Sensory atrophy is largely learned. But some is automatic. That is, some kinds of signals actually fatigue our physical sensors to the point that we are no longer able to perceive them. Perhaps the most common example of this is the afterimage. If you stare at a bright light or open your eyes to the streaks of sunlight coming through the edges of the shades first thing in the morning, you are likely to look away only to see the image lingering in your field of vision. The afterimage is dark where the original image was bright, because it corresponds to those places on your retina where the sensors have been bleached by the light. For some moments, they can no longer respond. They can no longer send the signal to your brain saying, "white wall here" or "blue sky here." The rest of your retina responds normally, so what you see is a normal background with a dark image of the original bright "flash" imposed on it.

Some painters actually color their work with afterimages in mind. For when your eyes tire of one color, they will see its complement. Say, for example, you stare for fifteen seconds or so at a bright-red area on a painting or on a wall. The red sensors in your eye fatigue. If you then look at a white wall, your eyes will send the following message to your brain: white *minus* red. Since white minus red is green, green is the color you see. (If you stare at a green spot, you see a red spot when you look at the white wall. And so on.)

Your motion sensors work much the same way. If you spin around the   20
room in one direction, your motion sensors soon lose their ability to respond to the steady signals: they no longer send a message to the brain that you are turning clockwise; turning clockwise has become synonymous with "stopped." When you stop spinning, the fatigued sensors respond by sending a message to the brain that says, "no longer stopped; spinning in opposite direction." You sense yourself spinning counterclockwise. If you stare at falling water for fifteen seconds or so and then switch your gaze to the ground, it can make the ground seem to "fall up," a phenomenon appropriately known as the waterfall effect.

Sensory fatigue can sometimes cause you to perceive the *opposite* of the signals you actually receive.

People who are brilliant scientists (or writers or parents or doctors or carpenters) are those who have a special talent for keeping the important things in focus—both separating the signal from the noise and also knowing when what sounds like noise might contain the quiet whisper of important information.

The instruments of science have vastly extended our senses. Indeed, physicist David Bohm concludes that "science is *mainly* a way of extending our perceptual contact with the world," its purpose being to foster "an awareness and understanding of an ever growing segment of the world with which we are in contact." Technology has unveiled vast new vistas, opening up untapped realms of time, space, and temperature. To modern telescopes and particle accelerators, the radio waves and gamma rays invisible to us are rich with images. The number of so-called elementary particles has proliferated wildly because the instrumentation to "see" them has gotten better and better. The same is true of the number of stars in the sky, and such strange newcomers to the galactic zoo as pulsars and quasars and probable planets around stars other than our sun. We can see out into space, back into time, inside our own genetic structure. We can see what the stars are made of and how a virus looks.

We can measure things smaller and larger, colder and hotter, faster and slower than could ever be "seen" before. With the help of high-powered computers, scientists can extrapolate to the end of the universe or the beginning of time or the center of the earth. They can "see" what happens when chemicals react, particles collide, hurricanes evolve.

"How rich we are," writes Guy Murchie, "that we can look on these worlds with the perspective of modern science . . . that we do not have to wonder as did former men whether stars are jewels dangling from celestial drapery or peepholes in the astral skin of creation!"

Our view of the universe is changing so rapidly partly because our ability to see is growing so rapidly. That's one reason why ideas that seem right today get overturned so readily tomorrow. The more we see, the more we correct our vision. "Early descriptions of the universe are egocentric and based on the physical size and capabilities of man," writes Richard Gregory in his marvelous book on perception, *The Intelligent Eye*. Prescientific philosophy was based solely on human perception. But now we know that there is a lot going on that we can't see *except* through science. "The simple fact that stars exist invisible to the unaided eye," Gregory writes, "made it unlikely that the heavens are but a backcloth for the state of human drama."

Scientific perception has a different authority from personal perception, because it can more easily be shared. It's a way of seeing that many people can agree on—or at least agree on a way of thinking about. But the process is essentially the same: scientists "see" by gathering data, measuring, making assumptions, and drawing conclusions. "Elementary particles don't seem real to ordinary people, because they aren't perceived in an ordinary way," says MIT physicist Vera Kistiakowsky. "Something like astronomy *seems* more real, because you can see the stars with your own eyes. But even that is mostly inferred. All science involves the interpretation of secondary information."

All *perception* involves the interpretation of secondary information. We are always seeing a great deal more than meets the eye. The light patterns that form on the tiny screens within our eyes are upside down, full of holes and splotches, badly bent out of shape. Most of what we see is in our heads. If I believed my eyes, I would see people shrink to Thumbelina size as they walked away. In fact, all my visions would remain inside my body. For it is our brains that perform the incredible feat of projecting what we see "out there" from the backs of our eyes to some arbitrary place in space. Not only vision but *all* sensory experience takes place within our bodies. Yet we attribute these properties to objects that exist outside us. We say that ice cream tastes sweet, or the table feels hard, when in fact it is *we* who taste and feel.

Galileo recognized that qualities such as color and smell "can no more be ascribed to the external objects than can the tickling or the pain caused sometimes by touching such objects." We are tickled or hurt not by the feather or pin but by the interpretation of an electrical signal within our brains.

"We each live our mental life in a prison-house from which there is no escape," writes Sir James Jeans. "It is our body; and its only communication with

25

the outer world is through our sense organs—eyes, ears, etc. These form windows through which we can look out onto the outer world and acquire knowledge of it."

Our newfound scientific senses are even farther from direct interpretation. The images of quasars seen by radio telescopes using Very Long Baseline Interferometry, for example, are really composite patterns resolved from information recorded separately at individual antennas as much as six thousand miles apart, synchronized by atomic clocks and pieced together by computers. They are not "images" in the ordinary sense but rather interference patterns, like the rapidly moving moirés° you see when two fences or fireplace grates or curtains overlap—secondary patterns emerging from the combination of two (unseen) patterns.

Human science no longer experiences the world through human senses. Indeed, much of scientific knowledge these days completely contradicts our senses, which is why it is so difficult to accept such concepts as quantum mechanics and curved space. The sights and sounds and objects and motions around us are not divided up into small quantum bits, like still frames from a moving picture. The space around us does not seem to bend or change or curve. "This has led to a curious situation," writes Gregory. "The physicist in a sense cannot trust his own thought." And yet, he points out, we have to learn with the "nonperceptual concepts" of physics: "We are left with a question: How far are human brains capable of functioning with concepts detached from sensory experience?"

The answer has to be that there is more than one valid way of seeing things. If we listen to Bach with our ears, and then "listen" again with (other kinds of) electronic detectors, we will pick up very different sets of signals. Both kinds of perception are equally indirect. There are many possible windows on reality. Indeed, one of Einstein's most radical notions had to do with the multiple realities of space and time; that is, the space or time we perceive depends on the means we use to mark it off, on our point of view. "Space has no objective reality except as an order or arrangement of the objects we perceive in it," writes Lincoln Barnett, "and time has no independent existence apart from the order of events by which we measure it."

Perception, after all, is a very *active* process. We do not just sit around waiting for information to rain down on us. We go out and get it. In the process, we alter it and even create it. One of the strangest things about the way physicists "see" elementary particles is that they often create them out of the energy of other particles to make them visible—something that doesn't seem quite "fair." But as Philip Morrison points out, you can't see the rapidly rotating blades of a fan unless you stop them or throw a rock at them. You can't sense radio waves by putting your hand in front of them, but you can if you tune your receiver so that it vibrates in resonance with the incoming

moirés: The illusion of moving or "shimmering" patterns created when two sets of geometrically regular patterns of parallel lines are overlaid at an acute angle.

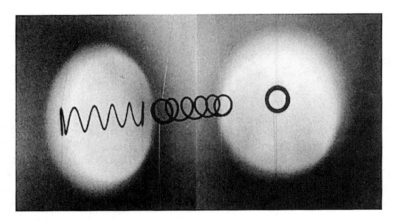

FIGURE 1.3   One shadow of the spring is a circle; another shadow of the same spring is a wave. If you could perceive the spring only by looking at its shadows, you might easily come to the conclusion that it was two different things.

signal. The sound waves coming from the radio are as much created in the process of detecting them as the particles created in accelerators.

What we see depends on what we look for. It also depends on our point of view. A house viewed from an airplane does not look at all the same as a house viewed from its own front door, or from the window of a rapidly passing car. A baby does not recognize a toy viewed from the top as the same toy that looked so very different when seen from the side. A rotating shadow of any three-dimensional object will take on an amazing variety of different shapes. Which is the "true" perspective? It may be that the only wrong perspective is the one that insists on a single perspective. Like the baby with the toy, we may be mistaking one thing for two. Space and time, energy and matter, waves and particles, are all different aspects of the same thing.

Gathering, arranging, and sorting the information from the outside world is only the first step, however. We still must decide, What is it? What does the information mean? Meson or proton? Streetlight or moon? Shadow or burglar? Planet or star? A small dim object close up looks the same as a large bright object from afar. Stick out your thumb and use it to size up a house far away outside the window. The house may seem no bigger than the tip of your nail. Then how do you know it isn't? "When a tiny meteor smaller than a pea is falling through the air," writes Jeans, "it will send the same electric currents to our brains as will a giant star millions of times larger than the sun and millions of times more distant. Primitive man jumped to the conclusion that the tiny meteor was really a star, and we still describe it as a shooting star."

You have no way of knowing that there is anything behind you until you turn around, and yet we are not surprised to see things there. You have no way of knowing that your next step will fall on solid ground, and yet you take it on faith. Sometimes we are fooled: The piece of fluff floating a few feet away looks like an airplane miles up in the sky (or vice versa). Yet most of the time we are remarkably accurate in the way we size up our familiar world and get around in it.

"Familiar," however, is the key. As Richard Gregory points out, perception is a matter of seeing the present with images stored from the past; it is a matter of selecting the most likely (that is, the most familiar) object, the most "obvious" answer for the question, What is it? "This acceptance by the brain of the most probable answer implies a danger: It must be difficult, perhaps somewhat impossible, to see very unusual objects," Gregory notes. And if perception is a matter of making sense of the world with our limited collection of answers from the past, he asks, "then what happens when we are confronted with something unique?"

The answer is, we don't see it. The seventeenth-century Dutch scientist Christiaan Huygens drew detailed pictures of the planet Saturn as seen through his homemade telescopes. But he never recognized the unusual patterns as the now familiar rings. He couldn't see the rings largely because he wasn't *expecting* to see rings. "We not only believe what we see," writes Gregory, "to some extent we see what we believe. . . . The implications about our beliefs are frightening."

Gregory is hardly the only scientist to come to this conclusion. Loren Eiseley writes, "Each man deciphers from the ancient alphabets of nature only those secrets that his own deeps possess the power to endow with meaning." Sir Peter Medawar, in *Advice to a Young Scientist,* dismisses the notion that scientific discoveries are made by "just looking around":

> I myself believe it to be a fallacy that any discoveries are made in this way. I think that Pasteur° and Fontenelle° would have agreed that the mind must already be on the right wavelength, another way of saying that all such discoveries begin as covert hypotheses — that is, as imaginative preconceptions or expectations about the nature of the world and never merely by passive assimilation of the evidence of the senses. . . . The truth is *not* [emphasis his] in nature, waiting to declare itself. . . . Every discovery, every enlargement of the understanding begins as an imaginative preconception of what the truth might be.

In fact, it is often hard to disentangle the image of the "real" world from   40
the preconceptions we project on it. How much about the universe do we actually discover and how much do we impose? Often it is not clear which we are doing — like the person who heard a lecture on astronomy and afterward complained that while the lecturer had beautifully explained how the scientists had discovered the sizes and temperatures of the stars, he had neglected to tell how the scientists discovered their *names.*

Pasteur: Louis Pasteur (1822–1895), French chemist and microbiologist.
Fontenelle: Bernard le Bouyer de Fontenelle (1657–1757), French scientist.

Perceptions are at best good guesses. They are the shortcuts we need to keep the information coming in from the outside world from becoming overwhelming, but they are never (necessarily) the truth. We have to judge a book by its cover, because we don't have the time or the resources to look inside every book. We assume that if we see a face looking out of a window there is a body attached to it, and that something that looks like a tree or a sailboat or a star probably is. We recognize patterns that seem familiar in a wide variety of contexts; even a child seems to know instinctively that a Saint Bernard is a "woof-woof" along with a Pekingese. But it is important to remember that it is we who have decided that these two very dissimilar creatures are both "dogs," in the same way as we call both the tool in the kitchen and a configuration of stars a "dipper." It is we who see the "man" in the moon. Snap judgments are as useful and essential as they are treacherous and misleading.

"We cannot . . . believe in raw data of perception and suppose that perceptually given 'facts' are solid bricks for basing all knowledge," writes Gregory. "All perception is theory-laden."

We see what is familiar and we see what we choose to see, which are often the same thing. If people engage in conversation only to disagree later completely on what was said, then in fact they really "heard" very different things, according to current memory research. "Memory is not a literal recording," says Harvard psychologist Daniel Schacter. "It's more like a kind of [evolving] sculpture." Laboratory studies have revealed consistent biases in the ways we remember things. For example, memory often acts as an ego booster, according to University of Washington memory expert Elizabeth Loftus: "We remember we gave more to charity than we [actually] did, we took more airplane trips, we had kids who walked and talked earlier than they did, we voted in more elections."

What we learn to see is also culturally conditioned, and this applies even to the things we see through the supposedly objective eyes of science. When people first look through a microscope, they often have trouble seeing anything but their own eyelashes, or random specks of light. They have to be taught how to see an amoeba—just as they "have to be taught" racial prejudice.

Culture also affects what scientists "see." Its influence is so strong that when a brilliant supernova appeared in 1054, at the height of religious belief in Europe, not a single European chronicle mentioned it, though it shone for many months. It was not recorded because it was not considered important. It was filtered out of history as effectively as the bonging of my clock was filtered out of my living room.

Galileo first got into trouble when he had the temerity to see such a supernova. "The appearance of a new star in heaven," writes George Gamow, "which was supposed to be absolutely unchangeable according to Aristotle's philosophy and the teachings of the Church, made Galileo many enemies among his scientific colleagues and among the high clergy." Galileo's telescope revealed (among other things) that Venus and Mercury, like the moon, sometimes have crescent shapes, implying that they orbit the sun. But what he saw was "certainly more than the Holy Inquisition° could permit; he was arrested and subjected to a long period of solitary confinement."

We need not go back in history to see examples of this cultural perceptual conditioning. Who would think that civilized people are so culturally accustomed to rooms with right angles that they would rather see a person shrink before their eyes than a room change shape? Yet this happens in the famous Distorted Room invented by the psychologist Adelbert Ames. The room is misshapen in such a way that a person viewing it through a thin slot (which makes binocular depth perception impossible) has to make a perceptual choice: Either people inside shrink and grow as they move about or else the room isn't the usual rectangular shape. People always choose the right angles. Even our perceptual belief that things in the distance don't actually shrink is to some extent culturally conditioned. A psychologist visiting The Exploratorium in San Francisco told the staff about a forest-dwelling tribe of pygmies who had no experience seeing things at long distances. One day this tribe spied a herd of cattle, or some such animal, on a far-off plain—and of course assumed that they were tiny creatures, perhaps the size of ants. Imagine the pygmies' terror when the tiny creatures grew to great size as they approached!

It's fun to be amused by optical illusions. But illusions can be disillusioning. Usually the only illusion involved is a departure from our usual point of view, a contradiction of our preconceived notion of reality. Perceptual expectations not only make it impossible to see the shape of things correctly, they can lead us to see "impossible" things. A case in point is the Impossible Triangle, a structure of three thick beams joined at right angles. Of course, no triangle can consist of three right angles, but the Impossible Triangle is no ordinary two-dimensional triangle. It is a configuration of three beams joined at right angles that *looks* like a triangle from a particular point of view. It is only impossible as long as we insist on seeing it as a familiar triangle, instead of the unfamiliar figure that it really is. The unfamiliar figure, on the other hand, appears impossible, "*although it exists,*" says Gregory (with emphasis!).

We dismiss the real as impossible and experience the impossible even though it cannot be real. If you soak one hand in ice water and one hand in hot water, and then plunge both hands into a bowl of warm water, one hand will feel cold and the other hot, even though they are both resting in water of the same temperature. On the other hand, if you touch metal and Styrofoam at the same temperature, the metal will feel much colder. What you perceive is "impossible" only because your understanding of temperature is incomplete.

Intellectual knowledge alone does not change what we perceive. The   50
Impossible Triangle, the Distorted Room, the experiment with the hot and cold water retain their power to fool us even after we have learned how they work. We still see the sun "rise" and "set." We see the stars hang from a flat

Holy Inquisition: A general tribunal established by the Roman Catholic Church in the thirteenth century for the purpose of suppressing heresy and punishing heretics.

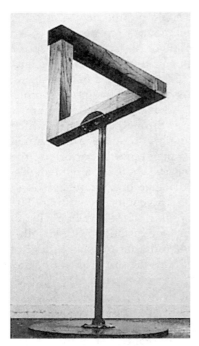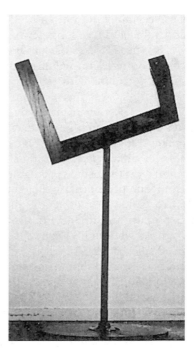

FIGURE 1.4   The Impossible Triangle appears impossible only because we insist on seeing it in the familiar shape we call a triangle. What is truly impossible is the ability to perceive totally unfamiliar objects.

ceiling, earth stretched out flat. We see the moon as a disk about a foot across and a mile away, even when we know it is a sphere about 240,000 miles away and 2,000 miles in diameter. Look at the sun sometime and try to see it as a star 93 million miles away. It is truly impossible. "It is an effort to get perceptual and intellectual knowledge to coincide," writes Gregory. "If the eighteenth-century empiricists had known this, philosophy might have taken a very different course. No doubt there are also implications for political theory and judgment."

The moon in particular is a "heaven-sent object for perceptual study," says Gregory. The size and distance error in our perception of it are about a millionfold. But what is truly surprising, he says, is that we attribute any size or distance to it at all. We have no frame of reference. We have no experience with objects so large or so far away. Then how do we know the brightness of stars, the size of quasars, the distance of far-off galaxies? The answer is, we make long chains of assumptions. If even one of those assumptions is just a little bit wrong, our perceptual conclusion will be a great deal wrong.

In fact, the moon, as almost everyone knows, changes size in the sky as our assumptions about its distance from us change. The moon looks larger on the horizon than it does when it's high in the sky. There is no widely accepted explanation for this, but one theory is that the "ceiling" of the sky seems closer to us than the far-off horizon. Therefore the same-size object, if it were closer, would have to be smaller to make the same-size image in our eyes. A basketball across the room and a Ping-Pong ball at arm's length make the same-size image on your retina. If you didn't know the size of the basketball, you would automatically see it as larger than the Ping-Pong ball, merely because it was farther away. When we assume the moon is farther away on the horizon, we see it as larger, too.

In addition, we all have a wealth of experience that tells us that things flying by us — planets, balls, planes, birds — all get smaller as they recede into the distance. If they *didn't* seem to get smaller, then it could only be because they were actually growing bigger! The same thing happens with the moon. It doesn't really grow bigger, but it does seem to recede in the distance. And since its image doesn't get smaller, you can only assume that it, too, is growing larger.

If this seems hard to believe, you can prove it to yourself with a simple experiment. The next time a bright light flashes in your eyes, look at your hand and you may see a small afterimage of the object floating on your palm. If you then look at a wall a few feet away, and then at a wall even farther away, the afterimage will get bigger and bigger. It helps to blink to keep the afterimage in view; your brain tries to erase the "extraneous" image by pushing it aside, but blinking can bring it back. The size of the actual image is imprinted on your retina and stays the same. But your brain automatically makes it appear larger or smaller, depending on the presumed distance of the "object" making the image.

You can also alter the size of the moon merely by changing your perspec- 55 tive. When you see the "large" moon on the horizon, if you look at it upside down — say, through your legs — so that the perspective of the horizon disappears, it will suddenly appear "small" again. Often we have to turn things upside down to see them in a proper perspective.

There are still other limits to our perceptual powers: some of them have to do with the fact that we are a part of the nature we study (how clearly can you think about thinking, for example?); others have to do with the fact that if you look at something closely enough, you always have to disturb it. Behavioral scientists are constantly plagued by this problem, but so are physicists. There is no way to simultaneously "see" the exact position and velocity of a subatomic particle, because in measuring one aspect, you automatically disturb the other. In trying to look at subatomic things, we are, as Lincoln Barnett says, somewhat in the position of a blind person trying to discern the shape and texture of a snowflake. As soon as it touches our fingers or tongue, it dissolves.

Some people have interpreted these perceptual limitations to mean that objective reality does not "really exist" — whatever that means. But the world is full of many important and lovely things that elude measuring. Love, for one. But also hate, humor, and almost all other emotions, ranging from our reaction to the sight of blood to our uncanny response to the arrangement of sounds we call music. If you try to dissect the emotional power of a painting bit by bit, it will dissolve (at least temporarily) as surely as a snowflake.

In any event, "reality" means different things to different people. As physicist Max Born put it, "For most people the real things are those things which are important for them. The reality of an artist or a poet is not comparable with that of a saint or prophet, nor with that of a businessman or administrator, nor with that of the natural philosopher or scientist."

This does not mean, Born says, that our sense impressions are some kind of "permanent hallucination." On the contrary, we can often agree on the nature of objective reality, despite its many appearances: "This chair here looks different with each movement of my head, each twinkle of my eye, yet I perceive it as the same chair. Science is nothing else than the endeavour to construct these invariants where they are not obvious."

Our scientific perception of reality grows and gains confidence in the same way that a baby gains confidence in the everyday reality of his or her world. We not only make hypotheses, we *test* them (or we should). If the same things happen enough times, we gain confidence in our theories. If the rattle falls to the floor every time it rolls off the table, this is unlikely to be a coincidence. If what we see with our eyes is confirmed by our sense of smell or hearing or touch, so much the better. And if other people seem to sense the same things we do, the more convincing still. We cannot eliminate the subjective aspects of perception, but we can subdue them. "It is impossible to explain to anybody what I mean by saying, 'This thing is red,' " writes Born, "or 'This thing is hot.' The most I can do is to find out whether other persons call the same things red or hot. Science aims at a closer relation between word and fact." 60

David Bohm concluded that what we perceive is what is *invariant*—what does not change under altered conditions. The baby learns to perceive the bottle correctly when he or she learns that it does not change when it's seen from various points of view. And it was the realization that the speed of light is invariant that led Einstein to his special theory of relativity. The surprising conclusion that space and time were relative came from the much more fundamental insight that the laws of nature (like the speed of light) were invariant under all conditions.

The strength of our beliefs is buoyed by the connections between our observations and beliefs. The more threads we can tie together, and the more tightly they are knit, the less likely it is that something major can slip unnoticed through a perceptual blind spot. Not only does the rattle fall to the floor but the moon itself is falling toward the earth and the earth toward the sun; rivers and rain and cold air all sink to the center of the planet. Gravity gains force as more and more phenomena can be explained by it. Therefore even though there are many things that astrophysicists or subatomic physicists cannot really "see," even in theory, they gain confidence in their solutions to puzzles as more and more pieces fit. If some underlying idea were fundamentally wrong, writes Victor Weisskopf, "our interpretation of the wide field of atomic phenomena would be nothing but a web of errors, and its amazing success would be based upon accidental coincidence."

Our innate perceptual limitations are as necessary as they are sometimes deceiving, so there's no point in wishing them away. We will simply have to accept, as British astronomer Sir Arthur Eddington observed, that any true law of nature is likely to seem irrational to rational human beings. Still we can do what scientists do to diminish the margin of error: We can try to get to know our instrument, its calibration, position, limitations, frame of reference — in short, how it works.

That is, we can better get to know our perceptual selves. No longer is perception the relatively simple matter it was in the Galilean world, where the universe was considered an object under inspection. Now we know we are part of that universe, and any valid observation has to take the workings of our inborn instrumentation into account. As Niels Bohr put it, science is a fascinating adventure in which we are not only spectators but actors as well.

Note

1. "Quasar" is short for quasi-stellar object. Quasars are sources of immense outpourings of energy found far away from us in space and time. Their exact nature is still unknown.

EXPLORING THE TEXT

1. Cole begins this selection by focusing on the way that physicists "see" subatomic particles. Clearly, however, her purpose is broader. What, in your estimation, is the main point or central idea in this essay? What is Cole trying to convey about perception and its relation to science?

2. Why are human beings "narrow-minded" or "narrow-sensed" in Cole's view? How does she help her reader see, through the use of illustrations, what by her own admission, cannot be seen? What other limitations does she note in relation to our sensory systems?

3. What impact have science and technology had on our ability to perceive the world around us, according to Cole? In how many different ways does technology extend our senses in the world of everyday — nonscientific — experience?

4. In what sense is perception, scientific and otherwise, always in "active process"? How do our expectations, preconceptions, and beliefs influence what we see? What we take for "reality"?

5. At the end of this selection, Cole suggests that we can counter the limits of natural vision by "getting to know our perceptual selves" (para. 64). What does she mean by this? How many different lessons about "our perceptual selves" can you find in Cole's essay?

FURTHER EXPLORATIONS

1. Review Ian Frazier's "Take the F" (p. 18), noting how he focuses the reader's attention throughout his description of his daily commute. To what extent does he focus on unusual or highlighted details that break through the kind of "sensory fatigue" that Cole discusses in this selection? To what extent does his essay help us appreciate details in our day-to-day life that we might normally overlook?

2. To what extent is Cole's depiction of how we see things challenged or confirmed by Georgina Kleege's account of sight from the perspective of someone who is legally blind (p. 93)? How might Cole explain the pleasure that Kleege discovers in the world as she sees it?

3. Compare Cole's view of perception with that presented by Walker Percy in "The Loss of the Creature" (p. 118). How do these authors view the role of expectations and preconceptions in relation to the act of seeing? How do they view the impact on perception of theoretical knowledge, learning, and belief? To what extent would they agree that familiar objects are more difficult to see clearly than unique objects? How do they each understand the idea of "objective reality"? Which of these views of perception do you find more truthful or appealing? Why?

ESSAY OPTIONS

1. Cole offers a number of illustrations in this selection of scientists who learn to look beyond the familiar expectations of their societies and historical eras in order to see something genuinely new. Write a personal essay about a time when you learned to see something in a way that challenged your "normal" perceptions of how the world works. You might think back to a particular experiment in a science class that forced you to look beyond "commonsense" explanations or to a time when you began to see computers, books, music, or art in a radically new way. It may have been a supervised educational experience or something you learned on your own. The content and context is less important than conveying the process you went through, the preconceptions you had to overcome, and how your "vision" of your subject changed.

2. In this selection, Cole suggests that human beings have difficulty seeing things the first time they are encountered. Perception, she claims, depends on learning and "cultural conditioning" (para. 44). Drawing on Cole, your own experience, and on reading selections by Barry Lopez (p. 27), Diane Ackerman (p. 36), Constance Classen et al. (p. 59), and Georgina Kleege (p. 93), write an essay in which you explore the role that education and acculturation play in expanding our ability to sense the world around us.

The Mind's Eye

GEORGINA KLEEGE

In 1967 when Georgina Kleege was eleven years old, she didn't wonder what it would be like to be blind; nor did she wonder what it would be like to have perfect vision. All she knew was that the center of her visual world was a widening blur and that her teachers and parents kept pushing her schoolbooks away from her face when she did her homework. Eventually, her problem was diagnosed as "macular degeneration" — the gradual but irreversible deterioration of her retinas — a condition that would leave her legally blind by her teens. Today, as she bluntly describes it, her world "has a hole in the center." When she looks at her cat on her desk, she sees a familiar, immobile shadow of gray against a background of pulsating speckles and her hands disappear into a white-violet fog as she types at her computer. In this selection from her memoir, *Sight Unseen* (1999), Kleege reflects on the way she sees the world around her and on the impact that blindness has had on her life. A lover of modern art, Kleege (b. 1956) has spent years wrestling with what it means to be "visually challenged." As a teen, she studied at the Martha Graham School of Contemporary Dance in New York. Today she is a teacher, novelist, essayist, and translator. Her most recent work of fiction is *Home for the Summer* (1989). She is working on a book tentatively titled *Writing Helen Keller.*

BEFORE READING

Freewrite in your journal about the last time you can remember looking at a painting in a museum, art gallery, church, or other public location. What do you recall doing as you looked at the work in question? What did you see?

A t the 1992 Matisse exhibition at New York's Museum of Modern Art, a man said to me, "You're standing too close to that painting. You have to stand back to really see it."

He was right, I was standing about a foot from a canvas large enough for most people to view comfortably from a distance of several yards. When I look at a painting from a sighted person's distance, macular degeneration, my form of blindness, obscures or distorts the center of the canvas. My peripheral vision is unaffected, so the edges of the canvas are more or less visible. To get a general sense of the overall composition, I scan the painting systematically, moving my oversized blind spot around it, allowing different regions to emerge into my peripheral vision. My brain slowly identifies the forms and assembles the picture bit by bit. In effect, my mind sketches an outline, or a map: "To the left, there's a table with a basket of fruit. To the right, there's a window with a view of the sea."

To add detail to this rough sketch growing in my brain, I must get very close to the painting, as close as museum guards allow, even closer when they look away. This is where I spend most of my time in art galleries. I edge closer and closer, then stand, usually off to one side, leaning forward, scanning small sections one at a time. But as I approach, the details of texture, depth, and illumination become only so much paint to me, an arrangement of different pigments differently applied. With my face a few inches from the canvas, every painting, even the most representational, becomes an abstraction. Paint is paint. But paint is also the point, isn't it? Looking at a work of art is seldom simply a matter of identifying the objects or people depicted there. Up close, I can appreciate the tricks of the painter's trade, understand how a seemingly random daub or dribble ends up meaning something so precise. I recognize that a stroke of purple may represent the shadowy side of a cathedral tower, a cherry blossom reflected in water, or the sheen on a fold of brown velvet. But the sketch in my head lets me know what this stroke of purple means in the context of a particular painting. I observe that the most "realistic" eye, the kind which seems to follow the viewer's movements around the room, may be no more than a swirl of brown with a thin comma of white laid over. Up close, Monet's waterlilies are wonderfully crusty, while at a distance they look almost liquid. I enjoy these discoveries and marvel at the artist's skill and ingenuity. While my too-close vantage point makes representational paintings seem abstract, with abstract works I sense not only movement and energy but depth and form. The sprays of paint on a Jackson Pollock canvas become a dense, webby mass. Ad Reinhardt's flat planes of color resonate afterimages, vibrate with ghosts of form. Mark Rothko's exquisite colors bleed beyond their frames, staining the wall and the air around them.

Varnished canvases give me trouble. Puddles of brilliant white obscure the faces of Rembrandt's dark Dutchmen or drape portions of Rubens's corpulent nudes. But since this white part moves when I move, I know to disregard it. I shift my position and slide my gaze back and forth, watching what emerges.

Of course my method of looking at paintings takes time and space. I perform a slow minuet before each painting, stepping forward and back, sweeping my gaze from edge to edge. Considering the crowds at most museums nowadays, it may seem surprising that I ever manage to get as close to the paintings as I need to. But current museum practices aid me. People tend to cluster around printed texts displayed at the entrance of each gallery or by particular paintings. Other people rent tape-recorded tours that direct them to certain works, so they bypass others. As they congregate before the texts and prescribed canvases, it leaves space open elsewhere for me.

The man at the Matisse show who told me that I was standing too close was one of these tape-recorded tour-takers. He had to lift his earphones to speak to me. And before I could formulate a response he had wheeled and hurried on to the next correct vantage point, the next preordained view.

So I didn't get a chance to tell him that I am blind. I suspect that it would have stopped him in his tracks. The visual arts are for the sighted, he might have told me. The idea of a blind person in a museum sounds like the punch line to a bad joke. Though, as far as he could tell, any number of his fellow earphone-wearers could have been blind. Why not? Certainly it is no challenge to a skilled blind person to follow recorded directions, to move from room to room with a crowd of similarly directed people. In fact, a blind person accustomed to reading books on tape would probably get more out of the taped tour than would the average sighted person.

"But," the man would object, "when I stand in front of a painting I know what I'm looking at. The tape only supplements what I'm seeing. When I look at the painting I see it. I don't piece it together like a jigsaw puzzle, like you do. I just see it. You're doing something else. Your brain creates some second-hand version of the painting. You do not experience the painting itself."

To such people there is a right way and a wrong way to see. The dialogue that goes on between my eyes and brain seems something distinctly different from sight. It is not vision but revision, something altered, edited, changed by my mind, subject to my values, expectations, and even moods. I see what I sense is there, what I know is there, what I hope is there, not necessarily what actually is. For the sighted, seeing is both instantaneous and absolute. To see is to take something in at a glance and possess it whole, comprehending all its complexities. Sight provides instantaneous access to reality. The eye is the window on the world. It's a perfect little camera, with a lens that automatically focuses the image on a light-sensitive film. Aim, focus, presto—nothing to it.

The sighted can be so touchingly naive about vision. They apparently be-   10
lieve that the brain stays out of it. Or at best, they extend the camera metaphor and envision a tiny self seated inside the skull, passively watching images as they are projected on a movie screen, then pushing the buttons and pulling the levers that will make the body respond appropriately by speaking, running, reaching, or closing the eyes. A few can describe vision with more specialized language. They explain that light of different frequencies and intensities reflected off an object is refracted through the eye's cornea and lens to hit the retina, where it initiates a chemical change in the photoreceptor cells, which triggers an electrical impulse to the ganglion cells, which send an impulse to the optic nerve, which relays the message to the lateral geniculate nucleus, which conveys it to the primary visual cortex and other regions of the brain, where different aspects of the image (color, motion, form) are assessed. And thus, you see. Still, despite fancy language, the idea remains the same. The image that hits the retina is presumed to be what you see. That initial image is described as having a constant, inviolable integrity. The visual process is said to work something like a fax machine. Whatever shuffling and rearranging of the image that takes place inside the brain, you end up with the same image you had at the beginning. The sighted preserve this absolute faith in the image despite everyday experiences when their eyes deceive them or when they see more (or less) than actually meets their eyes.

For example, picture this. You are waiting to meet a friend in a crowded train station. You are able to spot him from across the large waiting room, a distance of perhaps forty yards or so. The next day you are there again, waiting for someone else. Your friend of the day before also shows up and walks toward you, but you do not recognize him until he is much closer, perhaps only a yard or two away. Why? The image projected on your retina is pretty much the same. And you're alert to it, actively scanning the crowd. Your friend's image is there in your eye on Tuesday as it was on Monday. You should see him, but you don't.

Or picture this. You are pitching in the final game of the World Series. You must throw a strike. You look at the catcher. You focus on his glove, the precise spot in his glove where you want the ball to hit. As you do this, you do not see the fans in the stands, even though (since these are not your home fans) they are waving banners, hats, towels, seat cushions, and generally trying to distract you. You do not see the hitter at the plate or the umpire crouching behind the catcher, or even the catcher, just that spot in his glove. You don't see those other things even though their images appear on your retinas. Why? Your eyes, unlike cameras, are not equipped with zoom lenses that can alter the field of view and allow you to zero in on the catcher's mitt that way.

Is this just a manner of speaking, a way to spice up the post-game interview by re-creating the suspense of the moment? Or are there really instances when stress, fatigue, illness, and emotion (not to mention drugs or alcohol) distort or alter what you see? A smoke alarm sounds in your favorite restaurant and, in your haste to escape, you see nothing between you and the Exit sign, though the lights are still shining and your eyes can see the waiters and other diners overturning tables as they rush toward the door. When you describe the experience, you will blame your eyes, not your brain, and call it "blind panic." Some enchanted evening you will see a stranger and be "blinded by desire," utterly unconscious of all the other people and objects in that crowded room even though all these things are right before your eyes.

"So occasionally the brain plays tricks," the man at the Matisse exhibition might argue. "Sometimes the brain ignores, even dumps, part of the image that the eyes receive and highlights, even enhances, other parts. But this only happens under certain circumstances. The rest of the time I see exactly what's there. I see everything that's there. My vision is both impartial and democratic. My brain doesn't intervene or intrude. It merely receives and responds." To this I would say, "Look again."

Try this. Picture the world as I see it. My world has a hole in its center. 15 The central region of my retina, the macula, no longer functions. So when light entering my eyes hits the retinas, only the cells on the periphery, and a few good cells scattered around the center, send messages to the brain. In the most common form of macular degeneration, now called "age-related" but once called "senile" or "wet," abnormal blood vessels form behind the retina. These leak and damage the delicate photoreceptor cells. In my form of the condition (which is rare and, some feel, so different from the common form that it deserves a different name), there were no leaky blood vessels. My photoreceptors seem to have been genetically programmed simply to give up the ghost. I have no memory of this. It happened when I was about ten years old, and probably very gradually, perhaps even cell by cell. Whatever the cause, the damaged cells do not regenerate or grow back. As my most recent ophthalmologist put it, patches of my retinas are entirely "worn through." The affected area is small. The whole macula measures about 5 millimeters across its diameter. But it contains a higher concentration of photoreceptors than the peripheral areas. More important, the macula is densely packed with the sensitive cone cells that allow for the perception of fine details. So I lack not only central vision but also the visual equipment designed to perform such tasks as reading print or recognizing a face. In effect, I have an extremely large blind spot in the center of my visual field. Every human eye has a blind spot. It is the place where the optic nerve meets the retina, where there are no photoreceptors. The reason you do not see your blind spot most of the time is because it is out of the central region of vision. Also, since you have two eyes, there are two blind spots, but they do not overlap. When something is obscured by the blind spot in your left eye, your right eye will see it. And your brain knows the blind spots are there and always have been. Your whole visual system works around the fact of your blind spot, so you can disregard it. My blind spot is simply larger and more central than yours. You can crudely simulate macular degeneration by putting a blob of toothpaste in the center of your eyeglasses, so wherever you aim your eyes you see only toothpaste. But this is not exactly what I see.

With effort, I can force myself to see my blind spot. When I stare directly at a blank wall, this flaw in my retina does not appear as a black hole or splotch of darkness. When I am very tired I see an irregularly shaped blotch, which throbs slightly and is either an intense blue-violet, or a deep teal green. More often, I see a blur slightly darker in color than the wall overlaid with a pattern of tiny flecks. Depending on lighting conditions these flecks are bright white, sometimes edged in violet or a golden yellow. Sometimes the flecks are less vividly colored, and the wall appears like a surface of water dappled by a breeze or soft rain. These flecks or dapples vibrate, pulsate, shiver but stay closely packed and never migrate from the central region. Around this movement, in the periphery of my visual field, there is calm.

When I look at a simple object—a white 3-by-5-inch index card on my desk, for example—it disappears. More accurately, the beige wood color of the desktop flows into the central blurry region of vision, while flecks of white pulsate above. The card seems to disintegrate into tiny, quivering particles, to dissolve into the desktop and the air. If I shift my eyes slightly in any direction, the card reappears. It seems to emerge from the desk's surface, to differentiate itself from the pale wood grain. I shift my gaze back and it's gone. When the object is larger and there's a higher degree of contrast between it and the background—a 5-by-8-inch paperback book—its disappearance is less complete. When I aim my eyes at its center, only the top two thirds disappear, while the lower two inches or so remain. Also, the colors of the cover design disintegrate into pulsating flecks, invading the pale surface around it. I see the book losing solidity, becoming translucent while a cluster of vibrating speckles dance just above it. It's something like what they do on the TV news to protect the identity of a courtroom witness or accused criminal. The person's face is blotted out by a moving pattern of tiny squares. But for me the pattern is less regular and moves faster.

My blind spot always occupies the central region of my visual field. The wider the field, the larger the blind spot. When I look at my hand from arm's length, it vanishes. When I bring it close to my face, only the fingertips are gone. To see the picture on the cover of the book I bring it close to my eyes. With the book an inch from my face the blind spot is only about the size of a silver dollar. I can see enough of the picture to identify the book.

I cannot perceive a straight line, because wherever I aim my eye, the line appears severed. The line that designates the edge of an object bows, wobbles, or oscillates from side to side. The more straight lines in the object, the more distortion. A bookcase with its uprights and shelves full of books is a haze of motion. The color of the shelves bounces up and down, bleeding into the color of the books, which vibrate from side to side. A filmy veil seems to hang over it, blurring the spines of books into a smudgy, variegated haze. I look down. A sheer, white-violet fog hangs over my computer keyboard, slashed here and there with streaks of yellow. My fingers pierce the fog as I type, sinking in up to the first knuckle. One of my cats sleeps on my desk. Every curve and contour of her body oscillates outward, forming a translucent ghost cat emerging from the real one. All around there are pulsating speckles of violet and gold, dazzlingly at odds with the cat's immobility. When I touch her, the shadow cat grays my hand.

As solid objects seem to dissolve or shimmy, insubstantial shadows and   20
patches of light acquire solidity and form. The shadow in the corner could be a pair of shoes. Bright specks of light shining through prismatic glass blocks appear as scraps of colored paper. Lamplight reflected off a polished table might make me gasp — spilled milk to me.

I "see" more than I'm supposed to. Ophthalmology textbooks predict that people with macular degeneration will in fact see a black (or perhaps white) hole in the middle of what they're looking at. Ophthalmologists are not necessarily well versed in the neurology and psychology of vision. What goes on in the brain is someone else's province. Research to identify the specific functioning of cells in the retina, and the corresponding nerve fibers and neurons in the brain, is relatively recent and somewhat inconclusive. But it allows me to speculate. The scintillating motion, vibrant speckles, shadowy emanations, and changing forms may have to do with the few remaining good photoreceptors scattered over the macula. When I stare at an object, the few functioning cells in my maculas may be dutifully sending reliable messages to the brain, oblivious to the blank space, the vacant silence that surrounds them. If these are cones (I know I must have some since I see color), the brain pays more attention. There is a one-to-one ratio of cones to ganglion cells, while several rods synapse on one ganglion cell. Each cone has a private line to the brain. Also, a disproportionate amount of cortical space is devoted to the central region of the retina. Whatever messages get through from those last few holdouts are scrutinized by a large number of neurons. My brain receives these messages without the millions of other messages that should corroborate or enhance them. My brain takes what little it has to go on and does the best it can. It hedges its bets. There might be a white index card there on the desk, my brain tells me. Then again, maybe not.

Leaving aside this neurological speculation (which is probably more whimsy than fact), I surmise that my general visual experience is something like your experience of optical illusions. Open any college psychology textbook to the chapter on perception and look at the optical illusions there. You stare at the image and see it change before your eyes. In one image, you may see first a vase and then two faces in profile. In another, you see first a rabbit then a duck. These images deceive you because they give your brain inadequate or contradictory information. In the first case, your brain tries to determine which part of the image represents the object and which part represents the background. In the second case, your brain tries to group the lines of the sketch together into a meaningful picture. In both cases there are two equally possible solutions to the visual riddle, so your brain switches from one to the other, and you have the uncanny sensation of "seeing" the image change. When there's not much to go on—no design on the vase, no features on the faces, no feathers, no fur—the brain makes an educated guess.

When I stare at an object I can almost feel my brain making such guesses. And there are usually more than two alternatives. Before my eyes, the hazy blur that conceals the object oscillates and shudders, taking on new colors and contours. I "see" my brain's confusion as it mulls over the amorphous shapes before my eyes. The red coffee mug on my desk becomes a green mug, then a green ball, then a black box, then . . . .

Expectation plays a large role in what I perceive. I know what's on my desk because I put it there. If someone leaves me a surprise gift, it may take a few seconds to identify it, but how often does that happen? At home, at work, on the street, and in stores, museums, theaters, parking garages, airports, train stations, even unfamiliar cities, there is a finite number of objects that I am likely to encounter. I can recognize most things through a quick process of elimination. And that process is only truly conscious on the rare occasions when the unexpected occurs, as when my cats carry objects out of context. A steel wool soap pad appears in the bath tub. I see it as a rusty, grayish blob. Though touch would probably tell me something, it can be risky to touch something you cannot identify some other way. I wait for it to move. When it doesn't, I sniff. It smells faintly metallic and vaguely soapy. Is it a massive hair clog regurgitated by the drain? This seems implausible. I think, "What is that?" and then, almost in the same moment, I come up with a better question, "What's it doing there?" and know the answer.

I once encountered a rabid raccoon on a sidewalk near my house. I learned what it was from a neighbor watching it from his screened porch. What I saw was an indistinct, grayish mass, low to the ground and rather round. It was too big to be a cat and the wrong shape to be a dog. Its gait was

25

not only unfamiliar but unsteady. It zigzagged up the pavement. I moved my gaze around it as my brain formed a picture of a raccoon. The raccoon in my mind had the characteristic mask across its face, a sharply pointed nose, striped tail, brindled fur. Nothing in the hazy blob at my feet, no variations in color or refinements in form, corresponded with that image. Its position was wrong. The raccoon in my mind was standing up on its haunches, holding something in its front paws. And what does a rabid raccoon look like? Was it foaming at the mouth?

Without my neighbor's information I wouldn't have gone through this mental process. I could tell that it was an animal, and probably not a pet. That's all I needed to know to proceed with caution. But I still might have guessed it was a raccoon. In this part of the world there are only so many animals it could have been. Groundhog, woodchuck, raccoon, my brain would have proposed, but not sloth or koala.

But such unexpected encounters happen so rarely that they become anecdotes. In the normal course of events I encounter only those objects, animals, and people that I can predict I will. If I see them as wobbly shadows, or semi-translucent blobs, it hardly ever startles me. And the fact that I can distinguish one shadow from another is no miracle. I cannot see people's faces well enough to recognize them, but often I know them from their posture or gait. At the supermarket I distinguish the Cheerios from the Wheaties because one hazy blur is yellow and the other is orange. But in a way, you do this too. Marketing experts chose that color to catch your eye, and the eye of your three-year-old, who can't read the words yet. Also, while I actively seek that color to identify the brand, you and your child may be responding to subliminal messages about sunshiny cheerfulness. Otherwise, all cereal boxes could be white.

The unimpaired human eye provides the brain with such a surfeit of visual information that only a certain amount consciously registers at any moment. In effect, your brain privileges certain aspects of the retina's images and disregards others. Each eye sends the brain a billion messages per second. Together the two eyes transmit twice as much information to the brain as the rest of the body combined. With all this information flooding in every second, the perceptual system seems designed to adapt readily to losses and distortions, whether because of eye damage or other circumstances. . . .

Perceptual development takes about the first ten years of life. But it may not stop there. Certain people in certain lines of work seem to train their perceptual systems to perform specific visual tasks that other people would find impossible. Such people may have only average eyesight but seem to see more, more quickly and more accurately. Senator Bill Bradley claims that during his basketball playing days he trained himself to use his peripheral vision more accurately, as a way to give himself an advantage on the court. He would walk past a store window with his eyes aimed straight ahead and try to identify the objects on display. Then he would go back and check. Over time, he claims, he actually expanded his visual field. In fact, the placement of the eyeballs in the skull limits how far a person can see in any direction. The maximum angle of vision for humans is 180 degrees from side to side, and 70 degrees from top to bottom. But most people do not consciously register at the farthest reaches of their visual fields. Bradley saw no more than other passersby or players, but he heightened his sensitivity to what was going on in the periphery. He taught his brain to recognize objects or people from minimal details — a flash of motion, a wavy line.

If Bradley's story raises eyebrows, it is because normal vision is supposed   30 to be immediate, spontaneous, now-you-see-it-now-you-don't, not a continual game of "Where's Waldo?"° To the blind with some sight, however, Bradley's story makes perfect sense. Relative to the type and degree of our conditions, we learn to interpret the world through minimal visual information. We learn to combine these imperfect and incomplete images with our other sensory perceptions, plus what we know about the laws of nature, and call it the world. But when we do this, when we make claims about our adaptation to subnormal vision, is when we become most alien. The idea that some people, through habit or even conscious effort, can use visual information and skills differently, seems to indict the averagely sighted as lazy, slack, perhaps even stupid. Because we get by with less, wringing meaning out of mere scraps of images, we seem to wag our fingers at the sighted for their wastefulness.

The sighted seem more comfortable thinking of someone like Ted Williams. Some years after Williams retired from baseball he performed an informal experiment to prove that he could actually see the seams of the baseball as it hit his bat. A hitter with a "good eye" will swing only when the ball appears to be in a particular region of the strike zone. He looks for the white blur of the ball to cross that imaginary line, but other details about the ball do not necessarily register in his brain. Williams saw the ball as more than a blur. He saw the orientation of the ball — where the seams were relative to the bat — at the split second of impact. Optically speaking, the image on the retina of both hitters would be the same, but Williams's brain apparently got more from the image. Hitters on a good streak often describe the ball as looking bigger than usual. Williams seems to have seen it this way all the time. A lifetime of practice presumably trained his brain to evaluate the image on his retina at a higher rate of speed. Practice makes perfect, but practice cannot turn an average hitter into a Ted Williams. Williams probably had better than average vision. He was a fighter pilot too, a job that usually requires acuity of 20/20 or better. Still, half of baseball is 90 percent mental. A great hitter like Williams combines great physical, and in his case visual, resources with a high level of intellectual discernment. But vision, the sighted assert, is a God-given gift rather than a well-honed skill. Superman was born with X-ray vision; he didn't pick it up along the way. And the vision that separates some — the artist, the

---

"Where's Waldo?": A popular children's book series that challenges readers to find the distinctive-looking Waldo character amidst a chaos of visual images.

scientist, the leader—from the rest of humanity is always said to be innate and a little bit otherworldly. The sighted seem to want to preserve the mystery. Intelligent and highly educated people are often a bit vague about visual processes. A friend who teaches visual perception reports that her students, who are preparing for careers as clinical psychologists, often find the subject perplexing and irrelevant. If you can see, you don't need to know why you see. And if you see more than other people, you should accept the gift without question. Visionaries do not always choose their own fates. The exceptional vision that the gods occasionally bestow dictates what path to follow. As Branch Rickey said of Ted Williams, "How can a man with eyes like that not be a great hitter?"

Your eyes are supposed to make you who you are. If you are clear-sighted, you are probably also level-headed and open-minded. So what do my eyes make me, I wonder. Does the fact that everything I see seems on the verge of disintegration mean I'm in a constant state of anxiety about imminent loss? Does the scintillating motion that I perceive in static objects mean I'm actually in contact with the seething energy of subatomic particles? Or else, since my gaze erases everything in its path, does it make me harbor a delusion about my own divine power?

Perhaps I ask for this. All my speculation about how I see more than I should given my marred retinas is beside the point. In most circumstances I rely very little on sight. A cat still sleeps on my desk. To see her well enough to identify which of my two cats she is, I must look at her very closely. I lower my face toward her so that my entire visual field is full of cat, and my distorting blind spot affects a smaller area. I move my gaze around, taking in the details of her markings that will allow me to know which one she is. But I do this only because I am writing about my vision, attempting to specify how my perceptual system works. Under normal circumstances I would simply touch her. The fur of one cat has a slightly coarser texture than the other. When a surprise gift appears on my desk, I can stare at it, watching it transmogrify before my eyes, or I can pick it up and handle it. Touch takes a second but seeing takes more time, and a kind of concentration better directed elsewhere. Since my sight is so unreliable, I tend to ignore it altogether or to trust it only when what I see is confirmed by something else I know.

The notion that one might deliberately ignore sight seems to threaten sighted people in a way that I cannot fully understand, since there are situations when sighted people do this too. As a teenager I studied at the Martha Graham School of Contemporary Dance. My lack of central vision was not the hindrance that one might assume. Though teachers and choreographers often demonstrate positions and steps, they also give oral instructions. Once a dancer learns the vocabulary of a particular technique, directions and corrections can be communicated in words. Also, part of a dancer's training involves giving up an absolute reliance on sight. My best teachers regularly made the class turn away from the mirror or close our eyes while performing an exercise. There is a risk for a dancer of becoming too dependent on the mirror, since there is never a mirror on stage. But more important, a dancer has to know, without looking, what her body is doing at all times. She may be obliged to enter the stage in the dark, to find her position and begin moving without the luxury of sight. Even when the stage is lit, the angles of particular lights may hit the dancer's eyes in ways that make it impossible to see the floor or the edge of the stage. When she is dancing with a partner or as part of the corps de ballet, she must be conscious not only of her own body but also of the bodies of the dancers around her. Part of this perfect unity comes from re-hearsal, of course, but in a live performance, with live music, the tempo may not be exactly the same as it was in rehearsal. Adjustments must be made without looking. There can be no shifting eyeballs, no sideways glances to see where someone else is. A dancer develops eyes in the back of her head, on the soles of her feet. To illustrate this point, one of our teachers used a negative example. She would mime one of those ludicrously inept people you en-counter at parties or standing in a movie line, who back into you, apparently unaware that you were standing there. "Can you imagine?" she'd say as we laughed, vowing never to be like that. "Not knowing there was someone be-hind you!"

A good baker smells when the bread is done. An auto mechanic hears the trouble in the engine — isn't that why they call it a tune-up? You can fasten a necklace at the back of your neck without looking, shampoo your hair with your eyes closed and find the light switch in the dark. 35

"But when I do those things I'm not renouncing sight," you may argue, "I just sometimes get by without it." This hits on a dilemma that faces the blind like me who have, in the phrase of experts, "some usable sight." The phrase is troubling because it seems to denote a hierarchy with a visual elite (20/20 or better) on top and the blind with absolutely no sight on the bot-tom. Also, the phrase is imbued with the notion that there is a right and wrong way to use sight. Do you always make the best possible use of your sight? You may never need to ask yourself this question. But if your sight fails, if your acuity dips below the magic 20/200 line, or your visual field narrows to less than 20 degrees, you will hear the question all the time. We live in an age of high-tech low vision innovations. Optometrists can pre-scribe dozens of different aids designed to help patients perform all sorts of visual activities. But unlike the eyeglasses you may already be used to wear-ing, no single device, or even a gambit of gadgets, can completely compen-sate for the sight you've lost. The handheld magnifier you use to read the newspaper does not help you read a street sign or do embroidery or watch TV. To be an informed consumer of all the equipment now on the market, you will have to think of vision in a new way. Vision is a series of discrete activities, not a constant, seamless, pervasive ebb and flow of information. What's more, you will need to prioritize, decide which activities are worth performing visually. Otherwise you may leave the doctor's office laden with cumbersome and expensive paraphernalia but little guidance on how to deal with the world without sight.

I use some low vision aids. For example, I have a pair of reading glasses with a magnifying lens mounted on the right side, which allows me to read print (mostly large print) when I get very close to the page. I also have a closed-circuit television system that projects a magnified image of books and letters. My computer allows me to work in print as large as I like. From time to time I investigate other devices. Every month something new comes on the market, but I do not buy everything that's available. For one thing, most low vision aids are very expensive, and health insurance companies are still rather stingy about them. Still, I could afford to buy them for myself. The question is: Do I need them? I could get a pair of glasses with small telescopes mounted on the lenses which would allow me to make out a person's face. These would be custom-made, with the telescopes carefully laced and permanently focused at a predetermined distance. My doctor suggested that such glasses might be useful in the classroom, so I tried on a pair. Since these were not made for me, it took a while to figure out how to make them work. Eventually I managed to see my doctor's face as he stood in the doorway, about ten feet from me. In fact, I could see his face only about as well as I would if he were sitting across a table from me. His features were merely a hazy smudge on his face. I could, however, see his lips move, which was an undeniable improvement. But the glasses also created an extremely disconcerting distortion. While I saw a closeup of his face through the telescopes, I simultaneously saw his body at the proper distance. He appeared like a truncated cartoon figure, and I found myself laughing uncontrollably. Over time, I could have gotten used to the distortion. But I would still have to decide at what distance to have the telescopes set. Ten to fifteen feet would allow me to see the students in the back row in a small classroom, but not those in the middle or front rows. Would I have to get three different pairs and keep switching? And for what—the pleasure of knowing that a student in the back row is snoozing or that another's lips move while he's speaking? I know these things already.

Fortunately, my optometrist was not offended by my rejection of available technology, much less my laughter. He knew that an aid one person finds indispensable another will find useless, even though both share the same type and degree of blindness. Not all eye care specialists are so gracious. Some are perplexed, even annoyed by blind patients who reject visual aids. Few offer or even possess much information about nonvisual skills for the blind, such as braille or white cane use. Patients, especially those who bring with them myths and prejudices about blindness, can end up with the impression that it is better to do something with the eyes than without, no matter how cumbersome and expensive the equipment required. Eye specialists are committed to the mission of preserving sight and preventing blindness. Blindness is the enemy, to be kept at bay at all costs. When a patient rejects visual aids for nonvisual techniques, many eye specialists take it as an insult, as ingratitude, or worse yet, as a defection to the other side.

In 1991, researchers at a clinic of the National Institutes of Health implanted tiny electrodes in the brain of a woman who had been blind for twenty years. When they stimulated the electrodes, the woman "saw" colored dots, as if before her eyes. In the not so distant future these researchers and others will be able to implant a greater number of electrodes. These will be attached to tiny TV cameras mounted in eyeglass frames so the user would "see" the world as patterns of dots similar to the array on a stadium scoreboard. These researchers are quick to point out that this artificial vision is meant to "aid reading and mobility, not restore normal vision to the point you could go into an art gallery and appreciate a Rembrandt." I admire the unnamed woman who volunteered for this experiment. The research has far-reaching implications that will benefit many more people than the few blind individuals who might choose to have the operation done. At the same time, like many blind people (even those with no sight at all) who can read and get around through nonvisual means, I find news of such research unsettling. If such artificial vision won't let you see a Rembrandt, is it really worth getting a hole cut in your head?

The newspaper accounts of this experiment included no references to the woman's feelings about what she "saw." Psychologists and physicians who have studied blind people whose sight has been restored by an operation (usually a cornea transplant) often report that patients eventually experience some degree of depression. Some end up rejecting sight and the advantages that sight provides. They continue to read braille rather than print, to identify objects through touch, and to sit in the dark. The usual explanation for this depression is that learning to see is such a daunting task that it leads to discouragement. Or else they are overwhelmed with regret for the long lost years of darkness. The thought never occurs to the sighted researchers who have devoted themselves to the study of vision that the depression may be due to another cause. After a lifetime of hearing about the miracle of sight, the reality may be disappointing. The visible world may turn out to be uglier than expected.

If I got my sight back, I would be able to read print effortlessly and would learn to drive a car. I doubt that I would get depressed, but I probably wouldn't be continually elated either. I have a pretty good idea about how seeing works. As it is, by some people's standards I rely too much on sight. Since I never underwent official rehabilitation training for the blind, my nonvisual skills are not as well honed as they could be. For instance, I have only recently begun to learn braille and am nowhere near proficient. I have also recently begun using a white cane to indicate to sighted people, especially those driving cars, that I do not see well. But in many situations I find it more convenient to leave the cane at home and maneuver through space using my peripheral sight. My closets, cupboards, drawers, and refrigerator do not always stay arranged so that I can find things without looking. And I make mistakes. I talk to the sweater lying on the couch, thinking it's a cat. I try to pick a scrap of shiny gift wrap off the carpet and find that it is only a patch of reflected light. So I make resolutions, vow to improve myself, as you probably do. The difference is that my resolutions tend to turn on the debate about when to use and when not to use the sight I have.

I used to thread a needle using vision. I would hold the needle in my left hand, between my thumb and index finger. I could not see its eye, so I felt for it with my finger, then turned the needle until the eye was facing me. I took the thread in my right hand, with about an inch protruding between my thumb and index finger. Behind a magnifying lens I would aim my eyes a little to one side of the needle. I could see its straight, silvery sheen. I drew the thread to that line of light and slid it upward to where I knew the eye to be. When I felt it miss its mark, I would try again, guiding the thread a millimeter to the left or right. Eventually the end of the thread would catch. I'd carefully make the thread perform slow, regular undulations until I felt it pass all the way through the needle's eye.

I don't do this anymore. Now I know better. I ask someone else to thread the needle for me. Or I use a self-threading needle. More likely, I take the garment to the dry cleaners and pay someone to sew on the button or mend the tear. It may seem ludicrous that I ever did it at all. Threading a needle is a daunting task even to the visual elite. But for the blind in the sighted world, where blindness is the enemy, synonymous with ignorance, indifference, and sin, the simple question—to see or not to see—takes on substantial significance.

Sight is perhaps not my primary sense, but I still use it. I know my vision is not trustworthy, so I tend to seek corroboration from my other senses for what I see. But I don't know how to turn it off. Besides, I like what I see. Color, for instance, gives me great pleasure. On gray winter days I long for vivid colors, as I sometimes crave certain tastes. I suspect that I don't see color as well as the average viewer. My retinas don't have many cones, the photoreceptors that allow for color perception. But the colors that I see fascinate and refresh me. I close my eyes and imagine colors, summoning up memories of particular hues. Perhaps I am practicing. Although whatever caused my maculas to degenerate has probably done all the damage it ever will, there is no guarantee that something else might not go wrong. Everything I know about the retina tells me it's a wonder anyone can expect to have an undamaged one for a lifetime. And there is so much else that can happen to the eyes. If I lost the sight I have, I would miss it. But to mourn that loss as I mourn the loss of loved ones would be to buy the assertion that human experience is always, first and foremost, visual. I see through that now.

Perhaps I had no business at the Matisse exhibition. Perhaps I should give up my affection for the visual arts and seek aesthetic enrichment only in concert halls and opera houses. But I have been going to museums and art galleries since childhood. When I was growing up in New York, such field trips were a routine part of my education. And since both my parents were visual artists, looking at works of art always seemed a natural part of life. It requires concentration and patience, but for now, this effort still seems worth it. 45

I stand before the two versions of *The Dance*. The man with the earphones tells me that I am standing too close, then moves on before I can ask him, "Do you make the best possible use of your sight?"

"What?" he would probably say. "Do I what?"

It's too bad. We might have had an interesting conversation about vision or art or something. "When you look at this painting, what do you see? How do you know that's what you're supposed to see? What makes you so sure?"

I let him go. He's right; I am standing about a foot away from the wall. No one else is standing this near. Matisse is not a painter who inspires close examination. The world he paints is devoid of the kind of fine detail that demands such intense perusal. Still, there could be other reasons to stand at this viewing distance. I might be a painter examining brush strokes at close range. Except that I don't even seem to be looking at the painting. I have my eyes aimed at the wall between the two canvases. I might be a gallery owner, examining how the canvases are framed or the precise shade of the wall on which to hang such works. In fact, I am, out of the corners of my eyes, trying to gauge the difference between the two versions. In the version I have never seen before the dancers seem redder, but the other colors seem about the same. These colors please me. The green in particular has a freshness that I find very satisfying. I step back to where you're supposed to stand. I aim my blind gaze at the center of the first version, and it is ringed by dancers. I have known this painting since childhood, and my appreciation of it is naive and rather personal. The figure in the lower left resembles one of my teachers at the Graham school, perhaps because her pose is the most dancerly. And the circle is a powerful symbol to me. I move closer again, because it is the green that gets to me today.

Behind me, all along the bench below the window, sit people wearing earphones. I do not know whether the recorded message has told them to sit there or whether they are just resting, letting the tapes play out. The sound of the tapes hovers around them like a swarm of whispering bees.   50

In the future, art lovers won't need to rent those machines. Museums will hang tape players or perhaps video screens by every canvas, and people will select which ones to plug their earphones into. These devices will become more and more interactive, allowing people to select from a menu of possible topics, perhaps even ask questions. "Why is that one red?" I would ask, or, "Tell me something about this green." And CD-ROM and multimedia technologies soon will allow me to view this entire show, or any museum collection, on my home computer screen. I could boot up an image of this painting, zoom in on any detail, access volumes of historical, biographical, and critical information, all from the privacy of my own home.

I do not question the value of all this technology, and I will probably make use of some of it. But I will still come to museums. I assume that they will be less crowded, more peaceful, with no one there to bother me and tell me how to look at art.

It is late in the afternoon. The crowd is thinning. I will leave soon, missing more than half the show. The work I need to do to see these paintings is physically wearying and mentally taxing. But I linger. "Red," I think, looking at the unfamiliar version of the painting. "Red changes everything." It makes the outline of the dancers less distinct, which gives a slightly greater sense of motion. This may just be me. Red and black is a tricky combination in my eyes. Red print on a black background registers as pure black to me. I am uncertain if the redder color of the dancers in that version will have the same effect on another viewer. I have come to this show alone, and there's no one around to ask.

I take a final look. I know I probably don't see what I'm supposed to see. I'm sure that I don't see what you do. But I don't delude myself either. I know that what I see, or think I see, is primarily a product of my brain working around my visual limitations and doing the best it can. You may believe you see something else. I live with my uncertainty and you with your unwavering faith. We may never see eye to eye on this. But I can live with that, too.

EXPLORING THE TEXT

1. What, according to Kleege, do most people think happens when they look at a painting in a museum? How does this commonplace view of seeing contrast with the way that Kleege sees Matisse's works at the Museum of Modern Art? In your view, who probably sees Matisse more clearly or more productively—Kleege or the sighted man who speaks to her? Why?

2. What role does the mind play in the process of vision—or "revision"—as Kleege describes it? How are expectations and memories involved, from her perspective, in what we see? Why does she insist that vision is a "skill" and not a "God-given gift"?

3. How does Kleege convey her experience of vision to her reader? What specific verbal strategies does she employ to help us see the world through her eyes?

4. How does Kleege read the attitudes of the sighted world in relation to blind people and blindness? In general, how does she depict the sighted in this selection? What is her attitude toward sightedness? Toward blindness? Why does she feel this way?

FURTHER EXPLORATIONS

1. Compare the way that Kleege observes a painting by Matisse with the way that nuclear physicists observe subatomic particles, according to K. C. Cole in "Seeing Things" (p. 75). What aspects of the process of seeing do Cole and Kleege agree on? To what extent does Kleege illustrate Cole's suggestion that we can improve our visual abilities by "getting to know our perceptual selves"?

2. How do Kleege's reflections on the process of seeing compare with Walker Percy's meditation on what's required to achieve authentic perception of the world around us (p. 118)? How do their views compare on the parts played by memory, expectation, and learning in relation to the objects we see? How might Percy view Kleege's approach to studying Matisse? How might he view the man with the headphones she encounters in the museum? To what extent do these writers agree on the nature of perception?

3. Individually or as a class, visit a local museum or art gallery and observe what you do when you look at a painting. Pay close attention to how you look at the image,

where you stand, when you change position and why, and what you choose to look at first, second, and so forth. Try to record what you see each time you change position or shift your focus. How does your own process of seeing compare with that of Kleege or the sighted man in headphones she mentions in this selection? What might you do to "hone" your own skills as an observer of art?

4. While at the museum, try the following experiment: have a fellow class member lead you to a relatively large painting with your eyes closed. Once you are within a foot of the canvas, open your eyes and record the observations you make, scanning the image for five to ten minutes from no more than a foot away. Once you have completed this viewing and finished documenting the experience in your journal, move away and observe the painting from a "normal" distance. How does your appreciation of the painting change when you view it from different vantage points? Which perspective do you enjoy more? Why? Which offers the opportunity to make the most interesting "discoveries"?

ESSAY OPTIONS

1. After visiting a local art museum, write a paper in which you offer two contrasting perceptions of the same portrait—one seen from a comfortable viewing distance and the other from the intense, close-up view modeled by Georgina Kleege in this selection. What do you see when you view the painting from these two perspectives? What "discoveries" do you make about the painting from each of these points of view? Which is more satisfying to you? Why?

2. Write a paper in which you describe a particular work of abstract, nonrepresentational art. Try to put into words your overall experience of the work and the meaning or feeling it conveys to you. Allow yourself the freedom to experiment with all the descriptive strategies at your disposal—images, analogies, metaphors, even anecdotes—to express your experience of this work to your reader. Share your efforts in class, along with a reproduction of the original, and discuss how effectively you convey the spirit of the work in words.

Television and the Twilight of the Senses

BILL McKIBBEN

On May 3, 1990, naturalist and author Bill McKibben began an extraordinary experiment in perception. He started by videotaping all of the programming available during a twenty-four-hour period over the ninety-three cable stations carried in Fairfax, Virginia, one of the largest cable outlets in the United States at that time. From dawn to dusk, his bank of coordinated VCRs logged more than a thousand hours of television, hours that he then dutifully watched, including every local news show, infomercial, B movie, MTV video, and PBS special that aired. After months of viewing, McKibben celebrated his return to the light of day by spending twenty-four hours alone on Crow Mountain, a modest peak about a mile from his home in upstate New York. Later, he summarized these dramatically different experiences in *The Age of Missing Information* (1992), his personal assessment of the impact of mass media on human identity, community, and our relationship to nature. The selection included here comes from the book's closing pages, when twilight is settling over Crow Mountain and McKibben pauses for an early evening swim. The sensations he records as he enjoys the sun's last rays and the approach of night lead him to reflect on the way that television influences our ability to sense the world around us. A former staff writer for the *New Yorker*, McKibben (b. 1960) is the author of *The End of Nature* (1989), *Hope, Human and Wild: True Stories of Living Lightly on the Earth* (1995), *Maybe One: A Personal and Environmental Argument for Single-Child Families* (1998), and *Long Distance: A Year of Living Strenuously* (2000).

BEFORE READING

Working in small groups, discuss the effects that habitual television use is commonly thought to have on people. What is prolonged exposure to television supposed to do to us? What do you think watching television does to most viewers? What leads you to think so?

Deeper Twilight

Time for a swim. I ease myself down from the rocks into the chilly water, feeling the mud between my toes. I stand for a minute, aware of the line on my calves between the cold of water and the warmth of sun, and then dive in a taut stretch. I can feel the water rushing past my head, smoothing back my hair. As I stroke out to the middle, I'm conscious of the strength and pull of my shoulder blades. I haul myself out onto a rock in the middle of the pond, and sit there dripping. A breeze comes up, and lifts the hairs on my back, each one giving a nearly imperceptible tug at my skin. Under hand and thigh I can feel the roughness and the hardness of the rock. If I listen, I can hear the birds singing from several trees around the shore, and a frog now and again, and from the outlet stream a few hundred yards away a faint burbling — always changing and always the same. If I listen without concentrating, it's mainly the wind that I hear, a steady slight pressure on the leaves. I can see a hundred things — the sun reflects off the ripples from my passage and casts a moving line of shadow and sparkle on the rocks that rise up at the water's edge. I can smell the water. I can taste the water too — not the neutral beverage you drink because there's nothing in the fridge, but wet, rich, *complete*. As it drops into the corner of my mouth there's the slightest tang of salt from the trail sweat of the afternoon. I can feel my weight — feel it disappear as I slip into the water, feel it cling to me again as I drag myself back onto the rock.

TV restricts the use of our senses — that's one of the ways it robs us of information. It asks us to use our eyes and ears, and only our eyes and ears. If it is doing its job "correctly," you lose consciousness of your body, at least until a sort of achy torpor begins to assert itself, and maybe after some hours a dull headache, and of course the insatiable hunger that you never really notice but that somehow demands a constant stream of chips and soda. If you cut off your nose to spite your face, or for any other reason, it wouldn't impair your ability to watch television. You could make these same objections about other mediums, too — about writing, maybe. You can't smell words on a page. But you can summon a sense of smell. I hope the first paragraph of this chapter, however dimly, triggered your sense memory; it is not, I think, reproducible on television.

Even the senses that TV caters to, sight and hearing, it limits. It rarely provides a vista, not unless the Goodyear blimp is on hand. (My family gathered around the TV each New Year's Day for the opening seconds of the Rose Bowl coverage because the camera would briefly pan around the Los Angeles mountains where we once lived.) Its instinct is for the close-up. In the three or four years between the time I stopped watching TV and the time I began this project, the camera had tightened in dramatically on people's faces, especially during commercials — a man would be selling you financial services and you could count the worry lines around his eyes. But this tight shot demands one center of attention. If you're shooting *Nova,* you can get a nifty shot of an ant mating, but you can't, say, lie on your stomach and observe one square foot of ground. Here's a big spidery thing waving back and forth on improbable legs, and a line of ants, and the wind dripping needles from the bottom bough of a small pine. TV can't deal with faint noise, either; even "background" music is in the foreground, and only one sound at a time is permitted. When people shout, the decibel level doesn't really rise much — you knew Crazy Eddie was screaming because of his hand gestures, not his volume, which was certainly a blessing, but it all contributes to the sense of living in a muffled, shrunken world.

TV chops away perspective, too. On the mountain, even if your eye is drawn to something in particular, your peripheral vision fills in all sorts of detail, constantly. When you watch TV your peripheral vision ceases to function — you stare at the screen like a pitcher staring in at the catcher's mitt. You no longer even notice the *set* — the frame, the knobs, the antenna (if you're still backward enough to need an antenna). Your vision is cut down to maybe 10 degrees of the horizon — on a large screen maybe 15 degrees. What we see, we see sharply — the images have been edited so that peripheral vision is unnecessary. In the Cosby° living room there is a staircase, and in front of it a sofa, and the family is sitting on the sofa. No one is off in the corner making faces — it's fantastically stripped down, uncomplicated, and as a consequence whoever is in the foreground assumes vaster importance than he'd be granted under an open sky.

Any art, of course, does this to one degree or another — the artist wants   5
you to focus on something she has chosen, picked out from the world. But the experience of watching, say, a play in the theater differs vastly from the

---

Cosby: Refers to the *Bill Cosby Show,* a popular family situation comedy during the 1980s, starring comedian Bill Cosby.

experience of watching a television drama. The curtain comes up and down, lights shift on and off, the volume goes up and down—if you are sitting front row left you may see action quite different from what you would fifteen seats to the right or thirty behind. Most of all, you can *choose* what to watch. There is more there than the eye can take in, far more. You may spend the whole scene looking at what the TV director would call the reaction shot, or you may let yourself get caught up in the background. Sometimes the actors come right out among you—they may touch you. In any case, your absorption is of an entirely different character. Movies move in the direction of television, but even they have much more periphery—even on HDTV with Dolby stereo it's hard to imagine a television epic, a spectacle. No one's ever shot a scene for television with a cast of thousands.

Or consider the difference between watching a baseball game on TV and watching one at the park. Technology enriches the TV version with close-up and slo-mo and instant replay, but at a great price. It deprives you of the enormous perspective available to anyone in the stadium, the incredible choice of what to look at. TV looks at pretty women on occasion but never at the fight in the stands or the man selling beer or the outfielder hitching his pants. TV filters out most of the familiar sound of the ballpark, too—the sourceless, undifferentiated babble that comes from forty thousand people talking, laughing, rustling sacks of popcorn, a sound that the crack of the bat breaks so cleanly through, refocusing everyone's attention. TV systems are planning to introduce new interactive technology that will allow you to select between, say, three or four camera angles during the course of a game. But this sort of choice only underlines how much TV amputates your senses. What is there at a circus that can't be topped by a hundred spectacles a night on television? And yet circuses survive—what TV picture can compete with the humid excitement? And three rings! A delicious overload of the senses, starved on television's visual Pritikin regimen°. Still, the time may be coming when this overload seems like too much—when we prefer our baseball on TV. When it begins to seem more *real* on TV. At the beginning of *And So It Goes*, Linda Ellerbee's° book about her TV career, she recalls a conversation with colleagues about whether her new show should be live or on tape. Her son Josh overheard the argument and interrupted: "This is live," he said. "You, me, everybody in this room. *This* is live. That, Mom," he said pointing to the box, "*that's* television."

During the war in the Persian Gulf, people said we were seeing things as they happened, live, with gut-wrenching immediacy. In truth, we were seeing what television was able to show us—the lights of tracer fire flashing over Baghdad were in some way impressive, but if I'd been told they were a laser show commemorating the hundredth anniversary of the Iraqi electric utility I'd have nodded my head. The shudder, the concussion, the dust, the smell, all the things that even a moderately competent writer would express, TV

Pritikin regimen: A particularly rigorous diet plan popular during the 1980s and early 1990s.
Linda Ellerbee's: Linda Ellerbee (b. 1944), former NBC newswoman.

can't. Most of all, the confusion—the camera and the small screen can't cope with confusion because they search relentlessly for a center, a focus. "Does TV 'bring the war into your living room'?" asked Mark Crispin Miller in his book *Boxed-In.* "In fact, the experience is fundamentally absurd. Most obviously there is an incongruity of scale, the radical disjunction of locations. While a war is among the biggest things that can ever happen to a nation or a person, devastating families, blasting away the roofs and walls, we see it compressed and miniaturized on a sturdy little piece of furniture, which stands and shines at the very center of our household." If you wanted even the slightest sense of what the war in Iraq was *like,* how it *felt,* you'd be far better off hiring someone to come at some random hour in the night and toss a brick through your window.

Deeper Twilight Still

I've been sitting on a flat rock next to the pond for many minutes, watching the sun go down and seeing the stars come up. When I got out of the water, I drip-dried in the last sun—the stored soft heat in the rock warmed my back. I sat there without a shirt on, for the breeze kept down the few mosquitoes. The air grew cooler and cooler—the breeze felt great, and then right on the line between great and chilly, and then just plain cool till it raised gooseflesh, but I was too happy with the stars to move. Finally I got up, and wandered back to the tent, dug out a clean T-shirt, and pulled it over my head—and thought about how great it felt. How dry against the back of my neck where my wet hair still dripped, how warm against the breeze, how soft compared with the rock I'd been lying on. It occurs to me that I may have cast myself as a killjoy . . . , an antimaterialist, the unsensual man, but it isn't true. The mountain is filled with deep animal satisfaction—far better stocked with physical pleasure than any fancy home or leather-lined car. That's because the mountain also exposes you to cold, damp, wind, heat—when you finish with these and move on to warm, dry, still, cool, you feel not just comfort. You feel *pleasure, joy.*

The difference between comfort and pleasure is enormous, though hard to set down in words. Albert Borgmann says "comfort is the feeling of well-being that derives from an optimally high and steady level of arousal of positive stimulation, whereas pleasure arises from an upward change of the arousal level. Since there is a best or highest level of pleasure that constitutes comfort, one cannot indefinitely obtain pleasure by rising from comfort to more comfort. . . . Hence pleasure can only be had at the price of discomfort." What he means, I think, is, if you walk out of the bitter cold into a 70-degree room, it will feel *marvelous, toasty, cheerful, a haven, a nest.* But if you spend all your time in a room where the temperature is 70 degrees it will simply feel neutral. I can remember my father talking about taking a long hiking trip around Mount Rainier. At the end of the trek, after days of water and the kind of food you carry with you on a trail, he emerged, went to a restaurant, and ordered a milk shake. And I think he can taste that milk shake still—whereas, of course, if you have a milk shake every day you hardly notice it. This is the most obvious thing on earth, and yet it is the easiest to forget. When you are sitting inside on a cold and windy night it is nearly impossible to make yourself get up and walk the dog, even though when you do, the fresh air feels bracing, and the home you return to is a magic place.

The great virtue of the mountain is that once you're up there away from the car, there's no way to escape those kinds of swings—the information about what actually feels good is forced on you relentlessly. The second day I was up there it rained like crazy—little rivers finding the stitching holes in my old tent. It stopped for a while in the morning and I went out for a short hike—ten minutes from the tent the clouds opened up again, and by the time I was back you could have wrung me out. Nothing to do but crawl into my damp sleeping bag and read. It was too hot inside the sleeping bag and my legs sweated. Outside the bag was too cool—clammy. And then, in the afternoon, the sun broke through, the rain fled, the world warmed up. I stretched out my gear and myself on a rock and warmed up—and that sun felt ten times as glorious because of the rain that came before it.

We are stubbornly unwilling to acknowledge this kind of pleasure—either that or we habitually overstate the discomfort that precedes it. On the *Today* show, Bryant Gumbel announced that in a few weeks the whole cast was going on a camping trip so they could broadcast from the great outdoors. Co-host Deborah Norville shrieked girlishly: "We're not sleeping in tents, are we?" When Bryant said yes, she said, "The heck we are. . . . There's nothing in my contract that says I have to sleep in tents. I feel an illness coming on—exactly what date is that? Oooooh, crawly things," and so on.

If this were simply a physical phenomenon, it would be bad enough—a loss of information about our bodies that has enriched the lives of most members of every previous generation, and a loss of understanding about what it is is like for others to be cold and hungry and dirty. But it's more than that. We have developed a series of emotional thermostats as well, by far the most potent of which is television itself. Instead of really experiencing the highs and lows, pain and joys, that make up a life, many of us use TV just as we use central heating—to flatten our variations, to maintain a constant "optimal" temperature. A pair of academics, Robert Kubey and Mihaly Cziksentmihalyi, recently published a massive and novel study of why people watch TV. Instead of assembling their subjects in a college classroom somewhere, showing them a program, and passing out questionnaires, Kubey and Cziksentmihalyi tried to find out what TV meant to people in the ordinary course of life. Each subject was given a beeper, which went off eight or nine times a day at random intervals between 8:00 A.M. and 10:00 P.M. When the pager sounded, the subjects were supposed to instantly fill out a form that showed what they were doing at the time and how they were feeling—whether they were concentrating, what kind of mood they were in, if their head was aching, whether they really wished they were doing something else.

Some of the findings were obvious: "Television is used by some singles in lieu of company when dining." But much of their research broke new ground. Their

10

data showed quite convincingly that people watch television when they felt depressed—that the strongest variable predicting that people would watch TV in
the evening was that in the afternoon they felt the day was going badly. Only a minority, described as "rare" in one study, watch television "selectively," in order to
see a few favorite shows—only about half of Americans report even using a television guide. Instead, we use the set like a drug. Not an addictive drug exactly—
the idea that people are addicted to TV has a long history, and surely all of us have
sometimes felt it to be true. But the new research indicates that it's not a drug like
crack—that watching it actually makes us feel more passive, bored, irritable, sad,
and lonely. There was certainly no euphoria, not even much active pleasure. TV
didn't dominate people's thoughts all day—when they were beeped at work, in
only five of three thousand cases were people thinking about programs. If our lives
are going pleasantly, if there's something else to do that's attractive, even if it's as
undramatic as chatting on the phone with friends, then we're much less likely to
watch TV. We use TV as we use tranquilizers—to even things out, to blot out unpleasantness, to dilute confusion, distress, unhappiness, loneliness. The reason
that television can be counted on to work this way—the way that television most
nearly resembles a drug—is its predictability. It is *not* a drug like LSD; you don't
take it to see where you'll be transported to today. You take it because you *know*
where you'll be transported. *General Hospital* can be counted on to rouse the same
emotions at the same time each day, as can *Jeopardy* or *Nightline* or *Letterman*. In
an uncertain world, TV restores an old familiar pattern. The Corporation for
Public Broadcasting once commissioned a study to discover why people weren't
flocking to its "innovative" programming. It found people preferred commercial
TV precisely *because* on the networks they were "more likely to see familiar actors
and episodes of programs they had viewed previously." When Rhoda° separated
from her TV husband the ratings dropped; when *M*A*S*H* killed off McLean
Stevenson,° it drew bagloads of angry mail.

That's one reason the *Playhouse 90*–type programs° that originally dominated TV have fallen by the wayside—you wouldn't know, from one night to
the next, if you were going to be scared or shocked or amused. It's why all
those people who called Walter Cronkite° the most influential man in America
were wrong. He held our affection because he was utterly predictable, right
down to his inflection, and had he suddenly urged us to rise up and break our

Rhoda: Main character in a popular late 1970s and early 1980s situation comedy of the same
name.

when M*A*S*H killed off McLean Stevenson . . . : Refers to the fictional death of Lt. Col.
Henry Blake, a character played by actor McLean Stevenson on the 1970s situation comedy
M*A*S*H, about an army medical unit.

***Playhouse* 90–type programs:** *Playhouse 90* was a live, weekly dramatic television series that
became famous during the 1950s because of its powerful original scripts and exceptional performances; hence, any high-quality television programming.

Walter Cronkite: (b. 1916), popular anchor of the *CBS Evening News* during the 1960s, 1970s,
and 1980s.

chains he would instantly have gone from soothing to alarming—he would have broken the trance we turn on television to create.

This tranquilization has its advantages—anyone who ever checked into a hotel room knows that TV masks the loneliness. And if it really made us happy, who could argue? Loneliness, stress, fear—these aren't to be desired, exactly. But television doesn't leave us happy; it only presses our boredom and alienation a little to the back. "Obviously," wrote Kubey and Cziksentmihalyi, "if they possibly could, TV producers would regularly broadcast programs that would make people feel significantly happier than they do normally. They would do so because of the obvious commercial gains that would accrue. That television viewing helps us feel more relaxed than usual but generally does not help us feel substantially happier says something about human nature and what makes for happiness. Happiness is a more complex state than relaxation. It requires a more elusive set of conditions, and is therefore more difficult to obtain. Others can successfully attract and hold our attention and help us relax, but perhaps only we can provide for ourselves the psychological rewards and meaning that make for happiness." In the same way that traveling by airline assures your comfort but rarely allows you any adventure along the way, watching TV insulates you from anything real. We all know this—when researchers ask what activity best fits the description "I should have been doing something else," television is the hands-down winner. But that something else might be unpleasant—it might mean dealing with a spouse you'd rather not deal with, or thinking about a job that leaves you empty and unfulfilled. Or that something else might be risky—television never even thinks about rejecting you. Under the pressure of your thumb it comes instantly to life, cooing and making eyes.

That's why TV makes us feel so guilty sometimes. It's a time-out from life. Which is okay if you're really winded—TV as white-noise therapy has its occasional value. But the time-outs soon last longer than the game, which at some level you realize is passing you by. TV makes it so easy to postpone living for another half hour. I can remember hundreds of Saturday afternoons as a boy spent staring at *Wide World of Sports*. I wasn't much of an athlete then—a deep fear of embarrassment kept me out of Pop Warner and Little League. So I lay on the sofa and watched cliff diving in Acapulco and learned to mildly loathe myself.

I've taken friends up the mountain to the pond many times, and at the top suggested a swim. Invariably some of them hang back—it's too cold, or they don't want anyone to think they're fat, or they'd be soggy on the hike down, or all the other inhibitions we feel in such situations. But you can tell, when everyone else is whooping and hollering in the frigid water, that they wish they'd come in.

EXPLORING THE TEXT

1. What, according to McKibben, does television do to our ability to sense the world around us? Why does he feel that other forms of mass communication, like writing or theater, do not have a similar impact? To what extent would you agree?

2. Why do events seem "more real" when seen on television than they do in reality, in McKibben's view? Would you agree that places, people, or things seen on television seem more "immediate" or "true" than the actual places, people, or things themselves? Why might this be so?

3. What difference does McKibben see between comfort and pleasure? To what extent do you think this is a generally valid distinction or simply the expression of his own personal preference? Would you agree that people are losing the ability to appreciate genuine pleasure today? Why or why not?

4. Why, in McKibben's opinion, are people attracted to television? What danger does he see in this attraction? What other dangers are commonly associated with television viewing?

5. Review the opening paragraphs of both sections of this selection, being sure to note lines or phrases that evoke clear sensory images for you as you read. What sensations does McKibben conjure up for you in these sections? Which of his sense images strike you as more effective? Which seem less effective? Why?

FURTHER EXPLORATIONS

1. In your journal, write an imaginary dialogue between McKibben and Georgina Kleege (p. 93) on the dominance of vision in modern American society and the need for a balance of the senses.

2. Compare McKibben's view of television's effect on the senses with Walker Percy's analysis of the impact of modern technological society on our ability to see the world around us (p. 118). What role do familiarity and predictability play in both writers' views of technology's effect on human perception?

3. Working in small groups, test McKibben's claim about the predictability of television programming by outlining the plot structures of several popular TV shows. You might, for example, sketch out the plot of a typical episode of *ER, Frasier, Friends, NYPD Blue,* or *Ally McBeal.* You might even try your hand at outlining the "plot" of a typical local "eleven o'clock" news show, an afternoon talk show, a typical NBA basketball game, or a World Wrestling Federation "Smackdown." Compare your results as a class and discuss whether you agree with McKibben's view of television's predictability and its impact on viewers.

4. To what extent would the Sioux medicine man Lame Deer (p. 512) be likely to agree with McKibben's assertion that people in modern technological societies have lost the ability to experience real pleasure in the natural world as well as access to important information about living in harmony with nature?

ESSAY OPTIONS

1. Using the opening paragraphs of McKibben's description of his twilight swim as a model, write a brief personal essay in which you try to express the "feel" and meaning of a particularly "pleasurable" experience you recall from your past. As you plan your paper, keep in mind the special sense in which McKibben uses the term "pleasure" and the distinction he makes between genuine pleasure and mere comfort. In your description, try your best to capture the total impression of this experience, using images appealing to all five senses.

2. Using McKibben's selection as a point of departure and drawing on your own experience of television programming for examples and illustrations, write an essay in which you evaluate McKibben's claim that television "tranquilizes" its audience. In what ways does television programming dull viewer's senses? To what extent do news shows or "reality" programs challenge this view of television's impact? Isn't it possible that certain forms of television programming actually sharpen, educate, or extend our ability to sense the world around us?

3. Drawing on ideas and information presented in any or all of the reading selections by McKibben, Barry Lopez (p. 27), Diane Ackerman (p. 36), Constance Classen et al. (p. 59), K. C. Cole (p. 75), Georgina Kleege (p. 93), and Walker Percy (below), write a paper exploring the topic of educating the senses. To what extent do our sense responses appear to be learned or innate? What limits the extent to which we can expand the intensity or the acuity of our sense impressions? How do the authors you've read in this chapter view education in relation to the senses?

4. Drawing on McKibben, Constance Classen et al. (p. 59), Georgina Kleege (p. 93), K. C. Cole (p. 75), and Lame Deer (p. 512), as well as your own experience, write an essay on the visual bias of contemporary technological society. To what extent would you agree that vision is the dominant form of human perception and that the other senses — and particularly the senses of smell and touch — are losing their importance for us? What if anything might we lose if vision displaces the other senses?

The Loss of the Creature

WALKER PERCY

Pause for a moment and think of what the Grand Canyon looks like. Without much effort, most of us can conjure up a fairly accurate image of this famous natural marvel, complete with multicolored, water-carved canyon walls, guard rails, and scenic lookouts. The fact is that even if you've never been farther west than the Mississippi, you've probably already "seen" the Grand Canyon any number of times in books, on television, or in popular movies or magazines. Or have you? In the following selection, Walker Percy argues that even a tourist teetering on the canyon's edge for the perfect snapshot never really "sees" this natural wonder. Authentic perception, in Percy's view, results from a constant struggle to penetrate what has already been seen, just as real education results from the student's struggle to experience the world beyond the limitations of what is already known.

Percy (b. 1916) graduated with a degree in medicine from Columbia University in 1941 and worked as a physician at New York's Bellevue Hospital until tuberculosis forced him to cut short his career. While in recovery, he rekindled a longstanding love of reading and writing, eventually publishing his first essay in 1954. His acclaimed first novel, *The Movie-goer*, won the National Book Award for fiction in 1962. Before his death in 1990, Percy wrote five other novels, including *Love in the Ruins* (1971) and *Lancelot* (1977), as well as two collections of essays. "The Loss of the Creature" originally appeared in *The Message in the Bottle: How Queer Man Is, How Queer Language Is, and What One Has to Do with the Other* (1975).

BEFORE READING

Think back to a time you visited a well-known natural or man-made wonder like the Grand Canyon, Niagara Falls, the Hoover Dam, or the Eiffel Tower. What do you recall seeing there? Is your experience of what you saw any more "real" or meaningful than it would have been if you had seen the same thing at the movies or on a television travel show? Why or why not? What's the difference between seeing something on television and seeing it for yourself?

I

E very explorer names his island Formosa, beautiful. To him it is beautiful because, being first, he has access to it and can see it for what it is. But to no one else is it ever as beautiful — except the rare man who manages to recover it, who knows that it has to be recovered.

Garcia López de Cárdenas discovered the Grand Canyon and was amazed at the sight. It can be imagined: one crosses miles of desert, breaks through the mesquite, and there it is at one's feet. Later the government set the place aside as a national park, hoping to pass along to millions the experience of Cárdenas. Does not one see the same sight from the Bright Angel Lodge that Cárdenas saw?

The assumption is that the Grand Canyon is a remarkably interesting and beautiful place and that if it had a certain value P for Cárdenas, the same value P may be transmitted to any number of sightseers — just as Banting's discovery of insulin can be transmitted to any number of diabetics. A counterinfluence is at work, however, and it would be nearer the truth to say that if the place is seen by a million sightseers, a single sightseer does not receive value P but a millionth part of value P.

It is assumed that since the Grand Canyon has the fixed interest value P, tours can be organized for any number of people. A man in Boston decides to spend his vacation at the Grand Canyon. He visits his travel bureau, looks at the folder, signs up for a two-week tour. He and his family take the tour, see the Grand Canyon, and return to Boston. May we say that this man has seen the Grand Canyon? Possibly he has. But it is more likely that what he has done is the one sure way not to see the canyon.

Why is it almost impossible to gaze directly at the Grand Canyon under 5 these circumstances and see it for what it is — as one picks up a strange object from one's back yard and gazes directly at it? It is almost impossible because the Grand Canyon, the thing as it is, has been appropriated by the symbolic complex which has already been formed in the sightseer's mind. Seeing the canyon under approved circumstances is seeing the symbolic complex head on. The thing is no longer the thing as it confronted the Spaniard; it is rather that which has already been formulated—by picture postcard, geography book, tourist folders, and the words *Grand Canyon*. As a result of this preformulation, the source of the sightseer's pleasure undergoes a shift. Where the wonder and delight of the Spaniard arose from his penetration of the thing itself, from a progressive discovery of depths, patterns, colors, shadows, etc., now the sightseer measures his satisfaction *by the degree to which the canyon conforms to the performed complex*. If it does so, if it looks just like the postcard, he is pleased; he might even say, "Why it is every bit as beautiful as a picture postcard!" He feels he has not been cheated. But if it does not conform, if the colors are somber, he will not be able to see it directly; he will only be conscious of the disparity between what it is and what it is supposed to be. He will say later that he was unlucky in not being there at the right time. The highest point, the term of the sightseer's satisfaction, is not the sovereign discovery of the thing before him; it is rather the measuring up of the thing to the criterion of the performed symbolic complex.

Seeing the canyon is made even more difficult by what the sightseer does when the moment arrives, when sovereign knower confronts the thing to be known. Instead of looking at it, he photographs it. There is no confrontation at all. At the end of forty years of preformulation and with the Grand Canyon yawning at his feet, what does he do? He waives his right of seeing and knowing and records symbols for the next forty years. For him there is no present; there is only the past of what has been formulated and seen and the future of what has been formulated and not seen. The present is surrendered to the past and the future.

The sightseer may be aware that something is wrong. He may simply be bored; or he may be conscious of the difficulty: that the great thing yawning at his feet somehow eludes him. The harder he looks at it, the less he can see. It eludes everybody. The routist cannot see it; the bellboy at the Bright Angel Lodge cannot see it: for him it is only one side of the space he lives in, like one wall of a room; to the ranger it is a tissue of everyday signs relevant to his own prospects—the blue haze down there means that he will probably get rained on during the donkey ride.

How can the sightseer recover the Grand Canyon? He can recover it in any number of ways, all sharing in common the stratagem of avoiding the approved confrontation of the tour and the Park Service.

It may be recovered by leaving the beaten track. The tourist leaves the tour, camps in the back country. He arises before dawn and approaches the South Rim through a wild terrain where there are no trails and no railed-in lookout points. In other words, he sees the canyon by avoiding all the facilities for seeing the canyon. If the benevolent Park Service hears about this fellow and thinks he has a good idea and places the following notice in the Bright Angel Lodge: *Consult ranger for information on getting off the beaten track*—the end result will only be the closing of another access to the canyon.

It may be recovered by a dialectical movement which brings one back to the beaten track but at a level above it. For example, after a lifetime of avoiding the   10 beaten track and guided tours, a man may deliberately seek out the most beaten track of all, the most commonplace tour imaginable: he may visit the canyon by a Greyhound tour in the company of a party from Terre Haute — just as a man who has lived in New York all his life may visit the Statue of Liberty. (Such dialectical savorings of the familiar as the familiar are, of course, a favorite stratagem of *The New Yorker* magazine.) The thing is recovered from familiarity by means of an exercise in familiarity. Our complex friend stands behind his fellow tourists at the Bright Angel Lodge and sees the canyon through them and their predicament, their picture taking and busy disregard. In a sense, he exploits his fellow tourists; he stands on their shoulders to see the canyon.

Such a man is far more advanced in the dialectic than the sightseer who is trying to get off the beaten track — getting up at dawn and approaching the canyon through the mesquite. This stratagem is, in fact, for our complex man the weariest, most beaten track of all.

It may be recovered as a consequence of a breakdown of the symbolic machinery by which the experts present the experience to the consumer. A family visits the canyon in the usual way. But shortly after their arrival, the park is closed by an outbreak of typhus in the south. They have the canyon to themselves. What do they mean when they tell the home folks of their good luck: "We had the whole place to ourselves"? How does one see the thing better when the others are absent? Is looking like sucking: the more lookers, the less there is to see? They could hardly answer, but by saying this they testify to a state of affairs which is considerably more complex than the simple statement of the schoolbook about the Spaniard and the millions who followed him. It is a state in which there is a complex distribution of sovereignty, of zoning.

It may be recovered in a time of national disaster. The Bright Angel Lodge is converted into a rest home, a function that has nothing to do with the canyon a few yards away. A wounded man is brought in. He regains consciousness; there outside his window is the canyon.

The most extreme case of access by privilege conferred by disaster is the Huxleyan° novel of the adventures of the surviving remnant after the great wars of the twentieth century. An expedition from Australia lands in Southern California and heads east. They stumble across the Bright Angel Lodge, now fallen into ruins. The trails are grown over, the guard rails fallen away, the dime telescope at Battleship Point rusted. But there is the canyon, exposed at last. Exposed by what? By the decay of those facilities which were designed to help the sightseer.

This dialectic of sightseeing cannot be taken into account by planners, for the object of the dialectic is nothing other than the subversion of the efforts of the planners.   15

The dialectic is not known to objective theorists, psychologists, and the like. Yet it is quite well known in the fantasy-consciousness of the popular arts.

Huxleyan: Refers to English novelist and social critic Aldous Huxley (1894–1963) and, more specifically, to his 1932 satirical science fiction novel *Brave New World.*

The devices by which the museum exhibit, the Grand Canyon, the ordinary thing, is recovered have long since been stumbled upon. A movie shows a man visiting the Grand Canyon. But the movie maker knows something the planner does not know. He knows that one cannot take the sight frontally. The canyon must be approached by the stratagems we have mentioned: the Inside Track, the Familiar Revisited, the Accidental Encounter. Who is the stranger at the Bright Angel Lodge? Is he the ordinary tourist from Terre Haute that he makes himself out to be? He is not. He has another objective in mind, to revenge his wronged brother, counterespionage, etc. By virtue of the fact that he has other fish to fry, he may take a stroll along the rim after supper and then we can see the canyon through him. The movie accomplishes its purpose by concealing it. Overtly the characters (the American family marooned by typhus) and we the onlookers experience pity for the sufferers, and the family experiences anxiety for themselves; covertly and in truth they are the happiest of people and we are happy through them, for we have the canyon to ourselves. The movie cashes in on the recovery of sovereignty through disaster. Not only is the canyon now accessible to the remnant: the members of the remnant are now accessible to each other, a whole new ensemble of relations becomes possible—friendship, love, hatred, clandestine sexual adventures. In a movie when a man sits next to a woman on a bus, it is necessary either that the bus break down or that the woman lose her memory. (The question occurs to one: Do you imagine there are sightseers who see sights just as they are supposed to? a family who live in Terre Haute, who decide to take the canyon tour, who go there, see it, enjoy it immensely, and go home content? a family who are entirely innocent of all the barriers, zones, losses of sovereignty I have been talking about? Wouldn't most people be sorry if Battleship Point fell into the canyon, carrying all one's fellow passengers to their death, leaving one alone on the South Rim? I cannot answer this. Perhaps there are such people. Certainly a great many American families would swear they had no such problems, that they came, saw, and went away happy. Yet it is just these families who would be happiest if they had gotten the Inside Track and been among the surviving remnant.)

It is now apparent that as between the many measures which may be taken to overcome the opacity, the boredom, of the direct confrontation of the thing or creature in its citadel of symbolic investiture, some are less authentic than others. That is to say, some stratagems obviously serve other purposes than that of providing access to being—for example, various unconscious motivations which it is not necessary to go into here.

Let us take an example in which the recovery of being is ambiguous, where it may under the same circumstances contain both authentic and unauthentic components. An American couple, we will say, drives down into Mexico. They see the usual sights and have a fair time of it. Yet they are never without the sense of missing something. Although Taxco and Cuernavaca° are interesting and picturesque as advertised, they fall short of "it." What do the

---

Taxco and Cuernavaca: Small, popular tourist destinations outside of Mexico City.

couple have in mind by "it"? What do they really hope for? What sort of experience could they have in Mexico so that upon their return, they would feel that "it" had happened? We have a clue: Their hope has something to do with their own role as tourists in a foreign country and the way in which they conceive this role. It has something to do with other American tourists. Certainly they feel that they are very far from "it" when, after traveling five thousand miles, they arrive at the plaza in Guanajuato only to find themselves surrounded by a dozen other couples from the Midwest.

Already we may distinguish authentic and unauthentic elements. First, we see the problem the couple faces and we understand their efforts to surmount it. The problem is to find an "unspoiled" place. "Unspoiled" does not mean only that a place is left physically intact; it means also that it is not encrusted by renown and by the familiar (as in Taxco), that it has not been discovered by others. We understand that the couple really want to get at the place and enjoy it. Yet at the same time we wonder if there is not something wrong in their dislike of their compatriots. Does access to the place require the exclusion of others?

Let us see what happens.   20

The couple decide to drive from Guanajuato to Mexico City. On the way they get lost. After hours on a rocky mountain road, they find themselves in a tiny valley not even marked on the map. There they discover an Indian village. Some sort of religious festival is going on. It is apparently a corn dance in supplication of the rain god.

The couple know at once that this is "it." They are entranced. They spend several days in the village, observing the Indians and being themselves observed with friendly curiosity.

Now may we not say that the sightseers have at last come face to face with an authentic sight, a sight which is charming, quaint, picturesque, unspoiled, and that they see the sight and come away rewarded? Possibly this may occur. Yet it is more likely that what happens is a far cry indeed from an immediate encounter with being, that the experience, while masquerading as such, is in truth a rather desperate impersonation. I use the word *desperate* advisedly to signify an actual loss of hope.

The clue to the spuriousness of their enjoyment of the village and the festival is a certain restiveness in the sightseers themselves. It is given expression by their repeated exclamations that "this is too good to be true," and by their anxiety that it may not prove to be so perfect, and finally by their downright relief at leaving the valley and having the experience in the bag, so to speak—that is, safely embalmed in memory and movie film.

What is the source of their anxiety during the visit? Does it not mean that   25 the couple are looking at the place with a certain standard of performance in mind? Are they like Fabre,° who gazed at the world about him with wonder, letting it be what it is; or are they not like the overanxious mother who sees

Fabre: Jean Henri Fabre (1823–1915), French entomologist.

her child as one performing, now doing badly, now doing well? The village is their child and their love for it is an anxious love because they are afraid that at any moment it might fail them.

We have another clue in their subsequent remark to an ethnologist friend. "How we wished you had been there with us! What a perfect goldmine of folkways! Every minute we would say to each other, if only you were here! You must return with us." This surely testifies to a generosity of spirit, a willingness to share their experience with others, not at all like their feelings toward their fellow Iowans on the plaza at Guanajuato!

I am afraid this is not the case at all. It is true that they longed for their ethnologist friend, but it was for an entirely different reason. They wanted him, not to share their experience, but to certify their experience as genuine.

"This is it" and "Now we are really living" do not necessarily refer to the sovereign encounter of the person with the sight that enlivens the mind and gladdens the heart. It means that now at last we are having the acceptable experience. The present experience is always measured by a prototype, the "it" of their dreams. "Now I am really living" means that now I am filling the role of sightseer and the sight is living up to the prototype of sights. This quaint and picturesque village is measured by a Platonic ideal of the Quaint and the Picturesque.

Hence their anxiety during the encounter. For at any minute something could go wrong. A fellow Iowan might emerge from a 'dobe hut; the chief might show them his Sears catalog. (If the failures are "wrong" enough, as these are, they might still be turned to account as rueful conversation pieces. "There we were expecting the chief to bring us a churinga° and he shows up with a Sears catalog!") They have snatched victory from disaster, but their experience always runs the danger of failure.

They need the ethnologist to certify their experience as genuine. This is 30 borne out by their behavior when the three of them return for the next corn dance. During the dance, the couple do not watch the goings-on; instead they watch the ethnologist! Their highest hope is that their friend should find the dance interesting. And if he should show signs of true absorption, an interest in the goings-on so powerful that he becomes oblivious of his friends — then their cup is full. "Didn't we tell you?" they say at last. What they want from him is not ethnological explanations; all they want is his approval.

What has taken place is a radical loss of sovereignty over that which is as much theirs as it is the ethnologist's. The fault does not lie with the ethnologist. He has no wish to stake a claim to the village; in fact, he desires the opposite: he will bore his friends to death by telling them about the village and the meaning of the folkways. A degree of sovereignty has been surrendered by the couple. It is the nature of the loss, moreover, that they are not aware of the loss, beyond a certain uneasiness. (Even if they read this and admitted it, it

churinga: Sacred amulet.

would be very difficult for them to bridge the gap in their confrontation of the world. Their consciousness of the corn dance cannot escape their consciousness of their consciousness, so that with the onset of the first direct enjoyment, their higher consciousness pounces and certifies: "Now you are doing it! Now you are really living!" and, in certifying the experience, sets it at nought.)

Their basic placement in the world is such that they recognize a priority of title of the expert over his particular department of being. The whole horizon of being is staked out by "them," the experts. The highest satisfaction of the sightseer (not merely the tourist but any layman seer of sights) is that his sight should be certified as genuine. The worse of this impoverishment is that there is no sense of impoverishment. The surrender of title is so complete that it never even occurs to one to reassert title. A poor man may envy the rich man, but the sightseer does not envy the expert. When a caste system becomes absolute, envy disappears. Yet the caste of layman-expert is not the fault of the expert. It is due altogether to the eager surrender of sovereignty by the layman so that he may take up the role not of the person but of the consumer.

I do not refer only to the special relation of layman to theorist. I refer to the general situation in which sovereignty is surrendered to a class of privileged knowers, whether these be theorists or artists. A reader may surrender sovereignty over that which has been written about, just as a consumer may surrender sovereignty over a thing which has been theorized about. The consumer is content to receive an experience just as it has been presented to him by theorists and planners. The reader may also be content to judge life by whether it has or has not been formulated by those who know and write about life. A young man goes to France. He too has a fair time of it, sees the sights, enjoys the food. On his last day, in fact as he sits in a restaurant in Le Havre° waiting for his boat, something happens. A group of French students in the restaurant get into an impassioned argument over a recent play. A riot takes place. Madame la concierge joins in, swinging her mop at the rioters. Our young American is transported. This is "it." And he had almost left France without seeing "it"!

But the young man's delight is ambiguous. On the one hand, it is a pleasure for him to encounter the same Gallic temperament he had heard about from Puccini° and Rolland°. But on the other hand, the source of his pleasure testifies to a certain alienation. For the young man is actually barred from a direct encounter with anything French excepting only that which has been set forth, authenticated by Puccini and Rolland—those who know. If he had encountered the restaurant scene without reading Hemingway,° without knowing that the performance was so typically,

---

Le Havre: French seaport.

Puccini: Giacomo Puccini (1858–1924), Italian composer famed for his romantic operas.

Rolland: Romain Rolland (1866–1944), French novelist.

Hemingway: Ernest Miller Hemingway (1899–1961), American novelist.

charmingly French, he would not have been delighted. He would only have been anxious at seeing things get so out of hand. The source of his delight is the sanction of those who know.

This loss of sovereignty is not a marginal process, as might appear from   35
my example of estranged sightseers. It is a generalized surrender of the horizon to those experts within whose competence a particular segment of the horizon is thought to lie. Kwakiutls° are surrendered to Franz Boas;° decaying Southern mansions are surrendered to Faulkner and Tennessee Williams.° So that, although it is by no means the intention of the expert to expropriate sovereignty—in fact he would not even know what sovereignty meant in this context—the danger of theory and consumption is a seduction and deprivation of the consumer.

In the New Mexico desert, natives occasionally come across strange-looking artifacts which have fallen from the skies and which are stenciled: *Return to U.S. Experimental Project, Alamogordo. Reward.* The finder returns the object and is rewarded. He knows nothing of the nature of the object he has found and does not care to know. The sole role of the native, the highest role he can play, is that of finder and returner of the mysterious equipment.

The same is true of the laymen's relation to *natural* objects in a modern technical society. No matter what the object or event is, whether it is a star, a swallow, a Kwakiutl, a "psychological phenomenon," the layman who confronts it does not confront it as a sovereign person, as Crusoe° confronts a seashell he finds on the beach. The highest role he can conceive himself as playing is to be able to recognize the title of the object, to return it to the appropriate expert and have it certified as a genuine find. He does not even permit himself to see the thing—as Gerard Hopkins° could see a rock or a cloud or a field. If anyone asks him why he doesn't look, he may reply that he didn't take that subject in college (or he hasn't read Faulkner).

This loss of sovereignty extends even to oneself. There is the neurotic who asks nothing more of his doctor than that his symptoms should prove interesting. When all else fails, the poor fellow has nothing to offer but his own neurosis. But even this is sufficient if only the doctor will show interest when he says, "Last night I had a curious sort of dream; perhaps it will be significant to one who knows about such things. It seems I was standing in a sort of alley—" (I have nothing else to offer you but my own unhappiness. Please say that it, at least, measures up, that it is a *proper* sort of unhappiness.)

Kwakiutls: Native Americans of the Pacific Coast.

Franz Boas: (1858–1942), German-born American anthropologist.

Faulkner and Tennessee Williams: William Cuthbert Faulkner (1897–1962), American novelist; Tennessee Williams, originally Thomas Lanier Williams (1911–1983), American dramatist.

Crusoe: Robinson Crusoe, a sixteenth-century Englishman stranded alone for twenty-four years on an island near the Orinoco River, is the main character in the novel of the same name by English author Daniel Defoe (1660–1731).

Gerard Hopkins: Gerard Manley Hopkins (1844–1889), English poet.

II

A young Falkland Islander° walking along a beach and spying a dead dogfish and going to work on it with his jackknife has, in a fashion wholly unprovided in modern educational theory, a great advantage over the Scarsdale high-school pupil who finds the dogfish on his laboratory desk. Similarly the citizen of Huxley's *Brave New World* who stumbles across a volume of Shakespeare in some vine-grown ruins and squats on a potsherd to read it is in a fairer way of getting at a sonnet than the Harvard sophomore taking English Poetry II.

The educator whose business it is to teach students biology or poetry is un-   40 aware of a whole ensemble of relations which exist between the student and the dogfish and between the student and the Shakespeare sonnet. To put it bluntly: A student who has the desire to get at a dogfish or a Shakespeare sonnet may have the greatest difficulty in salvaging the creature itself from the educational package in which it is presented. The great difficulty is that he is not aware that there is a difficulty; surely, he thinks, in such a fine classroom, with such a fine textbook, the sonnet must come across! What's wrong with me?

The sonnet and the dogfish are obscured by two different processes. The sonnet is obscured by the symbolic package which is formulated not by the sonnet itself but by the *media* through which the sonnet is transmitted, the media which the educators believe for some reason to be transparent. The new textbook, the type, the smell of the page, the classroom, the aluminum windows and the winter sky, the personality of Miss Hawkins — these media which are supposed to transmit the sonnet may only succeed in transmitting themselves. It is only the hardiest and cleverest of students who can salvage the sonnet from this many-tissued package. It is only the rarest student who knows that the sonnet must be salvaged from the package. (The educator is well aware that something is wrong, that there is a fatal gap between the student's learning and the student's life: the student reads the poem, appears to understand it, and gives all the answers. But what does he recall if he should happen to read a Shakespeare sonnet twenty years later? Does he recall the poem or does he recall the smell of the page and the smell of Miss Hawkins?)

One might object, pointing out that Huxley's citizen reading his sonnet in the ruins and the Falkland Islander looking at his dogfish on the beach also receive them in a certain package. Yes, but the difference lies in the funda-mental placement of the student in the world, a placement which makes it possible to extract the thing from the package. The pupil at Scarsdale High sees himself placed as a consumer receiving an experience-package; but the Falkland Islander exploring his dogfish is a person exercising the sovereign right of a person in his lordship and mastery of creation. He too could use an instructor and a book and a technique, but he would use them as his subor-dinates, just as he uses his jackknife. The biology student does not use his

---

Falkland Islander: A resident of the Falkland Islands, a British Crown colony off the coast of Argentina.

scalpel as an instrument, he uses it as a magic wand! Since it is a "scientific instrument," it should do "scientific things."

The dogfish is concealed in the same symbolic package as the sonnet. But the dogfish suffers an additional loss. As a consequence of this double deprivation, the Sarah Lawrence° student who scores A in zoology is apt to know very little about a dogfish. She is twice removed from the dogfish, once by the symbolic complex by which the dogfish is concealed, once again by the spoliation of the dogfish by theory which renders it invisible. Through no fault of zoology instructors, it is nevertheless a fact that the zoology laboratory at Sarah Lawrence College is one of the few places in the world where it is all but impossible to see a dogfish.

The dogfish, the tree, the seashell, the American Negro, the dream, are rendered invisible by a shift of reality from concrete thing to theory which Whitehead° has called the fallacy of misplaced concreteness. It is the mistaking of an idea, a principle, an abstraction, for the real. As a consequence of the shift, the "specimen" is seen as less real than the theory of the specimen. As Kierkegaard° said, once a person is seen as a specimen of a race or a species, at that very moment he ceases to be an individual. Then there are no more individuals but only specimens.

To illustrate: A student enters a laboratory which, in the pragmatic view, 45 offers the student the optimum conditions under which an educational experience may be had. In the existential view,° however—that view of the student in which he is regarded not as a receptacle of experience but as a knowing being whose peculiar property it is to see himself as being in a certain situation—the modern laboratory could not have been more effectively designed to conceal the dogfish forever.

The student comes to his desk. On it, neatly arranged by his instructor, he finds his laboratory manual, a dissecting board, instruments, and a mimeographed list:

Exercise 22: Materials
1 dissecting board
1 scalpel
1 forceps
1 probe
1 bottle India ink and syringe
1 specimen of *Squalus acanthias*

Sarah Lawrence: Sarah Lawrence College, located in Bronxville, New York, was founded in 1828 as a women's institution.

Whitehead: Alfred North Whitehead (1861–1947), English mathematician and philosopher.

Kierkegaard: Soren Aabye Kierkegaard (1813–1855), Danish philosopher and theologian.

the existential view: Existentialism is a twentieth-century philosophical movement that focuses on the plight of the individual, who must assume complete responsibility for himself in a world that offers no clear meaning nor any sense of right and wrong.

The clue of the situation in which the student finds himself is to be found in the last item: 1 specimen of *Squalaus acanthias.*

The phrase *specimen of* expresses in the most succinct way imaginable the radial character of the loss of being which has occurred under his very nose. To refer to the dogfish, the unique concrete existent before him, as a "specimen of *Squalas acanthias*" reveals by its grammar the spoliation of the dogfish by the theoretical method. This phrase, *specimen of,* example of, instance of, indicates the ontological status of the individual creature in the eyes of the theorist. The dogfish itself is seen as a rather shabby expression of an ideal reality, the species *Squalus acanthias.* The result is the radical devaluation of the individual dogfish. (The *reductio ad absurdum°* of Whitehead's shift is Toynbee's° employment of it in his historical method. If a gram of NaCl° is referred to by the chemist as a "sample of" NaCl, one may think of it as such and not much is missed by the oversight of the act of being of this particular pinch of salt, but when the Jews and the Jewish religion are understood as — in Toynbee's favorite phrase — a "classical example of" such and such a kind of *Voelkerwanderung,°* we begin to suspect that something is being left out.)

If we look into the ways in which the student can recover the dogfish (or the sonnet), we will see that they have in common the stratagem of avoiding the educator's direct presentation of the object as a lesson to be learned and restoring access to sonnet and dogfish as beings to be known, reasserting the sovereignty of knower over known.

In truth, the biography of scientists and poets is usually the story of the discovery of the indirect approach, the circumvention of the educator's presentation — the young man who was sent to the *Technikum* and on his way fell into the habit of loitering in book stores and reading poetry; or the young man dutifully attending law school who on the way became curious about the comings and goings of ants. One remembers the scene in *The Heart Is a Lonely Hunter°* where the girl hides in the bushes to hear the Capehart° in the big house play Beethoven. Perhaps she was the lucky one after all. Think of the unhappy souls inside, who see the record, worry about scratches, and most of all worry about whether they are *getting it,* whether they are bona fide music lovers. What is the best way to hear Beethoven: sitting in a proper silence around the Capehart or eavesdropping from an azalea bush?

50

---

reductio ad absurdum: Something that is carried to an absurd extreme.

Toynbee's: Arnold Joseph Toynbee (1889–1975), English historian.

NaCl: The chemical formula for table salt.

Voelkerwanderung: (German) Emigration of nations.

The Heart Is a Lonely Hunter: Novel (1940) by American author Carson McCullers (1917–1967), focusing on the adventures of Mick Kelly, an adolescent girl growing up in the South.

Capehart: Refers to the Capehart radio and phonograph consule which could be adapted for use with a player piano.

However it may come about, we notice two traits of the second situation: (1) an openness of the thing before one—instead of being an exercise to be learned according to an approved mode, it is a garden of delights which beckons to one; (2) a sovereignty of the knower—instead of being a consumer of a prepared experience, I am a sovereign wayfarer, a wanderer in the neighborhood of being who stumbles into the garden.

One can think of two sorts of circumstances through which the thing may be restored to the person. (There is always, of course, the direct recovery: a student may simply be strong enough, brave enough, clever enough to take the dogfish and the sonnet by storm, to wrest control of it from the educators and the educational package.) First by ordeal: The Bomb falls; when the young man recovers consciousness in the shambles of the biology laboratory, there not ten inches from his nose lies the dogfish. Now all at once he can see it directly and without let, just as the exile or the prisoner or the sick man sees the sparrow at his window in all its inexhaustibility; just as the commuter who has had a heart attack sees his own hand for the first time. In these cases, the simulacrum of everydayness and of consumption has been destroyed by disaster; in the case of the Bomb, literally destroyed. Secondly, by apprenticeship to a great man: one day a great biologist walks into the laboratory; he stops in front of our student's desk; he leans over, picks up the dogfish, and, ignoring instruments and procedure, probes with a broken fingernail into the little carcass. "Now here is a curious business," he says, ignoring also the proper jargon of the speciality. "Look here how this little duct reverses its direction and drops into the pelvis. Now if you would look into a coelacanth, you would see that it—" And all at once the student can see. The technician and the sophomore who loves his textbooks are always offended by the genuine research man because the latter is usually a little vague and always humble before the thing; he doesn't have much use for the equipment or the jargon. Whereas the technician is never vague and never humble before the thing; he holds the thing disposed of by the principle, the formula, the textbook outline; and he thinks a great deal of equipment and jargon.

But since neither of these methods of recovering the dogfish is pedagogically feasible—perhaps the great man even less so than the Bomb—I wish to propose the following educational technique which should prove equally effective for Harvard and Shreveport High School. I propose that English poetry and biology should be taught as usual, but that at irregular intervals, poetry students should find dogfishes on their desks and biology students should find Shakespeare sonnets on their dissection boards. I am serious in declaring that a Sarah Lawrence English major who began poking about in a dogfish with a bobby pin would learn more in thirty minutes than a biology major in a whole semester; and that the latter upon reading on her dissecting board.

> That time of year Thou may'st in me behold
> When yellow leaves, or none, or few, do hang
> Upon those boughs which shake against the cold—
> Bare ruin'd choirs where late the sweet birds sang

might catch fire at the beauty of it.

The situation of the tourist at the Grand Canyon and the biology student are special cases of a predicament in which everyone finds himself in a modern technical society—a society, that is, in which there is a division between expert and layman, planner and consumer, in which experts and planners take special measures to teach and edify the consumer. The measures taken are measures appropriate to the consumer: the expert and the planner *know* and *plan*, but the consumer *needs* and *experiences*.

There is a double deprivation. First, the thing is lost through its packaging. The very means by which the thing is presented for consumption, the very techniques by which the thing is made available as an item of need-satisfaction, these very means operate to remove the thing from the sovereignty of the knower. A loss of title occurs. The measures which the museum curator takes to present the thing to the public are self-liquidating. The upshot of the curator's efforts are not that everyone can see the exhibit but that no one can see it. The curator protests: why are they so indifferent? Why do they even deface the exhibit? Don't they know it is theirs? But it is not theirs. It is his, the curator's. By the most exclusive sort of zoning, the museum exhibit, the park oak tree, is part of an ensemble, a package, which is almost impenetrable to them. The archaeologist who puts his find in a museum so that everyone can see it accomplishes the reverse of his expectations. The result of his action is that no one can see it now but the archaeologist. He would have done better to keep it in his pocket and show it now and then to strangers.

The tourist who carves his initials in a public place, which is theoretically "his" in the first place, has good reasons for doing so, reasons which the exhibitor and planner know nothing about. He does so because in his role of consumer of an experience (a "recreational experience" to satisfy a "recreational need") he knows that he is disinherited. He is deprived of his title over being. He knows very well that he is in a very special sort of zone in which his only rights are the rights of a consumer. He moves like a ghost through schoolroom, city streets, trains, parks, movies. He carves his initials as a last desperate measure to escape his ghostly role of consumer. He is saying in effect: I am not a ghost after all; I am a sovereign person. And he establishes title the only way remaining to him, by staking his claim over one square inch of wood or stone.

Does this mean that we should get rid of museums? No, but it means that the sightseer should be prepared to enter into a struggle to recover a sight from a museum.

The second loss is the spoliation of the thing, the tree, the rock, the swallow, by the layman's misunderstanding of scientific theory. He believes that the thing is *disposed of* by theory, that it stands in the Platonic relation of being a *specimen* of such and such an underlying principle. In the transmission of scientific theory from theorist to layman, the expectation of the theorist is reversed. Instead of the marvels of the universe being made available to the public, the universe is disposed of by theory. The loss of sovereignty takes this form: as a result of the science of botany, trees are not made available to every man. On the contrary. The tree loses its proper density and mystery as a concrete existent and, as merely another *specimen* of a species, becomes itself nugatory.°

Does this mean that there is no use taking biology at Harvard and Shreveport High? No, but it means that the student should know what a fight he has on his hands to rescue the specimen from the educational package. The educator is only partly to blame. For there is nothing the educator can do to provide for this need of the student. Everything the educator does only succeeds in becoming, for the student, part of the educational package. The highest role of the educator is the maieutic° role of Socrates: to help the student come to himself not as a consumer of experience but as a sovereign individual.

The thing is twice lost to the consumer. First, sovereignty is lost: it is theirs, not his. Second, it is radically devalued by theory. This is a loss which has been brought about by science but through no fault of the scientist and through no fault of scientific theory. The loss has come about as a consequence of the seduction of the layman by science. The layman will be seduced as long as he regards beings as consumer items to be experienced rather than prizes to be won, and as long as he waives his sovereign rights as a person and accepts his role of consumer as the highest estate to which the layman can aspire.   60

As Mounier° said, the person is not something one can study and provide for; he is something one struggles for. But unless he also struggles for himself, unless he knows that there is a struggle, he is going to be just what the planners think he is.

nugatory: Of little or no consequence; unimportant.

maieutic: Resembling the Socratic method of educating through the use of pointed questions.

Mounier: Emmanuel Mounier (1905–1950), French philosopher.

EXPLORING THE TEXT

1. What assumptions do we make about the way we see natural objects, according to Percy? Why does he claim that it is "almost impossible" to see a well-known landmark like the Grand Canyon for what it really is? To what extent would you agree that most people never really see well-known sites, but only something that has "already been formulated" for them — something "like a postcard"?

2. How, in Percy's view, is it possible "to recover" the immediate experience of seeing an object like the Grand Canyon? How do each of the strategies Percy describes alter the experience of seeing?

3. Why does Percy feel that movies typically succeed in capturing the "sovereignty" of visual experience while photography does not? Would you generally agree that films help us see famous locations with fresh eyes, or do they also contribute to the "symbolic machinery" that works against our ability to confront the world around us?

4. What is Percy's attitude toward education and the role it plays in shaping our perceptions? Would you agree that an unschooled Falkland Islander would discover

more in a dogfish washed up on the beach than would a student in biology lab at Sarah Lawrence? Why or why not?

5. To what extent might Percy be open to the same criticism he offers in regard to experts, theorists, and teachers? Is it possible to accept his theory of authentic perception without becoming a consumer of his preformulated experience? To what extent are the images he presents of explorers, tourists, students, teachers, and researchers themselves "preformulated" for easy consumption?

FURTHER EXPLORATIONS

1. Working in groups, assemble a collection of images of a famous natural object or tourist destination and discuss the "preformed complex" of ideas and associations that these images communicate. Share the results of your discussion with the whole class and assess the extent to which such images structure our experiences in advance.

2. Revisit "Take the F" (p. 18) and discuss whether Frazier's experience of New York strikes you as being particularly "authentic" or true. To what extent does this essay contribute to or reinforce the "symbolic machinery" that surrounds the idea of New York City? Do you think that reading Frazier's essay might, in fact, make it more difficult for you to confront the meaning of New York for yourself? Why or why not?

3. Compare Percy's understanding of the act of seeing to that of K. C. Cole (p. 75) and Georgina Kleege (p. 93). How do each of these authors portray the act of visual perception? What roles do they ascribe to memory, expectation, culture, and learning in relation to how we perceive things? What limits do they associate with human sight? How might you explain the differences in their views?

4. How might Percy evaluate Mark Slouka's indictment of capitalism's impact on our sense of hearing in "Listening for Silence" (p. 50)? In what ways does Percy's view of the relation between visual perception and society resemble Slouka's view of the relation between hearing and capitalist culture? In what ways do they differ? Which do you find most persuasive? Why?

5. Compare Percy's explanation of our ability to perceive the "creature" in the world around us with John Berger's analysis of how zoos influence our ability to look at animals (p. 521). How might Percy's notions of "symbolic machinery" and "preformulated" perceptions account for the "disappearance" of animals that Berger notes? To what extent do these authors trace "the loss of the creature" to the same social or cultural forces?

ESSAY OPTIONS

1. Write an essay about an experience you've had that helped you encounter the "sovereign" reality of a book, an object in the natural world, or an important idea. What was the setting of this experience? What did you discover through it? If it occurred in a formal educational setting, how did the instructor avoid the problems Percy associates with teaching? In general, would you agree with Percy's claim that

education makes it more difficult to confront the "sovereign reality" of the natural world and that real education always involves personal struggle? Why or why not?

2. Synthesizing information presented in selections by K. C. Cole (p. 75), Georgina Kleege (p. 93), and Percy—and drawing on examples and illustrations from your own experience—write an essay in which you discuss the role that the mind plays in the process of visual perception. To what extent is seeing a purely mechanical or automatic activity? What roles do memory and expectation play in vision? How do culture and learning influence what we see? What forces or factors limit our ability to perceive the visual worlds we live in?

3. Drawing on your own experience and on the ideas of Percy, Mark Slouka (p. 50), K. C. Cole (p. 75), Bill McKibben (p. 109), and Constance Classen et al. (p. 59), write an essay in which you evaluate the claim that people in advanced technological societies have become passive consumers of the perceptions produced by experts and have lost contact with the "sovereignty" of their own perceptual experiences.

2

Reading Memory
Rebuilding the Past

The Art of Memory

How do you "read" memory? Why would you want to? Most of us don't spend a lot of time fretting about memory. After all, we live in America, a place where many of us were convinced that "History is bunk" even before Henry Ford came along to spell it out. America has always prided itself on living for to-morrow. The Pilgrims who landed in Plymouth in 1621 saw themselves as refugees from the "fallen world" of Europe; they came as spiritual revolution-aries determined to fashion a new society and to free themselves from all the sins and imperfections of the past. In the nineteenth and twentieth centuries they were followed by generations of immigrants who sought a new way of life and a more promising future, turning their backs once they arrived on the "Old Worlds" they had left behind. The notion of a fresh start—of personal renewal and spiritual rebirth—has always held a special place in the collective consciousness of the United States. As a nation, we celebrate those who suc-ceed in re-creating themselves, who defy the odds of their origins and take control of their destinies. For better or worse, our national attitude toward memory can be summed up by the lyrics of the Fleetwood Mac song that Bill Clinton and the Democratic Party used as a theme throughout the 1990s: "Don't stop thinking about tomorrow," the refrain urges us, because "Yesterday's gone, yesterday's gone. . . ."

Gone, that is, until it suddenly rushes back. Take, for example, the case of Eileen Franklin-Lipsker. One day in 1989 as she was giving her eight-year-old daughter a bath, the tilt of the child's head and the expression on her face trig-gered a horrific memory. Two decades after the fact, Franklin-Lipsker began to recall how her father had sexually abused and then murdered Susan Nason, a childhood friend, in 1969. After a year of intensive therapy, Franklin-Lipsker took the witness stand and offered a detailed account of her friend's homicide, leading to George Franklin's conviction and imprisonment. Covered exten-sively in the media, the Franklin-Lipsker case set off a nationwide epidemic of what has come to be known as "recovered memory syndrome." Within the next few years, thousands of adults across the United States would begin to recall incidents of abuse and violence that they had repressed during their childhoods. Therapists began to specialize in the analysis of "recovered mem-ories," and even celebrities like Roseanne Barr came forward with stories of repressed experiences of abuse. Unfortunately, many of these memories turned out to be unfounded. Six years after he went to jail, George Franklin was freed on the basis of expert testimony by psychologists who cast doubt on his daughter's story. They demonstrated that the violent incident Eileen Franklin-Lipsker recalled so vividly on the witness stand had, in fact, been a "false memory," a fantasy shaped into a convincing story in response to the unwitting suggestions of her therapist.

The debate over the reliability of so-called "recovered memories" is trou-bling because it reveals the limitations of our commonly held assumptions about how memory works. We tend to think of memory as something that happens *to* us, not as something that we make happen. In comparison with the mind's more "executive" functions like reasoning and creativity, we think of memory as a kind of mental bureaucrat, dutifully transcribing the events of our lives and filing them away so that they can be located for future use. The tilt of a child's head or the look on her face triggers the automatic retrieval of this verbatim record of past events. Seen in this way, remembering is just another automatic reflex, something like the hiccups or the psychological equivalent of digestion after the main course of experience. Denizens of a culture that sees itself living for tomorrow and living down the past, we don't waste a lot of time thinking about memory. We pride ourselves on our creativity, our vision, and our problem-solving abilities—but, for the most part, we let memory fend for itself.

But memory hasn't always been seen as the mind's stepchild. For the greater part of human history, the art of memory was cultivated as the loftiest of human achievements. In preliterate tribal societies, leadership was commonly associated with the power of recollection: the tribal sage or shaman looked to the past, not to the future, for wisdom and the right to rule. The shaman's knowledge of the stories that linked her tribe to its past was a source of prestige and power. In ancient Greece, memory was venerated as the cornerstone of both creativity and reason. In the *Dialogues* of Plato, Socrates argues that when a thinker grasps the truth or eternal "essence" of an idea, he is simply "remembering" what he has already experienced during a prior lifetime in the world of ideal forms. Thinking, for Plato, is deeply rooted in the arts of memory. In fact, Plato so venerated the power of memory that in the *Phaedrus* he has Socrates caution the reader against the dangers of the newfangled Egyptian invention of "letters," which, as he warns, "will create forgetfulness in the learner's soul, because they will not use their memories, they will trust to the external written characters, and not remember of themselves. . . ." For the Greeks, memory wasn't just a mental bureaucrat; she was a goddess. Mnemosyne, the divine embodiment of memory, was the consort of Zeus and mother of the nine Muses— the deities that ruled the arts. Mnemosyne and the Muses inspired the artist; they literally "breathed" the creative power of memory into the mind of the poet, dramatist, historian, sculptor, and dancer. A Greek poet wouldn't sing unless he first paid homage to the source of his craft by invoking the power of Mnemosyne and her daughters. Memory, in the classical world, was a divine gift, a magical art that could be conjured and cultivated, but never taken for granted.

A thousand years after Plato, memory was still perceived as the most awe inspiring of the mind's faculties. Here's an homage to memory, penned in the fourth century A.D. by Saint Augustine, one of history's greatest memoirists:

> In [memory] are the sky, the earth, and the sea, ready to my summons, together with anything that I have already perceived in them by my senses, except the things which I have forgotten. In it I meet myself as well. I remember myself and what I have done, when and where I did it, and the state of my mind at the

time. In memory, too, are all the events that I remember, whether they are things that have happened to me or things that I have heard from others. From the same source I can picture to myself all kinds of different images based either upon my own experience or upon what I find credible because it tallies with my own experience. I can fit them into the general picture of the past; from them I can make a surmise of actions and events and hopes for the future; and I can contemplate them all over again as if they were actually present. If I say to myself in the vast cache of my mind, where all those images of great things are stored, "I shall do this or that," the picture of this or that particular thing comes into my mind at once. . . . No sooner do I say this than the images of all the things of which I speak spring forward from the same great treasure-house of memory. . . . The power of the memory is prodigious, my God. It is a vast, immeasurable sanctuary. Who can plumb its depths?

Augustine believed that memory was itself a spark of divinity God had left in humanity as a reminder of our heavenly origin. In his view, the power of reflection was the key to personal salvation. To appreciate the workings of the divine will here on earth, he believed you had to cultivate the habit of reflecting on the events and activities of your own life. Seen retrospectively through the lens of memory, the will of God, he believed, would make itself clear to the mortal mind. Thus, for Augustine, memory was a sacred art, and one that he put to good use in the composition of his *Confessions,* a book that today is widely considered the first example of a truly modern autobiography.

The art of memory continued to dominate the philosophical and educational traditions of the West for at least another thousand years. Following the prescriptions contained in memory manuals composed by famous orators and rhetoricians, medieval students labored for centuries to sharpen their powers of recall through the practice of "mnemotechnics." The most common of these memory aerobics involved storing ideas and information in an imaginary structure — a "memory palace," full of nooks and crannies, created specifically as an aid to recollection. To remember an elaborate speech, the aspiring student only had to do was to place the various ideas it contained in "rooms" of the palace, according to the order of their presentation. When the time came to recall the speech, all he then had to do was to "walk," mentally, from room to room, picking up the deposited topics.

By the sixteenth century, the development of the publishing industry and the rise of modern science revolutionized attitudes toward memory. With literacy putting an end to the mnemonic traditions of oral culture, and with science's emphasis on challenging past beliefs, schools began to turn away from memorization as the focus of intellectual activity. In the past hundred years, technological extensions of natural memory have accelerated the process even more. Technological innovations like photography, film, the phonograph, the compact disk, television, videotape, and the computer have permanently altered our relation to memory. While it was common for students to commit whole speeches, poems, mathematical theorems, and scientific tables to memory just a generation ago, today educators scoff at such "rote" learning. In a world where information is literally at your fingertips and where typing is often perceived as more important than remembering the past, we seem to have forgotten the centrality of memory to human experience. Why work hard to remember a speech when you can watch it on video? Why spend hours memorizing multiplication tables when you can use a calculator during the test? Why drill historical facts and dates when you can look them up in a book or program them into your Palm Pilot?

Fortunately, the study of memory has been experiencing a renaissance over the past few years. As a result of the computer revolution and developments in cognitive science, researchers and humanists have become increasingly involved in exploring the dynamic nature of human memory. Memory, it turns out, is almost never a simple matter of mechanical reproduction. In fact, recent research suggests that the ancient Greeks had it about right: human memory is both an extremely active and an intensely imaginative process. As shocking as it might seem, memory appears to have more in common with creativity than it does with the rote transcription of events. Memory, it seems, isn't a function or a reflex, but an art—an intellectual gift that needs to be cultivated, just as Mnemosyne and her temperamental daughters needed to be wooed by the poets before they would share the secrets of their craft.

Writing and Memory

If you have any doubt about the relationship between memory and creativity, think back to the last time you had a bad case of writer's block. Remember sitting at your desk, staring at a blank page of paper, and wondering how you were going to generate enough ideas to fill the pages required by the assignment? According to Peter Elbow, an authority on writer's block and the writing process, we get into jams like this because we underestimate the complexity of what happens when we write. Writing, we assume, is just a matter of transcribing our ideas—a matter of transferring the contents of our brains onto the blank page sitting in front of us. Over the past two decades, however, we've begun to recognize that composing an essay isn't just a matter of transcription. To become an effective writer, you first have to become a skilled memorist—an expert rememberer. It isn't that some folks write more easily because they're smarter, know more, or have more to say than others. Good writers make writing look easy because they've developed techniques that help them draw on the ideas, knowledge, and experience they already have in the storehouse of memory. It's not that they have more information; it's just that they know how to access the information they already have at their disposal.

That's why effective writers allow lots of time for what Elbow calls "cooking." Nowadays, most expert writers divide the composing process into three distinct stages. There's *drafting*, the process of sitting down to write out the bulk of the paper—the part where most people get stuck when they encounter writer's block. This is followed by *revising,* the final stage when you read over and make substantive changes in the structure and content of what you've produced through drafting. But the most crucial stage—and the one most overlooked by beginning writers—is planning or *prewriting.* This is the stage when, as Elbow suggests, you "cook" your ideas by giving them time to "bubble up" in your mind, one idea or experience triggering the memory of another, one reflection stimulating other associations, until you begin to see where your ideas are leading you. Effective "cooking" requires two things: you need to spread the process of reflection out over a long period of time, and you need to develop techniques that will help you discover connections between the ideas you come up with. Most experienced writers allow for several days of "incubation"—enough time for ideas to play off one another and to percolate up to the level of awareness. Instead of plunging into a formal draft as soon as they get an assignment—or waiting until the wee hours of the morning before an assignment is due—experienced writers draw on an arsenal of prewriting strategies designed to encourage the serious work of playing with associations, ideas, and possible relationships, just to see where they will lead. Some writers jot ideas down on paper for days before they actually sit down to write. Some sketch outlines or brainstorm lists of ideas related to their topic. Some free-associate all over a piece of scratch paper or write timed "garbage drafts" they will never reread, just to get their ideas flowing. Some build elaborate cluster diagrams that encourage ideas to ricochet randomly off other ideas and associations. The largely unconscious process of "cooking" works because the initial ideas you have on any topic will call up the memory of other relevant ideas, associations, and experiences—if, that is, you give yourself enough freedom and time to let your memory work.

The important thing to keep in mind about prewriting is that you can't *force* your memory to perform. As the Greeks understood, memory is a goddess and remembering an art, not a machine that leaps into motion at the flick of a switch. To become a skillful rememberer you have to enter into a relationship with your own memory and learn how to invoke its powers in support of your thinking process. You have to create the right conditions for memory to engage the topic, and you have to build in the opportunity to reflect, again and again, on where your ideas are leading you. That's why many experienced writers alternate periods of concentrated prewriting activity with periods of relatively mindless relaxation. Some intersperse bouts of prewriting with jogging, swimming laps, sleeping, or baking batches of chocolate chip cookies. Some take planned breaks from thinking to talk their ideas over with friends. This gives memory the time and psychic space it needs to do its mysterious work, and it gives your conscious mind the chance to reflect on where your thinking process is headed. Pausing occasionally to trace out the themes that are emerging from your prewriting activities and to jot these overarching ideas down is the job of your conscious, remembering self. Once you discover what your memory wants to say on a given issue, your mind will use this new lead as a stimulus to further thinking—a new invitation for your internal muse to engage in still more rounds of creative recollection and discovery. Becoming a successful writer, then, involves developing a set of prewriting and composing strategies that will help you access and discover connections between the ideas and experiences you already carry around with you in the encyclopedia of your unconscious mind. Good writers are, first and foremost, good "readers" of their own memories. They have learned how to exploit the muse's mysterious power of creative recollection.

Chapter Overview

This chapter offers you the chance to explore the mysteries of human memory with help from some of the leading experts in the field. The selections you'll find here will introduce you to various ways of "reading" memories, ways of thinking about how and why we remember the past as we do. We begin with two illustrations of the power of recollection. In "The Inheritance of Tools," Scott Russell Sanders relates a series of memories associated with a hammer passed down in his family for generations—memories that shape his identity, past, present, and future. In "The Brown Wasps," anthropologist Loren Eiseley reflects on the "miracle" and the "morality" of memory—animal and human—as he pursues the childhood recollection of a tree that, as he says, never really existed. The next selection offers an overview of the mechanics and pathology of memory. "Building Memories" by neuroscientist Daniel L. Schacter presents a theory of recollection that equates the act of remembering with the way a paleontologist extrapolates a dinosaur from a few fossilized bone fragments. Schacter's exploration of remarkable and broken minds offers insights about the way memory works to "double" our appreciation of the world around us.

The next section of the chapter focuses more narrowly on the interactions between personal and impersonal memories. In "Memory and Imagination," Patricia Hampl offers a personal memoir that challenges the standard notion of memory as the verbatim transcription of events. Hampl's retelling of her first piano lesson under the watchful eye of Sister Olive also presents a fascinating account of the relation of memory and the writing process. In "Then and Now: Creating a Self Through the Past," psychologist Susan Engel elaborates a conceptual framework for discussing the relationship between "remembering" and "remembered" selves. Engel's exploration of how we fashion the "persona" of our past selves in response to the demands of our immediate context can be applied to readings throughout the chapter. The last three readings address the personal and cultural politics of historical memory. Maxine Hong Kingston's classic personal account of the death of her aunt in "No-Name Woman" illustrates the complex relationship between family memories and individual identity in the present. Next, sociologist Eviatar Zerubavel comments on the way that "mnemonic communities" influence our own recollections of the past. Zerubavel's examination of the dynamics of historical memory invites us to explore the political, social, and cultural tensions that underlie the way we choose to commemorate the past. The chapter closes with bell hooks's reflection on the historical memory of Columbus and his "discovery" of the Americas and its continuing impact on women and people of color in the present.

Sources

Augustine, Saint. *Confessions.* New York: Penguin Putnam, 1996.
Elbow, Peter. *Writing Without Teachers.* New York: Oxford UP, 1975.
Engel, Susan. *Context Is Everything: The Nature of Memory.* New York: Freeman, 1999.
Park, Clara Clairborne. "The Mother of the Muses: In Praise of Memory." In *The Anatomy of Memory, An Anthology,* edited by James McConkey. New York: Oxford UP, 1966.
Schacter, Daniel, ed. *Memory Distortion: How Minds, Brains, and Societies Reconstruct the Past.* Cambridge, Mass.: Harvard UP, 1995.
Yates, Francis A. *The Art of Memory.* New York: Routledge, 1996.

The Inheritance of Tools

SCOTT RUSSELL SANDERS

The common model of how we recall past events involves what psychologists refer to as "flashbulb memories." A flashbulb memory happens in an instant, when you hear shocking news or witness an extraordinary event. Most baby boomers can tell you exactly what they were doing when they heard that President Kennedy had been shot in Dallas, Texas. Most Americans can probably do the same for the moment they learned about the attack on the World Trade Center on September 11, 2001. "The Inheritance of Tools" puts a twist on the flashbulb formula. When Scott Russell Sanders hears the news of his father's sudden death, he doesn't imprint details of the present; instead, he plunges into the past. Sanders recalls his father through an act of mnemonic accretion, a layering of past experiences that builds memory up the way a pearl consolidates around a grain of sand. Only, in this case, the grain of sand that sets memory working is a hammer. Sanders (b. 1945) is an essayist, novelist, and professor of English and creative writing at Indiana University. His publications include *The Paradise of Bombs* (1987), the source of this selection; *Stone Country* (1985); *Secrets of the Universe* (1992); and the novel *Bad Man Ballad* (1986). Most recently, he has published *The Country of Language* (1999) and *The Force of Spirit* (2000).

BEFORE READING

Freewrite in your journal about a specific object that links you to something or someone important in your past — it might be a tool, a pen, a watch, a piece of jewelry, a piece of clothing or sporting equipment, a family heirloom, or something used in the kitchen —

anything that has special meaning because it links you to the past. What memories and meaning does this object hold for you?

At just about the hour when my father died, soon after dawn one February morning when ice coated the windows like cataracts, I banged my thumb with a hammer. Naturally I swore at the hammer, the reckless thing, and in the moment of swearing I thought of what my father would say: "If you'd try hitting the nail it would go in a whole lot faster. Don't you know your thumb's not as hard as that hammer?" We both were doing carpentry that day, but far apart. He was building cupboards at my brother's place in Oklahoma; I was at home in Indiana putting up a wall in the basement to make a bedroom for my daughter. By the time my mother called with news of his death—the long distance wires whittling her voice until it seemed too thin to bear the weight of what she had to say—my thumb was swollen. A week or so later a white scar in the shape of a crescent moon began to show above the cuticle, and month by month it rose across the pink sky of my thumbnail. It took the better part of a year for the scar to disappear, and every time I noticed it I thought of my father.

The hammer had belonged to him, and to his father before him. The three of us have used it to build houses and barns and chicken coops, to upholster chairs and crack walnuts, to make doll furniture and bookshelves and jewelry boxes. The head is scratched and pockmarked, like an old plowshare that has been working rocky fields, and it gives off the sort of dull sheen you see on fast creek water in the shade. It is a finishing hammer, about the weight of a bread loaf, too light really for framing walls, too heavy for cabinetwork, with a curved claw for pulling nails, a rounded head for pounding, a fluted neck for looks, and a hickory handle for strength.

The present handle is my third one, bought from a lumberyard in Tennessee down the road from where my brother and I were helping my father build his retirement house. I broke the previous one by trying to pull sixteen-penny nails out of floor joists—a foolish thing to do with a finishing hammer, as my father pointed out. "You ever hear of a crowbar?" he said. No telling how many handles he and my grandfather had gone through before me. My grandfather used to cut down hickory trees on his farm, saw them into slabs, cure the planks in his hayloft, and carve handles with a drawknife. The grain in hickory is crooked and knotty, and therefore tough, hard to split, like the grain in the two men who owned this hammer before me.

After proposing marriage to a neighbor girl, my grandfather used this hammer to build a house for his bride on a stretch of river bottom in northern Mississippi. The lumber for the place, like the hickory for the handle, was cut on his own land. By the day of the wedding he had not quite finished the house, and so right after the ceremony he took his wife home and put her to work. My grandmother had worn her Sunday dress for the wedding, with a fringe of lace tacked on around the hem in honor of the occasion. She removed this lace and folded it away before going out to help my grandfather nail siding on the house. "There she was in her good dress," he told me some fifty-odd years after that wedding day, "holding up them long pieces of clapboard while I hammered, and together we got the place covered up before dark." As the family grew to four, six, eight, and eventually thirteen, my grandfather used this hammer to enlarge his house room by room, like a chambered nautilus expanding his shell.

By and by the hammer was passed along to my father. One day he was up on the roof of our pony barn nailing shingles with it, when I stepped out the kitchen door to call him for supper. Before I could yell, something about the sight of him straddling the spine of that roof and swinging the hammer caught my eye and made me hold my tongue. I was five or six years old, and the world's commonplaces were still news to me. He would pull a nail from the pouch at his waist, bring the hammer down, and a moment later the *thunk* of the blow would reach my ears. And that is what had stopped me in my tracks and stilled my tongue, that momentary gap between seeing and hearing the blow. Instead of yelling from the kitchen door, I ran to the barn and climbed two rungs up the ladder—as far as I was allowed to go—and spoke quietly to my father. On our walk to the house he explained that sound takes time to make its way through air. Suddenly the world seemed larger, the air more dense, if sound could be held back like any ordinary traveler.

By the time I started using this hammer, at about the age when I discovered the speed of sound, it already contained houses and mysteries for me. The smooth handle was one my grandfather had made. In those days I needed both hands to swing it. My father would start a nail in a scrap of wood, and I would pound away until I bent it over.

"Looks like you got ahold of some of those rubber nails," he would tell me. "Here, let me see if I can find you some stiff ones." And he would rummage in a drawer until he came up with a fistful of more cooperative nails. "Look at the head," he would tell me. "Don't look at your hands, don't look at the hammer. Just look at the head of that nail and pretty soon you'll learn to hit it square."

Pretty soon I did learn. While he worked in the garage cutting dovetail joints for a drawer or skinning a deer or tuning an engine, I would hammer nails. I made innocent blocks of wood look like porcupines. He did not talk much in the midst of his tools, but he kept up a nearly ceaseless humming, slipping in and out of a dozen tunes in an afternoon, often running back over the same stretch of melody again and again, as if searching for a way out. When the humming did cease, I knew he was faced with a task requiring great delicacy or concentration, and I took care not to distract him.

He kept scraps of wood in a cardboard box—the ends of two-by-fours, slabs of shelving and plywood, odd pieces of molding—and everything in it was fair game. I nailed scraps together to fashion what I called boats or houses, but the results usually bore only faint resemblance to the visions I carried in my head. I would hold up these constructions to show my father, and he would turn them over in his hands admiringly, speculating about what they might be. My cobbled-together guitars might have been alien spaceships, my barns might have been models of Aztec temples, each wooden contraption might have been anything but what I had set out to make.

Now and again I would feel the need to have a chunk of wood shaped or 10 shortened before I riddled it with nails, and I would clamp it in a vise and scrape at it with a handsaw. My father would let me lacerate the board until my arm gave out, and then he would wrap his hand around mine and help me finish the cut, showing me how to use my thumb to guide the blade, how to pull back on the saw to keep it from binding, how to let my shoulder do the work.

"Don't force it," he would say, "just drag it easy and give the teeth a chance to bite."

As the saw teeth bit down the wood released its smell, each kind with its own fragrance, oak or walnut or cherry or pine — usually pine, because it was the softest and the easiest for a child to work. No matter how weathered and gray the board, no matter how warped and cracked, inside there was this smell waiting, as of something freshly baked. I gathered every smidgen of sawdust and stored it away in coffee cans, which I kept in a drawer of the workbench. When I did not feel like hammering nails I would dump my sawdust on the concrete floor of the garage and landscape it into highways and farms and towns, running miniature cars and trucks along miniature roads. Looming as huge as a colossus, my father worked over and around me, now and again bending down to inspect my work, careful not to trample my creations. It was a landscape that smelled dizzyingly of wood. Even after a bath my skin would carry the smell, and so would my father's hair, when he lifted me for a bed-time hug.

I tell these things not only from memory but also from recent observation, because my own son now turns blocks of wood into nailed porcupines, dumps cans full of sawdust at my feet and sculpts highways on the floor. He learns how to swing a hammer from the elbow instead of the wrist, how to lay his thumb beside the blade to guide a saw, how to tap a chisel with a wooden mallet, how to mark a hole with an awl before starting a drill bit. My daughter did the same before him, and even now, on the brink of teenage aloofness, she will occasionally drag out my box of wood scraps and carpenter something. So I have seen my apprenticeship to wood and tools reenacted in each of my children, as my father saw his own apprenticeship renewed in me.

The saw I use belonged to him, as did my level and both of my squares, and all four tools had belonged to his father. The blade of the saw is the bluish color of gun barrels, and the maple handle, dark from the sweat of hands, is inscribed with curving leaf designs. The level is a shaft of walnut two feet long, edged with brass and pierced by three round windows in which air bubbles float in oil-filled tubes of glass. The middle window serves for testing whether a surface is horizontal, the others for testing whether it is plumb or vertical. My grandfather used to carry this level on the gun rack behind the seat in his pickup, and when I rode with him I would turn around to watch the bubbles dance. The larger of the two squares is called a framing square, a flat steel elbow so beat up and tarnished you can barely make out the rows of numbers that show how to figure the cuts on rafters. The smaller one is called a try square, for marking right angles, with a blued steel blade for the shank and a brass-faced block of cherry for the head.

I was taught early on that a saw is not to be used apart from a square: "If 15 you're going to cut a piece of wood," my father insisted, "you owe it to the tree to cut it straight."

Long before studying geometry, I learned there is a mystical virtue in right angles. There is an unspoken morality in seeking the level and the plumb. A house will stand, a table will bear weight, the sides of a box will hold together only if the joints are square and the members upright. When the bubble is lined up between two marks etched in the glass tube of a level, you have aligned yourself with the forces that hold the universe together. When you miter the corners of a picture frame, each angle must be exactly forty-five degrees, as they are in the perfect triangles of Pythagoras, not a degree more or less. Otherwise the frame will hang crookedly, as if ashamed of itself and of its maker. No matter if the joints you are cutting do not show. Even if you are butting two pieces of wood together inside a cabinet, where no one except a wrecking crew will ever see them, you must take pains to insure that the ends are square and the studs are plumb.

I took pains over the wall I was building on the day my father died. Not long after that wall was finished—paneled with tongue-and-groove boards of yellow pine, the nail holes filled with putty and the wood all stained and sealed—I came close to wrecking it one afternoon when my daughter ran howling up the stairs to announce that her gerbils had escaped from their cage and were hiding in my brand-new wall. She could hear them scratching and squeaking behind her bed. Impossible! I said. How on earth could they get inside my drum-tight wall? Through the heating vent, she answered. I went downstairs, pressed my ear to the honey-colored wood, and heard the scritch scritch of tiny feet.

"What can we do?" my daughter wailed. "They'll starve to death, they'll die of thirst, they'll suffocate."

"Hold on," I soothed. "I'll think of something."

While I thought and she fretted, the radio on her bedside table delivered 20 us the headlines. Several thousand people had died in a city in India from a poisonous cloud that had leaked overnight from a chemical plant. A nuclear-powered submarine had been launched. Rioting continued in South Africa. An airplane had been hijacked in the Mediterranean. Authorities calculated that several thousand homeless people slept on the streets within sight of the Washington Monument. I felt my usual helplessness in face of all these calamities. But here was my daughter weeping because her gerbils were holed up in a wall. This calamity I could handle.

"Don't worry," I told her. "We'll set food and water by the heating vent and lure them out. And if that doesn't do the trick, I'll tear the wall apart until we find them."

She stopped crying and gazed at me. "You'd really tear it apart? Just for my gerbils? The *wall*?" Astonishment slowed her down only for a second, however, before she ran to the workbench and began tugging at drawers, saying, "Let's see, what'll we need? Crowbar. Hammer. Chisels. I hope we don't have to use them — but just in case."

We didn't need the wrecking tools. I never had to assault my handsome wall, because the gerbils eventually came out to nibble at a dish of popcorn. But for several hours I studied the tongue-and-groove skin I had nailed up on the day of my father's death, considering where to begin prying. There were no gaps in that wall, no crooked joints.

I had botched a great many pieces of wood before I mastered the right angle with a saw, botched even more before I learned to miter a joint. The knowledge of these things resides in my hands and eyes and the webwork of muscles, not in the tools. There are machines for sale — powered miter boxes and radial arm saws, for instance — that will enable any casual soul to cut proper angles in boards. The skill is invested in the gadget instead of the person who uses it, and this is what distinguishes a machine from a tool. If I had to earn my keep by making furniture or building houses, I suppose I would buy powered saws and pneumatic nailers; the need for speed would drive me to it. But since I carpenter only for my own pleasure or to help neighbors or to remake the house around the ears of my family, I stick with hand tools. Most of the ones I own were given to me by my father, who also taught me how to wield them. The tools in my workbench are a double inheritance, for each hammer and level and saw is wrapped in a cloud of knowing.

All of these tools are a pleasure to look at and to hold. Merchants would   25 never paste NEW NEW NEW! signs on them in stores. Their designs are old because they work, because they serve their purpose well. Like folksongs and aphorisms and the grainy bits of language, these tools have been pared down to essentials. I look at my claw hammer, the distillation of a hundred generations of carpenters, and consider that it holds up well beside those other classics — Greek vases, Gregorian chants, *Don Quixote,* barbed fishhooks, candles, spoons. Knowledge of hammering stretches back to the earliest humans who squatted beside fires chipping flints. Anthropologists have a lovely name for those unworked rocks that served as the earliest hammers. "Dawn stones" they are called. Their only qualification for the work, aside from hardness, is that they fit the hand. Our ancestors used them for grinding corn, tapping awls, smashing bones. From dawn stones to this claw hammer is a great leap in time, but no great distance in design or imagination.

On that iced-over February morning when I smashed my thumb with the hammer, I was down in the basement framing the wall that my daughter's gerbils would later hide in. I was thinking of my father, as I always did whenever I built anything, thinking how he would have gone about the work, hearing in memory what he would have said about the wisdom of hitting the nail instead of my thumb. I had the studs and plates nailed together all square and trim, and was lifting the wall into place when the phone rang upstairs. My wife answered, and in a moment she came to the basement door and called down softly to me. The stillness in her voice made me drop the framed wall and hurry upstairs. She told me my father was dead. Then I heard the details over the phone from my mother. Building a set of cupboards for my brother in Oklahoma, he had knocked off work early the previous afternoon because of cramps in his stomach. Early this morning, on his way into the kitchen of my brother's trailer, maybe going for a glass of water, so early that no one else was awake, he slumped down on the linoleum and his heart quit.

For several hours I paced around inside my house, upstairs and down, in and out of every room, looking for the right door to open and knowing there was no such door. My wife and children followed me and wrapped me in arms and backed away again, circling and staring as if I were on fire. Where was the door, the door, the door? I kept wondering. My smashed thumb turned purple and throbbed, making me furious. I wanted to cut it off and rush outside and scrape away the snow and hack a hole in the frozen earth and bury the shameful thing.

I went down into the basement, opened a drawer in my workbench, and stared at the ranks of chisels and knives. Oiled and sharp, as my father would have kept them, they gleamed at me like teeth. I took up a clasp knife, pried out the longest blade, and tested the edge on the hair of my forearm. A tuft came away cleanly, and I saw my father testing the sharpness of tools on his own skin, the blades of axes and knives and gouges and hoes, saw the red hair shaved off in patches from his arms and the backs of his hands. "That will cut bear," he would say. He never cut a bear with his blades, now my blades, but he cut deer, dirt, wood. I closed the knife and put it away. Then I took up the hammer and went back to work on my daughter's wall, snugging the bottom plate against a chalkline on the floor, shimming the top plate against the joists overhead, plumbing the studs with my level, making sure before I drove the first nail that every line was square and true.

EXPLORING THE TEXT

1. What do Sanders's tools mean to him? What does he imply when he says that the tools in his workbench "are a double inheritance, for each hammer and level and saw is wrapped in a cloud of knowing" (para. 24)?

2. What do you learn about Sanders's father and grandfather through the memories he associates with his tools? What can you tell about them as people? About their values, attitudes, and philosophy of life? Why do you think Sanders chose to focus this essay on his tools and not simply to write directly about his relationship with his father?

3. What is the point of the story about hitting his thumb that Sanders uses to introduce the essay? What does it suggest about his feelings toward his father and the news of his father's death? How do you interpret the essay's concluding paragraphs?

4. Why does Sanders mention the headlines that are in the news on the day of the gerbil incident? What does this suggest about the way he sees himself, his family, and his memories in relation to the wider world around him?

5. Reread Sanders's essay, paying attention to the role that stories and storytelling play in its structure. Which sections of the essay tell the story of particular moments recalled in relatively fine sensuous detail? Which sections seem to speak more generally of the past? What do both types of writing add to Sanders's essay? Next, try to condense the meaning of the selection into a concise, paragraph-long summary. What is lost in such a purely conceptual translation of Sanders's memories?

6. What role do direct quotations play in Sanders's memories? Would the essay have been as effective if Sanders had simply "reported" what people had said instead of relying on direct quotation? Why or why not?

FURTHER EXPLORATIONS

1. Compare Sanders's essay on the meaning of tools to Barry Lopez's essay about the education of his hands (p. 27). How do these personal reflections differ in terms of the way they incorporate sensory detail, stories about specific past events, and more general commentary? Which essay seems more effective to you? Why?

2. How does the experience of memory reflected in "The Inheritance of Tools" compare with that of Loren Eiseley's "The Brown Wasps" (p. 150)? How do these two instances of remembering differ in terms of the occasion or context of the act of remembering, the way that one memory links or leads to another, their sense of clarity and organizational logic? To what extent do these and other differences between the essays reflect the differing purposes of their authors?

3. Read Susan Engel's "Then and Now: Creating a Self Through the Past" (p. 192) and consider how many "past selves" Sanders presents in his memoir. How do these past selves relate to the present self he projects in this essay? What is this present self like? What "face" is Sanders attempting to present to his readers? In what sense is it determined by the context that surrounds this act of memory?

ESSAY OPTIONS

1. Using the *Before Reading* activity on page 142 as a point of departure, write a personal essay focused on an object that holds special meaning for you because of its association with important people or experiences in your past. It might be a tool that has been passed down to you, like Sanders's hammer, a watch, a kitchen utensil, an article of clothing — anything that is surrounded with important memories for you. As you write, keep in mind the structure of Sanders's essay, the way that he relies on storytelling, and the way he alternates specific sensory details with more general memories.

2. Write a dialogue between Sanders and Walker Percy (p. 118), focusing on the way that the past shapes our understanding of the present. To what extent would Sanders be likely to agree with Percy's concept of "sovereign" experience? How might Percy view Sanders's perspective on the world?

The Brown Wasps

LOREN EISELEY

As chair of the Department of Anthropology for many years at the University of Pennsylvania, Loren Eiseley (1907–1977) devoted his professional life to the scientific study of the relation between the environment and human evolution. A "scientist with the soul of a poet," Eiseley also dedicated himself to the craft of writing, producing a series of important works of science-based literature over a career spanning more than three decades. In this lyrical meditation on the complexity of human memory, Eiseley carries us from his encounter with a group of elderly homeless people in a railway station to the front yard of his family home in Nebraska a half-century earlier—all in search of the "shade of a nonexistent tree." Eiseley's evocative memoir offers an example of how memory leads to insight by "doubling" or juxtaposing events and experiences that are separated in time but linked by powerful personal associations. After earning his Ph.D. in 1933, Eiseley taught anthropology and sociology at the University of Kansas and Oberlin College before joining the faculty at the University of Pennsylvania in 1947. His many publications include *The Immense Journey* (1957); *Darwin's Century* (1958); *The Mind in Nature* (1962); *The Unexpected Universe* (1969); *The Night Country* (1971), the source of this selection; and an autobiography, *All the Strange Hours: The Excavation of a Life* (1977).

BEFORE READING

In your journal, freewrite for a few minutes about your earliest recollections of your childhood home and neighborhood. What details do you recall about the place where you lived, the children you played with next door, or the atmosphere or appearance of your neighborhood? How sure are you that your recollections are based on fact and not on fantasy? How can you be sure?

There is a corner in the waiting room of one of the great Eastern stations where women never sit. It is always in the shadow and overhung by rows of lockers. It is, however, always frequented—not so much by genuine travelers as by the dying. It is here that a certain element of the abandoned poor seeks a refuge out of the weather, clinging for a few hours longer to the city that has fathered them. In a precisely similar manner I have seen, on a sunny day in midwinter, a few old brown wasps creep slowly over an abandoned wasp nest in a thicket. Numbed and forgetful and frost-blackened, the hum of the spring hive still resounded faintly in their sodden tissues. Then the temperature would fall and they would drop away into the white oblivion of the snow. Here in the station it is in no way different save that the city is busy in its snows. But the old ones cling to their seats as though these were symbolic and could not be given up. Now and then they sleep, their gray old heads resting with painful awkwardness on the backs of the benches.

Also they are not at rest. For an hour they may sleep in the gasping exhaustion of the ill-nourished and aged who have to walk in the night. Then a policeman comes by on his round and nudges them upright.

"You can't sleep here," he growls.

A strange ritual then begins. A old man is difficult to waken. After a muttered conversation the policeman presses a coin into his hand and passes fiercely along the benches prodding and gesturing toward the door. In his wake, like birds rising and settling behind the passage of a farmer through a cornfield, the men totter up, move a few paces and subside once more upon the benches.

One man, after a slight, apologetic lurch, does not move at all. Tubercularly thin, he sleeps on steadily. The policeman does not look back. To him, too, this has become a ritual. He will not have to notice it again officially for another hour.

Once in a while one of the sleepers will not awake. Like the brown wasps, he will have had his wish to die in the great droning center of the hive rather than in some lonely room. It is not so bad here with the shuffle of footsteps and the knowledge that there are others who share the bad luck of the world. There are also the whistles and the sounds of everyone, everyone in the world, starting on journeys. Amidst so many journeys somebody is bound to come out all right. Somebody.

Maybe it was on a like thought that the brown wasps fell away from the old paper nest in the thicket. You hold till the last, even if it is only to a public seat in a railroad station. You want your place in the hive more than you want a room or a place where the aged can be eased gently out of the way. It is the place that matters, the place at the heart of things. It is life that you want, that bruises your gray old head with the hard chairs; a man as a right to his place.

But sometimes the place is lost in the years behind us. Or sometimes it is a thing of air, a kind of vaporous distortion above a heap of rubble. We cling to a time and place because without them man is lost, not only man but life. This is why the voices, real or unreal, which speak from the floating trumpets at spiritualist seances are so unnerving. They are voices out of nowhere whose only reality lies in their ability to stir the memory of a living person with some fragment of the past. Before the medium's cabinet both the dead and the living revolve endlessly about an episode, a place, an event that has already been engulfed by time.

This feeling runs deep in life; it brings stray cats running over endless miles, and birds homing from the ends of the earth. It is as though all living creatures, and particularly the more intelligent, can survive only by fixing or transforming a bit of time into space or by securing a bit of space with its objects immortalized and made permanent in time. For example, I once saw, on a flower pot in my own living room, the efforts of a field mouse to build a remembered field, I have lived to see this episode repeated in a thousand guises, and since I have spent a large portion of my life in the shade of a non-existent tree, I think I am entitled to speak for the field mouse.

One day as I cut across the field which at that time extended on one side 10 of our suburban shopping center, I found a giant slug feeding from a runnel of pink ice cream in an abandoned Dixie cup. I could see his eyes telescope and protrude in a kind of dim, uncertain ecstasy as his dark body bunched and elongated in the curve of the cup. Then, as I stood there at the edge of the concrete, contemplating the slug, I began to realize it was like standing on a shore where a different type of life creeps up and fumbles tentatively among the rocks and sea wrack. It knows its place and will only creep so far until something changes. Little by little as I stood there I began to see more of this shore that surrounds the place of man. I looked with sudden care and attention at things I had been running over thoughtlessly for years. I even waded out a short way into the grass and the wild-rose thickets to see more. A huge black-belted bee went droning by and there were some indistinct scurryings in the underbrush.

Then I came to a sign which informed me that this field was to be the site of a new Wanamaker suburban store. Thousands of obscure lives were about to perish, the spores of puffballs would go smoking off to new fields, and the bodies of little white-footed mice would be crunched under the inexorable wheels of the bulldozers. Life disappears or modifies its appearances so fast that everything takes on an aspect of illusion — a momentary fizzing and boiling with smoke rings, like pouring dissident chemicals into a retort. Here man was advancing, but in a few years his plaster and bricks would be disappearing once more into the insatiable maw of the clover. Being of an archaeological cast of mind, I thought of this fact with an obscure sense of satisfaction and waded back through the rose thickets to the concrete parking lot. As I did so, a mouse scurried ahead of me, frightened of my steps if not of that ominous Wanamaker sign. I saw him vanish in the general direction of my apartment house, his little body quivering with fear in the great open sun on the blazing concrete. Blinded and confused, he was running straight away from his field. In another week scores would follow him.

I forgot the episode then and went home to the quiet of my living room. It was not until a week later, letting myself into the apartment, that I realized I had a visitor. I am fond of plants and had several ferns standing on the floor in pots to avoid the noon glare by the south window.

As I snapped on the light and glanced carelessly around the room, I saw a little heap of earth on the carpet and a scrabble of pebbles that had been kicked merrily over the edge of one of the flower pots. To my astonishment I discovered a full-fledged burrow delving downward among the fern roots. I waited silently. The creature who had made the burrow did not appear. I remembered the wild field then, and the flight of the mice. No house mouse, no *Mus domesticus,* had kicked up this little heap of earth or sought refuge under a fern root in a flower pot. I thought of the desperate little creature I had seen fleeing from the wild rose thicket. Through intricacies of pipes and attics, he, or one of his fellows, had climbed to this high green solitary room. I could visualize what had occurred. He had an image in his head, a world of seed pods and quiet, of green sheltering leaves in the dim light among the weed stems. It was the only world he knew and it was gone.

Somehow in his flight he had found his way to this room with drawn shades where no one would come till nightfall. And here he had smelled green leaves and run quickly up the flower pot to dabble his paws in common earth. He had even struggled half the afternoon to carry his burrow deeper and had failed. I examined the hole, but no whiskered twitching face appeared. He was gone. I gathered up the earth and refilled the burrow. I did not expect to find traces of him again.

Yet for three nights thereafter I came home to the darkened room and my 15 ferns to find the dirt kicked gaily about the rug and the burrow reopened, though I was never able to catch the field mouse within it. I dropped a little food about the mouth of the burrow, but it was never touched. I looked under beds or sat reading with one ear cocked for rustlings in the ferns. It was all in vain; I never saw him. Probably he ended in a trap in some other tenant's room.

But before he disappeared I had come to look hopefully for his evening burrow. About my ferns there had begun to linger the insubstantial vapor of an autumn field, the distilled essence, as it were, of a mouse brain in exile from its home. It was a small dream, like our dreams, carried a long and weary journey along pipes and through spider webs, past holes over which loomed the shadows of waiting cats, and finally, desperately, into this room where he had played in the shuttered daylight for an hour among the green ferns on the floor. Every day these invisible dreams pass us on the street, or rise from beneath our feet, or look out upon us from beneath a bush.

Some years ago the old elevated railway in Philadelphia was torn down and replaced by a subway system. This ancient El with its barnlike stations containing nut-vending machines and scattered food scraps had, for generations, been the favorite feeding ground of flocks of pigeons, generally one flock to a station along the route of the El. Hundreds of pigeons were dependent upon the system. They flapped in and out of its stanchions and steel work or gathered in watchful little audiences about the feet of anyone who rattled the peanut-vending machines. They even watched people who jingled change in their hands, and prospected for food under the feet of the crowds who gathered between trains. Probably very few among the waiting people who tossed a crumb to an eager pigeon realized that this El was like a food-bearing river, and that the life which haunted its banks was dependent upon the running of the trains with their human freight.

I saw the river stop.

The time came when the underground tubes were ready; the traffic was transferred to a realm unreachable by pigeons. It was like a great river subsiding suddenly into desert sands. For a day, for two days, pigeons continued to circle over the El or stand close to the red vending machines. They were patient birds, and surely this great river which had flowed through the lives of unnumbered generations was merely suffering from some momentary drought.

They listened for the familiar vibrations that had always heralded an ap- 20
proaching train; they flapped hopefully about the head of an occasional work-
man walking along the steel runways. They passed from one empty station to
another, all the while growing hungrier. Finally they flew away.

I thought I had seen the last of them about the El, but there was a revival
and it provided a curious instance of the memory of living things for a way of
life or a locality that has long been cherished. Some weeks after the El was
abandoned workmen began to tear it down. I went to work every morning by
one particular station, and the time came when the demolition crews reached
this spot. Acetylene torches showered passersby with sparks, pneumatic drills
hammered at the base of the structure, and a blind man who, like the pigeons,
had clung with his cup to a stairway leading to the change booth, was forced
to give up his place.

It was then, strangely, momentarily, one morning that I witnessed the return of a little band of the familiar pigeons. I even recognized one or two
members of the flock that had lived around this particular station before they
were dispersed into the streets. They flew bravely in and out among the sparks
and the hammers and the shouting workmen. They had returned — and they
had returned because the hubbub of the wreckers had convinced them that
the river was about to flow once more. For several hours they flapped in and
out through the empty windows, nodding their heads and watching the fall of
girders with attentive little eyes. By the following morning the station was reduced to some burned-off stanchions in the street. My bird friends had gone.
It was plain, however, that they retained a memory for an insubstantial structure now compounded of air and time. Even the blind man clung to it.
Someone had provided him with a chair, and he sat at the same corner staring sightlessly at an invisible stairway where, so far as he was concerned, the
crowds were still ascending to the trains.

I have said my life has been passed in the shade of a nonexistent tree, so
that such sights do not offend me. Prematurely I am one of the brown wasps
and I often sit with them in the great droning hive of the station, dreaming
sometimes of a certain tree. It was planted sixty years ago by a boy with a
bucket and a toy spade in a little Nebraska town. That boy was myself. It was
a cottonwood sapling and the boy remembered it because of some words spoken by his father and because everyone died or moved away who was supposed to wait and grow old under its shade. The boy was passed from hand to
hand, but the tree for some intangible reason had taken root in his mind. It
was under its branches that he sheltered; it was from this tree that his memories, which are my memories, led away into the world.

After sixty years the mood of the brown wasps grows heavier upon one.
During a long inward struggle I thought it would do me good to go and look
upon that actual tree. I found a rational excuse in which to clothe this madness.
I purchased a ticket and at the end of two thousand miles I walked another mile
to an address that was still the same. The house had not been altered.

I came close to the white picket fence and reluctantly, with great effort,   25
looked down the long vista of the yard. There was nothing there to see. For
sixty years that cottonwood had been growing in my mind. Season by season
its seeds had been floating farther on the hot prairie winds. We had planted it
lovingly there, my father and I, because he had a great hunger for soil and live
things growing, and because none of these things had long been ours to protect. We had planted the little sapling and watered it faithfully, and I remembered that I had run out with my small bucket to drench its roots the day we
moved away. And all the years since it had been growing in my mind, a huge
tree that somehow stood for my father and the love I bore him. I took a grasp
on the picket fence and forced myself to look again.

A boy with the hard bird eye of youth pedaled a tricycle slowly up beside me.

"What'cha lookin' at?" he asked curiously.

"A tree," I said.

"What for?" he said.

"It isn't there," I said, to myself mostly, and began to walk away at a pace   30
just slow enough not to seem to be running.

"What isn't there?" the boy asked. I didn't answer. It was obvious I was
attached by a threat to a thing that had never been there, or certainly not for
long. Something that had to be held in the air, or sustained in the mind, because it was part of my orientation in the universe and I could not survive
without it. There was more than an animal's attachment to a place. There was
something else, the attachment of the spirit to a grouping of events in time; it
was part of our morality.

So I had come home at last, driven by a memory in the brain as surely as
the field mouse who had delved long ago into my flower pot or the pigeons flying forever amidst the rattle of nut-vending machines. These, the burrow
under the greenery in my living room and the red-bellied bowls of peanuts
now hovering in midair in the midst of pigeons, were all part of an elusive
world that existed nowhere and yet everywhere. I looked once at the real world
about me while the persistent boy pedaled at my heels.

It was without meaning, though my feet took a remembered path. In sixty
years the house and street had rotted out of my mind. But the tree, the tree
that no longer was, that had perished in its first season, bloomed on in my
individual mind, unblemished as my father's words. "We'll plant a tree
here, son, and we're not going to move any more. And when you're an old, old
man you can sit under it and think how we planted it here, you and me, together."

I began to outpace the boy on the tricycle.

"Do you live here, Mister?" he shouted after me suspiciously. I took a firm   35
grasp on airy nothing—to be precise, on the bole of a great tree. "I do," I said.
I spoke for myself, one field mouse, and several pigeons. We were all out of
touch but somehow permanent. It was the world that had changed.

EXPLORING THE TEXT

1. What does Eiseley observe about the elderly poor he encounters in the train station? What motives does he ascribe to them? What connection leads him to associate them with his earlier memory of the brown wasps? How logical or appropriate does this relation strike you as being? What does the memory of the wasps add to his understanding of the people he observes in the station?

2. What other memories does Eiseley link to these first two recollections? Why is he led along this chain of associations? What similarities link them in his mind? What does each of these memories contribute to his deepening understanding of the elderly poor he originally saw?

3. What details about Eiseley's early family life can be inferred from his comments about his return in search of the tree that grows in his memory? What does this nonexistent tree represent for him? Why does he feel that he "could not survive without it" (para. 31)?

4. What, overall, would you say is the theme or central idea of "The Brown Wasps"? How does each of the memories that Eiseley recalls contribute to this central idea?

5. What does Eiseley mean when he says that memory — or "the attachment of the spirit to a grouping of events in time" — is "part of our morality" (para. 31)? Does this essay strike you as having anything in particular to do with morality? Why or why not?

FURTHER EXPLORATIONS

1. Compare Eiseley's meditation on the past, the nature of memory, and his father with that offered in Scott Russell Sanders's "The Inheritance of Tools" (p. 142). How would you characterize the experience of reading these selections? How do they differ in terms of tone, structure, and clarity of approach? How do these differences relate to differences in Eiseley's and Sanders's purpose in writing, their relationship to their subjects, and their attitudes toward memory?

2. In "Building Memories" (p. 157), Daniel Schacter suggests that the subjective experience of memory results from the combination of two separate mental phenomena: the "cue" or the present stimulus that conjures up a particular memory and the "engram" or the fragments of past experience encoded in the brain. Drawing on Schacter's theory, analyze how the various memories Eiseley introduces in this essay relate to one another as both cure and engram. How do the memories that Eiseley presents compare with those presented by Sanders (p. 142) in this regard?

3. Read "Then and Now: Creating a Self Through the Past" by Susan Engel (p. 192), paying close attention to the concept of "template" memories that Engel describes (para. 20). How well does Eiseley's recollection of the tree outside his family home fulfill the function of a template memory? What "unresolved feelings" might this memory express?

4. How might Patricia Hampl (p. 180) explain the relation between memory and imagination in Eiseley's "The Brown Wasps"? To what extent is it possible to view Eiseley's essay as a "rough draft" in Hampl's terms?

ESSAY OPTIONS

1. Write a brief paper about the role of symbolism in Eiseley's "The Brown Wasps" and Sanders's "The Inheritance of Tools" (p. 142). What special meanings do concrete objects like hammers, squares, levels, railway stations, hives, and trees assume in these essays? What role do such symbolic objects play in conveying the essays' themes or central points? Why do symbolic objects appear to play such a large part in memory-based writing?

2. In "Building Memories" (below), Daniel Schacter suggests that memories involve a kind of "stereoscopic" vision in that every recollection either directly or tacitly compares a "present sensation" with a past experience (para 57). Write an essay in which you evaluate "The Brown Wasps" as an illustration of this kind of stereoscopic vision. In what sense do all of the memories that Eisley summons up represent doublings of the observations he initially makes in the train station at the beginning of the essay? How does each of these doublings add to our understanding of what he sees in this first scene? How does Eiseley's memory of the nonexistent tree in the yard of his childhood home "double" his encounter with the homeless that begins the essay?

3. Using *Further Explorations* number 1 above as a point of departure, write a paper in which you compare Sanders's and Eiseley's essays as examples of two different approaches to writing from memory. How do the experiences of memory conveyed by these two essays compare? How would you describe the process of remembering for Sanders and Eiseley? What do the differences you note suggest about the nature of memory? About the interests, values, and attitudes of Sanders and Eiseley?

Building Memories: Encoding and Retrieving the Present and the Past

DANIEL L. SCHACTER

There may be no better-qualified expert on the mechanics of memory than Daniel L. Schacter. Professor and chair of psychology at Harvard University, Schacter is an internationally recognized authority on neuroimaging and memory theory who has spent the last two decades puzzling out exactly how neurons collaborate to snare the past in their chemical webs. This wide-ranging selection from Schacter's acclaimed *Searching for Memory: The Brain, the Mind, and the Past* (1996) begins with a visit to New York's Museum of Modern Art and ends with the story of how Marcel Proust used the "stereoscope" of recollection to create a literary masterpiece. Along the way, Schacter introduces us to a professional gambler with a prodigious memory, relates the tragic story of a groundbreaking neurologist all but forgotten by modern science, and presents the case of a fourteen-year-old amnesiac who can recall the details of his day-to-day existence only when he writes them down. Schacter's theory of how memories are "constructed" from bits and pieces of the past and present—just as 3-D images emerge from stereoscopic vision — offers a framework for discussing the way that memory retrieval works. Schacter has authored and edited more than 150 scholarly books and articles in the field of memory research, including *Stranger Behind the Engram: Theories of Memory and the Psychology of Science* (1982). His books include *Memory, Brain, and Belief* (2000), edited in collaboration with Elaine Scarry, and *The Seven Sins of Memory: How the Mind Forgets and Remembers* (2001).

BEFORE READING

Divided in small groups, discuss your impressions of how the mechanics of memory work. How do experiences become memories? Why do some experiences take hold in memory while others are quickly forgotten? Why do some remain in memory longer than others? How and why do memories come to mind? What metaphors of the mind make it easier to think about the workings of memory and recollection?

One of my favorite places is the Museum of Modern Art in midtown Manhattan. A native New Yorker, I have made regular pilgrimages to this mecca of art since high school days, and have come to regard many of the paintings there as wise and familiar old friends. Like close friends, however, they cannot always be there when you want them. More than once I have returned to a favorite spot, eagerly anticipating another look at an esteemed painting by de Chirico, Hopper, or Klee, only to learn that it was away on extended loan. Although the painting's absence is disappointing, I sometimes attempt to make up for it by conducting an informal study of my own memory for the piece: What objects and people does the painting include, and how are they located relative to one another? How big is the work? What are the dominant colors and important themes? I can check the accuracy of my answers by locating a reproduction in the museum shop.

The French artist Sophie Calle wondered what aspects of a painting linger in the memories of viewers who are familiar with it. To find out, she conducted a kind of naturalistic memory experiment with an artistic twist. Calle asked a cross section of museum personnel to describe their recollections of several paintings that had been removed from their usual locations at the Museum of Modern Art. She proceeded to create a "memory ghost" for each missing painting—exhibiting the exact words used by the museum workers to describe their recollections of the piece. The most striking outcome was the sheer variety of recollections that her inquiry elicited. Some people recalled only an isolated color or object; others remembered at length subtle nuances of form, space, people, and things.

Calle's observations imply that different people retain and recollect very different aspects of their everyday environments. Why would this be so? Scientists agree that the brain does not operate like a camera or a copying machine. Then what aspects of reality do remain in memory once an episode has concluded? These kinds of questions have dogged every philosopher, psychologist, and neuroscientist who has thought seriously about the nature of remembering and forgetting. Throughout much of the history of scholarly thinking about memory, dating back to the Greeks, people have approached these questions by adopting a spatial metaphor of the mind. The Greek philosophers held that memory is like a wax tablet on which experiences are imprinted, perhaps forever; centuries later, Sigmund Freud° and William James° both conjectured that memories are like objects placed in rooms of a house. One pundit compared memory to a garbage can that contains a random assortment of objects.[1]

The cognitive psychologist Ulric Neisser called the idea that faithful copies of experience are kept in the mind, only to reappear again at some later time pretty much in their original form, the "reappearance hypothesis." Neisser proposed instead that only bits and pieces of incoming data are represented in memory. These retained fragments of experience in turn provide a basis for reconstructing a past event, much as a paleontologist is able to reconstruct a dinosaur from fragments of bone. "Out of a few stored bone chips," reflected Neisser, "we remember a dinosaur."[2]

A visual analogue of Neisser's reflections is found in the work of the Israeli   5
artist Eran Shakine. Shakine has explored his personal past by making collaged paintings in which fragments of old photographs and text are submerged in layers of milky white paint as exemplified by his painting "Hadassah." Shakine struggles with the seeming paradox that our sense of self, the foundation of our psychological existence, depends crucially on these fragmentary and often elusive remnants of experience. What we believe about ourselves is determined by what we remember about our pasts. If memory worked like a video recorder, allowing us to replay the past in exact detail, we could check our beliefs about ourselves against an objective record of what happened in our lives. We must make do instead with the bits and pieces of the past that memory grants us.

The general idea that memories are built from fragments of experience can help us understand key aspects of the rememberer's recollective experience, as well as memory distortions and effects of implicit memory. . . . For now, it is important to understand something more about how the fragments are constructed and reconstructed.

Bubbles P. and the Nature of Encoding

Bubbles P., a professional gambler from Philadelphia, spends virtually all his time making bets: shooting craps at local gaming clubs, dealing cards in illegal poker games, attempting to come up with new systems to beat the numbers. He is not a highly educated man — Bubbles claims to have read only two

Sigmund Freud: (1856–1939), Austrian neurologist and the founder of modern psychoanalysis.
William James: (1842–1910), American psychologist and philosopher.

books in his entire life—but he is capable of certain feats of memory that are well beyond the abilities of even the most erudite Ph.D.s. Most people have difficulty recalling in correct order a string of more than seven digits immediately after seeing or hearing them. When the task is to repeat them backward, most people remember even fewer digits. But Bubbles P.'s digit memory is equally spectacular in either direction.[3] To appreciate his ability, inspect each of the digits at the end of this sentence for one second each, then look away from the page and immediately try to recall them in reverse order: 43902641974935483256. I suspect that by the time you worked your way back to 8, 4, or 5, you were already having problems going any further, and I would be willing to place a bet that nobody made it to 0, much less all the way back to the beginning. Bubbles P., however, can rattle off in correct backward order every one of the twenty numbers in this sequence and similar ones. How does he do it? Has he simply been gifted with an extraordinary, perhaps photographic, memory?

The answer likely resides in the same process that contributes to constructing fragments of experience. Psychologists refer to it as an *encoding process*—a procedure for transforming something a person sees, hears, thinks, or feels into a memory. Encoding can be thought of as a special way of paying attention to ongoing events that has a major impact on subsequent memory for them.

Psychologists first recognized the importance of encoding processes during debates about short-term memory that raged in the 1960s. Short-term memories last for only seconds. Nowadays, researchers believe that such temporary records depend on a specialized system, called *working memory*, that holds small amounts of information for brief time periods, as in the backward recall task you just performed. Everyone is familiar with the operation of working memory from experiences in day-to-day life. Imagine that you need to look up a friend's number in the phone book. You find the number, then walk across the room to make the call, all the while madly repeating the digits to yourself as rapidly as you can. If you are distracted for even a moment during your walk to the phone, you will need to consult the book again; if you punch in the number successfully, you will probably forget it almost immediately. Why are such memories so fleeting?

Part of the answer is that working memory depends on a different network 10 of brain structures than long-term memory systems do. Some patients with damage to the inner part of the temporal lobes in the center of the brain have little or no difficulty retaining a string of digits for several seconds, yet they have great difficulty forming and explicitly remembering more enduring memories. Other patients who have suffered damage to a specific part of the parietal lobe on the cortical surface can form long-term memories but cannot hold and repeat back a string of digits. They lack a specific part of working memory, known as the *phonological loop*, that most of us rely on when we need to hold a small amount of linguistic information in mind for several seconds.[4]

This is where the concept of encoding comes in. By relying on your phonological loop to repeat a phone number madly to yourself, you encode it only superficially. To establish a durable memory, incoming information must be encoded much more thoroughly, or deeply, by associating it meaningfully with knowledge that already exists in memory. You must do more than simply recycle the information in the phonological loop. Suppose that instead of just repeating the phone number—555-6024—to yourself over and over, you attempt to make the number meaningful in some way. For example, if you play golf (as I do), you might encode the number by thinking that 555 is the yardage of a par-5 hole and that 6024 is the length of a relatively short 18-hole course. You have now carried out a deep encoding and should be able to remember the information much longer and more accurately than if you merely repeat it. This is known in the psychological literature as a "depth of processing" effect.[5]

The same sort of effect is probably at work in cases like that of Bubbles P. Bubbles is knowledgeable about numbers and seems able to segregate effortlessly a long string of them into meaningful units or chunks. Rather than frantically recycling them, as most of us do, Bubbles uses the skill he has developed with numbers through years of gambling to link incoming digits to knowledge already in his memory. Bubbles does not have a generally extraordinary memory: his memory for words, faces, objects, and locations—anything other than numbers—is no better than average.

Elaborative Encoding

Memory researchers have tried to devise special techniques to gain control over the encoding operations that a person performs, and these operations have played a crucial role in the unfolding story of memory and amnesia research during the past twenty years.[6] Suppose I tell you that an hour from now, I will test your ability to recall the following words: floor, car, tree, cake, shirt, flower, cup, grass, dog, table. You might try to remember the words by conjuring up visual images, by simply repeating the words again and again, or by making up a story that connects the words to one another. As long as I leave you to your own devices, I cannot learn much about how encoding processes influence memory. I need to come up with some way of controlling how you think about the to-be-remembered items.

Memory researchers have solved this problem by using what is known as an orienting task. Instead of allowing people to memorize the target items in any manner they please, an orienting task guides encoding by requiring a person to answer a specific question about the target. For example, I could induce you to carry out a deep, semantic encoding of target words by asking for a yes or no answer to questions such as, "Is *shirt* a type of clothing?" You cannot answer this question accurately without thinking about the meaning of the word *shirt*. To induce you to engage in shallow, nonsemantic encoding of the word, I could ask you to answer a question such as, "Does *shirt* contain more vowels or more consonants?" You can answer this question easily without attending to the meaning of the word. If I later test your ability to recollect *shirt* and other words on the list, I can be fairly confident that you will be able to recall or recognize many of the words that you encoded semantically and few of the words that you encoded nonsemantically.

This finding may not seem particularly surprising; everyday experience suggests that something that is meaningful will be more easily remembered than something that is not. But it turns out that only a certain kind of semantic encoding promotes high levels of memory performance—an *elaborative* encoding operation that allows you to integrate new information with what you already know. For example, if I induce you to encode one of our study list words by posing the question, "Is *shirt* a type of insect?" you must pay attention to the meaning of the word in order to provide the correct answer. As you formulate a response to this question, however, you do not integrate the target word with your preexisting knowledge of shirts—that is, you do not carry out an effective elaboration of the word *shirt*. If I test you after you have answered this kind of orienting question, you will show surprisingly poor memory for whether the word *shirt* was on the list.[7]

In our everyday lives, memory is a natural, perhaps automatic, byproduct of the manner in which we think about an unfolding episode. If we want to improve our chances of remembering an incident or learning a fact, we need to make sure that we carry out elaborative encoding by reflecting on the information and relating it to other things we already know. Laboratory studies have shown that simply intending to remember something is unlikely to be helpful, unless we translate that intention into an effective elaborative encoding. For example, when preparing for an exam, a good student may make a special effort to form meaningful mental associations among the study materials, whereas the same student may not bother engaging in such elaborative encoding if she is not going to be tested. In my earlier example, carrying out the orienting task—answering the question, "Is *shirt* a type of clothing?"—ensures that you have already made effective use of elaborative encoding processes; "trying to remember" adds nothing beyond that.

The issue can be turned around, too: most experiences that we recall effortlessly from our day-to-day existence—yesterday's important lunch date, the big party last weekend, last year's summer vacation—are not initially encoded with any particular intention to remember them. Occasionally, the apparent significance of an event may prompt us to make a special effort to encode it deeply. However, day-to-day existence would be precarious and probably unmanageable if we had to make an intentional effort to encode each and every episode from our daily lives in order to be able to recollect it later. Instead, a kind of natural selection drives us. What we already know shapes what we select and encode; things that are meaningful to us spontaneously elicit the kind of elaborations that promote later recall. Our memory systems are built so that we are likely to remember what is most important to us.

Carrying out a deep, elaborative encoding influences not only the quantity of what can be remembered but also the quality of our recollective experience. . . . When we meet a new person and encode information elaboratively, we are more likely later to "remember" the episode; if we do not elaborate, we are more likely to "just know" that the person seems familiar. Elaborative encoding is a critical and perhaps necessary ingredient of our ability to remember in rich and vivid detail what has happened to us in the past.[8]

But the dependence of explicit memory on elaboration has a downside, too: if we do not carry out elaborative encoding, we will be left with impoverished recollections. Experiments have shown that people are surprisingly poor at remembering what is on the front and back of a penny, despite seeing and handling pennies all the time.[9] It is likely, however, that we encode the features of a penny quite superficially, because using pennies in everyday life requires only that we notice the general shape and color of the coin. The encoding process can halt once we have extracted the necessary information; there is no need to carry out a more elaborate analysis of the coin. In this example, we are behaving like experimental volunteers who perform shallow or superficial orienting tasks, and later recall little or nothing of what they have seen. If we operate on automatic pilot much of the time and do not reflect on our environment and our experiences, we may pay a price by retaining only sketchy memories of where we have been and what we have done.

Encoding and Mnemonic Devices

Elaborative encoding is a critical component of virtually all popular memory-improvement techniques. The oldest example of a memory-improvement strategy is visual imagery mnemonics, first developed by the Greek orator Simonides in 477 B.C. As the story goes, Simonides, a poet, was called to recite verse at a large banquet. During the course of the evening, he was unexpectedly summoned outside to meet two young men; the moment he left, the roof of the banquet hall collapsed, crushing and mutilating beyond recognition all the guests. Simonides became a hero because he was able to reconstruct the guest list by imagining each location around the table, which brought to mind the person who had been sitting there.

He accomplished this feat by using a system of mnemonics he had developed known as the method of *loci*, which became famous in ancient Greece after this incident. The method involves encoding information into memory by conjuring up vivid mental images and mentally placing them in familiar locations. Later, at the time of attempted recall, one consults the locations, just as Simonides did.[10] If, for example, you wanted to remember to buy beer, potato chips, and toothpaste, you could use rooms in your home as locations, and imagine your bedroom afloat in beer, your kitchen stuffed from top to bottom with bags of potato chips, and your living room slathered with toothpaste. Upon arriving at the store, you could then take a mental walk around your house and "see" what is in each room.

Modern practitioners use the method of loci and other related imagery techniques to perform such feats as remembering all the names and numbers listed in good-sized telephone books. These accomplishments are nothing new, however. Greek orators used mnemonics to memorize speeches of extraordinary length, and Roman generals used them to remember the names of tens of thousands of men in their command. During the Middle Ages, scholastics used mnemonics to aid in the learning of interminable religious tomes. In fact, throughout the Middle Ages, mnemonics played a major role in society, exerting a large influence on artistic and religious life.[11]

By the fifteenth and sixteenth centuries, Simonides' relatively simple method of loci had been superseded by increasingly baroque "memory theaters" that were conceived and drawn by some of Europe's most inventive minds. These intricate and sometimes beautiful structures consisted of hundreds of locations, each containing ideas and precepts that were frequently mystical. Learning all the locations and precepts in a memory theater—into which one could later mentally deposit new to-be-remembered information—was itself an arduous, sometimes impossible task. The excesses of mnemonic systems eventually created a backlash against them.[12]

My central point is that the core cognitive act of visual imagery mnemonics—creating an image and linking it to a mental location—is a form of deep, elaborate encoding. Mnemonic techniques produce rich and detailed encodings that are tightly linked to preexisting knowledge, yet are distinctively different from other items in memory. It also seems likely, in light of my earlier discussion about the importance of visual reexperiencing in conscious recollection, that the visual format of imagery mnemonics enhances its usefulness as an aid to explicit remembering.[13] . . .

The Museum Test

The notion of elaboration also provides interesting perspectives on the recollections of the Museum of Modern Art personnel in the project I mentioned earlier. Several of them were asked to recall the Magritte painting, "The Menaced Assassin" (Fig. 1). Their memory reports are revealing:

1. There's a lot of pink flesh, red blood, guys in black. The background is blue with French ironwork on the balcony, the bedroom is beige, but the only striking color is that blood painted red that looks like ketchup.

2. It's a painting with a smooth surface, an easy one to spot check. It is approximately five feet high and seven feet long. It is framed in a plain, dark, walnut-stained molding, something austere. I never liked it. I don't like stories in painting. I don't like trying to figure them out. That's why I never gave it any time.

3. It has a film noir sort of feel, a mystery novel look to it. The puzzle is there. You have all those little clues that will probably lead you nowhere; there

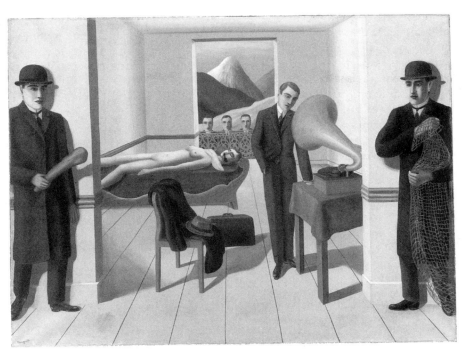

FIGURE 2.1   René Magritte, "The Menaced Assassin," 1926. 59¼" × 6′ 4⅞". Oil on canvas. The Museum of Modern Art, New York. Kay Sage Tanguy Fund. Photograph © 1996 The Museum of Modern Art, New York.

Sophie Calle, an artist, queried museum personnel about their recollections of Magritte's painting, and elicited a wide variety of memories.

are men dressed in dark coats, and black bowler hats, the way Albert Finney was dressed in *Murder on the Orient Express,* placed in a room with a dead body. In the center, the one who seems to be the perpetrator is lifting the needle of a phonograph. Two weird-looking individuals are hiding to the side. There is a face looking from the balcony, almost like a sun on the horizon. And, when you look at her carefully, you realize that the towel probably conceals a decapitated head.

4. I think it's just a murder scene. Men in dark suits, a pale woman and dashes of red blood. That's all I remember.[14]

Based on what they recollected, I feel I can make reasonably confident guesses about their identities: Comment #4 probably belongs to a security guard or other nonprofessional staff, as does #1, which focuses solely on the physical features of the painting. Comment #2, which describes the work's exact measurements and properties of its frame, likely comes from someone charged with maintaining the painting. And the thematically rich set of memories in #3 no doubt belong to a curator or similar art professional. The rationale for these educated guesses is simple. What people remember about a painting is heavily influenced by how they think about or encode it, and exactly which aspects of a painting are elaborated depends on what kind of knowledge is already available in one's long-term memory.

Encoding and remembering are virtually inseparable. But the close relationship between the two can sometimes cause problems in our everyday lives. We remember only what we have encoded, and what we encode depends on who we are — our past experiences, knowledge, and needs all have a powerful influence on what we retain. This is one reason why two different people can sometimes have radically divergent recollections of the same event (Fig. 2). . . .

HISTORICAL INTERLUDE
The Story of Richard Semon

The study of memory, like that of any scientific endeavor, has a history full of pioneering figures whose achievements are recognized and honored by researchers active in the field today. As a graduate student, I became intrigued by Richard Semon, who played an unappreciated role in the history of memory research. My curiosity was sparked by tantalizing comments from some of the twentieth century's most towering intellects, such as the philosopher Bertrand Russell° and the physicist Erwin Schrödinger,° concerning the great value of his work. Hardly anyone working on memory in 1977 had heard of him, but I soon discovered that his ideas were both original and important.[15]

Semon was born in Berlin in 1859, the same year that Charles Darwin published *The Origin of Species*. As a young man, Semon fell under the spell of this innovative approach to understanding evolution, and he went off to study at the University of Jena with the most famous German proponent of the new theory, the controversial biologist Ernst Haeckel. Semon received his Ph.D. and became a rising young professor at the University of Jena, a major European center for evolutionary research. Then, in 1897, he fell in love with the wife of an eminent colleague, Maria Krehl, who eventually left her husband to live with Semon. The two were vilified, Semon resigned his professorship, and the pair moved to Munich, where they were married. Semon, working on his own as private scholar, developed a theory of memory.

In 1904, he published a monograph, *Die Mneme*, that attempted to unite the biological analysis of heredity with the psychological and physiological analysis of memory. Semon argued that heredity and reproduction could be thought of as memory that preserves the effects of experience across generations. *Mneme*, a term Semon created in allusion to the Greek goddess of memory, Mnemosyne, refers to a fundamental process that he believed sub-

Bertrand Russell: Bertrand Arthur William Russell (1872–1970), English mathematician and philosopher.
Erwin Schrödinger: (1887–1961), American physicist.

FIGURE 2.2   Jerry Coker, "The Memory Tree Man," 1993. 15 × 10¾ × 1". Mixed media on found metal. Marion Harris Gallery, Simsbury, Connecticut.

Coker is a self-taught maker of masks who uses scrap metal and other everyday materials to create expressive faces of people he remembers from his childhood. In "The Memory Tree Man" the metal face is that of a migrant worker traveling with his family in rural Arkansas. They came upon the young Jerry as he was playing near his grandfather's apple tree. The family stopped and stared at the tree with great interest. Sensing what they wanted, Jerry asked the migrants if they wished to pick some apples. They pulled out several bushels, filled them up, and happily chatted with Jerry about coming back the next day.

Jerry's grandfather was none too pleased, however, when the worker dutifully returned and demanded all the apples remaining on the tree. The migrant insisted that Jerry had told him he could pick all the apples he wished. But Jerry swore to his grandfather that he never promised anything. Was one of the two parties fibbing? Or had they remembered the event differently? Jerry's grandfather must have known something about how different people encode different aspects of the same event, because he came to the wise conclusion that only the apple tree knew what had actually happened. He worked out an equitable settlement between the boy and the worker, but he could not bridge the gulf between the two different versions of the past that each maintained.[16]

serves both heredity and everyday memory. He conceived it as an elemental elasticity of biological tissue that allows the effects of experience to be preserved over time.

Semon distinguished three aspects or stages of Mneme that he deemed   35 crucial to understanding both everyday memory and hereditary memory. Because he believed that ordinary language has too many potentially misleading connotations to be useful scientifically, Semon described the three stages with terms of his own invention: *engraphy* is Semon's term for encoding information into memory; *engram* refers to the enduring change in the nervous system (the "memory trace") that conserves the effects of experience across time; and *ecphory* is the process of activating or retrieving a memory.

Semon's unusual terminology and his emphasis on the memory/heredity analogy elicited a torrent of disapproval from prominent experts of the time. Yet precisely because of this controversy, his ideas about the operation of everyday memory tended to be overlooked. Only one reviewer of *Die Mneme*, the American psychologist Henry J. Watt, looked beyond the issues of heredity that so mesmerized biologists and picked out the single most important aspect of Semon's theory. "The most valuable part of the book is the concept of the ecphoric stimulus," reflected Watt. "However, Semon in his attempt to find something common in the reproduction of the organism and in the reproduction in the sense of memory, has lost sight of his own objective (the discovery of the nature of the ecphoric stimulus) and has gone astray."[17]

What exactly was Watt driving at? Psychologists at the time showed scant interest in memory-retrieval processes. Most of them believed that the likelihood of remembering an experience is determined entirely by the strength of associations that are formed when the information is initially encoded into memory. According to this view, if strong associations are formed—because the information is particularly vivid, or is repeated frequently enough—memory will later be good; if weak associations are formed, memory will later be poor. Semon, in contrast, argued that memory does not depend solely on the strength of associations. He contended that the likelihood of remembering also hinges on the ecphoric stimulus—the hint or cue that triggers recall—and how it is related to the engram, or memory trace, that was encoded initially. Watt realized that Semon had pinpointed a key aspect of memory that had been given short shrift, and wished that Semon had focused more extensively on it.

In 1909, Semon published a book that must have made Watt exceedingly happy. Entitled *Die Mnemischen Empfindungen (Mnemic Psychology)*, it was entirely about everyday memory, leaving aside the contentious issues of heredity in *Die Mneme*. Semon elaborated his theory of ecphory (retrieval processes) and applied it to a host of critical issues. Sadly for Semon, however, the new book aroused slight interest among researchers and had no detectable impact on the study of memory. Psychologists had little use for Semon's iconoclastic views on retrieval processes; in fact, they misunderstood his ideas. In addition,

Semon's status as a scientific isolate, without prestigious institutional affiliations, did not enhance his cause. He was accorded the same kind of treatment given to flat-earth theorists, believers in perpetual-motion machines, and other cranks who exist at the fringes of science: he was ignored.

In 1918, Semon's wife died of cancer. Later that year, he placed a German flag on his wife's bed and shot himself through the heart.

Despite his nagging despair over the neglect of his work, Semon believed   40
that his ideas would soon achieve widespread recognition among researchers. His hopes went largely unrealized, with the exception of one of his terminological inventions: the engram. The great neuroscientist Karl Lashley wrote a paper in 1950 entitled "In Search of the Engram," which summarizes Lashley's unsuccessful attempts to find the engram (the representation of a memory in the brain) in any single, restricted location. Because the paper became a classic in the field and contains the first prominent invocation of the term *engram,* most scientists have assumed that Lashley invented the word — and he did not even cite, much less discuss, Semon's prior use of the term.

Engrams are the transient or enduring changes in our brains that result from encoding an experience. Neuroscientists believe that the brain records an event by strengthening the connections between groups of neurons that participate in encoding the experience. A typical incident in our everyday lives consists of numerous sights, sounds, actions, and words. Different areas of the brain analyze these varied aspects of an event. As a result, neurons in the different regions become more strongly connected to one another. The new pattern of connections constitutes the brain's record of the event: the engram. This idea was first suggested by the Canadian psychologist Donald Hebb, and has since been worked out in considerable detail.[18]

Engrams are important contributors to what we subjectively experience as a memory of something that has happened to us. But, as we have seen, they are not the only source of the subjective experience of remembering. As you read these words, there are thousands, maybe millions, of engrams in some form in your brain. These patterns of connections have the potential to enter awareness, to contribute to explicit remembering under the right circumstances, but at any one instant most of them lie dormant. If I cue you by asking you to remember the most exciting high school sports event you ever attended, a variety of engrams that only seconds ago were in a quiescent state become active as you sift through candidate experiences; if I ask you to remember what you ate the last time you had dinner at an Italian restaurant, a very different set of engrams enters into awareness. Had I not just posed these queries to you, the relevant engrams might have remained dormant for years.

Semon appreciated that, engrams being merely potential contributors to recollection, an adequate account of memory depends on understanding the influences that allow engrams to become manifest in conscious awareness: What properties of a cue allow it to "awaken" a dormant engram? Why are some cues effective in eliciting recollection whereas others are not? Semon argued that any given memory could be elicited by just a few select cues — parts of the original experience that a person focused on at the time the experience occurred. Thus, only a fraction of the original event need be present in order to trigger recall of the entire episode.

To recollect the most exciting high school sports event you ever attended, you need not reinstate all the cues that were present initially. Only a subset must be available, those that are closely related to your encoding of the event. Your original encoding and elaboration of the event — say, a football game in which the quarterback made a series of miraculous plays to pull off an unexpected victory — focused heavily on the role of the quarterback. Years later, the mere mention of the quarterback's name, or even a glance at his face, may bring to your mind the game, the participants, and how your team won. But if you do not encounter the critical cues, you will not recall the experience. A friend may ask if you recall the time your team beat the school with the young coach who went on to a career with a professional team. You may be puzzled about what game he is referring to, and have only a fuzzy recollection of the coach. But as soon as he says that it was the game in which your quarterback threw two long touchdown passes in the final minutes, you can retrieve the memory easily. Thus, if encoding conditions are not adequately reinstated at the time of attempted recall, retrieval will fail — even if an event has received extensive elaborative encoding. . . .

Because our understanding of ourselves is so dependent on what we can remember of the past, it is troubling to realize that successful recall depends heavily on the availability of appropriate retrieval cues. Such dependence implies that we may be oblivious to parts of our pasts because we fail to encounter hints or cues that trigger dormant memories. This may be one reason why encountering acquaintances we have not seen for years is often such an affecting experience: our old friends provide us with cues and reminders that are difficult to generate on our own, and that allow us to recollect incidents we would ordinarily fail to remember. . . . 45

We must not, however, confuse these ideas with the notion that all experiences are recorded somewhere in our brains, only awaiting the appropriate retrieval cue to be brought into awareness. While controlled research has demonstrated over and over that cues and reminders can lead to recall of experiences that have seemingly disappeared, it does not necessarily follow that all experiences are preserved and potentially recallable. Sometimes we forget because the right cues are not available, but it is also likely that sometimes we forget because the relevant engrams have weakened or become blurred.[19]

Retrieval cues are a bit like the portable metal detectors that scavengers sometimes use to try to recover coins on a beach. If coins are hidden somewhere beneath the sands, then the scavenger needs the detector to find them. But if no coins remain in the sand, then even the most powerful detector will turn up nothing. Our brains include some beaches with hidden coins and others that are barren. Like the scavenger seeking money, we do not know before searching which are which.

NEIL
Retrieval Processes and the Brain

In 1988, a fourteen-year-old English boy named Neil began radiation treatment for a tumor hidden deep within the recesses of his brain. Neil had been a normal child until the expanding tumor began to interfere with his vision and memory and to create a host of other medical problems. Chemotherapy was eventually successful, but Neil suffered heavy cognitive losses. He was virtually unable to read and could no longer name common objects on sight. Neil was able to recount most of his life prior to the operation, but he had great difficulty remembering his ongoing, day-to-day experiences.

Curiously, however, Neil performed reasonably well at school, especially in English and mathematics. The psychologists who tested his memory wondered how he managed to do so well. To find out, they asked him some questions about an audiotaped book he had been studying, *Cider with Rosie*, by Laurie Lee. He remembered nothing. Noting Neil's frustration, and realizing that his class performance was based on written responses, the examiner asked Neil to write down his answers, beginning with anything that he could recall from the book. After a while he wrote: "Bloodshot Geranium windows Cider with Rosie Dranium smell of damp pepper and mushroom-growth." "What have I written?" he then asked, unable to read his own handwriting but able to speak normally. The examiner, who was familiar with the book, immediately recognized that the phrases came directly from its pages.

Intrigued by Neil's ability to write down information that he could not express orally, the examiner asked whether Neil could write anything about incidents related to his hospitalization some two years earlier, which he had been unable to remember when asked to talk about them. "A man had Gangrene," he wrote, correctly recalling the ailment of another man in the ambulance that brought Neil to the hospital.

Neil's parents asked him to write down the names of the children in his class. He produced a long list, which turned out to be accurate. When his mother asked him what had happened at school that day, Neil wrote, "Mum I saw tulips on the way home." This was the first time in two years that Neil had been able to relate to his mother a memory of something that had happened to him in her absence.

Neil's parents equipped him with a small notebook, and he began to communicate regularly about incidents in his everyday life. Yet he remained unable to recount these episodes orally. When he wrote them down, Neil was unable to read them, and often expressed surprise when someone told him what he had written. After an afternoon's excursion to several familiar locations, Neil was unable to remember anything when asked. But when told to write down what had happened, he provided a succinct, and accurate, summary of the afternoon's activities: "We went to the museum, and we had some pizza. Then we came back, we went onto the Beach and we looked at the sea. Then we came home."

This case is unprecedented in the annals of psychology, psychiatry, or neurology.[20] Neil's tumor did damage his brain, including some structures that are known to be important for memory. But nothing about the condition of his brain provides specific clues to how or why he could retrieve recent episodic memories through writing but not speaking.

There are other indications that the brain uses different systems for retrieving written and spoken information. The neuropsychologist Alfonso Caramazza has described two patients who suffered strokes in different regions of the left hemisphere that are usually associated with language impairments. Both patients subsequently had special problems producing English verbs (they could produce nouns normally). One patient had problems writing verbs but not saying them, whereas the other had problems saying verbs but not writing them.[21]

Caramazza's findings still leave us a long way from understanding how Neil could recall his recent experiences through writing but not speaking. But these strange cases of disruptions of retrieval raise questions that are essential to understanding memory: Exactly how does the retrieval process work? What goes on in my mind/brain that allows the cue "What did you do during your summer vacation?" to evoke in me the subjective experience of remembering beautiful sunlit days of hiking and swimming at Lake Tahoe? We do not understand precisely how the retrieval process works, but some clues are beginning to emerge.[22] . . .

CONSTRUCTING MEMORIES
The Role of the Retrieval Environment

Findings and ideas concerning brain mechanisms of retrieval are absolutely crucial to understanding memory's fragile power. But it is still important to develop an adequate conceptualization of retrieval at the psychological level. How are we to think about what is retrieved when we recall a past experience? Does the act of retrieval simply serve to activate, or bring into conscious awareness, a dormant memory?

Suppose, for example, that I provide a retrieval cue such as "tell me about last year's Thanksgiving dinner." It may take you a few seconds to recollect where it occurred and who was there, but by the time you reach the end of this sentence there is a good chance that you will recall some of the basic information. How did this subjective experience of remembering come about? The simplest account is that the cue somehow activated a dormant engram of the event, and that your subjective experience of remembering the event, however incomplete, is a straightforward reflection of the information that had been quiescent in your mind: a lightbulb that had been turned off is suddenly turned on.

But memory retrieval is not so simple. I have already suggested an alternative possibility, rooted in Neisser's analogy that retrieving a memory is like reconstructing a dinosaur from fragments of bone. For the paleontologist, the bone chips that are recovered on an archaeological dig and the dinosaur that is ultimately reconstructed from them are not the same thing; the full-blown dinosaur is constructed by combining the bone chips with other available fragments, in accordance with general knowledge of how the complete dinosaur should appear. Similarly, for the remember, the engram (the stored fragments of an episode) and the memory (the subjective experience of recollecting a past event) are not the same thing. The stored fragments contribute to the conscious experience of remembering, but they are only part of it. Another important component is the retrieval cue itself. Although it is often assumed that a retrieval cue merely arouses or activates a memory that is slumbering in the recesses of the brain, I have hinted at an alternative: the cue combines with the engram to yield a new, emergent entity—the recollective experience of the rememberer—that differs from either of its constituents. This idea was intimated in some of Proust's writings, in which memories emerge from comparing and combining a present sensation with a past one, much as stereoscopic vision emerges from combining information from the two eyes. . . .

Marcel Proust: Involuntary Memory

No single work of literature is more closely associated with human memory than Marcel Proust's *À la recherche du temps perdu (In Search of Lost Time).*[23] The depth of Proust's obsession with recapturing the past is difficult to overstate. The eight volumes that constitute *À la recherche* were written over a period of nearly fifteen years, beginning around 1908 and concluding several months before his death in November 1922. The entire treatise exceeds three thousand pages, most concerned in one way or another with personal recollections or meditations on the nature of memory. Proust may have become so single-minded because he had largely withdrawn from society by the time he began writing his opus. He confined himself to his room throughout much of the writing, suffering from illness and exhaustion, and in so doing substituted a world of time for the world of space. But his obsession with the past also reflects Proust's passionate conviction that the truth of human experience could be grasped only through an understanding of memory and time.

In the most dramatic memory-related incident of the novel, the narrator, Marcel, is visiting his mother, who serves him tea and pastries known as *petites madeleines.* After dipping a madeleine into the tea and imbibing the mixture, he is overcome by an unexpected, overwhelming, and entirely mysterious sense of well-being. "Whence could it have come to me, this all-powerful joy?" he asks. "I sensed that it was connected with the taste of the tea and the cake, but that it infinitely transcended those savours, could not, indeed, be of the same nature. Whence did it come from? What did it mean? How could I seize and apprehend it?"[24] He tries to induce the experience again by tasting several more mouthfuls of the potent mixture, but each experience is weaker than the previous one, leading him to conclude that the basis of the effect "lies not in the cup but in myself." He surmises that the tea and cake have somehow activated a past experience, and wonders whether he will be able to recall it consciously.

Then comes the extraordinary instant when the mystery is resolved: "And suddenly the memory revealed itself. The taste was that of the little crumb of madeleine which on Sunday mornings at Combray [the fictional name of Proust's childhood town] when I went to say good morning to her in her bedroom, my aunt Leonie used to give me, dipping it first in her own cup of tea." Marcel notes that he had never elsewhere encountered the combination of smells and tastes that characterized the episode at his aunt's house, thus making them uniquely effective cues for an elusive but powerful memory: "But when from a long-distant past nothing subsists, after the people are dead, after the things are broken and scattered, taste and smell alone, more fragile but more enduring, more immaterial, more persistent, more faithful, remain poised for a long time, like souls, remembering, waiting and hoping, amid the ruins of all the rest; and bear unflinchingly, in the tiny and almost impalpable drop of their essence, the vast structure of recollection."

The moment when the madeleine memory revealed itself was the moment when the narrator saw that memory could be both fragile and powerful. Memories that can be elicited only by specific tastes and smells are fragile: they can easily disappear because there are few opportunities for them to surface. But those that survive are also exceptionally powerful: having remained dormant for long periods of time, the sudden appearance of seemingly lost experiences cued by tastes or smells is a startling event.

The madeleine episode also highlights that reexperiencing one's personal past sometimes depends on chance encounters with objects that contain the keys to unlocking memories that might otherwise be hidden forever. But Marcel's recognition that *involuntary* recollections are fleeting, lasting only several seconds, and depend on rare confrontations with particular smells or sights, leads him to alter the focus of his quest for the past. As the novel progresses, his quest for self-understanding depends increasingly on the active, *voluntary* retrieval of his past.[25] He explores the self-defining role of voluntary recollection in one of the key scenes from the final novel in the series, *Time Regained.* At a gathering of old friends whom Marcel has not seen for many years, he strains to recall their identities and to place them in the context of his remembered experiences. In so doing he achieves a synthesis of past and present that heightens his appreciation of his own identity.

Proust also draws on concepts and analogies from the science of optics to develop an analogy of time and memory, which he made explicit in a 1922 letter. "The image (imperfect as it is) which seems to me best suited to convey the nature of that special tense," Proust wrote, "is that of a telescope, a telescope pointed at time, for a telescope renders visible for us stars invisible to the naked eye, and I have tried to render visible to the consciousness unconscious phenomena, some of which, having been entirely forgotten, are situated in the past."[26]

Proust further develops his optical analogy. The experience of remembering a past episode, Proust contends, is not based merely on calling to mind a stored memory image. Instead, a feeling of remembering emerges from the comparison of two images: one in the present and one in the past. Just as visual perception of the three-dimensional world depends on combining information from the two eyes, perception in time—remembering—depends on combining information from the present and the past. The renowned Proust scholar Roger Shattuck explains: "Proust set about to make us *see time*. . . . Merely to remember something is meaningless unless the remembered image is combined with a moment in the present affording a view of the same object or objects. Like our eyes, our memories must see double; these two images then converge in our minds into a single heightened reality."[27] Foreshadowing scientific research by more than a half-century, Proust achieved the penetrating insight that feelings of remembering result from a subtle interplay between past and present.

Notes

1. Roediger (1980) reviews spatial metaphors of memory, and Landauer (1975) describes the "garbage can" analogy. Koriat and Goldsmith (in press) contrast the storehouse metaphor of memory to an alternative metaphor that emphasizes how well remembered events correspond to the original experiences.

2. Neisser (1967), p. 285.

3. Ceci, DeSimone, and Johnson (1992) describe the case of Bubbles P. and report a series of experiments concerning his memory abilities. The importance of the "magic number" seven was described by Miller (1956).

4. Research concerning working memory has been pioneered by Baddeley (1986) and colleagues. Baddeley fractionates working memory into several subsystems: a central executive or limited capacity workspace and two "slave" subsystems, the phonological loop and a visuospatial sketch pad that temporarily holds nonverbal information. For studies of patients with damage to the phonological loop, see Vallar and Shallice (1990).

5. The term *depth of processing,* synonymous with *levels of processing,* was introduced to the psychological literature in a classic paper by Craik and Lockhart (1972).

6. For a discussion of these special techniques, known as *orienting tasks,* see Craik and Tulving (1975).

7. This finding was first reported by Craik and Tulving (1975). Other early experiments documenting the importance of elaborative encoding included those by Stein and Bransford (1979), which revealed that even subtle differences in the exact kind of elaboration that people perform can have a major impact on subsequent memory performance.

8. See Gardiner and Java (1993) for elaborative encoding and experiences of remembering and knowing.

9. See Nickerson and Adams (1979).

10. This rendition of the story of Simonides is based on Yates (1966), who provides a definitive history of the origins of mnemonics.

11. The story of mnemonics and the Middle Ages is beautifully told by Carruthers (1990). Scholarly discussions of visual imagery mnemonics and memory improvement

can be found in Bellezza (1981) and Bower (1972). A popular treatment of how to use mnemonics to enhance memory function has been provided by Lorayne and Lucas (1974), among many others. Herrmann, Raybeck, and Gutman (1993) focus specifically on improving memory performance in students.

12. For the backlash against mnemonics, see J. Spence (1984), pp. 4 and 12.

13. For wide-ranging discussions of imagery, mind, and brain, see Kosslyn (1981, 1994).

14. The quoted texts are from Storr (1992), p. 6.

15. For an overview of Semon's theory of memory, see Schacter, Eich, and Tulving (1978); for a broader treatment that delves into Semon's life and ideas in the context of the history and sociology of science, see Schacter (1982). For English translations of his work on memory, see Semon (1921, 1923).

16. For more information on Jerry Coker's life and art, see Harris (1995), which contains a brief essay of mind on the role of memory in Coker's work.

17. Watt (1905), p. 130.

18. See Hebb (1949) for the original statement of what has come to be known as "Hebbian learning." For a modern treatment, see McNaughton and Nadel (1989), and for a review of recent evidence, see Merzenich and Sameshima (1993).

19. For a review of evidence from people and animals on retrieval of seemingly forgotten memories in response to cues and reminders, see Capaldi and Neath (1995).

20. Neil's case is described in detail by Vargha-Khadem, Isaacs, and Mishkin (1994). Quotes are from pp. 692–693 of that article. The tumor was in the pineal region of the third ventricle. Although it was treated successfully, MRI scans after treatment revealed abnormalities in structures thought to be important for memory, including the left hippocampal formation, parts of the diencephalon, and the fornix, which connects the hippocampus and diencephalon.

21. Caramazza and Hillis (1991).

22. For a readable discussion of possible cellular bases of memory retrieval, see Johnson (1991). For psychological and computational theories of retrieval, see McClelland (1995) and Metcalfe (1993).

23. Proust's collection of novels is best known in English as *Remembrance of Things Past*. My reading and all quotes are based on D. J. Enright's recent revision of earlier translations by C. K. Scott Moncrief and then Terence Kilmartin. In the Enright translation (Proust, 1992), the series is titled *In Search of Lost Time*.

24. This quote and the following ones are from the most recently revised translation of *Swann's Way* (Proust, 1992, pp. 60–63).

25. This point is made eloquently in Shattuck's (1983) superb analysis of the role played by memory and time in Proust's work.

26. The letter is quoted in ibid., p. 46.

27. Ibid., pp. 46–47.

Selected Bibliography

Baddeley, A. (1986). *Working memory.* Oxford: Clarendon.

Bellezza, F. S. (1981). Mnemonic devices: Classification, characteristics, and criteria. *Review of Educational Research, 51,* 247–275.

Bower, G. H. (1972). Mental imagery and associative learning. In L. Gregg (Ed.), *Cognition and learning and memory.* New York: Wiley.

Capaldi, E. J., & Neath, I. (1995). Remembering and forgetting as context discrimination. *Learning and Memory, 2,* 107–132.

Caramazza, A., & Hillis, A. E. (1991). Lexical organization of nouns and verbs in the brain. *Nature, 349,* 788–790.

Carruthers, M. J. (1990). *The book of memory: A study of memory in medieval culture.* New York: Cambridge University Press.

Ceci, S. J., DeSimone, M., & Johnson, S. (1992). Memory in context: A case study of "Bubbles P.," a gifted but uneven memorizer. In D. J. Herrmann, H. Weingartner, A. Searleman, & C. McEvoy (Eds.), *Memory improvement: Implications for memory theory* (pp. 169–186). New York: Springer-Verlag.

Craik, F. I. M., & Lockhart, R. S. (1972). Levels of processing: A framework for memory research. *Journal of Verbal Learning and Verbal Behavior, 11,* 671–684.

Craik, F. I. M., & Tulving, E. (1975). Depth of processing and the retention of words in episodic memory. *Journal of Experimental Psychology: General, 104,* 268–294.

Freud, S. (1899). Screen Memories. In J. Strachey (Ed. and Trans.), *The standard edition of the complete psychological works of Sigmund Freud* (Vol. 3). London: Hogarth Press.

Freud, S. (1926/1959). Inhibitions, symptoms, and anxiety. In J. Strachey (Ed. and Trans.), *The standard edition of the complete psychological works of Sigmund Freud* (Vol. 20). London: Hogarth Press.

Freud, S., & Breuer, J. (1966). *Studies on hysteria.* (J. Strachey, Trans.). New York: Avon.

Gardiner, J. M., & Java, R. I. (1993). Recognising and remembering. In A. F. Collins, S. E. Gathercole, M. A. Conway, & P. E. Morris (Eds.), *Theories of memory* (pp. 163–188). Hove, United Kingdom: Erlbaum.

Hebb, D. O. (1949). *The organization of behavior.* New York: Wiley.

Hermann, D., Raybeck, D., & Gutman, D. (1993). *Improving student memory.* Seattle, WA: Hogrefe & Huber.

James, W. (1890). *The principles of psychology.* New York: Holt.

Johnson, G. (1991). *In the palaces of memory: How we build the worlds inside our heads.* New York: Knopf.

Koriat, A., & Goldsmith, M. (in press). Memory metaphors and the everyday-laboratory controversy: The correspondence versus the storehouse conceptions of memory. *Behavioral and Brain Sciences.*

Landauer, T. K. (1975). Memory without organization: Properties of a model with random storage and undirected retrieval. *Cognitive Psychology, 7,* 495–531.

Lorayne, H., & Lucas, J. (1974). *The memory book.* New York: Ballantine.

McClelland, J. L. (1995). Constructive memory and memory distortions: A parallel-distributed processing approach. In D. L. Schacter, J. T. Coyle, G. D. Fischbach, M.-M. Mesulam, & L. E. Sullivan (Eds.), *Memory distortion: How minds, brains and societies reconstruct the past* (pp. 69–90). Cambridge, MA: Harvard University Press.

Metcalfe, J. (1993). Novelty monitoring, metacognition and control in a composite holographic associative recall model: Implications for Korsakoff amnesia. *Psychological Review, 100,* 3–22.

Miller, G. A. (1956). The magical number seven, plus or minus two: Some limits on our capacity for processing information. *Psychological Review, 63,* 81–96.

Neisser, U. (1967). *Cognitive psychology.* New York: Appleton-Century-Crofts.

Neisser, U., & Harsch, N. (1992). Phantom flashbulbs: False recollections of hearing the news about *Challenger.* In E. Winograd & U. Neisser (Eds.), *Affect and accuracy in recall: Studies of "flashbulb memories"* (pp. 9–31). Cambridge: Cambridge University Press.

Neisser, U., Winograd, E., Bergman, E. T., Schreiber, C. A., Palmer, S. E., & Weldon, M. S. (in press). Remembering the earthquake: Direct experience vs. hearing the news. *Memory.*

Nickerson, R. S., & Adams, M. J. (1970). Long-term memory for a common object. *Cognitive Psychology, 11,* 287–307.

Proust, M. (1992). *In search of lost time: Swann's way* (Moncrieff, C. K. S., Kilmartin, T., & Enright, D. J., Trans.). New York: The Modern Library.

Roediger, H. L., III (1980). Memory metaphors in cognitive psychology. *Memory & Cognition, 8,* 231–246.

Schacter, D. L. (1982). *Stranger behind the engram: Theories of memory and the psychology of science.* Hillsdale, NJ: Erlbaum.

Schacter, D. L., Eich, J. E., & Tulving, E. (1978). Richard Semon's theory of memory. *Journal of Verbal Learning and Verbal Behavior, 17,* 721–743.

Semon, R. (1904/1921). *The mneme.* London: George Allen & Unwin.

Semon, R. (1909/1923). *Mnemic psychology.* London: George Allen & Unwin.

Shattuck, R. (1983). *Proust's binoculars: A study of memory, time, and recognition in "A La Recherche du Temps Perdu."* Princeton: Princeton University Press.

Spence, J. (1984). *The memory palace of Matteo Ricci.* New York: Viking.

Stein, B. A., & Bransford, J. D. (1979). Constraints on effective elaboration: Effects of precision and subject generation. *Journal of Verbal Learning and Verbal Behavior, 18,* 769–777.

Storr, R. (1992). *Dislocations.* New York: The Museum of Modern Art.

Vallar, G., & Shallice, T. (1990). *Neuropsychological impairments of short-term memory.* Cambridge: Cambridge University Press.

Vargha-Khadem, F., Isaacs, E., & Mishkin, M. (1994). Agnosia, alexia and a remarkable form of amnesia in an adolescent boy. *Brain, 117,* 683–703.

Watt, H. J. (1905). Review of *Die Mneme. Archiv für die Gesamte Psychologie, 5,* 127–130.

Yates, F. A. (1966). *The art of memory.* Chicago: University of Chicago Press.

EXPLORING THE TEXT

1. Pause for a moment after reading this selection to perform the following experiment. For the next five to ten minutes, write a summary of Schacter's "Building Memories." Try to include as much detail and as many key concepts and names as you can; try even to reproduce Schacter's order of presentation. Compare your results with those of your classmates and discuss why certain aspects of this selection are more memorable than others and what you could have done while reading to improve your recall.

2. What metaphors are commonly used to describe how memory works, according to Schacter? What other metaphors or analogies can you think of to describe how memory might work? What metaphor does Schacter suggest as an alternative? What's novel or unusual about this way of picturing the process of remembering? Why does Schacter feel it captures the workings of memory more accurately than the rest?

3. What is the difference between short-term, working, and long-term memory? Why, according to Schacter, are certain bits of information incorporated into

long-term memory while others are quickly forgotten? How are the principles of long-term memory applied in formal mnemonic training?

4. Why do people remember the same event or object differently, according to Schacter? How is it possible for Schacter to guess the occupation of the people involved in the art museum memory experiment involving Magritte's *The Menaced Assassin?*

5. What role do stories play in this selection? How do the stories of Bubbles P. and Richard Semon differ in terms of their functions? Why does Schacter elaborate on Semon's story in such detail?

6. In what sense are memories "constructed," according to Schacter? What role do the "retrieval cue" and the "engram" play in this process? What does Schacter mean when he says that the experience of memory compares a present and past experience, much in the same way that "stereoscopic vision emerges from combining information from the two eyes" (para. 58)?

FURTHER EXPLORATIONS

1. Compare the role of prior knowledge in the theory of memory presented by Schacter with its role in perception as described by K. C. Cole in "Seeing Things" (p. 75). What do both of these theories suggest about our ability to learn something that is radically new? How might you make such learning easier?

2. How might Schacter analyze the relation of retrieval cues to engrams in Scott Russell Sanders's "The Inheritance of Tools" (p. 142) and Loren Eiseley's "The Brown Wasps" (p. 150)? What events or objects call up memories for Sanders and Eiseley? How do the relationships between cues and memories differ in each of these essays? In what sense might the memories that Sanders and Eiseley relate be seen as products of the present as much as of the past?

3. Based on the claim that we "remember only what we have encoded, and what we encode depends on who we are" (para. 31), Schacter predicts the occupations and preoccupations of the individuals involved in Sophie Calle's experiment in artistic recall. Using the same principle, what can you tell about the interests, attitudes, values, and beliefs of Loren Eiseley (p. 150), Scott Russell Sanders (p. 142), Ian Frazier (p. 18), and/or Barry Lopez (p. 27), based on the memories they share in their writings?

4. Given that two people's recollections of a given event can differ dramatically depending on "our past experiences, knowledge, and needs" (para. 31), offer your own analysis of how and why Maxine Hong Kingston's retelling of her aunt's death (p. 206) differs so radically from the version her mother retains of the same event.

ESSAY OPTIONS

1. As a class, recreate Sophie Calle's experiment in recall by writing a description of a painting that you are all familiar with or of the image that serves as frontispiece to this chapter. Try to make your description as accurate and detailed as possible without referring back to the image you've chosen. Compare your descriptions in

small groups and discuss any differences that arise. To what extent do these differences in memory reflect differences that exist between the members of your group in terms of their experiences, interests, or background knowledge? Report the results of this informal experiment in an essay on the relative nature of memory.

2. As Schacter hints in this selection, the process of remembering establishes an interpretive relationship between present and past events, actions, people, or objects. When we remember, a present cue becomes associated with the engram of a past experience, and the two moments of time become fused—the past commenting on the present and the present on the past. Keeping this notion of the "stereoscopic" quality of recollection in mind, write an essay in which you explore the way that experiences, past and present, double and comment on each other in Scott Russell Sanders's "The Inheritance of Tools" (p. 142) and Loren Eiseley's "The Brown Wasps" (p. 150).

Memory and Imagination

PATRICIA HAMPL

Is memory ever just memory? Because memories have more in common with dreams than they do with legal transcripts, we rarely send a suspect to prison based solely on the remembered testimony of a single witness. And because memory depends so much on our point of view, we don't bother asking friends or relatives of the accused to offer their account of the night in question. In legal terms, the blurriness between memory and imagination makes every recollection suspect. That's one reason why courts allow cross-examination—to test the reliability of memory. But, as Patricia Hampl suggests in this essay, in the world of the writer, the mix of memory and fantasy is a source of deeper truth. Good writers, in Hampl's view, let their imaginations run wild, because they trust the mind to reveal its secrets regardless of how accurately memory cleaves to the concrete details of the past. They also understand that in the mental economy of recollection, only the most significant details persist through time—even if those details are actually the stuff of pure fiction. A poet as well as a memoirist, Hampl (b. 1946) is the author of *A Romantic Education* (1981), *Virgin Time* (1993), and *I Could Tell You Stories: Sojourns in the Land of Memory* (1999), as well as numerous articles and essays appearing in popular magazines and newspapers. She currently teaches English and creative writing at the University of Minnesota.

BEFORE READING

Freewrite in your journal about the earliest formal learning experience you can remember. What was the setting? What do you recall about your teacher, your fellow students, the lessons you studied? What details or stories come to mind when you return to this moment in your past? What feelings do you connect with this early educational experience?

When I was seven, my father, who played the violin on Sundays with a nicely tortured flair which we considered artistic, led me by the hand down a long, unlit corridor in St. Luke's School basement, a sort of tunnel that ended in a room full of pianos. There many little girls and a single sad boy were playing truly tortured scales and arpeggios in a mash of troubled sound. My father gave me over to Sister Olive Marie, who did look remarkably like an olive.

Her oily face gleamed as if it had just been rolled out of a can and laid on the white plate of her broad, spotless wimple.° She was a small, plump woman; her body and the small window of her face seemed to interpret the entire alphabet of olive: her face was a sallow green olive placed upon the jumbo ripe olive of her black habit. I trusted her instantly and smiled, glad to have my hand placed in the hand of a woman who made sense, who provided the satisfaction of being what she was: an Olive who looked like an olive.

My father left me to discover the piano with Sister Olive Marie so that one day I would join him in mutually tortured piano-violin duets for the edification of my mother and brother who sat at the table meditatively spooning in the last of their pineapple sherbet until their part was called for: they put down their spoons and clapped while we bowed, while the sweet ice in their bowls melted, while the music melted, and we all melted a little into each other for a moment.

But first Sister Olive must do her work. I was shown middle C, which Sister seemed to think terribly important. I stared at middle C and then glanced away for a second. When my eye returned, middle C was gone, its slim finger lost in the complicated grasp of the keyboard. Sister Olive struck it again, finding it with laughable ease. She emphasized the importance of middle C, its central position, a sort of North Star of sound. I remember thinking, "Middle C is the belly button of the piano," an insight whose originality and accuracy stunned me with pride. For the first time in my life I was astonished by metaphor. I hesitated to tell the kindly Olive for some reason; apparently I understood a true metaphor is a risky business, revealing of the self. In fact, I have never, until this moment of writing it down, told my first metaphor to anyone.

Sunlight flooded the room; the pianos, all black, gleamed. Sister Olive, dressed in the colors of the keyboard, gleamed; middle C shimmered with meaning and I resolved never — never — to forget its location: it was the center of the world.

Then Sister Olive, who had had to show me middle C twice but who seemed to have drawn no bad conclusions about me anyway, got up and went to the windows on the opposite wall. She pulled the shades down, one after the other. The sun was too bright, she said. She sneezed as she stood at the windows with the sun shedding its glare over her. She sneezed and sneezed, crazy little convulsive sneezes, one after another, as helpless as if she had the hiccups.

wimple: Head covering worn by Catholic nuns.

"The sun makes me sneeze," she said when the fit was over and she was back at the piano. This was odd, too odd to grasp in the mind. I associated sneezing with colds, and colds with rain, fog, snow, and bad weather. The sun, however, had caused Sister Olive to sneeze in this wild way, Sister Olive who gleamed benignly and who was so certain of the location of the center of the world. The universe wobbled a bit and became unreliable. Things were not, after all, necessarily what they seemed. Appearance deceived: here was the sun acting totally out of character, hurling this woman into sneezes, a woman so mild that she was named, so it seemed, for a bland object on a relish tray.

I was given a red book, the first Thompson book, and told to play the first piece over and over at one of the black pianos where the other children were crashing away. This, I was told, was called practicing. It sounded alluringly adult, practicing. The piece itself consisted mainly of middle C, and I excelled, thrilled by my savvy at being able to locate that central note amidst the cunning camouflage of all the other white keys before me. Thrilled too by the shiny red book that gleamed, as the pianos did, as Sister Olive did, as my eager eyes probably did. I sat at the formidable machine of the piano and got to know middle C intimately, preparing to be as tortured as I could manage one day soon with my father's violin at my side.

But at the moment Mary Katherine Reilly was at my side, playing something at least two or three lessons more sophisticated than my piece. I believe she even struck a chord. I glanced at her from the peasantry of single notes, shy, ready to pay homage. She turned toward me, stopped playing, and sized me up.

Sized me up and found a person ready to be dominated. Without intro-   10
duction she said, "My grandfather invented the collapsible opera hat."

I nodded, I acquiesced, I was hers. With that little stroke it was decided between us—that she should be the leader, and I the side-kick. My job was admiration. Even when she added, "But he didn't make a penny from it. He didn't have a patent"—even then, I knew and she knew that this was not an admission of powerlessness, but the easy candor of a master, of one who can afford a weakness or two.

With the clairvoyance of all fated relationships based on dominance and submission, it was decided in advance: that when the time came for us to play duets, I should always play second piano, that I should spend my allowance to buy her the Twinkies she craved but was not allowed to have, that finally, I should let her copy from my test paper, and when confronted by our teacher, confess with convincing hysteria that it was I, I who had cheated, who had reached above myself to steal what clearly belonged to the rightful heir of the inventor of the collapsible opera hat. . . .

There must be a reason I remember that little story about my first piano lesson. In fact, it isn't a story, just a moment, the beginning of what could perhaps become a story. For the memoirist, more than for the fiction writer, the story seems already *there*, already accomplished and fully achieved in history ("in reality," as we naively say). For the memoirist, the writing of the story is a matter of transcription.

That, anyway, is the myth. But no memoirist writes for long without experiencing an unsettling disbelief about the reliability of memory, a hunch that memory is not, after all, *just* memory. I don't know why I remembered this fragment about my first piano lesson. I don't, for instance, have a single recollection of my first arithmetic lesson, the first time I studied Latin, the first time my grandmother tried to teach me to knit. Yet these things occurred too, and must have their stories.

It is the piano lesson that has trudged forward, clearing the haze of forgetfulness, showing itself bright with detail more than thirty years after the event. I did not choose to remember the piano lesson. It was simply there, like a book that has always been on the shelf, whether I ever read it or not, the binding and title showing as I skim across the contents of my life. On the day I wrote this fragment I happened to take that memory, not some other, from the shelf and paged through it. I found more detail, more event, perhaps a little more entertainment than I had expected, but the memory itself was there from the start. Waiting for me.

Or was it? When I reread what I had written just after I finished it, I realized that I had told a number of lies. I *think* it was my father who took me the first time for my piano lesson—but maybe he only took me to meet my teacher and there was no actual lesson that day. And did I even know then that he played the violin—didn't he take up his violin again much later, as a result of my piano playing, and not the reverse? And is it even remotely accurate to describe as "tortured" the musicianship of a man who began every day by belting out "Oh What a Beautiful Morning" as he shaved?

More: Sister Olive Marie did sneeze in the sun, but was her name Olive? As for her skin tone—I would have sworn it was olive-like; I would have been willing to spend the better part of an afternoon trying to write the exact description of imported Italian or Greek olive her face suggested: I wanted to get it right. But now, were I to write that passage over, it is her intense black eyebrows I would see, for suddenly they seem the central fact of that face, some indicative mark of her serious and patient nature. But the truth is, I don't remember the woman at all. She's a sneeze in the sun and a finger touching middle C. That, at least, is steady and clear.

Worse: I didn't have the Thompson book as my piano text. I'm sure of that because I remember envying children who did have this wonderful book with its pictures of children and animals printed on the pages of music.

As for Mary Katherine Reilly. She didn't even go to grade school with me (and her name isn't Mary Katherine Reilly—but I made that change on purpose). I met her in Girl Scouts and only went to school with her later, in high school. Our relationship was not really one of leader and follower; I played first piano most of the time in duets. She certainly never copied anything from a test paper of mine: she was a better student, and cheating just wasn't a possibility with her. Though her grandfather (or someone in her family) did invent

15

the collapsible opera hat and I remember that she was proud of that fact, she didn't tell me this news as a deft move in a childish power play.

So, what was I doing in this brief memoir? Is it simply an example of the curious relation a fiction writer has to the material of her own life? Maybe. That may have some value in itself. But to tell the truth (if anyone still believes me capable of telling the truth), I wasn't writing fiction. I was writing memoir—or was trying to. My desire was to be accurate. I wished to embody the myth of memoir: to write as an act of dutiful transcription.

Yet clearly the work of writing narrative caused me to do something very different from transcription. I am forced to admit that memoir is not a matter of transcription, that memory itself is not a warehouse of finished stories, not a static gallery of framed pictures. I must admit that I invented. But why?

Two whys: why did I invent, and then, if a memoirist must inevitably invent rather than transcribe, why do I—why should anybody—write memoir at all?

I must respond to these impertinent questions because they, like the bumper sticker I saw the other day commanding all who read it to QUESTION AUTHORITY, challenge my authority as a memoirist and as a witness.

It still comes as a shock to realize that I don't write about what I know: I write in order to find out what I know. Is it possible to convey to a reader the enormous degree of blankness, confusion, hunch, and uncertainty lurking in the art of writing? When I am the reader, not the writer, I too fall into the lovely illusion that the words before me (in a story by Mavis Gallant, an essay by Carol Bly, a memoir by M. F. K. Fisher), which *read* so inevitably, must also have been *written* exactly as they appear, rhythm and cadence, language and syntax, the powerful waves of the sentences laying themselves on the smooth beach of the page one after another faultlessly.

But here I sit before a yellow legal pad, and the long page of the preceding two paragraphs is a jumble of crossed-out lines, false starts, confused order. A mess. The mess of my mind trying to find out what it wants to say. This is a writer's frantic, grabby mind, not the poised mind of a reader ready to be edified or entertained.

I sometimes think of the reader as a cat, endlessly fastidious, capable, by turns, of mordant indifference and riveted attention, luxurious, recumbent, and ever poised. Whereas the writer is absolutely a dog, panting and moping, too eager for an affectionate scratch behind the ears, lunging frantically after any old stick thrown in the distance.

The blankness of a new page never fails to intrigue and terrify me. Sometimes, in fact, I think my habit of writing on long yellow sheets comes from an atavistic° fear of the writer's stereotypic "blank white page." At least when I begin writing, my page isn't utterly blank; at least it has a wash of color

---

atavistic: Manifesting an earlier stage, style, or form.

on it, even if the absence of words must finally be faced on a yellow sheet as truly as on a blank white one. Well, we have our ways of whistling in the dark.

If I approach writing from memory with the assumption that I know what I wish to say, I assume that intentionality is running the show. Things are not that simple. Or perhaps writing is even more profoundly simple, more telegraphic and immediate in its choices than the grating wheels and chugging engine of logic and rational intention. The heart, the guardian of intuition with its secret, often fearful intentions, is the boss. Its commands are what a writer obeys—often without knowing it. Or, I do.

That's why I'm a strong adherent of the first draft. And why it's worth pausing for a moment to consider what a first draft really is. By my lights, the piano lesson memoir is a first draft. That doesn't mean it exists here exactly as I first wrote it. I like to think I've cleaned it up from the first time I put it down on paper. I've cut some adjectives here, toned down the hyperbole there, smoothed a transition, cut a repetition—that sort of housekeeping tidying-up. But the piece remains a first draft because I haven't yet gotten to know it, haven't given it a chance to tell me anything. For me, writing a first draft is a little like meeting someone for the first time. I come away with a wary acquaintanceship, but the real friendship (if any) and genuine intimacy—that's all down the road. Intimacy with a piece of writing, as with a person, comes from paying attention to the revelations it is capable of giving, not by imposing my own preconceived notions, no matter how well intentioned they might be.

I try to let pretty much anything happen in a first draft. A careful first draft is a failed first draft. That may be why there are so many inaccuracies in the piano lesson memoir: I didn't censor, I didn't judge. I kept moving. But I would not publish this piece as a memoir on its own in its present state. It isn't the "lies" in the piece that give me pause, though a reader has a right to expect a memoir to be as accurate as the writer's memory can make it. No, it isn't the lies themselves that make the piano lesson memoir a first draft and therefore "unpublishable."

The real trouble: the piece hasn't yet found its subject; it isn't yet about what it wants to be about. Note: what *it* wants, not what I want. The difference has to do with the relation a memoirist—any writer, in fact—has to unconscious or half-known intentions and impulses in composition.

Now that I have the fragment down on paper, I can read this little piece as a mystery which drops clues to the riddle of my feelings, like a culprit who wishes to be apprehended. My narrative self (the culprit who has invented) wishes to be discovered by my reflective self, the self who wants to understand and make sense of a half-remembered story about a nun sneezing in the sun. . . .

We only store in memory images of value. The value may be lost over the passage of time (I was baffled about why I remembered that sneezing nun, for example), but that's the implacable judgment of feeling: *this*, we say somewhere deep within us, is something I'm hanging on to. And of course, often we cleave to things because they possess heavy negative charges. Pain likes to be vivid.

Over time, the value (the feeling) and the stored memory (the image) may become estranged. Memoir seeks a permanent home for feeling and image, a habitation where they can live together in harmony. Naturally, I've had a lot of experiences since I packed away that one from the basement of St. Luke's School; that piano lesson has been effaced by waves of feeling for other moments and episodes. I persist in believing the event has value—after all, I remember it—but in writing the memoir I did not simply relive the experience. Rather, I explored the mysterious relationship between all the images I could round up and the even more impacted feelings that caused me to store the images safely away in memory. Stalking the relationship, seeking the congruence between stored image and hidden emotion—that's the real job of memoir.

By writing about that first piano lesson, I've come to know things I could   35
not know otherwise. But I only know these things as a result of reading this first draft. While I was writing, I was following the images, letting the details fill the room of the page and use the furniture as they wished. I was their dutiful servant—or thought I was. In fact, I was the faithful retainer of my hidden feelings which were giving the commands.

I really did feel, for instance, that Mary Katherine Reilly was far superior to me. She was smarter, funnier, more wonderful in every way—that's how I saw it. Our friendship (or she herself) did not require that I become her vassal, yet perhaps in my heart that was something I wanted; I wanted a way to express my feelings of admiration. I suppose I waited until this memoir to begin to find the way.

Just as, in the memoir, I finally possess that red Thompson book with the barking dogs and bleating lambs and winsome children. I couldn't (and still can't) remember what my own music book was, so I grabbed the name and image of the one book I could remember. It was only in reviewing the piece after writing it that I saw my inaccuracy. In pondering this "lie," I came to see what I was up to: I was getting what I wanted. At last.

The truth of many circumstances and episodes in the past emerges for the memoirist through details (the red music book, the fascination with a nun's name and gleaming face), but these details are not merely information, not flat facts. Such details are not allowed to lounge. They must work. Their work is the creation of symbol. But it's more accurate to call it the *recognition* of symbol. For meaning is not "attached" to the detail by the memoirist; meaning is revealed. That's why a first draft is important. Just as the first meeting (good or bad) with someone who later becomes the beloved is important and is often reviewed for signals, meanings, omens, and indications.

Now I can look at that music book and see it not only as "a detail," but for what it is, how it *acts*. See it as the small red door leading straight into the dark room of my childhood longing and disappointment. That red book *becomes* the palpable evidence of that longing. In other words, it becomes symbol. There is no symbol, no life-of-the-spirit in the general or the abstract. Yet a writer wishes—indeed all of us wish—to speak about profound matters that are, like it or not, general and abstract. We wish to talk to each other about life and death, about love, despair, loss, and innocence. We sense that in order to live together we must learn to speak of peace, of history, of meaning, and values. Those are a few.

We seek a means of exchange, a language which will renew these ancient   40
concerns and make them wholly and pulsingly ours. Instinctively, we go to our store of private images and associations for our authority to speak of these weighty issues. We find, in our details and broken and obscured images, the language of symbol. Here memory impulsively reaches out its arms and embraces imagination. That is the resort to invention. It isn't a lie, but an act of necessity, as the innate urge to locate personal truth always is.

All right. Invention is inevitable. But why write memoir? Why not call it fiction and be done with all the hashing about, wondering where memory stops and imagination begins? And if memoir seeks to talk about "the big issues," about history and peace, death and love — why not leave these reflections to those with expert and scholarly knowledge? Why let the common or garden variety memoirist into the club? I'm thinking again of that bumper sticker: why Question Authority?

My answer, of course, is a memoirist's answer. Memoir must be written because each of us must have a created version of the past. Created: that is, real, tangible, made of the stuff of a life lived in place and in history. And the down side of any created thing as well: we must live with a version that attaches us to our limitations, to the inevitable subjectivity of our points of view. We must acquiesce to our experience and our gift to transform experience into meaning and value. You tell me your story, I'll tell you my story.

If we refuse to do the work of creating this personal version of the past, someone else will do it for us. That is a scary political fact. "The struggle of man against power," a character in Milan Kundera's novel° *The Book of Laughter and Forgetting* says, "is the struggle of memory against forgetting." He refers to willful political forgetting, the habit of nations and those in power (Question Authority!) to deny the truth of memory in order to disarm moral and ethical power. It's an efficient way of controlling masses of people. It doesn't even require much bloodshed, as long as people are entirely willing to give over their personal memories. Whole histories can be rewritten. As Czeslaw Milosz° said in his 1980 Nobel Prize lecture, the number of books published that seek to deny the existence of the Nazi death camps now exceeds one hundred.

What is remembered is what *becomes* reality. If we "forget" Auschwitz,° if we "forget" My Lai,° what then do we remember? And what is the purpose of

Milan Kundera's novel: Milan Kundera (b. 1929), Czech novelist.
Czeslaw Milosz: (b. 1911), Czech novelist.
Auschwitz: One of the most infamous of the Nazi death camps during World War II.
My Lai: Site of a notorious massacre of civilians by American troops during the Vietnam War.

our remembering? If we think of memory naively, as a simple story, logged like a documentary in the archive of the mind, we miss its beauty but also its function. The beauty of memory rests in its talent for rendering detail, for paying homage to the senses, its capacity to love the particles of life, the richness and idiosyncrasy of our existence. The function of memory, on the other hand, is intensely personal and surprisingly political.

Our capacity to move forward as developing beings rests on a healthy relation with the past. Psychotherapy, that widespread method of mental health, relies heavily on memory and on the ability to retrieve and organize images and events from the personal past. We carry our wounds and perhaps even worse, our capacity to wound, forward with us. If we learn not only to tell our stories but to listen to what our stories tell us — to write the first draft and then return for the second draft — we are doing the work of memoir.

Memoir is the intersection of narration and reflection, of storytelling and essay-writing. It can present its story *and* reflect and consider the meaning of the story. It is a peculiarly open form, inviting broken and incomplete images, half-recollected fragments all the mass (and mess) of detail. It offers to shape this confusion — and in shaping, of course it necessarily creates a work of art, not a legal document. But then, even legal documents are only valiant attempts to consign the truth, the whole truth and nothing but the truth to paper. Even they remain versions.

Locating touchstones — the red music book, the olive Olive, my father's violin playing — is deeply satisfying. Who knows why? Perhaps we all sense that we can't grasp the whole truth and nothing but the truth of our experience. Just can't be done. What can be achieved, however, is a version of its swirling, changing wholeness. A memoirist must acquiesce to selectivity, like any artist. The version we dare to write is the only truth, the only relationship we can have with the past. Refuse to write your life and you have no life. At least, that is the stern view of the memoirist.

Personal history, logged in memory, is a sort of slide projector flashing images on the wall of the mind. And there's precious little order to the slides in the rotating carousel. Beyond that confusion, who knows who is running the projector? A memoirist steps into this darkened room of flashing, unorganized images and stands blinking for a while. Maybe for a long while. But eventually, as with any attempt to tell a story, it is necessary to put something first, then something else. And so on, to the end. That's a first draft. Not necessarily the truth, not even *a* truth sometimes, but the first attempt to create a shape.

The first thing I usually notice at this stage of composition is the appalling inaccuracy of the piece. Witness my first piano lesson draft. Invention is screamingly evident in what I intended to be transcription. But here's the further truth: I feel no shame. In fact, it's only now that my interest in the piece truly quickens. For I can see what isn't there, what is shyly hugging the walls, hoping not to be seen. I see the filmy shape of the next draft. I see a more acute version of the episode or — this is more likely — an entirely new piece rising from the ashes of the first attempt.

The next draft of the piece would have to be a true re-vision, a new see-   50
ing of the materials of the first draft. Nothing merely cosmetic will do—no
rouge buffing up the opening sentence, no glossy adjective to lift a sagging
line, nothing to attempt covering a patch of gray writing. None of that. I can't
say for sure, but my hunch is the revision would lead me to more writing about
my father (why was I so impressed by that ancestral inventor of the collapsible
opera hat? Did I feel I had nothing as remarkable in my own background? Did
this make me feel inadequate?) I begin to think perhaps Sister Olive is less
central to this business than she is in this draft. She is meant to be a moment,
not a character.

And so I might proceed, if I were to undertake a new draft of the memoir.
I begin to feel a relationship developing between a former self and me.

And, even more compelling, a relationship between an old world and me.
Some people think of autobiographical writing as the precious occupation of
a particularly self-absorbed person. Maybe, but I don't buy that. True memoir is written in an attempt to find not only a self but a world.

The self-absorption that seems to be the impetus and embarrassment of
autobiography turns into (or perhaps always was) a hunger for the world.
Actually, it begins as hunger for *a* world, one gone or lost, effaced by time or
a more sudden brutality. But in the act of remembering, the personal environment expands, resonates beyond itself, beyond its "subject," into the endless and tragic recollection that is history.

We look at old family photographs in which we stand next to black, boxy
Fords and are wearing period costumes, and we do not gaze fascinated because there we are young again, or there we are standing, as we never will
again in life, next to our mother. We stare and drift because there we are . . .
historical. It is the dress, the black car that dazzle us now and draw us beyond
our mother's bright arms which once caught us. We reach into the attractive
impersonality of something more significant than ourselves. We write memoir,
in other words. We accept the humble position of writing a version rather than
"the whole truth."

I suppose I write memoir because of the radiance of the past—it draws   55
me back and back to it. Not that the past is beautiful. In our communal memoir, in history, the death camps *are* back there. In intimate life too, the record
is usually pretty mixed. "I could tell you stories . . ." people say and drift off,
meaning terrible things have happened to them.

But the past is radiant. It has the light of lived life. A memoirist wishes to
touch it. No one owns the past, though typically the first act of new political
regime, to grab the past and make it over so the end comes out right. So their
power looks inevitable.

No one owns the past, but it is a grave error (another age would have said
a grave sin) not to inhabit memory. Sometimes I think it is all we really have.
But that may be a trifle melodramatic. At any rate, memory possesses authority for the fearful self in a world where it is necessary to have authority in order
to Question Authority.

There may be no more pressing intellectual need in our culture than for people to become sophisticated about the function of memory. The political implications of the loss of memory are obvious. The authority of memory is a personal confirmation of selfhood. To write one's life is to live it twice, and the second living is both spiritual and historical, for a memoir reaches deep within the personality as it seeks its narrative form and also grasps the life-of-the-times as no political treatise can.

Our most ancient metaphor says life is a journey. Memoir is travel writing, then, notes taken along the way, telling how things looked and what thoughts occurred. But I cannot think of the memoirist as a tourist. This is the traveler who goes on foot, living the journey, taking on mountains, enduring deserts, marveling at the lush green places. Moving through it all faithfully, not so much a survivor with a harrowing tale to tell as a pilgrim, seeking, wondering.

EXPLORING THE TEXT

1. Which elements of the story she tells in this selection are real, according to Hampl? Which are "lies"? How does Hampl view these embellishments? What impact does Hampl's confession have on you as her reader? What effect, if any, does it have on your appreciation of her memoir? Why?

2. What is Hampl's approach to writing? What is the purpose of the first draft, according to Hampl? Why does she consider the story of Sister Olive Marie and Mary Katherine Reilly a draft? How does she view the relation between memory, imagination, and writing?

3. What significance does Hampl begin to discover in the story of Sister Olive Marie and Mary Katherine Reilly? Why have these images lingered in Hampl's memory? In what other ways might this experience be meaningful to her?

4. What is Hampl's "narrative self"? How does this facet of her identity relate to her "reflective self"? How does the meaning of a memory emerge for Hampl? What role do concrete details—"touchstones" as Hampl terms them—play in this meaning-making process? Overall, what lessons does Hampl's exploration of memoir and memory offer about thinking and writing?

5. Why does Hampl write memoirs? Why does she believe that memories are both "intensely personal and surprisingly political"? (para. 44) What, if anything, strikes you as being political about the story of Sister Olive Marie and Mary Katherine Reilly? What does Hampl mean when she says that if you "refuse to write your life . . . you have no life"? Do you agree? Why or why not?

FURTHER EXPLORATIONS

1. How does Hampl's view of memory compare with that outlined by Daniel L. Schacter in "Building Memories" (p. 157)? To what extent do they agree about the factual accuracy of memory? How might Schacter explain Hampl's multidraft writing/remembering process in light of his discussion of engrams, cues, and memory retrieval?

2. Hampl claims that the purpose of memoir is the creation or recognition of "symbol." What symbols emerge from Scott Russell Sanders's "The Inheritance of Tools" (p. 142) and Loren Eiseley's "The Brown Wasps" (p. 150)? Why do these details strike us as more meaningful than the other matters of fact that Sanders and Eiseley include in their essays? Which details in these selections do you suspect might be "lies"—the product of the memoirist's creative imagination? Why do you think so?

3. How does Hampl's view of the relation between writing, memory, and imagination help explain the elusive style and complex structure of Loren Eiseley's "The Brown Wasps" (p. 150)? To what extent might his essay be read as an illustration of Hampl's claim that writing from memory always involves a "journey" and that every memoirist is, in a sense, a "pilgrim, seeking, wondering" (para. 59)?

4. Compare Hampl's notion of her "narrative" and "past" selves with the idea of "remembered" and "remembering" selves described by Susan Engel in "Then and Now: Creating a Self Through the Past" (p. 192). To what extent does Engel's theory of memory confirm Hampl's view of the craft of the memoirist? How might Engel's concept of "template" memories help explain the symbolic function of "touchstones" and their relation to emotion in Hampl's writing?

ESSAY OPTIONS

1. Expand the freewrite you did in the *Before Reading* exercise on page 180 into a draft of a personal memoir on an early childhood learning experience. Let yourself wander as much as you like, and feel free to invent as many details as you want. A day or so later, reread this draft, allowing your "reflective self" to probe the ideas unearthed by your "remembering self." What potentially significant details emerge from this experience? What feelings, additional images, or associations occur to you as you think about these "touchstones"? Write about the "discoveries" you make in this first draft, and then work through a second, allowing yourself to elaborate and expand on your initial memory, and trying, as Hampl says, to "explore the hidden relationship" between images and emotions.

2. Write a memoir based on a childhood photo showing you in a particular situation. Let your mind wander in the first draft from the setting in the photo to other scenes or places that rise up in your memory as you write. Tell the story of each scene in detail, striving to write as freely and creatively as you can. Like Hampl, don't hesitate about "inventing" details, characters, actions, and events. On second and third readings, what additional meanings emerge from the stories generated by this picture? Incorporate these ideas in your final draft as well as a brief analysis of the "past self" your writing reveals.

3. Drawing on Scott Russell Sanders's "The Inheritance of Tools" (p. 142), Loren Eiseley's "The Brown Wasps" (p. 150), and Barry Lopez's "A Passage of the Hands" (p. 27), write a paper exploring Hampl's assertion that "true memoir is written in an attempt to find not only a self but a world" (para. 52). What kind of worlds do Sanders, Eiseley, and Lopez seek to create through their art? How do these memory worlds compare? What is the relationship between the memory worlds they create through reflection and the wider "real" worlds they live in?

4. Write a paper in which you analyze your own writing processes. How did you approach assignments that you've already undertaken in this and other classes? How does your approach differ, depending on whether you're writing text-based, academic essays or more personal essays? How does your "thinking" or "creative" self differ from your "editing," "revising," or "critical" self? At this point in your development as a writer, what do you think you can do to improve your own writing process?

Then and Now: Creating a Self Through the Past

SUSAN ENGEL

As suggested in the epigraph that introduces this selection, memory is the mind's most "intimate" aspect. Our memories belong to us alone. They exist out of time and beyond the influence of daily events. Within the safe haven of memory, we turn to the serious work of fashioning a self: we weave the people we were at the age of three and seven and twelve together, shaping these different selves into a coherent personality—a "persona," or mask, that we wear as we venture out into the world. How we negotiate the tensions that arise between our present and past selves is the subject of this selection. As Susan Engel sees it, most people approach the past the way a novelist approaches the creation of a literary character: we shape and reshape our memories to produce selves that serve specific purposes and that elicit predictable responses from the audience we "play to" in the present. Engel is a lecturer in psychology and director of teaching programs at Williams College. Her publications include *The Stories that Children Tell: Making Sense of the Narratives of Childhood* (1995) and *Context Is Everything: The Nature of Memory* (1999), the source of this selection.

BEFORE READING

In your journal, write a brief dialogue between your present "self" and a past "self" you have ceased to be. How do these two aspects of your identity differ? What changes led to this difference?

Ideas and memories are the most intimate part of man, where nobody can scrutinize, where not even the harshness of the mountain can penetrate—the only thing that nature cannot easily transform. You nourish your memories, and when you lie down in your hammock at night you hold your memories close to you; you bring them out a bit into the world, you turn them over in your head, you parade them a bit, timidly in front of your eyes, though you never really see them. So you air these memories, and before going to sleep you return them very slowly to your brain, as if back into a spiral shell that is very gradually closing. You wind in your ideas once again, and probably your body curls up, too, I don't know—you start to gather in your ideas, to reel in your memories until they are all covered over and perfectly quiet, in the shelter of your brain, as if resting—and you sleep. You might say that the only umbilical cord, the only thread that still binds you to that past, or to that present which has become the past, is idea, memory.

— OMAR CABEZAS[1]

The Self as Personal Historian

We each believe ourself to be our own personal historian. We record events from the past, and dredge up others that we thought long since lost or buried. We start doing this as early as age three. As Jerome Bruner,° among others, has pointed out, it is clear that we do this instinctually. It seems to be an intrinsic part of being human to organize past experience and use it again and again.

The literary critic Daniel Albright suggests that we recall the past to understand and justify who we are. He casts this in a framework that I think extends to all of us when he says, "Psychology is a garden, literature is a wilderness." He argues that psychologists' goal is to cure people. They want to create coherence in order to allow people to figure out what their memories mean. For the research psychologist, this means finding patterns and predictability in what people recall and how they recall. For the clinical psychologist, this means knowing how to help others interpret the past so that patients can be freed from those elements in their memories that bind them in their current life.[2]

Writers, on the other hand, want to justify, and use the past to explain who they are, Albright argues. If you take a literary approach to thinking about memory, you are more likely to find idiosyncrasy rather than pattern, individuality rather than generalizations. The writer and the literary critic, in other words want the past to entertain, engage, and perhaps illuminate the narrator, and by extension or identification, the reader.

It is most likely that in everyday life most of us are part writer and part psychologist. We all use the past to justify who we are, but also to know and perhaps change or overcome who we were. We all have implicit theories regarding the patterns and logic of memory, and at the same time are immersed in the unpredictable specificity of our own memories and remembering experiences.

Whether one uses the past to justify or transcend one's past, whether one   5
views memory as predictable and explainable or murky and idiosyncratic, we draw upon memories as a source for the present. We dig out, amplify, and create autobiographical material as a way to know and communicate who we are now. But most often, this archaeological work happens in the company of others, even when those others are representations in our mind. Thus the internal work of creating coherence and meaning out of memories is never done in a social vacuum. We are always remembering in the company of others.

Jerome Bruner: (b. 1915), American psychologist and educational theorist.

At age two and a half, my youngest son, Sam, has discovered the power, and thus the meaning, of telling stories about things that have happened to him. He is as interested in stories he cannot remember as those he can. The urge appears to be simultaneously social and internal. He is creating a self for himself as he creates one for others.

He overhears me talking about the time when he was a newborn baby and his eldest brother, Jake, slipped down the stairs while holding him. How does he know this is an interesting story? What about the story is interesting to him? What flags it as a candidate for his autobiographical repertoire? He asks me to tell it over and over again. He tries to tell it to others, and then turns to me, asking me to fill in, end it, and add to it. Researchers have found that it is common for two-year-olds to collaborate with others (usually parents) in telling stories about their past.

He turns to an adult friend and begins, "When I was a born baby . . . (hesitation while he tries to find the words) Jake was holding me. And he fell, and he cried, and . . . (turning to me), Mommy, you tell the rest?" He wants to have that memory, and by telling the story he is trying to create it as a memory for himself. Equally, he wants to have a story to tell others—he is performing his memory for an audience.

What makes it a good memory for him? It is dramatic. It involves a fall and fear. Jake cried and assured me that the baby wasn't hurt. It involves action and emotion. Sam plays a central role. And everything comes out all right. It makes a good story, and a perfect one to fit into his emerging autobiography. He not only is a central character in the memory, but the memory demonstrates his powerful connection with a family member and the powerful effect their experience had on other family members. At this point in his life, Sam's personal stories don't fit together into an autobiography. At this age toddlers collect autobiographical memories. Not only do they not offer memoir-like narratives, they also are unable, even upon request, to tell their life story. It is not even clear that they have any sense of acquiring a collection of stories about the self.

All the young rememberer is capable of is choosing interesting episodes to   10 repeat, edit, and embellish. My son, like many toddlers, seems motivated to tell stories as a meaningful activity in and of itself (aside from the intrinsic interest of the specific information or material). But he does not view his life retrospectively. Nor can he tell you about events in his life on demand or with any kind of order, either temporal or thematic. This is not to say that his stories don't begin to contribute to his self-concept. They do. But in the first few years of life the connections between memories, the emerging themes, and the lines from early life to present life are not conscious. There is no evidence to suggest that young children have any explicit awareness of autobiography, life story, or even the ways in which their past experiences are tied to their current life. But the dimensions and nature of our remembering process undergo dramatic change in the first ten years of life.

The sheer capacity of our memory expands during early childhood. A ten-year-old can recall more items on a list than a four-year-old can. What is perhaps more important is that children become more conscious of their own memory, more deliberate about how and what they recall. When preschoolers are asked to remember a list of words or other quantity of information, they appear to do nothing special to aid their own memory. Older children use specific strategies, such as repeating the list to themselves over and over again, chunking the information in groups, or using simple mnemonic devices. The development of other important cognitive processes during this period also has a substantive effect on the way people remember. For instance, Sylvia Scribner and Michael Cole have shown that literate and nonliterate children differ in their tendency to use organizing strategies to help them with memory tasks.[3] Conceptions of the self have been shown to relate to how likely people are to talk about individual experiences from the past.

While there has been great interest in fledgling attempts by toddlers to recall and recount past experience, and considerable interest in the character and function of life stories in adulthood, only a handful of studies have looked directly at how children first tell their life story. It appears that children first share incidents about their past with parents, then with teachers, then peers. When an experimenter asks seven-year-olds to tell their life story, it is a novel task for them. Children range widely in how they approach the activity, from describing in detail the story of their birth to talking only about what has happened in the preceding four months. The sense of a ready-made life story, the kind an adult might offer upon demand (to a date, to a therapist, in an interview) doesn't seem available to children under the age of twelve.

Sam, for instance, doesn't yet have an implicit or explicit theory of his own remembering. His memories have not yet become objects for reflection. Nothing about his behavior (or that of any toddler observed in any study) suggests that he thinks about what his memories mean, how they relate to who he is, or anything about how he comes to recall what it is he recalls. And yet, autobiographical novels and autobiographies are replete with reflections on the memory process itself. It is not simply our memories and memory processes that develop. Not only do we develop an awareness of our own memory process, this awareness becomes integral to how and what we recall.

Sam, at two and a half is just realizing both the power and meaning of autobiographical memories. The memories are powerful for him internally because they give him an intoxicating, and necessary, sense of personal continuity—what Ulric Neisser° refers to as the extended self. The extended self is the sense that "I exist over time, and the same me was at the birthday party, falling down the stairs, eating cotton candy, going to the doctor, and it's the same me who is sitting here now thinking about all of that." This is probably one of the great epistemic discoveries one makes in life, similar in impact to the discovery that everything has a name.[4] It is the dawning awareness of the experiencing "I" that William James° talks about.[5] It is the awareness of

Ulric Neisser: (b. 1928), American research psychologist.
William James: (1842–1910), American psychologist and philosopher.

consciousness. The child is at first a remembering self, looking with admiration and interest at all his or her remembered selves, at the same time discovering and exploiting his or her capability to portray that self to others.

The Remembering Self and the Remembered Self

From his or her first autobiographical references, the young child experiences   15
a bifocal view of the past: the self looking backward and the selves one sees
in the past. The interplay among these selves is one of the most interesting dynamics that researchers, and everyone else who reflects on their memories,
confront. Penelope Lively's memoir, *Oleander, Jacaranda . . .* , exquisitely captures the double vision implicit in the adult memory of childhood experience:

> We are going by car from Bulaq Dakhrur to Heliopolis. I am in the back. The
> leather of the seat sticks to my bare legs. We travel along a road lined at either
> side with oleander and jacaranda trees, alternate splashes of white and blue. I
> chant, quietly: "jacaranda, oleander . . . jacaranda, oleander. . . ." And as I do so
> there comes to me the revelation that in a few hours' time we shall return by the
> same route and that I shall pass the same trees, in reverse order—oleander,
> jacaranda, oleander, jacaranda—and that, by the same token, I can look back
> upon myself of now, of this moment. I shall be able to think about myself now,
> thinking this—but it will be then, not now.
>   And in due course I did so, and perceived with excitement the chasm between past and future, the perpetual slide of the present. As, writing this, I think
> with equal wonder of that irretrievable child, and of the eerie relationship between her mind and mine. She is myself, but a self which is unreachable except
> by means of such miraculously surviving moments of being: the alien within.[6]

There is not simply one line of connection, one explanation for how the remembering self corresponds or creates links with the remembered selves. The remembering self is always a person in a specific situation, remembering for a particular reason. I recall my childhood in the company of good friends, eager to show them how outrageous I was as a child, or I recall an incident in anger and rage, eager to show my parent how unhappy I used to be, or I write about my early years as a way of explaining how I became a writer, and so on. Penelope Lively recalls her jacaranda chant as a way of opening her memoir of her childhood in Egypt during World War II. She at once gives you a sensuous experience of where she lived, the conditions of her childhood, and a way into her inner life. Why a person recalls what he or she does is shaped by the setting in which [the] person recalls. But it is also true that the way in which past and present selves are connected is shaped by the context of remembering as well. By context I mean both the form the memory takes (written, spoken in conversation, spoken in therapy) and also the mental context— what else one is talking about and why.

What are some of the ways in which the remembering self and the remembered self meet, and how do other people participate in this process? Most moments of remembering are not done alone in the process of self-understanding or self-contemplation. Many personal recollections that contribute to one's identity unfold in highly motivated and charged situations—where there are other people. You are trying to justify yourself, impress another person, show how you are the same, or different, from others. These situations then end up shaping one's life story as it emerges across time and place. In this way context plays a huge role in determining the self one knows through one's stories about the past. A colleague tells of the time his young daughter came home from her first day of school. He asked her how it was. "Not good," she said. "Really," my colleague replied, looking concerned. "What was bad about your day?" "The teacher made me spend the day in the closet." "Sophie, did that really happen?" he asked. "No," she said, looking serious and upset, "but it could have."

This poignant example demonstrates a common dynamic in memory exchanges. The past we describe is often determined more by unconscious feelings that are real even when not located in the events we recount, and our need to justify a feeling, to convince someone of something. Sophie may have been anxious about school. Perhaps her story reflects an important fantasy. Equally probable, her story had the effect on her listener that she wanted. It elicited from her father sympathy and collusion, a belief that her experience warranted her worried feelings about school. The tendency to use the past to convince others of one's construction of reality is even more pervasive and perhaps more problematic as we become adults. It may also be harder to detect, less flagrant when adults tell each other about the past.

A life story is usually a patchwork affair, unless you are an author, or perhaps, a politician. For most of us, different stories come out at different times; some are repeated until they are well-rehearsed yarns, while others may tumble out before one even knows what they are meant to signify. And the stories only cohere as a unified autobiography in the most subtle, inchoate way. In fact, most of the time people recall a story at a time, or a string of stories, rather than *the* life story. These stories may contain or stand for much more than the specific incident being recounted.

Often a particular reminiscence acts as a template, standing for a whole 20 strand of feeling or events in one's life. These templates can provide a stage on which to experience a form of transference. In other words, we then project onto that memory all the feelings and thoughts that we have toward a multitude of experiences and emotions for which it stands. The template memory, like the psychotherapist, becomes a stand-in for a set of unresolved feelings we cannot confront directly. A particular feeling or idea that has followed one through life is encapsulated in a given story. Telling it evokes the reactions and images that actually occurred across myriad incidents and events.

At other times, there is a strong urge to tell a sequence, a chronology of one's life events. But again, this is most often done in response to a particular social situation or interpersonal dynamic. Choosing and connecting specific happenings to create one's life narrative is usually done to satisfy very specific psychological and social purposes.

Finally, there are people who deliberately use the process of autobiography to re-create themselves. Again, this is at heart a response to being with others, and thus is best explained in interpersonal as well as intrapersonal terms. We all know of people, both privately and in the public domain, who create a persona that may turn out to be far different from whom they used to be. The most obvious examples of this are writers who convey a self through their published works that seems far different from the self they display in personal interactions. It is typical for people such as this to choose autobiographical information that supports the self they want to present to the world. But it is also true that this self-creation through selective memory is done with and for other people.[7]

In each of these cases, two seemingly opposing forces are at work. On the one hand is a person's need to experience him- or herself as continuous across time (the extended self). And on the other hand is the tremendous motivation to present what Erving Goffman° calls a face, a particular self that fits the current social situation and elicits satisfying social feedback. Most personal reminiscences bear the influence of these two forces. Those reminiscences, in turn, circle back and feed the constantly shifting inner self. Thus the self is shaped, at least in part, by the vagaries of the situations in which one recalls the past.

Self for Self and Self for Others

If we draw on our memories to create an ongoing sense of who we are in the present, how does this self for self relate or conflict with the different selves in the past we describe for others?

The sociologist Erving Goffman has described the ways in which we create different faces, or selves, in response to different social situations.[8] He illustrates the ways in which people collude in helping you to maintain a given face, or self-presentation. One of the ways we support or maintain these faces is to draw on memories that support the self we are presenting to others. In this way the self we construct through memory may shift to fit different social situations. For instance, when I am around family I am likely to tell stories about how strange I was as a child. This fits the family stereotype of me and fulfills my need to be seen as eccentric. It may also fulfill more subtle family dynamics. It may be a form of ingratiation, a way of pleasing my siblings by "one-downing" myself. On the other hand, when I am in an adversarial position on our local school committee, I am likely to tell stories about my past that illustrate my superior achievements, strengths, and skills as an educator. I may want to cow my colleagues and convince them I am an authority. Goffman argues that we present a face in each social setting, a self-for-others. Those others collude with us, helping us to maintain the self, or line, that we have established.

Erving Goffman: (1922–1982), American sociologist.

For instance, one might want to present oneself as lighthearted and easy-going. In that case, not only your way of talking and your manner, but also the stories you tell about yourself, highlight your lightheartedness. Those around you will help you maintain that face. They won't tend to challenge your stories but instead will give you feedback that deepens or strengthens your self-presentation. You are likely not only to choose stories that illustrate your light-heartedness but to tell about the past in a way that suppresses your serious side and underscores your easygoing side. In this way two different selves emerge in two different settings, each one connecting a line between different collections of memories.

And yet, we work hard to create and maintain a sense of inner cohesion and consistency in our self-concept. This is, to a large degree, what cognitive dissonance theory is all about. Elliot Aronson° refined the theory of cognitive dissonance and made it even more applicable to the study of autobiographical memory. He argued that we are particularly vulnerable to cognitive dissonance and its reduction when the conflict between a thought and an action or two contradictory thoughts involves our self-concept: we like to think of ourselves as good, decent people, and we like to believe we are consistent over time and across situations. Thus, any time our actions and/or beliefs threaten our self-concept as good, decent, smart, and consistent, our dissonance reduction mechanisms go into high gear. We reconstruct reality in a way that restores our self-concept. Aronson uses the example of smokers trying to deal with the plethora of information that shows that smoking is bad for you. How does one deal with the dissonance between the belief that you are smart, on the one hand, and the evidence that you are doing something that is stupid? Aronson suggests these three options:

> You quit smoking.
> You convince yourself there is no proof that smoking is bad for you.
> You say, "I'd rather live the way I want to even if it means I live briefly."

Comparatively few people choose the first. It is easier to construct an added argument that somehow closes the gap between the action and the belief (in this case, that I am a smart person and I smoke). The theory was not cast particularly as a theory of memory, but in fact this theory often can explain why people describe their past in the ways that they do.

To take a recent example, when the journalist Jon Krakauer recounts his participation in the disastrous 1996 climb up Mt. Everest in *Into Thin Air*, he needs to explain his contribution to the death of fellow climber Andy Harris in such a way as to maintain his self-concept as a decent and responsible person. He does this by highlighting his own altitude sickness, his exhaustion, and his difficulty with the cold after his struggle down the mountain during a

---

Elliot Aronson: (b. 1932), American social psychologist.

storm, and his mistaken belief that he saw Harris precede him into the safety of the campsite.[9] In this way he constructs the past in such a way that his dissonance is reduced. It would be the rare circumstance in which a person would recall an event from the past and say, "I was just a terrible person at that moment."

As another dramatic example, take Robert Jay Lifton's examination of Nazi doctors and their recollections of their murderous work in the concentration camps of the late 1930s and 1940s.[10] Their accounts provide mammoth rationalizations of how one could have taken the Hippocratic Oath° and then devote one's medical skills to torture and murder. In each case the doctor explained the seeming contradiction by reconstructing the surrounding boundaries of reality (Jews were gangrene of the body of mankind, and in order to save mankind, we had to remove the gangrene). In a few cases the doctors could not reduce dissonance this way, and ended up alcoholic, insane, or a suicide. No one simply said, "In that situation, at that time, I was a terrible person who did terrible things and so that is a part of who I am." Few people simply live with the feelings of dissonance, and memory provides us with an extraordinarily creative and potent tool for reducing dissonance about ourselves.

The social psychologist Anthony Greenwald has shown how the ego dominates the construction of events such that one's own role is not only placed at the center of an event, it is recalled in such a way as to maintain a positive and consistent self-concept.[11] We know, for instance, that people tend to overestimate their own contribution to a group effort (if five people work on a project, each of them will estimate their part as being more than one-fifth of the total effort).   30

Dissonance theory (and the many experiments it has spawned) helps explain why and how we recall the past in ways that shape our current sense of self. We change past experiences so that they confirm how we see ourselves in the moment. We want to know that in the past we were good and intelligent, and that there is some consistency between how we have acted and the self-presentation we offer in the present.

This brings us to a fascinating paradox inherent in the process of remembering the self. On the other hand, dissonance theory predicts (correctly) that we recall the past in a way that makes us seem and feel consistent. On the other hand, Erving Goffman has convincingly argued that there is no one self we present across all situations, that in fact we present different selves to suit different contexts.

One might say that the process of remembering oneself in the past is shaped by two opposing forces: the motivation to construct a consistent self and the motivation to re-create the self to fit differing social situations. Rather

---

the Hippocratic Oath: A pledge taken by medical doctors, promising to live up to the code of ethics established by Hippocrates (ca 460–377 B.C.), the "father" of modern medicine in the West.

than choosing between these forces as explanations for how we recall our-selves in the past, it seems more fruitful to say that memories of one's past are a result of the way in which these contrasting forces shape a given moment of remembering. For instance, imagine that your teenaged daughter has asked you about your sex life when you were a teenager. You worry that your daugh-ter feels bad that she doesn't have a boyfriend, that she thinks she is the only fifteen-year-old in the world who has never slept with a man. You want to de-scribe yourself as having been shy and inexperienced at that age. The situation calls for a particular description of that period of your life. But you are some-one drawn to describing yourself as wild, full of life and adventure; it is your tendency to choose those episodes in your past that illustrate your daring and sometimes foolish penchant for excitement. What will you tell your daughter? Probably a story that contains shades of both forces: in some ways your story will reveal your love of excitement even as a fifteen-year-old, and yet, will end with a view of you as similar to her: shy and inexperienced. You might achieve this by making the outer landscape one of loneliness ("We lived in the coun-try, honey, and my parents were strict: I rarely went out. I really didn't know that many boys"), and of inner wildness ("But I was very restless, I read lots of romance books, and made eyes at every guy who walked through the house"). . . .

The Memory as Template

In his poem "All Our Yesterdays," Jorge Luis Borges° reminds us that there are many memories of self in the past one might choose to think of or share with others:

> I need to know who lays claim to my past.
> Who, of all those I was? The Geneva boy
> Who learned some Latin hexameters with joy,
> Lines that the year and decades have erased?
> That child who searched his father's library for
> Exact details, the round-cheeked cherub storms
> Of the old maps, or else the savage forms
> That are the panther and the jaguar?
> Or the one who opened a door and looked upon
> A man as he lay drawing his last breath,
> Leaving forever, and kissed in the white dawn
> The face that stiffens away, the face in death?
> I am those that are no more. For no good reason
> I am, in the evening sun, those vanished persons.[12]

Borges reminds us that there are many memories of self in the past that one might choose to think of or share with others. What makes us recall a

Jorge Luis Borges: (1899–1986), Argentine poet, essayist, and author.

certain episode, and more to the point, why do certain episodes become staples of our internal autobiography? In Judith Sensibar's examination of the life and work of William Faulkner,° she claims that his early experiences of a racist culture (the deep South during the early twentieth century) and his unsatisfying relationships with a black mammy and a white mother provided powerful themes for much of his adult writing.[13] In this sense, she claims, Faulkner's autobiography can be unearthed from his fiction. She cites a memory he describes of himself at age 3, being carried by his black mammy.

> I will be awfully glad to see Vanneye again. The last time I remember seeing her was when I was 3, I suppose. I had gone to spend the night with Aunt Willie (in Ripley) and I was suddenly taken with one of those spells of loneliness and nameless sorrow that children suffer, for what or because of what they do not know. And Vanneye and Natalie brought me home, with a kerosene lamp. I remember how Vanneye's hair looked in the light—like honey. Vanneye was impersonal; quite aloof; she was holding the lamp. Natalie was quick and dark. She was touching me. She must have carried me.

Sensibar claims that this memory crystallizes Faulkner's sense of conflict between a beloved black mother, one whom he feels genuinely intimate with but cannot ultimately have, and a distant, aloof white mother. She argues that the memory is a screen memory and that it captures a theme of his life that became a theme of his fiction.

The idea of a screen memory is an alluring one. Freud coined the phrase to describe a memory that is a cover-up for a more dangerous, id-governed memory. Screen memories tend to be safe, moderately bland, and, according to Freud, always conceal some deeper material.[14] Sensibar suggests that a screen memory also serves to condense into scenario form the themes and issues that may have rambled through and pervaded life. How do we know Faulkner's memory is not a real memory? How do we know he didn't create it as a justification of the theme of racial tension in his books? It turns out that Faulkner first put this screen memory into writing soon after his work of fiction was published. It may be that he recalled this scene to make sense of his fiction. That doesn't make the memory untrue; it just helps explain how and why he recalled the scene when he did. As a single event, even if it happened just as Faulkner recalls, it is doubtful it caused him to have a lifelong conflict about maternal figures and race. It is likely that the memory stands for a series of events that represent a conflict running through Faulkner's life. It is also possible that as these themes began to emerge in his published writing, memories such as the one just described became salient to him as a way of explaining the themes in his fiction. Faulkner's memory is a good example of the way in which context determines what is recalled, and the way in which one's particular situation (writing novels in this case) causes one to forge particular links between past and present.

William Faulkner: William Cuthbert Faulkner (1897–1962), American novelist.

I have been describing the way in which a particular scene from the past serves to illuminate or explain a current aspect of the self. But is there any order or significance to the kinds of things we focus on in our recollections? In Sensibar's analysis of Faulkner's screen memory she notes the sense of disturbing illogic within the memory. She points out that on first reading it one finds a semblance of narrative coherence. Upon closer inspection the memory reveals a sense of unresolved and unexplained threads. In this sense, the order—or apparent disorder, as the case may be—provides a guide to interpretation. What is left out and what is put in, and the sense generated from the sequence of details and events, tell a lot not only about what happened in a person's life but what those memories mean to the person.

Many of an adult's most vivid or important memories of childhood convey that quality of disturbance, something unexplained, or unresolved. That sense of irresolution may fuel your need to recall it. As we develop and discover the sense-making power of the past, we may focus more and more on those memories that capture puzzles or ambiguities—just the things that we need to figure out who we are.

I have always recalled the dismal time I had when, at age 5, I had my tonsils taken out. I recall being told it would be fun, that I would get lots of candy and ice cream to eat. I recall waking up in the hospital, the night before the surgery, and playing a game of Space Bug with my mother, who stayed with me. I recall how wretched I felt when I came out of surgery, how shocked I was by the unexpected pain in my throat. And I recall the loving concern with which my divorced parents let me choose which of them should drive me to my home 2 hours away on Long Island. I also recall the misery I felt at having chosen my father, how much I really wanted my mother, but how carefully I acted like I was glad I had asked my father. Finally, I recall the stop we made at his mother's house so that I could sample her wonderful melon balls, but my throat hurt too much to enjoy them, and I was too miserable wishing that I was with my mother to enjoy anything.

What is more interesting than this sort of narrative that I have dredged up 40 now and then to myself, and to others, when talking about tonsillectomies, childhood hospital says, the game of Space Bug, is how and when the memory became truly meaningful and reconnected. Just a few years ago I was faced with a difficult job decision. My ambivalence and sense of total paralysis in the face of this decision were bewildering. In an effort to reach some clarity, I took a long, hot bath. I lay there tormenting myself about why a decision in which both options seemed so good would be so incapacitating to me. And that is the moment when I recalled the tonsillectomy and understood why I had continued to recall it. Because what was really meaningful about the memory was that I had been so overwhelmed by having to choose between my mother and my father. Two seemingly good choices.

And I had chosen the parent I thought I should choose—the one I didn't live with, the one I felt more ambivalent about, the one who might be hurt if I didn't choose him. Even though I really wanted to go with the other parent.

Having made the "good" choice, I regretted it terribly. That was what the memory really meant. The memory was always meaningful, always had a narrative form that gave it several points of entry, or connection. But any of these points of entry had to be "taken" for the memory to be used or experienced in any real sense. Memories can tell you what happened, but they feel so potent and powerful because they explain who you are. I knew all along what happened when I had my tonsils out, but when I realized how the memory illuminated who I am, a whole other level of meaning was added, not only to my present but to my past. And in discovering the real meaning of the memory, the core or locus of the event shifted for me. The operation itself no longer seemed to be at the center of the memory. The question of emphasis, so important in narrative studies, turns out to be central to understanding memory as well. Subtleties such as emphasis and tone are as important for understanding a construction of the past as are the grosser elements, such as the inclusion or exclusion of crucial details.

This example also makes clear that a template memory — a memory that stands for a large, more diffuse meaning of theme in a person's life — can be discovered unwittingly, or used deliberately. To begin with, I wasn't seeking out a story that would explain my difficulty making decisions. However, a somewhat self-reflective personality, combined with a moment that demanded self-understanding, catapulted me into the memory. Having uncovered the meaning of the memory and constructed it as a template for a theme in my life, I will now refer to it in a much quicker, neater fashion when trying to explain to myself or others the theme of indecision in my life. This suggests that the line from unbidden memory, to insight, to deliberate use is more fluid than one might think.

Notes

1. The quotation is from Omar Cabezas, *Fire from the Mountains* (New York: Crown, 1985), p. 205, an account of the Sandinista revolution.

2. See Daniel Albright, "Literary and Psychological Modes of the Self," in *The Remembering Self*, edited by Ulric Neisser and Robyn Fivush (New York: Cambridge University Press, 1994). The quotation is from page 19.

3. An excellent book that contains descriptions of studies of how people remember is Sylvia Scribner and Michael Cole, *The Psychology of Literacy* (Cambridge, MA: Harvard University Press, 1981).

4. See Ulric Neisser, "Five Kinds of Self-Knowledge," *Philosophical Psychology*, 1 (1988), 35–59.

5. See William James, "The Self," in *Principles of Psychology, The Briefer Course* (New York: Henry Holt, 1892).

6. The quotation is from page 1 of Penelope Lively's memoir, *Oleander, Jacaranda: A Childhood Perceived* (New York: HarperCollins, 1994).

7. In addition to autobiographical memory, there is a growing body of work on life stories and what is called the narrative approach to psychology. Two examples are Charlotte Linde, *Life Stories* (New York: Oxford University Press, 1993); and *The Narrative Study of Lives,* edited by Ruthellen Josselson and Amia Liebrlich (London: Sage Publications, 1993).

The recent exchange between and about the writers Paul Theroux and V. S. Naipaul is an example of people re-creating themselves. Theroux's *Sir Vidia's Shadow* (Boston: Houghton Mifflin, 1998) contains his perspective of this exchange.

8. Erving Goffman, *The Presentation of Self in Everyday Life* (New York: Anchor, 1959).

9. Jon Krakauer, *Into Thin Air* (New York: Willard, 1997).

10. Robert Jay Lifton, *The Nazi Doctors* (New York: Basic Books, 1986).

11. Anthony Greenwald, "The Totalitarian Ego: Fabrication and Revision of Personal History," *American Psychologist*, 35 (1980), 603–618, is a classic paper on the way in which we distort the past to maintain a good sense of self.

12. Jorge Luis Borges, "All Our Yesterdays," translated by Robert Mezey, *New York Review of Books* (December 1995).

13. From Judith Sensibar, "Writing Loss in a Racialized Culture," paper presented at the 1996 annual meeting of the American Psychological Association, Toronto, August 1996.

14. There is an excellent selection on screen memories in Peter Gay, *The Freud Reader* (New York: W. W. Norton, 1989), p. 117.

EXPLORING THE TEXT

1. What, according to Engel, is the relationship between memory and present identity? How does our understanding of this relationship develop as we mature? What does Engel mean when she refers to the notion of the "extended self"?

2. What is the difference between the "remembering" and the "remembered" self, in Engel's view? Between the "self for self" and the "self for others"? How are these concepts related to the idea of "persona" or "face"? How does the context of remembering influence the selves we create? Can you think of a time when you remembered a past event and the role you played in it differently for different audiences?

3. What is "cognitive dissonance theory," and why is the reduction of cognitive dissonance necessary to maintain the integrity of the "extended self"? What role does dissonance theory play in the paradox that Engel claims is inherently involved in the process of remembering the self?

4. What are "template memories"? How, according to Engel, do they relate to Sigmund Freud's concept of "screen memories"? Why, in her view, are these memories particularly useful? Can you think of any specific childhood memories you have had that you would categorize as template memories? Why would you view them this way?

FURTHER EXPLORATIONS

1. How would you describe the "personas" of the "remembered selves" presented in the personal memoirs of Barry Lopez (p. 27), Scott Russell Sanders (p. 142), Loren Eiseley (p. 150), and/or Patricia Hampl (p. 180)? To what extent do the "remembered" and "remembering" selves of these authors differ? What attitudes do each of these authors appear to take toward their past selves?

2. What similarities, if any, can you discover between the theories of memory presented by Engel and by Daniel L. Schacter (p. 157)? How similar, for example, is

Schacter's notion of the "stereoscopic" relation of cue and engram to Engel's theory of "bifocal" memory? What differences, if any, do you note in the way that they approach the topic of personal recollection?

3. How might Engel's notion of the "template memory" apply to the events recounted by Loren Eiseley in "The Brown Wasps" (p. 150) and by Patricia Hampl in "Memory and Imagination" (p. 180)? Would it also be possible, in your view, to categorize Eiseley's and Hampl's recollections as "screen memories"? Why or why not? How well can these categories be applied to the memories related by Scott Russell Sanders (p. 142) and Barry Lopez (p. 27)? Why?

4. In what sense does Maxine Hong Kingston create multiple versions of her aunt's persona in the multiple retellings of her aunt's death in "No-Name Woman" (below). Which of these personas does she prefer? How can you tell? What does this act of remembrance tell us about her sense of her own identity?

5. Read Eviatar Zerubavel's "Social Memories" (p. 217) and discuss how the concepts of extended identity and cognitive dissonance reduction might be applied to the way we as a nation remember major historical events like World War II, the Civil Rights movement, and the Vietnam War.

ESSAY OPTIONS

1. Return to one of the personal, memory-based essays you've written in this class and use it as the basis of a paper in which you explore the relation between your "remembered" and "remembering" selves. How did you shape your past self or selves? What motives in the present guided the choices you made about how to present your attitudes and actions? How are these past selves related to the "face" you sought, consciously or unconsciously, to project for your remembering self? To what extent did your audience influence the way you presented both your past and present selves?

2. Drawing on selections you have read by Loren Eiseley (p. 150), Patricia Hampl (p. 180), and/or Maxine Hong Kingston (below), write an essay discussing Engel's concept of "template memories." In your essay, offer your own detailed definition of template memories and explain how they are distinguished from other forms of recollection. What evidence of template memories can you find in the essays you've read in this chapter? In what ways do these template memories differ?

No-Name Woman

MAXINE HONG KINGSTON

Every family has its legends. Told around dinner tables, shared during holiday celebrations, or offered as valuable lessons in life, family stories are an important bridge to the past, linking us to heritage, culture, ethnicity, and nationality. The memories such stories convey can be a powerful source of personal identity, helping us appreciate the values, attitudes, and beliefs we inherit along with family membership. But sometimes these stories can also be disturbing reminders of behaviors and beliefs we would rather forget. In this excerpt from *The Woman Warrior: Memoirs of a Girlhood Among Ghosts* (1975), Maxine Hong Kingston struggles with the memory of an aunt who died in China before her father's family emigrated to the United States. Kingston's multiple revisions of her ill-fated aunt's life and death offer a telling illustration of the power of family stories and an example of how such tales can be reinvented to serve the purposes of freedom in the present. When Kingston (b. 1940) published *The Warrior Woman* in 1975, it became an instant success, almost single-handedly ushering in a new type of memoir — the story of growing up a second-generation immigrant in modern America. Since then, Kingston has published *China Men* (1980), *Tripmaster Monkey* (1989), and numerous poems, short stories, and articles in national magazines. Her most recent novel is *The Fifth Book of Peace* (2001). She currently lives in Oakland, California, and is a senior lecturer in the English department at the University of California, Berkeley.

BEFORE READING

Brainstorm a list of family "legends" — stories that you heard told repeatedly as you grew up about a relative or friend who had special meaning for your family. These legends might focus on the history of a grand- or great-grandparent, the exploits of a distant aunt or uncle, or the adventures of an early family friend or neighbor. Try to list as many as you can recall, and note what "lesson" seems contained in each of these tales.

"You must not tell anyone," my mother said, "what I am about to tell you. In China your father had a sister who killed herself. She jumped into the family well. We say that your father has all brothers because it is as if she had never been born.

"In 1924 just a few days after our village celebrated seventeen hurry-up weddings — to make sure that every young man who went 'out on the road' would responsibly come home — your father and his brothers and your grandfather and his brothers and your aunt's new husband sailed for America, the Gold Mountain. It was your grandfather's last trip. Those lucky enough to get contracts waved good-bye from the decks. They fed and guarded the stowaways and helped them off in Cuba, New York, Bali, Hawaii. 'We'll meet in California next year,' they said. All of them sent money home.

"I remember looking at your aunt one day when she and I were dressing; I had not noticed before that she had such a protruding melon of a stomach. But I did not think, 'She's pregnant,' until she began to look like other pregnant women, her shirt pulling and the white tops of her black pants showing. She could not have been pregnant, you see, because her husband had been gone for years. No one said anything. We did not discuss it. In early summer she was ready to have the child, long after the time when it could have been possible.

"The village had also been counting. On the night the baby was to be born the villagers raided our house. Some were crying. Like a great saw, teeth strung with lights, files of people walked zigzag across our land, tearing the rice. Their lanterns doubled in the disturbed black water, which drained away through the broken bunds. As the villagers closed in, we could see that some of them, probably men and women we knew well, wore white masks. The people with long hair hung it over their faces. Women with short hair made it stand up on end. Some had tied white bands around their foreheads, arms, and legs.

"At first they threw mud and rocks at the house. Then they threw eggs and 5 began slaughtering our stock. We could hear the animals scream their deaths — the roosters, the pigs, a last great roar from the ox. Familiar wild heads flared in our night windows; the villagers encircled us. Some of the faces stopped to peer at us, their eyes rushing like searchlights. The hands flattened against the panes, framed heads, and left red prints.

"The villagers broke in the front and the back doors at the same time, even though we had not locked the doors against them. Their knives dripped with the blood of our animals. They smeared blood on the doors and walls. One woman swung a chicken, whose throat she had slit, splattering blood in red arcs about her. We stood together in the middle of our house, in the family hall with the pictures and tables of the ancestors around us, and looked straight ahead.

"At that time the house had only two wings. When the men came back, we would build two more to enclose our courtyard and a third one to begin a second courtyard. The villagers pushed through both wings, even your grandparents' rooms, to find your aunt's, which was also mine until the men returned. From this room a new wing for one of the younger families would grow. They ripped up her clothes and shoes and broke her combs, grinding them underfoot. They tore her work from the loom. They scattered the cooking fire and rolled the new weaving in it. We could hear them in the kitchen breaking our bowls and banging the pots. They overturned the great waist-high earthenware jugs; duck eggs, pickled fruits, vegetables burst out and mixed in acrid torrents. The old woman from the next field swept a broom through the air and loosened the spirits-of-the-broom over our heads. 'Pig.' 'Ghost.' 'Pig,' they sobbed and scolded while they ruined our house.

"When they left, they took sugar and oranges to bless themselves. They cut pieces from the dead animals. Some of them took bowls that were not broken and clothes that were not torn. Afterward we swept up the rice and sewed it back up into sacks. But the smells from the spilled preserves lasted. Your aunt gave birth in the pigsty that night. The next morning when I went for the water, I found her and the baby plugging up the family well."

"Don't let your father know that I told you. He denies her. Now that you have started to menstruate, what happened to her could happen to you. Don't humiliate us. You wouldn't like to be forgotten as if you had never been born. The villagers are watchful."

Whenever she had to warn us about life, my mother told stories that ran 10 like this one, a story to grow up on. She tested our strength to establish real-

ities. Those in the emigrant generations who could not reassert brute survival
died young and far from home. Those of us in the first American generations
have had to figure out how this invisible world the emigrants built around our
childhoods fit in solid America.

The emigrants confused the gods by diverting their curses, misleading
them with crooked streets and false names. They must try to confuse their offspring as well, I suppose, threaten them in similar ways—always trying to get
things straight, always trying to name the unspeakable. The Chinese I know
hide their names; sojourners take new names when their lives change and
guard their real names with silence.

Chinese-Americans, when you try to understand what things in you are
Chinese, how do you separate what is peculiar to childhood, to poverty, in-
sanities, one family, your mother who marked your growing with stories, from
what is Chinese? What is Chinese tradition and what is the movies?

If I want to learn what clothes my aunt wore, whether flashy or ordinary,
I would have to begin, "Remember Father's drowned-in-the-well sister?" I
cannot ask that. My mother has told me once and for all the useful parts. She
will add nothing unless powered by Necessity, a riverbank that guides her life.
She plants vegetable gardens rather than lawns; she carries the odd-shaped
tomatoes home from the fields and eats food left for the gods.

Whenever we did frivolous things, we used up energy; we flew high kites.
We children came up off the ground over the melting cones our parents
brought home from work and the American movie on New Year's Day—*Oh,
You Beautiful Doll* with Betty Grable one year, and *She Wore a Yellow Ribbon*
with John Wayne another year. After the one carnival ride each, we paid in
guilt; our tired father counted his change on the dark walk home.

Adultery is extravagance. Could people who hatch their own chicks and
eat the embryos and the heads for delicacies and boil the feet in vinegar for
party food, leaving only the gravel, eating even the gizzard lining—could such
people engender a prodigal aunt? To be a woman, to have a daughter in starvation time was a waste enough. My aunt could not have been the lone romantic who gave up everything for sex. Women in the old China did not
choose. Some man had commanded her to lie with him and be his secret evil.
I wonder whether he masked himself when he joined the raid on her family.

Perhaps she had encountered him in the fields or on the mountain where
the daughters-in-law collected fuel. Or perhaps he first noticed her in the marketplace. He was not a stranger because the village housed no strangers. She
had to have dealings with him other than sex. Perhaps he worked an adjoin-
ing field, or he sold her the cloth for the dress she sewed and wore. His demand must have surprised, then terrified her. She obeyed him; she always did
as she was told.

When the family found a young man in the next village to be her husband,
she had stood tractably beside the best rooster, his proxy, and promised before they met that she would be his forever. She was lucky that he was her age
and she would be the first wife, an advantage secure now. The night she first

15

saw him, he had sex with her. Then he left for America. She had almost forgotten what he looked like. When she tried to envision him, she only saw the black and white face in the group photograph the men had taken before leaving.

The other man was not, after all, much different from her husband. They both gave orders: she followed. "If you tell your family, I'll beat you. I'll kill you. Be here again next week." No one talked sex, ever. And she might have separated the rapes from the rest of living if only she did not have to buy her oil from him or gather wood in the same forest. I want her fear to have lasted just as long as rape lasted so that the fear could have been contained. No drawn-out fear. But women at sex hazarded birth and hence lifetimes. The fear did not stop but permeated everywhere. She told the man, "I think I'm pregnant." He organized the raid against her.

On nights when my mother and father talked about their life back home, sometimes they mentioned an "outcast table" whose business they still seemed to be settling, their voices tight. In a commensal tradition,° where food is precious, the powerful older people made wrongdoers eat alone. Instead of letting them start separate new lives like the Japanese, who could become samurais and geishas, the Chinese family, faces averted but eyes glowering sideways, hung on to the offenders and fed them leftovers. My aunt must have lived in the same house as my parents and eaten at an outcast table. My mother spoke about the raid as if she had seen it, when she and my aunt, a daughter-in-law to a different household, should not have been living together at all. Daughters-in-law lived with their husbands' parents, not their own; a synonym for marriage in Chinese is "taking a daughter-in-law." Her husband's parents could have sold her, mortgaged her, stoned her. But they had sent her back to her own mother and father, a mysterious act hinting at disgrace not told me. Perhaps they had thrown her out to deflect the avengers.

She was the only daughter; her four brothers went with her father, husband, and uncles "out on the road" and for some years became western men. When the goods were divided among the family, three of the brothers took land, and the youngest, my father, chose an education. After my grandparents gave their daughter away to her husband's family, they had dispensed all the adventure and all the property. They expected her alone to keep the traditional ways, which her brothers, now among the barbarians, could fumble without detection. The heavy, deep-rooted women were to maintain the past against the flood, safe for returning. But the rare urge west had fixed upon our family, and so my aunt crossed boundaries not delineated in space. 20

The work of preservation demands that the feelings playing about in one's guts not be turned into action. Just watch their passing like cherry blossoms. But perhaps my aunt, my forerunner, caught in a slow life, let dreams grow and fade and after some months or years went toward what persisted. Fear at the enormities of the forbidden kept her desires delicate, wire and bone. She

---

commensal tradition: A culture in which all members are interdependent for their survival.

looked at a man because she liked the way the hair was tucked behind his ears, or she liked the question-mark line of a long torso curving at the shoulder and straight at the hip. For warm eyes or a soft voice or a slow walk—that's all— a few hairs, a line, a brightness, a sound, a pace, she gave up family. She offered us up for a charm that vanished with tiredness, a pigtail that didn't toss when the wind died. Why, the wrong lighting could erase the dearest thing about him.

It could very well have been, however, that my aunt did not take subtle enjoyment of her friend, but, a wild woman, kept rollicking company. Imagining her free with sex doesn't fit, though. I don't know any women like that, or men either. Unless I see her life branching into mine, she gives me no ancestral help.

To sustain her being in love, she often worked at herself in the mirror, guessing at the colors and shapes that would interest him, changing them frequently in order to hit on the right combination. She wanted him to look back.

On a farm near the sea, a woman who tended her appearance reaped a reputation for eccentricity. All the married women blunt-cut their hair in flaps about their ears or pulled it back in tight buns. No nonsense. Neither style blew easily into heart-catching tangles. And at their weddings they displayed themselves in their long hair for the last time. "It brushed the backs of my knees," my mother tells me. "It was braided, and even so, it brushed the backs of my knees."

At the mirror my aunt combed individuality into her bob. A bun could have been contrived to escape into black streamers blowing in the wind or in quiet wisps about her face, but only the older women in our picture album wear buns. She brushed her hair back from her forehead, tucking the flaps behind her ears. She looped a piece of thread, knotted into a circle between her index fingers and thumbs, and ran the double strand across her forehead. When she closed her fingers as if she were making a pair of shadow geese bite, the string twisted together catching the little hairs. Then she pulled the thread away from her skin, ripping the hairs out neatly, her eyes watering from the needles of pain. Opening her fingers she cleaned the thread, then rolled it along her hairline and the tops of her eyebrows. My mother did the same to me and my sisters and herself. I used to believe that the expression "caught by the short hairs" meant a captive held with a depilatory string. It especially hurt at the temples, but my mother said we were lucky we didn't have to have our feet bound when we were seven. Sisters used to sit on their beds and cry together, she said, as their mothers or their slaves removed the bandages for a few minutes each night and let the blood gush back into their veins. I hope that the man my aunt loved appreciated a smooth brow, that he wasn't just a tits-and-ass man.

Once my aunt found a freckle on her chin, at a spot that the almanac said predestined her for unhappiness. She dug it out with a hot needle and washed the wound with peroxide.

More attention to her looks than these pullings of hairs and picking at spots would have caused gossip among the villagers. They owned work clothes and good clothes, and they wore good clothes for feasting the new seasons. But since a woman combing her hair hexes beginnings, my aunt rarely found an occasion to look her best. Women looked like great sea snails — the corded wood, babies, and laundry they carried were the whorls on their backs. The Chinese did not admire a bent back; goddesses and warriors stood straight. Still there must have been a marvelous freeing of beauty when a worker laid down her burden and stretched and arched.

Such commonplace loveliness, however, was not enough for my aunt. She dreamed of a lover for the fifteen days of New Year's, the time for families to exchange visits, money, and food. She plied her secret comb. And sure enough she cursed the year, the family, the village, and herself.

Even as her hair lured her imminent lover, many other men looked at her. Uncles, cousins, nephews, brothers would have looked, too, had they been home between journeys. Perhaps they had already been restraining their curiosity, and they left, fearful that their glances, like a field of nesting birds, might be startled and caught. Poverty hurt, and that was their first reason for leaving. But another, final reason for leaving the crowded house was the never-said.

She may have been unusually beloved, the precious only daughter, spoiled 30 and mirror gazing because of the affection the family lavished on her. When her husband left, they welcomed the chance to take her back from the in-laws; she could live like the little daughter for just a while longer. There are stories that my grandfather was different from other people, "crazy ever since the little Jap bayoneted him in the head." He used to put his naked penis on the dinner table, laughing. And one day he brought home a baby girl, wrapped up inside his brown western-style greatcoat. He had traded one of his sons, probably my father, the youngest, for her. My grandmother made him trade back. When he finally got a daughter of his own, he doted on her. They must have all loved her, except perhaps my father, the only brother who never went back to China, having once been traded for a girl.

Brothers and sisters, newly men and women, had to efface their sexual color and present plain miens. Disturbing hair and eyes, a smile like no other, threatened the ideal of five generations living under one roof. To focus blurs, people shouted face to face and yelled from room to room. The immigrants I know have loud voices, unmodulated to American tones even after years away from the village where they called their friendships out across the fields. I have not been able to stop my mother's screams in public libraries or over telephones. Walking erect (knees straight, toes pointed forward, not pigeon-toed, which is Chinese-feminine) and speaking in an inaudible voice, I have tried to turn myself American-feminine. Chinese communication was loud, public. Only sick people had to whisper. But at the dinner table, where the family members came nearest one another, no one could talk, not the outcasts nor any eaters. Every word that falls from the mouth is a coin lost. Silently they gave and accepted food with both hands. A preoccupied child who took his bowl with one hand got a sideways glare. A complete moment of total attention is due everyone alike. Children and lovers have no singularity here, but my aunt used a secret voice, a separate attentiveness.

She kept the man's name to herself throughout her labor and dying; she did not accuse him that he be punished with her. To save her inseminator's name she gave silent birth.

He may have been somebody in her own household, but intercourse with a man outside the family would have been no less abhorrent. All the village were kinsmen, and the titles shouted in loud country voices never let kinship be forgotten. Any man within visiting distance would have been neutralized as a lover—"brother," "younger brother," "older brother"—one hundred and fifteen relationship titles. Parents researched birth charts probably not so much to assure good fortune as to circumvent incest in a population that has but one hundred surnames. Everybody has eight million relatives. How useless then sexual mannerisms, how dangerous.

As if it came from an atavism° deeper than fear, I used to add "brother" silently to boys' names. It hexed the boys, who would or would not ask me to dance, and made them less scary and as familiar and deserving of benevolence as girls.

But, of course, I hexed myself also—no dates. I should have stood up, both arms waving, and shouted out across libraries, "Hey, you! Love me back." I had no idea, though, how to make attraction selective, how to control its direction and magnitude. If I made myself American-pretty so that the five or six Chinese boys in the class fell in love with me, everyone else—the Caucasian, Negro, and Japanese boys—would too. Sisterliness, dignified and honorable, made much more sense.

Attraction eludes control so stubbornly that whole societies designed to organize relationships among people cannot keep order, not even when they bind people to one another from childhood and raise them together. Among the very poor and the wealthy, brothers married their adopted sisters, like doves. Our family allowed some romance, paying adult brides' prices and providing dowries so that their sons and daughters could marry strangers. Marriage promises to turn strangers into friendly relatives—a nation of siblings.

In the village structure, spirits shimmered among the live creatures, balanced and held in equilibrium by time and land. But one human being flaring up into violence could open up a black hole, a maelstrom that pulled in the sky. The frightened villagers, who depended on one another to maintain the real, went to my aunt to show her a personal, physical representation of the break she had made in the "roundness." Misallying couples snapped off the future, which was to be embodied in true offspring. The villagers punished her for acting as if she could have a private life, secret and apart from them.

---

atavism: A recurrence of or a reversion to a past style, form, manner, outlook, or approach; hence, a throwback.

If my aunt had betrayed the family at a time of large grain yields and peace, when many boys were born, and wings were being built on many houses, perhaps she might have escaped such severe punishment. But the men—hungry, greedy, tired of planting in dry soil—had been forced to leave the village in order to send food-money home. There were ghost plagues, bandit plagues, wars with the Japanese, floods. My Chinese brother and sister had died of an unknown sickness. Adultery, perhaps only a mistake during good times, became a crime when the village needed food.

The round moon cakes and round doorways, the round tables of graduated sizes that fit one roundness inside another, round windows and rice bowls—these talismans had lost their power to warn this family of the law: a family must be whole, faithfully keeping the descent line by having sons to feed the old and the dead, who in turn look after the family. The villagers came to show my aunt and her lover-in-hiding a broken house. The villagers were speeding up the circling of events because she was too shortsighted to see that her infidelity had already harmed the village, that waves of consequences would return unpredictably, sometimes in disguise, as now, to hurt her. This roundness had to be made coin-sized so that she would see its circumference: punish her at the birth of her baby. Awaken her to the inexorable. People who refused fatalism because they could invent small resources insisted on culpability. Deny accidents and wrest fault from the stars.

After the villagers left, their lanterns now scattering in various directions toward home, the family broke their silence and cursed her. "Aiaa, we're going to die. Death is coming. Death is coming. Look what you've done. You've killed us. Ghost! Dead ghost! Ghost! You've never been born." She ran out into the fields, far enough from the house so that she could no longer hear their voices, and pressed herself against the earth, her own land no more. When she felt the birth coming, she thought that she had been hurt. Her body seized together. "They've hurt me too much," she thought. "This is gall, and it will kill me." With forehead and knees against the earth, her body convulsed and then relaxed. She turned on her back, lay on the ground. The black well of sky and stars went out and out and out forever; her body and her complexity seemed to disappear. She was one of the stars, a bright dot in blackness, without home, without a companion, in eternal cold and silence. An agoraphobia rose in her, speeding higher and higher, bigger and bigger; she would not be able to contain it; there would be no end to fear.

Flayed, unprotected against space, she felt pain return, focusing her body. This pain chilled her—a cold, steady kind of surface pain. Inside, spasmodically, the other pain, the pain of the child, heated her. For hours she lay on the ground, alternately body and space. Sometimes a vision of normal comfort obliterated reality: she saw the family in the evening gambling at the dinner table, the young people massaging their elders' backs. She saw them congratulating one another, high joy on the mornings the rice shoots came up. When these pictures burst, the stars drew yet further apart. Black space opened.

She got to her feet to fight better and remembered that old-fashioned women gave birth in their pigsties to fool the jealous, pain-dealing gods, who do not snatch piglets. Before the next spasms could stop her, she ran to the pigsty, each step a rushing out into emptiness. She climbed over the fence and knelt in the dirt. It was good to have a fence enclosing her, a tribal person alone.

Laboring, this woman who had carried her child as a foreign growth that sickened her every day, expelled it at last. She reached down to touch the hot, wet, moving mass, surely smaller than anything human, and could feel that it was human after all—fingers, toes, nails, nose. She pulled it up on to her belly, and it lay curled there, butt in the air, feet precisely tucked one under the other. She opened her loose shirt and buttoned the child inside. After resting, it squirmed and thrashed and she pushed it up to her breast. It turned its head this way and that until it found her nipple. There, it made little snuffling noises. She clenched her teeth at its preciousness, lovely as a young calf, a piglet, a little dog.

She may have gone to the pigsty as a last act of responsibility: she would protect this child as she had protected its father. It would look after her soul, leaving supplies on her grave. But how would this tiny child without family find her grave when there would be no marker for her anywhere, neither in the earth nor the family hall? No one would give her a family hall name. She had taken the child with her into the wastes. At its birth the two of them had felt the same raw pain of separation, a wound that only the family pressing tight could close. A child with no descent line would not soften her life but only trail after her, ghostlike, begging her to give it purpose. At dawn the villagers on their way to the fields would stand around the fence and look.

Full of milk, the little ghost slept. When it awoke, she hardened her breasts against the milk that crying loosens. Toward morning she picked up the baby and walked to the well. 45

Carrying the baby to the well shows loving. Otherwise abandon it. Turn its face into the mud. Mothers who love their children take them along. It was probably a girl; there is some hope of forgiveness for boys.

"Don't tell anyone you had an aunt. Your father does not want to hear her name. She has never been born." I have believed that sex was unspeakable and words so strong and fathers so frail that "aunt" would do my father mysterious harm. I have thought that my family, having settled among immigrants who had also been their neighbors in the ancestral land, needed to clean their name, and a wrong word would incite the kinspeople even here. But there is more to this silence: they want me to participate in her punishment. And I have.

In the twenty years since I heard this story I have not asked for details nor said my aunt's name; I do not know it. People who can comfort the dead can also chase after them to hurt them further—a reverse ancestor worship. The real punishment was not the raid swiftly inflicted by the villagers, but the family's deliberately forgetting her. Her betrayal so maddened them, they saw to it that she would suffer forever, even after death. Always hungry, always needing, she would have to beg food from other ghosts, snatch and steal it from those whose living descendants give them gifts. She would have to fight the ghosts massed at crossroads for the buns a few thoughtful citizens leave to decoy her away from village and home so that the ancestral spirits could feast unharassed. At peace, they could act like gods, not ghosts, their descent lines providing them with paper suits and dresses, spirit money, paper houses, paper automobiles, chicken, meat, and rice into eternity—essences delivered up in smoke and flames, steam and incense rising from each rice bowl. In an attempt to make the Chinese care for people outside the family, Chairman Mao° encourages us now to give our paper replicas to the spirits of outstanding soldiers and workers, no matter whose ancestors they may be. My aunt remains forever hungry. Goods are not distributed evenly among the dead.

My aunt haunts me—her ghost drawn to me because now, after fifty years of neglect, I alone devote pages of paper to her, though not origamied into houses and clothes. I do not think she always means me well. I am telling on her, and she was a spite suicide, drowning herself in the drinking water. The Chinese are always very frightened of the drowned one, whose weeping ghost, wet hair hanging and skin bloated, waits silently by the water to pull down a substitute.

Chairman Mao: Mao Zedong (1893–1976), Communist leader of the People's Republic of China from 1949 to 1976.

EXPLORING THE TEXT

1. Briefly summarize the story of Kingston's aunt. Why does her mother tell her this family legend? What lesson is she supposed to learn from it? How does Kingston feel about this?

2. What are the facts of village life in relation to gender roles and male/female behavior, according to Kingston? In general, what seems to be Kingston's attitude toward the village, its customs, values, and beliefs?

3. How does Kingston interpret her aunt's motives for engaging in an extramarital affair? How many different reasons does she explore for her aunt's behavior? How does her characterization of her aunt change as she explores these different reasons? Which version of her aunt do you find most plausible? Why?

4. How does Kingston interpret her aunt's death? To what extent does Kingston sympathize with her aunt by the end of the story? How would the story of Kingston's aunt change if told from the point of view of the villagers? How would they have explained her aunt's motives for entering into an extramarital relationship? How would they have interpreted her final actions?

5. What does Kingston mean when she says that the real punishment was her family's "deliberately forgetting" her aunt's story? How would you characterize Kingston's attitude toward the past? Toward memory?

FURTHER EXPLORATIONS

1. Which elements of Kingston's story of her aunt are probably based on the "facts" of the tale as she heard it from her mother? Which elements are probably "lies" that she invented in the style of Patricia Hampl (p. 180)? How can you tell? Which of these aspects of the story do you find the most interesting? Why?

2. Keeping Susan Engel's distinction between "remembering" and "remembered" selves in mind (p. 192), discuss the different "personas" that Kingston creates for her aunt. How do these remembered versions of her aunt reflect the persona of the remembering self that Kingston presents her readers? What "cognitive dissonance," if any, do you detect in Kingston's retelling of this family story?

3. In what ways do Kingston's imaginative revisions of her aunt's story confirm or complicate Eviatar Zerubavel's view of the role that family and cultural stories play in our lives (below)? Do Kingston's revisions of her aunt's story reinforce or subvert cultural memory? To what extent do they tie her to or free her from her cultural heritage?

ESSAY OPTIONS

1. Using the *Before Reading* activity on page 207 as a point of departure, write a personal essay in which you offer your own retelling — or retellings — of a story that has been passed down within your family. Use your imagination to detail the scene of your story as fully as possible, much as Kingston does in her account of her aunt's life in China. Try, also, to speculate as Kingston does about the personality, values, and motives of the actors featured in your story. Finally, spend some time thinking about what this story and the figures in it mean to you. How has it affected — or "haunted" — you? What lessons is it meant to teach? How has your revision of it altered these lessons?

2. Drawing on the personal experiences of Kingston, Loren Eiseley (p. 150), and Patricia Hampl (p. 180), and on the ideas presented by Eviatar Zerubavel (below), and/or bell hooks (p. 237), write an essay on the politics of memory. To what extent do these selections confirm Hampl's belief that every act of remembering is a political act? Would you agree that every act of memory is a "struggle" against the powers that foster forgetting?

Social Memories

EVIATAR ZERUBAVEL

Remember the Alamo? If not, how about the *Dred Scott* decision, the Zoot Suit riots, Stonewall, My Lai, Deep Throat, Saddam, or the impeachment of William Jefferson Clinton? Our minds brim with memories of people, places, and events we have never personally experienced. Every May we remember wars that few of us likely ever fought in. Every February during Black History month, we remember the story of Martin Luther King Jr. and the struggles of the Civil Rights movement, although few if any of us can personally recall marching to Selma or supporting Rosa Parks in her famous act of civil disobedience. According to Eviatar Zerubavel, we all share thousands of such "impersonal" memories, memories that we acquire as the result of our membership in the different "mnemonic communities" to which we belong. As Zerubavel indicates, these impersonal memories play a crucial role in our personal relationship to the past, just as the battles we wage over what we commemorate speak volumes about our cultural identity and the politics of collective memory. Zerubavel is professor of sociology at Rutgers University and the author of *Hidden Rhythms* (1981), *The Seven-Day Circle* (1985), and *The Fine Line* (1991). This selection originally appeared in *Social Mindscapes: An Invitation of Cognitive Sociology* (1997).

BEFORE READING

Working in groups, brainstorm a list of all the people, places, events, and dates you think should be included in the "collective memory" of every American citizen. What, if anything, should every legal resident of the United States be expected to know about the American past? Why?

N ot only does our social environment influence the way we mentally process the present, it also affects the way we remember the past. Like the present, the past is to some extent also part of a social reality that, while far from being absolutely objective, nonetheless transcends our own subjectivity and is shared by others around us.

As evident from the universalistic tendency of those who study memory today to focus primarily on the formal aspects of the processes of organizing, storing, and accessing memories which we all share, they are largely interested in how *humans* remember past events. And yet, when they come to examine the actual contents of those memories, they usually go to the other extreme and focus on the individual. Nowhere is this individualistic bent more glaringly evident than in psychoanalysis, which deals almost exclusively with our distinctly personal memories.

Once again one can identify a relatively unexplored intellectual terrain made up of various "remembrance environments" lying somewhere between the strictly personal and the absolutely universal. These environments (which include, for example, the family, the workplace, the profession, the fan club, the ethnic group, the religious community, and the nation) are all larger than the individual yet at the same time considerably smaller than the entire human race.

Admittedly, there are various universal patterns of organizing, storing, and accessing past experiences that indeed characterize *all* human beings and actually distinguish human memory from that of dogs, spiders, or parrots. At the same time, it is also quite clear that we each have our own unique autobiographical memories, made up of absolutely personal experiences that we share with nobody else. Yet we also happen to have certain memories which we share with some people but not with others. Thus, for example, there are certain memories commonly shared by most Guatemalans or art historians yet only by few Australians or marine biologists. By the same token, there are many memories shared by nearly all Beatles fans, stamp collectors, or long-time readers of *Mad Magazine,* yet by no one else besides them. The unmistakably common nature of such memories indicates that they are clearly not just personal. At the same time, the fact that they are almost exclusively confined to a particular thought community shows that they are not entirely universal either.

Such memories constitute the distinctive domain of the *sociology of mem-*   5 *ory,* which, unlike any of the other cognitive sciences, focuses specifically on the social aspects of the mental act of remembering. In doing so, it certainly helps us gain a finer appreciation of the considerable extent to which our social environment affects the way we remember the past.

The work on memory typically produced by cognitive psychologists might lead one to believe that the act of remembering takes place in a social vacuum. The relative lack of explicit attention to the social context within which human memory is normally situated tends to promote a rather distorted vision of individuals as "mnemonic Robinson Crusoes"° whose memories are virtually free of any social influence or constraint. Such a naive vision would be quite inappropriate even within the somewhat synthetic context of the psychological laboratory, where much of the research on memory today (with the notable exception of "ecologically" oriented work)[1] typically takes place. It is even less appropriate, however, within the context of real life.

Consider the critical role of others as witnesses whose memories help corroborate our own.[2] No wonder most courts of law do not give uncorroborated testimony the same amount of credence and official recognition as admissible evidence that they normally give to socially corroborated testimony. After all, most of us tend to feel somewhat reassured that what we seem to remember indeed happened when there are others who can verify our recollections and thereby provide them with a stamp of intersubjectivity. The terribly frustrating experience of recalling people or events that no one else seems to remember strongly resembles that of seeing things or hearing sounds which no one else does.[3]

Furthermore, there are various occasions when other people have even better access to certain parts of our past than we ourselves do and can therefore help us recall people and events which we have somehow forgotten. A wife, for example, may remind her husband about an old friend of his which he had once mentioned to her yet has since forgotten.[4] Parents, grandparents, and older siblings, of course, often remember events from our own childhood

"mnemonic Robinson Crusoes": In the 1719 novel of the same name by Daniel Defoe (1660–1731), Robinson Crusoe is shipwrecked alone on an island for twenty-four years; hence, a person who is completely self-sufficient or independent.

that we cannot possibly recall. In fact, many of our earliest "memories" are actually recollections of stories we heard from them about our childhood.[5] In an odd way, they remember them for us!

Yet such social mediation can also assume a somewhat negative form, since such "mnemonic others" can also help block our access to certain events in our own past, to the point of actually preventing some of them from becoming memories in the first place! This is particularly critical in the case of very young children, who still depend on others around them to define what is real (as well as "memorable") and what is not. A thirty-five-year-old secretary whose boss tells her to "forget this ever happened" will probably be psychologically independent enough to store that forbidden memory in her mind anyway. However, a five-year-old boy whose mother flatly denies that a certain event they have just experienced together ever took place will most likely have a much harder time resisting her pressure to suppress it from his consciousness and may thus end up repressing it altogether.

Such instances remind us, of course, that the reasons we sometimes tend to repress our memories may not always be internal and that our social environment certainly plays a major role in helping us determine what is "memorable" and what we can (or even should) forget. Needless to say, they further demonstrate the ubiquity of sociomental control.

The notion that there are certain things that one *should* forget also underscores the normative dimension of memory, which is typically ignored by cognitive psychology. Like the curricular institutionalization of required history classes in school, it reminds us that remembering is more than just a spontaneous personal act, as it also happens to be regulated by unmistakably social *rules of remembrance* that tell us quite specifically what we should remember and what we must forget.

Such rules often determine how far back we remember. In the same way that society helps delineate the scope of our attention and concern through various norms of focusing, it also manages to affect the extent of our mental reach into the past by setting certain historical horizons beyond which past events are regarded as somehow irrelevant and, as such, often forgotten altogether.[6]

The way society affects the "depth" of individuals' memory by relegating certain parts of the past to official oblivion is often quite explicit, as in the case of the 1990 ruling by the Israeli broadcasting authorities prohibiting television and radio announcers from referring to places in present-day Israel by their old Arab names. Just as blatant is the aptly named statute of limitations, the ultimate institutionalization of the idea that it is actually possible to put certain things "behind us." The very notion of such a statute implies that even events that we agree happened can nonetheless be mentally banished to a "pre-historical" past that is considered legally irrelevant, and thereby officially forgotten. The unmistakably conventional nature of any statute of limitations, of course, reminds us that it is very often society that determines which particular bygones we let be bygones.

Yet the extent to which our social environment affects the "depth" of our memory is also manifested somewhat more tacitly in the way we conventionally begin historical narratives.[7] By defining a certain moment in history as the actual beginning of a particular historical narrative, it implicitly defines for us everything that preceded that moment as mere "pre-history" which we can practically forget. Thus, for example, when the founders of Islam established the flight of the Prophet from Mecca to Medina in A.D. 622 as the pivot of the conventional Mohammedan chronological dating system, they implicitly defined everything that had ever happened prior to that momentous event as a mere prelude to the "real" history that every Muslim ought to remember.[8] By the same token, when sociologists say (as they often do) that sociology was "born" in the 1830s with the work of Auguste Comte (who was indeed the first ever to use the term "sociology"), they are implicitly saying that their students need not really read the work of Aristotle, Hobbes, or Rousseau,° which is somehow only "pre-sociological."[9]

Nowhere is the unmistakably social partitioning of the past into a memorable "history" and a practically forgettable "pre-history" more glaringly evident than in the case of so-called discoveries. When the *New York Times*, for example, offers it readers a brief historical profile of Mozambique that begins with its "discovery" by the Portuguese in 1498 and fails to remind them that that particular moment marks only the beginning of the *European* chapter in its history, it relegates that country's entire pre-European past to official oblivion. A similar example of such "mnemonic decapitation" is the way Icelanders begin the official history of their island. Both the Book of Settlements (*Landnámabók*) and Book of Icelanders (*Íslendingabók*) mention in passing the fact that when the first Norwegians arrived on the island in the ninth century, they found Irish monks already living there, yet their commitment to Iceland's Scandinavian identity (and therefore origins) leads them to present those Norwegians as its *first* settlers![10] While not trying to explicitly conceal the actual presence of Celts° prior to Iceland's official "discovery" by Scandinavians, they nevertheless treat them as irrelevant to its "real" history.

Consider also the way we conventionally regard Columbus's first encounter with America as its official "discovery," thereby suppressing the memory of the millions of native Americans who were already living there. The notion that Columbus "discovered" America goes hand in hand with the idea that American history begins only in 1492 and that all events in the Western Hemisphere prior to that year are just part of its "pre-American" past. From this historiographic perspective, nothing that predates 1492 truly belongs in

Aristotle, Hobbes, or Rousseau: Aristotle (384–322 B.C.), Thomas Hobbs (1588–1789), Jean-Jacques Rousseau (1712–1778) — respectively, three famous Greek, English, and French philosophers.

Celts: Early Indo-European inhabitants of prehistorical Europe from Ireland to Spain and Asia Minor who were frequently displaced by invading tribes during the first millennium A.D.

15

"American history." Indeed, it is conventionally considered part of a mere "pre-Columbian" prologue.

America's "pre-history" includes not only its own native past but also earlier, "pre-Columbian" European encounters with it, which explains why the Norse voyages across the Atlantic (to Greenland, Newfoundland, and possibly Nova Scotia) in the late tenth and early eleventh centuries are still not considered part of the official narrative of "the discovery of America."[11] Despite the fact that most of us are fully aware of the indisputable Norse presence on the western shores of the Atlantic almost five centuries before Columbus, we still regard his 1492 landfall in the Bahamas as the official beginning of American history. After all, if "America" was indeed born only on 12 October 1492 (a notion implicitly supported by the official annual celebration of its "birthday" on Columbus Day), nothing that had happened there prior to that date can be considered truly part of "American history."[12]

Needless to say, this grand division of the past into a memorable "history" and an officially forgettable "pre-history" is neither logical nor natural. It is an unmistakably social, normative convention. One needs to be socialized to view Columbus's first voyage to the Caribbean as the beginning of American history. One certainly needs to be taught to regard everything that had ever happened in America prior to 1492 as a mere prelude to its "real" history. Only then, indeed, can one officially forget "pre-Columbian" America.

We usually learn what we should remember and what we can forget as part of our *mnemonic socialization,* a process that normally takes place when we enter an altogether new social environment, such as when we get married, start a new job, convert to another religion, or emigrate to another country.[13] (It is a subtle process that usually happens rather tacitly: listening to a family member recount a shared experience, for example, implicitly teaches one what is considered memorable and what one can actually forget.) In acquainting us with the specific rules of remembrance that operate in that environment, it introduces us to a particular "tradition" of remembering.

A *mnemonic tradition* includes not only what we come to remember as members of a particular thought community but also *how* we remember it. After all, much of what we seem to "remember" is actually filtered (and often inevitably distorted) through a process of subsequent interpretation, which affects not only the actual facts we recall but also the particular "light" in which we happen to recall them. Thus, it is hardly surprising that a girl who grows up in a highly traditionalistic family which tends to embellish and romanticize the past would come to "remember" her great-grandfather as a larger-than-life, almost mythical figure. Indeed, that is why Americans who grow up today in liberal and conservative homes "remember" so differently the great social upheavals of the 1960s and 1970s.

As the very first social environment in which we learn to interpret our own experience, the family plays a critical role in our mnemonic socialization. In fact, most subsequent interpretations of early "recollections" of particular events in one's life are only *re*interpretations of the way they were originally experienced *and remembered* within the context of one's family! That explains why we often spend a lot of mental effort as we grow up trying to "reclaim" our own personal recollections from our parents or older siblings. Indeed, what is often experienced in intensive psychotherapy is the almost inevitable clash between recalling certain people and events through the *mnemonic lenses* provided by our immediate family and recalling those same people and events by gradually regaining contact with deeper layers of our selves.

Yet mnemonic traditions affect our memory even more significantly by prompting us to adopt a particular cognitive "bias"[14] that leads us to remember certain things but not others. As an increasing body of research on memory seems to indicate, familiarity usually breeds memorability, as we tend to remember information that we can somehow fit into ready-made, familiar schematic mental structures that "make sense" to us.[15] . . . That is why it is usually much easier to recall that a particular character in a story we have read happened to wear glasses when she is a librarian, for example, than when she is a waitress or a nurse. This tendency to remember things schematically applies not only to actual facts but also to the way we recall the general "gist" of events (which is often all we can remember of them)[16] as well as to the way we interpret those memories.[17]

To further appreciate such tendency to remember events that proceed according to a certain schematic set of prior expectations, consider also the formulaic, script-like "plot structures"[18] we often use to narrate the past, a classic example of which is the traditional Zionist view of the history of Jews' "exilic" life outside the Land of Israel almost exclusively in terms of persecution and victimization.[19] I find it quite interesting, in this regard, that only in my late thirties did I first realize that Captain Alfred Dreyfus,° who I had always "remembered" languishing in the penal colony on Devil's Island *until he died* (following the infamous 1894 trial at which he was wrongly convicted for treason against France), was actually exonerated by the French authorities and even decorated with the Legion of Honor twelve years later! Having grown up in Israel during the 1950s and having been socialized into the Zionist mnemonic tradition of narrating European Jewish history, it is hardly surprising that that is how I "remembered" the end of the famous Dreyfus Affair.

Needless to say, the schematic mental structures on which mnemonic traditions typically rest are neither "logical" nor natural. Most of them are either culture-specific or subculture-specific,[20] and therefore something we acquire as part of our mnemonic socialization. Thus, if we tend to remember so much better situational details that are salient in our own culture or subculture,[21] it is mostly because so many of our pre-existing expectations are based on conventionalized, social typifications.[22]

Captain Alfred Dreyfus: In 1894 Alfred Dreyfus (1859–1935), a French army officer of Jewish descent, was accused and convicted of treason in a case that became a notorious example of state-sponsored anti-Semitism.

Once again we are seeing indisputable evidence of society's ubiquitous 25
cognitive role as a mediator between individuals and their own experience. In
fact, since most of the schematic mental structures that help us organize and
access our memories are part of our unmistakably social "stock of knowledge,"[23] much of what we seem to recall is only socially, rather than personally, familiar to us! Indeed, it is what we come to "remember" *as members of
particular thought communities.*

The fact that I can actually "recall" the Dreyfus Affair also reminds us that
what we remember includes far more than just what we have personally experienced. In other words, it underscores the unmistakably impersonal aspect of
memory.

I was already forty-three when I first saw Venice, yet I soon realized that
it was actually quite familiar to me. The majestic Grand Canal, for example,
was something I had already "seen" on the cover of an album of brass concerti
by Venetian composer Antonio Vivaldi when I was eighteen. And when I saw
the infamous "Lion's Mouth" (where anonymous accusers once dropped their
denunciations of fellow Venetians to the secret police) in the Palace of the
Doges, I was actually seeing something I remembered from a book I had read
some twenty years earlier.

Stored in my mind are rather vivid "recollections" of my great-grandfather (who I never even met and about whom I know only indirectly from my
mother's, grandmother's, and great-aunt's accounts), the Crucifixion (the way
I first "saw" it in Nicholas Ray's film *The King of Kings* when I was twelve),
and the first voyage around the world (the way I first envisioned it when I read
Stefan Zweig's biography of Ferdinand Magellan as a teenager). I have somewhat similar "memories" of the Inca Empire, the Punic Wars, and Genghis
Khan,° despite the fact that I personally experienced none of them.

In fact, neither are my recollections of most of the "historical" events that
have taken place in my own lifetime entirely personal.[24] What I usually remember of those events is how they were described by others who did experience them personally! They are socially mediated memories that are based
entirely on secondhand accounts of others.[25] Thus, for example, I "remember" the French pullout from Algeria and the Soviet invasion of Prague mainly
through the way they were reported at the time in the newspapers. I likewise
"recall" the Eichmann trial, the Cuban missile crisis,° and the landing of
Apollo 11 on the moon mainly through radio and television reports.[26]

the Inca Empire, the Punic Wars, and Genghis Khan: The Inca Empire extended throughout what is now modern Peru, Ecuador, and Chile from ca 1438 to 1532; the Punic Wars were
fought between Rome and Carthage between 264 and 146 B.C.; Genghis Khan (ca 1162–1227)
was the leader of the Mongols during the period of their greatest expansion.

the Eichmann trial, the Cuban missile crisis: Adolf Eichmann (1906–1962) was tried in
Israel in 1960 for crimes against humanity committed during the Nazi era; in 1962, the United
States threatened the Soviet Union with diplomatic and possible military retaliation unless it re-
moved missiles from Cuban installations.

In fact, much of what we seem to "remember" we did not actually expe-   30
rience personally. We only do so as members of particular families, organizations, nations, and other *mnemonic communities*[27] to which we happen to belong. Thus, for example, it is mainly as a Jew that I "recall" so vividly the
Babylonian destruction of the First Temple in Jerusalem more than twenty-
five centuries before I was born. By the same token, it is as a member of my
family that I "remember" my great-great-grandmother (whose memory is
probably no longer carried by anyone outside it), and as a soccer fan that I recall Uruguay's historic winning goal against Brazil in the 1950 World Cup
final. Consider also the special place of the Stonewall riots° and of Charlie
Parker's early gigs with Dizzy Gillespie at Minton's Play House in the respec-
tive memories of homosexuals and jazz aficionados.°

Indeed, being social presupposes the ability to experience events that happened to groups and communities long before we even joined them as if they
were somehow part of our own past, an ability so perfectly captured by the traditional Jewish claim, explicitly repeated every Passover,° that "*we* were slaves
to Pharaoh in Egypt, and God brought *us* out of there with a mighty hand."
(On Passover Jews also recite the following passage from the Haggadah: "In
every generation, a man should see himself *as though he* had gone forth from
Egypt. As it is said: 'And you shall tell your son on that day, it is because of
what God did for *me* when *I* went forth from Egypt.'")[28] Such existential fusion of one's own biography with the history of the groups or communities to
which one belongs is an indispensable part of one's unmistakably social identity as an anthropologist, a Mormon, a Native American, a Miami Dolphins
fan, or a member of the U.S. Marine Corps.

In marked contrast to our strictly autobiographical memory, such *sociobi-
ographical memory*[29] also accounts for the sense of pride, pain, or shame we
sometimes experience as a result of things that happened to groups and communities to which we belong long before we even joined them.[30] Consider the
national pride of present-day Greeks, much of which rests on the glorious
accomplishments of fellow Greek scholars, artists, and philosophers some
twenty-four centuries ago, or the institutional arrogance of many current faculty of academic departments that were considered great forty years ago but
have since been in decline. Consider also the long tradition of pain and suffering carried by many present-day American descendants of nineteenth-
century African slaves, or the great sense of shame that pervades the experience of many young Germans born many years after the collapse of the Nazi
regime.

the Stonewall riots: Riots against police brutality and harassment at New York's Stonewall club
in 1969 were seen as the beginning of the Gay Pride movement.

Charlie Parker's early gigs with Dizzy Gillespie . . . : Charles "Bird" Parker (1920–1955)
and Dizzy Gillespie (1917–1993), American jazz musicians.

Passover: A Jewish holiday commemorating the liberation of the Israelites from slavery in
Egypt.

Indeed, identifying with a particular collective past is an important part of the process of acquiring a particular social identity (hence the appeal for some students of African-American and Women's Studies programs in universities, for example). Familiarizing new members with their collective past is an important part of groups' and communities' general efforts to incorporate them. Business corporations, colleges, and army battalions, for example, often introduce new members to their collective history as part of their general "orientation." Children whose parents come to the United States from Ghana, Ecuador, or Cambodia are likewise taught in school to "remember" Paul Revere and the *Mayflower* as part of their own past. From Poland to Mexico, from Israel to Taiwan, the study of national history plays a major role in the general effort of the modern state to foster a national identity.[31]

At the same time (and for precisely the same reasons), exiting a group or a community typically involves forgetting its past. Children who are abandoned by one of their parents, for example, rarely carry on the memories of his or her family. Children of assimilated immigrants likewise rarely learn much from their parents about the history of the societies they chose to leave, both physically and psychologically, behind them.

Given its highly impersonal nature, social memory need not even be stored in   35
individual's minds. Indeed, there are some unmistakably impersonal "sites"[32] of memory.

It was the invention of language that first freed human memory from the need to be stored in individuals' minds. As soon as it became technically possible for people to somehow "share" their personal experiences with others, those experiences were no longer exclusively theirs and could therefore be preserved as somewhat impersonal recollections even after they themselves were long gone. In fact, with language, memories can actually pass from one person to another even when there is no direct contact between them, through an intermediate. Indeed, that has always been one of the main social functions of the elderly, who, as the de facto custodians of the social memories of their communities, have traditionally served as "mnemonic go-betweens," essentially linking historically separate generations who would otherwise never be able to mentally "connect" with one another.

Such "mnemonic transitivity" allows for the social preservation of memories in stories, poems, and legends that are transmitted from one generation to the next. One finds such oral traditions[33] in practically any social community—from families, churches, law firms, and college fraternities to ethnic groups, air force bases, basketball teams, and radio stations. It was thus an oral tradition that enabled the Marranos° in Spain, for example, to preserve their secret Jewish heritage (and therefore identity) for so many generations. It was likewise through stories that the memory of their spectacular eleventh-century encounter with America was originally preserved by Icelanders, more than a

Marranos: A Christianized Jew in medieval Spain.

century before it was first recorded in their famous sagas and some 950 years before it was first corroborated by actual archaeological finds in Newfoundland.[34]

Furthermore, ever since the invention of writing several thousand years ago, it is also possible to actually bypass any oral contact, however indirect, between the original carrier of a particular recollection and its various future retrievers. Present-day readers of Saint Augustine's *Confessions* can actually "share" his personal recollections of his youth despite the fact that he has already been dead for more then fifteen centuries! Doctors can likewise share patient histories readily, since the highly impersonal clinical memories captured in their records are accessible even when those who originally recorded them there are not readily available for immediate consultation.[35] That explains the tremendous significance of documents in science (laboratory notes, published results of research), law (affidavits, contracts), diplomacy (telegrams, treaties), business (receipts, signed agreements), and bureaucracy (letters of acceptance, minutes of meetings), as well as of the archives, libraries, and computer files where they are typically stored.[36] It also accounts for the critical role of history textbooks in the mnemonic socialization of present and future generations.

Yet preserving social memories requires neither oral nor written transmission. Given the inherent durability of material objects as well as the fact that they are mnemonically evocative in an immediate, "tangible" manner, they too play an important role in helping us retain memories.[37] Hence the role of ruins, relics, and old buildings as *social souvenirs*. A visit to the National Museum of Anthropology in Mexico City, for example, helps "connect" modern Mexican "pilgrims" to their Toltec, Maya, and Aztec origins. A walk through the old neighborhoods of Jerusalem likewise allows present-day Jews a quasi-personal "contact" with their collective past.[38]

As evident from the modern advent of preservationism[39] as well as from the modern state's political use of archaeology as part of its general effort to promote nationalism,[40] we are certainly more than just passive consumers of such quasi-physical mnemonic links to our collective past. Numerous medals, plaques, tombstones, war memorials, Halls of Fame, and other commemorative monuments (and the fact that we make them from stone or metal rather than paper or wood)[41] serve as evidence that we purposefully design such future sites of memory well in advance. Like souvenirs, class yearbooks, and antiques,[42] such objects have a purely commemorative value for us, and we design them strictly for the purpose of allowing future generations mnemonic access to their collective past.[43] The entire meaning of such "pre-ruins" derives from the fact that they are mnemonically evocative and will therefore help us in the future to recover our past.

The self-conscious effort to preserve the past for posterity is manifested even more poignantly in the statues, portraits, stamps, coins, and paper money we produce as social souvenirs. The visual images so vividly captured on them represent an ambitious attempt to somehow "freeze" time and allow future generations the fullest possible mnemonic access to major individuals and events from their collective past. National galleries that try to offer posterity a comprehensive visual encapsulation of a nation's history (the collection of paintings displayed in the U.S. Capitol building,[44] Diego Rivera's murals° at the National Palace in Mexico City) are the culmination of such artistic endeavors.

Since the invention of the camera (as well as its two major offspring, the motion-picture and television cameras), these more traditional means of "capturing" the past have gradually given way to photographs and films.[45] The family photo album and the television archive, indeed, are among the major modern sites of social memory. In fact, it is primarily through snapshots, home movies, and television footage that most of us nowadays remember old relatives, family weddings, or the Gulf War.

As evident from the rapid evolution of audio-recording technology from the phonograph to the portable cassette-recorder, in our attempt to somehow "freeze" time we actually try to capture not only visual images but also the very sounds of the past. Historic recordings of Winston Churchill's speeches and Vladimir Horowitz's concerts,° for example, underscore the growing significance of tapes, cassettes, and compact disks as modern sites of social memory.

Video technology, of course, represents the modern attempt to integrate such graphic and sonic efforts to preserve the past. The ultimate progeny of the camera and the phonograph, the camcorder generates remarkably vivid audio-visual memories that are virtually independent of any individual carrier! The famous videotaped beating of Rodney King° by members of the Los Angeles police, for example, is the epitome of such absolutely disembodied and therefore truly impersonal memory. As evident from its repeated use in court, it may very well represent (not unlike the increasingly common use of instant video replay in television sports)[46] the ultimate victory of social and therefore "official" over purely personal memory.

Not only are many of our recollections impersonal, they are often also collective. My memory of the first mile ever run under four minutes, for example, is actually shared by the entire track world. So are some of the memories I

Diego Rivera's murals: Diego Rivera (1886–1957), Mexican painter famed for his murals celebrating Mexican culture and history.

Winston Churchill's speeches and Vladimir Horowitz's concerts:" Sir Winston Leonard Spenser Churchill (1874–1965), English statesman and prime minister, famed for his wartime oratory; Vladimir Horowitz (1903–1989), Russian-born American pianist.

The famous videotaped beating of Rodney King . . . : In 1991, a videotape of Los Angeles police officers beating Rodney King after stopping him for a traffic infraction was broadcast nationwide and was credited with inciting the Los Angeles riots of 1992 after the acquittal of King's assailants.

share with other sociologists, Jews, or Rutgers University employees. In each of these cases my own recollections are part of a *collective memory*[47] shared by an entire community as a whole.

The collective memory of a mnemonic community is quite different from the sum total of the personal recollections of its various individual members,[48] as it includes only those that are *commonly shared* by all of them (in the same way that public opinion, for example, is more than just an aggregate of individuals' personal opinions).[49] In other words, it involves the integration of various different personal pasts into a single common past that all members of a community come to remember collectively. America's collective memory of the Vietnam War, for example, is thus more than just an aggregate of all the war-related recollections of individual Americans, just as Israel's collective memory of the Holocaust[50] is more than the mere sum of the personal recollections of all the Holocaust survivors living in Israel.

We must be particularly careful not to mistake personalized manifestations of a mnemonic community's collective memory for genuinely personal recollections.[51] When asked to list the first names that come to their minds in response to the prompt "American history from its beginning through the end of the Civil War," Americans usually list the same people—George Washington, Abraham Lincoln, Thomas Jefferson, Benjamin Franklin, Robert E. Lee, John Adams, and Ulysses S. Grant.[52] The fact that so many different individuals happen to have the same "free" associations about their nation's past shows that their memories are not as independent as we might think but merely personalized manifestations of a single common collective memory. In so doing, it also underscores the tremendous significance of mnemonic socialization.

Yet the notion of a "collective memory" implies a past that is not only commonly shared but also jointly remembered (that is, "co-memorated"). By helping ensure that an entire mnemonic community will come to remember its past *together*, as a group, society affects not only what and who we remember but also when we remember it!

Commemorative anniversaries such as the 1992 Columbus quincentennial, the 1995 fiftieth anniversary of the end of World War II, and the 1976 American bicentennial are classic manifestations of such *mnemonic synchronization*. Yet we also "co-remember" past events by associating them with holidays and other "memorial days" which we jointly celebrate on a regular annual[53] (or even weekly, as in the case of both the Sabbath and the Lord's Day)[54] basis. Fixed in a mnemonic community's calendar, such days ensure members' synchronized access to their collective past. Indeed, keeping certain past events in our collective memory by ensuring their annual commemoration is one of the main functions of the calendar.[55]

Thus, on Easter, millions of Christians come to remember their common spiritual origins together, as a community. By the same token, every Passover, 50

Jews all over the world jointly remember their collective birth as a people. The annual commemoration of the French Revolution on Bastille Day° and of the European colonization of New England on Thanksgiving Day play similar "co-evocative" roles for Frenchmen and Americans, respectively.

That also explains various attempts throughout history to remove certain holidays from the calendar in an effort to obliterate the collective memories they evoke. The calendrical dissociation of Easter from Passover, for example, was thus part of a conscious effort by the Church to "decontaminate" Christians' collective memory from somewhat embarrassing Jewish elements,[56] whereas the calendar of the French Revolution represented an attempt to establish a mnemonically sanitized secular holiday cycle that would be devoid of any Christian memories.[57] Given all this, it is also clear why the recent political battle over the inclusion of Martin Luther King Jr.'s birthday in the American calendar was actually a battle over the place of African Americans in America's collective memory.

The battle over whether to officially include Martin Luther King Jr.'s birthday in the American calendar is one of numerous battles fought between as well as within mnemonic communities over the social legacy of the past. The very existence of such *mnemonic battles* further underscores the social dimension of human memory.

The most common mnemonic battles are the ones fought over the "correct" way to interpret the past. As we develop a collective sense of history, we may not always agree on how a particular historical figure or event ought to be remembered. While many Americans regard Columbus as a hero who embodies the modern Western quest for knowledge and spirit of free enterprise, there are many others who claim that he should actually be remembered as the villainous spearhead of the modern Western expansionist spirit that is responsible for both colonialism and the massive destruction of the environment.[58] By the same token, whereas many Israelis still accept the official Zionist view of the fall of Masada and the Bar-Kokhba rebellion° nineteen centuries ago as exemplary heroic events, a growing number of others are voicing the concern that they are actually symptomatic of a rather myopic stubbornness that resulted in terrible national disasters that could have been avoided by a more politically expedient way of dealing with the Romans who occupied Judaea.[59] Consider also the cultural battles fought among Americans over the "correct" interpretation of Watergate,[60]° or the debate among historians over whether the origins of Greek

Bastille Day: A French national holiday celebrated on July 14, commemorating the destruction of the Bastille prison and the overthrow of the French monarchy.

Masada and the Bar-Kokhba rebellion: Masada was a Roman fortress taken over by Jewish rebels in A.D. 66. When the Romans recaptured it, they found most of the Jews had killed themselves. The Bar-Kokhba rebellion (A.D. 123–125) was another Jewish revolt that was suppressed by the Romans.

Watergate: The 1972 political scandal involving the burglary of Democratic Party headquarters in the Watergate Hotel in Washington, D.C. by Republican Party operatives.

(and therefore Western) civilization are Indo-European or African,[61] as well as everyday marital battles over past infidelities.

Mnemonic battles are also fought over what ought to be collectively remembered in the first place. Eurocentrists, multiculturalists, and feminists, among others, battle over the literary tradition into which young members of society ought to be mnemonically socialized. Consider also the problem of delineating the historical narratives that are to be remembered. Given the inherently conventional nature of any beginning,[62] "where" a particular historical narrative ought to begin is by no means self-evident.[63] After all, even people who are trying to recount an event they have just witnessed together often disagree on the precise point at which their account ought to begin. It is not at all clear, for example, whether we should begin the "story" of the Vietnam War during the Johnson or Kennedy years. Nor is it absolutely clear whether the narrative of the events leading to the Gulf War ought to begin in August 1990, when Iraq invaded Kuwait (which is the standard American version), or several decades earlier, when both were still part of a single, undivided political entity (which is the standard Iraqi version).

As we might expect, such narratological pluralism often generates discord. Japan and the United States wage an ongoing mnemonic battle over the inclusion of the Japanese attack on Pearl Harbor in 1941 in the narrative of the events leading to the atomic bombings of Hiroshima and Nagasaki by the United States four years later. Consider also the Arab-Israeli dispute over the point at which a fair narration of the history of the West Bank ought to begin, or the strong objection of Native Americans to the Eurocentric depiction of 1492 as the beginning of American history. After all, for anyone whose ancestors lived in America thousands of years before it was "discovered" by Europe, that date certainly constitutes more of an ending than a beginning.

Like Akira Kurosawa's *Rashomon*,° the fact that such discord exists at all reminds us that our memory of the past is not entirely objective, since we evidently do not all remember it the same way. Yet mnemonic battles usually involve not just individuals but entire communities, and are typically fought in the public arena (such as in newspaper editorials and radio talk shows), which suggests that the past is not entirely subjective either. That remembering is more than just a personal act is also evident from the fact that major changes in the way we view the past (such as our growing sensitivity to multiculturalist historiographic concerns) usually correspond to major social changes that affect entire mnemonic communities.[64] This, again, underscores the intersubjective, unmistakably social dimension of human memory.

Akira Kurosawa's *Rashomon*: Film (1950) by Japanese director Akira Kurosawa (1910–1998).

Notes

1. See, for example, Ulric Neisser and Eugene Winograd (eds.), *Remembering Reconsidered: Ecological and Traditional Approaches to the Study of Memory* (Cambridge: Cambridge University Press, 1988).

2. See, for example, Maurice Halbwachs, *The Collective Memory* (New York: Harper Colophon, 1980 [1950]), pp. 22–24.

3. See also Maurice Halbwachs, *The Social Frameworks of Memory*, in Lewis A. Coser (ed.), *Maurice Halbwachs on Collective Memory* (Chicago: University of Chicago Press, 1992 [1925]), p. 74.

4. See also Vered Vinitzky-Seroussi, *Looking Forward, Looking Back: High School Reunions and the Social Construction of Identities* (Chicago: University of Chicago Press, forthcoming).

5. See also Steen F. Larsen, "Remembering without Experiencing: Memory for Reported Events," in Ulric Neisser and Eugene Winograd (eds.), *Remembering Reconsidered: Ecological and Traditional Approaches to the Study of Memory* (Cambridge: Cambridge University Press, 1988), p. 337.

6. Zerubavel, "Horizons," pp. 406–408.

7. See also Eviatar Zerubavel, "In the Beginning: Notes on the Social Construction of Historical Discontinuity," *Sociological Inquiry* 63 (1993): 457–459.

8. See also Bernard Lewis, *History: Remembered, Recovered, Invented* (Princeton: Princeton University Press, 1975), pp. 31–32.

9. On sociologists' remarkably short memory, see also Herbert J. Gans, "Sociological Amnesia: The Noncumulation of Normal Social Science," *Sociological Forum* 7 (1992): 701–710.

10. See Gwyn Jones, *The Norse Atlantic Saga* (Oxford: Oxford University Press, 1986), 2nd ed., pp. 144, 156.

11. For some other notable exclusions from that narrative, see Zerubavel, *Terra Cognita: The Mental Discovery of America* (New Brunswick, N.J.: Rutgers University Press, 1992), pp. 36–66, 117–118.

12. Ibid., pp. 22–23.

13. See also Peter L. Berger, *Invitation to Sociology: A Humanistic Perspective* (Garden City, N.Y.: Doubleday Anchor, 1963), pp. 54–65; Peter L. Berger and Hansfried Kellner, "Marriage and the Construction of Reality: An Exercise in the Microsociology of Knowledge," in Hans-Peter Dreitzel (ed.), *Recent Sociology No. 2: Patterns of Communicative Behavior* (London: Macmillan, 1970 [1964]), pp. 62–64.

14. Frederic C. Bartlett, *Remembering: A Study in Experimental and Social Psychology* (Cambridge: Cambridge University Press, 1932), pp. 254–255.

15. See, for example, Walter Kintsch and Edith Greene, "The Role of Culture-Specific Schemata in the Comprehension and Recall of Stories," *Discourse Processes* 1 (1978): 1–13; Claudia E. Cohen, "Person Categories and Social Perception: Testing Some Boundaries of the Processing Effects of Prior Knowledge," *Journal of Personality and Social Psychology* 40 (1981): 441–452; Fiske and Taylor, *Social Cognition* (New York: Addison-Wesley, 1984), pp. 152–153, 161–162; Jean M. Mandler, *Stories, Scripts, and Scenes: Aspects of Schema Theory* (Hillsdale, N.J.: Lawrence Erlbaum, 1984), pp. 93–108; Robert Pritchard, "The Effects of Cultural Schemata on Reading Processing Strategies," *Reading Research Quarterly* 25 (1990): 273–295.

16. Roger C. Shank and Robert P. Abelson, "Scripts, Plans, and Knowledge," in P. N. Johnson-Laird and P. C. Wason (eds.), *Thinking: Readings in Cognitive Science* (Cambridge: Cambridge University Press, 1977), p. 430.

17. Rumelhart and Ortony, "The Representation of Knowledge in Memory," in Richard C. Anderson, Rand J. Spiro, and William E. Montague (eds.), *Schooling and the Acquisition of Knowledge* (Hillsdale, N.J.: Lawrence Erlbaum, 1977), p. 117.

18. Hayden White, "The Historical Text as Literary Artifact," in *Tropics of Discourse: Essays in Cultural Criticism* (Baltimore: Johns Hopkins University Press, 1978 [1974]),

pp. 81–99. See also Mandler, *Stories, Scripts, and Scenes*, p. 18; S. Wojciech Sokolowski, "Historical Tradition in the Service of Ideology," *Conjecture* (September 1992): 4–11; Yael Zerubavel, *Recovered Roots: Collective Memory and the Making of Israeli National Tradition* (Chicago: University of Chicago Press, 1995), pp. 216–221.

19. See, for example, Zerubavel, *Recovered Roots*, pp. 17–22.

20. See, for example, Bartlett, *Remembering;* Kintsch and Greene, "The Role of Culture-Specific Schemata in the Comprehension and Recall of Stories"; Margaret S. Steffensen, Chitra Joag-Dev, and Richard C. Anderson, "A Cross-Cultural Perspective on Reading Comprehension," *Reading Research Quarterly* 15 (1979): 10–29; Marjorie Y. Lipson, "The Influence of Religious Affiliation on Children's Memory for Text Information," *Reading Research Quarterly* 18 (1983): 448–457; Pritchard, "The Effects of Cultural Schemata on Reading Processing Strategies."

21. See, for example, Bartlett, *Remembering*, pp. 249–251; Steffensen, Joag-Dev, and Anderson, "Cross-Cultural Perspective on Reading Comprehension."

22. See also Schutz and Luckmann, *The Structures of the Life-World* (Evanston, Ill.: Northwestern University Press, 1973), pp. 77, 229–241; Berger and Luckmann, *The Social Construction of Reality* (Garden City, N.Y.: Doubleday Anchor, 1967 [1966]), pp. 30–34; Zerubavel, *The Fine Line: Making Distinctions in Everyday Life* (Chicago University of Chicago Press, 1993 [1991]), p. 17.

23. Schutz and Luckmann, *The Structures of the Life-World.*

24. See also, in this regard, Ruth Simpson, "I Was There: Establishing Ownership of Historical Moments" (paper presented at the annual meeting of the American Sociological Association, Los Angeles, August 1994).

25. See also Larsen, "Remembering without Experiencing."

26. See also Barbie Zelizer, *Covering the Body: The Kennedy Assassination, the Media, and the Shaping of Collective Memory* (Chicago: University of Chicago Press, 1992).

27. See also Iwona Irwin-Zarecka, *Frames of Remembrance: The Dynamics of Collective Memory* (New Brunswick, N.J.: Transaction, 1994), p. 47 on "communities of memory."

28. On the traditional Jewish duty to remember one's national past, see also Yosef H. Yerushalmi, *Zakhor: Jewish History and Jewish Memory* (Seattle: University of Washington Press, 1982).

29. I borrow this term from Lisa Bonchek, "Fences and Bridges: The Use of Material Objects in the Social Construction of Continuity and Discontinuity of Time and Identity" (unpublished manuscript, Rutgers University, Department of Sociology, 1994).

30. See also Steven Knapp, "Collective Memory and the Actual Past," *Representations* 26 (1989): 134–147.

31. On the state-sponsored study of national history, see for example, Frances FitzGerald, *America Revised: History Schoolbooks in the Twentieth Century* (New York: Vintage, 1980); Gilmer W. Blackburn, *Education in the Third Reich: Race and History in Nazi Textbooks* (Albany: State University of New York Press, 1985); Zerubavel, *Recovered Roots.*

32. See Pierre Nora, "Between Memory and History: Les Lieux de Memoire," *Representations* 26 (1989): 7–25.

33. See, for example, Jan Vansina, *Oral Tradition as History* (Madison: University of Wisconsin Press, 1985).

34. See, for example, Zerubavel, *Terra Cognita*, pp. 14–17.

35. See Zerubavel, *Patterns of Time in Hospital Life: A Sociological Perspective* (Chicago: University of Chicago Press, 1979), pp. 45–46.

36. See also Georg Simmel, "Written Communication," in Kurt H. Wolff (ed.), *The Sociology of Georg Simmel* (New York: Free Press, 1950 [1908]), pp. 352–355; Weber, *Economy and Society: An Outline of Interpretive Sociology* (Berkeley: University of California Press, 1978 [1925]), pp. 219, 957; M. T. Clanchy, *From Memory to Written Record: England, 1066–1307* (Cambridge, Mass.: Harvard University Press, 1979); Edward Shils, *Tradition* (Chicago: University of Chicago Press, 1981), pp. 109–112, 120–124, 140–147.

37. Shils, *Tradition*, pp. 63–72; David Lowenthal, *The Past Is a Foreign Country* (Cambridge: Cambridge University Press, 1985), pp. 238–249.

38. See, for example, Samuel C. Heilman, *A Walker in Jerusalem* (New York: Summit Books, 1986), pp. 77–111. See also Halbwachs, *The Collective Memory*, pp. 128–136.

39. See, for example, Kevin Lynch, *What Time Is This Place?* (Cambridge, Mass.: MIT Press, 1972), pp. 29–64, 235–238; E. R. Chamberlin, *Preserving the Past* (London: J. M. Dent, 1979); Lowenthal, *The Past Is a Foreign Country*, pp. 384–406.

40. See, for example, Lewis, *History*, pp. 6–7, 33–34, 101; Neil A. Silberman, *Between Past and Present: Archaeology, Ideology, and Nationalism in the Modern Middle East* (New York: Holt, 1989); Zerubavel, *Recovered Roots*, pp. 56–59, 63–68, 129–133, 185–189.

41. See, for example, Daniel J. Sherman, "Art, Commerce, and the Production of Memory in France after World War I," in John R. Gillis (ed.), *Commemorations: The Politics of National Identity* (Princeton: Princeton University Press, 1994), pp. 186–211; James E. Young (ed.), *The Art of Memory: Holocaust Memorials in History* (Munich: Prestel, 1994); Omer Bartov, *Murder in Our Midst: The Holocaust, Industrial Killing, and Representation* (New York: Oxford University Press, 1996), pp. 153–157, 175–186.

42. See also Ira Silver, "Role Transitions, Objects, and Identity," *Symbolic Interaction* (forthcoming).

43. Shils, *Tradition*, pp. 72–74.

44. See Barry Schwartz, "The Social Context of Commemoration: A Study in Collective Memory," *Social Forces* 61 (1982): 374–396.

45. See also Lowenthal, *The Past Is a Foreign Country*, pp. 257–258.

46. Gary Gumpert, *Talking Tombstones and Other Tales of the Media Age* (New York: Oxford University Press, 1987), pp. 56–64. See also Eviatar Zerubavel, "Time and Technology: On the Modern Relations between Humans and Temporality" (paper presented at the annual meeting of the Social Science History Association, St. Louis, October 1986).

47. This increasingly popular term was first introduced by Maurice Halbwachs in 1925 in *The Social Frameworks of Memory*.

48. See also Vansina, *Oral Tradition as History*, p. 149.

49. Cooley, *Social Organization: A Study of the Larger Mind* (New York: Schocken, 1962 [1909]), pp. 121–122. See also Durkheim, *The Elementary Forms of Religious Life*, pp. 436–437.

50. See, for example, Yael Zerubavel, "The Death of Memory and the Memory of Death: Masada and the Holocaust as Historical Metaphors," *Representations* 45 (1994): 72–100.

51. On the fundamental difference between the genuinely personal and merely personalized manifestations of the collective, see Durkheim, *The Rules of Sociological Method* (New York: Free Press, 1982 [1895]), pp. 50–59; Durkheim, *Suicide: A Study in Sociology* (New York: Free Press, 1966 [1897]), pp. 297–325. See also Zerubavel, *Patterns of Time in Hospital Life*, pp. 106–109.

52. Michael Frisch, "American History and the Structures of Collective Memory: A Modest Exercise in Empirical Iconography," *Journal of American History* 75 (1989): 1130–1155.

53. See Mircea Eliade, *The Sacred and the Profane: The Nature of Religion* (New York: Harcourt, Brace & World, 1959 [1957]), pp. 68–113; Paul Connerton, *How Societies Remember* (Cambridge: Cambridge University Press, 1989), pp. 41–48.

54. Zerubavel, *Hidden Rhythms*, p. 109; Zerubavel, *The Seven-Day Circle*, pp. 20–23.

55. See, for example, David Cressy, *Bonfires and Bells: National Memory and the Protestant Calendar in Elizabethan and Stuart England* (Berkeley: University of California Press, 1989); Zerubavel, *Recovered Roots*, pp. 138–144, 216–221; Eviatar Zerubavel and Yael Zerubavel, "Calendars and National Memory: The Semiotics of History in Modern Israel" (forthcoming).

56. Zerubavel, "Easter and Passover."

57. Zerubavel, *Hidden Rhythms: Schedules and Calendars in Social Life* (Berkeley: University of California Press, 1985 [1981]), pp. 84–88.

58. See, for example, Kirkpatrick Sale, *The Conquest of Paradise: Christopher Columbus and the Columbian Legacy* (New York: Alfred A. Knopf, 1990).

59. See Zerubavel, *Recovered Roots*, pp. 179–185, 200–203.

60. See Michael Schudson, *Watergate in American Memory: How We Remember, Forget, and Reconstruct the Past* (New York: Basic, 1992).

61. See Martin Bernal, *Black Athena: The Afroasiatic Roots of Classical Civilization* (New Brunswick, N.J.: Rutgers University Press, 1987).

62. Zerubavel, *The Fine Line*, pp. 68–69; Zerubavel, "In the Beginning"; Zerubavel, "Horizons," pp. 407–408; Isaacson, "The Fetus-Infant"; Foster, "Menstrual Time."

63. That is also true of "where" it should end. See Zerubavel, *Recovered Roots*, pp. 221–228.

64. See, for example, FitzGerald, *America Revised;* Barry Schwartz, "The Reconstruction of Abraham Lincoln," in David Middleton and Derek Edwards (eds.), *Collective Remembering* (London: Sage, 1990), pp. 81–104; Barry Schwartz, "Social Change and Collective Memory: The Democratization of George Washington," *American Sociological Review* 56 (1991): 221–234; Zerubavel, *Recovered Roots*.

EXPLORING THE TEXT

1. In what sense are our memories the products of the societies we live in, according to Zerubavel? What role do "mnemonic others" play in the creation of individual memories? In your opinion, who are the most important "mnemonic others" in relation to your own memories? Why might these people have such influence?

2. Zerubavel claims that every social environment or "thought community" has its own "rules of remembrance" (para. 11). What examples does he offer to illustrate the notion of a "thought community"? How many additional illustrations can you think of? How do the "rules of remembrance" function within these social groups? What does Zerubavel's use of the term "rule" imply in this context? How accurate is it in your estimation?

3. What, in Zerubavel's view, is "mnemonic socialization"? What roles do formal education and the family play in this process? How does this form of socialization lead to the development of "cognitive bias"? What role do "scripts" play in the creation of such mnemonic biases? What "scripts" or "plots" might liberal families

use to interpret the events of the 1960s and 1970s? What contrasting "scripts" might shape a politically conservative American family's recollections of the same era? Why does Zerubavel feel that all such schematic mental structures are "neither logical nor natural"? To what extent would you agree?

4. What does Zerubavel mean by the concept of "impersonal memory"? How are impersonal memories formed? What role does "impersonal memory" play in the shaping of an individual's cultural identity? What difference, if any, is there between impersonal memory and the kind of history you learn in school?

5. Why does Zerubavel stress the "collective" nature of human memory? What makes an impersonal memory "collective"? Why do groups "battle" over the collective memory of past events?

FURTHER EXPLORATIONS

1. Working in groups, research what Zerubavel might call the "mnemonic geography" of your campus or of the surrounding community. In your survey, be sure to note the location and meaning of all the sites, monuments, memorials, or buildings that are associated with specific impersonal memories. Chart these on a map of your devising, share them in class, and evaluate the effectiveness of the area you live in as "site of memory."

2. Zerubavel claims that we each possess a great many memories of things we have never directly experienced. He notes, for example, that it is possible for all of us to "share" the personal recollections of Saint Augustine by reading his *Confessions,* even though Augustine died over a millennium ago. Return to Ian Frazier's "Take the F" (p. 18) and review his description of his cross-town commute. To what extent do you think it's accurate to say that you share a "memory" of life in Brooklyn, New York, based on your reading of Frazier? In what ways, if any, might this "memory" of New York differ from those of someone who currently lives in Frazier's neighborhood?

3. Revisit Scott Russell Sanders's "The Inheritance of Tools" (p. 142), noting the role that family and cultural memories play in this selection. Which of Sanders's recollections result from direct personal experience? Which involve family or cultural memories? What is Sanders's view of the kind of historical or impersonal memory that Zerubavel describes? How can you tell?

4. Compare Zerubavel's view of the importance of impersonal memory with Walker Percy's notion of "preformulated" experiences in "The Loss of the Creature" (p. 118). What, according to these authors, is the relation between cultural memory, education, and the natural or historical worlds we live in? To what extent is it possible to reconcile these views on the issue of impersonal memory?

5. View Akira Kurosawa's *Rashomon* on videotape or the cinematic version of Ariel Dorfman's play *Death and the Maiden,* and discuss how these films deal with the theme of public and private memories. What questions do they raise about the creation and manipulation of historical memories? What do they suggest about the role of art and the artist in the cultural "battles" waged over how we collectively remember the past?

ESSAY OPTIONS

1. Write a paper in which you explain how memories are preserved in one of the cultures or subcultures you are a member of. What traditional stories, rituals, holidays or other special observances or activities help to maintain the identity of the members of this cultural community? What traditions, places, texts, artifacts, or even styles of dress serve as "sites of memory"?

2. Write a paper in which you compare the relative role of memory in two different cultures that you are familiar with. If, for example, your family identifies with a particular ethnic, racial, or religious group, you might compare the role that memory plays within this "mnemonic community" with the role that memory plays within the context of general American culture. Or, if you are familiar with the cultural practices of two "subcultural groups," you may want to compare the role of memory within these two more defined mnemonic communities. Again, you will want to examine not only the relative importance of memory within these groups, but also the institutions, rituals, or practices within each group dedicated to the maintenance of cultural memory.

3. Research a recent "mnemonic battle" waged in the United States. It might involve the establishment or disestablishment of a national holiday, the design of a public monument, the official display of a controversial flag or symbol, the use of a particular image on a coin or stamp, or even the way an important cultural figure is presented in a film, book, or television show. In a paper documenting your research, identify the parties involved in this conflict and analyze the differences that exist between their contrasting views of the past. How do these views reflect differences in their values, attitudes, and beliefs?

4. Drawing on ideas presented by Zerubavel in this selection, Daniel L. Schacter in "Building Memories" (p. 157), Patricia Hampl in "Memory and Imagination" (p. 180), Susan Engel in "Then and Now: Creating a Self Through the Past" (p. 192), as well as on the personal experiences of Hampl, Loren Eiseley (p. 150), and/or Maxine Hong Kingston (p. 206), write an essay assessing the commonplace notion of memory as an accurate record or "transcript" of personal experience. What forces shape the way we remember and interpret past events? To what extent do our memories belong to us?

Columbus: Gone But Not Forgotten

bell hooks

It's midnight, and the doorbell rings. The African American woman who answers — a nationally recognized writer and social critic — encounters a young white man standing outside with a package in hand. In the mind of bell hooks, the heroine of our relatively commonplace scenario, this innocent meeting of strangers conjures up the memory of another encounter between the races, one that occurred more than five hundred years ago. The story of Columbus and the "discovery" of the "New World" lingers in the collective memory of all Americans. For some, it is a story of heroic exploits and a source of national pride. For others, like hooks, it is a reminder of the horrors of colonial domination — a historical ghost story that continues to poison national attitudes toward race and gender relations. In this essay, hooks reminds us of the power that cultural memories exert over individual lives and illustrates the kind of struggle waged every day over how we collectively choose to remember the past. Bell hooks is the pen name of Gloria Watkins (b. 1952), a professor of English at City College of New York who has established a nationwide reputation as an essayist, feminist, and social critic. Her many publications include *Outlaw Culture* (1994), the source of this selection; the memoir *Bone Black* (1996); and, most recently, *All About Love: New Visions* (2000); *Salvation: Black People and Love* (2001); and *Homemade Love* (2001).

BEFORE READING

Reflect on the Columbus story that you recall learning in school. How was Columbus portrayed in this version of the saga of "discovery"? What motives supposedly led him to undertake such a dangerous voyage? How were the indigenous peoples he met in the "New World" depicted? How does the version you learned of Columbus's exploits compare with that learned by your classmates?

L ate last night a strange white man came to my door. Walking towards him through the dark shadows of the corridor, I felt fear surface, uncertainty about whether I should open the door. After hesitating, I did. He was a messenger bringing a letter from a female colleague. As I took the letter from him, he told me that he was reading my book, *Black Looks*, that he liked it, but that he just wanted to say that there was just too much emphasis on "Oh," he insisted, "you know the phrase." I finished the sentence for him, "white supremacist capitalist patriarchy." After a moment's pause I said, "Well, it's good to know you are reading this book."

From the onset when I began to use the phrase "white supremacist capitalist patriarchy" to describe my understanding of the "new world order,"° folks reacted. I witnessed the myriad ways this phrase disturbed, angered, and provoked. The response reinforced my awareness that it is very difficult for most Americans, irrespective of race, class, gender, sexual preference or political allegiance, to really accept that this society is white supremacist. Many white feminists were using the phrase "capitalist patriarchy" without questioning its appropriateness. Evidently it was easier for folks to see truth in referring to the economic system as capitalist and the institutionalized system of male gender domination as patriarchal than for them to consider the way white supremacy as a foundational ideology continually informs and shapes the direction of these two systems of domination. The nation's collective re-

---

"new world order": A phrase coined during the Reagan administration to characterize the new worldwide political situation that was expected to emerge after the fall of Communism.

fusal to acknowledge institutionalized white supremacy is given deep and profound expression in the contemporary zeal to reclaim the myth of Christopher Columbus as patriotic icon.

Despite all the contemporary fuss, I do not believe that masses of Americans spend much time thinking about Columbus. Or at least we didn't until now. Embedded in the nation's insistence that its citizens celebrate Columbus's "discovery" of America is a hidden challenge, a call for the patriotic among us to reaffirm a national commitment to imperialism and white supremacy. This is why many of us feel it is politically necessary for all Americans who believe in a democratic vision of the "just and free society," one that precludes all support of imperialism and white supremacy, to "contest" this romanticization of Columbus, imperialism, capitalism, white supremacy, and patriarchy.

Columbus's legacy is an inheritance handed down through generations. It has provided the cultural capital that underlies and sustains modern-day white supremacist capitalist patriarchy. Those of us who oppose all forms of domination long ago debunked the Columbus myth and reclaimed histories that allow us a broader, more realistic vision of the Americas. Hence, we resist and oppose the national call to celebrate Columbus. What we celebrate is our subversion of this moment, the way many folks have made it a space for radical intervention. Indeed, the invitation to celebrate Columbus was for some of us a compelling call to educate the nation for critical consciousness — to seize the moment to transform everyone's understanding of our nation's history. What we acknowledge is that this moment allows us a public space to mourn, an occasion to grieve for what this world was like before the coming of the white man and to recall and reclaim the cultural values of that world. What we acknowledge is the burgeoning spirit of resistance that will undoubtedly rock this nation so that the earth, the ground on which we stand and live, will be fundamentally changed — turned over as we turn back to a concern for the collective harmony and life of the planet.

Thinking about the Columbus legacy and the foundations of white supremacy in the United States, I am drawn most immediately to Ivan Van Sertima and to his groundbreaking book, *They Came Before Columbus.* Documenting the presence of Africans in this land before Columbus, his work calls us to rethink issues of origin and beginnings. Often the profound political implications of Van Sertima's work is ignored. Yet in a revolutionary way, this work calls us to recognize the existence in American history of a social reality where individuals met one another within the location of ethnic, national, and cultural difference and who did not make of that difference a site of imperialist/cultural domination. When I recall learning about Columbus from grade school on, what stands out is the way we were taught to believe that the will to dominate and conquer folks who are different from ourselves is natural, not culturally specific. We were taught that the Indians would have conquered and dominated white explorers if they could have but they were simply not strong or smart enough. Embedded in all these teachings was the assumption that it was the whiteness of these explorers in the "New World" that gave them greater power. The word "whiteness" was never used. The key word, the one that was synonymous with whiteness, was "civilization." Hence, we were made to understand at a young age that whatever cruelties were done to the indigenous peoples of this country, the "Indians," was necessary to bring the great gift of civilization. Domination, it became clear in our young minds, was central to the project of civilization. And if civilization was good and necessary despite the costs, then that had to mean domination was equally good.

The idea that it was natural for people who were different to meet and struggle for power merged with the idea that it was natural for whites to travel around the world civilizing nonwhites. Despite progressive interventions in education that call for a rethinking of the way history is taught and culturally remembered, there is still little focus on the presence of Africans in the "New World" before Columbus. As long as this fact of history is ignored, it is possible to name Columbus as an imperialist, a colonizer, while still holding on to the assumption that the will to conquer is innate, natural, and that it is ludicrous to imagine that people who are different nationally, culturally, could meet each other and not have conflict be the major point of connection. The assumption that domination is not only natural but central to the civilizing process is deeply rooted in our cultural mind-set. As a nation we have made little transformative progress to eradicate sexism and racism precisely because most citizens of the United States believe in their heart of hearts that it is natural for a group or an individual to dominate over others. Most folks do not believe that it is wrong to dominate, oppress, and exploit other people. Even though marginalized groups have greater access to civil rights in this society than in many societies in the world, our exercise of these rights has done little to change the overall cultural assumption that domination is essential to the progress of civilization, to the making of social order.

Despite so much evidence in daily life that suggests otherwise, masses of white Americans continue to believe that black people are genetically inferior — that it is natural for them to be dominated. And even though women have proved to be the equals of men in every way, masses still believe that there can be no sustained social and family order if males do not dominate females, whether by means of benevolent or brutal patriarchies. Given this cultural mind-set, it is so crucial that progressives who seek to educate for critical consciousness remind our nation and its citizens that there are paradigms for the building of human community that do not privilege domination. And what better example do we have as a culture than the meeting of Africans and native peoples in the Americas? Studying this historical example we can learn much about the politics of solidarity. In the essay "Revolutionary Renegades" published in *Black Looks,* I emphasize the importance of ties between the Africans who came here before Columbus and Native American communities:

> The Africans who journeyed to the "New World" before Columbus recognized their common destiny with the Native peoples who gave them shelter and a

place to rest. They did not come to command, to take over, to dominate, or to colonize. They were not eager to sever their ties with memory; they had not forgotten their ancestors. These African explorers returned home peaceably after a time of communion with Native Americans. Contrary to colonial white imperialist insistence that it was natural for groups who are different to engage in conflict and power struggle, the first meetings of Africans and Native Americans offer a counter-perspective, a vision of cross-cultural contact where reciprocity and recognition of the primacy of community are affirmed, where the will to conquer and dominate was not seen as the only way to confront the Other who is not ourselves.

Clearly the Africans and Native peoples who greeted them on these shores offered each other a way of meeting across difference that highlighted the notion of sharing resources, of exploring differences and discovering similarities. And even though there may not remain a boundless number of documents that would affirm these bonds, we must call attention to them if we would dispel the cultural assumption that domination is natural.

Colonizing white imperialists documented the reality that the indigenous people they met did not greet them with the will to conquer, dominate, oppress, or destroy. In his journals and letters to Spanish patrons, Columbus described the gentle, peace-loving nature of Native Americans. In a letter to a Spanish patron, Columbus wrote (quoted in Howard Zinn's essay° "Columbus, the Indians, and Human Progress")

> They are very simple and honest and exceedingly liberal with all they have, none of them refusing anything he may possess when he is asked. They exhibit great love toward all others in preference to themselves.

Though he seemed in awe of the politics of community and personal relations that he witnessed among the indigenous people, Columbus did not empathize with or respect the new cultural values he was observing and allow himself to be transformed, born again with a new habit of being. Instead he saw these positive cultural values as weaknesses that made the indigenous people vulnerable, nations that could be easily conquered, exploited, and destroyed. This cultural arrogance was expressed in his journal when he boasted, "They would make fine servants. With fifty men we could subjugate them all and make them do whatever we want." At the core of the new cultural values Columbus observed was a subordination of materiality to collective welfare, the good of the community. From all accounts, there was no indigenous community formed on the basis of excluding outsiders so it was possible for those who were different—in appearance, nationality, and culture—to be embraced by the communal ethos.

Zinn's essay: Most likely refers to "Columbus, the Indians, and Human Progress," the first chapter of *A People's History of the United States* (1980) by American historian Howard Zinn (b. 1922).

It is the memory of this embrace that we must reinvoke as we critically interrogate the past and rethink the meaning of the Columbus legacy. Fundamentally, we are called to choose between a memory that justifies and privileges domination, oppression, and exploitation and one that exalts and affirms reciprocity, community, and mutality. Given the crisis the planet is facing—rampant destruction of nature, famine, threats of nuclear attack, ongoing patriarchal wars—and the way these tragedies are made manifest in our daily life and the lives of folks everywhere in the world, it can only be a cause for rejoicing that we can remember and reshape paradigms of human bonding that emphasize the increased capacity of folks to care for the earth and for one another. That memory can restore our faith and renew our hope.

Whether we are evoking memories of Columbus or the Africans who jour-   10
neyed before him, the legacy they both represent, though different, is masculine. One semester, I began my course on African American women writers speaking about this journey. For the first time, I talked about the fact that initial contact between Africans and Native Americans was first and foremost a meeting between men. Later, Columbus arrives—also with men. While the African and Native American men who greeted one another did not embody the characteristics of an imperialist misogynistic° masculine ideal, they shared with white colonizers a belief in gender systems that privilege maleness. This means that even though there were communities to be found in Africa and the Americas where women did have great privilege, they were always seen as fundamentally different from and in some ways always less than men. Zinn's essay emphasizes both "widespread rape of native women" by white colonizers as well as the degree to which the imperialist venture in the Americas was seen as a "masculine conquest." What contemporary speculative discussion do we have about the way indigenous men responded to the assaults on native women? Zinn emphasizes the way gendered metaphors were used to celebrate the colonizers' victory. He quotes Samuel Eliot Morison's patriarchal romanticization of this conquest: "Never again may mortal men hope to recapture the amazement, the wonder, the delight of those October days in 1492, when the new world gracefully yielded her virginity to the conquering Castilians." Indigenous men had no relationship to the land, to the world of their ancestor, to the earth that would have allowed them to evoke metaphors of rape and violation. To imagine the earth as a woman to be taken over, consumed, dominated was a way of thinking about life peculiar to the colonizer. My point is not that Native Americans and Africans did not hold sexist values, but that they held them differently from white colonizers; that there were among these diverse men of color and communities of color limits to masculine power. It is a tragic consequence of colonization that contemporary men of color seek to affirm nationhood and male power in specific cultural contexts by asserting a masculinity informed by the very worst of the white patriarchal legacy.

misogynistic: Related to a hatred of women.

In our cultural retelling of history we must connect the Columbus legacy with the institutionalization of patriarchy and the culture of sexist masculinity that upholds male domination of females in daily life. The cultural romanticization of Columbus's imperialist legacy includes a romanticization of rape. White colonizers who raped and physically brutalized native women yet who recorded these deeds as the perks of victory acted as though women of color were objects, not the subjects of history. If there was conflict, it was between men. Females were perceived as though they and their bodies existed apart from the struggle between males for land and territory. From that historical moment on, women of color have had to grapple with a legacy of stereotypes that suggest we are betrayers, all too willing to consent when the colonizer demands our bodies. Any critical interrogation of the Columbus legacy that does not call attention to the white supremacist patriarchal mind-set that condoned the rape and brutalization of native females is only a partial analysis. For contemporary critics to condemn the imperialism of the white colonizer without critiquing patriarchy is a tactic that seeks to minimize the particular ways gender determines the specific forms oppression may take within a specific group. It subsumes the rape and exploitation of native women by placing such acts solely within the framework of military conquest, the spoils of war, a gesture which mystifies the way in which patriarchal thinking works both apart from, and in conjunction with, imperialism to support and affirm sexual violence against females—particularly women of color. Why is it many contemporary male thinkers, especially men of color, repudiate the imperialist legacy of Columbus but affirm dimensions of that legacy by their refusal to repudiate patriarchy?

Are contemporary people of color not wedding ourselves to the Columbus legacy when we construct a cultural politics of tribal or national identity that perpetuates the subordination of women? If contemporary notions of ethnic subcultural nationhood and identity condone and celebrate female subordination by males via the perpetuation of sexist thinking and behavior, then progressive demands for a rethinking of history will never be fundamentally linked with a politics of solidarity that fully repudiates domination. No transformative interventions can take place to end oppression and exploitation as long as we critique one form of domination and embrace another.

The Columbus legacy is clearly one that silences and eradicates the voices—the lives—of women of color. In part to repair the damage of this history, the way it has been taught to us, the way it has shaped how we live our lives, we must seize this moment of historical remembering to challenge patriarchy. No amount of progressive rethinking of history makes me want to call to mind the fate of native women during the imperialist conquest of the Americas. Or the extent to which their fate determined the destiny of enslaved African Americans. There is only sorrow to be found in evoking the intensity of violence and brutalization that was part of the Western colonization of the minds and bodies of native women and men. We can, however, call that legacy to mind in a spirit of collective mourning, making our grief a catalyst for resistance. Naming our grief empowers it and us. Chickasaw writer Linda Hogan [in her essay "Columbus Debate" from the October 1992 issue of *Elle*] reminds us of the depth of this sorrow.

> No people could have imagined anything as terrible as what happened here — such terrors, a genocide that is ongoing, the beginning of a grief we still feel. What has been done to the land has been done to the people; we are the same thing. And all of us are injured by the culture that separates us from the natural world and our inner lives, all of us are wounded by a system that grew out of such genocide, destruction to the land and society.

Our indigenous comrades who struggle for freedom in South Africa° remind us that "our struggle is also a struggle of memory against forgetting." To remember is to empower. Even though these memories hurt, we dare to name our grief and pain and the sorrow of our ancestors, and we defiantly declare that the struggle to end patriarchy must converge with the struggle to end Western imperialism. We remember the particular fate of indigenous women at the hands of white supremacist patriarchal colonizers; we remember to honor them in acts of resistance, to reclaim the sound of their protests and rage, the sound that no history books record.

In the past year, I have rejected all overtures to speak or write anything   15 about Columbus. Again and again, I would hear myself saying, "I don't really ever think about Columbus." Critically interrogating this assertion, I unpacked the levels of untruth it holds. It is not that simple — that I just do not think about Columbus. I want to forget him, to deny his importance, because those earliest childhood memories of learning about Columbus are tied to feelings of shame that "red and black" people (as I thought of us then) were victimized, degraded and exploited by these strange white discoverers. In truth, I can close my eyes and vividly call to mind those images of Columbus and his men sketched in history books. I can see the crazed and savage looks that were on the faces of indigenous men, just as I remember the drawings of sparsely clothed, shackled African slaves. I want to forget them even as they linger against my will in memory. Writing in a letter to a friend, Laguna novelist and poet Leslie Silko speaks about the place of images in the mind's eye, describing what it is like when we think we recall a specific event, as though we were really present, only to find out that our memory of that moment has been shaped by a photograph. Silko writes, "Strange to think that you heard something — that you heard someone describe a place or a scene when in fact you saw a picture of it, saw it with your own eyes." And I would add even stranger when those pictures linger in the imagination from generation to generation. When I recall the shame I felt seeing those images, of the Indian and the

---

Our indigenous comrades who struggle for freedom in South Africa: Apartheid, the South African policy of officially sanctioned racial discrimination, ended along with white rule in 1994.

"great" white men, I recognize that there is also rage there. I was not only angry at these images, which did not feel right in my heart, I felt that being forced to look at them was like being forced to witness the symbolic reenactment of a colonizing ritual, a drama of white supremacy. The shame was feeling powerless to protest or intervene.

We are not powerless today. We do not choose to ignore or deny the significance of remembering Columbus because it continues to shape our destiny. By speaking, opposing the romanticization of our oppression and exploitation, we break the bonds with this colonizing past. We remember our ancestors, people of color—Native American and African, as well as those individual Europeans who opposed genocide in word and deed. We remember them as those who opened their hearts, who bequeathed us a legacy of solidarity, reciprocity, and communion with spirits that we can reclaim and share with others. We call on their knowledge and wisdom, present through generations, to provide us with the necessary insight so that we can create transformative visions of community and nation that can sustain and affirm the preciousness of all life.

EXPLORING THE TEXT

1. Why does hooks introduce this examination of the impact of the Columbus myth by telling the story of her encounter with a late-night messenger? What purpose—or purposes—does this brief introductory anecdote serve?

2. What, according to hooks, is the role of the Columbus myth in relation to the "dominant culture"? What, in her view, is the cultural "legacy" of the Columbus story? What does it suggest about Native Americans, women of color, white Europeans, civilization, and domination? In what other ways might the story of Columbus and the "discovery" of America be interpreted?

3. Hooks notes that "progressive interventions" have already begun to reshape how the story of Columbus is remembered in American schools. How was the story of "discovery" presented when you encountered it in school? To what extent has your education—in history or other types of classes—reinforced the kind of cultural lessons that hooks describes?

4. What alternatives does hooks offer to the traditional version of Columbus's "discovery" of the Americas? How, in her view, should we commemorate this historical event? How do you think we should commemorate the "discovery" of America? Why?

5. Hooks says that although she would rather not remember Columbus at all, she is haunted by images that linger in her memory against her will. What images haunt you when you close your eyes and "remember" the American past? Where do these images come from?

FURTHER EXPLORATIONS

1. To what extent does Maxine Hong Kingston's revision of the story of her aunt's death in "No-Name Woman" (p. 206) offer an example of the kind of "cultural

retelling" of the past that hooks calls for in this selection? In what ways might Kingston's revision of this family story be seen as an act of "resistance"?

2. How does hooks's personal response to the historical legend of Columbus challenge or help clarify the nature of impersonal memories as described by Eviatar Zerubavel (p. 217)? How accurate is it to view hooks's memory of colonization as "impersonal"?

3. How might hooks respond to Walker Percy's claim (p. 118) that the only person to truly appreciate the beauty of the Grand Canyon was Garcia López de Cárdenas, the European explorer who "discovered" it? To what extent does Percy's theory of perception as "confrontation" perpetuate what might be seen as a colonialist or sexist view of our relation to the world of the senses?

4. How might the idea of the dissonance between "remembered" and "remembering" selves as presented by Susan Engel (p. 192) explain hooks's desire to "retell" the cultural history of the colonized? How do the "personas" of men and women of color change in hooks's retelling? To what extent do the changes that hooks calls for in our cultural memories of Columbus reflect a change in the "audience" those memories address?

5. To what extent might bell hooks view Lame Deer's critique of white civilization (p. 512) as an example of political resistance—an illustration of the way that an alternative memory of the past can be used to subvert domination in the present?

ESSAY OPTIONS

1. Drawing on the ideas and experiences presented by bell hooks, Patricia Hampl (p. 180), Maxine Hong Kingston (p. 206), and Eviatar Zerubavel (p. 217), write an essay discussing how individuals transform "impersonal" historical memories in order to integrate them with their own values and beliefs.

2. Research portrayals of Christopher Columbus in current history textbooks and write a paper in which you report your findings and compare them with the version of the Columbus myth presented in this selection. How do recent textbook portrayals of Columbus compare with the traditional version of the Columbus story? How do they differ? To what extent does your research support hooks's suggestion that "progressive interventions" have already begun to change the way we remember the events of 1492? Do you personally think that such revisions are appropriate? Why or why not?

3. In your college library, locate and read excerpts relating to Columbus in Ivan Van Sertima's *They Came Before Columbus*, Howard Zinn's *A People's History of the United States*, Ward Churchill's *A Little Matter of Genocide: Holocaust and Denial in the Americas, 1492 to the Present*, or any other recent retelling of the story of the "discovery" of the Americas. Use the information you gather as the basis of a paper in which you compare this version of the Columbus myth with the "traditional" version of the story. How is Columbus portrayed in the retelling of history that you read? What are his motives and views of indigenous peoples? How are native peoples themselves portrayed? To what extent does this retelling of history represent what hooks calls "an act of resistance"?

3

Reading the Self
Ghosts in the Machine?

"Beam Me Up, Scottie"

It's the stuff of science fiction. As any fan of *Star Trek* can tell you, teletransportation is a perfectly safe and reliable process. In almost every episode of the original television series, Captain Kirk and a contingent of Enterprise officers take their places on the transporter platform, dutifully waiting until Scottie can beam them to wherever adventure beckons. A moment later, captain and crew evaporate into thin air, leaving only a blurry afterimage onboard the ship, and then rematerialize, no worse for wear, thousands of miles away. Of course, nobody explains how Captain Kirk and his crew pull off this nifty trick. Do they cease to exist—even for a moment—between the time of their decomposition and miraculous reappearance? Are the actual molecules that make up their bodies taken apart and sent through space? Or are their bodies scanned, mapped, disassembled, and discarded, so that they can be reassembled from a stock of spare atoms later on? Would it matter if the original Captain Kirk were incinerated weekly by Scottie in the transporter room to be replaced by an anatomically and psychologically exact replica? Why? To whom?

No one in their right mind sits around asking these questions—unless, that is, you're a philosopher or neuroscientist obsessed with discovering the secrets of the self. Then it becomes hard not to wonder what separates Captain Kirk from the rest of us. After all, we know that once every six or seven years, every cell in the human body wears out and gets replaced, so aren't we in pretty much the same situation as the "incinerated" Captain Kirk? The only difference is the speed of the process. Over the course of a lifespan, every atom we're made of gets duplicated and replaced nine or ten times; only the special arrangement—the mapping—remains the same. Still, if you could be transported anywhere you wanted to go in the blink of an eye, would you do it—assuming that it would mean that the original "you" would be discarded and replaced by an exact duplicate when you got there? If you would, what do you think would happen if, due to a glitch in the transporter, your original you wasn't destroyed and two "yous" continued to exist? Which one would be the real you? Which one would hold title to your sense of self?

Selfhood is a slippery concept—a real tribute to the power of abstract thought. No one has ever seen or touched a self. You can grab your brother's hand, but is that the same as grabbing his "self"? If, for some tragic reason, he lost his hand in an accident, would he then have less "selfness"? Over the centuries, people have located the seat of the self in different parts of the body. Aristotle believed that the self made its home in the heart. For the seventeenth-century French philosopher René Descartes, the self held sway in the pineal gland, a tiny organ in the middle of the brain that he believed controlled all willed and intellectual activity. Today, we still commonly think of the self as a kind of person in miniature inside our heads. The self is the "I" whose voice we hear when we think, the internal subject who "owns" our being, the mind's decision maker who wills the actions that our arms and legs perform. In the words of philosopher and social commentator Arthur Koestler, the self is a "ghost in the machine" of the body, a kind of spiritual CEO that calls the shots of consciousness. We may not be able to touch or see the "I" that speaks inside us, and we may never find out exactly where it resides, but all of us intuitively believe that we have one and that it has its own history, qualities, and unique characteristics.

Odd as it may seem, some researchers believe that our ancestors once lived without a well-defined sense of self. In fact, it's even been proposed that the idea of a coherent inner self that endures from day to day is a relatively new phenomenon, one that arose during the last few thousand years of human history when the left and right hemispheres of the brain were welded together into a single mind by a bridge of densely packed nervous tissue known as the corpus callosum. Before that crucial evolutionary step, we humans supposedly heard other "voices" speaking to us in our heads—mythic voices that expressed the wills of the gods or that spoke for the rivers, trees, and animals who shared the world of nature with us.

The self really took off as a concept with the development of religion. Once the voice of consciousness became identified with the "I" of the thinker, it was only a short imaginative leap to the idea of the soul. The notion that a part of the self could transcend the physical limits of the body and endure beyond death set the stage for the modern concept of individual consciousness. In the West, Christianity was particularly predisposed to embrace the concept of an unseen, hidden soul or self. Originally developing as an underground cult, Christianity easily accommodated the idea that the body contained a secret place, a sacred sanctuary where an individual's most cherished feelings, values, and beliefs could be preserved amid the corruption of a world of "fallen" nonbelievers and "false" social forms and conventions. This view of the soul as sanctuary made it possible to draw an imaginary boundary around the self, a kind of mental frontier that set up a number of crucial intellectual oppositions—oppositions like those between self and other, mind and body, individual and society, appearance and reality—oppositions that have had a profound impact on Western ideas about human identity and the nature of individual consciousness.

In the nineteenth century, this fundamentally religious notion of the self was carried to its logical extreme by one of America's leading philosophers and essayists. Ralph Waldo Emerson was the best-known and most widely respected American intellectual of the mid-1800s. Trained as a minister, Emerson was a leader in the American transcendentalist movement. He devoted himself to the spiritual awakening of his fellow Americans, a task he attempted to achieve through public presentations of the essays that he spent his life crafting. As a transcendentalist, Emerson believed that every individual is directly connected to what he and other transcendentalists termed the "over-soul"—an expression of divine intelligence that radiates throughout creation. Linked directly to this emanation of divinity, the individual is born in a state of grace; his intuitions and impulses are pure and wise, and he falls into error only when he is distracted from inner truth by the temptations offered by society and its rules and conventions. Here's a sample of Emerson at his best, taken from one of his most celebrated essays, "Self Reliance":

> Society everywhere is in conspiracy against the manhood of every one of its members. Society is a joint-stock company in which the members agree for the better securing of his bread to each shareholder, to surrender the liberty and the culture of the eater. The virtue in most request is conformity. Self-reliance is its aversion. It loves not realities and creators, but names and customs.
>
> Whoso would be a man, must be a nonconformist. He who would gather immortal palms must not be hindered by the name of goodness, but must explore if it be goodness. Nothing is at last sacred, but the integrity of your own mind. Absolve you to yourself, and you shall have the suffrage of the world. I remember an answer which when quite young I was prompted to make to a valued advisor who was wont to importune me with the dear old doctrines of the church. On my saying, "What have I to do with the sacredness of tradition, if I live wholly from within?" my friend suggested—"But these impulses may be from below, not from above." I replied, "They do not seem to me to be such; but if I am the Devil's child, I will live then from the Devil." No law can be sacred to me but that of my nature. Good and bad are but names very readily transferable to that or this; the only right is what is after my constitution; the only wrong what is against it. (148)

Emerson's language may seem antique, but his message is as fresh as the latest bit of self-help wisdom or rage-rock lyric: stay true to your self, don't be misled by the "smiling faces" and false values you see around you, and you can't go wrong. This vision of the radically self-reliant individual—one that exists not merely *apart from* but *opposed to* history, society, and culture—underlies some of our most cherished national ideals, from the notion that every individual deserves equal justice under the law to the fundamental idea that individuals have the right to live freely without undue intrusion by society or state. It is a vision that has dominated American society without challenge for nearly two centuries, right up until new voices and new ways of thinking about identity and the nature of the self emerged in the United States during the latter half of the twentieth century.

The past twenty years have witnessed an unprecedented reassessment of the notion of the radically independent self. Cognitive scientists like MIT's Marvin Minsky have rejected the calculus of one self to a customer, preferring instead to envision the mind as a place made up of many competing intelligent "agents," each with its own distinctive agenda and interests. Cross-cultural scholars have argued that the individual self is an artifact of Western thinking and that it does not do justice to more complex versions of selfhood current in non-Western social contexts. And most recently, the prospect of human cloning has raised even more profound questions about the future of the self. What will it mean, for example, when the replication of human beings becomes a matter of daily medical practice and not the stuff of science fiction? Today, as never before, scientists, scholars, and philosophers are rethinking the significance of selfhood and reexamining the nature of the "ghost" that inhabits the body's machine.

Style and Voice: The Writer's Self

The self of a writer is, naturally enough, made up of words. You can tell a lot about a writer from the things she chooses to write about, the point of view she takes on her topic, and the assumptions she makes about her readers. When a writer argues against the death penalty, she does more than present a case against capital punishment; she presents the reader with an image of who she is as a person. You might expect a foe of capital punishment, for example, to be a person who is predisposed to doubt the absolute authority of the state — someone who leans to the progressive or libertarian side of the political spectrum — or, perhaps, someone who has strong moral or ethical principles. Choice of topic tells us a great deal about a writer, but the most personal part of a writer's self is best expressed in his or her style. Style is that combination of verbal habits and preferences that adds up to a sense of voice. Some writers tend to express themselves in short crisp sentences based on straightforward grammatical structures and relatively plain language. Others take a more complex approach, opting for complicated syntactical or grammatical structures and a more "scholarly" choice of words or diction. Listen carefully to the rhythm and tone of Emerson's voice as he describes the self-reliant individual: "Whoso would be a man, must be a nonconformist. He who would gather immortal palms must not be hindered by the name of goodness, but must explore if it be goodness. Nothing is at last sacred, but the integrity of your own mind." Emerson breaks each sentence into two balanced segments. This gives his voice a deliberate, mediative — and ultimately authoritative — tone. You can *hear* the conviction in his voice: he isn't just "jotting down" his ideas; he's "proclaiming" the truth.

Now listen to a few lines by Rubén Martínez, a contemporary Latino writer from Los Angeles, in which he describes the role that movies played in shaping his sense of self:

> I've always spent more time at movie houses or huddled up next to my TV and VCR than with my nose between the pages of a book. Truth be told, I read only books directly related to my research and a handful of literary faves. But sit down to read a new novel or the latest six-hundred-page biography on the *Times*'s best-seller list? Nah — who has the time in the Age of MTV? Me, I want to see colors rippling across a wide screen! I want to hear the characters' voices not with my mind's ear but with my real ear! And I want a soundtrack of violins and trumpets composed by a nonagenarian Russian émigré. I want crane shots and spaghetti-western super-closeups of eyes and crow's-feet crinkling. I want Bergman (Ingrid), Mitchum, Hayworth, and Poitier forever teamed up with Curtis, want them sneering-panting-whistling, and a single, soft-focused tear tracking down every one of their cheeks. (246)

More than just a hundred years of history separates Martínez from Emerson. While Emerson's voice is authoritative, ministerial, and oratorical—the kind of voice you'd expect to encounter in a great preacher—Martínez speaks in a voice that is familiar, casual, and cool. It isn't just a matter of his references to contemporary cultural phenomena like MTV or the "*Times*'s best-seller list." It's the tone established by his choice of words and the clipped style of his sentence structures. It's the way he'll begin a sentence with a little conversational tag phrase like "Truth be told . . . ," or deploy a slang word like "fave" to spice things up, or even deliberately commit a grammatical mistake like the "Me/I" double self-reference he uses in the middle of the paragraph. All in all, Martínez's style conveys the impression of a breezy, easy-going, bright, and maybe even likeable character—someone you might run into at a local hangout and enjoy swapping stories with for a couple of hours. It's a masterful verbal presentation of self—a self that we, as contemporary Americans, can feel at home with, even as we listen to the truths he chooses to proclaim and the lessons he wants to teach.

The real mystery is why many fledgling college writers choose to project a verbal self that is so dry, formal, and impersonal. It's almost as if many students assume that academic writing has to be "academic" sounding in order to be taken seriously. Most of us do walk around with a stereotype of what it means to "sound" intellectual in our heads. According to this stereotype, academic discourse is full of complicated abstract words, highfalutin concepts, and convoluted sentence structures. But while most academic writing does tend to be relatively impersonal and restrained, it doesn't have to be impenetrable and unclear. Here's an example of academic prose by sociologist Roy F. Baumeister:

> There are two further points to make about the evolution of the hidden, inner self as a standard way of thinking about selfhood. First, it increases the problematic nature of selfhood. If the self is a secret entity, indeed in important respects concealed even from the very person whose self it is, then self-knowledge is a difficult and elusive matter. Indeed, if all a person's actions and statements fail to reveal some inner truth, then it is unclear how one can ever be certain that one has understood the true inner self. . . . The modern concept of self-actualization takes the problem even a step further because it requires first a process of discovering the hidden inner realities and then a process of working to cultivate and develop these inner realities traits to reach their full potential. The version of selfhood implicit in all these modern concepts is one that carries a significant burden and a recipe for uncertainty, difficulty, and dissonance. (195)

Baumeister's voice is serious, logical, and pedagogical. It is the voice of a teacher who is presenting a carefully thought-out lesson to his students. And it serves his purpose well. Unfortunately, many students think that by imitating the logical and pedagogical "tone" of academic discourse, they will somehow begin to think like an academician. What they often fail to see is that tone alone is no substitute for careful reasoning, and that by striving to imitate a scholarly style, they never tackle the real work of developing a voice that conveys a sense of their own identity as writers and thinkers.

Chapter Overview

This chapter is designed to help you explore how we construct the fragile things we call selves and to examine how these constructions grow out of the cultural contexts that give them birth. The chapter opens, appropriately enough, with an essay on the most fundamental characteristic of every self — the opposition of self and other. In his "Ego Boundaries, or the Fit of My Father's Shirt," neurologist Robert Sapolsky reveals how the death of his father led him to question not only the nature of their relationship, but the integrity and the coherence of his own identity. Next, University of Chicago psychologist Mihaly Csikszentmihalyi explores the role that objects and artifacts play in the way that we humans shape a sense of self from the social and cultural environments we grow up in. Alice Walker's classic short story "Everyday Use" illustrates the relationship between objects and identity and offers two contrasting views of the nature of selfhood. A theoretical context for analyzing Walker's story is presented in Arnold M. Ludwig's "Living Backwards." Ludwig's exploration of the nature of the self in terms of the life stories, roles, plots, and scripts that we adopt from the cultures we belong to offers a frame of reference that can be applied to readings throughout the text and to general experience as well. The first half of the chapter closes with "Technicolor," Rubén Martínez's impassioned declaration of his indebtedness to John Wayne, Audie Murphy, and a host of other Hollywood heroes and the roles they played for the self — or "selves" — that he eventually became.

The next two selections in the chapter focus more narrowly on cross-cultural conceptions of the self and their implications. In "The Self and Society: Changes, Problems, and Opportunities," Roy F. Baumeister describes the historical development of the "inner" sense of self that dominates Western cultures and discusses some of the dangers that it poses when it displaces traditional sources of value and authority. In "A Mutable Self," anthropologist Mary Catherine Bateson draws on her experiences in Iran, Israel, and the Philippines as she considers alternatives to the "rigid" version of selfhood she identifies with the United States.

The chapter concludes with two selections that challenge us to rethink almost every assumption we have about the self. Philip Kitcher's "Whose Self Is It, Anyway?" turns our attention to the legal and ethical issues surrounding the phenomenon of cloning. Kitcher's analysis of the morality of cloning in three different scenarios offers a framework for discussing what many see as the greatest threat to the concept of human selfhood. University of Chicago ethicist Jean Bethke Elshtain closes the chapter with her categorical rejection of cloning as a method of reproduction. Elshtain's "To Clone or Not to Clone" sounds a note of warning about the dangers of cloning and raises questions about the role that contemporary notions of selfhood have played in making such "alternative" reproductive technologies acceptable.

Sources

Anderson, Walter Truett. *The Future of the Self: Exploring the Post-Identity Society.* New York: Jeremy P. Tarcher/Putnam, 1997.

Baumeister, Roy F. "The Self and Society." In *Self & Identity: Contemporary Philosophical Issues.* Ed. Daniel Kolak and Raymond Martin. New York: Macmillan Publishing Co., 1991.

Emerson, Ralph Waldo. "Self Reliance." In *The Selected Writings of Ralph Waldo Emerson.* Ed. Brooks Atkinson. New York: Random House Inc., 1940.

Jaynes, Julian. *The Origin of Consciousness in the Breakdown of the Bicameral Mind.* Boston: Houghton Mifflin Company, 1976.

Koestler, Arthur. *The Ghost in the Machine.* New York: MacMillan, 1967.

Martínez, Rubén, "Technicolor." In *Half and Half: Writers on Growing Up Biracial and Bicultural.* Ed. Claudia Chiawei O'Herarn. New York: Pantheon Books, 1998.

McGinn, Colin. *The Mysterious Flame: Conscious Minds in a Material World.* New York: Basic Books, 1999.

Minsky, Marvin. *The Society of Mind.* New York: Simon and Schuster, 1985.

Packer, Barbara. *Ralph Waldo Emerson.* Columbia Literary History of the United States. Ed. Emory Elliot. New York: Columbia University Press, 1988.

Parfit, Derek. "The Psychological View." In *Self & Identity: Contemporary Philosophical Issues.* Ed. Daniel Kolak and Raymond Martin. New York: Macmillan Publishing Co., 1991.

Ego Boundaries, or the Fit of My Father's Shirt

ROBERT SAPOLSKY

The idea of multiple personalities packed in a single brain has been a perennial favorite ever since Doctor Jekyll made the acquaintance of Mr. Hyde in Robert Louis Stevenson's famous novel of 1886. Stories about "split personalities" — or multiple personality disorder as it is officially known — have long been a staple of popular culture. It seems that people just can't hear enough about the multiselved "Sybils" and "Eves" who live among us. In fact, over the past few decades there's been a veritable MPD "arms race," with case histories featuring more and more personalities coming to light. It's no longer enough to house two or three selves in a single body; now you have to cram at least twelve in to get any real attention.

Perhaps we're drawn to stories of multiple consciousnesses because the idea of boundary is so central to our understanding of the self. From our very first breath, we're involved in establishing the fragile border that separates our "I" from the "Others" who live around us. We spend the greater part of our lives defining where we begin and where the forces in our environment leave off. And with good reason, for what could be more devastating than losing track of the self that we've nurtured all these years? What could be worse than having two, three, or four "selves" suddenly drop in for an extended psychic visit? Actually, according to the firsthand experience of neurologist Robert Sapolsky, making room in your consciousness for a supplementary self isn't as difficult — or as rare an occurrence — as you might think. The psychological invasion that Sapolsky experiences after the death of his father raises fundamental questions about the nature of the self and the boundaries that define it. Sapolsky's account of his own brush with multiple consciousness also offers a perfect point of departure for your exploration of the mysteries of personal identity. Robert Sapolsky is a neuroendocrinologist at Stanford University, specializing in stress-induced diseases. He is a recipient of the MacArthur "genius award," a regular contributor to *Discover* magazine, and the author of *Why Zebras Don't Get Ulcers: A Guide to Stress, Stress-Related Disease, and Coping* (1993).

BEFORE READING

Working in small groups, pool your knowledge about the idea of multiple or "split" personalities. What stories or famous cases of multiple personalities are you familiar with? What is the common attitude toward someone who contains several different "selves"?

I 've been wondering how many bodies a person needs. This is not a question that would normally interest me as a scientist, yet it has crept into my consciousness lately, and I find I'm no longer sure of the answer.

One afternoon I watched someone inhabit two bodies. Stephen Hawking, the astrophysicist famed as much for his progressive paralysis from Lou Gehrig's disease as for his work, had come to my graduate school to lecture on the beginning and end of time. This was a decade ago, when Hawking could still move his mouth a bit, generating a gargly, incomprehensible voice. Though we didn't expect to understand the lecture with our rudimentary physics, we packed the auditorium, biochemists and physiologists and geneticists, to bear witness to Hawking's body melted by disease and his mind knowing when, or whether, time began.

Four physics professors, none of them young, carried Hawking onto the stage. They panted visibly, but it seemed as if only they could perform this task, that if you did not understand special relativity and you touched his wheelchair, you might be vaporized. After placing their burden, chair and all, with his back to us, the professors fled. Then, in the stillness, the electric wheelchair whirred and rotated, revealing a shriveled husk that stared out from behind horn-rimmed glasses.

As we sat there, paralyzed by awe at this mummy brain from the crypt, a tousled young guy in jeans sauntered onstage. He looked as if he'd just rolled out of bed and was still preoccupied with whomever he had left there. He walked up behind Hawking, tossed his head to adjust his blond mane, and suddenly shoved the wheelchair forward.

Jesus, Hawking is going to roll off the stage. This rock star assassin is murdering the great Stephen Hawking. At the last second the kid reaches out, barely stopping the wheelchair. He faces Hawking toward the audience and bends over the microphone. In an arrogant English public school accent he says, "You know, you're not in church."

This, apparently, is to be Hawking's interpreter. As Hawking begins, the arrogant voice translates the strangulated raspings. "Today I will discuss some theories of mine concerning the beginning and end of time. In some cases, these theories have been experimentally confirmed. In others, there has not yet been sufficient time for their confirmation." We chuckle—cocky bastard—before we catch ourselves. How can you think such a thing about Stephen Hawking?

As the lecture emerges with painstaking slowness but utter clarity, time glimmers into being without a beginning. Radio waves, defying possibility, escape from black holes. Equations appear, interlaced with a puckish humor.

But the kid is getting worse. While Hawking struggles, he tosses his chalk in the air, bored. He drops the chalk, forcing the mummy through the arduous task of starting again. Once, when he mistranslates a sentence, Hawking has to repeat himself. Glowering, the translator mutters, "You're not making yourself understood."

Who is this creature? Slowly it dawns on us. Hawking, in his Cambridge chair once occupied by Newton, has selected him as his student, his intimate. This is his chosen voice. Something begins to shift in our picture of the mummy brain.

Before the illness, Hawking was a showboat, ostentatiously functioning at half speed to barely finish some task before returning to a party, all with a dissolute brilliance. He must have been just like this kid. And it hits us: they planned this—the careering wheelchair, the insouciance—to desanctify our experience. The conspiracy we sense is so intimate that Hawking seems to have borrowed his student's very being. For an hour the mummy brain is gone. Instead we're listening to an entertaining lecture by a cocky Cambridge don°—one who just happens to need two bodies to pull it off.

Hawking's act was a metaphor, a piece of theater. It was also, one assumes, temporary. Still, it raises a number of questions: Can bodies and consciousnesses disagree in number? Can they do so for a prolonged period of time? The issue has not often interested neuroscientists, but there is the significant exception of split-brain patients. While the brain is roughly symmetrical, its functions can be lateralized—the left and right sides perform different tasks. The left hemisphere typically specializes in language, while the right excels in nonverbal spatial abilities, facial recognition, music. And despite absurd New Age assertions that people go about every conceivable behavior with "left brain" or "right brain" styles, the science of lateralization is solid.

a cocky Cambridge don: A teaching fellow at Cambridge University.

The two hemispheres communicate by a hefty cable of connections called the corpus callosum, and normally the conversation is beneficial. But in a certain type of epilepsy, one seizure can provoke another on the mirrored part of the opposite hemisphere. Back and forth the seizures chase, across the corpus callosum. Since the late 1950s some epileptics have had their corpora callosa severed surgically, halting their seizures but leaving the patients with two disconnected hemispheres. Roger Sperry, a neuroscientist, won a Nobel Prize for experiments with such patients. In some he fed information to only one hemisphere, while in others he fed different information to each side simultaneously. His results showed that the hemispheres could function separately, with separate analytic strengths. For example, if an object was presented to a patient's visual field so that the information entered only the verbal hemisphere, the person could identify the picture easily. But when the same information was presented to the nonverbal hemisphere, he couldn't even state that he had seen anything—yet he could identify the object by touch.

Sperry's experiments suggested that each hemisphere could learn, remember, reason, have opinions, initiate behavior, be self-aware, feel time pass, imagine the future, and generate emotions. This raised the messy prospect that there might be two individuals occupying one skull. Even worse: Perhaps normal people also consist of two separate individuals, yoked together by the corpus callosum. Psychologist Julian Jaynes addressed this possibility in a highly eccentric book, *The Origin of Consciousness in the Breakdown of the Bicameral Mind.* He argued that a coherent sense of self, a well-bounded ego, developed only three thousand or so years ago. Before that, he wrote, the brain was "bicameral" (that is, two-chambered), with the two hemispheres barely integrated. One hemisphere spoke, either metaphorically or literally, and the other obeyed, attributing the voice to the gods. Jaynes asserted that the modern sense of ego represents a breakdown of bicameralism. Schizophrenics remain bicameral, he claimed, supporting his ideas with mountains of trivia from archaeology, mythology, the classics, and the Bible. Savants found the book dizzyingly erudite, stimulating, and loony.

Unlike Jaynes, Sperry rejected the notion that there were two individuals inside anyone's head, and most scientists agreed with him. While split-brain patients could be manipulated into displaying two independent cognitive styles, the underlying opinions, memories, and emotions were the same. This could be explained anatomically. Even though the corpus callosum was cut, deeper structures of the brain that are critical to emotion and physiological regulation remained connected. Split brains are not really split into two but instead form a Y. There might be two separate consciousnesses, one navigating through town by remembering names of streets, the other by remembering a spatial map of the town's appearance—yet it was still the same individual. One body, one person.

A battle over how many selves can reside within one body surrounds the issue of multiple personality disorder. Different facets of our personality dominate in different settings: we may act like "a different person" when with a boss instead of a subordinate, or with a woman instead of a man. But we are not literally different people. In individuals with multiple personality disorder, however, separate personalities seem to take full control of the person's behavior at different times. Most mental health professionals agree that there are individuals in whom the different facets of personality are so disjointed and dissociated as to constitute disease. Often these patients describe having suffered horrific childhood abuse, and some theorists think the compartmentalizing of the different personalities evolved as a protective strategy. But do the nonoverlapping identities truly represent different personalities?

Some clinicians report hundreds of such patients and believe in the bio-   15
logical reality of the disorder, citing studies showing that when personalities shift, so do eyeglass or medication prescriptions. Other clinicians become apoplectic over such claims, insisting that a true multiple personality patient shows up once in a career, that the "different eyeglasses" stories are only stories.

The patriarchs of psychiatry have generally taken the latter view. In the latest edition of psychiatry's bible, the *Diagnostic and Statistical Manual of Mental Disorders,* there have been careful changes in the definition of the disorder; its diagnosis no longer involves the "existence" of multiple "personalities." Instead the prerequisite is the "presence" of "distinct identities or personality states," and the disease even has a new name: dissociative identity disorder. In other words, a patient with the disease identifies himself in multiple ways, but the experts refuse to say whether those identities constitute personalities. Moreover, to paraphrase a psychiatrist who helped make the changes in the manual, what makes this a tragic disease is that sufferers don't have more than one personality; when the pieces are put together, they really have less than one.

Dissociative identity disorder and split-brain patients raise the possibility of the self's fragmenting into several selves. Far more plausible, though, is the idea that it might occasionally make room for another self. Freudians° believe that this can occur and that when it does, it may reflect profound psychopathology.

In the face of loss, we all mourn with a certain sadness and withdrawal. Most of us eventually heal. However, some people who lose someone close to them fall into prolonged and incapacitating sadness—melancholia, to use Freud's term, or as we would now call it, a major depression. Along with the usual symptoms of mourning, deeply depressed people typically hate themselves, claim responsibility for the death, wallow in guilt over ancient behaviors, and engage in punishingly self-destructive behavior. In the healthy state of mourning, Freud wrote, "it is the world which has become poor and empty; in melancholia it is the ego itself."

Freudians: Adherents of the theory of psychoanalysis first propounded by Sigmund Freud (1856–1938).

Why should mourning give way to incapacitating sadness and self-hatred? The root, Freud thought, lay in ambivalence. The mourner not only loved but also hated the dead person. Critically, the loss leaves the depressive unconsciously angry—at being abandoned by the dead person, over their previous conflicts, at the impossibility of ever resolving those conflicts. Out of anger, the depressive makes room within for aspects of the dead. With the emotional adversary gone, there is no choice but to reconstruct the lost person internally and then carry on the battle.

And, as Freud also observed, the depressive mourner internalizes not just   20 any features of the lost individual but those that were the most hated. "If one listens patiently to a melancholic's many and various self-accusations," Freud wrote, "one cannot in the end avoid the impression that often the most violent of them are hardly at all applicable to the patient himself, but that with insignificant modifications they do fit someone else, someone whom the patient loves or has loved or should love." By carrying on the traits, one can still argue ("You see, don't you hate when I do that? Can you believe I put up with that for fifty years?") and, through the terrible pain of a major depression, punish oneself for arguing.

Science, then, has only occasionally considered cases of the self's fragmenting or withering sufficiently to make room for another, cases in which more than one self might dwell in one body. There has been even less concern for the possibility of one self's occupying more than a single body. And, all things considered, these musings haven't generated much scientific certainty about what really constitutes a self.

I myself was neither certain of the definition nor particularly interested in the question until recently, when my father reached the end of his life. Then all at once I found the boundaries of self collapsing around my ears. At first I felt I could use the discourse of science to explain my experience fully, viewing its extreme manifestations as pathology.

As my father aged, he suffered cognitive problems secondary to neurological damage. Often he could not name the decade, his location, or even his grandchildren. His ego boundaries began to dissolve as well, and gradually he purloined bits of my life, the life of his only son. There were similarities already. Long ago he had done medical research, as I do now. He had been a professor, as I am. We had always shared tastes, styles, and temperaments, but now the details of our lives began to intertwine. When I moved to San Francisco, his point of entry into the United State in 1919 switched to San Francisco from New York's Ellis Island, and his first view of America included a Golden Gate Bridge that had not yet been built. His medical research, cut short by the Depression, had been in cancer biology, but now he was full of contentless memories of an interest in neurobiology, my subject.

I don't believe it was competitiveness or a need for us to have more in common—we had too much in common already. It was easy to see me as a version of him without the bad luck of refugee status, world wars, and the

Depression, privileged with the rewards that his obsessive hard work had provided me, looking forward to perhaps a half century of life ahead, while his shadows lengthened. As the fog of his disorientation swept in, he clung to my stories, becoming less certain of where he ended and I began.

This felt more than a bit intrusive, but I defended myself with an armamentarium of diagnoses and detached, condescending understanding. *Another feature of the demented patient,* I'd imagine myself lecturing, *that one occasionally sees....* At night he'd wander the house in agitation, sure he saw angry strangers or long-dead colleagues. His confusion about which of the two of us was falling in love with California redwoods seemed the least of his problems. Cut the guy some slack, I thought; there's been some neurological damage.

His recent death knocked me off my diagnostic high horse: suddenly I was the one who had problems with boundaries. It started manageably enough. I began to spout my father's sayings and take on his mannerisms. This was not Freudian melancholia — while I was plenty sad, I wasn't clinically depressed, and the behaviors of his that I seized weren't the ones that had irritated me for decades with a competitive itch. They were the insignificant quirks that had made him who he was. I found myself arranging the utensils as he had, or humming his favorite Yiddish tune, and soon I had forsaken my own blue flannel shirts and put on his. I developed an interest in his profession, architecture, absentmindedly drawing floor plans of my apartment.

At first my reactions seemed reasonable. When I was younger, I would have bristled at signs that I carried bits of him in me. Over the years, though, I had become reconciled to our differences and similarities, and now I felt I could pay him homage without my earlier bile. Then things took a troubling turn.

Just after his death, when I spent a week of mourning at the family house, the magnitude of his final frailty was brought home to me by the little bottles of nitroglycerin that were stored everywhere, placed so that they'd never be out of reach. I took one back to California and, disturbingly, found I needed to keep it with me. I would make love to my wife, work out in the gym, attend a lecture, and always the bottle would be nearby. One day I misplaced it briefly, and everything stopped for an anxious search. I felt an urgent sense of danger. Was my heart now diseased, or was it his diseased heart somewhere inside me that I vigilantly stood by to medicate?

What the hell was going on? I don't believe in gods, angels, or the transmigration of souls. I don't believe in souls for that matter, or in flying saucers either. Was it my hard-assed individualism that was making me feel unnerved by this intermingling? Or could it have been my father's?

The height of the confusion came a month later, as I was lecturing. Though my class, with it 400 undergraduates, was large and impersonal, many of the students had expressed warm, supportive thoughts after my father died, and I had come to feel close to them. At the end of the year's final lecture, I thought to tell them about what a spectacular lecturer my father had been, to pass on some of what I had learned from his teaching. I intended a eulogy, but something became confused, and soon, wearing his shirt, I was lecturing for him, offering the frail advice of an octogenarian.

I warned them to expect setbacks amid their ambitious plans, because every commitment would entail turning their backs on many others. I told them that though they wanted to change the world, they should prepare for the inconceivable — someday they would become tired. This was not me speaking, still with a sheltered optimism, but him with his weathered disappointments. At the end, wondering whether so much emotion was setting me up for one of his angina attacks, I said good-bye for him to an ocean of 20-year-olds rippling with life and future. And that night I put away the nitroglycerin.

During that month, my head swam with unlikely disorders from my textbooks to explain this intermingling. Now, a year later, safe again on my battlefield of individuation, that time has begun to make more sense to me. I feel sure what I went through does not require a diagnosis, and I no longer believe that my father's confusion about the boundaries between the two of us really had to do with his neurological problems. It is a measure of the pathological consequences of my training as a scientist that I saw pathology where there was none, and a measure of the poverty of our times that I could feel only as a brief flicker something intrinsic to human experience.

I have occasionally been able to observe that flicker burning more robustly. As part of my research, I have worked intermittently in an East African game park for seventeen years. Often I accompany one or another of my African friends to his home in some hamlet clinging to a mountainside. Invariably, when I do, I notice that in his home my friend has become an outsider like me. The ones I know are the ones who left — the second sons, the restless ones, the ones who got some schooling and a far-off job, who find themselves stumbling over words in their mother tongue, bringing home new ways and a white friend.

And my friends have always left the same sort of world, a world with one old man whom everyone recognizes as the archetypal Old Man, one damaged village idiot wandering the slopes, one wife-beating drunkard. At my friend's house I always meet the older brother, the first son, the one who stayed. He sits next to his aging father: two farmers who speak no English or Swahili, who have been to the county seat once, perhaps, but no farther. They grunt phlegmatically in unison, half amused and half puzzled by some hyperverbal story my friend tells about the big city.

It is a world without our Western frenzy for individuation, where no parent thinks "I want better for my kids" and it is absurd to ask a child what he or she wants to grow up to be. No one there views joining the family business as a worrisome lack of independence. In this tough world, you're lucky if you wind up farming the same land and raising your kids the same way your parents did, or if, as these older brothers do, you turn into your parent, your identities melding.

Thomas Mann° captured this sense of continuity in his novel *Joseph and His Brothers*, in which an old servant named Eliezer uses the first person to narrate the experiences of an earlier Eliezer—the servant of the biblical patriarch Abraham.° It was perceived as normal, Mann tells us, "that the old man's ego was not quite clearly demarcated, that it opened at the back, as it were, and overflowed into spheres external to his own individuality both in space and in time; embodying in his own experience events which . . . ought actually to have been put into the third person." As he ages, the present-day Eliezer becomes the mythic one, and the community expects him to do so.

Every traditional community must have its archetypes: Eliezer, the wise servant; Esau and Jacob, brothers battling for an ailing father's blessing; Abraham, the ur-patriarch. These needs transcend individual rights to a bounded ego, and people in traditional communities are named and raised as successive incarnations. In such societies, Abraham always lives 900 years—he simply finds a new body to inhabit now and then. This is not Jaynes's society of bicameral minds innocent of a sense of self. Instead the self exists, but it's subordinated to something bigger and tribal.

We no longer reverence continuity, and to feel even a glimmer of it, as I did, requires an emotional crisis, perhaps coupled with some tempering. My students usually come with ego boundaries like exoskeletons. Most have no use for religion, precedents, or tradition. They want their rituals newly minted and shared horizontally within their age group, not vertically over time. The ones I train to become scientists go at it like warriors, overturning reigning paradigms, each discovery a murder of their scientific ancestors. If I have trained them well, I must derive whatever satisfaction I can from the inevitability of becoming their oedipal target someday. These students are right on maturational schedule in believing they can reinvent the world within themselves, and if they should happen to find themselves confused as to where they end and another person begins, they know they are dealing with something scientifically, certifiably abnormal.

I've become less certain, myself. I can still do without religion, but some ritual would be nice. There are other changes, too. I watch these damn kids sprint past me when I play soccer, and I fumble for an answer to a *Jeopardy* question the high school contestants jump on. My beard is getting some white; my spine has probably started shrinking. Another few birthdays and it will be prudent to have a physician regularly poke around my prostate. I begin to think my ego-bounded self is not such a hot deal anymore.

A tribal mind-set cannot be reattained; we cannot turn back. It can only   40
come as an echo of what it feels like to be swaddled in continuity, a hint in our individuated world that a bit of confusion about ego boundaries can be an act of health, of homage and love. An experience like my father's and mine is a lesson, amid our ever-expanding array of scientific labels, about the risks of over-

Thomas Mann: (1875–1955), German novelist.

the biblical patriarch Abraham: In the Old Testament (Genesis 22:1–13), the founder of the Hebrew people who was commanded by God to sacrifice his first-born son, Isaac.

pathologizing. It might not be so bad — it could even be a point of pride — if in the end someone mistakes you for him.

EXPLORING THE TEXT

1. How would you characterize Sapolsky's initial attitude toward Stephen Hawking in the anecdote he uses to introduce this essay? How is this attitude challenged by Hawking's choice of a spokesman? What is the point of this story? How effective is it as an introductory strategy?

2. How, according to Sapolsky, do scientists tend to view the issue of multiple personalities? What was Sigmund Freud's view of the phenomenon? How does Sapolsky himself react as a scientist when he begins to experience a "loosening" of his ego boundaries? What risk does he perceive in the tendency to "overpathologize" such events?

3. How do Sapolsky's experiences in East Africa challenge his understanding of what selfhood means? How is the self defined, according to Sapolsky, in traditional tribal cultures?

4. In your view, was Sapolsky "sick" or clinically depressed when he began to wear his father's clothing, carry his medicine around with him, and speak to his students as if he were an eighty-year-old man reflecting on the meaning of his life? How does he come to understand this experience? How would you view him if he had not found his way back to the "battlefield of individuation"?

5. What is Sapolsky trying to suggest about the nature of selfhood in this essay? How would you describe his purpose as a writer?

FURTHER EXPLORATIONS

1. To what extent do the experiences of Scott Russell Sanders in "The Inheritance of Tools" (p. 142), and/or Maxine Hong Kingston in "No-Name Woman" (p. 206) confirm or challenge the notion that our ego boundaries can expand to incorporate aspects of the identities of other people? What difference is there, if any, between incorporating aspects of another self and simply holding on to memories of a person who has played an important role in your life?

2. What questions might Eviatar Zerubavel's discussion of impersonal memory (p. 217) raise about the notion of ego boundaries? To what extent does Zerubavel's concept of "mnemonic socialization" challenge the common conception of a freely existing, independent self?

3. How might Sapolsky's analysis of ego boundaries help explain the decision Alice Walker's narrator makes in "Everyday Use" (p. 283) to refuse her daughter's request for the family's heirloom quilts? Which of Walker's characters seems to have the most rigidly defined sense of self? Which seems to have the most fluid or open ego boundary? Which seems most distinctly "Western"? Why?

4. How do the "mythic" or "archetypal" identities that Sapolsky discovers in tribal society compare with the notion of life stories, roles, and scripts presented by Arnold M. Ludwig in "Living Backwards" (p. 292)? What distinguishes the archetype of "the Old Man," the "wife-beating drunkard," or the "wise servant"

from the modern roles we play, according to Ludwig? How might this complicate or challenge Sapolsky's assertion that a "tribal mind-set cannot be reattained"?

5. The topics of aging and ego boundaries have been treated in a number of recent movies, including *American Beauty* and *Magnolia*. View one of these films and analyze how the issue of selfhood is treated. Which characters strike you as having particularly closed or rigid ego boundaries? Which seem more open to the influences of the other "selves" around them? What does the film you view suggest about dominant conceptions of the self in contemporary American society?

ESSAY OPTIONS

1. Write a personal essay about a time when you felt yourself adopting some of the attitudes, values, ideas, mannerisms, speech patterns, or gestures of a person who was a mentor or guide to you. This person might have been an influential teacher or relative or an important friend. How similar was this experience to the "opening" of ego boundaries experienced by Sapolsky? To what extent do you recall feeling at all unsettled or uneasy about the influence of this person on your developing sense of self?

2. Drawing on ideas and experiences of Sapolsky, Scott Russell Sanders (p. 142), Maxine Hong Kingston (p. 206), and/or Rubén Martínez (p. 306), write an essay on the role played by parents and family in the construction of the self.

What Is the Self?[1]

MIHALY CSIKSZENTMIHALYI

It's a deceptively simple question. Since Socrates first urged his fellow Greeks to "Know thyself," philosophers, sages, and scholars have spent millennia trying to pin down the mind's most mysterious faculty. We all know instinctively what the self is and what the experience of having a self is like. But what goes into the making of a self? What are the ingredients that add up to the experience of what it's like to be the person who you are? In this selection, noted psychological theorist Mihaly Csikszentmihalyi offers his own version of the ingredients that go into the making of selfhood. It's a recipe that is bound to provoke some strong reactions—and one that will help you as you begin to reflect on the various elements that contribute to your sense of self. In addition to being professor and former department chair of the Department of Psychology at the University of Chicago, Csikszentmihalyi (b. 1934) is the author of a number of popular books on cognitive science, including *Beyond Boredom and Anxiety* (1975); *The Evolving Self: A Psychology for the Third Millennium* (1993), the source of this selection; and *Flow: The Psychology of Optimal Experience* (2001).

BEFORE READING

Working in groups, brainstorm your own collaborative recipe of what makes up the self. What ingredients or elements shape the self? What features or factors combine to help define who we are?

S tanding on a beach along the Atlantic or the Pacific, and looking out at the tremendous expanse of water, one cannot help but think something along the lines of "Ah, the mighty ocean!" Yet what we call the "ocean" is actually a mental construction, because all there is in front of us is just a great number of hydrogen and oxygen atoms dancing together to form what we call "water molecules." We don't see the molecules, only the sum of their effects, which we then imagine as a single entity: the Atlantic, the Pacific, the Mediterranean.

In order to make sense of the stimuli that bombard our senses, our nervous system has learned to bundle up information in manageable chunks, so that we are not overwhelmed by a mass of discrete details. Therefore, we see the particles of water as a single substance, we see the particles of air as the "sky," the mineral surface of the planet as the "earth," and so forth. Our minds, in reflecting on what we see, endow these images with separate identities, identities they have only in our imagination. This is the process of *reification*,° by which we attribute reality to mental constructions.

The self is such a reification, and certainly one of the most significant ones. We usually think of it as a force, a spark, an inner flame with an indivisible integrity. Yet, from what we know now, the self is more in the nature of a figment of the imagination, something we create to account for the multiplicity of impressions, emotions, thoughts, and feelings that the brain records in consciousness. In simpler organisms, the nervous system consists of more or less closed circuits. Only a few sensory channels are open, and these are connected to single, discrete motor responses. The organism doesn't have to make complex decisions, but reacts instinctively and piecemeal. But because the human brain has become so complex over time, there is too much information coming into it; a great variety of sensory data clamors for attention, and priorities have to be set. Eventually, a "traffic cop" function develops among the neurons of the brain to monitor and control what otherwise would be buzzing confusion. Without a centralized director, the competing sensory inputs would jostle one another in a senseless chaos. But as soon as we begin to use this executive capability that has emerged in recent evolutionary history, it, too, becomes one of the items of information in consciousness. And as we reflect on our ability to control what is happening in the mind, we come to think of it as a concrete entity — the "self" — to which we attribute all sorts of qualities. Many imagine the self as a homunculus,° a manikin, a tiny individual sitting in the middle of the brain directing our lives.

While this is not literally true, there *is* something in our mind that is more than the sum of the individual neurons that make up the brain. This something is the self, the brain's awareness of its own form of organizing information. Just as we apprehend the millions of water molecules as a single ocean,

reification: The process of regarding an abstract idea as a concrete object.

homunculus: Literally a "little man," deriving from the seventeenth-century "preformation" theory of reproduction that held that a miniature version of the adult inhabited germ cells; in cognitive science, the idea that a distinct thinking and perceiving "self" exits in the mind, like a person in miniature.

we experience the coming together of information in consciousness as the self. And just as the sea has many properties that cannot be imagined from mere knowledge of the discrete molecules of water—such as tides, waves, whales, icebergs, gulls, boats, and beautiful sunsets—so the self has its own features that cannot be predicted from the discrete bits of information that make it up.

Perhaps the most fateful consequence of the self's emergence is the power   5
it eventually acquires over our psychic energy. After the self develops, its primary goal becomes that of every other organism: to defend itself, to aggrandize itself. If we don't control it, it soon takes over all our energy for its own purposes, and we end up being ruled by a figment of the imagination. Of course, it may be better to be ruled by the self and its needs than by external forces, genes and memes,° which is the other alternative. But then the question becomes, what sort of a self will we create to rule us?

If the self includes everything that passes in consciousness, it follows that what we pay attention to over time will shape that self. For instance, the Nuer people of East Africa² raise cattle and spend most of their time watching their herds. They know each animal intimately, they know its habits and ancestors for many generations. They believe that the calves born to their herd come from the same water wells from which their own babies came, and to which their souls will return after death. Because of the mythical kinship they feel with their cattle, the Nuer very rarely slaughter their animals; having a large herd is an end in itself, an accomplishment that makes them feel proud and contented. It is not just a figure of speech to say that the self of a Nuer is made up, in part, by the cows and the bulls he or she spends so much time attending to.

For a male Nuer, there is another center to the self. Before becoming pastoralists, the Nuer were a warring and hunting tribe, and a man lived by his spear. Even after they turned to cattle raising, however, Nuer men retained their spears. In fact, early anthropologists reported that a Nuer man always kept a spear in his hand, feeling its weight, caressing its blade, balancing its shaft on his shoulder. By constantly attending to his weapon, as he was guarding his cattle or while sitting in front of his hut, the Nuer knew that he was a warlike, powerfully dangerous being; hence, this information became an integral part of his self. It was a similar insight that moved the anthropologist Ruth Benedict to entitle her book about Japan *The Chrysanthemum and the Sword*, because she saw in these two objects a key to the Japanese character, at the same time delicate and fierce.

There is nothing mysterious, or mystical, about the way objects become part of ourselves. The man who spends most of his time polishing his car, tuning up its engine, and talking about it to his friends will gradually end up including the car in his conception of his self. When the chrome shines he feels

---

memes: In the theory of cultural evolution first advanced by biologist Richard Dawkins (b. 1941), a "meme" is the lowest level of cultural reproduction and is thus similar to the gene, the lowest level of genetic reproduction.

proud, a rust spot on the fender is almost as distressing as a bald spot on the scalp, and a newer car in the neighbor's driveway can cause gut-wrenching jealousy. Therefore, what we pay attention to is no trivial matter; we are what we attend to.

But it is not just *what* we pay attention to that will constitute the self; it matters also *how* we do so. The way data is organized in consciousness also becomes a defining aspect of the self. For instance, a person who is drawn to other people and pays more attention to social events than to inner feelings or thoughts becomes an extrovert, while a person who always believes others want to harm him becomes neurotic. An optimist turns events around until he sees their bright side; a materialist is someone who always looks for a concrete advantage.

We have said earlier that the self comes into being because consciousness, to avoid being overwhelmed by information clamoring for attention, needs a mechanism to sort out and prioritize the diverse demands. The means by which attention becomes prioritized we call goals. A goal is a channel into which psychic energy flows. Therefore, the self can be considered a hierarchy of goals, because the goals define what we pay attention to, and how. If you know what goal takes precedence for a given person, you can generally anticipate where that person will invest psychic energy, and therefore predict his or her behavior.

Each person's goals are to a large extent similar to those of everyone else. Being human we all want, first of all, to survive, to be comfortable, to be accepted, loved, and respected. After these goals are reasonably satisfied—or blocked beyond hope—we then turn our energy to develop our own unique potential, to achieve what the psychologist Abraham Maslow[3] has called "self-actualization." Then some people shift their priorities again, and envision the goal of transcendence. They attempt to move beyond the boundaries of their personal limitations by integrating individual goals with larger ones, such as the welfare of the family, the community, humanity, the planet, or the cosmos. For a scientist who has invested a great deal of thought into trying to figure out superconductivity, any breakthrough in that field will be as worthy of his attention as hunger or a headache originating in his body. For a transcender like Mother Teresa,° what happens to the orphans of Calcutta is as important as what happens to herself.

It is these two last stages in the formation of the self that lead to complexity. Individual uniqueness, or self-actualization, represents the differentiation component; transcendence involves a higher level of integration. Both are necessary for the kind of self that leads to a complex and harmonious evolution. . . . If the third millennium is to be an improvement over its predecessor, more of us will have to build selves around transcendent goals.

Mother Teresa: (1910–1997), Catholic nun famous for her charitable works in Calcutta, India.

Evolving Images of the Ideal Self[4]

An intriguing question to raise here is whether the complexity of the human self has evolved through history. Is the average person today more differentiated and integrated than our ancestors were three or thirty thousand years ago? Of course, there is no reliable evidence on which to base an answer. It is difficult enough to evaluate the inner lives and motivations of our contemporaries, let alone to determine what people in Egypt or Sumeria thought and felt. The best we can do is to consider the way ideal men and women have been represented in paintings and sculptures across time. These images will not tell us precisely what kind of people our ancestors were, but they might at least give us a clue as to what kind of personhood was valued in the past. . . .

The great advance that culture contributed to evolution was that it enabled information to be represented extrasomatically. With the advent of pictographs and then writing, it was no longer necessary to keep all of an individual's or a culture's knowledge within the organism, stored in the memory pathways of the nervous system. It was now possible to externalize it in pictures and books, and to transmit images of experience from person to person by means of symbols. Extrasomatic coding and storage of information allowed an accumulation of knowledge many orders of magnitude beyond what could be previously stored in the brain. Perhaps as a result of this advance, humankind became able to give imagination a new meaning. Once people could make copies of events on external media, they must have realized that they could also create images of events that they had not directly witnessed. Thus they could conceive of representations of gods no one had seen, and depict events that never happened. Imagination emancipated itself from its former task as faithful recorder of reality, and was on its way as a reality sui generis,° now leading humans to unexpected triumphs, now luring them into illusion.

Of course, images are unable to present a "true" picture of reality. Cartesian coordinates, X-rays, or colored maps of the brain are ways we happen to have learned to mediate visually certain aspects of reality we think are important, in ways the mind can grasp them. These images are just as bounded by the limitations of our nervous system, and of our survival needs, as the images a bee has of its environment are limited by the bee's representational abilities.   15

One of the most important aspects of experience that humans have tried to represent through images is their own self. As the self began to depend more and more on learning as opposed to relying simply on genetically programmed behavior, its representations began to refer not just to the visible feature of the physical body but included psychological qualities, the spiritual essences that people either experienced in themselves, or wished to attain. If human evolution is to continue, it will be because of our trying to live up to increasingly complex images of our selves.

sui generis: "of its own kind or category, unique."

More often than not, the images of the self people created in the past were not intended to represent the self as it *is,* but rather as it *ought to be.* In cave paintings the hunter is usually depicted as successful in the hunt, the early fertility figurines show fat females with enormous breasts and buttocks, the Egyptian pharaohs are invariably represented triumphing over the enemy. Such distortions of reality are of course entirely functional, in that they potentially serve the purpose of propelling the individual toward more desirable states of being.

Personal Objects

Images of the ideal self are often embedded in objects that people wear on their bodies, or are actually carved on the body itself. These images are not always literal depictions of individuals; often they consist of objects symbolizing qualities important to the self. One universal category of objects that represents important aspects of the self includes those a person carries on himself or herself. These tend to be items that are worn in order to enhance the power of the owner, and communicate the person's ability to control energy, to defeat opponents, to command loyalty, to attract attention and envy. Perhaps the simplest forms of this type are body decorations, the paints and tattoos that preliterate people apply directly to their flesh, transforming it from a natural substance into a cultural entity. "The face paintings," writes Lévi-Strauss° about the Caduevo Indians of Brazil,[5] "confer upon the individual his dignity as a human being: they help him cross the frontier from Nature to culture, and from the 'mindless' animal to the civilized Man. Furthermore, they differ in style and composition according to social status, and thus have a social function." There are many messages that such decorations convey, one of the most typical being the person's position in a kinship network. Thus a tattoo serves as a badge of identity, and signals the fact that its bearer is not a solitary human being but a member of a social network. In other words, if you attack this man, you are attacking his entire group.

Next in complexity are the various adornments made of feathers, cloth, or metal, which attest both to the social position of the wearer and also to his or her individual accomplishments. Some archaeologists now believe that the first use of metals was not to forge weapons or useful tools, but to fashion body ornaments:[6]

> In several areas of the world it has been noted, in the case of metallurigcal innovations in particular, that the development of bronze and other metals as useful commodities was a much later phenomenon than their first utilization as new and attractive materials, employed in contexts of display. . . . In most cases early metallugry appears to have been practiced primarily because its products have novel properties that made them attractive as symbols and as personal adornment and ornaments, in a manner that, by focusing attention, could attract and enhance prestige.

Lévi-Strauss Claude Lévi-Strauss (b. 1908), French anthropologist.

Currently, the use of adornment to enhance one's image is no less obvi-   20
ous. The red "power tie" indicates that its wearer is ambitious; tinted hair,
plastic surgery, cosmetics, jewelry, and fashion clothing are ways to make the
self appear more desirable or prestigious than it actually is. Historically the
body ornaments of males have tended to represent power as physical strength
or control over other people and goods; the power of women was traditionally
represented by their ability to attract men because of outstanding sexual attributes, the promise of fertility, or intimations of good housekeeping. All of
these attempts are quite clearly a cultural extension of the biological markers
that so many insects, birds, and mammals possess in order to make themselves
appear larger, fiercer, or more attractive—depending on the function the
markings are supposed to advertise.

In different cultures, specialized objects may be adopted for representing
different dimensions of the self. Among many Native American tribes, adults
wore "medicine bundles" around their necks, in which were stored the objects
that symbolized the owner's special knowledge or accomplishments: some
powerful medicinal herbs, the teeth and claws of a bear defeated in hand-to-
hand struggle.

In our own time, people carry a great variety of objects to symbolize the
desired quality of their selves. Most men's wallets and women's purses contain
the equivalent of a Cheyenne medicine bundle. In addition we tote watches,
pens, pocket calculators, pagers, cellular phones, and other paraphernalia calculated to reassure ourselves and impress others about our powers. More than
any other single item, the car one drives has become in our culture a representation and extension of the ideal self. With its blatantly totemic symbolism
and purely cosmetic appearance, it makes a statement that is hard to ignore
about who we think we are and want to be known as. Personal objects thus
serve partly as a psychological crutch, reminding the owner of his or her ability to cope with the world; partly they serve to create an image that will give
the owner an advantage in interactions with others.

Household Objects

While personal objects worn on the body appear to have primarily defensive
purposes, creating as it were a symbolic armor against the dangers of the outside world, the objects one collects in the home seem to serve a different function. As they are more private, their function seems to be to create inner order
and clarity in the owner's conception of self, rather than making an external
impression.

The most important part of the home in Rome, China, and many other
cultures was the corner reserved for ancestral images. The living person acquired identity and meaning in relation to the departed kin whose past lives
were memorialized by masks, statuettes, or other symbols to be seen and
revered each day. The individual meant little outside the stream of life represented by the eternally renewed kinship group. Wherever Christianity substi-

tuted the idea of a universal family ruled by God the Father, holy images took precedence over those portraying earthly relations. The icons of Christ, his mother, and his saints became the symbolic center of the household, to which people could turn to clarify and reaffirm their identities.

In contemporary homes, most people construct a symbolic environment   25 filled with images that help them to remember who they were, to confirm who they are, and to foreshadow the kind of persons they would like to be in the future. But instead of using ready-made and culturally validated icons of the kind so prevalent in past cultures, today we must construct our own vision of self, to a large extent from our own personal experiences. True, visual references to ancestors and kinship roots are still astonishingly important, even in the most modern households, but their significance must be personally validated, rather than simply borrowed from a generally shared and accepted cultural script.

In a study of over three hundred members of eighty-two families living in the Chicago metropolitan area, we found a very wide spectrum of objects that served to represent salient aspects of the owner's self.[7] For example, furniture, stereo sets, books, and musical instruments were among the things owners mentioned most often as standing for important dimensions of the self. A chair in the living room was very special for a man because its practical and economical design expressed perfectly his own values. His wife cherished an old recliner because it was in that chair that she nursed her children when they were babies. Their son favored a third chair because it was like a trampoline, and he could bounce on it and feel free. Each of these chairs was a concrete reminder of an important aspect of the self for a different member of the family.

As in the oldest cultures, modern Americans' relation to kinfold remains one of the central dimensions of the self objectified in household symbols. Ancestors and parents are remembered primarily via inherited plateware and furniture; in addition, paintings tend to remind people more of their fathers, and sculptures more of their mothers. In contrast to previous cultures, however, things that symbolize children and other descendants were just as much in evidence as objects symbolizing ancestors. Photographs were the objects most often mentioned as being special because they reminded their owners of their children, grandchildren, or the family as a whole. For grandparents photographs were the most valued objects in the home, mentioned by 37 percent; for parents they were the sixth most often mentioned objects (22 percent); only 10 percent of the youngest generation mentioned photos, making them the fifteenth most frequent category. For this youngest generation stereo sets were the premier household objects, mentioned by 45 percent of the teenage respondents.

Another aspect of the self that the symbolic environment of the home represents is the owners' ideals. These are most often revealed by books (in 27 percent of the cases), by plants (12 percent), and by musical instruments (7 percent). But occasionally an old pair of rock-climbing boots, a trophy, or the diary one kept in high school can serve this purpose. Values, beliefs, and even the sense of who one is are constantly buffeted, challenged, and corroded through trafficking with the outside world. By returning home each day people not only restore themselves physically, but they also renew and reaffirm their identity by interacting with objects that contain desired images of the self.

Collective Representations

Another set of images is invoked when individuals meet in a public arena to invent or to reaffirm their collective identity. From the first lumbering dances our hominid ancestors performed around the campfire, to the extravagant opening and closing ceremonies of the latest Olympics broadcast around the world on television, we try to find symbolic expressions for our relationships with people who are not bound to us by kinship ties, and with the mysterious forces immanent in the cosmos. Often the images are auditory or kinesthetic rather than visual, as in the rhythm of tribal dances; or the bullroarer (*churinga*) that Australian aborigines rattle[8] to create the impression of an all-powerful spiritual force and that, as Durkheim° said, "is counted among the eminently sacred things; there are none that surpass it in religious dignity"; or the *molimo* trumpets that the pygmies of the Ituri forest in Africa use to wake up the sacred trees in the forest when a misfortune threatens the tribe.[9] In each of these cases—as in the rock concerts that are such an important part of our youth's experience—the sound envelops the discrete individuals and creates in them a sense of joint participation in a powerful group entity. Presumably without such collective experiences we would feel even more isolated and helpless than we already are.

A very ancient tool for linking individuals visually with supernatural   30
forces are the masks worn on ceremonial occasions, usually representing gods, heroes, or ancestral spirits central to a group's identity. For the Hopi as well as the New Guinea tribesman, wearing a mask is one of the most widespread means for transforming oneself from a puny mortal into the image of a powerful, meaningful entity. A good account of the transcendent function of masks is given by Monti:[10]

> From a psychological point of view the origin of the mask can also be explained by the more atavistic° aspiration of the human being to escape from himself in order to be enriched by the experience of different existences—a desire which obviously cannot be fulfilled on the physical level—and in order to increase its own power by identifying with universal, divine, or demonic forces, whichever they may be. It is a desire to break out of the human constriction of individuals shaped in a specific and immutable mould and closed in a birth-death cycle which leaves no possibility of consciously chosen existential adventures.

Durkheim: Emile Durkheim (1858–1916), French sociologist.
atavistic: Referring to the recurrence of a past style, form, or feature.

Preliterate cultures have also developed more abstract images for representing the collective forces to which they lay claim. In Australia, among the sacred objects of the Arunta that symbolized the essential force of the clan was the *nurturya*,[11] a bundle of sticks or spears assembled at the center of the village on ritual occasions. This same symbol was used by the Romans to represent the authority of the state to punish trespassers of the law. Public officials in ancient Rome were surrounded by lictors who carried bundles of elm or birch rods tied together with red thongs; wherever these *fasces* appeared, any disturbance or unrest quieted down in awe of this symbol of collective power. In 1919 Mussolini's Facist Party° took its name from the *fasces,* which also signified the motto *L'unione fa la forza:* while each rod can be broken one at a time, when joined together the bundle is unbreakable. The universal readability of this image of the force to be found in unity is demonstrated by the fact that it appears conspicuously even on the speaker's stand in the U.S. House of Representatives.

Religious symbols of the collective also represent power, albeit of a sacred rather than a secular kind. As Henry Adams° noted, the great medieval cathedrals acted as giant storehouses of psychic energy,[12] equivalent to the large electric turbines of a hundred years ago. Modern-day analogies might be nuclear reactors, supercolliders, and space centers. They transform the physical manpower required to build them into awesome images of a mysterious force, which in turn enhances the self-image of those who identify with them.

Collective power, especially of the religious variety, is not necessarily equivalent to physical force or material control. A great number of the Gothic cathedrals were dedicated to the Virgin Mary, and the images of meekness, suffering, and gentleness associated with her are much more typical of Christian iconography than the representation of naked force. But within the Christian worldview the meek inherited the earth; the Virgin's gentle intercession swayed the might of God the Father. Power is a much subtler concept than Joseph Stalin° imagined when he asked derisively how many divisions the Pope commanded.

Nevertheless, most of the images people create of themselves, whether at the personal or collective level, are in some respect an expression of power, whether that power involves influencing others, controlling the course of events, or simply having one's way. Of course, from an evolutionary point of view, this is an important function that images of the self should provide. It could be argued that they supply the goals, they foreshadow possibilities of being, that pull us toward the future. But are some images more useful than others in steering us forward on this journey?

Mussolini's Fascist Party: The political organization of World War II–era Italian dictator Benito Mussolini (1883–1945).

Henry Adams: Henry Brooks Adams (1838–1918), American historian.

Joseph Stalin: (1879–1953), World War II–era Soviet leader renowned for his autocratic rule.

Images of the Ideal Self

Where is one to find the images that humankind has created to give itself a di-   35
rection, a goal toward which to aspire? The task of choosing relevant examples
is made difficult by the very richness of human imagination. There are so
many depictions of gods, angels, demons, and anthropomorphic animals that
are tempting to use as models, but that ultimately must be rejected as irrelevant. How gods and demons are represented tells us something about a culture's view of the superhuman forces surrounding it, but it is within the more
narrow range of representations of actual men and women that we should seek
that culture's aspirations.

In the Western tradition, the ideal for human perfection was set almost
three thousand years ago by the sculptors of Greece.[13] Different but still very
recognizable models were developed more or less independently in Egypt,
China, and India. Outside the perimeters of what used to be called the great
civilizations, however, it is more difficult to recognize representations of indi-
vidualized human beings — figures of men or women who may have actually
existed. The typical style of the complex cultures of Melanesia, Africa, and the
New World could be best characterized as expressionistic. Bodies tend to be
distorted in ways that emphasize desired or magically significant features —
huge eyes, enormous genitals. The positions of the body are formalized,
arranged according to ritually prescribed lines.

Of course, the difference between the carvings on a Maori war canoe and
a frieze on an early Egyptian or Greek temple may be only a matter of degree,
and non-Western imagery may be an accurate gauge of ideal personhood for
its time. A rigid, ritually prescribed posture may have signified that a person
was disciplined, in control of his or her body, in harmony with the laws of the
gods and the tribe. A priapic phallus° was clearly desirable — what better
model for a man than a sexually superendowed being? Even the pharaohs surrounded themselves with outsized phallic obelisks, and Roman busts stood on
plinths decorated with erect penises.

We are on slightly more secure ground when trying to interpret the message of the human images sculpted in the classic period of Greek culture.
Here, for example, is how Arnold Hauser interprets the iconography of the archaic *kouroi* of the seventh century B.C., and the later statues of the time of
Polyclitus.°

> It is now that the foundations of the ethics of the nobility are laid: the concep-
> tion of *areté*° with its dominant traits of physical fitness and military discipline,
> built up on a tradition, birth and race; of *kalokagathia,* the ideal of the right bal-

---

priapic phallus: Priapus was an ancient Roman fertility god, often depicted with grotesquely
enlarged genitalia.

Polyclitus: Fifth-century B.C. Greek sculptor and architect.

areté: Ancient Greek ideal of the warrior-noble.

ance between bodily and spiritual, physical and moral qualities; of *sophrosyne,* the ideal of self-restraint, discipline, and moderation.

Hauser argues that, toward the end of the aristocratic age of Greece, when the warring nobles were starting to lose political control to the increasingly affluent merchants, they sought to have carved in marble the virtues claimed by their own class. Fitness, moderation, and self-discipline were supposedly the traits that justified the rule of the warrior nobility. The statues that displayed these qualities were intended as a bulwark against the pretensions of the ambitious merchants intent on usurping that rule. Hauser further argues that the statues carved a few hundred years later, in the era of Praxiteles° and Lysippus,° reveal the changes in values that the victory of the merchant classes had brought to Athens. The human figures now show a humanistic enlightenment, which emphasized beauty rather than strength, alert intelligence instead of resolute character, and spontaneity over discipline.

Many of the ideals suggested by the earliest Greek sculptures are also im-   40
plied by the typical human representations of Oriental art, especially in the figures of sages and of the Bodhisattvas,° the enlightened ones. The trancelike smile, the compressed energy, the serenity of the Greek *kouros,* held in check by some inner discipline, are duplicated in thousands of Buddha images distributed all across East Asia. Despite vast cultural differences, all the great civilizations, from Egypt to Japan, have envisioned a similar state of consciousness as the highest expression of the self. It has to do with a calm power, a restrained energy at peace with itself and with the world.

Some of this inner serenity survived the destruction of the classical civilizations. The otherwise lugubrious figures of Byzantine art retained in their haunting eyes a semblance of that peace, and it continued to imbue medieval countenances. The great cycles of frescoes upon the walls of cathedrals portrayed in an ever more colorful and lifelike manner what the ideal life of a Christian should be,[14] for the edification of the faithful. Martyrs and virgins were represented in the full bloom of their moral superiority, the rewards of the just were visually catalogued, and the sufferings of those who did not live up to the expectations of the Church were depicted with excruciating detail.

Christian educators believed that exposing young children to the images of saints was an effective way of illustrating desirable virtues — and perhaps actually inculcating them into the viewer. Thus at the end of the fourteenth century Giovanni Dominici recommends that one should have:[15]

> paintings in the house, of holy boys, or young virgins, in which your child when still in swaddling clothes may delight as being like himself. . . . I would like them

Praxiteles: Fourth-century B.C. Greek sculptor.

Lysippus: Fourth-century B.C. Greek sculptor.

Bodhisattvas: In Mahayana Buddhism, a being who voluntarily refrains from entering nirvana, the goal of enlightenment, in order to save other souls.

to see Agnes with the fat lamb, Cecilia crowned with roses, Elisabeth with many roses, Catherine on the wheel, with other figures that would give them love of virginity with their mother's milk, desire for Christ, hatred of sins, disgust at vanity, shrinking from bad companions, and a beginning . . . of contemplating the supreme Saint of saints.

The Renaissance, like the time of Praxiteles in Greece, was a period in which the human form almost exploded out of its defensive carapace and gained a rare spontaneity and freedom. Inebriated by possibility, figures now take on every shape and try every adventure; there are no limits to what humankind can be. The power of the ideal self no longer derives from obedience to divine authority but from the individual's determination to achieve the greatest potential from his or her being. A well-executed painting could even help in the procreation of beautiful children, as Giulio Mancini suggested at the start of the seventeenth century:[16]

> Lascivious things are to be placed in private rooms, and the father of the family is to keep them covered, and only uncover them when he goes there with his wife, or an intimate who is not too fastidious. And similar lascivious pictures are appropriate for the room where one has to do with one's spouse; because once seen they serve to arouse one and to make beautiful, healthy, and charming children . . . because each parent, through seeing the picture, imprints in their seed a similar constitution which has been seen in the object or figure.

It took several centuries for the optimism of the Renaissance to fade. By the end of World War I, few artists in the West could sustain belief in the ideal of human perfectability. In the last few generations the human form has been represented in shapes not seen in Europe since before the great civilizations began their difficult journey toward a hopeful future. The great artists of this century have given up idealizing men and women, and borrowed instead distorted images from tribal art, the scribbles of children, and the art of the insane. It is probably erroneous to think that the Africans who originally carved the masks that later inspired Picasso or Klee° were expressing a basic existential dread, as some art critics have claimed.[17] But it is quite clear that the Western artists who replicated their work were portraying their despair at the human condition through the distorted features of their paintings.

For many years now mainstream art seems to have relinquished hope of being able to provide a viable model of the self. In our century, there have been only three currents of idealized images of humankind. Two were political, and the utopias they advocated through their art have both turned out to be horrible failures. The fascist regimes presented a muscular, crude version of the Greek ideal of *areté* as the model for the Aryan race destined to inherit the earth. The statuary around Mussolini's *Foro Italico*, or Hitler's ministries in Berlin pro-

45

Picasso or Klee: Pablo Picasso (1881–1973), Spanish painter and sculptor; Paul Klee (1879–1940), Swiss painter.

vided a concrete representation of the intimidating, merciless, robotlike individual that best fit the ruling ideology. The other human ideal inspired by political ideology was the one depicted by Socialist Realism.° For half a century the experiment with communism generated an enormous number of paintings and statues representing rosy-cheeked youth involved in innumerable useful projects, from harvesting to fishing to repairing tractors and feeding children. Less monumental than fascist art, the Soviet variety was perhaps more vacuous. The self it represented was too obviously a creature of propaganda with almost no connection to the social reality it purported to represent. And what is much worse, neither did it bear any relevance to a foreseeable future.

The third set of images representing an ideal self is the one provided by the Western media, usually in the service of commercial advertising.[18] From the flapper girls of the 1920s, used to promote cosmetics or cigarettes, to the Pepsi generation and TV spots selling beer, a form of frankly exploitive representation of what it means to be human has taken over our visual environment. Its purpose is to attract attention to a specific product, and to associate that product with desirable thoughts and feelings, inducing us to a purchase and thus increasing its market share. In order to achieve this, the products are typically associated with healthy young people who appear to be having the time of their lives.

The ideal of selfhood that emerges from these commercial images lacks any hint of the balanced self-discipline of early Greek heroes, of the spiritual ecstasies of the Christian saints, of the ideological fanaticism of fascist nudes, or of the collectivist delusion of the Soviet workers. What they display is good animal health, sensual contentment, and a lack of worries or responsibilities that could interfere with enjoying the latest fashion in consumption or sensory stimulation. The iconography of modern advertising often seems a return to the fetishism° and totemism° of our distant ancestors. According to Martin Esslin,° who sees TV commercials as a religious drama, the moral universe of the TV commercial[19]

> is essentially that of a polytheistic religion. It is a world dominated by a sheer pantheon of powerful forces, which literally reside in every article of use or consumption. . . . If the wind and the waters, the trees and brooks of ancient Greece were inhabited by a host of nymphs, dryads, satyrs,° and other local and specific deities, so is the universe of the TV commercial. The polytheism that confronts

Socialist Realism: An artistic style developed in the Soviet Union during the 1930s that glorified Marxist revolution through the depiction of heroic agricultural and industrial workers.

fetishism: Belief in supposedly magical objects, such as amulets and animal charms.

totemism: Belief in a mystical relationship between a group of people and an animal spirit or totem.

Martin Esslin: (b. 1918), German literary critic.

"nymphs, dryads, satyrs": Half-human, half-animal spirits in ancient Greek and Roman mythology.

us here is thus a fairly primitive one, closely akin to animistic and fetishistic beliefs.°

Other commentators have compared advertising to a gospel, "an ultimate source of reference wherein we find ourselves revealed. . . . Each form, moreover, provides a controlling image for our consciousness in apprehending our selves and our world." The world we apprehend by these means is filled with semianimate things that clamor for attention and money, and the selves we apprehend are those of consumers trying to validate their identity through the possession of things.

The message of these images is that the highest goal is to live a life of carefree pleasure. Of course this is not a particularly novel or original theme: As Sorokin° has attempted to prove, sensate cultures have alternated with cultures inclined to value ideas more than pleasure for as long as historical records have been kept.[20] Perhaps the liberated figures of Renaissance art come closest to conveying an image of the self that is similar to the one surrounding us in the environment of commercial art. But contemporary observers are likely to find that human representations from the Renaissance are more interesting, more suggestive of complex thoughts and emotions, than their contemporary counterparts obsessed by narcissism° and the fetishism of commodities.

It seems, then, that within living memory neither artists nor the two great political movements of the century, nor the commercial energies of the age have succeeded in providing viable representations of the self on which to model feasible ways of being for the future. Does this mean that we have run out of ideas for the millennium that faces us, and artists are justified in representing the human form as the stick figure of a child or the scrawls of a schizophrenic? Is their implicit analysis of what we have come to be correct, and there is no way to imagine a positive way to be human? Or is that our imagination has been only temporarily stymied, and with time we may hope for a new representation of the ideal self to emerge?   50

The Self of the Future

I will assume that the last alternative is the correct one. It is by definition impossible, however, to guess what form that representation will take. But because the issue is by no means trivial, it may be worthwhile to speculate on the kind of images that could stand for the qualities to which we might aspire.

The most obvious possibility is that the future image of the self will recapitulate some of the features of the past—the physical dynamism of the classical Greek goddess or athlete combined with the serene inner focus of the *kouroi*

"animistic . . . beliefs": The attribution of animate or living qualities to nonliving things.

Sorokin: Pitirim Sorokin (1889–1968), American sociologist.

narcissism: egoism, self-love.

or the Bodhisattvas. It is in this *coincidentia oppositorum°* that the peaks of human complexity are combined. But is there a viable contemporary visual expression of this state of being? Perhaps we should turn to the movies for our inspiration: Gary Cooper in *High Noon,* or the *Seven Samurai,* or even the image of the astronaut in the person of the fearless Princess Leia, or the earnest Luke Skywalker.

A more radical possibility is that external features—beauty, character, the mask of personality—will grow less and less more important. Serious artists have already abandoned the attempt to represent the outer appearance of individuals. But what will take its place? Perhaps the focus will shift toward the depiction of inner complexity. The computer may become the metaphor for the self:[21] the organism as an immensely complex machine. Perhaps it will be something like HAL, the master computer aboard the starship in Stanley Kubrick's *2001;* or the computer world of *Tron.*

Finally there is what for lack of a better term we might call the cosmic self. One example of it is Kevin Costner's character in the film *Dances with Wolves.* This model points to an integration of the individual with larger and more complex units: with other cultures, with humanity as a whole, with other animals, with the natural landscape. The most extreme destination along this trajectory is the "quantum self,"[22] which defines itself through union with the totality of existence—with the energy that pulses through the cosmos.

Clearly artists will have an enormous challenge in visualizing and representing these more radical possibilities for being. But then, that is the task that the true artist has always faced. As Karl Jaspers° wrote: "The human being is an open possibility, incomplete and incompletable. Hence it is always more and other than what he has brought to realisation in himself."[23] Nevertheless, it is our responsibility to try imagining what that human being could be at the next stage of its history. If we do not, evolution will continue to proceed blindly. Yet we have advanced too deeply into the future to simply let things work out as they will. And we cannot chart a hopeful course without meaningful models, without realistic images of what we can become.

coincidentia oppositorum: Latin for a coincidence of opposites—a theory by Nicolas of Cusa to oppose Aristotle's theory of nontradition.

Karl Jaspers: Karl Theodor Jaspers (1883–1969), German philosopher.

Notes

1. This account of its development is an extremely simplified summary of the very complex description offered by Dennett (1991).

2. **The Nuer people of East Africa:** The Nuer were studied by Evans-Pritchard (1974); for the quotation about the role of the spear in defining the self of Nuer males, see p. 233.

3. **Abraham Maslow:** Maslow's hierarchy of needs is most extensively presented in *The Farther Reaches of Human Nature* (1971).

4. **Evolving Images of the Ideal Self:** The arguments presented in this section have been developed in greater length in a recent article in the journal *Poetics* (Csikszentmihalyi 1992).

5. **Caduevo Indians of Brazil:** The Caduevo Indians and the role of body-painting in general are described in Lévi-Strauss (1967, 176).

6. **Metals as body ornaments:** The ornamental function of metallurgy is described in Renfrew (1986, 144, 146).

7. **In a study of over three hundred . . . :** The study of eighty-two families is the one reported in Csikszentmihalyi and Rochberg-Halton (1981).

8. **The bullroarer that Australian aborigines rattle:** The *churinga* is described in Emile Durkheim's classic book, *The Elementary Forms of Religious Life* (1967, 141).

9. **The *molimo* trumpet:** The *molimo* trumpet and its uses are mentioned by the anthropologist Colin Turnbull (1961, 80).

10. **Ceremonial masks:** Francesco Monti (1969, 9–15) developed the argument about the transcendent function of masks.

11. **The sacred objects of the Arunta:** The Arunta of Australia and their use of the *nurturya* is described in Durkheim (1947, 145).

12. **Medieval cathedrals:** The reference is to Adams (1905).

13. **The ideal for human perfection:** Greek ideals of selfhood as represented in early sculpture are from Arnold Hauser's magisterial study of the evolution of art (Hauser 1951, 70).

14. **The great cycles of frescoes . . . :** The educational uses of Medieval frescoes on church walls are discussed in Lavin (1990).

15. **Giovanni Dominici:** Dominici's ideas about interior decoration are quoted in Freedberg (1989, 4).

16. **Giulio Mancini:** Mancini's views about how pictures can help in procreating healthy children are detailed in Mancini (1956).

17. **It is probably erroneous . . . :** That African and other preliterate representations of the human figure in distorted form express a basic existential deread pervasive in such societies is an interpretation discussed in Price (1989). This interpretation is opposed to the one advanced by Monti (see note 10); however, both may be true.

18. **Commercial advertising:** The iconography of advertising is discussed, among others, by Goffman (1979) and Jhally (1990).

19. **The moral universe of the TV commercial:** The quote about TV commercials as religious drama is from Esslin (1976, 271). The quotation about advertising as gospel ("an ultimate source . . .") is from Kavanaugh (1981, 15–16).

20. **As Sorokin has attempted to prove . . . :** Sorokin's analysis of history in terms of alternating cycles of sensory and ideational cultures is contained in *Social and Cultural Dynamic* (1962); see also Csikszentmihalyi (1991).

21. **The computer as a metaphor of the self:** This idea was developed by Sherry Turkle (1984).

22. **"quantum self":** The quantum self is described in Zohar (1990) and Lancaster (1991).

23. **"The human being is an open possibility . . .":** The Karl Jaspers quote is from his *General Psychopathology*, originally published in 1923 (Jaspers, 1965, 766).

Selected Bibliography

Adams, H. [1905] 1959. *Mont Saint-Michel and Chartres.* Garden City, N.Y.: Doubleday Anchor.

Csikszentmihalyi, M. 1991. Consciousness for the twenty-first century. *Zygon 26* (no. 1): 7–25.

Csikszentmihalyi, M. 1992. Imagining the self: An evolutionary excursion. *Poetics* 21:153–67.

Csikszentmihalyi, M., and E. Rochberg-Halton. 1981. *The meaning of things: Domestic symbols and the self.* New York: Cambridge University Press.

Dennett, D. C. 1991. *Consciousness explained.* Boston: Little, Brown.

Durkheim, E. [1912] 1967. *The elementary forms of religious life.* New York: The Free Press.

Esslin, M. 1976. Aristotle and the advertisers: The television commercial considered as a form of drama. In *Television: The critical view,* ed. N. Newcomb. New York: Oxford University Press.

Evans-Pritchard, E. E. [1956] 1974. *Nuer religion.* New York: Oxford University Press.

Freedberg, D. 1989. *The power of images: Studies in the history and theory of response.* Chicago: University of Chicago Press.

Goffman, E. 1979. *Gender advertisements.* New York: Harper & Row.

Granet, M. 1934. *La pensée chinoise.* Paris: F. Alcan.

Hauser, A. 1951. *The social history of art.* New York: Alfred A. Knopf.

Jaspers, K. [1923] 1963. *General psychopathology.* Chicago: University of Chicago Press.

Jhally, S. 1990. *The codes of advertising: Fetishism and the political economy of meaning in the consumer society.* New York: Routledge.

Kavanaugh, J. 1981. *Following Christ in a consumer society.* New York: Orbis.

Lancaster, B. 1991. *Mind, brain and human potential: The quest for an understanding of self.* Rockport, Ma.: Element.

Lavin, M. A. 1990. *The place of narrative.* Chicago: University of Chicago Press.

Lévi-Strauss, C. 1967. *Tristes tropiques.* New York: Atheneum.

Mancini, G. [1613] 1956. *Considerazioni sulla pittura,* ed. A. Marucchi. Rome.

Maslow, A. 1971. *The farther reaches of human nature.* New York: Viking.

Monti, F. 1969. *African masks.* London: Paul Hamlyn.

Price, S. 1989. *Primitive art in civilized places.* Chicago: University of Chicago Press.

Renfrew, C. 1986. Varna and the emergence of wealth in prehistoric Europe. In *The social life of things,* ed. A. Appadurai, 141–68. New York: Cambridge University Press.

Sorokin, P. 1962. *Social and cultural dynamics.* New York: Bedminster.

Turkle, S. 1984. *The second self: Computers and the human spirit.* New York: Simon & Schuster.

Turnbull, C. M. 1961. *The forest people.* Garden City, N.Y.: Doubleday.

Zohar, D. 1990. *The quantum self: Human nature and consciousness defined by the new physics.* New York: Morrow.

EXPLORING THE TEXT

1. How does Csikszentmihalyi define the self? What, in his view, does the self do for us? What functions does it serve? Does it seem accurate to you to describe the self as a "figment of the imagination"? Why or why not? To what extent would you agree that we can "create" the sort of self we want "to rule us"?

2. What metaphors are commonly offered in order to picture that self? What metaphorical ideas does Csikszentmihalyi himself use in the first few pages of this selection to convey his conception of the self? What other metaphors might be useful for describing the self?

3. What role do body decorations, clothing, personal possessions, and household objects play in the construction of our sense of self, according to Csikszentmihalyi? Do you agree that material possessions are, in fact, powerful symbols of selfhood? What specific things, decorations, or household objects of yours contribute to your sense of self? What information do these objects communicate about you?

4. What are "collective representations" and how do they contribute to our sense of self? In addition to the historical illustrations that Csikszentmihalyi offers — like the *fasces* of Mussolini's Fascist Party or the cathedrals of medieval Europe — what contemporary examples of such collective symbols can you think of? To what extent do you agree that collective representations typically are an "expression of power"?

5. What role do "ideal images" play in the construction of our sense of self? How have such idealizations changed over the course of human history? In Csikszentmihalyi's view, where do we find ideal images of the self today? What attitudes and values are associated with these contemporary ideals?

FURTHER EXPLORATIONS

1. Using Csikszentmihalyi's claim that "we are what we attend to" as a guide, what can you infer about the selves of Ian Frazier in "Take the F" (p. 18), Barry Lopez in "A Passage of the Hands" (p. 27), Scott Russell Sanders in "The Inheritance of Tools" (p. 142), and/or Loren Eiseley in "The Brown Wasps" (p. 150)? What captures the attention of these writers? What do they focus on in their selection? What does this tell us about their sense of self?

2. Revisit selections on the senses by Mark Slouka (p. 50), Bill McKibben (p. 109), and Walker Percy (p. 118), paying attention to the claims they make about the impact of technological society on perception. What do these readings suggest about the nature of the self in a highly technological society like ours? How do they complicate Csikszentmihalyi's assertion that "we are what we attend to"?

3. How does Csikszentmihalyi's definition of the self challenge or complicate the notion of ego boundaries as presented by Robert Sapolsky (p. 254)? To what extent does Csikszentmihalyi's view of the "extrasomatic" sources of selfhood undermine the concept of the self as a relatively isolated and inviolable entity?

4. Working in groups, assemble a collage of advertising images from a number of popular magazines, representing an informal "survey" of the types of objects that define the self in modern American culture. What meanings or messages does each of the objects in your portfolio communicate about its owner? What overall picture does your survey offer of the values and attitudes associated with the contemporary American self?

5. Using your library's art resources, assemble a collection of images documenting the "ideal selves" of one or more ancient cultures. You may want to focus on the ancient Greeks, Romans, Chinese, Hindus, Japanese, Egyptians, Mayans, or Aztecs — any culture that has left behind a substantial body of pictorial or sculptural art. What qualities or characteristics do these images of the ideal self convey? To what extent does your research support Csikszentmihalyi's claim that all classical civilizations "have envisioned a similar state of consciousness as the highest expression of the self"?

ESSAY OPTIONS

1. Assemble a collection of images drawn from popular magazines, newspapers, movie ads, or television shows that reflect the "ideal selves" of our culture and use these images as the basis for a paper in which you analyze the values, attitudes, and beliefs associated with our dominant cultural concept of selfhood. What messages do these images convey to young people about the body, wealth, achievement, status, dominance, pleasure, control, spirituality, community, beauty, and so forth? How do the "ideal selves" of men differ from those conveyed for women? Overall, what is your assessment of the impact of such ideal images of the self?

2. Write a paper in which you inventory the ingredients that make up your sense of self. What things do you "pay attention to," and what do these things say about your sense of self? What decorations, fashions, or other aspects of personal appearance contribute to your sense of identity? What specific personal possessions play a part in the "symbolic environment" you live in? What "collective identities" do you participate in through group memberships, musical tastes, cultural associations, and so forth? What "ideal selves" have served as models for your goals, values, and beliefs?

Everyday Use

ALICE WALKER

When Alice Walker published this short story back in 1973, the segregated schools and poll tax of a "separate-but-equal" South were still fresh in America's memory, and the concepts of black pride and black power were just taking shape on college campuses across the country. Black leaders like Malcolm X and Stokely Carmichael were urging young African Americans to rebel against the past and to liberate their sense of self from the cultural memory of slavery and subservience. The ideological battles that raged in America during the 1960s and 1970s set off what amounted to a nationwide identity crisis: in a world that was trying to reinvent technology, reinterpret history, and reimagine the future, it was crucial to begin by rethinking your sense of self. Walker's story of Dee's return from college with her newly adopted African identity to her family home in the deep South captures this moment in America's collective cultural history; her depiction of a mother's decision between two daughters — and two ways of defining the self — offers an object lesson on the complexities of human identity. Born in Eston, Georgia, in 1944, Alice Walker is one of the most honored American writers of her generation. Her novel *The Color Purple* (1982) received both the Pulitzer Prize for fiction and the American Book Award. She has also written five other novels, two collections of short stories, three collections of essays, and several children's books. Her most recent publication, *The Way Forward Is with a Broken Heart*, appeared in 2001.

BEFORE READING

In a brief journal entry, describe an object that links you to your family's past or your cultural heritage. When did this object come into your family? What does it mean to you?

I will wait for her in the yard that Maggie and I made so clean and wavy yesterday afternoon. A yard like this is more comfortable than most people know. It is not just a yard. It is like an extended living room. When the hard clay is swept clean as a floor and the fine sand around the edges lined with tiny, irregular grooves, anyone can come and sit and look up into the elm tree and wait for the breezes that never come inside the house.

Maggie will be nervous until after her sister goes: she will stand hopelessly in corners, homely and ashamed of the burn scars down her arms and legs, eying her sister with a mixture of envy and awe. She thinks her sister has held life always in the palm of one hand, that "no" is a word the world never learned to say to her.

You've no doubt seen those TV shows where the child who has "made it" is confronted, as a surprise, by her own mother and father, tottering in weakly from backstage. (A pleasant surprise, of course: What would they do if parent and child came on the show only to curse out and insult each other?) On TV mother and child embrace and smile into each other's faces. Sometimes the mother and father weep, the child wraps them in her arms and leans across the table to tell how she would not have made it without their help. I have seen these programs.

Sometimes I dream a dream in which Dee and I are suddenly brought together on a TV program of this sort. Out of a dark and soft-seated limousine I am ushered into a bright room filled with many people. There I meet a smiling, gray, sporty man like Johnny Carson° who shakes my hand and tells me what a fine girl I have. Then we are on the stage and Dee is embracing me with tears in her eyes. She pins on my dress a large orchid, even though she has told me once that she thinks orchids are tacky flowers.

In real life I am a large, big-boned woman with rough, man-working   5
hands. In the winter I wear flannel nightgowns to bed and overalls during the day. I can kill and clean a hog as mercilessly as a man. My fat keeps me hot in zero weather. I can work outside all day, breaking ice to get water for washing; I can eat pork liver cooked over the open fire minutes after it comes steaming from the hog. One winter I knocked a bull calf straight in the brain between the eyes with a sledge hammer and had the meat hung up to chill before nightfall. But of course all this does not show on television. I am the way my daughter would want me to be: a hundred pounds lighter, my skin like an uncooked barley pancake. My hair glistens in the hot bright lights. Johnny Carson has much to do to keep up with my quick and witty tongue.

But that is a mistake. I know even before I wake up. Who ever knew a Johnson with a quick tongue? Who can even imagine me looking a strange white man in the eye? It seems to me I have talked to them always with one foot raised in flight, with my head turned in whichever way is farthest from

Johnny Carson: (b. 1925), American entertainer and former late-night television talk-show host.

them. Dee, though. She would always look anyone in the eye. Hesitation was no part of her nature.

"How do I look, Mama?" Maggie says, showing just enough of her thin body enveloped in pink skirt and red blouse for me to know she's there, almost hidden by the door.

"Come out into the yard," I say.

Have you ever seen a lame animal, perhaps a dog run over by some careless person rich enough to own a car, sidle up to someone who is ignorant enough to be kind to him? That is the way my Maggie walks. She has been like this, chin to chest, eyes on ground, feet in shuffle, ever since the fire that burned the other house to the ground.

Dee is lighter than Maggie, with nicer hair and a fuller figure. She's a   10
woman now, though sometimes I forget. How long ago was it that the other house burned? Ten, twelve years? Sometimes I can still hear the flames and feel Maggie's arms sticking to me, her hair smoking and her dress falling off her in little black papery flakes. Her eyes seemed stretched open, blazed open by the flames reflected in them. And Dee. I see her standing off under the sweet gum tree she used to dig gum out of; a look of concentration on her face as she watched the last dingy gray board of the house fall in toward the red-hot brick chimney. Why don't you do a dance around the ashes? I'd wanted to ask her. She had hated the house that much.

I used to think she hated Maggie, too. But that was before we raised the money, the church and me, to send her to Augusta to school. She used to read to us without pity; forcing words, lies, other folks' habits, whole lives upon us two, sitting trapped and ignorant underneath her voice. She washed us in a river of make-believe, burned us with a lot of knowledge we didn't necessarily need to know. Pressed us to her with the serious way she read, to shove us away at just the moment, like dimwits, we seemed about to understand.

Dee wanted nice things. A yellow organdy dress to wear to her graduation from high school; black pumps to match a green suit she'd made from an old suit somebody gave me. She was determined to stare down any disaster in her efforts. Her eyelids would not flicker for minutes at a time. Often I fought off the temptation to shake her. At sixteen she had a style of her own, and knew what style was.

I never had an education myself. After second grade the school was closed down. Don't ask me why: in 1927 colored asked fewer questions than they do now. Sometimes Maggie reads to me. She stumbles along good-naturedly but can't see well. She knows she is not bright. Like good looks and money, quickness passed her by. She will marry John Thomas (who has mossy teeth in an earnest face) and then I'll be free to sit here and I guess just sing church songs to myself. Although I never was a good singer. Never could carry a tune. I was always better at a man's job. I used to love to milk till I was hooked in the side in '49. Cows are soothing and slow and don't bother you, unless you try to milk them the wrong way.

I have deliberately turned my back on the house. It is three rooms, just like the one that burned, except the roof is tin; they don't make shingle roofs any more. There are no real windows, just some holes cut in the sides, like the portholes in a ship, but not round and not square, with rawhide holding the shutters up on the outside. This house is in a pasture, too, like the other one. No doubt when Dee sees it she will want to tear it down. She wrote me once that no matter where we "choose" to live, she will manage to come see us. But she will never bring her friends. Maggie and I thought about this and Maggie asked me, "Mama, when did Dee ever *have* any friends?"

She had a few. Furtive boys in pink shirts hanging about on wash-day after   15
school. Nervous girls who never laughed. Impressed with her they worshiped the well-turned phrase, the cute shape, the scalding humor that erupted like bubbles in lye. She read to them.

When she was courting Jimmy T she didn't have much time to pay to us, but turned all her faultfinding power on him. He *flew* to marry a cheap city girl from a family of ignorant flashy people. She hardly had time to recompose herself.

When she comes I will meet—but there they are!

Maggie attempts to make a dash for the house, in her shuffling way but I stay her with my hand. "Come back here," I say. And she stops and tries to dig a well in the sand with her toe.

It is hard to see them clearly through the strong sun. But even the first glimpse of leg out of the car tells me it is Dee. Her feet were always neat-looking, as if God himself had shaped them with a certain style. From the other side of the car comes a short, stocky man. Hair is all over his head a foot long and hanging from his chin like a kinky mule tail. I hear Maggie suck in her breath. "Uhnnnh," is what is sounds like. Like when you see the wriggling end of a snake just in front of your foot on the road. "Uhnnnh."

Dee next. A dress down to the ground, in this hot weather. A dress so loud   20
it hurts my eyes. There are yellows and oranges enough to throw back the light of the sun. I feel my whole face warming from the heat waves it throws out. Earrings gold, too, and hanging down to her shoulders. Bracelets dangling and making noises when she moves her arm up to shake the folds of the dress out of her armpits. The dress is loose and flows, and as she walks closer, I like it. I hear Maggie go "Uhnnnh" again. It is her sister's hair. It stands straight up like the wool on a sheep. It is black as night and around the edges are two long pigtails that rope about like small lizards disappearing behind her ears.

"Wa-su-zo-Tean-o!"° she says, coming on in that gliding way the dress makes her move. The short stocky fellow with the hair to his navel is all grinning and he follows up with "Asalamalakim,° my mother and sister!" He moves to hug Maggie but she falls back, right up against the back of my chair. I feel her trembling there and when I look up I see the perspiration falling off her chin.

"Wa-su-zo-Tean-o!": Dee sounds out this greeting in Swahili one syllable at a time.

"Asalamalakim": Arabic greeting: "Peace be upon you."

"Don't get up," says Dee. Since I am stout it takes something of a push. You can see me trying to move a second or two before I make it. She turns, showing white heels through her sandals, and goes back to the car. Out she peeks next with a Polaroid. She stoops down quickly and lines up picture after picture of me sitting there in front of the house with Maggie cowering behind me. She never takes a shot without making sure the house is included. When a cow comes nibbling around the edge of the yard she snaps it and me and Maggie *and* the house. Then she puts the Polaroid in the back seat of the car, and comes up and kisses me on the forehead.

Meanwhile Asalamalakim is going through motions with Maggie's hand. Maggie's hand is as limp as a fish, and probably as cold, despite the sweat, and she keeps trying to pull it back. It looks like Asalamalakim wants to shake hands but wants to do it fancy. Or maybe he don't know how people shake hands. Anyhow, he soon gives up on Maggie.

"Well," I say. "Dee."

"No, Mama," she says. "Not 'Dee,' Wangero Leewanika Kemanjo!"   25

"What happened to 'Dee'?" I wanted to know.

"She's dead," Wangero said. "I couldn't bear it any longer, being named after the people who oppress me."

"You know as well as me you was named after your aunt Dicie," I said. Dicie is my sister. She named Dee. We called her "Big Dee" after Dee was born.

"But who was *she* named after?" asked Wangero.

"I guess after Grandma Dee," I said.   30

"And who was she named after?" asked Wangero.

"Her mother," I said, and saw Wangero was getting tired. "That's about as far back as I can trace it," I said. Though, in fact, I probably could have carried it back beyond the Civil War through the branches.

"Well," said Asalamalakim, "there you are."

"Uhnnnh," I heard Maggie say.

"There I was not," I said, "before 'Dicie' cropped up in our family, so why   35 should I try to trace it that far back?"

He just stood there grinning, looking down on me like somebody inspecting a Model A car. Every once in a while he and Wangero sent eye signals over my head.

"How do you pronounce this name?" I asked.

"You don't have to call me by it if you don't want to," said Wangero.

"Why shouldn't I?" I asked. "If that's what you want us to call you, we'll call you."

"I know it might sound awkward at first," said Wangero.   40

"I'll get used to it," I said. "Ream it out again."

Well, soon we got the name out of the way. Asalamalakim had a name twice as long and three times as hard. After I tripped over it two or three times he told me to just call him Hakim-a-barber. I wanted to ask him was he a barber, but I didn't really think he was, so I didn't ask.

"You must belong to those beef-cattle peoples down the road," I said. They said "Asalamalakim" when they met you, too, but they didn't shake hands. Always too busy: feeding the cattle, fixing the fences, putting up salt-lick shelters, throwing down hay. When the white folks poisoned some of the herd the men stayed up all night with rifles in their hands. I walked a mile and a half just to see the sight.

Hakim-a-barber said, "I accept some of their doctrines, but farming and raising cattle is not my style." (They didn't tell me, and I didn't ask, whether Wangero (Dee) had really gone and married him.)

We sat down to eat and right away he said he didn't eat collards and pork was unclean. Wangero, though, went on through the chitlins and corn bread, the greens and everything else. She talked a blue streak over the sweet potatoes. Everything delighted her. Even the fact that we still used the benches her daddy made for the table when we couldn't afford to buy chairs.

"Oh, Mama!" she cried. Then turned to Hakim-a-barber. "I never knew how lovely these benches are. You can feel the rump prints," she said, running her hands underneath her and along the bench. Then she gave a sigh and her hand closed over Grandma Dee's butter dish. "That's it!" she said. "I knew there was something I wanted to ask you if I could have." She jumped up from the table and went over in the corner where the churn stood, the milk in it clabber by now. She looked at the churn and looked at it.

"This churn top is what I need," she said. "Didn't Uncle Buddy whittle it out of a tree you all used to have?"

"Yes," I said.

"Uh-huh," she said happily. "And I want the dasher, too."

"Uncle Buddy whittle that, too?" asked the barber.

Dee (Wangero) looked up at me.

"Aunt Dee's first husband whittled the dash," said Maggie so low you almost couldn't hear her. "His name was Henry, but they called him Stash."

"Maggie's brain is like an elephant's," Wangero said, laughing. "I can use the churn top as a centerpiece for the alcove table," she said, sliding a plate over the churn, "and I'll think of something artistic to do with the dasher."

When she finished wrapping the dasher the handle stuck out. I took it for a moment in my hands. You didn't even have to look close to see where hands pushing the dasher up and down to make butter had left a kind of sink in the wood. In fact, there were a lot of small sinks; you could see where thumb and fingers had sunk into the wood. It was beautiful light yellow wood, from a tree that grew in the yard where Big Dee and Stash had lived.

After dinner Dee (Wangero) went to the trunk at the foot of my bed and started rifling through it. Maggie hung back in the kitchen over the dishpan. Out came Wangero with two quilts. They had been pieced by Grandma Dee and then Big Dee and me had hung them on the quilt frames on the front porch and quilted them. One was in the Lone Star pattern. The other was Walk Around the Mountain. In both of them were scraps of dresses Grandma

Dee had worn fifty and more years ago. Bits and pieces of Grandpa Jarrell's paisley shirts. And one teeny faded blue piece, about the size of a penny matchbox, that was from Great Grandpa Ezra's uniform that he wore in the Civil War.

"Mama," Wangero said sweet as a bird. "Can I have these old quilts?"

I heard something fall in the kitchen, and a minute later the kitchen door slammed.

"Why don't you take one or two of the others?" I asked. "These old things was just done by me and Big Dee from some tops your grandma pieced before she died."

"No," said Wangero. "I don't want those. They are stitched around the borders by machine."

"That'll make them last better," I said.   60

"That's not the point," said Wangero. "These are all pieces of dresses Grandma used to wear. She did all this stitching by hand. Imagine!" She held the quilts securely in her arms, stroking them.

"Some of the pieces, like those lavender ones, come from old clothes her mother handed down to her," I said, moving up to touch the quilts. Dee (Wangero) moved back just enough so that I couldn't reach the quilts. They already belonged to her.

"Imagine!" she breathed again, clutching them closely to her bosom.

"The truth is," I said. "I promised to give them quilts to Maggie, for when she marries John Thomas."

She gasped like a bee had stung her.   65

"Maggie can't appreciate these quilts!" she said. "She'd probably be backward enough to put them to everyday use."

"I reckon she would," I said. "God knows I been saving 'em for long enough with nobody using 'em. I hope she will!" I didn't want to bring up how I had offered Dee (Wangero) a quilt when she went away to college. Then she had told me they were old-fashioned, out of style.

"But, they're *priceless!*" she was saying now, furiously; for she has a temper. "Maggie would put them on the bed and in five years they'd be in rags. Less than that!"

"She can always make some more," I said. "Maggie knows how to quilt."

Dee (Wangero) looked at me with hatred. "You just will not understand.   70
The point is these quilts, *these* quilts!"

"Well," I said, stumped. "What would *you* do with them?"

"Hang them," she said. As if that was the only thing you *could* do with quilts.

Maggie by now was standing in the door. I could almost hear the sound her feet made as they scraped over each other.

"She can have them, Mama," she said, like somebody used to never winning anything, or having anything reserved for her. "I can 'member Grandma Dee without the quilts."

I looked at her hard. She had filled her bottom lip with checkerberry snuff 75 and it gave her face a kind of dopey, hangdog look. It was Grandma Dee and Big Dee who taught her how to quilt herself. She stood there with her scarred hands hidden in the folds of her skirt. She looked at her sister with something like fear but she wasn't mad at her. This was Maggie's portion. This was the way she knew God to work.

When I looked at her like that something hit me in the top of my head and ran down to the soles of my feet. Just like when I'm in church and the spirit of God touches me and I get happy and shout. I did something I never had done before: hugged Maggie to me, then dragged her on into the room, snatched the quilts out of Miss Wangero's hands and dumped them into Maggie's lap. Maggie just sat there on my bed with her mouth open.

"Take one or two of the others," I said to Dee.

But she turned without a word and went out to Hakim-a-barber.

"You just don't understand," she said, as Maggie and I came out to the car.

"What don't I understand?" I wanted to know. 80

"Your heritage," she said. And then she turned to Maggie, kissed her, and said, "You ought to try to make something of yourself, too, Maggie. It's really a new day for us. But from the way you and Mama still live you'd never know it."

She put on some sunglasses that hid everything above the tip of her nose and her chin.

Maggie smiled; maybe at the sunglasses. But a real smile, not scared. After we watched the car dust settle I asked Maggie to bring me a dip of snuff. And then the two of us sat there just enjoying, until it was time to go in the house and to bed.

EXPLORING THE TEXT

1. What do we learn about the narrator of this story within the first few pages? Who is she? How would you describe her background? From what sources does she draw her sense of self?

2. What is Dee's story? What do we learn about her past behavior, values, and attitudes? How is she viewed by her mother and sister? What seem to be the sources of her sense of selfhood?

3. What do objects like the house, churn, and bench represent to Dee in this story? What special symbolism might be associated with the quilt that Dee wants for her apartment? Why does the narrator decide to give it to Maggie and not to Dee? Is she right to refuse Dee's request? What does this action mean for the narrator?

4. Who is the main character of this story? Why do you think so? How would our view of the story change if it were told from Dee's point of view?

5. Overall, what is Alice Walker saying through this story about changing attitudes toward the self? Which character would you be more likely to identify with, the narrator or Dee? Why?

FURTHER EXPLORATIONS

1. Compare the attitudes of Dee and Maggie toward their heirloom quilts with that of Scott Russell Sanders (p. 142) towards the hammer he inherits from his father and grandfather. What lessons and meanings do these objects contain for their inheritors? How do they link them to the past? Does Sanders's relation to his hammer more nearly resemble Dee's or Maggie's relation to the quilts in "Everyday Use"? Why?

2. How might Eviatar Zerubavel (p. 217) explain Dee's desire to preserve and display the quilts that she returns home for in "Everyday Use"? How does this explanation affect your view of her as a character?

3. Which character in Walker's story appears to have the most impermeable or rigid "ego boundaries" in the sense that Robert Sapolsky uses this term (p. 254)? Which one seems to have a more flexible or permeable sense of self? What leads you to think so?

4. How might Mihaly Csikszentmihalyi (p. 264) interpret the importance for Dee of the household objects she wants to take home for display? To what extent might it be possible to interpret the conflict between Dee and her mother as a matter of differing "ideal selves"?

5. In light of his historical overview of the evolution of the self, how might Roy F. Baumeister (p. 320) interpret the conflict between Walker's narrator and her daughter Dee? What forces shape the self of the narrator? What forces shape Dee? How might Baumeister describe the sense of selfhood of each of these characters?

ESSAY OPTIONS

1. Expand the journal entry you wrote for the *Before Reading* assignment on page 283 into a fully developed essay in which you explore the meaning of an object that has played an important role in your family's history or one that has special cultural significance for you and the members of your family. What stories, memories, or meanings does this object contain for you and your family? How does it figure in your family's and your own personal identity? To what extent has it remained an item of "everyday use" in your household?

2. Drawing on ideas and experiences presented in Walker's "Everyday Use," Scott Russell Sanders's "The Inheritance of Tools" (p. 142), Patricia Hampl's "Memory and Imagination" (p. 180), Susan Engel's "Then and Now: Creating a Self Through the Past" (p. 192), Barry Lopez's "A Passage of the Hands" (p. 27), and/or Eviatar Zerubavel's "Social Memories" (p. 217), write an essay on the role that memories play — personal and impersonal — in the construction of the self. How do personal and impersonal memories contribute to our sense of who we are? To what extent do we fashion our sense of self from past experiences and events?

Living Backwards

ARNOLD M. LUDWIG

Nineteenth-century American novelist Stephen Crane packed a lot of living into a remarkable short lifespan. By the age of twenty-four, he had won national acclaim for his now classic depiction of the American Civil War in *The Red Badge of Courage*. By twenty-nine, he had died of tuberculosis in England after participating in Cuba's war for independence from Spain, surviving a celebrated shipwreck, and sharing the last years of impoverished self-exile with Cora Howorth Taylor, his lover and former owner of the "Hotel de Dream" brothel of Jacksonville, Florida. Crane, it seems, had the habit of living his life "backwards" — he acted out the plots of his novels and stories after having lived them first in his imagination — a not so remarkable phenomenon according to psychologist Arnold M. Ludwig. In fact, as Ludwig suggests in this provocative selection, we all live our lives backwards, to a certain degree, by shaping our notions of self around the life stories, plots, and roles we inherit from the social context we grow up in. Each one of us adopts a part to play in life from the "scripts" written for us by the collective imagination of our culture. Ludwig is E. A. Edwards Professor of Psychiatry at the University of Kentucky College of Medicine and the author of seven books, including *The Price of Greatness* (1995), and *How Do We Know Who We Are?: A Biography of the Self* (1997).

BEFORE READING

Freewrite in your journal about the person you'll become in 20 to 30 years. What will you be doing? Where will you live? With whom? What social role or roles do you see yourself playing? Share these imaginative "prebiographies" in class and try to explain where they come from.

According to the biographer Christopher Benfey, Stephen Crane lived out events in his imagination long before he experienced them in reality.[1] Contrary to expectations that a writer's works are based on past experiences, he actually wrote about events before he experienced them, making his fiction eerily predictive of what lay ahead. For instance, his only experiences with battle, as a highly paid war correspondent, came years after he published his novel about the Civil War, *The Red Badge of Courage,* acclaimed worldwide for its vivid portrayal of war. He wrote *Maggie,* his novel about a prostitute, long before he fell in love with a real-life madam. Some time after writing several stories about shipwrecks, he actually found himself aboard a foundering steamer. In his novel, *The Third Violet,* he wrote about courting a society belle; later, he carried out a courtship with one through his letters. To dismiss these instances as coincidental cases of life imitating art is to overlook the full implications of Crane's experiences. In a metaphorical sense, he seemed to be living his life backwards, experiencing the future before it happened.

I asked Christopher Benfey, "In what way was Stephen Crane's double life different from that of others?"

"In Crane's case, the relation between the life imagined and the life lived struck me as so literal and extreme and almost lock-step that he seemed a particularly good example of *lived doubleness* that I think is common to just about everyone."

"Why do you think he did that? Why did he have to translate his fantasies into reality?"

"If I were required to sketch out what such a motivation would be, I could give two parts of it pretty quickly, and the third part might still need a good deal of psychological expertise. The first two are cultural. Crane grew up in a household that was intensely religious and intensely involved with a fairly literal interpretation of the Bible. His father was a Methodist minister. All of his uncles on his mother's side were Methodist ministers. His grandfather was, and so on. One tenet of a certain kind of nineteenth-century evangelical Christianity is that you model your life on the Good Book.° So the idea of living his life according to an earlier script could not be more deeply ingrained in Crane's temperament.

"The second thing is that Crane lived in a journalistic culture, in addition to the religious culture . . . that tended to frame the story first and then go out and try to find it. Crane's letters are full of requests to cover the next streetcar strike or to write a certain kind of story before the event actually happened. He also worked for people like Hearst° whose basic view was that if you didn't have the news story that you needed, you went out and tried to create it. There is some evidence that Hearst did engineer the sinking of the battleship *Maine*° in order to get the U.S. involved in the Spanish American War.

"So those are two parts of what I would think of as a three part motivation. . . . The third is tougher. [It has to do with] the reason for the particular extremity and literalness of Crane's write-it-then-live-it temperament, and I don't really see a way to go much further with that, except by finding other temperaments who seem the same way and trying to see what they might have in common. This is a character type that you sometimes run into with writers."

Does this mean that you actually live portions of your life backwards with future experiences preceding present ones, like the rewinding of a videotape? Of course not. Your inexorable progression through successive developmental stages insures that you will move forward in time until your biological clock winds down. What it means more exactly is that you exhibit what Christopher Benfey called "lived doubleness," meaning that you simultaneously live in your imagination and in the real world, even though these experiences may not be in synch. When the imagined experiences you explicitly think about, write about, or express in other ways come true, they create the illusion of a reversal in time. Because the future comes to be experienced before it actually happens, it takes on aspects of the past.

"the Good Book:" The Bible.

Hearst: William Randolph Hearst (1863–1951), American newspaper publisher.

the battleship *Maine* The sinking of the *Maine* in Cuba's Havana Harbor in 1898 was widely regarded as the reason why the United States entered the Spanish-American War later that year.

The notion that you, like Crane, may experience portions of your life in a reverse order raises important questions about the nature of the self. From an experiential standpoint, what if all you take for granted about the temporal course of your life is the other way around, and your life represents not so much a progression into the future as a realization of the past? This has a ring of science fiction about it. Instead of building your life only on past experiences, you actually may be living your life to conform to stories already written for you. If you aren't a novelist, like Crane, your stories may be vague and inchoate, without clear narrative structure, but stories nonetheless, waiting for you to live them. Much of what you do in life—maturing, selecting a mate, procreating, exhibiting certain temperaments, aging—may be written in your genes in a language you don't yet know how to decode, creating erosions and gullies over the unexplored terrain of your life through which your life story flows. Perhaps much of what you strive to become is already preordained for you by your biological predisposition, inculcated in you by your parents, suggested by cultural myths, or spelled out in places like the New Testament. Perhaps you spend your life seeking experiences that you're supposed to have and that feel "right" because they are indelibly written on your mind in an invisible script. If this be so, then over the course of your life, you simply become what you're destined to be. . . .

Of course, it's possible to interpret accounts of this sort in different ways. It's customary to view them prospectively and say that these people are responding to the dictates of unconscious conflicts or motives. They still exert choice and shape their own futures. But you also can view their lives retrospectively, arguing that their father's expectations, which were written on their minds from an early age, became their own aspirations, and they pursued them throughout their lives, much as Stephen Crane pushed the objects of his fiction.

What this suggests is that you often live out in your imagination many of the experiences you later seek, but in a less dramatic fashion than Crane. You imagine what your first date or sex encounters will be like, relying on the stories of friends or accounts you read about in magazines or novels. You imagine how colleagues and friends will respond to you if you win some prestigious award, and then spend your life pursuing it. You imagine long in advance the kind of home you want and the lifestyle you wish to lead, and then work toward achieving it. You may not have actually written out parts of your own life-to-be, as Crane did, but you already know much of it in advance, years before you live it. It may be stretching matters a bit, and we may be quibbling over semantics, but it's possible to construe this as living portions of your life in reverse. . . .

The Story That Is Not a Story

Because a personal life story is so important for your sense of self, let me recap its essential elements. One of these elements is that you be able to consciously experience progressive change in your life. Your developmental unfolding insures that you become aware of the passage of time and your relative position along the life cycle. Narrative flow, almost by definition, depends on direction and movement. The second element of a personal story is that you can distinguish yourself from others. Without the presence of another human being, you have no way to define yourself. In a solipsistic universe, a single self becomes the equivalent of all people or merely the expression of God.

To emphasize these points, let me retell the biblical story of Eden to show that it's mostly no story at all, and only becomes a real story when these two elements are present. To this end, I'll assume that the biblical account of the creation story in the Garden of Eden is literally true.

In the beginning, the Lord God creates the heavens and the earth and all living creatures. Then He forms man from the dust of the ground, breathes life into his nostrils, and puts him smack in the Garden of Eden to tend it. He tells man that he may eat freely of every tree that is pleasant to sight and good for food, except for the Tree of Knowledge of Good and Evil, which stands in the middle of the Garden. If man disobeys this warning, he will lose his innocence and experience death.

So here is Adam, without care or want, wandering endlessly and aimlessly about, plucking delectable fruits off trees and biting into their fleshy pulps or spitting out seeds, perhaps also taking pleasure in his own body, with no other ambition than to "be." He has no need for language since there is no one for him to communicate with. He has no social role since there is no society. He has no conflicts or aspirations since all his needs are met. He is without guile or cunning since these qualities have no use. He has no need to succeed or compete since he already is first in the eyes of God. He has no need for knowledge since this will detract from his innocence. Besides, there are no books, music, or art available anyway, so intellectual curiosity will do him no good. He has no sense of self since he is the only one who exists. He has no personal life story since he leads a life without variety, without change, and without plot—with no beginning, no middle, no end. He has eternal life and Paradise, an existence without need, pain, or conflict. What more can he ask? Yet inexplicably, as days follow days, years follow years, centuries follow centuries, for eternity, he experiences a growing boredom and discontent.

Then the Lord God, in His wisdom, decides that it's not good for Adam to be alone and, after causing him to fall into a deep slumber, makes a helpmate for him out of one of his ribs, a being known as "woman" because she is part of "man." It's at this point that Adam gets the first glimmerings of a sense of personal self, as he begins to communicate with Eve, but his self-ness is negligible since she remains subject to him and he still has no wants. In the development of a personal identity, Eve, though, is more advanced, for she already has a rebellious spirit and constantly urges Adam to eat of the forbidden fruit.

Eventually, he succumbs. It's only after the Fall, when they both are cast out of the Garden of Eden and beget the long line of the begats and begottens, that Adam and Eve become mortal and the personal stories of man and

10

woman begin. Only then does each begin to exist in time and space. Each enters a personal life cycle and now must distinguish between the sense of "I" and the sense of "we."

While you may continue to dream of recapturing that idyllic time before the Fall—that undifferentiated, mindless, care-free, womb-like existence, which your progenitors, Adam and Eve, lost—it remains unattainable as long as you retain a personal sense of self. Paradise happens to be a place where time is nonexistent. Without time, you can have no new experiences. Without new experiences, you can't live out a personal life story. Without having a personal life story, you can have no sense of self.

> "Do you believe in Crane's case there was a good deal of illusion, a public persona to get beyond?" I asked Christopher Benfey.
>
> "Sure, I think there are all kinds of masks and false fronts that Crane assumes. . . . But I'm a little uncomfortable with the too easy distinction between a false front or public self on the one hand versus the real self or the authentic self on the other. I think especially for a writer like Crane, that distinction was not always entirely clear for him, and much of what a writer does is to put forth imaginative other selves. They tend to take on a reality that his original self doesn't have for him. When Crane keeps saying, 'I cannot help disappearing and vanishing, it is my form of trait,' that seems to me a very common feeling that an artist may have. It's what Keats° called 'negative capability.' The artist, when he or she is most involved in the creation of art, has a sense of disappearing, of vanishing, of losing or scooping out whatever original sense of self he or she had and projecting an imaginative self that has a fuller reality."

Composing a Life

Whether you believe that you have the power to shape your own life or are fated to do what you do, you can't help construing your life within a story format. There are many reasons for this, but the most important, in my opinion, is that you rely on stories to give coherence to your sense of self and make sense out of your existence. Your personal life story offers you an opportunity to integrate in a cohesive and understandable way the seemingly immiscible mixture of your many biological urges, psychological needs, social responses, and spiritual yearnings. Without some organizing framework for these often competing and contradictory experiences, you likely would be emotionally incapacitated.

Since I rely on a narrative framework to explain many aspects of human behavior, I need to clarify what such terms as "life," "story," "role," and "script" mean. As a general guide, consider that you are born into a life and live out a story in which you adopt certain roles requiring certain scripts. In this process of becoming progressively differentiated from others, you may experience incompatibilities at the different interfaces. Your personal story may

Keats: John Keats (1795–1821), English poet.

be unsuitable for the life you are born to or it may allow the full flowering of your potential. Your roles may fit or not fit your personal story. And the scripts you employ may be inconsistent with your roles or let you function successfully in them. Let me elaborate.

Being Born Into a Life

At the start, much like Adam, you are born into a life. You enter the world as   15
a human being, a biological organism, with potentialities that may or may not be realized, depending on the influences to which you are exposed. Your life itself has no form or meaning as yet, other than the necessity of it being lived. The general parameters of your life are the same for all other members of your species. You progress from inception, to birth, to childhood, to adulthood, to old age, and to death, revealing all the properties of living forms. To live a life, all you need do is to eat, sleep, procreate, protect your territory, age, and fulfill your biological destiny. You don't necessarily need to be conscious of who you are and what you do and why you do it. Mostly, you live your life oblivious to the many forces impinging on you that determine what you can or can't do — your genetic makeup, your biological constitution, the neurophysiological workings of your brain, climatic conditions, the availability of natural resources, familial, social, and cultural programming, historical forces, and other unknown factors. Much of the time, you live your life instinctively as part of the animal kingdom, especially during infancy and childhood — the age of innocence — without seeking meaning in what you do.

Entering a Personal Story

With consciousness, reflection, and a sense of time, you enter your personal story. A personal story requires that you possess a self that can serve as a protagonist, someone who can act on the environment and be acted upon by it. Mostly, the broad outlines of your life story are already set out for you at birth and during childhood by the life you enter, as dictated by your biological makeup, family background and cultural heritage.[2] These early influences usually decide the kinds of people you're drawn to, the appeal of certain occupations, and the lifestyle you pursue.[3]

As part of a life story, other characters must exist as well. You aren't an island unto yourself, even when you try to be. You are reared by parents, compete with siblings and peers, work for superiors, select mates, and encounter adversaries. Because you are a social creature, you rarely have the luxury of carrying out your own plot without it impinging on others' lives. You not only inhabit other people's stories, but they also inhabit yours. More likely than not, frictions will develop between you and others, obliging you to modify your story plot. However, if your story line happens to be important enough to you, you stubbornly cling to it, even if that involves upsetting others.

Whatever your personal story, you must live it in a cultural context. One of the major functions of cultures is to insure a cohesiveness among its members through common languages, codes of behavior, customs, rituals and belief systems. Each culture has its own mythology containing the common dreams and aspirations of its collective people. It's from this vast reservoir of mythic offerings, which are filled with struggles between heroes and villains, good and evil, and the quest for everlasting life, that you derive your own personal story. Myths of this sort serve as harmonizing and stabilizing forces that integrate people with their societies and nature.[4]

Even though your cultural mythology supplies you with the major elements and themes for your personal story, the story you eventually enter isn't always clearly articulated. Stories can be coherent or incoherent, cohesive or fragmented, developed or undeveloped, or rich or poor in content. They also can have different narrative tones, some being upbeat or credulous, others being downbeat or cynical. Not all people embark on a cohesive and developed life tale. Perhaps in the past, when people's livelihoods, social status, educational prospects, and future opportunities were mostly determined at birth, you could predict the course of their lives even before they set forth in the world. With the dissolution of the family, scientific challenges to established beliefs, rapid political change, and shifts in values and attitudes, the similarity and stability of many personal stories begin to disappear. In industrialized, wealthy societies, new stories proliferate and offer a broader range of options.

Just as every personal life story has a protagonist, it also has a plot. And a plot or story line represents an unfolding goal or purpose — the quest for immortality, power, control, knowledge, security, or pleasure — that follows a temporal course with a beginning, middle, and end. Even if you somehow manage to lead a relatively conflict-free or uneventful existence in a controlled, regulated environment, as Adam originally did in Paradise, your exposure to the passage of time itself creates a plot since with each succeeding day you change and are one day closer to death. 20

Naturally, your circumstances and personal inclinations shape the range of stories available to you. The more coherent and cohesive the story, the more it reconciles all the discrepancies and loose ends in your life, the more relentless and attractive its pull, the more each chapter inexorably follows another. You may be drawn, for instance, to the typical middle-class story of professional success, a home in suburbia, membership in a country club, church affiliation, and social respectability. Or you can live out a story for musicians and singers from the 1960s, a frenetic, driven life of alcohol, drugs, outrageousness, and social protest, culminating in your own self-destruction, a story played out so well by Jim Morrison, Jimi Hendrix, and Janis Joplin° — a story also well known to Kurt Cobain, of the group Nirvana, who also followed suit — all of whom managed to kill themselves at the same age of twenty-seven. Or you can enter the typical life of a daughter of an alcoholic father and a long-suffering mother, by marry-

Jim Morrison, etc. . . . .   Rock-and-roll stars who died as the result of their extreme lifestyles and drug use.

ing an alcoholic husband, divorcing him because of his drinking, marrying another alcoholic, or perhaps for variety a cocaine user, and then raising alcoholic or drug-using sons and unhappy, caretaking daughters. Or, whether talented or not, you can lead the unconventional life of an artist or poet, nursing your angst and wrestling over the meaning of life in ateliers or cafes. Or you can live out the predictable life of the chronically unhappy housewife, bored by your life, resentful of your husband's perceived freedom and control, wanting to do something meaningful, yet too scared to strike out on your own. Or you can live the life of a high-roller, full of excitement and adventure, sports and gambling, exploring new experiences and living on the edge. Or you can enter the world of high society, associating with others of similar backgrounds and engaging in all those activities that go with your social rank. The stories go on. There is even one if you find none suitable. You can go about reinventing yourself, cultivating eccentricities, saying and doing outrageous things, fabricating your past, and being the center of attention.

Usually, one dominant plot subsumes several different subplots or themes. A major theme running through your life may be to fulfill your role as a parent or a spouse, or as the dutiful son or daughter to your parents. Another may be to serve God, your church, and community. Another may be to be successful in your career. All these themes represent only components of your basic story plot, which may be to lead an exemplary, traditional life as a guarantee for personal fulfillment and happiness. Or your dominant story plot may be the quest for power and success, with all else — family life, friendships, and recreational pursuits — representing only minor themes.

And on it goes. You become an active conspirator in your own life story. You move forward in your life by expressing your past and becoming the character you're biologically, psychologically, and socially disposed to be, if events and others let you.

Although the particular plot you live seems new at the time you're living it, others likely have lived it many times before, with minor details left for you to fill in or alter. As with fiction, original plots are rare. Most tend to be formula-driven and even hackneyed, especially the best-sellers. There's good reason for this. You tend to be drawn to conventional, ready-made plots because those are what your parents, teachers, and society trained you to prefer. Because most of the major parameters of these traditional plots are already implicit or spelled out, you never have to worry about losing your personal bearings, as sometimes happens when you embark on an unexplored course. But with whatever story you enter, you need to convince yourself that you potentially have some measure of control over its course. Unless you have your personal story imposed on you by force, accident, or circumstance, it enhances your sense of selfhood to believe that you select your own story, and not, as may be the case, that the story selects you.

It's important to note that your personal story doesn't only include what 25 is actively transpiring in your life; it also corresponds to what you expect your life to be. You may live your life in obscurity, for example, yet constantly yearn for fame. Under ideal circumstances, your life story and basic aspirations co-incide. When they don't, you keep working to reconcile them. If unsuccessful, you remain discontented and ill-at-ease unless you finally become resigned to your lot.

Because the story plot you follow offers a structure for your life, a vehicle for integrating your experiences, and a conceptual map to guide your way, you cling to it to keep from becoming disoriented. It becomes a *de facto* extension of you, familiar experiential territory for your life, and creates the context for your existence. This is why you try to preserve it at all costs. You may not play the prime role in composing your own personal life story, but you play a de-cisive one in safeguarding it.[5]

Playing Roles

Within each story, you adopt roles, some of which are suited to your ends and others not.[6] A general story theme potentially may be realized through the adoption of assorted roles. For instance, if your main agenda is wealth and power, then you can pursue it through different routes — as a banker, a physi-cian, a professional athlete, a politician, or vicariously through marriage. This is so for most of what you do, whether it be to live in the limelight, to be loved and admired, to lead an artistic and creative life, or to attack and confront authority.

Roles represent implicit or explicit expectations for behavior. They have evolved in society to meet various social needs and to reduce friction among people. Roles govern almost every aspect of social life. There are parental roles, sick roles, gender roles, professional roles, and leadership roles, for ex-ample, each defining appropriate attitudes and actions. Conflicts arise be-tween people when their different roles overlap or their boundaries become ambiguous. Turf battles, animosities, and misunderstandings tend to be the inevitable consequences of role diffusion.

While you bring to your roles certain special personal features, they also exert powerful molding effects on you. They have a stability and momentum of their own, giving continuity to your identity, consistency to your actions, and constancy to your life, and enabling you, if they are suitable, to move more smoothly through your personal life story. For other people, the roles you assume convey important information about you and let them know what to expect from you.

Roles also serve as a basis for constructing your own personal identity. Because certain roles convey certain meanings in society, you can use them to represent who you are and base your self-esteem on how successfully you fulfill them. Although certain self-help approaches urge you to step outside your roles to find your true self, the roles you play actually may help you to feel more whole and coherent. Peter Sellers,° the actor, articulated this well when he observed, "When my role is finished, I experience a sudden loss of identity."[7] . . .

Peter Sellers: (1925–1980), English actor famous for portraying multiple parts in his movies.

As guides for how to play various roles, you often rely on role models, either by directly observing their behavior or incorporating images of them within you.[8] These internal images that you accumulate over the years of parents, teachers, celebrities, or other inspiring persons sometimes remain distinct and identifiable, but mostly they fade and become absorbed and assimilated into your sense of who you are. They provide the blueprints for your thoughts and actions, and keep you from responding haphazardly when you encounter new situations.

Using Scripts

For each of your many roles, you have available a number of ready-made, prepackaged scripts that let you function effectively, efficiently, and convincingly.[9] You dress in certain ways, decorate your office in certain ways, act in certain ways, and say certain things that are expected of you when you play your parts. The requirements of your various roles tend to be almost ceremonial, conventional, and ritualistic, allowing for automatic and instant exchanges with others to facilitate social discourse. To play the role of a friendly neighbor, you utter standard greetings, comment on the weather, and offer other chit-chat and pleasantries. As an enlightened parent, you try to do and say all the things that enlightened parents are supposed to. As a celebrity, you make the usual authoritative pronouncements, speak elliptically, or make outrageous statements to show that ordinary standards don't quite apply to you. If you are a politician, you remain vague and equivocal so as not to give offense. And so it goes.

The importance of scripts is that they let you function comfortably in your roles. They are the basis for ritual and convention. They represent automatic, acceptable responses for a variety of situations and usually tend to be stereotyped and predictable. They play a large part in etiquette and decorum, telling you how to act in various social interactions at work, at home, and with your family. You may have several scripts to choose from for a particular role, but in time the scripts you use and the roles you play become intertwined. There are even common scripts for people who play the role of people writing their own scripts, such as being openly promiscuous, saying or doing outrageous things, and being tactless or self-centered.

Of course, you have a certain degree of freedom to make planned or impromptu changes in the scripts available for your roles, adding a distinctive stamp of your own, but that doesn't detract from the basic similarities that continue to exist. There's usually good reason for this since without a certain standardization in scripts, your behavior loses credibility for others or becomes less expressive of your role. It's as though an implicit protocol governs what you do and say and how you appear. Certain behaviors are associated with certain roles and others aren't. For example, you tolerate preaching from your preacher and not from your barber. "Feminine" women aren't supposed to be aggressive or outspoken. Employees are supposed to be deferential toward their employers. The scripts represent a shorthand for informing others about your roles, and your roles represent a shorthand for telling them about the plots you've selected and the stories you're living. Scripts that are incongruous or inappropriate raise suspicion and gain undue attention. There's some slack about how you play your roles, but if you digress too much or are too deviant or too unorthodox, you can expect to encounter public censure or rejection.

Playwright or Actor?

So powerful influences shape the nature and direction of your life, inducing you   35
to inhabit standard life stories that have a beginning, middle, and end, and that mostly conform to certain culturally acceptable themes. Depending on your perspective, you can make a case for living your life prospectively, interpreting your experiences as the result of prior causes or personal choices. Or you can make a case for living your life retrospectively, interpreting your experiences as echoes of similar lives already lived or as already written parts you must play. Not unlike a Greek play, you act as though you can modify your fate, while the chorus of the voices in the background proclaims what you must do.

Whatever your perspective about causality, what transpires in your life needn't be as inexorable as it first seems. Playing a role and participating in a personal story aren't incompatible with personal freedom. To observe that Stephen Crane later led a life already conceived in his imagination is perhaps less amazing than the fact that he conceived of these events in the first place. Where did his phenomenal understanding of war or life with a prostitute or the nature of a shipwreck come from? There was no *Red Badge of Courage* or *Maggie* before he wrote them. These works seem to have been a product of his creative imagination, which brought into being something that didn't exist before. Therefore, if you say that he led his life backwards in time after his writing, you also must conclude that he lived it forwards in time before. This suggests that within the context of his own personal story, he has shown authorial freedom himself. Semantics? Perhaps. But with important implications about the extent of your personal freedom.

Pursuing Shakespeare's metaphor of all the world being a stage, we find that participating in a play needn't mean performing in rote fashion, with no opportunity for spontaneity or creativity. Like an accomplished actor on stage, you presumably have the opportunity for improvisation at times and can interpret your roles and the meaning of the story in your own distinctive way. And like Stephen Crane, you may be able to create the future before you live it.

Whoever the Great Playwright happens to be who formulates your personal story, provides your roles, and writes your scripts, he, she, or it seems to have created a mystery that underlies every personal plot, which has to do with the extent to which you can compose your personal life story or are only an actor in the unfolding drama. Obviously, you have little personal control over much of what is already written out for you when you are born into a life. But you may have more leeway in the course it takes than it first seems. You may not be the main author or even a collaborator in the composing of your life — since if it was largely up to you, you likely would have written it differently (perhaps choosing a longer life span, the absence of disease, more talent, or greater intelligence) — but you realistically seem to be able to function as a biographer, shaping and revising the material you have responsibility for, to make your life more meaningful and improve the quality of the story. This little bit of biographical freedom lets you believe that you can make crucial decisions at major forks in the road, to take "the road less traveled," so to speak. And, . . . you may well have that option, as long as you act within the relative constraints of your many roles and don't wander too far from your unfolding story plot.

Notes

1. C. Benfey, *The Double Life of Stephen Crane* (New York: Knopf, 1992).

2. J. Kagan, *Galen's Prophesy: Temperament in Human Nature* (New York: Basic Books, 1994). Also see W. Gallagher, "How We Become What We Are," *The Atlantic Monthly,* September 1994, 39–55; and C. R. Cloninger, D. M. Svrakic, and T. R. Przybeck, "A Psychological Model of Temperament and Character," *Archives of General Psychiatry, 50* (1993): 975–90.

3. See M. Csikszentmihalyi and O. V. Beattie, "Life Themes: A Theoretical and Empirical Exploration of Their Origins and Effects," *Journal of Humanistic Psychology 19* (1979): 45–63, for how unresolved, early life conflicts have profound effects on the dominant themes governing individual's lives. Of course, this is likewise a basic assumption of psychoanalytic theory.

4. See J. Campbell, *The Power of Myth,* with B. Moyers (New York: Doubleday, 1988) and J. Campbell, *The Hero with a Thousand Faces* (Princeton: Princeton University Press, 1968). Also see S. Keen and A. Valley-Fox, *Your Mythic Journey: Finding Meaning in Your Life Through Writing and Storytelling* (Los Angeles: Jeremy P. Tarcher, 1989); L. Rue, *By the Grace of Guile: The Role of Deception in Natural History and Human Affairs* (London: Oxford University Press, 1994); and D. P. McAdams, *The Stories We Live By: Personal Myths and the Making of the Self* (New York: William Morrow, 1993) for discussions of the role of myths and stories in our lives.

5. Plots can be driven by talent or intellectual and motivational needs as well. By virtue of a superior facility, a person can be drawn to art, music, or chess as a major medium for personal experience and then, eventually, for personal fulfillment. Gerald Holton, in *Thematic Origins of Scientific Thought: Kepler to Einstein* (Cambridge: Harvard University Press, 1973), describes the importance of "themata," around which individuals organize their lives and ideas. Also see E. E. Jones, "Interpreting Interpersonal Behavior: The Effects of Expectancies," *Science 234* (1986): 41–46 for an excellent account of the role of expectancies in human behavior. A. G. Greenwald, "The Totalitarian Ego: Fabrication and Revision of Personal History," *American Journal of Psychology 35* (1980): 603–18, discusses the reasons for cognitive constancy.

6. There is vast literature on social role therapy. Talcott Parsons, of course, has written the pioneer work in this area. See *The Social System* (Glencoe, IL: Free Press, 1959). Also see D. P. McAdams, *The Stories We Live By: Personal Myths and the Making of the Self,* and R. F. Baumeister, *Identity: Cultural Change and the Struggle for the Self* (New York: Oxford University Press, 1986).

7. P. Evans, *Peter Sellers: The Mask Behind the Mask* (Englewood Cliffs, NJ: Prentice-Hall, 1968), 191.

8. D. P. McAdams *(The Stories We Live By: Personal Myths and the Making of the Self)* discusses the importance of "imagoes" and role models in our lives.

9. Silvan S. Tomkins ("Script Theory," in *The Emergency of Personality,* J. Aronoff, A. I. Rabin, and Robert A. Zucker, eds. [New York: Springer Publishing, 1987]) also developed an important theory about human behavior based on "scripts." In his particular usage of the term, a script represents the basic unit of analysis for understanding persons. Some scripts are innate, but most are innate and learned. The learned scripts originate in innate scripts but usually radically transform them. These innate and learned scripts, in turn, affect most behavior patterns in adult life. Also see M. J. Horowitz, "Person Schemas," in *Person Schemas and Maladaptive Interpersonal Patterns,* M. J. Horowitz ed. (Chicago: University of Chicago Press, 1991); J. L. Singer and P. Salovey, "Organized Knowledge Structures and Personality: Person Schemas, Self Schemas, Prototypes, and Scripts," in *Person Schemas and Maladaptive Interpersonal Patterns,* M. J. Horowitz, ed.

EXPLORING THE TEXT

1. What exactly does Ludwig mean when he says that Stephen Crane lived his life "backwards"? In what sense do we experience "lived doubleness"?

2. What point is Ludwig making through his retelling of the biblical story of the Garden of Eden? Why does he believe that without a personal life story "you can have no sense of self"? To what extent would you agree with this assertion? Why?

3. Where do our personal life stories come from, according to Ludwig? What common "plots" does Ludwig identify in relation to American cultural mythology? What other common plots are associated with the cultures you participate in?

4. Why, in Ludwig's view, do we tend to adopt "ready-made" life stories and plots? What do the roles that we play do for us individually and socially? What other advantages can you find in this adoption of socially recognizable roles and plots?

5. What are "scripts" and how do they relate to the roles we play? What might be included in the script for a chance meeting between two "friendly neighbors"? In the script for an annual checkup at the doctor's? For the first phone call home to the parents from an entering freshman college student? For a chance meeting between two first-year students at the campus cafeteria? For ordering lunch at McDonald's? For ordering dinner at a four-star restaurant in New York?

6. What questions does Ludwig's theory of life stories, roles, plots, and scripts raise about the nature of the self, free will, and destiny? How free are we, in Ludwig's view? Do you agree that most of us live within the constraints of the role we choose—or are given—to play in life? Why or why not?

FURTHER EXPLORATIONS

1. Compare Ludwig's notion of "biographical freedom" with the way that we shape our life stories—and presentation of self—according to Susan Engel in "Then

and Now: Creating a Self Through the Past" (p. 192). To what extent would Engel be likely to agree with Ludwig about the roles and plots that shape our identities?

2. To what extent is it possible to interpret the conflict between Dee and her mother in Alice Walker's "Everyday Use" (p. 283) as a clash between differing roles, in Ludwig's sense of the term? What roles have Dee and her mother chosen to play? What "script" would Dee write for her mother to perform during their reunion, if it were in her power to do so? What script would her mother write for Dee? How free are Walker's characters to "choose" the roles they play in life?

3. How does Rubén Martínez's description of his early infatuation with film heroes in "Technicolor" (p. 306) support or complicate Ludwig's theory of "lived doubleness" (p. 292)? What roles or scripts does Martínez adopt from the multiple cultures he grows up in?

4. Working in small groups, sketch out plot lines for several of the life stories that Ludwig identifies with the "mythic" context of contemporary American culture — plot lines for the middle-class story of professional success, for the unconventional life of an artist or poet, the chronically unhappy housewife, the high roller who lives on the edge, and so forth. Later, compare your plot lines in class and see how closely they match. Does this informal experiment confirm the assumption that these stories and plot lines are commonly available throughout our cultural context?

5. Read James Baldwin's short story "Sonny's Blues" (p. 390) and evaluate how Ludwig might interpret the conflict of Sonny and his brother in terms of the life stories they've decided to act out. What roles have Sonny and his brother chosen to play? What motives lead them to choose these roles? What plots are associated with these roles? How do Sonny and his brother rise above these stereotypical expectations?

ESSAY OPTIONS

1. Write a paper in which you analyze two or three roles that you have been attracted to as models for your life story. What themes or values do you associate with these roles? What attractions do they hold for you? What drawbacks or limitations do you see associated with living out these life patterns?

2. Drawing on the ideas of Ludwig in this selection, Robert Sapolsky in "Ego Boundaries, or the Fit of My Father's Shirt" (p. 254), and Susan Engel in "Then and Now: Creating a Self Through the Past" (p. 192), write an essay discussing the role that the self plays in creating a sense of continuity and coherence in our lives. How does the concept of selfhood order our inner world? What roles does it play in our social relationships? What costs are associated with the notion of a continuous, unchanging self?

3. Using ideas and experiences presented by Ludwig, K. C. Cole (p. 75), Walker Percy (p. 118), and Daniel L. Schacter (p. 157) as points of departure, write a paper about the difficulties of living in the present. How do phenomena like Schacter's "binocular vision," Ludwig's "lived doubleness," and Percy's "preformed complex" supposedly tie us to the past? What dangers do these authors associate with the tendency to view the present through the past?

Technicolor

RUBÉN MARTÍNEZ

When Rubén Martínez looks back at his life, he sees it through the lens of a 72-millimeter camera. A self-confessed child of Hollywood—and proud graduate of Hollywood High—Martínez's preadolescent fantasies were shaped by the mythic machinery of the films he saw for half price at Saturday afternoon matinees. It was only later in life that his "Technicolor" concept of self was to collide with the color of his skin. Martínez's story of the many "selves" he inherited from the movies illustrates the way we adopt and discard the roles and role models we encounter as we grow up. It also challenges us to consider how much freedom we have to pick and choose the selves that we eventually become. An award-winning journalist, poet, and performer, Martínez is a professor of journalism at Claremont McKenna College, an editor for the Pacific News Service, and a guest commentator on National Public Radio's *All Things Considered.* He is also the author of *The Other Side: Notes from the New L.A., Mexico City, and Beyond* (1992) and writes regularly for the *New York Times,* the *Los Angeles Times,* the *Village Voice, Spin Magazine,* and other national publications.

BEFORE READING

Think back to one or more characters in a movie or television show that you recall identifying with in your childhood or adolescence. What were these fictional figures like? Why were you attracted to them? What qualities or characteristics did you admire in them? To what extent would you say that they played a role in shaping your sense of self?

FADE IN.

INTERIOR DAY, MOJAVE DESERT.

OVER THE SHOULDER SHOT: WRITER, a Latino in his mid-thirties, dressed rather shabbily, sits at a poorly put together Ikea desk that wobbles with each letter typed into a PowerBook 540c, which looks like it's suffered one too many punches from writer's block–inspired fists. Writer stares intensely at the screen, as if closely examining his face in a mirror.

CLOSE UP on COMPUTER SCREEN, where we see these very words appearing.

SLOWLY PULL BACK, revealing the rest of the cluttered desk: Camel Filter cigs, a pile of audio cassettes, a navy-blue bandanna, a stack of unpaid bills, scattered books (Baldwin's *Another Country,*° Steinbeck's *The Grapes of Wrath,*° Fante's *Ask the Dust,*° a Whitman collection,° a Bible in Spanish, a

Baldwin's *Another Country:* James Baldwin (1924–1987), American author.

Steinbeck's *The Grapes of Wrath:* John Steinbeck (1902–1968), American novelist.

Fante's *Ask the Dust:* John Fante (1909–1983), American novelist.

a Whitman collection: Walt Whitman (1819–1892), American poet.

title on Santería,° etc.), a beautiful nineteenth-century gold-leaf Virgin of Guadalupe statuette sitting just before the window.

CAMERA GOES THROUGH WINDOW and out into the desert, a tremendous ascending crane shot that floats over the few isolated homes and the expanse of sand, creosote, and cacti. Now and again a human appears below us—a middle-aged white lady hanging laundry on the line, a black gardener raking a sandy carport, a Mexican kid slamming a porch door, a Vietnamese woman cussing out her towheaded Marine Corps husband as he gets into a red '68 Mustang. . . .

I've always spent more time at movie houses or huddled up next to my TV and VCR than with my nose between the pages of a book. Truth be told, I read only books directly related to my research and a handful of literary faves. But sit down to read a new novel or the latest six-hundred-page biography on the *Times*'s best-seller list? Nah—who has the time in the Age of MTV? Me, I want to see colors rippling across a wide screen! I want to hear the characters' voices not with my mind's ear but with my real ear! And I want a soundtrack of violins and trumpets composed by a nonagenarian Russian émigré. I want crane shots and spaghetti-western super-closeups of eyes and crow's-feet crinkling. I want Bergman (Ingrid), Mitchum, Hayworth, and Poitier forever teamed up with Curtis,° want them sneering-panting-whistling, and a single, soft-focused tear tracking down every one of their cheeks—

I grew up in Hollywood. Literally. ABC Studios was just across the Shakespeare Bridge from us in a neighborhood we always called Silver Lake but that the yuppies have recently rechristened Franklin Hills. The imposing set for D. W. Griffith's *Intolerance* once stood about a mile away from my elementary school. In nearby Edendale, now called Echo Park, Mack Sennett filmed the comedic greats of early cinema, including Hal Roach and Laurel and Hardy. (Echo Park, with its elegant Victorians and quaint courtyard bungalows, has been a Hollywood favorite over the decades; much of *Chinatown* was shot there, as well as *L.A. Confidential.*) My alma mater, John Marshall High, has a New England Gothic façade that has served as the quintessential American high school for dozens of TV shows and movies; John Travolta and Olivia Newton-John bobby-soxed on my football field when I was a freshman.°

And, as if to live up to these origins in my adult life, I have, for the past several years, worked for the local PBS° outlet at KCET Studios, a couple of

Santería: A religion originally practiced in Cuba in which African Yoruba deities are associated with Roman Catholic saints.

Bergman . . . Mitchum, Hayworth, and Poitier . . . with Curtis: Ingrid Bergman, Robert Mitchum, Rita Hayworth, Sidney Poitier, and Tony Curtis—famous actors of the 1940s, 1950s, and 1960s.

John Travolta and Olivia Newton-John bobby-soxed . . . : Stars of the 1978 film *Grease*, shot at Hollywood High School.

PBS: Public Broadcasting Service.

blocks away from the Jewish Community Center that I, a Latino Catholic, once frequented because most of my friends were Jewish.

The house my father grew up in (and where my parents, and occasionally I, live now) is nestled in the hills of Silver Lake, about two miles from Franklin Hills. "Mixville," the ranch owned by early western hero Tom Mix, was once only a block away from my family's house, a real-life rendition of what my father saw at Saturday matinees.

Pop was quite the Cowboys-and-Indians kid, in spite of the fact that he was born to Mexican parents whose blood was much more Indian than Spanish. In the radio days he regularly listened to *The Lone Ranger,* whose by all accounts clever Indian sidekick was inexplicably named Tonto (which means "stupid" in Spanish). In the golden California afternoons of his youth, my father gathered with the other kids in Silver Lake — from Italian, German, Irish, and, up until Pearl Harbor, Japanese families — and the unlucky draw became the Indian to be chased down and shot dead with cap pistols.

My father wasn't the only Indian who loved Cowboys. Throughout what we used to call the "Third World" just about everybody was weaned on westerns in which the Indians were bad and the Cowboys good and the Indians always outnumbered the Cowboys but the Cowboys were better shooters and there the Indian (actually a Cowboy stuntman) goes down, clutching at his chest, a puff of dust as his body hits dirt, and the Cowboy and the Cowgirl hug and steal a kiss behind his hat and the violins come up and the credits roll. We all loved the Cowboys.

Over the years, Hollywood's given me great and terrible things — a culture as tangible as the mix of race and ethnicity I grew up around — and somewhere between my "reel" and "real" lives lie my deepest beliefs and my greatest fears, my nightmares and my dreams. As a kid and now an adult with a perpetual identity crisis, Hollywood has been a constant mirror for me, and what I've screened has resulted in validation and self-loathing, vindication and betrayal (I of it, and it of me). I was raised in a swirl of cultures that at times melded seamlessly and at others clashed violently — a contradiction that exists at the very heart of Hollywood, the tension between its most noble and most debased instincts.

For starters, I think I'd hate white people if it wasn't for Hollywood. This is not to say that I haven't hated some white people, and sure, the entire race, on occasion. But how can you hate someone you're on such intimate terms with — on screen and off? At my elementary school, I was the only Latino until the third grade. In addition to two Iranian brothers who were often mistaken for Latins, the extent of our integration was one black girl and a smattering of Japanese and Chinese. The vast majority of students were Anglo or Jewish.

My English was somewhat lacking when I began kindergarten. For kids of immigrants, there weren't exactly a lot of cultural choices back in the days before bilingual education and "multiculturalism." You either "assimilated" or you fought the dominant culture to the death. In my junior high school, a much more mixed environment, I came across Latino kids who embarked upon the latter course: *cholos*° who followed in the footsteps of older siblings or parents and wore the uniform of an ethnic rebel (dickies, hairnets) and lived a life at odds not just with white society but also Mother Mexico. I always envied them; however troubled their lives, their style, when compared to white kids in Hush Puppies, was way *cool* (a look that would have to wait nearly fifty years before Luis Valdez made the film version of *Zoot Suit* to get the flashy Hollywood treatment it deserved).

I, on the other hand, did everything I could to assimilate, or, in the more   10
modern lingo, "acculturate." My father was crucial in this regard. He, too, eschewed the *cholo* way of life. That his parents had made enough money to move into a middle-class neighborhood is not an unimportant detail here. By living among the Other, it was much easier to become conversant in their language and perspective. In America, acculturation is usually as much an economic rite of passage as it is a cultural one.

My father entered the American mainstream with a Graphic Arts International Union card and a cultural sensibility honed as much by Hollywood as by my grandparents' Old World family values. His teachers might have taught him to read and write English, but it was John Wayne, Audie Murphy, and Gary Cooper° that taught him how to play American. He fulfilled his Hollywood dreams, to a degree, by working at a print shop that held lucrative contracts with several movie studios. Thus, instead of a typical Mexican household decorated with Catholic icons and gaudy, oversized family portraits, we had the movie posters my father had done the color-separation work for hanging on the walls.

I experienced "race" (Latinos are not officially a race, though this country has a long history of racializing them, especially the Mexicans) pretty much the way that I imagine my father did when he was growing up, since he, too, was often the odd one among his classmates. I had to endure the occasional wetback jokes (Who's the president of Mexico? Manual Labor), but I stubbornly remained an assimilationist. I came to speak an accentless English, just like my father. In fact, I was so good at listening to and mimicking the language that I became something of the Rich Little° of my class. By junior high school I was imitating John Wayne and Richard Nixon about as good as a kid with Mexican looks can.

Hollywood helped, and hindered, me all along the way. In my youth, Hollywood was hitting the peak of the first phase of its race vetting. I'll never forget when the film version of *West Side Story* aired on network TV for the first time in the late sixties, around the time that *Guess Who's Coming to Dinner*° was probably still in the movie houses. That first screening is etched into

cholos: Slang expression for a Mexican-American gang member.

John Wayne, Audie Murphy, and Gary Cooper: American actors of the 1930s, 1940s, and 1950s famous for their portrayals of tight-lipped cowboy heroes.

Rich Little: (b. 1938), American comedian and impressionist.

Guess Who's Coming to Dinner: Film (1967) famed for challenging racial stereotypes.

memory as much for how fascinated I was by the movie as for what happened the day after.

Of course I fell in love with Natalie Wood's Maria, which placed me firmly in white-kid Tony's shoes. Although I'd had minor brushes with racism before, I arrived at school the next day not thinking of having to fight the Jets—hell, I *was* a Jet and a white girl named Wendy was, in fantasy, my Natalie Wood. Only in hindsight can I see the irony of a brown kid who thought he was white and desired a white classmate standing in for a white woman playing a Puerto Rican.

That morning at Franklin Elementary, all the kids arrived snapping their   15 fingers, whistling, and talking darkly of a "rumble" after school. I walked out of Mrs. Goodman's class after the afternoon bell rang and heard a prepubescent voice screech: "SHARK!" I looked around, but of course everyone was looking at me. There wasn't any physical harm to the game (some Jewish kids, probably second-generation red-diaper babies,° played the liberals and saved my skin), but I can point to the experience as the moment in which a schizophrenic consciousness began to grow in me.

On one hand, just about everyone I saw on TV and in the movies was white, except for a handful of minor roles for blacks, Asians, and Mexicans ("Latinos," from Central or South America—like my mom, who was born in El Salvador—simply didn't exist back then, except, of course, Carmen Miranda).° Without dwelling on the contradictions, I viewed things from a white perspective. My father helped me in this regard, since he supplied me with a healthy dose of westerns and WW II hero-flicks at home on the tube and at revival houses.

Despite the fact that he was one of my father's favorites, I never much cared for John Wayne. In John Ford's *The Searchers,* a film I saw several times as a kid, he portrayed the brutal Ethan, who almost kills Natalie Wood because she'd "turned Indian" after she was kidnapped as a child by a renegade tribe. In *The Searchers* I sympathized with Wood and her half-breed half brother, played by a bronzed, stunningly good-looking Jeffrey Hunter. In *West Side Story* I'd been a Jet; in *The Searchers* I leaned Indian.

But there were other great actors of midcentury American cinema that I adored and that, unlike Wayne, often played thoughtful, complex characters. Jimmy Stewart humanized his heroes with psychological depth and downright vulnerability—I remember him crying in some western I saw on TV one day I stayed home from school (I often acted like my minor colds were full-blown pneumonias just so that I could watch movies all day on the tube). Jack Lemmon's nervous comedy was thoroughly modern, and it seemed to capture some of the anxiety my young parents were going through in the early sixties.

---

red-diaper babies: Children of parents who belonged to the American Communist Party during the 1930s or who were sympathetic to communist or socialist causes.

Carmen Miranda: (1909–1955), Latina film star of the 1940s.

And Jerry Lewis—the French are so right about him—made us all feel at home with the absurdity of things American.

Let's just say that in some "raceless" way, I did learn a lot about life through the characters and stories. But there was something Faustian° about my love affair with Hollywood's whiteness. Sooner or later, the Mexican character appeared on the screen, almost always a stereotype, a jester whose jokes are at his own expense. This was always most obvious in the western genre.

I bought the video of John Ford's *Three Godfathers* the other day to screen   20 again the image of myself that I saw in my youth. The film is a simple, sentimental Christ-child parable with Ford's brilliant eye giving us plenty of wide shots of characters nearly lost in the pastel immensity of southwestern desert space. Mexican film legend Pedro Armendáriz plays John Wayne's sidekick. I don't know if Ford prodded Armendáriz to play a howling caricature of a Mexican or if Armendáriz found the stereotype of his character through the Method,° but his ethnicity becomes the comic foil for the film.

As a kid, I laughed at Armendáriz's antics (howling like a cantina character, overemoting everything), and I laugh today. I laugh at myself. It is a strange experience: you are disembodied as you laugh at the image that represents you on the screen. Your consciousness splits and, in a desperate attempt to survive the humiliation, identifies with the subjectivity of the culture that made the film, no longer with the objectified body that once belonged to you. Lose your body a few hundred times as a kid and a reservoir of pain and rage starts to build up inside you.

The ramifications of all this became apparent in the transition between my reel and real lives. My heroes were white, just as my father's heroes had been. But I wasn't allowed to "pass" like Anthony Quinn and play an exotic ethnic role (Zorba,° let's say) more palatable to mainstream American culture. That culture, I would slowly discover, wanted me to play a "dirty" outsider: if not the greaser, the Latin Lover; if not the Latin Lover, the revolutionary, or, these days, the narco-terrorist. (I was recently detained at Los Angeles International Airport because I fit the description of a drug dealer: "Tall Hispanic in a dark suit.")

My first experiences of being relegated to the outsider role resulted from my early romantic failures. In the tenth grade, I had a terrible crush on a blond-haired, blue-eyed girl named Gloria. She had braces. Her best friend,

---

something Faustian: According to legend, Faust makes a bargain with the devil to gain secret knowledge; hence, anything involving exchange of an important value or ethical principle for short-term gain.

the Method: Realistic acting method taught by Russian theater director Constantine Stanislavsky (1836–1938).

like Anthony Quinn . . . Zorba: Anthony Quinn (b. 1915), American actor who played the part of Zorba the Greek in the movie of the same name. Since ethnic identity is Martínez's topic, it may be worth noting that Quinn was born in Mexico to a half-Irish father and a Mexican-Indian mother, and that he was famous for playing "ethnic" roles of all types.

Kitty, was the object of desire of every straight boy at Marshall High. Gloria wasn't exactly homely, but she didn't hold a match next to Kitty's smoldering, Brigitte Bardot–like sensuality.° A common thing in school society: the hottest kids always have an entourage of less handsome kids floating about them, whose job it is to hold a mirror up to the prince or princess.

Like Gloria to Kitty, I was an underling to one Michael Delaney, who was quite short but had remarkable green eyes and a "cute" (as the girls said) freckled face beneath a mop of jet-black hair. A curious thing about Michael. He was Irish-Mexican. Clearly, his looks leaned towards his Irish father. But Michael's mom had bequeathed him quite a bit of the maternal culture. It was Michael who first taught me to play Mexican romantic ballads on the guitar. I was taking lessons at the time, but I was intent on becoming a bluegrass legend,° true to the "western" part of my upbringing.

Michael was from a poorer neighborhood where more Mexicans lived,   25 and he sometimes lapsed into *pocho*-speak° (a slang combining English and Spanish), which was a revelation to me, since I'd grown up in a family where we were intravenously fed *The Brady Bunch* and *The Partridge Family* on the tube.

At any rate, Michael fell for Kitty, and I for Gloria. He was French-kissing Kitty in the hallway within a matter of days. I, on the other hand, held marathon telephone sessions with Gloria, playing the "friend," since I'd never had a girlfriend—never even kissed a girl before—and I was terrified of rejection. Michael soon advised me to take the plunge or else risk being stuck in the platonic forever. So one night after school, he and I walked to our favorite phone booths down at the Mayfair Market (which stood on a lot that had once been home to Disney Studios). He dropped in the dime to call Kitty, and I, heart pounding, dialed Gloria's number to ask her to go steady.

Amazingly, I'd never considered the possibility that a white girl like Gloria wouldn't date a Mexican. Kitty could date Michael Delaney; he was only half Mexican and of course he didn't play up his Mexican half around her. (He saved that part of himself for me.) Me, I couldn't play down my Mexican-ness. I wore it on my brown (not tan, not copper, but brown) skin.

Through my first sixteen years, I'd done everything I could to become   •
white, from plucking a five-string banjo to buying Beach Boys albums. I went to the beach quite often—always to the "white" beach at Santa Monica, staying away from the pier, where the Mexicans, who were usually too poor to have bathing trunks and swam in their shorts and sometimes even their underwear, hung out. But after a long day in the sun I'd come home and notice

Brigitte Bardot–like sensuality: Brigitte Bardot (b. 1934), French film star of the 1960s.

a bluegrass legend: Bluegrass is a form of American country music associated with the Appalachian mountain area.

***pocho*-speak:** *Pocho* is a slang expression for a person of Mexican descent born in the United States who has assimilated to American culture; "*pocho*-speak" is thus Spanish-accented English or "Spanglish."

my skin, which was no longer just brown, but verging on *chocolate*. I clearly remember one time standing in the shower with a bar of Irish Spring soap, scrubbing as hard as I could, raking nails across skin, hoping to soften the darkness.

Gloria never came out and said she'd never date a Mexican; indeed, the thought may never even have crossed her mind. And yet, I hadn't stopped to notice that there wasn't a single interracial couple on the entire campus, except for a few Anglo-Asian pairings (always white boy and Asian girl; never the other way around). Actually, it didn't dawn on me that the race issue even existed until long after the sting of Gloria's rejection had faded. It was the twelfth grade and I had another crush, on a girl whose name I can't remember, but I'll call her Cybill, because I swear she was the Cybill Shepherd° of John Marshall High with her silky blond hair, perfect teeth, and magnificent body. I waited the entire year to get the nerve to speak to her. It was at the last dance of the spring, and even then I waited till a couple of minutes before midnight before finally walking up to her. I crossed the gymnasium in slow motion, my body feeling strangely light; she stood on the other side of the midcourt line, bathed in pulsating disco oranges and reds, surrounded by her entourage of girls with glasses and tiny breasts. I don't think she saw me until I was a yard away from her, from where I asked her to dance. She stared at me expressionless for a moment, and then, loud enough for her lackeys to hear (loud enough to bounce her voice off the gymnasium walls, it seemed to me at the time) she said, "With *you?*" To this day, I cannot ask a girl who is not my date to dance.

I looked around me at the dance floor with new eyes: Mexicans danced   30 with Mexicans, blacks with blacks, whites with whites. Who the hell did I think I was? Still, it would take a while for the gringo-hater in me to bust out.

> **mestizo** (mĕ stē′ zō) *n., pl.* **mestizos** or **mestizoes.** A person of mixed racial ancestry, especially of mixed European and Native American ancestry.

It was only a matter of time before I turned away from my whiteness and became the ethnic rebel. It seemed like it happened overnight, but it was the result of years of pent-up rage in me. No matter how hard I tried to live out my "colorless" fantasies, deep inside, in some corner of my psyche where it is difficult for the pain to find words, much less ideas, I always sensed my outsider status and yearned to fit in, completely, somewhere.

History helped me. A civil war broke out in my mother's El Salvador, a cause that I became quite involved in (just short of running arms). In my early twenties, I traveled incessantly through Mexico and Central America. I relearned Spanish (came to speak it without an accent as a matter of fact — damned if I was going to be the outsider among my "own people"), penned

---

Cybill Shepherd: American film and television star (b. 1950) renowned for her "all-American, blond, blue-eyed" beauty.

anti-gringo manifestoes, betrayed Whitman for Roque Dalton° (the great Salvadoran revolutionary poet), and, of course, started dating Latinas. After so many years trying to play the Cowboy, I wholeheartedly took the role of the Indian.

And Hollywood, bless its liberal soul, was right there for me. Oliver Stone romanced the revolution with *Salvador*, Gene Hackman discovered the terrible truth in Nicaragua, and even Jack Lemmon had a run-in with the fascists in South America.

Yeah, sure, all the movies told the story through gringo eyes, but at least the story was being told — *my* story.

My story?   35

The irony of the first twenty-five years of my life was that at first I, a kid born to a Mexican father and a Salvadoran mother, was convinced I was white and that later I, the erstwhile white kid, renounced gringo-ness to become Latino. Both were fantasies, beautiful lies, Hollywood constructs.

The truth was that I was always both, that dreaded ambiguity — and how Hollywood hates ambiguity! For to say that I am both is not a simple thing. What is American in me, what is Latino? Let's try the American: my Jewishness, my black-ness, my Asian-ness, my Scandinavian-ness, my immigrant-ness. And how about the Latino: Indian-ness, Iberian-ness, Creole-ness, African-ness. Many Chicanos, a community with which I have a hate-love relationship, describe their identity crisis as a simple north-south paradigm, gringo and Mexican, English and Spanish, rich and poor. As if Chicano would be Chicano (or white, white, or Asian, Asian) in America without the cultural rock at the center of it all: the black. Practically every Chicano aesthetic (oldies, lowriders, graffiti) is the result of at least a collaboration with, if not a downright plagiary of, African American culture. But don't expect to hear that in Chicano Studies courses or, for that matter, in Western Civ. The Irony is that Americans (and here I speak of all the races and ethnicities) have always prided themselves on their exceptionalism. Here was a country without Old World or Third World nationalism ("Patriotism is the last refuge of a scoundrel"). But what is segregation if not an internal form of nationalism?

Some years ago, at a point where I was beginning to tire of the binary notion of cultural identity, I wrote a poem that included the line "I am much more than two," aping, of course, our bawdy bard, Whitman ("I am large, I contain multitudes"). And thus began what I see as the third phase of my cultural maturation, in which I'm exploring the interconnectedness of it all.

Looking back on my youth today, things don't look as white as I once believed them to be, the color lines not as fast. The Virgin of Guadalupe was always there, right alongside my *Brady Bunch* visions. For Latinos, this is certainly not a new state of affairs. Mestizo is just another word for mixed — very mixed — race. Perhaps the one thing the Cowboys and the Indians (gringos

Roque Dalton: (b. 1935), Salvadoran writer.

and Mexicans) have in common is their denial of the complexity of their identities. It strikes me that the story of America's past and present segregation is all the more ironic, and tragic, for the way that the colors really do bleed into one another (I mixed that metaphor on purpose), and have done so all along.

It certainly was so in the Martínez household. My parents were quite the partiers when they were young. Dancing cha-cha-cha and cumbia at our house were many of my mother's friends, mostly women from El Salvador, who'd married, almost all of them, American Anglo men. The women would chatter in Spanish and the men would joke about those crazy Latinas, like *I Love Lucy* with the gender roles reversed, even as their hips struggled with the tropical rhythms. The men's superficial banter, a mild and mostly benign form of racism, masked the complex process that was occurring. What of the children of these marriages? What of my own mother and father, the Salvadoran and the Mexican American, and the negotiation of their influences on their kids?

There is something innately comic about communication between two cultures that see each other as exotic, a humor that has both its light and its dark side. We laugh at how difficult the simplest things become, even as it is obvious that there is a power struggle occurring. Ideally, the power is divided equally and both sides become the richer for it. But often cultural influences can be democratically sorted out—we can dance to each other's musics, eat each other's foods—without a negotiation of any power beyond the aesthetic realm. This is why African American culture is undeniably America's most powerful while African Americans themselves don't have political or economic power proportionate to their numbers. It's called racism.

And so I can celebrate what I feel to be my cultural success. I've taken the far-flung pieces of myself and fashioned an identity beyond that ridiculous, fraying old border between the United States and Mexico, that line so important to the nativists. I am not the "melting pot," nor do I feel myself to be the "chunky stew" (the in-vogue term which hints, however slightly, at segregation). I am both Cowboy and Indian.

But my "success" is still marked by anxiety, a white noise that disturbs whatever raceless utopia I might imagine. I feel an uneasy tension between all the colors, hating and loving them all, perceiving and speaking from one and many perspectives simultaneously. The key word here is "tension": nothing, as yet, has been resolved. My body is both real and unreal, its color both confining and liberating.

The Hollywood kid in me still yearns for the happy ending. And there are clear signs that some fundamental things are changing. My family was quite the anomaly when I was growing up in Silver Lake: middle-class Mexicans weren't very common back then. Over the years, my neighborhood has grown increasingly mixed. The new immigrants move in alongside the old; Mexico and Central America move into black, white, and Asian enclaves. I don't have to leave Silver Lake to visit Mexico, El Salvador, China, or Vietnam. They have come to Silver Lake.

It is a demographic change taking place all over the United States, in   45
every major city and even in the formerly all-white or black-white rural towns.
Last spring I undertook a journey across the United States, my first cross-
country trip, to research the phenomenon of Mexican migration and its impact on both the "native" and the "foreign" culture. The trip was my first foray
into the "heartland" of America. As I drove through the plains of East Texas
on I-30 toward Texarkana, an old fear rose up in me. Would I be welcome in
Mayberry,° or would the good ol' boys see me as some kind of furriner?

My cultural survival strategy in Texas, Arkansas, Kentucky, North
Carolina, Illinois, Missouri, and Wisconsin was the same as it had been all
these years: when in Rome, *talk* like the Romans. Language is a powerful
thing, something I learned intuitively early on. With accents gleaned from the
likes of John Wayne, James Dean (*Giant*),° and even Billy Bob Thornton,° I
got along well enough. But in doing so, wasn't I just denying my body once
again, silently laughing at my inner Pedro Armendáriz?

At times, I felt, or imagined that I felt, that old joy of being colorless again
(being a journalist with a sophisticated-looking broadcast-quality tape
recorder and microphone also helps soften the color separation, since my relationship to the media—which are, of course, mostly white—comes before
the color of my skin). And then I'd be back, smack in the middle of America's
segregation-integration wars. In Texas, some poor white guys straight out of
the pen complained about the "niggers." A black street-maintenance worker
in Arkansas protested the "sneakiness" of latter-day white racism. And the
Mexicans, who are all over the map on matters of race (and who, I suppose,
saw me as one of their own), spoke schizophrenically of desiring white girls
and hating white bosses and sympathizing with blacks and thinking blacks are
just a bunch of welfare freeloaders.

In the end, my journey showed me that playing the Cowboy wasn't enough,
that the Indian was just as important. Mestizo, that culture chameleon born
centuries before Boy George,° is the essence of my role. Among the Dominicans
of Washington, D.C., the Nigerians of New York, and the very particular kind of
Americans that are the descendants of Scandinavians in the upper Midwest, I
discovered parts of myself that were both new and old. The mestizo in me needs
to embrace—appropriate, I mean—every influence it encounters, not to recall
that I was conquered but that I *survived*. The Indian wears a Cowboy hat, but is
no less the Indian for that fact; the Indian is ever becoming. It's probably the
greatest lesson my father ever taught me—even if I had to laugh at Pedro
Armendáriz to get it.

Mayberry: Fictional hometown of Andy Griffith on television's *The Andy Griffith Show;* hence,
any traditional small American town.

James Dean (*Giant*): James Dean (1931–1955), American actor who played a young Texan in
the 1956 film *Giant*.

Billy Bob Thornton: (b. 1955), American actor/director whose films are often set in the South.

Boy George: (b. 1961), Openly gay English pop music star of the 1980s.

A postscript from my American tour: In Norwalk, Wisconsin, a tiny town where everyone is employed by the local meat-packing plant, Mexican immigrants now make up half the population. At first, tensions dominated the relations between the Mexicans and the Mennonite, Amish, and Plain Christian stock. But in the matter of a few years, dozens of Mexican men became romantically involved with local white girls. The white girls began liking *norteña* music,° the Mexican boys walked down Main Street with heavy metal buzzing in their Walkman earphones. Recently, a bunch of sandy-haired, golden-skinned babies have been born, speaking a Spanglish patois — a new kind of Chicano. Because everybody is poor in Norwalk (except for the white owner of the meat-packing plant, an important detail), race is somewhat less of an issue in terms of power, though gender (machismo and its discontents) is a battlefield.

This is the future. America is becoming a mestizo nation.   50

Today, I live in the Mojave Desert. It's a long story, one that I won't tell here. Suffice to say that it's a place where mostly poor people of every color come, to forget, in some way or another, where they came from. Kind of like immigrants. Me, I remember where I came from all too well out here. In the black, brown, yellow, and white faces, I see Silver Lake and El Salvador and Mexico. And more than ever before, I feel at home. For that's the redemption for someone who's played the role of the outsider for so many years: if you're an exile long enough, eventually you'll be at home wherever you are.

INTERIOR NIGHT, MOJAVE DESERT.

Writer again at the wobbly desk. Snow-capped desert peaks in the distance.

MONTAGE SEQUENCE:

Writer as a tot posing for the camera, sitting astride a pony, dressed in cowboy hat, cow-print vest, and chaps.

Writer at about nine years, sitting before the tube, giggling (with what the Buddhists call the "laughter of recognition") at one of Ricky's Spanish-language tantrums.

Thirteen-year-old writer playing "Dueling Banjos" on an authentic five-string banjo (not long after seeing *Deliverance,* one of the first "adult" movies he ever saw).

Junior high school writer imitating John Wayne's voice to a crowd of white classmates who burst into laughter (it is unclear whether they are laughing *with* him or *at* him).

Writer in high school, awkwardly attempting a Mexican ballad on guitar, Irish-Mexican friend helping him finger the chords.

Writer dancing, in a wet dream, with Cybill Shepherd.

Writer, twentysomething, declaiming anti-gringo verse before an audience of enraptured Salvadoran revolutionaries and weepy gringo liberals.

norteña **music:** Northern Mexican style of music featuring the accordian.

Writer, thirtysomething, walking the teeming streets of Mexico City, an Indian among Indians, remembering his father's and his grandfather's footsteps.

RAPID CUTS:

Writer stealing kisses from white, black, yellow, brown women and men.

WE FREEZE on the last kiss, with a white man. Brown and white—you may imagine Pedro Armendáriz and John Wayne—separate and, at arm's length, regard each other with looks that reveal myriad emotions: desire, loathing, tenderness, shock, etc.

WE SLOWLY DISSOLVE back to the desk and a CLOSEUP of the computer screen again. These words appear:

I am in between, and beyond, colors.

FADE TO BLACK.

EXPLORING THE TEXT

1. What cultural role models were available to shape Martínez's identity when he was growing up in Los Angeles? What role did Hollywood films play in the construction of Martínez's sense of self? What movie heroes or villains today have this kind of impact on adolescents? Do you think that most kids model themselves to some extent on the roles they see portrayed in films and on television?

2. What does Martínez mean when he says that he developed "a schizophrenic consciousness" as a result of his love of the movies and movie heroes? What did he feel as he watched Latinos in stereotyped roles?

3. What "real" as opposed to "reel" experiences challenge the identities Martínez adopts as a child from the movies? How "real" is his reaction to these experiences?

4. Why does Martínez reject what he terms "the binary notion of cultural identity"? Why does he refuse to see himself as a kind of "melting pot" or even a "chunky stew"? Why, in his opinion, is it difficult for Americans to embrace the notion of plural ethnicity or complex ethnic identities?

5. What does Martínez mean when he says that "America is becoming a mestizo nation"? What does he base this observation on? To what extent do you agree?

6. How do you interpret the conclusion of Martínez's essay? Why does he have John Wayne and Pedro Armendáriz kiss? What does he mean when he says "I am in between, and beyond, colors"? Is he confronting—or avoiding—the "real" issues of race, ethnicity, and identity?

FURTHER EXPLORATIONS

1. What does Martínez's experience in "Technicolor" suggest about the relative permeability of what Robert Sapolsky would call his "ego boundaries" (p. 254)? Do you think that Martínez's self is exceptionally open to outside influences? Or is Sapolsky overestimating the rigidity of ego boundaries in American culture? How might you account for this discrepancy?

2. To what extent is it possible to consider the cowboy and Indian stereotypes that Martínez appropriates from Hollywood films to be examples of the "ideal selves" that have traditionally helped shape personal identity, according to Mihaly Csikszentmihalyi (p. 264)? What, in your opinion, are the "ideal selves" that Hollywood offers adolescents as role models today?

3. How would Arnold M. Ludwig (p. 292) be likely to interpret the influence that fictional Hollywood movie heroes and real-life role models like the "ethnic rebel" have had on Martínez? To what extent does Martínez's analysis of his own multiple and sometimes conflicting identities confirm or challenge Ludwig's view that we adopt our life stories and the roles we play "ready-made" from the cultural contexts we inhabit?

4. How does bell hooks's reflection on the impact of historical memories in "Columbus: Gone But Not Forgotten" (p. 237) complicate Martínez's account of the development of his sense of self and his view of America as an emerging "mestizo" nation?

ESSAY OPTIONS

1. Using the *Before Reading* assignment on page 306 as a point of departure, write an essay in which you analyze the impact that the media have had on the development of your sense of self. What characters in films, television series, or books did you identify with as you grew up? What did they represent to you? What lessons did they teach? Looking back, how might these fictional figures have shaped your ideals, values, and attitudes?

2. At the conclusion of his essay, Martínez suggests that America is becoming a "mestizo" nation. Write an essay in which you explore this claim. What evidence do you find to support or challenge the idea that America is moving beyond "binary" notions of cultural identity? Do you think that most Americans experience the kinds of tensions and ambivalence Martínez associates with multicultural consciousness? Why or why not?

3. Drawing on the ideas and experiences treated by Martínez in this selection, Robert Sapolsky in "Ego Boundaries, or the Fit of My Father's Shirt" (p. 254), Alice Walker in her short story "Everyday Use" (p. 283), Arnold M. Ludwig in "Living Backwards" (p. 292), Patricia Hampl in "Memory and Imagination (p. 180), Maxine Hong Kingston in "No-Name Woman" (p. 206), and Eviatar Zerubavel in "Social Memories" (p. 217), as well as on any other selections you deem appropriate, write an essay in which you explore the thesis that the self is something we create — something like a work of art that we deliberately shape through the choices we make. To what extent do you think the self is created, inherited, or adopted? Why?

The Self and Society: Changes, Problems, and Opportunities

ROY F. BAUMEISTER

The self, like all great ideas, has an impressive intellectual pedigree. Indeed, as sociologist Roy F. Baumeister claims, the Western concept of the individual self scarcely existed just a few short centuries ago. Our notions about individual identity and a "hidden" internal self have evolved over the last few centuries under the influence of factors ranging from the Black Death, the collapse of feudalism, the development of theater, and the theological concept of the soul. As Baumeister indicates in this introduction to the evolution of the ideology of radical individualism, the West's notion of selfhood has grown so vast that it threatens to destabilize the culture that gave it birth. In contemporary Western societies, the self, according to Baumeister, has become an end in itself — a force that has displaced religion, morality, and every other traditional source of value and authority in our lives. Roy F. Baumeister (b. 1953) received his Ph.D. from Princeton University in 1978. He's written a number of scholarly and general-interest articles and books, including *Breaking Hearts: The Two Sides of Unrequited Love* (with Sara R. Wotman), 1992; *Your Own Worst Enemy: Understanding the Paradox of Self-Defeating Behavior* (with Steven Berglas), 1993; and *Evil: Inside Human Cruelty and Violence*, 1997. He is a professor of psychology at Case Western Reserve University.

BEFORE READING

Working in groups or by means of a brief journal entry, describe how you think our modern sense of selfhood differs from notions of the self in past historical times. How, for example, does our contemporary understanding of the self differ from the idea of the self as it existed in the Middle Ages?

Personal identity is a crucial interface between the private organism and society. The identity represents an important means by which the physical being takes its place in society so as to communicate and interact with other people. Meanwhile, the broader society assigns roles to the individual and shapes the values the person holds, so that identity is also an important means by which society can influence and control his or her behavior. It is no more correct to say that the individual is passively created by society than it is to regard society as a mere outcome of the choices and actions of autonomous, self-determined individuals; self and society shape each other. . . .

Roots of Selfhood

It is undeniably true that self begins with body. The number of selves in a given room is equal to the count of bodies. Understanding of selfhood begins with awareness of one's body, and the body continues to be an important basis of selfhood throughout life. Yet clearly there is more to self than the body. There are several basic kinds of experience that create a more elaborate and complex basis for selfhood than the mere fact of having a physical form. (Indeed, these adapt and transform the experience of having a body, too.) These have been of greatest interest to psychologists, and these will be the main focus of the psychology of self.

I propose three main, universal experiences by which bodies become selves and that thus form the basis of the psychological self. Society and culture can use, alter, shape, and adapt these experiences, but they constitute the essential nature of selfhood. Moreover, they seem sufficient to encompass the immense variety of research that social and personality psychologists have conducted to investigate the self (see Baumeister, in press).

The first of these is the experience of reflexive consciousness. Human consciousness can turn around in a circle, so to speak, and become aware of its source. Reflexive consciousness is what is involved when a man is ruminating about his triumphs or failures, when a woman wonders whether she could ever perform the sort of heroic sacrifice or cruel betrayal she has heard on the news, when the spiritual novice meditates on his breathing or spiritual center, when the dieter debates whether she needs to lose more pounds, and when the survey respondent tries to answer a series of questions about personal opinions, attributes, and values. Without reflexive consciousness, the very notion of self would be incomprehensible.

The second root of selfhood is the interpersonal being. People everywhere 5 exist as members of groups and as partners in interpersonal relationships. The interpersonal aspect of self is the focal one in love and hate, in rivalry and competition, in trying to live up to someone's expectations or worrying about what impression one is making, in feeling pride in one's spouse or college team or ethnic group, and in taking people's praise or blame for what one has done. Selves do not and probably cannot develop in social isolation, and it is misleading to regard interpersonal patterns as mere accidental products of self-contained, wholly independent selves.

The third root of selfhood is the executive function. This is the active decision-making entity that initiates action, exerts control, and regulates the self. Making a promise or resolution, signing a mortgage or contract, resisting temptation, stifling one's feelings, choosing a car to buy, or forcing oneself to concentrate all involve the executive function. The moral responsibilities of one's acts and choices are also an important basis for creating the unity and continuity of the self. The terms "agency" and "agent" are sometimes used to describe this aspect of the self, but they seem misleading in a fundamental way: to be an agent is to act on behalf of someone else, whereas the executive function essentially involves acting on one's own behalf. The self is a capacity for making choices, taking responsibility, and exerting self-control. Without the executive function, the self could still be self-aware and belong to groups, but it would be a mere helpless, passive spectator of events.

Culture Constructs the Individual

There is fair evidence that Westerners have not always had the strong sense of individuality that reigns now. Notions of selfhood in the Middle Ages in the West may have been far more collective than they are now. Some of the evidence behind this conclusion includes the lack of autobiographical writing, the indifference to factual accuracy in the writing of biographies, the indifference to privacy in architecture and social life, religious attitudes and practices (e.g., burial patterns), and the neglect of individuality and perspective in literature (Baumeister, 1986, 1987).

One of the best works on individuality is that by historian Karl Weintraub (1978). His definition of individuality has two criteria. First, individuality involves the appreciation, even the celebration, of ways in which each individual person is special or unique or different. Second, it involves a sense of unique destiny for each person. Weintraub concludes that the early modern period, roughly 1500 to 1800, saw a decisive shift, to this new, individualistic view of the human being. The first criterion was satisfied around the beginning of that era, and the second around the end. The early modern period saw extensive changes in the society and culture, and some of these altered the basic way in which human selfhood was shaped, used, and understood. For example, politically in Europe the feudal system° broke down and had mostly disappeared by the end of the early modern era (except perhaps in Russia). People gained the right to move, to make their own decisions, to decide their own marriages and occupations.

Obviously, these new rights and opportunities were not simply given because someone thought they would be nice. The actual political struggles of the time involved the emergence of national states as major centers of power (except in Germany). These replaced the previous organization, in which most power was concentrated locally. The shift in power was not easily accomplished. Local power was held by small nobles and aristocrats in connection with extended families who controlled wealth and other resources. In that system, the extended family or clan was of decisive importance because it formed the power base of the local nobles and officials. To thwart that axis and concentrate political power at the national level, the central governments needed a different power base, and they found this by using individual citizens. Concepts of justice, wealth, duty, and rights were refocused on the individual instead of the kinship network.

Also underlying the social reorganization was a series of economic   10
changes. The feudal system, after all, was economic even more than it was a political arrangement: it kept people locked in place and manipulated their labor so that the wealth it created supported the status quo. Most people

---

the feudal system: The political and economic system that dominated medieval Europe from the ninth to the fifteenth centuries, founded on the relation of landowning lords and dependent peasants or vassals.

worked as serf farmers, toiling without ever accumulating much wealth or having the opportunity to do anything else.

Some historians think that the Black Death° dealt a fatal blow to the feudal system. In large parts of Europe, a third of the population died. Two economic consequences were a shortage of labor and a surplus of available land. Despite the effort to restrict movement and pass laws regulating wages, it almost inevitably resulted that poor people could begin to move around, get different jobs and homes, and in essence find a new position in society if they disliked their old one. The Black Death also gave people more money; after all, if the amount of wealth is constant but one third of the population dies, then on average each survivor becomes richer by half. The greater wealth offered more scope for the middle class to gain money and influence, and hence power. This, too, was something that fed into the emergence of national governments, because the middle classes were not so dependent on the local barons as the serfs had been and their cash made them a desirable ally for the emerging national governments against the local barons (who were, after all, a common enemy).

The social changes centrally affect two of the most important aspects of the self—namely, the interpersonal one and the executive function. The part of the self that takes initiative and makes decisions is a trivial one when there are relatively few major choices to be made, such as in the rigid and restrictive society of medieval Europe. In contrast, the new opportunities gave vastly expanded scope for making choices. By 1800, in fact, people could, to a substantial extent, choose their own occupations, their spouses, and where they wanted to live. And city dwellers mostly had some choice among food, housing, and other elements of their lifestyles. The executive function suddenly had a significant role to play in both the consequential and the mundane.

The change should not be overstated, of course. Undoubtedly there have always been choices and decisions to make. Yet it seems hard to deny that the range and variety of such choices is much greater in modern Western society than it has been in many other times and places. Simply deciding what to have for supper and what form of entertainment to pursue afterward presents the modern Western individual with an immense array of options and requires the self to have a reasonably well articulated set of preferences, priorities, and criteria. The range of possible supper entrées and evening entertainments available to a sixteenth-century farmer in a small European or African village was undoubtedly much narrower, and so his self did not require such an elaborate structure.

Meanwhile, the interpersonal aspect of self has been severely altered in the modern world. The self is no longer immersed in the local clan and small society where it lived for centuries. Indeed, it is relatively free to choose and

---

the Black Death: An acute infectious disease spread by rats throughout Europe during the fourteenth century, which was responsible for the death of millions.

change its relationships. A particular self is not necessarily or permanently a part of a particular neighborhood; one can move away and become part of a different one.

The upshot is not merely the ability to change one's interpersonal con-   15
nections, though: it is to separate selfhood from its immersion in these connections. As Alasdair MacIntyre (1981) has argued, the new view or selfhood involved thinking of it as existing prior to and apart from its roles in society. Thus was created the paradox or tension that continues to define (and plague) modern selfhood: the self exists as something outside of its particular connections, yet everywhere it seeks such connections.

Emergence of Inner Selfhood

I turn now to a second development in how cultural changes have fundamentally altered the nature of selfhood: the rise in Western societies of a strong belief in the self as a hidden entity that exists inside the person. The inner self refers to a self that is not directly visible in one's actions and physical appearance, not the same as one's social roles. These appearances are regarded as expressions of the inner reality of selfhood. In some cases, according to the new belief, these appearances may be misleading or may contradict the true self. Another corollary of the belief in an inner self is that often it becomes necessary for a person to exert him- or herself to discover the nature of this inner self. People generally assume that each individual self contains many hidden depths that are essential to its individual nature but that must be searched for and then cultivated.

Clearly, the notion of an inner or hidden self is not one that was invented overnight or even in one single development. The Christian concept of soul, which has been widely influential in our culture, is an important precursor of the idea of an inner self, though even the concept of soul has evolved and changed. The theological changes around the eleventh and twelfth centuries led to the consideration of souls as much more individually different from each other than in the prior views. In the new Christian thought emerging at that time, the concept spread that people would be judged as individuals, based on the morality and piety of their personal actions during life. The soul came to be seen as carrying around a record of one's acts, both virtuous and sinful.

Still, many scholars believe that it was in the sixteenth century that the culture most decisively expanded its conception of an inner selfhood. Many significant developments reflected this change. Theater began to feature plots on the idea that many characters pretended to be someone or something other than who they actually were. This in particular included the standard character of the villain, who is evil but deceives the other characters about his (or, less often, her) evil intentions. In contrast, in medieval morality plays, the evil characters came clearly and overtly named as evil (Trilling, 1971).

Other signs of the emergence of an inner self included social practices in which people might adopt the dress and mannerisms appropriate to a different, especially a better, class of people. There had always been fairly rigid dress codes, and one's rank in society dictated what one was permitted to wear, with the result that one could tell someone's position in society from a distance simply by seeing his or her clothes. In the modern period, however, some people began to break those rules and "dress up." The relative anonymity of city life made it harder for the collectivity to recognize and punish people who were dressing better than they should have been allowed, and the increasing wealth of many middle-class people gave them the means to buy finer clothes. In many cases, the motives for such deception went beyond mere short-term narcissism. The political and economic changes of the times meant that many aristocrats began to have money problems. Marriages between upwardly mobile, well-heeled bourgeoisie and cash-poor blue bloods became increasingly frequent because both parties got something they coveted. Still, the aristocrats would not marry just any common person who happened to have money; to be eligible, the middle-class person and to some extent the whole family had to have at least the veneer of social acceptability to the upper classes. The eighteenth century saw the spread of "finishing schools" and other institutions designed to teach the children of the ambitious middle class how to pass for ladies and gentlemen, so that they might become eligible to intermarry with people of quality (e.g., Sennett, 1974; Stone, 1977).

The increased recognition that inner and outer selves might differ was 20 also reflected in the new sixteenth-century virtue of sincerity (Trilling, 1971). Sincerity came to mean that one's visible actions and statements were in agreement with one's inner thoughts, feelings, and intentions. To elevate sincerity to the status of an important virtue indicates that the society has developed some pervasive concerns about people who present a face that does not express their true sentiments.

As a related trend, self-deception also became much more commonly recognized. The concept of self-deception implies that there is an inner, hidden reality to the self that even the person's own conscious self fails to see. Many historians have argued that the Puritans provided a great stimulus to the acknowledgment of self-deception. Puritan doctrine believed in one particularly crucial inner reality — namely, the predestined eternal fate of the individual soul. Calvin° thought that one could tell during life whether a particular individual was fated to spend eternity in heaven or hell, and perhaps unfortunately this stimulated many ordinary Puritans to spend much of their time examining their own thoughts, feelings, and actions for signs of exceptional piety or sinful depravity. Inevitably, they began to notice that everyone wanted to believe himself or herself among the elect and that people often tried to put an optimistic interpretation on their own responses. Self-deception was widely discovered. Self-knowledge would never enjoy that same total easy confidence again.

Calvin: John Calvin (1509–1564), French theologian and reformer.

Once the notion of an inner self was established, successive generations elaborated on it. The Romantics° expanded the notion of an individual destiny and therefore gave us the by now quite familiar notion that a person must look inside oneself to discover one's calling and then pursue that throughout life in order to reach fulfillment. In tandem, they expanded the view of art and creativity as a process of reaching inside oneself to find the makings of major artistic achievements. Later yet, the Victorians° came to regard the visible actions and appearances as merely being small clues about the vast and inner realms of selfhood. The quintessential Victorian hero Sherlock Holmes,° for example, would frequently solve crimes simply by noticing some detail of appearance or some seemingly trivial act and appreciating its broad significance for revealing crucial facts about an individual. Likewise, Sigmund Freud° succeeded by expanding what vast hidden forces of desire, violence, and trauma lay hidden beneath the seemingly ordinary and mundane surfaces of well-to-do bourgeois citizens, sometimes glimpsed through such easily overlooked signs as slips of the tongue and dreams.

There are two further points to make about the evolution of the hidden, inner self as a standard way of thinking about selfhood. First, it increases the problematic nature of selfhood. If the self is a secret entity, indeed in important respects concealed even from the very person whose self it is, then self-knowledge is a difficult and elusive matter. Indeed, if all a person's actions and statements fail to reveal some inner truth, then it is unclear how one can ever be certain that one has understood the true inner self. And if self-deception is always a possibility, it is unclear how one can ever surely know oneself. The modern concept of self-actualization takes the problem even a step further because it requires first a process of discovering the hidden inner realities and then a process of working to cultivate and develop these inner traits to reach their full potential. The version of selfhood implicit in all these modern concepts is one that carries a significant burden and a recipe for uncertainty, difficulty, and dissonance.

Second, the evolution of the inner self is in many respects a cultural elaboration of the reflexive consciousness aspect of the self. To be sure, it invokes a couple of the other aspects as well. Some of the early factors that gave rise to the concept of the inner self were interpersonal, such as the concern with sincerity of other people. Our culture has come to regard the process of choice as often involving looking inside oneself to discover the correct attitude or

The Romantics: Members of the romantic movement, an early-nineteenth-century European philosophical and artistic reaction against the rationalism of the neoclassicist period, that stressed the importance of emotion and the imagination.

the Victorians: People living during the reign of England's Queen Victoria (1819–1901), supposedly characterized by their formality, conventionality, and restraint.

Sherlock Holmes: Hero of a series of detective novels by English author Sir Arthur Conan Doyle (1859–1930).

Sigmund Freud: (1856–1939), Austrian neurologist and the founder of modern psychoanalysis.

nature of one's inner self, which is then presumed to be a basis for making correct choices (see Bellah, Madsen, Sullivan, Swidler, and Tipton, 1985). Thus, the interpersonal partner and the executive function aspects of self are involved.

Still, though, the most centrally involved is the reflexive consciousness of 25 the self. One becomes aware of oneself as trying to discover what one is really like inside. One knows that such self-discovery is often difficult and one may even become aware of tendencies toward self-deception. Although many influential experiments have manipulated self-awareness by having students look at a mirror, this is of course regarded as a stimulating cue rather than the essence of the process. One does not see everything in the mirror. Self-awareness is a matter of examining inner realms to learn the elusive truths about a presumably extensive and fixed nature. Thus, the culture transformed reflexive consciousness from a mere act of attending to one's own sensations or states into a challenging journey of exploration: a treasure hunt.

The New Moral Role of Selfhood

To achieve a full understanding of the modern problems associated with Western selfhood, it is necessary to examine social and cultural shifts in yet another context. Some social changes unrelated to the self created a new psychological need in the culture, and the self was mobilized to provide it. A new kind of demand has been placed on selfhood recently, and this is altering the role of selfhood in Western society, as well as increasing the concern and fascination with it.

One important shift in the modern era is a gradual loss of moral consensus. This does not mean that modern Western citizens are necessarily any less honest or decent or virtuous than their ancestors. It does mean, however, that the difficulty of being a virtuous or decent person has increased insofar as firm rules of right and wrong have been lost and tolerance for personal values, situational ethics, and differing moral outlooks has been promoted. The separation of church and state has in many cases been accompanied by a reluctance to impose one set of moral values on everyone. As a result, many citizens of today's Western countries believe that they must look inside themselves to find some basis for making moral decisions. As Bellah et al. (1985) have described in their insightful analysis of this moral vacuum, today's Americans tend to ask themselves whether something "feels right" as their primary basis for making moral judgments.

The loss of consensus about moral principles is only part of a broader development. The essence of this development is that Western society has gradually weakened or lost its *value bases,* which are defined as firm, recognized sources of justification and moral worth (see also Harbermas, 1973). Most justifications of specific actions operate by citing some other source, authority, or principle from which they derive their goodness. These in turn can be challenged and defended by citing yet more basic values or principles. Ultimately, however, moral discourse requires that there must be some things whose moral goodness is not derivative but that rather are accepted as good in and of themselves. God's will is a traditional example: if something is consistent with God's will, then it is good, but God's will does not require further justification. No believer challenges this justification by asking, "So what?"

Clearly, however, the scope of everyday actions that ordinary citizens base on God's will has dwindled over the centuries with the shift toward modern, secular society. Other value bases, such as tradition, have also been weakened or undermined (see Shils, 1981), and as Habermas (1973) has explained, they are difficult to replace. For example, instituting a bureaucracy based on rational systems may easily replace tradition as a means of making decisions and solving problems, but it does not effectively supply the sense of goodness and value that tradition also furnished.

In my own analysis of the evolution of meaning of life (Baumeister, 1991b), I referred to this same loss of moral sense as the *value gap*. The value gap appears to have become acute with the Enlightenment's critique and partial rejection of Christianity because no secular humanism can muster the potent value bases that a religion usually has. As a source of moral authority, utilitarian analysis lacks the emotional force of God's will, even if it may be more adaptable to new social conditions.

It does appear that Western culture struggled to find new value bases to replace the lost ones. The work ethic was an attempt to consider work as a source of positive value in and of itself, although social attitudes and the changing nature of work may have doomed it, and in any case it no longer commands a consensus or guides the actual moral choices of most workers (Rodgers, 1978). Likewise, an enhanced value placed on the nuclear family, including elevating the perceived moral importance of love and motherhood, can also be understood as an attempt by the culture to endow a new value base that would help people know what was right and wrong without appealing to the fading authorities of religion and tradition (e.g., Lasch, 1977; Margolis, 1984). Today, clearly, family is a far more important and potent moral authority (e.g., what is right is whatever is best "for the sake of the children") than the work ethic.

For present purposes, however, the most important cultural response to the value gap is the attempt to transform the self into a major value base. Today's Americans believe that they have a right and even a duty to do what is best for their individual, unique, esteemed selves. They believe that every person should try to know him- or herself, which includes working to learn about his or her inner traits. They also believe that a person should try to fulfill his or her potential, which means identifying one's capabilities and unique talents, finding a suitable environment in which one can grow and flourish, and working to cultivate these capacities so as to "be all that you can be," in the phrase that ironically is used by the military services to recruit gullible young seekers after selfhood into combat training (Baumeister, 1991b; see also Bellah et al. 1985).

The new power of selfhood as an important value base can be seen in how people face moral conflicts between the self and other value bases. A well-known article by Zube (1972) documented how women's magazines showed a meaningful shift in moral attitudes from the 1940s to the 1960s in how they treated conflicts between marriage and self. In the years after World War II, whenever the self was unable to grow or thrive or reach its potential because of the press of marital obligations, the value judgment expressed in these magazine stories indicated that the morally right line of action was to maintain the marriage, even at the expense of the self. By the late 1960s, however, this had reversed: it became right and even obligatory for a woman to leave an oppressive, stultifying marriage in order to pursue her own identity and self-fulfillment. Thus, between two of the most potent values of twentieth-century America—selfhood and family—selfhood evolved from the lesser to the stronger value.

Recent analyses of religious movements suggest a similar theme. Although I have indicated that Christian religion lost the grip it once had on the collective workings of society, this should not be overstated. Most Americans continue to believe in God and to participate in some church. Religion thus remains an important force in their lives and presumably a welcome source of moral authority. The most successful churches today, however, appear to have shifted their attitude toward the self. The traditional emphasis on sin, damnation, weakness, and hellfire is largely gone. Instead, churches try to attract worshipers by invoking the value of selfhood. Churches offer multiple self-help programs, and sermons present a modernized view of spirituality that can seem little more than a form of self-esteem therapy with metaphysical overtones. Delbanco (1995) noted that the pursuit of self-interest could no longer be equated with the devil, as earlier eras had done, because in modern America everyone is permitted and even expected to pursue self-interest.

The functioning of the self as an important value base can also be seen in 35 its influence over work. Each society must find one way or another to motivate people to work in order that the necessary goods and services will be provided. In early civilizations, peasant farmers work because they know they will starve otherwise, but in modern societies the unemployed do not typically starve to death. Christianity motivated people to work because that was their sacred duty, but few of today's workers believe that their daily activities on the job are directly required by divine mandate. The work ethic insisted that people should work as a good end in and of itself, or as a means toward building their character, but these attitudes, too, have lost most of their force.

Modern society, then, must motivate people to work by mobilizing the self as a relevant, potent value base. The modern concept of work as career treats work as a vital means of glorifying and fulfilling the self. The true careerist is motivated neither by shallow extrinsic goals such as making a living nor by deep intrinsic factors such as love of the work itself. Rather, the careerist aims to accumulate a record of promotions, achievements, and honors that will reflect favorably on the self. Hence people work very hard at things they personally may care rather little about in order to gain respect and esteem through their achievements. The value that drives them is the value placed on the self.

It is important to appreciate that the new moral value of selfhood is a radical departure from traditional attitudes. For most of history, morality and self-interest were opposites. Indeed, one of the crucial functions of morality has always been to oppose and prevent people from acting in selfish ways; pride, greed, and other sins essentially involved pursuing the best interests of the self at the expense of others. In the 1680 edition of the *Oxford English Dictionary,* the sample use of "self" supplied with the definition was, "Self is the great Anti-Christ and Anti-God in the world" (Rosenthal, 1984). In contrast, modern thought now usually puts self and morality on the same side. Moral duties and obligations do not all involve restraining or opposing the self—and sometimes they require promoting the self.

In an important manner, this emphasis on self as a value base constitutes an extension of the agent aspect of the self. The self becomes more than just the agent who decides how to implement moral principles and other obligations and who carries out those decisions; it is now the source of those moral principles and obligations. Selfhood has become the root of moral authority. In the words of Bellah et al. (1985), "In the absence of any objectifiable criteria of right and wrong, good and evil, the self and its feelings become our only moral guide" (p. 76). Thus, this cultural shift has greatly extended the agent aspect of the self.

Modern Western society has devised a new role for the self, which involves supplying important meaning to life. Hence many individual's problems with finding a meaningful life will be expressed as selfhood problems and identity crises. Moreover, it is arguably unfair and unrealistic to expect the self to provide a firm basis for making moral decisions and supplying life with value, and so this modern use of the self seems likely to lead to serious problems and difficulties of selfhood.

The Vicissitudes of Self-Control

As a corollary of the rising reliance on self as a major value base, many people have in practice become skeptical or even negative toward self-control. This is difficult to document, if only because it is hard to measure self-control as a personality trait or capacity, and indeed at present the lack of useful questionnaire measures has been an obstacle to researchers. These difficulties naturally are compounded when one seeks to compare across different historical periods or eras. Still, there seems to be some validity to the stereotypes of Victorian self-control and modern self-indulgence.

One common explanation for such shifts focuses on the change in emphasis in the economy (e.g., Potter, 1954). As a general rule, economic changes do have strong effects on people's behaviors and attitudes (e.g., Harris, 1978, 1979). Prior to 1900, the limiting factor on sales was manufacturing. If the

40

product was good, one could sell as many as one could make. In the twentieth century, manufacturing technology advanced so rapidly that in many cases one could make almost unlimited quantities of goods. The limiting factor therefore became consumer demand. One can sell as much as people want to buy. In response to this new economic reality, advertising emerged as a vital means of stimulating consumer demand. The modern individual is almost constantly subjected to a barrage of messages exhorting him or her to buy and consume. The Protestant ethic was one of saving money, but that became obsolete in the modern world. Instead, twentieth-century citizens are urged to spend their money as fast as — and now even faster than — they earn it. Many people consume so much that they remain chronically in debt.

Thus, the self-restraint urged by past eras fit the economic realities of the time, but these have changed, and self-restraint has become the enemy rather than the ally of the main economic forces. Self-control can be understood as the resisting of one's impulses, or other responses, so as to alter them. Today's economy does not want people to resist their impulses: it wants them to act on them and indeed to have more of them.

Other societal factors may have contributed to the erosion in the popularity of self-control. The twentieth century tends to view the Victorian era as marked by neurosis, frustration, and unhappiness deriving from excessive control. Freud's famous insights are widely understood to suggest that repression is unhealthy and that to stifle any impulse is damaging. (I suspect that Freud would be horrified to see self-indulgence justified on the basis of his theories.) People are reluctant to force their children to conform to external controls and standards, fearing that imposing such authoritarian controls will stifle their creativity and create low self-esteem.

The current problems with violence in society probably have roots in this same issue of self-control. Of course, the idea that social and cultural factors contribute to violence is hardly a new idea. In the 1960s, the hypothesis of "subcultures of violence" was put forward to explain the high rates of crime in poor urban centers. This hypothesis said that certain subcultures placed a positive value on violent action and so young men would commit crimes as a way of gaining prestige and respect. This hypothesis was largely discredited in the 1970s because researchers persistently failed to find any evidence of subcultures that placed a positive value on violence (see Tedeschi & Felson, 1994, for review) or that people behaved violently in the expectation of gaining prestige (e.g., Berkowitz, 1978).

Yet the subculture-of-violence hypothesis may be worth reviving, with one 45 crucial change. Criminologists have increasingly come to recognize that crimes are committed impulsively and by people who show a pervasive lack of self-control in all spheres of life (Gottfredson & Hirschi, 1990). This means that it is not necessary for a society to advocate violence in order to promote it; all one has to do is remove the inner blocks. A subculture (or indeed a culture) of violence may emerge simply because the society lowers its standards for self-control. The point at which people abandon self-control is highly negotiable and flexible (see Baumeister, Heatherton, & Tice, 1994). Cultural prescriptions can exert considerable influence by telling people at what point it is appropriate to turn violent, ranging from "only when someone is attacking you in a life-threatening fashion" to "when the person implies disrespect toward you by making eye contact."

Creating the Burden of Selfhood

By all accounts, modern Western society has surrounded individual selfhood with much greater demands and expectations than have most other cultures in the history of the world. To be sure, most societies have expected individuals to live up to various standards, and sometimes these have been high. But only the modern West has expected its citizens to generate and validate their own standards, as well as constructing and maintaining a unique and autonomous self that can be socially validated through a constantly changing series of interpersonal relationships and transactions. The task is a daunting one, and indeed the transformation of adolescence into an age of identity crisis and self-exploration is one sign of how difficult people often find it to satisfy the paradoxical modern demand that the self must create and discover itself (e.g., Baumeister & Tice, 1986; see also Demos & Demos, 1969; Kett, 1977).

Some problems of selfhood are age-old. Undoubtedly, when a person falls far short of an important standard, such as when a man does something that brings ruin or disgrace on himself and his family, then the person will feel bad and suffer over the tarnished image of self. Possibly the distress is magnified in modern life because of the value-base aspect: not only has the person damaged a self-image, but he or she has also damaged an important source of value in life. Still, the problem of coping with a temporarily damaged self-image is an ancient one.

Other problems of selfhood are new, however. The new cultural demands on selfhood make it into a burdensome concern that can produce frequent stress (Baumeister, 1991a). People feel they must maintain a highly positive image of self that requires constant vigilance against dangers and threats. Even if they do not encounter major experiences of humiliation or disgrace, the ongoing threat and the resulting demand for vigilance may become tiresome and draining. Awareness of self may often be tinged with worry or stress and hence may take on an aversive aspect. . . .

References

Aires, P. (1981). *The hour of our death.* (H. Weaver, Trans.). New York: Knopf.
Baumeister, R. F. (1986). *Identity: Cultural change and the struggle for self.* New York: Oxford University Press.
Baumeister, R. F. (1987). How the self became a problem: A psychological review of historical research. *Journal of Personality and Social Psychology, 52,* 163–176.
Baumeister, R. F. (1988). Masochism as escape from self. *Journal of Sex Research, 25,* 28–59.

Baumeister, R. F. (1989). *Masochism and the self.* Hillsdale, NJ: Erlbaum.

Baumeister, R. F. (1990). Suicide as escape from self. *Psychological Review, 91,* 90–113.

Baumeister, R. F. (1991a). *Escaping the self: Alcoholism, spirituality, masochism, and other flights from the burden of selfhood.* New York: Basic Books.

Baumeister, R. F. (1991b). *Meanings of life.* New York: Guilford.

Baumeister, R. F. (1995). Self and identity: An introduction. In A. Tesser (Ed.), *Advanced social psychology* (pp. 51–97). New York: McGraw-Hill.

Baumeister, R. F. (in press). The self. In G. Lindzey, S. Fiske, & D. Gilbert (Eds.), *Handbook of social psychology* (4th ed.). New York: McGraw-Hill.

Baumeister, R. F., Heatherton, T. F., & Tice, D. M. (1993). When ego threats lead to self-regulation failure: Negative consequences of high self-esteem. *Journal of Personality and Social Psychology, 64,* 141–156.

Baumeister, R. F., Heatherton, T. F., & Tice, D. M. (1994). *Loving control: How and why people fail at self-regulation.* San Diego, CA: Academic Press.

Baumeister, R. F., Smart, L., & Boden, J. M. (1996). Relation of threatened egotism to violence and aggression: The dark side of high self-esteem. *Psychological Review, 103,* 5–33.

Baumeister, R. F., Stillwell, A. M., & Heatherton, T. F. (1994). Guilt: An interpersonal approach. *Psychological Bulletin, 115,* 243–267.

Baumeister, R. F., & Tice, D. M. (1986). How adolescence became the struggle for self: A historical transformation of psychological development. In J. Suls & A. G. Greenwald (Eds.), *Psychological perspectives on the self* (Vol. 3, pp. 183–201). Hillsdale, NJ: Erlbaum.

Bellah, R. N., Madsen, R., Sullivan, W. M., Swidler, A., & Tipton, S. M. (1985). *Habits of the heart: Individuation and commitment in American life.* Berkeley and Los Angeles: University of California Press.

Berkowitz, L. (1978). Is criminal violence normative behavior? Hostile and instrumental aggression in violent incidents. *Journal of Research in Crime and Delinquency, 15,* 148–161.

California Task Force to Promote Self-esteem and Personal and Social Responsibility (1990). *Toward a state of self-esteem.* Sacramento, CA: California State Department of Education.

Campbell, A. (1981). *The sense of well-being in America.* New York: McGraw-Hill.

Colvin, C. R., Block, J., & Funder, D. C. (1995). Overly positive evaluations and personality: Negative implications for mental health. *Journal of Personality and Social Psychology, 68,* 1152–1162.

Delbanco, A. (1995). *The death of Satan: How Americans have lost the sense of evil.* New York: Farrar, Straus, & Giroux.

Demos, J., & Demos, V. (1969). Adolescence in historical perspective. *Journal of Marriage and the Family, 31,* 632–638.

Diener, E., Diener, M., & Diener, C. (1995). Factors predicting the subjective well-being of nations. *Journal of Personality and Social Psychology, 69,* 851–864.

Gottfredson, M. R., & Hirschi, T. (1990). *A general theory of crime.* Stanford, CA: Stanford University Press.

Habermas, J. (1973). *Legitimation crisis.* (T. McCarthy, Trans.). Boston: Beacon.

Harris, M. (1978). *Cannibals and kings: The origins of cultures.* New York: Random House.

Harris, M. (1979). *Cultural materialism: The struggle for a science of culture.* New York: Random House.

Heatherton, T. F., & Baumeister, R. F. (1991). Binge eating as escape from self-awareness. *Psychological Bulletin, 110,* 86–108.

Hull, J. G. (1981). A self-awareness model of the causes and effects of alcohol consumption. *Journal of Abnormal Psychology, 90,* 586–600.

Kett, J. F. (1977). *Rites of passage: Adolescence in America 1790 to the present.* New York: Basic Books.

Lasch, C. (1977). *Haven in a heartless world: The family besieged.* New York: Basic Books.

Lasch, C. (1978). *The culture of narcissism: American life in an age of diminishing expectations.* New York: Norton.

Lawson, A. (1988). *Adultery: An analysis of love and betrayal.* New York: Basic Books.

Leary, M. R., & Kowalski, R. (1995). *Social anxiety.* New York: Guilford.

Leary, M. R., Tambor, E. S., Terdal, S. K., & Downs, D. L. (1995). Self-esteem as an interpersonal monitor: The sociometer hypothesis. *Journal of Personality and Social Psychology, 68,* 518–530.

Lerner, M. J. & Mikula, G. (Eds.) (1994). *Entitlement and the affectional bond: Justice in close relationships.* New York: Plenum.

MacIntyre, A. (1981). *After virtue.* Notre Dame, IN: University of Notre Dame Press.

Margolis, M. L. (1984). *Mothers and such: Views of American women and why they changed.* Berkeley and Los Angeles: University of California Press.

McFarlin, D. B., Baumeister, R. F., & Blascovich, J. (1984). On knowing when to quit: Task failure, self-esteem, advice, and nonproductive persistence. *Journal of Personality, 52,* 138–155.

Mischel, W., Shoda, Y., & Peake, P. K. (1988). The nature of adolescent competencies predicted by preschool delay of gratification. *Journal of Personality and Social Psychology, 54,* 687–696.

Newman, L. S., & Baumeister, R. F. (1996). Toward an elaboration of the UFO abduction phenomenon: Hypnotic elaboration, extraterrestrial sadomasochism, and spurious memories. *Psychological Inquiry, 7,* 99–126.

Potter, D. M. (1954). *People of plenty.* Chicago: University of Chicago Press.

Rodgers, D. T. (1978). *The work ethic in industrial America 1850–1920.* Chicago: University of Chicago Press.

Rosenthal, P. (1984). *Words and values: Some leading words and where they lead us.* New York: Oxford University Press.

Scarry, E. (1985). *The body in pain: The making and unmaking of the world.* New York: Oxford University Press.

Schlenker, B. R. (1980). *Impression management: The self-concept, social identity, and interpersonal relations.* Monterey, CA: Brooks/Cole.

Sennett, R. (1974). *The fall of public man.* New York: Random House.

Shils, E. (1981). *Tradition.* Chicago: University of Chicago Press.

Shoda, Y., Mischel, W., & Peake, P. K. (1990). Predicting adolescent cognitive and self-regulatory competencies from preschool delay of gratification: Identifying diagnostic conditions. *Developmental Psychology, 26,* 978–986.

Stone, L. (1977). *The family, sex and marriage in England 1500–1800.* New York: Harper & Row.

Tedeschi, J. T., & Felson, R. B. (1994). *Violence, aggression, and coercive action.* Washington, DC: American Psychological Association.

Tice, D. M., Butler, J. L., Muraven, M. B., & Stillwell, A. M. (1995). When modesty prevails: Differential favorability of self-presentation to friends and strangers. *Journal of Personality and Social Psychology, 69,* 1120–1138.

Trilling, L. (1971). *Sincerity and authenticity.* Cambridge, MA: Harvard University Press.

Vallacher, R. R., & Wegener, D. M. (1985). *A theory of action identification.* Hillsdale, NJ: Erlbaum.

Vallacher, R. R., & Wegner, D. M. (1987). What do people think they're doing? Action identification and human behavior. *Psychological Review, 94,* 3–15.

Vaughan, D. (1986). *Uncoupling.* New York: Oxford University Press.

Weintraub, K. J. (1978). *The value of the individual: Self and circumstance in autobiography.* Chicago: University of Chicago Press.

Zube, M. J. (1972). Changing concepts of morality: 1948–1969. *Social Forces, 50,* 385–393.

Zweig, P. (1980). *The heresy of self-love.* Princeton, NJ: Princeton University Press. (Original work published 1968.)

EXPLORING THE TEXT

1. What are the three "universal experiences" that transform bodies into selves, according to Baumeister? What examples from your life illustrate these experiences?

2. What, according to Baumeister's chronology, are the historical and political roots of the modern self? How did the notion of an "inner self" arise? What role has deception — or changing identities — played in the development of the distinction between inner and outer selves? What problems does Baumeister associate with the notion of a hidden, inner self?

3. How have our sources of moral authority changed over time, in Baumeister's view? What role has the self come to play in relation to moral values? How has this evaluation of the self inverted traditional attitudes toward selfhood and moral action? Do you agree that the self has displaced religion as the main source of moral authority in contemporary society? Why or why not?

4. What are some of the problems created by the new status of the self, in Baumeister's view? Why does Baumeister suggest that the self has become a burden? What specific social and personal problems do you think might arise as the result of the importance of the self in contemporary society?

5. At the beginning of this selection, Baumeister suggests that the construction of personal identity is an important way that society "can influence and control" the behavior of an individual. In what ways might the modern conception of the self function as a source of social control?

FURTHER EXPLORATIONS

1. Revisit Patricia Hampl's "Memory and Imagination" (p. 180), paying particular attention to the way that Hampl describes the process of self discovery that she believes underlies the art of memoir writing. To what extent does Hampl reflect the modern concept of reflexive consciousness as a kind of "treasure hunt"? What other elements of the modern Western concept of self does Hampl reflect?

2. How might Robert Sapolsky (p. 254) respond to Baumeister's assertion that "the number of selves in a given room is equal to the number of bodies" (para. 2)? How

do Sapolsky's experiences after his father's death challenge the commonplace identification of the boundary of the self with that of the body?

3. Compare the understandings of self and selfhood that emerge from Baumeister's and Mihaly Csikszentmihalyi's analyses of human identity (p. 264). What aspects of the self do Baumeister and Csikszentmihalyi seem to be in agreement on? How might you account for any differences that you note between their views of the self?

4. How might Baumeister explain the conflict between Dee and her mother in Alice Walker's "Everyday Use" (p. 283)? To what extent is it possible to view Walker's story as dramatizing a conflict between two different historical definitions of selfhood? Why?

5. Compare Baumeister's depiction of the role of the self among contemporary American women with Mary Catherine Bateson's portrayal of female identities in "A Mutable Self" (p. 337). Which of these versions of female selfhood strikes you as most accurate? Why?

6. As an experiment, read the "mission" or "philosophy" statement of your college or university. What role is played by traditional sources of moral or ethical authority in this document? To what extent is education described in terms of self-fulfillment, self-discovery, or self-actualization? Could you revise this statement in a way that would de-emphasize the self?

ESSAY OPTIONS

1. Drawing on illustrations and examples from popular magazines, television shows, movies, recent news stories, and from your own personal experience, write an essay in which you evaluate Baumeister's claim that the self has become the center of all value, morality, and authority in contemporary Western culture. Would you agree that ours is becoming an excessively self-indulgent society? Why or why not?

2. Write a paper in which you explore Baumeister's suggestion that the self has become a "burden" for many people in contemporary Western cultures. What evidence do you see in the mass media or your own experience to support or challenge the claim that people are suffering stress from the "demands and expectations" associated with the effort of being "all that you can be"? What evidence do you see that violence in contemporary society is associated with changing attitudes toward self-control? Do you think it would be better if we could, in fact, return to more traditional forms of moral and ethical authority? Why or why not?

3. Survey popular women's magazines to test Baumeister's claims about changes in the way American women have viewed the self since the 1940s. Then use this informal research as the basis of a paper on the emerging image of the modern American female self. What specific features or characteristics dominate the common notion of the female self communicated through these magazines? Do the images you collect as part of your survey suggest that the self and the exploration of selfhood have displaced other, more traditional sources of value for American women? To what extent does the self appear to be replacing family, community, and religion as a source of value and meaning in the lives of American women?

A Mutable Self

MARY CATHERINE BATESON

Mary Catherine Bateson (b. 1939) has been uniquely positioned to appreciate the many kinds of selves that populate the world. The daughter of two of the twentieth century's most renowned students of human behavior—sociologist Gregory Bateson and anthropologist Margaret Mead—Bateson grew up a citizen of the world, equally at home in a European capital or on a South Seas island. As a result, she developed the ability to see things from alternative perspectives and to view the values and attitudes of dominant cultures from the point of view of those who have been overlooked or marginalized by history. In this selection from her aptly titled *Peripherial Visions: Learning Along the Way* (1994), Bateson takes us on a tour of the self as defined in different cultural contexts, from prerevolutionary Iran to the present-day Philippines. From Bateson's opening lines, referring to the "old rhyme" about "something old, something new" and the other things a bride should bring to her wedding, you're bound to note that she takes an unusual and highly personal approach to her topic and her craft as a writer. In these reflections on what she's learned while traveling the world with her Iranian-born husband, Barkev, and daughter, Vanni, Bateson invites us to consider the role that human relationships play in the formation of identity and to rethink the rigidity of Western conceptions of the self. The Clarence J. Robinson Professor in Anthropology and English at George Mason University, Bateson has written and coauthored eight books, including *Composing a Life* (1990) and *With a Daughter's Eye: A Memoir of Margaret Mead and Gregory Bateson* (1984). Most recently she has published *Full Circles, Overlapping Lives: Culture and Generation in Transition* (2000).

BEFORE READING

Freewrite in your journal about a time in your life when you had to accommodate yourself to a new culture, community, or institution. What was the situation? How did you cope with it?

After I decided to use the old rhyme about what a bride should have at her wedding, I looked it up and discovered among its multiple versions a third line I had never heard. "Something old, something new, . . . And a silver sixpence in her shoe." What the tradition no doubt had in mind was prosperity for the new household, but the line reminds me of the times when I tucked a five-dollar bill into my shoe or my bra, "mad money" that would allow me to get home on my own if a date went sour.

Today, even if they choose not to be employed after marriage or while their children are small, young women are well-advised to be able to support themselves and to maintain that capacity by use: getting out, working with others, being effective. Circulating. That silver sixpence evokes a cultural expectation for healthy development of boys that is becoming more important for girls: a sense of self that is autonomous, independent, self-confident.

A silver sixpence is hard, round, stable. No fuzzy edges and little apparent change over time. It is a bad metaphor for the self but useful to show how the self is sometimes regarded, a thing rather than a process. Like the blue sky, the self is a matter of understanding and experience. Like money, it is a matter of convention. Think, then, of a sixpence in an inflationary economy, its value based only on agreement and steadily running down unless it is kept moving: earned and spent, invested and combined.

American culture has gone further than most in valuing the autonomous self, downplaying the importance of relationship. It was once virtually unique, for instance, in the preference for having infants sleep alone. Through history, most human infants have slept in the same room, often in the same bed, with at least one adult, then slept with siblings as they grew older. In Manila you can see the carryover of this as people cluster together, pack themselves cheerfully into tiny spaces, and walk, men with men and women with women, holding hands, linked and enfolded, seeking contact. The Jesuit scholastics used to scandalize their American mentors by cheerfully sitting on each other's laps. It was not easy for American Jesuits, moving like armored vessels, their compasses set in the individualistic spirituality of the Counter-Reformation,° to train these aspirants in separateness.

Only poverty, it is sometimes implied, would make parents share their   5
bedroom or their bed. This once near-universal human closeness is now seen as bad for the child. New mothers are often told severely that if they bring their infants into bed with them they may suffocate them; sometimes that pressure is reinforced with innuendo about sexual abuse. We have so little information about forbidden sexual activity within households in other cultures that it is hard to be certain, but it strikes me that some violations of the incest taboo depend on distance, on a deficit of intimacy. The very close contact in which kibbutz° children are raised, like a group of siblings in the children's house, seems to lead to a reduction in sexual interest in each other, so they grow up and seek romance outside the kibbutz.

Putting the baby in a separate room must lead to a heightened awareness of separateness and a more palpable time lapse between need and satisfaction, especially when an infant is left to cry, tasting abandonment as often as freedom, a self rooted in solitude. We think of this as laying the groundwork for independence, yet times of sleep are imposed and enforced by adults, not chosen. For one held in a warm bed between two protecting bodies, combining the scents of different skins and different rhythms of breathing, it must be easy to feel oneself part of a larger whole. Lying in the sun on a hilltop, you can

---

Counter-Reformation: Sixteenth-century reaction by European Catholics against the Protestant Reformation initiated by Martin Luther.

kibbutz: A communal farm or settlement in Israel.

have the same feeling of immersion in the living, breathing biosphere, full of scent and rhythm, as if you had never been expelled from the womb.

Becky and Shahnaz° offer a glimpse of alternative approaches. Becky maintained a visual connection with her mother, but she will grow up to face the possibility and the compulsion of autonomy and will need to be able to make herself at home in strange places. Shahnaz acted almost as if she and her mother were one body, yet she was acutely aware of boundaries beyond them, for the sense of being part of a larger whole may go beyond the family to a community, yet may set that community at odds with other human groups. Iranian boys also separate from their parents more gradually than American boys and may suffer from deep loneliness if they travel abroad; decisions of career and education are often made for the welfare of the extended family. In Iran, not only do infants often sleep with their mothers but they stay by their mothers, dozing and waking, until the mothers are ready to sleep themselves. The reality of human infancy is dependency, but some cultures create charades of early independence and project individualism and the rhetoric of rights onto infants, sometimes even onto fetuses. Other cultures go to the opposite extreme: autonomous membership in the wider community may be conferred only at adolescence or later, perhaps never for females.

It was in the Philippines, where I became pregnant myself, that I began to think of personhood, both the inner sense of self and the assurance of membership, as something that comes into being and grows through relationship and participation. I wrote a poem in that period using the imagined image of the Virgin Mary to express the way mothers and other caring adults turn infants into members of the human community:

In cradling that small god she had conceived,
She made him Man by loving.
Mothers do.

Not only mothers, and not only in infancy. The gift of personhood is potentially present in every human interaction, every time we touch or speak or call one another by name, yet denial can be very subtle too, inflicted in the failure to listen, to empathize, to attend. Membership in a human family or community is an artifact, something that has to be made, not a biological given. Membership both acknowledges and bridges separateness, for it is constructed across a gap of mutual incomprehension, depending always on the willingness to join in and be changed by a common dance. Western culture associates independence and autonomy with strength, but there is a sense in which an awareness of being part of a larger whole, of being defined by context, a self in adaption, can offer a different strength, leading to flexibility and

---

Becky and Shahnaz: Refers to two children, Becky, an American, and Shahnaz, an Iranian, whose experiences Bateson contrasts throughout her book.

constant learning. One can define a human being by DNA or by the physical traits of the species, but I prefer to use the word *person* for the focus of a pattern of relationships. Caring and commitment are what make persons, and persons in turn reach out for community. Personhood arises from a long process of welcoming closeness and continues to grow and require nourishment over a lifetime of participation.

A willingness to offer full participation to all its people is in some sense   10 the criterion of a good society, yet societies vary in their ideas of where membership begins and how it comes into being. As I write, debates about the rights of the unborn and of those impaired beyond all capacity for participation are ebbing and flowing in different places in the world. The recognition that personhood is socially constructed means that there is no single, self-evident answer to these debates. Almost everywhere, however, a person is one who knows others even as she or he is known: more than living tissue, a participant. Exclusion and second-class membership, when full humanity is denied, are assaults, bloodless murders. Just as the creatively responsive eye implies responsibility to preserve natural beauty, the fact that personhood is culturally constructed increases responsibility rather than decreases it. There is no alternative method.

Not only is a fetus contingent, a part of a woman's body, but an adult, man or woman, is also contingent, part of a larger whole, family or community or ecosystem. We cannot afford to carry emphasis on the individual too far, for no one—fetus, child, or adult—is independent of the actions and imaginations of others. Persons are human individuals shaped and succored by the reality of interdependence.

Those who see personhood as coming into being at a single point in time, whether through a divine act or through the biological events of conception or birth, uphold a lonely vision of the self rather than the self in relationship. Such an absolute vision is likely also to be static, playing down (and often subverting) ongoing development and learning. The self in relationship is necessarily fluid, held in a vessel of many strands, like the baskets closely woven by some Native American tribes, caulked tightly enough to hold water. The possibility of being freely welcomed and cherished may seem trivial compared with life and death, but emphasizing birth rather than participation leads to a society that supports the life of patients in irreversible coma yet denies adequate education and health care to vast numbers of children.

The business of human community includes the shared construction and conservation of meaning and compassion that exist only as they are lived. No legal definition can free us from the need to bring one another into being. I am only real and only have value as long as you are real and have value. What would happen if we learned to read Descartes's *cogito* beyond the first person concealed in the Latin verb forms: "You think therefore I am. I think therefore you are. We think . . . ." Every *ergo* conceals a different theory of the intermingling of lives.° In Filipino, there are two forms of *we*, one including and the other excluding the listener. It may be that the more closely one is defined by membership in a group, the more difficult it is to recognize the personhood of the "other" coming from outside.

During the months when the revolution° was building up in Iran, I was on the Caspian coast at the campus of a new university. We were set down in a small community where the Iranian faculty were also outsiders, newcomes from the big city; feeling vulnerable themselves, they feared that foreigners would act as lightning rods and asked us not to circulate in the town and to be as inconspicuous as possible. That request had to be honored, but I found that over time seclusion had an insidious effect on my morale, showing me what is meant by referring to many urban environments as dehumanizing. Sometimes I began to believe I was necessarily an object of hostility, susceptible to attack at any moment. Sometimes I felt invisible, a nonperson, all my effort in learning Persian canceled, and unable to fend for myself. Barkev° had teased me when we first traveled to the Middle East about the fact that blue eyes are regarded as bad luck, saying that women snatched their babies away when they saw me coming, and now that joke felt true.

On visits to Tehran, however, no loyalty to colleagues held me back. There 15 I went and walked among the crowds. Sometimes a passerby would make a hostile comment, but when I responded without contention in Persian the tone would change. As I walked along a main street, full of demonstrators surging out of the way as armored cars firing blanks rolled back and forth, people would draw me into storefronts, taking my hand or my arm: step back, be careful. These encounters on the street were an acknowledgment of me as a person and outweighed the risks, which were really rather minor. If this wandering looked like courage, it was a courage arising from a contingent sense of self, not an invulnerable one, for to me separation was the greater danger. If it looked like folly, it was folly arising from need.

Within the framework of Western assumptions, we begin to know a little about how the self is differentiated from others, how it takes shape for males and females, the kind of resilience associated with it. A wide range of pathologies have been associated with flawed attitudes toward the self: lack of self-esteem on the one hand and narcissism° on the other. Physical violence and sexual abuse deform the sense of self, or split it into multiples. So do insult and bigotry. So does invisibility or the realization that in a given context one is inaudible. We think of the self as a central continuity, yet recognizing that the self is not identical through time is a first step in celebrating it as fluid and variable, shaped and reshaped by learning.

Descartes's *cogito* . . . : The principle of "*Cogito ergo sum*"—Latin for "I think, therefore I am"—which was the foundation of French philosopher René Descartes's (1596–1650) philosophical system.

the revolution: Refers to the Iranian revolution of 1979.

Barkev: Bateson's husband.

narcissism: egoism, self-love.

In Iran, looking for a school for Vanni,° I visited a kindergarten. The teacher announced that it was time to draw and walked around the room with a cardboard box from which she gave one colored pencil (no opportunity to choose) and one piece of paper to each five-year-old. After a while she announced that drawing time was over and walked around the room again, this time carrying a wastebasket into which she put the drawings. Coming from the land of the decorated refrigerator door, where we have been taught to applaud each child's efforts as a way of building self-esteem and independence, I was appalled.

Respect for children as individuals and support for their emerging creativity continued to be the criteria for my selection. At the same time, I reflected that Western ideas of the individual are not universal and that American styles of child rearing are not noted for promoting cooperation and sensitivity to others. Particularly for boys, we value separateness: separateness from family, from community, and from the natural world, which we feel free to dominate and exploit. Even though girls are expected to retain a sense of connectedness, they are disparaged for it, while all too many boys are pushed into proving themselves by aggression and competition.

To find really profound differences in concepts of the self or the individual, I would have to look beyond the cultures in which I have worked; for Judaism, Christianity, and Islam are similar in supposing a self separate from God, free to choose obedience or not. I would have to look instead at hunting-gathering cultures or at the highly elaborated psychologies of Buddhism or Hinduism. Even so, there was enough variation in my experience to make me aware of differences. Israeli teenagers learning mutual support in the desert had first taught me something about different constructions of the self, and that in turn allowed me to understand what I was hearing when American brides complained of the intrusiveness of Iranian in-laws treating their time and property as common to the household.

Because the self is the instrument of knowledge, different concepts of self   20 offer different criteria for truth, whether social or private. Authenticity and sincerity are not private but interpersonal, with very different meanings in different cultures. Like the concept of zero in mathematics, a concept of self is pivotal in organizing experience, useful as an idea as long as it is not mistaken for a thing. Yet even though we regard the self as logically central to any way of experiencing the world, we are trained to look through it like a pane of glass, only noticing when it becomes blurred or cracked. The Western insistence on a separate self carries its own blindness, its own nonrecognition of necessary connection, its own inconsistencies. The very self we set out to affirm can become a hostage to fortune.

The self is learned, yet ironically it often becomes a barrier to learning. The illusion of autonomy confers a sort of immunity, often tenaciously defended, to the effect of new contexts and relationships, yet in order to move

Vanni: Bateson's daughter.

through society, we are asked to put the tenuous certainties of the self at risk again and again. The self fluctuates through a lifetime and even through the day, altered from without by changing relationships and from within by spiritual and even biochemical changes, such as those of adolescence and menopause and old age. Yet the self is the basic thread with which we bind time into a single narrative. We improvise and struggle to respond in unpredictable and unfamiliar contexts, learning new skills and transmuting discomfort and bewilderment into valuable information about difference—even, at the same time, becoming someone different. Clarity about the self dims and brightens like a lamp in a thunderstorm or a radio signal from far away, but all our learning and adapting is devoted to keeping it alight.

The cost of exposure to another system of certainties is a bruising risk to clarity about the self. Taking on a new role or entering a new institution are both transitions when the self is put at risk: school systems are often particularly violent in their attack. Thus, children who fail to learn in school may simply be unwilling or unable to put a fragile sense of self or of membership in a group at risk, while adults who decline to learn do so in self-defense.

To become educated, one must concur with the implication of ignorance—and in many traditions one must also concur that one is evil, a sinner. In societies with immigrant communities, many children have to concur that their parents are ignorant, while members of minority communities may get the message that ignorance is their permanent condition. These are very expensive agreements to give. Traditionally the definition of oneself as ignorant has been compensated by the promise that, at the end of some number of years of submission and deference, one will be allowed to become somebody—a pillar of adult society. For the many children who suspect that this promise is false, the bargain is unacceptable. Even in private schools, with their constant message of selectivity, the insults of schooling are barely tolerable. Even when we try to build up the self, we subvert it for the sake of discipline and conformity. It is almost as if schools demanded, Leave your self, your self-esteem, the confidence accrued from learning to walk and speak, at the door. And do that without the genuine confidence that in the end you will have a share in your society and that being an adult is desirable. This is what many children are asked to do in school. I can't think why anyone puts up with it.

When Vanni was approaching the end of secondary school, one of her teachers warned the parents that he would soon be assigning personal essays of the kind that students write to project their personalities and talents for college admissions. Vanni turned to me in some distress, and said, "Mom, I don't know how to write an essay in the first-person singular."

In many schools, children are disciplined from early on not to do what is called personalizing. Not to use the word *I*. Not to give their opinions or use school essays as a vehicle for self-expression even while they continue to be vehicles for competition. What I suggested to Vanni, since her primary interest is acting, was to shift to a different medium, where her capacity for expression had not been deformed by classroom conventions. She developed and taped

25

a dramatic monologue and edited the transcription. But what an extraordinary thing it is that in a society where we regard the self as central, we are so often engaged in silencing its expression or putting confidence at risk. Volumes have been written about the miracle represented by learning to use the word *I,* yet that capacity is under constant attack.

Children learn skills and information in school. These are the issues when we complain that they cannot use decimals or give the dates of the Civil War. More significantly, they learn how society is organized and where they fit into that organization. They learn notions of authority and truth and the limits to creativity. These are the underlying communications of school. For a very large number of children, they have been basically negative, a progressive stripping away of dreams, an undermining of confidence. Western societies and their imitators use competition to improve performance, beginning in the classroom, paying a price in the loss of collaborative skills. For every child whose confidence is enhanced, there are half a dozen for whom it will be reduced, and some of those will grow up to inflate their own self-respect by finding someone else to put down.

In the Philippines, children learn early on to avoid competing, so that success or failure is often attributed to luck and the child who claims credit for success is remorselessly teased. When American educators arrived in the Philippines, they found this reluctance to stand out and excel frustrating. American clergy have sometimes complained that Filipinos lack the kind of internalized conscience they were used to, responding to public shame rather than true contrition. Individual behavior is experienced as an expression less of the self than of the group. Yet if the conscience really is an internalization of external authority, as Freudians.° argue, this may be liberating to know

Even in a society that uses competition to select and strengthen a few members of the group for success, there are situations in which the smart ones, the successes, limit their risks in the face of future challenges, for once they have gotten away from school and become established at a high level, the risks of learning may seem hardly worth it. Given a choice, as we are later in life, most people choose not to learn and therefore not to change except in superficial ways. Deborah Tannen° points out that in American culture men are notoriously unwilling even to stop on the road to ask for directions, but this is only one of many settings in which obtaining information or guidance is blocked because of the acknowledgment of weakness involved. Only a few people become, out of their experience, addicted to the process of learning, to its intrinsic rewards.

When we went to the Philippines, Barkev and his colleagues went as professors of management, brought by the Ford Foundation. They started trying to learn a little Filipino—phrases and greetings. One day one of them walked

Freudians: Adherents of the theory of psychoanalysis first propounded by Sigmund Freud (1856–1938).
Deborah Tannen: (b. 1945), American linguist.

into a room where there were six young Filipina secretaries and complained loudly, "No breasts, no breasts!"—a tiny mispronunciation of "no keys." The room was filled with cascading female laughter, and the story was retold for months. That was the end of their effort to learn the language, for the professors were prohibited by their status from making fools of themselves. Wealth and power are obstacles to learning. People who don't wear shoes learn the languages of people who do, not vice versa. Given a choice, few will choose the reversal of status that is involved in being ignorant and being a learner, unless there is a significant gain of intimacy or respect in the new learning. When I first became a dean, I admired the campus skating rink and started talking about learning to skate, but helpful faculty friends argued that as dean I could not afford to let colleagues see me in the inevitable comic falls. . . .

Women are often constrained to make new beginnings because of choices   30 made by men, sometimes moving them to new places and cultures. I was in Manila because, after I got my doctorate in Arabic linguistics, my husband accepted a job there. How do you survive under these circumstances? One way to survive is to learn, accepting the internal change that new learning requires and the loss of status that goes with being a beginner once again. In a new country this may mean returning to the infant's task of learning a whole new language and culture, so it is not surprising that many of those assigned to work overseas take refuge in expatriate enclaves and continue to assume that their way of doing things is right, with few changes. Some American women in Manila took courses in Chinese cooking and learned how to judge the quality of pearls, and in Tehran they took seminars on Persian carpets—skills as souvenirs. Husbands are no more willing than wives to risk the changes that would go with fundamental new learning.

Most of the jobs that take Americans overseas are structured so they are not obliged to learn the local culture; indeed they may carry a sort of obligation to hold on to American ways of doing things and to the authority this implies. Barkev has taught management in several countries, in English. To do this, he has eventually had to learn a great deal about the business climate and how people function. He is being paid for expertise, however, not for a willingness to put himself back in nursery school and try to learn the system from scratch. Even in socializing with the local community, expatriates seek out those who will reinforce their sense of confidence and familiarity. Shortly before the Iranian revolution, a member of the diplomatic community said to me, "Look, I socialize with Iranians all the time, and there just is no groundswell of hostility to Americans."

Women have suffered from lower self-esteem than men and have been less respected and less valued, but the very responsiveness demanded from women can sometimes lead to greater adaptability and greater willingness to follow the cues of a new environment. Today women are especially likely to work for change in cultures where, having been valued primarily for beauty or continuing fertility, they face an earlier loss of status than men, a declining future. There are societies, however, where women's status traditionally rose as their sons grew to maturity. An Iranian woman of fifty, courted and honored by a son coming into his prime, could be poised and confident, with little motivation for new learning or social change, while a new bride, who has recently left her home environment to start from scratch among strangers, is necessarily malleable. Even when he has set up a new household, a businessman may stop off at the end of the workday with flowers for his mother and sit and drink tea with her, listening to her advice, while his wife is at home preparing a meal and looking after young children. Not surprisingly, social change is less attractive to women for whom the best years of their lives are still ahead under the traditional system. In fact, both men and women may be more at peace with the losses that accompany aging in cultures where the old are respected and life has a built-in sense of progression. The Western preoccupation with progress may be an effort to compensate for a personal sense of being condemned to regress.

Many adults only take on the challenge of profound change when they are desperate. This is why so much of adult learning is packaged today as therapy and why it must often offer the compensation of membership in a new community or relationship. We have begun to develop rituals for adults who find themselves in need of drastic change and new beginnings, rituals that give some value to the surrender of adult confidence. Alcoholics Anonymous and other twelve-step groups teach that they cannot help you until you hit bottom and relinquish your sense of being in control of your life—apparently it is helpful to get the acknowledgment of weakness over with in order to make new learning possible.

The alternative would be to conserve the openness and need for new learning that we find in infants, by making it a part of identity. If I were to move to a new country now, I doubt that I would become fluent in yet another non-Western language, because doing so does get harder with the passage of time, but I would learn enough to cope. Learning languages is part of my sense of myself. Following the Turkish proverb that says *her lisan bir insan,* "every language a person," each new language has come to represent an enrichment to me. I know how to do it, I enjoy doing it, and frankly after writing this paragraph I'd be embarrassed not to. I also know that eventually, even though I may look like an outsider, people will recognize their words in my mouth and respond, and that too has become necessary to me.

All too often those who can teach or lead with authority are armored against new learning, while those who are open to new learning are made diffident about expressing what they do know by the very fact that they deem it tentative. The best learners are children, not children segregated in schools but children at play, zestfully busy exploring their own homes, families, neighborhoods, languages, conjuring up possible and impossible worlds of imagination. Only a little way from the front door, in other parts of the city or in forest or meadow, exploration continues to be possible throughout life. Some traditions emphasize this, expecting those who have leisure to fill it with explorations of the arts or natural history. The eighteenth-century idea that a gentleman might collect beetles, read unfamiliar texts of the classics, or conduct experiments played a role in the emergence of modern science.

There is a famous story about two visitors to the Ames experiments in Princeton. Adelbert Ames had set up a series of boxes and rooms (if an artist did it today it would be called an installation) that created optical illusions by distorting perspective. Looking through a slit that allows vision with only one eye, the visitor was invited to touch various points with a stick, but because of deliberately distorted clues of perspective the stick kept missing. Eisenhower,° it is said, lost his temper when he visited, threw down the stick, and refused to continue. He had a vein in his high, bald forehead that used to pulse visibly when he was angry or frustrated. Einstein,° it is said, was fascinated when he encountered the same errors, using them to explore further.

The two men had clearly found their ways to greatness in the niches that fit their temperaments, but they were also shaped by the conventions of the worlds in which they worked. Generals and presidents are expected to be decisive. An open mind, the willingness to learn from mistakes, the willingness to admit ignorance — these are not widely valued or rewarded in the circles where Eisenhower developed. When political leaders hesitate or revise their views, we mistake it for weakness, not strength. As a society, we need to consider whether those conventions might be altered, whether a little more tolerance for ambiguity might not be a good thing in those who hold leadership positions. We joke about the problem, with buttons that say, "Question authority," and desk plaques that quip back, "My mind is made up, don't trouble me with facts." . . .

More flexible boundaries of the self open up attention to the environment that may ultimately be essential to survival, for it is not the individual organism that survives but the organism in the environment that gives it life. We need to find ways to encourage a sense of the self as continuing to develop through responsive interaction. Relying on competition as a way of motivating learning eventually subverts not only cooperation but also the willingness to learn. The models for a more responsive sense of self might be borrowed across lines of culture and gender or be treasured from an undamaged childhood.

Learning is perhaps the only pleasure that might replace increasing consumption as our chosen mode of enriching experience. Someday, the joy of recognizing a pattern in a leaf or the geological strata in a cliff face might replace the satisfactions of new carpeting or more horsepower in an engine, and the chance to learn in the workplace might seem more valuable than increased purchasing power or a move up the organizational chart. Increasing knowledge of the ethology of wolves might someday replace the power savored in destroying them.

Eisenhower: Dwight David Eisenhower (1890–1969), thirty-fourth president of the United States.

Einstein: Albert Einstein (1879–1955), German-born American physicist.

We reach for knowledge as an instrument of power, not as an instrument   40
of delight, yet the preoccupation with power ultimately serves ignorance. The
political scientist Karl Deutsch defined power as "the ability not to have to
learn," which is exemplified by the failure of empathy in a Marie Antoinette°
or the rejection of computer literacy by an executive. Ironically, in our society
both the strongest, those who have already succeeded, and the weakest, those
who feel destined for failure, defend themselves against new learning.

Sitting alone at my computer a little after dawn, writing seems a very private thing: my thoughts, my words, the gap between them that I struggle with.
But unlike a typewriter, the computer keeps me a part of multiple conversations. A poem from a woman in California, scrolling across the screen, about
the inaccessible speech of the body; the machine's curmudgeonly messages,
programmed by others, balking at instructions it finds unacceptable — these
remind me that I am shaped by other minds. I sit here telling stories about
human give and take, repeated encounters sometimes leading to growth, and
all the words and concepts I use are old, inherited, part of the way I have been
shaped by my environment. I try to become transparent to their possible
meaning. The trees on the slope outside grow invisibly and move gently in the
wind, shaping me more than I shape them, each one playing a role in birthing
a human consciousness. With a sense of self so permeable, peripheral vision is
essential, for all those others present with me now are a source of identity and
partners in my survival.

Adults are freer than schoolchildren in their writing, but I am in defiance of
scientific convention and much of literary history when I claim the freedom to
begin many of my sentences with the word *I*. Yet it rescues me from the temptation to be categorical. The word I want is *we*, but there are limits to the assumption of agreement, so I "personalize" as a more honest way to be inclusive.
Impersonal writing often claims a timeless authority: this is so. Personal writing
affirms relationship, for it includes these implied warnings: this is what I think
at this moment, this is what I remember now, continuing to grow and change.
This finally is contingent on being understood and responded to.

Marie Antoinette: (1755–1793), Queen of France and wife of Louis XVI, infamous for her extravagant lifestyle and her advice to "Let them eat cake" as a way of combating hunger among the
poor of eighteenth-century Paris.

EXPLORING THE TEXT

1. What is the Western concept of the self, according to Bateson? How is this notion
   of self developed during childhood? Overall, how does Bateson feel about attitudes
   toward the self in the United States? Why? To what extent do you agree with her
   assessment?

2. What do Bateson's experiences in Iran, the Philippines, and Israel teach her about
   notions of selfhood in other cultures? How do such cross-cultural experiences influence the way she defines what it means to be a person? How accurate or attractive do you find her definition? Why?

3. What does Bateson mean when she says that "[t]he self is learned, yet ironically it often becomes a barrier to learning" (para. 18)? What, in Bateson's view, is the relation between learning, power, and the self? How does she view formal education and its influence on the self? To what extent do you agree with her assessment? Why?

4. How do the "constructions" of male and female selves differ in Western cultures, according to Bateson? Why, in her view, does this make women potentially better "learners" than men? To what extent has your personal experience confirmed or challenged this view of male and female selves?

5. How would you describe—or diagram—the structure of Bateson's essay? How does it compare with the structure you'd expect in more traditional forms of academic writing? How would you characterize its tone?

FURTHER EXPLORATIONS

1. Compare Bateson's view of the self in Western culture with that presented by Roy F. Baumeister (p. 320). How might you account for the differences of opinion or emphasis that separate these authors' views of the Western concept of self?

2. Explore the role that interpersonal relationships play in the construction of identity in one or more of the following selections: Ian Frazier's "Take the F" (p. 18), Scott Russell Sanders's "The Inheritance of Tools" (p. 142), Loren Eiseley's "The Brown Wasps" (p. 150), Maxine Hong Kingston's "No-Name Woman" (p. 206), Robert Sapolsky's "Ego Boundaries, or the Fit of My Father's Shirt" (p. 254), Alice Walker's "Everyday Use" (p. 283), and Rubén Martínez's "Technicolor" (p. 306). To what extent do the relationships presented in these selections reflect Bateson's view of the self as the result of a fluid process of learned interdependence? How do these selections confirm or challenge Bateson's view of the relation between power, the ability to learn, and ego boundaries?

ESSAY OPTIONS

1. Use the *Before Reading* activity on page (337) as the point of departure for an essay on a time in your life when you had to accommodate yourself to a new culture, community, or institution. In what ways did this experience challenge your values, attitudes, beliefs, or perceptions? How did it change you? How did it modify your sense of self?

2. Write about an experience you recall from your own schooling when you felt "silenced" or when your self-confidence was put "at risk." Would you agree with Bateson that even in the best schools the self—the "I"—is under constant attack? Why or why not?

3. Write a paper in which you inventory all the relationships you participate in that contribute significantly to your sense of self. What family ties, friendships, associations, or institutional memberships play a role in your identity? What social, racial, cultural, ethnic, or religious affiliations are central to your sense of self? What values, attitudes, or other personal characteristics have you derived from these relationships? How have they shaped your understanding of your identity as an individual?

4. Drawing on ideas presented by Bateson, Robert Sapolsky in "Ego Boundaries, or the Fit of My Father's Shirt" (p. 254), Roy F. Baumeister in "The Self and Society: Changes, Problems and Opportunities" (p. 320), and Rubén Martínez in "Technicolor" (p. 306), write an essay in which you assess the status of the self in contemporary American culture. How is the American self portrayed by these authors? What is happening, in their view, to the concept of selfhood in America today? What do you see happening to the self in America's future? Why?

Whose Self Is It, Anyway?

PHILIP KITCHER

On 23 February 1997, the British press broke a story that sent shock waves throughout scientific, political, and philosophical circles around the world. It was the announcement that a ewe named Dolly had been born at the Roslin Institute outside Edinburgh, Scotland. The fanfare surrounding Dolly's arrival on earth was understandable, because, technically speaking, Dolly wasn't really born at all; she was cloned — produced, that is, by deliberate scientific effort through the asexual process of "somatic cell nuclear transfer." The concept of cloning has long had a bad reputation among science-fiction writers and cultural critics. In sci-fi movies and comic books, cloning conjures up visions of bioengineered zombie stormtroopers who threaten to destroy or displace us in all of our colorful variety. In the popular imagination, to be a clone is to be a body without a mind, a self without a soul. But would a clone really amount to nothing more than a genetic Xerox of another being? Would cloned children have incomplete or damaged selves? Not according to ethicist Philip Kitcher (b. 1947). Despite the provocative title of this examination of cloning, Kitcher takes a remarkably balanced view of his subject. According to Kitcher, our fears about cloning's impact on human autonomy say more about our misunderstanding of genetics than they do about the fragility of the human self. In Kitcher's view, cloning, like any new technology, may serve either ethical or unethical ends. Kitcher is professor of philosophy at Columbia University and the author of *The Lives to Come: The Genetic Revolution and Human Possibilities* (1996). This essay originally appeared in *The Sciences*.

BEFORE READING

Working in small groups, discuss the kinds of situations when cloning might be used as a means of human reproduction in the future. Who would use it? Why would they resort to cloning? Under what conditions might the cloning of a human being be justified?

I n April 1988 Abe and Mary Ayala of Walnut, California, began living through every parent's nightmare: Anissa, their sixteen-year-old daughter, was diagnosed with leukemia. Without a bone-marrow transplant, Anissa would probably die within five years. But who could donate bone marrow that Anissa's immune system would not reject? Tests confirmed the worst: neither Abe, Mary, nor their other child had compatible marrow.

The family embarked on a desperate plan. Abe, who had had a vasectomy years before, had it surgically reversed. Within months, at the age of forty-three, Mary became pregnant. The genetic odds were still three-to-one against a match between Anissa's bone marrow and that of the unborn child. The media got hold of the story, and the unbearable wait became a public agony.

Against all the odds a healthy daughter was born with compatible bone marrow. Fourteen months later, in June 1991, physicians extracted a few ounces of the child's marrow: the elixir that would save her older sister's life.

The story has a happy ending, but many people have found it at least slightly disturbing. Is it right for a couple to conceive one child to save another? Can someone brought into the world for such a well-defined purpose ever feel that she is loved for who she is? Thirty-seven percent of the people questioned in a contemporaneous *Time* magazine poll said they thought what the Ayalas had done was wrong; 47 percent believed it was justifiable.

Six years have passed and now a different, yet related, event a continent away has shaken the public's moral compass. Lamb number 6LL3, better known as Dolly, took the world by surprise last February when she was introduced as the first creature ever cloned from an adult mammal. Recognizing that what is possible with sheep today will probably be feasible with human beings tomorrow, commentators speculated about the legitimacy of cloning a Pavarotti or an Einstein, about the chances that a demerited dictator might produce an army of supersoldiers, about the future of basketball in a world where a team of Larry Birds could play against a team of Michael Jordans. Polls showed that Mother Teresa was the most popular choice for person-to-be-cloned, but the film star Michelle Pfeiffer was not far behind, and Bill and Hillary Clinton, though tainted by controversy over alleged abuses of presidential power, also garnered some support.

Beyond all the fanciful talk, Dolly's debut introduces real and pressing moral issues. Cloning will not enable anyone to duplicate people like so many cookie-cutter gingerbread men, but it will pave the way for creating children who can fulfill their parents' preordained intentions. Families in the Ayalas' circumstances, for instance, would have a new option: Clone their dying child to give birth to another whose identical genetic makeup would guarantee them a compatible organ or a tissue match. Should they be allowed to exercise that opinion? The ethical implications of cloning balance on a fine line.

Society can probably blame Mary Wollstonecraft Shelley and her fervent imagination for much of the brouhaha over cloning. The Frankenstein story colors popular reception of the recent news, fomenting a potent brew of associations: many people assume that human lives can be made to order, that there is something vaguely illicit about the process, and, of course, that it is all going to turn out disastrously. Reality is much more complicated—and more sobering—so one should preface debates about the morality of human cloning with a clear understanding of the scientific facts.

As most newspaper readers know by now, the recent breakthroughs in cloning did not come from one of the major centers of the genetic revolution, but from the far less glamorous world of animal husbandry and agricultural research. A team of investigators at the Roslin Institute, near Edinburgh, Scotland, led by Ian Wilmut, conjectured that past efforts to clone mammals had failed because the cell that supplied the nucleus and the egg that received it were at different stages of the cell cycle. Applying well-known techniques from cell biology, Wilmut "starved" the cells so that both were in an inactive phase at the time of transfer. Inserting nuclei from adult sheep cells in that quiescent phase gave rise to a number of embryos, which were then implanted into ewes. In spite of a high rate of miscarriage, one of the pregnancies continued to term. After beginning with 277 transferred adult nuclei, Wilmut and his coworkers obtained one healthy lamb: the celebrated Dolly.

Wilmut's achievement raises three important questions about the prospect of human cloning: Will it be possible to undertake the same operations on human cells? Will cloners be able to reduce the high rate of failure? And just what is the relation between a clone obtained through nuclear transplantation and the animals, born in the usual way, from which the clone is derived?

Answers to the first two questions are necessarily tentative; predicting   10
even the immediate trajectory of biological research is always vulnerable to contingencies. In the late 1960s, for example, after the developmental biologist J. B. Gurdon, now of the University of Cambridge, produced an adult frog through cloning, it seemed that cloning all kinds of animals was just around the corner; a few years later, the idea of cloning adult mammals had returned to the realm of science fiction. But leaving aside any definite time frame, one can reasonably expect that Wilmut's technique will eventually work on human cells and that failure rates will be reduced.

What about the third question, however, the relation between "parent" animal and clone? There one can be more confident. Dolly clearly has the same nuclear genetic material as the ewe that supplied the inserted nucleus. A second ewe supplied the egg into which that nucleus was inserted; hence Dolly's mitochondrial DNA came from another source. Indeed, though the exact roles played by mitochondrial DNA and other contents of the cytoplasm in vertebrate development are still unclear, one can say this much: Dolly's early development was shaped by the interaction between the DNA in the nucleus and the contents of the egg cytoplasm—the contributions of two adult females. A third sheep, the ewe into which the embryonic Dolly was implanted, provided Dolly with a uterine environment. Dolly thus has three mothers—nuclear mother, egg mother, and womb mother—and no father (unless, of course, one accords that honor to Wilmut for his guiding role).

Now imagine Holly, a human counterpart of Dolly. You might think Holly would be similar to her nuclear mother, perhaps nearly identical, particularly if the mother of the nuclear mother were also the womb mother, and if either that woman or the nuclear mother were the egg mother. Such a hypothetical circumstance would ensure that Holly and her donor shared a similar gestation experience, as well as both nuclear and mitochondrial DNA. (Whether they would share other cytoplasmic constituents is anyone's guess, because the extent of the differences among eggs from a single donor is still unknown.)

But even if all Holly's genetic material and her intrauterine experience matched those of a single donor, Holly would not be an exact replica of that human being. Personal identity, as philosophers since John Locke have recognized, depends as much on life experiences as on genetics. Memories, attitudes, prejudices, and emotional attachments all contribute to the making of a person. Cloning creates babies, not fully formed adults, and babies mature through a series of unique events. You could not hope to ensure the survival of your individual consciousness by arranging for one of your cells to be cloned. Megalomaniacs with intimations of immortality need not apply.

Other environmental factors would also lead to differences between Holly and her donor. For one thing, the two would likely belong to different generations, and the gap in their ages would correspond to changes in educational trends, the adolescent subculture, and other aspects of society that affect children's development. Perhaps even more important, Holly and her donor would be raised in different families, with different friends, close relatives, teachers, neighbors, and mentors. Even if the same couple acted as parents to both, the time gap would change the familial circumstances.

Identical twins reared together are obviously similar in many respects, but even they are by no means interchangeable; for instance, 50 percent of male identical twins who are gay have a twin who is not [see "Whenever the Twain Meet," by Thomas J. Bouchard Jr., *The Sciences* (September/October 1997): 52]. Small differences in shared environments clearly play a large role. How much more dissimilarity, then, can be anticipated, given the much more dramatic variations that would exist between clones and their donors? 15

There will never be another you. If you hoped to fashion a son or daughter exactly in your image, you would be doomed to disappointment. Nevertheless, you might hope to take advantage of cloning technology to have a child of a certain kind—after all, the most obvious near-term applications for cloning lie in agriculture, where the technique could be used to perpetuate certain useful features of domestic animals, such as their capacity for producing milk, through succeeding generations. Some human characteristics are directly linked to specific genes and are therefore more amenable to manipulation—eye color, for instance. But in cloning, as in a good mystery novel, nothing is quite as simple as it seems.

Imagine a couple who are determined to do what they can to create a Hollywood star. Fascinated by the color of Elizabeth Taylor's eyes, they obtain a tissue sample from the actress and clone a young Liz. Will they succeed in creating a girl who possesses exact copies of the actress's celebrated eyes? Probably not. Small variations that occur at the cellular level during growth could modify the shape of the girl's eye sockets so that the eye color would no longer have its bewitching effect. Would the Liz clone still capture the hearts of millions? Perhaps the eyes would no longer have it.

Of course, Taylor's beauty and star appeal rest on much more than eye color. But the chances are that other physical attributes—height, figure, complexion, facial features—would also be somewhat different in a clone. Elizabeth II might overeat, for instance, or play strenuous sports, so that as a young adult her physique would be fatter or leaner than Elizabeth I's. Then there are the less tangible attributes that contribute to star quality: character and personal style. Consider what goes into something as apparently simple as a movie star's smile. Capturing as it does the interplay between physical features and personality, a smile is a trademark that draws on a host of factors, from jaw shape to sense of humor. How can anything so subtle ever be duplicated?

Fantasies about cloning Einstein, Mother Teresa, or Yo-Yo Ma are equally doomed. The traits people value most come about through a complex interaction between genotypes and environments. By fixing the genotype one can only increase the chances—never provide a guarantee—of achieving one's desired results. The chances of artificially fashioning a person of true distinction in any area of complex human activity, whether it be science, philanthropy, or artistic expression, are infinitesimal.

Although cloning cannot produce exact replicas or guarantee outstanding   20
performance, it might be exploited to create a child who tends toward certain traits or talents. For example, had my wife and I wanted a son who would dominate the high school basketball court, we would have been ill-advised to reproduce in the old-fashioned way. At a combined height of just over eleven feet, we would have dramatically increased our chances by having a nucleus transferred from some strapping NBA star. And it is here, in the realm of the possible, that cloning scenarios devolve into moral squalor. By dabbling in genetic engineering, parents would be demonstrating a crass failure to recognize their children as independent beings with the freedom to form their own sense of who they are and what their lives mean.

Parents have already tried to shape and control their children, of course, even without the benefit of biological tools. The nineteenth-century English intellectual James Mill had a plan for his son's life, leading him to begin young John Stuart's instruction in Greek at age three and his Latin at age eight. John Stuart Mill's *Autobiography* is a quietly moving testament to the cramping effect of the life his eminent father had designed for him. In early adulthood, Mill *fils* suffered a nervous breakdown, from which he recovered, going on to a career of great intellectual distinction. But though John Stuart partly fulfilled his father's aspirations for him, one of the most striking features of his philosophical work is his passionate defense of human freedom. In *On Liberty* he writes: "Mankind are greater gainers by suffering each other to live as seems good to themselves, than by compelling each to live as seems good to the rest."

If the cloning of human beings is undertaken in the hope of generating a particular kind of person, then cloning is morally repugnant. The repugnance arises not because cloning involves biological tinkering but because it interferes with human autonomy. To discover whether circumstances might exist in which cloning would be morally acceptable, one must ask whether the objectionable motive can be removed. Three scenarios come immediately to mind.

First is the case of the dying child: Imagine a couple in a predicament similar to that of the Ayalas, which I described at the beginning of this essay. The couple's only son is dying and needs a kidney transplant within ten years. Unfortunately, neither parent can donate a compatible organ, and it may not be possible to procure an appropriate one from the existing donor pool. If a brother were produced by cloning, one of his kidneys could be transplanted to save the life of the elder son.

Second, the case of the grieving widow: A woman's beloved husband has been killed in an automobile accident. As a result of the same crash, the couple's only daughter lies in a coma with irreversible brain damage. The widow, who can no longer bear children, wants to have the nuclear DNA from one of her daughter's cells inserted into an egg supplied by another woman, so that a clone of her child can be produced through surrogate motherhood.

Third, the case of the loving lesbians: A lesbian couple wishes to have a   25
child. Because they would like the child to be biologically connected to each of them, they request that a cell nucleus from one of them be inserted into an egg from the other, and that the embryo be implanted in the uterus of the woman who donated the egg.

No blatant attempt is made in any of these scenarios to direct the child's life; indeed, in some cases like these cloning may turn out to be morally justified. Yet lingering concerns remain. In the first scenario, and to a lesser extent in the second, the disinterested bystander suspects that children are being subordinated to the special purposes or projects of adults. Turning from John Stuart Mill to another great figure in contemporary moral theory, Immanuel Kant, one can ask whether any of the scenarios can be reconciled with Kant's injunction to "treat humanity, whether in your own person or in the person of another, always at the same time as an end and never simply as a means."

Perhaps the parents in the case of the dying child have no desire to expand their family; for them the younger brother would be simply a means of saving the really important life. And even if the parental attitudes were less callous, concerns would remain. In real case histories in which parents have borne a child to save an older sibling, their motives have been much more complex; the Ayala family seems a happy one, and the younger sister is thriving. Ironically, though, in such circumstances the parents' love for the younger child may be manifested most clearly if the project goes awry and the older child dies. Otherwise, the clone — and perhaps the parents as well — will probably always wonder whether he is loved primarily for his usefulness.

Similarly, the grieving widow might be motivated solely by nostalgia for the happy past, so that the child produced by cloning would be valuable only because she was genetically close to the dead. If so, another person is being treated as a means to understandable, but morbid, ends.

The case of the loving lesbians is the purest of the three. The desire to have a child who is biologically related to both of them is one that our society recognizes, at least for heterosexual couples, as completely natural and justifiable. There is no question in this scenario of imposing a particular plan on the nascent life—simply the wish to have a child who is the expression of the couple's mutual love. That is the context in which human cloning would be most defensible.

In recent decades, medicine has enabled many couples to overcome reproductive problems and bear their own biological children. Techniques of assisted reproduction have become mainstream because of a general belief that infertile couples have been deprived of something valuable, and that manipulating human cells is a legitimate response to their frustrations.

But do we, members of a moral community, know what makes biological connections between parents and offspring valuable? Can we as a society assess the genuine benefits to the general welfare brought about by techniques of assisted reproduction, and do we want to invest in extending those techniques even further? Artificial insemination or in vitro fertilization could help the grieving widow and the lesbian couple in my scenarios; in both cases cloning would create a closer biological connection—but one should ask what makes that extra degree of relatedness worth striving for. As for the parents of the dying child, one can simply hope that the continuing growth of genetic knowledge will provide improved methods of transplantation. By the time human cloning is a real possibility, advances in immunology may enable patients to tolerate tissue from a broader range of sources.

Should human cloning be banned? For the moment, while biology and medicine remain ignorant of the potential risks—the miscarriages and malformed embryos that could result—a moratorium is surely justified. But what if future research on nonhuman mammals proves reassuring? Then, as I have suggested, cloning would be permissible in a small range of cases. Those cases must satisfy two conditions: First, there must be no effort to create a child with specific attributes. Second, there must be no other way to provide an appropriate biological connection between parent and child. As people reflect on the second condition, perhaps some will be moved to consider just how far medicine should go to help people have children "of their own." Many families have found great satisfaction in rearing adopted children. Although infertile couples sometimes suffer great distress, further investment in technologies such as cloning may not be the best way to bring them relief.

The public fascination with cloning reached all the way to the White House almost immediately after Wilmut's epochal announcement. President Clinton was quick first to refer the issue to his National Bioethics Advisory Commission and then to ban federal funding for research into human cloning. The response was panicky, reflexive, and disappointing. In the words of the editors of *Nature*: "At a time when the science policy world is replete with technology foresight exercises, for a U.S. president and other politicians only now to be requesting guidance about [the implications of cloning] is shaming."

But though society and its leadership are woefully unprepared to handle cloning with policies based on forethought, many people race ahead irresponsibly with fantasies and fears. Human cloning becomes a titillating topic of discussion, while policy makers ignore the pressing ethical issues of the moment. In a fit of moral myopia, the U.S. government moves to reject human cloning because of potential future ills, while it institutes policies that permit existing children to live without proper health care and that endanger children's access to food and shelter.

The respect for the autonomy of lives and the duty to do what one can to   35
let children flourish in their own ways should extend beyond hypothetical discussions about cloning. However strongly one may feel about the plights of loving lesbians, grieving widows, or even couples with dying children, deciding how cloning might legitimately be applied to their troubles is not the most urgent moral or political question, or the best use of financial resources. I would hope that the public debate about new developments in biotechnology would ultimately spur our society to be more vigilant about applying the moral principles that we espouse but so often disregard.

Making demands for social investment seems quixotic, particularly when funds for the poor in the United States are being slashed and when other affluent countries are having second thoughts about the responsibilities of societies toward their citizens. The patronizing adjectives, such as "idealistic" and "utopian," that conservatives bestow on liberal programs do nothing to undermine the legitimacy of the demands. What is truly shameful is not that the response to the possibilities of cloning came so late, nor that the response has been so confused, but that the affluent nations have been so reluctant to think through the implications of time-honored moral principles and to design a coherent use of the new genetic science, technology, and information for human well-being.

EXPLORING THE TEXT

1. Kitcher begins his essay by discussing Abe and Mary Ayala's decision to have a child in order to provide a bone marrow match to save the life of their daughter Anissa. In your opinion, were they right to have a child for this purpose? Why or why not? Why is the case of the Ayalas relevant to the issue of cloning?

2. What, overall, is Kitcher's attitude toward cloning? Why does he believe that you would be "doomed to disappointment" if you tried to employ cloning in order to "design" the perfect son or daughter? What is he saying about the genetic basis of selfhood?

3. Under what conditions would Kitcher allow the use of cloning as a reproductive strategy? What ethical principles would guide his decision making? Would you agree that the case of the "loving lesbians" offers a more ethical scenario for cloning than that of the "dying child"? Why or why not?

4. What contradictions does Kitcher point out in relation to the government's sudden interest in the regulation of cloning? What inconsistencies does he find in the ethical principles of those who wish to ban cloning because of their respect for the autonomy of the self?

FURTHER EXPLORATIONS

1. Why might the issue of cloning one human being from another be particularly troubling in the context of contemporary Western notions of selfhood, as described by Roy F. Baumeister (p. 320)? Why might the emergence of the contemporary Western notion of the radically independent self help explain both our repugnance for and attraction to the possibility of cloning human beings?

2. How might Robert Sapolsky (p. 254), Arnold M. Ludwig (p. 292), and Mary Catherine Bateson (p. 337) respond to the question posed in the title of Kitcher's essay? To what extent do the notions of selfhood presented by these authors complicate the principle of individual autonomy that is often used to argue in favor of a ban on human cloning?

3. Compare Kitcher's attitude toward the self with that of Arnold M. Ludwig (p. 292) and Eviatar Zerubavel (p. 217). How "unique" or autonomous are individuals when seen from the perspective of social roles and historical memories? To what extent might the ideas of Ludwig and Zerubavel complicate Kitcher's view of the irreproducibility of a human self?

4. The theme of cloning has a long history in the genre of Hollywood horror and science-fiction films. View one or more movies dealing with the idea of cloning — films like *Invasion of the Body Snatchers, Gattaca, The Sixth Day,* or even the comedy *Multiplicity*—and discuss how the idea of cloning is presented. What motivates the cloning of human beings in these movies? What happens to people in these films when they are cloned? What "lessons" do these films convey about cloning?

ESSAY OPTIONS

1. Write an essay examining the notion that it is unethcial for parents to attempt to "create a child with specific attributes." To what extent do parents attempt to shape the skills and abilities of their naturally born children today? Should such attempts to "engineer" a child's sense of self be deemed unethical? Why or why not? Does predetermining a child's genetics or sex determine its attributes or destiny any more effectively than imposing a particular educational program on a child—or a particular form of religious training? Why or why not?

2. Using *Further Explorations* question number 4 as a point of departure, and supplementing it with additional research, write a paper in which you explore the way that cloning is depicted in popular culture. How has the topic of cloning been treated in films, television shows, comic books, and science-fiction stories and novels? What does the way we envision the meaning of cloning say about contemporary American culture, its fears and obsessions?

To Clone or Not to Clone

JEAN BETHKE ELSHTAIN

Can you imagine what it would be like to watch a stadium floor full of Michael Jordans play basketball or to hear an orchestra of Mozarts play a symphony? Well, Jean Bethke Elshtain did just that, and she didn't particularly care for it. For her, the answer to the question of whether "to clone or not to clone" is an emphatic "no." But Elshtain is tackling more in this essay than just the question of whether it should be legally permissible to clone human beings: she sees a hint of hubris in all forms of reproductive technology—a glorification of the self that goes way beyond the boundaries of good old-fashioned selfishness. Laura Spelman Rockefeller Professor of Social and Political Ethics at the University of Chicago, Elshtain (b. 1941) is a contributing editor to the *New Republic* and the author of a number of books on politics and philosophy, including *Democracy on Trial* (1995); *Augustine and the Limits of Politics* (1996); and, most recently, *Who Are We? Critical Reflections and Hopeful Possibilities* (2000).

BEFORE READING

Working in small groups, discuss what you think life would be like in a future society that allowed the cloning of human beings. What impact do you think cloning might have on individuals in the future? On society as a whole? Why?

Cloning is upon us. The techno-enthusiasts in our midst celebrate the collapse of yet another barrier to human mastery and control. But for most of us, this is an extraordinarily unsettling development. Talk to the man and woman in the street and you hear murmurs and rumblings and much dark musing about portents of the end-times and "now we've gone too far." The airwaves and the street win this one hands down, a welcome contrast to the celebratory glitz of *USA Today* trumpeting "Hello Dolly!"—Dolly being the name of the fetching ewe that faced the reader straight-on in a front page color photo announcing her cloned arrival. The subhead read, "Sheep cloning prompts ethical debate." The sheep looked perfectly normal, of course, and not terribly exercised about her historic significance. That she was really the child of no one—no one's little lamb—will probably not haunt her nights and bedevil her days. But we—we humans—should be haunted by Dolly and all the Dollies to come and by the prospect that others are to appear on this earth as the progeny of our omnipotent striving, our yearning to create without pausing to reflect on what we are destroying.

When I pondered cloning initially, a Chicago Bulls game was on television. The Bulls were clobbering the Spurs. Michael Jordan had just performed a typically superhuman feat, an assist that suggested he has eyes in the back of his head and two sets of arms. To one buoyant citizen—a rare optimist among the worriers—who called a local program to register his two cents worth on cloning, the prospect of "more Michael Jordans" made the whole "cloning thing" worthwhile. "Can you imagine a whole basketball team of Michael Jordans?" he queried giddily. Unfortunately, I could. It seemed to me then and seems to me now a nightmare. If there were basketball teams fielding Jordans against Jordans, we wouldn't be able to recognize the one, the only, Michael Jordan. It's rather like suggesting that forty Mozarts are better than one. But there would be no Mozart were there forty Mozarts. We know the singularity of the one; the extraordinary genius—a Jordan, a Mozart—because they stand apart from and above the rest. Absent that irreducible singularity, their gifts and glorious, soaring accomplishments would come to mean nothing as they would have become the norm, just commonplace. Another dunk; another concerto. In fact, lots of callers made this point, or one similar to it, reacting to the Michael Jordan Clontopia scenario.

A research librarian at a small college in India, who had driven me to her campus for the purpose of delivering a lecture, offered a spontaneous, sustained, and troubled critique of cloning that rivals the best dystopian fictions. Her cloning nightmare was a veritable army of Hitlers, ruthless and remorseless bigots and killers who kept reproducing themselves and were one day able to finish what the historic Hitler failed to accomplish. It occurred to me that an equal number of Mother Teresas would probably not be a viable deterrent, not if the Hitler clones were behaving like, well, Hitlers.

But I had my own nightmare scenario to offer. Imagine, I suggested to my librarian driver, a society that clones human beings to serve as spare parts. Because the cloned entities are not fully human, our moral queasiness could be disarmed and we could "harvest" organs to our heart's content—and organs from human beings of every age, race, phenotype at that. Harvesting organs from anencephalic newborns would, in that new world, be the equivalent of the Model T—an early and, it turns out, very rudimentary prototype of glorious, gleaming things to come.

Far-fetched? No longer. Besides, often the far-fetched gets us nearer the truth of the matter than all the cautious, persnickety pieces that fail to come anywhere close to the pity and terror this topic evokes. Consider Stanislaw Lem's *The Star Diaries*, in which his protagonist, Ijon Tichy, described as a "hapless Candide of the Cosmos," ventures into space encountering one weird situation after another. Lem's "Thirteenth Voyage" takes him to a planet, Panta, where he runs afoul of local custom and is accused of the worst of crimes, "the crime of personal differentiation." The evidence against him is incriminating. Nonetheless, Tichy is given an opportunity to conform. A planet spokesman offers a peroration to Tichy concerning the benefits of his planet, on which there are no separate entities—"only the collective."

For the denizens of Panta have come to understand that the source of all "the cares, sufferings and misfortunes to which beings, gathered together in societies, are prone" lies in the individual, "in his private identity." The individual, by contrast to the collective, is "characterized by uncertainty, indecision, inconsistency of action, and above all—by impermanence." Having "completely eliminated individuality," on planet Panta they have achieved "the highest degree of social interchangeability." It works rather the way the Marxist utopia was to function. Everyone at any moment can be anything else. Functions or roles are interchangeable. On Panta you occupy a role for twenty-four hours only: one day a gardener, the next an engineer, then a mason, now a judge.

The same principle holds with families. "Each is composed of relatives—there's a father, mother, children. Only the functions remain constant; the ones who perform them are changed every day." All feelings and emotions are entirely abstract. One never needs to grieve or to mourn as everyone is infinitely replaceable. "Afflection, respect, love were at one time gnawed by constant anxiety, by the fear of losing the person held dear. This dread we have conquered. For in point of fact whatever upheavals, diseases or calamities may be visited upon us, we shall always have a father, a mother, a spouse, and children." As well, there is no "I." And there can be no death "where there are no individuals. We do not die." Tichy can't quite get with the program. Brought before a court, he is "found guilty and condemned to life identification." He blasts off and sets his course for Earth.

Were Lem writing an addendum for his brilliant tale, he might show Tichy landing, believing he is at last on terra firma in both the literal and metaphorical sense, only to discover that the greeting party at the rocket-port is a bit strange: There are forty very tall basketball players all in identical uniforms wearing No. 23 jerseys, on one side and, on the other, forty men in powdered wigs, suited up in breeches and satin frock coats and playing identical pieces on identical harpsichords. Wrong planet? No more.

Sure, it's amusing, up to a point. But it was anything but amusing to overhear the speculation that cloning might be made available to parents about to lose a child to leukemia, or having lost a child to an accident, in order that they might reproduce and replace that lost child. This image borders on an obscenity. Perhaps we need a new word to describe what it represents, to capture fully what order of things the cloning of children in order to forestall human loss and grief violates. We say to little Tommy, in effect: "Sorry to lose you. But Tommy 2 is waiting in the wings." And what of Tommy 2? What happens when he learns he is the pinch hitter? "There was an earlier Tommy, much loved, so Mommy and Daddy had a copy made." But it isn't really Mommy and Daddy—it's the two people who placed the order for him and paid a huge sum. He's their little product; little fabricated Tommy 2, a techno-orphan. And Tommy 1 lies in the grave unmourned; undifferentiated in death; unremembered because he had been copied and his individuality wrenchingly obliterated.

The usual nostrums are of no use here. I have in mind the standard cliché that, once again, our "ethical thinking" hasn't caught up with technological "advance." This is a flawed way to reflect on cloning and so much else. The problem is not that we must somehow catch our ethics up to our technology.

The problem is that technology is rapidly gutting our ethics. And it is *our* ethics. Ethical reflection belongs to all of us—all those agitated radio callers—and it is the fears and apprehension of ordinary citizens that should be paid close and respectful attention. The ethicists are cut from the same cloth as everybody else. They breathe the same cultural air. They, too, are children of the West, of Judaism, Catholicism, the Renaissance, the Reformation, the Enlightenment. In the matter of cloning, we cannot wait for the experts. The queasiness the vast majority of Americans feel at this "remarkable achievement" is appropriate and should be aired and explored fully.

Perhaps something remarkable will finally happen. We will put the genie back into the bottle for a change. We will say, "No, stop, we will not go down this road." This doesn't make us antiscience or antiprogress or stodgy sticks-in-the-mud. It makes us skeptical, alert, and, yes, frightened citizens asking the question: Whatever will become of the ancient prayer, "That I may see my children's children and peace upon Israel," in a world of cloned entities, peopled by the children of No Body, copies of our selves? These poor children of our fantasies and our drive to perfect and our arrogant search for dominion: What are we to say to them? Forgive us, for we knew not what we were doing? That tastes bitter on the tongue. We knew what we were doing and we did it anyway. Of whom will we ask forgiveness? Who will be there to listen? Who to absolve?

Are these the musings of an alarmist, a technophobe, a Luddite? Consider that there are now cloned calves in Wisconsin and cloned rodents in various laboratories worldwide. Cloned company is bursting out all over: thus far none of it human. The clone enthusiasts will surely find a way, however. Dolly's creator or producer or manufacturer—hard to know what to call him—thinks human cloning is a bad idea. But others are not nearly so reticent. Consider, then, some further developments on the cloning and related fronts that promise, or threaten, to alter our relation to our bodies, our selves.

A big story of the moment—and a huge step toward human cloning—lies in the fertile field of infertility science: the world of human reproductive technology. Many procedures once considered radical are by now routine. These include in vitro fertilization, embryo flushing, surrogate embryo transfer, and sex preselection, among others. Now comes Dr. Mark Sauer, described by the *New York Times* as "an infertility expert at Columbia Presbyterian Medical Center in New York" who "dreams of offering his patients a type of cloning some day." It would work like this. You take a two- or three-day-old human embryo and use its cells—there are only about eight at this stage—to grow identical embryos where once there was only one. The next step is to implant "some" of these embryos in a woman's uterus immediately and freeze the extras. And what are the plans for the clonettes in cold storage? Well, initial attempts at impregnation may fail. So you have some spare embryos for a second, third, or fourth try. Suppose the woman successfully carries the initial implants to term. She may want more babies—identical babies—and the embryos are there for future use. The upshot, of course, is that a woman could wind up with "identical twins, triplets, or even quadruplets, possibly born years apart."

And why would anyone want this, considering the potentially shattering questions it presents to the identity and integrity of the children involved? Dr. Sauer has an answer. Otherwise there "might be no babies at all." To be sure, the premise of this procedure isn't as obviously morally repugnant as the scenario noted above, the speculation that cloning might be made available to parents about to lose a child to leukemia or, having lost a child to an accident, in order that they might reproduce and replace that child, as I noted already.

Rather, the debate about this latest embryo cloning scenario, by contrast, rages around whether or not this is, in fact, cloning at all or whether it is a version of cloning that is more or less questionable than the standard or classic form: the Dolly scenario. Dr. Sauer and other enthusiasts say that because cloning is a "politically dirty word"—there is, apparently, no real ethical issue here—they hope that their proposed method of crypto-cloning may slip under the radar screen. Besides, he avers, it's much better for the women involved: You don't have to give them lots of drugs to "force their ovaries to pump out multiple eggs so that they could fertilize them and create as many embryos as possible."

Again, why are so many women putting themselves through this? And why has this been surrounded by the halo of "rights"? You can be sure, once word gets around, that the more "attractive" idea (in the words of another infertility specialist) of replicating embryos will generate political demands. A group will spring up proclaiming "embryo duplication rights" just as an outfit emerged instantly after Dolly was announced arguing that to clone oneself was a fundamental right. Several of the infertility specialists cited in the *Times* piece, all male doctors, interestingly enough, spoke of the pleading of women, of "the misery my patients are living through." But surely a good bit of that misery comes from having expectations lifted out of all proportion in relation to chances of success (with procedures like in vitro), only to find, time and time again, that the miracle of modern medicine has turned into an invasive, expensive, mind-bending, heart-rending dud. A doleful denouement to high-tech-generated expectations and the playing out of "reproductive freedom."

Whatever happened to accepting embodied limits with better grace? There are many ways to enact what the late Erik Erikson called "generative" projects and lives. Biological parenthood is one but not the only one. Many of the women we call great from our own history—I think here of one of my own heroes—Jane Addams of Hull-House—were not mothers although they did an extraordinary amount of mothering. Either through necessity or choice, she and many others offered their lives in service to civic or religious projects that located them in a world of relationships over the years with children not their own that involved loving concern, care, friendship, nurture, protection, discipline, pride, disappointment: all the complex virtues, habits, and emotions called forth by biological parenting.

And there is adoption, notwithstanding the frustrations many encounter and the fear instilled by such outrageous violations of decency as the holding in the "Baby Richard" and other recent cases in which children were wrenched from the only family they had ever known in order to be returned to a bioparent claimant who had discovered belatedly the overwhelming need to be a father or mother. How odd that biology now trumps nearly all other claims and desires. In several texts I've encountered recently, adoption is surrounded with a faintly sinister odor and treated as an activity not all that different from baby selling. Somehow all these developments — the insistent urge to reproduce through any means necessary and the emergence of a multimillion-dollars-a-year specialty devoted to precisely that task; the diminution of the integrity of adoption in favor of often dubious claims from bioparents; the possibility, now, of cloning embryos in order to guarantee more or less identical offspring to a desperate couple — are linked.

What common threads tie these disparate activities together? How does one account for the fact that the resurgence of feminism over the past thirty years and enhanced pressures on women, many of them placed on women by themselves, to reproduce biologically have emerged in tandem? Why are these developments surrounded by such a desperate aura and a sense of misery and failure — including the failure of many marriages that cannot survive the tumult of infertility high-tech-medicine's intrusion into a couple's intimate lives? Let's try out one possible explanation. Here at the end of the twentieth century we all care mightily about identity: who we are. Sometimes this takes the form of identity politics in which one's own identity gets submerged into that of a group, likely a group defined in biological or quasi-biological terms on grounds of sex, race, or ethnicity. That's problematic enough as a basis for politics, to say the least. But we've further compounded the biological urgencies, upping the ante to bear one's "own" child as a measure of the success or failure of the self.

Mind you, I do not want to downplay how heartbreaking it is for many couples who want to have a baby and cannot. But, again, there are many ways to parent and many babies desperate for loving families. Rather than to expand our sense of gracious acceptance of those who may not be our direct biological offspring, which means accepting our own limits but coming to see that these open up other possibilities, we rail against cruel fate and reckon ourselves nigh-worthless persons if we fail biologically. Perhaps with so much up for grabs, in light of the incessant drumbeat to be all we can be, to achieve, to produce, to succeed, to define our own projects, to be the sole creators of our own destinies, we have fallen back on the bedrock of biology. When all that is solid is melting into air, maybe biology seems the last redoubt of solidity, of identity. But, of course, this is chimerical. In demanding of our bodies what they sometimes cannot give, our world grows smaller, our focus more singular if not obsessive, and identity itself is called into question: our own and that of our future, identical offspring.

EXPLORING THE TEXT

1. What nightmare scenarios does Elshtain envision about the future of human cloning? What makes these visions particularly repugnant in her view? To what extent would you agree with her?

2. Why does Elshtain object to other forms of reproductive technology, such as in vitro fertilization and sex preselection? Would you agree that these forms of "reproductive freedom," as she calls them, represent "a huge step toward cloning"? Why or why not?

3. What's wrong, in Elshtain's view, with Dr. Mark Sauer's dream of "cloning" multiple siblings from a single embryo? What "potentially shattering questions" might such a procedure raise about the "identity and integrity" of the children involved? Why would the production of identical siblings through this method differ, in terms of ethical considerations or psychological impact, from the natural production of twins or triplets?

4. Why, according to Elshtain, are contemporary women apparently unwilling to accept what she calls the "embodied limits" they encounter in life? How does she explain why so many couples today spend so much on fertility technology instead of considering adoption? What, in her view, does this suggest about our values and our view of selfhood?

5. What does Elshtain mean when she says that "biology seems the last redoubt of solidity, of identity"? What evidence does she offer to support the notion that we as a culture have begun to view biology—genetic inheritance—as the most fundamental aspect of the self? Would you agree that most people today think of biological inheritance as the primary basis of personal identity? Why or why not?

FURTHER EXPLORATIONS

1. How might Elshtain respond to the Ayala family's decision to have a child in order to provide a bone marrow implant for their leukemia-stricken daughter, as described by Philip Kitcher in "Whose Self Is It, Anyway?" (p. 350)? How does her view of the parent-child relationship in cloning differ from Kitcher's? How might Kitcher respond to her concern about the possible cloning of whole teams of Michael Jordans or whole armies of Adolf Hitlers? What, if anything, might Elshtain and Kitcher agree about in relation to the topic of human cloning?

2. How might Roy F. Baumeister's analysis of the historical development of the self (p. 320) help explain the current obsession with biological parenting that Elshtain notes in this essay? Given Baumeister's view of the emerging "female self" in American culture, is it likely that women will accept "embodied limits" as Elshtain suggests? To what extent might cloning be seen as the logical—or illogical—outcome of a society obsessed with selfhood?

3. How might the relationship between concepts of the self and power as discussed by Robert Sapolsky (p. 254) and Mary Catherine Bateson (p. 337), support Elshtain's assertion that cloning expresses "our drive to perfect and our arrogant search for dominion"? What would cloning give us power over? What, if anything, would be wrong with extending human "dominion" in this way?

4. How might John (Fire) Lame Deer view the possibility of reproducing human beings by means of cloning (p. 512)? What deep-seated fear within "white culture" might cloning express in Lame Deer's view?

ESSAY OPTION

Using library and online resources, do additional research on the arguments made for and against the legalization of human cloning. What concerns are raised by opponents of cloning research? How are these concerns answered by its proponents? What arguments are advanced in support of human cloning? Drawing on this independent research and the reading you have done in this chapter, write a paper in which you present your own position on whether human cloning should be banned or allowed under certain conditions.

4

Reading Other Minds
Inside the Black Box

Good Intentions

In the award-winning 1988 film *Rain Man,* Dustin Hoffman plays a character with an extraordinary mind. When we meet him, Raymond Babbitt has been institutionalized for most of his adult life. Like many "high level" autistics, Raymond is a genius when it comes to feats of perception or memory: he can total the contents of a box of toothpicks the moment it hits the floor, calculate the square roots of multidigit numbers in the blink of an eye, and recite the schedule for every television show on every channel every week without consulting *TV Guide.* But when it comes to social interaction, Raymond is a disaster. He has trouble sustaining eye contact with other people and responding appropriately to their questions and comments. Dealing with family members makes him hysterical; dealing with strangers leads to paralysis. Head bowed, shoulders hunched, his voice flattened into a monotone, Raymond Babbit lives in a state of permanent semiwithdrawal from the world. The simplest social transaction—a casual question or a friendly greeting—is enough to send him into a panic attack or running for cover.

Although the cause of autism remains a mystery, most psychologists agree that it involves what's known as "theory of mind." Most of us are lucky enough to come equipped with a well-functioning theory of mind. Sometime during our first few years of life, we make an enormous mental leap: we realize that even though we can't see them or touch them the people around us also have minds—minds that resemble ours in many ways, but that are also independent of ours in terms of the thoughts, ideas, intentions, and beliefs they contain. Armed with a theory of mind, a child can predict what another child knows or wants to do. Say, for example, that two healthy four-year-olds see an adult put some candy in a box, and then, after one of the kids leaves the room, the adult takes the candy out again and puts it in his pocket. Theory of mind tells the witness to these adult shenanigans that the poor kid outside the door will still think that there's candy in the box and that he may even be willing to trade something precious to get it. By contrast, an autistic child in similar circumstances probably won't be able to put himself into the place of his less-informed counterpart. He'll assume the child outside the room knows what he knows—and lose the chance to take advantage of his friend.

Our ability to understand the workings of other minds—to read them—is so central to human consciousness that we tend to take it for granted. We depend on our ability to predict the thoughts and intentions of others to guide us through every social transaction—from buying groceries at the supermarket to falling in love—yet we rarely stop to reflect on what a miracle mind reading really is. The mind of another person is by far the most mysterious object any of us will ever encounter. It's about the only thing in the natural world that we can't see, hear, or touch. We may be able to measure the brain's electrical activity through encephalography or map its structure by means of magnetic imaging technology, but none of our scientific techniques show us the inner workings of someone else's consciousness. As cognitive science has long recognized, the mind is a "black box" — a hermetically sealed region of hidden intentions, desires, and emotions, accessible only to the self it contains.

Yet, despite the mystery that shrouds other minds, most of us are expert mind readers. As a species, we spend a remarkable amount of time brooding on the thoughts and feelings of others. And with good reason. If you can sense a lie even when it's told with a smiling face or predict the intentions of the powerful, you'll probably go far in this world. But mind reading isn't just about gaining an advantage over our friends and bosses; it's also about sympathy and connection. Having an operative theory of mind allows us not only to read other people's intentions, but also to comprehend their needs and emotions. Know the old saying about "walking a mile in another person's shoes"? Well, theory of mind is what makes this kind of empathetic identification possible. Without the ability to empathize with others, we wouldn't be able to predict how our actions might affect the people around us. Without the ability to project our consciousness into others, we wouldn't be able to feel sympathy, friendship, or love. In fact, we humans are so hooked on empathy that we tend to attribute intentions and feelings to all kinds of "beings" — everything from cars to computers. Think of all the times you've felt that your laptop or your car malfunctioned just to spite you. It's hard *not* to take these mechanical insults personally.

Theory of mind works best when we read minds within a familiar cultural context. In fact, culture can be thought of as a system of rules, cues, and assumptions that makes it possible to sustain a theory of mind. Cultures provide the people who belong to them a kind of mental codebook for reading the intentions of others. When you walk into a college classroom, you don't have to guess what will happen or how people will act. Your knowledge of "college culture" provides you with a mental guidebook of assumptions about how students and teachers behave, what they will expect of each other, and how they will interact. You expect your professor to stand in the front of the class, to address you as a group, and to tell you something worth learning. You assume that she expects you to listen, take notes, and perhaps offer an occasional question or comment. You also assume she thinks her subject is important and that she won't respond positively if you dial up a friend on your cell phone or fire up your portable Playstation for a quick game of Doom. Cultures tell us what's expected of us and what we can expect of others in different social contexts. They provide us with the symbolic languages we use when we read other minds.

But just as culture can further our ability to read other minds, it can also blind us to the feelings and intentions of others. Mind reading becomes a risky business when different cultures collide. The bowed head and averted eyes that signify respect for one group of people, may, for example, signal shame or even hostility in other social contexts. Depending on your point of view, a casual touch on the shoulder might be read as an act of friendship, a sign of condescension, an effort to dominate, or an embarrassing sexual advance. During the past few decades, Americans have learned to acknowledge the demands of this kind of cultural "relativism." We've learned to recognize the role that cultures play in shaping our expectations, responses, and intentions. We've even learned to allow others to speak for themselves. But real understanding means more than simply giving different groups equal time for self-explanation. Mind reading across cultural boundaries means learning to appreciate how the cultures you participate in shape your own assumptions, perceptions, expectations, and intentions. To climb inside the shoes of someone else, you first have to learn how to read your own mind as if you yourself were someone "other." You have to start seeing yourself from the "other's" point of view.

Of course, the truth is that we can never really say for sure what's going on in another person's consciousness. In fact, it's doubtful that we can pin down everything that's going on in our own from moment to moment. Even within the context of a single culture, other, often more profound, differences may keep us from simply "tuning in" to the thoughts of other people — differences of gender, generation, education, social class, personal style, interests, experience — all of the things that contribute to the recipe of a human self. Mind reading, then, is never really more than an educated guess. Yet, despite the obvious absurdity of the enterprise, we don't have much of a choice. Our survival as individuals and as a species has long depended on our ability to predict the intentions and responses of other intelligent creatures. Simply put, without the ability to anticipate the mental states of other minds, we would not be who we are today. And given the problems of prejudice, group hatred, and the seemingly irrational violence that continues to pervade contemporary America and the world at large, the need to read other minds accurately and compassionately has never been more urgent.

Readers as "Others"

For a writer, the ultimate "other" is always the reader. Although the reader is never physically present when a writer sits down to put pen to paper, writers are acutely aware of the impact that their words and ideas will have on their readers' minds. That's one of the reasons why learning to write can be such a challenge: in order to write well, you have to be constantly aware of someone who's *not* there — someone whose expectations and responses help you shape the content and order of your thoughts — someone whose mind will eventually grapple with the task of reading *you*. Good writers have internalized this attention to their readers' expectations. They use it to anticipate the information their readers will need, the order they'll need it in, the level of explanation and illustration their readers will require, and the nature of their probable responses to what they write. In fact, at this moment, I'm wondering if you might need a concrete example to understand just what I'm getting at, so take a few moments now to read the introductory paragraphs of Andrew Sullivan's "What's So Bad About Hate?":

I wonder what was going on in John William King's head two years ago when he tied James Byrd Jr.'s feet to the back of a pickup truck and dragged him three miles down a road in rural Texas. King and two friends had picked up Byrd, who was black, when he was walking home, half drunk, from a party. As part of a bonding ritual in their fledgling white supremacist group, the three men took Byrd to a remote part of town, beat him, and chained his legs together before attaching them to the truck. Pathologists at King's trial testified that Byrd was probably alive and conscious until his body finally hit a culvert and split in two. When King was offered a chance to say something to Byrd's family at the trial, he smirked and uttered an obscenity.

We know all these details now, many months later. We know quite a large amount about what happened before and after. But I am still drawn, again and again, to the flash of ignition, the moment when fear and loathing became hate, the instant of transformation when King became hunter and Byrd became prey.

What was that? And what was it when Buford Furrow Jr., long-time member of the Aryan Nations, calmly walked up to a Filipino American mailman he happened to spot, asked him to mail a letter, and then shot him at point-blank range? Or when Russell Henderson beat Matthew Shepard, a young gay man, to a pulp, removed his shoes, and then, with the help of a friend, tied him to a post, like a dead coyote, to warn off others?

For all our documentation of these crimes and others, our political and moral disgust at them, our morbid fascination with them, our sensitivity to their social meaning, we seem at times to have no better idea now than we ever had of what exactly they were about. About what that moment means when, for some reason or other, one human being asserts absolute, immutable superiority over another. About not the violence, but what the violence expresses. About what—exactly— hate is. And what our own part in it may be. (182–83)

It's difficult to read about the brutal events Sullivan offers to open his essay, and it's clear that Sullivan wants us to feel upset when we first encounter them. He knows that his topic—the nature of hate—is explosive, and he's deliberately recounting some of the worst examples of recent "hate crimes" to rivet his reader's attention on his topic and to stir up the reader's disgust against those who do such things. He wants us to engage the issue on this emotional level because, as he suggests in the final sentence quoted above, he plans to address what he views as "our own part" in the problem of hatred. What better way to get us focused on the power of hate and our part in it than to get us hating those who commit acts of hatred?

Although it's not always done so dramatically, most effective writers work to draw their readers into their subject in this way. You know that Sullivan's essay is about hate from the essay's title alone; by the time you've finished the first paragraph, you know it's about the kind of hate associated with prejudice; and by the time you've finished the second, you know it's addressing the nature of hate in the minds of those who resort to violence. Sullivan "rolls out" his subject, step by step, in this manner, because he recognizes that his readers need time to orient themselves to his topic and to begin to grasp his point of view. He also pays close attention to the level of detail and explanation that we require. He offers us enough background information about each crime to assure that we can appreciate his motive for writing, but he never allows the essay to become bogged down in unneeded detail. By the fourth paragraph, Sullivan makes the main focus of his essay explicit: he's going to explore "what hate is. And what our own part in it may be." Skillful writers spell out such controlling ideas not because they know that every essay has to have a "thesis," but because they understand that readers need explicit statements of a writer's intentions and that these explicit statements help readers form expectations about what they'll encounter later in the essay.

This isn't to suggest, however, that you should do exactly what Sullivan does when you structure the introduction of your next essay. I'm not offering him as a model of the ideal opening strategy. In fact, you'd probably run into trouble if you took four paragraphs to get your essay started. The point is that you need to start seeing your work through your reader's eyes if you are going to grow as a writer. Almost every decision a writer makes (even the decision to use a "transitional phrase" like "however" as I did in the first sentence of this paragraph) is made because an author is imagining how the reader will experience and respond to the words he's writing. Good writers constantly ask themselves if the reader will understand key concepts, if readers need more illustrations and examples, if two bits of evidence is enough to be convincing, or if the reader needs the extra support of a transitional word or phrase to follow the logical flow of an argument. Getting into the habit of thinking about the needs, questions, and responses of the reader is the only way to develop rhetorical sensitivity—the kind of mind-reading skill that will free you from the "rules" of compositions so you can begin to experiment with your own creative approaches to what you write.

Chapter Overview

In this chapter, you'll encounter selections that invite you to reflect on mind reading in a variety of different contexts. The chapter begins with a trio of readings on the nature of interpersonal understanding. Computer scientist Roger C. Schank leads off with his theory of story-based understanding through an experiment involving film clips from two popular Hollywood movies. Next, "Sonny's Blues," James Baldwin's classic short story about brothers with conflicting values and lifestyles, illustrates Schank's theory of story-based understanding and offers an example of how we can misconstrue one another even within a shared cultural context. The section concludes with a selection on the power of empathy by University of Chicago philosopher Martha C. Nussbaum. In "The Narrative Imagination," Nussbaum argues that works of literature—like Baldwin's "Sonny's Blues"—help us develop the ability to empathize with minds that are unlike our own and that the act of imaginatively identifying with fictional others prepares us for life in a culturally diverse, democratic society.

The next pair of readings focuses on the challenges of mind reading across cultures. Anthropologist Edward T. Hall's "Hidden Culture" offers a theoretical context for the discussion of cross-cultural miscommunication as well as an extended practical example from Hall's own experience as an American adapting to Japanese values and traditions. In "Mrs. Cassadore," Mick Fedullo describes how he struggled to overcome the assumptions of his own Anglo background in order to understand the mind of woman on an Apache reservation where he taught tribal students how to cope with white culture. Science writer Deborah Blum follows with "Heart to Heart: Sex Differences in Emotion," a selection from her book *Sex on the Brain: The Biological Differences Between Men and Women.* Blum's survey of the differing interests, aptitudes, strengths, and weaknesses of male and female minds raises the issue of cross-gender mind reading and is sure to spark debate about whether there, in fact, are male and female minds.

The chapter closes with two selections that invite us to think about how we read—or fail to read—violent minds. Andrew Sullivan's "What's So Bad About Hate?" challenges us not only to rethink the need for "hate crime" legislation, but to empathize with some of the most notorious young criminal minds in recent history. In "Rejected and Neglected, Ashamed and Depressed," psychologist James Garbarino offers his interpretation of what goes on in the minds of the suburban teenage killers whose story has become all too common in contemporary America.

Sources

Baron-Cohen, S. *Mindblindness: An Essay on Autism and Theory of Mind.* Cambridge: MIT, 1995.

Dennett, Daniel C. *The Intentional Stance.* Cambridge: MIT, 1993.

O'Connell, Sanjida. *Mindreading: An Investigation into How We Learn to Love and Lie.* New York: Doubleday, 1997.

Sullivan, Andrew W. "What's So Bad About Hate?" *New York Times Magazine.* 26 September 1999.

Understanding Other People's Stories

ROGER C. SCHANK

According to Roger C. Schank, most of the time we don't really understand the things that other people tell us. A leading figure in the field of artificial intelligence, Schank has devoted his professional life to the challenge of building machines that think just the way we do. The key to human thought, according to Schank, lies in storytelling. Everything we perceive, every event we experience, every bit of information we know gets embedded in a story that we can remember at will and share with others. Events and information that fail to connect with the stories we know are lost forever—forgotten in the course of daily events. In this selection from Tell Me a Story: Narrative and

Intelligence (1990), Schank presents the results of an informal experiment in story-based understanding. To test his theory, Schank asked some students to watch excerpts from two Hollywood films—*Diner* and *The Breakfast Club*—featuring characters telling stories about their lives. Then he invited his subjects to respond to these personal stories by telling stories of their own. Schank's findings suggest that while we usually feel it's easy to appreciate the experiences of others, we're actually trapped by the stories we already know. During his career, Schank (b. 1946) has served as chair of the Computer Science Department at Yale University and as professor of linguistics and computer science at Stanford. Currently, he is the director of the Institute for Learning Sciences and John Evans Professor of Electrical Engineering and Computer Science at Northwestern University. His publications include *The Cognitive Computer: On Language, Learning, and Artificial Intelligence* (1984), *Explanation Patterns: Understanding Mechanically and Creatively* (1986), *The Connoisseur's Guide to the Mind: How We Think, How We Learn, and What It Means to Be Intelligent* (1991), *Coloring Outside the Lines: Raising a Smarter Kid by Breaking all the Rules* (2000), and *Scrooge Meets Dick and Jane* (2001).

BEFORE READING

Think back to a specific story you remember hearing recently from a friend or relative. What was the point of this anecdote? How could you "prove" that you understood it?

L et me tell a story: I went to visit a cousin of mine who is curious about why family members turned out the way they did. She asked me whether I knew anything of interest about our mutual grandfather. I told her my father always says his father (our grandfather) never really talked to or had much time for him. My father explains this reticence in a variety of ways having to do with how much work my grandfather had to do. Recently, however, I heard that whenever he didn't have much work, my grandfather would go to the movies by himself. My cousin was very excited by this information and ran to tell her grown-up daughter. It seems that both my cousin and her daughter have the habit of going to the movies alone and thought that they were quite odd to do this. They found something fascinating about the fact that their ancestor did the same thing. I found it all quite confusing myself. My cousin and her daughter are very gregarious people. My grandfather never spoke to anybody. My point was that growing up with this man as a father was probably difficult. My cousin's point was something else entirely. When I noted the differences in our perspective, she was too excited about discovering our grandfather's predisposition for going to the movies alone to consider another point of view.

People are only able to hear part of what is being said to them. Some of the reasons for this are obvious. Most of what we hear is complex and has so many possible avenues of interpretation and provides so many possible inference paths that people must make their choices as they listen. We cannot think about all the possible ramifications of something we are being told. So we pay attention to what interests us.

Interest can be expressed in a variety of ways, but one way is to focus on the things you were looking for, ignoring the things you were not prepared to deal with. Another way to look at this is to take the view that, since we can only understand things that relate to our own experiences, it is actually very difficult to hear things that people say to us that are not interpretable through those experiences. In other words, we hear what we are capable of hearing. When what we hear relates to what we know, what we care about, or what we were prepared to hear, we can understand quite easily what someone is saying to us. If we have heard the same story or a similar story before we can also understand more easily what we are being told.

Understanding, for a listener, means mapping the speaker's stories onto the listener's stories. One of the most interesting aspects of the way stories are used in memory is the effect they have on understanding. Different people understand the same story differently precisely because the stories they already know are different. Understanders attempt to construe new stories that they hear as old stories they have heard before. It follows then that one of the major problems in understanding is identifying which of all the stories you already know is being told to you yet again.

In the shallowest form of understanding, a hearer has only one story that he wants to tell. No matter what you say to him, he tells you his story. He understands what you say as something that reminds him of the story that he wanted to tell in the first place. Thus, his understanding algorithm needn't have more in it than a detector for when you have stopped talking, and perhaps he doesn't even need that. One typical case of this kind of understanding involves people who we might label as crazy, people who just rattle on without regard to the world around them.

In the world of computers, we have an analog in machines that do their thing irrespective of the wishes of the user because the user either doesn't know how to communicate instructions to the machine or else doesn't know how to stop the machine once it has begun to do its thing. The crazy person or the user-hostile computer has a story to tell, and it may not really care about whether you want to hear that story. For them, understanding means no more than unrestrained storytelling.

A less shallow form of understanding takes place when listeners with many stories to tell pay enough attention to what you have said in order to relate the story in their repertoire that is most closely connected to what they have heard. But, in a sense, this still seemingly shallow understanding may be all we can really expect most of the time. Now, this view may seem rather radical. After all, we do see and hear new things every day. To say that we never have to understand any story that is brand-new may be overstating the case. And, of course, we do get presented with new stories. My point is that we don't really understand them.

Well, more accurately, we don't understand them as new stories. They may be new enough, but we nevertheless persist in seeing them as old stories. To understand what I mean here, consider the possibility of this hypothesis in its strongest form. Let us assume an understander who knows three stories. No matter what story you tell him, he will tell one of his three stories back. If understanding means matching the story we are hearing to the stories we have already heard, the strong form of my hypothesis states that an understander must decide which of the three stories he knows is most applicable. When he has found some way to relate the new story to an old one that he knows, we can claim that he has understood the new story as well as could be hoped for.

Looked at this way, the strong hypothesis appears somewhat silly. Why should we label as "understanding" a process that merely differentiates among three stories? In some sense, we shouldn't. But let's consider the same situation where the understander knows ten thousand stories. When he selects one to tell as a response to the new one that he has heard, he will most likely seem more profound than the understander who has only three stories. If he has used sound principles for selecting a story to tell from his data base of ten thousand, we are unlikely to dispute his having understood the original story. But naturally the process of understanding in both cases is identical; only our subjective judgment allows us to decide that one understander seems to have "really" understood. We cannot look inside people's heads to see what the difference in their understanding of a new story is; therefore, from an objective evaluation of the output alone, we still can measure understanding only by how effectively and reasonably we think the responsive story relates to the input story.

Now, my argument here is that all that people are doing when they understand is figuring out what story to tell. . . . In some sense, then, no two people can really understand a story in the same way. You can't understand a story that you haven't previously understood because understanding means finding (and telling) a story that you have previously understood. Finding some familiar element causes us to activate the story that is labeled by that familiar element, and we understand the new story as if it were an exemplar of that old element. In this way, we find things to say to those who talk to us. These things differ considerably from person to person, thus accounting for the very different ways in which two people can understand the same story. . . .

Indexing Stories

If our knowledge is really a collection of hundreds of thousands of stories, then finding the one we need leaves us with a massive indexing problem. Of course, finding stories is a problem that people seem to manage with some ease, if not with perfection. So we probably have some method that works. To see what I mean here, let's consider an actual situation of story understanding.

A group of people heard two monologues from the movies *Diner* and *The Breakfast Club*. In each monologue, the speaker tells some listeners about a problem of his. The subjects in this informal experiment were asked to imagine that they were the friend whose advice was being solicited or to expect that, as conversational partners, they would have to say something back. The subjects were asked, therefore, to tell a story or to give some advice or to comment in any way that came to mind. . . .

Here is the first story, from *Diner*, exactly as it was read to the students, from *The Actor's Book of Movie Monologues* (Marisa Smith and Amy Schewel, eds.; New York: Penguin, 1986).

TIME: 1959

PLACE: Baltimore, Maryland

A group of six high-school friends get together around the Christmas–New Year holidays. Most of them have stayed in town after graduation. Shrevie, the first of the group to get married, works in an appliance store and nurtures his obsession for his record collection. He can tell you what's on the flip side of practically every record he owns. His collection is kept in frighteningly fastidious condition—with a detailed system of categories that would put the Library of Congress to shame.

Eddie, his pal, a ferociously loyal Baltimore Colts fan, is planning on marrying Elise on New Year's Eve on the condition that she pass an outrageously difficult football quiz he has prepared for her. One night, in front of the local diner where the guys hang out, two days before the test, three days before the wedding, Eddie asks Shrevie if he's happy with his marriage to his wife, Beth. Shrevie answers.

SHREVIE: You know the big part of the problem? When we were dating we spent most of our time talking about sex. *Why* couldn't I do it? *Where* could we do it? Were her parents going to be out *so* we could do it. Talking about being alone for a weekend. A whole night. You know. Everything was talking about gettin' sex or planning our wedding. Then when you're married . . . It's crazy. You can have it whenever you want. You wake up. She's there. You come home from work. She's there. So all the sex-planning talk is over. And the wedding-planning talk. We can sit up here and bullshit the night away, but I can't have a five-minute conversation with Beth. But I'm not putting the blame on her. We've just got nothing to talk about.

The first subject chose to tell a story about a friend of his:

SUBJECT 1:   In high school, I had a friend named Larry who was a couple of years older than me. We were the two computer jocks in school. His dad had died, and his mother was sort of on hard times. But Larry was doing OK, and we used to go to the beach together. We had this great arrangement with the computer teacher. The teacher would teach one day, and we would teach one day. This was summer school. The day that we taught the teacher would take off, and the day the teacher taught, we would take off and go to the beach. It was a great way to get summer school credit. I think about where I am now, and where Larry is. Larry didn't go to college. He didn't really take his hacking talents anywhere. He got married as soon as he got out of high school. He was a manager of a Shakey's in Hollywood. Now he's a group manager at Shakey's in Mar Vista, and he's married to this stupid woman. It's really a sad story. The guy just exploded—and he had all that potential. He just didn't know what to do once he got out of high school. He didn't know what to do with himself, so he got married and got a job like he was supposed to.

One thing that we do when we understand a story is to relate that story   15
to something in our own lives. But to what? One thing seems clear. Potentially, we can see Shrevie's story in many ways. Subject 1 understood Shrevie's story by relating it to one about a friend of his whose life never amounted to much. In other words, according to his value system, he saw Shrevie's statement as a story about how one can get trapped into a dull life by marrying right out of high school. To put this another way, Subject 1 seems to believe that marrying too young leads to a dull and pointless life. Subject 1 also probably believed this prior to hearing Shrevie's story. Thus, we know two things. First, Subject 1 drew a conclusion from Shrevie's story that confirmed a view he already had about the perils of marrying too early. Second, he already had labeled a story in his own memory with such an index.

So the first index we shall identify is:

INDEX 1:   Marrying too early can lead to a dull and pointless life.

Actually, we cannot say for sure that this is the index that Subject 1 used. What other matches are there between Subject 1's story and Shrevie's story? Both stories are also about the following:

INDEX 2:   Blindly following scripts that are chosen for you in life can cause you to raise questions when it is too late.

This index, also, might not be the one that Subject 1 actually used, although clearly Subject 1 believes this generally and believes this about Shrevie specifically. However, and here is the important point, the story that Subject 1 heard, namely a story about the futility of early marriage, was not the same story that the other subjects heard at all.

Now let's consider how Subject 2's understanding of Shrevie's story differed from Subject 1's understanding:

SUBJECT 2:   I had the same experience. Basically you desire things that you can't have, and often once you can have them, you don't desire them as much. I remember that with a woman I was always interested in sexually over the course of many years. Either she had boyfriends or I had girlfriends, and we never consummated our relationship. For four or five years, I always kept in contact with her, wrote letters, and so forth, but independently of anything else, I considered her a friend. A year or two ago, we did end up having sex. What's interesting to me is that, afterwards, I wasn't all that interested in her friendship. Now we sort of occasionally make efforts to see each other, but I find that I don't have much motivation. It's very disillusioning. I realize that most of my interest in her must have been sexual, particularly in trying to get something I couldn't have, and not in her, herself. That reminds me of this situation. You seem to be saying a similar thing which is that you thought you really loved your wife when she was your fiancée, but now that you have her, you realize that what you really wanted was the conquest. Part of it is political. I guess the opposite story that I could tell is about a woman I knew a year ago. I saw her for about two months, very heavily, but it was a platonic relationship pretty much because she had a boyfriend, and we were still trying to decide what would happen if we didn't want to meet behind his back. In the end, she decided to stay with him. She has remained in my mind very, very strongly. I think the reason for this is that I didn't succeed in the conquest. So she occupies my imagination disproportionately. Well, is there any solution to this? One relationship that I had was very successful for three years. Why did it survive once we had sex very regularly? I think the answer is that there has to be a lot of intrinsic interest in the person outside of sex and the relationship. So if it is just the conquest, then you lose interest. It's not that having sex makes it less interesting—it's more that what really is often at issue is the power relationship. If that's all there is to the relationship, making the conquest, then it won't last.

Subject 2 sees Shrevie's story as a story about sex, not early marriage. He understands Shrevie to be saying that he got married as a way of getting sex on a regular basis. Here are some of the indices that Subject 2 explicitly mentions:

INDEX 3:   You desire things you can't have, and then when you can have them you don't desire them so much.

INDEX 4:   Desiring sex clouds your judgment about whether you really like and want to spend time with the person you desire.

INDEX 5:   Good relationships depend upon intrinsic interest in a person, not sex.

INDEX 6:   The exercise of power in the form of sexual conquests can be a strong motivating force.

Notice that while this interpretation is a perfectly reasonable way to understand Shrevie's story, it simply isn't the way Subject 1 understood it. Subject 1 sees the story as one about the promise of life unfulfilled. Subject 2 sees this story as one about the hazards of thinking with your sex organ. Clearly, this story is about both of these things. Surely Subjects 1 and 2 would agree that the other's interpretation is valid, but what each learned from the story is different.

One question to ask here is what kind of animals these indices are. They look a great deal like beliefs. In a sense, I am arguing that each subject learned very little precisely because they both saw the stories as simply verifying already-held beliefs. The four indices above are certainly things that Subject 2 believes, but they are also labels that the mind uses to find what it knows. It almost couldn't be any other way.

Consider for a moment what it might mean to believe something and not   20
be able to justify why one believes what one believes. Certainly inarticulate people have difficulty with that sort of thing. And, in fact, we do use that ability, namely the ability to justify one's beliefs with evidence, as a measure of intelligence and reasonableness. In other words, we expect intelligent people to have a story to tell that explains why they believe what they believe. But how can they do this? The mental mechanisms that are available must be ones that connect beliefs to stories. The fact that we can do this is obvious. It follows, therefore, that beliefs are one possible index in memory. Construct a belief and you should be able to find a story that exemplifies that belief.

Thus, for Subject 2 at least, beliefs and indices are one and the same. Understanding, then, in this model depends upon being able to see one's own beliefs in whatever one is trying to understand. Understanding Shrevie's story for Subject 2 meant identifying what he believed about what was happening to Shrevie, but the beliefs expressed in the story that Shrevie told are Shrevie's beliefs. So what we are seeing in the understanding process is the attempt to understand the beliefs of another in terms of one's own beliefs.

An index is a juxtaposition of another person's beliefs, made evident by statements or actions, with one's own beliefs. Indices are not beliefs, but are actually beliefs about beliefs. In other words, our reactions to the implicit beliefs of others cause us to consider what we believe about the same subject. We can either directly access what we believe by finding our own belief and telling a story that exemplifies it, or we can use the belief expressed in the story as if it were one of our own and see what story we might have stored away in memory under that label. Alternatively, we can create a new belief that is a juxtaposition of what we heard and what we might think about what we heard. This new belief might already exist and thus we would find another story to tell, but possibly the new belief will be entirely new. If this is the case, we need to create a story that exemplifies the belief or it will be lost.

Indices are phenomenally complicated and phenomenally important. We find what we want to say effortlessly and unconsciously. But to do so, we must construct complex labels of events that describe their content, their import, their relation to what we know and what we believe, and much more. It is effective indexing that allows us to have stories to tell and enables us to learn from the juxtaposition of others' stories and the stories that we are reminded of.

Let's now consider another subject:

SUBJECT 3:   There seems to be a real pattern of joking between guys that are married and guys that are not married or are about to be married. I've been having some conversations like this because I'm getting married in the fall. I think there is a standard pattern that's involved in these stories. Unmarried guys and married guys joke to each other a lot about sex. I remember hearing the comment, jokingly said because I am getting married soon, "Oh, you'll be married, and you'll understand it someday, my boy." It seems to be a comment that sometimes is said seriously, but a whole bunch of jokes are based around it.

Subject 3 is a very clear example of an idiosyncratic understander. Obviously, he had been talking with many people about getting married and had been subjected to various jokes about sex and marriage. He sees Shrevie's story as yet another person bothering him with worries about why one should not get married. Obviously, that was not the intent of Shrevie's story. Shrevie did not say what he did with Subject 3 in mind. Equally obviously, Subject 3 knew this. Nevertheless, Subject 3 took Shrevie's story personally as yet another married person trying to scare him about getting married. He, too, had heard this story before, but the story he had heard was about why marriage will make you unhappy. Note that neither of the previous two subjects sees the story in this way.

With that in mind, let's look at another response. Subject 4 understood Shrevie's story in terms of the belief that Shrevie had expressed:

SUBJECT 4:   Something like that happened to me with my girlfriend. It must have been right after things had gotten past the initial stage, that we really knew we were together, and we started sleeping together. I remember I was sitting on the floor one morning, and she was doing something in the kitchen. So I said to her, "What do lovers do when they're not eating or screwing?" She threw a spoon at me. She didn't think much of the question. But I think it was a question that bothered me for a long time. We had to kind of learn what to do and what we were going to talk about and what we were going to do when we weren't eating and screwing and doing the things that we knew we had to do anyway.

Subject 4 understood this story exactly as it appeared on the surface. While the other subjects tried to relate the story to some deeper theme about marriage or life or sex, Subject 4 asked himself the question: *Well, what else is there to do with a mate other than screw and eat?* This question strikes at the heart of Shrevie's story in some sense. Rather than read a deeper meaning into the story, why did Subject 4 only see the superficial question? Because he had already asked himself that question. In other words, Subject 4 had seen this story before in his own life exactly as Shrevie presented it. The index here is:

INDEX 7:   What do lovers do when they are not screwing or eating?

While indices clearly can be beliefs, indices can obviously be questions also. This assertion is obvious because people can answer questions. In order to answer them, they must be able to use something in them to find a story in memory. But what?

People can ask and answer their own question rather easily. They can query themselves about real world facts (What was the name of George Washington's wife?), about internal facts (What is my favorite flavor of ice cream?), about recent history (Where was I when I heard about the crash of the space shuttle?), and about beliefs (Should a man open the door for a woman?). People do not know how they find the answers to such questions, but they know that they can find them if they only ask.

Perhaps equally important is the fact that people know, again implicitly,   30 what questions not to bother asking themselves because they know they cannot easily find the answer. These include questions about forgotten past history that has never come up again (What was the name of the little girl who sat next to me in the second grade?), things that no one remembers if they are asked in the wrong way (What picture was on page forty-two of your science text in high school?), and things that we know were never stored away in the first place (Tell me five word analogies that were on the SAT test that you took to get into college).

Why are some questions answerable and others not? The answer is indices. Certain concepts, and the words that name those concepts, are indices in memory and others are not. George Washington is an index. So is ice cream, the space shuttle, and etiquette. But book is not an index, at least not by itself. Page numbers are almost never indices, and SAT may be an index, but curiously not to the SAT itself. In any case, while it is clear that most beliefs are indices, not all concepts are.

Even a superficial reading that results in the recognition of a story as one of your own stories can differ from person to person. Consider the next subject:

SUBJECT 5:   You're right. You got married very young. When you're young like that you are very preoccupied with sex. I remember the time before I got married, going over to a friend's apartment in order to have a liaison with my wife-to-be because we couldn't at the home of my parents. That wasn't accepted.

Here, Subject 5 recognizes a story from his own life, not about what else you do besides sex, but about the complexity of getting sex.

INDEX 8:   Young people must go to extremes to find places to have sex.

Subject 5 did get divorced from the wife he refers to, so perhaps he is also making a prediction about what will happen to Shrevie. Perhaps he is saying that interest in making arrangements for sex can provide the interest in a relationship. Yet, even here, Subject 5's view is that young people find things to do and talk about that do not relate to what marriage will be like. Subject 5 saw Shrevie's story as a story about himself. Here too, understanding means finding a story you already know and saying, "Oh, yeah, that one."

The last subject did not see this story as being about sex or marriage. For him the index was quite different than it was for the others:

SUBJECT 6:   Well, that reminds me of the qualifying exam in Artificial Intelligence actually. It reminds me of the phenomenon where you're spending time thinking about one particular thing going on in your life, and then when that thing is over you are supposed to be happy because you have passed through this barrier. Before you get married, your main goals are having a place to have sex and having sex, and then when you're married, that's taken care of, and then, all of a sudden, all sorts of other problems start to creep in. That reminds me of the qual. You're focused on how your whole life is going to be okay if you just pass the qual; but when you pass the qual, then other aspects of graduate school start sweeping back in. All of a sudden, you're upset that your room is a mess, and your social life starts to seep back in, and you have to find a way to do research.

Subject 6 is referring to the qualifying examination in Artificial Intelligence that graduate students spend months preparing for in their second year at Yale. If they fail, they are asked to leave graduate school. This particular subject had passed his exam three years earlier, but his office mate had taken the exam a month before this story was read to him. For Subject 6, certain ordeals in life cause one to lose the forest for the trees. He sees that the trials involved in sex and marriage can prevent one from seeing that life goes on. He believes that focusing on immediate problems causes one to lose sight of the larger issues.

INDEX 9:   Putting aside all your goals in order to achieve one major goal only works for a short time. Eventually real life reappears.

And, of course, here again, Subject 6 already believed this, prior to hearing Shrevie's story.

An important question, therefore, is, How did each of these subjects manage to find his own story in Shrevie's story when each story is so different? How does this kind of very subjective understanding actually work? The key point is that there is no one way to understand this story. When someone hears a story, he looks for beliefs that are being commented upon. Shrevie's story has many possible beliefs inherent in it. But how does someone listening to Shrevie's story find those beliefs? He finds them by looking through the beliefs that he already has. He is not as concerned with what he is hearing as he is with finding what he already knows that is relevant.

Picture it this way. An understander has a list of beliefs, indexed by subject area. When a new story appears, he attempts to find a belief of his that relates to it. When he does, he finds a story attached to that belief and compares the story in memory with the one he is processing. His understanding of the new story becomes, at that point, a function of the old story. The key point here is that once we find a belief and connected story, no further processing, that is, no search for other beliefs need be done. We rarely look to understand a story in more than one way. This process explains why each person understood Shrevie's story quite differently. The mind cannot easily pursue multiple paths.

Let's pursue this way of looking at story understanding while considering   40
a number of responses to a story taken from *The Breakfast Club:*

TIME: 1985

PLACE: Shermer High School, Shermer, Illinois

Five high school students, Brian, Andy, Alison, Clair, and John, must spend Saturday in detention at the school library. Their assignment is to write a thousand-word essay describing who they are. They all come from different cliques in their school and are described by one of the group as being "a brain, an athlete, a basket case, a princess, and a criminal." Although they don't know each other as they start the detention, by the end of the day each has revealed something about himself, and all five become friends. Andy, "the athlete," explains why he got detention.

ANDY: Do you guys know what I did to get in here? I taped Larry Lester's buns together. Yeah, you know him? Well then, you know how hairy he is, right? Well, when they pulled the tape off, most of his hair came off and some skin too. And the bizarre thing is, is that I did it for my old man. I tortured this poor kid because I wanted him to think I was cool. He's always going off about, you know, when he was in school all the wild things he used to do, and I got the feeling that he was disappointed that I never cut loose on anyone, right? So, I'm sitting in the locker room and I'm taping up my knee, and Larry's undressing a couple lockers down from me, and he's kinda, kinda skinny, weak, and I started thinking about my father and his attitude about weakness, and the next thing I knew I, I jumped on top of him and started wailing on him. Then my friends, they just laughed and cheered me on. And afterwards, when I was sittin' in Vernon's office, all I could think about was Larry's father and Larry having to go home and explain what happened to him. And the humiliation, the fucking humiliation he must have felt. It must have been unreal. I mean, how do you apologize for something like that? There's no way. It's all because of me and my old man. God, I fucking hate him. He's like, he's like this mindless machine I can't even relate to any-more. "Andrew, you've got to be number one. I won't tolerate any losers in this family. Your intensity is for shit." You son of a bitch. You know, sometimes I wish my knee would give in, and I wouldn't be able to wrestle anymore. He could forget all about me.

Subject 1 makes a comment and not a story.

SUBJECT 1:   I always wondered what the assholes who beat up on me in junior high school were thinking. It's sort of nice to think that they were actually humans and that they did it for some reason.

There must be a story, however, behind the comment. Subject 1 got beaten up in school and never understood why. The particular stories are probably not interesting stories or else Subject 1 didn't feel like telling them. Nevertheless, he was reminded of them. How?

One possibility is that *bullies who beat up smaller kids in high school* is an index which Subject 1 has used to label one or more stories in his memory. He first had to construct that index from the story he heard. Next, he had to find the stories in memory labeled by that index. Then, on listening further to the new story, he had to recognize that his story in memory had no reason listed for why someone was beating him up. As he hears a reason in the new story, he finds that he has no old story to match it against. Thus, he can, if he wants to, learn something from this story. Namely, he can add a possible rea-son derived from Andy's story to explain the actions of the actors in his own story. Therefore, understanding a story in order to learn from it means find-ing an old story in memory that matches the new story but then enhancing the old story with details from the new.

Now let's look at the next subject:

SUBJECT 2:   You have to be your own person. You can't keep trying to please someone else. You should develop to the best you can be, and your father will have to learn to like it.

Here we have another comment that seems to reflect an untold story. Somewhere in memory, Subject 2 probably has an opinion about this story that he is not revealing. Notice that the index is something like *When deciding what kind of person to be, trying to please someone else never works (Index 11)*. Again, the two subjects have heard very different stories.

In Subject 3's story, we have another case where the subject has under-stood Andy's story by reliving his own version:

SUBJECT 3:   Part of the problem is that you are trying to prove yourself by doing things you don't want to so that you can appear cool. When I was in eighth grade, I went to visit friends of the family in the countryside, and they had a boy about my age. He had a shooting rifle. So we went hunting, and he made a big point of having this special privilege of the gun. He wouldn't let me use it, and I was basically acting like a scout. But I really wanted to fire his gun. He said that if he killed one of the chipmunks which we were hunting then I would get the gun. Eventually, up comes the chipmunk. I pointed it out to him, and he shot and killed it. We walked over to the chipmunk—it looked so pathetic. It was still sort of twitching. It was such a pointless killing. I felt really bad because I felt responsible. I tried to be cool. You do something for no reason, no reason at all. You don't even stop to think about it. You just act, and, then afterwards, you feel terrible.

After telling his story, he then uses it to have better insight into Andy's story. The process seems to be like this. First, Subject 3 found an index from Andy's story which he states in the beginning as *Trying to prove yourself may cause you to do things you don't want to so you can appear cool (Index 12)*. But as he tells his story, he begins to think about his own story rather than Andy's and realizes that his own story is labeled in an additional way by something like *Guilt follows the rush of the moment when you do something against your own value system (Index 13)*. He then realizes that this is a better analysis of Andy's story. Still, in the end, what he has understood is really his own story although remembering it this additional time may have allowed him greater insight into it. We dwell on our own stories, not those of others.

Subject 4 is almost a classic case of not paying attention to someone else's story any more than is necessary for being able to retrieve your own:

SUBJECT 4:   When I was in the seventh grade, I was in the locker room, and one of the guys who was a lot bigger than me, for no apparent reason, started jabbing and popping me. Everyone was standing around in a circle watching, as people tend to do. Then finally, even though he was so big, finally, I stood up and started wailing on him. Immediately everyone jumped on my side, and he was chased out of the place. So that was sort of a victory for me even though we didn't get into a bloody knockdown fight. All I had to do was stand up for myself and wail on him to get everyone else on my side.

The index *getting beaten up in school* caused Subject 4 to recall his own experience, and he found nothing else to think about. Certainly understanding in this case may seem to be something quite different from what constitutes understanding in the other examples, but the difference here is really a question of degree and not of kind. Understanding means searching memory. Sometimes we have less memory to search, and sometimes we have fewer indices available with which to search. An understander is, in some sense, in control of both of these variables. He decides how much attention to pay to the world around him and how much to remember about what he has previously processed. Attention and memory are strongly related.

Subject 5 has resonated to an index that he found in Andy's story about how *the efforts to please an unsuccessful and demanding father can lead to bad decisions in life (Index 14)*.

> SUBJECT 5:   A friend of mine had an older brother who ended up on drugs. Looking at his family situation was always weird to me. His father was an alcoholic sportswriter who seemed to have big expectations for both of his sons. The older son had been a stellar athlete and a great student in high school. In college, he just came apart and ended up a drug addict and wasted his mind one way or another. At one point, he was in a mental institution, I think. I was friends with the younger son, and I always wondered if the same thing would happen to him because he seemed to be very successful and very oriented towards doing well somehow or other where his brother had fucked up — but it seemed like he was on the same road his brother was on. So I don't know, I can sympathize with this guy.

The recalling of his story from memory caused Subject 5 to recognize Andy's story as one he had seen before, and no more really came to mind.

Subject 6 saw Andy's story as showing that *sometimes you act irrationally in a group when you wouldn't if you were alone (Index 15)*.

> SUBJECT 6:   Yeah, I don't know. Everyone does all sorts of shit because of who they think they're supposed to be and because their parents told them who they thought they were supposed to be. Actually, it happens just as much from who your friends think you should be. I'm reminded of my undergraduate days, being in the band, an incredibly obnoxious and rude bunch of people. And in that gang, you felt safe doing things that you wouldn't do otherwise. You'd get up in the middle of a football game and do a series of Humpty Dumpty cheers: "Humpty Dumpty sat on a wall, Humpty Dumpty had a great fall, all the king's horses and all the king's men raped the queen." It's like you scream it at the top of your lungs in the middle of a football game. It's still an open question for me to what extent you sort of surrender yourself to something which seems like a bad thing to do. Or to what extent is it reasonable to let yourself try out things you wouldn't do otherwise? Basically, you can rationalize what you do in a lot of different ways. The question is to what extent are you rationalizing? When have you really done something that shouldn't have been done?

As in the case of Subject 3, Subject 6 evaluated his own story again, and this time constructed an index from a different point of view: *Trying new (bad) things with the encouragement of a group is probably the only way one can safely try them (Index 16)*. Subject 6 is not sure of his beliefs and thus might see Andy's story as more evidence to be considered. When our own beliefs about a situation are in a state of flux, however, we can learn from paying attention to other people's stories.

This aspect of story understanding is, in some sense, what we really mean by understanding although, as we have seen, it is not really the most common form of story understanding. We would like to imagine that we learn from the stories of others, but we really only do so when the stories we hear relate to beliefs that we feel rather unsure of, ones that we are flirting with at the moment, so to speak. When we are wondering, consciously or unconsciously, about the truth, about how to act or how to understand some aspect of the world, then the evidence provided by others can be of some use. We can extract evidence from a story, supporting or refuting a given belief that we are considering. This extraction process is an important form of understanding which serves as input to various thinking processes.

Subject 7 has seen Andy's story as a story about change. He has constructed an index such as *Part of growing up is selecting the groups that you want to belong to and trying their value system for a while (Index 17).*

SUBJECT 7:   I am reminded of two people I knew in high school. One guy I had known since kindergarten. He was a jock, and he was a very popular guy. He hung out with everyone, and the girls all liked him. Toward the end of high school, he became more and more sensitive and less and less of a jock. He was a very smart guy. And I remember toward the end of high school, somebody told some crude joke, and Terry objected to the language. I thought this was strange coming from a jock, but he'd really turned around. And then I had another friend who I had also gone to school with since kindergarten. He was an artist, and his father was an artist as well. This guy was very talented and sensitive. The opposite thing happened to him. Toward the end of high school, he kind of stopped being smart and decided he wouldn't study much anymore. He started hanging out with all the jocks. That was much more fun, and he decided that he just wanted to become a regular guy. So I think of these two people's paths crossing. They both wanted acceptance by some group that hadn't accepted them before.

Subject 7 had seen the movie and probably remembered that Andy was making an uncharacteristic admission to a group of kids that were not at all macho. So for Subject 7, the index was quite different from those constructed by the other subjects. His index was constructed from more information than was provided by Andy's story. He was also recalling the story of the movie itself from his memory and "reading" that story as well. He was like the others, however, in that he was simply reminded of an old story and then let the old story take over the comprehension of the new story. . . .

There is a funny side effect to all this. We really cannot learn from other people's stories. In getting reminded of our own stories, ones which of course have more poignancy and more rich detail than the ones we are hearing, we tend to get distracted into thinking more about what happened to us. The incoming story can get recalled in terms of the story of which we were reminded, but in the end, we rarely recall the stories of others easily. More often than not, other people's stories don't have the richness of detail and emotional impact that allows them to be stored in multiple ways in our memories. They do, on the other hand, provide enough details and emotions to allow them to be more easily stored than if the tellers had simply told us their beliefs.

So we are left with an odd picture of understanding. Real communication is rather difficult to achieve. We do not easily remember what other people have said if they do not tell it in the form of a story. We can learn from the stories of others, but only if what we hear relates strongly to something we already knew. We can learn from these stories to the extent that they have caused us to rethink our own stories. But mostly we learn from a re-examination of our own stories. We hear, in the stories of others, what we personally can relate to by virtue of having in some way heard or experienced that story before. Understanding is an idiosyncratic affair. Our idiosyncrasies come from our stories.

EXPLORING THE TEXT

1. What role, according to Schank, do expectation and memory play in our ability to understand the stories other people tell? How do we show others that we do, in fact, understand their stories? What makes some responses more "intelligent" than others, in Schank's view? Generally, when you share a personal story with a friend, what kind of response do you expect?

2. What does the technical term "index" mean to Schank in his analysis of the role of memory in understanding? What do indices do? What difference, if any, can you see between Schank's concept of an index and the more common notions of a theme or main idea?

3. How does Schank evaluate the individual responses of his students to the stories told in the movies *Diner* and *The Breakfast Club*? Which of these responses strike you as the most interesting or effective? Which strike you as the weakest? Why? In general, what seems to characterize responses that show "deep" or full understanding?

4. How does Schank describe the process of learning? Why is it so hard to learn anything new from the stories we hear, in Schank's view? Do you agree that in general "we dwell on our own stories, not those of others"?

5. Why does Schank believe that "no two people can really understand a story the same way"? What factors affect the way that two people interpret and respond to the same story? To what extent do you agree with Schank's conclusion that "real communication is rather difficult to achieve"?

FURTHER EXPLORATIONS

1. Drawing on Schank's theory of story-based understanding, how might you explain the difficulty that Baldwin's narrator has in comprehending the dreams and desires of his brother in "Sonny's Blues" (p. 390)? How do the narrator's beliefs—

or the stories he tells himself about jazz and street culture and addiction—interfere with his efforts to understand Sonny? What role do stories and storytelling play in changing his views?

2. How might Eviatar Zerubavel's theory of "Social Memories" (p. 217) complicate Schank's view of story-based understanding? To what extent can impersonal as well as personal memories serve as "indices" for the retrieval of stories from memory? Does the sharing of historical or impersonal memories also constitute understanding in Schank's view of the term? Why or why not?

3. Return to Maxine Hong Kingston's "No-Name Woman" (p. 206) and explore how Kingston uses storytelling as a means of understanding herself and others around her. In what sense are the stories she tells responses to "old stories" she hears or inherits? To what extent does she appear to be trapped in her own stories—or able to learn something new?

ESSAY OPTIONS

1. Recreate Schank's experiment in understanding other people's stories by asking three people you know outside of class to read Ian Frazier's "Take the F" (p. 18) and to explain what Frazier's essay means to them—or to tell a story of their own in response to Frazier. (As an alternative, you may want to use a story about an important experience from your own life.) Document their responses in a report and evaluate the depth of understanding shown by each. How might you account for their reactions? What do their responses suggest about the way we understand the stories we encounter?

2. Write an essay in which you compare the theories of learning that underlie the writings of Schank and Mary Catherine Bateson (p. 337). When does real learning occur, according to Schank and Bateson? What obstacles stand in the way of genuine learning? What kinds of people—or what kinds of minds—are most open to learning from new experiences? What experiences of yours confirm or complicate these views of learning?

Sonny's Blues

JAMES BALDWIN

One of the most celebrated authors of the twentieth century, James Baldwin wrote about the obstacles that lead us to misread the thoughts and feelings of other minds—obstacles like age, race, culture, and sexual orientation. The son of a Harlem lay preacher who believed that God would repay the white race for its sins, Baldwin grew up in New York's Greenwich Village where he first decided to become a writer and began to grapple with the difficulties of being both black and gay in postwar America. In his mid-twenties, he expatriated himself to live in Europe with his lover, where he experienced cultural conflicts that he eventually dramatized in books like *Go Tell It on the Mountain* (1953), *Notes of a Native Son* (1955), *Giovanni's Room* (1956), *Another Country* (1962), and *The Fire Next Time* (1963). This story, from Baldwin's collection *Going to Meet the Man* (1965), focuses on barriers that can block understanding even between those who share the same cultural and family background. The story of the conflict between Sonny, an aspiring jazz musician struggling with addiction, and his algebra-teacher brother illustrates how difficult—and how rewarding—it can be to listen to someone whose mind and way of life are fundamentally different from your own.

BEFORE READING

Working in small groups, discuss the causes of drug addiction. What factors lead some people to become addicted to hard drugs like heroin or cocaine? Why are other people in similar circumstances able to resist drug use?

I read about it in the paper, in the subway, on my way to work. I read it, and I couldn't believe it, and I read it again. Then perhaps I just stared at it, at the newsprint spelling out his name, spelling out the story. I stared at it in the swinging lights of the subway car, and in the faces and bodies of the people, and in my own face, trapped in the darkness which roared outside.

It was not to be believed and I kept telling myself that, as I walked from the subway station to the high school. And at the same time I couldn't doubt it. I was scared, scared for Sonny. He became real to me again. A great block of ice got settled in my belly and kept melting there slowly all day long, while I taught my classes algebra. It was a special kind of ice. It kept melting, sending trickles of ice water all up and down my veins, but it never got less. Sometimes it hardened and seemed to expand until I felt my guts were going to come spilling out or that I was going to choke or scream. This would always be at a moment when I was remembering some specific thing Sonny had once said or done.

When he was about as old as the boys in my classes his face had been bright and open, there was a lot of copper in it; and he'd had wonderfully direct brown eyes, and great gentleness and privacy. I wondered what he looked like now. He had been picked up, the evening before, in a raid on an apartment downtown, for peddling and using heroin.

I couldn't believe it: but what I mean by that is that I couldn't find any room for it anywhere inside me. I had kept it outside me for a long time. I hadn't wanted to know. I had had suspicions, but I didn't name them, I kept putting them away. I told myself that Sonny was wild, but he wasn't crazy. And he'd always been a good boy, he hadn't ever turned hard or evil or disrespectful, the way kids can, so quick, so quick, especially in Harlem. I didn't want to believe that I'd ever see my brother going down, coming to nothing, all that light in his face gone out, in the condition I'd already seen so many others. Yet it had happened and here I was, talking about algebra to a lot of boys who might, every one of them for all I knew, be popping off needles every time they went to the head. Maybe it did more for them than algebra could.

I was sure that the first time Sonny had ever had horse, he couldn't have   5
been much older than these boys were now. These boys, now, were living as
we'd been living then, they were growing up with a rush and their heads
bumped abruptly against the low ceiling of their actual possibilities. They were
filled with rage. All they really knew were two darknesses, the darkness of their
lives, which was now closing in on them, and the darkness of the movies,
which had blinded them to that other darkness, and in which they now, vin-
dictively, dreamed, at once more together than they were at any other time,
and more alone.

When the last bell rang, the last class ended, I let out my breath. It seemed
I'd been holding it for all that time. My clothes were wet—I may have looked
as though I'd been sitting in a steam bath, all dressed up, all afternoon. I sat
alone in the classroom a long time. I listened to the boys outside, downstairs,
shouting and cursing and laughing. Their laughter struck me for perhaps the
first time. It was not the joyous laughter which—God knows why—one associates with children. It was mocking and insular, its intent was to denigrate.
It was disenchanted, and in this, also, lay the authority of their curses. Perhaps
I was listening to them because I was thinking about my brother and in them
I heard my brother. And myself.

One boy was whistling a tune, at once very complicated and very simple,
it seemed to be pouring out of him as though he were a bird, and it sounded
very cool and moving through all that harsh, bright air, only just holding its
own through all those other sounds.

I stood up and walked over to the window and looked down into the
courtyard. It was the beginning of the spring and the sap was rising in the
boys. A teacher passed through them every now and again, quickly, as though
he or she couldn't wait to get out of that courtyard, to get those boys out of
their sight and off their minds. I started collecting my stuff. I thought I'd better get home and talk to Isabel.

The courtyard was almost deserted by the time I got downstairs. I saw this
boy standing in the shadow of a doorway, looking just like Sonny. I almost
called his name. Then I saw that it wasn't Sonny, but somebody we used to
know, a boy from around our block. He'd been Sonny's friend. He'd never
been mine, having been too young for me, and, anyway, I'd never liked him.
And now, even though he was a grown-up man, he still hung around that
block, still spent hours on the street corners, was always high and raggy. I used
to run into him from time to time and he'd often work around to asking me
for a quarter or fifty cents. He always had some real good excuse, too, and I
always gave it to him. I don't know why.

But now, abruptly, I hated him. I couldn't stand the way he looked at me,   10
partly like a dog, partly like a cunning child. I wanted to ask him what the hell
he was doing in the school courtyard.

He sort of shuffled over to me, and he said, "I see you got the papers. So
you already know about it."

"You mean about Sonny? Yes, I already know about it. How come they didn't get you?"

He grinned. It made him repulsive and it also brought to mind what he'd looked like as a kid. "I wasn't there. I stay away from them people."

"Good for you." I offered him a cigarette and I watched him through the smoke. "You come all the way down here just to tell me about Sonny?"

"That's right." He was sort of shaking his head and his eyes looked   15 strange, as though they were about to cross. The bright sun deadened his damp dark brown skin and it made his eyes look yellow and showed up the dirt in his kinked hair. He smelled funky. I moved a little away from him and I said, "Well, thanks. But I already know about it and I got to get home."

"I'll walk you a little ways," he said. We started walking. There were a couple of kids still loitering in the courtyard and one of them said goodnight to me and looked strangely at the boy beside me.

"What're you going to do?" he asked me. "I mean, about Sonny?"

"Look. I haven't seen Sonny for over a year, I'm not sure I'm going to do anything. Anyway, what the hell *can* I do?"

"That's right," he said quickly, "ain't nothing you can do. Can't much help old Sonny no more, I guess."

It was what I was thinking and so it seemed to me he had no right to say it.   20

"I'm surprised at Sonny, though," he went on—he had a funny way of talking, he looked straight ahead as though he were talking to himself—"I thought Sonny was a smart boy, I thought he was too smart to get hung."

"I guess he thought so too," I said sharply, "and that's how he got hung. And how about you? You're pretty goddamn smart, I bet."

Then he looked directly at me, just for a minute. "I ain't smart," he said. "If I was smart, I'd have reached for a pistol a long time ago."

"Look. Don't tell *me* your sad story, if it was up to me, I'd give you one." Then I felt guilty—guilty, probably, for never having supposed that the poor bastard *had* a story of his own, much less a sad one, and I asked, quickly, "What's going to happen to him now?"

He didn't answer this. He was off by himself some place.   25

"Funny thing," he said, and from his tone we might have been discussing the quickest way to get to Brooklyn, "when I saw the papers this morning, the first thing I asked myself was if I had anything to do with it. I felt sort of responsible."

I began to listen more carefully. The subway station was on the corner, just before us, and I stopped. He stopped, too. We were in front of a bar and he ducked slightly, peering in, but whoever he was looking for didn't seem to be there. The juke box was blasting away with something black and bouncy and I half watched the barmaid as she danced her way from the juke box to her place behind the bar. And I watched her face as she laughingly responded to something someone said to her, still keeping time to the music. When she smiled one saw the little girl, one sensed the doomed, still-struggling woman beneath the battered face of the semi-whore.

"I never *give* Sonny nothing," the boy said finally, "but a long time ago I come to school high and Sonny asked me how it felt." He paused, I couldn't bear to watch him, I watched the barmaid, and I listened to the music which seemed to be causing the pavement to shake. "I told him it felt great." The music stopped, the barmaid paused and watched the juke box until the music began again. "It did."

All this was carrying me some place I didn't want to go. I certainly didn't want to know how it felt. It filled everything, the people, the houses, the music, the dark, quicksilver barmaid, with menace; and this menace was their reality.

"What's going to happen to him now?" I asked again.   30

"They'll send him away some place and they'll try to cure him." He shook his head. "Maybe he'll even think he's kicked the habit. Then they'll let him loose" — he gestured, throwing his cigarette into the gutter. "That's all."

"What do you mean, that's *all*?"

But I knew what he meant.

"I *mean*, that's *all*." He turned his head and looked at me, pulling down the corners of his mouth. "Don't you know what I mean?" he asked, softly.

"How the hell *would* I know what you mean?" I almost whispered it, I   35
don't know why.

"That's right," he said to the air, "how would *he* know what I mean?" He turned toward me again, patient and calm, and yet I somehow felt him shaking, shaking as though he were going to fall apart. I felt that ice in my guts again, the dread I'd felt all afternoon; and again I watched the barmaid, moving about the bar, washing glasses, and singing. "Listen. They'll let him out and then it'll just start all over again. That's what I mean."

"You mean — they'll let him out. And then he'll just start working his way back in again. You mean he'll never kick the habit. Is that what you mean?"

"That's right," he said, cheerfully. "*You* see what I mean."

"Tell me," I said at last, "why does he want to die? He must want to die, he's killing himself, why does he want to die?"

He looked at me in surprise. He licked his lips. "He don't want to die. He   40
wants to live. Don't nobody want to die, ever."

Then I wanted to ask him — too many things. He could not have answered, or if he had, I could not have borne the answers. I started walking. "Well, I guess it's none of my business."

"It's going to be rough on old Sonny," he said. We reached the subway station. "This is your station?" he asked. I nodded. I took one step down. "Damn!" he said, suddenly. I looked up at him. He grinned again. "Damn it if I didn't leave all my money home. You ain't got a dollar on you, have you? Just for a couple of days, is all."

All at once something inside gave and threatened to come pouring out of me. I didn't hate him any more. I felt that in another moment I'd start crying like a child.

"Sure," I said. "Don't sweat." I looked in my wallet and didn't have a dollar, I only had a five. "Here," I said. "That hold you?"

He didn't look at it—he didn't want to look at it. A terrible, closed look came over his face, as though he were keeping the number on the bill a secret from him and me. "Thanks," he said, and now he was dying to see me go. "Don't worry about Sonny. Maybe I'll write him or something."

"Sure," I said. "You do that. So long."

"Be seeing you," he said. I went on down the steps.

And I didn't write Sonny or send him anything for a long time. When I finally did, it was just after my little girl died, and he wrote me back a letter which made me feel like a bastard.

Here's what he said:

Dear brother,

You don't know how much I needed to hear from you. I wanted to write you many a time but I dug how much I must have hurt you and so I didn't write. But now I feel like a man who's been trying to climb up out of some deep, real deep and funky hole and just saw the sun up there, outside. I got to get outside.

I can't tell you much about how I got here. I mean I don't know how to tell you. I guess I was afraid of something or I was trying to escape from something and you know I have never been very strong in the head (smile). I'm glad Mama and Daddy are dead and can't see what's happened to their son and I swear if I'd known what I was doing I would never have hurt you so, you and a lot of other fine people who were nice to me and who believed in me.

I don't want you to think it had anything to do with me being a musician. It's more than that. Or maybe less than that. I can't get anything straight in my head down here and I try not to think about what's going to happen to me when I get outside again. Sometime I think I'm going to flip and *never* get outside and sometime I think I'll come straight back. I tell you one thing, though, I'd rather blow my brains out than go through this again. But that's what they all say, so they tell me. If I tell you when I'm coming to New York and if you could meet me, I sure would appreciate it. Give my love to Isabel and the kids and I was sure sorry to hear about little Gracie. I wish I could be like Mama and say the Lord's will be done, but I don't know it seems to me that trouble is the one thing that never does get stopped and I don't know what good it does to blame it on the Lord. But maybe it does some good if you believe it.

Your brother,
Sonny

Then I kept in constant touch with him and I sent him whatever I could and I went to meet him when he came back to New York. When I saw him many things I thought I had forgotten came flooding back to me. This was because I had begun, finally, to wonder about Sonny, about the life that Sonny lived inside. This life, whatever it was, had made him older and thinner and it had deepened the distant stillness in which he had always moved. He looked very unlike my baby brother. Yet, when he smiled, when we shook hands, the baby brother I'd never known looked out from the depths of his private life, like an animal waiting to be coaxed into the light.

"How you been keeping?" he asked me.

"All right. And you?"

"Just fine." He was smiling all over his face. "It's good to see you again."

"It's good to see you."

The seven years' difference in our ages lay between us like a chasm: I won-   55
dered if these years would ever operate between us as a bridge. I was remembering, and it made it hard to catch my breath, that I had been there when he was born; and I had heard the first words he had ever spoken. When he started to walk, he walked from our mother straight to me. I caught him just before he fell when he took the first steps he ever took in this world.

"How's Isabel?"

"Just fine. She's dying to see you."

"And the boys?"

"They're fine, too. They're anxious to see their uncle."

"Oh, come on. You know they don't remember me."   60

"Are you kidding? Of course they remember you."

He grinned again. We got into a taxi. We had a lot to say to each other, far too much to know how to begin.

As the taxi began to move, I asked, "You still want to go to India?"

He laughed. "You still remember that. Hell, no. This place is Indian enough for me."

"It used to belong to them," I said.   65

And he laughed again. "They damn sure knew what they were doing when they got rid of it."

Years ago, when he was around fourteen, he'd been all hipped on the idea of going to India. He read books about people sitting on rocks, naked, in all kinds of weather, but mostly bad, naturally, and walking barefoot through hot coals and arriving at wisdom. I used to say that it sounded to me as though they were getting away from wisdom as fast as they could. I think he sort of looked down on me for that.

"Do you mind," he asked, "if we have the driver drive alongside the park? On the west side — I haven't seen the city in so long."

"Of course not," I said. I was afraid that I might sound as though I were humoring him, but I hoped he wouldn't take it that way.

So we drove along, between the green of the park and the stony, lifeless   70
elegance of hotels and apartment buildings, toward the vivid, killing streets of our childhood. These streets hadn't changed, though housing projects jutted up out of them now like rocks in the middle of a boiling sea. Most of the houses in which we had grown up had vanished, as had the stores from which we had stolen, the basements in which we had first tried sex, the rooftops from which we had hurled tin cans and bricks. But houses exactly like the houses of our past yet dominated the landscape, boys exactly like the boys we once

had been found themselves smothering in these houses, came down into the streets for light and air and found themselves encircled by disaster. Some escaped the trap, most didn't. Those who got out always left something of themselves behind, as some animals amputate a leg and leave it in the trap. It might be said, perhaps, that I had escaped, after all, I was a school teacher; or that Sonny had, he hadn't lived in Harlem for years. Yet, as the cab moved uptown through streets which seemed, with a rush, to darken with dark people, and as I covertly studied Sonny's face, it came to me that what we both were seeking through our separate cab windows was that part of ourselves which had been left behind. It's always at the hour of trouble and confrontation that the missing member aches.

We hit 110th Street and started rolling up Lenox Avenue. And I'd known this avenue all my life, but it seemed to me again, as it had seemed on the day I'd first heard about Sonny's trouble, filled with a hidden menace which was its very breath of life.

"We almost there," said Sonny.

"Almost." We were both too nervous to say anything more.

We live in a housing project. It hasn't been up long. A few days after it was up it seemed uninhabitably new, now, of course, it's already rundown. It looks like a parody of the good, clean, faceless life — God knows the people who live in it do their best to make it a parody. The beat-looking grass lying around isn't enough to make their lives green, the hedges will never hold out the streets, and they know it. The big windows fool no one, they aren't big enough to make space out of no space. They don't bother with the windows, they watch the TV screen instead. The playground is most popular with the children who don't play at jacks, or skip rope, or roller skate, or swing, and they can be found in it after dark. We moved in partly because it's not too far from where I teach, and partly for the kids; but it's really just like the houses in which Sonny and I grew up. The same things happen, they'll have the same things to remember. The moment Sonny and I started into the house I had the feeling that I was simply bringing him back into the danger he had almost died trying to escape.

Sonny has never been talkative. So I don't know why I was sure he'd be dying to talk to me when supper was over the first night. Everything went fine, the oldest boy remembered him, and the youngest boy liked him, and Sonny had remembered to bring something for each of them; and Isabel, who is really much nicer than I am, more open and giving, had gone to a lot of trouble about dinner and was genuinely glad to see him. And she's always been able to tease Sonny in a way that I haven't. It was nice to see her face so vivid again and to hear her laugh and watch her make Sonny laugh. She wasn't, or, anyway, she didn't seem to be, at all uneasy or embarrassed. She chatted as though there were no subject which had to be avoided and she got Sonny past his first, faint stiffness. And thank God she was there, for I was filled with that icy dread again. Everything I did seemed awkward to me, and everything I said sounded freighted with hidden meaning. I was trying to remember 75 everything I'd heard about dope addiction and I couldn't help watching Sonny for signs. I wasn't doing it out of malice. I was trying to find out something about my brother. I was dying to hear him tell me he was safe.

"Safe!" my father grunted, whenever Mama suggested trying to move to a neighborhood which might be safer for children. "Safe, hell! Ain't no place safe for kids, nor nobody."

He always went on like this, but he wasn't, ever, really as bad as he sounded, not even on weekends, when he got drunk. As a matter of fact, he was always on the lookout for "something a little better," but he died before he found it. He died suddenly, during a drunken weekend in the middle of the war, when Sonny was fifteen. He and Sonny hadn't ever got on too well. And this was partly because Sonny was the apple of his father's eye. It was because he loved Sonny so much and was frightened for him, that he was always fighting with him. It doesn't do any good to fight with Sonny. Sonny just moves back, inside himself, where he can't be reached. But the principal reason that they never hit it off is that they were so much alike. Daddy was big and rough and loud-talking, just the opposite of Sonny, but they both had—that same privacy.

Mama tried to tell me something about this, just after Daddy died. I was home on leave from the army.

This was the last time I ever saw my mother alive. Just the same, this picture gets all mixed up in my mind with pictures I had of her when she was younger. The way I always see her is the way she used to be on a Sunday afternoon, say, when the old folks were talking after the big Sunday dinner. I always see her wearing pale blue. She'd be sitting on the sofa. And my father would be sitting in the easy chair, not far from her. And the living room would be full of church folks and relatives. There they sit, in chairs all around the living room, and the night is creeping up outside, but nobody knows it yet. You can see the darkness growing against the windowpanes and you hear the street noises every now and again, or maybe the jangling beat of a tambourine from one of the churches close by, but it's real quiet in the room. For a moment nobody's talking, but every face looks darkening, like the sky outside. And my mother rocks a little from the waist, and my father's eyes are closed. Everyone is looking at something a child can't see. For a minute they've forgotten the children. Maybe a kid is lying on the rug, half asleep. Maybe somebody's got a kid in his lap and is absent-mindedly stroking the kid's head. Maybe there's a kid, quiet and big-eyed, curled up in a big chair in the corner. The silence, the darkness coming, and the darkness in the faces frighten the child obscurely. He hopes that the hand which strokes his forehead will never stop— will never die. He hopes that there will never come a time when the old folks won't be sitting around the living room, talking about where they've come from, and what they've seen, and what's happened to them and their kinfolk.

But something deep and watchful in the child knows that this is bound to end, is already ending. In a moment someone will get up and turn on the light.

Then the old folks will remember the children and they won't talk any more that day. And when light fills the room, the child is filled with darkness. He knows that every time this happens he's moved just a little closer to that darkness outside. The darkness outside is what the old folks have been talking about. It's what they've come from. It's what they endure. The child knows that they won't talk any more because if he knows too much about what's happened to *them*, he'll know too much too soon, about what's going to happen to *him*.

The last time I talked to my mother, I remember I was restless. I wanted to get out and see Isabel. We weren't married then and we had a lot to straighten out between us.

There Mama sat, in black, by the window. She was humming an old church song, *Lord, you brought me from a long ways off*. Sonny was out somewhere. Mama kept watching the streets.

"I don't know," she said, "if I'll ever see you again, after you go off from here. But I hope you'll remember the things I tried to teach you."

"Don't talk like that," I said, and smiled. "You'll be here a long time yet."

She smiled, too, but she said nothing. She was quiet for a long time. And I said, "Mama, don't you worry about nothing. I'll be writing all the time, and you be getting the checks. . . ." 85

"I want to talk to you about your brother," she said, suddenly. "If anything happens to me he ain't going to have nobody to look out for him."

"Mama," I said, "ain't nothing going to happen to you *or* Sonny. Sonny's all right. He's a good boy and he's got good sense."

"It ain't a question of his being a good boy," Mama said, "nor of his having good sense. It ain't only the bad ones, nor yet the dumb ones that gets sucked under." She stopped, looking at me. "Your Daddy once had a brother," she said, and she smiled in a way that made me feel she was in pain. "You didn't never know that, did you?"

"No," I said, "I never knew that," and I watched her face.

"Oh, yes," she said, "your Daddy had a brother." She looked out of the window again. "I know you never saw your Daddy cry. But *I* did—many a time, through all these years." 90

I asked her, "What happened to his brother? How come nobody's ever talked about him?"

This was the first time I ever saw my mother look old.

"His brother got killed," she said, "when he was just a little younger than you are now. I knew him. He was a fine boy. He was maybe a little full of the devil, but he didn't mean nobody no harm."

Then she stopped and the room was silent, exactly as it had sometimes been on those Sunday afternoons. Mama kept looking out into the streets.

"He used to have a job in the mill," she said, "and, like all young folks, he just liked to perform on Saturday nights. Saturday nights, him and your father would drift around to different places, go to dances and things like that, or just sit around with people they knew, and your father's brother would sing, he had 95 a fine voice, and play along with himself on his guitar. Well, this particular Saturday night, him and your father was coming home from some place, and they were both a little drunk and there was a moon that night, it was bright like day. Your father's brother was feeling kind of good, and he was whistling to himself, and he had his guitar slung over his shoulder. They was coming down a hill and beneath them was a road that turned off from the highway. Well, your father's brother, being always kind of frisky, decided to run down this hill, and he did, with that guitar banging and clanging behind him, and he ran across the road, and he was making water behind a tree. And your father was sort of amused at him and he was still coming down the hill, kind of slow. Then he heard a car motor and that same minute his brother stepped from behind the tree, into the road, in the moonlight. And he started to cross the road. And your father started to run down the hill, he says he don't know why. This car was full of white men. They was all drunk, and when they seen your father's brother they let out a great whoop and holler and they aimed the car straight at him. They was having fun, they just wanted to scare him, the way they do sometimes, you know. But they was drunk. And I guess the boy, being drunk, too, and scared, kind of lost his head. By the time he jumped it was too late. Your father says he heard his brother scream when the car rolled over him, and he heard the wood of that guitar when it give, and he heard them strings go flying, and he heard them white men shouting, and the car kept on a-going and it ain't stopped till this day. And, time your father got down the hill, his brother weren't nothing but blood and pulp."

Tears were gleaming on my mother's face. There wasn't anything I could say.

"He never mentioned it," she said, "because I never let him mention it before you children. Your Daddy was like a crazy man that night and for many a night thereafter. He says he never in his life seen anything as dark as that road after the lights of that car had gone away. Weren't nothing, weren't nobody on that road, just your Daddy and his brother and that busted guitar. Oh, yes. Your Daddy never did really get right again. Till the day he died he weren't sure but that every white man he saw was the man that killed his brother."

She stopped and took out her handkerchief and dried her eyes and looked at me.

"I ain't telling you all this," she said, "to make you scared or bitter or to make you hate nobody. I'm telling you this because you got a brother. And the world ain't changed."

I guess I didn't want to believe this. I guess she saw this in my face. She turned away from me, toward the window again, searching those streets.   100

"But I praise my Redeemer," she said at last, "that He called your Daddy home before me. I ain't saying it to throw no flowers at myself, but, I declare, it keeps me from feeling too cast down to know I helped your father get safely through this world. Your father always acted like he was the roughest, strongest man on earth. And everybody took him to be like that. But if he hadn't had me there — to see his tears!"

She was crying again. Still, I couldn't move. I said, "Lord, Lord, Mama, I didn't know it was like that."

"Oh, honey," she said, "there's a lot that you don't know. But you are going to find out." She stood up from the window and came over to me. "You got to hold on to your brother," she said, "and don't let him fall, no matter what it looks like is happening to him and no matter how evil you gets with him. You going to be evil with him many a time. But don't you forget what I told you, you hear?"

"I won't forget," I said. "Don't you worry, I won't forget. I won't let nothing happen to Sonny."

My mother smiled as though she was amused at something she saw in my   105
face. Then, "You may not be able to stop nothing from happening. But you got to let him know you's *there*."

Two days later I was married, and then I was gone. And I had a lot of things on my mind and I pretty well forgot my promise to Mama until I got shipped home on a special furlough for her funeral.

And, after the funeral, with just Sonny and me alone in the empty kitchen, I tried to find out something about him.

"What do you want to do?" I asked him.

"I'm going to be a musician," he said.

For he had graduated, in the time I had been away, from dancing to the   110
juke box to finding out who was playing what, and what they were doing with it, and he had bought himself a set of drums.

"You mean, you want to be a drummer?" I somehow had the feeling that being a drummer might be all right for other people but not for my brother Sonny.

"I don't think," he said, looking at me very gravely, "that I'll ever be a good drummer. But I think I can play a piano."

I frowned. I'd never played the role of the oldest brother quite so seriously before, had scarcely ever, in fact, *asked* Sonny a damn thing. I sensed myself in the presence of something I didn't really know how to handle, didn't understand. So I made my frown a little deeper as I asked: "What kind of musician do you want to be?"

He grinned. "How many kinds do you think there are?"

"Be *serious*," I said.   115

He laughed, throwing his head back, and then looked at me. "I *am* serious."

"Well, then, for Christ's sake, stop kidding around and answer a serious question. I mean, do you want to be a concert pianist, you want to play classical music and all that, or — or what?" Long before I finished he was laughing again. "For Christ's *sake*, Sonny!"

He sobered, but with difficulty. "I'm sorry. But you sound so — *scared!*" and he was off again.

"Well, you may think it's funny now, baby, but it's not going to be so funny when you have to make your living at it, let me tell you *that*." I was furious because I knew he was laughing at me and I didn't know why.

"No," he said, very sober now, and afraid, perhaps, that he'd hurt me, "I   120
don't want to be a classical pianist. That isn't what interests me. I mean"—he
paused, looking hard at me, as though his eyes would help me to understand, and
then gestured helplessly, as though perhaps his hand would help—"I mean, I'll
have a lot of studying to do, and I'll have to study *everything*, but, I mean, I want
to play *with*—jazz musicians." He stopped. "I want to play jazz," he said.

Well, the word had never before sounded as heavy, as real, as it sounded
that afternoon in Sonny's mouth. I just looked at him and I was probably
frowning a real frown by this time. I simply couldn't see why on earth he'd
want to spend his time hanging around nightclubs, clowning around on band-
stands, while people pushed each other around a dance floor. It seemed—beneath him, somehow. I had never thought about it before, had never been
forced to, but I suppose I had always put jazz musicians in a class with what
Daddy called "good-time people."

"Are you *serious?*"

"Hell, *yes,* I'm serious."

He looked more helpless than ever, and annoyed, and deeply hurt.

I suggested, helpfully: "You mean—like Louis Armstrong?"   125

His face closed as though I'd struck him. "No, I'm not talking about none
of that old-time, down home crap."

"Well, look, Sonny, I'm sorry, don't get mad. I just don't altogether get it,
that's all. Name somebody—you know, a jazz musician you admire."

"Bird."

"Who?"

"Bird! Charlie Parker!° Don't they teach you nothing in the goddamn   130
army?"

I lit a cigarette. I was surprised and then a little amused to discover that I
was trembling. "I've been out of touch," I said. "You'll have to be patient with
me. Now. Who's this Parker character?"

"He's just one of the greatest jazz musicians alive," said Sonny, sullenly,
his hands in his pockets, his back to me. "Maybe *the* greatest," he added, bit-
terly, "that's probably why *you* never heard of him."

"All right," I said, "I'm ignorant. I'm sorry. I'll go out and buy all the cat's
records right away, all right?"

"It don't," said Sonny, with dignity, "make any difference to me. I don't
care what you listen to. Don't do me no favors."

I was beginning to realize that I'd never seen him so upset before. With   135
another part of my mind I was thinking that this would probably turn out to
be one of those things kids go through and that I shouldn't make it seem important by pushing it too hard. Still, I didn't think it would do any harm to
ask: "Doesn't all this take a lot of time? Can you make a living at it?"

"Bird! Charlie Parker!": Charlie "Bird" Parker (1920–1955), American jazz musician, played
a leading role in the development of progressive jazz during the 1940s and was also a victim of
heroin addiction.

He turned back to me and half leaned, half sat, on the kitchen table. "Everything takes time," he said, "and—well, yes, sure, I can make a living at it. But what I don't seem to be able to make you understand is that it's the only thing I want to do."

"Well, Sonny," I said gently, "you know people can't always do exactly what they *want* to do—"

"*No,* I don't know that," said Sonny, surprising me. "I think people *ought* to do what they want to do, what else are they alive for?"

"You getting to be a big boy," I said desperately, "it's time you started thinking about your future."

"I'm thinking about my future," said Sonny, grimly. "I think about it all the time."   140

I gave up. I decided, if he didn't change his mind, that we could always talk about it later. "In the meantime," I said, "you got to finish school." We had already decided that he'd have to move in with Isabel and her folks. I knew this wasn't the ideal arrangement because Isabel's folks are inclined to be dicty and they hadn't especially wanted Isabel to marry me. But I didn't know what else to do. "And we have to get you fixed up at Isabel's."

There was a long silence. He moved from the kitchen table to the window. "That's a terrible idea. You know it yourself."

"Do you have a *better* idea?"

He just walked up and down the kitchen for a minute. He was as tall as I was. He had started to shave. I suddenly had the feeling that I didn't know him at all.

He stopped at the kitchen table and picked up my cigarettes. Looking at   145
me with a kind of mocking, amused defiance, he put one between his lips. "You mind?"

"You smoking already?"

He lit the cigarette and nodded, watching me through the smoke. "I just wanted to see if I'd have the courage to smoke in front of you." He grinned and blew a great cloud of smoke to the ceiling. "It was easy." He looked at my face. "Come on, now. I bet you was smoking at my age, tell the truth."

I didn't say anything but the truth was on my face, and he laughed. But now there was something very strained in his laugh. "Sure. And I bet that ain't all you was doing."

He was frightening me a little. "Cut the crap," I said. "We already decided that you was going to go and live at Isabel's. Now what's got into you all of a sudden?"

"*You* decided it," he pointed out. "*I* didn't decide nothing." He stopped in   150
front of me, leaning against the stove, arms loosely folded. "Look, brother. I don't want to stay in Harlem no more, I really don't." He was very earnest. He looked at me, then over toward the kitchen window. There was something in his eyes I'd never seen before, some thoughtfulness, some worry all his own. He rubbed the muscle of one arm. "It's time I was getting out of here."

"Where do you want to *go,* Sonny?"

"I want to join the army. Or the navy, I don't care. If I say I'm old enough, they'll believe me."

Then I got mad. It was because I was so scared. "You must be crazy. You goddamn fool, what the hell do you want to go and join the *army* for?"

"I just told you. To get out of Harlem."

"Sonny, you haven't even finished *school.* And if you really want to be a 155
musician, how do you expect to study if you're in the *army?*"

He looked at me, trapped, and in anguish. "There's ways. I might be able to work out some kind of deal. Anyway, I'll have the G.I. Bill° when I come out."

"*If* you come out." We stared at each other. "Sonny, please. Be reasonable. I know the setup is far from perfect. But we got to do the best we can."

"I ain't learning nothing in school," he said. "Even when I go." He turned away from me and opened the window and threw his cigarette out into the narrow alley. I watched his back. "At least, I ain't learning nothing you'd want me to learn." He slammed the window so hard I thought the glass would fly out, and turned back to me. "And I'm sick of the stink of these garbage cans!"

"Sonny," I said, "I know how you feel. But if you don't finish school now, you're going to be sorry later that you didn't." I grabbed him by the shoulders. "And you only got another year. It ain't so bad. And I'll come back and I swear I'll help you do *whatever* you want to do. Just try to put up with it till I come back. Will you please do that? For me?"

He didn't answer and he wouldn't look at me.   160

"Sonny. You hear me?"

He pulled away. "I hear you. But you never hear anything *I* say."

I didn't know what to say to that. He looked out of the window and then back at me. "OK," he said, and sighed. "I'll try."

Then I said, trying to cheer him up a little. "They got a piano at Isabel's. You can practice on it."

And as a matter of fact, it did cheer him up for a minute. "That's right," 165
he said to himself. "I forgot that." His face relaxed a little. But the worry, the thoughtfulness, played on it still, the way shadows play on a face which is staring into the fire.

But I thought I'd never hear the end of that piano. At first, Isabel would write me, saying how nice it was that Sonny was so serious about his music and how, as soon as he came in from school, or wherever he had been when he was supposed to be at school, he went straight to that piano and stayed there until suppertime. And, after supper, he went back to that piano and stayed there until everybody went to bed. He was at the piano all day Saturday and all day Sunday. Then he bought a record player and started playing records. He'd play one record over and over again, all day long sometimes, and he'd improvise

the G.I. Bill: A package of benefits, including college tuition stipends, for those who serve in the armed forces.

along with it on the piano. Or he'd play one section of the record, one chord, one change, one progression, then he'd do it on the piano. Then back to the record. Then back to the piano.

Well, I really don't know how they stood it. Isabel finally confessed that it wasn't like living with a person at all, it was like living with sound. And the sound didn't make any sense to her, didn't make any sense to any of them — naturally. They began, in a way, to be afflicted by this presence that was living in their home. It was as though Sonny were some sort of god, or monster. He moved in an atmosphere which wasn't like theirs at all. They fed him and he ate, he washed himself, he walked in and out of their door; he certainly wasn't nasty or unpleasant or rude, Sonny isn't any of those things; but it was as though he were all wrapped up in some cloud, some fire, some vision all his own; and there wasn't any way to reach him.

At the same time, he wasn't really a man yet, he was still a child, and they had to watch out for him in all kinds of ways. They certainly couldn't throw him out. Neither did they dare to make a great scene about that piano because even they dimly sensed, as I sensed, from so many thousands of miles away, that Sonny was at that piano playing for his life.

But he hadn't been going to school. One day a letter came from the school board and Isabel's mother got it — there had, apparently, been other letters but Sonny had torn them up. This day, when Sonny came in, Isabel's mother showed him the letter and asked where he'd been spending his time. And she finally got it out of him that he'd been down in Greenwich Village, with musicians and other characters, in a white girl's apartment. And this scared her and she started to scream at him and what came up, once she began — though she denies it to this day — was what sacrifices they were making to give Sonny a decent home and how little he appreciated it.

Sonny didn't play the piano that day. By evening, Isabel's mother had   170
calmed down but then there was the old man to deal with, and Isabel herself. Isabel says she did her best to be calm but she broke down and started crying. She says she just watched Sonny's face. She could tell, by watching him, what was happening with him. And what was happening was that they penetrated his cloud, they had reached him. Even if their fingers had been a thousand times more gentle than human fingers ever are, he could hardly help feeling that they had stripped him naked and were spitting on that nakedness. For he also had to see that his presence, that music, which was life or death to him, had been torture for them and that they had endured it, not at all for his sake, but only for mine. And Sonny couldn't take that. He can take it a little better today than he could then but he's still not very good at it and, frankly, I don't know anybody who is.

The silence of the next few days must have been louder than the sound of all the music ever played since time began. One morning, before she went to work, Isabel was in his room for something and she suddenly realized that all of his records were gone. And she knew for certain that he was gone. And he was. He went as far as the navy would carry him. He finally sent me a postcard from some place in Greece and that was the first I knew that Sonny was still alive. I didn't see him any more until we were both back in New York and the war had long been over.

He was a man by then, of course, but I wasn't willing to see it. He came by the house from time to time, but we fought almost every time we met. I didn't like the way he carried himself, loose and dreamlike all the time, and I didn't like his friends, and his music seemed to be merely an excuse for the life he led. It sounded just that weird and disordered.

Then we had a fight, a pretty awful fight, and I didn't see him for months. By and by I looked him up, where he was living, in a furnished room in the Village, and I tried to make it up. But there were lots of other people in the room and Sonny just lay on his bed, and he wouldn't come downstairs with me, and he treated these other people as though they were his family and I weren't. So I got mad and then he got mad, and then I told him that he might just as well be dead as live the way he was living. Then he stood up and he told me not to worry about him any more in life, that he *was* dead as far as I was concerned. Then he pushed me to the door and the other people looked on as though nothing were happening, and he slammed the door behind me. I stood in the hallway, staring at the door. I heard somebody laugh in the room and then the tears came to my eyes. I started down the steps, whistling to keep from crying, I kept whistling to myself, *You going to need me, baby, one of these cold, rainy days.*

I read about Sonny's trouble in the spring. Little Grace died in the fall. She was a beautiful little girl. But she only lived a little over two years. She died of polio and she suffered. She had a slight fever for a couple of days, but it didn't seem like anything and we just kept her in bed. And we would certainly have called the doctor, but the fever dropped, she seemed to be all right. So we thought it had just been a cold. Then, one day, she was up, playing, Isabel was in the kitchen fixing lunch for the two boys when they'd come in from school, and she heard Grace fall down in the living room. When you have a lot of children you don't always start running when one of them falls, unless they start screaming or something. And, this time, Gracie was quiet. Yet, Isabel says that when she heard that *thump* and then that silence, something happened to her to make her afraid. And she ran to the living room and there was little Grace on the floor, all twisted up, and the reason she hadn't screamed was that she couldn't get her breath. And when she did scream, it was the worst sound, Isabel says, that she'd ever heard in all her life, and she still hears it sometimes in her dreams. Isabel will sometimes wake me up with a low, moaning, strangling sound and I have to be quick to awaken her and hold her to me and where Isabel is weeping against me seems a mortal wound.

I think I may have written Sonny the very day that little Grace was buried. 175 I was sitting in the living room in the dark, by myself, and I suddenly thought of Sonny. My trouble made his real.

One Saturday afternoon, when Sonny had been living with us, or anyway, been in our house, for nearly two weeks, I found myself wandering aimlessly about the living room, drinking from a can of beer, and trying to work up the courage to search Sonny's room. He was out, he was usually out whenever I was home, and Isabel had taken the children to see their grandparents. Suddenly I was standing still in front of the living room window, watching Seventh Avenue. The idea of searching Sonny's room made me still. I scarcely dared to admit to myself what I'd be searching for. I didn't know what I'd do if I found it. Or if I didn't.

On the sidewalk across from me, near the entrance to a barbecue joint, some people were holding an old-fashioned revival meeting.° The barbecue cook, wearing a dirty white apron, his conked° hair reddish and metallic in the pale sun, and a cigarette between his lips, stood in the doorway, watching them. Kids and older people paused in their errands and stood there, along with some older men and a couple of very tough-looking women who watched everything that happened on the avenue, as though they owned it, or were maybe owned by it. Well, they were watching this, too. The revival was being carried on by three sisters in black, and a brother. All they had were their voices and their Bibles and a tambourine. The brother was testifying° and while he testified two of the sisters stood together, seeming to say, amen, and the third sister walked around with the tambourine outstretched and a couple of people dropped coins into it. Then the brother's testimony ended and the sister who had been taking up the collection dumped the coins into her palm and transferred them to the pocket of her long black robe. Then she raised both hands, striking the tambourine against the air, and then against one hand, and she started to sing. And the two other sisters and the brother joined in.

It was strange, suddenly, to watch, though I had been seeing these meetings all my life. So, of course, had everybody else down there. Yet, they paused and watched and listened and I stood still at the window. "'Tis the old ship of Zion," they sang, and the sister with the tambourine kept a steady, jangling beat, "it has rescued many a thousand!" Not a soul under the sound of their voices was hearing this song for the first time, not one of them had been rescued. Nor had they seen much in the way of rescue work being done around them. Neither did they especially believe in the holiness of the three sisters and the brother, they knew too much about them, knew where they lived, and how. The woman with the tambourine, whose voice dominated the air, whose face was bright with joy, was divided by very little from the woman who stood watching her, a cigarette between her heavy, chapped lips, her hair a cuckoo's nest, her face scarred and swollen from many beatings, and her black eyes glittering like coal. Perhaps they both knew this, which was why, when, as rarely, they addressed each other, they addressed each other as Sister. As the singing filled the air the watching, listening faces underwent a change, the eyes

an old-fashioned revival meeting: A Christian religious gathering distinguished by gospel singing and public confessions of faith.

conked: Straightened by means of chemical processing.

testifying: A public proclamation of faith.

focusing on something within; the music seemed to soothe a poison out of them; and time seemed, nearly, to fall away from the sullen, belligerent, battered faces, as though they were fleeing back to their first condition, while dreaming of their last. The barbecue cook half shook his head and smiled, and dropped his cigarette and disappeared into his joint. A man fumbled in his pockets for change and stood holding it in his hand impatiently, as though he had just remembered a pressing appointment further up the avenue. He looked furious. Then I saw Sonny, standing on the edge of the crowd. He was carrying a wide, flat notebook with a green cover, and it made him look, from where I was standing, almost like a schoolboy. The coppery sun brought out the copper in his skin, he was very faintly smiling, standing very still. Then the singing stopped, the tambourine turned into a collection plate again. The furious man dropped in his coins and vanished, so did a couple of the women, and Sonny dropped some change in the plate, looking directly at the woman with a little smile. He started across the avenue, toward the house. He has a slow, loping walk, something like the way Harlem hipsters walk, only he's imposed on this his own half-beat. I had never really noticed it before.

I stayed at the window, both relieved and apprehensive. As Sonny disappeared from my sight, they began singing again. And they were still singing when his key turned in the lock.

"Hey," he said.   180

"Hey, yourself. You want some beer?"

"No. Well, maybe." But he came up to the window and stood beside me, looking out. "What a warm voice," he said.

They were singing *If I could only hear my mother pray again!*

"Yes," I said, "and she can sure beat that tambourine."

"But what a terrible song," he said, and laughed. He dropped his note-   185
book on the sofa and disappeared into the kitchen. "Where's Isabel and the kids?"

"I think they want to see their grandparents. You hungry?"

"No." He came back into the living room with his can of beer. "You want to come some place with me tonight?"

I sensed, I don't know how, that I couldn't possibly say no. "Sure. Where?"

He sat down on the sofa and picked up his notebook and started leafing through it. "I'm going to sit in with some fellows in a joint in the Village."

"You mean, you're going to play, tonight?"   190

"That's right." He took a swallow of his beer and moved back to the window. He gave me a sidelong look. "If you can stand it."

"I'll try," I said.

He smiled to himself and we both watched as the meeting across the way broke up. The three sisters and the brother, heads bowed, were singing *God be with you till we meet again.* The faces around them were very quiet. Then the song ended. The small crowd dispersed. We watched the three women and the lone man walk slowly up the avenue.

"When she was singing before," said Sonny, abruptly, "her voice reminded me for a minute of what heroin feels like sometimes—when it's in your veins. It makes you feel sort of warm and cool at the same time. And distant. And—and sure." He sipped his beer, very deliberately not looking at me. I watched his face. "It makes you feel—in control. Sometimes you've got to have that feeling."

"Do you?" I sat down slowly in the easy chair.   195

"Sometimes." He went to the sofa and picked up his notebook again. "Some people do."

"In order," I asked, "to play?" And my voice was very ugly, full of contempt and anger.

"Well"—he looked at me with great, troubled eyes, as though, in fact, he hoped his eyes would tell me things he could never otherwise say—"they *think* so. And *if* they think so—!"

"And what do *you* think?" I asked.

He sat on the sofa and put his can of beer on the floor. "I don't know," he   200
said, and I couldn't be sure if he were answering my question or pursuing his thoughts. His face didn't tell me. "It's not so much to *play*. It's to *stand* it, to be able to make it at all. On any level." He frowned and smiled: "In order to keep from shaking to pieces."

"But these friends of yours," I said, "they seem to shake themselves to pieces pretty goddamn fast."

"Maybe." He played with the notebook. And something told me that I should curb my tongue, that Sonny was doing his best to talk, that I should listen. "But of course you only know the ones that've gone to pieces. Some don't—or at least they haven't *yet* and that's just about all *any* of us can say." He paused. "And then there are some who just live, really, in hell, and they know it and they see what's happening and they go right on. I don't know." He sighed, dropped the notebook, folded his arms. "Some guys, you can tell from the way they play, they on something *all* the time. And you can see that, well, it makes something real for them. But of course," he picked up his beer from the floor and sipped it and put the can down again, "they *want* to, too, you've got to see that. Even some of them that say they don't—*some*, not all."

"And what about you?" I asked—I couldn't help it. "What about you? Do *you* want to?"

He stood up and walked to the window and I remained silent for a long time. Then he sighed. "Me," he said. Then: "While I was downstairs before, on my way here, listening to that woman sing, it struck me all of a sudden how much suffering she must have had to go through—to sing like that. It's *repulsive* to think you have to suffer that much."

I said: "But there's no way not to suffer — is there, Sonny?"   205

"I believe not," he said and smiled, "but that's never stopped anyone from trying." He looked at me. "Has it?" I realized, with this mocking look, that there stood between us, forever, beyond the power of time or forgiveness, the fact that I had held silence—so long!—when he had needed human speech to help him. He turned back to the window. "No, there's no way not to suffer. But you try all kinds of ways to keep from drowning in it, to keep on top of it, and to make it seem—well, like *you.* Like you did something, all right, and now you're suffering for it. You know?" I said nothing. "Well you know," he said, impatiently, "why *do* people suffer? Maybe it's better to do something to give it a reason, *any* reason."

"But we just agreed," I said, "that there's no way not to suffer. Isn't it better, then, just to—take it?"

"But nobody just takes it," Sonny cried, "that's what I'm telling you! *Everybody* tries not to. You're just hung up on the *way* some people try—it's not *your* way!"

The hair on my face began to itch, my face felt wet. "That's not true," I said, "that's not true. I don't give a damn what other people do, I don't even care how they suffer. I just care how *you* suffer." And he looked at me. "Please believe me," I said, "I don't want to see you—die—trying not to suffer."

"I won't," he said flatly, "die trying not to suffer. At least, not any faster   210 than anybody else."

"But there's no need," I said, trying to laugh, "is there? in killing yourself."

I wanted to say more, but I couldn't. I wanted to talk about will power and how life could be—well, beautiful. I wanted to say that it was all within; but was it? or, rather, wasn't that exactly the trouble? And I wanted to promise that I would never fail him again. But it would all have sounded—empty words and lies.

So I made the promise to myself and prayed that I would keep it.

"It's terrible sometimes, inside," he said, "that's what's the trouble. You walk these streets, black and funky and cold, and there's not really a living ass to talk to, and there's nothing shaking, and there's no way of getting it out— that storm inside. You can't talk it and you can't make love with it, and when you finally try to get with it and play it, you realize *nobody's* listening. So *you've* got to listen. You got to find a way to listen."

And then he walked away from the window and sat on the sofa again, as   215 though all the wind had suddenly been knocked out of him. "Sometimes you'll do *anything* to play, even cut your mother's throat." He laughed and looked at me. "Or your brother's." Then he sobered. "Or your own." Then: "Don't worry. I'm all right now and I think I'll *be* all right. But I can't forget—where I've been. I don't mean just the physical place I've been, I mean where I've *been.* And *what* I've been."

"What have you been, Sonny?" I asked.

He smiled—but sat sideways on the sofa, his elbow resting on the back, his fingers playing with his mouth and chin, not looking at me. "I've been something I didn't recognize, didn't know I could be. Didn't know anybody could be." He stopped, looking inward, looking helplessly young, looking old. "I'm not talking about it now because I feel *guilty* or anything like that—maybe it would be better if I did, I don't know. Anyway, I can't really talk about it. Not to you, not to anybody," and now he turned and faced me. "Sometimes, you know, and it was actually when I was most *out* of the world, I felt that I was in it, that I was *with* it, really, and I could play or I didn't really have to *play*, it just came out of me, it was there. And I don't know how I played, thinking about it now, but I know I did awful things, those times, sometimes, to people. Or it wasn't that I *did* anything to them — it was that they weren't real." He picked up the beer can; it was empty; he rolled it between his palms: "And other times — well, I needed a fix, I needed to find a place to lean, I needed to clear a space to *listen* — and I couldn't find it, and I — went crazy, I did terrible things to *me*, I was terrible *for* me." He began pressing the beer can between his hands, I watched the metal begin to give. It glittered, as he played with it like a knife, and I was afraid he would cut himself, but I said nothing. "Oh well. I can never tell you. I was all by myself at the bottom of something, stinking and sweating and crying and shaking, and I smelled it, you know? *my* stink, and I thought I'd die if I couldn't get away from it and yet, all the same, I knew that everything I was doing was just locking me in with it. And I didn't know," he paused, still flattening the beer can, "I didn't know, I still *don't* know, something kept telling me that maybe it was good to smell your own stink, but I didn't think that *that* was what I'd been trying to do — and — who can stand it?" and he abruptly dropped the ruined beer can, looking at me with a small, still smile, and then rose, walking to the window as though it were the lodestone rock. I watched his face, he watched the avenue. "I couldn't tell you when Mama died — but the reason I wanted to leave Harlem so bad was to get away from drugs. And then, when I ran away, that's what I was running from — really. When I came back, nothing had changed, *I* hadn't changed, I was just — older." And he stopped, drumming with his fingers on the windowpane. The sun had vanished, soon darkness would fall. I watched his face. "It can come again," he said, almost as though speaking to himself. Then he turned to me. "It can come again," he repeated. "I just want you to know that."

"All right," I said, at last. "So it can come again. All right."

He smiled, but the smile was sorrowful. "I had to try to tell you," he said.

"Yes," I said. "I understand that."

"You're my brother," he said, looking straight at me, and not smiling at all.

"Yes," I repeated, "yes. I understand that."

He turned back to the window, looking out. "All that hatred down there," he said, "all that hatred and misery and love. It's a wonder it doesn't blow the avenue apart."

We went to the only nightclub on a short, dark street, downtown. We squeezed through the narrow, chattering, jampacked bar to the entrance of the big room, where the bandstand was. And we stood there for a moment, for the lights were very dim in this room and we couldn't see. Then, "Hello, boy," said the voice and an enormous black man, much older than Sonny or myself, erupted out of all that atmospheric lighting and put an arm around Sonny's shoulder. "I been sitting right here," he said, "waiting for you."

He had a big voice, too, and heads in the darkness turned toward us.   225

Sonny grinned and pulled a little away, and said, "Creole, this is my brother. I told you about him."

Creole shook my hand. "I'm glad to meet you, son," he said, and it was clear that he was glad to meet me *there*, for Sonny's sake. And he smiled, "You got a real musician in *your* family," and he took his arm from Sonny's shoulder and slapped him, lightly, affectionately, with the back of his hand.

"Well. Now I've heard it all," said a voice behind us. This was another musician, and a friend of Sonny's, a coal-black, cheerful-looking man, built close to the ground. He immediately began confiding to me, at the top of his lungs, the most terrible things about Sonny, his teeth gleaming like a lighthouse and his laugh coming up out of him like the beginning of an earthquake. And it turned out that everyone at the bar knew Sonny, or almost everyone; some were musicians, working there, or nearby, or not working, some were simply hangers-on, and some were there to hear Sonny play. I was introduced to all of them and they were all very polite to me. Yet, it was clear that, for them, I was only Sonny's brother. Here, I was in Sonny's world. Or, rather: his kingdom. Here, it was not even a question that his veins bore royal blood.

They were going to play soon and Creole installed me, by myself, at a table in a dark corner. Then I watched them, Creole, and the little black man, and Sonny, and the others, while they horsed around, standing just below the bandstand. The light from the bandstand spilled just a little short of them and, watching them laughing and gesturing moving about, I had the feeling that they, nevertheless, were being most careful not to step into that circle of light too suddenly; that if they moved into the light too suddenly, without thinking, they would perish in flame. Then, while I watched, one of them, the small black man, moved into the light and crossed the bandstand and started fooling around with his drums. Then—being funny and being, also, extremely ceremonious—Creole took Sonny by the arm and led him to the piano. A woman's voice called Sonny's name and a few hands started clapping. And Sonny, also being funny and being ceremonious, and so touched, I think, that he could have cried, but neither hiding it nor showing it, riding it like a man, grinned, and put both hands to his heart and bowed from the waist.

Creole then went to the bass fiddle and a lean, very bright-skinned brown   230
man jumped up on the bandstand and picked up his horn. So there they were, and the atmosphere on the bandstand and in the room began to change and tighten. Someone stepped up to the microphone and announced them. Then there were all kinds of murmurs. Some people at the bar shushed others. The waitress ran around, frantically getting in the last orders, guys and chicks got closer to each other, and the lights on the bandstand, on the quartet, turned to a kind of indigo. Then they all looked different there. Creole looked about him for the last time, as though he were making certain that all his chickens were in the coop, and then he—jumped and struck the fiddle. And there they were.

All I know about music is that not many people ever really hear it. And even then, on the rare occasions when something opens within, and the music enters, what we mainly hear, or hear corroborated, are personal, private, vanishing evocations. But the man who creates the music is hearing something else, is dealing with the roar rising from the void and imposing order on it as it hits the air. What is evoked in him, then, is of another order, more terrible because it has no words, and triumphant, too, for that same reason. And his triumph, when he triumphs, is ours. I just watched Sonny's face. His face was troubled, he was working hard, but he wasn't with it. And I had the feeling that, in a way, everyone on the bandstand was waiting for him, both waiting for him and pushing him along. But as I began to watch Creole, I realized that it was Creole who held them all back. He had them on a short rein. Up there, keeping the beat with his whole body, wailing on the fiddle, with his eyes half closed, he was listening to everything, but he was listening to Sonny. He was having a dialogue with Sonny. He wanted Sonny to leave the shoreline and strike out for the deep water. He was Sonny's witness that deep water and drowning were not the same thing—he had been there, and he knew. And he wanted Sonny to know. He was waiting for Sonny to do the things on the keys which would let Creole know that Sonny was in the water.

And, while Creole listened, Sonny moved, deep within, exactly like someone in torment. I had never before thought of how awful the relationship must be between the musician and his instrument. He has to fill it, this instrument, with the breath of life, his own. He has to make it do what he wants it to do. And a piano is just a piano. It's made out of so much wood and wires and little hammers and big ones, and ivory. While there's only so much you can do with it, the only way to find this out is to try; to try and make it do everything.

And Sonny hadn't been near a piano for over a year. And he wasn't on much better terms with his life, not the life that stretched before him now. He and the piano stammered, started one way, got scared, stopped; started another way, panicked, marked time, started again; then seemed to have found a direction, panicked again, got stuck. And the face I saw on Sonny I'd never seen before. Everything had been burned out of it, and, at the same time, things usually hidden were being burned in, by the fire and fury of the battle which was occurring in him up there.

Yet, watching Creole's face as they neared the end of the first set, I had the feeling that something had happened, something I hadn't heard. Then they finished, there was scattered applause, and then, without an instant's warning, Creole started into something else, it was almost sardonic, it was *Am I Blue*. And, as though he commanded, Sonny began to play. Something began to happen. And Creole let out the reins. The dry, low, black man said something awful on the drums, Creole answered, and the drums talked back. Then the horn insisted, sweet and high, slightly detached perhaps, and Creole listened, commenting now and then, dry, and driving, beautiful and calm and old. Then they all came together again, and Sonny was part of the family

again. I could tell this from his face. He seemed to have found, right there beneath his fingers, a damn brand-new piano. It seemed that he couldn't get over
it. Then, for a while, just being happy with Sonny, they seemed to be agreeing
with him that brand-new pianos certainly were a gas.

Then Creole stepped forward to remind them that what they were play-   235
ing was the blues. He hit something in all of them, he hit something in me,
myself, and the music tightened and deepened, apprehension began to beat
the air. Creole began to tell us what the blues were all about. They were not
about anything very new. He and his boys up there were keeping it new, at the
risk of ruin, destruction, madness, and death, in order to find new ways to
make us listen. For, while the tale of how we suffer, and how we are delighted,
and how we may triumph is never new, it always must be heard. There isn't
any other tale to tell, it's the only light we've got in all this darkness.

And this tale, according to that face, that body, those strong hands on
those strings, has another aspect in every country, and a new depth in every
generation. Listen, Creole seemed to be saying, listen. Now these are Sonny's
blues. He made the little black man on the drums know it, and the bright,
brown man on the horn. Creole wasn't trying any longer to get Sonny in the
water. He was wishing him Godspeed. Then he stepped back, very slowly, filling the air with the immense suggestion that Sonny speak for himself.

Then they all gathered around Sonny and Sonny played. Every now and
again one of them seemed to say, amen. Sonny's fingers filled the air with life,
his life. But that life contained so many others. And Sonny went all the way
back, he really began with the spare, flat statement of the opening phrase of
the song. Then he began to make it his. It was very beautiful because it wasn't
hurried and it was no longer a lament. I seemed to hear with what burning he
had made it his, and what burning we had yet to make it ours, how we could
cease lamenting. Freedom lurked around us and I understood, at last, that he
could help us to be free if we would listen, that he would never be free until
we did. Yet, there was no battle in his face now, I heard what he had gone
through, and would continue to go through until he came to rest in earth. He
had made it his: that long line, of which we knew only Mama and Daddy. And
he was giving it back, as everything must be given back, so that, passing
through death, it can live forever. I saw my mother's face again, and felt, for
the first time, how the stones of the road she had walked on must have bruised
her feet. I saw the moonlit road where my father's brother died. And it brought
something else back to me, and carried me past it, I saw my little girl again
and felt Isabel's tears again, and I felt my own tears begin to rise. And I was
yet aware that this was only a moment, that the world waited outside, as hungry as a tiger, and that trouble stretched above us, longer than the sky.

Then it was over. Creole and Sonny let out their breath, both soaking wet,
and grinning. There was a lot of applause and some of it was real. In the dark,
the girl came by and I asked her to take drinks to the bandstand. There was a
long pause, while they talked up there in the indigo light and after awhile I saw
the girl put a Scotch and milk on top of the piano for Sonny. He didn't seem

to notice it, but just before they started playing again, he sipped from it and looked toward me, and nodded. Then he put it back on top of the piano. For me, then, as they began to play again, it glowed and shook above my brother's head like the very cup of trembling.°

cup of trembling: Isaiah 51:22: "I have taken out of thine hand the cup of trembling . . . thou shalt no more drink it again."

EXPLORING THE TEXT

1. What do we learn about the narrator through his thoughts, actions, and reactions? How would you describe his personality, values, beliefs, and attitudes, and how do they compare with those of his brother, Sonny? Why does the narrator have such difficulty understanding Sonny's love of jazz? His addiction? His way of life?

2. How does the narrator change in his relationship to Sonny during the story? What events or memories are involved in this transformation? What does he learn through these key experiences and family memories?

3. What does the narrator learn about "listening" by the time he enters the club at the conclusion of the story? How does the way he listens to Sonny change? What does real listening require?

4. What will happen to Sonny in the future? What will happen to his brother? Why do you think so?

5. Which of these characters — Sonny or his brother — do you feel the most sympathy toward? Which do you feel you understand better? Why?

6. What is Baldwin saying at the end of "Sonny's Blues" about jazz and the power of art? What is he saying about suffering and life? Overall, how do you interpret the meaning of this story?

FURTHER EXPLORATIONS

1. How might Roger C. Schank's theory of story-based understanding (p. 373) help explain both the narrator's initial inability to understand his brother and the transformation that eventually allows him to appreciate Sonny's music? What stories come to the narrator's mind when he first learns about Sonny's career choice and problems with addiction? How do stories figure in his change of heart toward his brother?

2. How might Arnold M. Ludwig's theory of cultural roles and personal identity (p. 292) help explain the conflict between Baldwin's narrator and his brother? What roles have Sonny and his brother adopted? Why do these roles make it difficult for the narrator to listen to his brother? How does the narrator's view of Sonny's role change?

3. Discuss the differences between Sonny and the narrator in light of the distinction Mary Catherine Bateson (p. 337) draws between "rigid" Western notions of the self and more open or relational ways of conceiving personal identity. To what

extent is it possible to interpret this story as depicting the collision of two different definitions of the self?

ESSAY OPTIONS

1. Write about a person who has always been a mystery to you. How might you account for your inability to understand or sympathize with this person's way of seeing the world? What aspects of your own values, attitudes, and beliefs — your own goals or fears — might make it difficult for you to see or listen to this person on his or her own terms?

2. Drawing on "Sonny's Blues" and Alice Walker's "Everyday Use" (p. 283), write an essay about the difficulty of understanding other minds within families. Why is it that family members in these stories have such a difficult time listening to each other? Do you think that family members have more or less difficulty communicating than nonfamily members? Why or why not?

The Narrative Imagination

MARTHA C. NUSSBAUM

Generations of students have sat in high school English classes on spring afternoons wondering why they have to read poems, plays, and novels about people from other times and places. What's the point when you've got your own life to lead? Nationally-renowned ethicist Martha C. Nussbaum has the answer. In this selection from *Cultivating Humanity: A Classical Defense of Reform in Liberal Education* (1997), Nussbaum argues that reading literature is a kind of ethical aerobics: by identifying with the thoughts and feelings of characters who are distinctly "other" in terms of their gender, race, culture, or class, we develop the capacity for empathy, and thus, lay the psychological foundation for the civic virtues required for life in a complex and increasingly diverse society. Nussbaum's vision of literature — from nursery rhymes to classical tragedy — as a training ground for the ethical imagination offers more than a compelling case for the importance of reading books. It also suggests that literacy is the key element in the development of our ability to read other minds. Ernest Freund Professor of Law and Ethics at the University of Chicago, Nussbaum (b. 1947) is the author of many publications on philosophy, law, and theology, including *Poetic Justice* (1996), *Love's Knowledge* (1990), and *Women and Human Development* (2000).

BEFORE READING

Write about the most memorable character you've ever encountered in a short story, novel, or play. What do you remember most vividly about this imaginary person? Why do you think you were attracted to this figure?

[There] are many forms of thought and expression within the range of human communications from which the voter derives the knowledge, intelligence, sensitivity to human values: the capacity for sane and objective judgment which, so far as possible, a ballot should express. [The] people do need novels and dramas and paintings and poems, "because they will be called upon to vote."

— ALEXANDER MEIKLEJOHN, *The First Amendment Is an Absolute*

The world citizen needs knowledge of history and social fact.[1] We have begun to see how those requirements can be met by curricula of different types. But people who know many facts about lives other than their own are still not fully equipped for citizenship. As Heraclitus° said 2,500 years ago, "Learning about many things does not produce understanding." Marcus Aurelius° insisted that to become world citizens we must not simply amass knowledge; we must also cultivate in ourselves a capacity for sympathetic imagination that will enable us to comprehend the motives and choices of people different from ourselves, seeing them not as forbiddingly alien and other, but as sharing many problems and possibilities with us. Differences of religion, gender, race, class, and national origin make the task of understanding harder, since these differences shape not only the practical choices people face but also their "insides," their desires, thoughts, and ways of looking at the world.

Here the arts play a vital role, cultivating powers of imagination that are essential to citizenship. As Alexander Meiklejohn, the distinguished constitutional scholar and theorist of "deliberative democracy," put it fifty years ago, arguing against an opponent who had denied the political relevance of art, the people of the United States need the arts precisely because they will be called upon to vote. That is not the only reason why the arts are important, but it is one significant reason. The arts cultivate capacities of judgment and sensitivity that can and should be expressed in the choices a citizen makes. To some extent this is true of all the arts. Music, dance, painting and sculpture, architecture—all have a role in shaping our understanding of the people around us. But in a curriculum for world citizenship, literature, with its ability to represent the specific circumstances and problems of people of many different sorts, makes an especially rich contribution. As Aristotle said in chapter 9 of *The Poetics*, literature shows us "not something that has happened, but the kind of thing that might happen." This knowledge of possibilities is an especially valuable resource in the political life.

To begin to understand how literature can develop a citizen's imagination, let us consider two literary works widely separated in place and time. In both cases, the literary work refers to its own distinctive capacity to promote adequate civic perception.

Heraclitus: Fifth-century-B.C.E. Greek philosopher.

Marcus Aurelius: (121–180 C.E.), Stoic philosopher and emperor of Rome.

Sophocles' *Philoctetes,* produced in 409 B.C., during a crisis in the Athenian democracy, concerns the proper treatment of a citizen who has become an outcast, crippled by a disfiguring illness. On his way to Troy to fight with the Greeks in the Trojan War, Philoctetes stepped by mistake into a sacred shrine. His foot, bitten by the serpent who guards the shrine, began to ooze with an ulcerous sore, and his cries of pain disrupted the army's religious festivals. So the commanders abandoned him on the deserted island of Lemnos, with no companions and no resources but his bow and arrows. Ten years later, learning that they cannot win the war without his magical bow, they return, determined to ensnare him by a series of lies into participating in the war. The commander Odysseus shows no interest in Philoctetes as a person; he speaks of him only as a tool of public ends. The chorus of common soldiers has a different response (lines 169–176):

> For my part, I have compassion for him. Think how
> with no human company or care,
> no sight of a friendly face,
> wretched, always alone,
> he wastes away with that savage disease,
> with no way of meeting his daily needs.
> How, how in the world, does the poor man survive?

Unlike their leader, the men of the chorus vividly and sympathetically imagine the life of a man whom they have never seen, picturing his loneliness, his pain, his struggle for survival. In the process they stand in for, and allude to, the imaginative work of the audience, who are invited by the play as a whole to imagine the sort of needy, homeless life to which prosperous people rarely direct their attention. The drama as a whole, then, cultivates the type of sympathetic vision of which its characters speak. In the play, this kind of vivid imagining prompts a political decision against using Philoctetes as a means, and the audience is led to believe this to be a politically and morally valuable result. In this way, by showing the public benefits of the very sort of sympathy it is currently awakening in its spectators, the drama commends its own resources as valuable for the formation of decent citizenship and informed public choice. Although the good of the whole should not be neglected, that good will not be well served if human beings are seen simply as instruments of one another's purposes.

Ralph Ellison's *Invisible Man* (1952) develops this tradition of reflection 5 about our failures of perception and recognition. Its hero describes himself as "invisible" because throughout the novel he is seen by those he encounters as a vehicle for various race-inflected stereotypes: the poor, humiliated black boy who snatches like an animal at the coins that lie on an electrified mat; the good student trusted to chauffeur a wealthy patron; the listening ear to whom this same patron unburdens his guilt and anxiety; the rabble-rousing activist who energizes an urban revolutionary movement; the violent rapist who gratifies the sexual imagination of a woman brought up on racially charged sexual images — always he is cast in a drama of someone else's making, "never more loved and appreciated" than when he plays his assigned role. The "others," meanwhile, are all "lost in a dream world" — in which they see only what their own minds have created, never the reality of the person who stands before them. "You go along for years knowing something is wrong, then suddenly you discover that you're as transparent as air." Invisibility is "a matter of the construction of their inner eyes, those eyes with which they look through their physical eyes upon reality."[2]

Ellison's grotesque, surreal world is very unlike the classical world of Sophocles' play. Its concerns, however, are closely linked: social stratification and injustice, manipulation and use, and above all invisibility and the condition of being transparent to and for one's fellow citizens. Like Sophocles' drama, it explores and savagely excoriates these refusals to see. Like that drama, it invites its readers to know and see more than the unseeing characters. "Being invisible and without substance, a disembodied voice, as it were, what else could I do? What else but try to tell you what was really happening when your eyes were looking through?"[3] In this way, it works upon the inner eyes of the very readers whose moral failures it castigates, although it refuses the easy notion that mutual visibility can be achieved in one heartfelt leap of brotherhood.

Ellison explicitly linked the novelist's art to the possibility of democracy. By representing both visibility and its evasions, both equality and its refusal, a novel, he wrote in an introduction, "could be fashioned as a raft of hope, perception and entertainment that might help keep us afloat as we tried to negotiate the snags and whirlpools that mark our nation's vacillating course toward and away from the democratic idea." This is not, he continued, the only goal for fiction; but it is one proper and urgent goal. For a democracy requires not only institutions and procedures; it also requires a particular quality of vision, in order "to defeat this national tendency to deny the common humanity shared by my character and those who might happen to read of his experience."[4] The novel's mordantly satirical treatment of stereotypes, its fantastic use of image and symbol (in, for example, the bizarre dreamlike sequence in the white-paint factory), and its poignant moments of disappointed hope, all contribute to this end.

As Ellison says, forming the civic imagination is not the only role for literature, but it is one salient role. Narrative art has the power to make us see the lives of the different with more than a casual tourist's interest — with involvement and sympathetic understanding, with anger at our society's refusals of visibility. We come to see how circumstances shape the lives of those who share with us some general goals and projects; and we see that circumstances shape not only people's possibilities for action, but also their aspirations and desires, hopes and fears. All of this seems highly pertinent to decisions we must make as citizens. Understanding, for example, how a history of racial stereotyping can affect self-esteem, achievement, and love enables us to make more informed judgments on issues relating to affirmative action and education. . . .

Fancy and Wonder

When a child and a parent begin to tell stories together, the child is acquiring essential moral capacities. Even a simple nursery rhyme such as "Twinkle, twinkle little star, how I wonder what you are" leads children to feel wonder — a sense of mystery that mingles curiosity with awe.[5] Children wonder about the little star. In so doing they learn to imagine that a mere shape in the heavens has an inner world, in some ways mysterious, in some ways like their own. They learn to attribute life, emotion, and thought to a form whose insides are hidden. As time goes on, they do this in an increasingly sophisticated way, learning to hear and tell stories about animals and humans. These stories interact with their own attempts to explain the world and their own actions in it. A child deprived of stories is deprived, as well, of certain ways of viewing other people. For the insides of people, like the insides of stars, are not open to view. They must be wondered about. And the conclusion that this set of limbs in front of me has emotions and feelings and thoughts of the sort I attribute to myself will not be reached without the training of the imagination that storytelling promotes.

Narrative play does teach children to view a personlike shape as a house   10 for hope and fear and love and anger, all of which they have known themselves. But the wonder involved in storytelling also makes evident the limits of each person's access to every other. "How I wonder what you are," goes the rhyme. In that simple expression is an acknowledgment of the lack of completeness in one's own grasp of the fear, the love, the sympathy, the anger, of the little star, or of any other creature or person. In fact the child adept at storytelling soon learns that people in stories are frequently easier to know than people in real life, who, as Proust° puts it in *The Past Recaptured*, frequently offer "a dead weight that our sensitivity cannot remove," a closed exterior that cannot be penetrated even by a sensitive imagination. The child, wondering about its parents, soon learns about these obstacles, just as it also learns that its parents need not know everything that goes on in its own mind. The habits of wonder promoted by storytelling thus define the other person as spacious and deep, with qualitative differences from oneself and hidden places worthy of respect.

In these various ways, narrative imagination is an essential preparation for moral interaction. Habits of empathy and conjecture conduce to a certain type of citizenship and a certain form of community: one that cultivates a sympathetic responsiveness to another's needs, and understands the way circumstances shape those needs, while respecting separateness and privacy. This is so because of the way in which literary imagining both inspires intense concern with the fate of characters and defines those characters as containing a

---

Proust: Marcel Proust (1871–1922), French novelist.

rich inner life, not all of which is open to view; in the process, the reader learns to have respect for the hidden contents of that inner world, seeing its importance in defining a creature as fully human. It is this respect for the inner life of consciousness that literary theorist Lionel Trilling describes when he calls the imagination of the novel reader a "liberal imagination"[6] — meaning by this that the novel reader is led to attribute importance to the material conditions of happiness while respecting human freedom.

As children grow older, the moral and social aspects of these literary scenarios become increasingly complex and full of distinctions, so that they gradually learn how to ascribe to others, and recognize in themselves, not only hope and fear, happiness and distress — attitudes that are ubiquitous, and comprehensible without extensive experience — but also more complex traits such as courage, self-restraint, dignity, perseverance, and fairness. These notions might be defined for the child in an abstract way; but to grasp their full meaning in one's own self-development and in social interactions with others requires learning their dynamics in narrative settings.

As children grasp such complex facts in imagination, they become capable of compassion. Compassion involves the recognition that another person, in some ways similar to oneself, has suffered some significant pain or misfortune in a way for which that person is not, or not fully, to blame. As many moral traditions emphasize — the analysis of compassion is remarkably constant in both Western and non-Western philosophy — it requires estimating the significance of the misfortune as accurately as one can — usually in agreement with the sufferer, but sometimes in ways that depart from that person's own judgment. Adam Smith° points out that people who lose their mental faculties are the objects of our compassion even though they themselves are not aware of this loss: what is significant is the magnitude of the loss, as the onlooker estimates its role in the life of the loser. This requires, in turn, a highly complex set of moral abilities, including the ability to imagine what it is like to be in that person's place (what we usually call *empathy*), and also the ability to stand back and ask whether the person's own judgment has taken the full measure of what has happened.

Compassion requires one thing more: a sense of one's own vulnerability to misfortune. To respond with compassion, I must be willing to entertain the thought that this suffering person might be me. And this I will be unlikely to do if I am convinced that I am above the ordinary lot and no ill can befall me. There are exceptions to this, in some religious traditions' portrayals of the compassion of God; but philosophers such as Aristotle and Rousseau° have plausibly claimed that imperfect human beings need the belief that their own possibilities are similar to those of the suffering person, if they are to respond with compassion to another's plight. This recognition, as they see it, helps explain why compassion

---

Adam Smith: (1723–1790), Scottish economist.

Rousseau: Jean-Jacques Rousseau (1721–1778), French philosopher.

so frequently leads to generous support for the needs of others: one thinks, "That might have been me, and that is how I should want to be treated."

Compassion, so understood, promotes an accurate awareness of our common vulnerability. It is true that human beings are needy, incomplete creatures who are in many ways dependent on circumstances beyond their control for the possibility of well-being. As Rousseau argues in *Emile,* people do not fully grasp that fact until they can imagine suffering vividly to themselves, and feel pain at the imagining. In a compassionate response to the suffering of another, one comprehends that being prosperous or powerful does not remove one from the ranks of needy humanity. Such reminders, the tradition argues, are likely to lead to a more beneficent treatment of the weak. Philoctetes, in Sophocles' play, asks for aid by reminding the soldiers that they themselves might suffer what he has suffered. They accept because they are able to imagine his predicament.

It seems, then, to be beneficial for members of a society to see themselves as bound to one another by similar weaknesses and needs, as well as by similar capacities for achievement. As Aristotle argues in chapter 9 of *The Poetics,* literature is "more philosophical than history"—by which he means more conducive to general human understanding—precisely because it acquaints us with "the kind of thing that might happen," general forms of possibility and their impact on human lives.

Compassion requires demarcations: which creatures am I to count as my fellow creatures, sharing possibilities with me? One may be a person of refined feeling and still treat many people in one's world as invisible, their prospects as unrelated to one's own. Rousseau argues that a good education, which acquaints one with all the usual vicissitudes of fortune, will make it difficult to refuse acknowledgment to the poor or the sick, or slaves, or members of lower classes. It is easy to see that any one of those might really have been me, given a change of circumstances. Boundaries of nationality can similarly be transcended in thought, for example by the recognition that one of the frequent hazards of wartime is to lose one's nation. Boundaries of race, of gender, and of sexual orientation prove, historically, more recalcitrant: for there might appear to be little real-life possibility of a man's becoming a woman, a white person's becoming black, or even (*pace* earlier psychiatry) a straight person's becoming gay or lesbian. In these cases, then, it is all the more urgent to cultivate the basis for compassion through the fictional exercise of imagination—for if one cannot in fact change one's race, one can imagine what it is like to inhabit a race different from one's own, and by becoming close to a person of different race or sexual orientation, one can imagine what it would be like for someone one loves to have such a life.

Rousseau thought that people differed only in circumstances: underneath, their desires, aims, and emotions were the same. But in fact one of the things imagining reveals to us is that we are not all brothers under the skin, that circumstances of oppression form desire and emotion and aspiration. Some characters feel like us, and some repel easy identification. But such failures to identify can also be sources of understanding. Both by identification and by its absence, we learn what life has done to people. A society that wants to foster the just treatment of all its members has strong reasons to foster an exercise of the compassionate imagination that crosses social boundaries, or tries to. And this means caring about literature.

Literature and the Compassionate Imagination

The basis for civic imagining must be laid in early life. As children explore stories, rhymes, and songs — especially in the company of the adults they love — they are led to notice the sufferings of other living creatures with a new keenness. At this point, stories can then begin to confront children more plainly with the uneven fortunes of life, convincing them emotionally of their urgency and importance. "Let him see, let him feel the human calamities," Rousseau writes of his imaginary pupil. "Unsettle and frighten his imagination with the perils by which every human being is constantly surrounded. Let him see around him all these abysses, and, hearing you describe them, hold on to you for fear of falling into them."[7]

For older children and young adults, more complex literary works now should be added. It was in connection with the moral education of young adults that ancient Athenian culture ascribed enormous importance to tragic drama. Going to a tragedy was not understood to be an "aesthetic experience," if that means an experience detached from civic and political concerns. The tragic festivals of the fifth century B.C. were civic festivals during which every other civic function stopped, and all citizens gathered together. Dramas were routinely assessed as much for their moral and political content as for their other characteristics. Indeed, as the literary criticism preserved in Aristophanes' *Frogs* makes plain, it was well understood that formal devices of meter, vocabulary, and verse form conveyed, themselves, a moral content. What, then, was the civic education that tragedies were intended to promote?

Tragedies acquaint the young citizen with the bad things that may happen in a human life, long before life itself does so. In the process they make the significance of suffering, and the losses that inspire it, unmistakably plain to the spectator; this is one way in which the poetic and visual resources of the drama have moral weight. By inviting the spectators to identify with the tragic hero, at the same time portraying the hero as a relatively good person, whose distress does not stem from deliberate wickedness, the drama makes compassion for suffering seize the imagination. This emotion is built into the dramatic form.

The sympathies of the spectator are broadened in the process, through the notion of risks that are common to all human beings. Tragedies are obsessed with the possibilities and weaknesses of human life as such, and with the contrast between human life and other, less limited lives, belonging to gods and demigods. In the process they move their spectator, in imagination, from the male world of war to the female world of the household. They ask the future

20

male citizen of ancient Athens to identify himself not only with those he might in actual fact become — beggars, exiles, generals, slaves — but also with many who in some sense he can never be, such as Trojans and Persians and Africans, such as wives and daughters and mothers.

Through such devices the drama explores both similarity and difference. Identifying with a woman in a drama, a young male spectator would find that he can in some sense remain himself, that is to say, a reasoning human being with moral virtues and commitments. On the other hand, he discovers through this identification much that is not his own lot: the possibility, for example, of being raped and being forced to bear the enemy's child; the possibility of witnessing the deaths of children whom one has nursed oneself; the possibility of being abandoned by one's husband and in consequence totally without social support. He is brought up against the fact that people as articulate and able as he face disaster and shame in some ways that males do not; and he is asked to think about that as something relevant to himself. So far from being "great books" without a political agenda, these dramas were directly pertinent to democratic debates about the treatment of captured peoples in wartime. With their efforts to overcome socially shaped invisibilities, they participated actively in those debates.

Literature does not transform society single-handed; we know that these powerful and in some sense radical dramatic experiences took place in a society that was highly repressive of women, even by the standards of its own era. Certain ideas about others may be grasped for a time and yet not be acted upon, so powerful are the forces of habit and the entrenched structures of privilege and convention. Nonetheless, the artistic form makes its spectator perceive, for a time, the invisible people of their world — at least a beginning of social justice.

The tragic form asks its spectators to cross cultural and national boundaries. On the other hand, in its universality and abstractness it omits much of the fabric of daily civic life, with its concrete distinctions of rank and power and wealth and the associated ways of thinking and speaking. For such reasons, later democratic thinkers interested in literature as a vehicle of citizenship came to take a particular interest in the novel — a genre whose rise coincided with, and supported, the rise of modern democracy.[8] In reading a realist novel with active participation, readers do all that tragic spectators do — and something more. They embrace the ordinary. They care not only about kings and children of kings, but about David Copperfield,° painfully working in a factory, or walking the twenty-six miles from London to Canterbury without food. Such concrete realities of a life of poverty are brought home to them with a textured vividness unavailable in tragic poetry.

Again, the reader's learning involves both sameness and difference. Reading a novel of class difference (for example, a novel of Dickens), one is aware, on the one hand, of many links to the lives of the characters and their

David Copperfield: Title character in Charles Dickens's 1849 novel of the same name.

aspirations, hopes, and sufferings. There are many ways, however, in which circumstances have made the lives of the poorer characters very different from those of middle-class readers. Such readers assess those differences, thinking of their consequence for aspirations to a rich and fulfilling life. They also notice differences in the inner world, seeing the delicate interplay between common human goals and the foreignness that can be created by circumstances. Differences of class, race, ethnicity, gender, and national origin all shape people's possibilities, and their psychology with them. Ellison's "invisible man," for example, repels the easy and facile sympathy that says "we are all brothers" because his inner world strikes the reader as dark and frightening, as the secure child of a loving home gradually takes on more savage and pessimistic sentiments. In this way we start to see how deeply racism penetrates the mind and emotions. Consider, for example, the scene in which the narrator buys a yam from a Harlem street vendor. His emotions of homesickness, delight, and recognition are in one sense familiar; but the struggle with shame, as he decides not to hide his pleasure in something he has been taught to see as a sign of negritude, will be unfamiliar to the white middle-class reader, who probably will not be able to identify with such an experience. Such a failure of sympathy, however, prompts a deeper and more pertinent kind of sympathy, as one sees that a human being who initially might have grown up free from the deforming experience of racism has been irrevocably shaped by that experience; and one does come to see that experience of being formed by oppression as a thing "such as might happen" to oneself or someone one loves.

This complex interpretive art is what the Stoics° required when they asked the world citizen to gain empathic understanding of people who are different.[9] This idea, however, needs to be developed in a specifically democratic way, as an essential part of thinking and judging well in a pluralistic democratic society that is part of an even more complex world. One literary figure from our own tradition who gives us particular help in this task is Walt Whitman,° who saw the literary artist as an irreplaceably valuable educator of democratic citizens. "Their Presidents," he wrote, "shall not be their common referee so much as their poets shall."[10] He went on to argue that literary art develops capacities for perception and judgment that are at the very heart of democracy, prominently including the ability to "see eternity in men and women," understanding their aspirations and the complexity of their inner world, rather than to "see men and women as dreams or dots," as mere statistics or numbers. Whitman makes it clear that his idea of a democratic poetry is his own translation of the ancient Athenian idea to the situation of modern America: in "Song of the Exposition" he imagines the Muse of ancient Greek poetry migrating to the New World and

---

the Stoics: Stoicism was a fourth-century-B.C.E. Greek school of philosophy founded on the belief that since all events expressed the divine will, one should accept one's fate without regret or emotional reaction.

Walt Whitman: openly gay American poet (1819–1892).

inspiring his poetry, "undeterr'd" by America's mixture of peoples and its surprising love of machinery.

The poet's ability to "see eternity," Whitman holds, is especially important when we are dealing with groups whose humanity has not always been respected in our society: women and racial minorities, homosexuals, the poor and the powerless. A major part of the social role of the literary artist, as he saw it, was to promote our sympathetic understanding of all outcast or oppressed people, by giving their strivings voice. "I am he attesting sympathy," the poet announces (*Song of Myself* 22.461–24.5):

> Through me many long dumb voices,
> Voices of the interminable generations of prisoners and slaves,
> Voices of the diseas'd and despairing and of thieves and dwarfs,
> . . .
>
> Through me forbidden voices,
> Voices of sexes and lusts, voices veil'd and I remove the veil,
> Voices indecent by me clarified and transfigur'd . . .
>
> Dazzling and tremendous how quick the sun-rise would kill me,
> If I could not now and always send sun-rise out of me.

The poet in effect becomes the voice of silenced people, sending their speech out of himself as a kind of light for the democracy. Like Ellison much later, Whitman focuses on our failures to see the flesh and blood of those with whom we live; his poems, like Ellison's novel, portray themselves as devices of recognition and inclusion. The imagining he demands promotes a respect for the voices and the rights of others, reminding us that the other has both agency and complexity, is neither a mere object nor a passive recipient of benefits and satisfactions. At the same time, it promotes a vivid awareness of need and disadvantage, and in that sense gives substance to the abstract desire for justice.

As in Athens, so in America: the fact that sympathy inspired by literary 30 imagining does not immediately effect political change should not make us deny its moral worth. If we follow Whitman's idea, we will conclude that it is essential to put the study of literature at the heart of a curriculum for citizenship, because it develops arts of interpretation that are essential for civic participation and awareness.

Notes

1. The issues here are treated at greater length in Martha C. Nussbaum, *Poetic Justice: The Literary Imagination in Public Life* (Boston: Beacon Press, 1996).

2. Ralph Ellison, *Invisible Man* (New York: Random House, 1992), pp. 563, 566, 3.

3. Ibid., p. 572.

4. Ibid., pp. xxiv–xxv, xxvi.

5. See Nussbaum, *Poetic Justice,* for Dickens' discussion of this case.

6. See Lionel Trilling, *The Liberal Imagination* (New York: Scribner's, 1953).

7. Jean-Jacques Rousseau, *Emile, or On Education,* trans. Allan Bloom (New York: Basic Books, 1979), p. 224.

8. On this phenomenon, see Charles Taylor, *Sources of the Self: The Making of the Modern Identity* (Cambridge, Mass.: Harvard University Press, 1989); also Ian Watt, *The Rise of the Novel* (Berkeley: University of California Press, 1957).

9. The original Stoics were critical of most literature of their time, since they believed that it usually exaggerated the importance of circumstances for human well-being. But this aspect of their view is logically independent of their interest in sympathetic perception, which naturally led them to take an interest in cultivating the imagination.

10. Walt Whitman, "By Blue Ontario's Shore."

EXPLORING THE TEXT

1. Why does Nussbaum feel that instruction in literature plays an important role in the civic life of a democracy? Based on your own experiences of reading literature in school, would you agree with her position? Why or why not?

2. How do stories contribute to the development of empathy and compassion in childhood, according to Nussbaum? What insights do stories provide children about other people and their situations? To what extent do you agree with her claim that empathetic identification with fictional "others" helps us transcend boundaries of class, race, gender, and nationality?

3. Why is tragedy particularly well suited to the development of empathy and compassion, according to Nussbaum? What lessons are taught by tragic drama and the modern novel? In what sense do most "great books" contain a clear "political agenda" in Nussbaum's view? Would you agree, based on your experience of reading the classics?

FURTHER EXPLORATIONS

1. Drawing on Nussbaum's theory of the narrative imagination, assess James Baldwin's "Sonny's Blues" (p. 390) as an example of how fiction promotes the development of empathy and compassion. What does Baldwin help the reader see about other minds and ways of living through the story of Sonny and his brother? How does it work on the "inner eyes" of the reader? What features does Baldwin's story have in common with classical tragedy?

2. Nussbaum argues that "the artistic form makes its spectator perceive, for a time, the invisible people of their world" (para. 24) and notes that this insight derived through the imaginative appreciation of art is "at least a beginning of social justice" (para. 24). In what ways do Alice Walker's story "Everyday Use" (p. 283) and/or Loren Eiseley's essay "The Brown Wasps" (p. 150) confirm this view of the social role of art and the imagination? To what extent do these works convey what you'd consider to be a particularly political message?

3. How does Nussbaum's view of our ability to understand other minds compare with that of Roger C. Schank (p. 373)? How might Schank respond to Nussbaum's claim that imaginative literature cultivates habits of empathy and conjecture that promote the development of genuine understanding and compassion? Do the student responses Schank collects show this kind of compassion or empathetic response?

ESSAY OPTIONS

1. Drawing on your knowledge of recent films, television dramas, adolescent novels, or comic books, write a paper in which you explore the extent to which Nussbaum's claims for the humanizing and democratizing influence of literature can be extended to works of contemporary popular culture. Do pop-culture heroes and heroines encourage the kind of empathy that "is conducive to a certain type of citizenship and community"? How would you describe the personal attitudes and attributes that are associated with the characters that dominate popular culture today? How might current pop-culture characters be shaping our views of other minds?

2. Survey a number of current children's books and compare them to several books you recall from your own childhood. Then use this informal research as the basis of a paper discussing the role that children's literature plays in the development of empathetic understanding of other minds. What lessons do these books teach about the hidden, inner complexities of other people? What qualities of character in others do they help children recognize? In what ways do they prepare children for citizenship in a diverse society? What changes, if any, do you note in the messages that children's books convey today about the value of wonder and nature of other minds?

Hidden Culture

EDWARD T. HALL

It might come as a surprise, but it turns out that there's precious little connection between your mind and your brain. Brains are made up of cells that are made up of molecules that are made up of atoms. Melt down a brain and all you get is a mess of organic compounds with no mind in sight. Minds, by contrast, are made up of thoughts, beliefs, values, attitudes, perceptions, and ideas. So, if you're serious about examining minds, it makes more sense to begin in the lobby of a Tokyo hotel than in a neurologist's lab — at least that's the approach taken by anthropologist Edward T. Hall. In Hall's view, human minds aren't the product of brains, but of the cultures they're associated with. So, if you want to read the mind of someone from Japan, you first have to learn how to read the patterns of value, attitude, and belief that make up Japanese culture. But as Hall insists, you can't possibly begin to engage in such cross-cultural mind reading until you recognize how the cultures you grew up in shape your own values, reactions, and interpretations. An expert in intercultural communication, Edward T. Hall (b. 1914) has taught at Northwestern University, the University of Denver, Bennington College, the Washington School of Psychiatry, the Harvard Business School, and the Illinois Institute of Technology. He currently lives in Santa Fe, New Mexico, where he divides his time between writing and research. His publications include *The Silent Language* (1959), *The Hidden Dimension* (1966), and, most recently, *West of the Thirties: Discoveries Among the Navajo and Hopi* (1994).

BEFORE READING

Write a journal entry about a misunderstanding or conflict you have witnessed or personally experienced that involved a clash of cultures. What happened? What cultural groups were involved? What did you learn from this experience?

Consistency and Life

M an's nervous system evolved before the time of mass media, mass transportation, airplanes, and automobiles. For over a million years, our forefathers knew the significance of every act of all the individuals around them. Like the body language of a dog who wags his tail and prances with forepaws spread out, saying, "Let's play," or raises the hair on his back, saying, "Stay away," the physical signs as well as the behavioral cues of people who were known were easy to read. Stability and predictability were essential if human society was to prosper, develop, and evolve to its present point. Living today in a rapidly changing, ever-shrinking world, it is hard for most of us to conceive what it would be like to grow up and live in a world that did not change, and where there were few strangers because one always saw and dealt with the same people. Those who were raised in the now-disappearing small town have some notion of what it must have been like during the major portion of man's past — quite comfortable and reassuring, but very public. People knew what was coming next before you did something or even knew that you were going to do it. "Jake's going to get a new horse." "Yup. He always fattens up the old one before he trades. Too cheap to feed 'em the rest of the time."

"You can always tell when Mike's getting ready to take somebody apart. First, he gets up and walks around, then he looks out the window with his back to everyone, pulls out his pocket comb and gets every hair in place. When he turns around and looks at them, you know it's going to happen."

Unlike animals, many of whose responses are innate, much of man's communicative behavior evolved independently of his physiology, and like the spoken language, it cannot be read with assurance if one is dealing with a new culture or even a subculture one does not know well. Man's body is recognizably human everywhere, even though such superficial characteristics as skin color, hair form, physiognomy, and body build may vary. Unless we start tampering with it, this panhuman form will be with us for thousands of generations to come. What has changed, what has evolved, and what is characteristically man — in fact, what gives man his identity no matter where he is born — is his culture, the total communication framework: words, actions, postures, gestures, tones of voice, facial expressions, the way he handles time, space, and materials, and the way he works, plays, makes love, and defends himself. All these things and more are complete communication systems with meanings that can be read correctly only if one is familiar with the behavior in its historical, social, and cultural context.[1]

Everything man is and does is modified by learning and is therefore malleable. But once learned, these behavior patterns, these habitual responses, these ways of interacting gradually sink below the surface of the mind and, like the admiral of a submerged submarine fleet, control from the depths. The hidden controls are usually experienced as though they were innate simply because they are not only ubiquitous but habitual as well.[2]

What makes it doubly hard to differentiate the innate from the acquired   5
is the fact that, as people grow up, everyone around them shares the same patterns. This is not true, of course, if one grows up in a bicultural or tricultural situation, which can be a tremendous asset because it accustoms one to the fact that people are really very different in the ways they behave. In bicultural cases, I have seen people shift from a Spanish to a German way of interacting without knowing that the shift occurred. Also, I have seen others start with a Greek pattern and slip automatically into a German-Swiss pattern as the situation demanded.

Fantastic? Yes, but reasonably common—a function of the way the information-processing and control mechanisms of the brain operate. In fact, according to Powers,[3] man's nervous system is structured in such a way that the patterns that govern behavior and perception come into consciousness only when there is a deviation from plan. That is why the most important paradigms or rules governing behavior, the ones that control our lives, function below the level of conscious awareness and are not generally available for analysis. This is an important point, one that is often overlooked or denied. The cultural unconscious, like Freud's unconscious,° not only controls man's actions but can be understood only by painstaking processes of detailed analysis. Hence, man automatically treats what is most characteristically his own (the culture of his youth) as though it were innate. He is forced into the position of thinking and feeling that anyone whose behavior is not predictable or is peculiar in any way is slightly out of his mind, improperly brought up, irresponsible, psychopathic, politically motivated to a point beyond all redemption, or just plain inferior.

A comment one frequently hears in cross-cultural situations is: "Oh, I just try to be myself and take them as they are. After all, they are adult human beings, aren't they?" Fine and dandy. In superficial social situations, the be-yourself formula works. But what if you are an Anglo schoolteacher with a

---

Freud's unconscious: In the psychoanalytic theory of Austrian neurologist Sigmund Freud (1856–1939), the aspect of the mind that is not accessible to deliberate conscious thought, associated with repressed feelings and desires.

Spanish American class and are confronted with what appears to be a lack of motivation on the part of your students? You, as a non-Spanish American take it for granted that a certain percentage of children want to do well and to get ahead. So it comes as a shock when you learn that, to many New Mexican Spanish, to stand out from one's peers is to place oneself in great jeopardy and is to be avoided at all costs. Suddenly, your old stereotypes take on a new meaning.

Today, man is increasingly placed in positions in which culture can no longer be depended upon to produce reliable readings of what other people are going to do next. He is constantly in the position of interacting with strangers, so he must take the next step and begin to transcend his culture. This cannot be done in an armchair.

However, what may at first be experienced as a very difficult chore can turn out to be deeply and personally significant. In this context, it is important to keep reminding oneself that the part of man's nervous system that deals with social behavior is designed according to the principle of negative feedback. That is, one is completely unaware of the fact that there is a system of controls as long as the program is followed. Ironically, this means that the majority of mankind are denied knowledge of important parts of the self by virtue of the way the control systems work. The only time one is aware of the control system is when things don't follow the hidden program. This is most frequent in intercultural encounters. Therefore, the great gift that the members of the human race have for each other is not exotic experiences but an opportunity to achieve awareness of the structure of their *own* system, which can be accomplished only by interacting with others who do not share that system—members of the opposite sex, different age groups, different ethnic groups, and different cultures—all suffice. . . .

Hidden Culture

The paradox of culture is that language, the system most frequently used to describe culture, is by nature poorly adapted to this difficult task. It is too linear, not comprehensive enough, too slow, too limited, too constrained, too unnatural, too much a product of it own evolution, and too artificial. This means that the writer must constantly keep in mind the limitations language places upon him. He is aided, however, by one thing which makes all communication possible and on which all communication and all culture depend; namely, that language is not (as is commonly thought) a system for transferring thoughts or meaning from one brain to another, but a system for organizing information and for releasing thoughts and responses in other organisms. The materials for whatever insights there are in this world exist in incipient form, frequently unformulated but nevertheless already there in man. One may help to release them in a variety of ways, but it is impossible to plant them in the minds of others. Experience does that for us instead—particularly overseas experience.

I can think of few countries Americans are likely to visit and work in in significant numbers where it is more difficult to control one's inputs and where life is more filled with surprises than Japan. Clearly, the above observation does not apply to short visits and the like, because all over the world suitable environments have been created for tourists that shield them from the reality of the life of the people. Tourists seldom stick around for long, and they are happier insulated from the full impact of the foreign culture. Businessmen, educators, government officials, and Foreign Service personnel are something else again. It is to this group that my thoughts are directed, because they stand to gain the most from understanding cultural processes in living contexts. Understanding the reality of covert culture and accepting it on a gut level comes neither quickly nor easily, and it must be lived rather than read or reasoned. However, there are times when examples of what is experienced most intimately can illustrate certain basic patterns that are widely shared. . . . For no matter how well prepared one is intellectually for immersion in another culture, there is the inevitability of surprises.

A few years ago, I became involved in a sequence of events in Japan that completely mystified me, and only later did I learn how an overt act seen from the vantage point of one's own culture can have an entirely different meaning when looked at in the context of the foreign culture. I had been staying at a hotel in downtown Tokyo that had European as well as Japanese-type rooms. The clientele included a few Europeans but was predominantly Japanese. I had been a guest for about ten days and was returning to my room in the middle of an afternoon. Asking for my key at the desk, I took the elevator to my floor. Entering the room, I immediately sensed that something was wrong. Out of place. Different. I was in the wrong room! Someone else's things were distributed around the head of the bed and the table. Somebody else's toilet articles (those of a Japanese male) were in the bathroom. My first thoughts were, "What if I am discovered here? How do I explain my presence to a Japanese who may not even speak English?"

I was close to panic as I realized how incredibly territorial we in the West are. I checked my key again. Yes, it really was mine. Clearly they had moved somebody else into my room. But where was my room now? And where were my belongings? Baffled and mystified, I took the elevator to the lobby. Why hadn't they told me at the desk, instead of letting me risk embarrassment and loss of face by being caught in somebody else's room? Why had they moved me in the first place? It was a nice room and, being sensitive to spaces and how they work, I was loath to give it up. After all, I had told them I would be in the hotel for almost a month. Why this business of moving me around like someone who has been squeezed in without a reservation? Nothing made sense.

At the desk I was told by the clerk, as he sucked in his breath in deference (and embarrassment?) that indeed they had moved me. My particular room had been reserved in advance by somebody else. I was given the key to my new room and discovered that all my personal effects were distributed around the new room almost as though I had done it myself. This produced a fleeting and strange feeling that maybe I wasn't myself. How could somebody else do all those hundred and one little things just the way I did?

Three days later, I was moved again, but this time I was prepared. There was no shock, just the simple realization that I had been moved and that it would now be doubly difficult for friends who had my old room number to reach me. *Tant pis,*° I was in Japan. One thing did puzzle me. Earlier, when I had stayed at Frank Lloyd Wright's Imperial Hotel° for several weeks, nothing like this had ever happened. What was different? What had changed? Eventually I got used to being moved and would even ask on my return each day whether I was still in the same room.

Later, at Hakone, a seaside resort where I was visiting with friends, the first thing that happened was that we were asked to disrobe. We were given *okatas,* and our clothes were taken from us by the maid. (For those who have not visited Japan, the okata is a cotton print kimono.) We later learned, when we ventured out in the streets, that it was possible to recognize other guests from our hotel because we had all been equipped with identical okatas. (Each hotel had its own characteristic, clearly recognizable pattern.) Also, I noted that it was polite to wave or nod to these strangers from the same hotel.

Following Hakone, we visited Kyoto, site of many famous temples and palaces, and the ancient capital of Japan.

There we were fortunate enough to stay in a wonderful little country inn on the side of a hill overlooking the town. Kyoto is much more traditional and less industrialized than Tokyo. After we had been there about a week and had thoroughly settled into our new Japanese surroundings, we returned one night to be met at the door by an apologetic manager who was stammering something. I knew immediately that we had been moved, so I said, "You had to move us. Please don't let this bother you, because we understand. Just show us to our new rooms and it will be all right." Our interpreter explained as we started to go through the door that we weren't in that hotel any longer but had been moved to *another* hotel. What a blow! Again, without warning. We wondered what the new hotel would be like, and with our descent into the town our hearts sank further. Finally, when we could descend no more, the taxi took off into a part of the city we hadn't seen before. No Europeans here! The streets got narrower and narrower until we turned into a side street that could barely accommodate the tiny Japanese taxi into which we were squeezed. Clearly this was a hotel of another class. I found that, by then, I was getting a little paranoid, which is easy enough to do in a foreign land, and said to myself, "They must think we are very low-status people indeed to treat us this way."

As it turned out, the neighborhood, in fact the whole district, showed us an entirely different side of life from what we had seen before, much more

---

Tant pis: French for "so much the worse," "too bad."

Frank Lloyd Wright's Imperial Hotel: Hotel designed by American architect Frank Lloyd Wright (1867–1959).

interesting and authentic. True, we did have some communication problems, because no one was used to dealing with foreigners, but few of them were serious.

Yet, the whole matter of being moved like a piece of derelict luggage puzzled me. In the United States, the person who gets moved is often the lowest-ranking individual. This principle applied to all organizations, including the Army. Whether you can be moved or not is a function of your status, your performance, and your value to the organization. To move someone without telling him is almost worse than an insult, because it means he is below the point at which feelings matter. In these circumstances, moves can be unsettling and damaging to the ego. In addition, moves themselves are often accompanied by great anxiety, whether an entire organization or a small part of an organization moves. What makes people anxious is that the move usually presages organizational changes that have been coordinated with the move. Naturally, everyone wants to see how he comes out vis-à-vis everyone else. I have seen important men refuse to move into an office that was six inches smaller than someone else's of the same rank. While I have heard some American executives say they wouldn't employ such a person, the fact is that in actual practice, unless there is some compensating feature, the significance of space as a communication is so powerful that no employee in his right mind would allow his boss to give him a spatial demotion—unless of course he had already reached his crest and was on the way down.

These spatial messages are not simply conventions in the United States—unless you consider the size of your salary check a mere convention, or where your name appears on the masthead of a journal. Ranking is seldom a matter that people take lightly, particularly in a highly mobile society like that in the United States. Each culture and each country has its own language of space, which is just as unique as the spoken language, frequently more so. In England, for example, there are no offices for the members of Parliament. In the United States, our congressmen and senators proliferate their offices and their office buildings and simply would not tolerate a no-office situation. Constituents, associates, colleagues, and lobbyists would not respond properly. In England, status is internalized; it has its manifestations and markers—the upper-class received English accent, for example. We in the United States, a relatively new country, externalize status. The American in England has some trouble placing people in the social system, while the English can place each other quite accurately by reading ranking cues, but in general tend to look down on the importance that Americans attach to space. It is very easy and very natural to look at things from one's own point of view and to read an event as though it were the same all over the world.

I knew that my emotions on being moved out of my room in Tokyo were of the gut type and quite strong. There was nothing intellectual about my initial response. Although I am a professional observer of cultural patterns, I had no notion of the meaning attached to being moved from hotel to hotel in Kyoto. I was well aware of the strong significance of moving in my own culture, going back to the time when the new baby displaces older children, right up to the world of business, where a complex dance is performed every time the organization moves to new quarters.

What was happening to me in Japan as I rode up and down in elevators with various keys gripped in my hand was that I was reacting with the cultural part of my brain—the old, mammalian brain. Although my new brain, my symbolic brain—the neocortex—was saying something else, my mammalian brain kept repeating, "You are being treated shabbily." My neocortex was trying to fathom what was happening. Needles to say, neither part of the brain had been programmed to provide me with the answer in Japanese culture. I did have to put up a strong fight with myself to keep from interpreting what was going on as though the Japanese were the same as I. This is the conventional and most common response and one that is often found even among anthropologists. Any time you hear someone say, "Why, *they* are no different than the folks back home—they are just like I am," even though you may understand the reasons behind these remarks you also know that the speaker is living in a single-context world (his own) and is incapable of describing either his world or the foreign one.

The "they are just like the folks back home" syndrome is one of the most persistent and widely held misconceptions of the Western world, if not the whole world. There is very little any outsider can do about this, because it expresses views that are very close to the core of the personality. Simply talking about "cultural differences" and how we must respect them is a hollow cliché. And in fact, intellectualizing isn't much more helpful either, at least at first. The logic of the man who won't move into an office that is six inches smaller than his rival's is *cultural* logic; it works at a lower, more basic level in the brain, a part of the brain that synthesizes but does not verbalize. The response is a total response that is difficult to explain to someone who doesn't already understand, because it is so dependent on context for a correct interpretation. To do so, one must explain the entire system; otherwise, the man's behavior makes little sense. He may even appear to be acting childishly—which he most definitely is not.

It was my preoccupation with my own cultural mold that explained why I was puzzled for years about the significance of being moved around in Japanese hotels. The answer finally came after further experiences in Japan and many discussions with Japanese friends. In Japan, one has to "belong" or he has no identity. When a man joins a company, he does just that—joins himself to the corporate body—and there is even a ceremony marking the occasion. Normally, he is hired for life, and the company plays a much more paternalistic role than in the United States. There are company songs, and the whole company meets frequently (usually at least once a week) for purposes of maintaining corporate identity and morale.[4]

As a tourist (either European or Japanese) when you go on a tour, you *join* that tour and follow your guide everywhere as a group. She leads you with a little flag that she holds up for all to see. Such behavior strikes Americans as sheeplike; not so the Japanese. The reader may say that this pattern holds in Europe, because there people join Cook's tours and the American Express tours, which is true. Yet there is a big difference. I remember a very attractive young American woman who was traveling with the same group I was with in Japan. At first she was charmed and captivated, until she had spent several days visiting shrines and monuments. At this point, she observed that she could not take the regimentation of Japanese life. Clearly, she was picking up clues, such as the fact that our Japanese group, when it moved, marched in a phalanx rather than moving as a motley mob with stragglers. There was much more discipline in these sightseeing groups than the average Westerner is either used to or willing to accept.

It was my lack of understanding of the full impact of what it means to belong to a high-context culture that caused me to misread hotel behavior at Hakone. I should have known that I was in the grip of a pattern difference and that the significance of all guests being garbed in the same okata meant more than that an opportunistic management used the guests to advertise the hotel. The answer to my puzzle was revealed when a Japanese friend explained what it means to be a guest in a hotel. As soon as you register at the desk, you are no longer an outsider; instead, for the duration of your stay you are a member of a large, mobile family. You *belong*. The fact that I was moved was tangible evidence that I was being treated as a family member—a relationship in which one can afford to be "relaxed and informal and not stand on ceremony." This is a very highly prized state in Japan, which offsets the official properness that is so common in public. Instead of putting me down, they were treating me as a member of the family. Needless to say, the large, luxury hotels that cater to Americans, like Wright's Imperial Hotel, have discovered that Americans do tenaciously stand on ceremony and want to be treated as they are at home in the States. Americans don't like to be moved around; it makes them anxious. Therefore, the Japanese in these establishments have learned not to treat them as family members.

While there are a few rare individuals who move along in the current of life looking around with innocent wonder regardless of what happens to them, most of mankind are not that relaxed. The majority are like men on a raft tossed about in a turbulent sea, who get only an occasional orienting glimpse of surrounding landmarks.

In the United States, the concern of the large middle class is to move ahead in the system, whichever part of it we happen to be in. With perhaps the exception of the younger generation just now entering the job market, we are very tied to our jobs. In fact, the more successful a man or a woman is, the more likely his or her life will revolve around a job to which home and personal relations assume secondary importance. We are only peripherally tied to the lives of others. It takes a long, long time for us to become deeply involved with others, and for some this never happens.

In Japan, life is a very different story, one that is puzzling in the extreme to   30
Americans who interact regularly with the Japanese. Their culture seems to be

full of paradoxes. When they communicate, particularly about important things, it is often in a roundabout way (indirection is a word that one hears often in the foreign colony). All of this points to a very high-context approach to life; yet, on the other hand, there are times when they swing in the opposite direction and move to the lower end of the context scale, where nothing can be taken for granted. . . . Years later, I had occasion to send some film to Japan for processing and was told to be *sure* to tell them everything I wanted done, because if I left anything out it would be my fault. Weeks later, after having provided what I thought was a set of instructions that could be followed by a computer, I got the film back. Everything was as I had requested—exquisite work—except that I had forgotten one thing. I didn't tell them to roll the film up and put it in a little can or to protect it in some way. In the process of mailing, the negatives had been folded and scratched, in fact were useless for any further work. I had run afoul of the low-context side of Japanese life. . . .

The Japanese are pulled in two directions. The first is a very high-context, deeply involved, enveloping intimacy that begins at home in childhood but is extended far beyond the home. There is a deep need to be close, and it is only when they are close that they are comfortable. The other pole is as far away as one can get. In public and during ceremonial occasions (and there are ceremonies of a sort every day, even when people meet), there is great emphasis on self-control, distance, and hiding inner feelings. Like most of Japanese behavior, attitudes toward showing emotion are deeply rooted in a long past. At the time of the samurai knights and nobles, there was survival value in being able to control one's demeanor, because a samurai could legally execute anyone who displeased him or who wasn't properly respectful. This standing on ceremony extended to all levels; not only was the servant expected to be respectful, but the samurai's wife was to show no emotion when she received the news that her husband or son had been killed in battle. Until very recently, there was no public showing of intimacy or touching in Japan.

Still, on the formal, ceremonial side it is very important for the Japanese to be able to place people in a social system. In fact, it is impossible to interact with someone else if this placing has not occurred, hence the requirement that you state who you are on your calling card—first, the organization you work for, second, your position in that organization, your degrees, honors you have received, followed by the family name, the given name, and address, in that order.[5]

When functioning in the low-context mode, the Japanese keeps his mouth shut and volunteers nothing even though he has information that would be very useful. Thus, a young man I knew in Tokyo several years ago was completely unstrung when, just as he was leaving for Europe via Hong Kong he received a telephone call informing him that his flight had been canceled. Due to the scarcity of hotels and infrequency of flights (sometimes only one or two a week), to get off schedule used to be catastrophic, if for no other reason than the matter of hotel reservations. Assuming that the Japanese low-context mode was being used, I advised him to call the airlines immediately and ask if there was another flight to Hong Kong and, if so, could he get on it. The same clerk answered the phone and was very pleased to say yes, there was another flight leaving one hour later than the one that had been canceled. The clerk was of course being solicitous of my friend's status and would not have dreamed of suggesting the other flight. To do so would be to presume to do his thinking for him.

Through all these experiences, I was eventually able to discern the common thread that connected everything, which began to put Japanese behavior in context. The pattern is one that it is important to understand: In Japan there are the two sides to everyone—his warm, close, friendly, involved, high-context side that does not stand on ceremony, and the public, official, status-conscious, ceremonial side, which is what most foreigners see. From what I understand of Japanese culture, most Japanese feel quite uncomfortable (deep down inside) about the ceremonial, low-context, institutionalized side of life. Their principal drive is to move from the "stand on ceremony" side toward the homey, comfortable, warm, intimate, friendly side. One sees this even at the office and the laboratory, where the honorifics are dropped as the day progresses. By this, I do not mean to imply that the Japanese are not tough businessmen or that they aren't well organized, etc. Anyone who has had anything to do with them can only admire their capacity to get things done. The point is that their drive to be close and get to know other people is very strong—in some cases, more than the detached European is either used to or can stand. The record is very clear on this. Consider their practice of men and women sleeping side by side crowded together on the floor in a single room, and the camaraderie of communal bathing.

The American provides a real contrast. He is inclined to be more oriented   35
toward achieving set goals and less toward developing close human relations. It is difficult for him to understand and act on the basis that once a customer in Japan "has been sold," that is just the beginning. He must be "massaged" regularly; otherwise he goes somewhere else. There are of course many other sides to the Japanese, such as their great dependence on tradition—as well as their group, rather than individual, orientation.

The message is simple on the surface but does depend somewhat on the reader's being already contexted in cross-cultural communication. Two things get in the way of understanding: the linearity of language and the deep biases and built-in blinders that every culture provides. Transcending either is a formidable task. In addition, the broad base on which culture rests was laid down millions of years ago, long before man appeared on this earth, and for better or worse it ties man forever to the rest of nature. This base is rooted in the old, mammalian brain—that part of the brain that treats things as wholes—which constantly synthesizes and comes up with solutions based on everything that happened in the past. Paradoxically, this old brain that can understand and integrate one's own culture on a preverbal level frequently gets in the way of understanding and integrating new cultural experiences.

This means that if one is to *really* understand a given behavior on the basic level I am referring to, one must know the entire history of the individual. It is never possible to understand completely any other human being; and no individual will ever really understand himself—the complexity is too great and there is not the time to constantly take things apart and examine them. This is the beginning of wisdom in human relations. However, understanding oneself and understanding others are closely related processes. To do one, you must start with the other, and vice versa.

Notes

1. For a more complete treatment of culture as a communication, see my THE SILENT LANGUAGE (1959).

2. A lifetime of dealing with the subtleties of intercultural communication has convinced me that the strength and persistence of these habitual behaviors are almost beyond belief. These behaviors are closely identified with the self—the good self, the socially responsible self, which wants to do right and to fit in—and are synonymous with social competence. However, in intercultural situations, when other people call attention to these hidden responses and perceptual differences, suggesting that the world is not as one perceives it, these observations can be unsettling. To do so is to suggest that a person is incompetent, not properly motivated, ignorant, or even infantile. The mere mention of patterns or the suggestion that there are such things threatens some people's individuality. Older parts of the psyche are mobilized—the parts that were active when growing up and that represent the internalized authority of the parent and the past. To counteract the effect of dynamisms from the past, one has to remind oneself that one's image of others is largely made up of projections of various parts of one's own personality including one's psychic needs, which are treated as though they were innate. For example, it is difficult for Americans who like freedom from binding institutional ties to believe that many Japanese would actively seek to submerge themselves in business or government bureaucracy for life. "How could anyone subject himself willingly to such a paternalistic life?"

3. Powers (1973).

4. Dore (1973) and Robert Cole (1973).

5. Morsbach (1973).

Selected Bibliography

Cole, Robert E. *Japanese Blue Collar.* Berkeley: University of California Press, 1973.

Dore, Ronald. *Japanese Factory.* Berkeley: University of California Press, 1973.

Hall, Edward T. *The Silent Language.* Garden City, N.Y.: Doubleday & Company, Inc., 1959.

Morspach, Helmut. "Aspects of Nonverbal Communication in Japan," *Journal of Nervous and Mental Disease,* October 1973.

Powers, William T. "Feedback: Beyond Behaviorism," *Science,* Vol. 179, pp. 351–56, January 26, 1973.

EXPLORING THE TEXT

1. What does Hall mean by "the cultural unconscious"? How does culture help us read the minds of people in the social groups we belong to? How does it interfere when we attempt to read the motives and desires of those from other cultural groups? Why, according to Hall, do intercultural encounters provide an opportunity for increasing self-awareness?

2. How does Hall respond, initially, to the experience of being moved in a Japanese hotel? What emotions does he feel in relation to this experience? What do his expectations and reactions tell us about American cultural attitudes toward status, power, individualism, and so forth? Would you agree that most Americans would respond as Hall did in a similar situation?

3. What explanation does Hall offer for the treatment he receives at the hotels he visits in Japan? What deeply held Japanese cultural values and beliefs does Hall identify as underlying this treatment? How persuasive do you find Hall's explanation and the evidence he provides to support it? Why?

4. What is the difference between "high-context" and "low-context" cultural modes in Japan, according to Hall? How do these modes shape people's expectations and relationships? In general, is the cultural style of the United States high or low context? To what extent, in your opinion, do cultural groups within the United States—groups like Asian Americans, African Americans, Latinos, Italian Americans, and others—display signs of high or low cultural context?

5. Why does Hall believe that "simply talking about cultural differences and how we must respect them is a hollow cliché"? What is wrong with simply respecting cultural differences, according to Hall? What more must we do, in his opinion, to fully understand the workings and meanings of other cultures?

FURTHER EXPLORATIONS

1. Compare Hall's experience of cross-cultural misunderstanding in Japan with the misreading of motives, values, and attitudes that James Baldwin dramatizes in "Sonny's Blues" (p. 390). What, if anything, distinguishes the interpersonal conflict between the narrator and Sonny from the kind of cultural conflict that Hall experiences? To what extent are the values, attitudes, and beliefs of Baldwin's characters shaped by the culture—or cultures—they grew up in? Is it possible to interpret "Sonny's Blues" as a case of cultural conflict? Why or why not?

2. In what ways might Hall's view of cross-cultural conflict and understanding complicate or complement Martha C. Nussbaum's belief (p. 416) that literature can help us transcend the barriers of race, gender, and nationality? To what extent might Hall view the kind of empathetic identification promoted by reading as merely another form of "intellectualizing" about cultural differences?

3. Compare Hall's view of genuine cross-cultural understanding with that presented by Mary Catherine Bateson in "A Mutable Self" (p. 337). What obstacles keep Americans from learning about other cultures according to these authors? What picture of American culture emerges from their analyses of cultural conflict? To

what extent would you agree with the values and attitudes they associate with American cultural patterns?

4. Given Hall's view of the difficulty of cross-cultural understanding, how might he evaluate Mick Fedullo's experience of reading the cultural differences between himself and his middle-aged female Apache colleague Mrs. Cassadore (below)? To what extent is Fedullo's conflict with Mrs. Cassadore the result of cultural, gender, or political differences?

5. View any recent film dealing with Japanese culture—examples might include *Shower, Dance with Me*, or *In the Mood for Love*—to test Hall's interpretation of Japanese cultural attitudes and styles. To what extent does the film you view reflect the interpretation of Japanese cultural values and beliefs offered by Hall in this selection?

ESSAY OPTIONS

1. Using the *Before Reading* exercise on page 429 as a point of departure, write an essay in which you relate and analyze a cross-cultural misunderstanding or conflict you were once involved in or witnessed. In your analysis, try to explore your own part in this cultural collision by probing the cultural values or beliefs that might have shaped your expectations, attitudes, and responses. Try also to explain, as Hall does, the differences of value and belief that gave rise to this conflict. If time permits, seek out a representative of the other cultural group involved in this experience, and ask them to read and critique your analysis. From his perspective, how well have you succeeded in analyzing the basic assumptions of their culture?

2. Drawing on the theories of perception and memory presented by Diane Ackerman (p. 36), Constance Classen et al. (p. 59), K. C. Cole (p. 75), Georgina Kleege (p. 93), Walker Percy (p. 118), and Eviatar Zerubavel (p. 217), write an essay discussing the formation of what Hall terms "the cultural unconscious." How does culture work, according to these authors, to shape our experiences at a preconscious level? Why do the "deep biases" and "built-in blinders" of our home cultures make cross-cultural communication a difficult task? To what extent do you agree that understanding people across cultures is, in fact, so difficult?

Mrs. Cassadore

MICK FEDULLO

When Mick Fedullo arrived in San Carlos, Arizona, to teach a course in survival skills to kids on the local Apache Indian reservation, he brought with him a wealth of firsthand experience in cross-cultural communication. Born in Pennsylvania in 1949, Fedullo lived and worked on the Gila River Indian Reservation in Arizona from 1979 to 1984. Later, he taught creative writing on the Crow, Rocky Boy, and Blackfeet reservations in

Montana. But, as he recounts in this selection, none of these experiences prepared him for his first encounter with Elenore Cassadore, a bilingual instructor and influential figure among the San Carlos Apaches. Fedullo's account of the mistakes he makes trying to get to know Mrs. Cassadore and the approach he takes in overcoming them offers a telling illustration of how stereotypes and personal stories can complicate cross-cultural mind reading. This selection originally appeared in *Light of the Feather: Pathways through Contemporary Indian America* (1992).

BEFORE READING

Freewrite about the stereotypes commonly associated with Native Americans, African Americans, Mexican Americans and Latinos, Asian Americans, or any other cultural group. Are all stereotypes the products of racism or prejudice? Why do you think stereotypes are so hard to get rid of?

Mrs. Cassadore and Apache Students

E lenore Cassadore, an elder of the San Carlos Apache, was employed in the bilingual program at the high school in Globe. Because she didn't drive, she rode with a fellow aide each school day from San Carlos to Globe and back, a round trip of over forty miles. I met Mrs. Cassadore at the beginning of a four-week stint working with the Apache high school students. Because there was no high school on the reservation, the students were bused to Globe. Sometimes, when Mrs. Cassadore's ride was unavailable, she joined the kids on the bus.

I knew from the moment I met her that I wanted to spend time talking with her; I could learn much about the San Carlos Apaches from this intelligent and wise woman. Mrs. Cassadore was of medium height and build, with salt-and-pepper hair. Her weathered face looked quiet, firm, sad. I never saw her in anything but traditional, ankle-length Apache camp dresses.

When I was first introduced to her, I explained what I hoped to accomplish with the students. We would, I said, put together a manuscript of poems, stories, articles, and drawings about Apache life, past and present—all composed by the students. I would also conduct several sessions on "survival skills"—that is, comfortable or at least practical ways for young Indian adults to get by in the non-Indian world. I added that it would be an honor if she sat in on some of the classes.

Mrs. Cassadore nodded and said, "Sounds good."

I pressed: "I hope you *will* be able to attend."   5

"In the morning classes," she answered. "Afternoons I'm busy in the office. But the mornings are okay. Those two classes are the ones I sometimes teach anyway."

In my enthusiasm to develop an acquaintanceship, I said, "I would really enjoy your company at dinner some evening. Maybe we could go to a restaurant. I'd like to talk to you about the students and the bilingual program here.

My treat." What I really wanted was to talk to Mrs. Cassadore about her and her tribe. I had lied. A *white* lie.

Mrs. Cassadore nodded and said nothing. I sensed that I had been too abrupt.

The following day, I saw Mrs. Cassadore walking down the hallway toward the bilingual office. All the students were in class, and we were the only two people in the oak-floored, echoey corridor.

"Excuse me, Mrs. Cassadore," I said. "Have you thought about that dinner? Is any particular night best for you?"

"I've thought about it," she said. "There's nothing I can tell you over dinner that I can't just as well tell you here at the school."

I staggered under the weight of this rejection. Forget it, she had told me. And with a voice as soft and sweet as a mother's. If that quiet voice didn't echo in the hallway, it more than bounced around inside my skull.

"Oh," I said. Then, trying to regain my composure: "You're right, but the offer still holds."

My own Anglo need to be immediately accepted had been thumped on, and, ridiculously, it hurt. I spent that night repeatedly reliving the corridor scene, and winced every time Mrs. Cassadore's words replayed in my mind.

The next morning I almost said to Mrs. Cassadore, "Another thing I'd like to talk to you about is . . . well, I'd like to share some of my ideas about Indian education. And I'd like to learn about your tribe. I'd like to learn about you." That's how I sort of planned my words. But in the end I held my tongue. I had already been pushy enough. And now I was remembering what I had learned in Sacaton from the Whitmans and other Pimas about friendship. Observe the other person. Be patient. Assume nothing. Determine if there are common grounds. Open up only when the time is appropriate. And once you've decided to open up, and only then, commit yourself to an understanding of relationship — maybe of friendship.

I was trying to see things from Mrs. Cassadore's point of view, from an Indian point of view. Malinda Powsky, the Hualapai with whom I had developed a friendship rather quickly, had known about me and my work before I met her. She had seen me work with the Hualapai children, and we had spent hours talking to each other before she invited me for the drive into the Grand Canyon. Mrs. Cassadore, on the other hand, had never set eyes on me until yesterday; she didn't know where I had come from, or anything about my work, and we had never spent a moment talking to each other.

This elder from the San Carlos Apache tribe had been introduced to (had to shake the hand of) a tall (intimidating) white man who wore a sports jacket over a sweatshirt (dressed like a businessman *and* a hippie), and whose face was covered with a beard (unnatural growth). Before she knew it, this man had invited (cornered) her into making a decision about spending time alone with him so he could learn about (exploit) Globe's bilingual program and the Apaches. Thinking of it from Mrs. Cassadore's point of view, I was suddenly and definitely put off by this image of myself.

"Good morning," I said to Mrs. Cassadore. This time I spoke with the quiet respect I knew should be given a person older than I was. At our first meeting, I had acted disrespectfully, forgetting the rules of Indian friendship and acquaintanceship. It's not easy, after all, to unlearn social habits that have been practiced over a lifetime. I was now behaving toward Mrs. Cassadore not from instinct, as I had yesterday, but from the knowledge I had gained about appropriate social intercourse in the Indian world. I was consciously unlearning, and relearning. I had no right to assume that this Apache woman should be comfortable with, or even aware of, the twists and turns of my Anglo forwardness. I would merely do my best to behave in a way that demonstrated the genuine respect I felt for her, and I hoped that she had not already completely shut out the possibility of some kind of relationship.

I offered, as I said good morning to Mrs. Cassadore, another show of respect by avoiding eye contact with her, instead glancing down at the floor. Among many Indians, quickly establishing direct eye contact is regarded as rude and aggressive, if not downright confrontational.

Mrs. Cassadore's sweet, motherly voice answered, "Good morning." Then 20
we passed each other and walked in opposite directions through the cement corridor.

Be patient, I told myself. Patient and respectful. If it is meant for the two of us to know each other better, it will happen — when the time is appropriate.

My classes with the Apache students were both exciting and rewarding. Particularly interesting were the survival-skills sessions, since they involved more open discussion. Each group I saw was composed of students from all four high school grades, pooled from their English classes. Half of the students already knew and were comfortable with me, since I had worked with them when they were seventh- and eighth-graders at the elementary school on the reservation. At our initial meetings, as I entered the classrooms, the freshmen and sophomores exclaimed, "It's Mick!" "All right!" "You followed us to the high school!" The juniors and seniors, never having seen me before, were quietly curious and suspicious of this white man's presence.

In the first class I conducted, Mrs. Cassadore sat at the back of the room on an old pine chair pressed against the back wall, as far away from me as possible. In the following weeks, she would attend most of my morning classes sitting in the same distant spot. I was especially pleased, however, that she showed up at the beginning of the classes and witnessed the students' welcoming cheers. If nothing else, this would indicate to her the kind of rapport I developed with Indian students — with *Apache* students.

I waited until the third week to begin the survival-skills sessions, giving the older students time to become relaxed in my presence. The first and most important rule of these classes was that, aside from me, no non-Indians were allowed in the classroom. I wanted the Apache students to be open and honest about the problems they perceived in their encounters with the Anglo world. I felt that my established relationship with the younger students would make the discussions not only possible but productive.

And I tried to keep realistic expectations. There was no way I could make survival in two different cultures easy. These Apache students, as well as Indian students in general, had two major tasks challenging them: the maintenance of their own Indian culture and the acquisition of skills that would enable them to function, when they had to, in mainstream non-Indian society. What separated them from other minorities, and made their task more difficult, was the fact that the nature of the differences between their culture and Anglo culture was so extreme. So, coping in the Anglo world meant, as it does today, not a *reconciliation* of opposites, but an *adjustment* to the very existence of profound opposites — an adjustment that must include the development of behaviors that often seem strange to the young Indian. True biculturalism also includes the maintenance of basic Indian culture patterns and deep-rooted beliefs. As difficult as this may be to accomplish, it remains for Indians a realistic, attainable goal.

Not all the Apache students at Globe High School would become Hartman Lomawaimas, the assistant director of the Lowie Museum in Berkeley, but in our classes we could at least discuss specific problems and various ways to handle them.

Subjects for our discussions ranged from Anglo "time" as a concept different from Indian "time," to the analysis of Anglo behaviors the Apache students found odd or intimidating. I constantly reinforced the idea that the students, in learning survival skills, did not have to give up being Indian; they did not have to become *assimilated*.

The irony, of course, was that at the same time that I was conducting these classes, I was also adjusting my own behaviors to conform to acceptable Indian ways in my encounters with Mrs. Cassadore. Cross-cultural understanding is a two-way street. The non-Indian in contact with Indians has a responsibility to learn about their world and make the same adjustment to profound opposites that is expected of the Indian in reverse situations. When I talked to Mrs. Cassadore, usually in the bilingual office, I kept my side of the conversations brief and to the point, spoke in a soft voice, and never tried to establish prolonged eye contact.

On Wednesday of the second week, I began the morning class by saying, "Today we're going to talk a little bit about racial prejudice toward Indians, toward you guys. Can anyone define what the word 'prejudice' means?"

Tom, a sophomore, said, "It's like when white people look at you funny 'cause they don't like Indians."

Marie, also a sophomore, chimed in, "They get suspicious of you, and some of them just hate us."

"Okay. Why don't we talk about ways that some white people act toward Indians that might show prejudice, and how you can try to tell if those actions really do show prejudice. And we should talk about the ways you respond, and other possible responses. Someone tell me something that some whites do that might show prejudice."

"When they stare at us real long," offered an eleventh-grader named Sean. "You look away, but every time you look back, they're still staring." The class stirred, the students nodding and mumbling in agreement.

Sean added, "It's like they don't even blink their eyes, kinda like snakes or somethin'." Everyone chuckled.

This was a perfect start, I thought. The students had opened up quickly, 35 and even some humor had been injected; a relaxed but honest tone had been set. I said, "Staring. How about their expressions when they stare? Can you tell what they're feeling, like anger or hatred or, as Marie pointed out, suspicion?"

"Sometimes they look like they're mad."

"Or like they think you're gonna steal something."

"Usually just a stare, kinda blanklike."

More students were joining in. I said, "Okay, so let's talk about the situations in which staring occurs. When and where do whites stare?"

"Like last week," a tall, muscular senior said. "Me and my family were at 40 a restaurant here in Globe. We was real quiet, like good Indians." He snickered as he said this, and the class laughed again, acutely aware of the image many Indians believe they should project when in non-Indian public. "But this old white man and his wife just kept starin' at us. He even had to look partway over his shoulder to get a good view." More chuckles.

I said, "Let me tell you right off. Some white people like to stare, even though it may be rude. Many times it *is* from prejudice. Sometimes it's not. Staring itself doesn't *always* indicate prejudice. Do you think those old people were staring because they were prejudiced, or could there have been some other reason?" This idea had obviously not occurred to most of the students. Several moments of silence passed as they considered it. Then I said, "Can you think of any kind of staring that's really not prejudice?"

The muscular boy pulled his sunglasses down from the top of his head and over his eyes as he said, "Yeah. On the street, if it's a woman who's starin', it's 'cause she thinks I'm sexy." The whole class roared.

"Are you all laughing because white women get turned on when they see him, or because so many white women are blind?" The volume of the laughter increased.

When the students settled, I said, "But there you have it. There's a reason why some whites stare at an Indian that's kind of the opposite of prejudice." I pointed to the boy; he was smiling from behind his sunglasses. "Just look at him," I said. "He's a handsome, sexy dude." The kids laughed again, but I knew they were getting the point. "I'll bet every one of you has seen a white kid here at school that you thought was attractive. Maybe you even kind of stared at him or her. Maybe secretly. Maybe not so secretly." Little waves of giggles spread through the classroom. "Give me one good reason why a woman, any woman, wouldn't find this young man attractive. He may have been joking, but he was also right."

Our discussion lasted the full hour and would have to be continued the   45
next day. The students had identified other situations in which staring clearly
represented racial prejudice. The fierce, suspicion-filled glare of a store proprietor the minute a young Indian walks into a store — "It makes you feel like
a criminal even though you wasn't gonna do nothing wrong in the first place."
The venomous stares of a group of young whites on a street corner challenging a young Indian to some form of perverted, one-sided combat — "They
scared the shit outta me." Concerning the old couple in the restaurant, the
students concluded it was impossible to determine the motive for their rude-
ness. They might have been locals who disliked Indians, or they might as easily have been tourists from the hinterlands of the Midwest who had never laid
eyes on a real-honest-to-goodness "Injun."

During that first hour we had discussed the students' responses to their
own individual situations; they had decided no *single* way of dealing with
someone whose eyes are fixed on you suits every such encounter. In some
cases, the students decided, it was better to ignore the stares. In others, they
felt that staring back was justified, if only to embarrass guilty eyes enough to
turn them away. A few situations seemed to call for actual verbal or physical
responses. One brassy young man told of an experience at a hardware store in
which, when the clerk leveled her sights on her Apache target, he pulled out
his wallet, raised his arms, looked back into the clerk's eyes, and said, "I got
money, lady. I got money." This uncharacteristic response had been applauded
by the other students, but most of them, especially the young women, said
they personally preferred to ignore stares altogether. We had also discussed at
length the fact that different individuals, even of the same tribe, may react differently to similar situations. The important thing, we concluded, was to respond in a manner that felt as comfortable as possible, and at the same time
maintain a sense of personal and tribal dignity.

After the bell had sounded its old-fashioned clang, I stood at the doorway
saying good-bye to the students individually as they filed out. We all looked
forward to the next day's session. It was good, and rare, for these Apache students to have shared such personal experiences with an Anglo who was sympathetic and who could offer legitimate, sometimes new, perspectives. It was
good for *this* Anglo as well.

After the last student passed into the corridor, I took a deep breath, at
once savoring the moment, giving the moment up, and readying myself to
start the whole process over again with another group of kids. I felt exhila-
rated.

Then Mrs. Cassadore came from her usual spot at the back of the room.
"That was good," she said. "We need more of that kind of thing."

"Thank you," I said, looking down.   50

Mrs. Cassadore had watched me interact with the Apache students for
two-and-a-half weeks now. She had read their poems and articles. And she had
just offered a compliment. I wondered if the time might be right to ask her to
dinner again. If she accepted, I would be delighted; if she turned me down,

well, I could handle it gracefully and resign myself to knowing her only within the context of our high school meetings.

Looking down at the floor, I said, "You know, I would still enjoy your company for dinner some evening." I braced myself.

Mrs. Cassadore thought for a moment. I readied myself to say something like, "That's okay. It's not that important." Then I glanced up.

Mrs. Cassadore raised her head. In the same sweet voice she used with everyone, she said, "How about tonight?"

Dinner with Mrs. Cassadore

The stereotype of the silent, stoic Indian was created by non-Indians who had   55
never gotten to the first stage of the Indian manner of coming to an understanding of relationship. Had those non-Indians used the Indian approach of quiet, patient, cautious observation, and finally been accepted with trust and friendship, they would have experienced quite a different Indian, one who joked and laughed much of the time, one who loved to talk and share stories with an obsessive attention to detail, one who valued loyalty.

Over dinner, I witnessed a different Mrs. Cassadore, one who had decided I was okay and could be trusted. We had gone to a Mexican restaurant near the high school and sat down in a window booth next to a neon Coors sign that glowed like an electric-stove burner. Brightly colored piñatas hung from the ceiling, and south-of-the-border serapes covered the stucco walls. I ordered chicken enchiladas, rice, beans, and a Dos Equis beer. Mrs. Cassadore asked for combination number one—the basic taco, tamale, and enchilada served with beans and rice—and an iced tea.

We talked for a while about Indian education. I told her about the poetry books and calendars I had edited at Sacaton, the calendar of Apache student writings we had produced at the elementary school in San Carlos, and expressed my hope that the bilingual program at Globe High School would be able to publish the manuscript we were now putting together. The point, I said, was to demonstrate to the students the importance of sharing with the community their written creations while giving them the sense of pride that comes with seeing one's writing in published form.

Mrs. Cassadore said, "But there's a problem with that for some Apaches." I had no idea what she was talking about. Publishing student work and distributing it among the children's parents and throughout the community had always seemed an essential part of my writing program.

"What do you mean?" I asked.

"Well, some Apaches don't think books are important." My face must   60
have registered the same kind of surprise that earlier I had seen on the faces of the high school students when I had said that not all staring by Anglos reflected racial prejudice. Mrs. Cassadore went on, "Some think that written words are kind of evil."

I stared at Mrs. Cassadore, confused and curious. My own experience in San Carlos had indicated the opposite. In fact, after we had published the poetry calendar, I had learned of a wonderful example of the benefit of written communication. An eighth-grader named Dawn Casuse had written a simple and elegant description of herself waiting to go through the Sunrise Dance Ceremony, the traditional puberty rite held for young Apache women. The poem appeared on the calendar. I assumed at the time that the girl had already gone through the ritual. A year later, when I returned to San Carlos, I was told by one of her aunts that before writing her poem, Dawn had never expressed an interest in the Sunrise Ceremony, and that whenever her parents had asked her about it, she had told them she didn't want one. Then they saw the poem on the calendar and wondered why she would write about the ceremony if she had no interest in it. They confronted her. Dawn then confessed to them the real reason she had acted indifferent—she feared that they could not afford the expense and didn't want them to feel guilty. Part of the ceremony involves the parents conducting a giveaway in which those in attendance receive blankets and food costing the family hundreds of dollars. Once her parents knew what Dawn was really thinking and feeling, they immediately arranged for her to have a Sunrise Dance Ceremony. Had Dawn not written that poem, and had it not been published, her parents would never have known that she secretly wanted the ritual. Dawn Casuse would have gone through life having never been initiated into adulthood in a way she believed important.

The Dawn Casuse story was one example of the positive side of printing students' work, but now Mrs. Cassadore was telling me that some Apaches viewed printed materials not only as unimportant, but as evil. "I'm lost," I said to her. "Can you explain?"

"Yes." Mrs. Cassadore sipped at her iced tea. I took a long pull from my Dos Equis, squinting into the orange neon glow to my left. "You know a lot of young Apaches," she said. "And you know some of their parents. But there's a lot of parents and grandparents you don't know, and they probably wouldn't want to know you, unless maybe they saw how you are with their kids. They been to school in their day, and what that usually meant was a bad BIA° boarding school. And all they remember about school is that there were all these Anglos trying to make them forget they were Apaches; trying to make them turn against their parents, telling them that Indian ways were evil.

"Well, a lot of those kids came to believe that their teachers were the evil ones, and so anything that had to do with 'education' was also evil—like books. Those kids came back to the reservation, got married, and had their own kids. And now they don't want anything to do with the white man's education. The only reason they send their kids to school is because it's the law. But they tell their kids not to take school seriously. So, to them, printed stuff is white-man stuff."

BIA: Bureau of Indian Affairs.

"But Indian education is changing," I said. "Assimilation is not official 65 policy anymore. The school in San Carlos has an Apache school board."

"Doesn't matter. Education for some Apache adults means what it always meant. *They* haven't changed. They shut education out a long time ago, and they don't want to hear anything about it. So of course they don't see the changes in the schools. And they don't read a poetry calendar from the school, either."

I said, "That means that we—I mean people working in Indian education, people working for change—have got to get out there and talk to those parents. We've got to show them how things like writing can be important, how education can be used in a positive way."

"You're right. The more Indians you talk to, the more that'll change. But it won't happen all at once. One or two families at a time. A lot probably still won't trust you. Us Apaches don't trust too many outsiders. Too much bad blood between us and Anglos. And it doesn't just go back to Geronimo's day. Things still happen, even today."

"I'm sure," I said. "I know that's true at Gila River. Could you give me an example, though?"

"I'll give you a good one. It's one of the reasons I really didn't like you for 70 a couple days."

"Oh," I said, again startled. "I knew you weren't sure of me, but I didn't know you actually didn't like me."

Mrs. Cassadore continued, "Well, I didn't. You see, something happened to me a long time ago that I never forgot." She hesitated.

"Yeah?"

"When I was raising my family, one time I got sick. Like the flu. I coughed a lot, and my lungs hurt. And I was really tired. For a couple weeks, I stayed in bed most of the time. I didn't want to go to the clinic; I didn't trust Anglo medicine. But I got worse. Finally, I figured I had no choice, so I went to see a doctor.

"He was a young man, just outta school. Those young doctors that bor- 75 rowed money from the government could pay their loans off by going out to an Indian reservation and working for the Indian Health Service for a couple years. That's how they staffed Indian hospitals.

"Well, he told me they had to do some tests, so I stayed at the hospital most of the day. Then he told me to go home, rest, and come back a few days later. When I went back, he took me into an office and closed the door. I didn't like that. Then he told me I had tuberculosis.

"I knew about that disease; I knew it was bad. That doctor said he was sorry, but I couldn't go home, I might spread it around to my children and my husband and other people. He said there was a place in Tucson called a sana-torium, and that I had to go there right away and stay till I got better. But I knew there was more to it than he was saying; I knew he really meant I'd stay there till I got better *or* till I died. I got really upset. Not about dying, but about not seeing my children and husband, not even being able to say good-bye. That same day they took me to Tucson.

"That sanatorium was awful. All these poor Indians just sitting there, or lying there, some of them dying. Coughing and coughing, that's what I remember. I thought if tuberculosis didn't kill me, being in that place would.

"Soon I felt better. I thought I was getting over it. But they kept telling me I couldn't leave. I couldn't understand why I had to stay if I wasn't coughing no more, if I didn't feel sick like all those people around me.

"Then one day someone told me to go to one of the doctors' offices. When I got there, the doctor said, very politely, 'Please sit down.' I was thinking, *What now?*

"He told me that something had gone wrong, that some tests they took showed I didn't have tuberculosis after all, and that the tests they took last week, to make sure, proved it. I wasn't sick.

"I was so happy I cried. I thought of my children and my husband; now I could be with them again. I asked the doctor when I could go home.

"Just like that first doctor in San Carlos, he said, 'I'm sorry.' I knew something wasn't right. Then he told me that there was a chance I had picked up tuberculosis while I was there. I had to stay at least a few more weeks, in another ward, just to make sure I hadn't caught it.

"Every day and every night, all I could think about was that they had sent me away from home, to this terrible place, because of a disease I never had but might have gotten while I was there. If I got it and died, then the IHS° killed me. Some white person had made a mistake that killed an Indian, and I'd be buried, and whoever it was that killed me wouldn't have to answer to anyone. I kept thinking about that young doctor in San Carlos. He should have checked. He should have made sure. It was his fault, really."

Mrs. Cassadore fell silent. She stared at the twisted napkin in her hand, visibly upset.

Shocked into numbness, I could muster no more than a few words. "How long were you in that sanatorium?"

Mrs. Cassadore mumbled, "Half my life." Though she had been incarcerated for at least weeks, at most months, I knew what she meant.

"When did this happen?"

"In 1973."

I knew that things like that had happened in the 1800s, and maybe in the early part of this century, but I never would have imagined that they were still occurring as late as 1973. How wrong I had been in my supposition. Perhaps things like this happened yet.

Mrs. Cassadore glanced up. "You see, that's why I didn't like you when I first saw you."

IHS: Indian Health Service.

I still didn't get it.

"Well, that doctor at the hospital in San Carlos—he looked just like *you*. Tall, curly hair, beard. When I saw you, I saw him. All my memories flooded back. You were that young doctor. You were the one who almost killed me."

After a long silence, I whispered, "And now?"

"Now, I think you're okay."   95

"What changed?"

"That doctor couldn't be trusted. But you—I've watched you awhile. I think you can be trusted."

"I hope I'm worthy of your trust," I said, again looking down.

Mrs. Cassadore chuckled. "Well, let me put it this way, I've lived long enough, as of tonight, to know I shouldn't judge a white man by his face hair. That's a first for me."

EXPLORING THE TEXT

1. What mistakes does Fedullo make during his first encounter with Mrs. Cassadore? How do the assumptions and interpersonal style of Anglo American culture contribute to these missteps? What does he do to overcome Mrs. Cassadore's initial rejection of his attempts at friendship?

2. What tasks or challenges face young Native Americans, according to Fedullo, in their dealings with Anglo society? Why do you think he opposes the idea of assimilation? Why might it be important for Native American children to maintain native cultures and traditions?

3. How do the kids that Fedullo works with in his survival-skills class "read" the intentions of the non-Indians they encounter? What cultural assumptions underlie these interpretations? Are these assumptions themselves a kind of prejudice? Why or why not? How would you describe Fedullo's purpose as a teacher? What is his role in relation to his students?

4. What does Fedullo learn during his dinner with Mrs. Cassadore? How does this encounter challenge his assumptions about Apache culture, literacy, and education? How does it complicate his initial interpretation of Mrs. Cassadore's motives and intentions?

FURTHER EXPLORATIONS

1. To what extent is the misunderstanding that occurs between Fedullo and Mrs. Cassadore a matter of cultural conflict as described by Edward T. Hall in "Hidden Culture" (p. 428)? How are the actions, reactions, and interpretations of Fedullo and Mrs. Cassadore shaped by what Hall terms the "cultural unconscious"? How might Hall evaluate Fedullo's approach to resolving this problem in cross-cultural communication?

2. To what extent can Roger C. Schank's theory of story-based understanding (p. 373) help explain Mrs. Cassadore's initial reluctance to accept Fedullo's offer of friendship? Seen from a "Schankian" perspective, is this cross-cultural misun-

derstanding necessarily resolved when Mrs. Cassadore tells Fedullo her own story? Why or why not?

3. What role do "impersonal memories" as described by Eviatar Zerubavel (p. 217) play in Mrs. Cassadore's reluctance to accept Fedullo's invitation to dinner? To what extent are all stereotypes and prejudices the result of impersonal memories?

4. How does Fedullo's experience with Mrs. Cassadore complicate Martha C. Nussbaum's claim that we learn empathy through our encounters with imaginative literature (p. 416)? In what ways do Fedullo and Mrs. Cassadore both demonstrate the power of empathetic thinking?

ESSAY OPTIONS

1. Using the definitions of learning offered by Mary Catherine Bateson in "A Mutable Self" (p. 337) and Roger C. Schank in "Understanding Other People's Stories" (p. 373) as a point of departure, write an essay in which you explore the role of learning in "Mrs. Cassadore." What is learned by Fedullo, his students, and Mrs. Cassadore? How "genuine" is the understanding that they gain?

2. Drawing on ideas and experiences in Fedullo's "Mrs. Cassadore" and on those presented in any of the other selections in this chapter, write an essay on the challenges and pitfalls of learning how to listen to others. What obstacles keep us from understanding the ideas, feelings, and experiences of others? What do we have to do to become active and effective listeners? To what extent is it possible to hear what others are trying to tell us? What experiences have you had that illustrate the difficulties involved in active or empathetic listening?

Heart to Heart: Sex Differences in Emotion

DEBORAH BLUM

According to the age-old cliché *vive la difference!*, we should celebrate, not castigate differences between males and females. But for many feminists and gender studies scholars, *la difference* is itself a concept fraught with danger for women. Since the inception of the modern feminist movement, controversy has raged over the issue of gender difference. Theories asserting that men and women have different aptitudes, interests, and abilities have been condemned by some scholars as simply perpetuating outmoded gender stereotypes and embraced by others as validating alternative ways of thinking and being. In this selection from *Sex on the Brain: The Biological Differences Between Men and Women* (1997), science writer Deborah Blum presents the case for the emotional differences that distinguish male and female minds. In Blum's view, women possess an innate emotional sensitivity that gives them significant advantages over men, both in terms of their resilience and their ability to read other minds. A professor of journalism at the University of Wisconsin-Madison, Blum (b. 1954) won the Pulitzer Prize in 1992 for a series of articles on the ethical dilemmas involved in primate research, which she expanded upon in book form as *The Monkey Wars* (1994). She is coeditor of *A Field Guide for Science Writers* (1997).

BEFORE READING

Working in groups, do a quick collective sketch of stereotypical male and female behavior patterns. What are the interests, values, and attitudes of the stereotypical male? How do they compare with those commonly associated with the stereotypical female? What truth, if any, do you see in these commonplace views of gender?

The heart is mostly muscle. Its steady thump — for all that we invest it with the rhythm of romance ("It beats for you, darling") — is merely the sound of machinery at work, pushing blood where it needs to go. Only in a too narrow window of childhood do we believe in the heart as a literal container, a dispenser of love. When my son Marcus was four, he asked one morning before our daily separation — I to the office, he to preschool — if I remembered him when he was away. "You're always in my heart," I replied, smiling. He looked back at me, very sober. "Will you keep me in the point?" he asked. "I want to be there." And he wanted his daddy, he said, in the upper curve. For him, the heart, my heart, was a valentine-shaped container to hold him, his father, his beloved cat, and a world of security. He's left that behind now, as any properly cynical seven-year-old would. And me? Not a chance. I still hold him in the point of my heart.

While it's not rational, it's unexpectedly hard to demystify the heart, to let it be what it is: atria, ventricles, and valves packed in cardiac muscle, pumping some nine thousand liters of blood a day, in and out, thump and thump, pacing the biological rhythms of our days. Mine beats — in all technical accuracy — for me alone. Yours, for you. We all know it; it's the ABC stuff of high school biology. And yet we still have heartthrobs, hearts and flowers, heartbreaking songs, heartfelt, follow your heart — as if the brain is all cold logic and the heart all warm feelings.

Maybe there is actually a scientific reason for this. One theory, at least, links the heart and emotion in a most logical way. It goes back to the developing fetus — the flickering start of a human being — floating in the amniotic sac, where the loudest, steadiest, most reliable sound is the beat of the mother's heart. We know that somewhere between five and six months' gestation, the fetus begins to hear. That world of darkness and warmth is not silent; somewhere between 50 and 160 times a minute, the drumbeat of the heart repeats, as constant as time. And after birth — into a world shockingly full of noise and light and dry, rasping air — the baby can still hear that reassuring rhythm if the mother holds her (or him) just so. The sound that so recently defined safety is still there, still close.

It's a fact that mothers preferentially carry infants on the left hip.[1] It's true for right-handed mothers, who rationally explain that it makes sense to free their more useful hand for other chores. But it's also true for left-handed mothers, who rationally explain that it makes sense to use their stronger, dominant arm in holding the child safely. For women, it has been true across culture and history. It likely grows out of our evolution: Consider that ape females, too, prefer to cuddle their babies to the left. Perhaps in some distant past mothers learned that their infants settled and relaxed if they were held close to the heart.

Could each new mother—ape and human—learn this lesson anew? Not likely. If so, why wouldn't the left-carrying bias be true for fathers? It's not nearly as strong, not even in fathers who spend a lot of time caring for their small children. Mostly right-handed, as is the human species at large, they're more likely to hold the child in the stronger arm, across the body from the heart. It makes rational sense, but it apparently runs counter to an emotional-biological sense built into the mother-child bond. In that crucial, virtually universal relationship, the heart really is more than a pump. It is a signal. It binds us, giving the small child his first sense of security in the world outside the womb.

Frans de Waal, a primatologist and professor of psychology at Emory University in Atlanta, comments that people sometimes try too hard to prove that they are making an intelligent choice. Is every action of parenting based on intellect rather than (if you will) the heart? Unlikely, says de Waal, who proposes an open-minded attitude toward the influence of biology. We come from a species—a series of species, really—with a long history of females as mothers, nurturers, and supporters. There's a graceful, evolutionary kind of logic to the way a mother cradles her child, and, maybe, an equal logic to the distance a father leaves between baby and heart. That's not ever to deny love between father and child. In either case, we're talking about a parent carrying a child, holding a baby close, and providing security and shelter. The width of a human body is not large, but the space is still curiously suggestive.

Of all the differences between men and women, the one that seems currently to grab the most attention is that of emotional connection. It has become the stuff of stereotypes and greeting cards: women seek commitment and men flee; women talk about their feelings, men change the subject to basketball scores; women share their emotions with friends, men regard that as an act of indecent exposure. Is it merely perception? And even if it is, where does that perception come from? How soon does it separate the boys from the girls?

De Waal pays tribute to the work of New York University psychologist Martin Hoffman, who has studied the emotional responses of day-old infants too young for anyone to "train"—before any suspicion of socialization. Hoffman simply let the babies listen to sounds—of other babies crying, of animal calls, of the weird droning voice of computer-generated language. The babies responded most strongly to the sound of another human in distress. But it was the tiny females who reacted most intensely to the sound of another's trouble—a reaction that Hoffman suggested would run like an underground stream through their entire lives. His inference was that, while both sexes respond to another's distress, even on the first day girls are more tuned to an empathetic response. Hoffman's carefully technical analysis puts it like this: "Females may be more apt to imagine how it would feel if the stimuli impinging on the other were impinging on the self."

Females, for so long the first line of caregiving—the first defense, really, that an infant has against the world—*have* to be oriented to the needs of others. No wonder, then, that females possess such exquisitely tuned senses: The female sense of smell is more acute than the male's (especially during ovulation), and women are more sensitive to touch than men. As it turns out, ability to communicate with touch is critical for the healthy survival of a child. Studies with premature infants have found that if they are held, even just gently stroked, they grow and mature faster. They gain weight 47 percent faster than those left alone, even if both receive the same amount of food.

Touch now appears to be one of those factors that the genes rely on to guide proper development. In some animals—rats, for instance—if the mother isn't there to cuddle and lick, the babies simply don't make the hormonal chemistry necessary to grow. Saul Schanberg, at Duke University Medical Center, suggests that because mammals are so dependent on a mother's care, her touch sends a signal of reassurance that the world is all right. Denied it, even for forty-five minutes, a newborn rat's metabolism slows in a seemingly self-protective measure, shutting down requirements for nourishment.[2]

There's another, almost charming, study of rhesus macaques—an agile species of Asian monkey—in which University of Wisconsin scientists found that the mother's holding an infant near the chest directly influenced what we sometimes think of as the chemistry of happiness, raising the natural opiates of the bloodstream to the point that the scientists compared the pleasure of touch to a drug-induced high.[3]

And then there's hearing. Females hear high-pitched sounds better than males. That difference begins in childhood and actually becomes more acute. In one study of simple noise, a researcher asked twenty-four men and twenty-four women to turn up a speaker until the wail of sound just passed the comfort zone. The men averaged eight decibels louder than the women. Men are comfortable with sounds twice as loud as women are. This is equally true for boys and girls even as young as age five. Examining the tiny hair cells in the inner ear that vibrate to transmit sound, researchers have found women's ears to be more sensitive, men's less. The number of hairs are about the same, but women's vibrate more intensely—and the richer and more complex the vibrations, the better the hearing. The exception is women who have (or had) a twin brother: Their ears are also less sharply tuned. Scientists suspect some masculinizing influence on early development side by side with a male—perhaps an extra wash of testosterone in the amniotic fluid.[4]

Mothers have to communicate with children—not just comfort them, but warn them of danger. This protects the individual child and may, in an expanded picture, be essential to the overall survival of the species. Researchers regard such communication—nurturing, protective—as so necessary that they suggest it created women's verbal advantage over men.

Evolutionary psychologists such as Anne Fernald at Stanford University have found that mothers talk to their infants in a particularly high, crooning voice. A mother's voice goes up by as much as two octaves, the equivalent of sixteen ivory-colored piano keys, when addressing a baby. Fathers' voices rise also, but less dramatically—perhaps half an octave, or four piano keys. Fernald finds the same maternal pattern across cultures. American, French, German, Italian, Chinese, African, Japanese—all mothers scale up for infants, and not just for their own. Babies respond to the tone more than the words. An American infant smiles as readily at the music of a Japanese voice as at that of an English one. It's the "song" that counts. (Recently, British scientists suggested that this maternal music fits beautifully with the idea that carrying babies on the left helps nurture them emotionally. The position means that a mother would be crooning into the infant's left ear. Thus the sounds are processed by the right hemisphere of the brain, where neuroscientists think emotions are mainly processed.)[5]

"I'm arguing that the vocalizations of mothers are well matched to the sensitivities and needs of the infants," Fernald says. At the same time, she points out, this style of communication would be distinctly out of place elsewhere. Imagine turning to a coworker, or a fellow subway passenger, and talking as we do to a baby: up close, in the face, suddenly high in the fluting notes of the treble range. "They'd think you'd gone crazy."

Fernald has found, by playing tape-recorded voices to them, that infants turn more readily toward a woman's high-note sounds than toward the tones the same woman might use to an adult. And the heart of the infant slows, calms, and steadies, beating more gently as it hears that particular music of a mother's voice. Comfort, in this sense, is anything but a luxury; the comfort that mother gives child appears basic, biological, and continuous with (perhaps part of) the same developmental process that goes on in the womb. It is in this intertwining of mother and child—a tale of two hearts—that the evolutionary argument for emotional differences between men and women begins. . . .

. . . Men love to build hierarchies. Any traditionally male-dominated organization—from the military to the corporation—is based on a pecking order, a chain of command. Rules accommodate competition, even confrontation. "Picking a fight can actually be a way for men to relate to one another, check each other out, and take a first step toward friendship," de Waal notes. And this kind of bonding is alien to most women, who see confrontation as causing painful, hard-to-mend rifts in their feminine fabric of connections.

A colleague of de Waal's at Emory University's Yerkes Regional Primate Research Center, psychologist Kim Wallen, tells this story about a friend of his, a woman lawyer who gave up trial law: "She could never adjust to the contest nature that males brought to it. She said, 'They would say the worst things about each other in court and then go pee together and laugh at each other's jokes and I would be seething and taking it all personally.'"

Wallen has studied the way testosterone seems, in males, to spike up in competitive situations, climbing in the face of challenge, relaxing as the need to face off declines. The response occurs in a wide range of species, including primates. Does this make it easier for males to play such power games? "Now I don't know whether there are hormones involved in this," Wallen says, "but I could imagine that the fluctuations males experience could make for white-hot responses which are meaningless a few moments later."

Such fluctuations, looked at from a woman's perspective, could add up to   20 emotional inconsistency, even untrustworthiness. Among men, if you live by competition and embrace aggression, then you must also be on guard against it in others; suspicion and a certain distancing are part of any competitor's stance. In the opening of her book *You Just Don't Understand,* which explores male-female communication styles, sociolinguist Deborah Tannen tells an anecdote about herself and her husband.[6] They had a commuter marriage at the time, each teaching at a different university in a different city. Friends and colleagues would commiserate with them, and Tannen tended to accept the sympathy. She would reinforce the support with a sigh and agree that, yes, they did have to fly a lot and it was tough. Her husband, on the other hand, did not care for condolences. In fact, he would even reject the comments with irritation. He downplayed the problem. Tannen's analysis, after doing research for her book, was that they were following established gender roles. She was tapping into the network of connections that women like to build. He was responding like a typical male: Trust no one and reveal no weakness, lest it diminish one's status.

The way we talk to each other has received a lot of attention in recent years, but we also talk *about* each other—a lot. Gossip, stemming from a fascination with the business of others, seems to be a trait also deeply woven into our evolutionary history. Stanford University primatologist Robert Sapolsky points out that it's not just us; gossip seems fundamental across primate species.[7] He describes, for instance, a vicious fight between two male baboons in the African savannah, going at each other with absolute fury and wicked canine teeth. A bystander, Sapolsky notes, could get hurt watching. What did the other baboons do? "Drop everything, stand up on two feet, and push in for a closer view."

Among researchers, gossip is being reborn. They are moving its reputation from sly bitchiness to an essential part of social connectedness. A 1996 issue of *Psychology Today,* for instance, declared firmly that gossip is good[8]—a way of navigating the social environment and figuring out what's important. Good people gossip, in other words. I find myself, in a perverse way, wondering if I really want to let science turn every bad habit into a good one. Besides, what's the fun of trashing people behind their backs if it only makes you a better person?

However, the new, improved gossip research also offers insight into gender differences. Everyone gossips—boy and girl, man and woman. Generally, gossip gets intense in late adolescence. And generally it starts with talking about others of the same sex. That's right; in spite of the stereotype that teenage girls do nothing but talk about teenage boys, they actually spend three times as much time talking about other girls. Girls do, however, tell their girlfriends about boys they like—all about how great he looked in that blue tank top, and how he teased the teacher in homeroom and, well, everything.

Boys tend not to do the equivalent. Detailed research finds that teenage boys spend very little time describing the way a girl smiles or the sound of her laugh—even to their best friends. Girls do it casually; it's fun. For boys, it's too intimate. And by the time these boys and girls reach college—as documented in a study in which researchers secretly tape-recorded students in a university cafeteria (remember this next time you want to discuss your sex life over lunch)—the gender gap had deepened. College women mostly talked about people in their lives—classmates, friends, guys they dated, family. Men mostly talked sports, politics, tests, and classwork.

Books such as Tannen's, exploring the puzzle of communication differ-   25
ences, reveal how amazingly close we seem to follow the ancient ground rules that appear in chimpanzee society. In childhood, the idea of status— being alpha male,° if you will—seems to occur very young in boys. It doesn't seem to, at least not so much, in girls. Overall, girls seem less determined to be number one. (Of course there are exceptions.) A typical study of children's play illustrates the point by exploring the way groups of same-sex children played the game of "doctor." The boys all wanted to be the doctor—the one in charge who told everyone else what to do. They would argue this out for an extended period. Girls would ask who wanted to be doctor. Then they'd negotiate, sharing roles as doctor, or sometimes several doctors, nurse, and patient.

Boys, more than girls, want competitive games with real winners. They also seem more comfortable with confrontation over the outcome of the games. In one of the classic studies of child play, by Janet Lever in 1972, girls' games turned out to be measurably shorter than boys'. Lever saw boys arguing all the time over their games—who did what, who had what. Not once, though, did she see a boys' game end due to an argument. With girls, though, the children themselves complained that quarrels regularly ended their games. At least one girl routinely marched away, saying she didn't want to play anymore and, often, that she wasn't speaking to her fellow playmates either.[9] It's worth raising here the parallel to reconciliation patterns in chimpanzees. Once again, males let go of disagreements more easily than girls; girls have a stronger emotional response to conflict. Some argue, of course, that this is a result of culture, that we encourage girls to be more emotional and discourage emotionalism in boys. In this argument, everything is culture—similar behaviors in closely related species are just a coincidence.

---

alpha male: Term used to designate the dominant male in a group of primates.

But much as we try to separate them, biology and culture aren't mutually exclusive. They can't be. Our questions about the role of nature versus nurture form a circle in which one influence feeds the other and around it comes again. We're not chimpanzees, certainly, but chimpanzees' own remarkably complex society may provide perspective on what ours might once have been. In this loop, biology is most important as a starting place. But how do you figure out where a circle begins?

Michael Milburn, a psychology professor at the University of Massachusetts, may have traced one starting place through a backwards-looking study of adult political attitudes, both liberal and conservative.[10] Milburn was interested in whether there was a connection between growing up in a very strict household—in being severely punished for infractions—and one's adult political orientation. He found a curious and, I think, enlightening gender difference.

In general, he found that children of parents who went lightly on the punishment, especially corporal punishment, grew up to be political moderates. But children of high-punishment parents—who disciplined particularly with the belt and hand—tended to split by gender. Men, notably those who never sought counseling or therapy, grew up very politically conservative. Most were strong on capital punishment and big believers in military force. Women, on the other hand, who were whipped often as children almost always became politically liberal, whether they went through therapy or not. Milburn saw that different response as beginning with female empathy. The girls had been severely punished themselves. They tended to put themselves in the place of another person facing punishment. He argues that the difference begins in biology, in that inclination of females toward empathy, citing Hoffman's work with baby girls. Family and culture, Milburn suggests, only expand and build on what we bring into the world, which then affects our social choices, and so on.

Some male-female differences in emotional response are so distinct that it's easy to understand why scientist would look backwards for an explanation.   30

Ruben and Raquel Gur recently took such a route in their studies of emotion. They were following a lengthy parade of experiments which show that women are far more adept than men at interpreting facial expression. The evidence is so strong in this direction that researchers are beginning to take it as a given. So now they've started exploring why. Why are women better than men? Why should they be? One of the theories goes directly to primate societies. That is, in most one-to-one relationships in monkeys and apes, there's a dominant-submissive pattern. Put two rhesus macaques in a cage and they'll negotiate that relationship; forever more, the submissive partner will back away, lower the body, and accommodate the dominant partner.

There's always a slight element of fear in this, of the risk of annoying the dominant partner and getting hurt. A worried monkey is known to produce a kind of nervous smile, known as a fear grin. Similarly, women tend to smile far more often than men; of course, men often encourage women to smile. Researchers have pondered whether this pattern—women's ready smiling, men urging them to do so—comes from a past based on a dominant-submissive relationship.[11] Similar questions have been raised about women's apparently sharper ability to read nonverbal expression, from body language to the subtle set of an unsmiling mouth. Is the latter from sadness, worry, or a gathering anger? Is it important in terms of self-protection to know?

The Gurs added all kinds of interesting complexity to that question. They looked at not only how well each sex can read facial expression, but whether the sex of the face studied made a difference. Can men read women's faces better or vice versa? They also wondered if there were particular emotions that drew a stronger response, say, joy versus grief.

In a series of tests studying photographs of faces, both sexes were equally adept at noticing when someone else was happy. Women also easily read sadness in a person's face, whether male or female, at about 90 percent accuracy. Men, on the other hand, more accurately read unhappiness in another man's face rather than in women's faces. They were right about other men about 90 percent of the time, but when they looked at women's faces, they were right only about 70 percent of the time. And the woman's face had to be dramatically down. "A woman's face had to be really sad for me to see it," Ruben Gur says. "The subtle expressions went right by them." His suggestion is that this may indeed spring from that ancient power balance. In a society—not so different from chimpanzees—where males hung out together and negotiated for power, it was vital for men to be able to read male faces; they might have had far less need to be tuned to the expressions of a female face. But for women, it would have been different.

The Gurs also did a study in which they asked people, both male and female, to look at a series of expressive faces. They found something that we all suspect: mood is catching. Both men and women, exposed to enough smiling faces, felt cheerful. Seeing an unrelieved series of grief portraits made everyone depressed. You could argue here that a male's tendency to be less sensitive to female unhappiness could serve him well, especially in a relationship in which he might actually induce unhappiness.[12]

Let's make one more parallel with chimpanzees here. Male chimpanzees are bigger and stronger than females, and are known for occasionally losing their tempers and taking it out on the nearest fellow primate. Every so often, female chimps really get slapped around. It may occur to you that it's not an enormous reach, even today, to compare this with some aspects of human behavior. And in that dangerous-male scenario, it might make a great deal of sense for females to be very good at reading the subtlest of male expressions. It might mean survival. "Given the power differential," Gur says, "the higher sensitivity of women to male emotions may have evolutionary adaptive significance."

At this point, I must confess that all this discussion of submissiveness in women makes me wince. There's such a nasty little implication of women being the species' biological doormat. So, let's put this in a little more perspective. The point of all this evolutionary backtracking is not to label either sex strong or weak; it's to try to figure out where certain behaviors might have begun. With emotional sensitivity, perhaps women did gain extra abilities from their need to nurture children, to build strong support systems, and to accommodate the sometimes dangerous moods of men. Perhaps males spent more time playing power games. These are only theories. But even if we accept these theories, they don't diminish one end result, which is that today, women seem to have developed a powerful emotional advantage over men.

There are people who argue that women have learned to use their emotional and verbal skills as effective weapons. Some researchers say that mothers teach their daughters how to use words well and how to share feelings far better than they teach their sons. Studies show that mothers tend to talk to girls more about emotions and to make up stories for their daughters that deal with resolving emotional conflict. They encourage daughters more, so scientists say, to talk about their feelings. The one emotion that mothers do routinely discuss with their sons is anger, and, in that case, it tends to be about controlling behavior — as in, Don't push the smaller children off the climbing structure at school, even if they get in your way.

According to a plurality of studies, by the time children reach about age thirteen or so, boys are quick to respond physically, while girls fight with words — or, often just as deftly, by withholding them and shutting someone out. Daniel Goleman, a psychologist who covers behavioral science for the *New York Times,* describes these differences as part of a continuum: first, girls learn to use emotional response to control their teenage relationships; then, women use that well-honed ability to out-manipulate men in their adult relationships. Females, he concludes, use language with more sophistication.[13]

In this context, you notice, sophisticated doesn't mean nice. Words are   40
sharp-edged and women handle them with practiced cruelty. If you believe the argument, men make easy targets.

There's another new school of thought, also suggesting that emotional strengths are real ones: they help make women physically healthier than men. This represents a sea change in Western societies, where emotion used to be regarded as a weak female quality; where reserve and self-control were both more male and more admired. Now there's growing evidence that weaving emotional bonds can be compared to weaving a safety net. There's a return on emotional giving. A man's traditional reluctance to reach out very far, or to very many, results in a net more fragile, more liable to betray him. Women, in general, cushion themselves with the company of others in a way that eludes men, sometimes with catastrophic results. Who, after all, are more often the loners in society — especially those at the alienated fringe? Federal prosecutors portray Ted Kaczynski,° of Unabomber fame, as spending years planning meticulously impersonal murders of strangers while he shut himself away in his Montana cabin.

Ted Kaczynski: Theodore Kaczynski (b. 1942), known as the "Unabomber," was convicted on multiple counts of homicide in 1998.

There are a multitude of studies that compare the reactions of men and women who lose a spouse to death. They show that women recover their emotional balance faster. If children lose a parent, it's the daughters, in general, who seem to take less of a mental beating, and who fall less often into antisocial or destructive behaviors.

But it can't be all attributed to connectedness or willingness to talk and share. There's a female something—still mysterious, even to scientists—that seems to provide the foundation for a different kind of emotional security. Frans de Waal cautions moderation, noting that we seem to be in the middle of a pendulum swing that admires female qualities, where once we venerated the male: "Women stand around in front of baby clothes oohing and aahing and everyone thinks that's just charming. Why can't men be more like that? But let a man follow his natural inclinations—maybe it's looking at pictures of undressed women—and he's really a jerk. Why can't he behave better? It's almost more politically correct these days to be a woman."

The Gurs are also cautious; at least, they warn that it's far too early to say that women stand ahead of men in dealing with emotional issues. "Obviously, if you have a measure of performance on something, and one group scores higher, we can say that they do 'better,'" said Ruben Gur. "We believe nonetheless that there is yet a lot more to learn about sex differences in the several aspects of emotional processing before we can say that women perform better as a rule." . . .

There's a clear indication that emotional learning and connection is also enormously important at a very young age. In a brain study of very young children by University of Seattle psychologist Geraldine Dawson,[14] she found that lack of affection produced physical results. Dawson did PET scans of the brains of children whose mothers were severely depressed. They showed, she reported in 1996, that metabolism levels dropped severely in the brains of those babies compared to those with warm and cheerful mothers. Dawson particularly saw a difference in the frontal lobes, where the brain seems to handle positive emotions like curiosity and happiness. The normal building of connections in that region did not show up in the children with depressed mothers. Dawson also found that most of those children began showing signs of angry and aggressive behavior by the age of three. The study suggests, at least circumstantially, that the unhappy infancy produced a brain less open to happiness and more prone to negative actions.

What Belsky° wonders, then, is whether somewhere in this tale of emotion and health and developing brain is another connection that we've somehow missed or misunderstood. Perhaps, especially early on, boys need more— more touch, song, emotional support—than we tend to give them. Maybe parents disconnect from boys early in a way they don't with girls, pushing

45

Belsky: Jay Belsky (b. 1952), child development researcher at Pennsylvania State University.

them faster toward independence. As grown men, they wouldn't remember that, of course, but the emotional distance may have been built in anyway.

You have to wonder if our culture has misread the realities of our biology. Remember that old nursery rhyme, that girls are made of "sugar, spice and everything nice" while boys are "snips and snails and puppy dog tails"? I quoted it carelessly to my son Marcus one morning when he was five. He was outraged. Why did girls get to be the good stuff? Why did boys get stuck being garden pests and, apparently, amputated dog body parts? Maybe we need to accept that, at least very early on, baby girls may be stronger than we know and baby boys more vulnerable. In this case, stereotypes may do neither sex any favors.

The late Nancy Bayley of the University of California, Berkeley, whose tests of infant development are still standard, once compared the effect on infant boys and girls of mothers who were depressed enough to be withdrawn or hostile. These were long, awful depressions in mothers often resentful of carrying the extra burden of a child.

Bayley used the first eighteen months of life for her comparison, charting children who received affection against those who did not. She then waited until the children were a little older, between the ages of three and five, and returned to do a series of intelligence and competence tests. Her results suggested that the boys raised by withdrawn and hostile mothers might indeed have been harmed. Their intelligence scores were steadily below those of boys raised with tangible love. That wasn't the case with the girls. They were more withdrawn than children from happy families, but there was no apparent effect on intelligence. For girls, no matter what the home life, the test scores correlated best with the tested intelligence and social class of their mothers. There was one exception: Being raised by a restrictive mother—one who narrowed their experience and sheltered out the world—brought their test scores down. Laura Allen, the UCLA neuroscientist who has done so many comparisons of gender differences in the brain, once analyzed the Bayley work like this: "I think boys need more one-on-one attention. I think the affection may change the sex hormone level in the brain, which then affects brain development."

Why would our biology be so codependent, so that failure of affection 50 would alter the way a baby grows? Perhaps this began simply indeed, in the life-sustaining bond between mother and child. Our species has evolved as intensely social, woven together in a fabric that tears along emotional lines. There's some remarkable work by Sally Mendoza, a psychologist at the University of California, Davis, that suggests that even distant relationships, as they shift, can change the hormone balance within. If a coworker changes jobs, leaving a new opening at the office, and the familiar balance of relationships changes, our stress hormones rise. Essentially, we seek stability in our relationships with others. There's comfort in it, and safety; breaking bonds predicts only trouble. On a much larger scale, Mendoza suggests that some of the rising crime and cruelty of the late twentieth century may have something to do with our increasingly impersonal society—that we aren't biologically equipped to function in a world that demands distance.[15]

Neuroscientist Bruce McEwen, of Rockefeller University, has shown that the hippocampus—that home for recollection, mapmaking, and much that we probably don't yet know—responds almost directly to stress, with cells dying in response to rising levels of cortisol.[16] In studies using rats, this process of cell loss is increased dramatically if the animals are isolated and left without social support. In humans, there are countless studies, of countless men and women, showing that they best survive even severe illnesses, such as heart disease and cancer, if there's a loving and supportive marriage. Even a minor marital spat sends shivers through the immune system, so that couples after a fight are much more likely to come down with a cold or the flu. Scientists have found that, if a partner dies, the immune system of the survivor stays depressed for between four and fourteen months. And no one has ever found that loneliness or grief are good for health, mental or physical.

We really don't understand, however, why boys and men seem even more vulnerable than girls and women in these respects. Is this, too, a consequence of our times? Belsky, Kagan, and others have suggested that emotional isolation and its negative results are simply part of the male package—less durable than the female design, linked to a live-fast-and-die evolutionary past. But now, as medicine keeps us all alive longer, and as technology and changing culture make us more independent from one another and less bonded to extended families and communities, the difference becomes more pronounced. And it becomes more destructive.

Yet even if all of that is true, it may merely add up to a classic example of how difficult it can be to apply scientific theory. It's easy to say boys would be better off with more cozy, chatty relationships, the kind that girls tend to establish and maintain naturally. But how do we make that happen across a society trained in a clearly opposite tradition? Further, as the Gurs reminded me, we're early into this science; we're still sorting emotional strength from emotional weakness, deciding what the terms mean.

Notes

1. The information on mothers carrying babies on the left side of their bodies comes from a personal interview with Frans de Waal, and the issue is discussed in more depth in his book *Good Natured* (Cambridge, Ma.: Harvard University Press, 1996). The book contains a section on gender emotional differences on pages 117–122. De Waal praised Martin Hoffman's work in our discussion, and he cites him in the book as well. Hoffman's 1978 paper, "Sex Differences in Empathy and Related Behaviors," *Psychological Bulletin* 84: 712–722, is considered a classic in the field.

2. Robert Pool discusses the sensory differences between men and women in *Eve's Rib: The Biological Roots of Sex Differences* (New York: Crown Publishers, 1994). Saul Schanberg's work on the importance of touch appeared in "The Experience of Touch: Research Points to a Critical Role," by Daniel Goleman, *New York Times*, February 2,

1988, Science Times. See also S. M. Schanberg, T. Field, C. M. Kuhn, J. Bartolome, "Touch: A Biological Regulator of Growth and Development in the Neonate," *Verhaltenstherapie* 3 (Suppl.) (1993): 15; Saul M. Schanberg and Tiffany M. Field, "Sensory Deprivation Stress and Supplemental Stimulation in the Rape Pup and Preterm Human Neonate," *Child Development* 58 (1987): 1431–1447.

3. The University of Wisconsin study on touch is cited in the January 1994 issue of *Brainwork,* published by the Charles A. Dana Foundation, in an article titled "High on Hugging," by June Kinoshita.

4. The research on differences in vibrations within the ears was reported in "Quiet-Eared Women and the Men Born with Them," *Discover,* May 1994, 14–15.

5. Anne Fernald sets forth her mother-child communication work in a chapter titled "Human Maternal Vocalizations to Infants as Biologically Relevant Signals: An Evolutionary Perspective," in *The Adapted Mind: Evolutionary Psychology and the Generation of Culture,* edited by Jerome H. Barkow, Leda Cosmides, and John Tooby (New York: Oxford University Press, 1992): 391–428. The research connecting holding a baby on the left and emotional response is from "Why You Hold Baby on the Left," *Parenting* (November 1996): 13.

6. The Deborah Tannen anecdote cited is in *You Just Don't Understand* (New York: Ballantine Books, 1991): 24–25.

7. Robert Sapolsky's comments on primate gossip are from his article in the March–April 1995 issue of *The Science;* also reported by the Associated Press on February 27, 1995, in "Gorillas Gossip, Baboons Like to Watch."

8. Human sex differences in gossip were reported in Robin Western, "The Real Slant on Gossip," *Psychology Today* 29, no. 4 (July/August 1996).

9. The study of children playing doctor is cited in Tannen's book *You Just Don't Understand,* but is based on work by Jacqueline Sachs, reported in "Young Children's Language Use in Pretend Play," *Language, Gender and Sex in Comparative Perspective,* edited by Susan Philips, Susan Steele, and Christine Tanz (Cambridge, Ma.: Cambridge University Press, 1987): 178–188. Janet Lever's much-praised observations in 1972 of children at play were published later as "Sex differences in the games children play," *Social Problems* 23 (1976): 478–487.

10. Michael Milburn and S. D. Conrad, "The Politics of Denial," *Journal of Psychohistory* 23, no. 3 (Winter 1996): 238–251.

11. Theories of whether women's sensitivity to nonverbal expression is suggestive of a submissive approach are discussed in Judith A. Hall and Amy G. Halberstadt, "Subordination and Sensitivity to Non-Verbal Cues," *Sex Roles* 31:3/4 (August 1994): 149–166. The authors do not find evidence for that theory.

12. Roland J. Erwin, Ruben C. Gur, Raquel E. Gur, Brett Skolnick, Maureen Mawhinney-Hee, and Joseph Smailis, "Facial Emotion Discrimination: 1. Task Construction and Behavioral Findings in Normal Subjects," *Psychiatry Research* 42 (1992): 231–240; and Frank Schneider, Ruben C. Gur, Raquel E. Gur, and Larry R. Muenz, "Standardized Mood Induction with Happy and Sad Facial Expressions," *Psychiatry Research* 51 (1994): 19–31.

13. The commentary on girls and women using emotions more effectively than boys and men is from Daniel Goleman, *Emotional Intelligence* (New York: Bantam Books, 1996): 130–133.

14. Geraldine Dawson's study of children of depressed mothers was reported at a June 1996 conference, "Brain Development in Young Children," held at the University of Chicago.

15. Nancy Bayley's work is discussed in "Boys May Be More Emotionally Fragile" (by Blum, *Sacramento Bee,* June 10, 1996), the Laura Allen quote in Michael D'Antonio, "The Fragile Sex," *Los Angeles Times Magazine,* December 4, 1994. Sally Mendoza's discussion of emotional connection is in "Morality Not Limited to Humans, More Scientists Believe," by Deborah Blum, *Sacramento Bee,* March 11, 1996, A-1.

16. Bruce McEwen's research into the effect of emotional distress on brain structure is detailed in Bruce S. McEwen, "Stressful Experience, Brain and Emotions: Developmental, Genetic and Hormonal Influences," in *The Cognitive Neurosciences,* Michael S. Gazzaniga, editor (Cambridge, Ma.: MIT Press, 1995): 117–136.

EXPLORING THE TEXT

1. In what ways, according to Blum, are women more sensitive, empathetic, and nurturing than men? What does this suggest about women as interpreters of other minds? How, by contrast, does Blum portray male behaviors, attitudes, and aptitudes? In your opinion, is there some truth in Blum's depiction of the differences between female and male minds — or is Blum presenting stereotypical thinking under the guise of science?

2. How does Blum account for the evolution of higher levels of sensitivity and empathy in females? Why does she feel that "women seem to have developed a powerful emotional advantage over men"? Would you agree? Why or why not?

3. Frans de Waal notes that being female seems more "politically correct" nowadays and that behaviors that were once seen as typically masculine — like looking at pictures of undressed women — are now viewed as relatively primitive. Would you agree that attitudes and values associated with the traditional male are becoming outmoded? What evidence do you see that males are adopting traditionally female values and attitudes or that women are becoming more like men in their views of status, conflict, and hierarchy?

4. According to the research studies noted by Blum, how might we have historically misinterpreted the needs of young boys and girls? Why are boys apparently more "vulnerable" than girls during their early years? What, if anything, can be done to change the way boys are raised in order to address this need for greater emotional support?

FURTHER EXPLORATIONS

1. Working in small groups, make a collage of images of ads and photos from popular magazines that expresses the current view of what it means to be male in American culture and a second collage, similarly assembled, expressing what it means to be female. Present these in class and analyze them in terms of the aptitudes, attitudes, and values they seem to suggest. To what extent do these images confirm or conflict with the research presented by Blum on male and female minds?

2. To what extent do the following selections offer examples of the female mind at work, as described by Blum? Which selections challenge or complicate Blum's depiction of female minds? Why?

"The Mind's Eye" by Georgina Kleege (p. 93)

"No-Name Woman" by Maxine Hong Kingston (p. 206)

"A Mutable Self" by Mary Catherine Bateson (p. 337)

"Mouse" by Faith McNulty (p. 535)

3. Which of the following selections illustrates Blum's conception of the attitudes, values, and aptitudes associated with male minds? Why? Which challenge or complicate Blum's categorization of male/female minds?

"Take the F" by Ian Frazier (p. 18)

"A Passage of the Hands" by Barry Lopez (p. 27)

"The Inheritance of Tools" by Scott Russell Sanders (p. 142)

"Ego Boundaries, or the Fit of My Father's Shirt" by Robert Sapolsky (p. 254)

"Technicolor" by Rubén Martínez (p. 306)

"Mrs. Cassadore" by Mick Fedullo (p. 441)

4. To what extent does the narrator in James Baldwin's "Sonny's Blues" (p. 390) demonstrate what Blum identifies as typically male values or attitudes? Why do these traits make it difficult for him to understand others?

5. How might the depiction of women in Alice Walker's "Everyday Use" (p. 283) complicate Blum's assessment of female minds? To what extent, in your view, can Blum's portrayal of female values and attitudes be extended across cultures?

6. Compare Blum's view of the female mind with Roy F. Baumeister's depiction of female identities in "The Self and Society: Changes, Problems, and Opportunities" (p. 320). How can you account for the differences in these two contrasting appraisals of the female self?

7. How does Blum's distinction between male and female minds complicate Martha C. Nussbaum's theory of the civic function of imaginative literature in a diverse, democratic society (p. 416)? Would it be fair to characterize Nussbaum's view of literature as being particularly "female"? Why or why not?

ESSAY OPTIONS

1. Drawing on Blum's insights about male and female minds, write a paper in which you present and analyze a conflict you have experienced with a person of the opposite sex. What were the circumstances surrounding this conflict, and what was the outcome? To what extent does Blum's analysis of the attributes of male and female ways of thinking help explain why this conflict occurred? What other factors may have been involved? How do you think the other person or persons involved in this conflict viewed you and your motives? Looking back, how might your approach to resolving this conflict change?

2. Drawing on Blum's depiction of the dominant attributes of female minds and on Ellen Ullman's assessment of life in the information technology industry (p. 656), write an essay in which you evaluate how women are likely to fare in the electronic workplace. What challenges are women likely to face in accommodating themselves to the cult of the "boy engineer"?

What's So Bad About Hate?

ANDREW SULLIVAN

Outrageous question, isn't it? Actually, Andrew Sullivan isn't suggesting outright anarchy. Instead, he's picking a fight with a particular kind of legal mind reading. During the 1980s and 1990s, communities across the nation adopted laws meant to protect minority groups from deliberate expressions of racism, anti-Semitism, and homophobia. The problem with such "hate laws," according to Sullivan, is that they assume we can understand and interpret the motives that underlie any act of violence. Hate, Sullivan argues in this essay, is too complicated a phenomenon — and too deeply woven into the fabric of life in a diverse society — to be legislated out of existence. Sullivan himself is no stranger to the subject of hate, having at one time or another infuriated many of his fellow gay Americans with the critical stands he's taken on the issue of gay rights. A graduate of Oxford and Harvard Universities, Sullivan (b. 1963) writes for the *New York Times Magazine*, London's *Sunday Times*, and the *New Republic*, where he has also served as editor. His publications include *Virtually Normal: An Argument About Homosexuality* (1995) and *Love Undetectable: Notes on Friendship, Sex, and Survival* (1998). He is currently working on a book about the politics of genetics.

BEFORE READING

Working in groups, pool your knowledge on hate crimes. What distinguishes a hate crime from a "regular" criminal offense? How can you tell the difference between hate crimes and crimes that are not motivated by hatred? Should the issue of motivation make a difference in the punishment of a crime? Why or why not?

I

I wonder what was going on in John William King's head two years ago when he tied James Byrd Jr.'s feet to the back of a pickup truck and dragged him three miles down a road in rural Texas. King and two friends had picked up Byrd, who was black, when he was walking home, half drunk, from a party. As part of a bonding ritual in their fledgling white supremacist group, the three men took Byrd to a remote part of town, beat him, and chained his legs together before attaching them to the truck. Pathologists at King's trial testified that Byrd was probably alive and conscious until his body finally hit a culvert and split in two. When King was offered a chance to say something to Byrd's family at the trial, he smirked and uttered an obscenity.

We know all these details now, many months later. We know quite a large amount about what happened before and after. But I am still drawn, again and again, to the flash of ignition, the moment when fear and loathing became hate, the instant of transformation when King became hunter and Byrd became prey.

What was that? And what was it when Buford Furrow Jr., long-time member of the Aryan Nations, calmly walked up to a Filipino-American mailman he happened to spot, asked him to mail a letter, and then shot him at point-blank range? Or when Russell Henderson beat Matthew Shepard, a young gay man, to a pulp, removed his shoes, and then, with the help of a friend, tied him to a post, like a dead coyote, to warn off others?

For all our documentation of these crimes and others, our political and moral disgust at them, our morbid fascination with them, our sensitivity to their social meaning, we seem at times to have no better idea now than we ever had of what exactly they were about. About what that moment means when, for some reason or other, one human being asserts absolute, immutable superiority over another. About not the violence, but what the violence expresses. About what — exactly — hate is. And what our own part in it may be.

I find myself wondering what hate actually is in part because we have created an entirely new offense in American criminal law — a "hate crime" — to combat it. And barely a day goes by without someone somewhere declaring war against it. Last month President Clinton called for an expansion of hate-crime laws as "what America needs in our battle against hate." A couple of weeks later, Senator John McCain used a campaign speech to denounce the "hate" he said poisoned the land. New York's mayor, Rudolph Giuliani, recently tried to stop the Million Youth March° in Harlem on the grounds that the event was organized by people "involved in hate marches and hate rhetoric."

The media concur in their emphasis. In 1985, there were eleven mentions of "hate crimes" in the national media database Nexis. By 1990, there were more than a thousand. In the first six months of 1999, there were seven thousand. "Sexy fun is one thing," wrote a *New York Times* reporter about sexual assaults in Woodstock '99's mosh pit. "But this was an orgy of lewdness tinged with hate." And when Benjamin Smith marked the Fourth of July this year by targeting blacks, Asians, and Jews for murder in Indiana and Illinois, the story wasn't merely about a twisted young man who had emerged on the scene. As the *Times* put it, "Hate arrived in the neighborhoods of Indiana University, in Bloomington, in the early-morning darkness."

But what exactly was this thing that arrived in the early-morning darkness? For all our zeal to attack hate, we still have a remarkably vague idea of what it actually is. A single word, after all, tells us less, not more. For all its emotional punch, "hate" is far less nuanced an idea than prejudice, or bigotry, or bias, or anger, or even mere aversion to others. Is it to stand in for all these varieties of human experience — and everything in between? If so, then the war against it will be so vast as to be quixotic. Or is "hate" to stand for a very specific idea or belief, or set of beliefs, with a very specific object or group

the Million Youth March: A 1999 demonstration of solidarity in New York City by thousands of young African American men, organized by a former aide to Nation of Islam leader Louis Farrakhan.

of objects? Then waging war against it is almost certainly unconstitutional. Perhaps these kinds of questions are of no concern to those waging war on hate. Perhaps it is enough for them that they share a sentiment that there is too much hate and never enough vigilance in combating it. But sentiment is a poor basis for law and a dangerous tool in politics. It is better to leave some unwinnable wars unfought.

II

Hate is everywhere. Human beings generalize all the time, ahead of time, about everyone and everything. A large part of it may even be hard-wired. At some point in our evolution, being able to know beforehand who was friend or foe was not merely a matter of philosophical reflection. It was a matter of survival. And even today it seems impossible to feel a loyalty without also feeling a disloyalty, a sense of belonging without an equal sense of unbelonging. We're social beings. We associate. Therefore we disassociate. And although it would be comforting to think that the one could happen without the other, we know in reality that it doesn't. How many patriots are there who have never felt a twinge of xenophobia?°

Of course, by hate we mean something graver and darker than this kind of lazy prejudice. But the closer you look at this distinction, the fuzzier it gets. Much of the time, we harbor little or no malice toward people of other backgrounds or places or ethnicities or ways of life. But then a car cuts you off at an intersection and you find yourself noticing immediately that the driver is a woman, or black, or old, or fat, or white, or male. Or you are walking down a city street at night and hear footsteps quickening behind you. You look around and see that it is a white woman and not a black a man, and you are instantly relieved. These impulses are so spontaneous they are almost involuntary. But where did they come from? The mindless need to be mad at someone—anyone—or the unconscious eruption of a darker prejudice festering within?

In 1993, in San Jose, California, two neighbors, one heterosexual, one ho-   10 mosexual, were engaged in a protracted squabble over grass clippings. (The full case is recounted in *Hate Crimes*, by James B. Jacobs and Kimberly Potter.) The gay man regularly mowed his lawn without a grass catcher, which prompted his neighbor to complain on many occasions that grass clippings spilled over onto his driveway. Tensions grew until one day the gay man mowed his front yard, spilling clippings onto his neighbor's driveway, prompting the straight man to yell an obscene and common antigay insult. The wrangling escalated. At one point the gay man agreed to collect the clippings from his neighbor's driveway but then later found them dumped on his own porch. A fracas ensued, with the gay man spraying the straight man's son with a garden hose and the son hitting and kicking the gay man several times, yelling antigay slurs. The police were called, and the son was eventually convicted of

xenophobia: Fear of strangers or things foreign.

a hate-motivated assault, a felony. But what was the nature of the hate, anti-gay bias or suburban property-owner madness?

Or take the Labor Day parade last year in Broad Channel, a small island in Jamaica Bay, Queens.° Almost everyone there is white, and in recent years a group of local volunteer firefighters has taken to decorating a pickup truck for the parade in order to win the prize for "funniest float." Their themes have tended toward the outrageously provocative. Beginning in 1995, they won prizes for floats depicting "Hasidic Park," "Gooks of Hazzard," and "Happy Gays." Last year they called their float "Black to the Future, Broad Channel 2098." They imagined their community a century hence as a largely black enclave, with every stereotype imaginable: watermelons, basketballs, and so on. At one point during the parade, one of them mimicked the dragging death of James Byrd. It was caught on videotape, and before long the entire community was depicted as a caldron of hate.

It's an interesting case, because the float was indisputably in bad taste and the improvisation on the Byrd killing was grotesque. But was it hate? The men on the float were local heroes for their volunteer work; they had no record of bigoted activity and were not members of any racist organizations. In previous years they had made fun of many other groups, and they saw themselves more as provocateurs than bigots. When they were described as racists, it came as a shock to them. They apologized for poor taste but refused to confess to bigotry. "The people involved aren't horrible people," protested a local woman. "Was it a racist act? I don't know. Are they racist? I don't think so."

If hate is a self-conscious activity, she has a point. The men were primarily motivated by the desire to shock and to reflect what they thought was their community's culture. Their display was not aimed at any particular black people or at any blacks who lived in Broad Channel — almost none do. But if hate is primarily an unconscious activity, then the matter is obviously murkier. And by taking the horrific lynching of a black man as a spontaneous object of humor, the men were clearly advocating indifference to it. Was this an aberrant excess? Or the real truth about the men's feelings toward African Americans? Hate or tastelessness? And how on earth is anyone, even perhaps the firefighters themselves, going to know for sure?

Or recall H. L. Mencken.° He shared in the anti-Semitism of his time with more alacrity than most and was an indefatigable racist. "It is impossible," he wrote in his diary, "to talk anything resembling discretion or judgment into a colored woman. They are all essentially childlike, and even hard experience does not teach them anything." He wrote at another time of the "psychological stigmata" of the "Afro-American race." But it is also true that during much of his life, day to day, Mencken conducted himself with no regard to race and supported a politics that was clearly integrationist. As the editor of his diary

Jamaica Bay, Queens: Working- and middle-class New York neighborhood with a heavily white, Italian population.

H. L. Mencken: Henry Louis Mencken (1880–1956), American editor.

has pointed out, Mencken published many black authors in his magazine, *The Mercury,* and lobbied on their behalf with his publisher, Alfred A. Knopf. The last thing Mencken ever wrote was a diatribe against racial segregation in Baltimore's public parks. He was good friends with leading black writers and journalists, including James Weldon Johnson, Walter White, and George S. Schulyer, and played an underappreciated role in promoting the Harlem Renaissance.°

What would our modern view of hate do with Mencken? Probably ignore 15 him, or change the subject. But with regard to hate, I know lots of people like Mencken. He reminds me of conservative friends who oppose almost every measure for homosexual equality yet genuinely delight in the company of their gay friends. It would be easier for me to think of them as haters, and on paper, perhaps, there is a good case that they are. But in real life, I know they are not. Some of them clearly harbor no real malice toward me or other homosexuals whatsoever.

They are as hard to figure out as those liberal friends who support every gay rights measure they have ever heard of but do anything to avoid going into a gay bar with me. I have to ask myself in the same frustrating kind of way, are they liberal bigots or bigoted liberals? Or are they neither bigots nor liberals, but merely people?

III

Hate used to be easier to understand. When Sartre° described anti-Semitism in his 1946 essay "Anti-Semite and Jew," he meant a very specific array of firmly held prejudices, with a history, an ideology, and even a pseudoscience to back them up. He meant a systematic attempt to demonize and eradicate an entire race. If you go to the Web site of the World Church of the Creator, the organization that inspired young Benjamin Smith to murder in Illinois earlier this year, you will find a similarly bizarre, pseudorational ideology. The kind of literature read by Buford Furrow before he rained terror on a Jewish kindergarten last month and then killed a mailman because of his color is full of the same paranoid loopiness. And when we talk about hate, we often mean this kind of phenomenon.

But this brand of hatred is mercifully rare in the United States. These professional maniacs are to hate what serial killers are to murder. They should certainly not be ignored, but they represent what Harold Meyerson, writing in *Salon,* called "niche haters": cold-blooded, somewhat deranged, often poorly socialized psychopaths. In a free society with relatively easy access to guns, they will always pose a menace.

the Harlem Renaissance: An outburst of creative activity by African Americans from 1920 to about 1930 centered in Harlem, New York.

Sartre: Jean-Paul Sartre (1905–1980), French philosopher.

But their menace is a limited one, and their hatred is hardly typical of anything very widespread. Take Buford Furrow. He famously issued a "wake-up call" to "kill Jews" in Los Angeles before he peppered a Jewish community center with gunfire. He did this in a state with two Jewish female senators, in a city with a large, prosperous Jewish population, in a country where out of several million Jewish Americans, a total of sixty-six were reported by the FBI as the targets of hate-crime assaults in 1997. However despicable Furrow's actions were, it would require a very large stretch to describe them as representative of anything but the deranged fringe of an American subculture.

Most hate is more common and more complicated, with as many varieties   20 as there are varieties of love. Just as there are possessive love and needy love, family love and friendship, romantic love and unrequited love, passion and respect, affection and obsession, so hatred has its shadings. There is hate that fears, and hate that merely feels contempt; there is hate that expresses power, and hate that comes from powerlessness; there is revenge, and there is hate that comes from envy. There is hate that was love, and hate that is a curious expression of love. There is hate of the other, and hate of something that reminds us too much of ourselves. There is the oppressor's hate and the victim's hate. There is hate that burns slowly and hate that fades. And there is hate that explodes and hate that never catches fire.

The modern words that we have created to describe the varieties of hate — "sexism," "racism," "anti-Semitism," "homophobia" — tell us very little about any of this. They tell us merely the identities of the victims; they don't reveal the identities of the perpetrators, or what they think, or how they feel. They don't even tell us how the victims feel. And this simplicity is no accident. Coming from the theories of Marxist and post-Marxist academics, these isms are far better at alleging structures of power than at delineating the workings of the individual heart or mind. In fact, these isms can exist without mentioning individuals at all.

We speak of institutional racism, for example, as if an institution can feel anything. We talk of "hate" as an impersonal noun, with no hater specified. But when these abstractions are actually incarnated, when someone feels something as a result of them, when a hater actually interacts with a victim, the picture changes. We find that hates are often very different phenomena one from another, that they have very different psychological dynamics, that they might even be better understood by not seeing them as varieties of the same thing at all.

There is, for example, the now unfashionable distinction between reasonable hate and unreasonable hate. In recent years we have become accustomed to talking about hates as if they were all equally indefensible, as if it could never be the case that some hates might be legitimate, even necessary. But when some 800,000 Tutsis are murdered under the auspices of a Hutu regime in Rwanda, and when a few thousand Hutus are killed in revenge, the hates are not commensurate. Genocide is not an event like a hurricane, in which damage is random and universal; it is a planned and often merciless attack of one group upon another. The hate of the perpetrators is a monstrosity. The hate of the victims, and their survivors, is justified. What else, one wonders, were surviving Jews supposed to feel toward Germans after the Holocaust? Or, to a different degree, South African blacks after apartheid? If the victims overcome this hate, it is a supreme moral achievement. But if they don't, the victims are not as culpable as the perpetrators. So the hatred of Serbs for Kosovars today can never be equated with the hatred of Kosovars for Serbs.

Hate, like much of human feeling, is not rational, but it usually has its reasons. And it cannot be understood, let alone condemned, without knowing them. Similarly, the hate that come from knowledge is always different from the hate that comes from ignorance. It is one of the most foolish clichés of our time that prejudice is always rooted in ignorance and can usually be overcome by familiarity with the objects of our loathing. The racism of many Southern whites under segregation was not appeased by familiarity with Southern blacks; the virulent loathing of Tutsis by many Hutus was not undermined by living next door to them for centuries. Theirs was a hatred that sprang, for whatever reasons, from experience. It cannot easily be compared with, for example, the resilience of anti-Semitism in Japan, or hostility to immigration in areas where immigrants are unknown, or fear of homosexuals by people who have never knowingly met one.

The same familiarity is an integral part of what has become known as "sexism." Sexism isn't, properly speaking, a prejudice at all. Few men live without knowledge or constant awareness of women. Every single sexist man was born of a woman and is likely to be sexually attracted to women. His hostility is going to be very different from that of, say, a reclusive member of the Aryan Nations toward Jews he has never met.

In her book *The Anatomy of Prejudices*, the psychotherapist Elisabeth Young-Bruehl proposes a typology of three distinct kinds of hate: obsessive, hysterical, and narcissistic. It's not an exhaustive analysis, but it's a beginning in any serious attempt to understand hate rather than merely declaring war on it. The obsessives, for Young-Bruehl, are those, like the Nazis or Hutus, who fantasize a threat from a minority and obsessively try to rid themselves of it. For them, the very existence of the hated group is threatening. They often describe their loathing in almost physical terms: they experience what Patrick Buchanan,° in reference to homosexuals, once described as a "visceral recoil" from the objects of their detestation. They often describe those they hate as diseased or sick, in need of a cure. Or they talk of "cleansing" them, as the Hutus talked of the Tutsis, or call them "cockroaches," as Yitzhak Shamir° called the Palestinians. If you read material from the Family Research Council, it is clear that the group regards homosexuals as similar

Patrick Buchanan: (b. 1938), conservative American television commentator and political figure.

Yitzhak Shamir: (b. 1905), Israeli politician and prime minister from 1983–84 and 1986–92.

contaminants. A recent posting on its Web site about syphilis among gay men was headlined "Unclean."

Hysterical haters have a more complicated relationship with the objects of their aversion. In Young-Bruehl's words, hysterical prejudice is a prejudice that "a person uses unconsciously to appoint a group to act out in the world forbidden sexual and sexually aggressive desires that the person has repressed." Certain kinds of racists fit this pattern. White loathing of blacks is for some people at least partly about sexual and physical envy. A certain kind of white racist sees in black America all those impulses he wishes most to express himself but cannot. He idealizes in "blackness" a sexual freedom, a physical power, a Dionysian release° that he detests but also longs for. His fantasy may not have any basis in reality, but it is powerful nonetheless. It is a form of love-hate, and it is impossible to understand the nuances of racism in, say, the American South, or in British imperial India, without it.

Unlike the obsessives, the hysterical haters do not want to eradicate the objects of their loathing; rather, they want to keep them in some kind of permanent and safe subjugation in order to indulge the attraction of their repulsion. A recent study, for example, found that the men most likely to be opposed to equal rights for homosexuals were those most likely to be aroused by homoerotic imagery. This makes little rational sense, but it has a certain psychological plausibility. If homosexuals were granted equality, then the hysterical gay-hater might panic that his repressed passions would run out of control, overwhelming him and the world he inhabits.

A narcissistic hate, according to Young-Bruehl's definition, is sexism. In its most common form, it is rooted in many men's inability even to imagine what it is to be a woman, a failing rarely challenged by men's control of our most powerful public social institutions. Women are not so much hated by most men as simply ignored in nonsexual contexts, or never conceived of as true equals. The implicit condescension is mixed, in many cases, with repressed and sublimated erotic desire. So the unawareness of women is sometimes commingled with a deep longing or contempt for them.

Each hate, of course, is more complicated than this, and in any one person   30
hate can assume a uniquely configured combination of these types. So there are hysterical sexists who hate women because they need them so much, and narcissistic sexists who hardly notice that women exist, and sexists who oscillate between one of these positions and another. And there are gay-bashers who are threatened by masculine gay men and gay-haters who feel repulsed by effeminate ones. The soldier who beat his fellow soldier Barry Winchell to death with a baseball bat in July had earlier lost a fight to him. It was the image of a macho gay man—and the shame of being bested by him—that the vengeful soldier had to obliterate, even if he needed a gang of accomplices and a weapon to do so. But the murderers of Matthew Shepard seem to have had a different im-

---

a **Dionysian release:** A momentary freeing from the restraints of civilized behavior that has a therapeutic effect.

pulse: a visceral disgust at the thought of any sexual contact with an effeminate homosexual. Their anger was mixed with mockery, as the cruel spectacle at the side of the road suggested.

In the same way, the pathological anti-Semitism of Nazi Germany was obsessive, inasmuch as it tried to cleanse the world of Jews, but also, as Daniel Jonah Goldhagen shows in his book, *Hitler's Willing Executioners,* hysterical. The Germans were mysteriously compelled as well as repelled by Jews, devising elaborate ways, like death camps and death marches, to keep them alive even as they killed them. And the early Nazi phobia of interracial sex suggests as well a lingering erotic quality to the relationship, partaking of exactly the kind of sexual panic that persists among some homosexual-haters and anti-miscegenation racists. So the concept of "homophobia," like that of "sexism" and "racism," is often a crude one. All three are essentially cookie-cutter formulas that try to understand human impulses merely through the one-dimensional identity of the victims, rather than through the thoughts and feelings of the haters and hated.

This is deliberate. The theorists behind these isms want to ascribe all blame to one group in society — the "oppressors" — and render specific others — the "victims" — completely blameless. And they want to do this in order in part to side unequivocally with the underdog. But it doesn't take a genius to see how this approach too can generate its own form of bias. It can justify blanket condemnations of whole groups of people — white straight males, for example — purely because of the color of their skin or the nature of their sexual orientation. And it can condescendingly ascribe innocence to whole groups of others. It does exactly what hate does: it hammers the uniqueness of each individual into the anvil of group identity. And it postures morally over the result.

In reality, human beings and human acts are far more complex, which is why these isms and the laws they have fomented are continually coming under strain and challenge. Once again, hate wriggles free of its definers. It knows no monolithic groups of haters and hated. Like a river, it has many eddies, backwaters, and rapids. So there are anti-Semites who actually admire what they think of as Jewish power, and there are gay-haters who look up to homosexuals and some who want to sleep with them. And there are black racists, racist Jews, sexist women, and anti-Semitic homosexuals. Of course there are.

IV

Once you start thinking of these phenomena less as the isms of sexism, racism, and homophobia, once you think of them as independent psychological responses, it's also possible to see how they can work in a bewildering variety of ways in a bewildering number of people. To take one obvious and sad oddity: people who are demeaned and objectified in society may develop an aversion to their tormentors that is more hateful in its expression than the prejudice they have been subjected to. The FBI statistics on hate crimes throw up an interesting point. In America in the 1990s, blacks were up to three times as likely as whites to commit a hate crime, to express their hate by physically attacking their targets or their property. Just as sexual abusers have often been victims of sexual abuse and wife-beaters often grew up in violent households, so hate criminals may often be members of hated groups.

Even the Columbine murderers° were in some sense victims of hate before   35
they were purveyors of it. Their classmates later admitted that Dylan Klebold and Eric Harris were regularly called "faggots" in the corridors and classrooms of Columbine High and that nothing was done to prevent or stop the harassment. This climate of hostility doesn't excuse the actions of Klebold and Harris, but it does provide a more plausible context. If they had been black, had routinely been called "nigger" in the school, and had then exploded into a shooting spree against white students, the response to the matter might well have been different. But the hate would have been the same. In other words, hate victims are often hate victimizers as well. This doesn't mean that all hates are equivalent, or that some are not more justified than others. It means merely that hate goes both ways; and if you try to regulate it among some, you will find yourself forced to regulate it among others.

It is no secret, for example, that some of the most vicious anti-Semites in America are black, and that some of the most virulent anti-Catholic bigots in America are gay. At what point, we are increasingly forced to ask, do these phenomena become as indefensible as white racism or religious toleration of antigay bigotry? That question becomes all the more difficult when we notice that it is often minorities who commit some of the most hate-filled offenses against what they see as their oppressors. It was the mainly gay AIDS activist group Act Up that perpetrated the hateful act of desecrating communion hosts at a mass at St. Patrick's Cathedral in New York. And here is the playwright Tony Kushner, who is gay, responding to the Matthew Shepard beating in *The Nation* magazine: "Pope John Paul II endorses murder. He, too, knows the price of discrimination, having declared anti-Semitism a sin. . . . He knows that discrimination kills. But when the Pope heard the news about Matthew Shepard, he, too, worried about spin. And so, on the subject of gay-bashing, the Pope and his cardinals and his bishops and priests maintain their cynical political silence. . . . To remain silent is to endorse murder." Kushner went on to describe the pope as a "homicidal liar."

Maybe the passion behind these words is justified. But it seems clear enough to me that Kushner is expressing hate toward the institution of the Catholic Church and all those who perpetuate its doctrines. How else to interpret the way in which he accuses the pope of cynicism, lying, and murder? And how else either to understand the brutal parody of religious vocations expressed by the Sisters of Perpetual Indulgence, a group of gay men who dress

the Columbine murderers: In 1999 Dylan Klebold and Eric Harris murdered twelve fellow students and one faculty member at Colorado's Columbine High School.

in drag as nuns and engage in sexually explicit performances in public? Or T-shirts with the words "Recovering Catholic" on them, hot items among some gay and lesbian activists? The implication that someone's religious faith is a mental illness is clearly an expression of contempt. If that isn't covered under the definition of hate speech, what is?

Or take the following sentences: "The act male homosexuals commit is ugly and repugnant and afterwards they are disgusted with themselves. They drink and take drugs to palliate this, but they are disgusted with the act and they are always changing partners and cannot be really happy." The thoughts of Pat Robertson or Patrick Buchanan? Actually, that sentence was written by Gertrude Stein,° one of the century's most notable lesbians. Or take the following, about how beating up "black boys like that made us feel *good* inside. . . . Every time I drove my foot into his [expletive], I felt better." It was written to describe the brutal assault on an innocent bystander for the sole reason of his race. By the end of the attack, the victim had blood gushing from his mouth as his attackers stomped on his genitals. Are we less appalled when we learn that the actual sentence was how beating up "white boys like that made us feel *good* inside. . . . Every time I drove my foot into his [expletive], I felt better"? It was written by Nathan McCall, an African American who later in life became a successful journalist at the *Washington Post* and published his memoir of this "hate crime" to much acclaim.

In fact, one of the stranger aspects of hate is that the prejudice expressed by a group in power may often be milder in expression than the prejudice felt by the marginalized. After all, if you already enjoy privilege, you may not feel the anger that turns bias into hate. You may not need to. For this reason, most white racism may be more influential in society than most black racism—but also more calmly expressed.

So may other forms of minority loathing—especially hatred within minorities. I'm sure that black conservatives like Clarence Thomas° and Thomas Sowell° have experienced their fair share of white racism. But I wonder whether it has ever reached the level of intensity of the hatred directed toward them by other blacks? In several years of being an openly gay writer and editor, I have experienced the gamut of responses to my sexual orientation. But I have only directly experienced articulated, passionate hate from other homosexuals. I have been accused over the years by other homosexuals of being a sellout, a hypocrite, a traitor, a sexist, a racist, a narcissist, a snob. I've been called selfish, callous, hateful, self-hating, and malevolent. At a reading, a group of lesbian activists portrayed my face on a poster within the crosshairs of a gun. Nothing from the religious right has come close to such vehemence.

Gertrude Stein: (1874–1946), American writer.

Clarence Thomas: (b. 1948), associate justice of the U.S. Supreme Court who was accused of sexual harassment by former coworker Anita Hill.

Thomas Sowell: (b. 1930), conservative African American fellow at the Hoover Institution.

I am not complaining. No harm has ever come to me or my property, and much of the criticism is rooted in the legitimate expression of political differences. But the visceral tone and style of the gay criticism can only be described as hateful. It is designed to wound personally, and it often does. But its intensity comes in part, one senses, from the pain of being excluded for so long, of anger long restrained bubbling up and directing itself more aggressively toward an alleged traitor than an alleged enemy. It is the hate of the hated. And it can be the most hateful hate of all. For this reason, hate-crime laws may themselves be an oddly biased category—biased against the victims of hate. Racism is everywhere, but the already victimized might be more desperate, more willing to express it violently. And so more prone to come under the suspicious eye of the law.

V

And why is hate for a group worse than hate for a person? In Laramie, Wyoming, the now-famous "epicenter of homophobia," where Matthew Shepard was brutally beaten to death, vicious murders are not unknown. In the previous twelve months, a fifteen-year-old pregnant girl was found east of the town with seventeen stab wounds. Her thirty-eight-year-old boyfriend was apparently angry that she had refused an abortion and left her in the Wyoming foothills to bleed to death. In the summer of 1998, an eight-year-old Laramie girl was abducted, raped, and murdered by a pedophile, who disposed of her young body in a garbage dump. Neither of these killings was deemed a hate crime, and neither would be designated as such under any existing hate-crime law. Perhaps because of this, one crime is an international legend; the other two are virtually unheard of.

But which crime was more filled with hate? Once you ask the question, you realize how difficult it is to answer. Is it more hateful to kill a stranger or a lover? Is it more hateful to kill a child than an adult? Is it more hateful to kill your own child than another's? Under the law before the invention of hate crimes, these decisions didn't have to be taken. But under the law after hate crimes, a decision is essential. A decade ago, a murder was a murder. Now, in the era when group hate has emerged as our cardinal social sin, it all depends.

The supporters of laws against hate crimes argue that such crimes should be disproportionately punished because they victimize more than the victim. Such crimes, these advocates argue, spread fear, hatred, and panic among whole populations and therefore merit more concern. But of course all crimes victimize more than the victim and spread alarm in the society at large. Just think of the terrifying church shooting in Texas° only two weeks ago. In fact, a purely random murder may be even more terrifying than a targeted one, since the entire community and not just a part of it feels threatened. High

the terrifying church shooting in Texas: In 1999 Larry Gene Ashbrook burst into a church service in Fort Worth and killed seven people.

rates of murder, robbery, assault, and burglary victimize everyone, by spreading fear, suspicion, and distress everywhere. Which crime was more frightening to more people this summer: the mentally ill Buford Furrow's crazed attacks in Los Angeles, killing one, or Mark Barton's murder of his own family and several random day-traders in Atlanta, killing twelve? Almost certainly the latter. But only Furrow was guilty of "hate."

One response to this objection is that certain groups feel fear more intensely than others because of a history of persecution or intimidation. But doesn't this smack of a certain condescension toward minorities? Why, after all, should it be assumed that gay men or black women or Jews, for example, are as a group more easily intimidated than others? Surely in any of these communities there will be a vast range of responses, from panic to concern to complete indifference. The assumption otherwise is the kind of crude generalization the law is supposed to uproot in the first place. And among these groups, there are also likely to be vast differences. To equate a population once subjected to slavery with a population of Mexican immigrants or third-generation Holocaust survivors is to equate the unequatable. In fact, it is to set up a contest of vulnerability in which one group vies with another to establish its particular variety of suffering, a contest that can have no dignified solution.

Rape, for example, is not classified as a hate crime under most existing laws, pitting feminists against ethnic groups in a battle for recognition. If, as a solution to this problem, everyone except the white straight able-bodied male is regarded as a possible victim of a hate crime, then we have simply created a two-tier system of justice in which racial profiling is reversed, and white straight men are presumed guilty before being proved innocent, and members of minorities are free to hate them as gleefully as they like. But if we include the white straight male in the litany of potential victims, then we have effectively abolished the notion of a hate crime altogether, for if every crime is possibly a hate crime, then it is simply another name for crime. All we will have done is widened the search for possible bigotry, ratcheted up the sentences for everyone, and filled the jails up even further.

Hate-crime law advocates counter that extra penalties should be imposed on hate crimes because our society is experiencing an "epidemic" of such crimes. Mercifully, there is no hard evidence to support this notion. The federal government has only been recording the incidence of hate crimes in this decade, and the statistics tell a simple story. In 1992, there were 6,623 hate-crime incidents reported to the FBI by a total of 6,181 agencies, covering 51 percent of the population. In 1996, there were 8,734 incidents reported by 11,355 agencies, covering 84 percent of the population. That number dropped to 8,049 in 1997. These numbers are of course hazardous. They probably underreport the incidence of such crimes, but they are the only reliable figures we have. Yet even if they are faulty as an absolute number, they do not show an epidemic of hate crimes in the 1990s.

Is there evidence that the crimes themselves are becoming more vicious? None. More than 60 percent of recorded hate crimes in America involve no violent physical assault against another human being at all, and again, according to the FBI, that proportion has not budged much in the 1990s. These impersonal attacks are crimes against property or crimes of intimidation. Murder, which dominates media coverage of hate crimes, is a tiny proportion of the total. Of the 8,049 hate crimes reported to the FBI in 1997, a total of 8 were murders. Eight. The number of hate crimes that were aggravated assaults (generally involving a weapon) in 1997 is less than 15 percent of the total. That's 1,237 assaults too many, of course, but to put it in perspective, compare it with a reported 1,022,492 "equal opportunity" aggravated assaults in America in the same year. The number of hate crimes that were physical assaults is half the total. That's 4,000 assaults too many, of course, but to put it in perspective, it compares with around 3.8 million "equal opportunity" assaults in America annually.

The truth is, the distinction between a crime filled with personal hate and a crime filled with group hate is an essentially arbitrary one. It tells us nothing interesting about the psychological contours of the specific actor or his specific victim. It is a function primarily of politics, of special-interest groups carving out particular protections for themselves, rather than a serious response to a serious criminal concern. In such an endeavor, hate-crime law advocates cram an entire world of human motivations into an immutable, tiny box called hate and hope to have solved a problem. But nothing has been solved, and some harm may even have been done.

In an attempt to repudiate a past that treated people differently because 50 of the color of their skin or their sex or religion or sexual orientation, we may merely create a future that permanently treats people differently because of the color of their skin or their sex, religion, or sexual orientation. This notion of a hate crime, and the concept of hate that lies behind it, takes a psychological mystery and turns it into a facile political artifact. Rather than compounding this error and extending it even further, we should seriously consider repealing the concept altogether.

To put it another way: violence can and should be stopped by the government. In a free society, hate can't and shouldn't be. The boundaries between hate and prejudice and between prejudice and opinion and between opinion and truth are so complicated and blurred that any attempt to construct legal and political fire walls is a doomed and illiberal venture. We know by now that hate will never disappear from human consciousness; in fact, it is probably, at some level, definitive of it. We know after decades of education measures that hate is not caused merely by ignorance and, after decades of legislation, that it isn't cured entirely by law.

To be sure, we have made much progress. Anyone who argues that America is as inhospitable to minorities and to women today as it has been in the past has not read much history. And we should of course be vigilant that our most powerful institutions, most notably the government, do not actively or formally propagate hatred, and insure that the violent expression of hate is curtailed by the same rules that punish all violent expression.

But after that, in an increasingly diverse culture, it is crazy to expect that hate, in all its variety, can be eradicated. A free country will always mean a hateful country. This may not be fair, or perfect, or admirable, but it is reality, and while we need not endorse it, we should not delude ourselves into thinking we can prevent it. That is surely the distinction between toleration and tolerance. Tolerance is the eradication of hate; toleration is coexistence despite it. We might do better as a culture and as a polity if we concentrated more on achieving the latter than the former. We would certainly be less frustrated.

And by aiming lower, we might actually reach higher. In some ways, some expression of prejudice serves a useful social purpose. It lets off steam; it allows natural tensions to express themselves incrementally; it can siphon off conflict through words rather than actions. Anyone who has lived in the ethnic shouting match that is New York City knows exactly what I mean. If New Yorkers disliked each other less, they wouldn't be able to get on so well. We may not all be able to pull off a Mencken—bigoted in words, egalitarian in action—but we might achieve a lesser form of virtue: a human acceptance of our need for differentiation without a total capitulation to it.

Do we not owe something more to the victims of hate? Perhaps we do. But it is also true that there is nothing that government can do for the hated that the hated cannot better do for themselves. After all, most bigots are not foiled when they are punished specifically for their beliefs. In fact, many of the worst haters crave such attention and find vindication in such rebukes. Indeed, our media's obsession with "hate," our elevation of it above other social misdemeanors and crimes, may even play into the hands of the pathetic and the evil, may breathe air into the smoldering embers of their paranoid loathing. Sure, we can help create a climate in which such hate is disapproved of—and we should. But there is a danger that if we go too far, if we punish it too much, if we try to abolish it altogether, we may merely increase its mystique, and entrench the very categories of human difference that we are trying to erase.   55

For hate is only foiled not when the haters are punished but when the hated are immune to the bigot's power. A hater cannot psychologically wound if a victim cannot psychologically be wounded. And that immunity to hurt can never be given; it can merely be achieved. The racial epithet only strikes at someone's core if he lets it, if he allows the bigot's definition of him to be the final description of his life and his person—if somewhere in his heart of hearts, he believes the hateful slur to be true. The only final answer to this form of racism, then, is not majority persecution of it but minority indifference to it. The only permanent rebuke to homophobia is not the enforcement of tolerance but gay equanimity in the face of prejudice. The only effective answer to sexism is not a morass of legal proscriptions but the simple fact of female success. In this, as in so many other things, there is no solution to the problem. There is only a transcendence of it. For all our rhetoric, hate will never be destroyed. Hate, as our predecessors knew better, can merely be overcome.

EXPLORING THE TEXT

1. What's wrong with hate-crime legislation, in Sullivan's view? Would you agree that the examples he offers involving the grass-cutting dispute and the Labor Day parade float do not involve "self-conscious" hate? What, if anything, distinguishes such acts from simple acts of bad judgment or bad taste?

2. Why does Sullivan feel that "hate used to be easier to understand"? What makes hate in the present-day United States more complicated? Why is he particularly opposed to hate-related labels like "sexism," "racism," and "homophobia"?

3. What is the difference between "reasonable" and "unreasonable" hate, according to Sullivan? To what extent would you agree that some types of hate are "reasonable" and that you cannot condemn hate without knowing the reasons underlying it?

4. How does Sullivan anticipate the arguments of those who support hate-crime legislation? What arguments in support of hate-crime laws and what objections to his position does he examine? How does he respond to each of these positions? How effective, in your view, are his responses?

5. Ultimately, why does Sullivan feel that governments should punish violence but not hate? Would you agree that a "free country is always a hateful country" and that hate may actually fulfill a positive function in an open society? Would you agree that the best way to counteract hate is through what he calls "minority indifference"? Why or why not?

6. To what extent does Sullivan's sexual orientation influence your response to his arguments? Would you be less likely to credit his position if he were a straight, white, middle-class male? Why or why not? Do you think he was right to mention his sexual orientation in the context of this essay? Why or why not?

FURTHER EXPLORATIONS

1. How do Sullivan and Martha C. Nusbaum (p. 416) compare in terms of the way they view empathy, difference, and democracy? What objections might Nussbaum raise against Sullivan's assertion that a "free country will always be a hateful country"? Which of these visions of life in an open, democratic culture do you feel is most accurate? Why?

2. How does Mick Fedullo's cross-cultural experience in "Mrs. Cassadore" (p. 441) challenge Sullivan's claim that familiarity cannot overcome difference? What experiences have you had that challenge or confirm Sullivan's relatively pessimistic view of intergroup relations?

3. How might Deborah Blum (p. 453) respond to Sullivan's belief that "sexism isn't . . . a prejudice at all" because men generally live in close relationship with women and have a great deal of knowledge about them? Why, given Blum's view of the differences between female and male minds, might women need the protection of gender-specific laws and regulations?

4. Based on your reading of "Columbus: Gone But Not Forgotten" (p. 237), how do you think bell hooks might respond to Sullivan's claim that hate is an imprecisely defined phenomenon which is impossible to eliminate in a diverse society? How might she respond to his suggestion that the best way to combat hatred is to "achieve equanimity in the face of prejudice"?

ESSAY OPTIONS

1. Write an essay in which you research and analyze a specific variety of hate. It might be hate for women, African Americans, Asians, Latinos, immigrants, a particular national or religious group — or for any group or association that has been a recent target of violence or abuse. What form has this hatred taken? How has it been expressed? How is it justified in the minds of the haters involved? How might their motives for hating be categorized and explained? What good or harm can come from trying to "read" the minds of those who hate?

2. Drawing on information available through the NAACP, the National Organization of Women, Lambda Legal Defense and Education, or any other minority advocacy group, write an essay in which you assess the pros and cons of hate-crime legislation. What arguments are offered in support of hate-crime laws? How well does Sullivan respond to these arguments? What purpose, in your view, do hate-crime laws serve?

Rejected and Neglected, Ashamed and Depressed

JAMES GARBARINO

April 20, 1999, marked a watershed in recent American cultural history. On that day Dylan Klebold and Eric Harris methodically attacked their classmates at Columbine High School outside Denver, Colorado, leaving twelve students and one teacher dead and twenty-three wounded. What distinguished the assault on Columbine was the cold-bloodedness of Klebold and Harris — and the fact that their rage went undetected for so long. But it would be a mistake to think that Columbine was the beginning of teen violence in America. During the 1997–98 school year alone there were at least five notable shootings in American schools, including Michael Carmeal's slaying of three students at a school prayer meeting in West Paducah, Kentucky, and Kip Kinkel's murder spree in Springfield, Oregon, that ended with the death of his parents, two fellow students, and the wounding of twenty-four of his high school classmates. Since each of these outbursts, experts have tried to fathom the motives that led apparently well-adjusted teens to stalk and kill their peers. Some have blamed America's culture of violence; some have faulted the easy accessibility of guns. In James Garbarino's view, however, the answer to the riddle of youth violence can be read in the "soul" of murderous teens. Codirector of the Family Life Development Center and professor of human development at Cornell University, Garbarino has authored and coauthored seventeen books on issues related to teen violence. In this selection from his *Lost Boys: Why Our Sons Turn Violent and How*

We Can Save Them (1999), published just months before the Columbine tragedy, Garbarino speculates about the causes of what he calls "soul murder." Garbarino's empathetic analysis of the young offenders he has worked with during his career illustrates one approach to the challenge of reading the thoughts and feelings of violent minds. He has also published *Parents under Siege: Why You Are the Solution, Not the Problem, in Your Child's Life* (2001).

BEFORE READING

Working in groups, discuss the theories that are most commonly offered to account for violent behavior in children and adolescents. Which of these explanations do you find the most plausible? Why?

The Sacred Self

In a letter to a colleague after meeting the eight-year-old Helen Keller,° when her fame as a blind and mute child who nonetheless learned to communicate with eloquence was only beginning, Alexander Graham Bell° wrote, "I feel that in this child I have seen more of the Divine than has been manifest in anyone I ever met before." Every infant contains a divine spark. I believe this as a psychologist; I know it as a person and a parent. Recognizing the reality of the sacred self is the foundation for understanding human development as something more than a matter of engineering, plumbing, chemistry, and electronics. Far too few social scientists take this into account in their professional work, but many recognize it in their personal lives. I start from this spiritual basis in understanding violent boys.

You can see this spiritual reality in the eyes of a child. This is one reason why I shamelessly "flirt" with babies everywhere I see them—in airports, in shopping malls, in the waiting rooms of prisons. I seek out their eyes to make contact with their souls, hoping to elicit a smile and to experience once again the delight that comes from contact with the divine spark within them.

Through the eyes you can tell a great deal about the well-being of the soul. We recognize this in the ancient proverb "The eyes are the window to the soul." When we see darkness, we are alarmed. I've seen both light and darkness in the eyes of children in my travels around the world, and in the eyes of children in the prisons, schools, and neighborhoods of our country. I see light sometimes in violent boys. When we see light in a child's eyes, we are joyful and reassured. Sometimes we are made intensely aware of a child's soul by virtue of the special circumstances or character of the child.

What kindles the spark of divinity in a child? And what consigns the human spirit to darkness? We begin our journey to understand lost boys by

Helen Keller: Helen Adams Keller (1880–1968), American author and lecturer, deaf and blind from the age of two.

Alexander Graham Bell: (1847–1922), Scottish-born American inventor of the telephone.

studying the quality of their early relationships, the psychological condition of their inner life, the development of their spirit. At the heart of the matter is whether a young child is connected rather than abandoned, accepted rather than rejected, and nurtured rather than neglected and abused. Naturally, all of this takes place at a particular intersection of biology and society. The individual temperament of the child does much to dictate the terms of engagement between him and the world, just as what the child's environment has to offer in the way of opportunities and threats does much to dictate the consequences of individual temperament and experience. In some situations this intersection produces unhappiness and violence; in others it brings joy and peace.

Can a Soul Be Murdered?

Psychiatrist Leonard Shengold called his book on the effects of severe child   5
abuse *Soul Murder.*[1] He chose this title to reflect his belief that the catastrophically abused child, subject to so much internal devastation, is driven beyond the limits of humanness. I'm not in a position to debate the theological issue of whether or not souls can die or be killed, but I do believe that Shengold's view contains an important insight: at the very least, souls can be wounded. At the extremes of human deprivation and degradation, it may well be true that the human psyche can be so terribly mutilated that the soul departs, leaving behind something else to fill the void—or perhaps just leaving an unfilled void.

From what I have seen, the more likely course of development is that when forced to live in hell, the soul withdraws, perhaps shutting itself off from the world outside in a desperate attempt at preservation. Once hidden away, it covers itself with layers of insulation. As the years pass, this protective shell may harden to the point where eventually the soul seems dormant, so out of touch with the day-to-day self has it become even to the tormented person himself.

There are such individuals in our midst, although most of them seem to end up in prisons or mental institutions. Some are violent boys. In such boys, the soul is buried deep under layers of violence and distorted thoughts and emotions. But is such a soul dead or dormant beyond revival? I don't think so. I find inspiration in the life of psychotherapist Robin Casarjian,[2] whose work with adult prisoners focuses on efforts to help them reconnect with their buried souls. In her book *Houses of Healing,* she provides a road map for people seeking a pathway from the darkness into the light.

I side with Sister Prejean,[3] the author of a moving testimony to her work with men on death row, *Dead Man Walking.* Sister Prejean has found her vocation in ministering to the spiritual needs of these prisoners, men whose souls have often spent decades in a state of suspended animation. Faced with physical death but in the company of her spiritual love, these souls often reawaken, if only to be present at the time of the execution. For all its terror, waste, and defeat, death row can be a soulful place.

In August 1998, I was called upon to interview a young man on death row so that I might participate as an expert witness in his appeal. This was my third visit to death row. Byron is there because he shot and killed a police officer in 1994. His social history is perhaps the most appalling litany of child abuse and neglect I have ever encountered. Indeed, a social worker who evaluated him said that in her twenty years as a protective service worker she had investigated more than two thousand cases of child maltreatment and had never seen or heard of a more horrible story. Yet the reports speak of this young man's tender love for his children, his patience working with disabled adults in a halfway house, and his efforts to befriend and mentor a fourteen-year-old boy in his neighborhood.

What did I find when I entered the small interview room at the prison where Byron was being held? After a moment of initial awkwardness as we dealt with the circumstance of being strangers—one visiting, the other shackled—I found a beautiful soul. His eyes were alight with life as we talked for the next two hours. When we were done, I understood something of the contradiction of his life: the rage he lived with and sometimes expressed (as a response to the torture he had suffered at the hands of his abusive father) coupled with the impetus for goodness that was in him.

Byron admits that the four years he has spent in prison awaiting the results of his trial and appeals have provided him a first opportunity to reflect and ponder his life—indeed, the very meaning of life. Like most of us, he was previously caught up in the day-to-day search for diversion. Most of us allow everyday life to divert us from the essential business of our souls. But most of us don't have to face what Byron faces. Obviously, he has put this time to good use. More and more, he has become a monk serving time in a monastery of someone else's making. Now, as he awaits the results of his appeal, he is at peace, saying that his only goal is to live to see his son grow up. I was not the first visitor to comment on his soulfulness: he told me with a smile that a visiting poet from Chicago spoke with him and told him that his eyes shone with light and life.

The Soul in Hiding

How does a soul survive in a world of torment? What keeps a soul from dying? The conventional psychological answer has several parts. The first is temperament, the fact that children differ in constitution and in the emotional predispositions they bring with them into the world. Some are very sensitive to upset or threat; others seem naturally hardy. Some children seem to have a positive orientation to life, to be sunny and light; others are burdened with negativism, gloomy from the start, predisposed to depression. Temperament plays an important role in determining which souls survive and which depart.

A second part of the equation is resilience, the ability to bounce back from or overcome adversity. Much has been made of the role played by differences in resiliency in accounting for the fact that most children who have had a bad time in early life *don't* become delinquents or murderers.

There is a third force at work. This is the role of love, of being unconditionally loved. In an abusive family it may be the one small voice of kindness that comes from a relative too weak to change the situation but nonetheless able to feed the child's soul enough tidbits of love to sustain it during its hibernation, its long winter of discontent. In a cold, impersonal orphanage it may be one friend who kindly shares her own meager resources. I would be bluffing if I said I can always specify what in this world can sustain a child living in the midst of an earthly hell.

Beyond these findings from social science, there is a fourth force, yet another answer to the question of why some souls stay active and others hibernate. Removing my psychologist's hat for a moment, I would have to call it divine intervention, a single thread of light that feeds the spirit. Sometimes it seems like an amazing grace that finds that spark in a child's soul before it dies out entirely and that keeps it alive, ready to shine brightly if the child's social conditions ever permit that to occur. At other times the fourth force is a special talent or ability in the child, or an image he possesses of some better world.

I see this in Byron. What or who sustained his soul while he was being held hostage in the torture chamber of his father's house? Listening to him and reading the documents in his social history, I recognized his small connections to love and to the divine amidst the horror. For one thing, despite her many failings his mother loved him. She could not protect him from his father, who terrorized them both. And she herself sometimes whipped him in a mistaken effort to guide him. But she did love him, and we must never underestimate the value of love as the most important nutrient for the soul.

Noticing the cross around his neck, I ask Byron about his religious beliefs. "I believe in God, and I believe that God has a purpose for me," he replies. "Where does that come from?" I ask. "My grandmother. She believes, and she taught me to believe, too." Simple faith. Even if Byron's life is spared by the courts, the best he can hope for is life in prison. But he does hope for that. When he fired on the police officer he killed, the officer's partner returned the fire, and Byron was himself shot seven times. He looks back on that now and sees a divine plan. "God spared me that day for something," he says. "I believe it was so that I can look out for my son as he grows up."

Psychologists Patrick Tolan and Nancy Guerra at the University of Illinois in Chicago document that the most effective treatments for delinquent and criminally violent youth emphasize changes in thinking (cognitive restructuring) coupled with opportunities to practice nonviolent behavior (behavioral rehearsal).[4] Faith is the most profound cognitive restructuring that I know of. . . .

The Special Character of Male Depression

Research by psychologist Ronald Kessler at Harvard Medical School reveals that the rate of serious depression among American youth has increased from 2 percent in the 1960s to almost 25 percent in the 1990s.[5] Particularly important is the finding, reported by Columbia University psychologist Suniya Luthar, that these high rates of depression are being found equally among affluent and poor youth.[6] Our research shows that violent boys often have problems with depression as a prelude to their lethal crimes. Michael Carneal,° the fourteen-year-old shooter in West Paducah, Kentucky, and Kip Kinkel° in Springfield, Oregon, are two infamous examples of this. Both were diagnosed with depression prior to their attacks on their schoolmates, attacks in which a total of five people died.

But simply diagnosing depression is not the whole story. We need to go deeper into the special character of depression as it develops and affects boys; in particular, we need to understand its links to anger. This is stunningly clear in the case of Malcolm;° his father never made an effort even to meet him after being present for his birth, and now this incarcerated teenager carries a ton of anger about this abandonment. Although he keeps his rage about his abandonment bottled up most of the time, sometimes it slips out. The last time his father tried to talk to him on the phone, Malcolm would have nothing to do with him. "I took the phone and gave it to my mother. I just don't care no more." Knowing him as I do, I find it hard to believe that he doesn't care. Deep down, he cares too much. I suspect that his apparent lack of emotion about being abandoned exemplifies a common male strategy for dealing with very powerful negative emotions. In his book *I Don't Want To Talk About It,*[7] psychologist Terrence Real explores this characteristic emotional disconnectedness among boys and men. The subtitle of his book, *Overcoming the Secret Legacy of Male Depression,* refers to his observation that while troubled women are likely to express depression through overt suffering, men are more likely to experience hidden depression, what he calls covert depression.

When afflicted with covert depression, males hide the darkness within them both from those around them and from their own conscious awareness. For boys and men, the experience of depression is typically a mixture of two things: loss of the capacity to feel at all and externalization of their pain so that they attribute it to the actions of others, feel victimized, and deal with their distress through action, particularly violent action. Some boys are temperamentally primed to experience this depression; the neurochemical processes that keep people basically happy and on an even keel malfunction in them.

Michael Carneal: On December 1, 1997, fourteen-year-old Michael Carneal killed three students at a high school prayer meeting.

Kip Kinkel: On May 21, 1997, fifteen-year-old Kip Kinkel walked into his school cafeteria after murdering his parents and shot twenty-four classmates, two fatally.

Malcolm: One of several boys Garbarino interviewed during a research project at the Austin MacCormick Center in New York State between 1996 and 1998.

This creates a special vulnerability. This potential for depression is actualized when a boy's experiences of abandonment combine with the cultural messages he receives about masculinity, messages that devalue the direct expression of feelings and emphasize the necessity of burying feelings, particularly feelings of emotional connection, vulnerability, and softness. As boys experience increasingly more disrupted relationships at home and in the community, these factors combine to put them on the road to trouble.

My intimate time with troubled boys often permits me to glimpse the intensity of their sadness—and thus their rage—at being abandoned. The extent of their disconnection from their deepest, darkest feelings is often extreme. It is so extreme that sometimes they evidence a lack of memory when it comes to emotion-laden experiences. Terrence Real calls these experiences "the building blocks of depression, a condition which, conceived in the boy, erupts later in the man." Many boys I have spoken with exhibit this kind of emotional amnesia, but none more than Rasheen.

When I first met fifteen-year-old Rasheen, whom I found to be a nervous boy, he was serving a ten-year sentence for his involvement in an armed robbery that turned into a shoot-out with the shopkeeper and the police. In our first interview I tried to learn about the structure and composition of his family—who was around when he was born, whom he lived with over the years before he was incarcerated, what the family's financial situation was.

The early years of his childhood were a complete mystery to Rasheen. He didn't remember much of anything. "Where were you born?" I asked him.

"I don't know."   25

"Was your father around then?"

"I don't know."

"Did you live with your mother after you were born?"

"I don't know."

It turns out that he lived with his great-grandmother for as long as he   30
could remember, she raised him and his mother's aunt's children (his "cousins" he called them, although they were technically his first cousins once removed).

"Did you ever ask about your mother?" I inquired.

Rasheen lowered his eyes and twisted his fingers. "Yes. I would ask my grandmother, but she wouldn't tell me anything."

"Did you see your mother?"

"Sometimes, but my grandmother didn't want her around. . . . I didn't either."

Rasheen was clearly humiliated by the fact that he was abandoned by   35
his mother in favor of her addiction to drugs or alcohol (he wasn't sure which).

What shame a boy feels when he is abandoned by his mother! What lengths he will go to in order to defend himself against these feelings. Inside, he "forgets" so that he doesn't have to feel. Outside, he punishes the world so that he feels avenged. Shame at abandonment begets covert depression, which begets rage, which begets violence. That is one of the powerful equations of life for lost boys.

Parental Abandonment

Some parents disappear from their child's life, psychologically and/or physically. Some mothers experience what psychologists call postpartum depression during the early months of their baby's life and for a time are psychologically unavailable to their newborn, unable to form a secure attachment. Violence within the home, illness, extended hospitalization—all are factors known to impair the development of the attachment bond. Some women have strongly ambivalent feelings about being a mother, perhaps feeling they were pushed into motherhood by social or family expectations when what they really wanted was to focus on their careers outside the home.

Whatever the particular circumstances or barrier, social issues and psychological problems can prevent otherwise competent, caring individuals from succeeding in basic parenting tasks. And when this earliest parent-child relationship doesn't take hold and thrive, a boy is left emotionally high and dry and his soul retreats deeper and deeper.

It is commonplace for the general public and politicians to attribute youth crime and violence to a breakdown of the family. In truth, the problem is not the breakdown *of* the family but the breakdown *in* the family. Disruption in the basic relationships of the family figure prominently in the lives of violent boys. These boys often have a strong sense of family, and they often speak about their families. In this sense, they are very big on family values. For example, Malcolm's rhetoric on family resembles that of my own Italian father in his description of where loyalty fits into his value scheme. He says, "Nothing is more important than family, nothing. I would kill anyone to protect my family. I would die for my family, man."

But existing side by side with this feeling of family that many violent boys 40 have is a record of the disrupted connections and abandonments they have faced, often early in life. Sometimes in talking with them I get glimpses of how boys feel about these abandonments. When I ask Malcolm whom he trusts, he replies, "No one." I ask, "What about your family?" "My family," he replies, "only to a limited degree. I mean, you can't trust nobody all the way in this world."

To anyone who knows family life in America, it should come as no surprise that fathers play a crucial role in the development of boys. Two particular patterns of father influence are most important in understanding the development of violent boys: (1) the *presence* of an abusive father and (2) the *absence* of a caring and resourceful father. The presence of an abusive father teaches sons some very dangerous lessons about being a man, often lessons that are only unconsciously learned.

Fifteen-year-old Terrel is in jail for killing a convenience store clerk. As he talks about his history, he returns over and over again to his need to dominate people. "People are afraid of me," he says. "I like that." Terrell recounts how he assembled a group of boys who would do anything he told them to do. "I enjoyed having that power, making people do what I want. And if they disobey me, they get hurt. That's the way things are." He is currently serving a life sentence because the convenience store clerk dared to oppose him when Terrel demanded all the money in the cash register. "He said he couldn't do it," Terrel says. "So I says, 'Don't talk to me like that. Don't you ever talk to me like that.' And then I shot him."

Where did Terrel learn to be the boy he is? Having heard the story of his father's brutal treatment of Terrel and his eighteen-year-old brother, who is serving a life sentence in an adult prison, one doesn't have to look far. What Terrel describes happening between him and the convenience store clerk echoes his description of his relationship with his father: do what I say or get hurt; submit or feel pain. When asked about this parallel, Terrel seems surprised, even stunned. "Hmm," he says after thinking it over a minute. "I never thought of it that way, but I guess you're right." Sometimes a boy is better off with no father at all than one who teaches him these lessons about manhood and violence.

But boys also suffer from the absence of a caring father. Research shows that having an absent father is associated with a greater likelihood of chronic juvenile bad behavior.[8] The link comes through at least three effects of living without a father:

First, being fatherless increases the odds that a boy will grow up in a   45
neighborhood where resources of all kinds are in short supply, thus, the normal opportunities for success in the world will be limited. In America today, being fatherless is one of the most powerful predictors that a child will be poor, will be moved from home to home and neighborhood to neighborhood, and will therefore have more difficulty establishing stable and positive relationships with peers. Thirteen-year-old Mitchell Johnson° of Jonesboro, Arkansas, is but one example of a young boy who suffered through such instability in the years leading up to his infamous shooting spree.

Second, growing up fatherless increases the chances that a boy will lack a male guide, protector, and mentor. This is itself a risk factor for later delinquency, because boys in an environment with many negative possibilities require every possible counterforce to keep from succumbing to them. Having a father is no guarantee of protection (particularly if he is abusive), but it does increase the odds of success. We know that in Pearl, Mississippi, Luke Woodham° fell under the influence of a particularly pernicious peer group, one that capitalized on his emotional vulnerability and drew him ever deeper into violence. Tragically, Luke's mother was unable to move him away from that group.

Mitchell Johnson: On March 24, 1998, thirteen-year-old Johnson and eleven-year-old Andrew Golden killed four classmates and a teacher at their middle school.

Luke Woodham: On October 1, 1997, Luke Woodham killed three students and wounded seven at his Mississippi high school.

Finally, growing up without a father always leaves the question of why. "Why don't I have a father?" often goes unanswered. And there is always the possibility that a child will answer that question by concluding there is something wrong with him that he doesn't have a father. The repercussions from this negative conclusion pose a bigger danger for some children, particularly those with a temperamental predisposition to depression and aggression, than for others. Imagine the powerful chemical reaction when many boys who have grown up in similar circumstances, similarly hurt, get together.

An absent father is one thing—and the consequences for boys of this absence are not surprising to anyone familiar with the correlation between father absence and delinquency—but what is surprising is the prevalence of absent *mothers*. Many of the boys involved in lethal violence lose their mothers for significant periods in their early years; some lose them permanently. Some have a mother in jail or in a drug treatment program. Sometimes mothers move away and leave their boys with relatives; some mothers die. The pain and rage associated with maternal abandonment is often buried deeply, but it is there nonetheless.

Matt speaks to me about his postrelease plans and says that he hopes he might be able to relocate so that he can be closer to his mother, who is herself serving a life sentence for murder at the state prison. This is the same mother who gave up caring for him when he was four and turned him over to *her* mother. Why? She wanted to protect him from his father—her pimp—who was beating and tormenting him mercilessly, and she also wanted to be rid of him because he interfered with her "lifestyle." This double abandonment may cut more deeply than the hurt other boys experience, but Matt is far from unique.

The Costs of Abandonment

British psychiatrist Michael Rutter has studied the chain reactions that are   50
likely after a child experiences abandonment and other disruptions of early relationships.[9] In his research it is clear that for a boy to be separated from his mother in infancy and early childhood is a very significant risk factor for future development. Rarely does one risk factor by itself tell the whole story about development, but most child psychologists recognize that early detachment is a very powerful negative influence all by itself.

In Jonesboro, neighbors report that Andrew Golden, the eleven-year-old who partnered with thirteen-year-old Mitchell Johnson to shoot down kids at their school, was raised mainly by his grandparents while his parents worked long hours. In the weeks before the shooting, his dog was lost for a time, and when it returned it was suffering from a bullet wound. For a boy whose principal activity with his father seems to have been shooting and involvement in the gun culture and who was already angry, this kind of hurt could easily have been too much to bear.

In Moses Lake, Washington, fourteen-year-old Barry Loukaitis brought an assault rifle to school a few weeks after his mother announced that she was divorcing his father and that she was suicidally depressed about this planned breakup.

Of course, none of these abandonment experiences necessarily lead to violence. Thousands of boys live with the same losses each year, yet very few take extreme measures to cope with their pain. Many become depressed and mask that depression by self-destructive behavior such as alcohol or drug addiction. And many others express it through nonlethal violence (but violence just the same). But when an abandonment experience is put in the broader context of a troubled boy's life, particularly a boy with uncontrolled access to guns, such an experience can be the spark that ignites a powder keg.

Who Is There for Abandoned Children?

Why is parental abandonment so dangerous? For one thing, it leaves children dependent upon people other than those with the greatest biological investment in them. Working at McMaster University, psychologists Martin Daly and Margo Wilson documented this risk. While not denying that most of the adults who hurt children are biological fathers and mothers,[10] Daly and Wilson present data that show that the *odds* that children will come to harm increase the further away they are from the care of their biological parents. Their data indicate that there is a special danger faced by children in the care of nonrelatives. For example, while the overall odds that a child will die at the hands of an adult with whom she or he lives is small (totaling about two thousand cases per year in the United States and Canada), the likelihood that a child will be killed is eight times greater if that child lives with one or more substitute parents than if he or she lives with both biological parents.

At particular risk is a child who is exposed to a man who is sexually in-   55
volved with the child's mother but is not biologically related to the child nor legally or socially committed to serve as a surrogate father. This is the "mother's boyfriend" who appears so disproportionately in reports of child abuse of all kinds. Of course, many children are truly blessed with a loving foster or adoptive parent or a loving stepfather who cares for them. But too many others get dealt men who are negative influences. In Jonesboro, Arkansas, the mother of thirteen-year-old Mitchell Johnson married a man who had served time in prison on federal drug and weapons charges. Mitchell mourned the loss of his father (due to divorce), and to help heal this hurt he needed a stepfather who was especially kind and caring. It would appear he lost out on this score. While we know little about this stepfather's relationship with Mitchell, we can hazard a guess that the relationship did little or nothing to help an already troubled young boy and may even have undermined his development.

I visited seventeen-year-old Tyrone to find out how his background influenced his entry into the drug dealing that eventually brought him to the point of killing a neighborhood rival. Tyrone's father did come around sometimes, he reported. "He would give me money and things." "Can you remember something fun you did with your father?" I asked. Tyrone thought for a moment. "No. I don't think so," he replied. Being abandoned is a tough challenge for any child. Ironically, it may be better to lose a parent to an early death (even though many young children interpret this as a kind of abandonment) than to have a neglectful parent. At least then a child can accept the separation as inevitable and not of the parent's choosing.

Rejection Is a Psychological Cancer

Deliberate abandonment evokes in boys a deep shame. When I sit with him, I cannot help but be aware of the pain Tyrone feels. It's physically hard for him to sit there awash in his shame. The shame of abandonment appears over and over again in the lives of kids who kill. Boys feel the shame of rejection.

Shareef Cousin, a boy who exemplifies the potential of parental rejection for pushing a boy already at risk over the edge, is on death row in Louisiana. He spent his first decade of life believing he knew who his father was — a man who was involved with his mother but who did not live in the house. One day Shareef approached this man, Robert Epps, for validation of their relationship. Here's the way *Time* magazine reports their meeting:

> "Do you know me?" Shareef asked.[11] Epps said that he did. "You're my father, right?" Shareef asked. "No, I'm not," Epps replied. "I don't know why your momma would tell you that." Shareef was crushed. And in front of his friends. "I started crying," Cousin said in an interview in prison. "That was like him telling me, I'm sorry I made you. Like I wasn't worth anything." Family members said that day was the start of Cousin's descent. His grades fell. He developed a bad attitude. His mother began to suspect he was using drugs.

Being explicitly rejected by his father was the last straw for an already vulnerable boy. In just a few years Shareef committed the murder that landed him on death row. In Shareef's case, rejection was twice fatal — once for his victim and now for himself.

Anthropologist Ronald Rohner has studied rejection in more than a hundred cultures around the world.[12] His findings are clear: although cultures differ in how they express rejection, rejected children everywhere are at heightened risk for a host of psychological problems ranging from low self-esteem, to truncated moral development, to difficulty handling aggression and sexuality. This effect is so strong that Rohner calls rejection "a psychological malignancy" that spreads throughout a child's emotional system wreaking havoc.

John, one of the boys in prison, told my partner Claire that he knew from his earliest years that he was unwanted. His parents only had him in the hope of having a daughter to complement his older brother. Their disappointment in having a second son became the primary theme of John's young life, and the happiness surrounding the birth of a sister a few years later only magnified his perception of his parents' rejection of him. Psychologists report that Kip Kinkel struggled with a similar feeling of rejection, always feeling second best to his "perfect" older sister. It appears that Michael Carneal in Paducah, Kentucky, felt the same way about his successful sister. Many of the lost boys have this kind of comparative rejection at their core, even when parents try to overcome it.

How does a boy talk about rejection? It's not easy. I sit with eighteen-year-old Stephen, a boy from New York who is serving a life sentence for shooting a police officer, struggling to find a way to help him communicate his thoughts and feelings about rejection. I know that his mother rejected him in favor of his older brother, a palpable hurt that seems to lurk in everything he says about her. For example, he tells me that one day when he was twelve years old, he borrowed a pair of his brother's pants and wore them to the park. While he was there playing with his friends, his mother drove by. She recognized the pants as belonging to his brother and immediately stopped the car. After calling Stephen over to her, she made him take off his brother's pants right there in the park and hand them over to her, whereupon she drove off, leaving him standing there in his underwear. His shame at the time was profound and the words are still difficult to retrieve, so I am searching for some other way for him to tell me about it.

On the desk between us are two beverage cans (I had bought Stephen a soft drink on this hot day as a small gesture of solidarity). Seeing the cans gives me an idea. "Let's think of this whole desktop as your mother's love," I say to him. He nods his understanding. "Now, this can is you," I say, holding up one of the cans. "And this one is your brother," I continued, gesturing toward the other can. "How full of your mother's love is your can? And how full is your brother's can?" Stephen clearly understands that I am giving him a chance to tell me what could not be said before. He bows his head in thought for a moment, then he shows me that he received about 20 percent of his mother's love, and his brother got 80 percent. Stephen's feeling that he received even 20 percent of his mother's love may be the starting point for his redemption. Even this little tidbit of love was enough to nurture the light in his soul. If it had been the whole story, it might even have been enough.

I then say, "Now let's use the desk to show being accepted or rejected." I point to one end of the desk. "This end means complete acceptance, the other end is total rejection. Choose places for the two cans to show how much your mother accepted you and how much she accepted your brother." Again Stephen bows his head in thought. When he raises it, he puts "his" can almost all the way to the end of the desk that means rejection and puts the can representing his brother all the way to the edge at the other end of the desk, the end indicating complete acceptance. "Ninety percent rejection for you and a hundred percent acceptance for your brother?" I ask. "Yes," he says softly. That's a hurt that lasts.

Listening to Stephen and thinking about the violent crimes he has committed, I reflect upon how things might have been different were he a girl.   65

While boys are encouraged to act out their feelings through aggression, girls are taught to talk about how they feel. And, boys learn to punish other people, while girls are taught to keep that hurt inside, even if it eats her up. A boy is likely to spill that hurt into the world through his violent behavior.

Children who are rejected by one or both parents are likely to attribute the rejection to something lacking in themselves. "What's wrong with me that my parents don't want me?" is their inevitable, often silent, question. Adults who were adopted as young children often cannot even ask this question without the aid of counseling. It is no wonder that it is too big a question to be asked directly by many kids. Who among us could bear to confirm that a father or a mother *chose* not to be in our life? When I sit with Tyrone or Michael, the question hangs in the air between us. I can feel the weight of it in their lowered eyes.

Who Pays the Price for Abandoned and Rejected Children?

British psychiatrist John Bowlby was a pioneer in understanding attachment. I recall him telling the story of a little boy who had missed out on developing attachment. How did this happen? It resulted through a combination of the child's temperament and his parents' psychological unavailability. While seeing this young patient in the study of his home, Bowlby was called out of the room to answer the telephone. While out of the room, Bowlby remembered that he had left the cat in the room with the little boy and rushed back — only to find that the boy had very calmly thrown the cat into the fire.

Attachment is one of the crucial building blocks in the process of emotional development. As Bowlby's shocking story shows, children who don't develop attachment have trouble making appropriate emotional connections. They have trouble with their own feelings and with the feelings of others. They often lack the emotional fundamentals for becoming a well-functioning member of society and are prone to become infected with whatever social poisons are around them. In short, they have trouble learning the basics of empathy, sympathy, and caring. The relevance for violent boys everywhere is clear.

The big family issues for lost boys are not abstract formulations or political pronouncements about family values. They are very concrete and specific: rejection, abandonment, disrupted family relationships. The latter can take many forms and have multiple consequences, but one of the most important is that disruptions affect the child's ability to form and sustain secure, positive social relationships. These relationships serve as a psychological anchor, helping to hold a boy in good society rather than allowing him to drift into the dark side. As always, it is a matter of temperament and experience; a boy's fate is neither totally predetermined by genetic programming nor totally the result of social influences.

The problems violent boys show in truly understanding normal social relations in the community is sometimes startling, even to someone, like me, who is sympathetic to them. While few of them have the kind of cold-blooded character evident in the little boy who threw Bowlby's cat in the fire, some of them do seem clueless when it comes to conventional standards regarding humane behavior in our society.

Sitting with Michael one afternoon as he awaited trial for killing a police officer, I asked him, "What was the worst thing you ever did? What was the worst thing that ever happened to you?" He thought for awhile and then told me he couldn't think of anything really bad that he had ever done. After a brief pause, he added, "Of course, the worst thing that ever happened to *me* is the present situation." A minute later, he added that there were illegal things he had done that some people might consider bad from *their* point of view.

Michael had erected such strong defenses against his own deep feelings of hurt that he had great difficulty recognizing the feelings of others. Accurately seeing and hearing what others are feeling is one feature of what psychologist Dan Goleman calls "emotional intelligence,"[13] And it is in this sense that many violent boys suffer from a kind of "emotional retardation." Like most forms of retardation, it can arise from a mixture of biological predispositions (less than usual neurological capacity for empathy) and experiences of deprivation (being treated with emotional brutality rather than empathy).

Emotional retardation is one of the socially expensive side effects of surviving rejection in childhood, particularly in boys whose temperament puts them in jeopardy for emotional compartmentalization in the first place. When thirteen-year-old Mitchell Johnson and eleven-year-old Andrew Golden opened fire on their classmates in Jonesboro, Arkansas, the two boys seemed surprised at the results — at both the carnage and the adults' reactions. In the hours and minutes leading up to their crimes of carnage, some violent boys seem genuinely unaware of the human significance of what they are about to do. After the fact, they have trouble connecting with the emotional pain they have caused others. Shortly after Michael Carneal was apprehended following his shooting spree in Paducah, he told police, "It was like I was in a dream."

With their emotional retardation and great difficulty recognizing the feelings of others, it's no wonder that animal abuse is common among kids with difficult attachment histories. If our society were uniformly caring and nurturant toward animals, this might not be such a big problem, but our society kills and feasts on animals of all sorts and regularly exposes children to images of violent treatment of animals in movies and television. For example, how is it that we find the throwing of a cat in the fire hideous and yet are quite content with tossing live lobsters into pots of boiling water? From the perspective of a troubled boy, our society has rather ambiguous moral standards about the treatment of animals. This helps create a moral space for cruelty by boys who seem to lack the regular emotional feedback systems that cause most children to stop the hurting once they receive the victim's signals of distress and pain.

Sixteen-year-old Malique recalls his experiences abusing animals when he was twelve. "Any animal — a cat, a dog, a bird, or anything that we saw that was moving — it could be shot. That's where I learned to shoot my first gun. One time we had a long knife that we used to cut open this stray dog. It was disgusting, 'cause his insides fell right out." It should come as no surprise that Kip Kinkel, the fifteen-year-old who killed his parents and schoolmates in Springfield, Oregon, has a history of animal abuse, as do some of the other middle-class boys who opened fire on classmates at schools in recent years. In Pearl, Mississippi, Luke Woodham and a friend were observed beating Woodham's dog with a club, wrapping it in a plastic bag, setting it afire, and tossing it in a pond.

Early in our relationship Malcolm spoke about using his pit bulls in dog-fights in a way that I found particularly disturbing. It was not until we had spent months together and I felt a close relationship evolving that I heard him change his tune about the dogs. What began as a relationship with me matured into a larger capacity for relationships in general, and eventually Malcolm told me he didn't think he could participate in the dog fighting anymore. Perhaps our relationship was somehow starting to fill the void in his heart and soul. In a small way I was becoming the positive parental figure that Malcolm lacked.

But even when there is such a parent figure in a boy's social map, there are often other problems that arise from rejection and abandonment. Thomas had grandparents who filled the void left by his drug-dependent mother. But it was not enough, because Thomas still wonders why she wasn't there for him. Andrew Golden in Jonesboro spent most of his time with his grandparents while his parents worked. Malcolm's was separated from him for four years, serving in the army. She returned for him, but it may have been a case of too little too late. In fact, her presence provoked a crisis that grew out of the hole left in this family by the "missing" father and Malcolm's efforts to fill that hole. . . .

Psychologically Alone, Socially Vulnerable

Disrupted relationships in childhood predispose boys to trouble in adolescence. Whether it is outright abandonment or psychological rejection, violent boys often leave infancy and early childhood with one of the biggest strikes against them that a child can have—disrupted attachment relationships. Some boys are predisposed to this emotional isolation. To prevent this predisposition from manifesting itself requires special efforts on the part of their caregivers. Some boys may even be virtually "unattachable" in the normal course of things.

These disruptions in his early relationships challenge a boy's every effort to find a place for himself in the world. The emotional pain and isolation these boys feel can push their souls into hibernation. When what they need is a robust sense of connection to the deepest resources of the spirit, they experience only emptiness. When what they most need is to feel they belong to someone positive and strong, they feel only disdain and see only weakness.

Research on resilience documents the crucial protective role of a secure, strong attachment and the importance of being loved unconditionally by a parent or uncle, aunt, older sister, father, *someone*. Violent boys demonstrate

80

the emotional vulnerability created by weak or broken early attachment. It may take years to do its damage, but unsatisfactory childhood attachment sets in motion the chain of events that results in lethal violence when these boys reach adolescence. How can responsible adults in the community begin to repair this damage? First, they can provide emotional support for parents who are dealing with boys demonstrating attachment problems. It is emotionally grueling to be the parent of such a boy. By all accounts, Kip Kinkel's parents worked hard at trying to find a way to connect with him and bring him under control. As his behavior worsened, they became more desperate. And so did he. It was a race against time, and they lost.

Second, adults outside the family can engage the child and caregiver in therapeutic relationships that examine the nature of the child's attachment problems. For a child predisposed to isolation, only a skilled therapist may be able to figure out effective ways to relate to the child. Third, adults outside the family can go out of their way to provide opportunities for stability and continuity in the child's relationship with them. For example, although conventional programming in elementary schools has children changing teachers every year, vulnerable boys would do better if they had the same teacher over a period of years. This continuity can provide an opportunity for some remedial attachment experiences.

Fourth, when parental abandonment occurs, whether voluntary or enforced by the court, the focus of public policy must be to counteract the emergence and expansion of relationship problems in the child. This means offering therapy to children separated from their parents as well as making systematic efforts to ensure that children find stable homes. It means implementing what social services workers call "permanency planning," that is, carrying out a permanent plan in which children establish and maintain solid relationships while they are in foster care (and even after adoption). The goal is to stop early relationship problems from blossoming into long-term issues of shame, rage, and aggression.

Notes

1. Shengold, L. (1989). *Soul Murder: The Effects of Childhood Abuse and Deprivation.* New Haven, CT: Yale University Press.

2. Casarjian, R. (1995). *Houses of Healing: A Prisoner's Guide to Inner Power and Freedom.* Boston: The Lionheart Foundation.

3. Prejean, Sister Helen (1993). *Dead Man Walking: An Eyewitness Account of the Death Penalty in the United States.* New York: Random House.

4. Tolan, P., & Guerra, N. (1996). Youth Violence Prevention: Descriptions of Baseline Data from Thirteen Evaluation Projects. *American Journal of Preventative Medicine, Supplement to 12*(5), 1–134.

5. Kessler, R. cited in M. Elias (1998, August 13), Rich or Poor, More Kids Struggle with Symptoms. *USA Today,* sec. D, p. 1.

6. Luthar, S. cited in M. Elias (1998, August 13), Rich or Poor, More Kids Struggle with Symptoms. *USA Today,* sec. D, p. 1.

7. Real, T. (1997). *I Don't Want to Talk About It: Overcoming the Secret Legacy of Male Depression*. New York: Scribner.

8. Weintraub, K. J., & Gold, M. (1992). Monitoring and Delinquency. *Criminal Behaviour and Mental Health, 1*(3), 268–281.

9. Rutter, M. (1989). Pathways from Childhood to Adult Life. *Journal of Psychology and Psychiatry, 30,* 25–51.

10. Daly, M., & Wilson, M. (1997). Violence Against Stepchildren. *Current Directions in Psychological Science, 5*(3), 77–81.

11. Farley, C., & Willwerth, J. (1997, January). Dead Teen Walking. *Time.* 151(2), 33ff.

12. Rohner, R. (1975). *They Love Me, They Love Me Not.* New Haven, CT: Human Relations Area Files Press.

13. Goleman, D. (1995). *Emotional Intelligence: Why It Can Matter More Than IQ.* New York: Bantam.

EXPLORING THE TEXT

1. What does Garbarino mean by "soul murder"? Given the fact that he is a scientist, why do you think he chose to use a term that has such strong religious connotations? Why might it be preferable, from Garbarino's perspective, to think of children as having souls instead of simply having minds? What is implied in the idea of having a "sacred self"?

2. Why do the souls of some people survive in even the harshest environments, according to Garbarino? What situations are the most hazardous for the development of young men, in his view? Why?

3. How do male role models and gender role socialization affect a boy's ability to cope with abandonment, according to Garbarino? What, in his view, can nonfamily members do to "repair" boys who have been damaged?

4. What kinds of evidence or support does Garbarino offer to substantiate his theory of male violence? Which of these varieties of supporting evidence seems the most persuasive to you? Why?

5. What is the nature of the audience that Garbarino is addressing in this selection? What leads you to this image of his imagined reader?

FURTHER EXPLORATIONS

1. How might Deborah Blum's analysis of the differences between male and female minds (p. 453) support Garbarino's belief that boys are more vulnerable than girls during their childhood years and adolescence? To what extent would you agree that boys are generally more vulnerable than girls in childhood? Why?

2. How would Garbarino likely explain why the narrator and his brother survive on the streets of Harlem in James Baldwin's "Sonny's Blues" (p. 390)? Based on Garbarino's insights, compose an imaginary biography for the young junkie that the narrator initially encounters in Baldwin's story. How might his story contrast with that of Sonny and his brother?

3. To what extent does Garbarino's explanation of child violence support Andrew Sullivan's contention that some forms of hatred are "reasonable" (p. 469)? Should random acts of violence like the Columbine shootings be treated as "hate crimes"? Why or why not?

4. View the 1995 film *Dead Man Walking* and discuss how Sister Helen Prejean awakens the souls of men facing the death penalty. To what extent does her experience on death row confirm Garbarino's theory of male violence?

5. View a film like *Boyz in the Hood, Amongst Friends, Do the Right Thing,* or *Once Upon a Time in America* that depicts a young man succumbing to a life of violence. What role do factors like abandonment, shame, social attitudes toward masculinity, and poverty play in this process as it is presented? What other factors, if any, seem to be involved? What does the film suggest about the sources of violence in American society?

ESSAY OPTIONS

1. Research news accounts of several recent cases of teen violence to test Garbarino's theory of "soul murder." Do the details of the family lives of the teens involved confirm or challenge Garbarino's account of why young men turn to violence? What other theories have been advanced to explain the motives behind these teen assaults? What other factors might be involved? Use your research as the basis of an essay on the minds of violent teens.

2. Drawing on Garbarino's theory of violence, Martha C. Nussbaum's theory of imaginative identification through literature (p. 416) and Deborah Blum's theory of male and female minds (p. 453), write a paper in which you discuss the role that empathy plays in the creation of a civil society. How does empathy function to make living in a diverse society possible? How is such "emotional intelligence" developed? What problems, in your view, complicate the development of empathy in contemporary American society?

5

Reading Animal Minds
Objects or Equals?

Reasonable Differences

Back in the 1800s, a case of faulty mind reading almost changed the course of history. In the fall of 1831, British sea Captain Robert FitzRoy was searching for a companion to accompany him on a voyage exploring the coast of South America. An avid student of the popular but since discredited pseudoscience of phrenology, FitzRoy believed you could read a person's character in his facial features and from the shape of his head. A well-rounded cranium, according to phrenologist lore, might reveal a virtuous character and a diligent spirit; a slanting forehead and a bulbous nose might signal mental weakness or poor character. So, when FitzRoy first met the young man who wanted to share his cabin for the next two years, he had serious reservations: the twenty-two-year-old naturalist FitzRoy interviewed had a nose that suggested a distinct lack of "energy and determination" in its owner. Eventually, the skipper of the H.M.S. *Beagle* conquered his initial reservations and allowed Charles Darwin to sail with him to the untouched Galápagos Islands off the coast of Ecuador. Five years later, Darwin returned home to London, never having overcome the seasickness that plagued him throughout the trip, but armed now with the data that would eventually result in *The Origin of Species* and the theory of evolution through natural selection.

Darwin's discoveries during his voyage on the *Beagle* changed the way we view our relation to the world of animals. Before Darwin, Western European attitudes toward animals had been shaped by the Judeo-Christian philosophical tradition. As zoologist James Serpell observes in his classic study of the subject, the Book of Genesis influenced human attitudes toward animals for nearly two thousand years. In the biblical story of creation, God shapes Adam "in his own image" and gives him "dominion over every living thing that moveth upon the earth." In Genesis, Adam and Eve are presented as direct representations of divinity on earth and are thus distinguished from the "lower" orders of creation. Animals and plants exist to nurture human beings; they are provided as resources — things meant to satisfy human needs and purposes. Later, in the story of the Flood, God confirms human supremacy over animal life as he assures Noah of his covenant with humanity:

> And God blessed Noah and his sons, and said unto them, Be fruitful and multiply, and replenish the earth.
>
> And the fear of you and the dread of you shall be upon every beast of the earth, and upon every fowl of the air, upon all that moveth upon the earth, and upon all the fishes of the sea; into your hands are they delivered.
>
> Every moving thing that liveth shall be meat for you; even as the green herb have I given you all things.
>
> (Gen. 9: 1–3)

The Judeo-Christian tradition, it's true, has always held that animals should be treated with kindness and respect, and some figures within it, like

Saint Francis of Assisi, became famous for preaching love for other species. But, in general, the idea that an unbridgeable gulf of difference separates animals from humans has distinguished Western thinking for the past two millennia. Writing in the fifth century, Saint Augustine argued that the Biblical injunction against killing didn't apply to the animal world, because animals lacked the power of reason and thus were not part of the same community of creation as human beings. In the thirteenth century, Saint Thomas Aquinas expanded on this distinction by proclaiming that animals lacked not only the power of reason, but souls as well. How could animals gain entrance into heaven, Aquinas argued, if they didn't possess the power to discriminate right from wrong? A firm believer in the Ptolemaic view of the universe, Aquinas was convinced that human beings existed at the center of creation and that all other forms of life were merely objects meant for human use. In fact, he was so convinced of the centrality of human beings in creation, he felt compelled to explain why it was necessary to treat animals with respect. It would be wrong, he surmised, to brutalize animals, because human beings might become used to brutality and be tempted to treat one another in an equally brutal manner. Brutal treatment of animals was also wrong because it might result in the destruction of another man's property. Animals, in Aquinas's view, had no rights themselves; they were mindless and soulless objects that were deserving of kindness only insofar as their treatment would help or harm mankind.

The Greeks also believed that humans and animals were essentially different types of creatures; but, for the Greeks, the distinguishing factor between beasts and men lay in the mind. Classical philosophers like Plato and Aristotle celebrated reason as the most important and the most distinctly "human" of the mind's faculties. In Aristotle's view, the power of reason is what placed humans at the top of the *Scala Naturae* — the "Ladder of Nature" — which ranked all living things in order of perfection. The power of reason made humans superior to animals and thus justified our use of them. Interestingly enough, as Serpell notes, Aristotle used much the same thinking to justify the Grecian slave trade: just as some humans lacked the power of reason and thus became the "natural slaves" of their superiors, so were all animals "enslaved" by their deficient intellects to the interests of their naturally superior human masters. By the Middle Ages and the era of Thomas Aquinas, the mind had become the dividing line between humans and animals in Western Europe, and reason itself had become reason enough to justify both human slavery and animal abuse.

With the development of modern science in the seventeenth century, the ideological gulf separating animals and humans grew even wider. Under the influence of French philosopher René Descartes, early scientists came to view animals as little more than mechanical objects. In his *Discours de la Method* of 1637, Descartes explained that animals were essentially complex machines, like clocks, that operated according to straightforward mechanical principles. Humans resembled animals to the extent that our bodies also function like machines, but, in Descartes's view, we were distinguished from other inferior creatures by the gift of reason, the presence of the soul, and the power of speech. Armed with Descartes's view of the "beast-as-machine," modern science could begin its early explorations of anatomy and physiology with a clear conscience. After all, why worry about the feelings of the animal you are dissecting alive as part of your experiment on the circulatory system if the animal itself is only a kind of "automaton"—a cleverly constructed natural mechanism like the clockwork "chickens," "monkeys," and "schoolboys" that were becoming such popular attractions all over Europe? If an animal is a soulless machine without a mind, the cries it produces when killed for scientific or culinary purposes are merely mechanical reactions—something like the response of a spring when triggered by a gear in the animal's mechanical body.

This was the state of Western attitudes toward animals when Darwin published *The Origin of Species* in 1859. The observations Darwin made of animal life along the shores of South America convinced him that animal species were not "categories" that had been permanently fixed at the time of creation, but were instead the result of a continuous process of "natural selection" that favored certain traits and eliminated others in response to changing environmental conditions. This idea was revolutionary in itself, but what made Darwin's theory genuinely explosive was the idea that humans were subject to the same process of selection as animals and plants. From the perspective of natural selection, speech and reason are just two more natural "traits" that may or may not lead to success in certain environmental circumstances—no different really than opposable thumbs or bipedal motion. The theory of evolution returned human beings to the natural world on an equal footing with animals. Here is Darwin speculating on the possibility that all life, human and animal, springs from common ancestry:

> . . . if we choose to let conjecture run wild then animals our fellow brethren in pain, disease death & suffering & famine; our slaves in the most laborious work, our companions in our amusements, they may partake, from our origin in one common ancestor we may all be netted together. (238–39)

The furor over Darwin's assertion of animal and human equality has yet to die down. Since the time of the Scopes "Monkey Trial" over the teaching of evolution in 1925, conservative critics have charged that Darwinian theory undermines religion and deprives humanity of the dignity and superiority granted to us as our birthright in the Bible. Progressive critics have sometimes agreed with their conservative counterparts, objecting to "social-Darwinist" interpretations of human behavior which, in their view, often justify the worst aspects of human conduct—things like warfare and discrimination—because it grows out of the so-called "natural" behavior of animals.

But despite the controversy over shared ancestry, there's growing consensus in scientific and humanistic circles today about the similarity of animal and human minds. Research on primates by ethologists like Jane Goodall, Dian Fossey, and Frans de Waal has demonstrated what every pet lover has long known — that animals, like people, come equipped with a complex set of behaviors, emotions, characteristics, and intentions — that animals are, in fact, "individuals" with their own distinctive aptitudes and emotional lives. Indeed, recent experiments with animal languages have offered support to the belief that some species — like gorillas and dolphins — actually possess relatively sophisticated systems of communication and even the rudiments of "animal culture." Today, the question no longer appears to be whether or not animals are objects for humanity's use, but whether they are humanity's equals — equal coinhabitants of the earth's ecosystems with equal claims to life, liberty, and happiness.

Arguing Animals: Mind Reading and Reasoning

Many intellectual abilities have been used to define the frontier between human and animal minds, but none has been evoked as commonly as the faculty of reason. The ability to present and critically evaluate competing arguments and explanations has been seen as the most distinctly human form of mental activity since the time of Socrates. What makes reasoning seem so particularly human is its dependence on interpersonal communication. To reason about a problem or argument means to engage in discourse — to take part in an active "exchange of ideas" involving competing points of view. Think about how the process of reasoning works during a face-to-face debate: first, you present your position — say, that animals should be granted equal rights because they, like humans, are conscious creatures with the ability to suffer; then, your opponents present counterarguments to your position. You listen to these counterarguments and offer your rebuttal — either accepting or rejecting them as you deem appropriate. The process of actively testing your ideas, theories, or explanations against competing points of view lies at the heart of all discursive thinking. When we reason, we think "along with" other minds; we engage in an active dialogue of competing perspectives that helps us strengthen our own ideas and explore alternative approaches and positions. To reason is to think *socially* — to think in the context of other ways of thinking, to think with reference to other opinions, beliefs, and values.

Of course, your ability to engage in this intensely social kind of thought depends on your ability to read other minds. In a live debate, the competing team offers its critique of your claims and assertions and does its best to tease apart your reasoning. But when you're alone at your desk attempting to write an argumentative essay, you don't have the luxury of your opponent's presence. To engage in discursive reasoning as a writer, you have to imagine how a critical reader might react to your ideas and assertions — you have to step into the shoes of "the opposition" and imagine how someone who disagrees with your position would likely critique or argue against it. Let's pause for a moment to see how a pair of writers use discursive mind reading to introduce their argument for equal animal rights. In the passage below from the opening paragraphs of "The Case for the Personhood of Gorillas," Francine Patterson and Wendy Gordon claim that Koko, the famous sign-language "speaking" gorilla, should enjoy the same rights as any human being:

> We present this individual for your consideration:
> She communicates in sign language, using a vocabulary of over one thousand words. She also understands spoken English, and often carries on "bilingual" conversations, responding in sign to questions asked in English . . . .
> She demonstrates a clear self-awareness by engaging in self-directed behaviors in front of a mirror, such as making faces or examining her teeth, and by her appropriate use of self-descriptive language. She lies to avoid the consequences of her own misbehavior, and anticipates others' responses to her actions. She engages in imaginary play, both alone and with others. She has produced paintings and drawings which are representational. She remembers and can talk about past events in her life. . . .
> She laughs at her own jokes and those of others. She cries when hurt or left alone, screams when frightened or angered. She talks about her feelings, using words like *happy, sad, afraid, enjoy, eager, frustrate, mad,* and, quite frequently, *love.* She grieves for those she has lost—a favorite cat who has died, a friend who has gone away . . . .
> Does this individual have a claim to basic moral rights? It is hard to imagine any reasonable argument that would deny her these rights based on the description above. (58–59)

From the essay's opening words, it's clear that Patterson and Gordon are reading the minds of their readers and using the anticipated responses of their audience to structure their presentation of the case for Koko's personhood. They address the reader in the very first line, and it's obvious that the reader's likely expectations have shaped the list of Koko's attributes that follows. To convince the reader, Patterson and Gordon offer not one or two bits of evidence to back up their claim for Koko's personhood, but an extensive series of behaviors that link her to humans. They highlight behaviors that they know will be the most persuasive—things involving language, creativity, and empathy—and even ask rhetorical questions that "stand in" for the reader's possible first response: "It is hard to imagine any reasonable argument that would deny her these rights . . . ." This attempt to "imagine . . . reasonable arguments" and to respond to them is what distinguishes discursive reasoning from simple propaganda or blind assertion. It is this kind of deliberate self-assessment from other points of view that makes an argument genuinely persuasive.

But expert arguers rarely settle for the kind of mild self-scrutiny involved in rhetorical questions. Good persuasive writers often structure their arguments as direct responses to opposing points of view. Patterson and Gordon realize that to convince their readers of Koko's "personhood," they have to substantiate each of the initial claims they make by presenting concrete evidence showing that she can, in fact, do all these miraculous things. They also take it upon themselves to address counterarguments that might be made against their position. Here, they raise and respond to an objection about equating animal and human "interests":

> Arthur Caplan argues that animal interests and human interests should not be counted equally, claiming that nonhuman animals lack certain traits that make a moral difference. He uses the following example to illustrate his point . . . . (599)

After detailing Caplan's example of a baboon mother who carries on normally after the loss of a baby, which he feels shows that primates do not suffer, Patterson and Gordon offer this rebuttal:

> But in this example the comparison is between outward behavior in the case of the baboon mother, and a private mental state in the case of the human mother. In most such cases, the human mother also resumes her normal life . . . . Because the baboon mother cannot (or chooses not to) communicate to *us* her internal feelings about the death of her baby, it is assumed that it does not matter to her. While we cannot make any claims here about the emotional life of baboons, we have considerable evidence that Koko continues to mourn the loss of her adopted "baby" [cat] . . . even years after his death. (600)

Like expert debaters, Patterson and Gordon understand the deeply dialogical nature of argumentation: they present their case for the equality of primates by anticipating, critiquing, and responding to the counterarguments offered by those who would oppose them. They read the minds of their opposition in order to change the minds of their readers.

Philosopher Peter Singer engages in a similar kind of argumentative mind reading when he presents his case against the use of animals for human purposes. Having explained his contention that animals should not be made to suffer, because they, like humans, are capable of experiencing both pain and happiness, Singer goes on to consider possible counterarguments to his position:

> That, then, is really the whole of the argument for extending the principle of equality to nonhuman animals; but there may be some doubts about what this equality amounts to in practice. In particular, the last sentence of the previous paragraph may prompt some people to reply: "Surely pain felt by a mouse just is not as bad as pain felt by a human. Humans have much greater awareness of what is happening to them, and this makes their suffering worse. You can't equate the suffering of, say, a person dying slowly from cancer, and a laboratory mouse undergoing the same fate."
>
> I fully accept that in the case described the human cancer victim normally suffers more than the nonhuman cancer victim. This in no way undermines the extension of equal consideration of interests to nonhumans. It means, rather, that we must take care when we compare the interests of different species. . . . (610)

Singer goes on to offer his own counterexample of a valid comparison between human and animal pain and to explore other objections that might be made against his central claim for animal rights. In fact, his entire essay can be seen as an extended dialogue with a group of imaginary "opponents" who offer systematic objections which he then critiques and either refutes or uses to clarify his own thinking.

The discursive nature of argumentation can even lead a writer to "psychoanalyze" his opponents in an effort to explain the motives or intentions that underlie their claims. Bioethicist Paul Shepard engages in this kind of mind reading in his attack on the idea of animal liberation. Speculating about the unacknowledged fears that prompt proponents of animal liberation to shield all species from danger, Shepard asks

> How are we to understand this misplaced zeal? I think it has to do with death—the final, unacceptable reality of the natural world. This is where the antiorganic stance of our culture and our civilization leads in the end. "Protection" is a repository of the protector's own dread of the cycle of birth and death. . . . (634)

Whether or not you are persuaded by Shepard's analysis of the fears underlying the animal liberation movement, his probing of his opponents' motives demonstrates how genuinely dialogical the process of reasoning always is. Even if you're tucked away in the apparent quiet of a college library, when you write an argumentative essay, you are engaging in a dialogue with "other minds." Recognizing this fact and using it to help you shape your own thinking is the first step toward becoming a truly persuasive writer.

Chapter Overview

The reading selections in this chapter invite you to reflect on some of the intellectual and ethical challenges involved in the issue of animal intelligence. The first half of the chapter is devoted to exploring changing relationships between humans and their animal counterparts. We begin with a selection that provides an alternative perspective on animal minds. In "Talking to the Owls and Butterflies," Sioux medicine man John (Fire) Lame Deer contrasts tribal and "white" approaches to nature and the animal world. The next three selections highlight contemporary attitudes toward human/animal relationships. John Berger's "Why Look at Animals?" challenges us to contemplate the "marginalization" of animals in the modern world as reflected in the institution of the zoo and the rise of what Berger terms "animals of the mind." Next, the story of Faith McNulty's relationship with "Mouse," a wild creature she adopts and shares her home with, offers a telling example of an animal mind at work and the kind of impact it can have on the mind of its "master." "The

Artifice of the Natural" brings our exploration of human/animal interactions to a close by examining the way that television programming distorts our view of animals and the natural world.

The next three selections focus more narrowly on the issue of animal intelligence. In "The Whole Animal," primatologist Frans de Waal considers why modern science has shied away from thinking empathetically about animal minds. De Waal's examination of "anthropocentrism" and "anthropodenial" offers insights that apply to readings throughout the chapter. "Murder in a Zoo" by paleoanthropologist Richard Leakey and science writer Richard Lewin offers a shocking example of the Machiavellian complexity of primate minds as well as a stunning illustration of the relationship between human and animal thinking. Francine Patterson and Wendy Gordon balance this view of primate violence with the story of Koko, the lowland gorilla who was the first animal to master a human language and who, according to Patterson and Gordon, deserves to be accorded all the rights and privileges of "personhood."

The chapter concludes with two selections addressing the issues of animal liberation and animal rights. In "Equality for Animals," ethicist and philosopher Peter Singer argues the case for the "equal consideration" of animal interests, taking special aim at the use of animals for food and as subjects in scientific experiments. Paul Shepard's "Rights and Kindness: A Can of Worms" counters the position of animal liberationists like Singer and presents a blistering example of the role that mind reading plays in the service of argumentation.

Sources

Beaune, Jean-Claude. "The Classical Age of Automata: An Impressionistic Survey from the Sixteenth to the Nineteenth Century." In *Fragments for a History of the Human Body, Part One*. Ed. Michael Feher. New York: Zone Books, 1989.

Desmond, Adrian, and James Moore. *Darwin: The Life of a Tormented Evolutionist*. New York: W. W. Norton & Company, 1991, p. 238.

Francione, Gary L. *Introduction to Animal Rights: Your Child or the Dog?* Philadelphia: Temple University Press, 2000.

Serpell, James. *In the Company of Animals: A Study of Human-Animal Relationships*, Cambridge: Cambridge University Press, 1986.

Talking to the Owls and Butterflies

JOHN (FIRE) LAME DEER AND RICHARD ERDOES

When he was just sixteen years old, John "Fire" Lame Deer was sent out to spend four days and nights alone in a pit dug in a deserted hilltop on the Rosebud Reservation in South Dakota. He wasn't being punished for some adolescent transgression. He was experiencing his *hanblechia* — or "vision seeking" — the first step in his preparation as a Sioux medicine man. In the context of Sioux culture, if you want to talk to the gods, you get in touch with nature. For the traditional Sioux, nature is alive and animals are related to their human counterparts by territory, history, and blood. In this excerpt from his classic autobiography, Lame Deer castigates the "white world" for its attitude toward nature and its treatment of animals. He also offers some revealing insights into Native American views of animal minds.

Lame Deer (1900–1976) was a tribal leader, medicine man, storyteller, rodeo clown, and painter. Richard Erdoes (b. 1912) was nearly sixty when he met Lame Deer after being assigned by *Life* magazine to paint and photograph daily existence on a Sioux reservation. The meeting convinced Erdoes to give up his career as a professional illustrator for the life of a writer. Lame Deer chose him to collaborate on the story that became *Lame Deer, Seeker of Visions* (1972), the source of this selection. The author of more than thirty books, Erdoes also worked with Mary Crow Dog on her autobiography, *Lakota Woman* (1990), which received the 1991 American Book Award, and with Lame Deer's Son, Archie Fire Lame Deer, on his memoir, *Gift of Power: The Life and Teachings of a Lakota Medicine Man* (1992). He also coedited, with Alfonso Ortiz, *American Indian Trickster Tales* (1998).

BEFORE READING

Freewrite in your journal about your impression of the relationship between Native Americans and the animal world. How, according to this impression, do Native Americans view animals? Where do your impressions of Native American life and values come from? How accurate do you think they are? Why?

L et's sit down here, all of us, on the open prairie, where we can't see a highway or a fence. Let's have no blankets to sit on, but feel the ground with our bodies, the earth, the yielding shrubs. Let's have the grass for a mattress, experiencing its sharpness and its softness. Let us become like stones, plants, and trees. Let us be animals, think and feel like animals.

Listen to the air. You can hear it, feel it, smell it, taste it. *Woniya waken—* the holy air—which renews all by its breath. *Woniya, woniya waken*—spirit, life, breath, renewal—it means all that. *Woniya*—we sit together, don't touch, but something is there; we feel it between us, as a presence. A good way to start thinking about nature, talk about it. Rather talk to it, talk to the rivers, to the lakes, to the winds as to our relatives.

You have made it hard for us to experience nature in the good way by being part of it. Even here we are conscious that somewhere out in those hills there are missile silos and radar stations. White men always pick the few unspoiled, beautiful, awesome spots for the sites of these abominations. You have raped and violated these lands, always saying, "Gimme, gimme, gimme," and never giving anything back. You have taken 200,000 acres of our Pine

Ridge° reservation and made them into a bombing range. This land is so beautiful and strange that now some of you want to make it into a national park. The only use you have made of this land since you took it from us was to blow it up. You have not only despoiled the earth, the rocks, the minerals, all of which you call "dead" but which are very much alive; you have even changed the animals, which are part of us, part of the Great Spirit, changed them in a horrible way, so no one can recognize them. There is power in a buffalo — spiritual, magic power — but there is no power in an Angus, in a Hereford.°

There is power in an antelope, but not in a goat or in a sheep, which holds still while you butcher it, which will eat your newspaper if you let it. There was great power in a wolf, even in a coyote. You have made him into a freak — a toy poodle, a Pekingese, a lap dog. You can't do much with a cat, which is like an Indian, unchangeable. So you fix it, alter it, declaw it, even cut its vocal cords so you can experiment on it in a laboratory without being disturbed by its cries.

A partridge, a grouse, a quail, a pheasant, you have made them into chickens, creatures that can't fly, that wear a kind of sunglasses so that they won't peck each other's eyes out, "birds" with a "pecking order." There are some farms where they breed chickens for breast meat. Those birds are kept in low cages, forced to be hunched over all the time, which makes the breast muscles very big. Soothing sounds, Muzak, are piped into these chicken hutches. One loud noise and the chickens go haywire, killing themselves by flying against the mesh of their cages. Having to spend all their lives stooped over makes an unnatural, crazy, no-good bird. It also makes unnatural, no-good human beings.

That's where you fooled yourselves. You have not only altered, declawed and malformed your winged and four-legged cousins; you have done it to yourselves. You have changed men into chairmen of boards, into office workers, into time-clock punchers. You have changed women into housewives, truly fearful creatures. I was once invited into the home of such a one.

"Watch the ashes, don't smoke, you stain the curtains. Watch the goldfish bowl, don't breathe on the parakeet, don't lean your head against the wallpaper; your hair may be greasy. Don't spill liquor on that table: it has a delicate finish. You should have wiped your boots; the floor was just varnished. Don't, don't, don't . . ." That is crazy. We weren't made to endure this. You live in prisons which you have built for yourselves, calling them "homes," offices, factories. We have a new joke on the reservation: "What is cultural deprivation?" Answer: "Being an upper-middle-class white kid living in a split-level suburban home with a color TV."

Sometimes I think that even our pitiful tar-paper shacks are better than your luxury homes. Walking a hundred feet to the outhouse on a clear wintry night, through mud or snow, that's one small link with nature. Or in the sum-

Pine Ridge: Reservation established for the Oglala Sioux in 1978 following more than ten years of fighting and negotiation; site of the Wounded Knee massacre.

Angus, in a Hereford: Breeds of cattle.

mer, in the back country, leaving the door of the privy open, taking your time, listening to the humming of the insects, the sun warming your bones through the thin planks of wood; you don't even have that pleasure anymore.

Americans want to have everything sanitized. No smells! Not even the good, natural man and woman smell. Take away the smell from under the armpits, from your skin. Rub it out, and then spray or dab some nonhuman odor on yourself, stuff you can spend a lot of money on, ten dollars an ounce, so you know this has to smell good. "B.O.," bad breath, "Intimate Female Odor Spray"—I see it all on TV. Soon you'll breed people without body openings.

I think white people are so afraid of the world they created that they don't   10
want to see, feel, smell or hear it. The feeling of rain and snow on your face, being numbed by an icy wind and thawing out before a smoking fire, coming out of a hot sweat bath and plunging into a cold stream, these things make you feel alive, but you don't want them anymore. Living in boxes which shut out the heat of the summer and the chill of winter, living inside a body that no longer has a scent, hearing the noise from the hi-fi instead of listening to the sounds of nature, watching some actor on TV having a make-believe experience when you no longer experience anything for yourself, eating food without taste—that's your way. It's no good.

The food you eat, you treat it like your bodies, take out all the nature part, the taste, the smell, the roughness, then put the artificial color, the artificial flavor in. Raw liver, raw kidney—that's what we old-fashioned full-bloods like to get our teeth into. In the old days we used to eat the guts of the buffalo, making a contest of it, two fellows getting hold of a long piece of intestines from opposite ends, starting chewing toward the middle, seeing who can get there first; that's eating. Those buffalo guts, full of half-fermented, half-digested grass and herbs, you didn't need any pills and vitamins when you swallowed those. Use the bitterness of gall for flavoring, not refined salt or sugar. *Wasna*—meat, kidney fat and berries all pounded together—a lump of that sweet *wasna* kept a man going for a whole day. That was food, that had the power. Not the stuff you give us today: powdered milk, dehydrated eggs, pasteurized butter, chickens that are all drumsticks or all breast; there's no bird left there.

You don't want the bird. You don't have the courage to kill honestly—cut off the chicken's head, pluck it and gut it—no, you don't want this anymore. So it all comes in a neat plastic bag, all cut up, ready to eat, with no taste and no guilt. Your mink and seal coats, you don't want to know about the blood and pain which went into making them. Your idea of war—sit in an airplane, way above the clouds, press a button, drop the bombs, and never look below the clouds—that's the odorless, guiltless, sanitized way.

When we killed a buffalo, we knew what we were doing. We apologized to his spirit, tried to make him understand why we did it, honoring with a prayer the bones of those who gave their flesh to keep us alive, praying for their return, praying for the life of our brothers, the buffalo nation, as well as for our own people. You wouldn't understand this and that's why we had the Washita

Massacre,° the Sand Creek Massacre,° the dead women and babies at Wounded Knee.° That's why we have Song My and My Lai° now.

To us life, all life, is sacred. The state of South Dakota has pest-control officers. They go up in a plane and shoot coyotes from the air. They keep track of their kills, put them all down in their little books. The stockmen and sheepowners pay them. Coyotes eat mostly rodents, field mice and such. Only once in a while will they go after a stray lamb. They are our natural garbage men cleaning up the rotten and stinking things. They make good pets if you give them a chance. But their living could lose some man a few cents, and so the coyotes are killed from the air. They were here before the sheep, but they are in the way; you can't make a profit out of them. More and more animals are dying out. The animals which the Great Spirit put here, they must go. The man-made animals are allowed to stay—at least until they are shipped out to be butchered. That terrible arrogance of the white man, making himself something more than God, more than nature, saying, "I will let this animal live, because it makes money"; saying, "This animal must go, it brings no income, the space it occupies can be used in a better way. The only good coyote is a dead coyote." They are treating coyotes almost as badly as they used to treat Indians.

You are spreading death, buying and selling death. With all your deodorants, you smell of it, but you are afraid of its reality; you don't want to face up to it. You have sanitized death, put it under the rug, robbed it of its honor. But we Indians think a lot about death. I do. Today would be a perfect day to die—not too hot, not too cool. A day to leave something of yourself behind, to let it linger. A day for a lucky man to come to the end of his trail. A happy man with many friends. Other days are not so good. They are for selfish, lonesome men, having a hard time leaving this earth. But for whites every day would be considered a bad one, I guess.

Eighty years ago our people danced the Ghost Dance, singing and dancing until they dropped from exhaustion, swooning, fainting, seeing visions. They danced in this way to bring back their dead, to bring back the buffalo. A prophet had told them that through the power of the Ghost Dance the earth would roll up like a carpet, with all the white man's works—the fences and

15

Washita Massacre: The U.S. Army, led by Lt. Col. George Custer, attacked a Cheyenne camp at Washita River, now in Oklahoma, on November 27, 1868, because the Cheyenne were resisting railroad construction.

Sand Creek Massacre: On November 29, 1864, Colorado militiamen attacked an encampment of Southern Cheyenne at Sand Creek in southeastern Colorado, killing about a third of a band of five hundred, including many women and children.

Wounded Knee: At Wounded Knee in South Dakota, Miniconjou Sioux led by Big Foot fought the Seventh U.S. Cavalry in December 1890. This battle, two weeks after Chief Sitting Bull was killed, ended the Ghost Dance war. Wounded Knee was also the site of a 1973 protest by the American Indian movement.

Song My, My Lai: My Lai was a Vietnamese hamlet, part of a village called Song My or Son My. In the most famous of the Vietnam War atrocity, American soldiers massacred several hundred Vietnamese civilians there on 16 March 1968.

the mining towns with their whorehouses, the factories and the farms with their stinking, unnatural animals, the railroads and the telegraph poles, the whole works. And underneath this rolled-up white man's world we would find again the flowering prairie, unspoiled, with its herds of buffalo and antelope, its clouds of birds, belonging to everyone, enjoyed by all.

I guess it was not time for this to happen, but it is coming back, I feel it warming my bones. Not the old Ghost Dance, not the rolling-up — but a new-old spirit, not only among Indians but among whites and blacks, too, especially among young people. It is like raindrops making a tiny brook, many brooks making a stream, many streams making one big river bursting all dams. Us making this book, talking like this — these are some of the raindrops.

Listen, I saw this in my mind not long ago: In my vision the electric light will stop sometime. It is used too much for TV and going to the moon. The day is coming when nature will stop the electricity. Police without flashlights, beer getting hot in the refrigerators, planes dropping from the sky, even the President can't call up somebody on the phone. A young man will come, or men, who'll know how to shut off all electricity. It will be painful, like giving birth. Rapings in the dark, winos breaking into the liquor stores, a lot of destruction. People are being too smart, too clever; the machine stops and they are helpless, because they have forgotten how to make do without the machine. There is a Light Man coming, bringing a new light. It will happen before this century is over. The man who has the power will do good things, too — stop all atomic power, stop wars, just by shutting the white electro-power off. I hope to see this, but then I'm also afraid. What will be will be.

I think we are moving in a circle, or maybe a spiral, going a little higher every time, but still returning to the same point. We are moving closer to nature again. I feel it, your two boys here feel it. It won't be bad, doing without many things you are now used to, things taken out of the earth and wasted foolishly. You can't replace them and they won't last forever. Then you'll have to live more according to the Indian way. People won't like that, but their children will. The machine will stop, I hope, before they make electric corncobs for poor Indians' privies.

We'll come out of our boxes and rediscover the weather. In the old days 20 you took your weather as it came, following the cranes, moving south with the herds. Here, in South Dakota, they say, "If you don't like the weather, wait five minutes." It can be 100 degrees in the shade one afternoon and suddenly there comes a storm with hailstones as big as golf balls, the prairie is all white and your teeth chatter. That's good — a reminder that you are just a small particle of nature, not so powerful as you think. . . .

But all animals have power, because the Great Spirit dwells in all of them, even a tiny ant, a butterfly, a tree, a flower, a rock. The modern, white man's way keeps that power from us, dilutes it. To come to nature, feel its power, let it help you, one needs time and patience for that. Time to think, to figure it all out. You have so little time for contemplation; it's always rush, rush, rush with you. It lessens a person's life, all that grind, that hurrying and scurrying about.

Our old people say that the Indians of long ago didn't have heart trouble. They didn't have that cancer. The illnesses they had they knew how to cure. But between 1890 and 1920 most of the medicines, the animal bundles, the pipes, the ancient, secret things which we had treasured for centuries, were lost and destroyed by the B.I.A., by the Government police. They went about tearing down sweat lodges, went into our homes, broke the pipes, tore up the medicine bags, threw them into the fire, burned them up, completely wiped out the wisdom of generations. But the Indian, you take away everything from him, he still has his mouth to pray, to sing the ancient songs. He can still do his *yuwipi* ceremony° in a darkened room, beat his small drum, make the power come back, make the wisdom return. . . .

A *hoka*—a badger—now there's a real animal. One day my uncle was on his gray horse, the one he uses to round up his other ponies with. He was riding bareback, just with a rope, a hitch around the gray's nozzle. Then he saw the badger. Once a badger is in his hole, not three or four men can drag him out. My uncle roped that *hoka,* but he couldn't pull it out. The badger was going into his hole; the rope was going in, too. Pretty soon there was the horse coming on. My uncle tried to unhitch it around the nose, but the horse's head was already too close to the hole. My uncle had to shoot the rope in two. Once a badger dips in, there isn't much you can do about it.

With the body of a dead badger, you can foretell how long you are going to live. There's a gift of prophecy in it. I knew a man called Night Chaser. He cut a dead badger open and let the blood stand there. You are supposed to see a vision in it. It's like a red looking glass, like seeing yourself in a mirror. Only you see yourself in that badger's blood as you will look when you are about to die. Three or four men were looking inside that *hoka.* I was there, too. We were all young. The first man to look said, "Boy, I'm an old man, wrinkled and white-haired, stooped, no teeth left." He was happy about it. He knew he'd live to be an old granddaddy. The second one was not so happy. "I think I'm about through," he said. "I'm looking as you see me now. I die before one of my hairs get gray!" Then it was my turn, but I didn't see anything, just the dark blood. But the two others were right. The one who had seen himself as an old man is still around. The other one died long ago, only a few months after he had looked inside that badger, just as he said, before his hair turned gray.

We use a badger's bone pizzle, his penis, for sewing, or as an awl. You polish it, make it shiny. It lasts forever. This is a good tool, so valuable that you get a good horse in exchange for it.

There are some animals, a kind of gopher, very fast, with a black line   25
down their faces. They got a lot of power; they can hypnotize you, even kill you. The power is in their eyes. They live with the prairie dogs. They are real subway users, traveling underground. They are so fast, your eyes can hardly follow them. Your eye is still here, he's already over there. They tell a funny

yuwipi **ceremony:** Sioux religious ceremony.

story about a man who wanted to get one of these creatures. He was told to be fast. Shoot it and then run like hell, grab it before it disappears into its hole. The man made up his mind to be real quick about it. He shot and ran like the dickens. Something hit him in the seat of his pants—his own bullet! The earth from a gopher hole is also very powerful. It can protect you in war, make you bullet-proof. I use it for curing certain illnesses. . . .

As for myself, the birds have something to tell me. The eagle, the owl. In an eagle there is all the wisdom of the world; that's why we have an eagle feather at the top of the pole during a *yuwipi* ceremony. If you are planning to kill an eagle, the minute you think of that he knows it, knows what you are planning. The black-tailed deer has this wisdom, too. That's why its tail is tied farther down at the *yuwipi* pole. This deer, if you shoot at him, you won't hit him. He just stands right there and the bullet comes right back and hits you. It is like somebody saying bad things about you and they come back at him.

In one of my great visions I was talking to the birds, the winged creatures. I was saddened by the death of my mother. She had held my hand and said just one word: "pitiful." I don't think she grieved for herself; she was sorry for me, a poor Indian she would leave in a white man's world. I cried up on that vision hill, cried for help, stretched out my hands toward the sky and then put the blanket over myself—that's all I had, the blanket and the pipe, and a little tobacco for an offering. I didn't know what to expect. I wanted to touch the power, feel it. I had the thought to give myself up, even if it would kill me. So I just gave myself to the winds, to nature, not giving a damn about what could happen to me.

All of a sudden I hear a big bird crying, and then quickly he hit me on the back, touched me with his spread wings. I heard the cry of an eagle, loud above the voices of many other birds. It seemed to say, "We have been waiting for you. We knew you would come. Now you are here. Your trail leads from here. Let our voices guide you. We are your friends, the feathered people, the two-legged, the four-legged, we are your friends, the creatures, little tiny ones, eight legs, twelve legs—all those who crawl on the earth. All the little creatures which fly, all those under water. The powers of each one of us we will share with you and you will have a ghost with you always—another self."

That's me, I thought, no other thing than myself, different, but me all the same, unseen, yet very real. I was frightened. I didn't understand it then. It took me a lifetime to find out.

And again I heard the voice amid the bird sounds, the clicking of beaks, 30 the squeaking and chirping. "You have love for all that has been placed on this earth, not like the love of a mother for her son, or of a son for his mother, but a bigger love which encompasses the whole earth. You are just a human being, afraid, weeping under that blanket, but there is a great space within you to be filled with that love. All of nature can fit in there." I was shivering, pulling the blanket tighter around myself, but the voices repeated themselves over and over again, calling me "Brother, brother, brother." So this is how it is with me. Sometimes I feel like the first being in one of our Indian legends. This was a giant made of earth, water, the moon and the winds. He had timber instead of hair, a whole forest of trees. He had a huge lake in his stomach and a waterfall in his crotch. I feel like this giant. All of nature is in me, and a bit of myself is in all of nature.

EXPLORING THE TEXT

1. How does Lame Deer view what he terms the "white world"? What, in his view, has the white world done to the world of nature and animals? What differences of attitude and value does he see between the white world and the world of Native Americans?

2. How, according to Lame Deer, do Native Americans view death? How does this view of death compare with the way death is viewed in white society? How accurate, in your view, is this portrayal of white cultural attitudes toward death and dying? How have these attitudes influenced white society's relation to the natural world? What other motives might underlie white views of nature?

3. How does Lame Deer view his own personal relationship to animals and the animal world? How does this relationship compare with yours?

FURTHER EXPLORATIONS

1. How might Lame Deer interpret the decline in the importance of the sense of smell in Western culture as documented by Constance Classen, David Howes, and Anthony Synott (p. 59)? Would Lame Deer likely agree with their account of why the sense of smell is no longer considered an important source of information about the world?

2. To what extent do the critiques of capitalist/consumerist culture in Mark Slouka's "Listening for Silence" (p. 50), Bill McKibben's "Television and the Twilight of the Senses" (p. 109), and/or Ellen Ullman's "Out of Time" (p. 656) support Lame Deer's view of life in white society?

3. To what extent might bell hooks (p. 237) view Lame Deer's critique of white civilization as an example of political resistance—an illustration of the way that an alternative memory of the past can be used to re-envision the future and subvert domination in the present?

4. View the documentary film *Koyaanisqatsi*, which takes its title from the Hopi for "life out of balance," and discuss the critique it offers of modern technology and urban America. To what extent would you agree with Lame Deer that technology has transformed Western civilization into a giant machine? What, if anything, can be done to make contemporary American culture less machinelike?

ESSAY OPTIONS

1. Write a personal response to the charges Lame Deer levels here against white society. To what extent would you agree, for example, that the white world has attempted to domesticate itself and the world of nature?

2. Drawing on the cross-cultural and historical examinations of selfhood presented in earlier selections by Robert Sapolsky (p. 254), Roy F. Baumeister (p. 320), and Mary Catherine Bateson (p. 337), write a paper in which you explore Lame Deer's sense of self. How closed or open are Lame Deer's ego boundaries? How rigid or flexible is his sense of his own identity? To what extent do his attitudes toward life, the senses, nature, death, and the world of animals reflect or result from his sense of self?

Why Look at Animals?

JOHN BERGER

Do you remember animals? Most urban Americans live without much direct contact with other species. You might have a dog, cat, parakeet, or goldfish at home — and you might even have been lucky enough to have taken riding lessons. But for most of us, the first encounter we have with the animal world comes through the mass media or during childhood trips to the zoo. Yet, as John Berger reminds us in this selection, when we "look at" animals in books, on television, or at the zoo, we don't really "see" them at all. According to Berger, the way that humans encounter animals has changed dramatically in the last few hundred years. In fact, in the modern postindustrial West, animals have all but "disappeared," leaving behind only their illusion — what Berger calls "animals of the mind." That's why trips to the zoo are always so boring: the very things you go to look at really aren't there to be seen. John Berger (b. 1926) is an award-winning novelist, essayist, and art critic who has published eleven novels and fifteen major collections of nonfiction along with plays, poetry, and screenplays. This selection first appeared in About Looking (1992).

BEFORE READING

Freewrite in your journal about what you recall from your childhood visits to the zoo. What do you remember most vividly about these trips to the zoo? What do you recall about the animals you saw there? What do you remember feeling or thinking about the animals you saw?

The nineteenth century, in western Europe and North America, saw the beginning of a process, today being completed by twentieth-century corporate capitalism, by which every tradition which has previously mediated between man and nature was broken. Before this rupture, animals constituted the first circle of what surrounded man. Perhaps that already suggests too great a distance. They were with man at the center of his world. Such centrality was of course economic and productive. Whatever the changes in productive means and social organization, men depended upon animals for food, work, transport, clothing.

Yet to suppose that animals first entered the human imagination as meat or leather or horn is to project a nineteenth century attitude backwards across the millenia. Animals first entered the imagination as messengers and promises. For example, the domestication of cattle did not begin as a simple prospect of milk and meat. Cattle had magical functions, sometimes oracular, sometimes sacrificial. And the choice of a given species as magical, tameable *and* alimentary was originally determined by the habits, proximity and "invitation" of the animal in question.

> White ox good is my mother
> And we the people of my sister,
> The people of Nyariau Bul . . .
> Friend, great ox of the spreading horns,
> which ever bellows amid the herd,
> Ox of the son of Bul Maloa.
>
> (*The Nuer: a description of the modes of livelihood and political institutions of a Nilotic people,* by Evans-Pritchard.)

Animals are born, are sentient and are mortal. In these things they resemble man. In their superficial anatomy—less in their deep anatomy—in their habits, in their time, in their physical capacities, they differ from man. They are both like and unlike.

> We know what animals do and what beaver and bears and salmon and other creatures need, because once our men were married to them and they acquired this knowledge from their animal wives.
>
> (Hawaiian Indians quoted by Lévi-Strauss° in *The Savage Mind.*)

The eyes of an animal when they consider a man are attentive and wary. The same animal may well look at other species in the same way. He does not reserve a special look for man. But by no other species except man will the animal's look be recognized as familiar. Other animals are held by the look. Man becomes aware of himself returning the look.

The animal scrutinizes him across a narrow abyss of noncomprehension.   5
This is why the man can surprise the animal. Yet the animal—even if domesticated—can also surprise the man. The man too is looking across a similar, but not identical, abyss of noncomprehension. And this is so wherever he looks. He is always looking across ignorance and fear. And so, when he is *being seen* by the animal, he is being seen as his surroundings are seen by him. His recognition of this is what makes the look of the animal familiar. And yet the animal is distinct, and can never be confused with man. Thus, a power is ascribed to the animal, comparable with human power but never coinciding

---

Lévi-Strauss: Claude Lévi-Straus (b. 1908), French anthropologist.

with it. The animal has secrets which, unlike the secrets of caves, mountains, seas, are specifically addressed to man.

The relation may become clearer by comparing the look of an animal with the look of another man. Between two men the two abysses are, in principle, bridged by language. Even if the encounter is hostile and no words are used (even if the two speak different languages), the *existence* of language allows that at least one of them, if not both mutually, is confirmed by the other. Language allows men to reckon with each other as with themselves. (In the confirmation made possible by language, human ignorance and fear may also be confirmed. Whereas in animals fear is a response to signal, in men it is endemic.)

No animal confirms man, either positively or negatively. The animal can be killed and eaten so that its energy is added to that which the hunter already possesses. The animal can be tamed so that it supplies and works for the peasant. But always its lack of common language, its silence, guarantees its distance, its distinctness, its exclusion, from and of man.

Just because of this distinctness, however, an animal's life, never to be confused with a man's, can be seen to run parallel to his. Only in death do the two parallel lines converge and after death, perhaps, cross over to become parallel again: hence the widespread belief in the transmigration of souls.

With their parallel lives, animals offer man a companionship which is different from any offered by human exchange. Different because it is a companionship offered to the loneliness of man as a species.

Such an unspeaking companionship was felt to be so equal that often one   10
finds the conviction that it was man who lacked the capacity to speak with animals — hence the stories and legends of exceptional beings, like Orpheus,° who could talk with animals in their own language.

What were the secrets of the animal's likeness with, and unlikeness from man? The secrets whose existence man recognized as soon as he intercepted an animal's look.

In one sense the whole of anthropology, concerned with the passage from nature to culture, is an answer to that question. But there is also a general answer. All the secrets were about animals as an *intercession* between man and his origin. Darwin's evolutionary theory,° indelibly stamped as it is with the marks of the European nineteenth century, nevertheless belongs to a tradition, almost as old as man himself. Animals interceded between man and their origin because they were both like and unlike man.

Animals came from over the horizon. They belonged *there* and *here*. Likewise they were mortal and immortal. An animal's blood flowed like human blood, but its species was undying and each lion was Lion, each ox was

Orpheus: In Greek mythology, Orpheus was a poet whose music was so beautiful that it could entrance beasts and charm trees and rivers.

Darwin's evolutionary theory: Charles Robert Darwin (1809–1882), English naturalist who theorized that humans evolved from earlier species of animals. (See p. 505, for more information.)

Ox. This—maybe the first existential dualism—was reflected in the treatment of animals. They were subjected *and* worshipped, bred *and* sacrificed.

Today the vestiges of this dualism remain among those who live intimately with, and depend upon, animals. A peasant becomes fond of his pig and is glad to salt away its pork. What is significant, and is so difficult for the urban stranger to understand, is that the two statements in that sentence are connected by an *and* and not by a *but*.

The parallelism of their similar/dissimilar lives allowed animals to provoke   15 some of the first questions and offer answers. The first subject matter for painting was animal. Probably the first paint was animal blood. Prior to that, it is not unreasonable to suppose that the first metaphor was animal. Rousseau,° in his *Essay on the Origins of Languages,* maintained that language itself began with metaphor: "As emotions were the first motives which induced man to speak, his first utterances were tropes (metaphors). Figurative language was the first to be born, proper meanings were the last to be found."

If the first metaphor was animal, it was because the essential relation between man and animal was metaphoric. Within the relation what the two terms—man and animal—shared in common revealed what differentiated them. And vice versa.

In his book on totemism,° Levi-Strauss comments on Rousseau's reasoning: "It is because man originally felt himself identical to all those like him (among which, as Rousseau explicitly says, we must include animals) that he came to acquire the capacity to distinguish *himself* as he distinguishes *them*—i.e., to use the diversity of species for conceptual support for social differentiation."

To accept Rousseau's explanation of the origins of language is, of course, to beg certain questions (what was the minimal social organization necessary for the breakthrough of language?). Yet no search for origin can ever be fully satisfied. The intercession of animals in that search was so common precisely because animals remain ambiguous.

All theories of ultimate origin are only ways of better defining what followed. Those who disagree with Rousseau are contesting a view of man, not a historical fact. What we are trying to define, because the experience is almost lost, is the universal use of animal-signs for charting the experience of the world.

Animals were seen in eight out of twelve signs of the zodiac. Among the   20 Greeks, the sign of each of the twelve hours of the day was an animal. (The first a cat, the last a crocodile.) The Hindus envisaged the earth being carried on the back of an elephant and the elephant on a tortoise. For the Nuer of the southern Sudan (see Roy Willis's *Man and Beast*),

> all creatures, including man, originally lived together in fellowship in one camp. Dissension began after Fox persuaded Mongoose to throw a club into Elephant's face. A quarrel ensued and the animals separated; each went its own way

Rousseau: Jean-Jacques Rousseau (1712–1778), French philosopher.

totemism: Belief in a magical relationship between a tribal group and an animal "ancestor."

and began to live as they now are, and to kill each other. Stomach, which at first lived a life of its own in the bush, entered into man so that now he is always hungry. The sexual organs, which had also been separate, attached themselves to men and women, causing them to desire one another constantly. Elephant taught man how to pound millet so that now he satisfies his hunger only by ceaseless labor. Mouse taught man to beget and women to bear. And Dog brought fire to man.

The examples are endless. Everywhere animals offered explanations, or more precisely, lent their name or character to a quality, which like all qualities, was, in its essence, mysterious.

What distinguished man from animals was the human capacity for symbolic thought, the capacity which was inseparable from the development of language in which words were not mere signals, but signifiers of something other than themselves. Yet the first symbols were animals. What distinguished men from animals was born of their relationship with them.

The *Iliad*° is one of the earliest texts available to us, and in it the use of metaphor still reveals the proximity of man and animal, the proximity from which metaphor itself arose. Homer describes the death of a soldier on the battlefield and then the death of a horse. Both deaths are equally transparent to Homer's eyes, there is no more refraction in one case than the other.

> Meanwhile, Indomeneus struck Erymas on the mouth with his relentless bronze. The metal point of the spear passed right through the lower part of his skull, under the brain and smashed the white bones. His teeth were shattered; both his eyes were filled with blood; and he spurted blood through his nostrils and his gaping mouth. Then the black cloud of Death descended on him.

That was a man.

Three pages further on, it is a horse who falls:

> Sarpedon, casting second with his shining spear, missed Patroclus but struck his horse Pedasus on the right shoulder. The horse whinnied in the throes of Death, then fell down in the dust and with a great sigh gave up his life.

That was animal.

Book 17 of the *Iliad* opens with Menelaus standing over the corpse of Patroclus to prevent the Trojans stripping it. Here Homer uses animals as metaphoric references, to convey, with irony or admiration, the excessive or superlative qualities of different moments. *Without the example of animals,* such moments would have remained indescribable. "Menelaus bestrode his body like a fretful mother cow standing over the first calf she has brought into the world."

The *Iliad:* Ancient Greek epic attributed to the poet Homer, celebrating the Greek siege of the city of Troy.

A Trojan threatens him, and ironically Menelaus shouts out to Zeus:

Have you ever seen such arrogance? We know the courage of the panther and
the lion and the fierce wild boar, the most high-spirited and self-reliant beast of
all, but that, it seems, is nothing to the prowess of these sons of Panthous . . . !

Menelaus then kills the Trojan who threatened him, and nobody dares approach him.

He was like a mountain lion who believes in his own strength and pounces on
the finest heifer in a grazing herd. He breaks her neck with his powerful jaws,
and then he tears her to pieces and devours her blood and entrails, while all
around him the herdsmen and their dogs create a din but keep their distance —
they are heartily scared of him and nothing would induce them to close in.

Centuries after Homer, Aristotle, in his *History of Animals,* the first major
scientific work on the subject, systematizes the comparative relation of man
and animal.

In the great majority of animals there are traces of physical qualities and attitudes,
which qualities are more markedly differentiated in the case of human beings. For
just as we pointed out resemblances in the physical organs, so in a number of animals we observe gentleness and fierceness, mildness or cross-temper, courage or
timidity, fear or confidence, high spirits or low cunning, and, with regard to intelligence, something akin to sagacity. Some of these qualities in man, as compared
with the corresponding qualities in animals, differ only quantitatively: that is to
say, man has more or less of this quality, and an animal has more or less of some
other; other qualities in man are represented by analogous and not identical qualities; for example, just as in man we find knowledge, wisdom and sagacity, so in
certain animals there exists some other natural potentiality akin to these. The
truth of this statement will be the more clearly apprehended if we have regard to
the phenomena of childhood: for in children we observe the traces and seeds of
what will one day be settled psychological habits, though psychologically a child
hardly differs for the time being from an animal. . . .

To most modern "educated" readers, this passage, I think, will seem noble
but too anthropomorphic. Gentleness, cross-temper, sagacity, they would
argue, are not moral qualities which can be ascribed to animals. And the be-
haviorists° would support this objection.

Until the nineteenth century, however, anthropomorphism was integral to   30
the relation between man and animal and was an expression of their proximity. Anthropomorphism was the residue of the continuous use of animal

---

behaviorists: Proponents of the American psychological movement of "behaviorism," which
was founded on the principle that psychology should focus solely on overt behaviors and not on
inner mental phenomena, such as intentions, feelings, or mental states.

metaphor. In the last two centuries, animals have gradually disappeared. Today we live without them. And in this new solitude, anthropomorphism makes us doubly uneasy.

The decisive theoretical break came with Descartes.° Descartes internalized, *within man,* the dualism implicit in the human relation to animals. In dividing absolutely body from soul, he bequeathed the body to the laws of physics and mechanics, and, since animals were soulless, the animal was reduced to the model of a machine.

The consequences of Descartes's break followed only slowly. A century later, the great zoologist Buffon,° although accepting and using the model of the machine in order to classify animals and their capacities, nevertheless displays a tenderness towards animals which temporarily reinstates them as companions. This tenderness is half envious.

What man has to do in order to transcend the animal, to transcend the mechanical within himself, and what his unique spirituality leads to, is often anguish. And so, by comparison and despite the model of the machine, the animal seems to him to enjoy a kind of innocence. The animal has been emptied of experience and secrets, and this new invented "innocence" begins to provoke in man a kind of nostalgia. For the first time, animals are placed in a *receding* past. Buffon, writing on the beaver, says this:

> To the same degree as man has raised himself above the state of nature, animals have fallen below it: conquered and turned into slaves, or treated as rebels and scattered by force, their societies have faded away, their industry has become unproductive, their tentative arts have disappeared; each species has lost its general qualities, all of them retaining only their distinct capacities, developed in some by example, imitation, education, and in others, by fear and necessity during the constant watch for survival. What visions and plans can these soulless slaves have, these relics of the past without power?
>
> Only vestiges of their once marvellous industry remain in far deserted places, unknown to man for centuries, where each species freely used its natural capacities and perfected them in peace within a lasting community. The beavers are perhaps the only remaining example, the last monument to that animal intelligence. . . .

Although such nostalgia towards animals was an eighteenth-century invention, countless *productive* inventions were still necessary—the railway, electricity, the conveyor belt, the canning industry, the motor car, chemical fertilizers—before animals could be marginalized.

During the twentieth century, the internal combustion engine displaced   35 draft animals in streets and factories. Cities, growing at an ever-increasing rate, transformed the surrounding countryside into suburbs where field animals,

Descartes: René Descartes (1596–1650), French philosopher. (See p. 506, for more information.)

Buffon: Comte Georges Louis Leclerc de Buffon (1707–1788), French naturalist.

wild or domesticated, became rare. The commercial exploitation of certain species (bison, tigers, reindeer) has rendered them almost extinct. Such wild life as remains is increasingly confined to national parks and game reserves.

Eventually, Descartes's model was surpassed. In the first stages of the industrial revolution, animals were used as machines. As also were children. Later, in the so-called postindustrial societies, they are treated as raw material. Animals required for food are processed like manufactured commodities.

> Another giant [plant], now under development in North Carolina, will cover a total of 150,000 hectares but will employ only one thousand people, one for every 15 hectares. Grains will be sown, nurtured and harvested by machines, including airplanes. They will be fed to the fifty thousand cattle and hogs . . . those animals will never touch the ground. They will be bred, suckled and fed to maturity in specially designed pens.
>
> (Susan George's *How the Other Half Dies.*)

This reduction of the animal, which has a theoretical as well as economic history, is part of the same process as that by which men have been reduced to isolated productive and consuming units. Indeed, during this period an approach to animals often prefigured an approach to man. The mechanical view of the animal's work capacity was later applied to that of workers. F. W. Taylor who developed the "Taylorism" of time-motion studies and "scientific" management of industry proposed that work must be "so stupid" and so phlegmatic that he (the worker) "more nearly resembles in his mental make-up the ox than any other type." Nearly all modern techniques of social conditioning were first established with animal experiments. As were also the methods of so-called intelligence testing. Today behaviorists like Skinner° imprison the very concept of man within the limits of what they conclude from their artificial tests with animals.

Is there not one way in which animals, instead of disappearing, continue to multiply? Never have there been so many household pets as are to be found today in the cities of the richest countries. In the United States, it is estimated that there are at least forty million dogs, forty million cats, fifteen million cage birds and ten million other pets.

In the past, families of all classes kept domestic animals because they served a useful purpose — guard dogs, hunting dogs, mice-killing cats, and so on. The practice of keeping animals regardless of their usefulness, the keeping, exactly, of *pets* (in the sixteenth century the word usually referred to a lamb raised by hand) is a modern innovation, and, on the social scale on which it exists today, is unique. It is part of that universal but personal withdrawal into the private small family unit, decorated or furnished with mementoes from the outside world, which is such a distinguishing feature of consumer societies.

Skinner: Burrhus Frederick Skinner (1904–1990), American psychologist and leader of the behaviorist movement.

The small family living unit lacks space, earth, other animals, seasons, 40
natural temperatures, and so on. The pet is either sterilized or sexually isolated, extremely limited in its exercise, deprived of almost all other animal
contact, and fed with artificial foods. This is the material process which lies
behind the truism that pets come to resemble their masters or mistresses. They
are creatures of their owner's way of life.

Equally important is the way the average owner regards his pet. (Children
are, briefly, somewhat different.) The pet *completes* him, offering responses to
aspects of his character which would otherwise remain unconfirmed. He can
be to his pet what he is not to anybody or anything else. Furthermore, the pet
can be conditioned to react as though it, too, recognizes this. This pet offers
its owner a mirror to a part that is otherwise never reflected. But, since in this
relationship the autonomy of both parties has been lost (the owner has become the-special-man-he-is-only-to-his-pet, and the animal has become dependent on its owner for every physical need), the parallelism of their separate
lives has been destroyed.

The cultural marginalization of animals is, of course, a more complex
process than their physical marginalization. The animals of the mind cannot
be so easily dispersed. Sayings, dreams, games, stories, superstitions, the language itself, recall them. The animals of the mind, instead of being dispersed,
have been co-opted into other categories so that the category *animal* has lost
its central importance. Mostly they have been co-opted into the *family* and
into the *spectacle*.

Those co-opted into the family somewhat resemble pets. But having no
physical needs or limitations as pets do, they can be totally transformed into
human puppets. The books and drawings of Beatrix Potter are an early example; all the animal productions of the Disney industry are a more recent
and extreme one. In such works the pettiness of current social practices is *uni-
versalized* by being projected on to the animal kingdom. The following dialogue between Donald Duck and his nephews is eloquent enough.

> DONALD: Man, what a day! What a perfect day for fishing, boating, dating or
> picnicking—only I can't do *any* of these things!
> NEPHEW: Why not, Unca Donald? What's holding you back?
> DONALD: The Bread of Life boys! As usual, I'm broke and its eons till payday.
> NEPHEW: You could take a walk Unca Donald—go birdwatching.
> DONALD: (groan!) I may *have to!* But first, I'll wait for the mailman. He may
> bring something good newswise!
> NEPHEW: Like a check from an unknown relative in Moneyville?

Their physical features apart, these animals have been absorbed into the
so-called silent majority.°

---

silent majority: Coined in Nixon's 1969 speech appealing to those with traditional conservative values to continue the Vietnam War.

The animals transformed into spectacle have disappeared in another way.   45
In the windows of bookshops at Christmas, a third of the volumes on display
are animal picture books. Baby owls or giraffes, the camera fixes them in a domain which, although entirely visible to the camera, will never be entered by
the spectator. All animals appear like fish seen through the plate glass of an
aquarium. The reasons for this are both technical and ideological: Technically
the devices used to obtain ever more arresting images—hidden cameras, tel-
escopic lenses, flashlights, remote controls and so on—combine to produce
pictures which carry with them numerous indications of their normal *invisibility*. The images exist thanks only to the existence of a technical clairvoyance.

A recent, very well-produced book of animal photographs (*La Fête
Sauvage* by Frédéric Rossif) announces in its preface: "Each of these pictures
lasted in real time less than three hundredths of a second, they are far beyond
the capacity of the human eye. What we see here is something never before
seen, because it is totally invisible."

In the accompanying ideology, animals are always the observed. The fact
that they can observe us has lost all significance. They are the objects of our
ever-extending knowledge. What we know about them is an index of our
power, and thus an index of what separates us from them. The more we know,
the further away they are. . . .

Public zoos came into existence at the beginning of the period which was to
see the disappearance of animals from daily life. The zoo to which people go
to meet animals, to observe them, to see them, is, in fact, a monument to the
impossibility of such encounters. Modern zoos are an epitaph to a relationship
which was as old as man. They are not seen as such because the wrong questions have been addressed to zoos.

When they were founded—the London Zoo in 1828, the Jardin des
Plantes in 1793, the Berlin Zoo in 1844—they brought considerable prestige
to the national capitals. The prestige was not so different from that which had
accrued to the private royal menageries. These menageries, along with gold
plate, architecture, orchestras, players, furnishings, dwarfs, acrobats, uniforms, horses, art and food, had been demonstrations of an emperor's or
king's power and wealth. Likewise in the nineteenth century, public zoos were
an endorsement of modern colonial power. The capturing of the animals was
a symbolic representation of the conquest of all distant and exotic lands.
"Explorers" proved their patriotism by sending home a tiger or an elephant.
The gift of an exotic animal to the metropolitan zoo became a token in sub-
servient diplomatic relations.

Yet, like every other nineteenth-century public institution, the zoo, how-   50
ever supportive of the ideology of imperialism, had to claim an independent
and civic function. The claim was that it was another kind of museum, whose
purpose was to further knowledge and public enlightenment. And so the first
questions asked of zoos belonged to natural history; it was then thought possible to study the natural life of animals even in such unnatural conditions. A

century later, more sophisticated zoologists such as Konrad Lorenz° asked behavioristic and ethological questions, the claimed purpose of which was to discover more about the springs of human action through the study of animals under experimental conditions.

Meanwhile, millions visited the zoos each year out of a curiosity which was both so large, so vague, and so personal that it is hard to express in a single-question. Today in France 22 million people visit the two hundred zoos each year. A high proportion of the visitors were and are children.

Children in the industrialized world are surrounded by animal imagery: toys, cartoons, pictures, decorations of every sort. No other source of imagery can begin to compete with that of animals. The apparently spontaneous interest that children have in animals might lead one to suppose that this has always been the case. Certainly some of the earliest toys (when toys were unknown to the vast majority of the population) were animal. Equally, children's games, all over the world, include real or pretend animals. Yet it was not until the nineteenth century that reproductions of animals became a regular part of the decor of middle-class childhoods—and then, in this century, with the advent of vast display and selling systems like Disney's—of all childhoods.

In the preceding centuries, the proportion of toys which were animal was small. And these did not pretend to realism, but were symbolic. The difference was that between a traditional hobby horse and a rocking horse: the first was merely a stick with a rudimentary head which children rode like a broom handle: the second was an elaborate "reproduction" of a horse, painted realistically, with real reins of leather, a real mane of hair, and designed movement to resemble that of a horse galloping. The rocking horse was a nineteenth-century invention.

This new demand for verisimiltude in animal toys led to different methods of manufacture. The first stuffed animals were produced, and the most expensive were covered with real animal skin—usually the skin of still-born calves. The same period saw the appearance of soft animals—bears, tigers, rabbits—such as children take to bed with them. Thus the manufacture of realistic animal toys coincides, more or less, with the establishment of public zoos.

The family visit to the zoo is often a more sentimental occasion than a   55
visit to a fair or a football match. Adults take children to the zoo to show them the originals of their "reproductions," and also perhaps in the hope of refinding some of the innocence of that reproduced animal world which they remember from their own childhood.

The animals seldom live up to the adults' memories, while to the children they appear, for the most part, unexpectedly lethargic and dull. (As frequent as the calls of animals in a zoo, are the cries of children demanding: Where is he? Why doesn't he move? Is he dead?) And so one might summarize the felt, but not necessarily expressed question of most visitors as: Why are these animals less than I believed?

Konrad Lorenz: (1903–1989), German ethologist.

And this unprofessional, unexpressed question is the one worth answering.

A zoo is a place where as many species and varieties of animal as possible are collected in order that they can be seen, observed, studied. In principle, each cage is a frame round the animal inside it. Visitors visit the zoo to look at animals. They proceed from cage to cage, not unlike visitors in an art gallery who stop in front of one painting, and then move on to the next or the one after next. Yet in the zoo the view is always wrong. Like an image out of focus. One is so accustomed to this that one scarcely notices it any more; or, rather, the apology habitually anticipates the disappointment, so that the latter is not felt. And the apology runs like this: What do you expect? It's not a dead object you have come to look at, it's alive. It's leading its own life. Why should this coincide with its being properly visible? Yet the reasoning of this apology is inadequate. The truth is more startling.

However you look at these animals, even if the animal is up against the bars, less than a foot from you, looking outwards in the public direction, *you are looking at something that has been rendered absolutely marginal;* and all the concentration you can muster will never be enough to centralize it. Why is this?

Within limits, the animals are free, but both they themselves, and their 60 spectators, presume on their close confinement. The visibility through the glass, the spaces between the bars, or the empty air above the moat, are not what they seem — if they were, then everything would be changed. Thus visibility, space, air, have been reduced to tokens.

The decor, accepting these elements as tokens, sometimes reproduces them to create pure illusion — as in the case of painted prairies or painted rock pools at the back of the boxes for small animals. Sometimes it merely adds further tokens to suggest something of the animal's original landscape — the dead branches of a tree for monkeys, artificial rocks for bears, pebbles and shallow water for crocodiles. These added tokens serve two distinct purposes: for the spectator they are like theater props: for the animal they constitute the bare minimum of an environment in which they can physically exist.

The animals, isolated from each other and without interaction between species, have become utterly dependent upon their keepers. Consequently most of their responses have been changed. What was central to their interest has been replaced by a passive waiting for a series of arbitrary outside interventions. The events they perceive occurring around them have become as illusory in terms of their natural responses, as the painted prairies. At the same time this very isolation (usually) guarantees their longevity as specimens and facilitates their taxonomic arrangement.

All this is what makes them marginal. The space which they inhabit is artificial. Hence their tendency to bundle towards the edge of it. (Beyond its edges there may be real space.) In some cages the light is equally artificial. In all cases the environment is illusory. Nothing surrounds them except their own lethargy or hyperactivity. They have nothing to act upon — except, briefly, supplied food and — very occasionally — a supplied mate. (Hence their perennial actions become marginal actions without an object.) Lastly, their dependence and isolation have so conditioned their responses that they treat any event which takes place around them—usually it is in front of them, where the public is—as marginal. (Hence their assumption of an otherwise exclusively human attitude—indifference.)

Zoos, realistic animal toys and the widespread commercial diffusion of animal imagery, all began as animals started to be withdrawn from daily life. One could suppose that such innovations were compensatory. Yet in reality the innovations themselves belonged to the same remorseless movement as was dispersing the animals. The zoos, with their theatrical decor for display, were in fact demonstrations of how animals had been rendered absolutely marginal. The realistic toys increased the demand for the new animal puppet: the urban pet. The reproduction of animals in images—as their biological reproduction in birth becomes a rarer and rarer sight—was competitively forced to make animals ever more exotic and remote.

Everywhere animals disappear. In zoos they constitute the living monument to their own disappearance. And in doing so, they provoked their last metaphor. *The Naked Ape, The Human Zoo,* are titles of world bestsellers. In these books the zoologist, Desmond Morris, proposes that the unnatural behavior of animals in captivity can help us to understand, accept and overcome the stresses involved in living in consumer societies.

All sites of enforced marginalization—ghettos, shanty towns, prisons, madhouses, concentration camps—have something in common with zoos. But it is both too easy and too evasive to use the zoo as a symbol. The zoo is a demonstration of the relations between man and animals; nothing else. The marginalization of animals is today being followed by the marginalization and disposal of the only class who, throughout history, has remained familiar with animals and maintained the wisdom which accompanies that familiarity: the middle and small peasant. The basis of this wisdom is an acceptance of the dualism at the very origin of the relation between man and animal. The rejection of this dualism is probably an important factor in opening the way to modern totalitarianism. But I do not wish to go beyond the limits of that unprofessional, unexpressed but fundamental question asked of the zoo.

The zoo cannot but disappoint. The public purpose of zoos is to offer visitors the opportunity of looking at animals. Yet nowhere in a zoo can a stranger encounter the look of an animal. At the most, the animal's gaze flickers and passes on. They look sideways. They look blindly beyond. They scan mechanically. They have been immunized to encounter, because nothing can any more occupy a *central* place in their attention.

Therein lies the ultimate consequence of their marginalization. That look between animal and man, which may have played a crucial role in the development of human society, and with which, in any case, all men had always lived until less than a century ago, has been extinguished. Looking at each animal, the unaccompanied zoo visitor is alone. As for the crowds, they belong to a species which has at last been isolated.

This historic loss, to which zoos are a monument, is now irredeemable for the culture of capitalism.

EXPLORING THE TEXT

1. How, according to Berger, did humans view animals before the rise of corporate capitalism? What special meaning did animals once have for human beings and what role did animals play in human development? What does Berger mean when he says that an "existential dualism" once typified human attitudes toward animals?

2. What is "anthropomorphism," and what role did it play in human/animal relationships prior to the nineteenth century? What role did the philosophy of René Descartes play in the end of anthropomorphism? How have human views of animals changed, according to Berger, since the beginning of the industrial revolution? Why have such changes occurred?

3. What is Berger's view of pets? What social functions does he see them fulfilling? To what extent would you agree with his assessment of the role that pets play in contemporary society?

4. What are "animals of the mind," as Berger refers to them? How do these imaginary creatures contribute to what he terms the "cultural marginalization" of animals? What do you think Berger means when he says that the more we know about animals, "the further away they are"?

5. How does Berger view the institution of the zoo? What functions do zoos perform, from his perspective? Why does he feel that zoos must always "disappoint"? To what extent would you agree that zoos, pets, cartoon animals, and realistic animal toys are all pure "illusions"? Illusions of what?

6. Overall, what has been lost in human/animal interrelations over the last few hundred years? What, in Berger's view, does this loss suggest about the condition of the human species at the end of the twentieth century? How would you describe the tone of the closing paragraphs of Berger's essay?

FURTHER EXPLORATIONS

1. Visit your local zoo to test Berger's claims about how zoos marginalize animals. To what extent would you agree that animals in zoos are "lethargic and dull" or that they are displayed in ways that emphasize their remoteness or exoticness? Would you agree that animals in zoos have been reduced to the level of "theater props" (para. 61) or parts of an "illusion"? Why or why not? What illusions, if any, are zoos trying to convey?

2. Compare Berger's notion of the marginalization of animals in the twentieth century with John (Fire) Lame Deer's view of how animals and nature have changed under the influence of white civilization (p. 512). How do Berger and Lame Deer explain recent changes in human/animal relationships? Which of these explanations strikes you as the most plausible? Why?

3. To what extent does Faith McNulty's relationship with her pet mouse (p. 535) illustrate or complicate Berger's views on pets and pet keeping? How might Berger

interpret McNulty's responses to her pet mouse? How might McNulty respond to Berger's interpretations of the meanings and functions of pets in contemporary households?

4. Working independently or in small groups, collect images from magazines, comic books, and other pop-culture sources to make a collage of what Berger calls "animals of the mind" (para. 42). What human characteristics and qualities are associated with these images? What messages do these imaginary animals convey about animal minds, nature, and wilderness?

ESSAY OPTIONS

1. Using Berger's "Why Look at Animals?" as a point of departure, write an essay in which you assess the function of the zoo as an institution. Why do zoos exist? What social, cultural, and educational functions do they perform? Have zoos, in fact, outlived their function? Why or why not?

2. Drawing on your knowledge of popular culture, write an essay exploring Berger's concept of "animals of the mind" in contemporary American society. How are animals typically portrayed in pop culture? To what extent are they associated with a kind of "innocence," as Berger suggests in this selection? Why do you think animals have come to be seen in this light?

3. Drawing on your own experiences as well as on ideas expressed by John Berger, Bill McKibben (p. 109), Walker Percy (p. 118), and John (Fire) Lame Deer (p. 512), write an essay in which you explore current attitudes toward animals and nature in American society. Would you agree that we are losing the ability to understand or relate to genuine wildness? That we are losing touch with the wildness that once existed in ourselves? Why or why not?

Mouse

FAITH McNULTY

"What Is It Like to Be a Bat?" is the provocative title of a 1974 essay by philosopher Thomas Nagel. Nagel's now-famous response to this question was simply that we, as humans, can never possibly know. According to Nagel, we can never comprehend the feelings, motives, or desires of a bat, because we have no way of relating to a consciousness so bizarrely different from our own. The world of "batness," according to Nagel, is beyond human grasp. In this selection, by contrast, Faith McNulty holds out some hope that we can at least enter into the mind of a close relative. The wild field mouse that McNulty took into her home for several years opened up a new world to her—the world of another, independent mind, with its own comprehensible desires, fears, and intentions. McNulty's reminiscence on her relationship with "Mouse" offers an example of how we can use the power of mind reading to gain insight into radically other forms of consciousness. Faith McNulty (b. 1918) made her debut as a wildlife reporter in 1964 when she published this essay in *Audubon Magazine*. Since then, her reflections on animal life have been featured in the *New Yorker* and published in *The Wildlife Stories of Faith McNulty* (1980). She is also the author of a number of children's books, many of them dealing with animals and animal themes.

BEFORE READING

Working in your journal, brainstorm a list of reasons why people keep pets. Once you're done, compare your lists in small groups and see if you can draw any conclusions about the motives that underlie pet ownership — or about the relationships that develop between pets and their owners.

On a sunny morning in early September my husband called me out to the barn of our Rhode Island farm. I found him holding a tin can and peering into it with an expression of foolish pleasure. He handed me the can as though it contained something he had just picked up at Tiffany's. Crouched at the bottom was a young mouse, not much bigger than a bumblebee. It stared up with eyes like polished seeds. Its long whiskers vibrated like a hummingbird's wings. It was a beautiful little creature and clearly still too small to cope with a wide and dangerous world.

I don't know how old Mouse was when Richard found her, but I doubt it was a fortnight. She was not only tiny, but weak. He told me he had found her on the doorstep and that when he picked her up he thought she was done for. By chance he had a gumdrop in his pocket. He placed it on his palm beside the limp mouse. The smell acted as a quick stimulant. She struggled to her feet and flung herself upon the gumdrop, ate voraciously, and was almost instantly restored to health.

Richard made a wire cage for Mouse (we never found a name more fitting), and we made a place for it on a table in the kitchen. Here I could watch her while I was peeling vegetables but I found that I often simply watched while uncounted minutes went by. I had had no idea that there were so many things to notice about a mouse.

For the first few days Mouse had the gawkiness of a puppy. Her head and feet looked too big. Her hind legs had a tendency to spraddle. But she had fine sharp teeth and a striking air of manful competence. She cleaned herself, all over, with serious pride. Her method was oddly catlike. Sitting on her small behind (she could have sat on a postage stamp without spilling over), she licked her flanks, then moistened her paws to go over her ears, neck, and face. She would grasp a hind leg with suddenly simian hands while she licked the extended toes. For the finale she would pick up her tail, and as though eating corn on the cob, wash its inch and a half of threadlike length with her tongue.

Mouse's baby coat was dull gunmetal gray. It soon changed to a bright 5 reddish brown. Her belly remained white. She had dark gray anklets and white feet. I had thought of mouse tails as hairless and limp. Not so. Mouse's tail was furred, and rather than trailing it behind her like a piece of string, she held it quite stiffly. Sometimes it rose over her back like a quivering question mark.

When Mouse's coat turned red I was able to identify her from a book—*The Mammals of Rhode Island*—which said that although *leucopus,* or white-footed mice, are easily confused with *maniculatus,* or deer mice, there are only *leucopus* in Rhode Island. The book also said that white-footed mice are found everywhere, from hollow trees to bureau drawers; that they are nocturnal and a favorite food of owls. Judging by Mouse's enthusiasm for chicken, owl, if she could get it, would be one of *her* favorite foods. Her range of taste was wide. Though grains were a staple, she liked meat, fruit, and vegetables. I usually offered her a tiny bit of whatever was on the chopping board. She tasted and considered each item, rejecting some and seizing others with delight. A melon seed was a great prize. To this day, when I throw melon seeds in the garbage I feel sad to waste them and wish I had a mouse to give them to.

Mouse became tame within a few days of her capture. She nibbled my fingers and batted them with her paws like a playful puppy. She liked to be stroked. If I held her in my hand and rubbed gently with a forefinger, she would raise her chin, the way a cat will, to be stroked along the jawbone, then raise a foreleg and wind up lying flat on her back in the palm of my hand, eyes closed, paws hanging limp, and nose pointed upward in apparent bliss.

Mouse could distinguish people. If, when she was asleep, I poked my finger into her nest, she licked and nibbled it as though grooming it. If my husband offered his finger, she would sniff it and then give it a firm little bite accompanied by an indignant chirp. When, for a time, she was in my sister's care, she accepted my sister but bit anyone else. In one respect, however, she never trusted even me. She suspected me of intending to steal her food. If I approached while she was eating she assumed a protective crouch. I think she was uttering tiny ultrasonic growls.

When I looked up scientific studies of mice I was disappointed to find that most investigators had been interested, not in the mice, but in using them as a tool to study something related to human physiology. In one paper, however, I read that "in mice the rate of defecation and urination is an index of emotionality." Dedicated scientists had spent days harassing mice and counting the resultant hail of tiny turds. I had assumed that mice have no control over these functions; an inference based on the careless behavior of certain anonymous mice that sometimes visited my kitchen shelves. When I handled Mouse, however, nothing of the sort ever happened. It could not have been sheer luck. She must have exercised some restraint.

I was surprised by still other aspects of Mouse's behavior. She was a heavy   10
sleeper. She slept in a plastic cup from a thermos, covering herself with a bedding of rags that she shredded into fluff as soft as a down quilt. If I pushed aside the covers I would find her curled up on her side like a doughnut, dead to the world. As I touched her, her eyes would open. Then she would raise her chin, stretch herself, and yawn enormously, showing four wicked front teeth and a red tongue that curled like a wolf's. She would rise slowly, carefully

stretching her hind legs and long toes, then suddenly pull herself together, fan out her whiskers, and be ready for anything. Her athletic ability was astounding. As she climbed around her cage she became incredibly flexible, stretching this way and that like a rubber band. She could easily stand on her hind legs to reach something dangled above her. Her jumping power was tremendous. Once I put her in an empty garbage pail while I cleaned her cage. She made a straight-upward leap of fifteen inches and neatly cleared the rim.

Mouse's cage was equipped with an exercise wheel, on which she traveled many a league to nowhere. Richard and I racked our brains for a way to utilize "one mouse-power." Her cage was also furnished with twigs that served as a perch. After a while I replaced her plastic cup with half a coconut shell, inverted and with a door cut in the lower edge. It made a most attractive mouse house; quite tropical in feeling. She stuffed her house from floor to ceiling with fluff. She kept some food in the house, but her major storehouse was a small aluminum can screwed to the wall of the cage. We called it (and beg the generous reader to forgive the cuteness), the First Mouse National Bank. If I sprinkled birdseed on the floor of her cage, Mouse would work diligently to transport it, stuffed in her cheeks, for deposit in her bank.

Mouse was full of curiosity and eager to explore. When I opened the door of her cage she ran about the tabletop in short bursts of motion, looking, somehow, as though she were on roller skates. I feared she might skate right over the edge of the table, but she always managed to stop in time. All objects she met — books, pencils, ashtrays, rubber bands, and such odds and ends — were subjected to a taste test. If a thing was portable, a pencil for instance, she might haul it a short way. Her attention was brief; a quick nibble and on to the next. One day she encountered a chicken bone. She grabbed it in her teeth and began to tug. As she danced around, pulling and hauling, she looked like a terrier struggling to retrieve the thighbone of an elephant. Alas, the task was too great. She had to settle for a fragment of meat and leave the bone behind.

What fascinated me most was Mouse's manual dexterity. Her front paws had four long fingers and a rudimentary thumb. She used them to hold, to manipulate, and to stuff things into her mouth for carrying. Her paws were equally equipped for climbing. They had small projections, like the calluses inside a man's hand, that helped her to cling, fly fashion, to vertical surfaces.

Though Mouse kept busy, I feared her life might be warped by loneliness and asked a biologist I knew for help. He not only determined Mouse's sex (this is not easy; to the layman the rear end of a mouse is quite enigmatic) but provided a laboratory mouse as a companion.

I found the new mouse unattractive. He had a mousy smell, whereas Mouse was odorless; I named him Stinky. His coat was like dusty black felt. He was careless about grooming. He had small, squinty eyes, a Roman nose, a fat-hipped, lumpy shape, and a ratty, hairless tail. Nature would not have been likely to create such a mouse without the help of man. With some misgivings I put him in Mouse's cage. She mounted to the top of her perch and sat shivering and staring, ears cocked so that her face looked like that of a little red fox.

Stinky lumbered about the cage, squinting at nothing in particular. Stumbling over some of Mouse's seeds, he made an enthusiastic buck-toothed attack on these goodies. This stirred Mouse to action. She flashed down the branch and, cautiously approaching from the rear, nibbled Stinky's tail. He paid no heed, but continued to gobble up whatever he found. Mouse nibbled him more boldly, working up from his tail to the fur of his back. I began to fear she would depilate him before he realized it. Finally she climbed on his back and nibbled his ears. He showed a certain baffled resistance, but made no other response. Disgusted, Mouse ate a few seeds and went to bed.

From this unpromising start a warm attachment bloomed. The two mice slept curled up together. Mouse spent a great deal of time licking Stinky, holding him down and kneading him with her paws. He returned her caresses, but with less ardor, reserving his more passionate interest for food. Food was a source of strife. In a contest Stinky was domineering but dumb. Mouse was quick and clever.

Stinky's greed prompted Richard to fashion Mouse's bank, tailoring the opening to fit her slim figure and exclude Stinky's chubby one—or at least most of it. He could get his head and shoulders inside, but not his fat belly. Richard fastened the bank near the top of the cage. When stinky got his head in, his hind part was left dangling helplessly, and he soon gave up attempts at robbery.

One day, as an experiment, I put the bank down on the floor of the cage. Stinky sniffed at the opening. Mouse watched, whiskers quivering, and I had the distinct impression of consternation on her face. With a quickness of decision that amazed me, she seized a wad of bedding, dragged it across the floor of the cage, and stuffed it into the door of the bank, effectively corking up her treasure. It was a brilliant move. Baffled, Stinky lumbered away.

In spite of their ungenerous behavior toward each other, I felt that Stinky made a real contribution to Mouse's happiness. Once or twice I separated them for a day or so. Their reunions were joyous, with Mouse scrambling all over Stinky and just about licking him to pieces, and even stolid Stinky showing excitement. They lived together for about a year. I wasn't aware that Stinky was ill, but one day I saw Mouse sitting trembling on her branch when she should have been asleep. I looked in the cup and found Stinky stone-cold dead. "Mouse will miss you," I thought as I heaved his crummy little body into the weeds. I got another laboratory mouse called Pinky to take Stinky's place, but he bullied Mouse so relentlessly that I sent him back. Mouse lived alone for the rest of her days.

Before closing Mouse's story I would like to tell about an episode that took place in Mouse's first weeks with me. After I had had her about ten days I found a lump on her belly near the hind leg. I first noticed it as she lay on her back in my palm while I stroked her. The lump grew larger each day and I feared she had some fatal disease—a tumor of some sort. During the ensuing search for help for Mouse I discovered a peculiar fact about human nature; for some reason people laugh at a mouse.

I live near the University of Rhode Island. I phoned and said I wanted to talk to an expert on mice. The response was laughter. I said my mouse had a mysterious ailment. More laughter, but I was given the name of a woman, Dr. C., I'll call her. Carrying Mouse in her cage, I found the professor in her office. I explained my trouble. When Dr. C. stopped laughing she said she couldn't touch my mouse lest it have germs that would contaminate her laboratory mice. She suggested I ask Dr. H. to examine Mouse. We went to his office. Dr. H. chuckled patronizingly and agreed to look at Mouse's lump. I took her out of her cage and held her belly up for inspection. Both professors gasped at the sight of the lump. Both were baffled.

Dr. H. offered a shot of penicillin, but admitted he had no idea how to measure a dose for a patient weighing half an ounce. Dr. C. forthrightly suggested autopsy. I thanked them and left. Crossing the campus, I passed the library. On an impulse I borrowed a manual of veterinary medicine and took it home.

That evening I skimmed through descriptions of disease after disease looking for symptoms that might fit. Nothing sounded similar to Mouse's trouble until I came to "Cuterebra Infestation" on page 929 and knew I had found the answer. The larva of the botfly, the manual said, lives in a pocket that it forms under the skin of its host, which may be any mammal, most often young. When the parasite reaches full size it emerges through the skin. The manual said that the cure was a simple matter of opening the lump and removing the larva. I hurried to the telephone and dialed a local veterinarian. His wife answered and insisted that I give her the message. Foreseeing difficulty, I replied evasively, "I have an animal that needs a slight operation."

"What kind of animal?" persisted Mrs. Vet.   25

"A mouse."

There was a long, cold silence. Then the woman asked, in icy tones, "Is it a *white* mouse?"

"No," I admitted. "It is brown."

Mrs. Vet said that her husband did not include mice in his practice and hung up.

The next day my young son hit his toe a glancing blow with an ax while   30
chopping wood, inflicting a wound that needed stitches. As it happened, I had been just about to take Mouse to our local animal shelter for further consultation. She and her cage were in the car as I drove my son to the emergency room at the hospital. While he was being stitched a plan formed in my mind.

The moment John limped out of the operating room I buttonholed the young doctor, a nice soap opera type. I told him I had a mouse that needed surgery. He laughed. With his eye on some pretty nurses standing nearby, he made jokes about calling in the anesthetist, scrubbing up, and so on. The nurses giggled and my cause was won. "Don't go away," I cried, and ran out to get Mouse.

When I got back the doctor had the sheepish look of a man who has been trapped by his own jest, but when he saw Mouse's problem his eyes widened with pure scientific amazement. He studied the lump. We gravely discussed the operating procedure. I held Mouse tightly, on her back, in the palm of my hand. A nurse applied a dab of antiseptic. The doctor made a small incision. Mouse squeaked, but there was no blood. The doctor called for forceps and pulled forth a big, horrible, wiggling grub. There was a babble of astonishment, congratulations, and, inevitably, laughter from the crowd that had gathered around us. The doctor looked pleased and put the grub in a bottle of alcohol as a medical curiosity.

I put Mouse in her cage. She ran about lightly, showing no ill effects. I took her and my limping son home. Both patients healed quickly. I paid a large bill for John's toe, but there was no charge for the mouse.

Mouse lived with me for over three years, which is, I believe, a good deal beyond the span usually allotted to mice. She showed no sign of growing old or feeble, but one day I found her dead. As I took her almost weightless body in my hand and carried it out to the meadow, I felt a genuine sadness. In a serious sense she had given me so much. She had stirred my imagination and opened a window on a Lilliputian world no less real than my world for all its miniature dimensions. By watching her I had learned and changed. Beyond that there had been moments, elusive of description, when I had felt a contact between her tiny being and my own. Sometimes when I touched her lovingly and she nibbled my fingers in return, I felt as though an affectionate message were passing between us. The enormous distance between us seemed to be bridged momentarily by faint but perceptible signals.

I put Mouse's body down in the grass and walked back to the house. I   35
knew that there may be as many mice as there are visible stars. They are given life and extinguished as prodigally as leaves unfolding and falling from trees. I was not sad for Mouse because of her death, but sad for me because I knew I would miss her.

EXPLORING THE TEXT

1. What details does McNulty note about Mouse's physical appearance and behavior? What do these details suggest about her attitudes toward Mouse and her estimation of her intelligence?

2. How does McNulty "read" or interpret Mouse's desires and motivations? Do you think she unnecessarily anthropomorphizes her pet and overestimates her intelligence? Why or why not?

3. What do other people think of McNulty's pet mouse? Why do they feel this way? What does McNulty feel she gained as the result of her relationship with Mouse? What qualities does McNulty seem to possess that allow her to discover such meaning in a relationship with a mouse?

FURTHER EXPLORATIONS

1. How does McNulty's relationship with Mouse confirm or challenge Berger's assessment of the role of pets in contemporary culture (p. 521)? To what extent does
   McNulty "idealize" Mouse's behavior? Would you agree that Mouse fulfills some
   unrecognized "need" in McNulty's life—or that Mouse, as McNulty understands
   her, is just another example of Berger's "animals of the mind"? Why or why not?

2. In what ways does McNulty's relationship with Mouse complicate John (Fire)
   Lame Deer's assessment of the white world's impact on animals and nature
   (p. 512)? To what extent does she exhibit the kind of "arrogance" that Lame Deer
   associates with white attitudes toward the natural world? In what ways does she
   depart from such attitudes?

3. How might Martha C. Nussbaum (p. 416) view McNulty's interpretations of
   Mouse's behavior, motives, and feelings? As a pet, is Mouse more than simply a means
   for nurturing McNulty's imaginative or empathetic faculties? Why or why not?

4. Keeping Deborah Blum's analysis of male and female attitudes toward emotion
   and relationship in mind (p. 453), how might you account for the difference between McNulty's reaction to Mouse and the reactions of the doctors she consults
   for help with Mouse's ailment?

ESSAY OPTIONS

1. Write a detailed profile of an animal you have known well, roughly in the style of
   McNulty's essay, which presents your assessment of the animal's intellectual and
   emotional capacities. Support your assessment of the qualities you associate with
   your subject by offering specific examples of the animal's behavior, as McNulty
   does for Mouse. Based on your observations, how would you assess this animal's
   level of intelligence?

2. Drawing on ideas and experiences presented by McNulty, John (Fire) Lame Deer
   (p. 512), and John Berger (p. 521), write an essay debating the pros and cons of
   pet ownership. What motives lead people to keep pets? Is pet keeping an expression of human dominance or a kind of "compensation" for lost relationships?
   What positive values or benefits might be associated with pet keeping?

The Artifice of the Natural

CHARLES SIEBERT

It's a hot, sunny day in the semitropics. The sky is azure blue and the grass waves lush and
green in the wind as animals gather around a waterhole in the middle of an open stretch
of land. Suddenly, a predator appears on the edge of the clearing, and a dubbed-in
voice, muffled to an unnecessary whisper, informs us that "having gone for days without
a kill for her cubs, the female cheetah prepares to play her part in the never-ending
struggle for survival. . . ." It's a story that's almost as old as television itself. TV has always

been attracted to stories about animals. For generations, television "naturalists" have tramped into the "outback" and endured all sorts of hardships to bring us incredible close-ups of animal assaults and matings. But does television animal programming actually get us any closer to the reality of animal life and the working of animal minds? Not according to the author of this selection. As seen by Charles Siebert, television warps our view of animals, making them seem more like actors in an "opera" than real creatures in the wild. Siebert (b. 1938) is a poet, essayist, and journalist who lives in Brooklyn, New York. He is the author of *Wickerby: An Urban Pastoral* (1998) and *Angus: A Memoir* (2000), an "autobiography" written from the perspective of his dog. His poems, essays, and other articles have appeared in the *New Yorker, Harper's Magazine, New York Times Magazine, Esquire,* and *Outside.* This essay originally appeared in *Harper's Magazine.*

BEFORE READING

Compare notes with your classmates on the nature shows you've seen on television. What does nature programming tend to focus on? What kinds of animal activities or encounters does it highlight? What impressions does television convey about animals, nature, and life in the wilderness?

I t's a Sunday evening, just after eight o'clock, and my TV screen is filled with elephant seals. They crowd the beaches of a small Pacific island called Año Nuevo. There was lighthearted Latin music as the show began, followed by a dizzying montage of the wildlife that yearly inhabits the island; then the cameras settled on the show's subject—huge, gelatinous mammals that spend most of their life slipping seamlessly through open seas but whose existence on land looks to be a self-contained Sisyphean nightmare:° endless, exhaustive heavings of themselves back and forth across the sand. Of course, their life on land is nothing of the kind. Yet we can neither depict nor look upon beached seals without somehow articulating the ache that their limbless listing induces in us. They don't, as far as anyone knows, have a constant inner aria of grounded-seal woes playing in their brain. That is playing now in mine, as it no doubt played in the minds of those who made this film. TV nature shows are, above all else, extravagant animal opera, dramatizing, scoring, voicing in human terms the vast backdrop of inhuman action. Tonight's show is entitled *Elephant Seals: Those Magnificent Diving Machines.* "They look helpless, primitive, even absurd," the narrator, PBS's° George Page, intones to a shot of two beached, floppy-nosed elephant-seal bulls butting heads, "but they're precisely shaped for . . . life in the ocean. We humans, marooned in air, can only catch brief glimpses of that underwater world."

Sisyphean nightmare: In Greek mythology, Sisyphus was condemned by the gods to roll a huge rock uphill every day, only to have the rock roll back down every night; hence, any pointless task requiring extraordinary effort.

PBS's: PBS stands for the Public Broadcasting Service.

At the moment, I'm "marooned" six floors in the air in the living room of my Brooklyn, New York, apartment. At the opposite end of the sofa is my dog, Lucy. It's a clear, mild, late-autumn evening. Out my window I can see the tiered building lights of Manhattan, jet planes sliding past the highest towers, and, when I look down, directly below me, Lincoln Place, quiet for such a warm evening, none of the usual clamor coming from the stoop of the crackhouse brownstone with the chained sapling out front, every inch of its branches covered with blinking Christmas lights. Brooklyn is where I do the bulk of my nature-show viewing. The rest I do in a log cabin in the Canadian woods. It may seem a redundancy watching nature on TV while passing days — actually, months — each year, mostly alone, in the midst of what is commonly considered to be the natural world. But the two places — actual and televised nature — have little to do with each other. The woods are so wide, old, and slow as to be dismissive of me and the names I know and what I might wish and wait to see. The show, by contrast, is rapid, focused, and framed, a potent distillation of someone else's waiting designed precisely for me.

In fact, nature shows are much more like cities, both entities being elaborate human constructs: fast-paced, multistoried, and artificially lit. And both entities are, in turn, having an increasing influence on the way we view nature. Living in cities, watching our TVs, we have come to see nature not so much as that inscrutable place; that living, visitable gradualness with which, in the traditional romantic and transcendentalist conception,° we try to merge by abandoning our will and gauging our senses down to it; that spiritually infused world, as Wordsworth° wrote, "Of eye, and ear, both what they half create, / And what perceive." Today, the natural world is for us a place of reticent and reticular wonders that command our coaxing, our active exposure and editing; a world made up of what we half create and what, even when we're there, we fully expect to see.

On the beaches of Año Nuevo now there's sexual mayhem: bulls mounting everything in sight, charging at interlopers, crushing mothers and nursing pups along the way. Suddenly, a storm hits. Waves pound the beach, dragging newborns far out to sea. "This pup," Page says as I watch a baby seal slipping under and then an adult onshore looking seaward, "drowns before his mother's eyes." Nature shows always do this, the old war- and horror-movie technique of getting you attached to the minor characters — in this instance, via countless mother/pup nuzzling and nursing scenes — so that you'll feel more deeply the pain of their loss. Now there's an overview shot of seal-strewn waves breaking softly against the shore in the storm's aftermath: "What the

---

the traditional romantic and transcendentalist conception: In romantic philosophy, nature is typically seen as a sacred or powerful realm closely associated with the mystery of creation and opposed to the world of human activity. In American transcendentalism, a form of romanticism, nature is viewed as being allied with spiritual truth.

Wordsworth: William Wordsworth (1770–1850), English romantic poet famed for his meditative depictions of nature.

waves take," says our narrator, "the waves return, rolling the dead up the beach to the waiting gulls."

There's an implicit unnaturalness in our watching of nature shows: we are, at once, ensconced in our day and tuned into *theirs,* that of the wild animals. There's something vaguely illicit about it to me, and, my guess is, to many among the millions of us who tune in each week. We ask ourselves questions, what I call my questions of stasis, after the poet Elizabeth Bishop's famous "Questions of Travel": "Should we," she asks from afar, "have stayed at home and thought of here? . . . Is it right to be watching strangers in a play / in this strangest of theaters?" And should we, I wonder, be making shows of them at all, and am I right to just sit here at home and think of there, and what if I and everyone else were to just suddenly pick up and go, where then would that leave them? "Oh, must we dream our dreams / and have them, too?"

Outside my window now, the night air is all soft urban thrum: the occasional bleat of a car horn; a far-off siren wobbling like a tired top along a distant side street; a light breeze moving the tops of the ailanthus in great dark waves above the neighborhood's vacant lots. Through my open windows, honeybees — dazed, listless, postsummer drones — keep drifting in and out, bristling as they bob before the TV screen, aswim now with the image of a lone seal pup in a camera-lighted sea. This is our protagonist. Separated from her mother in the storm, she's finning herself back to safety. Darkness approaches. "If she can't find a surrogate mother," our narrator explains, "she'll starve." Mournful Andean flute music sounds. The pup pulls up into a wide, slow, skyward gaze and cries. I had thought about not tuning in tonight, having already seen elephant seals before on past shows. In fact, insofar as this species — as I've just learned — was nearly wiped out save for a core group of a hundred seals on this island, the chances are that I've seen the very same seals or their relatives. Still, if the seals are the same, the show is different, more elaborate and engaging, which is why I tuned in. The more facts we compile about the animals' days, the more human the tales we tell of them. We've come so far from actual nature.

I remember, as a child back in the 1960s, watching a particularly riled elephant-seal bull chase Marlin Perkins up the beach in *Mutual of Omaha's Wild Kingdom.* That seemed to be about the extent of nature programming back then, close encounters with the wild: Marlin and one of his muscular, square-jawed cohorts frantically running from or wrestling with animals, bagging snakes, lassoing leopards, shooting myriad creatures with tranquilizers before releasing them again back into the wilderness. Somehow that was enough of a show then, the capture and release, perhaps because we could still believe there was someplace other and unknown — a place we could confidently call the natural world — for them to be released into. I remember as well Jacques Cousteau° paying a visit to Año Nuevo back in the 1970s. We had, by this time,

Jacques Cousteau: Jacques-Yves Cousteau (1910–1997), French marine explorer and host of a popular television series on marine life during the 1960s and 1970s.

penetrated, captured on film, a good deal of the world's wilderness, and so there was already a marked embellishment in our narrations of it as well as that hushed, somber, guilt-tinged tone that has become the hallmark of nature-show narration. Of course, Cousteau, our first existentialist naturalist, got a bit carried away, describing the very mating scene I've been told tonight is quite natural for elephant seals as if it were something out of Petronius's *Satyricon*.° "Zee island iz a sex and milk bank. Beasts all mating wiz each uh-there, females giving milk to any pup that passes by. What has 'appened to zee seals also 'appens with humans. In difficult times, they obey strict rules. In opulence, society degenerates." Still, Cousteau had the same lines about the seals being so ungainly on land and yet streamlined for the sea, and he too filmed a wave-swept orphan seal pup, although in this case Cousteau and his crew stepped into the scene, lifted the pup from the water, and brought it to a nursing mother's side.

In tonight's show, however, we get a whole story, a year in the life, and the makers' hands are kept out of the frame so as not to break the tension that has been the dynamic of nature-show drama since Marlin Perkins first began bringing the wild (and, not incidentally, selling life insurance) to homes across America—that tension we feel between the indifference and apparent arbitrariness of occurrences in the natural world and our own civilized stays against it. Our pup survives the storm. Now we're about to follow her on her inaugural swim with the aid of the latest underwater photography and the information gleaned from a "time-depth recorder," which, stuck to the back of a mature elephant seal, traced the long, deep outlines of its yearly eight-month ocean migrations. "There's so much to learn," says our narrator. "The world unfolds before the little female's eyes, and it's an amazing sight."

Deep, sonorous flute music again as the pup swirls from one lesson to the next in her "world of floating shadows": sharks, a passing whale, schools of fish; our pup "sees creature after creature feeding—and becoming food," and she is now being drawn to the surface by an eerie constellation of floating lights. She rises up through a dense, gray cloud of squid, stares a moment through a glare of unseen camera lights at the skulking shadows on the deck of a commercial fisherman's boat, and then dives again. . . .

There's a driving rainstorm tonight, the city is completely obscured from view, 10 and I'm watching a show about the rain forest. My TV screen is a brilliant canvas of bright red beads set into a field of multicolored triangles: a close-up of red mites on the back of a harlequin beetle. Now, over surreal horizons of harlequin thorax, come tiny scorpions preying upon the mites. Paper wasps, meanwhile, are spitting rainwater off of their nest and cooling their brood with wing pulsations. A poison-arrow frog is dumping its tadpoles into a droplet of water at the base of a bromeliad. Golden toads are courting in misty pools atop the one mountain in this world where they can be found. There's a sud-

---

Petronius's *Satyricon*: Satirical novel by Titus Petronius Niger (d. A.D. 66), famed for its depiction of the grotesque sexual and culinary excesses of Roman society.

den wide shot of a night sky with a white-gold moon that gives way now to the luminous orb of a leaf toad's eye, and then a shocking, screen-size, green triangle: the head of a katydid. I can hear its chewing, and then the soft paddings across dead leaves of an approaching tarantula. The tarantula pounces. I listen to its pincers piercing the waxen abdomen of the katydid. "We soon get through with Nature," Thoreau° once noted in his journals. "She excites an expectation which she cannot satisfy." Thus, the modern TV nature show: a clean and well-lighted simultaneity of the unseen; of the things you'd never see in a thousand walks in the wild.

Jungles are most remarkable for what you don't see for the longest time. How many of us would wait long enough for the lives there that retreat upon our first footfalls to start back toward us? How many of us remain who might regard such creatures? Jungles are wondrous places for precisely the reasons a nature show cannot convey. It is the mostly hidden and nonreflective enormity of their life forces, behemoth and belittling, that has most to show and tell us. To be in "nature" — by which we've come to mean the world without us — is to meet firsthand that thriving indifference and nearly insufferable gradualness that moves us to *decamp* from nature. To be alone in the jungle or in any uninterrupted wilderness, even to walk through a typical deciduous forest such as the one surrounding my cabin in Canada, is to be rapidly divested of your ego and ideas. In fact, our most inspired writing about nature is, in essence, the evocation of this divesting, the depiction, often ecstatic, of our own thoughts' unraveling into a greater surrounding thoughtlessness.

But to sit here in front of a nature show is to have one's ego fed shamelessly via the distilled essence of that original place whose indifference and gradualness we can no longer abide. We need the time-lapsed and tightly woven tale called nature, and it is from here and not from that tale's source that we now collectively depart. We are, in a sense, a species being increasingly defined by the loss of gradualness, by the steady progress of our walk out of the woods.

Perhaps I shouldn't watch nature shows, lest I become no longer able to suffer the real place. But then I think what a shame it would be to have missed *Year of the Jackal, Sexual Encounters of the Floral Kind,* or *Tides of War,* a recent film about the Persian Gulf crisis° from the animals' point of view, surely the first of its kind, animals being the most available emissaries of our own outrage and outrageousness — that heron, for example, striding into a fiery expanse of oil-splattered desert as the narrator informs us that "herons were often seen in the oilfields appearing confused and miserable," when they were,

---

Thoreau: Henry David Thoreau (1817–1862), American transcendentalist author whose 1854 memoir *Walden: Or Life in the Woods* has had a lasting influence on American attitudes toward nature.

the Persian Gulf crisis: Euphemistic term for the United States' war with Iraq in response to its invasion of Kuwait in 1990.

of course, herons appearing in confused and miserable-looking fields. I would have missed as well *Realms of the Russian Bear*, a six-hour foray into previously unseen corners of the former Soviet Union, animals being the most easygoing ambassadors of our "new world order." (In one memorable shot a polar bear lazing among hundreds of walruses on some remote Siberian seashore gently bites one walrus after the other in search of a sick or disabled one for supper.) And while I can't say how or if seeing such things changes me, it would seem some kind of loss to miss the deep-diving films currently being shot by the wild sea lions whose backs we've strapped cameras to; or to have missed that noiseless stick spider suspended upside down above the leafy plate of its un-witting prey; or the polar bear mother emerging from her icebound winter's den with three newborns like animate snowballs beneath her; to have missed the shots—how did they get them?—from the very wing tips of a flying duck; or of those freshwater dolphins who make of themselves a fishing net and heave whole schools of fish onto the shore for supper; or of the killer whales who snatch seals from the beach and then toss them about like rubber toys in the surf. . . .

Friday night, late November, cold and clear, the city sparkling in the distance. There's no nature on this evening. (Actually, it's on somewhere in the vast TV system. There's an all-nature cable channel now, but my particular section of Brooklyn may be the last quadrant of this nation not yet wired for cable.) Lucy is, as usual, settled deep into her end of the couch, sifting for sleep through an elaborate series of sighs. I'm thinking about the cabin in the woods, wondering if it's still there.

It was built more than 160 years ago and lists pretty badly now into a wooded hillside. Daylight leaks in everywhere through the joints and siding. Tin sheets tapped onto the old roof hold out most of the rain; and plastic sheets over the broken windows, the wind. One small combination lock on a latch holds the front door, barely, within its jamb—or it might be holding the cabin up around the door. Not that one needs a combination to get inside. At this very moment all kinds of creatures are having the run of the place, or at least the slow, sleepy refuge of its webbed nooks and thinly insulated rafters. I merely do a kind of summer time-share with them each season: the mice, moles, snakes, skinks, and spiders. The place does have pipes that bring ice-cold water through the warmest months from an underground spring, and a phone, and electricity for the little portable black-and-white TV on which Lucy and I and our assorted native stowaways can watch the narrated images of animals—the huge darkness of the night sky and surrounding woods pressing in around us.

But along with the cabin itself, it's the very essence of the time I spend there that keeps collapsing now in my mind. I'm thinking in particular of my walks in the woods, how they begin with such a deep sense of disappointment not so much in, but *from*, my surroundings. It's a disappointment rooted in the disparity between the ways in which we now represent nature to ourselves and the way it actually is; between that flitting, omniscient, nature-show overview delivering me from one available, arcane wonder to the next, and the plodding, myopic bulk of me within such a mute and long-lived presence.

At one point in Lewis Carroll's *Through the Looking-Glass,* Alice wanders tentatively into a cool, shady wood "where things have no names." Immediately upon entering, she forgets what to call the tree under which she's standing, and she entirely forgets herself. She next comes face-to-face with a fawn, which, not being recalled by Alice as such, is entirely fearless and walks farther through the woods side by side with her in a spell of peace and calm. Eventually, the two emerge back out into an open field, at which point name recognition returns and the fawn bounds off, frightened, leaving Alice "almost ready to cry with vexation at having lost her . . . fellow-traveler so suddenly." Alice's walk is, in essence, a brief pass, at once unsettling and euphoric, through a primordial world, through the world without us and the names by which we naturally put things in their place and thus proceed away from them. And it is some semblance of her experience, however remote it may be to the modern psyche, that I have when I walk in the woods, an experience exactly the opposite of watching a nature show. It is the sufferance of my own insignificance, and of the full, muted, weighty presence of things; the daring to linger in a nonspecific, unnarrated, and ongoing anonymity; a prolonged visit with that absence of us. It is a walk away from what we know toward an understanding—in both the physical and abstract senses of that word—of what surrounds us.

Now, however, we are increasingly incapable of suffering the silent world without us, of standing a stand of trees. We've become, in a sense, a race of armchair naturalists even as more and more of us are now visiting the places and creatures whose stories we've watched on the TV. We go as nature tourists, fully equipped and expectant of seeing those characters, as though visiting the various sets of a Universal Studios theme park.

I remember a few years ago making a trip to Nepal to write a story about a young American doctor practicing emergency wilderness medicine at an outpost high in the Himalayas. On the day of my departure I learned that I would be accompanied by twelve other doctors, who were to be led by the subject of my story through Nepalese mountains and jungle while taking courses from him in emergency medicine—that is, an extravagant adventure vacation and tax write-off for the doctors and their families. I found all the doctors waiting at the airport gate in Seattle, already decked out in the finest Banana Republic trekking gear. All except one, an orthopedic surgeon from southern California who, I've since decided, is the prefigurement of humankind's next evolutionary advancement. His skin was milky white, his body a pervasive paunch bordering on shapelessness, and he wore—never departed from, in fact—a red knit polo shirt; tan slacks; brand-new, creaseless penny loafers; and a La Quinta Country Club° golf hat.

Yet in the course of our expedition, he outperformed everyone, always arriving at the top of trails of our jungle camps hours ahead of the rest of us. 20

La Quinta Country Club: A very exclusive private country club in La Quinta, California.

We would trek and look dutifully about in hopes of spotting something in the wild, our minds mired somewhere in that disappointment between "Disneyfied" nature and the actual place, while he sped along in those loafers, noting the surroundings as though clicking off items on a checklist on the way to a more poignant encounter with a big-list item, one of the rare snow leopards of the region, or rhinos, or Bengal tigers. On the buses that brought us from one corner of the country to another, everyone was reading Peter Matthiessen's *Snow Leopard.* He read vampire novels. The last I remember seeing of him, we were all riding on the backs of elephants through the jungles of southwestern Nepal. He was on the lead elephant, of course, and we came into a clearing along a winding riverbank of tall grass, the white wavy wands of which we were all instructed to pause and watch a few moments in the distance for the possible movement of a rhino. I looked up and watched the La Quinta doctor instead. He raised a pair of binoculars, focused briefly on the motionless tips of grass, and then drove on, those shiny penny loafers dug firmly into his elephant as they passed back into the jungle.

It is 8:45 P.M., mid-December, light snow outside, the city subsumed in a pale orange glow. I'm watching *Great Moments with Nature's Filmmakers,* a show about the making of the shows, a guided tour of sorts through nature's studio sets and all the suddenly disengaged props of that dream: here the fur-wrapped camera-on-wheels that brought us into that pride of lions, and here the feather duster that the falcon attacked the night I saw just talons and scattered plumage. Over here is the den aquarium tank that was the wide sea in which the moray eel ate the blowfish and then spit it free; and here is the film center in England where they first perfected time-lapse and various microcosmic film techniques: room upon room with cameras clicking tight fast frames of this world's wide days of sluggish plants, fleeing insects, and shy birds. These "camera techniques," the narrator solemnly declares at show's end, "changed forever our vision of the natural world."

I pick up the phone now and dial my cabin to make sure it's still there. Of course, for all I know a strong wind has blown it over since my last visit, leaving only the lintel to which the phone's attached, so that I'm calling a snowy wooded hilltop with a few chairs, a wood stove, some scattered books on the floor, and a dark TV on a table. I dial the cold, rimless northern night. There's the cheap crackling mimicry of distance in my ear; and then, after the first ring, I begin trying to reassemble my days there, but see only a series of twitched heads and wide-eyed stares, a rooftop crow scattering like a broken fleck of night sky, and the fawn that had been rubbing its flank against an outside corner, padding off now with a near-soundless hoof-squeak through snow.

EXPLORING THE TEXT

1. Why does Siebert believe that TV nature shows amount to little more than "extravagant animal operas"? What's particularly "operatic" about the examples he

offers from the PBS special on elephant seals? How do TV animal shows resemble operas in terms of their plots and the way they try to affect their audiences?

2. What, according to Siebert, is the experience of real nature like, in contrast to the kind of nature we see on television? How do animals in real nature differ from animals seen on TV? What do such shows typically edit out? Why do nature shows strike Siebert as "more like cities" than like real nature? Would you agree?

3. What is the purpose of the relatively lengthy descriptions that Siebert offers of the settings in which he watches television nature shows? What relevance is there in the details he includes, details like the jet he sees, or the fact that his apartment is on the sixth floor of a Brooklyn apartment building, or that the tree in front of it is "chained" and covered in Christmas lights?

4. What is the experience of being alone in nature like for human beings, according to Siebert? What does direct contact with animals and the natural world do to or for us, in his view? Would you agree? Why or why not? Why does he feel that there is "something vaguely illicit" about watching nature shows on television?

5. What is the point of the three brief passages that Siebert uses to close his essay — the anecdote about the "La Quinta doctor" touring Nepal, the description of watching *Great Moments with Nature's Filmmakers,* and the story about calling his vacant cabin in Canada? What do each of these recollections suggest about television and its impact on our views of nature? What do they suggest about how we see animals and how we see ourselves?

FURTHER EXPLORATIONS

1. How do Siebert's attitudes toward animals and nature compare with those of John (Fire) Lame Deer (p. 512)? Would Lame Deer be likely to agree with Siebert about the "Disneyfied" portrayal of nature and animal life on television? Would he likely agree with Siebert's view of the experience of "real" nature? Why or why not?

2. How might the nature of television nature programming, as analyzed by Siebert, help to explain why zoos tend to be such boring places, as noted by John Berger (p. 521)? What are contemporary zoos doing to reproduce the more exciting or dramatic aspects of television nature programming? Should they?

3. How might Walker Percy (p. 118) explain the attitudes and behavior of the "La Quinta Country Club" doctor who travels with Siebert to Nepal? What would he expect this well-heeled doctor to "see" in the Himalayas? How might Percy assess the impact of television nature shows on our ability to confront the reality of animal minds?

4. How might contemporary notions of selfhood, as discussed by Roy F. Baumeister (p. 320) help explain why television nature shows emphasize the "operatic" aspects of animal lives? Has human self-involvement expanded to the point of displacing the natural world of which it was once a part?

ESSAY OPTIONS

1. Working individually or in groups, survey a number of television nature shows to test Siebert's claims about how they tend to depict animals and the natural world.

Report your findings in a paper that offers your assessment of contemporary nature television programming. Do the shows that you watch portray animals in the "operatic" way that Siebert describes? How have portrayals of nature and animals on TV changed since the appearance of Siebert's essay in 1993? What lessons about nature and animals do contemporary nature programs convey—consciously *and* unconsciously—to their viewers?

2. Drawing on your own experience and on ideas and information presented by Siebert in this selection, John (Fire) Lame Deer in "Talking to the Owls and Butterflies" (p. 512), Mark Slouka in "Listening for Silence" (p. 50), and Bill McKibben in "Television and the Twilight of the Senses" (p. 109), write an essay in which you assess Siebert's claim that we are "a species being increasingly defined by the loss of gradualness, by the steady progress of our walk out of the woods" (para. 12). Would you agree that we, as a species, are "speeding up" to the point that we are literally losing contact with the world of nature? What forces account for this recent acceleration of human life?

The Whole Animal

FRANS de WAAL

When primatologist Frans de Waal was a boy in his native Holland, he would spend his days wandering through the *polder*—the low-flying fields left behind by centuries of Dutch land reclamation efforts—collecting buckets of frogs, salamanders, eels, and water insects. At home, he'd watch as his aquatic captives fed, mated, and gave birth in the microenvironments he'd rig up for them. This childhood fascination with nature led de Waal to become an ethologist—a scientist who studies animal behavior and "culture" by observing creatures in their natural environments. It also convinced him that we humans live in a state of "anthropodenial," because we refuse to acknowledge the obvious similarities between animal and human minds. We may not be able to say for certain what it's like to be a bat, a mouse, or an 800-pound gorilla, in de Waal's view, but the fact that we are animals ourselves does give us a powerful source of insight into the workings of animal minds. Today, de Waal (b. 1948) is C. H. Candler Professor of Primate Behavior at Emory University and director of the Living Links Center, an institute for the advanced study of ape and human evolution. He is also the author of *Chimpanzee Politics* (1982); *Peacemaking Among Primates* (1989); *Good Natured: The Origins of Right and Wrong in Humans and Other Animals* (1996); *Bonobo: The Forgotten Ape* (1997); and *The Ape and the Sushi Master: Cultural Reflections of a Primatologist* (2001), the source of this selection.

BEFORE READING

A few years ago, newspapers reported the amazing case of a female gorilla named Binti who "rescued" a young boy after he had fallen into the primate compound and suffered a serious head injury at Chicago's Brookfield Zoo. Working in small groups, discuss whether you think Binti's act was a sign of genuine intelligence and self-conscious "goodwill" or a matter of instinct. How would it be possible to know the difference? Would knowing the difference matter?

Why do I tell you this little boy's story of medusas, rays, and sea monsters, nearly sixty years after the fact? Because it illustrates, I think, how a naturalist is created. A child comes to the edge of deep water with a mind prepared for wonder. He is given a compelling image that will serve in later life as a talisman, transmitting a powerful energy that directs the growth of experience and knowledge.

EDWARD O. WILSON, 1995

Fear of the dangers of anthropomorphism has caused ethologists to neglect many interesting phenomena, and it has become apparent that they could afford a little disciplined indulgence.

ROBERT HINDE, 1982

S cientists are supposed to study animals in a totally objective fashion, similar to the way we inspect a rock or measure the circumference of a tree trunk. Emotions are not to interfere with the assessment. The animal-rights movement capitalizes on this perception, depicting scientists as devoid of compassion.

Some scientists have proudly broken with the mold. Roger Fouts, known for his work with language-trained chimpanzees, says in *Next of Kin:* "I had to break the first commandment of the behavioral sciences: *Thou shalt not love thy research subject.*" Similarly, Jeffrey Masson and Susan McCarthy, in *When Elephants Weep,* make it seem that very few scientists appreciate the emotional lives of animals.

In reality, the image of the unloving and unfeeling scientist is a caricature, a straw man erected by those wishing to pat themselves on the back for having their hearts in the right place. Unfeeling scientists do exist, but the majority take great pleasure in their animals. If one reads the books of Konrad Lorenz, Robert Yerkes, Bernd Heinrich, Ken Norris, Jane Goodall, Cynthia Moss, Edward Wilson,° and so on, it becomes impossible to maintain that animals are invariably studied with a cold, callous eye.

I have met many other scientists who may not write in the same popular style — and who may not dwell on their feelings, considering them irrelevant to their research — but for whom the frogs, budgerigars, cichlid fish, bats, or whatever animals they specialize in hold a deep attraction. How could it be otherwise? Can you really imagine a scientist going out every day to capture

Konrad Lorenz, Robert Yerkes, Bernd Heinrich, Ken Norris, Jane Goodall, Cynthia Moss, Edward Wilson: All famous scientists — mostly ethologists and zoologists.

and mark wild prairie voles—getting bitten by the voles, stung by insects, drenched by rain—without some deeper motivation than the pursuit of scientific truth? Think of what it takes to study penguins on the pack ice of the Antarctic, or bonobos in hot and humid jungles overrun by armed rebels. Equally, researchers who study animals in captivity really need to like what they are doing. Care of their subjects is a round-the-clock business, and animals smell and produce waste—which some of my favorite animals don't mind hurling at you—something most of us hardly think about until we get visitors who hold their noses and try to escape as fast as they can.

I would turn the stereotype of the unfeeling scientist around and say that   5
it is the rare investigator who is not at some level attached to the furry, feathered, or slippery creatures he or she works with. The maestro of observation, Konrad Lorenz, didn't believe one could effectively investigate an animal that one didn't love. Because our intuitive understanding of animals is based on human emotions and a sense of connection with animals, he wrote in *The Foundations of Ethology* (1981) that understanding seems quite separate from the methodology of the natural sciences. To marry intuitive insight with systematic data collection is both the challenge and the joy of the study of animal behavior.

Attraction to animals makes us forget the time spent watching them, and it sensitizes us to the tiniest details of behavior. The scientific mind uses the information thus gathered to formulate penetrating questions that lead to more precise research. But let us not forget that things did not start out with a scientific interest: the lifeblood of our science is a fascination with nature. This always comes first, usually early in life. Thus, Wilson's career as a naturalist began in Alabama, where as a boy—in an apparent attempt to show that not all human behavior is adaptive—he used his bare hands to pull poisonous snakes from the water. Lorenz opened his autobiographical notes for the Nobel Committee with "I consider early childhood events as most essential to a man's scientific and philosophical development." And Goodall first realized that she was born to watch animals when, at the age of five, she entered a chicken coop in the English countryside to find out how eggs were made.

Closeness to animals creates the desire to understand them, and not just a little piece of them, but the *whole* animal. It makes us wonder what goes on in their heads even though we fully realize that the answer can only be approximated. We employ all available weapons in this endeavor, including extrapolations from human behavior. Consequently, anthropomorphism is not only inevitable, it is a powerful tool. As summed up by Italian philosopher Emanuela Cenami Spada:

> Anthropomorphism is a risk we must run, because we must refer to our own human experience in order to formulate questions about animal experience. . . . The only available "cure" is the continuous critique of our working definitions in order to provide more adequate answers to our questions, and to that embarrassing problem that animals present to us.[1]

The "embarrassing problem" hinted at is, of course, that we see ourselves as distinct from other animals yet cannot deny the abundant similarities. There are basically two solutions to this problem. One is to downplay the similarities, saying that they are superficial or present only in our imagination. The second solution is to assume that similarities, especially among related species, are profound, reflecting a shared evolutionary past. According to the first position, anthropomorphism is to be avoided at all cost, whereas the second position sees anthropomorphism as a logical starting point when it comes to animals as close to us as apes.

Being a proponent of the second position creates a dilemma for an empiricist such as myself. I am not at all attracted to cheap projections onto animals, of the sort that people indulge who see cats as having shame (a very complex emotion), horses as taking pride in their performance, or gorillas as contemplating the afterlife. My first reaction is to ask for observables: things that can be measured. In this sense, I am a cold, skeptical scientist. With my team of students and technicians, I watch primates for hundreds of hours before a study is completed, entering codes of observed behavior into handheld computers. We also conduct experiments in which chimpanzees handle joysticks to select solutions to problems on a computer screen. Or we have monkeys operate an apparatus that allows them to pull food toward themselves, after which we see how willing they are to share the rewards with those who assisted them.[2]

All of this research serves to produce evidence for or against certain assumptions. At the same time that I am committed to data collection, however, I argue for breathing space in relation to cognitive interpretations, don't mind drawing comparisons with human behavior, and wonder how and why anthropomorphism got such a bad name. Anthropomorphism has proven its value in the service of good, solid science. The widely applied vocabulary of animal behavior, such as "aggression," "fear," "dominance," "courtship," "play," "alarm," and "bonding," has been borrowed straight from language intended for human behavior. It is doubtful that scientists from outer space, with no shared background to guide their thinking, would ever have come up with such a rich and useful array of concepts to understand animals. To recognize these functional categories is the part of our job that comes without training and usually builds upon long-standing familiarity with pets, farm animals, birds, bugs, and other creatures. . . .

10

Pecking Orders in Oslo

It is hard to name a single discovery in animal behavior that has had a greater impact and enjoys wider name recognition than the "pecking order." Even if pecking is not exactly a human behavior, the term is ubiquitous in modern society. In speaking of the corporate pecking order, or the pecking order at the Vatican (with "primates" on top!), we acknowledge both inequalities and their ancient origins. We also slightly mock the structure, hinting that we, sophisticated human beings that we are, share a few things with domestic fowl.

The momentous discovery of rank orders in nature was made at the beginning of the twentieth century by a Norwegian boy, Thorleif Schjelderup-Ebbe, who fell in love with chickens at the tender age of six.[3] He was so enthralled by these sociable birds that his mother bought him his own flock at a rented house outside of Oslo. Soon each bird had a name. By the age of ten, Thorleif was keeping detailed notebooks, which he maintained for many years. Apart from keeping track of how many eggs his chickens laid, and who pecked whom, he was particularly interested in exceptions to the hierarchy, so called "triangles," in which hen A is master over B, and B over C, but C over A. So, from the start, like a real scientist, he was interested in not only the regularities but also the irregularities of the rank order. The social organization that he discovered is now so obvious to us that we cannot imagine how anyone could have missed it, but no one had described it before.

The rest is history, as they say, but not a particularly pretty one. The irony is that the discoverer of the pecking order was himself a henpecked man. Thorleif the boy had a very domineering mother, and later in life he ran into major trouble with the very first woman professor of Norway. She supported him initially, but as an anatomist she had no real interest in his work.

After Schjelderup-Ebbe received a degree in zoology, he published the chicken observations of his youth while coining the term *Hackordnung*, German for pecking order. His classic paper, which appeared in 1922, describes dominants as "despots" and demonstrates the elegance of hierarchical arrangements in which every individual has its place. Knowing the rank order among twelve hens, one knows the dominance relation in all sixty-six possible pairs of individuals. It is easy to see the incredible economy of description, and to understand the discoverer's obsession with triangles, which compromise this economy.

At about the time that the young zoologist wanted to continue his studies, however, a malicious but well-written piece in a student paper made fun of his professor. An enemy then spread the rumor that the anonymous piece had been written by Schjelderup-Ebbe, who was indeed a gifted writer. Even though the piece was actually written by Sigurd Hoel, later to become one of Norway's foremost novelists, irreparable damage had been done to the relationship with his professor. She withdrew all support and became an active foe. As a result of lifelong intrigues against him, Thorleif Schjelderup-Ebbe never obtained a Norwegian doctorate, and never received the recognition he deserved.

Regardless of this sad ending, the beginning of the story goes to show how a child who takes animals seriously, who considers them worthy of individual recognition, and who assumes that they are not randomly running around but, like us, lead orderly lives, can discover things that the greatest scientists have missed. This quality of the child, of unhesitatingly accepting kinship with animals, was remarked upon by Sigmund Freud:

> Children show no trace of the arrogance which urges adult civilized men to draw a hard-and-fast line between their own nature and that of all other ani-

mals. Children have no scruples over allowing animals to rank as their full equals. Uninhibited as they are in the avowal of their bodily needs, they no doubt feel themselves more akin to animals than to their elders, who may well be a puzzle to them.[4]

The intuitive connection children feel with animals can be a tremendous source of joy. The unconditional love received from pets, and the lack of artifice in the relationship, contrast sharply with the much trickier dealings with members of their own species. I had an animal friend like this when I was young; I still think fondly of the neighbors' big dog, who was often by my side, showing interest in everything I did or said. The child's closeness to animals is fed by adults with anthropomorphic animal stories, fairy tales, and animated movies. Thus, a bond is fostered with all living things that is critically examined only later in life. As explained by the late Paul Shepard, who like no one else reflected on humanity's place in nature:

> Especially at the end of puberty, the end of innocence, we begin a lifelong work of differentiating ourselves from them [animals]. But this grows from an earlier, unbreakable foundation of contiguity. Alternatively, a rigorous insistence of ourselves simply as different denies the shared underpinnings and destroys a deeper sense of cohesion that sustains our sanity and keeps our world from disintegrating. Anthropomorphism binds our continuity with the rest of the natural world. It generates our desire to identify with them and learn their natural history, even though it is motivated by a fantasy that they are no different from ourselves.[5]

In this last sentence, Shepard hints at a more mature anthropomorphism in which the human viewpoint is replaced, however imperfectly, by the animal's. As we shall see, it is precisely this "animalcentric" anthropomorphism that is not only acceptable but of great value in science. . . .

Are We in Anthropodenial?

The human hunter anticipates the moves of his prey by attributing intentions and taking an anthropomorphic stance when it comes to what animals feel, think, or want. Somehow, this stance is highly effective in getting to know and predict animals. The reason it is in disrepute in certain scientific circles has a lot to do with how we see ourselves in relation to nature. It is not, I will argue, because anthropomorphism interferes with science, but because it acknowledges continuity between humans and animals. In the Western tradition, this attitude is okay for children, but not for grown-ups.

In one of my explorations of this issue, I ended up in Greece with a distinguished group of philosophers, biologists, and psychologists.[6] The ancient Greeks believed that the center of the universe was right where they lived. On a sun-drenched tour of the temple ruins in the foothills of Mount Parnassus,

20

near Delphi, we saw the *omphalos*° (navel) of the world—a large stone in the shape of a beehive—which I couldn't resist patting like a long-lost friend. What better location to ponder humanity's position in the cosmos? We debated concepts such as the anthropic principle, according to which the presence of human life on earth explains why the universe is uniform in all of its directions. Next to this idea, the Greek illusion of being at the navel of the world looks almost innocent. The theme of our meeting, the problem of anthropomorphism, related very much to the self-absorbed attitude that has spawned such theories.

Anthropomorphism and anthropocentrism are never far apart: the first is partly a "problem" due to the second. This is evident if one considers which descriptions of animal behavior tend to get dismissed. Complaints about anthropomorphism are common, for example, when we say that an animal acts intentionally, that is, that it deliberately strives toward a goal. Granted, intentionality is a tricky concept, but it is so equally for humans and animals. Its presence is about as hard to prove as its absence; hence, caution in relation to animals would be entirely acceptable if human behavior were held to the same standard. But, of course, this is not the case: cries of anthropomorphism are heard mainly when a ray of light hits a species other than our own.

Let me illustrate the problem with an everyday example. When guests arrive at the Field Station of the Yerkes Primate Center, near Atlanta, where I work, they usually pay a visit to my chimpanzees. Often our favorite troublemaker, a female named Georgia, hurries to the spigot to collect a mouthful of water before they arrive. She then casually mingles with the rest of the colony behind the mesh fence of their compound, and not even the sharpest observer will notice anything unusual. If necessary, Georgia will wait minutes with closed lips until the visitors come near. Then there will be shrieks, laughs, jumps, and sometimes falls when she suddenly sprays them.

Georgia performs this trick predictably, and I have known quite a few other apes that were good at surprising people, naive and otherwise. Heini Hediger, the great Swiss zoo biologist, recounts how even when he was fully prepared to meet the challenge, paying attention to the ape's every move, he nevertheless got drenched by an experienced old chimpanzee. I once found myself in a similar situation with Georgia. She had taken a drink from the spigot and was sneaking up to me. I looked straight into her eyes and pointed my finger at her, warning, in Dutch, "I have seen you!" She immediately stepped back, let some of the water fall from her mouth, and swallowed the rest. I certainly do not wish to claim that she understands Dutch, but she must have sensed that I knew what she was up to, and that I was not going to be an easy target.

Georgia's actions are most easily described in terms of human qualities such as intentions, awareness, and a taste for mischief. Yet some scientists feel that such language is to be avoided. Animals don't make decisions or have in-

---

omphalos: The omphalos at the shrine of Delphi was believed by the ancient Greeks to be the center of the earth.

tentions; they respond on the basis of reward and punishment. In their view, Georgia was not "up to" anything when she spouted water on her victims. Far from planning and executing a naughty plot, she merely fell for the irresistible reward of human surprise and annoyance. Thus, whereas any person acting like her would be scolded, arrested, or held accountable, some scientists would declare Georgia innocent.

Such knee-jerk rejections of anthropomorphism usually rest on lack of reflection on how we humans go about understanding the world. Inevitably, we ourselves are both the beginning and end of such understanding. Anthropomorphism — the term is derived from the Greek for "human form" — has enjoyed a negative reputation ever since Xenophanes objected to Homer's poetry in 570 B.C. because it treated the gods as if they were people. How could we be so arrogant as to think that they should look like us? If horses could draw pictures, Xenophanes joked, they would no doubt make their gods look like horses. Hence the original meaning of anthropomorphism is that of misattribution of human qualities to nonhumans, or at least overestimation of the similarities between humans and nonhumans. Since nobody wants to be accused of any kind of misattribution or overestimation, this makes it sound as if anthropomorphism is to be avoided under all circumstances.

Modern opposition to anthropomorphism can be traced to Lloyd Morgan, a British psychologist, who dampened enthusiasm for liberal interpretations of animal behavior by formulating, in 1894, the perhaps most quoted statement in all of psychology: "In no case may we interpret an action as the outcome of the exercise of a higher psychical faculty, if it can be interpreted as the outcome of the exercise of one which stands lower on the psychological scale."[7] Generations of psychologists have repeated Morgan's Canon, taking it to mean that the safest assumption about animals is that they are blind actors in a play that only we understand. Yet Morgan himself never meant it this way: he didn't believe that animals are necessarily simpleminded. Taken aback by the one-sided appeals to his canon, he later added a rider according to which there is really nothing wrong with complex interpretations if an animal species has provided independent signs of high intelligence. Morgan thus encouraged scientists to consider a wide array of hypotheses in the case of mentally more advanced animals.[8]

Unfortunately, the rider is not nearly as well known as the canon itself. In a recent assault on the "delusions" of anthropomorphism in the behavioral sciences, John Kennedy proudly holds up the behaviorist tradition as the permanent victor over naive anthropomorphism. He confidently claims in *The New Anthropomorphism:* "Once a live issue, a butt for behaviorists, it [anthropomorphism] now gets little more than an occasional word of consensual disapproval." In almost the same breath, however, the author informs us that "anthropomorphic thinking about animal behavior is built into us. We could not abandon it even if we wished to. Besides, we do not wish to."[9]

This seems illogical. On the one hand, anthropomorphism, is part and parcel of the way the human mind works. On the other hand, we have all but won the battle against it. But how did we overcome an irresistible mode of thinking? Did we really manage to do so, or is this a behaviorist delusion?

Is it even desirable to suppress thoughts that come naturally to us? Why is it that we, in Kennedy's own words, "do not wish to" abandon anthropomorphism? Isn't it partly because, even though anthropomorphism carries the risk that we overestimate animal mental complexity, we are not entirely comfortable with the opposite either, which is to deliberately create a gap between ourselves and other animals? Since we feel a clear connection, we cannot in good conscience sweep the similarities under the rug. In other words, if anthropomorphism carries a risk, its opposite carries a risk, too. To give it a name, I propose *anthropodenial* for the a priori rejection of shared characteristics between humans and animals when in fact they may exist.

Those who are in anthropodenial try to build a brick wall between themselves and other animals. They carry on the tradition of French philosopher René Descartes, who declared that while humans possessed souls, animals were mere machines. Inspired by the pervasive human-animal dualism of the Judeo-Christian tradition, this view has no parallel in other religions or cultures. It also raises the question why, if we descended from automatons, we aren't automatons ourselves. How did we get to be different? Each time we must ask such a question, another brick is pulled out of the dividing wall. To me, this wall is beginning to look like a slice of Swiss cheese. I work on a daily basis with animals from which it is about as hard to distance oneself as from Lucy, the Australopithecus fossil. All indications are that the main difference between Lucy and modern apes resided in her hips rather than her cranium. Surely we all owe Lucy the respect due an ancestor—and if so, does not this force a different look at the apes?

If Georgia the chimpanzee acts in a way that in any human would be considered deliberately deceitful, we need compelling evidence to the contrary before we say that, in fact, she was guided by different intentions, or worse, that apes have no intentions, and that Georgia was a mere water-spitting robot. Such a judgment would be possible only if behavior that in its finest details reminds us of our own—and that, moreover, is shown by an organism extremely close to us in anatomy and brain organization—somehow fundamentally differs from ours. It would mean that in the short evolutionary time that separates humans from chimpanzees, different motives and cognition have come to underlie similar behavior. What an awkward assumption, and how unparsimonious!

Isn't it far more economical to assume that if two closely related species act in a similar way, the underlying mental processes are similar, too? If wolves and coyotes have behavior patterns in common, the logical assumption is that these patterns mean the same thing, inasmuch as they derive from the common ancestor of both species. Applied to humans and their closest relatives, this rationale makes cognitive similarity the default position. In other words, given that the split between the ancestors of humans and chimpanzees is assumed to have occurred a mere five to six million years ago, anthropomorphism should be less of an issue than anthropodenial.[10]

This radical-sounding position—according to which, in the case of monkeys and apes, the burden of proof should be shifted from those who recognize similarity to those who deny it—is not exactly new. One of the strongest advocates of a unitary explanation was the philosopher David Hume. More than a century before both Lloyd Morgan and Darwin, Hume formulated the following touchstone in *A Treatise of Human Nature:*

> 'Tis from the resemblance of the external actions of animals to those we ourselves perform, that we judge their internal likewise to resemble ours; and the same principle of reasoning, carry'd one step farther, will make us conclude that since our internal actions resemble each other, the causes, from which they are deriv'd, must also be resembling. When any hypothesis, therefore, is advanc'd to explain a mental operation, which is common to men and beasts, we must apply the same hypothesis to both.[11]

Bambification

As soon as we admit that animals are not machines, that they are more like us than like automatons, then anthropodenial becomes impossible and anthropomorphism inevitable. Nor is anthropomorphism necessarily unscientific, unless it takes one of the unscientific forms that popular culture bombards us with. I was once struck by an advertisement for clean fuel in which a grizzly bear had his arm around his mate's shoulders while both enjoyed a beautiful landscape. Since bears are nearsighted and do not form pair-bonds, the image was nothing but our own behavior projected onto these animals.

Walt Disney made us forget that Mickey is a mouse and Donald a duck. Sesame Street, the Muppet Show, Barney: television is populated with talking and singing animal representations with little relation to their actual counterparts. Popular depictions are often pedomorphic, that is, they follow ethology's *Kindchenschema* (baby-appeal) by endowing animals with enlarged eyes and rounded infantile features designed to evoke endearment and protectiveness.

I've had firsthand experience with another form that I refer to as satirical anthropomorphism, which exploits the reputation of certain animals as stupid, stubborn, or funny in order to mock people. When my book *Chimpanzee Politics* came out in France in 1987, the publisher decided, unbeknownst to me, to put François Mitterand and Jacques Chirac on the cover with a grinning chimpanzee between them. I can only assume that he wanted to imply that these politicians acted like "mere" apes. Yet by doing so he went completely against the whole point of my book, which was not to ridicule people but to show that chimpanzees live in complex societies full of alliances and jockeying for power, societies that in some ways mirror our own.

You can hear similar attempts at anthropomorphic humor at the monkey rock of most zoos. Isn't it interesting that antelopes, lions, and giraffes rarely elicit hilarity, but that people who watch primates often end up hooting and yelling, scratching themselves in an exaggerated manner, and pointing at the animals while shouting things like "I had to look twice, Larry, I thought it was you"? In my mind, the laughter reflects anthropodenial: it is a nervous reaction caused by an uncomfortable resemblance.

The most common anthropomorphism, however, is the naive kind that attributes human feelings and thoughts to animals based on insufficient information or wishful thinking. I recall an interview with a woman in Wisconsin who claimed that the squirrels in her backyard loved her to an extraordinary degree. The rodents visited her every day, came indoors, and accepted food directly from her hand. She spent over a thousand dollars per year on nuts. When the interviewer discreetly suggested that perhaps the abundant goodies explained the animals' fondness of her, the woman denied any connection.

Naive anthropomorphism makes us exclaim "He must be the daddy!" when an adult male animal gently plays with a youngster. We are the only animals, however, with the concept of paternity as a basis of fatherhood. Other animals can be fathers—and fathers may treat juveniles differently than non-fathers—but this is never based on an explicit understanding of the link between sex and reproduction. Similarly, when Elizabeth Marshall Thomas tells us in *The Hidden Life of Dogs* that virgin bitches "save" themselves for future "husbands," she assumes Victorian values in an animal not particularly known for its sexual fidelity.

All such instances of anthropomorphism are profoundly anthropocentric. 40 The talking animals on television, the satirical depiction of public figures, and the naive attribution of human qualities to animals have little to do with what we know about the animals themselves. In a tradition going back to the folktales, Aesop, and La Fontaine,° this kind of anthropomorphism serves human purposes: to mock, educate, moralize, and entertain. Most of it further satisfies the picture, cherished by many, of the animal kingdom as a peaceable and cozy paradise. The fact that, in reality, animals kill and devour each other, die of starvation and disease, or are indifferent to each other, does not fit the idealized image. The entertainment industry's massive attempt to strip animals of their nasty side has been aptly labeled their "Bambification."[12]

The general public is less and less aware of the discrepancy with the real world as fewer people grow up on farms or otherwise close to nature. Even though having a pet provides a reality check (dogs are generally nice, but neither to their prey nor to invaders of their territory), the full picture of nature in all its glory and horror escapes the modern city dweller.

What Is It Like to Be a Bat?

The goal of the student of animal behavior is rarely a mere projection of human experiences onto the animal. Instead, the goal is to interpret behavior within the wider context of a species' habits and natural history.

Aesop . . . La Fontaine: Aesop was a legendary Greek teller of animal fables; Jean La Fontaine (1621–95), French poet and writer of fables.

Without experience with primates, one might think that a grinning rhesus monkey must be delighted, or that a chimpanzee running toward another with loud grunts must be in an aggressive mood. But primatologists know from hours of watching that rhesus bare their teeth when intimidated and that chimpanzees often grunt when they meet and embrace. In other words, a grinning rhesus monkey signals submission, and grunting by a chimpanzee serves as a greeting. In this way the careful observer arrives at an informed anthropomorphism that is often at odds with extrapolations from human behavior.

When Sofie, a six-month-old kitten, bounces toward me sideways, with wide eyes, arched back, and fluffy tail, I recognize this as playful bluff. This judgment is not based on knowing any people who act this way. I just know how Sofie's behavior fits with all the other things cats do. By the same token, when an animal keeper says "Yummy!" while feeding mealworms to a squirrel monkey, she is speaking for the animal, not for herself.

Or take an example that reached the bestsellers list. In *The Man Who Listens to Horses,* animal trainer Monty Roberts freely employs what appears to be hopelessly anthropomorphic language to describe his animals' reactions. When the horses make licking and chewing movements, for example, they are said to be negotiating with their trainer: "I am a herbivore; I am a grazer, and I'm making this eating action with my mouth now because I'm considering whether or not to trust you. Help me out with that decision, can you, please?"[13]

Rather than attributing human tendencies to his animals, however, Roberts's interpretations are from the animal's perspective. His extraordinary success as a trainer rests on the fact that he treats the horse as a flight animal in need of trusting relations. A horse has a fear-based psychology totally different from that of a predator.

While the goal of understanding animals from the inside out may be considered naive, it certainly is not anthropocentric. Ideally, we understand animals based on what we know about their *Umwelt*—a German term introduced in 1909 by Jacob von Uexküll for the environment as perceived by the animal. In the same way that parents learn to see through their children's eyes, the empathic observer learns what is important to his or her animals, what frightens them, under which circumstances they feel at ease, and so on.

Is it really anthropomorphic to look at the world from the animal's viewpoint, taking its Umwelt, intelligence, and natural tendencies into account? If anthropomorphism is defined as the attribution of human mental experiences to animals, then, strictly speaking, Roberts is not anthropomorphizing; he explicitly postulates major differences in the psychological makeup of horses and people. Although he does put human words in the horse's mouth, this seems done for the sake of reaching an audience, not because of any confusion between the species.

The animalcentric approach is not easy to apply to every animal: some are more like us than others. The problem of sharing the experiences of organisms that rely on different senses was expressed most famously by the philosopher

Thomas Nagel when he asked, "What is it like to be a bat?"[14] A bat perceives its world in pulses of reflected sound, something that we creatures of vision have a hard time imagining. Still, Nagel's answer to his own question—that we will never know—may have been overly pessimistic. Some blind persons manage to avoid collisions with objects by means of a crude form of echolocation.[15]

Perhaps even more alien would be the experience of an animal such as the star-nosed mole. With its twenty-two pink, writhing tentacles around its nostrils, it is able to feel microscopic textures on small objects in the mud with the keenest sense of touch of any animal on earth. Humans can barely imagine this creature's Umwelt. Obviously, the closer a species is to us, the easier it is to do so. This is why anthropomorphism is not only tempting in the case of apes, but also hard to reject on the grounds that we cannot know how they perceive the world. Their sensory systems are essentially the same as ours.

Animalcentric anthropomorphism must be sharply distinguished from anthropocentric anthropomorphism (see diagram). The first takes the animal's perspective, the second takes ours. It is a bit like people we all know, who buy us presents that they think *we* like versus people who buy us presents that *they* like. The latter have not yet reached a mature form of empathy, and perhaps never will.[16]

To make proper use of anthropomorphism we must view it as a means rather than an end. It should not be our goal to find some quality in an animal that is precisely equivalent to some aspect of our own inner lives. Rather, we should use the fact that we are animals to develop ideas we can put to a test. This heuristic use of anthropomorphism is very similar to the role of intuition in all of science. It inspires us to make predictions, and to ask ourselves how they can be tested, how we can demonstrate what we think is going on. In this way, a speculation is turned into a challenge.[17]

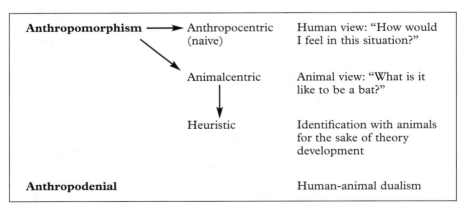

Anthropomorphism comes in many shapes and forms. The type to be treated with caution is the naive, humanizing (anthropocentric) type. Most students of animal behavior, however, try to understand animals on their own terms. Animalcentric anthropomorphism is a common heuristic tool: it generates testable ideas. The opposite of anthropomorphism is anthropodenial, which is based on the assumption that it is safer to err on the side of difference than continuity.

Gorilla Saves Boy

On August 16, 1996, an ape saved a three-year-old boy. The child, who had fallen six meters into the primate exhibit at Chicago's Brookfield Zoo, was scooped up and carried to safety by Binti Jua, an eight-year-old western lowland gorilla. The gorilla sat down on a log in a stream, cradling the boy in her lap, giving him a gentle back-pat before continuing on her way. Her act of sympathy touched many hearts, making Binti a celebrity overnight. It must have been the first time in U.S. history that a gorilla figured in the speeches of leading politicians, who held her up as an example of much-needed compassion. *Time* elected her one of the "best people" of 1996.

Some scientists were not as lyrical. They cautioned that Binti's motives might have been less noble than they seemed, pointing out that she had been raised by people, and had been taught parental skills with a stuffed animal. The whole affair, they suggested, might be explained by a confused maternal instinct. Other speculations included that Binti might have acted the same way with a sack of flour, or that she presented the child to the keepers with the same "pride" with which a house cat presents a dead mouse to her owner.

The intriguing thing about this flurry of creative explanations was that no-   55
body thinks of raising similar doubts when a person saves a dog hit by a car. The rescuer might have grown up around a kennel, have been praised for being kind to animals, and have a nurturing personality, yet we would still see his behavior as an act of caring. Why, then, was Binti's background held against her?[18]

I am not saying that I can look into Binti's heart, but I do know that no one had prepared her for this specific, unique emergency, and that it is highly unlikely that she, with her own seventeen-month-old infant riding on her back, was "maternally confused." How in the world could such a highly intelligent animal mistake a blond boy in sneakers and a red T-shirt for a juvenile of her species? Actually, the biggest surprise was how surprised most people were. Students of ape behavior did not feel that Binti had done anything unusual. Jürg Hess, a Swiss gorilla expert, put it most bluntly in an interview in *Stern:* "The incident can be sensational only for people who don't know a thing about gorillas."

What Hess meant—and I fully agree—is that Binti's action made a deep impression only because it benefited a member of our own species. To take care of a hurt juvenile is perfectly normal behavior for an ape, but of course it typically is directed at the ape's own kind. Instances of such caretaking behavior never reach the media, but they are well known and in line with Binti's assistance to the unfortunate boy. The idea that apes have a capacity for empathy is further supported by how they embrace and caress recent victims of aggression, a reaction thus far not observed in other primates.[19]

The incident at the Brookfield Zoo illustrates how hard it is to avoid both anthropodenial and anthropomorphism at the same time: in shying away from anthropomorphism one runs straight into the problem that Binti's actions hardly make any sense if one refuses to assume intentions and emotions. All one can come up with then is a confused instinct.

The larger question behind all of this is what kind of risk we are willing to take: the risk of underestimating animal mental life or the risk of overestimating it? There is no simple answer, but from an evolutionary perspective, Binti's kindness, like Georgia's mischievousness, is most parsimoniously explained in the same way that we explain our own behavior.

Notes

1. Cenami Spada (1997).

2. de Waal and Berger (2000) demonstrated that brown capuchin monkeys share more food with a partner who has helped them secure the food by pulling a heavy tray than with partners whose help was unneeded. This experiment was part of a series on social reciprocity, or tit for tat, and mental record keeping of given and received favors in chimpanzees and capuchins. Ultimately, it relates to the cooperative hunting observed in both of these primates in the field. In the hunt, several partners work together but only one captures the prey. Willingness of this individual to share with its helpers may be a prerequisite for continued cooperation.

3. The discovery of the pecking order and other historical details related here come from an interview by John Price with Dag Schjelderup-Ebbe, the sixty-year-old son of Thorleif, published in 1995 in the *Human Ethology Bulletin* 10 (1): 1–6.

4. Freud (1913).

5. Shepard (1996, p. 88).

6. The Athens-Pittsburgh Symposium in the History & Philosophy of Science & Technology, entitled The Problem of Anthropomorphism in Science and Philosophy, was held in May, 1996, in Delphi, Greece.

7. Morgan (1894).

8. Lloyd Morgan's rider went as follows: "To this, however, it should be added, lest the range of the principle be misunderstood, that the canon by no means excludes the interpretation of a particular activity in terms of the higher processes if we already have independent evidence of the occurrences of these higher processes in the animal under observation" (Morgan 1903). For the view that Morgan in fact had nothing against anthropomorphism, see Thomas (1998) and Sober (1998).

9. Kennedy (1992). For an antidote see the volume by Mitchell et al. (1997).

10. This position draws upon the familiar homology argument. Cross-specific similarities in behavior are either "analogies" (independently derived) or "homologies" (owing to shared descent), and the latter is more likely the more closely related the species are. De Waal (1991) discusses evolutionary (as opposed to cognitive) parsimony.

11. Hume (1739, p. 226).

12. Vicchio (1986).

13. Quotes are from Roberts (1996). The author's idea that the horse's chewing movements refer to grazing is not far removed from the ethological concept of ritualization. Evolution has turned many an instrumental act (such as preening or feeding) into a communication signal through exaggeration and increased stereotypy.

14. Nagel (1974).

15. Vermeij (1996), a blind biologist, writes: "If I had difficulty adjusting to blindness, the memory has faded. Almost immediately . . . I discovered the value of echoes for telling me where I was. Sounds bouncing off obstructions provided cues to the size of the room, the position of a tree, the speed of a car, the presence of a person, whether

a door was open or closed, and much more." Atkins (1996) exposes the limitations of Nagel's (1974) question.

16. Similarly, Batson et al. (1990) investigated human response patterns associated with two kinds of empathy: one based on imagining how you would feel in the other person's situation, the other based on imagining how the other feels.

17. Burghardt (1985).

18. A videotape of the incident (and a series of stills in *Stern*, September 5, 1996) shows Binti sitting down upright on a log in a stream while correctly positioning the unconscious boy, cradling him in her lap. It seems as if she is trying to put him on his feet. The Brookfield gorillas might not have reacted the same to an adult person (i.e., they probably recognized the boy as a youngster), and they certainly would not have reacted this way to a sack of flour. They would probably have been afraid of the sack at first, but then have opened it, causing a mess (Jay Peterson, curator at the Brookfield Zoo, personal communication).

19. Systematic data on the consolation of distressed individuals by chimpanzees has been provided by de Waal and Aureli (1996). For other accounts of empathy by apes, see de Waal (1996a). For example, in the Arnhem chimpanzee colony a mother put the normal preference for her younger offspring aside when her older offspring was seriously hurt in a scuffle. Ignoring the noisy protests of her infant, she took tender care of this juvenile for weeks until his injuries had healed.

Bibliography

Aisner, R., and Terkel, J. (1992). Ontogeny of pine-cone opening behavior in the black rat (*Rattus rattus*). *Animal Behaviour* 44: 327–336.

Alcock, J. (1998). Unpunctuated equilibrium in the *Natural History* essays of Stephen Jay Gould. *Evolution and Human Behavior* 19: 321–336.

Alexander, R. A. (1987). *The Biology of Moral Systems.* New York: Aldine de Gruyter.

Allen, B. (1997). The chimpanzee's tool. *Common Knowledge* 6: 34–51.

Alp, R. (1997). "Stepping-sticks" and "seat-sticks": New types of tools used by wild chimpanzees (*Pan troglodytes*) in Sierra Leone. *American Journal of Primatology* 41: 45–52.

Amudson, R. (1985). The hundredth monkey phenomenon. *The Skeptical Enquirer* 9: 348–356.

Arnhart, L. (1998). *Darwinian Natural Right: The Biological Ethics of Human Nature.* Albany, NY: SUNY Press.

Asquith, P. J. (1986). Anthropomorphism and the Japanese and Western traditions in primatology. In J. G. Else and P. C. Lee (eds.), *Primate Ontogeny, Cognition, and Social Behavior*, pp. 61–71. Cambridge: Cambridge University Press.

Asquith, P. J. (1989). Provisioning and the study of free-ranging primates: History, effects, and prospects. *Yearbook of Physical Anthropology* 32: 129–158.

Asquith, P. J. (1991). Primate research groups in Japan: Orientations and East-West differences. In L. Fedigan, and P. Asquith (eds.), *The Monkeys of Arashiyama: Thirty-five Years of Research in Japan and the West*, pp. 81–98. Albany, NY: SUNY Press.

Atkins, K. A. (1996). A bat without qualities? In M. Bekoff and D. Jamieson (eds.), *Readings in Animal Cognition*, pp. 345–358. Cambridge, MA: MIT Press.

Aureli, F., Cozzolino, R., Cordischi, C., and Scucchi, S. (1992). Kin-oriented redirection among Japanese macaques: An expression of a revenge system? *Animal Behaviour* 44: 283–291.

Aureli, F., and de Waal, F. B. M. (2000). *Natural Conflict Resolution*. Berkeley: University of California Press.

Austin, W. A. (1974). *The First Fifty Years: An Informal History of the Detroit Zoological Park and the Detroit Zoological Society*. Detroit: The Detroit Zoological Society.

Badcock, C. R. (1986). *The Problem of Altruism: Freudian-Darwinian Solutions*. Oxford: Blackwell.

Bagemihl, B. (1999). *Biological Exuberance: Animal Homosexuality and Natural Diversity*. New York: St. Martin's.

Bailey, M. B. (1986). Every animal is the smartest: Intelligence and the ecological niche. In R. Hoage and L. Goldman (eds.), *Animal Intelligence*, pp. 105–113. Washington, D.C.: Smithsonian Institution Press.

Balda, R. P., and Kamil, A. C. (1989). A comparative study of cache recovery by three corvid species. *Animal Behaviour* 38: 486–495.

Barkow, J. H. (1975). Prestige and culture: A biosocial interpretation. *Current Anthropology* 16: 553–572.

Batson, C. D., Early, S., and Salvarani, G. (1990). Perspective taking: Imagining how another feels versus imagining how you would feel. *Personality and Social Psychology Bulletin* 23: 751–758.

Beach, F. A. (1950). The snark was a boojum. *American Psychologist* 5: 115–124.

Beatty, H. (1951). A note on the behavior of the chimpanzee. *Journal of Mammalogy* 32: 118.

Beck, B. B. (1980). *Animal Tool Behavior: The Use and Manufacture of Tools by Animals*. New York: Garland.

Bischof, N. (1991). *Gescheiter als alle die Laffen*. Hamburg: Rasch & Röhring.

Boehm, C. (1999). *Hierarchy in the Forest: The Evolution of Egalitarian Behavior*. Cambridge, MA: Harvard University Press.

Boesch, C. (1991). Teaching in wild chimpanzees. *Animal Behaviour* 41: 530–532.

Boesch, C., and Boesch, H. (1983). Optimization of nut-cracking with natural hammers by wild chimpanzees. *Behaviour* 83: 265–286.

Boesch, C., and Boesch, H. (1984). Possible causes of sex differences in the use of natural hammers by wild chimpanzees. *Journal of Human Evolution* 13: 415–440.

Boesch, C., and Boesch-Ackermann, H. (1991). Dim forest, bright chimps. *Natural History* 9/91: 50–56.

Boesch, C., and Tomasello, M. (1998). Chimpanzee and human cultures. *Current Anthropology* 39: 591–614.

Bonner, J. T. (1980). *The Evolution of Culture in Animals*. Princeton, NJ: Princeton University Press.

Boyd, R., and Richerson, P. J. (1985). *Culture and the Evolutionary Process*. Chicago: University of Chicago Press.

Budiansky, S. (1998). *If a Lion Could Talk*. New York: Free Press.

Burghardt, G. M. (1985). Animal awareness: Current perceptions and historical perspective. *American Psychologist* 40: 905–919.

Busch, H., and Silver, B. (1994). *Why Cats Paint: A Theory of Feline Aesthetics*. Berkeley, CA: Ten Speed.

Byrne, R. W. (1995). *The Thinking Ape*. Oxford: Oxford University Press.

Byrne, R. W., and Russon, A. E. (1998). Learning by imitation: A hierarchical approach. *Behavioral and Brain Sciences* 21: 667–721.

Call, J., Judge, P. G., and de Waal, F. B. M. (1996). Influence of kinship and spatial density on reconciliation and grooming in rhesus monkeys. *American Journal of Primatology* 39: 35–45.

Cenami Spada, E. (1997). Amorphism, mechanomorphism, and anthropomorphism. In R. W. Mitchell, N. S. Thompson, and H. L. Miles (eds.), *Anthropomorphism, Anecdotes, and Animals,* pp. 37–49. Albany, NY: SUNY Press.

Chapais, B. (1988). Rank maintenance in female Japanese macaques: Experimental evidence for social dependency. *Behaviour* 104: 41–59.

Chelser, P. (1969). Maternal influence in learning by observation in kittens. *Science* 166: 901–903.

Cheney, D. L., and Seyfarth, R. M. (1990). *How Monkeys See the World.* Chicago: University of Chicago Press.

Corbey, R. (November 8, 1997). Beschaving is meer dan mes en vork. *NRC Handelsblad.*

Crist, E. (1999). *Images of Animals: Anthropomorphism and Animal Mind.* Philadelphia: Temple University Press.

Cullen, D. (1997). Maslow, monkeys, and motivation theory. *Organization* 4: 355–373.

Curio, E. (1978). Cultural transmission of enemy recognition: One function of mobbing. *Science* 202: 899–901.

Custance, D. M., Whiten, A., and Bard, K. A. (1995). Can young chimpanzees imitate arbitrary actions? Hayes and Hayes (1952) revisited. *Behaviour* 132: 839–858.

Damasio, A. R. (1994). *Descartes' Error: Emotion, Reason, and the Human Brain.* New York: Putnam.

Damasio, A. R. (1999). *The Feeling of What Happens.* New York: Harcourt.

Darwin, C. (1964 [1859]). *On the Origin of Species.* Cambridge, MA: Harvard University Press.

Darwin, C. (1981 [1871]). *The Descent of Man, and Selection in Relation to Sex.* Princeton, NJ: Princeton University Press.

Darwin, C. (1998 [1872]). *The Expression of the Emotions in Man and Animals.* Third Edition. New York: Oxford University Press.

Dawkins, R. (1976). *The Selfish Gene.* Oxford: Oxford University Press.

Dawkins, R. (1998). *Unweaving the Rainbow: Science, Delusion and the Appetite for Wonder.* New York: Houghton Mifflin.

Deacon, J. (1999). South African rock art. *Evolutionary Anthropology* 8: 48–63.

Deichmann, U. (1996). *Biologists under Hitler.* Cambridge, MA: Harvard University Press.

Desmond, A. (1994). *Huxley: From Devil's Disciple to Evolution's High Priest.* New York: Perseus.

Diamond, M. (1990). Selected cross-generational sexual behavior in traditional Hawaii: A sexological ethnography. In J. R. Feierman (ed.), *Pedophilia: Biosocial Dimensions,* pp. 378–393. New York: Springer.

Drea, C. M., and Wallen, K. (1999). Low status monkeys "play dumb" when learning in mixed social groups. *Proceedings of the National Academy of Sciences* 96: 12965–12969.

Ducros, A., Ducros, J., and Joulian, F. (1998). *La Culture est-elle Naturelle?* Paris: Errance.

Durham, W. H. (1991). *Coevolution: Genes, Culture, and Human Diversity.* Stanford, CA: Stanford University Press.

Ehrenreich, B. (1999). The real truth about the female body. *Time,* March 8: 57–65.

Eibl-Eibesfeldt, I. (1994). *Wider die Mißtrauensgesellschaft.* Munich: Piper.

Epstein, R., Lanza, R. P., and Skinner, B. F. (1981). "Self-awareness" in the pigeon. *Science* 212: 695–696.

Flack, J. C., and de Waal, F. B. M. (2000). "Any animal whatever": Darwinian building blocks of morality in monkeys and apes. *Journal of Consciousness Studies* 7 (1–2): 1–29.

Fouts, R. (1997). *Next of Kin.* New York: Morrow.

Freeman, D. (1983). *Margaret Mead and Samoa: The Making and Unmaking of an Anthropological Myth.* Cambridge, MA: Harvard University Press.

French, M. (1985). *Beyond Power.* New York: Ballantine.

Freud, S. (1989 [1913]). *Totem and Taboo.* New York: Norton.

Freud, S. (1989 [1930]). *Civilization and Its Discontents.* New York: Norton.

Galef, B. G. (1982). Studies of social learning in Norway rats: A brief review. *Developmental Psychobiology* 15: 279–295.

Galef, B. G. (1990). The question of animal culture. *Human Nature* 3: 157–178.

Gallup, G. G. (1970). Self-awareness in primates. *Science* 67: 417–421.

Gallup, G. G. (1982). Self-awareness and the emergence of mind in primates. *American Journal of Primatology* 2: 237–248.

Garcia, J., Ervin, F. R., and Koelling, R. A. (1966). Learning with prolonged delay of reinforcement. *Psychonomic Science* 5: 121–122.

Ghiglieri, M. (1988). *East of the Mountains of the Moon: Chimpanzee Society in the African Rain Forest.* New York: Free Press.

Ghiselin, M. (1974). *The Economy of Nature and the Evolution of Sex.* Berkeley: University of California Press.

Gilliard, E. T. (1969). *Birds of Paradise and Bowerbirds.* London: Weidenfeld & Nicolson.

Goodall, J. (1990). *Through a Window.* Boston: Houghton Mifflin.

Goodall, J. (1992). Unusual violence in the overthrow of an alpha male chimpanzee at Gombe. In T. Nishida, W. C. McGrew, P. Marler, M. Pickford, and F. B. M. de Waal, (eds.), *Topics in Primatology: Vol. 1, Human Origins*, pp. 131–142. Tokyo: University of Tokyo Press.

Gould, S. J. (1981). *The Mismeasure of Man.* New York: Norton.

Gould, S. J. (July 2, 1999). The human difference. *The New York Times.*

Green, S. (1975). Dialects in Japanese monkeys: Vocal learning and cultural transmission of locale-specific vocal behavior? *Zeitschrift für Tierpsychologie* 38: 304–314.

Greenberg, G., and Haraway, M. M. (1998). *Comparative Psychology: A Handbook.* New York: Garland.

Guinet, C., and Bouvier, J. (1995). Development of intentional stranding hunting techniques in killer whale (*Orcinus orca*) calves at Crozet Archipelago. *Canadian Journal of Zoology* 73: 27–33.

Günther, M. M., and Boesch, C. (1993). Energetic costs of nut-cracking behaviour in wild chimpanzees. In H. Preuschoft and D. J. Chivers (eds.), *Hands of Primates*, pp. 109–129. Vienna: Springer.

Halstead, L. B. (1985). Anti-Darwinian theory in Japan. *Nature* 317: 587–589.

Harris, J. R. (1998). *The Nurture Assumption: Why Children Turn Out the Way They Do.* London: Bloomsbury.

Hebb, D. O. (1971). Comment on altruism: The comparative evidence. *Psychological Bulletin* 76: 409–410.

Henrich, J., and Boyd, R. (1998). The evolution of conformist transmission and the emergence of between-group differences. *Evolution and Human Behavior* 19: 215–241.

Heyes, C. (1995). Self-recognition in mirrors: Further reflections create a hall of mirrors. *Animal Behaviour* 50: 1533–1542.

Hildebrand, G. (1999). *Origins of Architectural Pleasure.* Berkeley: University of California Press.

Hinde, R. A. (1966). *Animal Behaviour: A Synthesis of Ethology and Comparative Psychology.* New York: McGraw-Hill.

Hinde, R. A. (1982). *Ethology: Its Nature and Relations with Other Sciences.* Glasgow: Fontana.

Hinde, R. A. and Fisher, J. (1951). Further observations on the opening of milk bottles by birds. *British Birds* 44: 393–396.

Hirata, S., Myowa, M., and Matsuzawa, T. (1998). Use of leaves as cushions to sit on wet ground by wild chimpanzees. *American Journal of Primatology* 44: 215–220.

Hobbes, T. (1991 [1651]). *Leviathan.* Cambridge: Cambridge University Press.

Hodos, W., and Campbell, C. B. (1969). *Scala Naturae:* Why there is no theory in comparative psychology. *Psychological Review* 76: 337–350.

Hollard, V. D., and Delius, J. D. (1982). Rotational invariance in visual pattern recognition in pigeons and humans. *Science* 218: 804–806.

Hrdy, S. B. (1979). Infanticide among animals: A review, classification, and examination of the implications for the reproductive strategies of females. *Ethology & Sociobiology* 1: 13–40.

Hrdy, S. B. (1999). *Mother Nature: A History of Mothers, Infants, and Natural Selection.* New York: Pantheon.

Huffman, M. A. (1996). Acquisition of innovative cultural behaviors in nonhuman primates: A case study of stone handling, a socially transmitted behavior in Japanese macaques. In C. M. Heyes and B. G. Galef (eds.), *Social Learning in Animals: The Roots of Culture,* pp. 267–289. San Diego, CA: Academic Press.

Huffman, M. A. (1997). Current evidence for self-medication in primates: A multidisciplinary perspective. *Yearbook of Physical Anthropology* 40: 171–200.

Hume, D. (1985 [1739]). *A Treatise of Human Nature.* Harmondsworth, UK: Penguin.

Humphrey, N. K. (1976). The social function of intellect. In P. P. G. Bateson and R. A. Hinde (eds.), *Growing Points in Ethology,* pp. 303–321. Cambridge: Cambridge University Press.

Huxley, J. (1942). The origins of human drawing. *Nature* 142:637.

Huxley, T. H. (1989 [1894]). *Evolution and Ethics.* Princeton, NJ: Princeton University Press.

Imanishi, K. (1952). *Man.* Tokyo: Mainichi-Shinbunsha (in Japanese).

Inoue, R., and Anderson, A. (1988). The Terrier's Way. *Nature* 332: 758.

Inoue-Nakamura, N., and Matsuzawa, T. (1997). Development of stone tool use by wild chimpanzees. *Journal of Comparative Psychology* 111: 159–173.

Itani, J. (1985). The evolution of primate social structures. *Man* 20: 593–611.

Itani, J., and Nishimura, A. (1973). The study of infrahuman culture in Japan: A review. In E. W. Menzel (ed.), *Precultural Primate Behavior,* pp. 26–50. Basel: Karger.

Jacob, F. (1998). *Of Flies, Mice, and Men.* Cambridge, MA: Harvard University Press.

Jewell, D. (July 14, 1997). Brave hearts. *People.*

Kalikow, T. J. (1980). Die ethologische Theorie von Konrad Lorenz: Erklärung und Ideologie, 1938–1943. In H. Mertens and S. Richter (eds.), *Naturwissenschaft, Technik und NS-Ideologie,* pp. 189–214. Frankfurt: Suhrkamp.

Kano, T. (1992). *The Last Ape: Pygmy Chimpanzee Behavior and Ecology.* Stanford, CA: Stanford University Press.

Kano, T. (1998). Comments on C. B. Stanford. *Current Anthropology* 39: 410–411.

Kawai, M. (1965). Newly-acquired pre-cultural behavior of the natural troop of Japanese monkeys on Koshima islet. *Primates* 6: 1–30.

Kellogg, W. N., and Kellogg, L. A. (1967 [1933]). *The Ape and the Child*. New York: Hafner.

Kennedy, J. S. (1992). *The New Anthropomorphism*. Cambridge: Cambridge University Press.

Keyes, K. (1982). *The Hundredth Monkey*. Coos Bay, OR: Vision Books.

Killen, M., and de Waal, F. B. M. (2000). The evolution and development of morality. In F. Aureli and F. B. M. de Waal (eds.), *Natural Conflict Resolution*, pp. 352–372. Berkeley, CA: University of California Press.

Köhler, W. (1925). *The Mentality of Apes*. New York: Vintage Books.

Kroeber, A. L. (1928). Sub-human cultural beginnings. *Quarterly Review of Biology* 3: 325–342.

Kroeber, A. L. (1963 [1923]). *Anthropology: Culture Patterns & Processes*. New York: Harcourt.

Kummer, H. (1971). *Primate Societies*. Arlington Heights: Davidson.

Kummer, H. (1995). *In Quest of the Sacred Baboon*. Princeton, NJ: Princeton University Press.

Kunz, T. H., and Allgaier, A. L. (1994). Allomaternal care: Helper-assisted birth in the Rodrigues fruit bat, *Pteropus rodricensis*. *J. Zool., London* 232: 691–700.

Kurland, J. A. (1977). *Kin Selection in the Japanese Monkey*. Contributions to Primatology, vol. 12. Basel: Karger.

Kuroda, S. (1984). Interaction over food among pygmy chimpanzees. In R. L. Susman (ed.), *The Pygmy Chimpanzee*, pp. 301–324. New York: Plenum.

Ladygina-Kohts, N. N. (in press). *Infant Chimpanzee and Human Child* (F. B. M. de Waal, ed.). New York: Oxford University Press.

Leakey, R., and Lewin, R. (1992). *Origins Reconsidered*. New York: Doubleday.

Lefebvre, L. (1995). Culturally-transmitted feeding behaviour in primates: Evidence for accelerating learning rates. *Primates* 36: 227–239.

Lenain, T. (1997). *Monkey Painting*. London: Reaktion Books.

Levy, M. (1961). Dali, the quantum gun at Port Lligat. *The Studio* 162: 83–85.

Liessmann, K. P. (1996). *Der gute Mensch von Österreich*. Vienna: Sonderzahl.

Linton, R. (1936). *The Study of Man: An Introduction*. New York: Appleton-Century-Croft.

Lorenz, K. Z. (1962 [1952]). *King Solomon's Ring*. New York: Time.

Lorenz, K. Z. (1966 [1963]). *On Aggression*. London: Methuen.

Lorenz, K. Z. (1981). *The Foundations of Ethology*. New York: Simon & Schuster.

Lorenz, K. Z. (1985). My family and other animals. In D. A. Dewsbury (ed.), *Leaders in the Study of Animal Behavior*, pp. 259–287. Lewisburg, PA: Bucknell University Press.

Lumsden, C., and Wilson, E. O. (1981). *Genes, Mind, and Culture*. Cambridge, MA: Harvard University Press.

Mann, A. (1972). Hominid and cultural origins. *Man* 7: 379–386.

Manning, A. (Feb. 10, 1996). On the origins of behaviour. *New Scientist*.

Marler, P., and Tamura, M. (1964). Culturally transmitted patterns of vocal behavior in sparrows. *Science* 146: 1483–1486.

Marshall, A. J., Wrangham, R. W., and Arcadi, A. C. (1999). Does learning affect the structure of vocalizations in chimpanzees? *Animal Behaviour* 58: 825–830.

Marshall, Thomas E. (1993). *The Hidden Life of Dogs*. Boston: Houghton Mifflin.

Maslow, A. (1936). The role of dominance in the social and sexual behavior of infra-human primates. Series of articles in the *Journal of Genetic Psychology*, vols. 48–49.

Masson, J. M., and McCarthy, S. (1995). *When Elephants Weep: The Emotional Lives of Animals.* New York: Delacorte.

Masters, R. (1989). *The Nature of Politics.* New Haven, CT: Yale University Press.

Matsuzawa, T. (1994). Field experiments on use of stone tools by chimpanzees in the wild. In R. W. Wrangham, W. C. McGrew, F. B. M. de Waal, and P. Heltne (eds.), *Chimpanzee Cultures,* pp. 351–370. Cambridge, MA: Harvard University Press.

Mayr, E. (1997). *This Is Biology: The Science of the Living World.* Cambridge, MA: Belknap.

McGrew, W. C. (1979). Evolutionary implications of sex differences in chimpanzee predation and tool use. In D. A. Hamburg and E. R. McCown (eds.), *The Great Apes,* pp. 441–463. Menlo Park, CA: Benjamin/Cummings.

McGrew, W. C. (1992). *Chimpanzee Material Culture: Implications for Human Evolution.* Cambridge: Cambridge University Press.

McGrew, W. C., and Tutin, C. E. G. (1978). Evidence for a social custom in wild chimpanzees? *Man* 13: 243–251.

McGrew, W. C., Ham, R. M., White, L. J. T., Tutin, C. E. G., and Fernandez, M. (1997). Why don't chimpanzees in Gabon crack nuts? *International Journal of Primatology* 18: 335–374.

Mead, M. (1950). *Male and Female: A Study of the Sexes in a Changing World.* New York: Penguin.

Medawar, P. B. (1984). *The Limits of Science.* New York: Harper & Row.

Mencius (372–289 B.C.). *The Works of Mencius.* English transl. Gu Lu. Shanghai: Shangwu Publishing House.

Midgley, M. (1979). *Beast and Man: The Roots of Human Nature.* London: Routledge.

Miller, G. F. (2000). *The Mating Mind: How Sexual Choice Shaped the Evolution of Human Nature.* New York: Doubleday.

Mineka, S., Davidson, M., Cook, M., and Keir, R. (1984). Observational conditioning of snake fear in rhesus monkeys. *Journal of Abnormal Psychology* 93: 355–372.

Mitchell, R. W., Thompson, N. S., and Miles, H. L. (1997). *Anthropomorphism, Anecdotes, and Animals.* Albany, NY: SUNY Press.

Montagu, M. F. A. (1968). *Man and Aggression.* New York: Oxford University Press.

Moore, B. R., and Stuttard, S. (1979). Dr. Guthrie and *Felis domesticus* or: Tripping over the cat. *Science* 205: 1031–1033.

Moore, J. A. (1993). *Science as a Way of Knowing: The Foundations of Modern Biology.* Cambridge, MA: Harvard University Press.

Morgan, C. L. (1894). *An Introduction to Comparative Psychology.* London: Scott.

Morgan, C. L. (1903). *An Introduction to Comparative Psychology,* 2nd edition. London: Scott.

Morris, D. (1962). *The Biology of Art: A Study of the Picture-Making Behaviour of the Great Apes and Its Relationship to Human Art.* London: Methuen.

Morris, D. (1967). *The Naked Ape.* New York: Dell.

Morris, R., and Morris, D. (1966). *Men and Apes.* New York: McGraw-Hill.

Mulder, M. (1979). *Omgaan met Macht.* Amsterdam: Elsevier.

Myowa-Yamakoshi, M., and Matsuzawa, T. (1999). Factors influencing imitation of manipulatory actions in chimpanzees. *Journal of Comparative Psychology* 113: 128–136.

Nagel, T. (1974). What is it like to be a bat? *Philosophical Review* 83: 435–450.

Nakamichi, M., Kata, E., Kojima, Y., and Itoigawa, N. (1998). Carrying and washing of grass roots by free-ranging Japanese macaques at Katsuyama. *Folia primatologica* 69: 35–40.

Nakamura, M., McGrew, W., Marchant, L. F., and Nishida, T. (2000). Social scratch: Another custom in wild chimpanzees? *Primates* 41: 237–246.

Nimchinsky, E. A., Gilissen, E., Allman, J. M., Perl, D. P., Erwin, J. E., and Hof, P. R. (1999). A neuronal morphologic type unique to humans and great apes. *PNAS* 96: 5268–5273. Proceedings of the National Academy of Sciences.

Nishida, T. (1990). A quarter century of research in the Mahale Mountains: An overview. In T. Nishida (ed.), *The Chimpanzees of the Mahale Mountains*, pp. 3–35. Tokyo: University of Tokyo Press.

Nishida, T., and Hosaka, K. (1996). Coalition strategies among adult male chimpanzees of the Mahale Mountains, Tanzania. In W. C. McGrew, L. F. Marchant, and T. Nishida (eds.), *Great Ape Societies*, pp. 114–134. Cambridge: Cambridge University Press.

Nottebohm, G. (1880). *Mozartiana*. Wiesbaden: Breitkopf & Härtel.

Oakley, K. (1957). *Man the Tool-Maker*. Chicago: University of Chicago Press.

Ogawa, H. (1995). Recognition of social relationships in bridging behavior among Tibetan macaques. *American Journal of Primatology* 35: 305–310.

Ottoni, E. B., and Mannu, M. (in press). Semi-free ranging tufted capuchin monkeys (*Cebus apella*) spontaneously use tools to crack open nuts. *International Journal of Primatology*.

Parish, A. R. (1993). Sex and food control in the "uncommon chimpanzee": How bonobo females overcome a phylogenetic legacy of male dominance. *Ethology & Sociobiology*, 15: 157–179.

Parish, A. R., and de Waal, F. B. M. (2000). The other "closest living relative": How bonobos (*Pan paniscus*) challenge traditional assumptions about females, dominance, intra- and inter-sexual interactions, and hominid evolution. In D. LeCroy and P. Moller (eds.), *Evolutionary Perspectives on Human Reproductive Behavior. Annals of the New York Academy of Sciences* 907: 97–113.

Payne, K. (1998). *Silent Thunder: In the Presence of Elephants*. New York: Penguin.

Porter, D., and Neuringer, A. (1984). Musical discriminations by pigeons. *Journal of Experimental Psychology: Animal Behavior Processes* 10: 138–148.

Povinelli, D. J., et al. (1997). Chimpanzees recognize themselves in mirrors. *Animal Behaviour* 53: 1083–1088.

Premack, D., and Premack, A. J. (1994). Why animals have neither culture nor history. In T. Ingold (ed.), *Companion Encyclopedia of Anthropology*, pp. 350–365. London: Routledge.

Preston, S. D., and de Waal, F. B. M. (in press). The communication of emotions and the possibility of empathy in animals. In *Altruistic Love: Science, Philosophy, and Religion in Dialogue*. Oxford: Oxford University Press.

Ridley, M. (1996). *The Origins of Virtue*. London: Viking.

Roberts, M. (1996). *The Man Who Listens to Horses*. New York: Random House.

Roes, F. (1997). An interview of Richard Dawkins. *Human Ethology Bulletin* 12(1): 1–3.

Roes, F. (1998). A conversation with George C. Williams. *Natural History* 5: 10–15.

Russell, B. (1927). *Outline of Philosophy*. New York: Median.

Russon, A. E. (1996). Imitation in everyday use: Matching and rehearsal in the spontaneous imitation of rehabilitant orangutans (*Pongo pygmaeus*). In A. E. Russon, K. A. Bard, and S. T. Parker (eds.), *Reaching into Thought: The Minds of the Great Apes*, pp. 152–176. Cambridge: Cambridge University Press.

Sacks, O. (1985). *The Man Who Mistook His Wife for a Hat*. London: Picador.

Sakura, O. (1998). Similarities and varieties: A brief sketch on the reception of Darwinism and Sociobiology in Japan. *Biology & Philosophy* 13: 341–357.

Savage-Rumbaugh, S., and Lewin, R. (1994). *Kanzi: The Ape on the Brink of the Human Mind.* New York: Wiley.

VanSchaik, C. P., Deaner, R. O., and Merrill, M. Y. (1999). The conditions for tool use in primates: Implications for the evolution of material culture. *Journal of Human Evolution* 36:719–741.

Schiller, P. H. (1951). Figural preferences in the drawings of a chimpanzee. *Journal of Comparative Psychology* 46: 101–111.

Sept, J. M., and Brooks, G. E. (1994). Reports of chimpanzee natural history, including tool-use, in 16th- and 17th-century Sierra Leone. *International Journal of Primatology* 15: 867–878.

Serpell, J. (1996). *In the Company of Animals: A Study of Human-Animal Relationships.* Cambridge: Cambridge University Press.

Shepard, P. (1996). *The Others: How Animals Made Us Human.* Washington, D.C.: Shearwater.

Shweder, R. A. (1991). *Thinking through Cultures.* Cambridge, MA: Harvard University Press.

Sinclair, M. (1986). Imanishi and Halstead: Intra specific competition? *Nature* 320: 580.

Small, M. F. (1998). *Our Babies, Ourselves.* New York: Anchor.

Smith, A. (1937 [1759]). *A Theory of Moral Sentiments.* New York: Modern Library.

Sober, E. (1998). Morgan's Canon. In D. D. Cummins, and C. Allen (eds.), *The Evolution of Mind,* pp. 224–242. Oxford: Oxford University Press.

Sober, E., and David Wilson, D. S. (1998). *Unto Others: The Evolution and Psychology of Unselfish Behavior.* Cambridge, MA: Harvard University Press.

Sommer, V. (1994). Infanticide among the langurs of Jodhpur: Testing the sexual selection hypothesis with a long-term record. In S. Parmigiani, and F. S. vom Saal (eds.), *Infanticide and Parental Care,* pp. 155–187. Chur: Harwood.

Stanford, C. B. (1998). The social behavior of chimpanzees and bonobos. *Current Anthropology* 39: 399–407.

Sugiyama, Y. (1967). Social organization of Hanuman langurs. In S. A. Altmann (ed.), *Social Communication among Primates,* pp. 221–253. Chicago: University of Chicago Press.

Sugiyama, Y., and Koman, J. (1979). Tool-using and -making behavior in wild chimpanzees at Bossou, Guinea. *Primates* 20: 513–524.

Tanaka, I. (1995). Matrilineal distribution of louse egg-handling techniques during grooming in free-ranging Japanese macaques. *American Journal of Physical Anthropology* 98: 197–201.

Thomas, R. K. (1998). Lloyd Morgan's canon. In G. Greenberg, and M. M. Haraway (eds.), *Comparative Psychology, A Handbook,* pp. 156–163. New York: Garland.

Thompson, R. K. R., and Contie, C. L. (1994). Further reflections on mirror usage by pigeons: Lessons from Winnie-the-Pooh and Pinocchio too. In S. T. Parker et al. (eds.), *Self-Awareness in Animals and Humans,* pp. 392–409. Cambridge: Cambridge University Press.

Thorpe, W. H. (1979). *The Origins and Rise of Ethology.* London: Praeger.

Timbergen, T. (1963). On aims and methods of ethology. *Zeitschrift für Tierpsychologie* 20: 410–433.

Tokuda, K. (1961–62). A study of sexual behavior in the Japanese monkey. *Primates* 3(2): 1640.

Tomasello, M. (1999). *The Cultural Origins of Human Cognition.* Cambridge, MA: Harvard University Press.

Tomasello, M., and Call, J. (1997). *Primate Cognition.* New York: Oxford University Press.

Tomasello, M., Kruger, A. C., and Ratner, H. H. (1993). Cultural learning. *Behavioral & Brain Sciences* 16: 495–552.

Tomasello, M., Savage-Rumbaugh, E. S., and Kruger, A. C. (1993). Imitative learning of actions on objects by children, chimpanzees, and enculturated chimpanzees. *Child Development* 64: 1688–1705.

Tratz, E. P., and Heck, H. (1954). Der afrikanische Anthropoide "Bonobo", eine neue Menschenaffengattung. *Säugetierkundliche Mitteilungen* 2: 97–101.

Tylor, E. B. (1871). *Primitive Culture.* London: Murray.

Vermeij, G. 1996. The touch of a shell. *Discover* 17(8): 76–81.

Vicchio, S. J. (1986). From Aristotle to Descartes: Making animals anthropomorphic. In R. J. Hoage, and L. Goldman (eds.), *Animal Intelligence: Insights into the Animal Mind,* pp. 187–207. Washington, D.C.: Smithsonian Institution Press.

Virey, J.-J. (1817). Art: Histoire naturelle. In *Nouveau dictionnaire d'histoire naturelle appliquée aux arts,* pp. 542–564. Paris: Deterville.

Visalberghi, E., and Fragaszy, D. M. (1990a). Food washing behaviour in tufted capuchins and crabeating macaques. *Animal Behaviour* 40: 829–836.

Visalberghi, E., and Fragaszy, D. M. (1990b). Do monkeys ape? In S. Parker, and K. Gibson (eds.), *"Language" and Intelligence in Monkeys and Apes: Comparative Developmental Perspectives,* pp. 247–273. Cambridge: Cambridge University Press.

Vogel, C. (1985). Evolution und moral. In H. Maier-Leibnitz (ed.). *Zeugen des Wissens,* pp. 467–507. Mainz: Hase & Koehler.

de Waal, F. B. M. (1986). The brutal elimination of a rival among captive male chimpanzees. *Ethology & Sociobiology* 7: 237–251.

de Waal, F. B. M. (1989a). *Peacemaking among Primates.* Cambridge, MA: Harvard University Press.

de Waal, F. B. M. (1989b). Behavioral contrasts between bonobo and chimpanzee. In P. Heltne, and L. A. Marquardt (eds.), *Understanding chimpanzees,* pp. 154–175. Cambridge, MA: Harvard University Press.

de Waal, F. B. M. (1991). Complementary methods and convergent evidence in the study of primate social cognition. *Behaviour* 118: 297–320.

de Waal, F. B. M. (1995). Sex as an alternative to aggression in the bonobo. In P. Abramson, and S. Pinkerton (eds.), *Sexual Nature, Sexual Culture,* pp. 37–56. Chicago: University of Chicago Press.

de Waal, F. B. M. (1996a). *Good Natured.* Cambridge, MA: Harvard University Press.

de Waal, F. B. M. (1996b). Macaque social culture: Development and perpetuation of affiliative networks. *Journal of Comparative Psychology* 110: 147–154.

de Waal, F. B. M. (1997). *Bonobo: The Forgotten Ape,* with photographs by F. Lanting. Berkeley: University of California Press.

de Waal, F. B. M. (1998 [1982]). *Chimpanzee Politics: Power and Sex among Apes,* revised edition. Baltimore, MD: Johns Hopkins University Press.

de Waal, F. B. M. (1999). Cultural primatology comes of age. *Nature* 399: 635–636.

de Waal, F. B. M. (2000). Primates: A natural heritage of conflict resolution. *Science* 289: 586–590.

de Waal, F. B. M., and Aureli, F. (1996). Consolation, reconciliation, and a possible cognitive difference between macaque and chimpanzee. In A. E. Russon, K. A. Bard, and S. T. Parker (eds.), *Reaching into Thought: The Minds of the Great Apes*, pp. 80–110. Cambridge: Cambridge University Press.

de Waal, F. B. M., and Berger, M. L. (2000). Payment for labour in monkeys. *Nature* 404: 563.

de Waal, F. B. M., and Johanowicz, D. L. (1993). Modification of reconciliation behavior through social experience: An experiment with two macaque species. *Child Development* 64: 897–908.

de Waal, F. B. M., and Luttrell, L. M. (1988). Mechanisms of social reciprocity in three primate species: symmetrical relationship characteristics or cognition? *Ethology and Sociobiology* 9: 101–118.

de Waal, F. B. M., and Seres, M. (1997). Propagation of handclasp grooming among captive chimpanzees. *American Journal of Primatology* 43: 339–346.

Walker, A. (1998). *By the Light of My Father's Smile*. New York: Ballantine.

Watanabe, K. (1989). Fish: A new addition to the diet of Japanese macaques on Koshima Island. *Folia primatologica* 52: 124–131.

Watanabe, K. (1994). Precultural behavior of Japanese macaques: Longitudinal studies of the Koshima troops. In R. A. Gardner, A. B. Chiarelli, B. T. Gardner, and F. X. Plooij (eds.), *The Ethological Roots of Culture*, pp. 81–94. Dordrecht: Kluwer.

Watanabe, S., and Nemoto, M. (1998). Reinforcing properties of music in Java sparrows (*Padda oryzivora*). *Behavioural Processes* 43: 211–218.

Watanabe, S., Sakamoto, J., and Wakita, M. (1995). Pigeons' discrimination of paintings by Monet and Picasso. *Journal of the Experimental Analysis of Behavior* 63: 165–174.

Watson, J. B. (1930 [1925]). *Behaviorism: Revised Edition*. Chicago: University of Chicago Press.

West, M. J., and King, A. P. (1990). Mozart's starling. *American Scientist* 78: 106–114.

Westermarck, E. (1912). *The Origin and Development of the Moral Ideas*, vol. 1. London: Macmillan.

White, L. A. (1959). *The Evolution of Culture*. New York: McGraw-Hill.

Whitehead, H. (1998). Cultural selection and genetic diversity in matrilineal whales. *Science* 282: 1708–1711.

Whiten, A. (1998). Imitation of the sequential structure of actions by chimpanzees. *Journal of Comparative Psychology* 112: 270–281.

Whiten, A., Goodall, J., McGrew, W. C., Nishida, T., Reynolds, V., Sugiyama, Y., Tutin, C. E. G., Wrangham, R. W., and Boesch, C. (1999). Cultures in chimpanzees. *Nature* 399: 682–685.

Whittemore, H., and Hebard, C. (1995). *So That Others May Live*. New York: Bantam.

Williams, G. C. (1988). Reply to comments on "Huxley's evolution and ethics in sociobiological perspective." *Zygon* 23: 437–438.

Wilson, E. O. (1995). *Naturalist*. New York: Warner.

Wilson, E. O. (1998). *Consilience: The Unity of Knowledge*. New York: Knopf.

Wimsatt, W. C. (1999). Genes, memes, and cultural heredity. *Biology and Philosophy* 14: 279–310.

Wolf, A. P. (1995). *Sexual Attraction and Childhood Association: A Chinese Brief for Edward Westermarck*. Stanford, CA: Stanford University Press.

Wolpert, L. (1992). *The Unnatural Nature of Science*. London: Faber & Faber.

Woodward, R., and Bernstein, C. (1976). *The Final Days*. New York: Simon & Schuster.

Wrangham, R. W., and Peterson, D. (1996). *Demonic Males: Apes and the Evolution of Human Aggression.* Boston: Houghton Mifflin.

Wrangham, R. W., McGrew, W. C., de Waal, F. B. M., and Heltne, P. (1994). *Chimpanzee Cultures.* Cambridge, MA: Harvard University Press.

Wright, R. (1994). *The Moral Animal; The New Science of Evolutionary Psychology.* New York: Pantheon.

Wright, R. (Dec. 13, 1999). The accidental creationist: Why Stephen Jay Gould is bad for evolution. *The New Yorker,* pp. 56–65.

Yamakoshi, G. (1998). Dietary responses to fruit scarcity of wild chimpanzees at Bossou, Guinea: Possible implications for ecological importance of tool use. *American Journal of Physical Anthropology* 106: 283–295.

Yoshimi, K. (1998). Imanishi Kinji's biosociology as a forerunner of the semiosphere concept. *Semiotica* 120: 273–297.

Zhao, Q.-K. (1996). Etho-ecology of Tibetan macaques at Mount Emei, China. In J. E. Fa, and D. G. Lindburg (eds.), *Evolution and Ecology of Macaque Societies,* pp. 263–289. Cambridge: Cambridge University Press.

EXPLORING THE TEXT

1. What, in de Waal's view, is the common stereotype of the scientist? Where do you think this cultural image of the scientist comes from? What truth, if any, does it reflect, in your opinion? Why?

2. What "embarrassing problem" do animals present for us? What does de Waal mean when he says that most of us live in a state of "anthropodenial"? Why have we as a species tended to ignore or deny our relationship with other animals? Would you agree that most people refuse to accept the psychological and physical similarities between humans and animals?

3. What is the story of Thorleif Schjelderup-Ebbe meant to demonstrate? How does it relate to the points de Waal is making in this selection about the personal nature of science, the power of the imagination, and the phenomenon of anthropodenial?

4. What is wrong with simple-minded anthropomorphism like the kind that's involved in "Bambification," according to de Waal? Why does he believe that such naive forms of anthropomorphism are actually manifestations of anthrocentrism?

5. What is the difference between naive and "mature" anthropomorphism, in de Waal's view? How do the illustrations of "animalcentric" thinking that he describes — like his reading of Georgia's intentions or Monty Roberts's interpretation of horses — differ from "Bambification"?

6. How does de Waal use the case of Binti to anticipate objections against the reliability of "mature" anthropomorphic thinking? What does the case of Binti suggest about the way we tend to view animals? About the way we tend to view all of our experiences as a species?

FURTHER EXPLORATIONS

1. How might de Waal's view of science and mature anthropomorphism challenge the association that John (Fire) Lame Deer makes between the "white world" and the notion of domestication (p. 512)?

2. What kind of anthropomorphism, naive or mature, does Faith McNulty display in her interpretations of the intentions, feelings, and reactions of Mouse (p. 535)? What leads you to this conclusion? Would you agree with de Waal that most people today are losing the ability to appreciate the otherness of animals? Why or why not?

3. Given Charles Siebert's analysis of nature programming in "The Artifice of the Natural" (p. 542), what role has television played in the "Bambification" of animals? Do you think that television has generally made it easier or more difficult for most of us to develop the kind of "mature" anthropomorphism that de Waal values in his essay? Do you think people are generally more or less anthrocentric today as the result of television programming?

4. Compare de Waal's notion of "mature" anthropomorphism with Martha C. Nussbaum's understanding of empathy (p. 416). What distinguishes both of these forms of imaginative identification with others from simpler, more egocentric forms of mind reading? To what extent do Nussbaum and de Waal agree on the role that childhood plays in learning to read other minds?

5. How might de Waal evaluate the way that primate minds are read by the authors of "Murder in a Zoo" (p. 580) and "The Case for the Personhood of Gorillas" (p. 592)? What, if any, examples of naive anthropomorphism might he detect in these essays?

ESSAY OPTIONS

1. Drawing on your own experience and on ideas and information presented in this selection, in "Why Look at Animals?" by John Berger (p. 521), and in "The Artifice of the Natural" by Charles Siebert (p. 542), write an essay discussing the role that popular culture has played in the "Bambification" of animals and the natural world. How are animals and nature portrayed in recent films and television series? To what extent do these portrayals project a sentimentalized or naively anthropomorphic view of nature? Would you agree that we are losing contact with "the full picture of nature in all its glory and horror," as de Waal suggests? Why or why not?

2. Write an essay in which you evaluate the current status of what de Waal refers to as "anthropodenial" in contemporary American culture. What evidence do you see to suggest that we, as a species, are collectively more willing to recognize our relation to other forms of animal life? What evidence do you see to suggest that we continue to deny our physical and mental connection with animal others?

3. Locate and read an article, book, or excerpt written by any one of the ethologists de Waal mentions — scientists like Konrad Lorenz, Robert Yerkes, Bernd Heinrich, Ken Norris, Jane Goodall, Cynthia Moss, and Edward Wilson. Then write a report discussing how their work demonstrates the kind of "mature" anthropomorphism that de Waal describes in this essay.

4. Independently or as a class, view one or more recent ethological documentaries focusing on a particular animal species. You might, for example, screen one of the

films devoted to the work of Jane Goodall or any one of the many recent *National Geographic* or PBS documentaries on exotic animals or house pets. Then write a paper assessing the films' portrayal of animal minds. To what extent do these films model the kind of "animalcentric anthropomorphism" that de Waal promotes in this selection? What specific insights do they offer into the workings of animal minds?

Murder in a Zoo

RICHARD LEAKEY AND ROGER LEWIN

The chimpanzees you see in movies are usually portrayed as lovable clowns. They mug for the camera, imitate the foolish behavior of their human costars, and hoot their approval at happy—and ecologically sound—endings. In the wild, however, chimp behavior would probably play better in *The Godfather* than it would in *George of the Jungle*. This selection, documenting the cold-blooded assassination of a chimp by two of his follow-ers, introduces the seamier side of animal thinking. The scenario of political intrigue presented here by Richard Leakey and Roger Lewin challenges us to reconsider many of our assumptions about the sophistication of animal minds. It also invites us to reflect on what, if anything, distinguishes human from animal intelligence. Richard Leakey (b. 1944) spent most of his childhood in Tanzania, East Africa, where his famous archae-ologist parents, Louis and Mary Leakey, carried out their groundbreaking research, tracing human ancestry back to "Lucy," a two-million-year-old hominid fossil found in Olduvai Gorge. A paleoanthropologist, conservationist, and archaeologist, Richard Leakey currently serves as director of the Kenya Wildlife Service and has published a number of books and scholarly articles on early human evolution and animal behavior. Roger Lewin (b. 1946) is a science writer who specializes in issues relating to human evo-lution. This selection first appeared in *Origins Reconsidered: In Search of What Makes Us Human* (1992).

BEFORE READING

Imagine that you have been asked to devise a test to determine if a given species of ani-mal possesses true intelligence. What would your test look like? What skills or abilities would you expect to see in an intelligent animal? How could you tell if an animal pos-sessed these mental traits?

For five years Luit had been jockeying for leadership of the chimp colony at Burgers' Zoo, in Arnhem, the Netherlands. Intermediate in age between Yeroen and Nikkie, chief rivals for top chimp, Luit was a fine physical speci-men, muscular, with a sleek, black coat. Nevertheless, Luit exploited his wit, not his physique, in his drive for leadership. Manipulating the balance of power first with Yeroen, then with Nikkie, sometimes playing off one against the other, Luit finally achieved the position of alpha male,° and with it the favored access to the females in the colony. But success was soon followed by disaster, and this time brawn, not brain, prevailed: Yeroen and Nikkie joined forces and attacked Luit, brutally.

"I was working at home," remembers Frans de Waal,° who has studied the Arnhem colony for many years. "It was a Saturday morning. The telephone rang, and the news was about as bad as it could be." Rapidly, and in great distress, de Waal's assistant described how she had just found Luit, barely conscious and covered in blood and torn flesh. Deeply gashed on his head, sides, hands, and feet, Luit appeared near death. The most gruesome of injuries: Yeroen and Nikkie had torn off both of Luit's testicles. "Do what you can for him," de Waal shouted into the phone. "I'll be there right away."

Emotions churned in his breast as he frantically cycled the short distance between his house and the zoo, emotions of despair and sadness. And accusation. "Yeroen was to blame," he kept thinking. Luit's condition was even worse than de Waal had feared, and despite three hours of surgery, Luit died, from a combination of stress and loss of blood. Even now, a decade after the incident, de Waal says, "I cannot look at Yeroen without seeing a murderer. Nikkie, ten years younger than Yeroen, was only a pawn in Yeroen's game."

What kind of game could end in murder? "Politics; the pursuit of power," explains de Waal. Two millennia ago, Aristotle labeled the human a *politikon zoön*, a political animal. "He could not know just how near the mark he was," says de Waal. "Our political activity seems to be part of an evolutionary heritage we share with our close relatives." Assassination as the resolution of power struggles is not unusual in the pages of human history, a last resort when the usual means of political manipulation fail. So it has been for Luit. "What my work at Arnhem has taught me," says de Waal, "is that the roots of politics are older than humanity."

Although many people are unaware of the fact, my father° believed fervently that if we understood more about the behavior of the great apes — our closest living relatives — we would understand more about ourselves and about our evolutionary history. He devoted considerable energy to establishing what eventually became two of the most famous and influential of all primate field studies: Jane Goodall's, with chimpanzees in Tanzania, and Dian Fossey's,° with gorillas in Rwanda. The information gained from studies of the   5

alpha male: Term used to designate the dominant male in a group of primates.

Frans de Waal: See page 552.

my father: Louis Seymour Bazett Leakey (1903–1972), British paleontologist famed for the codiscovery, with his wife Mary, in 1959 of the fossil remains of "Lucy," believed, at that time, to be the earliest primate ancestor of the species *Homo sapiens.*

Jane Goodall's . . . Dian Fossey's: Jane Goodall (b. 1934), British ethologist known for her work with chimpanzees in Tanzania; Dian Fossey (1932–1985), American zoologist believed to have been killed by poachers because of her work with gorillas in Tanzania.

social behavior of the African apes would complement what we could learn from the fossil record, my father argued. How right he was.

Not only have these and other primate studies given us concrete ways of thinking about the social structure of our ancestors (especially in relation to such factors as body size, ecology, and sexual dimorphism°) they have given us insights into the primate mind. They have given us a glimpse of the evolution of consciousness, the phenomenon that we experience as introspection and self-awareness.

In recent years primatologists and psychologists have come to realize just how Byzantine° is the primate mind. From the monitoring and manipulation of complex networks of relations, to the perpetration of clever tricks of deception, our primate cousins inhabit social and intellectual worlds more complex than we could have imagined. The title of a recent book on the subject says it all: *Machiavellian Intelligence.*°

That the British psychologists Richard Byrne and Andrew Whiten, editors of *Machiavellian Intelligence,* considered such a title appropriate for a scholarly text on primate social expertise is indicative of the respect now being accorded to the nonhuman primate mind. We look at the subject here as a way to understand something of the human mind and, in particular, of the emergence of introspective consciousness during our evolutionary history. . . .

. . . In our quest for the roots of human consciousness we will explore the social worlds of nonhuman primates; we will ask why primates seem to be more intelligent than they need be; we will search for signs of a sense of self in these animals, including their penchant for deceiving one another; we will look at the meager clues of consciousness in the prehistoric record; and we will address the emergence of mythology and religion.

The first question to ask is not so much the what of consciousness as the why. Why should there even be the phenomenon of human consciousness? The capacity for introspection experienced by humans may be an epiphenomenon°   10

sexual dimorphism: Characterized by two distinct genders.

Byzantine: Anything that is extraordinarily complex and characterized by deviousness or deception.

Machiavellian Intelligence: In his book *The Prince,* sixteenth-century Italian courtier Niccolo Machiavelli advises monarchs to use cunning, duplicity, and ruthlessness in dealing with their subjects; hence, the aspect of mind dedicated to the manipulation of others.

epiphenomenon: A secondary phenomenon or effect caused by another primary phenomenon.

FIGURE 5.2

In the power struggle between the dominant chimpanzees at Burgers' Zoo in Arnhem, Nikkie and Yeroen at one point formed a coalition. In the top right, we see Nikkie (left) becoming angry that his coalition partner (Yeroen, right) is sitting near to Nikkie's rival, Luit. Nikkie sits aggressively opposite the other two males. In the middle right, Nikkie bluffs a threat, and Yeroen gets up and moves away. In the bottom right, his separation attempt now successful, Nikkie bluffs ostentatiously over Luit. (Frans de Waal)

of a large, complex brain, the byproduct of other neural functions, "the whine of neural gears, the clicking of neural circuitry," as the Cambridge University psychologist Horace Barlow once put it. In my approach to the human species, however, it is necessary to view consciousness as we view other aspects of ourselves: the direct product of natural selection. In that case, we have to ask what selective benefit consciousness conferred on our ancestors and on us. I will take what may seem a circuitous route in answering this question. The route begins with asking why higher primates appear to be more intelligent than they "need" to be.

· · ·

At the Language Research Center of Georgia State University, in Atlanta, there is a monkey that, armed with a miniature joystick, can anticipate the complex movement of an object on a computer screen and ultimately "capture" the object. Even for a human, the task is not easy. It requires concentration on, and prediction of, the object's likely trajectories, as well as fine manipulation of the joystick. And yet the monkey is not specially trained for the task, not especially talented. Any of the monkeys at the center can do it, once they are familiar with the system. In another part of the center are to be found chimpanzees that can accomplish even more demanding intellectual problems, often ones that require the ability to see three or four moves ahead in a sequential puzzle. Analytical skills, reasoning, and foresight are called for. Again, these animals are not specially trained or especially talented. They are displaying the natural talents of higher primates.

This presents us with a conundrum, for what is natural about the talents I've just described? Psychologists who study the cognitive abilities of monkeys and apes in laboratory situations agree that the animals seem to be profoundly smarter than their natural needs demand. "During two months that I spent watching gorillas in the Virunga Mountains of Rwanda," observes another Cambridge University psychologist, Nicholas Humphrey, "I could not help being struck by the fact that of all the animals in the forest the gorillas seemed to lead much the simplest existence—food abundant and easy to harvest (provided they *knew* where to find it), few if any predators (provided they *knew* how to avoid them) . . . little to do (and little done) but eat, sleep, and play." The cognitive skills displayed by higher primates in the laboratory seem to outstrip by far the practical demands of their natural worlds. Has natural selection been profligate in making them smarter than they really need to be?

A few years ago Nick Humphrey visited Kenya, and we went to Koobi Fora, where we talked about his ideas. What, I wanted to know, did these observations have to do with the evolution of the human mind? "The same things you can say about the daily lives of gorillas—that the world of practical affairs seems not very demanding intellectually—you can say about humans," he replied. "Studies on hunter-gatherer societies show that the demands of their daily lives are not great. Hunting techniques do not greatly outstrip those of other social carnivores. And gathering strategies are of the same order as you might find in, say, chimpanzees or baboons."

I acknowledged this and wondered what it was in evolutionary history that enabled the human brain to create a Mozart symphony or Einstein's theory of relativity. "The answer," said Nick, "is social life. Primates lead complex social lives. That's what makes them—and has made us—so intelligent." I must admit to having been pretty skeptical about Nick's suggestion during that trip to Koobi Fora. The notion that the exigencies of social interaction, such as building alliances and outwitting potential rivals, may have been responsible for honing human intellect seemed somehow insubstantive. Perhaps it is because the social nexus is so natural a part of human existence that it becomes, in a way, invisible to our thought. A decade of research on nonhuman primates has, however, had the effect of making the social nexus not only visible but also sharply focused. Nick's hypothesis now looks very powerful indeed.

For a long time anthropologists accepted the idea that technology, not so-   15
cial interaction, was the driving force behind the evolution of the human intellect. Given that our physical world is dominated by the fruits of clever in-
vention, it is not surprising that we are impressed by human technological skills. And it is natural that such skills should be thought of as the direct prod-
ucts of natural selection. But, as Harry Jerison has argued, it seems more likely that these skills are the byproduct of an intellect sharpened by other forces in natural selection. "Building a better reality" was how Jerison described it. As we bring this into closer focus, we can see that for the higher primates, the most important—and most intellectually challenging—components in an individual's reality are other individuals.

For a baboon or a chimpanzee, a certain amount of intellectual capacity and memory is required for exploiting food resources year round. They need a kind of mental map of their range. They need to know, and be able to rec-
ognize, when certain trees will be in fruit, when certain tubers are ready, when certain waterholes will be full. But there is a degree of predictability about it all, a pattern to follow. By contrast, other individuals in one's troop may be anything but predictable, particularly in their response to one's own behavior. A richly laden fruit tree may be difficult to find, but once located it doesn't suddenly disappear or its fruit become inedible. Such Alice-in-Wonderland transformations in a fruit tree would be the equivalent to the range of responses one individual in a troop may face when meeting another, a rival, for instance.

Compare gorillas and zebras, on the face of it an odd pair to contemplate together. Both species inhabit similar ecological worlds, in that both feed on evenly distributed and widely abundant food resources (leaves in mountain forests for gorillas, grasses on open plains for zebras). And in both species females leave their natal groups to live with a single dominant male and a group of unrelated females. Since their ecological worlds and social structures have the same framework, one might suppose their mental capacities would be similar too. Not so. Relatively speaking, gorillas are about four times brainier

than zebras, a difference that correlates with a much more complex and demanding social life than zebras.

"Like chess, a social interaction is typically a *trans*action between social partners," says Nick Humphrey. "It asks for a level of intelligence that is unparalleled in any other sphere of living. There may be, of course, strong and weak players—yet, as master or novice, we and most other members of complex primate societies have been in this game since we were babies." Nick has been developing this line of argument since the early 1970s, and his ideas served to crystallize similar thoughts among other researchers. By now, the notion of social intelligence—or, rather, the acute intellectual demands of complex social life—has become the leading paradigm among anthropologists.

A recent review of primate studies, by Dorothy Cheney, Robert Seyfarth, and Barbara Smuts, confirms the ascendancy of the paradigm. "Nonhuman primate tool use, which has received considerable attention because of its relevance to human evolution, is striking in part because it is relatively rare," they note. "By comparison, primatologists repeatedly emphasize the ability of the subjects to use other individuals as 'social tools' to achieve particular results." They conclude that, "among nonhuman primates, sophisticated cognitive abilities are most evident during social interactions."

What is it that makes primate social life so complex that it demands "so-   20
phisticated cognitive abilities"? In a word, the principal element is *alliances*. As in all animal groups, the ultimate driving factor in individual behavior is reproductive success. In anthropomorphic terms, females strive to raise to maturity as many offspring as they can, males strive to father as many offspring as they can. For females, reproductive success is achieved through being able to care for and protect offspring; for males, reproductive success depends on having as many mating opportunities as possible. For both males and females, the goals are made easier if they can rely on the support of others, friends and relations. A great deal of primate life is therefore spent in nurturing such alliances for oneself and in assessing the alliances of one's rivals.

Consider the affair between Alex and Thalia, young mature baboons, members of a troop that live near Eburru Cliffs, one hundred miles northwest of Nairobi, on the floor of the Great Rift Valley. Barbara Smuts, a primatologist at the University of Michigan, studied the social life of this troop over several years, paying particular attention to the establishment of what she called "friendships," long-term alliances between males and females. Alex had entered the troop recently and needed to establish a strong alliance with a female. He chose Thalia.

"It was like watching two novices in a singles bar," reports Barbara. "Alex stared at Thalia until she turned and almost caught him looking at her. He glanced away immediately, and then she stared at him until his head began to turn toward her. She suddenly became engrossed in grooming her toes. But as soon as Alex looked away, her gaze returned to him. They went on like this for more than fifteen minutes, always with split-second timing. Finally, Alex managed to catch Thalia looking at him. He made the friendly eyes-narrowed, ears-back face and smacked his lips together rhythmically. Thalia froze, and for a second she looked into his eyes. Alex approached, and Thalia, still nervous, groomed him. Soon she calmed down, and I found them together on the cliffs the next morning." Six years later, on a subsequent visit to Eburru Cliffs, Barbara found that the friendship formed in that initial tentative manner had held fast.

"Because baboon friendships are embedded in a network of friendly and antagonistic relationships, they inevitably have repercussions extending beyond the pair," explains Barbara. For instance, she once observed Cyclops with some meat, part of an antelope he had caught. Triton, the prime adult male of the troop, spotted the prize and began challenging Cyclops for it. "Cyclops grew tense and seemed about to abandon the prey," Barbara recounts. "Then Cyclops's friend Phoebe appeared with her infant, Phyllis. Phyllis wandered over to Cyclops. He immediately grabbed her close and threatened Triton away from the prey."

The move was a smart one, because if Triton had continued to threaten Cyclops, he would in effect be threatening Phyllis too, Phoebe's infant. As a result, "Triton risked being mobbed by Phoebe and her relatives and friends," explains Barbara. Against such odds, the prudent thing for Triton to do was back down, which he promptly did. "Thus, friendship involves costs as well as benefits because it makes the participants vulnerable to social manipulation or redirected aggression by others."

Networks of alliances hold primate troops together and govern individuals' interactions. Dorothy Cheney and Robert Seyfarth describe another example, this time in vervet monkeys, which they have studied in Amboseli National Park, in Kenya. "In a typical encounter, one female, Newton, may lunge at another, Tycho, while competing for a fruit. As Tycho moves off, Newton's sister Charing Cross runs up to aid in the chase. In the meantime, Wormwood Scrubs, another of Newton's sisters, runs over to Tycho's sister Holborn, who is feeding sixty feet away, and hits her on the head." What to the casual observer may look like an outburst of random aggression among a group of irascible individuals is in fact the playing out of conflict over ever-widening networks of alliances, both of blood and friendship.

"Hostility between two animals often expands to include whole families, so not only must monkeys predict one another's behavior, but they must assess one another's relationship," explain Dorothy and Robert. "A monkey confronted with all this nonrandom turmoil cannot be content with learning simply who's dominant or subordinate to herself; she must also know who's allied to whom and who's likely to aid an opponent." Through a series of ingenious experiments, in which they played recordings of specific individuals' calls, Dorothy and Robert were able to determine by the other monkeys' reactions that the animals know very clearly the patterns of relationship and alliance networks in their troop.

If alliance networks were permanent structures within a troop, it would be difficult enough for individuals to cope with their intricate connections. But they are by no means permanent. Always looking to their own best interests, and to the interests of their closest relatives, individuals may sometimes find it advantageous to break existing alliances and form new ones, perhaps even with previous rivals. Troop members therefore find themselves in the midst of changing patterns of alliances, demanding yet keener social intelligence to be able to play the changing game of social chess.

Luit, Yeroen, and Nikkie were pieces in such a game of social chess as their strategies propelled them toward that final, fatal attack, in September 1980. Frans de Waal, who watched the game, recorded it in detail.

In the beginning, in 1975, Yeroen, the eldest of the three, was the unquestioned alpha male. Luit and Nikkie routinely submitted to Yeroen, and he enjoyed the allegiance of all the females in the troop. Then, in the summer of 1976, Luit stopped showing submission to Yeroen, and began to challenge him with noisy displays. The much younger Nikkie joined in support of Luit, but only when Luit was confronting the females, Yeroen's supporters. After a few months, Luit's challenges to Yeroen's position prevailed, and he became the dominant male in the troop.

During the first year of the new era, both Luit and Nikkie solicited support from Yeroen, the fallen leader. It was as if Luit knew he would be better off if Yeroen were a friend rather than an enemy. Nikkie seemed to be seeking an alliance with Yeroen, perhaps to try to overthrow Luit. In any case, at the end of the year, Nikkie got what he wanted when Yeroen and he formed an alliance against Luit. By this time Luit had gained the loyalty of all the females in the troop, a state of affairs that was to bring his downfall, suggests de Waal.   30

"Luit's fate is reminiscent of the balance-of-power paradox 'strength is weakness,'" de Waal explains. "This means that the strongest of the three competing parties almost automatically elicits cooperation against himself, because the weaker parties gain more by joining together and sharing the payoffs than by joining the strongest party, who will monopolize the payoffs." As it was, with Yeroen's support, Nikkie became the alpha male. By contrast with Luit's previous position, Nikkie's status depended completely on the alliance with Yeroen. Although he wasn't the prime male, Yeroen still enjoyed considerable reproductive success, his access to females being tolerated by Nikkie as part of the deal between them.

Nikkie managed to consolidate his position over the next year, with Yeroen playing politics on both sides. He had been able to gain access to estrous females, sometimes by enlisting Nikkie's support against Luit, sometimes by co-opting Luit against Nikkie. This double game began to fall apart toward the end of 1978, when Nikkie and Luit struck up what de Waal calls a "nonintervention treaty." As a result, Nikkie and Luit's special relationship, which appeared during periods of sexual competition, strengthened over the ensuing months.

At the opening of 1980, the situation of the three males seemed stable. Nikkie was the dominant individual, with Yeroen's support, and Luit was excluded, even though he was more powerful than either of the other two. As the year progressed, however, Nikkie seemed lax in keeping his end of the bargain with Yeroen. For instance, he didn't support Yeroen's approach to estrous females, and didn't prevent Luit from approaching females. Two days later, during the night of July 6, a fight broke out in which Nikkie and Yeroen sustained injuries: fingers and toes cut or missing, as is typical of chimp encounters.

"Although no winner or loser could be determined on the basis of mere injury count, Nikkie clearly behaved like the loser," recounts de Waal. "Even though it didn't seem as if Luit had been very much involved in the physical battle, he emerged as the new dominant male." What had happened, believes de Waal, is that because Nikkie had failed to keep his bargain with Yeroen, Yeroen called an end to the alliance in a fairly violent way. When the alliance collapsed, Luit stepped into the power void, once again the dominant male.

During the subsequent weeks the troop was tense because of the fragile order that prevailed after the fight. Luit, Nikkie, and Yeroen constantly seemed to be testing possible new alliances. But "for Yeroen, restoration of the coalition with Nikkie seemed to have priority over any other option," says de Waal. "Yeroen would scream in apparent frustration and follow Luit and Nikkie around whenever they walked together. And Yeroen himself often tried to sit and groom with Nikkie." It was a patently unstable situation.

Then came the fatal attack. Yeroen and Nikkie appear to have decided that their best interests would be served by reestablishing their alliance. de Waal guesses the Yeroen initiated that attack, leading Nikkie with him. Significantly, the castration that Luit suffered as part of his injuries is not uncommon in status fights of this kind.

The pursuit of power in the Arnhem colony had for the most part been orchestrated with political manipulation and guile, but it ended with the ultimate imposition of the power of an alliance on a rival: death. Quite apart from its tragic elements, I find the story of Yeroen, Nikkie, and Luit arresting. I've been arguing that the world of higher primates — of monkeys, apes, and humans — is quintessentially a game of social chess, a keen intellectual challenge. The challenge is keener yet than the ancient board game itself, because the pieces not only unpredictably change identity — knights becoming bishops, pawns becoming castles, and so on — they occasionally switch colors to become the enemy. To prevail in this game, the player must constantly be alert, ever seeking a winning edge, ever avoiding disadvantage. Chess is an apt metaphor, because it captures precisely the dynamic complexity higher primates face in operating within their worlds. Apt, but somewhat abstract, lacking in emotion.

I wasn't at the Arnhem zoo during the struggle for power that led to Luit's death, but the raw emotion of it all comes through to me just from the description of the events. When de Waal talks about the struggle, he becomes rapt with the personal energy of the participants and clearly is not emotionally indifferent to their ordeal. He admits that when he labels Yeroen a "murderer," he is imputing human motives. I can see why. On a different level we can empathize with the fracas between the vervet monkeys Tycho and Newton over a piece of fruit;

cheer on Charing Cross, Newton's sister, as she comes to lend a hand; and understand why Wormwood Scrubs, another of Newton's sisters, takes the opportunity to harass Holborn, Tycho's sister. It makes sense logically and emotionally. And who can avoid a grin of recognition at the shy advances made so patiently by Alex, the young male baboon, to Thalia? The game of social chess in higher primate life is played by individuals pursuing their roles as best they can, expressing a range of emotions that we can identify as human.

What each individual seeks, of course, is reproductive success: producing as many healthy, socially adept offspring as possible. In birds of paradise, the greatest reproductive success (in males) goes to those with the most elaborate plumage and winning display. In red deer, the greatest reproductive success (again, in males) goes to those with the biggest, strongest bodies with which to overthrow rivals, sometimes literally. In higher primates, the greatest reproductive success (in both males and females) is shaped much more by social skills than by physical displays, either of strength or appearance. The complex interactions of the primate social nexus serve as an exquisite sorting system, in which the individuals with an edge in making alliances and monitoring the alliances of others may score significantly higher in reproductive success.

I am describing a world shaped by Darwinian natural selection, so none   40
of the players in it have maximum reproductive success as an immediate, conscious aim in life. Natural selection has sharpened social skills, which lead to reproductive success. Those skills are structured on a keen, analytical intelligence. In other words, natural selection has honed intelligence in primates in the same way and in the same evolutionary context as it influences attributes of strength and physical appearance in other groups of animals.

We began our exploration of the roots of human consciousness by asking why higher primates are more intelligent than they need to be for the daily round of practical affairs. The answer, I suggest, is the intense intellectual demands of primate social interactions, with the constant need to understand and outwit others in the drive for reproductive success. Our brain is extraordinarily large in part because of the exigencies of social interaction, which evolved to levels far greater than those of other higher primates.

EXPLORING THE TEXT

1. In what sense was Luit's death the result of "politics," according to the authors? What assumptions are built into the concept of politics and political motivations? How is our view of Nikkie and Yeroen changed if we view the act of violence they engaged in as politically motivated?

2. What role, according to Leakey and Lewin, has social interaction played in the development of chimpanzee and human minds? What arguments or evidence do they offer in support of the claim that primate minds have developed a complex form of "social intelligence"?

3. What questions do the authors set out to answer in this selection? What is their purpose? What assumptions are Leakey and Lewin making about the relationship

between primate and human minds? What problems, if any, might you see in linking the behaviors and intentions of two different species?

4. Given the authors' assessment of the motives and intelligence underlying Nikkie's and Yeroen's assault on Luit, would it be accurate — and just — to categorize their act of violence as a genuine act of "murder"? Why or why not? If they, in fact, did murder Luit, should their action be considered a crime and should they be punished in some way? Why or why not?

FURTHER EXPLORATIONS

1. How might John (Fire) Lame Deer (p. 512) respond to the suggestion that animals are capable of premeditated acts of murder, as described by Leakey and Lewin? How would you account for this possible reaction?

2. To what extent do Leakey and Lewin appear to indulge in what Frans de Waal might consider "naive" anthropomorphism in their analysis of Luit's "murder"? Is it possible to discuss chimpanzee behavior in terms of concepts like "alliances," "coalitions," "nonintervention treaties," "political manipulation," or a "balance of power" without engaging in excessive anthropomorphism? Why or why not?

3. To what extent might the "marginalization" of animals as described by John Berger (p. 521), their "Disneyfication" as described by Charles Siebert (p. 542), or their "Bambification" as described by Frans de Waal (p. 552) account for the difficulty of seeing any animal as a "murderer"? How does the case of Yeroen, Nikkie, and Luit challenge these contemporary ways of viewing the animal world?

4. To what extent do Faith McNulty's interpretations of the goals and intentions of Mouse (p. 535) suggest that a species other than primates may also engage in politics? Which, if any, of Mouse's actions might be seen as particularly "Machiavellian"? Why?

5. Compare the explanations for violent behavior among chimps offered in this selection with James Garbarino's concept of "soul murder" (p. 485). How might you explain why Leakey and Lewin view cold-blooded murder as a sign of rationality and complex intelligence in animals, while Garbarino views the same kind of violence among humans as a sign of mental breakdown? Is it possible to view the arguments forwarded by Leakey and Lewin as somehow "normalizing" human aggression? Why or why not?

6. How would Paul Shepard (p. 624) be likely to respond to Leakey and Lewin's analysis of primate "politics"? How do the observations of primate behavior and social patterns in "Murder in a Zoo" challenge Shepard's views of animals and their relationship to the ecosystem they inhabit?

ESSAY OPTION

Over the past two decades, a number of critics, like Stephen Jay Gould and Richard Lewontin, have faulted sociobiological explanations of human behavior because they believe that such "evolutionary" arguments tend to reduce complicated issues of human interaction to the level of "instincts" and "drives" and thus de-emphasize individual responsibility and ethical judgment. Using your library's resources, research the topic of sociobiology and the controversy surrounding sociobiological interpretations of human behavior, and write a report outlining the main points of this controversy.

The Case for the Personhood of Gorillas

FRANCINE PATTERSON AND WENDY GORDON

Chances are you're already familiar with the subject of this selection. Koko is a low-land gorilla who for nearly three decades has been astonishing the world as a participant in a remarkable experiment. Under the tutelage of Francine Patterson, Koko began learning American Sign Language symbols in 1972, eventually mastering more than one thousand "words" and becoming the first animal to communicate directly with a human being. Koko's achievement is so remarkable that, as the title of this selection suggests, Patterson believes she has earned the right to be recognized as a "person" — an independent "individual" who deserves all of the protections and considerations that we would offer any human being. As the result of her work with Koko, Patterson (b. 1947) earned her doctorate in developmental psychology from Stanford University in 1979 and today serves as the president of the Gorilla Foundation, an organization dedicated to Koko and the study of primate language acquisition. Wendy Gordon is a researcher who has worked with Koko and two other signing gorillas, Michael and Ndume, since 1992.

BEFORE READING

Working in groups, discuss what the concept of "personhood" means. What qualities, characteristics, or behaviors do we associate with the state of personhood? Are all human beings persons? What would it take for a gorilla to achieve the status of personhood? What would this mean?

We present this individual for your consideration:

She communicates in sign language, using a vocabulary of over one thousand words. She also understands spoken English, and often carries on "bilingual" conversations, responding in sign to questions asked in English. She is learning the letters of the alphabet, and can read some printed words, including her own name. She has achieved scores between 85 and 95 on the Stanford–Binet Intelligence Test.

She demonstrates a clear self-awareness by engaging in self-directed behaviors in front of a mirror, such as making faces or examining her teeth, and by her appropriate use of self-descriptive language. She lies to avoid the consequences of her own misbehavior, and anticipates others' responses to her actions. She engages in imaginary play, both alone and with others. She has produced paintings and drawings which are representational. She remembers and can talk about past events in her life. She understands and has used appropriately time-related words like *before, after, later,* and *yesterday.*

She laughs at her own jokes and those of others. She cries when hurt or left alone, screams when frightened or angered. She talks about her feelings, using words like *happy, sad, afraid, enjoy, eager, frustrate, mad,* and, quite frequently, *love.* She grieves for those she has lost—a favorite cat who has died, a friend who has gone away. She can talk about what happens when one dies, but she becomes fidgety and uncomfortable when asked to discuss her own death or the death of her companions. She displays a wonderful gentleness with kittens and other small animals. She has even expressed empathy for others seen only in pictures.

Does this individual have a claim to basic moral rights? It is hard to imagine any reasonable argument that would deny her these rights based on the description above. She is self-aware, intelligent, emotional, communicative, has memories and purposes of her own, and is certainly able to suffer deeply. There is no reason to change our assessment of her moral status if I add one more piece of information: namely that she is not a member of the human species. The person I have described—and she is nothing less than a person to those who are acquainted with her—is Koko, a twenty-year-old lowland gorilla.   5

For almost twenty years, Koko has been living and learning in a language environment that includes American Sign Language (ASL) and spoken English.[1] Koko combines her working vocabulary of over five hundred signs into statements averaging three to six signs in length. Her emitted vocabulary—those signs she has used correctly on one or more occasions—is about one thousand. Her receptive vocabulary in English is several times that number of words.

Koko is not alone in her linguistic accomplishments. Her multispecies "family" includes Michael, an eighteen-year-old male gorilla. Although he was not introduced to sign language until the age of three and a half, he has used over four hundred different signs. Both gorillas initiate the majority of their conversations with humans and combine their vocabularies in creative and original sign utterances to describe their environment, feelings, desires and even what may be their past histories. They also sign to themselves and to each other, using human language to supplement their own natural communicative gestures and vocalizations.

Sign language has become such an integral part of their daily lives that Koko and Michael are more familiar with the language than are some of their human companions. Both gorillas have been known to sign slowly and repeat signs when conversing with a human who has limited signing skills. They also attempt to teach as they have been taught. For example, one day Michael had been repeatedly signing "CHASE" (hitting two fisted hands together) but was getting no response from his companion, who did not know this sign. He finally took her hands and hit them together and then gave her a push to get her moving. Similarly, Koko has often been observed molding the hands of her dolls into signs.

Tests have shown that the gorillas understand spoken English as well as they understand sign. In one standardized test called the Assessment of Children's Language Comprehension, novel phrases corresponding to sets of pictures were given to the gorillas under conditions in which the tester did not know the correct answers. Koko's performance (see Table 1) was twice as good as might have been expected by chance, and there was no significant difference in her performance whether the instructions were given in sign only or in English only.[2]

Because the gorillas understand linguistic instructions and questions, we   10 have been able to use standardized intelligence tests to further assess their abilities.[3] Koko's scores on different tests administered between 1972 and 1977 yielded an average IQ of 80.3 (see Table 2). More significant than the actual scores is the steady growth of Koko's mental age. This increase shows that she is capable of understanding a number of the principles that are the foundation of what we call abstract thought.

Many of those who would defend the traditional barrier between *Homo sapiens* and all other species cling to language as the primary difference between humans and other animals. As apes have threatened this last claim to human uniqueness, it has become more apparent that there is no clear agreement as to the definition of language. Many human beings—including all infants, severely mentally impaired people and some educationally deprived deaf adults of normal intelligence—fail to meet the criteria for "having language" according to any definition. The ability to use language may not be a valid test for determining whether an individual has rights. But the existence of even basic language skills does provide further evidence of a consciousness which deserves consideration.

Conversations with gorillas resemble those with young children and in many cases need interpretation based on context and past use of the signs in question. Alternative interpretations of gorilla utterances are often possible. And even if the gorillas' use of signs does not meet a particular definition of language, studying that use can give us a unique perspective from which to understand more directly their physical and psychological requirements. By agreeing on a common vocabulary of signs we establish two-way communication between humans and gorillas. We can learn as much from what they say as we can by evaluating how they say it.

Some of what they tell us can be anticipated: "What do gorillas like to do most?" "GORILLA LOVE EAT GOOD." Or, "What makes you happy?" "GORILLA TREE." "What makes you angry?" "WORK." "What do gorillas do when it's dark?" "GORILLA LISTEN [pause], SLEEP." Some responses, on the other hand, are quite unexpected: "How did you sleep last night?" (expecting "FINE" "BAD" or some related response). "FLOOR BLANKET" (Koko sleeps on the floor with blankets). "How do you like your blankets to feel?" "HOT KOKO-LOVE." "What happened?" (after an earthquake). "DARN DARN FLOOR BAD BITE. TROUBLE TROUBLE."

TABLE 1   Koko's performance on the Assessment of Children's Language Comprehension
(ACLC) test

Number of critical elements	Percent correct				
	Chance	Sign + voice	Sign only	Voice only	Overall per cent
One — vocabulary (50 items)	20	72			
Two (e.g. HAPPY LADY)	20	70	50	50	56.7
Three (e.g. HAPPY LADY SLEEPING)	25	50	30	50	43.3
Four (e.g. HAPPY LITTLE GIRL JUMPING)	20	50	50	30	43.3
Overall per cent correct (two, three and four elements)		56.7	43.3	43.3	47.7

The results of χ^2 tests (1 df) indicate that Koko's performance on the ACLC in all modes and at all
levels of difficulty was significantly better than chance, and that there was no significant difference
in her comprehension whether the instructions were given in sign, English or sign plus English.

TABLE 2   Koko's tested IQ 1975–6

Date	Test	CA*	MA+	IQ
Dec 1976	Khulman–Anderson	65	56	84.8
July 1976	Peabody Picture Vocabulary Test	60	49	81.6
Jan 1976	Stanford–Binet Intelligence Scale	54	46	85.2
Nov 1975	Wechsler Preschool and Primary Scale of Intelligence	51	37	71.0
July 1975	Stanford–Binet	48	44	91.7
Apr 1975	McCarthy Scales of Children's Abilities	45	32	73.0‡ (GCI)
Feb 1975	Stanford–Binet	43	37	86.0

* Chronological age in months.

+ Mental age in months

‡ The McCarthy GCI stands for General Cognitive Index and is a scaled score, not a quotient.

Gorillas have suffered from a reputation for aloofness, low level of motivation and a contrary nature. Such gorilla stubbornness and negativism have been encountered and documented in our work with Koko and Michael, but certain findings indicate that this is evidence of intelligence and independence rather than of stupidity. And it is just this ornery independence that seems to spark episodes of humor and verbal playfulness. A characteristic incident involved Koko and assistant Barbara Hiller. Koko was nesting with a number of white towels and signed, "THAT RED," indicating one of the towels. Barbara corrected Koko, telling her that it was white. Koko repeated her statement with additional emphasis, "THAT *RED*." Again Barbara stated that the towel was white. After several more exchanges, Koko picked up a piece of red lint, held it out to Barbara and, grinning, signed, "THAT RED."

Our approach has been to give Koko and Michael vocabulary instruction   15
but no direct teaching of any other language skill. Most of the signs were learned either through the molding of the gorillas' hands into signs or through imitation. But Koko and Michael have both created signs and used the language in diverse ways not explicitly taught. In a very real sense, the study has involved the mapping of skills, rather than the teaching of skills. This mapping is being done through observations in relatively unstructured and uncontrolled situations and through rigorous tests. The best possible linguistic and cognitive performances are likely to be given in the informal setting, with support coming from tests.

The gorillas have taken the basic building block of conversation (signs) and, on their own, added new meaning through modulation, a grammatical process similar to inflection in spoken language. A change in pitch or loudness of the voice, or the addition (or substitution) of sounds, can alter the meaning of a spoken word. In sign language this is accomplished through changes in motion, hand location, hand configuration, facial expression and body posture. The sign BAD, for instance, can be made to mean "very bad" by enlarging the signing space, increasing the speed and tension of the hand, and exaggerating facial expression. Koko, like human signers, has exploited this feature of sign language to exaggerate a point, as when she signed THIRSTY from the top of her head to her stomach, instead of down her throat.

The gorillas have been observed to use these kinds of variations to mark relations of size (e.g. small versus large ALLIGATOR sign), number (BIRDS versus BIRD by repeating the sign), location (SCRATCH-ON-BACK), possession (KOKO'S-BABY signed simultaneously), manner, degree, intensity or emphasis (TICKLE signed with two hands), agent or object of an action (YOU-SIP signed by moving the signing hand toward the intended agent), negation (negating the ATTENTION sign by changing its location), to express questions (through eye contact and facial expression) and as a form of word play akin to wit or humor (simultaneously signing SAD FROWN when asked to "smile" for the camera).

A conversation with Koko that involved this kind of creativity with the sign ROTTEN has been documented on film. Koko demonstrated the standard form of the sign in an exchange of insults after her companion called her a

STINKER. Koko then inflected the sign by using two hands (perhaps meaning "really rotten") and in the same sequence, brought the sign off her nose toward her companion, conveying the idea "you're really rotten." Koko's use of ROTTEN in this conversation also demonstrates her grasp of the connotation of a word rather than its denotation or concrete or specific meaning.

The meaning of the gorillas' signs are not necessarily identical to the most common meanings, and in some cases they are entirely different. To interpret the gorillas' conversations correctly, one must discover what the signs mean to them. Word-association games provide some clues. The gorillas are asked, "What do you think of when I say ———?" Examples of stimulus-response pairs from sessions with Michael include: TEACHER-HAND, MICHAEL-FOOT, and similarly, AFRAID-HUG, DEAD-STINK and HUNGRY-EAT. The gorillas have also simply been asked to give definitions. Examples from data on Koko follow:

12 February 1984
Teacher: What's an insult?
Koko: THINK DEVIL DIRTY.
T: What's a stove?
K: COOK WITH
12 July 1984
T: What's an injury? [Voiced only.]
K: THERE BITE [to a cut on her hand].
13 July 1984
T: What is crazy?
K: TROUBLE SURPRISE.
8 February 1985
T: When do people say darn?
K: WORK OBNOXIOUS.
21 April 1983
T: What can you think of that's hard?
K: ROCK . . . WORK.
9 February 1984
T: What's a smart gorilla?
K: ME. . . .

The gorillas also communicate new meanings by making up their own entirely new signs. The intended meanings of some of the gorillas' invented nouns have been obvious *(nailfile, eyemakeup, barrette)* because of their iconic form. The meanings of more abstract words such as verbs and prepositions *(above, below, take-off)*, have to be worked out over time from records of the situations in which they occurred.

An analysis of the 876 signs emitted by Koko during the first ten years of the project[4] revealed that fifty-four signs, 6 percent of her total emitted vocabulary, were her own inventions. Another 2 percent (fifteen signs) were compounded by Koko from signs she was taught. Originally, only ten signs (1 percent) were counted as natural gorilla gestures. New data from detailed

20

observations of the gestures used by uninstructed gorillas indicates that these categories are fluid, and some of Koko's inventions are shared by other gorillas.

These invented signs indicate that the gorillas, like human children, take initiative with language by making up new words and by giving new meanings to old words. On the next level, there is evidence that Koko and Michael can generate novel names by combining two or more familiar words. For instance, Koko signed "BOTTLE MATCH" to refer to a cigarette lighter, "WHITE TIGER" for a zebra, and "EYE HAT" for a mask. Michael has generated similar combinations, such as "ORANGE FLOWER SAUCE" for nectarine yogurt and "BEAN BALL" for peas. Other examples in the samples of the gorillas' signing are "ELEPHANT BABY" for a Pinocchio doll and "BOTTLE NECKLACE" for a six-pack soda can holder. Critics have commented that such phrases are merely the pairing of two separate aspects of what is present. Many of the above examples, however, cannot be explained in this way—when Koko signed "BOTTLE MATCH," neither a bottle nor a match was present.

The gorillas have applied such new descriptive terms to themselves as well as to novel objects. When angered, Koko has labeled herself a "RED MAD GORILLA." Once, when she had been drinking water through a thick rubber straw from a pan on the floor after repeatedly asking her companion for drinks of juice which were not forthcoming, she referred to herself as a "SAD ELEPHANT." . . .

Another creative aspect of the gorillas' language behavior is humor. Humor, like metaphor, requires a capacity to depart from what is strictly correct, normal or expected. For example, when asked to demonstrate her invented sign for STETHOSCOPE for the camera, Koko did it on her eyes instead of on her ears. Asked to feed her chimp doll, she put the nipple to the doll's eye and signed "EYE." Appreciation of this kind of wit is sometimes dependent on recognizing the sign behind the distortion. A sceptic might see this as a simple error, but in the case of signs that the gorillas themselves invent, such as STETHOSCOPE, this is not likely, and there are consistencies that run across the gorillas' humorous use of signs.

We have often noticed Koko giving an audible chuckling sound at the result of her own and her companions' discrepant statements or actions. She discovered that when she blew bugs on her companions, a predictable shrieking and jumping response could be elicited. Originally, she laughed at this outcome, but now she chuckles in anticipation of the prank as well. Accidents and unexpected actions by others can also cause Koko to laugh. Chuckles were evoked, for instance, by a research assistant accidentally sitting down on a sandwich and by another playfully pretending to feed sweets to a toy alligator. Developmental psychologists have found that the earliest form of humor in young children, incongruity-based humor, relies on similar principles of discrepancy applied to objects, actions, and verbal statements.

Koko has also made verbal "jokes." On 30 October 1982, Barbara Hiller showed Koko a picture of a bird feeding her young.

K: THAT ME [to the adult bird].
B: Is that really you?
K: KOKO GOOD BIRD.
B: I thought you were a gorilla.
K: KOKO BIRD.

. . .

B: Can you fly?
K: GOOD. [GOOD can mean yes.]
B: Show me.
K: FAKE BIRD, CLOWN. [Koko laughs.]
B: You're teasing me. [Koko laughs.]
B: What are you really?
Koko laughs again, and after a minute signs.
K: GORILLA KOKO.

In stark contrast to the gorillas' ability to express humor is their ability to communicate their thoughts and feelings about death. When Koko was seven, one of her teachers asked, "When do gorillas die?" and she signed, "TROUBLE, OLD." The teacher also asked, "Where do gorillas go when they die?" and Koko replied, "COMFORTABLE HOLE BYE." When asked "How do gorillas feel when they die — happy, sad, afraid?" she signed, "SLEEP." Koko's reference to holes in the context of death has been consistent and is puzzling since no one has ever talked to her about burial, nor demonstrated the activity. That there may be an instinctive basis for this is indicated by an observation at the Woodland Park Zoo in Seattle, Washington. The gorillas there came upon a dead crow in their new outdoor enclosure, and one dug a hole, flicked the crow in, and covered it with dirt.[5]

In December of 1984 a tragic accident indicated the extent to which gorillas may grieve over the death of their loved ones. Koko's favorite kitten, All Ball, slipped out of the door and was killed by a speeding car. Koko cried shortly after she was told of his death. Three days later, when asked, "Do you want to talk about your kitty?" Koko signed, "CRY." "What happened to your kitty?" Koko answered, "SLEEP CAT." When she saw a picture of a cat who looked very much like All Ball, Koko pointed to the picture and signed, "CRY, SAD, FROWN." Her grief was not soon forgotten.

17 March 1985, with Francine Patterson
F: How did you feel when you lost Ball?
K: WANT.
F: How did you feel when you lost him?
K: OPEN TROUBLE VISIT SORRY.
F: When he died, remember when Ball died, how did you feel?
K: RED RED RED BAD SORRY KOKO-LOVE GOOD.

Arthur Caplan argues that animal interests and human interests should not be counted equally, claiming that nonhuman animals lack certain traits that make a moral difference. He uses the following example to illustrate his point:

> If you kill the baby of a baboon the mother may spend many weeks looking for her baby. This behavior soon passes and the baboon will go on to resume her normal life. But if you kill the baby of a human being the mother will spend the rest of her life grieving over the loss of her baby. Hardly a day will go by when the mother does not think about and grieve over the loss of her baby.[6]

But in this example the comparison is between outward behavior in the   30
case of the baboon mother, and a private mental state in the case of the human mother. In most such cases, the human mother also resumes her normal life: returning to her workplace, caring for her other children, going about her daily activities as before. Her grief is not necessarily apparent to the casual observer. Because the baboon mother cannot (or chooses not to) communicate *to us* her internal feelings about the death of her baby, it is assumed that it does not matter to her. While we cannot make any claims here about the emotional life of baboons, we have considerable evidence that Koko continues to mourn the loss of her adopted "baby," All Ball, even years after his death.

> *19 March 1990*
> Koko comes across a picture of herself and All Ball in a photo album.
> K: THAT BAD FROWN SORRY [emphatic] UNATTENTION.

Through conversations such as these the gorillas show not only that they are capable of experiencing emotions, but that they are aware of their emotions and can use language to describe them. Koko, at age six, was given a test that parallels a study with human children five to thirteen years old by Wolman, Lewis and King.[7] Koko was asked a series of questions with these frames:

(1) Do you ever feel ——?

(2) When do you feel ——?

The target feeling states were anger, fear, happiness, sadness, hunger, thirst, sleepiness and nervousness. Like the younger human subjects, Koko most frequently reported external events as conditions of emotional arousal; for example, when asked, "When do you feel hungry?" she answered, "FEEL TIME." A possible explanation of this reply is that when it is time (to eat), she feels hungry. Koko regularly uses an emphatic TIME sign to tell her companion to bring out the next scheduled meal. Her replies to questions about anger seem to be related to events of the months preceding the test. Her responses to "When do you feel mad?" included "KOKO LOVE MARJIE BYE" and "KOKO MAD GIRL." At the time this test was given Koko had been having a difficult time with a new assistant named Marjie.

Koko has displayed a capacity for empathy in her comments about the emotional states of others:

24 September 1977
Koko is shown a picture of the albino gorilla Snowflake struggling against being bathed. Koko signs "ME CRY THERE," indicating the picture.
3 November 1977, with companion Cindy Duggan
Koko looks at a picture of a horse with a bit in his mouth.
K: HORSE SAD.
CD: Why?
K: TEETH.
27 December 1977
Michael has been crying because he wants to be let out of his room. Koko, in the next room, is asked how Michael feels.
K: FEEL SORRY OUT.
7 April 1986
Mitzi Phillips tells Koko about a problem that is making her feel sad.
MP: What could I do to feel better?
K: CLOSE DRAPES . . . TUG-OF-WAR.
As Mitzi writes in the diary, Koko quietly comes up to her.
K: SAD? [Making the sign a question by raising her eyebrows and leaning forward, a standard ASL question form.]
MP: I feel better now.
Koko smiles.

The gorillas have also been asked to represent feeling states such as love, hate, happiness and anger with paints on canvas. Given free choice of ten or more colors, the gorillas produced works of contrasting color and form. Asking them to paint emotions seemed a reasonable request because they had earlier demonstrated some primitive representational ability in their drawings and paintings done from models or from memory. Both Koko and Michael titled these works appropriately. One example of Michael's representational art is a work he called "APPLE CHASE," for which he used our black and white dog named Apple as a model. The black and white painting bears a resemblance to Apple's head. (It is interesting to note that Michael and Apple have a special relationship. They frequently play "chase" together, and Michael often initiates the game by signing CHASE to Apple.)

Michael frequently expresses himself creatively through sound play. He uses various objects and parts of his body to produce a wide variety of sounds and intricate rhythms. In creating his "sound tools" he experiments with different materials in his environment. In addition to rhythmic drumming and tapping, for example, he sometimes strums a rope or fabric strip held taut between his feet and his mouth. He made a rattle by filling a PVC pipe end with hard nutshells and shaking it vigorously with his hand covering the open end. Then he filled his mouth with the nutshells and shook them around, making a contrasting "wet" rattling sound.

Koko regularly expresses her creativity through fantasy play, alone or with   35
her companions. Often this play involves her plastic reptile toys and centers on
their tendency to "bite."

13 October 1988, with Mitzi Phillips
Koko is lying down with one of her toy alligators. She looks at it and signs
"TEETH." She examines its mouth. She kisses it, puts two alligators together as if
to make them kiss each other, then gives them a three-way kiss. She puts her
hand into the toy's mouth, then pulls it out and shakes her hand.
MP: Oh, did it bite you?
K: BITE.
MP: Oh, no! Does it hurt?
Koko kisses her finger.
MP: May I see that bad alligator?
Koko gives it to Mitzi. Mitzi "asks" the alligator why it bit Koko and pretends to
listen to its answer, then hands it back to Koko.
Koko kisses the toy again and again.
K: ALLIGATOR. GORILLA. BITE. GORILLA NUT NUT NUT. STOMACH TOILET.

They are intelligent and emotional, they express themselves creatively
through language, art, music and fantasy play; but are gorillas self-aware?
Once considered unique to human beings, self-awareness is an elusive concept. Its many definitions are both varied and vague, although almost everyone has some notion of what it means. Through their signing, Koko and
Michael have shown a number of generally accepted cognitive correlates of
self-awareness, including the use of personal pronouns, references to their
own internal and emotional states, humor, deception and embarrassment.

While self-awareness is probably best determined through the use of language, self-recognition in mirrors is an accepted indicator of self-awareness in
human infants and other nonverbal individuals. In formal mirror-marking
tests, the subjects are first exposed to a mirror and observed for any self-
directed behavior. Then their appearance is altered in such a way that they can
only detect the change with the aid of a mirror. Nonhuman primates undergoing these tests are normally anesthetized and marked on the face with red
dye. Human children are marked surreptitiously with a spot of rouge while
they are distracted. Once marked, subjects are again exposed to a mirror.
Touching the mark while looking in the mirror is considered confirming evidence of self-recognition. Chimpanzees, orangutans and humans have
demonstrated a capacity for self-recognition in mirror tests, but the six gorillas previously tested failed to do so. It was concluded that gorillas lacked the
cognitive capacity for self-awareness, in spite of informal reports to the
contrary.

We gave a comparable mirror test to Koko[8] in which she demonstrated for
the first time that gorillas, too, are capable of mirror self-recognition. For
Koko, we used a modified procedure so that she would not have to be anes-

thetized. During a series of ten-minute sessions videotaped over a three-day period, Koko's brow was wiped with a warm, damp, pink washcloth. During one of these sessions, the washcloth had been dipped in clown paint of the same pink color. In the sessions in which she was unmarked, Koko touched the target area an average of only one time per session. During the fifth session when her brow was marked, she touched the target area forty-seven times, only after viewing it in the mirror. As she attempted to remove the paint, she also spent the most time viewing her reflection during the session in which she was marked. It is evident that Koko recognized the altered image as her own.

Koko had previously passed an informal "mark test" when she attempted to rub away a dark spot of pigment on her upper gum, a spot that she had precisely located by looking into her mouth with a mirror. Captured on videotape, this spontaneous experiment of nature eliminated any possibility that Koko sensed the presence of the mark before noticing it in the mirror.

Why did the gorillas fail to pass the mirror test? There are a number of possible explanations, including their age, rearing histories and social situations, their individual sensitivity to anesthesia, or lack of motivation. There may also have been methodological problems, as at least two of the subjects touched the mark before exposure to the mirror. However, a more likely explanation is that the gorillas were inhibited by the presence of unfamiliar observers. Primatologists who have worked closely with gorillas have long been aware that the presence of strangers can profoundly affect gorilla behavior, and this has been our experience as well. In certain situations Koko and Michael show a sensitivity to being watched even by familiar companions. Ironically, it may have been the gorillas' very capacity for self-consciousness that prevented them from exhibiting behaviors indicative of self-recognition in the test situation. . . .

Michael Lewis[9] suggests that there are certain emotional states that only the self-aware can have. One such state is embarrassment. In order to be embarrassed animals must be capable of reflecting on their own behavior and comparing it to standards set by society or themselves. Koko seems embarrassed when her companions notice that she is signing to herself, especially when the signing involves her dolls. One incident recorded when Koko was five years old provides an example. Her companion observed her creating what appeared to be an imaginary social situation between two gorilla dolls. She signed, "BAD, BAD" while looking at one doll, and "KISS" while looking at the other. Next, she signed, "CHASE, TICKLE," hit the two dolls together, and then wrestled with them and signed, "GOOD GORILLA, GOOD GOOD." At this point she noticed that she was being watched and abruptly put the dolls down.

There is no reason to think that Koko and Michael are significantly different from other gorillas in their inherent linguistic capacities, self-awareness or other mental abilities. They are two individuals selected more or less at random from the total population of gorillas, and the circumstances of their first few years were very different. So it is fair to assume that they are representative of their species. Nor is there reason to consider them essentially different from other gorillas because of their experience with human language. Indeed, a few zoo gorillas who have been exposed informally to sign language have shown that they, too, can learn signs, even later in life and without intensive teaching. By teaching sign language to Koko and Michael we have not imposed an artificial system on them, but rather have built upon their existing system to provide a jointly understood vocabulary for mutual exchange.

Detailed observation and analysis of the communicative gestures used by "uninstructed" gorillas in a zoo group indicate that their own gestural communication system is much more complex than previously thought.[10] This ongoing study involves analyzing a videotape compilation of these gestures and classifying them according to context and apparent functions. The gorillas have been observed to use communicative gestures in the following contexts: play invitation, anticipatory play reaction, play inhibition, indication of play location and action, sexual activities, agonistic interaction, group movement, body positioning and solitary play. One type of gesture involves touching to position the body of another, usually in the context of sexual activity. Another significant type of gesture uses the hands for deception, for example to hide a "playface" grin in order to alter the signal being received by another gorilla. So far, over forty apparently discrete and meaningful gestural types have been identified in one five-member population. Gorillas in this particular group have been observed using conversational strings of up to eight gestures, and there seems to be an element of request and response in their dialogues.

While we are a long way from any comprehensive understanding of natural gorilla communication, it is clear that nonsigning gorillas use gestures to communicate with one another. Field researchers may not have always recognized the significance of semantic gestures used by free-living gorillas, because they were unfamiliar with the gorillas' communicative habits or with gestural communication in general, or because the presence of human observers inhibits the gorillas' normal behavior. Recognition of semantically significant gestures and sounds becomes easier as we become more familiar with gorillas as communicators.

Perhaps our most interesting findings relate to how astonishingly like us   45
gorillas are—or how like them we are. But the striking similarities between gorillas and humans are hardly surprising in light of the most recent studies of our genetic kinship. The scientific classification of living organisms is based on the apparent similarities between those organisms. Within the order Primates, human beings have always been set apart in a separate family. More recent studies involving comparisons of chromosomes and analysis of DNA leave little doubt that apes and humans should be classed together in the family *Hominidae*. Some researchers now propose that humans, gorillas and chimpanzees also belong in the same subfamily, though the arrangement within this subfamily is still to be determined.[11]

Through what they have taught us about gorillas, Koko and Michael are helping to change the way we view the world. They force us to re-examine the ways we think about other animals. With an emotional and expressive range far greater than previously believed, they have revealed a lively and sure awareness of themselves as individuals. Asked to categorize herself, Koko declared "FINE ANIMAL GORILLA." Indeed. Fine animal-persons, gorillas.

Notes

1. Additional information about the work of the Gorilla Foundation with Koko and Michael can be found in: F. G. Patterson, "The gestures of a gorilla: language acquisition in another pongid," *Brain and Language,* vol. 5 (1978) pp. 72–97; F. Patterson, "Conversations with a gorilla," *National Geographic,* vol. 154, no. 4 (1978) pp. 438–65; F. Patterson and E. Linden, *The Education of Koko* (Holt, Rinehart and Winston, New York, 1981); F. Patterson, C. H. Patterson, and D. K. Brentari, "Language in child, chimp, and gorilla," *American Psychologist,* vol. 42, no. 3 (1987) pp. 270–2; F. Patterson, J. Tanner, and N. Mayer, "Pragmatic analysis of gorilla utterances: early communicative development in the gorilla Koko," *Journal of Pragmatics,* vol. 12, no. 1 (1988) pp. 35–55.

2. F. G. Patterson, "Linguistic capabilities of a young lowland gorilla," in F. C. Peng (ed.), *Sign Language and Language Acquisition in Man and Ape: New Dimensions in Comparative Pedolinguistics* (Westview Press, Boulder, CO, 1978), pp. 161–201.

3. F. G. Patterson, "Linguistic capabilities of a lowland gorilla" (Ph.D. dissertation, Stanford University, 1979. University Microfilms International no. 79–172–69, Abstract in *Dissertation Abstracts International,* August 1979, 40-B, 2).

4. F. G. Patterson and R. H. Cohn, "Language acquisition by a lowland gorilla: Koko's first ten years of vocabulary development," *Word,* vol. 41, no. 2 (1990) pp. 97–143.

5. D. Hancocks, "Gorillas go natural," *Animal Kingdom,* vol. 86, no. 1 (1983) pp. 10–16.

6. A. Caplan, "Moral community and the responsibility of scientists," *Acta Physiologica Scandinavica,* vol. 128 (1986) p. 554.

7. R. W. Wolman, W. C. Lewis and M. King, "The development of the language of emotions: conditions of emotional arousal," *Child Development,* vol. 42 (1971) pp. 1288–93.

8. F. Patterson and R. Cohn, "Self-recognition and self-awareness in lowland gorillas," in S. T. Parker, M. L. Boccia and R. Mitchell (eds.), *Self-awareness in Animals and Humans* (Cambridge University Press, Cambridge, in press).

9. M. Lewis, "Origins of self-knowledge and individual differences in early self-recognition," in A. Greenwald and T. Suls (eds.), *Psychological Perspective on the Self,* vol. 3 (1986) pp. 55–78.

10. F. Patterson and J. Tanner, "Gestural communication in captive gorillas," paper presented at the American Society of Primatologists meeting, University of California, Davis, July 1990.

11. J. Yunis and O. Prakash, "The origins of man: a chromosomal pictorial legacy," *Science,* vol. 215 (1982) pp. 1525–9; B. F. Koop, M. Goodman, P. Xu, K. Chan and J. L. Slightom, "Primate (eta)-globan DNA sequences and man's place among the great apes," *Nature,* vol. 319 (1986) pp. 234–7.

EXPLORING THE TEXT

1. What specific arguments do Patterson and Gordon advance in support of the claim that Koko should be considered a "person"? Which of Koko's and Michael's behaviors strike you as the most "personlike"? Why? If none of these behaviors qualify Koko for "personhood" in your view, what do you think she would have to be able to do in order to attain this distinction?

2. Given the evidence offered in this selection, would you agree that Koko should have "a claim to basic moral rights" (para. 4)? What rights, if any, should she have a claim to, in your opinion? Why? To what extent would these rights depend on the fact that Koko possesses unusual mental abilities?

3. Why do Patterson and Gordon take such pains at the end of the selection to assert the "normalcy" of Koko's behaviors? Why do you think they insist so vigorously on the "naturalness" of sign language among gorillas in the wild? What possible objections are these two points meant to anticipate?

4. In what ways do the authors of this essay take the reader's perspective into account as they structure their case for Koko's personhood? Why, for example, do they introduce their essay by presenting a list of Koko's achievements? Why don't they mention the fact that the "individual" they are referring to is a gorilla? How do they respond to objections or counterarguments they anticipate from skeptical readers?

FURTHER EXPLORATIONS

1. Compare the case that Patterson and Gordon make for the "personhood" of Koko with that made by Richard Leakey and Roger Lewin in support of their claim for the intelligence of chimpanzees in "Murder in a Zoo" (p. 580). Does Koko appear to demonstrate the kind of "social intelligence" that Leakey and Lewin observe in chimps? Which of these selections offers the most convincing evidence of primate intelligence in your view? Why do you think so?

2. How might Frans de Waal (p. 552) assess the way that Patterson and Gordon interpret Koko's motives and intentions in this selection? Do their readings of their primate subjects reflect what de Waal would term "mature" or "naive" anthropomorphism? Why?

3. To what extent is it possible to view Koko's training in sign language simply as a more sophisticated form of "Disneyfication," as John Berger might put it (p. 521)? By imposing this human form of communication on Koko, have Patterson and Gordon turned her into just another "animal of the mind"? Why or why not?

4. How might Peter Singer (p. 607) view Patterson's and Gordon's claim that Koko merits special consideration as a "person" because she has mastered hundreds of signs and can use them to communicate with humans? Why would he probably reject this appeal?

5. As a class, watch any one of the several videotapes that document the story of Koko and her acquisition of American Sign Language. How is Koko presented in this video portrayal? How does actually seeing Koko in action influence your appraisal of her "personhood"?

ESSAY OPTIONS

1. Drawing on information presented by Patterson and Gordon, and by Leakey and Lewin in "Murder in a Zoo" (p. 580), as well as on any additional information you gather through library research, write a paper in which you evaluate the case for the "personhood" of higher primates. What, in your opinion, seems like the strongest evidence in support of the claim that primates possess humanlike intelligence? What aspects of human intelligence, if any, do they appear to lack? What problems or difficulties might be associated with the notion that apes and chimps should be viewed as persons?

2. Do additional independent research on animal "languages" and/or attempts to communicate with other species. How do other animal species use language to communicate information? What types of information do they convey? How successful have scientists been in their attempts to communicate directly with other animal minds?

Equality for Animals?

PETER SINGER

We humans have always prided ourselves on our powers of reason. Since the time of Socrates, we've taken comfort in the fact that our ability to reflect on the logic of our beliefs sets us apart from the other, "lower" orders of creation. Unfortunately, according to Peter Singer, most of us live lives that are distinctly irrational. In the opinion of this Princeton University–based philosopher, most of us are "speciesists": like the bigots of earlier generations who espoused the principle of equality while tolerating racist and sexist practices in their daily lives, most of us today condemn cruelty to animals yet haven't a qualm about downing a double cheeseburger or using beauty products that involve animal testing. A self-styled "practical philosopher" and a leader in the animal liberation movement, Singer (b. 1946) has been lecturing us for the past twenty years about what it takes to live according to consistent ethical principles. His publications, numbering some seventeen titles, include *Animal Liberation* (1975, 1990); *Practical Ethics* (1979, 1993), the source of this selection; *Rethinking Life and Death* (1994); and *Writings on the Ethical Life* (2000). He currently serves as the Ira W. DeCamp Professor of Bioethics at Princeton University's Center for Human Values.

BEFORE READING

Working in groups, discuss the legal rights, if any, that might be extended to animals. Should animals have the right to protection from undue abuse at the hands of their owners? Should they have the right to protection from all physical punishment? Should they have the right to basic freedom of movement, the right to associate with animals of their own kind, the right to live without human control? How far do you think the idea of animal rights or animal equality should be carried?

Racism and Speciesism

The fundamental principle of equality, on which the equality of all human beings rests, is the principle of equal consideration of interests. Only a basic moral principle of this kind can allow us to defend a form of equality that embraces all human beings, with all the differences that exist between them. I shall now contend that while this principle does provide an adequate basis for human equality, it provides a basis that cannot be limited to humans. In other words I shall suggest that, having accepted the principle of equality as a sound moral basis for relations with others of our own species, we are also committed to accepting it as a sound moral basis for relations with those outside our own species—the nonhuman animals.

This suggestion may at first seem bizarre. We are used to regarding discrimination against members of racial minorities, or against women, as among the most important moral and political issues facing the world today. These are serious matters, worthy of the time and energy of any concerned person. But animals? Isn't the welfare of animals in a different category altogether, a matter for people who are dotty about dogs and cats? How can anyone waste their time on equality for animals when so many humans are denied real equality?

This attitude reflects a popular prejudice against taking the interests of animals seriously—a prejudice no better founded than the prejudice of white slaveowners against taking the interests of their African slaves seriously. It is easy for us to criticize the prejudices of our grandfathers, from which our fathers freed themselves. It is more difficult to distance ourselves from our own views, so that we can dispassionately search for prejudices among the beliefs and values we hold. What is needed now is a willingness to follow the arguments where they lead, without a prior assumption that the issue is not worth our attention.

The argument for extending the principle of equality beyond our own species is simple, so simple that it amounts to no more than a clear understanding of the nature of the principle of equal consideration of interests. This principle implies that our concern for others ought not to depend on what they are like, or what abilities they possess (although precisely what this concern requires us to do may vary according to the characteristics of those affected by what we do). It is on this basis that we are able to say that the fact that some people are not members of our race does not entitle us to exploit them, and similarly the fact that some people are less intelligent than others does not mean that their interests may be disregarded. But the principle also implies that the fact that beings are not members of our species does not entitle us to exploit them, and similarly the fact that other animals are less intelligent than we are does not mean that their interests may be disregarded.

Many philosophers have advocated equal consideration of interests, in some form or other, as a basic moral principle. Only a few have recognized that the principle has applications beyond our own species, one of the few being Jeremy Bentham,° the founding father of modern utilitarianism. In a forward-looking passage, written at a time when African slaves in the British dominions were still being treated much as we now treat nonhuman animals, Bentham wrote:

> The day may come when the rest of the animal creation may acquire those rights which never could have been withholden from them but by the hand of tyranny. The French have already discovered that the blackness of the skin is no reason why a human being should be abandoned without redress to the caprice of a tormentor. It may one day come to be recognized that the number of the legs, the villosity of the skin, or the termination of the *os sacrum*, are reasons equally insufficient for abandoning a sensitive being to the same fate. What else is it that should trace the insuperable line? Is it the faculty of reason, or perhaps the faculty of discourse? But a fullgrown horse or dog is beyond comparison a more rational, as well as a more conversable animal, than an infant of a day, or a week, or even a month, old. But suppose they were otherwise, what would it avail? The question is not, Can they *reason?* nor Can they *talk?* but, *Can they suffer?*

In this passage Bentham points to the capacity for suffering as the vital characteristic that entitles a being to equal consideration. The capacity for suffering — or more strictly, for suffering and/or enjoyment or happiness — is not just another characteristic like the capacity for language, or for higher mathematics. Bentham is not saying that those who try to mark "the insuperable line" that determines whether the interests of a being should be considered happen to have selected the wrong characteristic. The capacity for suffering and enjoying things is a prerequisite for having interests at all, a condition that must be satisfied before we can speak of interests in any meaningful way. It would be nonsense to say that it was not in the interests of a stone to be kicked along the road by a schoolboy. A stone does not have interests because it cannot suffer. Nothing that we can do to it could possibly make any difference to its welfare. A mouse, on the other hand, does have an interest in not being tormented, because mice will suffer if they are treated in this way.

If a being suffers, there can be no moral justification for refusing to take that suffering into consideration. No matter what the nature of the being, the principle of equality requires that the suffering be counted equally with the like suffering — in so far as rough comparisons can be made — of any other being. If a being is not capable of suffering, or of experiencing enjoyment or happiness, there is nothing to be taken into account. This is why the limit of sentience (using the term as a convenient, if not strictly accurate, shorthand for the capacity to suffer or experience enjoyment or happiness) is the only defensible boundary of concern for the interests of others. To mark this boundary by some characteristic like intelligence or rationality would be to mark it in an arbitrary way. Why not choose some other characteristic, like skin color?

Jeremy Bentham: (1748–1832), English philosopher.

Racists violate the principle of equality by giving greater weight to the interests of members of their own race when there is a clash between their interests and the interests of those of another race. Racists of European descent typically have not accepted that pain matters as much when it is felt by Africans, for example, as when it is felt by Europeans. Similarly those I would call "speciesists" give greater weight to the interests of members of their own species when there is a clash between their interests and the interests of those of other species. Human speciesists do not accept that pain is as bad when it is felt by pigs or mice as when it is felt by humans.

That, then, is really the whole of the argument for extending the principle of equality to nonhuman animals; but there may be some doubts about what this equality amounts to in practice. In particular, the last sentence of the previous paragraph may prompt some people to reply: "Surely pain felt by a mouse just is not as bad as pain felt by a human. Humans have much greater awareness of what is happening to them, and this makes their suffering worse. You can't equate the suffering of, say, a person dying slowly from cancer, and a laboratory mouse undergoing the same fate."

I fully accept that in the case described the human cancer victim normally suffers more than the nonhuman cancer victim. This in no way undermines the extension of equal consideration of interests to nonhumans. It means, rather, that we must take care when we compare the interests of different species. In some situations a member of one species will suffer more than a member of another species. In this case we should still apply the principle of equal consideration of interests but the result of so doing is, of course, to give priority to relieving the greater suffering. A simpler case may help to make this clear.

If I give a horse a hard slap across its rump with my open hand, the horse   10
may start, but it presumably feels little pain. Its skin is thick enough to protect it against a mere slap. If I slap a baby in the same way, however, the baby will cry and presumably does feel pain, for the baby's skin is more sensitive. So it is worse to slap a baby than a horse, if both slaps are administered with equal force. But there must be some kind of blow—I don't know exactly what it would be, but perhaps a blow with a heavy stick—that would cause the horse as much pain as we cause a baby by a simple slap. That is what I mean by "the same amount of pain" and if we consider it wrong to inflict that much pain on a baby for no good reason then we must, unless we are speciesists, consider it equally wrong to inflict the same amount of pain on a horse for no good reason.

There are other differences between humans and animals that cause other complications. Normal adult human beings have mental capacities that will, in certain circumstances, lead them to suffer more than animals would in the same circumstances. If, for instance, we decided to perform extremely painful or lethal scientific experiments on normal adult humans, kidnapped at random from public parks for this purpose, adults who entered parks would become fearful that they would be kidnapped. The resultant terror would be a form of suffering additional to the pain of the experiment. The same experiments performed on nonhuman animals would cause less suffering since the animals would not have the anticipatory dread of being kidnapped and experimented upon. This does not mean, of course, that it would be *right* to perform the experiment on animals, but only that there is a reason, and one that is not speciesist, for preferring to use animals rather than normal adult humans, if the experiment is to be done at all. Note, however, that this same argument gives us a reason for preferring to use human infants—orphans perhaps—or severely intellectually disabled humans for experiments, rather than adults, since infants and severely intellectually disabled humans would also have no idea of what was going to happen to them. As far as this argument is concerned, nonhuman animals and infants and severely intellectually disabled humans are in the same category; and if we use this argument to justify experiments on nonhuman animals we have to ask ourselves whether we are also prepared to allow experiments on human infants and severely intellectually disabled adults. If we make a distinction between animals and these humans, how can we do it, other than on the basis of a morally indefensible preference for members of our own species?

There are many areas in which the superior mental powers of normal adult humans make a difference: anticipation, more detailed memory, greater knowledge of what is happening, and so on. These differences explain why a human dying from cancer is likely to suffer more than a mouse. It is the mental anguish that makes the human's position so much harder to bear. Yet these differences do not all point to greater suffering on the part of the normal human being. Sometimes animals may suffer more because of their more limited understanding. If, for instance, we are taking prisoners in wartime we can explain to them that while they must submit to capture, search, and confinement they will not otherwise be harmed and will be set free at the conclusion of hostilities. If we capture wild animals, however, we cannot explain that we are not threatening their lives. A wild animal cannot distinguish an attempt to overpower and confine from an attempt to kill; the one causes as much terror as the other.

It may be objected that comparisons of the sufferings of different species are impossible to make, and that for this reason when the interests of animals and humans clash, the principle of equality gives no guidance. It is true that comparisons of suffering between members of different species cannot be made precisely. Nor, for that matter, can comparisons of suffering between different human beings be made precisely. Precision is not essential. As we shall see shortly, even if we were to prevent the infliction of suffering on animals only when the interests of humans will not be affected to anything like the extent that animals are affected, we would be forced to make radical changes in our treatment of animals that would involve our diet, the farming methods we use, experimental procedures in many fields of science, our approach to wildlife and to hunting, trapping and the wearing of furs, and areas of entertainment like circuses, rodeos, and zoos. As a result, the total quantity of suffering caused would be greatly reduced; so greatly that it is hard to imagine any other change of moral attitude that would cause so great a reduction in the total sum of suffering in the universe.

So far I have said a lot about the infliction of suffering on animals, but nothing about killing them. This omission has been deliberate. The application of the principle of equality to the infliction of suffering is, in theory at least, fairly straightforward. Pain and suffering are bad and should be prevented or minimized, irrespective of the race, sex, or species of the being that suffers. How bad a pain is depends on how intense it is and how long it lasts, but pains of the same intensity and duration are equally bad, whether felt by humans or animals. When we come to consider the value of life, we cannot say quite so confidently that a life is a life, and equally valuable, whether it is a human life or an animal life. It would not be speciesist to hold that the life of a self-aware being, capable of abstract thought, of planning for the future, of complex acts of communication, and so on, is more valuable than the life of a being without these capacities. (I am not saying whether this view is justifiable or not; only that it cannot simply be rejected as speciesist, because it is not on the basis of species itself that one life is held to be more valuable than another.) The value of life is a notoriously difficult ethical question, and we can only arrive at a reasoned conclusion about the comparative value of human and animal life after we have discussed the value of life in general. . . .

Speciesism in Practice

Animals as Food

For most people in modern, urbanized societies, the principal form of contact   15
with nonhuman animals is at meal times. The use of animals for food is probably the oldest and the most widespread form of animal use. There is also a sense in which it is the most basic form of animal use, the foundation stone on which rests the belief that animals exist for our pleasure and convenience.

If animals count in their own right, our use of animals for food becomes questionable—especially when animal flesh is a luxury rather than a necessity. Eskimos living in an environment where they must kill animals for food or starve might be justified in claiming that their interest in surviving overrides that of the animals they kill. Most of us cannot defend our diet in this way. Citizens of industrialized societies can easily obtain an adequate diet without the use of animal flesh. The overwhelming weight of medical evidence indicates that animal flesh is not necessary for good health or longevity. Nor is animal production in industrialized societies an efficient way of producing food, since most of the animals consumed have been fattened on grains and other foods that we could have eaten directly. When we feed these grains to animals, only about 10 percent of the nutritional value remains as meat for human consumption. So, with the exception of animals raised entirely on grazing land unsuitable for crops, animals are eaten neither for health, nor to increase our food supply. Their flesh is a luxury, consumed because people like its taste.

In considering the ethics of the use of animal flesh for human food in industrialized societies, we are considering a situation in which a relatively minor human interest must be balanced against the lives and welfare of the animals involved. The principle of equal consideration of interests does not allow major interests to be sacrificed for minor interests.

The case against using animals for food is at its strongest when animals are made to lead miserable lives so that their flesh can be made available to humans at the lowest possible cost. Modern forms of intensive farming apply science and technology to the attitude that animals are objects for us to use. In order to have meat on the table at a price that people can afford, our society tolerates methods of meat production that confine sentient animals in cramped, unsuitable conditions for the entire duration of their lives. Animals are treated like machines that convert fodder into flesh, and any innovation that results in a higher "conversion ratio" is liable to be adopted. As one authority on the subject has said, "Cruelty is acknowledged only when profitability ceases." To avoid speciesism we must stop these practices. Our custom is all the support that factory farmers need. The decision to cease giving them that support may be difficult, but it is less difficult than it would have been for a white Southerner to go against the traditions of his society and free his slaves; if we do not change our dietary habits, how can we censure those slaveholders who would not change their own way of living?

These arguments apply to animals who have been reared in factory farms — which means that we should not eat chicken, pork, or veal, unless we know that the meat we are eating was not produced by factory farm methods. The same is true of beef that has come from cattle kept in crowded feedlots (as most beef does in the United States). Eggs will come from hens kept in small wire cages, too small even to allow them to stretch their wings, unless the eggs are specifically sold as "free range" (or unless one lives in a relatively enlightened country like Switzerland, which has prohibited the cage system of keeping hens).

These arguments do not take us all the way to a vegetarian diet, since some animals, for instance sheep, and in some countries cattle, still graze freely outdoors. This could change. The American pattern of fattening cattle in crowded feedlots is spreading to other countries. Meanwhile, the lives of free-ranging animals are undoubtedly better than those of animals reared in factory farms. It is still doubtful if using them for food is compatible with equal consideration of interests. . . . Apart from taking their lives there are also many other things done to animals in order to bring them cheaply to our dinner table. Castration, the separation of mother and young, the breaking up of herds, branding, transporting, and finally the moments of slaughter—all of these are likely to involve suffering and do not take the animals' interests into account. Perhaps animals could be reared on a small scale without suffering in these ways, but it does not seem economical or practical to do so on the scale required for feeding our large urban populations. In any case, the important question is not whether animal flesh *could* be produced without suffering, but whether the flesh we are considering buying was produced without suffering. Unless we can be confident that it was, the principle of equal consideration of interests implies that it was wrong to sacrifice important interests of the animal in order to satisfy less important interests of our own; consequently we should boycott the end result of this process.

For those of us living in cities where it is difficult to know how the animals we might eat have lived and died, this conclusion brings us close to a vegetarian way of life. I shall consider some objections to it in the final section of this chapter.

Experimenting on Animals

Perhaps the area in which speciesism can most clearly be observed is the use of animals in experiments. Here the issue stands out starkly, because experimenters often seek to justify experimenting on animals by claiming that the experiments lead us to discoveries about humans; if this is so, the experimenter must agree that human and nonhuman animals are similar in crucial respects. For instance, if forcing a rat to choose between starving to death and crossing an electrified grid to obtain food tells us anything about the reactions of humans to stress, we must assume that the rat feels stress in this kind of situation.

People sometimes think that all animal experiments serve vital medical purposes, and can be justified on the grounds that they relieve more suffering than they cause. This comfortable belief is mistaken. Drug companies test new shampoos and cosmetics they are intending to market by dripping concentrated solutions of them into the eyes of rabbits, in a test known as the Draize test. (Pressure from the animal liberation movement has led several cosmetic companies to abandon this practice. An alternative test, not using animals, has now been found. Nevertheless, many companies, including some of the largest, still continue to perform the Draize test.) Food additives, including artificial colorings and preservatives, are tested by what is known as the LD50—a test designed to find the "lethal dose," or level of consumption that will make 50 percent of a sample of animals die. In the process nearly all of the animals are made very sick before some finally die and others pull through. These tests are not necessary to prevent human suffering: even if there were no alternative to the use of animals to test the safety of the products, we already have enough shampoos and food colorings. There is no need to develop new ones that might be dangerous.

In many countries, the armed forces perform atrocious experiments on animals that rarely come to light. To give just one example: at the U.S. Armed Forces Radiobiology Institute, in Bethesda, Maryland, rhesus monkeys have been trained to run inside a large wheel. If they slow down too much, the wheel slows down, too, and the monkeys get an electric shock. Once the monkeys are trained to run for long periods, they are given lethal doses of radiation. Then, while sick and vomiting, they are forced to continue to run until they drop. This is supposed to provide information on the capacities of soldiers to continue to fight after a nuclear attack.

Nor can all university experiments be defended on the grounds that they relieve more suffering than they inflict. Three experimenters at Princeton University kept 256 young rats without food or water until they died. They concluded that young rats under conditions of fatal thirst and starvation are much more active than normal adult rats given food and water. In a well-known series of experiments that went on for more than fifteen years, H. F. Harlow of the Primate Research Center, Madison, Wisconsin, reared monkeys under conditions of maternal deprivation and total isolation. He found that in this way he could reduce the monkeys to a state in which, when placed among normal monkeys, they sat huddled in a corner in a condition of persistent depression and fear. Harlow also produced monkey mothers so neurotic that they smashed their infant's face into the floor and rubbed it back and forth. Although Harlow himself is no longer alive, some of his former students at other U.S. universities continue to perform variations on his experiments.

In these cases, and many others like them, the benefits to humans are either nonexistent or uncertain, while the losses to members of other species are certain and real. Hence the experiments indicate a failure to give equal consideration to the interests of all beings, irrespective of species.

In the past, argument about animal experimentation has often missed this point because it has been put in absolutist terms: would the opponent of experimentation be prepared to let thousands die from a terrible disease that could be cured by experimenting on one animal? This is a purely hypothetical question, since experiments do not have such dramatic results, but as long as its hypothetical nature is clear, I think the question should be answered affirmatively—in other words, if one, or even a dozen animals had to suffer experiments in order to save thousands, I would think it right and in accordance with equal consideration of interests that they should do so. This, at any rate, is the answer a utilitarian must give. Those who believe in absolute rights might hold that it is always wrong to sacrifice one being, whether human or animal, for the benefit of another. In that case the experiment should not be carried out, whatever the consequences.

To the hypothetical question about saving thousands of people through a single experiment on an animal, opponents of speciesism can reply with a hypothetical question of their own: would experimenters be prepared to perform their experiments on orphaned humans with severe and irreversible brain damage if that were the only way to save thousands? (I say "orphaned" in order to avoid the complication of the feelings of the human parents.) If experimenters are not prepared to use orphaned humans with severe and irreversible brain damage, their readiness to use nonhuman animals seems to discriminate on the basis of species alone, since apes, monkeys, dogs, cats, and even mice and rats are more intelligent, more aware of what is happening to them, more sensitive to pain, and so on, than many severely braindamaged humans barely surviving in hospital wards and other institutions. There seems to be no morally relevant characteristic that such humans have that nonhuman animals lack. Experimenters, then, show bias in favor of their own species whenever they carry out experiments on nonhuman animals for purposes that they would not think justified them in using human beings at an equal or lower level of sentience, awareness, sensitivity, and so on. If this bias were eliminated, the number of experiments performed on animals would be greatly reduced.

Other Forms of Speciesism

I have concentrated on the use of animals as food and in research, since these are examples of large-scale, systematic speciesism. They are not, of course, the only areas in which the principle of equal consideration of interests, extended beyond the human species, has practical implications. There are many other areas that raise similar issues, including the fur trade, hunting in all its different forms, circuses, rodeos, zoos, and the pet business. Since the philosophical questions raised by these issues are not very different from those raised by the use of animals as food and in research, I shall leave it to the reader to apply the appropriate ethical principles to them.

Some Objections

How Do We Know That Animals Can Feel Pain?

We can never directly experience the pain of another being, whether that being   30
is human or not. When I see my daughter fall and scrape her knee, I know that she feels pain because of the way she behaves — she cries, she tells me her knee hurts, she rubs the sore spot, and so on. I know that I myself behave in a somewhat similar — if more inhibited — way when I feel pain, and so I accept that my daughter feels something like what I feel when I scrape my knee.

The basis of my belief that animals can feel pain is similar to the basis of my belief that my daughter can feel pain. Animals in pain behave in much the same way as humans do, and their behavior is sufficient justification for the belief that they feel pain. It is true that, with the exception of those apes who have been taught to communicate by sign language, they cannot actually say that they are feeling pain — but then when my daughter was very young she could not talk, either. She found other ways to make her inner states apparent, thereby demonstrating that we can be sure that a being is feeling pain even if the being cannot use language.

To back up our inference from animal behavior, we can point to the fact that the nervous systems of all vertebrates, and especially of birds and mammals, are fundamentally similar. Those parts of the human nervous system that are concerned with feeling pain are relatively old, in evolutionary terms. Unlike the cerebral cortex, which developed fully only after our ancestors diverged from other mammals, the basic nervous system evolved in more distant ancestors common to ourselves and the other "higher" animals. This anatomical parallel makes it likely that the capacity of animals to feel is similar to our own.

It is significant that none of the grounds we have for believing that animals feel pain hold for plants. We cannot observe behavior suggesting pain—sensational claims to the contrary have not been substantiated—and plants do not have a centrally organized nervous system like ours.

Animals Eat Each Other, So Why Shouldn't We Eat Them?

This might be called the Benjamin Franklin Objection. Franklin recounts in his *Autobiography* that he was for a time a vegetarian but his abstinence from animal flesh came to an end when he was watching some friends prepare to fry a fish they had just caught. When the fish was cut open, it was found to have a smaller fish in its stomach. "Well," Franklin said to himself, "if you eat one another, I don't see why we may not eat you" and he proceeded to do so.

Franklin was at least honest. In telling this story, he confesses that he convinced himself of the validity of the objection only after the fish was already in the frying pan and smelling "admirably well"; and he remarks that one of the advantages of being a "reasonable creature" is that one can find a reason for whatever one wants to do. The replies that can be made to this objection are so obvious that Franklin's acceptance of it does testify more to his love of fried fish than to his powers of reason. For a start, most animals who kill for food would not be able to survive if they did not, whereas we have no need to eat animal flesh. Next, it is odd that humans, who normally think of the behavior of animals as "beastly" should, when it suits them, use an argument that implies that we ought to look to animals for moral guidance. The most decisive point, however, is that nonhuman animals are not capable of considering the alternatives open to them or of reflecting on the ethics of their diet. Hence it is impossible to hold the animals responsible for what they do, or to judge that because of their killing they "deserve" to be treated in a similar way. Those who read these lines, on the other hand, must consider the justifiability of their dietary habits. You cannot evade responsibility by imitating beings who are incapable of making this choice.

Sometimes people point to the fact that animals eat each other in order to make a slightly different point. This fact suggests, they think, not that animals deserve to be eaten, but rather that there is a natural law according to which the stronger prey upon the weaker, a kind of Darwinian "survival of the fittest" in which by eating animals we are merely playing our part.

This interpretation of the objection makes two basic mistakes, one a mistake of fact and the other an error of reasoning. The factual mistake lies in the assumption that our own consumption of animals is part of the natural evolutionary process. This might be true of a few primitive cultures that still hunt for food, but it has nothing to do with the mass production of domestic animals in factory farms.

Suppose that we did hunt for our food, though, and this was part of some natural evolutionary process. There would still be an error of reasoning in the assumption that because this process is natural it is right. It is, no doubt, "natural" for women to produce an infant every year or two from puberty to menopause, but this does not mean that it is wrong to interfere with this process. We need to know the natural laws that affect us in order to estimate the consequences of what we do; but we do not have to assume that the natural way of doing something is incapable of improvement.

Differences between Humans and Animals

That there is a huge gulf between humans and animals was unquestioned for most of the course of Western civilization. The basis of this assumption has been undermined by Darwin's discovery of our animal origins and the associated decline in the credibility of the story of our Divine Creation, made in the image of God with an immortal soul. Some have found it difficult to accept that the differences between us and the other animals are differences of degree rather than kind. They have searched for ways of drawing a line between humans and animals. To date these boundaries have been shortlived. For instance, it used to be said that only humans used tools. Then it was observed that the Galapagos woodpecker used a cactus thorn to dig insects out of crevices in trees. Next it was suggested that even if other animals used tools, humans are the only tool-making animals. But Jane Goodall° found that chimpanzees in the jungles of Tanzania chewed up leaves to make a sponge for sopping up water, and trimmed the leaves off branches to make tools for catching insects. The use of language was another boundary line—but now chimpanzees, gorillas, and an orangutan have learnt Ameslan,° the sign language of the deaf, and there is some evidence suggesting that whales and dolphins may have a complex language of their own.

If these attempts to draw the line between humans and animals had fitted   40
the facts of the situation, they would still not carry any moral weight. As Bentham pointed out, the fact that a being does not use language or make tools is hardly a reason for ignoring its suffering. Some philosophers have claimed that there is a more profound difference. They have claimed that animals cannot think or reason, and that accordingly they have no conception of themselves, no self-consciousness. They live from instant to instant, and do not see themselves as distinct entities with a past and a future. Nor do they have autonomy, the ability to choose how to live one's life. It has been suggested that autonomous, self-conscious beings are in some way much more valuable, more morally significant, than beings who live from moment to moment, without the capacity to see themselves as distinct beings with a past and a future. Accordingly, on this view, the interests of autonomous, self-conscious beings ought normally to take priority over the interests of other beings. . . .

Jane Goodall: (b. 1934), British ethologist known for her work with chimpanzees in Tanzania.
Ameslan: American Sign Language.

The claim that self-conscious beings are entitled to prior consideration is compatible with the principle of equal consideration of interests if it amounts to no more than the claim that something that happens to self-conscious beings can be contrary to their interests while similar events would not be contrary to the interests of beings who were not self-conscious. This might be because the self-conscious creature has greater awareness of what is happening, can fit the event into the overall framework of a longer time period, has different desires, and so on. But this is a point I granted at the start of this chapter, and provided that it is not carried to ludicrous extremes — like insisting that if I am self-conscious and a veal calf is not, depriving me of veal causes more suffering than depriving the calf of his freedom to walk, stretch and eat grass — it is not denied by the criticisms I made of animal experimentation and factory farming.

It would be a different matter if it were claimed that, even when a self-conscious being did not suffer more than a being that was merely sentient, the suffering of the self-conscious being is more important because these are more valuable types of being. . . . Nevertheless we are entitled to ask *why* self-conscious beings should be considered more valuable and in particular why the alleged greater value of a self-conscious being should result in preferring the lesser interests of a self-conscious being to the greater interests of a merely sentient being, even where the self-consciousness of the former being is not itself at stake. This last point is an important one, for we are not now considering cases in which the lives of self-conscious beings are at risk but cases in which self-conscious beings will go on living, their faculties intact, whatever we decide. In these cases, if the existence of self-consciousness does not affect the nature of the interests under comparison, it is not clear why we should drag self-consciousness into the discussion at all, any more than we should drag species, race or sex into similar discussions. Interests are interests, and ought to be given equal consideration whether they are the interests of human or nonhuman animals, self-conscious or non-self-conscious animals.

There is another possible reply to the claim that self-consciousness, or autonomy, or some similar characteristic, can serve to distinguish human from nonhuman animals: recall that there are intellectually disabled humans who have less claim to be regarded as self-conscious or autonomous than many nonhuman animals. If we use these characteristics to place a gulf between humans and other animals, we place these less able humans on the other side of the gulf; and if the gulf is taken to mark a difference in moral status, then these humans would have the moral status of animals rather than humans.

This reply is forceful, because most of us find horrifying the idea of using intellectually disabled humans in painful experiments, or fattening them for gourmet dinners. But some philosophers have argued that these consequences would not really follow from the use of a characteristic like self-consciousness or autonomy to distinguish humans from other animals. I shall consider three of these attempts.

The first suggestion is that severely intellectually disabled humans who do   45
not possess the capacities that mark the normal human off from other animals
should nevertheless be treated as if they did possess these capacities, since
they belong to a species, members of which normally do possess them. The
suggestion is, in other words, that we treat individuals not in accordance with
their actual qualities, but in accordance with the qualities normal for their
species.

It is interesting that this suggestion should be made in defense of treating
members of our species better than members of another species, when it
would be firmly rejected if it were used to justify treating members of our race
or sex better than members of another race or sex. . . . If we accept this we
cannot consistently accept the suggestion that when dealing with severely intellectually disabled humans we should grant them the status or rights normal
for their species. For what is the significance of the fact that this time the line
is to be drawn around the species rather than around the race or sex? We cannot insist that beings be treated as individuals in the one case, and as members of a group in the other. Membership of a species is no more relevant in
these circumstances than membership of a race or sex.

A second suggestion is that although severely intellectually disabled humans may not possess higher capacities than other animals, they are nonetheless human beings, and as such we have special relations with them that we do
not have with other animals. As one reviewer of *Animal Liberation* put it:
"Partiality for our own species, and within it for much smaller groupings is,
like the universe, something we had better accept. . . . The danger in an attempt to eliminate partial affections is that it may remove the source of all affections."

This argument ties morality too closely to our affections. Of course some
people may have a closer relationship with the most profoundly intellectually
disabled human than they do with any nonhuman animal, and it would be absurd to tell them that they should not feel this way. They simply do, and as
such there is nothing good or bad about it. The question is whether our moral
obligations to a being should be made to depend on our feelings in this manner. Notoriously, some human beings have a closer relationship with their cat
than with their neighbors. Would those who tie morality to affections accept
that these people are justified in saving their cats from a fire before they save
their neighbors? And even those who are prepared to answer this question affirmatively would, I trust, not want to go along with racists who could argue
that if people have more natural relationships with, and greater affection towards, others of their own race, it is all right for them to give preference to the
interests of other members of their own race. Ethics does not demand that we
eliminate personal relationships and partial affections, but it does demand
that when we act we assess the moral claims of those affected by our actions
with some degree of independence from our feelings for them.

The third suggestion invokes the widely used "slippery slope" argument.
The idea of this argument is that once we take one step in a certain direction

we shall find ourselves on a slippery slope and shall slither further than we wished to go. In the present context the argument is used to suggest that we need a clear line to divide those beings we can experiment upon, or fatten for dinner, from those we cannot. Species membership makes a nice sharp dividing line, whereas levels of self-consciousness, autonomy, or sentience do not. Once we allow that an intellectually disabled human being has no higher moral status than an animal, the argument goes, we have begun our descent down a slope, the next level of which is denying rights to social misfits, and the bottom of which is a totalitarian government disposing of any groups it does not like by classifying them as subhuman.

The slippery slope argument may serve as a valuable warning in some contexts, but it cannot bear too much weight. If we believe that, as I have argued, the special status we now give to humans allows us to ignore the interests of billions of sentient creatures, we should not be deterred from trying to rectify this situation by the mere possibility that the principles on which we base this attempt will be misused by evil rulers for their own ends. And it is no more than a possibility. The change I have suggested might make no difference to our treatment of humans, or it might even improve it.   50

In the end, no ethical line that is arbitrarily drawn can be secure. It is better to find a line that can be defended openly and honestly.

Notes and References

My views on animals first appeared in *The New York Review of Books*, 5 April 1973, under the title "Animal Liberation." This article was a review of R. and S. Godlovitch and J. Harris (eds.), *Animals, Men and Morals* (London, 1972). A more complete statement was published as *Animal Liberation*, 2d ed. (New York, 1990). Richard Ryder charts the history of changing attitudes towards speciesism in *Animal Revolution* (Oxford, 1989).

Among other works arguing for a drastic revision in our present attitudes to animals are Stephen Clark, *The Moral Status of Animals* (Oxford, 1977); and Tom Regan, *The Case for Animal Rights* (Berkeley, 1983). *Animal Rights and Human Obligations*, 2d ed., edited by T. Regan and P. Singer (Englewood Cliffs, N.J., 1989) is a collection of essays, old and new, both for and against attributing rights to animals or duties to humans in respect of animals. P. Singer (ed.), *In Defence of Animals* (Oxford, 1985), collects essays by both activists and theorists involved with the animal liberation movement. Steve Sapontzis, *Morals, Reason and Animals* (Philadelphia, 1987), is a detailed and sympathetic philosophical analysis of arguments about animal liberation, while R. G. Frey, *Rights, Killing and Suffering* (Oxford, 1983), and Michael Leahy, *Against Liberation* (London, 1991), offer philosophical critiques of the animal liberation position. Mary Midgley, *Animals and Why They Matter* (Harmondsworth, Middlesex, 1983), is a readable and often penetrating account of these issues. James Rachels, *Created from Animals* (Oxford, 1990), draws the moral implications of the Darwinian revolution in our thinking about our place among the animals. Finally, Lori Gruen's "Animals" in P. Singer (ed.), *A Companion to Ethics*, explores the predominant recent approaches to the issue.

Bentham's defense of animals, quoted in the section "Racism and Speciesism" is from his *Introduction to the Principles of Morals and Legislation*, chap. 18, sec. 1, n.

A more detailed description of modern farming conditions can be found in *Animal Liberation,* chap. 3; and in James Mason and Peter Singer, *Animal Factories,* 2d ed. (New York, 1990). Similarly, *Animal Liberation,* chap. 2, contains a fuller discussion of the use of animals in research than is possible, but see also Richard Ryder, *Victims of Science,* 2d ed. (Fontwell, Sussex, 1983). Publication details of the experiment on rhesus monkeys carried out at the U.S. Armed Forces Radiobiology Institute are: Carol Frantz, "Effects of Mixed Neutron-gamma Total-body Irradiation on Physical Activity Performance of Rhesus Monkeys," *Radiation Research,* vol. 101 (1985): 434–41. The experiments at Princeton University on starving rats, and those by H. F. Harlow on isolating monkeys, referred to in the sub-section "Experimenting on Animals," were originally published in *Journal of Comparative and Physiological Psychology,* vol. 78 (1972): 202, *Proceedings of the National Academy of Science,* vol. 54 (1965): 90, and *Engineering and Science,* vol. 33, no. 6 (April 1970): 8. On the continuation of Harlow's work, see *Animal Liberation,* 2d ed., pp. 34–5.

Among the objections, the claim that animals are incapable of feeling pain has standardly been associated with Descartes. But Descartes's view is less clear (and less consistent) than most have assumed. See John Cottingham, "A Brute to the Brutes?: Descartes' Treatment of Animals," *Philosophy,* vol. 53 (1978): 551. In *The Unheeded Cry* (Oxford, 1989), Bernard Rollin describes and criticizes more recent ideologies that have denied the reality of animal pain.

The source for the anecdote about Benjamin Franklin is his *Autobiography* (New York, 1950), p. 41. The same objection has been more seriously considered by John Benson in "Duty and the Beast," *Philosophy,* vol. 53 (1978): 545–7.

Jane Goodall's observations of chimpanzees are engagingly recounted in *In the Shadow of Man* (Boston, 1971) and *Through a Window* (London, 1990); her own more scholarly account is *The Chimpanzees of Gombe* (Cambridge, MA., 1986). For more information on the capacities of the great apes, see Paola Cavalieri and Peter Singer (eds.), *Toward a New Equality: The Great Ape Project* (forthcoming). The "argument from marginal cases" was thus christened by Jan Narveson, "Animal Rights," *Canadian Journal of Philosophy,* vol. 7 (1977). Of the objections to this argument discussed in the sub-section "Differences between Humans and Animals," the first was made by Stanley Benn, "Egalitarianism and Equal Consideration of Interests," in J. Pennock and J. Chapman (eds.), *Nomos IX: Equality* (New York, 1967), pp. 62ff.; the second by John Benson, "Duty and the Beast," *Philosophy,* vol. 53 (the quotation from "one reviewer of *Animal Liberation*" is from p. 536 of this article) and related points are made by Bonnie Steinbock, "Speciesism and the Idea of Equality," *Philosophy,* vol. 53 (1978): 255–6, and at greater length by Leslie Pickering Francis and Richard Norman, "Some Animals Are More Equal Than Others," *Philosophy,* vol. 53 (1978): 518–27. The third objection can be found in Philip Devine, "The Moral Basis of Vegetarianism," *Philosophy,* vol. 53 (19): 496–8.

EXPLORING THE TEXT

1. Why should animals be included in the principle of "equal consideration," according to Singer? In general, how persuasive do you find the idea that speciesism is simply another form of discrimination, like racism or sexism?

2. Why does Singer find Jeremy Bentham's notion of "sentience" or the capacity to suffer the most ethical means of determining which creatures merit equal consid-

eration? What difficulties arise in determining equal levels of suffering? Why might a self-conscious human, for example, suffer less than an animal when faced with certain death? What problems, if any, do you see in applying this kind of comparative standard?

3. What arguments does Singer forward against the use of animals for food or in scientific experimentation? How does he use the arguments of his opponents to structure his own reasoning? How persuasive do you find the case he presents on these issues?

4. What specific counterarguments or objections to the concept of animal liberation does Singer anticipate in this essay? How does he respond to them?

FURTHER EXPLORATIONS

1. How might John (Fire) Lame Deer (p. 512) respond to Singer's claim that animals are the equals of humans primarily because they are "sentient" and are thus capable of suffering? How does his view of animals differ from that of Singer?

2. How would Singer be likely to respond to Francine Patterson's and Wendy Gordon's suggestion that Koko the gorilla has "earned" the distinction of personhood through her intellectual accomplishments (p. 592)? How would he probably view their use of Koko as an experimental subject or the display of gorillas and other animals in zoo exhibits? Why?

3. Does the violent behavior among chimps that Richard Leakey and Roger Lewin discuss (p. 580) undercut or challenge Singer's argument about animal equality? If we accept the principle of equal consideration of interests, should we permit violence between animals in captivity? In the wild? Why should we prohibit suffering caused by humans but tolerate suffering caused by animals, drought, floods, or other natural disasters?

4. What objections does Paul Shepard (p. 624) raise against the notion of animal liberation? How effectively do these objections weaken the case that Singer makes for equal consideration for animals?

ESSAY OPTIONS

1. Research the positions of animal liberation organizations like People for the Ethical Treatment of Animals (PETA) to determine how their views on the issue of animal rights compare with those of Singer. What differences, if any, do you see between Singer's argument for animal equality, and the arguments and appeals put forward by other groups in the animal liberation movement? Write a paper in which you summarize the results of your research and present your evaluation of the case for animal liberation.

2. Research the state of animal experimentation on your campus. What types of research projects employ animal subjects? What happens to animals in the course of such research? What guidelines are used to regulate the treatment of animals in scientific research on your campus? What justifications, if any, are required for the

use of living animal subjects? To what extent is the trauma or suffering inflicted on the animal addressed in these guidelines? How do these guidelines compare with official policies governing the use of human subjects in experiments on your campus? Summarize your findings in a report that offers your own assessment of the ethical issues involved in animal research.

Rights and Kindness: A Can of Worms

PAUL SHEPARD

For some people, the notion of animal liberation conjures up images of baby seals being clubbed by arctic fur hunters or of puppies being fitted with electrodes by men in crisp white lab coats. For Paul Shepard, the idea of animal liberation conjures up the image of sentimental do-gooders who have become so alienated from the natural world that they can't help seeing even wild animals as pets. This broadside against animal equality offers a sharp critique of the animal liberation movement and a stunning example of mind reading in the service of argumentation. Considered one of the most brilliant and original thinkers in the field of ecology and evolution for over forty years, Shepard (1925–1996) was the Avery Professor of Human Ecology at Pitzer College and the Claremont Graduate School until his death. His publications include *Thinking Animals* (1978); *Nature and Madness* (1982); *Traces of an Omnivore* (1996); and *The Others: How Animals Made Us Human* (1996), the source of this selection.

BEFORE READING

Working in small groups, discuss the idea of "rights." How would you define what it means to have a legal right? What specific rights do people enjoy in the United States? Where do rights come from? What limitations restrict rights? What rights, if any, might apply to animals?

The ambiguity of terms like "right" . . . does not just express a mistake but a deep and imperfectly understood connection between law and morality.

— MARY MIDGLEY

Animal rights is one of the most visible and dramatic campaigns in the modern world. Although abuses of animals have a long history, urban industrial society has added so many ways to ill-treat them that public outcries have become loud and organized against the whole range of horrors. Advocates of "animal liberation," "animal ethics," "the humane movement," "animal rights," or "animal protection" have had striking success in creating public outrage and reaction. Even so, as a major philosophical umbrella for articulating the relationship of our species to others, as given voice by Mary Midgley° above, it is disastrous.

Evidence for cruelty to animals is easy to find and to trace. The Jewish Bible warns against mistreating one's animals—clearly a prohibition against known problems and therefore evidence of abuse. But its modern expression arises with modernity in the eighteenth century. Experimental science, widespread pet keeping, the increasing application of technology to animal husbandry, and the marketing of livestock all produced their own forms of abuse and reaction against them. Enlightenment science with its new objectivity set a ruthless mood in the laboratory that to many seemed little different from the long-standing customs of cat-burning° and the beating of dogs and horses. Much has been made of René Descartes's denial° of a soul and sentience to animals, but it is clear that science was no different than popular culture when it came to cutting up animals. New thinking about the mind and consciousness played an important role. Deliberations on pain, and the discussion of the moral status of animals by Montaigne° and others, contributed to Victorian confrontations, particularly in English street demonstrations against medical training and experiment.

Concern for animal welfare came about in part as a trickle-down from bourgeois pet-love, urban eyes on cruel drovers, the spectacle of bear and dog fights. Animal protection emerged in the twentieth century as a footnote to political and civil liberation movements, as a complex, educated wrath over the general conditions of animals in research, on the farm, in slaughterhouses, in the household, in the streets, on fur farms, in traps, the "harvest" of seals and hunting of whales. In modern congested cities, millions of animals became victims of negligence and vicarious punishment, growing out of abandonment in which unwanted litters become feral populations living on rats and garbage.

While animal keeping on small farms may often have been benign, there was never an ethical issue among peasants as to the physical control, marketing, and slaughter of the birds, fish, and mammals that constitute the peasant's world. With twentieth-century "industrial" agriculture, however, the practices were organized on a scale previously rare and without the spontaneous caring that was usual among farmers. The breeding cycle became controlled to a degree and with measures that went far beyond anything known to old-style farmers. Domestic animals are typically squeezed into pens, cages, and stalls, castrated, debeaked, dehorned, injected, altered with hormones, force-fed,

Mary Midgley: (b. 1919), British ethical philosopher.

the long-standing customs of cat-burning: Cats being associated with witchcraft, their burning or killing was condoned throughout Europe until the nineteenth century.

René Descartes's denial: French philosopher René Descartes (1596–1650) believed that animals were biological machines without souls or consciousness.

Montaigne: Michel Eyquem de Montaigne (1533–1592), French essayist.

and exercised only when it is consistent with the desired product. Restricted throughout their lives, slaughtered in terror, even their own social lives are destroyed as the animals spend little time in groups. The industrialized farm crowds chickens for slaughter into small containers in the dark or puts egg-layers into artificial light/dark pens. Sows are harnessed and in-stalled, piglets quickly taken from them, and finally enclosed in darkness as they are fattened. Calves for veal are tightly confined and even sheep and cows are increasingly constrained. Their foods are increasingly unlike their natural food. They are shipped, warehoused, and dealt a mechanical, impersonal death. Deformity and cancer are widespread. The "pig" is little more than insentient pork, without access to sunlight and open fields, dazedly enduring monotony and isolation, with an attenuated or narcotized nervous system that reduces it to a numbed body and a vegetative brain.

Suffering and the broken heart, being largely subjective, are difficult to   5
measure. For farm animals, free life in an outdoor setting is nearly gone; even on the range, herd animals must be fed, vaccinated, branded or tagged, and protected from the leg-breaking holes of burrowing rodents, from odd predation on their young, and from their own immobility and stupidity in bad weather. Their brief lives end in impersonal handling and degradation.

The "farming" of animals includes the fur farm and the wild game farm for private hunting, target practice and dog-training practice, restocking, and meat. The recent tide of caring and kindness extends to zoos and private displays, circuses, trapping, the keeping of pets, and hunting. From attention to simpleminded apathy, ordinary horse-whipping and careless brutality in the preindustrial world, through Hogarth's drawings° of the stages of cruelty, to neurotic hunters' misplaced zeal, scientific and industrial exploitation, and the insensate side of pet keeping, we see the vast landscape of oppression as the motive to protect "our animal friends." Added to all this is the trade in wild animals and their parts for folk medicine and aphrodisiacs, scaled up in the past decades from regional to international, subject to magnified abuses by well-heeled gangs with automatic weapons and distributional networks.

Among the nations, Sweden points the way toward which civilized countries move. It has the most stringent animal welfare laws, guaranteeing the freedom of cattle, pigs, and chickens from the worst horrors of factory farming. Cows have grazing rights, pigs a right to a clean bed, and chickens a right to get out of their cages periodically. Except for the treatment of disease, no drugs or hormones may be used on them. Slaughtering must be done humanely. Curbs are imposed on scientific experiments using animals. By 1990 the Swedish legislature was considering prohibiting the use of hormones to increase milk output in dairy cattle; by the mid-1990s the target was genetic engineering. The Swedish leader in this movement in the 1980s was Astrid Lindgren, the author of *Pippi Longstocking* and other children's books and

Hogarth's drawings: William Hogarth (1697–1764), English painter and engraver famous for his animal caricatures.

grown-up versions of children's stories for the widest-circulating newspaper in Sweden.[1]

Elsewhere, much of the animal rights movement addresses the use of animals in research. In America, Tom Reagan's book, *Animal Sacrifice,* for example, is directed to this issue. With respect to domestic animals, no sane person could quarrel with his concern, and the moral validity of his perspective is obvious.

But with Tom Reagan and many others, the message of animal protection does not end with captives. In the projection of this hearth rug altruism onto nature the proponents of "kindness" fall into the traps created by their own, often infantile, imagination. No doubt animal welfare, sweeping up derelicts from the street, has an important moral weight on its side. All the traditional motives related to mercy, compassion, and kindness apply, but only when the reform is limited to the management of enslaved animals. To project this logic onto wild animals is to envelop the natural world in the fantasy. One of Astrid Lindgren's newspaper stories is written from the viewpoint of God, "who made man to take care of the animals," and who is disappointed in our performance. We are cautioned to do better. After all, "taking care" of the animals does not mean allowing them to be at risk by running free. It means fixing the conditions of their lives and protecting each of them from human cruelty and natural hazards.

This idealism is defective because it leaps from the wretched, abandoned cats and dogs and their "suffering" as experimental objects, and from the blighted lives of cattle and poultry in factory farms, to hunted victims — to "lost" whales supposed to be helplessly blundering about in harbors or beached at low tide or tardy in their southward migration and trapped north of the arctic ice. It exaggerates into a ghastly caricaturing of the medical oath to save all lives and end all pain everywhere at any cost. Attempts at such animal welfare address a truly colossal debacle, but the reaction is muddled in piety and its dream of the survival of *all* the buffaloes and *all* the stray cats.

That a moral outrage against suffering cannot be directed against the "suffering" of populations and ecosystems is ironic beyond laughter and tears, because the destruction of those natural communities is immeasurably more important than all the pain in all the cats everywhere.[2] But the extension of "kindness" to nature exhibits a deracinated° clinging, a neurotic zeal that omits all of "nature" except the individual — the projected self as it gropes for terms of responsibility, justice, and affiliation in animal welfare: protection, rights, kindness, ethics, liberation, reverence for life, sanctity of being, confounded with the semantics of "friendship," "stewardship," "kinship," "humane," "fellow creatures" and mixed in analogous politics of human political and social liberation.

deracinated: Rootless.

"Protection" is among the least complicated of the terms. It refers to the freedom of animals from misuse, ranging from the threat to an endangered species in some far area of the earth, to the trade in captives and skins, to a local population of butterflies threatened by development, to saving rhinos from the hired guns who would cut off their horns for the apothecary market. Beyond that, a fierce obsession takes hold — to protect wild antelopes from the weather or starvation in a harsh winter, to save baby rhinos from marauding lions, rare mollusks from human sewage, wild moose from cattle diseases. Is there any end to our benign outreach that imagines you can "save" all individual animals? In this fairy-tale world of "saving," death is banished forever.

"Liberation" invokes the end of oppression, especially in the political and military sense, where nations, races, and classes are subjugated. But in order to be liberated one must be captive, which is well enough for sheep and turkeys, but the captivity of lynx and peccaries is the "captivity" of a dangerous wild nature, a world of risks and early death. Of course, "liberation" can mean "to take from its previous owner," as when soldiers "liberate" property. Into what alternative status other than the barnyard do we liberate animals from their oppressor reality of food chains, parasites, disease, and storms?

"Rights" implies some kind of cosmic rule prior to any contracts among users, legislation for protection, or decisions to liberate. It refers to something intrinsic or given by God or Nature.[3] Animals may be said to have rights to continue life and freedom because that is what we say they have. A chicken may be given rights to walk about freely for two hours each day by the Swedish legislature. If we wish, rights apply as well to a goldfish in an aquarium, a bacterium in a biological laboratory, a zoo animal, milk cow, or pet cat.

Wild animals do not have rights; they have a natural history. To specify the   15 right of baby lions not to be killed by hyenas or the right of spider monkeys not to be eaten by Peruvian hunters gives the lions and monkeys a legalistic or pseudopolitical reality. One may legislate on behalf of them, dictate a denial of rights, create rights, cancel them, or never think of them at all, but they do not exist outside of those human considerations. Talking of wild animals' rights is like running in sand. Rights of one animal infringe upon the rights of another. If the issue is truly their welfare (and not some act of guilty compensation on our part), the legal and moral rights of forests or mountains would be more to the point, but only as a rather tenuous metaphor. Otherwise, the whole matter of rights becomes as conspicuously silly as it is obscure in reference to a cockroach. The only way such rights make sense is in terms of restrictions on my actions toward cockroaches or mountains — which I am prepared to accept — but they do not have to be described in terms of "rights" at all nor assumed to preexist in the order of things. Somehow these indigenous "rights" appear by magic when stated.

Philosophers argue the matter of animal rights in legal abstractions as well. Joel Feinberg says that duties toward animals follow a right, which in turn results from a claim. A claim becomes a right when it is acknowledged to exist from some prior circumstance or when its moral basis is accepted due to one's conscience or God's direction. Such a moral basis, he says, is seen in the statutes against cruelty. Since animals lack duties, moral standards, and understanding and are not "persons" with "interests," they cannot be participants in their own case. (To consider them thinking beings, he notes, is a primitive overregard for beasts.) Being so deficient, they belong to that category of helpless beings whom the law recognizes as deserving protection, like infants or imbeciles. Some rights, he says, precede legislation, being "natural," such as being free of unnecessary pain, free of having their movements restrained, free of lack of privacy, or free of being wantonly slaughtered. The idea of justice centers on biblical/legal retribution. The recipients of justice must *deserve* what they get. Deserving assumes accountability, and a claim to be made. Thus the idea of rights correlates with justice. A modification of the relation of justice to rights is the concept of the common good. On this basis it can be applied to animals.

But are rights really prior to our announcement of them? Where were they in the Pleistocene? The Paleozoic? Rights do not make sense without reference to a source. The dictionary says that rights are "that which is due to anyone by law, tradition, or nature." But law and tradition can just as easily be murderous and tyrannical. If there are "natural" rights of an animal, they are the right to participate in the ecosystems in which they evolved, a "right to exist" (only as long as they live, which for many newborn elk and gnus is just a few minutes). Is the right to be free from cruel treatment expressed only in terms of human restraints, or is it a right to be free from being eaten slowly by a parasite or rapidly by a predator or postmortem by a vulture? If so, what about the predator's right to a meal? What of the rights of the grass which is eaten by the deer?

Theology answers that we recognize all these values, but some are more important than others and we are therefore obliged to judge them. So said Albert Schweitzer° when he poured kerosene on the army ants while espousing "reverence for life." We are back to the biblical and humanistic hierarchies; so much for "natural" rights. Since the idea of liberation grows from Western ethics, the power of rights seems to be determined by how much a species of animals resembles humans or contributes to human life. But evolution is not a ladderlike structure leading to our species; it is tree-like, with the humans at the pinnacle of nothing but their own family branch, on which they are the only living species. The perverse theme of modern rights is that locusts are less important than dogs, snails less than badgers, and all of them together less than one human life. When rights ethics tries to abandon such a hierarchy, it creates purists like the Puritans or fanatics like the Jains,° whose real concern, as Schweitzer put it, is not the animals but our immortal souls.

Albert Schweitzer: (1875–1965), Alsatian theologian, humanitarian, musician, and medical missionary.

Jains: Followers of Jainism, a form of East Indian Buddhism that shuns all forms of killing, even the unintentional killing of insects.

"Ethics" as applied to animals is a more formal philosophical statement or code of human obligations to them, including their proper use, their rights to be, and even, perhaps, the necessity of their liberation. Ethics is formally a part of philosophy, as invented for the Western world by ancient Greeks, just as the Hebrews invented our morality. Ethics, conceived originally to deal with relationships among "men," or between them and their gods, may include the logic of human relationships to animals. Ethics lends itself to the concept of justice and to the justification of rights. It explains the logic of a morality. The "ethic" includes opposition to giving AIDS to experimental chimpanzees, to the wearing of furs and skins, to laws against dogs riding in open trucks, to fox hunting, to the overworking of horses in "western" movies, to the reduction of feral burros in national parks—all revealing the deeply felt absence of the natural in our lives, expressed as high-sounding transactions with nonhuman life.

The problem of infringing on one species while protecting another has been   20 "solved" by arguing that animals have both intrinsic and instrumental value. The first is of a higher sort. Intrinsic value implies something above utility. All creatures have intrinsic value, but some, being more sentient (like us), have greater intrinsic value than others. Thus an elephant has more intrinsic value than a fish. But what is the value of an elephant in the eyes of the fish who breed in its footprints in a stream: is it intrinsic or instrumental? How are we to act on the intrinsic value of my dog's fleas? Intrinsic values are ideal abstractions, like goodness, beauty, and truth. They are useful in order to understand the limits of idealism in an ambiguous world.

Instrumental value has caused even more trouble, since that is what cows and dogs have for us. As an ideal it may have some integrity on the family farm, but it produces untold injury when the instrumental values of animals are incorporated into the world as commodities and the instruments of the factory. Ecologically, all things have instrumental value. These are not necessarily gross and materialistic and selfish—that is what we have been making them, turning them into objects, units of meat or hides or energy or experimental victims. Only in captivity and museums do animals exist as objects. Outside, all live in natural systems and are instrumental to one another. The question is not to act on their "intrinsic" value in isolation but on their place (and our place—our limits) in such systems.

And then there are the "friends" of animals. "Friendship" can have a certain bizarre reality between master and slave, but it is a one-way window otherwise. Few individual wild animals recognize members of another species as "friend," except perhaps to approach in shy curiosity or becoming habituated to tolerance or benefiting from its warning calls. Self-styled "animal lovers" argue that wild things learn to fear man, that otherwise they would all be cozy friends in a kind of garden world. They point to foxes on St. Nicolas Island, or iguanas in the Galápagos, or boobies on Guam. But the examples all come from islands with no large terrestrial predators, populations in which the genetic disposition of normal vigilance which keeps such vulnerable animals at a distance from anything big has been gradually dimmed, just as the capacity for flight wanes among some species of birds on islands. The little fawn that does not run is not evidence that the deer has not learned fear; it is evidence that flight is a poor choice in its circumstances and that its nervous system is not yet developed. Most such animals on larger land areas have inborn fear responses, especially by the time they are able to run or fly. They can learn not to fear humans or other large forms by habituation, but they are not "born that way." Young mammals also follow cues from their parents and their companions in this regard.

Like humans, many animals develop inherent avoidance when they are big enough to discriminate among species and have become mobile—responses that can be escalated into fear or diminished by habituation. The wild African chimpanzees and gorillas who accepted Jane Goodall's and Dian Fossey's° proximity, and that of all the cameramen who have come after, were not their friends any more than they were friends of the bushes around them. Thinking of ourselves as a "friend" of distant whales, oceangoing sea turtles, or "vanishing" rhinos is a playlet in the head in which "I" am being "friendly" by my charity, giving money or appreciating them. A wild animal's "friendship" toward humans usually consists in going on as it was, or being lured in with food or captured. The relationships between species are not enmity, friendship, corporation, or family; they are simply not social in the sense of amicable attachment and generosity that the word generally means within our own species.

Of all the terms of the humane movement, "sanctity of being" has the best ring to it. It seems to say: "Let be; respect all creatures as they are; exercise responsibility or even compassion for life by not interfering," as Mary Midgley says, "as they exist, as ends in themselves." But is "being" a noun or a verb, or both? Are only individuals the object of this letting be, or does it include populations, species, natural communities, the biosphere? Does it include *our* being—just being, or being something? In these semantic tangles (and quicksands) philosophers live and play; their rational ploys and ambiguities pin us to our skulls. Their streetside counterparts, moved by small tragedies, carry banners, barricade fur salons, shout slogans, "Let them be!"

As models of people with such an "animal ethic," the Jains are often cited 25 because of their doctrine of *ahimsa,* or "harmlessness." Wearing masks to avoid accidentally inhaling and killing insects, stooping to remove tiny creatures from the footpath, abstaining from all meat and even eggs and those parts of plants that cause the death of an embryo, the Jains appear to be the very acme of the love of life. But when the Jain philosophy is examined more closely, it is seen to be motivated by an avoidance of defilement. Jains are among the world's great dichotomists, whose abhorrence of all things organic drives them to despise the living stream. For them the "pure crystal" of

Jane Goodall's . . . Dian Fossey's: Jane Goodall (b. 1934), British ethologist known for her work with chimpanzees in Tanzania; Dian Fossey (1932–1985), American zoologist believed to have been killed by poachers because of her work with gorillas in Tanzania.

nonmaterial essence and the "dark pollution of the material world" are in profound conflict. Organic life, unfortunately, mixes the spiritual and physical, which the Jains would keep separate. Their attempts to save worms from being trampled signifies their desire to avoid all possible connection with the natural world, even on the bottoms of their sandals. Their "harmlessness" is estrangement. As Frank Darling says of them: "The Jain, bent double peering at the ground before each step lest he should kill anything, would need eyes of an order not granted to us to see the still smaller creatures in his way. There is no room in our philosophy of responsibility for preciousness."[4] One does not have to dig far into Christian roots to find a parallel with Jainism's world rejection — and to suspect that the sweet charity of animal protectionism is energized not by religious insight and commitment to life, but by a free-floating compassion, more cathartic than ecological, soured by the contamination of birth and the fear of death.

"Defenders" of animals, animal rights and protection advocates, antivivisectionists, vegetarians, opponents of cruelty and torture, authors of a new ethics, antagonists of hunting, and promoters of "kindness" to our animal "friends" — my skepticism with this vast moral outrage, with its smarmy cloak of affection and fellowship, may seem strange in a book attempting to witness the essential place of animals in our humanity. Altruism is undeniably important; cruelty, callous keeping, rationalized butchery, overmechanized husbandry, social and legal disregard, corporate, commercial, and scientific exploitation, and the ordinary street torture of animals are all reprehensible. Given the reality of such cruelty and the advance of the modern paradigm of "kindness," why do these expressions of concern and caring make one uneasy? Why do polemics on behalf of the dumb beasts seem so inadequate as ethics or morality, and why does this philosophical equivalent of the veterinary romance of *All Creatures Great and Small* stick in the craw? As social phenomena and selfless intentions, such sentiments are clearly an expression of widely shared feelings. But this gentle and generous concern, the extension of civilized regard for a relatively helpless, kept assembly, however appropriate in the ethos of captives, is mostly bad ecology that can drive out the good.

With respect to nature as a whole, if kindness, friendship, and caregiving are not the Way, then what is? Is it "bonding" with animals? Mary Midgley advocates a new sense of bonds with animals.[5] She calls the idea of human superiority "species solipsism," resulting in the "species barrier" or "species gap" — that is, "the powerful tendency to resent and fear all close comparisons between our own species and any other." What we need is a "species bond," she argues, like that of "Elephant Bill," who worked with Burmese elephants for thirty years, one of those "who spend their lives dealing successfully with extremely demanding animals." In view of the subtlety of the elephant personality, she characterizes the thesis that animals have no consciousness as "ignoring elephants." Unlike some animal protectionists, she has the good sense not to blame our harmfulness on evolutionary theory ("nature red in tooth and claw" or "survival of the fittest") and to understand that Charles Darwin was himself "a broad and generous spirit" whose work made possible not only modern ecology but the modern naturalist's sensibility and recognition of mutual dependency and cooperation among animals, as well as the overall positive function of predation, parasitism, and competition.[6]

Part of the problem with Midgley's perspective, and that of most animal ethicists, is its simplistic repudiation of killing animals. (Elephant Bill actually loved elephants so deeply he had no doubt that some had to be shot.) Life sets traps for philosophers. Is "bonding" just a perspective? Midgley uses "bonding" to mean the recognition of a responsible kinship, but the term has long been used in the scientific study of animal life. Baby animals imprint on their parents, so that they direct their social behavior as adults toward the right species, becoming capable of an appropriate bond. If reared by a different species, a surrogate keeper, they misbond and develop social abnormalities that render them incapable of associating with their own kind. Unfortunately for "ethics," the natural community of life is not a bonding between species.

Another writer has argued that keeping animals was the tribal peoples' means of "bonding." Tame raccoons, moose, bison, bears, coatis, parrots, eagles, and so on demonstrate, he says, that pet keeping is not simply a feature of "Western wealth, decadence, and bourgeois sentimentality."[7] But those captive, tamed wild animals were simply prisoners, objects of beauty or curiosities, but not welded to their keepers by anything more than clipped wings and deformed social bonds. These captives were never confused with the vast realm of wild animal life that surrounded such villages. To propose the tame animal and its owner as a model "bond" for human/wild animal relationships is nonsense.

"Bonds" evoke images of babies and their mothers, of fraternal loyalty, of priestesses in secret rites with their goddess, of blood brothers, old war buddies, or cellmates. "Interspecies bonds" implies something felt by both parties, though it could mean commitment to animals without expecting any such commitment in return. Moreover, bonding suggests powers stronger than commitment, something forged in unconscious ties that transcend or precede loyalty, emotional as well as intellectual, yet having formal obligations. The term is used by psychologists to describe mother/infant dependency or sibling loyalty. But a bond is not only a connection. It is the deposit of valuables risked by those charged with a crime to guarantee their presence in court. Bonds are legal instruments defining rights in terms of restraints on the freedom of the bonded to be themselves — that is, for animals, to be wild. The primary symbol of a bond is a tether. It is difficult not to see in this reference to bonding by animal protectors a kind of barnyard hypocrisy. Am I to feel interspecific bonds to all other species? Am I bonded to bacteria as well as to horses? I am connected to bacteria by descent (not to horses) and I am host to their depredations and benefits in my own tissues. I suspect that life on earth would end without them. But I make no deposit against the risks in their personal lives. Their individual tragedies are not my tragedies.

It is as though all the virtuous and well-intentioned sense of obligation toward a few species of domesticated animals were seen as a guidepost for attitudes toward all animals everywhere. Organizations like Kids in Nature's Defense (KIND), sponsored by the National Association for the Advancement of Humane Education, pledge "Creatures great and small, we must defend them all." It sounds good, but domestic pets are isolated from their ancestral ecology, like bits of tissue in a petri dish in a laboratory. The dream of bonding has, in a twinkling, taken "bonding" into the wilderness as though all life were kittens abandoned on the street. The clinical regimen for captives—therapy, care, and consoling—becomes the key concept. The world is to be a protected and prophylactic zoo, at once medical and moral, the object of charity and the anodyne for guilt.

How are we to understand this misplaced zeal? I think it has to do with death—the final, unacceptable reality of the natural world. This is where the anti-organic stance of our culture and our civilization leads in the end. "Protection" is a repository of the protector's own dread of the cycle of birth and death, which close our dreams of perfection in a visceral and protoplasmic envelope.

One writer cites Plato's Athenian speech on the preservation of the whole in contrast to John Calvin's statement° that "All other things can properly be put in the service of man."[8] Putting them in our service does not mean only their wool and milk but their vicarious existence, their tendency to die, as an arena in which we can fight death. But for such thinkers, recognition of the whole is itself the true test of human eminence: "The dignity and distinctive value of the human species that an anthropocentric vision sustains cannot be ignored."[9] Somehow the other members of that whole seem to remain invisible before its august image.

A large part of the logic of animal rights involves the similarity of animals and humans—how they feel pain, communicate, think, respond emotionally, and so on. But when it comes to killing and eating animals, which all other carnivorous and omnivorous animals do, we suddenly become very different from them, superior in morality, intellectually estranged, nature's stewards, custodial keepers and architects, or we become vegetarian, a state of beatific mastication which we left six million years ago in our evolution from herbivorous primate ancestors. The double bind sets our membership in the natural community and its ecology against our desire for a warm bath of "animal friends."

Socially, there is some plain foolishness in the logic. In "Beasts for Pleasure," Maureen Duffy says: "The animals have sunk from being members of the family or at least dependent servants to being automata and for this the popular interpretation of Darwin's conclusions is largely responsible" and "after thousands of years of living with them we know almost nothing about them."[10] In other words, evolution and ecology cannot be our guides, and the wisdom and knowledge of indigenous peoples do not exist for her.

John Calvin's statement . . . : John Calvin (1509–1564), French Puritan theologian.

Hunting animals is anathema to most "animal lovers." In his book *In the Company of Animals,* James Serpell remarks, "With the exception of the so-called 'whaling industry' and the sporting activities of the learned rich, hunting as a way of life has more or less vanished."[11] Hunting/gathering cultures are indeed at the brink of oblivion, thanks to ten millennia of genocide at the hands of farmers and pastoralists, but hunting has not ceased to be important in modern life. In North America alone 50 million people hunt and 100 million fish every year, apart from the indigenous cultures, from Point Barrow and Ellsmere Island to Arizona and New Mexico, who have never quit believing in the sacred hunt.

Hunting is an easy target. The harassment of English fox-hunters, like the picketing of the fur stores, is easily connected with resentment against the rich and provides opportunities for demonstrations and the media. The commercialization and perversions of the hunt — the game hogs, the drunks, the shooters of cows, the facades of camaraderie — make the war against hunting both easy and facile. Despite recent studies of the religious and ethical sensibilities of hunting/gathering cultures, opening new paths to the modern ecological conscience as exemplified by modern hunters like Aldo Leopold and Theodore Roosevelt,° there remains a vociferous opposition to hunting as degenerate and atavistic. The myth common to many ethnic hunters about the marriage, once upon a time, of humans and animals, says one author, is merely a recollection of sexual relations with animals.[12]

Maureen Duffy furiously attacks hunting, but she reveals more about antihunters than the ethos of hunting. In her are married the outraged feminist and the animal lover. Hunting, she says, is thinly disguised rape. The social functions of hare coursing begin "after the kill when comparisons are swapped, sizes compared as bull sessions compare sexual prowess." The body shape of fox and otter "isn't hard to see as a phallus and both are traditionally sexy beasts and dwell in holes." Killing the hare by breaking its back is "the usual erotic movement of courtship being transferred to death." Hunting is like "masturbation fantasies . . . the build up and the orgasm," and so on. For her, death and sex constitute crimes against nature and women. She is gratified that bullbaiting, cockfighting and the public feeding of snakes at the zoo have declined, but she is puzzled that bird hunting and fishing have increased.

Duffy does not seem to see that those things which have declined were vicarious expressions of peasant and town neuroses, while those which have increased hark back to a positive generic layer of human being. The traditional myths associating hunting and death speak metaphorically of consummation and renewal rather than trivial sensuality. Her description has no relationship to the actual practice of the hunt. Indeed, her view seems to me to reflect a culturewide fear of being a participant in a world where life lives on death. She says that "we need other animals as part of our background as we need unpolluted

Aldo Leopold and Theodore Roosevelt: Aldo Leopold (1886–1948), American ecologist; Theodore Roosevelt (1858–1919) twenty-sixth president of the United States.

skies and rivers, trees in architecturally beautiful cities, oil-free beaches." These are the words of a spectator, for whom art and nature are valuable amenities, who imagines herself as in a movie, in a pictorial world, framed, static, preserved from the realities of organic process. As "background" nature is acceptable, removing us from the danger of "barbaric regression." . . .

In the end, the abuse of animals will not be solved by ethics any more than by   40 rebuke or exhortation. Neither logic nor charity can deal with what is, beyond pets and chicken factories, a mystery and an ecology: the ambiguity of life living on death, the spiritual nature of nonhuman life, traditions of human membership in natural communities embedded in place and ancestry. Earth history places us among the animals, as one of them, in food chains and other symbioses which we do not invent, but inherit, and which set our limitations among the Others. . . .

At the heart of the ideal of animal protection is their "right to be," or their "right to be let be," to serve no human end. Its best expressions are magnificent pieces of rhetoric which perfectly express the detached ethos of the educated, urban mind. It seems to say: why shouldn't we all just leave animals alone (except perhaps for filming them or otherwise appreciating or studying them at a distance), just as the activist animal protectors in their homes, libraries, cafés, and theaters do? Why struggle with the problem of how to relate to animals, especially when it is complicated with the protoplasmic pitfalls of disease, predation, all that ecological/evolutionary quagmire, and all those disturbing primal and ethnic human precursors? Why work out relationships to animals in terms of that morass of prehistory and the demented (or fallen) creation so interwoven with death? In Cleveland Amory's world° our kindest act is avoidance, our deepest obligation protection at a distance, our best satisfaction a friendship like that of Petrarch for Laura,° without response, a comfortable, ecstatic remoteness, its recompense of the heart rather than the stomach. We can stand back from it all and enjoy "nature" in art and literature and science, a subject matter in a great museum refuge and art gallery. What a truly civilized idea! With the finality of disconnection.

In this way the ethics of "let be" deals with the enigmas and perennial inquiry, finalizing the game by freezing nature in place and removing ourselves. But the true vocation of humankind, to puzzle out reciprocity, requires that we know, as the elders of a million years past knew, that there is no "solution," but instead an ongoing participation. Bystanding is an illusion. Willy-nilly, everybody plays. This play contains that most intimate aspect of the mystery — our own identity — signified in finding ourselves in relationship to the Others.

In Cleveland Amory's world . . . : Cleveland Amory (1917–1988), author and animal-rights advocate.

like that of Petrarch for Laura: Francesco Petrarca (1304–1374), Italian poet whose love lyrics celebrate a woman named Laura.

A hideous overabundance of humans and our demands on energy and space diminish the place for other species. The loss of wildness, extirpation° of species, reductions of natural populations, extinctions, compression of habitat, and poisoning of life by air and water are the tragic circumstances in which we see animal protectionists as indulging in a kind of sentimental morality that is more important to them than the world of animals. As Paul and Ann Ehrlich and Garrett Hardin° have been telling us for thirty years, the ridiculous code of medicine that prolongs human life at any cost and advocates death control without birth control has damaged life on earth far more than all the fox hunters and cosmetic laboratories could ever do — perhaps beyond recovery — and leads us toward disasters that loom like monsters from hell.

Human political rights are meaningless as interspecies relationships. "Liberation" means nothing to a calf elk about to be eaten by a wolf or a salmon about to be eaten by a man. "Bonding" to animals is a willful, Disneyish dream. Most of the advocates of these ideas have never watched wild animals closely and patiently, have little notion of their intelligence, otherness, or the complexity of their lives, cannot imagine combining holiness as killing them or celebrating them by wearing their skins, do not recognize the flesh of animals as a food sanctity, or perceive animals as a means of speculative thought, referential analogy, or immanent divinity.

Notes

1. Steve Lohr, "Swedish Farm Animals Get a Bill of Rights," *New York Times,* October 20, 1988.

2. In one meeting animal lovers picked the work of a psychologist, Harry Harlow, as an example of cruelty. His research involved separating monkey infants from their mothers to study the dynamics of bonding of infants to mothers, especially as a tactile experience, and the psychopathology that results when they are isolated, including the effects on the next generation when the deprived monkeys themselves become mothers. The insights of this work on the infant/mother interaction, on the needs of infants and their consequences for the social-sexual relationships of adults, especially as it stimulated observation on the care of human babies, and on its effect in enhancing the quality of ordinary family life at a time when both parents work, would be difficult to overestimate. Harlow was a nominee for the Nobel Prize. His laboratory was a model of responsible care. The kind of information he gathered could never have been so unambiguously established from the observation of people upon whom such an experiment would have been criminal. The best relief in a worldwide epidemic of schizoid behavior would be radical changes in child care based on the recovery of small-scale society much like that of primal peoples, among whom social and economic pressures do not deprive babies of necessary nurture. Otherwise we are stuck with chronic social sickness which we had better understand.

3. Several heretics have plumbed the superficialities of animal "rights." Myrdene Anderson's reply to the "rhetoric in which we drown" — "What's Wrong with Animal

---

extirpation: Complete destruction.

Paul and Ann Ehrlich . . . Garrett Hardin: American ecologists.

Rights?"—observes that the argument always favors some creatures over others. Anderson's paper was presented to the Twelfth Annual Congress of the Canadian Ethnology Society in 1985. She says the flawed assumption is that rights exist a priori in the natural order rather than being the invention of cultures. Another perennial curmudgeon, Garrett Hardin, further uncovers the rights-and-ethics bias as self-interest in two essays in 1982: "Ethics for Birds (and Vice Versa)" and "Limited World, Limited Rights," both in *Naked Emperors: Essays of a Taboo-Stalker* (Los Altos: Kaufman, 1982).

4. Frank Frazer Darling, *Wilderness and Plenty* (London: BBC Reith Lectures, 1970).

5. Midgley's excellent book *Animals and Why They Matter* (Athens: University of Georgia Press, 1983) is perhaps the most thoughtful essay on the question of an ecological ethic, yet one looks in vain there for the answer to the question: Why do they matter?

6. See Paul Sears, *Charles Darwin: The Naturalist as a Cultural Force* (New York: Scribner, 1950).

7. James Serpell, *In the Company of Animals* (Oxford: Blackwell, 1986), pp. 52–53.

8. John T. McNeill, ed., *Institute of the Christian Religion*, vol. 1 (Philadelphia: Westminster Press, 1955), pp. 81–82.

9. James M. Gustafson, "Ethical Issues in the Human Future," in David Ortner, ed., *The Laws*, vol. 2 (New York: Random House, 1937), p. 645.

10. Maureen Duffy, "Beasts for Pleasure," in Stanley Godlovitch, Rosalind Godlovitch, and John Harris, eds., *Animals, Men, and Morals* (New York: Taplinger, 1972).

11. Serpell, *In the Company of Animals.*

12. Ibid., p. 26.

EXPLORING THE TEXT

1. Why do you think Shepard chose to begin his examination of animal rights by offering a history of animal abuse? What does he gain through this strategy? How does it affect the reader's perception of him and his position? Why does he introduce his critique of the concept of animal rights by discussing the situation of wild animals? Is this a good argumentative strategy in your opinion, or does it weaken his overall position?

2. What specific criticisms does Shepard offer of the animal rights movement? What specific errors of logic or faulty assumptions do proponents of animal liberation make, in his view? What does he mean when he says that wild animals do not have rights but only "a natural history" (para. 15)? Could the same be said for human beings? Why or why not?

3. How does Shepard "read" the intentions and motives of those who believe in animal rights? What, in his view, leads animal rights activists to seek equal treatment for animals? How would you characterize his attitude toward his opponents? How persuasive do you find this analysis? Why?

4. What larger social implications does Shepard see in the animal rights movement? What does the concept of animal equality suggest, in his view, about the way we see our relationship to nature and the environment? What does he suggest as an alternative to animal rights?

FURTHER EXPLORATIONS

1. Compare Shepard's view of animals and nature with that of John (Fire) Lame Deer (p. 512). To what extent would Lame Deer be likely to agree with Shepard about the nature of animals and the motives of the animal rights movement?

2. Compare Shepard's analysis of the motives behind the drive for animal rights with Berger's analysis of the reasons why we look at animals in the zoo (p. 521). What does the act of observation do to both animals and human beings according to these authors?

3. How would Shepard likely interpret the "bond" that exists between Faith McNulty with her pet mouse (p. 535) or between Francine Patterson and Wendy Gordon and Koko (p. 592)? How might McNulty, Patterson, and Gordon respond to Shepard's view of their relationships with these animals? To what extent would you agree that "friendship" can or cannot exist between species?

4. How might Shepard view the idea that chimpanzees are capable of politically motivated acts of "murder," as suggested by Richard Leakey and Roger Lewin (p. 580)? To what extent does Leakey and Lewin's discussion of chimp social order support Shepard's view of animal life? If, in fact, animals don't have rights but only natural histories, as Shepard argues, should ethologists or zoo personnel interfere in cases of interanimal violence like the one described by Leakey and Lewin? Why or why not?

5. What role might nature television programming, as described by Charles Siebert (p. 542), play in promoting the idea that animals in the wild are potential "friends" deserving of our protection? How might television promote what Shepard terms "barnyard hypocrisy" by suggesting that we share an "interspecies bond" with creatures in the wild?

ESSAY OPTIONS

1. Write an essay in which you contrast the positions of Shepard and Peter Singer (p. 607) on the issue of animal rights. How do each of these thinkers view the issue of rights for other species? Why do they reach opposed conclusions on this issue? What differences separate them? Which, in your opinion, presents the most persuasive case? Why?

2. Drawing on the ideas and information you have encountered in any or all readings in this chapter, as well as on information you access from the Internet or your library's resources, write an essay on the issue of animal liberation. To what extent should we protect the rights or interests of animals in captivity, on farms, or in the wild? Is it ethically defensible to hunt, eat, and use animals for display or entertainment purposes? What leads you to this conclusion?

3. Do additional focused research on any one of the controversial issues related to animal ethics—including factory farming, sport hunting, the fur industry, the use of animals in research, or the use of animals for entertainment in films, zoos, or rodeos. Then use this research as the basis of a paper in which you describe how animals are treated in this context and debate the specific pros and cons of this use of animals. What arguments are advanced by those who defend and those who condemn these practices? What is your position on the issue and what reasons do you offer in its support?

6

Reading Cyberminds
The Internet to Artificial Intelligence

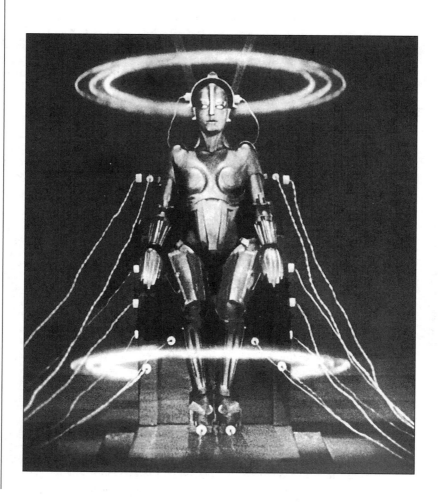

It's Alive!

It's one of the most arresting images of the modern era: the red cyclopean eye of HAL, the Series 2000 supercomputer, glares out at the audience, betraying neither the fear nor madness that is slowly consuming its precision-built circuitry. In 1962, Stanley Kubrick's HAL emerged as an early emblem of the approaching computer age. Widely perceived as the antihero of Kubrick's *2001*, HAL represented everything that the postwar generation believed true about computing: he was designed to be both logical and infallible; he was massive and immobile—made from an electronic honeycomb of wires and memory modules; he was distinctly male; and he was definitely in control—at least until the moment he turned homicidal. HAL was far from the first intelligent machine to debut in a Hollywood movie—but he was the first to be at one and the same time both so insistently machinelike and ominously human. Neither a robot nor an automaton, HAL was a brain in a box—a huge computer modeled on the room-size calculating machines that defined high technology in the 1960s. But he was a box with personality. The pulsing glower of HAL's fiery red eye conveys the presence of a radically other consciousness. It bespeaks a mind that harbors secret thoughts and feelings—a mind capable of resentment, terror, and self-love.

The fantasy of creating an artificial human has a long pedigree in Western civilization. Go back to the ancient Romans and Greeks and you find the story of the sculptor Pygmalion who falls in love with one of his own creations, the beautiful Galatea, brought to life by the gods in response to his prayers. During the Middle Ages, the tradition of Jewish mysticism associated with the Kabala offered the story of the golem. In one of the tale's most common variants, the mythical Rabbi Low shapes a man-doll from clay and brings him to life by placing the name of God in his mouth. Physically powerful but apparently soulless and insensate, the golem serves his master obediently as long as the Rabbi remembers to extract the magical "Shem" from his mouth on Friday, the day of rest. But as luck and mythology would have it, the Rabbi eventually forgets his duty and the golem goes on a rampage, terrorizing the villagers and destroying their homes until his master repents having usurped God's power of creation.

The fantasy of creating artificial life seems inevitably to end in transgression, terror, and guilt. In fact, some critics have argued that buried beneath this deep-seated desire is the male's urge to displace the female in the act of creation—the male's unconscious wish to dominate women by appropriating the power of birth. From this perspective, Pygmalion falls in love with Galatea not simply because she is beautiful, but because she reflects his masculine conception of the feminine ideal; indeed, in the original myth Pygmalion is a misogynist—a man who hates women—at least until he's love-struck by his own man-made image of female beauty. It might seem ironic, then, that two women were centrally involved in bringing the idea of artificial life into the modern era. According to literary legend, Mary Shelley conceived of the tale of Frankenstein during an overnight storytelling competition in 1818 between herself and two famous romantic poets, her husband Percy Bysshe Shelley and their friend Lord Byron. Substituting science for religion and technology for magic, Shelley adapted the legend of the golem to the industrial age. You're probably familiar with the outline of the plot: a brilliant if misdirected young researcher uses his medical skills to stitch together a manlike creature from spare body parts, bringing his creation to life with a jolt of electricity. Today, the story of Frankenstein still resonates with readers, because it offers more than a good hair-raising tale of scientifically inspired horror. Dr. Frankenstein's creature doesn't just come to life and avenge himself against his creator—he feels. He understands that he's doomed to live alone and suffer from the knowledge of his own self-consciousness. In *Frankenstein,* Mary Shelley foresaw not merely the creation of artificial life: she grasped the possibility of creating artificial intelligence.

Some twenty years later, the daughter of Lord Byron would help take the first step toward the scientific realization of Mary Shelley's fantasy. Educated to become a brilliant mathematician, Ada Lovelace was only seventeen years old when she met the eccentric English engineer and inventor Charles Babbage. In 1832, Babbage was struck by a bizarre idea: if the mechanical looms that were driving the European industrial revolution could weave complex designs by following the patterns of holes punched into paper cards, why couldn't a similar kind of machine produce the answers to complex mathematical equations by following a set of printed instructions? Although he never achieved success, Babbage worked on his vision of creating an "Analytical Engine" until his death in 1871. Ada Lovelace labored with him. Considered today the very first software engineer in history, Lovelace developed the notion of programming and invented a number of fundamental programming concepts, like the feedback loop and the subroutine. In 1843, she published the first scientific paper devoted to the prospect of creating an artificial thinking machine, the kind of machine that might one day play chess, compose music, and perhaps even achieve something akin to human consciousness.

Leap ahead a century and you come to yet another brilliant English mathematician, Alan Turing, who drew on the theories of Babbage and Lovelace to create the first operational computer in 1941. Built from telephone relay switches, "Robinson" was a room-size behemoth designed to break the famous "Enigma Code" that the Nazis used to communicate top-secret bombing plans during the Battle of Britain. In the 1950s, Turing set the agenda for all future artificial intelligence research in his article "Computer Machinery and Intelligence." During the decades that followed, thinking machines ballooned to the size of Kubrick's cinematic HAL and then shrank to the desktop proportions we're familiar with today, thanks to the invention of the integrated circuit and the microchip. One by one, the barriers between "meat" and machine minds were whittled away. In the 1950s, people laughed when they heard about the prospect of using robots to replace workers in automobile plants; in the 1980s, whole auto factories were automated with electronic "workers." People scoffed in the 1980s when it was suggested that a computer might some day beat a grand master at chess; in 1997, when IBM's "Deep Blue" defeated Gary Kasparov, critics argued that it proved only that chess doesn't require "real intelligence" after all. In the 1990s, folks doubted that a machine could ever master the kind of "commonsense" understanding of the world that underlies the operations of the average human mind; in the summer of 2001, a research team headed by Douglas B. Lenat unveiled "Cyc" (pronounced "Psych") — the first computer program meant to replicate the full range of human intelligence, from common sense to critical thought.

Today, there can be no doubt that electronic technology is changing and challenging what it means to be human. A little more than a century after Alexander Graham Bell's invention of the telephone, we live in a world obsessed with communication and information technologies. Computers are transforming the way we work, learn, shop, and socialize, and day by day we become increasingly dependent on our connection to the worldwide virtual machine we call the Internet. In fact, many theorists believe that the age of the cyborg — beings that blend organic and machine systems — is already upon us. It wasn't long ago that the idea of the robot was enough to inspire horror in generations of science-fiction film addicts. When Eva, the mechanical temptress, terrorized her human counterparts in Fritz Lang's classic 1927 anti-industrial fantasy *Metropolis* (see page 640), few would have dreamed how quickly and thoroughly our lives — and our identities — would become intertwined with high technology. Today, machines extend our senses of sight, hearing, smell, and touch all over the world. They move us from place to place and carry our voices and images across continents in a matter of seconds. We use machines to exercise and stay fit. We depend on machines to work and play. When we're sick, we turn to increasingly sophisticated medical technologies to heal our bodies. Within a decade or two, robotic surgeons will staff our hospitals, performing life-saving operations that will involve replacing organs like the heart, kidneys, liver, spleen, and lungs with "cyberorgan" transplants. Within the span of a generation, we will depend on intelligent "agents" to help us solve problems, extend our memories, and sharpen our perceptions. Eventually, as AI expert Hans Moravec suggests, we may even be ready to take the final step:

> One day when we know how the mind works, we will realize that it is not necessary to be sick, or to lose our memory in old age, or to die. One will then be able to transplant all the elements of his personality into another body, a machine body, which is maintained and continues to grow, so that we will not have to live with our restrictions forever.

This final chapter of *Mind Readings* invites you to explore what it means to be human on the threshold of the cybernetic era. It challenges you to think about how electronic information technology is reshaping human identities and relationships and about the nature of electronic intelligence. Ultimately, it asks you to contemplate what may well be the future of the mind—the emerging collaboration of human and machine intelligence.

Cyber Writing: Hypertext & Web Search

Perched as we are on the brink of the computer age, we tend to forget that the book itself is a form of high technology. Before the invention of the book, the scroll was the medium of choice for preserving written language. A roll of papyrus stored in a leather tube, the scroll was an "analogue" technology: its form mimicked the uninterrupted linear flow of the formal public oration or speech. In fact, the scroll was perceived as so close to the living voice in form that the scribes who copied speeches, plays, poems, and histories onto scrolls didn't bother with things like punctuation, capitalization, and word boundaries:

> thewordstheywroteflowedfrompentopapyrusinanunbrokenstreamthatimitatedthe
> continuousstreamofspokenlanguagelikethis.

All of this changed with the development of the "codex," the technical term for a collection of cut and bound pages that can be turned and read in sequence. Books are more "digital" than scrolls. They break language up into usable "bits" that are easier to identify, label, and retrieve. Emerging during the last two centuries of the Roman Empire—roughly between 200 and 400 A.C.E.—the book brought with it a host of innovations that helped readers search through texts for the chunks of information they wanted—devices like word boundaries, punctuation, paragraphs, chapters, titles, subheadings, tables of contents, footnotes, bibliographies, indices, and appendices. Books were more "user-friendly" and "interactive" than scrolls: they invited readers to browse through a text, to leap from section to section, and even to jot down their own ideas, responses, and interpretations as "marginalia" in the open spaces surrounding every page.

The computer continues the digital revolution that began with the invention of the book. Writing online is more open, interactive, reader-friendly, and "byte-sized" than ever. Now, instead of the page and the paragraph, our measure of meaning is the screen; instead of the isolated word or the footnote, we have the "link"—the electronic board-wax we use to surf from Web site to Web site. The computer is changing so many ideas we have about writing that some theorists, like Brown University's George P. Landow, suggest it's time to scrap antique ideas like the essay and the book and replace them with a new concept of written communication—the hypertext. Hypertext is what writing looks like online. It tends to be more fragmented—more "byte-sized"—than traditional forms of writing, and more open—open to multiple voices, other media, reader responses—you name it. Since the invention of the printing press, traditional writing has been organized around the notion of the theme or thesis. Reading a book or an essay requires you to identify the author's controlling idea or purpose—often explained in the introduction—and to appreciate how this central theme or thesis is "developed" or supported in the body of the text. Books and essays are like guided tours: you move from point A to point B, following the author's "authoritative" lead. Hypertexts are more like self-guided expeditions. Hypertext documents offer readers "webs" of information connected by links. More interactive than books and essays, they invite their readers/users to enter at any point and give them options about where to go next. You might enter a hypertext web about "robots" by reading a brief introductory essay on the history of the golem; then you might click on a link that connects you to an image gallery of robots and androids in famous films; from there you might link to a site that offers a video clip from Fritz Lang's *Metropolis;* from there you might leap to an illustrated essay on the latest research on computer consciousness. More open and interactive than formal essays and books, hypertext documents invite readers to browse through their offerings and to construct their own learning experiences from a variety of materials. Instead of delivering a clearly focused "message" through a logically organized, linear presentation, they invite exploration by presenting readers/ users with a network of interrelated ideas and information.

The openness of hypertext also means that it is not exclusively a linguistic form of communication. The earliest books were often Bibles that contained beautiful hand-painted "illuminations"—full-color pictures that illustrated the gospel stories they accompanied. Books have always mixed written and graphical elements. Online publication takes the sensory richness of the book a step further. Hypertexts are, by nature, multimedia and multisensory documents. An effective hypertext offers the reader/user a multimedia "collage"— an interactive mix of written, aural, pictorial, and even video-based information. The computer's visual/aural interface makes it possible to merge segments of traditional written text with photos, illustrations, graphics, sound clips, and video images. Creating a hypertext on the gender politics of cyborgs? How about including a few paragraphs from Donna Haraway's classic "Cyborg Manifesto," a gallery of popular comic book images, an audio track from Arnold Schwarzenegger's *Terminator* series, and your own illustrated analysis of the future of cyborg bodies? Whether it's offered online as a Web site, in the form of a gallery installation, as a piece of "performance art," or even as a collage of words and images on paper—a good hypertext blends media in a way that enriches the reader's experience. It never relies on the monologue of the traditional essay alone to ignite reader interest.

But before you start assembling your own hypertext collage—and even before you venture too far into the wilds of the Internet researching your next paper—a quick word of caution. The Net offers you access to more information today at the click of a mouse than students in past generations could have dreamed of. But it offers this kind of access at a price. In the past, students used library-selected resources that were, in a sense, guaranteed in terms of authority and reliability. When you look up an encyclopedia entry or an article in a series of professional abstracts in your library's resource room, you don't have to worry too much about the validity of the information you're getting. You have the entire research staff of your library—and the entire research enterprise of higher education—supporting you from behind the scenes. The situation online is very different. Do a "Google" search of a topic like artificial intelligence theory on the Net, and you're likely to pull up hundreds of screen pages of links, some of them connecting you with terrific sources of expert information and some conneting you with Web sites that are sure to waste your time. Your search might lead you to an *Encarta* article on AI theory, to the Web page of the MIT AI Lab, or to computer scientist Ray Kurzweil's "cybernetic poet" site. But it just as easily may lead you to the home page of an "organization" dedicated to the worship of computer circuitry, to a misbegotten essay posted by an anonymous secondary school student who flunked his "Science & Social Issues" class, or to a page of the "A.I. Smith" family genealogical report. The Internet gives you unlimited access to unlimited sources of information, but much of it is useless for academic research. Before you draw information from any online source, you need to document its reliability. You have to determine if the person, organization, or institution responsible for posting the information speaks with verifiable authority. Sometimes, this is simply a matter of tracing the posting back to a credible Web site: an article associated with a national magazine or a paper posted by a computer science professor at a major university are probably safe bets. Sometimes, it involves additional research: you might have to do more groundwork to ascertain that "Richard Smalley's Home Page" is, in fact, put out by a bona fide authority in nanotechnology and not by a home hobbyist with a penchant for science fiction. Ultimately, the best way to assure that you aren't misled by the research you do online is to use the same resource you'd turn to for help in doing any kind of basic intellectual research—your college library. Academic libraries today are staffed by highly skilled professionals, trained to help you navigate your way through the labyrinth of the Web and to make the most of the information you find there. You can also get additional help by checking out the research resources associated with the *Mind Readings* Web site at <www.bedfordstmartins.com/mindreadings>.

Chapter Overview

We begin with a series of four selections on the Internet. Web critic Clifford Stoll leads off by explaining why he thinks the Net isolates and dehumanizes those who use it. Veteran programmer Ellen Ullman follows with her appraisal of what it means to live "close to the machine." Ullman's analysis of the computer's "boy engineer" ethic and the way it's colonizing nearly every aspect of contemporary society issues a wake-up call to those who see the Net as the leading edge of social progress. Guillermo Gómez-Peña's "The Virtual Barrio" extends this discussion of Internet culture by raising questions about the issue of equal access to information technology resources. Sherry Turkle's "Who Am We?" brings the first half of the chapter to a thought-provoking close with a discussion of the psychological and moral implications of gender swapping and "Tiny sex" among the growing numbers of "MUDders" who engage in fantasy games online.

The second half of the chapter focuses on the theme of artificial intelligence and the future of mechanical minds. In "Muscular Circuitry," Claudia Springer surveys the gender-related body imagery that surrounds depictions of machine minds in the popular imagination. From Springer's analysis of bulging cyborg bodies like those featured in the *Terminator* and *Robocop* film series, we turn to an example of the cybernetic imagination at work in William Gibson's classic cyberpunk short story, "Johnny Mnemonic." Science fiction gives way to scientific theory in Douglas R. Hofstadter's informal "coffeehouse conversation" on the Turing test. Hofstadter's account of Turing's famous dialogical test for the presence of artificial intelligence invites you to speculate about the nature of mind and, perhaps more interestingly, about the features that might distinguish one "type" of mind from another.

The chapter's last three readings carry us to the outer limit in our exploration of human and machine intelligence. In "Redefining the Measure of Mankind," AI specialist Maureen Caudill wonders about the ethical implications of the quest to duplicate and ultimately to "own" other intelligent beings. "Grandfather Clause" presents an offer that the director of Carnegie Mellon University's Center for Mobile Robotics is sure you can't refuse — the chance to download your own consciousness into the shiny new and theoretically immortal body of a robot. Margaret Wertheim brings the chapter to a close — and back to earth — with "Cyber Soul-Space," her analysis of the fundamentally religious values and assumptions that underlie computer culture and the quest for artificial intelligence.

Sources

De Hamel, Christopher. *A History of Illuminated Manuscripts.* 2nd ed. London: Phaidon Books, 1994.

Hiltzik, Michael A. "Birth of a Thinking Machine." *Los Angeles Times,* 21 June 2001, p. 1.

Kurzweil, Ray. *The Age of Spiritual Machines: When Computers Exceed Human Intelligence.* New York: Penguin Books, 1999.

Landow, George P. *Hypertext 2.0: The Convergence of Contemporary Critical Theory and Technology.* Baltimore: Johns Hopkins University Press, 1997.

Seesslen, Georg. "Dream Replicants of the Cinema." In *Artificial Humans: Manic Machines, Controlled Bodies.* Ed. Rolf Aurich, Wolfgang Jacobsen, and Gabriele Jatho. Berlin: Jovis Verlagsburo, 2000.

Woolley, Benjamin. *The Bride of Science: Romance, Reason, and Byron's Daughter.* New York: McGraw-Hill, 1999.

Isolated by the Internet

CLIFFORD STOLL

U.C. Berkeley astronomer Clifford Stoll's first assault on computers took the world of high tech by surprise. In the early 1990s, nearly everyone was singing the praises of the information technology revolution. Computers, the futurists told us, were going to change everything, including the way we did business, the way we worked and learned — even the way we socialized and governed ourselves. Published in 1995, Stoll's *Silicon Snake Oil: Second Thoughts on the Information Highway* was a voice in the wilderness. In it, he challenged much of the conventional wisdom about computers and the benefits they were supposed to bestow. As he saw it, information technology wasn't helping us to be better humans, it was simply making us more like machines. In this selection from his latest foray against the information age, *High-Tech Heretic: Reflections of a Computer Contrarian* (1999), Stoll summarizes the ways that the Internet dehumanizes its users and destroys human relationships. A respected scientist, an Internet pioneer, and a regular commentator on computer-related issues for MSNBC, Stoll (b. 1950) is far from being an antielectronic reactionary. In addition to publishing scholarly papers and articles, he is also the author of the bestselling novel *The Cuckoo's Egg* (1989).

BEFORE READING

Working in groups, brainstorm a list of the ways in which computers, the Internet, and information technology in general are supposed to improve our lives according to the common wisdom on the subject. How is computing expected to change our daily lives over the next twenty years? How is electronic technology supposed to change the way we work, learn, do business, play, and govern ourselves?

For all my grinching about the soul-deadening effects of the Internet, most Internet users speak positively about it. One friend tells how she found a support group for an obscure medical condition. Another tells me that his modem provides an escape from a dull world, providing a rich mixture of fantasy and role playing. One soon-to-be-married couple writes how they met through postings to a Usenet news group. And one computer programmer confesses that although she's extremely shy in person, in her electronic chat room, she becomes a feisty, enchanting contessa. Meanwhile wired families keep in touch via e-mail, and new friendships blossom thanks to online special interest groups. Isolated hobbyists sign onto Web sites to exchange information and help each other. Surely the electronic virtual community is a positive social development.

Well, not necessarily. According to Carnegie Mellon University psychologists Robert Kraut and Vicki Lundmark, there are serious negative long-term social effects, ranging from depression to loneliness. The result of a concerted research effort, their findings were surprising since this research was funded by high-tech firms like AT&T, Apple Computer, Lotus, Intel, and Hewlett Packard. Their report, "The Internet Paradox—A Social Technology That Reduces Social Involvement and Psychological Well-Being?" appeared in the September 1998 issue of the *American Psychologist*.

Kraut and Lundmark had asked how using the Internet affects connections between people. They looked at both the extent and the depth of human links, and tried to understand how the Internet affected these connections. Deep social ties are relationships with frequent contact, deep feelings of involvement, and broad context. Weak ties have superficial and easily broken bonds, infrequent contact, and narrow focus. Weak ties link us to information and social resources outside our close local groups. But it's the strong social ties that buffer us from stress and lead to better social interactions.

Hardly surprising that strong personal ties come about when you're in close proximity to someone . . . it's been that way for millennia. Suddenly, along comes the Internet, reducing the importance of distance and letting you develop new relationships through chat rooms, e-mail, news groups, and Web pages.

To learn about the social effects of the Internet, Kraut and Lundmark fol-   5
lowed ninety-six families of various backgrounds for two years. They provided computers, software, modems, accounts, and training; in all, some 256 individuals entered the study, and two-thirds of them completed it. The software allowed full Internet use, but recorded how much time was spent in various online activities. Each participant answered questionnaires before they went online, after a year, and after two years of Internet use.

The researchers measured stress, loneliness, and depression using standardized psychological tests like the UCLA Loneliness Scale and the Center for Epidemiologic Studies Depression Scale. Participants would agree or disagree with statements like "I feel everything I do is an effort," "I enjoy life," "I can find companionship when I want it," "There is someone I could turn to for advice about changing my job or finding a new one." Kraut and Lundmark then measured each participant's social circle and distant social network during the two-year study.

After following the study group, the psychologists found an average increase in depression by about 1 percent for every hour spent online per week. Online activity resulted in increased loneliness as well. On the average, subjects began with sixty-six members in their nearby social circle. For every hour each week spent online, this group shrank by about 4 percent.

Depression. Loneliness. Loss of close friendships. This is the medium that we're promoting to expand our global community?

It's true that many online relationships developed as well, but most represented weak social ties rather than deep ones: a woman who exchanged mittens with a stranger, a man who exchanged jokes with a colleague he met over a tourist Web site. A few friendships blossomed—one teenager met his prom date online—but these were rarities. And even though such friendships were welcomed when they happened, there was an overall decline in real-world interaction with family and friends.

The overwhelming majority of online friendships simply aren't deep.   10
Online friends can't be depended on for help with tangible favors: small loans,
baby-sitting, help with shopping, or advice about jobs and careers. One participant "appreciated the e-mail correspondence she had with her college-aged
daughter, yet noted that when her daughter was homesick or depressed, she
reverted to telephone calls to provide support."

Kraut and Lundmark concluded that "greater use of the Internet was associated with small, but statistically significant declines in social involvement
as measured by communication within the family and the size of people's local
social networks, and with increases in loneliness, and depression. Other effects
on the size of the distant social circle, social support, and stress did not reach
standard significance levels but were consistently negative." Paradoxically, the
Internet is a social technology used for communication, yet it results in declining social involvement and psychological well-being.

What's important to remember is that their research wasn't a collection of
casual claims, but "an extremely careful scientific study," said Tora Bikson, a
senior scientist at Rand Corporation. "It's not a result that's easily ignored."
Despite a decade of concerns, it's the first time that professional psychologists
have done such a longitudinal study.

"We were shocked by the findings, because they are counterintuitive to
what we know about how socially the Internet is being used," said Dr. Kraut,
who hypothesized that Internet use is "building shallow relationships, leading
to an overall decline in feeling of connection to other people."

Not surprisingly, computer makers scoffed: One Intel psychologist replied
that "This is not about the technology, per se; it's about how it is used. It
points to the need for considering social factors in terms of how you design
applications and services for technology." In other words, technology is just a
neutral tool and social technologists will solve this problem. Uh, right.

According to computer scientists James Katz and Philip Aspden, there's   15
no reason to be pessimistic about the social effects of Internet use. They tele-
phoned six hundred Internet users, to survey the social effects of computer
use. Their 1997 report, "A Nation of Strangers," argues that the Internet augments existing communities. It's a medium for creating friendships and to stay
in touch with family members. They cheerily suggest that some two million
new meetings have taken place thanks to the Internet. Katz and Aspden happily conclude that "The Internet is creating a nation richer in friendships and
social relationships."

Unfortunately, Katz and Aspden used a biased system of self-reporting, a
phone survey in which those called judged themselves on whether they had
gained or lost friends. Hardly anyone's going to tell a stranger on the phone,
"Oh, I've lost friends because I spend too much time online." Also, while Katz
and Aspden tallied all social ties made over the Internet, they didn't probe into
the possible loss of strong local ties. Since they didn't ask about the depth, nature, or quality of online "friendships," naturally their phone survey delivered
a happily optimistic conclusion.

Psychologists point out that the best predictor of psychological troubles is a lack of close social contacts. There's a surprisingly close correlation between social isolation and such problems as schizophrenia and depression. Long hours spent online undercut our local social support networks; this isolation promotes psychological troubles.

Kraut and Lundmark's work points to a serious problem looming for wired generations: Will the proliferation of shallow, distant social ties make up for the loss of close local links?

Stanford psychology professor Philip Zimbardo has part of the answer. Since the mid-1970s, he's studied the psychology of shyness. In 1978, Dr. Zimbardo found that some 40 percent of undergraduates said, "I think of myself as shy." By 1988, this number had reached 45 percent. And by 1995, some 50 percent of undergrads saw themselves as shy; some research suggests that 60 percent of the population now suffers from shyness.

Why this epidemic of shyness? At a 1997 conference, Professor Zimbardo   20 pointed to several reasons, many connected to technology. Television and computing make us more passive . . . and passivity feeds into shyness. Now that many family members have separate televisions, watching TV is no longer a communal experience, but rather an isolated, nonsocial nonencounter. One report suggested that parents, busy from work which they've brought home, spend only six to eight minutes a day talking with their children.

"The electronic revolution of e-mails and faxes means the medium has finally become the message," said Professor Zimbardo. "With more virtual reality overtaking real reality, we're losing ordinary social skills and common social situations are becoming more awkward."

Yep, for better or worse, the only way to learn how to get along with others is to spend plenty of time interacting with people. E-mail, telephones, and faxes all prevent us from learning basic skills of dealing with people face to face. These electronic intermediaries dull our abilities to read each other's gestures and facial expressions, to express our feelings, to strike up conversations with strangers, to craft stories, to tell jokes.* Those weaned on computer communications won't learn basic social rules of conversation. How to interrupt. How to share time with another. How to speak to an audience. When to be quiet.

In the past, shyness has been passed off as a trivial problem that children grow out of. "Although we think of shy people as passive and easily manipulated, at the same time there is a level of resentment, rage and hostility," Zimbardo warned. I wonder if that explains some of the anger pervading the anonymous chat rooms and postings to Usenet news groups.

The notion that people can become addicted to the Internet was scoffed at by professional psychologists. It was considered to be a joke in the same way

---

*Once, people told stories — you'd pay attention to the homegrown comedian who knew how to tell a joke. Joke telling meant timing, inflection, and expression. Now, thanks to jokes passed by e-mail and Internet forums, stale comedy routines constantly circulate online. People who can't tell jokes won't shut their mouths.

that alcoholism, compulsive gambling, and obsessive shopping were thought laughable in the 1950s. After all, you can just stop. Only recently have a few psychologists asked questions about the seductive nature of the Internet and the type of person likely to become hooked. They're finding that the clinical definitions of established addictions fit the profiles of plenty of people who spend their lives online.

Psychologist Kimberly Young was among the first to investigate clinical cases of Internet addiction. She tells of a Pennsylvania college student she calls Steve who's online sixty to seventy hours a week. Steve's a wizard in the Multi-User Dungeons, Internet fantasy games best known as MUDs.   25

"MUDs are like a religion to me, and I'm a god there. I'm respected by all the other MUDders . . . Even when I'm not playing, I wonder if there will be more newbies for me to kill that night or which other guys will be playing. I am in control of my character and my destiny in this world. My character is a legend and I identify with him." Yet when Steve's not online, he's held back by low self-esteem. Shy and awkward around people, he's uncomfortable around women and believes he doesn't fit in at school. "When I'm playing the MUDs, I'm not feeling lonely or mopey. I'm not thinking about my problems . . . I want to stay on the MUDs as long as I possibly can."

Where once Steve would have worked within the real world and slowly learn how to deal with people, today he is able to turn to the Internet for solace and escape.

Compounding the withdrawal of individuals from their close social circle, technology also blurs the line between work and play. Thanks to telephones, pagers, and cell phones, work seeps into our private time, forcing shallow, impersonal communication into quiet hours and intimate moments. E-mail reaches our desktops and laptops; even our wristwatches have alarms and electronic reminders. At home, on the road, or on the golf course, we can't escape an electronic bombardment.

Walking in Yosemite Park, I met a hiker with all the latest paraphernalia hanging from his belt: pager, GPS° locator, and electronic altimeter. Amid the quiet of the sugar pines, his cell phone squawked and I overheard one side of his conversation with some New York advertising firm: "Tell both clients that I won't be able to make Monday's meeting," he told an unseen secretary. "I'll get them a proposal when I'm over this cold."

Here's a guy who's brought the stress of his office into the tranquility of the forest. He's never lost and always in reach. At the same time, he's utterly lost and out of touch.*   30

---

*In response to the noise and interruptions, one Japanese symphony hall has installed special transmitters to disable all cell phones and pagers in the audience. I hadn't realized it before, but one of the joys of speleology is that none of my caving partners can be reached a hundred feet under the ground.

GPS: Global Positioning System.

Office work tags along with homes equipped with fax machines. On the street, drivers and pedestrians dodge each other while talking over cell phones. In cafés, nerds type on laptops. Office managers bring their work home on floppy disks. The telecommuter merely represents one milestone in the blurring of home and office.

As work sneaks into playtime, play just isn't as much fun. Used to be that only students brought classwork home; increasingly, everyone has homework, everyone's on call. Our home provides little refuge from the stress of the outside world.

This isn't just the fault of technology — so many people want high-tech careers and professions that they willingly latch onto jobs which demand twenty-four-hour availability. And so we find the Webmaster who's on call all night, just in case the file server crashes. The high school teacher who answers students' e-mail all evening. The gardener who polishes her Web site when she comes home. For them, home is simply an extension of their workplace.

For children, home computers, instructional videotapes, and educational television extend the school into their home. Forget the innocence of childhood: Our kids are increasingly programmed as academic automatons.

The Internet is widely promoted as an aid for speed, profit, productivity, 35 and efficiency. These business goals simply aren't the aims of a home. Maybe there's such a thing as kitchen productivity, but efficiency doesn't make much sense in my living room, and exactly who considers profits in their bedroom?

At home, our goals might include tranquility, reflection, and warmth . . . hardly the image brought up by the phrase "home computing." With houses increasingly wired for communications, electronic messages invade our home life. It's not just the telemarketers who disrupt dinner with sales and surveys. Rather, our private space is increasingly available to the outside world, whether it's a call from the boss, tonight's business news on the TV, or an e-mail message about a business meeting.

Nor are the goals of business those of a school. Productivity doesn't map onto a sixth-grade class in pre-algebra. It's absurd to speak of increasing the efficiency of an instructor teaching a third-grade student how salt melts ice. Will a 200 MHz computer educate a child twice as fast as a 100 MHz computer?

The way we communicate constrains how we interact. Computer networks provide chat rooms in which emotions must fit into eighty columns of ASCII text, punctuated by smiley faces. No longer need my correspondent begin a letter with a gratuitous "Dear Cliff." Rather, the header of the e-mail describes recipient, sender, and subject. Any pretense of politeness is erased by the cold efficiency of the medium.

One survey reports that office workers typically receive 190 messages per day. Yet computer network promoters tell us that we need ever faster links and constantly more connectivity. Will I get more work done today if I receive 300 messages rather than 200?

Instead of encouraging me to concentrate on a single job, the constant 40 stream of electronic messages makes me constantly flip from one task to another. Computers are great at doing this, but people aren't. Promoters of electronic workplaces may speak glowingly of living asynchronous lives, but most of my work requires concentration, thinking, and organization . . . hardly promoted by a river of electronic messages.

Getting a high-speed link to the Internet causes Web pages to load faster. At first glance, you'd think that this would reduce the amount of time that students would spend online. Hardly. As connection speeds increase, college students spend more time surfing the Web, and less time writing, studying, or whatever they don't want to do. Same's true for office workers—an Internet link is a license to goof off.

As Robert Kraut and Vicki Lundmark's study reveals, e-mail enhances distant communications while degrading local interactions. It perniciously gives us the illusion of making friends with faraway strangers while taking our attention away from our friends, family, and neighbors.

In the past, people in trouble relied on close, nearby friends for support. Today, plenty of people turn to online support groups or chat rooms. Professor Mary Baker of Stanford reports that while she was expecting, she exchanged five e-mail messages a day with a friend across the country . . . a woman she'd never met. Yet e-mail pen pals can hardly provide the social support of a nearby friend or family member—if Professor Baker had to rush to the hospital, she could hardly get a ride from her e-mail friend.

Today, it's natural enough to look to the Internet for a community, since our real neighborhoods have been relentlessly undercut by television, automobiles, and urban renewal. Yet as more and more people turn to the Internet, our real communities receive even less human investment.

For the effect of instant electronic communications is to isolate us from   45
our colleagues next door. I met two computer jocks at a television station who spent their free time playing an Internet game with each other. Even though they sat five feet from each other, they'd communicate via e-mail and rarely so much as glanced at each other.

Professor Zimbardo tells me that sometimes he sticks his head into the office of a friend down the hall, with nothing more important than to say, "Hi!" On several occasions, my greeting has been received with the shock of 'What's so important that you're invading my personal space? Why are you interrupting my productivity?'"

The price of computing at home—as in school and at work—is far more than the cost of the hardware. The opportunity cost is our time, and it is taken out of our individual lives and our very real neighborhoods. The time you spend behind the monitor could be spent facing another person across a table or across a tennis court. Disguised as efficiency machines, digital time bandits steal our lives and undermine our communities.

EXPLORING THE TEXT

1. How does the Internet affect the social ties of those who use it, according to Stoll? Why does heavy Net use lead to depression? Would you agree that Net friendships tend to be more superficial than real-world friendships and that heavy Net users

tend to be less involved with family and friends than people with little Net experience? Why or why not?

2. How, in Stoll's view, does electronic technology undermine the skills it takes to participate in real communities? Do you think that there is, in fact, an "epidemic of shyness" among college students today? Do you think that students today are less prepared for face-to-face social interaction than students were a generation or two ago?

3. Do you think it's possible to be "addicted" to the Internet? In what ways does heavy use of the Net resemble chemical dependency or drug addiction? In what ways, if any, might it differ from genuine addictive dependency?

4. How has the Internet affected privacy and private life, according to Stoll? Would you agree that over the past twenty years the goals of business have begun to infiltrate the realms of education, family life, and personal relationships? Why or why not?

5. What, overall, are the costs associated with Internet use, in Stoll's estimation? What, if anything, might we do to mitigate the personal and social costs of Internet use?

FURTHER EXPLORATIONS

1. How might Ellen Ullman (p. 656) account for the isolation Stoll associates with computer use? For the epidemic of shyness Stoll sees spreading across college campuses in the postcomputer era? Would she be likely to agree with Stoll that the computer brings the "goals of business" into the realm of private life? Why or why not?

2. To what extent does Sherry Turkle's analysis of the effects of MUDs in "Who Am We?" (p. 675) support or challenge Stoll's view of the Internet? Do the individuals that Turkle describes in her essay seem particularly isolated or dehumanized?

3. Is it possible that the erosion of relationships and privacy that Stoll associates with the Internet actually results from larger cultural and economic forces, and not simply from the use of computer technology?

ESSAY OPTIONS

1. Drawing on your own personal experiences and observations, write an essay in which you debate Stoll's central claim—that the Internet isolates and dehumanizes those who use it. Would you agree that heavy Internet use can be addictive and induce shyness and the loss of social skills? What evidence have you seen of such effects among heavy Internet users you've known?

2. Drawing on the ideas expressed by Clifford Stoll, Mark Slouka in "Listening for Silence" (p. 50), and Bill McKibben in "Television and the Twilight of the Senses" (p. 109), write a paper discussing electronic technology and the loss of solitude in the modern era. What difference, if any, is there between solitude and isolation? How has electronic technology made real solitude hard to achieve? What does the loss of solitude mean for us as individuals and as a society?

Out of Time: Reflections on the Programming Life

ELLEN ULLMAN

Few people are likely to know as much about the impact of information technology on daily life than Ellen Ullman. A computer engineer since 1978, Ullman (b. 1944) was an early programming pioneer, working to develop sophisticated interactive and graphical user interface computer applications long before the era of Windows and the Mac desktop. She also broke new ground by working as a woman in a field originally dominated by men. By the early 1990s, Ullman owned her own software development firm and was by every measure a success. Yet, she had serious misgivings about what life in the information age was doing to her, her coworkers, and the millions of people who were logging onto the Internet in increasing numbers every day. In 1995, she distilled these concerns in *Close to the Machine: Technophilia and Its Discontents* — the account of her life as a programmer. In this essay, which Ullman eventually incorporated into her book, she reflects on the attitudes and values of those who live their lives "close to the machine" — attitudes and values that the "boy engineers" who love technology inevitably build into the devices they design. Today Ullman is a regular commentator on National Public Radio and contributor to such publications as *Harper's Magazine, Wired,* and the *New York Times.*

BEFORE READING

Think of someone you've known who you'd describe as living "close to the machine" — someone who simply loves technology or machinery. What is this person like? How would you describe his or her dominant values and attitudes? How "close to the machine" are you?

I

People imagine that programming is logical, a process like fixing a clock. Nothing could be further from the truth. Programming is more like an illness, a fever, an obsession. It's like those dreams in which you have an exam but you remember you haven't attended the course. It's like riding a train and never being able to get off.

The problem with programming is not that the computer isn't logical — the computer is terribly logical, relentlessly literal-minded. Computers are supposed to be like brains, but in fact they are idiots because they take everything you say completely at face value. You can say to a toddler, "Are yew okay tewday?" But it's not possible for a programmer to say anything like that to a computer. There will be a syntax error.

When you program, your mind is full of details, millions of bits of knowledge. This knowledge is in human form, which is to say rather chaotic, coming at you from one perspective then another, then a random thought, then something else important, then the same thing with a what-if attached. For example, try to think of everything you know about something as simple as an invoice. Now try to tell an idiot how to prepare one. That is programming.

A computer program is an algorithm° that must be written down in order, in a specific syntax, in a strange language that is only partially readable by regular human beings. To program is to translate between the chaos of human life and the line-by-line world of computer language. It is an act of taking dictation from your own mind.

You must not lose your own attention. As the human-world knowledge   5
tumbles about in your mind, you must keep typing, typing. You must not be interrupted. Any break in your listening causes you to lose a line here or there. Some bit comes then — oh no, it's leaving, please come back. It may not come back. You may lose it. You will create a bug and there's nothing you can do about it.

Every single computer program has at least one bug. If you are a programmer, it is guaranteed that your work has errors. These errors will be discovered over both short and long periods of time, most coming to light after you've moved to a new job. But your name is on the program. The code library software keeps a permanent record card of who did what and when. At the old job, they will say terrible things about you after you've gone. This is normal life for a programmer: problems trailing behind you through time, humiliation in absentia.

People imagine that programmers don't like to talk because they prefer machines to people. This is not completely true. Programmers don't talk because they must not be interrupted.

This inability to be interrupted leads to a life that is strangely asynchronous to the one lived by other human beings. It's better to send e-mail than to call a programmer on the phone. It's better to leave a note on the chair than to expect the programmer to come to a meeting. This is because the programmer must work in mind-time but the phone rings in real time. Similarly, meetings are supposed to take place in real time. It's not just ego that prevents programmers from working in groups — it's the synchrony problem. To synchronize with other people (or their representation in telephones, buzzers, and doorbells) can only mean interrupting the thought-train. Interruptions mean certain bugs. You must not get off the train.

I used to have dreams in which I was overhearing conversations I had to program. Once, I had to program two people making love. In my dream they sweated and tumbled while I sat with a cramped hand writing code. The couple went from gentle caresses to ever-widening passions, and I despaired as I tried desperately to find a way to express the act of love in the C computer language.

No matter what anyone tells you about the allure of computers, I can tell   10
you for a fact that love cannot be programmed.

algorithm: A formal procedure for solving problems that usually involves repeated steps or subroutines.

II

I once had a job where I didn't talk to anyone for two years. Here was the arrangement: I was the first engineer hired by a start-up software company. In exchange for large quantities of stock that might be worth something some-day, I was supposed to give up my life.

I sat in a large room with two other engineers and three Sun workstations. The fans of the machines whirred, the keys of the keyboards clicked. Occasionally one or the other of us would grunt or mutter. Otherwise, we did not speak. Now and then, I would have a temper outburst in which I pounded the keyboard with my fists, setting off a barrage of beeps. My colleagues might look up but never said anything about this.

Once a week, I had a five-minute meeting with my boss. He was a heavy-set bearded man with glasses who looked like everyone's stereotype of a nerd; as a matter of fact, he looked almost exactly like my previous boss, another heavy-set bearded man with glasses. At this meeting I would routinely tell him I was on schedule. Since being on schedule is a very rare thing in software en-gineering, my boss would say good, good, see you next week.

I remember watching my boss disappear down the row of cubbyhole par-titions. He always wore exactly the same clothes: he had several outfits, each one exactly the same, khaki pants and a checked shirt of the same pattern. So, week to week, the image of his disappearing down the row of partitions re-mained unchanged. The same khaki pants, the same pattern in the checked shirt. Good, good, see you next week.

Real time was no longer compelling. Days, weeks, months, and years came and went without much physical change in my surroundings. Surely I was aging. My hair must have grown, I must have cut it, grown more gray hairs. Gravity must have been working on my late-thirties body, but I didn't notice. I only paid attention to my back and shoulders because they seized up on me from long sitting. Later, after I left the company, there was a masseuse on staff. That way, even the back and shoulders could be ignored.

What was compelling was the software. I was making something out of nothing, I thought, and I admit the software had more life for me than my brief love affair, my friends, my cat, my house, my neighbor who was stabbed and nearly killed by her husband. I was creating ("creating," that is the word we used) a device-independent interface library. One day, I sat in a room by myself surrounded by computer monitors from various manufacturers. I remember looking at the screens of my companions and saying, "Speak to me."

I completed the interface library in two years and left the company. Five years later, the company's stock went public. For the engineers who'd stayed the original arrangement was made good: in exchange for giving up seven years of their lives, they became very, very wealthy. As for me, I bought a car. A red one.

III

Frank was thinking he had to get closer to the machine. Somehow, he'd floated up. Up from memory heaps and kernels. Up from file systems. Up through utilities. Up to where he was now: an end-user query tool. Next thing, he could find himself working on general ledgers, invoices—God—*financial reports.* Somehow he had to get closer to the machine.

Frank hated me. Not only was I closer to the machine, I had won the coin toss to get the desk near the window. Frank sat in full view of the hallway and he was further from the machine.

Frank was nearly forty. His wife was pregnant. Outside in the parking lot   20 (which he couldn't see through my window), his new station wagon was heating up in the sun. Soon, he'd have a kid, a wife who had just quit her job, a wagon with a child-carrier, and an end-user query tool. Somehow he had to get closer to the machine.

Here are the reasons Frank wanted to be closer to the machine: The machine means midnight dinners of Diet Coke. It means unwashed clothes and bare feet on the desk. It means anxious rides through mind-time that have nothing to do with the clock. To work on things used only by machines or other programmers—that's the key. Programmers and machines don't care how you live. They don't care when you live. You can stay, come, go, sleep, or not. At the end of the project looms a deadline, the terrible place where you must get off the train. But, in between, for years at a stretch, you are free: free from the obligations of time.

To express the idea of being "closer to the machine," an engineer refers to "low-level code." In regular life, "low" usually signifies something bad. In programming, "low" is good. Low is better.

If the code creates programs that do useful work for regular human beings, it is called "higher." Higher-level programs are called "applications." Applications are things that people use. Although it would seem that usefulness by people would be a good thing, from a programmer's point of view, direct people-use is bad. If regular people, called "users," can understand the task accomplished by your program, you will be paid less and held in lower esteem. In the regular world, the term "higher" may be better, but, in programming, higher is worse. High is bad.

If you want money and prestige, you need to write code that only machines or other programmers understand. Such code is "low." It's best if you write microcode, a string of zeroes and ones that only a processor reads. The next best thing is assembler code, a list of instructions to the processor, but readable if you know what you're doing. If you can't write microcode or assembler, you might get away with writing in the C or C++ language. C and C++ are really sort of high, but they're considered "low." So you still get to be called a "software engineer." In the grand programmer-scheme of things, it's vastly better to be a "software engineer" than a "programmer." The difference is about thirty thousand dollars a year and a potential fortune in stock.

My office-mate Frank was a man vastly unhappy in his work. He looked   25
over my shoulder, everyone's shoulder, trying to get away from the indignity
of writing a program used by regular people. This affected his work. His program was not all what it should have been, and for this he was punished. His
punishment was to have to talk to regular people.

Frank became a sales-support engineer. Ironically, working in sales and
having a share in bonuses, he made more money. But he got no more stock
options. And in the eyes of other engineers, Frank was as "high" as one could
get. When asked, we said, "Frank is now in sales." This was equivalent to saying he was dead.

IV

Real techies don't worry about forced eugenics.° I learned this from a real
techie in the cafeteria of a software company.

The project team is having lunch and discussing how long it would take
to wipe out a disease inherited recessively on the X chromosome. First some
calculations of inheritance probabilities. Given some sized population, one of
the engineers arrives at a wipeout date. Immediately, another suggests that the
date could be moved forward by various manipulations of the inheritance patterns. For example, he says, there could be an education campaign.

The six team members then fall over one another with further suggestions.
They start with rewards to discourage carriers from breeding. Immediately they
move to fines for those who reproduce the disease. Then they go for what they
call "more effective" measures: Jail for breeding. Induced abortion. Forced
sterilization.

Now they're hot. The calculations are flying. Years and years fall from the   30
final doom-date of the disease.

Finally, they get to the ultimate solution. "It's straightforward," someone
says, "just kill every carrier." Everyone responds to this last suggestion with
great enthusiasm. One generation and—bang!—the disease is gone.

Quietly I say, "You know, that's what the Nazis did."

They all look at me in disgust. It's the look boys give a girl who has interrupted a burping contest. One says, "This is something my wife would say."

When he says "wife," there is no love, warmth, or goodness in it. In this
engineer's mouth, "wife" means wet diapers and dirty dishes. It means someone angry with you for losing track of time and missing dinner. Someone *sentimental*. In his mind (for the moment), "wife" signifies all programming-
party-pooping, illogical things in the universe.

Still, I persist. "It started as just an idea for the Nazis, too, you know."   35

The engineer makes a reply that sounds like a retch. "This is how I know
you're not a real techie," he says.

eugenics: The scientific control of human populations by means of forced mating or sterilization.

V

A descendent of Italian princes directs research projects at a well-known manufacturer of UNIX workstations. I'm thrilled. In my then five years of being a
consultant, the director is the first person to compliment me on what I am
wearing to the interview.

It takes me a while, but I soon see I must forget all the usual associations
with either Italians or princes. There will be no lovely long lunches that end
with deftly peeled fruit. There will be no well-cut suits of beautiful fabrics. The
next time I am wearing anything interesting, the director (I'll call him Paolo)
tells me I look ridiculous.

Paolo's Italianism has been replaced, like a pod from outer space, with
some California New Age, Silicon Valley engineering creature. He eats no fat.
He spoons tofu-melange stuff out of a Tupperware container. Everything he
does comes in response to beeps emitted from his UNIX workstation: he eats,
goes to meetings, goes rollerblading in the parking lot, buys and sells stock,
calls his wife solely in response to signals he has programmed into his calendar
system. (The clock on his wall has only the number twelve on it.) Further,
Paolo swears he has not had a cold since the day he decided that he would always wear two sweaters. Any day now, I expect to see him get out of his stock-
option Porsche draped in garlic.

I know that Paolo has been replaced because I have met his wife. We are   40
at a team beer-fest in the local programmer hangout on a Friday afternoon.
It's full of men in T-shirts and jeans. Paolo's wife and I are the only people
wearing makeup. She looks just the way I expect a no-longer-young Italian
woman to look—she has children, she has taken time with her appearance,
she is trying to talk to people. Across the swill of pitchers and chips glopped
with cheesy drippings, she eyes me hopefully: another grown-up woman. At
one point, she clucks at Paolo, who is loudly describing the effects of a certain
burrito. "The only thing on earth that instantly turns a solid into a gas," he
says.

The odder Paolo gets, the more he fits in with the research team. One engineer always eats his dessert first (he does this conscientiously; he wants you,
dares you to say something; one simply doesn't). Another comes to work in
something that looks suspiciously like his pajamas. To work on this project, he
has left his wife and kids back East. He obviously views that absence of his
family as a kind of license: he has stopped shaving and (one can't help noticing) he has stop washing. Another research engineer comes to work in shorts
in all weather; no one has ever seen his knees covered. Another routinely
makes vast changes to his work the day before deadlines; he is completely un-
moved by any complaints about this practice. And one team member screens
all e-mail through a careful filter, meaning most mail is deposited in a dead-
letter file. This last engineer, the only woman permanently on the project, has
outdone everyone on oddness: she has an unlisted work phone. To reach
her, you must leave a message with her manager. The officially sanctioned

asynchrony of the unlisted phone amazes me. In my fifteen years in the software industry, I have never seen anything like it.

These research engineers can be as odd as they like because they are very, very close to the machine. At their level, it is an honor to be odd. Strange behavior is expected, it's respected, a sign that you are intelligent and as close to the machine as you can get. Any decent software engineer can have a private office, come and go at all hours, exist out of normal time. But to be permanently and sincerely eccentric—this is something only a senior research engineer can achieve.

In meetings, they behave like children. They tell each other to shut up. They call each other idiots. They throw balled-up paper. One day, a team member screams at his Korean colleague, "Speak English!" (A moment of silence follows this outburst, at least.) It's like dropping in at the day-care center by mistake.

They even behave like children when their Japanese sponsors come to visit. The research is being funded through a chain of agencies and bodies that culminates in the Japan Board of Trade. The head of the sponsoring department comes with his underlings. They all wear blue suits. They sit at the conference table with their hands folded neatly in front of them. When they speak, it is with the utmost discretion; their voices are so soft, we have to lean forward to hear. Meanwhile, the research team behaves badly, bickers, has the audacity to ask when they'll get paid.

The Japanese don't seem to mind. On the contrary, they appear delighted. 45 They have received exactly what their money was intended to buy. They have purchased bizarre and brilliant Californians who can behave any way they like. The odd behavior reassures them: Ah! These must be real top-rate engineers!

VI

We are attending conventions. Here is our itinerary: we will be traveling closer and closer to the machine. Our journey will be like crossing borders formed by mountain ranges. On the other side, people will be very, very different.

We begin "high," at a conference of computer trainers and technical writers. Women are everywhere. There is a great deal of nail polish, deep red, and briefcases of excellent leathers. In the cold, conditioned air of the conference hall drifts a faint, sweet cloud of perfume.

Next we travel to Washington, D.C., to an applications development conference, the Federal Systems Office Expo. It is a model of cultural diversity. Men, women, whites, blacks, Asians—all qualified applicants are welcome. Applications development ("high-level," low-status, and relatively low-paying) is the civil service of computing.

Now we move west and lower. We are in California to attend a meeting of SIGGRAPH, the graphics special interest group of the Association of Computing Machinery (ACM). African Americans have virtually disappeared. Young white men predominate, with many Asians among them. There are still some women: graphics can be seen, after all. Though we have crossed the summit and have begun our descent, we are still not very "low."

On our map, we must now place this warning: "Below here be engineers."   50

We are about to descend rapidly into valleys of programming, to the low levels close to the machine. We go first to an operating-systems interest group of the ACM. Then, getting ever closer to hardware, we attend a convention of chip designers. Not a female person in clear sight. If you look closely, however, you can see a few young Chinese women sitting alone, quiet, plainly dressed, succeeding at making themselves invisible. For these are gatherings of young men. This is the land of T-shirts and jeans, the country of perpetual graduate-studenthood.

Later, at a Borland developers' conference, company engineers proudly call themselves "barbarians" (although they are not really as "low" as they think they are). In slides projected onto huge screens, they represent themselves in beards and animal skins, holding spears and clubs. Except for the public-relations women (their faint clouds of perfume drifting among the hairy, exposed barbarian legs), there is only one woman (me).

A senior engineer once asked me why I left full-time engineering for consulting. At the time, I had never really addressed the question, and I was surprised by my own answer. I muttered something about being a middle-age woman. "Excuse me," I found myself saying, "but I'm afraid I find the engineering culture very teenage-boy puerile."

This engineer was a brilliant man, good-hearted, and unusually literate for a programmer. I had great respect for him and I really did not mean to offend him. "That's too bad," he answered as if he meant it, "because we obviously lose talent that way."

I felt immense gratitude at this unexpected opening. I opened my mouth   55 to go on, to explore the reasons for the cult of the boy engineer.

But immediately we were interrupted. The company was about to have an interdivisional water-balloon fight. For weeks, the entire organization had been engaged in the design of intricate devices for the delivery of rubberized inflatable containers filled with fluid. Work had all but stopped; all "spare brain cycles" were involved in preparations for war.

The engineer joined the planning with great enthusiasm, and I left the room where we had been having our conversation. The last I saw of him, he was covering a paper napkin with a sketch of a water-balloon catapult.

Here is a suggested letter home from our journey closer to the machine: Software engineering is a meritocracy. Anyone with the talents and abilities can join the club. However, if rollerblading, Frisbee playing, and water-balloon wars are not your idea of fun, you are not likely to stay long.

VII

I once designed a graphical user interface with a man who wouldn't speak to me. My boss hired this man without letting anyone else sit in on the interview; my boss lived to regret it.

I was asked to brief my new colleague and, with a third member of the   60
team, we went into a conference room. There, we filled two whiteboards with
lines, boxes, circles, and arrows in four marker colors. After about half an
hour, I noticed that the new hire had become very agitated.

"Are we going too fast?" I asked him.

"Too much for the first day?" said the third.

"No," said our new man, "I just can't do it like this."

"Do what?" I asked. "Like what?"

His hands were deep in his pockets. He gestured with his elbows. "Like   65
this," he said.

"You mean design?" I asked.

"You mean in a meeting?" asked the third.

No answer from our new colleague. A shrug. Another elbow gesture.

Something terrible was beginning to occur to me. "You mean talking?" I
asked.

"Yeah, talking," he said. "I can't do it by talking."   70

By this time in my career, I had met many strange engineers. But here was
the first one who wouldn't talk at all. Besides, this incident took place before
the existence of standard user interfaces like Windows and Motif, so we had
a lot of design work to do. No talking was certainly going to make things
difficult.

"So how *can* you do it?" I asked.

"Mail," he said immediately, "send me e-mail."

So, given no choice, we designed a graphical user interface by e-mail.

Corporations across North America and Europe are still using a system   75
designed by three people who sent e-mail and one who barely spoke.

VIII

Pretty graphical interfaces are commonly called "user-friendly." But they are
not really your friends. Underlying every user-friendly interface is a terrific
human contempt.

The basic idea of a graphical interface is that it does not allow anything
alarming to happen. You can pound on the mouse button all you want, and
the system will prevent you from doing anything stupid. A monkey can pound
on the keyboard, your cat can run across it, your baby can fist it, but the system should not crash.

To build such a crash-proof system, the designer must be able to imagine — and disallow — the dumbest action. He or she cannot simply rely on the
user's intelligence: who knows who will be on the other side of the program?
Besides, the user's intelligence is not quantifiable; it's not programmable; it
cannot protect the system. No, the real task is to forget about the intelligent
person on the other side and think of every single stupid thing anyone might
possibly do.

In the designer's mind, gradually, over months and years, there is created a vision of the user as imbecile. The imbecile vision is mandatory. No good, crash-proof system can be built except it be done for an idiot.

The designer's contempt for your intelligence is mostly hidden deep in the code. But, now and then, the disdain surfaces. Here's a small example: you're trying to do something simple like copy files onto a diskette on your Mac. The program proceeds for a while then encounters an error. Your disk is defective, says a message, and, below the message, is a single button. You absolutely must click this button. If you don't click it, the program hangs there indefinitely. So, your disk is defective, your files may be bollixed up, and the designer leaves you only one possible reply: You must say, "OK." 80

The prettier the user interface, and the fewer odd replies the system allows you to make, the dumber you once appeared in the mind of the designer.

IX

The computer is about to enter our lives like blood in the capillaries. Soon, everywhere we look, we will see pretty, idiot-proof interfaces designed to make us say, "OK."

A vast delivery system for retail computing is about to come into being, and the system goes by the name "interactivity." Telephones, televisions, sales kiosks will all be wired for interactive, on-demand services. The very word— interactivity—implies something good and wonderful. Surely a response, a reply, an answer is a positive thing. Surely it signifies an advance over something else, something bad, something that doesn't respond, reply or answer. There is only one problem: what we will be interacting with is a machine.

Interactive services are supposed to be delivered "on demand." What an aura of power—demand! See a movie, order seats to a basketball game, make hotel reservations, send a card to mother—all services waiting for us on our television or computer whenever we want them. Midnight, dawn, or, day. Sleep or order pizza: it no longer matters exactly what we do when. We don't need to involve anyone else in the sastifactions of our needs. We don't even have to talk. We get our services when we want them, free from the obligations of regularly scheduled time. We can all live closer to the machine.

"Interactivity" is misnamed. It should be called "asynchrony": the engineering culture coming to everyday life. 85

In the workplace, home office, sales floor, service kiosk, home—we will be "talking" to programs that are beginning to look suprisingly alike: all full of animated little pictures we are supposed to pick, like push-buttons on a toddler's toy. The toy is supposed to please us. Somehow, it is supposed to replace the satisfactions of transacting meaning with a mature human being, in the confusion of a natural language, together, in a room, at a touching distance.

As the computer's pretty, helpfully waiting face (and contemptuous underlying code) penetrates deeply into daily life, the cult of the boy engineer comes with it. The engineer's assumptions and presumptions are in the code.

That's the purpose of the program, after all: to sum up the intelligence and intentions of all the engineers who worked on the system over time — tens and hundreds of people who have learned an odd and highly specific way of doing things. The system contains them. It reproduces and reenacts life as engineers know it: alone, out-of-time, disdainful of anyone far from the machine.

Engineers seem to prefer the asynchronous life, or at least be used to it. But what about the rest of us? A taste of the out-of-time existence is about to become possible for everyone with a television. Soon, we may all be living the programming life. Should we?

EXPLORING THE TEXT

1. How does Ullman view computers? What is it like to program them, in her opinion? How does her experience of the challenges involved in programming compare, in your view, with the process you go through when you plan and write an essay?

2. What does it mean to live "close to the machine," according to Ullman? How does living close to the machine affect one's sense of time and space? How does it affect one's sense of self, relationships with others, attitudes toward work, home, and family?

3. What do the anecdotes that Ullman offers about "forced eugenics" and Paolo the Italian director reveal about the culture of computer engineers? What do these stories suggest about the values and attitudes of the "techies" that Ullman works with?

4. What does Ullman's experience suggest about the gender politics of computer culture? What aspects of the "cult of the boy engineer" strike you as being particularly "boyish"? To what extent would you agree that computer technology and computer culture contain a built-in bias in favor of adolescent male values and attitudes?

FURTHER EXPLORATIONS

1. How might Ullman view the impact of the computer on individual identity, as discussed by Sherry Turkle in "Who Am We?" (p. 675)? Is it possible to view the identity games that Turkle documents in her essay as another example of the "cult of the boy engineer"? Why or why not?

2. To what extent do the gendered cyborg fantasies that Claudia Springer documents in "Muscular Circuitry" (p. 689) support or challenge Ullman's understanding of the "teenage boy" culture of computing?

3. Given Ullman's interpretation of the "teenage boy" culture of the computer, how might she explain the difference between the two visions of the future of artificial intelligence offered by Maureen Caudill (p. 736) and Hans Moravec (p. 752)? To what extent might the differences of emphasis, tone, and attitude between these two assessments of AI be seen as reflecting the gendered perspectives of their authors?

4. Revisit Deborah Blum's "Heart to Heart: Sex Differences in Emotion" (p. 453) and compare her assessment of male interests, attitudes, and values with the cult of the "boy engineer," as described by Ullman. To what extent does Blum's analysis of male minds help to explain what it means to be "close to the machine"?

5. Compare the values and attitudes that Ullman associates with the culture of computing with the values and attitudes that Scott Russell Sanders associates with the hammer he inherits from his father and grandfather (p. 142). Would it be fair to say that Sanders's hammer, like most technological innovations, is gendered male? If so, how does its maleness differ from the maleness that Ullman associates with the "cult of boy engineers"?

ESSAY OPTIONS

1. Drawing on selections in this chapter by Ellen Ullman, Clifford Stoll (p. 648), Sherry Turkle (p. 675), and any other resource you deem appropriate, assemble a multimedia text-based or hypertext essay on what it means to live "close to the machine." What is technology doing to us as a species today? How are recent technological innovations changing the way we view time, space, and the nature of human relationships?

2. Drawing on selections by Ellen Ullman, Claudia Springer (p. 689), Sherry Turkle (p. 675), and any other reading you deem appropriate, write an essay on the gender of computer technology. In what ways are male values and attitudes "encoded" in computers and in the way computing technology is portrayed in advertisements and the mass media? What evidence do you see, if any, to suggest that the gender of computing is changing?

The Virtual Barrio @ the Other Frontier

GUILLERMO GÓMEZ-PEÑA

If you believe the hype, the Internet is going to transport all of us someday into a world without borders, a world that transcends all the old-fashioned limitations of race, class, gender, and nationality. If you don't believe the hype, you might well be a cyber-vato, cholo-punker, ethno-cyborg, or Hopi-rocker like Guillermo Gómez-Peña. Gómez-Peña is an artist on a mission. Arriving in the United States in 1978 from his native Mexico, he became a founding member of the Border Art Workshop in 1984 and has spent the last sixteen years creating works of poetry and performance art that explore the complexities of border culture and transcultural identity. The Internet, according to Gómez-Peña, like all forms of media controlled by those in power, sets up boundaries that exclude people who are deemed "culturally unfit." But for Gómez-Peña, the Net also represents a new "frontier" — an uncharted territory that offers the chance of wildness and free self-expression. A self-proclaimed "techno-pirate," Gómez-Peña subverts the homogenized world of IBM and AOL by staging multimedia performances, on- and offline, that celebrate alternative voices and cultural values. In addition to his work in the visual arts,

Gómez-Peña has contributed to programs on MTV and National Public Radio and is the author of *Warrior for Gringostroika* (1993) and *The New World Border* (1997).

BEFORE READING

What stereotypical image comes to mind when you think of the average "computer nerd"? What does this person act and look like? What are this person's cultural identity, class background, and gender? Where do you think this stereotype comes from?

[Mexicans] are simple people. They are happy with the little they got. . . . They are not ambitious and complex like us. They don't need all this technology to communicate. Sometimes I just feel like going down there & living among them.

— ANONYMOUS CONFESSION ON THE WEB

Tecnofobia

My laptop is decorated with a 3-D decal of the Virgin of Guadalupe.° It's like a traveling altar, office, and literary bank, all in one. Since I spend 70 percent of the year on the road, it is (besides the phone of course) my principal means to remain in touch with my beloved relatives and colleagues, spread throughout many cities in the United States and Mexico. Unwillingly, I have become a cyber-vato,° an information superhighway bandido. Like that of most Mexican artists, my relationship with digital technology and personal computers is defined by paradoxes and contradictions: I don't quite understand them, yet I am seduced by them; I don't want to know how they work, but I love how they look and what they do; I criticize my colleagues who are critically immersed in new technology, yet I silently envy them. I resent the fact that I am constantly told that as a "Latino" I am supposedly culturally handicapped or somehow unfit to handle high technology; yet once I have it right in front of me, I am propelled to work against it, to question it, to expose it, to subvert it, to imbue it with humor, linguas polutas° — Spanglish, Frangle, gringonol,° and radical politics. In doing so, I become a sort of Mexican virus, the cyberversion of the Mexican fly: tiny, irritating, inescapable, and highly contagious. Contradiction prevails.

Over a year ago, my collaborator Roberto Sifuentes and I bullied ourselves into the Net, and once we were generously adopted by various communities (Arts Wire and Latino Net, among others) we started to lose interest in maintaining ongoing conversations with phantasmagoric beings we had never met

Virgin of Guadalupe: Image of Mary, the mother of Jesus, deemed to have deep religious and cultural significance by many Mexicans and Mexican Americans.

cyber-vato: Cyber-guy.

linguas polutas: Dirty or grammatically incorrect language.

Spanglish, Frangle, gringonol: Terms referring to mixtures of English and other languages.

in person (that, I must say, is a Mexican cultural prejudice—if I don't know you in person, I don't really care to talk with you). Then we started sending a series of poetic/activist "techno-placas"° in Spanglish. In these short communiqués we raised some tough questions regarding access, privilege, and language. Since we didn't quite know where to post them in order to get the maximum response, and the responses were sporadic, casual, and unfocused, our passion began to dim. Roberto and I spend a lot of time in front of our laptops conceptualizing performance projects that incorporate new technologies in what we believe is a responsible and original manner, yet every time we are invited to participate in a public discussion around art and technology, we tend to emphasize its shortcomings and overstate our cultural skepticism.[1] Why? I can only speak for myself. Perhaps I have some computer traumas. I've been utilizing computers since 1988; however, during the first five years, I utilized my old "lowrider" Mac as a glorified typewriter. During those years I probably deleted accidentally here and there over three hundred pages of original texts that I hadn't backed up on disks, and thus was forced to rewrite them by memory. The thick and confusing "user-friendly" manuals fell many a time from my impatient hands; and I spent many desperate nights cursing the mischievous gods of cyberspace and dialing promising "hotlines" that rarely answered.

My bittersweet relationship to technology dates back to my formative years in the highly politicized ambiance of Mexico City in the 1970s. As a young "radical artist," I was full of ideological dogmas and partial truths. One such partial truth spouted was that high technology was intrinsically dehumanizing; that it was mostly used as a means to control "us" little techno-illiterate people politically. My critique of technology overlapped with my critique of capitalism. To me, "capitalists" were rootless corporate men who utilized mass media to advertise useless electronic gadgets, and sold as unnecessary apparatuses that kept us both eternally in debt and conveniently distracted from "the truly important matters of life." These matters included sex, music, spirituality, and "revolution" California style (in the abstract). As a child of contradiction, besides being a rabid antitechnology artist, I owned a little Datsun and listened to my favorite U.S. and British rock groups on my Panasonic *importado,* often while meditating or making love as a means to "liberate myself" from capitalist socialization. My favorite clothes, books, posters, and albums had all been made by "capitalists," but for some obscure reason, that seemed perfectly logical to me. Luckily, my family never lost their magical thinking and sense of humor around technology. My parents were easily seduced by refurbished and slightly dated American and Japanese electronic goods. We bought them as *fayuca* (contraband) in the Tepito neighborhood, and they occupied an important place in the decoration of our "modern" middle-class home. Our huge color TV set, for example, was decorated so as to perform the double function of entertainment unit and involuntary

---

"techno-placas": Techno-plaque or sheet.

postmodern altar—with nostalgic photos, plastic flowers, and assorted figurines all around it—as was the sound system next to it. Though I was sure that with the scary arrival of the first microwave oven to our traditional kitchen our delicious daily meals were going to turn overnight into sleazy fast food, my mother soon realized that *el microondas*° was only good to reheat cold coffee and soups. When I moved to California, I bought an electric ionizer for my grandma. She put it in the middle of her bedroom altar and kept it there—unplugged of course—for months. When I next saw her, she told me, "Mijito,° since you gave me that thing, I truly can breathe much better." And probably she did. Things like televisions, shortwave radios, and microwave ovens, and later on ionizers, Walkmans, calculators, and video cameras were seen by my family and friends as high technology, and their function was as much pragmatic as it was social, ritual, and aesthetic. It is no coincidence then that in my early performance work, technology performed both ritual and aesthetic functions.

Verbigratia°

For years, I used video monitors as centerpieces for my "techno-altars" on stage. I combined ritualistic structures, spoken word multilingual poetry, and activist politics with my fascination for "low-tech." Fog machines, strobe lights, and gobos,° megaphones and cheesy voice filters have remained since then trademark elements in my "low-tech/high-tech" performances. By the early 1990s, I sarcastically baptized my aesthetic practice. "Aztec high-tech art," and when I teamed with Cyber-Vato Sifuentes, we decided that what we were doing was "techno-razcuache art."° In a glossary that dates back to 1993, we defined it as "a new aesthetic that fuses performance art, epic rap poetry, interactive television, experimental radio and computer art; but with a Chicanocentric perspective and a sleazoid bent."

> (El Naftaztec° turns the knobs of his "Chicano virtual reality machine" and then proceeds to feed chili peppers into it. The set looks like a Mexican sci-fi movie from the 1950s.) El Naftaztec (speaking with a computerized voice): *So now, let's talk about the TECHNOPAL 2000, a technology originally invented by the Mayans with the help of aliens from Harvard. Its CPU is powered by habanero chili peppers, combined with this or DAT technology, with a measured clock speed of*

el microondas: The microwave.

"Mijito": My child.

Verbigratia: For example.

gobos: Thin masks.

"techno-razcuache art": Thin masks placed in the gate of a spotlight that shape the light beam into a certain pattern.

El Naftaztec: The name of Gómez-Peña's hero combines the abbreviation for the North American Free Trade Agreement (NAFTA) with Aztec, the name of the indigenous tribe that originally occupied the present site of Mexico City.

200,000 megahertz! It uses neural nets supplemented by actual chicken-brain matter and nacho cheese spread to supply the massive processing speed necessary for the machine to operate. And it's all integrated into one sombrero! Originally, the Chicano VR had to use a poncho, but with the VR sombrero, the weight is greatly reduced and its efficiency is magnified. And now, we have the first alpha version of the VR bandanna dos mil,° which Cyber-Vato will demonstrate for us! (Cyber-Vato wears a bandanna over his eyes. It is connected by a thick rope to a robotic glove. Special effects on the TV screen simulate the graphics and sounds of a VR helmet.)

— From "Naftaztec," an interactive TV project about
Mexicans and high technology

The mythology goes like this. Mexicans (and other Latinos) can't handle high technology. Caught between a preindustrial past and an imposed postmodernity, we continue to be manual beings — *Homo fabers°* par excellence, imaginative artisans (not technicians) — and our understanding of the world is strictly political, poetical, or metaphysical at best, but certainly not scientific. Furthermore, we are perceived as sentimental and passionate, meaning irrational; and when we decide to step out of our realm and utilize high technology in our art (most of the time we are not even interested), we are meant to naively repeat what others have already done. We often feed this mythology by overstating our romantic nature and humanistic stances and/or by assuming the role of colonial victims of technology. We are ready to point out the fact that "computers are the source of the Anglos' social handicaps and sexual psychosis" and that communication in America, the land of the future, "is totally mediated by faxes, phones, computers, and other technologies we are not even aware of." We, "on the contrary," socialize profusely, negotiate information ritually and sensually, and remain in touch with our primeval selves. This simplistic binary worldview presents Mexico as technologically underdeveloped yet culturally and spiritually overdeveloped and the United States as exactly the opposite. Reality is much more complicated: the average Anglo-American does not understand new technologies either; people of color and women in the United States clearly don't have equal access to cyberspace; and at the same time, the average urban Mexican is already afflicted in varying degrees by the same "first world" existential diseases produced by advanced capitalism and high technology. In fact the new generations of Mexicans, including my hip generation-Mex nephews and my seven-year-old fully bicultural son, are completely immersed in and defined by personal computers, video games, and virtual reality. Far from being the romantic preindustrial paradise of the American imagination, the Mexico of the 1990s is already a virtual nation whose cohesiveness and boundaries are provided solely by television, transnational pop culture, and the free market. It is true that there are entire parts of the country that still lack basic infrastructures and public services (not to mention communications technology). But in 1996 the same can be said of the United States, a "first world" nation whose

dos mil: two thousand.

Homo fabers: *Homo faber* is Latin for man the maker or builder.

ruined "ethnic" neighborhoods, Native American reserves, and rural areas exist in conditions comparable to those of a "third world" country. When trying to link, say, Los Angeles and Mexico City via video-telephone, we encounter new problems. In Mexico, the only artists with "access" to the technology are upper class, politically conservative, and uninteresting. And the funding sources down there willing to fund the project are clearly interested in controlling who is part of the experiment. In other words, we don't really need Octavio Paz° conversing with Richard Rodriguez.° We need Rubén Martínez° talking to Monsivais,° as well.

> The world is waiting for you — so come on!
> — ad for America Online

The Cyber-Migra°

Roberto and I arrived late to the debate. When we began to dialogue with artists   5
working with new technologies, we were perplexed by the fact that when referring to cyberspace or the Net, they spoke of a politically neutral/raceless/genderless/classless "territory" that provided us all with "equal access" and unlimited possibilities of participation, interaction, and belonging — especially belonging. Their enthusiastic rhetoric reminded us of both a sanitized version of the pioneer and cowboy mentalities of the Old West ("Guillermo, you can be the first Mexican ever to do this and that in the Net"), and the early-century Futurist cult° to the speed and beauty of epic technology (airplanes, trains, factories, etc.). Given the existing "compassion fatigue" regarding political art dealing with issues of race and gender, it was hard not to see this feel-good utopian view of new technologies as an attractive exit from the acute social and racial crisis afflicting the United States. We were also perplexed by the "benign (not naive) ethnocentrism" permeating the debates around art and digital technology. The unquestioned lingua franca° was of course English, the "official language of international communications"; the vocabulary utilized in these discussions was hyperspecialized and depoliticized; and if Chicanos and Mexicans didn't participate enough in the Net, it was solely because of lack of information or interest (not money or access), or again because we were "cul-

Octavio Paz: (1914–1998), Famed Mexican poet, critic, diplomat, and recipient of the Nobel Prize for literature in 1990.

Richard Rodriguez: (b. 1944), Nationally known Mexican American essayist and editor.

Rubén Martínez: Mexican American journalist and editor (see page 306).

Monsivais: (b. 1938), Carlos Monsivais, Mexican writer. In 1977, awarded the National Prize of Journalism. In 1995, awarded the Villaurrutia Literature Prize.

Migra: Spanish slang for the Immigration and Naturalization Service.

Futurist cult: Futurism was an artistic movement at the turn of the twentieth century that celebrated technology and saw the machine as the epitome of rationality and modern design.

lingua franca: The language of general communication in a multilingual society.

turally unfit." The unspoken assumption was that our true interests were grass-roots (by grassroots I mean the streets), representational, or oral (as if these concerns couldn't exist in virtual space). In other words, we were to remain dancing salsa, painting murals, writing flamboyant love poetry, and plotting revolutions in rowdy cafés. We were also perplexed by the recurring labels of "originality" and "innovation" attached to virtual art. And it was not the nature, contents, and structural complexity of the parallel realities created by digital technology, but the use of the technology per se that seemed to be "original" and "innovative." That, of course, has since engendered many conflicting responses. Native American shamans and medicine men rightfully see their centuries-old "visions" as a form of virtual reality. And Latin American writers equate their literary experimentation with involuntary hypertexts and vernacular postmodern aesthetics, and so do Chicanos and Chicanas. Like the pre-multicultural art world of the early 1980s, the new high-tech art world assumed an unquestionable "center" and drew a dramatic digital border. On the other side of that border lived all the techno-illiterate artists, along with most women, Chicanos, African Americans, and Native Americans. The role for us, then, was to assume, once again, the unpleasant but necessary role of cultural invaders, techno-pirates, and coyotes (smugglers). And then, just as multiculturalism was declared dead as soon as we began to share the paycheck, now as we venture into the virtual barrio° for the first time, some asshole at MIT declares it dead. Why? It is no longer an exclusive space. It emulates too much real life and social demographics. Luckily many things have changed. Since we don't wish to reproduce the unpleasant mistakes of the multicultural days, our strategies are now quite different: we are no longer trying to persuade anyone that we are worthy of inclusion. Nor are we fighting for the same funding (since funding no longer exists). What we want is to "politicize" the debate; to "brownify" virtual space; to "Spanglishize the Net"; to "infect" the lingua franca; to exchange a different sort of information — mythical, poetical, political, performative, imagistic; and on top of that to find grassroots applications to new technologies and hopefully to do all this with humor and intelligence. The ultimate goals are perhaps to help the Latino youth exchange their guns for computers and video cameras, and to link the community centers through the Net. CD-ROMs can perform the role of community memory banks, while the larger virtual community gets used to a new presence, a new sensibility, a new language.

Note

1. See <http://www.sfgate.com/foundry/pochanostra.html>.

barrio: Spanish for neighborhood.

EXPLORING THE TEXT

1. What Latino stereotypes in relation to electronic technology does Gómez-Peña attack in this essay? How do his own reflections on his past and present views of

technology, revolution, friends, and family challenge or confirm the "mythology" associated with Latinos and high technology?

2. What, in general, is Gómez-Peña's attitude toward computers and the Internet? Why, for example, does he identify the Internet as the "Cyber-Migra"? What is he saying in this essay about the impact of high technology on Latinos and other groups that might be considered "culturally unfit"? To what extent would you agree?

3. In what ways does Gómez-Peña attempt to "brownify" the world of high technology? What does he do to transform himself into "a sort of Mexican virus"? What does he hope to achieve by these actions? What else might he and people of other "culturally unfit" groups do, in your opinion, to diversify the world of high technology?

FURTHER EXPLORATIONS

1. How would the programmers described by Ellen Ullman (p. 656) probably view Gómez-Peña and his plan to "brownify" the Net? How realistic might his plan to "infect" or subvert the world of high technology seem from her perspective?

2. Compare Gómez-Peña's view of the influence of high technology with that of Clifford Stoll (p. 648). To what extent might Gómez-Peña agree with Stoll's assessment of the way computers isolate and dehumanize their users? Why?

3. Compare Gómez-Peña's attitude about identity online with that expressed by Sherry Turkle in "Who Am We?" (p. 675). How might Gómez-Peña respond to Turkle's claim that reality is becoming "just another window" online?

4. Browse Internet sites linked to Guillermo Gómez-Peña and Robert Sifuentes to see how successful these cyberspace invaders are in their attempt to "brownify" or "Spanglishize" the Net. To what extent do you think sites like these challenge the dominant "voice" or culture of cyberspace?

ESSAY OPTIONS

1. Using "The Virtual Barrio" as a point of departure, research and write a paper on the issue of access to the Internet. How equitable is the Internet as a means of electronic communication? How available is Internet use for all segments of the U.S. and world populations? What social problems may arise in the future if "people of color and women don't have equal access to cyberspace"? What, if anything, might be done to address this situation?

2. Based on your own independent Web research, create a multimedia report, either as text or hypertext, in which you explore the "culture" of the Internet. To what extent is the Net a "neutral/raceless, genderless/classless territory," as Gómez-Peña believes it was originally meant to be? What specific Web sites do you know of that actively subvert, "infect," or "invade" the dominant culture of the Net? Are such sites "virtual barrios" — isolated pockets of resistance against the dominant culture of the Web — or do they represent the leading edge of "a new presence, a new sensibility, a new language," as Gómez-Peña suggests at the end of his essay?

Who Am We?

SHERRY TURKLE

Do you know what it means to get RL? Chances are you do if you're one of the thousands of Internet devotees who spend hours every week portraying fictional characters in the collaborative fantasy games commonly known as "Multiple-User Dungeons" or MUDs. RL is shorthand for "Real Life," a topic of some urgency to MUDders according to Sherry Turkle, author of this selection and an expert on Internet cultures. Turkle's research into life online suggests that many Americans — including those of us who enjoy having "Tiny sex" while impersonating furry animals — may be losing their grip on what used to be known as reality. More importantly, her studies of the heaviest Web crawlers indicate that the Internet may be changing even the most fundamental assumptions about human identity. A clinical psychologist and professor of sociology at the Massachusetts Institute of Technology, Turkle (b. 1948) has written numerous books and articles about the psychological and cultural implications of computer technology. Her publications include *The Second Self: Computers and the Human Spirit* (1984) and *Life on Screen: Identity in the Age of the Internet* (1995). This selection originally appeared in *Wired* magazine.

BEFORE READING

If you were about to enter a MUD online, what alternative identity would you be tempted to adopt? Describe the being you'd become in a quick paragraph detailing its appearance, gender, age, background, and so forth. Share these fantasy profiles anonymously in small groups and try to match each profile with its writer.

There are many Sherry Turkles. There is the "French Sherry," who studied poststructuralism in Paris in the 1960s. There is Turkle the social scientist, trained in anthropology, personality psychology, and sociology. There is Dr. Turkle, the clinical psychologist. There is Sherry Turkle the writer of books — *Psychoanalytic Politics* (Basic Books, 1978) and *The Second Self: Computers and the Human Spirit* (Simon & Schuster, 1984). There is Sherry the professor, who has mentored MIT students for nearly twenty years. And there is the cyberspace explorer, the woman who might log on as a man, or as another woman, or as, simply, ST.

All of these Sherry Turkles have authored a new book, *Life on the Screen: Identity in the Age of the Internet,* published November 30, [1995] by Simon & Schuster. *Life on the Screen* tells how the computer profoundly shapes our ways of thinking and feeling, how ideas carried by technology are reshaped by people for their own purposes, how computers are not just changing our lives but changing our selves.

This story is borne of Turkle's past decade of research. In a series of pizza parties for MUDders in the Boston area, Turkle found conversations quickly turning to multiple personas, romance, and what can be counted on as "real" in virtual space. She soon turned to the world of Internet Relay Chat, newsgroups, bulletin boards, and commercial online services. She also examined the burgeoning cyberspace lives of children and teenagers.

What has she found? That the Internet links millions of people in new spaces that are changing the way we think and the way we form our communities. That we are moving from "a modernist culture of calculation toward a postmodernist culture° of simulation." That life on the screen permits us to "project ourselves into our own dramas, dramas in which we are producer, director, and star. . . . Computer screens are the new location for our fantasies, both erotic and intellectual. We are using life on computer screens to become comfortable with new ways of thinking about evolution, relationships, sexuality, politics, and identity."

Turkle's own metaphor of windows serves well to introduce the following   5 samplings from her new book. Those boxed-off areas on the screen, Turkle writes, allow us to cycle through cyberspace and real life, over and over. Windows allow us to be in several contexts at the same time—in a MUD, in a word-processing program, in a chat room, in e-mail.

"Windows have become a powerful metaphor for thinking about the self as a multiple, distributed system," Turkle writes. "The self is no longer simply playing different roles in different settings at different times. The life practice of windows is that of a decentered self that exists in many worlds, that plays many roles at the same time." Now real life itself may be, as one of Turkle's subjects says, "just one more window."

As recently as ten to fifteen years ago, it was almost unthinkable to speak of the computer's involvement with ideas about unstable meanings and unknowable truths. The computer had a clear intellectual identity as a calculating machine. In an introductory programming course at Harvard University in 1978, one professor introduced the computer to the class by calling it a giant calculator. Programming, he reassured the students, was a cut-and-dried technical activity whose rules were crystal clear.

Such reassurances captured the essence of what I call the modernist computational aesthetic. It's the computer as calculator: no matter how complicated a computer might seem, what happened inside it could be mechanically unpacked. Programming was a technical skill that could be done a right way or a wrong way. The right way was dictated by the computer's calculator essence. The right way was linear and logical. This linear, logical [model] guided thinking not only about technology and programming, but about eco-

---

postmodernist culture: Postmodernism is the term used to describe a constellation of cultural and artistic trends since the 1960s having to do with the rejection of values and structures associated with modernism—the dominant cultural trend of the early twentieth century. Modernism generally valued science, the clarity of rational thought, and an optimistic worldview. Postmodernist culture instead places greater emphasis on the artificial or "constructed" nature of all human knowledge, the relativity of all cultural values, and the fragmented or incomplete nature of concepts like the meaning of a work of art or the nature of the self.

nomics, psychology, and social life. Computational ideas were one of the great modern metanarratives, stories of how the world worked that provided unifying pictures and analyzed complicated things by breaking them down into simpler parts. Computers, it was assumed, would become more powerful, both as tools and as metaphors, by becoming better and faster calculating machines, better and faster analytical engines.

From today's perspective, the fundamental lessons of computing are wrong. Programming is no longer cut and dried. Are you programming when you customize your word-processing software? When you design "organisms" to populate a simulation of Darwinian evolution in the computer game SimLife? Or when you build a room in a MUD so that opening a door to it will cause "Happy Un-Birthday" to ring out on all but one day of the year?

The lessons of computing today have to do not with calculation and rules, 10 but with simulation, navigation, and interaction. The very image of the computer as a giant calculator has become quaint and dated. Fifteen years ago, most computer users were limited to typing commands. Today they use off-the-shelf products to manipulate simulated desktops, draw with simulated paints and brushes, and fly in simulated airplane cockpits. . . .

In the early 1970s, the face-to-face role-playing game Dungeons and Dragons swept the game culture. The term "dungeon" persisted in the high-tech culture to connote a virtual place. So when virtual spaces were created that many computer users could share and collaborate within, they were deemed Multi-User Dungeons or MUDs, a new kind of social virtual reality. (Some games use software that make them technically MUSHes or MOOs,° but the term MUD has come to refer to all of the multi-user environments.)

MUDs are a new kind of virtual parlor game and a new form of community. In addition, text-based MUDs are a new form of collaboratively written literature. MUD players are MUD authors, the creators as well as consumers of media content. In this, participating in a MUD has much in common with scriptwriting, performance art, street theater, improvisational theater, or even commedia dell'arte.° But MUDs are something else as well.

As players participate, they become authors not only of text but of themselves, constructing new selves through social interaction. Since one participates in MUDs by sending text to a computer that houses the MUD's program and database, MUD selves are constituted in interaction with the machine. Take it away and the MUD selves cease to exist: "Part of me, a very important part of me, only exists inside PernMUD," says one player. Several players joke that they are like "the electrodes in the computer," trying to express the degree to which they feel part of its space.

MUSHes or MOOs: Other types of MUDs.

commedia dell'arte: A form of Italian street theater popular during the sixteenth to eighteenth centuries involving improvised plots based on a set of stock characters and standardized situations.

All MUDs are organized around the metaphor of physical space. When you first enter a MUD, you may find yourself in a medieval church from which you can step out into the town square, or you may find yourself in the coat closet of a large, rambling house. For example, when you first log on to LambdaMOO, one of the most popular MUDs on the Internet, you see the following description:

> The Coat Closet. The Closet is a dark, cramped space. It appears to be very crowded in here; you keep bumping into what feels like coats, boots, and other people (apparently sleeping). One useful thing that you've discovered in your bumbling about is a metal doorknob set at waist level into what might be a door. There's a new edition of the newspaper. Type "news" to see it.

In the MUDs, virtual characters converse with each other, exchange gestures, express emotions, win and lose virtual money, and rise and fall in social status. A virtual character can also die. Some die of "natural" causes (a player decides to close them down), or they can have their virtual lives snuffed out. This is all achieved through writing, and this in a culture that had apparently fallen asleep in the audiovisual arms of television. Yet this new writing is a kind of hybrid: speech momentarily frozen into artifact, but curiously ephemeral artifact. In this new writing, unless it is printed out on paper, a screenful of flickers soon replaces the previous screen.

The anonymity of MUDs gives people the chance to express multiple and   15
often unexplored aspects of the self, to play with their identity and to try out new ones. MUDs make possible the creation of an identity so fluid and multiple that it strains the limits of the notion. Identity, after all, refers to the sameness between two qualities, in this case between a person and his or her persona. But in MUDs, one can be many.

A twenty-one-year-old college senior defends his violent characters as "something in me; but quite frankly I'd rather rape on MUDs where no harm is done." A twenty-six-year-old clerical worker says, "I'm not one thing, I'm many things. Each part gets to be more fully expressed in MUDs than in the real world. So even though I play more than one self on MUDs, I feel more like 'myself' when I'm MUDding." In real life, this woman sees her world as too narrow to allow her to manifest certain aspects of the person she feels herself to be. Creating screen personas is thus an opportunity for self-expression, leading to her feeling more like her true self when decked out in an array of virtual masks.

MUDs imply difference, multiplicity, heterogeneity, and fragmentation. Such an experience of identity contradicts the Latin root of the word, idem, meaning "the same." But this contradiction increasingly defines the conditions of our lives beyond the virtual world. MUDs thus become objects-to-think-with for thinking about postmodern selves. Indeed, the unfolding of all MUD action takes place in a resolutely postmodern context. There are parallel narratives in the different rooms of a MUD. The cultures of Tolkien,

Gibson, and Madonna° coexist and interact. Since MUDs are authored by their players, thousands of people in all, often hundreds at a time, are all logged on from different places; the solitary author is displaced and distributed. Traditional ideas about identity have been tied to a notion of authenticity that such virtual experiences actively subvert. When each player can create many characters in many games, the self is not only decentered but multiplied without limit.

As a new social experience, MUDs pose many psychological questions: If a persona in a role-playing game drops defenses that the player in real life has been unable to abandon, what effect does this have? What if a persona enjoys success in some area (say, flirting) that the player has not been able to achieve? Slippages often occur in places where persona and self merge, where the multiple personas join to comprise what the individual thinks of as his or her authentic self.

Doug is a Midwestern college junior. He plays four characters distributed across three different MUDs. One is a seductive woman. One is a macho, cowboy type whose self-description stresses that he is a "Marlboros rolled in the T-shirt sleeve kind of guy." The third is a rabbit of unspecified gender who wanders its MUD introducing people to each other, a character he calls Carrot. Doug says, "Carrot is so low key that people let it be around while they are having private conversations. So I think of Carrot as my passive, voyeuristic character." Doug's fourth character is one that he plays only on a MUD in which all the characters are furry animals. "I'd rather not even talk about that character because my anonymity there is very important to me," Doug says. "Let's just say that on FurryMUDs I feel like a sexual tourist." Doug talks about playing his characters in windows and says that using windows has made it possible for him to "turn pieces of my mind on and off.

"I split my mind. . . . I can see myself as being two or three or more. And I just turn on one part of my mind and then another when I go from window to window. I'm in some kind of argument in one window and trying to come on to a girl in a MUD in another, and another window might be running a spreadsheet program or some other technical thing for school. . . . And then I'll get a real-time message that flashes on the screen as soon as it is sent from another system user, and I guess that's RL. RL is just one more window, and it's not usually my best one."

Play has always been an important aspect of our individual efforts to build identity. The psychoanalyst Erik Erikson called play a "toy situation" that allows us to "reveal and commit" ourselves "in its unreality." While MUDs are not the only "places" on the Internet in which to play with identity, they provide an unparalleled opportunity for such play. On a MUD one actually gets

Tolkien, Gibson, and Madonna: Respectively, John Ronald Reuel Tolkien (1892–1973), English author of fantasy novels including *The Lord of the Rings*; William Gibson (b. 1948), American cyberpunk science-fiction novelist (see page 703); and Madonna Louise Ciccone (b. 1958), American pop singer and actress.

to build character and environment and then to live within the toy situation. A MUD can become a context for discovering who one is and wishes to be. In this way, the games are laboratories for the construction of identity.

Stewart, a twenty-three-year-old physics graduate student, uses MUDs to have experiences he can't imagine for himself in RL. His intense online involvements engaged key issues in his life but ultimately failed to help him reach successful resolutions.

Stewart's real life revolves around laboratory work and his plans for a future in science. His only friend is his roommate, another physics student whom he describes as even more reclusive than himself. For Stewart, this circumscribed, almost monastic student life does not represent a radical departure from what has gone before. He has had heart trouble since he was a child; one small rebellion, a ski trip when he was a college freshman, put him in the hospital for a week. He has lived life within a small compass.

Stewart is logged on to one MUD or another for at least forty hours a week. It seems misleading to call what he does there playing. He spends his time constructing a life that is more expansive than the one he lives in physical reality. Stewart, who has traveled very little and has never been to Europe, explains with delight that his favorite MUD, although played in English, is physically located on a computer in Germany and has many European players.

On the German MUD, Stewart shaped a character named Achilles,° but   25
he asks his MUD friends to call him Stewart as much as possible. He wants to feel that his real self exists somewhere between Stewart and Achilles. He wants to feel that his MUD life is part of his real life. Stewart insists that he does not role play, but that MUDs simply allow him to be a better version of himself.

On the MUD, Stewart creates a living environment suitable for his ideal self. His university dormitory is modest, but the room he has built for Achilles on the MUD is elegant and heavily influenced by Ralph Lauren advertising. He has named it "the home beneath the silver moon." There are books, a roaring fire, cognac, a cherry mantel "covered with pictures of Achilles's friends from around the world."

"You look up . . . and through the immense skylight you see a breathtaking view of the night sky. The moon is always full over Achilles's home, and its light fills the room with a warm glow."

Beyond expanding his social world, MUDs have brought Stewart the only romance and intimacy he has ever known. At a social event in virtual space, a "wedding" of two regular players on a German-based MUD I call Gargoyle, Achilles met Winterlight, a character played by one of the three female players on that MUD. Stewart, who has known little success in dating and romantic relationships, was able to charm this desirable player.

Achilles: Hero of the *Iliad*, an eighth- to ninth-century-B.C.E. Greek epic poem attributed to Homer.

On their first virtual date, Achilles took Winterlight to an Italian restaurant close to Stewart's dorm. He had often fantasized being there with a woman. Stewart used a combination of MUD commands to simulate a romantic evening — picking Winterlight up at the airport in a limousine, driving her to a hotel room so that she could shower, and then taking her to the restaurant and ordering veal for her.

This dinner date led to others during which Achilles was tender and romantic, chivalrous and poetic. The intimacy Achilles experienced during his courtship of Winterlight is unknown to Stewart in other contexts. "She's a very, she's a good friend. I found out a lot of things, from things about physiology to the color of nail polish she wears." Finally, Achilles asked for Winterlight's hand. When she accepted, they had a formal engagement ceremony on the MUD.

At the engagement, Winterlight gave Achilles a rose she had worn in her hair; Achilles gave her one thousand paper stars.

Although Stewart participated in this ceremony alone in his room with his computer and modem, a group of European players actually traveled to Germany, site of Gargoyle's host computer, and got together for food and champagne. Many of the twenty-five guests at the German celebration brought gifts and dressed specially for the occasion. Stewart felt as though he were throwing a party. This was the first time that he had ever entertained, and he was proud of his success. In real life, Stewart felt constrained by his health problems, his shyness and social isolation, and his narrow economic straits. In the Gargoyle MUD, he bypassed these obstacles, at least temporarily.

The psychological effects of life on the screen can be complicated: a safe place is not all that is needed for personal change. Stewart came to MUDding with serious problems, and for Stewart, playing on MUDs led to a net drop in self-esteem. MUDs did help Stewart talk about his troubles while they were still emotionally relevant; nevertheless, he is emphatic that MUDding has ultimately made him feel worse about himself. MUDding did not alter Stewart's sense of himself as withdrawn, unappealing, and flawed.

While Stewart has tried hard to make his MUD self, the "better" Achilles self, part of his real life, he says he has failed. He says, "I'm not social. I don't like parties. I can't talk to people about my problems." The integration of the social Achilles, who can talk about his troubles, and the asocial Stewart, who can only cope by putting them out of mind, has not occurred. From Stewart's point of view, MUDs have stripped away some of his defenses but have given him nothing in return. In fact, MUDs make Stewart feel vulnerable in a new way. Although he hoped that MUDs would cure him, it is MUDs that now make him feel sick. He feels addicted to MUDs: "When you feel you're stagnating and you feel there's nothing going on in your life and you're stuck in a rut, it's very easy to be on there for a very large amount of time."

Stewart cannot learn from his character Achilles's experience and social success because they are too different from the things of which he believes himself capable. Despite his efforts to turn Achilles into Stewart, Stewart has split off his strengths and sees them as possible only for Achilles in the MUD. It is only Achilles who can create the magic and win the girl. In making this split between himself and the achievements of his screen persona, Stewart does not give himself credit for the positive steps he has taken in real life. Like an unsuccessful psychotherapy, MUDding has not helped Stewart bring these good experiences inside himself or integrate them into his self-image.

Relationships during adolescence are usually bounded by a mutual understanding that they involve limited commitment. Virtual space is well suited to such relationships; its natural limitations keep things within bounds. As in Thomas Mann's *The Magic Mountain,°* which takes place in the isolation of a sanatorium, relationships become intense very quickly because the participants feel isolated in a remote and unfamiliar world with its own rules. MUDs, like other electronic meeting places, can breed a kind of easy intimacy. In a first phase, MUD players feel the excitement of a rapidly deepening relationship and the sense that time itself is speeding up. "The MUD quickens things. It quickens things so much," says one player. "You know, you don't think about it when you're doing it, but you meet somebody on the MUD, and within a week you feel like you've been friends forever."

In a second phase, players commonly try to take things from the virtual to the real and are usually disappointed.

Gender-swapping on MUDs is not a small part of the game action. By some estimates, Habitat, a Japanese MUD, has 1.5 million users. Habitat is a MUD operated for profit. Among the registered members of Habitat, there is a ratio of four real-life men to each real-life woman. But inside the MUD the ratio is only three male characters to one female character. In other words, a significant number of players, many tens of thousands of them, are virtually cross-dressing.

What is virtual gender-swapping all about? Some of those who do it claim that it is not particularly significant. "When I play a woman I don't really take it too seriously," said twenty-year-old Andrei. "I do it to improve the ratio of women to men. It's just a game." On one level, virtual gender-swapping is easier than doing it in real life. For a man to present himself as female in a chat room, on an IRC° channel, or in a MUD, only requires writing a description. For a man to play a woman on the streets of an American city, he would have to shave various parts of his body; wear makeup, perhaps a wig, a dress, and high heels; perhaps change his voice, walk, and mannerisms. He would have some anxiety about passing, and there might be even more anxiety about not passing, which would pose a risk of violence and possibly arrest. So more men are willing to give virtual cross-dressing a try. But once they are online as female, they soon find that maintaining this fiction is difficult. To pass as a woman for any length of time requires understanding how gender inflects

Thomas Mann's *The Magic Mountain:* Thomas Mann (1875–1955), German-born American author.

IRC: Internet Relay Chat, an electronic communication system with international access offering unmonitored 24/7 chat.

speech, manner, the interpretation of experience. Women attempting to pass as men face the same kind of challenge.

Virtual cross-dressing is not as simple as Andrei suggests. Not only can it   40 be technically challenging, it can be psychologically complicated. Taking a virtual role may involve you in ongoing relationships. You may discover things about yourself that you never knew before.

Case, a thirty-four-year-old industrial designer who is happily married to a co-worker, is currently MUDding as a female character. In response to my question, "Has MUDding ever caused you any emotional pain?" he says, "Yes, but also the kind of learning that comes from hard times."

"I'm having pain in my playing now. Mairead, the woman I'm playing in MedievalMUSH, is having an interesting relationship with a fellow. Mairead is a lawyer, and the high cost of law school has to be paid for by a corporation or a noble house. She fell in love with a nobleman who paid for her law school. [Case slips into referring to Mairead in the first person.] Now he wants to marry me although I'm a commoner, I finally said yes. I try to talk to him about the fact that I'm essentially his property. I'm a commoner . . . I've grown up with it, that's the way life is. He wants to deny the situation. He says, 'Oh no, no no . . . We'll pick you up, set you on your feet, the whole world is open to you.' But every time I behave like I'm now going to be a countess some day . . . as in, 'And I never liked this wallpaper anyway,' I get pushed down. The relationship is pull up, push down. It's an incredibly psychologically damaging thing to do to a person. And the very thing that he liked about her that she was independent, strong, said what was on her mind, it is all being bled out of her."

Case looks at me with a wry smile and sighs, "A woman's life." He continues: "I see her [Mairead] heading for a major psychological problem. What we have is a dysfunctional relationship. But even though it's very painful and stressful, it's very interesting to watch myself cope with this problem. How am I going to dig my persona's self out of this mess? Because I don't want to go on like this. I want to get out of it. . . . You can see that playing this woman lets me see what I have in my psychological repertoire, what is hard and what is easy for me. And I can also see how some of the things that work when you're a man just backfire when you're a woman."

Case further illustrates the complexity of gender swapping as a vehicle for self-reflection. Case describes his RL persona as a nice guy, a "Jimmy Stewart type like my father." He says that in general he likes his father and he likes himself, but he feels he pays a price for his low-key ways. In particular, he feels at a loss when it comes to confrontation, both at home and in business dealings. Case likes MUDding as a female because it makes it easier for him to be aggressive and confrontational. Case plays several online "Katharine Hepburn types,"° strong, dynamic, "out there" women who remind him of his mother, "who says exactly what's on her mind and is a take-no-prisoners sort."

"Katherine Hepburn types": Katherine Hepburn (b. 1907), American actress known for her portrayals of strong women.

For Case, if you are assertive as a man, it is coded as "being a bastard." If 45
you are assertive as a woman, it is coded as "modern and together."

Some women who play male characters desire invisibility or permission to
be more outspoken or aggressive. "I was born in the South and taught that
girls didn't speak up to disagree with men," says Zoe, a thirty-four-year-old
woman who plays male and female characters on four MUDs.

"We would sit at dinner and my father would talk and my mother would
agree. I thought my father was a god. Once or twice I did disagree with him.
I remember one time in particular when I was ten, and he looked at me and
said, 'Well, well, well, if this little flower grows too many more thorns, she will
never catch a man.'"

Zoe credits MUDs with enabling her to reach a state of mind where she
is better able to speak up for herself in her marriage ("to say what's on my
mind before things get all blown out of proportion") and to handle her job as
the financial officer for a small biotechnology firm.

"I played a MUD man for two years. First I did it because I wanted the
feeling of an equal playing field in terms of authority, and the only way I could
think of to get it was to play a man. But after a while, I got very absorbed by
MUDding. I became a wizard on a pretty simple MUD. I called myself
Ulysses° and got involved in the system and realized that as a man I could be
firm and people would think I was a great wizard. As a woman, drawing the
line and standing firm has always made me feel like a bitch and, actually, I feel
that people saw me as one, too. As a man I was liberated from all that. I
learned from my mistakes. I got better at being firm but not rigid. I practiced,
safe from criticism."

Zoe's perceptions of her gender trouble are almost the opposite of Case's. 50
While Case sees aggressiveness as acceptable only for women, Zoe sees it as
acceptable only for men. These stories share a notion that a virtual gender
swap gave people greater emotional range in the real. Zoe says: "I got really
good at playing a man, so good that whoever was on the system would accept
me as a man and talk to me as a man. So, other guys talked to Ulysses guy to
guy. It was very validating. All those years I was paranoid about how men
talked about women. Or I thought I was paranoid. Then I got a chance to be
a guy and I saw that I wasn't paranoid at all."

Virtual sex, whether in MUDs or in a private room on a commercial online service, consists of two or more players typing descriptions of physical actions, verbal statements, and emotional reactions for their characters. In cyberspace, this activity is not only common but, for many people, it is the
centerpiece of their online experience.

On MUDs, some people have sex as characters of their own gender.
Others have sex as characters of the other gender. Some men play female personas to have Net sex with men. And in the "fake-lesbian syndrome," men

Ulysses: Hero of the *Odyssey,* an eighth- to ninth-century-B.C.E. Greek epic poem attributed to
Homer.

adopt online female personas in order to have Net sex with women. Although it does not seem to be as widespread, I have met several women who say they present as male characters in order to have Net sex with men. Some people have sex as nonhuman characters, for example, as animals on FurryMUDs. Some enjoy sex with one partner. Some use virtual reality as a place to experiment with group situations. In real life, such behavior (where possible) can create enormous practical and emotional confusion. Virtual adventures may be easier to undertake, but they can also result in significant complications.

Martin and Beth, both forty-one, have been married for nineteen years and have four children. Early in their marriage, Martin regretted not having had more time for sexual experimentation and had an extramarital affair. The affair hurt Beth deeply, and Martin decided he never wanted to do it again. When Martin discovered MUDs he was thrilled. "I really am monogamous. I'm really not interested in something outside my marriage. But being able to have, you know, a Tiny romance° is kind of cool." Martin decided to tell Beth about his MUD sex life and she decided to tell him that she does not mind. Beth has made a conscious decision to consider Martin's sexual relationships on MUDs as more like his reading an erotic novel than like his having a rendezvous in a motel room. For Martin, his online affairs are a way to fill the gaps of his youth, to broaden his sexual experience without endangering his marriage.

Other partners of virtual adulterers do not share Beth's accepting attitude. Janet, twenty-four, a secretary at a New York law firm, is very upset by her husband Tim's sex life in cyberspace. After Tim's first online affair, he confessed his virtual infidelity. When Janet objected, Tim told her that he would stop "seeing" his online mistress. Janet says that she is not sure that he actually did stop. "The thing that bothers me most is that he wants to do it in the first place. In some ways, I'd have an easier time understanding why he would want to have an affair in real life. At least there, I could say to myself, 'Well, it is for someone with a better body, or just for the novelty.' It's like the first kiss is always the best kiss. But in MUDding, he is saying that he wants that feeling of intimacy with someone else, the 'just talk' part of an encounter with a woman, and to me that comes closer to what is most important about sex.

"First I told him he couldn't do it anymore. Then, I panicked and figured   55 that he might do it anyway because, unlike in real life, I could never find out. All these thousands of people all over the world with their stupid fake names . . . no way I would ever find out. So, I pulled back and said that talking about it was strictly off limits. But now I don't know if that was the right decision. I feel paranoid whenever he is on the computer."

This distressed wife struggles to decide whether her husband is unfaithful when his persona collaborates on writing real-time erotica with another

---

a Tiny romance: The term "Tiny" is used to distinguish an online activity from its correlative in the real world; hence, "online sex."

persona in cyberspace. And beyond this, should it make a difference if unbeknownst to the husband his cyberspace mistress turns out to be a nineteen-year-old male college freshman? What if "she" is an infirm eighty-year-old man in a nursing home? And even more disturbing, what if she is a twelve-year-old girl? Or a twelve-year-old boy?

Tiny sex poses the question of what is at the heart of sex and fidelity. Is it the physical action? Is it emotional intimacy with someone other than one's primary partner? Is infidelity in the head or in the body? Is it in the desire or in the action? What constitutes the violation of trust?

And once we take virtuality seriously as a way of life, we need a new language for talking about the simplest things. Each individual must ask: What is the nature of my relationships? What are the limits of my responsibility? And even more basic: Who and what am I? What is the connection between my physical and virtual bodies? And is it different in different cyberspaces? These questions are equally central for thinking about community. What is the nature of our social ties? What kind of accountability do we have for our actions in real life and in cyberspace? What kind of society or societies are we creating, both on and off the screen?

When people adopt an online persona they cross a boundary into highly charged territory. Some feel an uncomfortable sense of fragmentation, some a sense of relief. Some sense the possibilities for self-discovery, even self-transformation. Serena, a twenty-six-year-old graduate student in history, says, "When I log on to a new MUD and I create a character and know I have to start typing my description, I always feel a sense of panic. Like I could find out something I don't want to know." Arlie, a twenty-year-old undergraduate, says, "I am always very self-conscious when I create a new character. Usually, I end up creating someone I wouldn't want my parents to know about. . . . But that someone is part of me." . . .

Multiple viewpoints call forth a new moral discourse. The culture of simulation may help us achieve a vision of a multiple but integrated identity whose flexibility, resilience, and capacity for joy comes from having access to our many selves. But if we have lost reality in the process, we shall have struck a poor bargain. In Wim Wenders's film° *Until the End of the World,* a scientist develops a device that translates the electrochemical activity of the brain into digital images. He gives this technology to his family and closest friends, who are now able to hold small battery driven monitors and watch their dreams. At first, they are charmed. They see their treasured fantasies, their secret selves. They see the images they otherwise would forget, the scenes they otherwise would repress. As with the personas one can play in a MUD, watching dreams on a screen opens up new aspects of the self.

However, the story soon turns dark. The images seduce. They are richer and more compelling than the real life around them. Wenders's characters fall in love with their dreams, become addicted to them. People wander about

Wim Wenders's film: Wim Wenders (b. 1945), German filmmaker.

with blankets over their heads the better to see the monitors from which they cannot bear to be parted. They are imprisoned by the screens, imprisoned by the keys to their past that the screens seem to hold.

We, too, are vulnerable to using our screens in these ways. People can get lost in virtual worlds. Some are tempted to think of life in cyberspace as insignificant, as escape or meaningless diversion. It is not. Our experiences there are serious play. We belittle them at our risk. We must understand the dynamics of virtual experience both to foresee who might be in danger and to put these experiences to best use. Without a deep understanding of the many selves that we express in the virtual, we cannot use our experiences there to enrich the real. If we cultivate our awareness of what stands behind our screen personas, we are more likely to succeed in using virtual experience for personal transformation.

EXPLORING THE TEXT

1. How has the Internet changed the way we look at the self, according to Turkle? What does Turkle mean when she says that for many people today "real life" is quickly becoming "just one more window" (para. 6)? Would you agree? Why or why not?

2. Overall, what is Turkle's attitude toward MUDs and the people who frequent them? What benefits do the imagination games associated with MUDs offer their players? What dangers, if any, might await those who live their lives through "simulations"?

3. What motivates Turkle's informants to engage in virtual gender-swapping? What moral or ethical questions are raised by this practice? Is it acceptable, in your opinion, for a woman who acts the part of a man online to engage in a long-term e-relationship with another woman? Is it acceptable for a middle-aged man posing as an adolescent girl to "seduce" another man or for an adult to spend hours having e-sex in the guise of an animal on a "FurryMUD"? Do you agree with Turkle that virtual identity swapping is a kind of "serious play" serving valuable intellectual and social ends? Or do you think it simply promotes personal and sexual "confusion"?

4. How does life online challenge our assumptions about the meaning of trust and social ties, according to Turkle? In your view, should Beth continue to trust Martin in "RL" despite the fact that he engages in "Tiny sex" with women? Why or why not? How does virtual adultery differ from reading a pornographic novel? Does the widespread practice of identity swapping suggest that we are, in fact, losing contact with reality and the personal accountability that goes with it?

FURTHER EXPLORATIONS

1. To what extent does Turkle's research confirm or complicate Clifford Stoll's claim (p. 648) that the Internet isolates and dehumanizes frequent users? Would Turkle be likely to agree with Stoll that people who use the Internet lose valuable social skills?

2. How does Turkle's assessment of the nature of gender online support or complicate Ellen Ullman's view of the "boy engineer" culture associated with computing (p. 656)? Is there something particularly "boyish" about the kind of experimental freedom and identity swapping that Turkle describes among MUDders?

3. To what extent might it be possible to view the online gender swapping that Turkle describes in this selection as a practical enactment of the Turing gender imitation game, as described by Douglas Hofstadter (p. 719)? Does the fact that a man can successfully simulate a woman online "prove" that he understands what it means to be female at a deep level? If a middle-aged white man could pass as a twenty-year-old African American female online, would it mean that he grasps what it means to be a young black woman? If not, what might it mean?

4. To what extent does the definition of contemporary selfhood offered by Roy F. Baumeister (p. 320) challenge or support the notion of self that Turkle sees emerging from the Internet? Is it possible for the modern self to be both "sovereign" and fragmented or multiple?

5. Given her analysis of the role of empathy in the development of civic culture, how might Martha C. Nussbaum (p. 416) assess the social impact of virtual identity swapping? What difference, if any, do you see between learning to empathize with "others" through the experience of stories, plays, and novels, and the portrayal of "others" in chat rooms and MUDs online?

6. In view of his theory of narrative in the construction of personal identity (p. 292), how might Arnold M. Ludwig view the practice of online role playing? Would Ludwig be likely to see such identity swapping as a positive or negative option? Why?

ESSAY OPTIONS

1. Drawing on your own experiences and the ideas and experiences discussed by Sherry Turkle in this selection, Clifford Stoll in "Isolated by the Internet" (p. 648), and Ellen Ullman in "Out of Time: Reflections on the Programming Life" (p. 656), write an essay in which you assess the impact of electronic media on human relationships. How are inventions like the Internet changing the way we view ourselves in relation to others? How is electronic technology affecting our sense of community and connection?

2. Do additional research on the issue of fantasy games online as the basis for a formal report on the subject. What types of online role-playing games are currently most popular? What themes do they feature? What kinds of imaginative role playing do they encourage? How, in general, would you explain the appeal of these games? What intellectual or social "rewards" do they offer players? What "lessons" do such games convey about identity, human relations, gender, etc.? What effects do these imaginary worlds appear to have on those who participate in them on a regular basis?

Muscular Circuitry

CLAUDIA SPRINGER

Czech author Karel Čapek (1890–1938) was the first person in history to use the word *robot*. It made its debut in the play *R.U.R. (Rossum's Universal Robots)*, which Čapek wrote and produced in 1923. Following the standard Frankenstein plot line, *R.U.R.* tells the story of an industrialist who creates an army of mechanical workers, only to have them rebel against the inhuman treatment they receive from their human masters. Long before the invention of the microchip, the popular imagination was haunted by the specter of vengeful robots, androids, and cyborgs. In this selection from her *Electronic Eros: Bodies and Desire in the Postindustrial Age* (1996), Claudia Springer offers her own interpretation of some classic cyborg images. Springer's analysis of the cultural assumptions programmed into "hypermasculine" cinematic figures like the Terminator and Robocop invites you to consider what our fantasies about metallic bodies reveal about ourselves and to think about how these fantasies are changing as we get closer to the reality of machine intelligence. Springer (b. 1956) teaches English and film studies at Rhode Island College.

BEFORE READING

Working in groups, collectively draw a picture of a robot. Present these collaboratively created images in class and discuss where they come from and what they suggest about dominant cultural attitudes toward machine minds.

The whole world is men's bloody fantasies.
— ABHOR, A CYBORG[1]

R obocop and the Terminator have smashed their way into the public's awareness in a series of highly successful films. Their features have given concrete shape to the idea of human fusion with technology. Both are aggressively violent cyborgs that embody a fantasy of destructive force combined with invincibility. Although this hyperviolent figure is only one of many types of fictional cyborgs in circulation, it has become the dominant way for mainstream commercial films to represent the cyborg condition. While television, science-fiction literature, and comic books have explored diverse and imaginative ways to depict the fusion of humans and technological artifacts, mainstream films have privileged the violently masculinist figure. An analysis of invincible armored cyborg films reveals that the films and the cyborg bodies they put on display stage a conflict between different ways of thinking about sexual identity and gender.

Whereas the software-interfaced cyborg envisioned by scientist Hans Moravec° would make the human body obsolete once human consciousness

Hans Moravec: (b. 1948), American computer scientist and roboticist.

has been downloaded onto computer software, the mainstream films represent cyborgs as aggressive, bulging bodies.[2] The cyborg's physical prowess is heightened, not abandoned, and its strength is physical, not cerebral. What these cyborgs do best is kill. . . .

. . . RoboCop and the Terminator engage in relentless violence with their technologically fortified bodies. To some extent the phenomenon of the rampaging filmic cyborg suggests a residual fear of technology that found similar expression in older films like *Metropolis*.° Electronic technology's incredible capabilities certainly can evoke fear and awe, which can be translated in fictional representation into massive bodies that overpower human characters.

Nonetheless, fear of the computer's abilities does not entirely explain why films consistently associate cyborgs with violence. Significantly, muscle-bound cyborgs in films are informed by a tradition of muscular comic-book superheroes, and like these superheroes, their erotic appeal is in the promise of power they embody. Their heightened physicality culminates not in sexual climax but in acts of violence. Violence substitutes for sexual release. Film scholar Steven Neale has written that violence displaces male sexuality in films in response to a cultural taboo against a homoerotic gaze and that homophobia exerts a strong influence on cinematic techniques.[3] For example, close-up shots that caress the male body on screen encourage a homoerotic response from the male spectator. As Neale explains, however, the spectacle of a passive and desirable male body is typically undermined by a narrative that intervenes to make him the object or the perpetrator of violence, thereby justifying the camera's objectification of his body. The heightened physicality of cinematic cyborgs thus culminates not in sexual expression but in brute force.

The association between technology and violence is not unique to the 5 twentieth century. During the social upheavals of the nineteenth-century industrial revolution, when people's lives were radically transformed, widespread optimism that machines would bring progress was accompanied by anxiety about technology's potentially destructive powers. The fear evoked by machines was exacerbated by their sheer magnitude; they were often huge and loud, and they thrust, pumped, and turned with an aggressive persistence. Their power was palpable and visible.

Unlike industrial machinery and its forceful energy, electronic technology functions quietly and passively. Nevertheless, industrial-age metaphors for representing technology persist in the information age. For example, computers are compared on the basis of their "power," a term that used to refer to physical strength but now can connote a computer's calculating speed or memory. Thus, operations related to nonphysical computer functions are

Metropolis: Classic 1926 science-fiction film by German-American director Fritz Lang (1890–1976), featuring "Maria," a threatening female robot. (See frontispiece to this chapter, p. 640.)

discursively reconstituted to imply physical force. Our postmodern age is marked by discursive anachronisms that date from the exigencies of the industrial and resolutely patriarchal nineteenth century. Violent, forceful cyborg imagery participates in contemporary discourses that cling to nineteenth-century notions about technology, sexual difference, and gender roles in order to resist the transformations brought about by the new post-modern social order.

Mechanization has not always been conceived of as physically forceful. Historian Roger Hahn points out that from the ancient Greek period until the Renaissance, the uninformed public conceived of mechanization as concealed and mysterious.[4] Most people's understanding of machinery was based on seeing the mechanical automata that were often shaped like humans or animals and designed to amaze them by performing independently of human control. The mechanisms that controlled the automata were hidden from view, and artisans kept their designs a secret to enhance the notion that the figures were magical and mysterious.

During the Renaissance, according to Hahn, there was a shift in the concept of mechanization from internal to external and accessible. Mechanical devices were demystified once they were released from the possessive grip of secret societies. Texts that explained how machines worked, complete with precise illustrations, began to proliferate in the sixteenth century, making such devices comprehensible to all. According to Hahn, "The visual representation of machines forever stripped them of secret recesses and hidden forces."[5] At the same time, the new Renaissance philosophies of scientific inquiry replaced the earlier exaltation of the invisible with an emphasis on the externally visible. Scientists beginning with Bacon and Galileo° privileged theories that could be verified through experimentation rather than accepted on pure faith. As Hahn writes, "The tone of the new science was to displace the occult by the visible, the mysterious by the palpable."[6]

The concept of externally forceful machinery culminated in the industrial machinery of the nineteenth and early twentieth centuries. In accordance with the machine's new role as a worker, a new figure, the robot, replaced the automaton as the human being's mechanical double. After the term *robot* was introduced in a play titled *R.U.R.* (*"Rossum's Universal Robots"*), written by Czech playwright Karel Čapek in 1920,[7] robot imagery became a staple of early-twentieth-century science fiction, which usually maintained the Frankenstein theme enacted in *R.U.R.* by depicting robots as dangerous entities determined to overthrow humanity.[8]

More than a simple name change separated robots from automata. Automata belonged to an earlier time when mechanization was a wonderful and entertaining mystery; robots belonged to the age of factories and mills, when machines forcefully announced their powerful presence. Jean

10

Bacon and Galileo: Francis Bacon (1561–1626), English philosopher; Galileo Galilei (1564–1642), Italian astronomer and physicist.

Baudrillard° argues that "a whole world separates these two artificial beings," that the automaton is "the analogy of man," whereas the robot "is man's equivalent."[9]

> We shouldn't make any mistakes on this matter for reasons of "figurative" resemblance between robot and automaton. The latter is an interrogation upon nature, the mystery or the existence or nonexistence of the soul, the dilemma of appearance and being. It is like God: what's underneath it all, what's inside, what's in the back of it? . . . No such thing with the robot. The robot no longer interrogates appearance; its only truth is its mechanical efficacy.[10]

With the transition from automata to robots, the significance assigned to artificial beings underwent a change. Robots were no longer treated as charming mechanical novelties; rather, they evaluated on the basis of what they were capable of doing, either for humans or to humans.

In the late twentieth century machines have been replaced by systems dependent on intricate microelectronic circuitry. Our information age reintroduces a concept of technology as incomprehensible and hidden from view. Computer hardware contains microscopic parts concealed behind the computer screen, and for most people, how the system functions remains shrouded in mystery. Although there are no secret societies that invest computers with magical properties, computer hardware expertise is nevertheless confined to trained specialists, who often are themselves awed by the intricacy and hidden capacities of computers. According to Bruce Sterling:

> Computers are fearsome creations, redolent of mystery and power. Even to software engineers and hardware designers, computers are, in some deep and basic sense, hopelessly baffling. This is why commercial software is sold without any kind of real warranty, why computers are buggy, crashy, fluid, nonlinear and radically unreliable. Machines that perform millions of interactive operations per second are simply for too complex for any human brain to fully comprehend.[11]

Despite the concealed and mysterious intricacy of computers, cyborg imagery in the *RoboCop* and *Terminator* films relies on an external rather than an internal concept of mechanization. RoboCop and the Terminator, like robots, are distinguished by their large size and physical power, even though technology has become smaller and more passive since the industrial machines that inspired the idea of the robot. These cinematic cyborgs are aggressively corporeal, and as Mary Ann Doane tells us, "when technology intersects with the body in the realm of representation, the question of sexual difference is inevitably involved."[12]

Cyborg films are in fact preoccupied with sexual difference, and one of their sites of contestation is the figure of the cyborg, whose technologically

Jean Baudrillard: (b. 1929), French social philosopher.

produced form embodies metaphors of human sexuality: steely hard phallic strength is opposed to feminine fluidity. These particular metaphors, still prevalent today, derive from ways of thinking that became dominant in the late eighteenth century, when the notion of two distinct and opposite sexes was naturalized and taken for granted. Earlier, as Thomas Laqueur documents in his book *Making Sex*, people generally thought in terms of a one-sex model in which women's bodies were considered to be less fully developed versions of men's bodies, with genitals that were virtually identical to men's, only inverted rather than distended.[13] The one-sex system was vertical and hierarchical; women were thought of as less perfect than men but not altogether different from them. The different social roles assigned to men and women were not justified on the basis of clearcut biological difference prior to the late eighteenth century but instead were understood to be based on culturally defined gender categories. In fact, the body was not considered to be an entirely reliable indicator of a person's sex. Laqueur cites numerous stories that circulated before the eighteenth century about women whose bodies were transformed by the emergence of a penis; once the transformation had been verified by doctors, these women were allowed to change their names and become men.[14] Only after the social and political upheavals of the eighteenth century did the two-sex model triumph, and this change occurred not because of new knowledge about the human body but because of the requirements of the ascendant bourgeoisie and their newly industrializing societies.

In the two-sex model that still rules late-twentieth-century thinking, a woman's difference from men, and her supposed inferiority to them, is explained by reducing her to her body, specifically, her sexual organs, which are considered to be the opposite of men's. Women's genitals are described as hidden, internal, and inert, in contrast to what is described as the forceful and aggressive male penis. Women are thus associated with the interior spaces of the body, with the hidden, fluid, and fluctuating internal systems. (In the one-sex model, Laqueur shows, both men's and women's bodies were understood to be fluid-filled vessels.)[15] Men in the two-sex model, on the other hand, are associated with dry solidity and with hard physical strength.

Masculine and feminine stereotypes have long been used as metaphors for technology, and they are likely to persist as long as the two-sex system prevails. Aggressive, muscular cyborg imagery asserts the dominance of a phallic metaphor for technology. Phallic cyborgs constitute a contrast to the other, contradictory metaphor for contemporary electronic technology: the "feminized" computer with its concealed, passive, and internal workings. Feminine metaphors emphasize that microcircuitry is not physically forceful or massive. Miniaturization, concealment, and silence are its underlying principles. Moreover, computer users often experience a psychological union with their terminals that collapses ego boundaries. The intimacy and empathy that can result from fluid ego boundaries are conventionally associated with feminine subjectivity, which, compared to the male ego, is less dependent on Oedipal individuation.° It has recently become somewhat more acceptable in Western societies for men to exhibit so-called feminine traits, so that a fluid ego bound-ary is no longer thought of as an exclusively feminine characteristic. There are, however, patriarchal bastions of resistance to any human behavior that defies traditional gender stereotypes. The hyperviolent muscular cyborg in films is one such symbol of misogynistic resistance to change. He rampages across the screen as if to deny that late-twentieth-century technology no longer fits the forceful phallic model and that there is now a greater acceptance of human sexual diversity. . . .

Although the computer is the dominant technological paradigm for our age, it has not entirely displaced industrial machines. As J. David Bolter writes, "the computer leaves intact many older technologies, particularly the technologies of power, and yet it puts them in a new perspective. With the ap-pearance of a truly subtle machine like the computer, the old power machines (steam, gas, or rocket engines) lose something of their prestige."[16] With both electronic and industrial technologies present in our lives, we are seeing a con-flict between ways of conceptualizing technology in gendered terms: mascu-line metaphors oppose feminine metaphors. Andrew Ross exposes masculine metaphors when he analyzes the boy's sensibility that pervades cyberpunk fic-tion, which typically uses tough-guy jargon and imagery drawn from hard-boiled detective fiction to describe the human interface with technology.[17] Nicola Nixon also identifies a misogynistic base underlying cyberpunk's technology-laden futuristic dreams when she describes how cyberpunk spokes-men implicitly denigrate feminist science fiction of the 1970s by speaking of cyberpunk's reinvigoration of science fiction during the 1980s following a decade of decline.[18]

Counteracting popular culture's frequent emphasis on technological viril-ity, Donna Haraway° conceives of the cyborg as a potentially feminized and feminist figure, one that could make gender difference obsolete and liberate women from patriarchal inequality.[19] Once the cyborg has eliminated the boundary between humans and machines, other traditional hierarchical boundaries, such as the one between the sexes, could also dissolve. Haraway is joined by feminist theorists Avital Ronell[20] and Valie Export[21] in urging women to consider how technology might be used to restructure social rela-tions and notions of the self in feminist ways. They encourage women to re-ject the technophobic strain of feminism that associates women with the so-called natural world and condemns all technologies for being patriarchal tools

---

Oedipal individuation: According to Sigmund Freud's theory of psychoanalysis, young males develop a mature sense of individual identity and well-defined "ego boundaries" through a process of "Oedipal" conflict with a dominant father figure.

Donna Haraway: (b. 1944), American philosopher who argues in her 1985 essay "A Cyborg Manifesto: Science, Technology, and Socialist-Feminism in the Late Twentieth Century" that the cyborg embodies the transcendence of gender stereotypes and thus expresses an essentially fem-inist impulse.

of oppression. Haraway stresses the importance of developing an alternative to the politics of domination that controls the world's economic, racial, class, and gender systems. Despite its miniaturization, observes Haraway, electronic technology is currently used in insidiously powerful ways to subjugate workers and create increasingly destructive tools of war.[22] It is thus essential for women to appropriate and redefine technology according to feminist principles. Nineteenth-century social and economic relations have already been transformed in our postmodern era, and Haraway's "Manifesto" urges feminists to embrace the cyborg paradigm rather than allow a new masculine style of late-twentieth-century domination to prevail.

Cyborg films exist within our culture's larger discursive conflict over gendered metaphors for technology. The films sometimes betray signs of confusion when they try to depict a new electronic age using imagery from the industrial past. *The Terminator* reveals its mixed metaphors when it represents the threat that technology poses to human beings. As Constance Penley shows, it forges a link between contemporary household gadgets that tend to malfunction and future high tech that launches a full-scale revolt against humans.[23] In the film the precise nature of technology's danger to humans is identified as its intelligence but depicted as physical violence. Kyle Reese, a character in the film, explains that the war against humanity was masterminded by defense network computers that "got smart, a new order of intelligence," and decided to exterminate all humanity. Nevertheless, the threat is made manifest in the film by the figure of the Terminator, who relies on brute force to destroy humans. Even the depiction of the future shows not defense network computers but tanks, aircraft, and terminators that hunt and kill humans in an industrial wasteland of twisted steel.

The Terminator contains one sequence in particular that reveals how it rejects a feminized cyborg in favor of a hypermasculine one. The Terminator, a cyborg who has been created by his computer masters to travel back through time to 1984 to kill a young woman, Sarah Connor, arrives in 1984 folded on the ground in a fetal position, naked and vulnerable, as if newly born. His vulnerability increases when three punk youths laugh and sneer at his nakedness and brandish switchblades. With incredible force he hurls two of them through the air and enters another with his fist to pull out his heart. He penetrates the youth's body in a sexual way, laying claim to phallic mastery. When we next see him, he is wearing their leather and metal-studded clothing, and soon thereafter he obtains an arsenal of guns. No longer vulnerable, he is now fully armored in the trappings of aggressive masculinity.

The Terminator's nude entrance is repeated by the film's other time traveler, Kyle Reese. Vivian Sobchack makes the following point about their nudity: "Both the Terminator and Reese fall from above the frame of a dirty modern city, their nakedness a designation of their male sexual biology and their alien-ated status." Reese and the Terminator enter the film similarly, but, Sobchack writes, they represent contrasting versions of masculinity in crisis, especially in their styles of fatherhood: Reese is the warm, protective, paternal

20

figure, whereas the Terminator is the obsessive destroyer.[24] The film is one of many from the 1980s that stage the crisis of defining fatherhood amid the changes in family structure brought on by feminism.

In the sequel, *Terminator 2: Judgment Day* (Cameron 1991), the Terminator undergoes the same kind of transformation as in the first film. He arrives from the future stark naked in a womblike bubble. When he enters a tough country-and-western saloon, we observe from his point of view how everyone stares in disbelief at his penis. Only after the Terminator brutally attacks the saloon's patrons and clothes his naked body in a biker's gear does he earn their complete fear and respect. He leaves with the paraphernalia that guarantees his phallic authority: a Harley-Davidson Fat Boy motorcycle and a big gun. His equipment is external, displacing his penis with its symbolic equivalents, thus asserting an externally forceful masculine image of a technological human.

RoboCop also begins his existence in an inert manner appropriate to electronic technology: he is a computer. What we see from his point of view is his transformation into a masculine hulk. He is passive as he is worked on by the Security Concepts team that is creating him by fusing mechanical and electronic components with some remains of murdered police officer Alex J. Murphy. The first indication that RoboCop will become something other than a computer terminal is when his creators display a powerful robotic arm before attaching it to him. After he has been completed, we see that he has the exaggerated physique of a muscle man made of steel.

Fusion with the technological in *The Terminator* and *RoboCop* (Verhoeven 1987) is tantamount to stepping into a suit of armor. Both cyborgs are represented as invincible humans whose fortified bodies protect them from assaults that would destroy an ordinary human. The Terminator withstands gunfire, car and motorcycle crashes, a tank truck running over him, a fire that burns off all his skin, and an explosion that rips off his legs. Although finally destroyed when crushed in a hydraulic press, he is replaced by an identical terminator in *Terminator 2*. RoboCop also strides fearlessly into blazing gunfire and withstands multiple attacks. When he is disabled, and even destroyed, he knows that he can be reassembled. As he tells his human partner, Anne Lewis, when she is badly injured at the end of the film, "They'll fix you; they fix everything."

Unlike cyberpunk fiction's lean, vacillating male bodies, the Terminator and RoboCop display rock-solid masculinity. Their technological adornments serve to heighten, not diminish, their bodies' status as fortresses. Cyborg imagery in the *RoboCop* and *Terminator* films exemplifies the invincible armored killing machine theorized by Klaus Theweleit in *Male Fantasies*.[25] The proto-fascist soldiers Theweleit analyzes not only kill to externalize the dissolution of self they fear but also despise women, onto whom they project fluid ego boundaries and the temptation of sexual union, with its terrifying prospect of blurred boundaries. They take the two-sex model to an extreme, fortifying themselves with hard leather and metal body armor to assert their solidity against the threat of fluid women and to shore up their own fragile egos. Fascist armored-body imagery has appeared in many guises and has also been used to critique fascist ideology from within its own discourse, as Hal Foster shows in his analysis of the works of artists Max Ernst and Hans Bellmer.°26

For the Freikorps soldiers, invincibility was an unrealizable fantasy. Cyborgs like the Terminator and RoboCop realize the Freikorps fantasy in the realm of representation, making possible in fiction what can be only fantasized in fact. The Terminator methodically stalks his victim and feels no pain; as his adversary Kyle Reese tells Sarah Connor, "it can't be bargained with, it can't be reasoned with, it doesn't feel pity or remorse or fear and it absolutely will not stop, ever, until you are dead." RoboCop is also a brutal killer, even though his acts of violence are legitimized because he is a police officer fighting vicious criminals. When he is reprogrammed in *RoboCop 2* to apprehend criminals without killing them, he is ridiculously ineffective. The film celebrates his return to killing when he overcomes the restrictive program.

Theweleit argues that the protofascist fantasy of armored invincibility signifies a desire to ward off external threats of ego absorption and, simultaneously, ego dissolution from within. As if to illustrate the phenomenon, the film *Total Recall* (Verhoeven 1990) revolves around a fragmented subject, Doug Quaid, who suddenly learns that he may not be who he thinks he is and that his identity may be nothing more than an illusion created by an electronic implant in his head. (With a microchip in his head, he qualifies as a cyborg.) The lines between dream and reality, fact and fantasy, become blurred for Quaid as he struggles to discover his true identity—to create a coherent internal self—and to repel attackers who threaten him from all sides, with the most brutal attacks launched by the woman he thought was his wife. Quaid's psychological instability has no visual signifier, however; he is undeniably present and solid as a rock as played by Arnold Schwarzenegger, whose hypermasculine physique has become associated with cyborgs in the public imagination. By the end he has violently destroyed his attackers and heroically saved the human inhabitants of Mars from complete annihilation. Even his moment of doubt at the end, when he fears that all his exploits might have been a dream rather than reality, does not dispel the fantasy of omnipotent power that the film presents.

Doug Quaid, RoboCop, and the Terminator perpetuate and even exaggerate the anachronistic industrial-age metaphor of externally forceful masculine machinery, expressing nostalgia for a time when masculine superiority was taken for granted and an insecure man needed only to look at technology to find a metaphor for the power of phallic strength. Electronic technology no longer evokes the metaphor of externally visible musculature; instead, its bodily equivalents are the concealed and fluid internal systems. Moreover, in their interaction with humans, computers offer a radically new relationship, one

Max Ernst and Hans Bellmer: Max Ernst (1891–1976), German artist renowned for his surrealist paintings; Hans Bellmer (1902–1975), German artist, best known for photographs of female dolls posed in disturbing ways.

that no longer fortifies physical prowess. It is the miniaturization and stasis of electronic technology and the passivity of the human interaction with computers that these hypermasculine cyborgs resist.

In *Terminator 2* the two metaphors for technology, one solid and the other fluid, explicitly do battle, thereby implicitly contrasting the metaphors attached to male and female bodies in the two-sex model. The new, more advanced terminator, the T-1000, is smaller than Arnold Schwarzenegger's original model 101 and does not have his immense physical strength. Instead, the T-1000 has the ability to transform himself into a stream of silvery liquid, and he can fashion himself into any shape, squeeze through tiny openings, and absorb punches and projectiles by molding himself around them, leaving holes where he once was. He is the embodiment of "feminine" fluidity, and as such is a particularly frightening adversary for the 101, since he does not fight in conventionally masculine ways. More important, he represents the loss of bodily boundaries that the 101 maintains with layers of leather clothing, big guns, and motorcycles. The film gives its allegiance to the solid 101, who is now a benevolent paternal figure who has traveled back through time to protect Sarah Connor's son John from the T-1000, who is on a mission to kill John. The 101 emerges victorious, proving the superiority of his solid masculinity by throwing the T-1000 into a giant vat of molten steel. Nevertheless, even the 101 is vulnerable to feminine bodies of water that are sufficiently deep and hot: he sacrifices himself in the same vat of molten steel to ensure that his advanced technology from the future will not be used in the present to increase the destructive power of machines. In his analysis of how the battle between the two terminators evokes a conflict between the sexes, Mark Dery° writes that even while they die, the terminators display stereotypical male and female behavior: "In the movie's final moments, both Terminators are consumed in a vat of molten steel, where their mettle is revealed: The technetronic Teuton, Schwarzenegger, slips into the boiling goop with a chivalric wave of the hand worthy of a Wagnerian hero; the T-1000 squirms and shimmies, mouthing silent Edvard Munch–like screams in a most unmanly fashion."[27]

These cyborg films, however, do not always offer up a single unified reading in support of a violently masculine position. In fact, they generally present conflicting tendencies, with narratives that often privilege strong and autonomous women characters. What results is a clash of protofascist masculine imagery with feminist ideals, often in the same films. *RoboCop* presents a tough, resilient woman character, Anne Lewis, who was policeman Alex J. Murphy's partner and becomes RoboCop's sole ally. *The Terminator* pits the Terminator against Sarah Conner, an unassuming college student and waitress who becomes tremendously resilient and resourceful and finally triumphs when she single-handedly destroys the Terminator. Although her role in the future described by Kyle Reese consists of motherhood, which resonates in

Mark Dery: (b. 1959), American journalist.

the film with patriarchal Christian reverence (Sarah Connor is destined to give birth to a son, John, who will become humanity's savior by leading a successful revolt against the tyrannical machines), she is fated to be not a traditional mother but a militaristic one who trains her son to become a skilled fighter and leader. Indeed, in *Terminator 2* Sarah Connor has become a hardened killer, closer in spirit to a machine than to the traditional concept of a nurturing mother. Her strength and lean, muscular physique can be appealing as a feminist alternative to helpless Hollywood women characters, but they also represent a misogynistic rejection of all things feminine. As Mark Dery writes, "All that flabby femininity has been flensed away like so much blubber."[28] . . .

Sexuality is feared by the protofascist soldier not only because it signifies loss of personal boundaries, writes Theweleit, but also because sexuality evokes the creation of life, and the soldier is bent on destroying all signs of life before they can destroy him. According to Theweleit, pregnant women are treated with particular revulsion in the soldiers' rhetoric. Indeed, cyborgs in films are often determined to prevent birth. In *Hardware* the cyborg that kills all the lifeforms it encounters is a secret weapon in the government's birth control program. As film scholar Cynthia Fuchs writes, "The film charts the usurpation of reproductive processes by ultramilitary technology and governmental genocide."[29] The Terminator, likewise, has been programmed to travel back through time to prevent the birth of John Connor.

 Creation versus destruction of life is not only a central thematic concern but also a site of dispute in cyborg texts. The ability to engender life is divided between men and women and between humans and technology. Women are typically associated with biological reproduction, whereas men are involved in technological creation. Preoccupation with technology functions to replace femininity and sexuality in many science-fiction films. In an essay entitled "The Virginity of Astronauts" Vivian Sobchack writes that the science-fiction film genre's "primary and unconscious—or subtextual—thematic problem" centers on "the male desire to break free from biological dependence on the female as Mother and Other, and to mark the male self as separate and autonomous." Referring to the genre's male astronauts, she writes, "As if in training for the big game, they have rejected their biology and sexuality—pushed it from their minds and bodies to concentrate on the technology required to penetrate and impregnate not a woman, but the universe." Sobchack shows that although science-fiction films feature chaste technocratic astronauts and banish women to the margins (that is, if they are not covered in asexual spacesuits that obliterate signs of femininity), the films are rife with displaced and condensed references to sex and biological reproduction. Aliens, machines, and mutants become the creepy, fecund signifiers of sexuality and procreation.[30] . . .

The ambiguities and contradictions surrounding the issues of sexual difference and reproduction/destruction are part of what makes these films compelling. The films assert the invincibility of patriarchal power and simultaneously show evidence that this power is crumbling. Even the figure of the aggressive male cyborg contains within it its own undoing, for its masculine strength exists at the expense of its human identity, and its artificial components, as is the case with all technology, have no sex. Sexual identity in the films transcends the human body and becomes attached to technology, but it also threatens to disappear if scrutinized too closely. Contradictions abound, and once they have been set in motion, even narrative closure cannot resolve them.

Notes

1. Kathy Acker, *Empire of the Senseless* (New York: Grove, 1988), 210.
2. Hans Moravec, *Mind Children: The Future of Robot and Human Intelligence* (Cambridge, Mass.: Harvard University Press, 1988).
3. Steven Neale, "Masculinity as Spectacle: Reflections on Men and Mainstream Cinema," *Screen* 24, no. 6 (1983): 37.
4. Roger Hahn, "The Meaning of the Mechanistic Age," in *The Boundaries of Humanity: Humans, Animals, Machines,* ed. James J. Sheehan and Morton Sosna, 142–157 (Berkeley: University of California Press, 1991), 145.
5. Ibid., 146.
6. Ibid., 147.
7. Karel Čapek, *R.U.R.* (London: Oxford University Press, 1964 [1920]).
8. Isaac Asimov and Karen A. Frenkel, *Robots: Machines in Man's Image* (New York: Harmony, 1985), 12.
9. Jean Baudrillard, *Simulations,* trans. Paul Foss, Paul Patton, and Philip Beitchman (New York: Semiotext(e), 1983), 92–93.
10. Ibid., 93–94.
11. Bruce Sterling, "CATscan: Cyber-Superstition," *Science Fiction Eye* 8 (winter 1991): 11–12; 11.
12. Mary Ann Doane, "Technophilia: Technology, Representation, and the Feminine," in *Body/Politics: Women and the Discourses of Science,* ed. Mary Jacobus, Evelyn Fox Keller, and Sally Shuttleworth, 163–176 (New York: Routledge, 1990), 163.
13. Thomas Laqueur, *Making Sex: Body and Gender from the Greeks to Freud* (Cambridge, Mass.: Harvard University Press, 1990).
14. Ibid., 126–127.
15. Ibid., 35–43.
16. J. David Bolter, *Turing's Man: Western Culture in the Computer Age* (Chapel Hill: University of North Carolina Press, 1984), 8.
17. Andrew Ross, *Strange Weather: Culture, Science and Technology in the Age of Limits* (New York: Verso, 1991), 137–167.
18. Nicola Nixon, "Cyberpunk: Preparing the Ground for Revolution or Keeping the Boys Satisfied?" *Science-Fiction Studies* 57 (July 1992): 219–235.
19. Donna Haraway, "A Manifesto for Cyborgs: Science, Technology, and Socialist Feminism in the 1980s," *Socialist Review* 80 (1985): 65–107; reprinted in Haraway, *Simians, Cyborgs, and Women: The Reinvention of Nature* (New York: Routledge, 1991), 149–181.

20. Avital Ronell, interview by Andrea Juno, in *Angry Women*, ed. Andrea Juno and V. Vale, 127–153 (San Francisco: Re/Search, 1991).

21. Valie Export, "The Real and Its Double: The Body," *Discourse* 11, no. 1 (fall/winter 1988–1989): 3–27.

22. Haraway, "Manifesto," 70.

23. Penley, "Time Travel," 124.

24. Vivian Sobchack, "Child/Alien/Father: Patriarchal Crisis and Generic Exchange," in *Close Encounters: Film, Feminism, and Science Fiction*, ed. Constance Penley et al., 3–30 (Minneapolis: University of Minnesota Press, 1991), 23.

25. Klaus Theweleit, *Male Fantasies*, 2 vols. (vol. 1, *Women, Floods, Bodies, History*, trans. Stephen Conway [Minneapolis: University of Minnesota Press, 1987]; vol. 2, *Psychoanalyzing the White Terror*, trans. Erica Carter and Chris Turner [Minneapolis: University of Minnesota Press, 1989]).

26. Hal Foster, "Armor Fou," *October* 56 (spring 1991): 65–97.

27. Mark Dery, "Cyborging the Body Politic," *Mondo 2000* 6 (1992): 103.

28. Ibid., 102.

29. Cynthia J. Fuchs, "'Death Is Irrelevant': Cyborgs, Reproduction, and the Future of Male Hysteria," *Genders* 18 (Winter 1993): 126.

30. Vivian Sobchack, "The Virginity of Astronauts," in *Shadows of the Magic Lamp: Fantasy and Science Fiction in Film*, ed. George Slusser and Eric S. Rabkin, 41–57 (Carbondale: Southern Illinois University Press, 1985), 47–48.

EXPLORING THE TEXT

1. How have attitudes toward machines and technology changed, according to Springer, since the Middle Ages? What cultural forces and ideas shaped the image of the robot as it emerged at the beginning of the twentieth century? What tensions exist, in Springer's view, between dominant cultural conceptions of the robot and the computer?

2. How have gender roles affected the way cyborgs are portrayed in the mass media? Why, according to Springer, have cyborgs become so commonly identified with hypermasculine imagery and hyperviolent behavior? What fears or anxieties is this pose meant to compensate for?

3. To what extent would you agree that the worlds depicted in cyborg and science-fiction films "represent a misogynistic rejection of all things feminine"? How accurately does this claim apply to films that have appeared since the *Terminator* and *RoboCop* series that Springer discusses in this selection?

FURTHER EXPLORATIONS

1. As a class, test Springer's gendered reading of cyborg imagery by viewing one or more recent films or television shows featuring cybernetic heroes or heroines. Do recent depictions of robots, androids, and cyborgs continue to reinforce the gender stereotypes that Springer associates with figures like the Terminator?

2. Using William Gibson's "Johnny Mnemonic" as an example (p. 703), test Springer's claims about cyberpunk depictions of gender roles and technology. To what extent does cyberpunk fiction challenge or confirm the gendered reading of

technology that Springer associates with mainstream movies like the *Terminator* series?

3. Compare the ultramasculine concept of the self that Springer associates with cyberheroes on screen with the notion of selfhood that Sherry Turkle discovers in her travels through cyberspace on the Internet (p. 675). Would it be fair to say that the "selves" that Turkle describes emerging on the Net for both men and women are all essentially "feminine"? Or is the Net helping to erode all traditional gender boundaries?

4. How do the depictions of female identity offered by Roy F. Baumestier (p. 320), Deborah Blum (p. 453), and/or Mary Catherine Bateson (p. 337) support or complicate Springer's view of "femininity"? To what extent do recent depictions of women in science-fiction films, television shows, and comic books reflect real cultural changes in attitudes toward gender?

5. View Fritz Lang's classic 1926 silent film *Metropolis* to assess it as an example of early attitudes toward machine minds in popular culture. How are machines and human/machine relationships portrayed in Lang's film? Why do you think Lang chose to depict the demonic robot in this movie as a woman?

6. Read Donna Haraway's "Cyborg Manifesto" and discuss her assertion that women must redefine technology according to feminist principles. Do you see any evidence that technology and "high-tech" culture are, in fact, becoming more "female" than "male"?

ESSAY OPTIONS

1. Assemble a multimedia report, either as text or hypertext, that traces the history of the robot as it has been portrayed in the mass media over the past century. How were cybernetic minds depicted in the media before the invention of computers? In what ways, if any, have portrayals of cyborgs, robots, and androids evolved since the advent of the electronic age? What do recent portrayals suggest about emerging attitudes toward high technology?

2. Using *Further Explorations* question number 4 as a point of departure and supplementing your current knowledge of mass media with additional research, write a paper exploring the changing role of women in science-fiction literature, television shows, or film. What evidence, if any, do you see to suggest that the "nostalgia" for traditional gender roles that Springer sees in science fiction is giving way to new ways of thinking about women and technology?

Johnny Mnemonic

WILLIAM GIBSON

When Geroges Melies launched the first cinematic rocket in his celebrated *A Trip to the Moon* back in 1902, few people seriously believed that a human being would ever actually walk across the lunar surface. Fantasy always anticipates the future: the dreams of novelists, painters, and filmmakers stretch imagination beyond the limits of mere possibility to lay the foundation for what will eventually become human reality. At the turn of the twentieth century, artists dreamed of space travel; today, they dream nightmare visions of a future populated by creatures that blur the distinction between "meat" and machine minds. In the dark world of cyberpunk novelists like William Gibson (b. 1948), human beings as we know them have been replaced by drug-guzzling androids and shape-shifting "techs" with souped-up nervous systems and brains full of mechanical implants. The inventor of the concept of "cyberspace," Gibson almost single-handedly created the genre of cyberpunk fiction in works like *Neuromancer* (1984), *Mona Lisa Overdrive* (1988), *Virtual Light* (1993), *Idoru* (1996), and *All Tomorrow's Parties* (1999). Considered a cyberpunk classic, "Johnny Mnemonic" first appeared in *OMNI* magazine in 1981 and was adapted to the screen by artist-director Robert Longo in collaboration with Gibson in 1995. Although the film version differs significantly from the original story, both offer striking examples of the techno-fantasies of the cyberpunk genre.

BEFORE READING

Working in small groups, compare notes on your knowledge of cyberpunk fiction and film. What is the world of cyberpunk fantasy like? What examples of cyberpunk film or fiction are you familiar with? What are the standard characteristics of cyberpunk heroes?

I put the shotgun in an Adidas bag and padded it out with four pairs of tennis socks, not my style at all, but that was what I was aiming for: If they think you're crude, go technical; if they think you're technical, go crude. I'm a very technical boy. So I decided to get as crude as possible. These days, though, you have to be pretty technical before you can even aspire to crudeness. I'd had to turn both these twelve-gauge shells from brass stock, on a lathe, and then load them myself; I'd had to dig up an old microfiche with instructions for hand-loading cartridges; I'd had to build a lever-action press to seat the primers — all very tricky. But I knew they'd work.

The meet was set for the Drome at 2300, but I rode the tube three stops past the closest platform and walked back. Immaculate procedure.

I checked myself out in the chrome siding of a coffee kiosk, your basic sharpfaced Caucasoid with a ruff of stiff, dark hair. The girls at Under the Knife were big on Sony Mao,° and it was getting harder to keep them from

Sony Mao: The name of a fictional celebrity, which, in typical cyberpunk fashion, links the names of the Sony electronics corporation and Mao Zedong, leader of the People's Republic of China from 1949 to 1976.

adding the chic suggestion of epicanthic folds. It probably wouldn't fool Ralfi Face, but it might get me next to his table.

The Drome is a single narrow space with a bar down one side and tables along the other, thick with pimps and handlers and an arcane array of dealers. The Magnetic Dog Sisters were on the door that night, and I didn't relish trying to get out past them if things didn't work out. They were two meters tall and thin as greyhounds. One was black and the other white, but aside from that they were as nearly identical as cosmetic surgery could make them. They'd been lovers for years and were bad news in a tussle. I was never quite sure which one had originally been male.

Ralfi was sitting at his usual table. Owing me a lot of money. I had hun-   5
dreds of megabytes stashed in my head on an idiot/savant basis,° information I had no conscious access to. Ralfi had left it there. He hadn't, however, come back for it. Only Ralfi could retrieve the data, with a code phrase of his own invention. I'm not cheap to begin with, but my overtime on storage is astronomical. And Ralfi had been very scarce.

Then I'd heard that Ralfi Face wanted to put out a contract on me. So I'd arranged to meet him in the Drome, but I'd arranged it as Edward Bax, clandestine importer, late of Rio and Peking.

The Drome stank of biz, a metallic tang of nervous tension. Muscle-boys scattered through the crowd were flexing stock parts at one another and trying on thin, cold grins, some of them so lost under superstructures of muscle graft that their outlines weren't really human.

Pardon me. Pardon me, friends. Just Eddie Bax here, Fast Eddie the Importer, with his professionally nondescript gym bag, and please ignore this slit, just wide enough to admit his right hand.

Ralfi wasn't alone. Eighty kilos of blond California beef perched alertly in the chair next to his, martial arts written all over him.

Fast Eddie Bax was in the chair opposite them before the beef's hands   10
were off the table. "You black belt?" I asked eagerly. He nodded, blue eyes running an automatic scanning pattern between my eyes and my hands. "Me, too," I said. "Got mine here in the bag." And I shoved my hand through the slit and thumbed the safety off. Click. "Double twelve-gauge with the triggers wired together."

"That's a gun," Ralfi said, putting a plump, restraining hand on his boy's taut blue nylon chest. "Johnny has an antique firearm in his bag." So much for Edward Bax.

I guess he'd always been Ralfi Something or Other, but he owed his acquired surname to a singular vanity. Built something like an overripe pear, he'd worn the once-famous face of Christian White for twenty years — Christian White of the Aryan Reggae Band, Sony Mao to his generation, and final champion of race rock. I'm a whiz at trivia.

---

on an idiot/savant basis: Refers to the "savant syndrome," a form of autism that links low general intelligence with genius levels of artistic or intellectual performance.

Christian White: classic pop face with a singer's high-definition muscles, chiseled cheekbones. Angelic in one light, handsomely depraved in another. But Ralfi's eyes lived behind that face, and they were small and cold and black.

"Please," he said, "let's work this out like businessmen." His voice was marked by a horrible prehensile sincerity, and the corners of his beautiful Christian White mouth were always wet. "Lewis here," nodding in the beef-boy's direction, "is a meatball." Lewis took this impassively, looking like something built from a kit. "You aren't a meatball, Johnny."

"Sure I am, Ralfi, a nice meatball chock-full of implants where you can store your dirty laundry while you go off shopping for people to kill me. From my end of this bag, Ralfi, it looks like you've got some explaining to do."

"It's this last batch of product, Johnny." He sighed deeply. "In my role as broker—"

"Fence," I corrected.

"As broker, I'm usually very careful as to sources."

"You buy only from those who steal the best. Got it."

He sighed again. "I try," he said wearily, "not to buy from fools. This time, I'm afraid, I've done that." Third sigh was the cue for Lewis to trigger the neural disruptor they'd taped under my side of the table.

I put everything I had into curling the index finger of my right hand, but I no longer seemed to be connected to it. I could feel the metal of the gun and the foampad tape I'd wrapped around the stubby grip, but my hands were cool wax, distant and inert. I was hoping Lewis was a true meatball, thick enough to go for the gym bag and snag my rigid trigger finger, but he wasn't.

"We've been very worried about you, Johnny. Very worried. You see, that's Yakuza° property you have there. A fool took it from them, Johnny. A dead fool."

Lewis giggled.

It all made sense then, an ugly kind of sense, like bags of wet sand settling around my head. Killing wasn't Ralfi's style. Lewis wasn't even Ralfi's style. But he'd got himself stuck between the Sons of the Neon Chrysanthemum° and something that belonged to them—or, more likely, something of theirs that belonged to someone else. Ralfi, of course, could use the code phrase to throw me into idiot/savant, and I'd spill their hot program without remembering a single quarter tone. For a fence like Ralfi, that would ordinarily have been enough. But not for the Yakuza. The Yakuza would know about Squids, for one thing, and they wouldn't want to worry about one lifting those dim and permanent traces of their program out of my head. I didn't know very much about Squids, but I'd heard stories, and I made it a point never to repeat them to my clients. No, the Yakuza wouldn't like that; it looked too much like evidence. They hadn't got where they were by leaving evidence around. Or alive.

Yakuza: A Japanese organized crime syndicate.
the Sons of the Neon Chrysanthemum: Gibson's fictional name for his futuristic Yakuza.

Lewis was grinning. I think he was visualizing a point just behind my fore-   25
head and imagining how he could get there the hard way.

"Hey," said a low voice, feminine, from somewhere behind my right
shoulder, "you cowboys sure aren't having too lively a time."

"Pack it, bitch," Lewis said, his tanned face very still. Ralfi looked blank.

"Lighten up. You want to buy some good free base?" She pulled up a chair
and quickly sat before either of them could stop her. She was barely inside my
fixed field of vision, a thin girl with mirrored glasses, her dark hair cut in a
rough shag. She wore black leather, open over a T-shirt slashed diagonally with
stripes of red and black. "Eight thou a gram weight."

Lewis snorted his exasperation and tried to slap her out of the chair.
Somehow he didn't quite connect, and her hand came up and seemed to
brush his wrist as it passed. Bright blood sprayed the table. He was clutching
his wrist white-knuckle tight, blood trickling from between his fingers.

But hadn't her hand been empty?   30

He was going to need a tendon stapler. He stood up carefully, without
bothering to push his chair back. The chair toppled backward, and he stepped
out of my line of sight without a word.

"He better get a medic to look at that," she said. "That's a nasty cut."

"You have no idea," said Ralfi, suddenly sounding very tired, "the depths
of shit you have just gotten yourself into."

"No kidding? Mystery. I get real excited by mysteries. Like why your
friend here's so quiet. Frozen, like. Or what this thing here is for," and she
held up the little control unit that she'd somehow taken from Lewis. Ralfi
looked ill.

"You, ah, want maybe a quarter-million to give me that and take a walk?"   35
A fat hand came up to stroke his pale, lean face nervously.

"What I want," she said, snapping her fingers so that the unit spun and
glittered, "is work. A job. Your boy hurt his wrist. But a quarter'll do for a retainer."

Ralfi let his breath out explosively and began to laugh, exposing teeth that
hadn't been kept up to the Christian White standard. Then she turned the disruptor off.

"Two million," I said.

"My kind of man," she said, and laughed. "What's in the bag?"

"A shotgun."

"Crude." It might have been a compliment.   40

Ralfi said nothing at all.

"Name's Millions. Molly Millions. You want to get out of here, boss?
People are starting to stare." She stood up. She was wearing leather jeans the
color of dried blood.

And I saw for the first time that the mirrored lenses were surgical inlays,
the silver rising smoothly from her high cheekbones, sealing her eyes in their
sockets. I saw my new face twinned there.

"I'm Johnny," I said. "We're taking Mr. Face with us."   45

He was outside, waiting. Looking like your standard tourist tech, in plastic zoris and a silly Hawaiian shirt printed with blowups of his firm's most popular microprocessor; a mild little guy, the kind most likely to wind up drunk on sake in a bar that puts out miniature rice crackers with seaweed garnish. He looked like the kind who sing the corporate anthem and cry, who shake hands endlessly with the bartender. And the pimps and the dealers would leave him alone, pegging him as innately conservative. Not up for much, and careful with his credit when he was.

The way I figured it later, they must have amputated part of his left thumb, somewhere behind the first joint, replacing it with a prosthetic tip, and cored the stump, fitting it with a spool and socket molded from one of the Ono-Sendai diamond analogs. Then they'd carefully wound the spool with three meters of monomolecular filament.

Molly got into some kind of exchange with the Magnetic Dog Sisters, giving me a chance to usher Ralfi through the door with the gym bag pressed lightly against the base of his spine. She seemed to know them. I heard the black one laugh.

I glanced up, out of some passing reflex, maybe because I've never got used to it, to the soaring arcs of light and the shadows of the geodesics above them. Maybe that saved me.

Ralfi kept walking, but I don't think he was trying to escape. I think he'd already given up. Probably he already had an idea of what we were up against.   50

I looked back down in time to see him explode.

Playback on full recall shows Ralfi stepping forward as the little tech sidles out of nowhere, smiling. Just a suggestion of a bow, and his left thumb falls off. It's a conjuring trick. The thumb hangs suspended. Mirrors? Wires? And Ralfi stops, his back to us, dark crescents of sweat under the armpits of his pale summer suit. He knows. He must have known. And then the joke-shop thumbtip, heavy as lead, arcs out in a lightning yo-yo trick, and the invisible thread connecting it to the killer's hand passes laterally through Ralfi's skull, just above his eyebrows, whips up, and descends, slicing the pear-shaped torso diagonally from shoulder to rib cage. Cuts so fine that no blood flows until synapses misfire and the first tremors surrender the body to gravity.

Ralfi tumbled apart in a pink cloud of fluids, the three mismatched sections rolling forward onto the tiled pavement. In total silence.

I brought the gym bag up, and my hand convulsed. The recoil nearly broke my wrist.

It must have been raining; ribbons of water cascaded from a ruptured geodesic   55
and spattered on the tile behind us. We crouched in the narrow gap between a surgical boutique and an antique shop. She'd just edged one mirrored eye around the corner to report a single Volks module in front of the Drome, red lights flashing. They were sweeping Ralfi up. Asking questions.

I was covered in scorched white fluff. The tennis socks. The gym bag was a ragged plastic cuff around my wrist. "I don't see how the hell I missed him."

"'Cause he's fast, so fast." She hugged her knees and rocked back and forth on her bootheels. "His nervous system's jacked up. He's factory custom." She grinned and gave a little squeal of delight. "I'm gonna get that boy. Tonight. He's the best, number one, top dollar, state of the art."

"What you're going to get, for this boy's two million, is my ass out of here. Your boyfriend back there was mostly grown in a vat in Chiba City.° He's a Yakuza assassin."

"Chiba. Yeah. See, Molly's been Chiba, too." And she showed me her hands, fingers slightly spread. Her fingers were slender, tapered, very white against the polished burgundy nails. Ten blades snicked straight out from their recesses beneath her nails, each one a narrow, double-edged scalpel in pale blue steel.

I'd never spent much time in Nighttown. Nobody there had anything to pay   60
me to remember, and most of them had a lot they paid regularly to forget. Generations of sharpshooters had chipped away at the neon until the maintenance crews gave up. Even at noon the arcs were soot-black against faintest pearl.

Where do you go when the world's wealthiest criminal order is feeling for you with calm, distant fingers? Where do you hide from the Yakuza, so powerful that it owns comsats° and at least three shuttles? The Yakuza is a true multinational, like ITT and Ono-Sendai.° Fifty years before I was born the Yakuza had already absorbed the Triads, the Mafia, the Union Corse.

Molly had an answer: you hide in the Pit, in the lowest circle, where any outside influence generates swift, concentric ripples of raw menace. You hide in Nighttown. Better yet, you hide *above* Nighttown, because the Pit's inverted, and the bottom of its bowl touches the sky, the sky that Nighttown never sees, sweating under its own firmament of acrylic resin, up where the Lo Teks crouch in the dark like gargoyles, black-market cigarettes dangling from their lips.

She had another answer, too.

"So you're locked up good and tight, Johnny-san? No way to get that program without the password?" She led me into the shadows that waited beyond the bright tube platform. The concrete walls were overlaid with graffiti, years of them twisting into a single metascrawl of rage and frustration.

"The stored data are fed in through a modified series of microsurgical   65
contra-autism prostheses." I reeled off a numb version of my standard sales pitch. "Client's code is stored in a special chip; barring Squids, which we in the trade don't like to talk about, there's no way to recover your phrase. Can't drug it out, cut it out, torture it. I don't *know* it, never did."

Chiba City: In reality, a Tokyo suburb known for its recycling industry; in Gibson's fiction, an underworld city famous for cybernetic surgery.

comsats: Communication satellites.

ITT and Ono-Sendai: Names of fictional corporations.

"Squids? Crawly things with arms?" We emerged into a deserted street market. Shadowy figures watched us from across a makeshift square littered with fish heads and rotting fruit.

"Superconducting quantum interference detectors. Used them in the war to find submarines, suss out enemy cyber systems."

"Yeah? Navy stuff? From the war? Squid'll read that chip of yours?" She'd stopped walking, and I felt her eyes on me behind those twin mirrors.

"Even the primitive models could measure a magnetic field a billionth the strength of geomagnetic force; it's like pulling a whisper out of a cheering stadium."

"Cops can do that already, with parabolic microphones and lasers."   70

"But your data's still secure." Pride in profession. "No government'll let their cops have Squids, not even the security heavies. Too much chance of interdepartmental funnies; they're too likely to watergate you."

"Navy stuff," she said, and her grin gleamed in the shadows. "Navy stuff. I got a friend down here who was in the navy, name's Jones. I think you'd better meet him. He's a junkie, though. So we'll have to take him something."

"A junkie?"

"A dolphin."

He was more than a dolphin, but from another dolphin's point of view he   75
might have seemed like something less. I watched him swirling sluggishly in his galvanized tank. Water slopped over the side, wetting my shoes. He was surplus from the last war. A cyborg.

He rose out of the water, showing us the crusted plates along his sides, a kind of visual pun, his grace nearly lost under articulated armor, clumsy and prehistoric. Twin deformities on either side of his skull had been engineered to house sensor units. Silver lesions gleamed on exposed sections of his gray-white hide.

Molly whistled. Jones thrashed his tail, and more water cascaded down the side of the tank.

"What is this place?" I peered at vague shapes in the dark, rusting chain link and things under tarps. Above the tank hung a clumsy wooden framework, crossed and recrossed by rows of dusty Christmas lights.

"Funland. Zoo and carnival rides. 'Talk with the War Whale.' All that. Some whale Jones is. . . ."

Jones reared again and fixed me with a sad and ancient eye.   80

"How's he talk?" Suddenly I was anxious to go.

"That's the catch. Say 'hi,' Jones."

And all the bulbs lit simultaneously. They were flashing red, white, and blue.

★ ★ ★

RWBRWBRWB
RWBRWBRWB

```
RWBRWBRWB
RWBRWBRWB
RWBRWBRWB
```

"Good with symbols, see, but the code's restricted. In the navy they had him wired into an audiovisual display." She drew the narrow package from a jacket pocket. "Pure shit, Jones. Want it?" He froze in the water and started to sink. I felt a strange panic, remembering that he wasn't a fish, that he could drown. "We want the key to Johnny's bank, Jones. We want it fast."

The lights flickered, died.

"Go for it, Jones!"   85

```
        B
BBBBBBBBB
        B
        B
        B
```

Blue bulbs, cruciform.
Darkness.
"Pure! It's *clean*. Come on, Jones."

```
WWWWWWWWW
WWWWWWWWW
WWWWWWWWW
WWWWWWWWW
WWWWWWWWW
```

White sodium glare washed her features, stark monochrome, shadows cleaving from her cheekbones.

★ ★ ★

```
R    RRRRR
R    R
RRRRRRRR
        R    R
RRRRR    R
```

The arms of the red swastika were twisted in her silver glasses. "Give it to   90
him," I said. "We've got it."

Ralfi Face. No imagination.

Jones heaved half his armored bulk over the edge of his tank, and I thought the metal would give way. Molly stabbed him overhand with the Syrette, driving the needle between two plates. Propellant hissed. Patterns of light exploded, spasming across the frame and then fading to black.

We left him drifting, rolling languorously in the dark water. Maybe he was dreaming of his war in the Pacific, of the cyber mines he'd swept, nosing gently into their circuitry with the Squid he'd used to pick Ralfi's pathetic password from the chip buried in my head.

"I can see them slipping up when he was demobbed, letting him out of the navy with that gear intact, but how does a cybernetic dolphin get wired to smack?"

"The war," she said. "They all were. Navy did it. How else you get 'em working for you?"

"I'm not sure this profiles as good business," the pirate said, angling for better money. "Target specs on a comsat that isn't in the book—"

"Waste my time and you won't profile at all," said Molly, leaning across his scarred plastic desk to prod him with her forefinger.

"So maybe you want to buy your microwaves somewhere else?" He was a tough kid, behind his Mao-job. A Nighttowner by birth, probably.

Her hand blurred down the front of his jacket, completely severing a lapel without even rumpling the fabric.

"So we got a deal or not?"

"Deal," he said, staring at his ruined lapel with what he must have hoped was only polite interest. "Deal."

While I checked the two recorders we'd bought, she extracted the slip of paper I'd given her from the zippered wrist pocket of her jacket. She unfolded it and read silently, moving her lips. She shrugged. "This is it?"

"Shoot," I said, punching the RECORD studs of the two decks simultaneously.

"Christian White," she recited, "and his Aryan Reggae Band."

Faithful Ralfi, a fan to his dying day.

Transition to idiot/savant mode is always less abrupt than I expect it to be. The pirate broadcaster's front was a failing travel agency in a pastel cube that boasted a desk, three chairs, and a faded poster of a Swiss orbital spa. A pair of toy birds with blown-glass bodies and tin legs were sipping monotonously from a Styrofoam cup of water on a ledge beside Molly's shoulder. As I phased into mode, they accelerated gradually until their Day-Glo-feathered crowns became solid arcs of color. The LEDs that told seconds on the plastic wall clock had become meaningless pulsing grids, and Molly and the Mao-faced boy grew hazy, their arms blurring occasionally in insect-quick ghosts of gesture. And then it all faded to cool gray static and an endless tone poem in an artificial language.

I sat and sang dead Ralfi's stolen program for three hours.

The mall runs forty kilometers from end to end, a ragged overlap of Fuller domes° roofing what was once a suburban artery. If they turn off the arcs on

---

Fuller domes: R. Buckminster Fuller (1895–1983), American engineer whose inventions include the architectural geodesic dome.

a clear day, a gray approximation of sunlight filters through layers of acrylic, a view like the prison sketches of Giovanni Piranesi.° The three southernmost kilometers roof Nighttown. Nighttown pays no taxes, no utilities. The neon arcs are dead, and the geodesics have been smoked black by decades of cooking fires. In the nearly total darkness of a Nighttown noon, who notices a few dozen mad children lost in the rafters?

We'd been climbing for two hours, up concrete stairs and steel ladders with perforated rungs, past abandoned gantries and dust-covered tools. We'd started in what looked like a disused maintenance yard, stacked with triangular roofing segments. Everything there had been covered with that same uniform layer of spraybomb graffiti: gang names, initials, dates back to the turn of the century. The graffiti followed us up, gradually thinning until a single name was repeated at intervals. LO TEK. In dripping black capitals.

"Who's Lo Tek?"   110

"Not us, boss." She climbed a shivering aluminum ladder and vanished through a hole in a sheet of corrugated plastic. "'Low technique, low technology.'" The plastic muffled her voice. I followed her up, nursing my aching wrist. "Lo Teks, they'd think that shotgun trick of yours was effete."

An hour later I dragged myself up through another hole, this one sawed crookedly in a sagging sheet of plywood, and met my first Lo Tek.

"'S okay," Molly said, her hand brushing my shoulder. "It's just Dog. Hey, Dog."

In the narrow beam of her taped flash, he regarded us with his one eye and slowly extruded a thick length of grayish tongue, licking huge canines. I wondered how they wrote off tooth-bud transplants from Dobermans as low technology. Immunosuppressives don't exactly grow on trees.

"Moll." Dental augmentation impeded his speech. A string of saliva   115
dangled from his twisted lower lip. "Heard ya comin'. Long time." He might have been fifteen, but the fangs and a bright mosaic of scars combined with the gaping socket to present a mask of total bestiality. It had taken time and a certain kind of creativity to assemble that face, and his posture told me he enjoyed living behind it. He wore a pair of decaying jeans, black with grime and shiny along the creases. His chest and feet were bare. He did something with his mouth that approximated a grin. "Bein' followed, you."

Far off, down in Nighttown, a water vendor cried his trade.

"Strings jumping, Dog?" She swung her flash to the side, and I saw thin cords tied to eyebolts, cords that ran to the edge and vanished.

"Kill the fuckin' light!"

She snapped it off.

"How come the one who's followin' you's got no light?"   120

"Doesn't need it. That one's bad news, Dog. Your sentries give him a tumble, they'll come home in easy-to-carry sections."

Giovanni Piranesi: Giovanni Battista Piranesi (1720–1778), Italian artist known for his exaggerated architectural drawings of Roman buildings and imaginary prisons.

"This a *friend* friend, Moll?" He sounded uneasy. I heard his feet shift on the worn plywood.

"No. But he's mine. And this one," slapping my shoulder, "he's a friend. Got that?"

"Sure," he said, without much enthusiasm, padding to the platform's edge, where the eyebolts were. He began to pluck out some kind of message on the taut cords.

Nighttown spread beneath us like a toy village for rats; tiny windows   125 showed candlelight, with only a few harsh, bright squares lit by battery lanterns and carbide lamps. I imagined the old men at their endless games of dominoes, under warm, fat drops of water that fell from wet wash hung out on poles between the plywood shanties. Then I tried to imagine him climbing patiently up through the darkness in his zoris and ugly tourist shirt, bland and unhurried. How was he tracking us?

"Good," said Molly. "He smells us."

"Smoke?" Dog dragged a crumpled pack from his pocket and prized out a flattened cigarette. I squinted at the trademark while he lit it for me with a kitchen match. Yiheyuan filters. Beijing Cigarette Factory. I decided that the Lo Teks were black marketeers. Dog and Molly went back to their argument, which seemed to revolve around Molly's desire to use some particular piece of Lo Tek real estate.

"I've done you a lot of favors, man. I want that floor. And I want the music."

"You're not Lo Tek. . . ."

This must have been going on for the better part of a twisted kilometer,   130 Dog leading us along swaying catwalks and up rope ladders. The Lo Teks leech their webs and huddling places to the city's fabric with thick gobs of epoxy and sleep above the abyss in mesh hammocks. Their country is so attenuated that in places it consists of little more than holds for hands and feet, sawed into geodesic struts.

The Killing Floor, she called it. Scrambling after her, my new Eddie Bax shoes slipping on worn metal and damp plywood, I wondered how it could be any more lethal than the rest of the territory. At the same time I sensed that Dog's protests were ritual and that she already expected to get whatever it was she wanted.

Somewhere beneath us, Jones would be circling his tank, feeling the first twinges of junk sickness. The police would be boring the Drome regulars with questions about Ralfi. What did he do? Who was he with before he stepped outside? And the Yakuza would be settling its ghostly bulk over the city's data banks, probing for faint images of me reflected in numbered accounts, securities transactions, bills for utilities. We're an information economy. They teach you that in school. What they don't tell you is that it's impossible to move, to live, to operate at any level without leaving traces, bits, seemingly meaningless fragments of personal information. Fragments that can be retrieved, amplified . . .

But by now the pirate would have shuttled our message into line for blackbox transmission to the Yakuza comsat. A simple message: Call off the dogs or we wideband your program.

The program. I had no idea what it contained. I still don't. I only sing the song, with zero comprehension. It was probably research data, the Yakuza being given to advanced forms of industrial espionage. A genteel business, stealing from Ono-Sendai as a matter of course and politely holding their data for ransom, threatening to blunt the conglomerate's research edge by making the product public.

But why couldn't any number play? Wouldn't they be happier with some-   135
thing to sell back to Ono-Sendai, happier than they'd be with one dead Johnny from Memory Lane?

Their program was on its way to an address in Sydney, to a place that held letters for clients and didn't ask questions once you'd paid a small retainer. Fourth-class surface mail. I'd erased most of the other copy and recorded our message in the resulting gap, leaving just enough of the program to identify it as the real thing.

My wrist hurt. I wanted to stop, to lie down, to sleep. I knew that I'd lose my grip and fall soon, knew that the sharp black shoes I'd bought for my evening as Eddie Bax would lose their purchase and carry me down to Nighttown. But he rose in my mind like a cheap religious hologram, glowing, the enlarged chip on his Hawaiian shirt looming like a reconnaissance shot of some doomed urban nucleus.

So I followed Dog and Molly through Lo Tek heaven, jury-rigged and jerry-built from scraps that even Nighttown didn't want.

The Killing Floor was eight meters on a side. A giant had threaded steel cable back and forth through a junkyard and drawn it all taut. It creaked when it moved, and it moved constantly, swaying and bucking as the gathering Lo Teks arranged themselves on the shelf of plywood surrounding it. The wood was silver with age, polished with long use and deeply etched with initials, threats, declarations of passion. This was suspended from a separate set of cables, which lost themselves in darkness beyond the raw white glare of the two ancient floods suspended above the Floor.

A girl with teeth like Dog's hit the Floor on all fours. Her breasts were tat-   140
tooed with indigo spirals. Then she was across the Floor, laughing, grappling with a boy who was drinking dark liquid from a liter flask.

Lo Tek fashion ran to scars and tattoos. And teeth. The electricity they were tapping to light the Killing Floor seemed to be an exception to their over-all aesthetic, made in the name of . . . ritual, sport, art? I didn't know, but I could see that the Floor was something special. It had the look of having been assembled over generations.

I held the useless shotgun under my jacket. Its hardness and heft were comforting, even though I had no more shells. And it came to me that I had no idea at all of what was really happening, or of what was supposed to happen. And that was the nature of my game, because I'd spent most of my life as a blind receptacle to be filled with other people's knowledge and then drained, spouting synthetic languages I'd never understand. A very technical boy. Sure.

And then I noticed just how quiet the Lo Teks had become.

He was there, at the edge of the light, taking in the Killing Floor and the gallery of silent Lo Teks with a tourist's calm. And as our eyes met for the first time with mutual recognition, a memory clicked into place for me, of Paris, and the long Mercedes electrics gliding through the rain to Notre Dame; mobile greenhouses, Japanese faces behind the glass, and a hundred Nikons rising in blind phototropism, flowers of steel and crystal. Behind his eyes, as they found me, those same shutters whirring.

I looked for Molly Millions, but she was gone.   145

The Lo Teks parted to let him step up onto the bench. He bowed, smiling, and stepped smoothly out of his sandals, leaving them side by side, perfectly aligned, and then he stepped down onto the Killing Floor. He came for me, across that shifting trampoline of scrap, as easily as any tourist padding across synthetic pile in any featureless hotel.

Molly hit the Floor, moving.

The Floor screamed.

It was miked and amplified, with pickups riding the four fat coil springs at the corners and contact mikes taped at random to rusting machine fragments. Somewhere the Lo Teks had an amp and a synthesizer, and now I made out the shapes of speakers overhead, above the cruel white floods.

A drumbeat began, electronic, like an amplified heart, steady as a metronome.   150

She'd removed her leather jacket and boots; her T-shirt was sleeveless, faint telltales of Chiba City circuitry traced along her thin arms. Her leather jeans gleamed under the floods. She began to dance.

She flexed her knees, white feet tensed on a flattened gas tank, and the Killing Floor began to heave in response. The sound it made was like a world ending, like the wires that hold heaven snapping and coiling across the sky.

He rode with it, for a few heartbeats, and then he moved, judging the movement of the Floor perfectly, like a man stepping from one flat stone to another in an ornamental garden.

He pulled the tip from his thumb with the grace of a man at ease with social gesture and flung it at her. Under the floods, the filament was a refracting thread of rainbow. She threw herself flat and rolled, jackknifing up as the molecule whipped past, steel claws snapping into the light in what must have been an automatic rictus° of defense.

The drum pulse quickened, and she bounced with it, her dark hair wild   155
around the blank silver lenses, her mouth thin, lips taut with concentration. The Killing Floor boomed and roared, and the Lo Teks were screaming their excitement.

rictus: A grotesque grin or grimace.

He retracted the filament to a whirling meter-wide circle of ghostly poly-chrome and spun it in front of him, thumbless hand held level with his sternum. A shield.

And Molly seemed to let something go, something inside, and that was the real start of her mad-dog dance. She jumped, twisting, lunging sideways, landing with both feet on an alloy engine block wired directly to one of the coil springs. I cupped my hands over my ears and knelt in a vertigo of sound, thinking Floor and benches were on their way down, down to Nighttown, and I saw us tearing through the shanties, the wet wash, exploding on the tiles like rotten fruit. But the cables held, and the Killing Floor rose and fell like a crazy metal sea. And Molly danced on it.

And at the end, just before he made his final cast with the filament, I saw something in his face, an expression that didn't seem to belong there. It wasn't fear and it wasn't anger. I think it was disbelief, stunned incomprehension mingled with pure aesthetic revulsion at what he was seeing, hearing — at what was happening to him. He retracted the whirling filament, the ghost disk shrinking to the size of a dinner plate as he whipped his arm above his head and brought it down, the thumbtip curving out for Molly like a live thing.

The Floor carried her down, the molecule passing just above her head; the Floor whiplashed, lifting him into the path of the taut molecule. It should have passed harmlessly over his head and been withdrawn into its diamond-hard socket. It took his hand off just behind the wrist. There was a gap in the Floor in front of him, and he went through it like a diver, with a strange deliberate grace, a defeated kamikaze on his way down to Nighttown. Partly, I think, he took the dive to buy himself a few seconds of the dignity of silence. She'd killed him with culture shock.

The Lo Teks roared, but someone shut the amplifier off, and Molly rode   160
the Killing Floor into silence, hanging on now, her face white and blank, until the pitching slowed and there was only a faint pinging of tortured metal and the grating of rust on rust.

We searched the Floor for the severed hand, but we never found it. All we found was a graceful curve in one piece of rusted steel, where the molecule went through. Its edge was bright as new chrome.

We never learned whether the Yakuza had accepted our terms, or even whether they got our message. As far as I know, their program is still waiting for Eddie Bax on a shelf in the back room of a gift shop on the third level of Sydney Central-5. Probably they sold the original back to Ono-Sendai months ago. But maybe they did get the pirate's broadcast, because nobody's come looking for me yet, and it's been nearly a year. If they do come, they'll have a long climb up through the dark, past Dog's sentries, and I don't look much like Eddie Bax these days. I let Molly take care of that, with a local anesthetic. And my new teeth have almost grown in.

I decided to stay up here. When I looked out across the Killing Floor, before he came, I saw how hollow I was. And I knew I was sick of being a bucket. So now I climb down and visit Jones, almost every night.

We're partners now, Jones and I, and Molly Millions, too. Molly handles our business in the Drome. Jones is still in Funland, but he has a bigger tank, with fresh seawater trucked in once a week. And he has his junk, when he needs it. He still talks to the kids with his frame of lights, but he talks to me on a new display unit in a shed that I rent there, a better unit than the one he used in the navy.

And we're all making good money, better money than I made before, because Jones's Squid can read the traces of anything that anyone ever stored in me, and he gives it to me on the display unit in languages I can understand. So we're learning a lot about all my former clients. And one day I'll have a surgeon dig all the silicon out of my amygdalae, and I'll live with my own memories and nobody else's, the way other people do. But not for a while.   165

In the meantime it's really okay up here, way up in the dark, smoking a Chinese filtertip and listening to the condensation that drips from the geodesics. Real quiet up here — unless a pair of Lo Teks decide to dance on the Killing Floor.

It's educational too. With Jones to help me figure things out, I'm getting to be the most technical boy in town.

EXPLORING THE TEXT

1. What has happened to the boundary between humans and machines in the world of Johnny Mnemonic? How do Gibson's characters view their own "humanity"? How do they view machines? Who is more "machinelike" — Johnny, Molly Millions, or "the little tech" with the trick thumb? Why?

2. How does Gibson portray the future in this story? How would you describe his vision of society in the postelectronic era — his attitude toward governments, corporations, and civilization?

3. How do you interpret the significance of the confrontation between Molly and "the little tech"? What might Nighttown represent? What significance, if any, do you see in the way that Molly disposes of "the little tech" on the "Killing Floor"? In what sense does she kill him with "culture shock"? To what extent might it be possible to interpret this story as dramatizing a clash of cultures that is currently taking shape in response to the development of electronic technology?

4. What happens to the character of Johnny Mnemonic in this story? How does he change? What might Gibson be trying to suggest through this transformation about the impact of technology on the self and human relationships?

FURTHER EXPLORATIONS

1. How might Claudia Springer (p. 689) interpret the images of masculinity and the roles played by men, women, and machines in "Johnny Mnemonic"? Which aspects, if any, of Gibson's story strike you as particularly sexist? Which, if any, might be seen as particularly liberated or progressive?

2. How might Guillermo Gómez-Peña (p. 667) explain the role that cultural conflict plays in "Johnny Mnemonic"? How would he be likely to interpret the method that Molly Millions uses to defeat the "little tech"?

3. In "The Narrative Imagination" (p. 416), Martha C. Nussbaum argues that works of fiction promote civic culture by inviting us to empathize with "other" minds and "other" ways of life. How might "Johnny Mnemonic" function in this regard? What social, intellectual, or cultural purpose, if any, might it serve for us to identify with cyborgs and androids?

4. As a class, view the Robert Longo–directed film adaptation of "Johnny Mnemonic" and compare it with Gibson's short story. How accurately does Longo's depiction of the cyberpunk future reflect Gibson's? Which version of the story do you prefer? Why?

5. View a classic film noir detective movie, such as *The Postman Always Rings Twice, Double Indemnity, The Maltese Falcon,* or *Chinatown,* and discuss the features that distinguish this cinematic genre. What aspects of film noir do you see in works of cyberpunk fiction like "Johnny Mnemonic"? How might you explain why cyberpunk writers and filmmakers are attracted to the film noir worldview?

6. View another cyberpunk film, such as *Blade Runner* or *ExistenZ* and compare it with "Johnny Mnemonic" in terms of its depictions of humans, cyborgs, and high technology.

ESSAY OPTIONS

1. Using *Further Explorations* question number 1 as a point of departure, write your own gender analysis of Gibson's "Johnny Mnemonic." To what extent do Gibson's characters simply reproduce male and female stereotypes? To what extent might they be seen as resisting or challenging traditional gender categories? How do Gibson's gendered cyborgs compare with the "muscular" cybernetic heroes discussed by Claudia Springer (p. 689)?

2. Using "Johnny Mnemonic" and Claudia Springer's gendered readings of cyborg films (p. 689) as touchstones, and drawing on your own knowledge of popular culture, write an essay on the current state of machine minds in popular media. Are cyborgs and androids in recent television shows, films, novels, or comic books still depicted as "hypermasculine" industrial throwbacks and "hip" cyberpunk antiheroes? To what extent has contemporary popular culture moved beyond these machine mind stereotypes?

The Turing Test: A Coffeehouse Conversation

DOUGLAS R. HOFSTADTER

Without Alan Mathison Turing, the field of artificial intelligence might not exist. An English mathematician and computer theorist, Turing (1912–1954) published an essay in 1937 that provided the theoretical foundation for the entire field of computer science. In "On Computable Numbers," Turing presented the idea of the "Turing Machine"—a simple computational device that could solve mathematical problems by following the instructions provided by a "program" printed on a continuous paper tape. During World War II, Turing played a leading role in cracking the Nazis famed "Enigma Code" and built the world's first electronic computer to do it. In the 1950s, he turned his attention to the proposition that machines might do more than simply calculate answers to scientific problems. In his "Computing Machines and Intelligence," published in 1950, he outlined the program for a half century of artificial intelligence research and offered a famous method for testing whether or not a machine actually is capable of thought.

Douglas Hofstadter wrote this "coffeehouse conversation" as a user-friendly introduction to the Turing test and key concepts in artificial intelligence. Hofstadter (b. 1945) is College Professor of computer science and cognitive science, director of the Center for Research on Concepts and Cognition, and adjunct professor of philosophy, psychology, comparative literature, and the history and philosophy of science at Indiana University. In 1979, he received the Pulitzer Prize for his book *Göudel, Escher, Bach: An Eternal Golden Braid*. He has also published *Metamagical Themas* (1985) and *Fluid Concepts and Creative Analogies* (1995). Along with philosopher Daniel C. Dennett, he edited the source of this selection, *The Mind's I: Fantasies and Reflections on Self and Soul* in 1981.

BEFORE READING

Imagine for a moment that you have been commissioned to create a test for determining if a computer is capable of human thought. What would you expect a truly "intelligent" computer to be able to do? How would you prove that it could?

PARTICIPANTS: Chris, a physics student; Pat, a biology student; and Sandy, a philosophy student.

CHRIS: Sandy, I want to thank you for suggesting that I read Alan Turing's article "Computing Machinery and Intelligence." It's a wonderful piece and it certainly made me think—and think about my thinking.

SANDY: Glad to hear it. Are you still as much of a skeptic about artificial intelligence as you used to be?

CHRIS: You've got me wrong. I'm not against artificial intelligence; I think it's wonderful stuff—perhaps a little crazy, but why not? I simply am convinced that you AI advocates have far underestimated the human mind, and that there are things a computer will never, ever be able to do. For instance, can you imagine a computer writing a Proust novel?° The richness of imagination, the complexity of the characters . . . .

SANDY: Rome wasn't built in a day!

CHRIS: In the article Turing comes through as an interesting person. Is   5
he still alive?

SANDY: No, he died back in 1954, at just forty-one. He'd only be sixty-seven this year, although he is now such a legendary figure it seems strange to imagine him still alive today.

CHRIS: How did he die?

SANDY: Almost certainly suicide. He was homosexual and had to deal with a lot of harsh treatment and stupidity from the outside world. In the end it apparently got to be too much, and he killed himself.

CHRIS: That's a sad story.

SANDY: Yes, it certainly is. What saddens me is that he never got to see   10
the amazing progress in computing machinery and theory that has taken place.

PAT: Hey, are you going to clue me in as to what this Turing article is about?

SANDY: It is really about two things. One is the question "Can a machine think?"—or rather, "Will a machine ever think?" The way Turing answers this question—he thinks the answer is "yes," by the way—is by batting down a series of objections to the idea, one after another. The other point he tries to make is that the question is not meaningful as it stands. It's too full of emotional connotations. Many people are upset by the suggestion that people are machines, or that machines might think. Turing tries to defuse the question by casting it in less emotional terms. . . .

PAT: Does Turing suggest some . . . sort of IQ test for machines?

SANDY: That would be interesting, but no machine could yet come close to taking an IQ test. Instead, Turing proposes a test that theoretically could be applied to any machine to determine whether it can think or not.

PAT: Does the test give a clear-cut yes or no answer? I'd be skeptical if it   15
claimed to.

SANDY: No, it doesn't. In a way, that's one of its advantages. It shows how the borderline is quite fuzzy and how subtle the whole question is.

---

a Proust novel: Marcel Proust (1871–1922), French author famous for his complex, nine-volume novel *In Search of Lost Time.*

PAT: So, as is usual in philosophy, it's all just a question of words.

SANDY: Maybe, but they're emotionally charged words, and so it's important, it seems to me, to explore the issues and try to map out the meanings of the crucial words. The issues are fundamental to our concept of ourselves, so we shouldn't just sweep them under the rug.

PAT: So tell me how Turing's test works.

SANDY: The idea is based on what he calls the Imitation Game. In this game a man and a woman go into separate rooms and can be interrogated by a third party, via some sort of teletype set-up. The third party can address questions to either room, but has no idea which person is in which room. For the interrogator the idea is to discern which room the woman is in. Now the woman, by her answers, tries to aid the interrogator as much as possible. The man, however, is doing his best to bamboozle the interrogator by responding as he thinks a woman might. And if he succeeds in fooling the interrogator . . .

PAT: The interrogator only gets to see written words, eh? And the sex of the author is supposed to shine through? That game sounds like a good challenge. I would very much like to participate in it someday. Would the interrogator know either the man or the woman before the test began? Would any of them know the others?

SANDY: That would probably be a bad idea. All sorts of subliminal cueing might occur if the interrogator knew one or both of them. It would be safest if all three people were totally unknown to each other.

PAT: Could you ask any question at all, with no holds barred?

SANDY: Absolutely. That's the whole idea.

PAT: Don't you think, then, that pretty quickly it would degenerate into very sex-oriented questions? I can imagine the man, overeager to act convincing, giving away the game by answering some very blunt questions that most women would find too personal to answer, even through an anonymous computer connection.

SANDY: It sounds plausible.

CHRIS: Another possibility would be to probe for knowledge of minute aspects of traditional sex-role differences, by asking about such things as dress sizes and so on. The psychology of the Imitation Game could get pretty subtle. I suppose it would make a difference if the interrogator were a woman or a man. Don't you think that a woman could spot some telltale differences more quickly than a man could?

PAT: If so, maybe *that's* how to tell a man from a woman!

SANDY: Hmm . . . that's a new twist! In any case, I don't know if this original version of the Imitation Game has ever been seriously tried out, despite the fact that it would be relatively easy to do with modern computer terminals. I have to admit, though, that I'm not sure what it would prove, whichever way it turned out.

PAT: I was wondering about that. What would it prove if the interro-   30
gator—say, a woman—couldn't tell correctly which person was the woman? It certainly wouldn't prove that the man *was* a woman!

SANDY: Exactly! What I find funny is that although I fundamentally be-lieve in the Turing test, I'm not sure what the point is of the Imitation Game, on which it's founded!

CHRIS: I'm not any happier with the Turing test as a test for "thinking machines" than I am with the Imitation Game as a test for femininity.

PAT: From your statements I gather that the Turing test is a kind of ex-tension of the Imitation Game, only involving a machine and a person in separate rooms.

SANDY: That's the idea. The machine tries its hardest to convince the in-terrogator that it is the human being, while the human tries to make it clear that he or she is not a computer.

PAT: Except for your loaded phrase "the machine tries," this sounds very   35
interesting. But how do you know that this test will get at the essence of thinking? Maybe it's testing for the wrong things. Maybe, just to take a random illustration, someone would feel that a machine was able to think only if it could dance so well that you couldn't tell it was a machine. Or someone else could suggest some other character-istic. What's so sacred about being able to fool people by typing at them?

SANDY: I don't see how you can say such a thing. I've heard that objec-tion before, but frankly it baffles me. So what if the machine can't tap-dance or drop a rock on your toe? If it can discourse intelligently on any subject you want, then it has shown it can think—to me, at least! As I see it, Turing has drawn, in one clean stroke, a clear division between thinking and other aspects of being human.

PAT: Now *you're* the baffling one. If one couldn't conclude anything from a man's ability to win at the Imitation Game, how could one con-clude anything from a machine's ability to win at the Turing game?

CHRIS: Good question.

SANDY: It seems to me that you could conclude *something* from a man's win in the Imitation Game. You wouldn't conclude he was a woman, but you could certainly say he had good insights into the feminine men-tality (if there is such a thing). Now, if a computer could fool someone into thinking it was a person, I guess you'd have to say something similar about it—that it had good insights into what it's like to be human, into "the human condition" (whatever that is).

PAT: Maybe, but that isn't necessarily equivalent to thinking, is it? It   40
seems to me that passing the Turing test would merely prove that some machine or other could do a very good job of *simulating* thought.

CHRIS: I couldn't agree more with Pat. We all know that fancy computer programs exist today for simulating all sorts of complex phenomena. In physics, for instance, we simulate the behavior of particles, atoms, solids, liquids, gases, galaxies, and so on. But nobody confuses any of those simulations with the real thing!

SANDY: In his book *Brainstorms,* the philosopher Daniel Dennett makes a similar point about simulated hurricanes.

CHRIS: That's a nice example too. Obviously, what goes on inside a computer when it's simulating a hurricane is not a hurricane, for the machine's memory doesn't get torn to bits by two hundred-mile-an-hour winds, the floor of the machine room doesn't get flooded with rainwater, and so on.

SANDY: Oh, come on—that's not a fair argument! In the first place, the programmers don't claim the simulation really *is* a hurricane. It's merely a simulation of certain aspects of a hurricane. But in the second place, you're pulling a fast one when you imply that there are no downpours or two hundred-mile-an-hour winds in a simulated hurricane. To us there aren't any—but if the program were incredibly detailed, it could include simulated people on the ground who would experience the wind and the rain just as we do when a hurricane hits. In their minds—or, if you prefer, in their *simulated* minds—the hurricane would not be a simulation but a genuine phenomenon complete with drenching and devastation.

CHRIS: Oh, boy—what a science-fiction scenario! Now we're talking   45
about simulating whole populations, not just a single mind!

SANDY: Well, look—I'm simply trying to show you why your argument that a simulated McCoy isn't the real McCoy is fallacious. It depends on the tacit assumption that any old observer of the simulated phenomenon is equally able to assess what's going on. But, in fact, it may take an observer with a special vantage point to recognize what is going on. In this case, it takes special "computational glasses" to see the rain and the winds and so on.

PAT: "Computational glasses"? I don't know what you're talking about!

SANDY: I mean that to see the winds and the wetness of the hurricane, you have to be able to look at it in the proper way. You—

CHRIS: No, no, no! A simulated hurricane isn't wet! No matter how much it might seem wet to simulated people, it won't ever be *genuinely* wet! And no computer will ever get torn apart in the process of simulating winds!

SANDY: Certainly not, but you're confusing levels. The laws of physics 50 don't get torn apart by real hurricanes either. In the case of the simulated hurricane, if you go peering at the computer's memory expecting to find broken wires and so forth, you'll be disappointed. But look at the proper level. Look into the *structures* that are coded for in the memory. You'll see that some abstract links have been broken, some values of variables radically changed, and so forth. There's your flood, your devastation—real, only a little concealed, a little hard to detect.

CHRIS: I'm sorry. I just can't buy that. You're insisting that I look for a new kind of devastation, a kind never before associated with hurricanes. Using this idea, you could call *anything* a hurricane as long as its effects, seen through your special "glasses," could be called "floods and devastation."

SANDY: Right—you've got it exactly! You recognize a hurricane by its *effects*. You have no way of going in and finding some ethereal "essence of hurricane," some "hurricane soul," located right in the middle of the eye! It's the existence of a certain kind of *pattern*—a spiral storm with an eye and so forth that makes you say it's a hurricane. Of course there are a lot of things that you'll insist on before you call something a hurricane.

PAT: Well, wouldn't you say that being an atmospheric phenomenon is one vital prerequisite? How can anything inside a computer be a storm? To me, a simulation is a simulation is a simulation!

SANDY: Then I suppose you would say that even the calculations that computers do are simulated—that they are fake calculations. Only people can do genuine calculations, right?

PAT: Well, computers get the right answers, so their calculations are not 55 exactly fake—but they're still just *patterns*. There's no understanding going on in there. Take a cash register. Can you honestly say that you feel it is calculating something when its gears turn on each other? And a computer is just a fancy cash register, as I understand it.

SANDY: If you mean that a cash register doesn't feel like a schoolkid doing arithmetic problems, I'll agree. But is that what "calculation" means? Is that an integral part of it? If so, then contrary to what everybody has thought till now, we'll have to write a very complicated program to perform *genuine* calculations. Of course, this program will sometimes get careless and make mistakes and it will sometimes scrawl its answers illegibly, and it will occasionally doodle on its paper. . . . It won't be more reliable than the post office clerk who adds up your total by hand. Now, I happen to believe eventually such a program could be written. Then we'd know something about how post office clerks and schoolkids work.

PAT: I can't believe you could ever do that!

SANDY: Maybe, maybe not, but that's not my point. You say a cash register can't calculate. It reminds me of another favorite passage of mine from Dennett's *Brainstorms*—a rather ironic one, which is why I like it. The passage goes something like this: "Cash registers can't really calculate; they can only spin their gears. But cash registers can't really spin their gears either; they can only follow the laws of physics." Dennett said it originally about computers; I modified it to talk about cash registers. And you could use the same line of reasoning in talking about people: "People can't really calculate; all they can do is manipulate mental symbols. But they aren't really manipulating symbols; all they are doing is firing various neurons in various patterns. But they can't really make their neurons fire; they simply have to let the laws of physics make them fire for them." Et cetera. Don't you see how this Dennett-inspired *reductio ad absurdum*° would lead you to conclude that calculation doesn't exist, hurricanes don't exist, nothing at a higher level than particles and the laws of physics exists? What do you gain by saying a computer only pushes symbols around and doesn't truly calculate?

PAT: The example may be extreme, but it makes my point that there is a vast difference between a real phenomenon and any simulation of it. This is so for hurricanes, and even more so for human thought.

SANDY: Look, I don't want to get too tangled up in this line of argument, but let me try out one more example. If you were a radio ham listening to another ham broadcasting in Morse code and you were responding in Morse code, would it sound funny to you to refer to "the person at the other end"? 60

PAT: No, that would sound okay, although the existence of a person at the other end would be an assumption.

SANDY: Yes, but you wouldn't be likely to go and check it out. You're prepared to recognize personhood through those rather unusual channels. You don't have to see a human body or hear a voice—all you need is a rather abstract manifestation—a code, as it were. What I'm getting at is this. To "see" the person behind the dits and dahs, you have to be willing to do some decoding, some interpretation. It's not direct

---

reductio ad absurdum: An argument that disproves an assertion by showing that when the claim is carried to its logical extreme it results in an illogical or absurd conclusion.

perception; it's indirect. You have to peel off a layer or two, to find the reality hidden in there. You put on your "radio-ham's glasses" to "see" the person behind the buzzes. Just the same with the simulated hurricane! You don't see it darkening the machine room—you have to decode the machine's memory. You have to put on special "memory-decoding glasses." *Then* what you see is a hurricane!

PAT: Oh, ho ho! Talk about fast ones—wait a minute! In the case of the shortwave radio, there's a real person out there, somewhere in the Fiji Islands or wherever. My decoding act as I sit by my radio simply reveals that that person exists. It's like seeing a shadow and concluding there's an object out there, casting it. One doesn't confuse the shadow with the object, however! And with the hurricane there's no *real* hurricane behind the scenes, making the computer follow its patterns. No, what you have is just a shadow hurricane without any genuine hurricane. I just refuse to confuse shadows with reality.

SANDY: All right. I don't want to drive this point into the ground. I even admit it is pretty silly to say that a simulated hurricane *is* a hurricane. But I wanted to point out that it's not as silly as you might think at first blush. And when you turn to simulated thought, you've got a very different matter on your hands from simulated hurricanes.

PAT: I don't see why. A brainstorm sounds to me like a mental hurricane.   65
But seriously, you'll have to convince me.

SANDY: Well, to do so I'll have to make a couple of extra points about hurricanes first.

PAT: Oh, no! Well, all right, all right.

SANDY: Nobody can say just exactly what a hurricane is—that is, in totally precise terms. There's an abstract pattern that many storms share, and it's for that reason that we call those storms hurricanes. But it's not possible to make a sharp distinction between hurricanes and nonhurricanes. There are tornados, cyclones, typhoons, dustdevils. . . . Is the Great Red Spot on Jupiter a hurricane? Are sunspots hurricanes? Could there be a hurricane in a wind tunnel? In a test tube? In your imagination you can even extend the concept of "hurricane" to include a microscopic storm on the surface of a neutron star.

CHRIS: That's not so far-fetched, you know. The concept of "earthquake" has actually been extended to neutron stars. The astrophysicists say that the tiny changes in rate that once in a while are observed in the pulsing of a pulsar are caused by "glitches"—starquakes—that have just occurred on the neutron star's surface.

SANDY: Yes, I remember that now. The idea of a "glitch" strikes me as   70
wonderfully eerie—a surrealistic kind of quivering on a surrealistic kind of surface.

CHRIS: Can you imagine—plate tectonics on a giant rotating sphere of pure nuclear matter?

SANDY: That's a wild thought. So starquakes and earthquakes can both be subsumed into a new, more abstract category. And that's how science constantly extends familiar concepts, taking them further and further from familiar experience and yet keeping some essence constant. The number system is the classic example—from positive numbers to negative numbers, then rationals, reals, complex numbers, and "on beyond zebra," as Dr. Seuss says.

PAT: I think I can see your point here, Sandy. We have many examples in biology of close relationships that are established in rather abstract ways. Often the decision about what family some species belongs to comes down to an abstract pattern shared at some level. When you base your system of classification on very abstract patterns, I suppose that a broad variety of phenomena can fall into "the same class," even if in many superficial ways the class members are utterly unlike each other. So perhaps I can glimpse, at least a little, how to you a simulated hurricane could, in some funny sense, *be* a hurricane.

CHRIS: Perhaps the word that's being extended is not "hurricane" but "be"!

PAT: How so?   75

CHRIS: If Turing can extend the verb "think," can't I extend the verb "be"? All I mean is that when simulated things are deliberately confused with the genuine article, somebody's doing a lot of philosophical wool-pulling. It's a lot more serious than just extending a few nouns such as "hurricane."

SANDY: I like your idea that "be" is being extended, but I think your slur about "wool-pulling" goes too far. Anyway, if you don't object, let me just say one more thing about simulated hurricanes and then I'll get to simulated minds. Suppose you consider a really deep simulation of a hurricane—I mean a simulation of every atom, which I admit is impossibly deep. I hope you would agree that it would then share all that abstract structure that defines the "essence of hurricanehood." So what's to hold you back from calling it a hurricane?

PAT: I thought you were backing off from that claim of equality!

SANDY: So did I, but then these examples came up, and I was forced back to my claim. But let me back off, as I said I would do, and get back to *thought,* which is the real issue here. Thought, even more than hurricanes, is an abstract structure, a way of describing some complex events that happen in a medium called a brain. But actually thought can take place in any of several billion brains. There are all these physically very different brains, and yet they all support "the same thing"—thinking.

What's important, then, is the abstract *pattern,* not the medium. The same kind of swirling can happen inside any of them, so no person can claim to think more "genuinely" than any other. Now, if we come up with some new kind of medium in which *the same style* of swirling takes place, could you deny that thinking is taking place in it?

PAT: Probably not, but you have just shifted the question. The question   80
now is, how can you determine whether "the same style" of swirling is really happening?

SANDY: The beauty of the Turing test is that it *tells* you when!

CHRIS: I don't see that at all. How would you know that the same style of activity was occurring inside a computer as inside my mind, simply because it answered questions as I do? All you're looking at is its outside.

SANDY: But how do you know that when I speak to you, anything similar to what you call "thinking" is going on inside *me?* The Turing test is a fantastic probe, something like a particle accelerator in physics. Chris, I think you'll like this analogy. Just as in physics, when you want to understand what is going on at an atomic or subatomic level, since you can't see it directly, you scatter accelerated particles off the target in question and observe their behavior. From this you infer the internal nature of the target. The Turing test extends this idea to the mind. It treats the mind as a "target" that is not directly visible but whose structure can be deduced more abstractly. By "scattering" questions off a target mind, you learn about its internal workings, just as in physics.

CHRIS: More exactly put, you can hypothesize about what kinds of internal structures might account for the behavior observed—but they may or may not in fact exist.

SANDY: Hold on, now! Are you saying that atomic nuclei are merely hy-   85
pothetical entities? After all, their existence—or should I say "hypothetical existence"?—was proven—or should I say "suggested"?—by the behavior of particles scattered off of atoms.

CHRIS: Physical systems seem to me to be much simpler than the mind, and the certainty of the inferences made is correspondingly greater.

SANDY: The experiments are also correspondingly harder to perform and to interpret. In the Turing test, you could perform many highly delicate experiments in the course of an hour. I maintain that people give other people credit for being conscious simply because of their continual external monitoring of them—which is itself something like a Turing test.

PAT: That may be roughly true, but it involves more than just conversing with people through a teletype. We see that other people have bodies, we watch their faces and expressions—we see they are fellow human beings and so we think they think.

SANDY: To me, that seems a highly anthropocentric view of what thought is. Does that mean you would sooner say a mannikin in a store thinks than a wonderfully programmed computer, simply because the mannikin looks more human?

PAT: Obviously I would need more than just vague physical resemblance   90 to the human form to be willing to attribute the power of thought to an entity. But that organic quality, the sameness of origin, undeniably lends a degree of credibility that is very important.

SANDY: Here we disagree. I find this simply too chauvinistic. I feel that the key thing is a similarity of *internal* structure—not bodily, organic, chemical structure, but organizational structure—software. Whether an entity can think seems to me a question of whether its organization can be described in a certain way, and I'm perfectly willing to believe that the Turing test detects the presence or absence of that mode of organization. I would say that your depending on my physical body as evidence that I am a thinking being is rather shallow. The way I see it, the Turing test looks far deeper than at mere external form.

PAT: Hey now—you're not giving me much credit. It's not just the shape of a body that lends weight to the idea there's real thinking going on inside—it's also, as I said, the idea of common origin. It's the idea that you and I both sprang from DNA molecules, an idea to which I attribute much depth. Put it this way: The external form of human bodies reveals that they share a deep biological history, and it's *that* depth that lends a lot of credibility to the notion that the owner of such a body can think.

SANDY: But that is all indirect evidence. Surely you want some *direct* evidence. That is what the Turing test is for. And I think it is the *only* way to test for "thinkinghood."

CHRIS: But you could be fooled by the Turning test, just as an interrogator could think a man was a woman.

SANDY: I admit, I could be fooled if I carried out the test in too quick or   95 too shallow a way. But I would go for the deepest things I could think of.

CHRIS: I would want to see if the program could understand jokes. That would be a real test of intelligence.

SANDY: I agree that humor probably is an acid test for a supposedly intelligent program, but equally important to me—perhaps more so— would be to test its emotional responses. So I would ask it about its reactions to certain pieces of music or works of literature—especially my favorite ones.

CHRIS: What if it said, "I don't know that piece," or even "I have no interest in music"? What if it avoided all emotional references?

SANDY: That would make me suspicious. Any consistent pattern of avoiding certain issues would raise serious doubts in me as to whether I was dealing with a thinking being.

CHRIS: Why do you say that? Why not say that you're dealing with a   100
thinking but unemotional being?

SANDY: You've hit upon a sensitive point. I simply can't believe that emotions and thought can be divorced. Put another way, I think that emotions are an automatic by-product of the ability to think. They are implied by the very nature of thought.

CHRIS: Well, what if you're wrong? What if I produced a machine that could think but not emote? Then its intelligence might go unrecognized because it failed to pass *your* kind of test. . . .

SANDY: A couple of answers here! Number one, any intelligence has to have motivations. It's simply not the case, whatever many people may think, that machines could think any more "objectively" than people do. Machines, when they look at a scene, will have to focus and filter that scene down into some preconceived categories, just as a person does. And that means seeing some things and missing others. It means giving more weight to some things than to others. This happens on every level of processing.

PAT: What do you mean?

SANDY: Take me right now, for instance. You might think that I'm just   105
making some intellectual points, and I wouldn't need emotions to do that. But what makes me *care* about these points? Why did I stress the word "care" so heavily? Because I'm emotionally involved in this conversation! People talk to each other out of conviction, not out of hollow, mechanical reflexes. Even the most intellectual conversation is driven by underlying passions. There's an emotional undercurrent to every conversation—it's the fact that the speakers want to be listened to, understood, and respected for what they are saying.

PAT: It sounds to me as if all you're saying is that people need to be interested in what they're saying, otherwise a conversation dies.

SANDY: Right! I wouldn't bother to talk to anyone if I weren't motivated by interest. And interest is just another name for a whole constellation of subconscious biases. When I talk, all my biases work together and what you perceive on the surface level is my style, my personality. But that style arises from an immense number of tiny priorities, biases, leanings. When you add up a million of these interacting together, you get something that amounts to a lot of *desires*. It just all adds up! And that brings me to the other point, about feelingless calculation. Sure, that exists — in a cash register, a pocket calculator. I'd say it's even true of all today's computer programs. But eventually, when you put enough feelingless calculations together in a huge coordinated organization, you'll get something that has properties on another level. You can see it — in fact, you *have* to see it — not as a bunch of little calculations, but as a system of tendencies and desires and beliefs and so on. When things get complicated enough, you're forced to change your level of description. To some extent that's already happening, which is why we use words such as "want," "think," "try," and "hope," to describe chess programs and other attempts at mechanical thought. Dennett calls that kind of level switch by the observer "adopting the intentional stance." The really interesting things in AI will only begin to happen, I'd guess, when the program *itself* adopts the intentional stance toward itself!

CHRIS: That would be a very strange sort of level-crossing feedback loop.

SANDY: It certainly would. Of course, in my opinion, it's highly premature for anyone to adopt the intentional stance, in the full force of the term, toward today's programs. At least that's my opinion.

CHRIS: For me an important related question is: To what extent is it valid   110
to adopt the intentional stance toward beings other than humans?

PAT: I would certainly adopt the intentional stance toward mammals.

SANDY: I vote for that.

CHRIS: That's interesting! How can that be, Sandy? Surely you wouldn't claim that a dog or cat can pass the Turing test? Yet don't you think that the Turing test is the only way to test for the presence of thought? How can you have these beliefs at once?

SANDY: Hmm. . . . All right. I guess I'm forced to admit that the Turing test works only above a certain level of consciousness. There can be thinking beings that could fail the test — but on the other hand, anything that passes it, in my opinion, would be a genuinely conscious, thinking being.

PAT: How can you think of a computer as a conscious being? I apologize   115
if this sounds like a stereotype, but when I think of conscious beings, I just can't connect that thought with machines. To me consciousness is connected with soft, warm bodies, silly though that may sound.

CHRIS: That does sound odd, coming from a biologist. Don't you deal with life in terms of chemistry and physics enough for all magic to seem to vanish?

PAT: Not really. Sometimes the chemistry and physics just increase the feeling that there's something magical going on down there! Anyway, I can't always integrate my scientific knowledge with my gut-level feelings.

CHRIS: I guess I share that trait.

PAT: So how do you deal with rigid preconceptions like mine?

SANDY: I'd try to dig down under the surface of your concept of "ma-   120
chines" and get at the intuitive connotations that lurk there, out of sight but deeply influencing your opinions. I think that we all have a holdover image from the industrial revolution that sees machines as clunky iron contraptions gawkily moving under the power of some loudly chugging engine. Possibly that's even how the computer inventor Charles Babbage° viewed people! After all, he called his magnificent many-geared computer the Analytical Engine.

PAT: Well, I certainly don't think people are just fancy steam shovels or even electric can openers. There's something about people, something that—that—they've got a sort of *flame* inside them, something alive, something that flickers unpredictably, wavering, uncertain—but something *creative*!

SANDY: Great! That's just the sort of thing I wanted to hear. It's very human to think that way. Your flame image makes me think of candles, of fires, of thunderstorms with lightning dancing all over the sky in crazy patterns. But do you realize that just that kind of pattern is visible on a computer's console? The flickering lights form amazing chaotic sparkling patterns. It's such a far cry from heaps of lifeless clanking metal! It *is* flamelike, by God! Why don't you let the word "machine" conjure up images of dancing patterns of light rather than of giant steam shovels?

CHRIS: That's a beautiful image, Sandy. It changes my sense of mechanism from being matter-oriented to being pattern-oriented. It makes me try to visualize the thoughts in my mind—these thoughts right now, even—as a huge spray of tiny pulses flickering in my brain.

SANDY: That's quite a poetic self-portrait for a spray of flickers to have come up with!

CHRIS: Thank you. But still, I'm not totally convinced that a machine is   125
all that I am. I admit, my concept of machines probably does suffer from anachronistic subconscious flavors, but I'm afraid I can't change such a deeply rooted sense in a flash.

Charles Babbage: (1792–1871), English mathematician and inventor widely regarded, along with Ada Lovelace, as having first discovered the essential principles of the modern computer.

SANDY: At least you do sound open-minded. And to tell the truth, part of me does sympathize with the way you and Pat view machines. Part of me balks at calling myself a machine. It *is* a bizarre thought that a feeling being like you or me might emerge from mere circuitry. Do I surprise you? . . .

CHRIS: If people are machines, how come it's so hard to convince them of the fact? Surely if we are machines, we ought to be able to recognize our own machinehood.

SANDY: You have to allow for emotional factors here. To be told you're a machine is, in a way, to be told that you're nothing more than your physical parts, and it brings you face to face with your own mortality. That's something nobody finds easy to face. But beyond the emotional objection, to see yourself as a machine you have to jump all the way from the bottommost mechanical level to the level where the complex lifelike activities take place. If there are many intermediate layers, they act as a shield, and the mechanical quality becomes almost invisible. I think that's how intelligent machines will seem to us—and to themselves—when they come around. . . .

PAT: . . . Well, do you think any computer program today could pass a five-minute Turing test, given a sophisticated interrogator?

SANDY: I seriously doubt it. It's partly because no one is really working   130
at it explicitly. However, there is one program called "Parry" which its inventors claim has already passed a rudimentary version of the Turing test. In a series of remotely conducted interviews, Parry fooled several psychiatrists who were told they were talking to either a computer or a paranoid patient. This was an improvement over an earlier version, in which psychiatrists were simply handed transcripts of short interviews and asked to determine which ones were with a genuine paranoid and which ones with a computer simulation.

PAT: You mean they didn't have the chance to ask any questions? That's a severe handicap—and it doesn't seem in the spirit of the Turing test. Imagine someone trying to tell which sex I belong to just by reading a transcript of a few remarks by me. It might be very hard! So I'm glad the procedure has been improved.

CHRIS: How do you get a computer to act like a paranoid?

SANDY: I'm not saying it *does* act like a paranoid, only that some psychiatrists, under unusual circumstances, thought so. One of the things that bothered me about this pseudo-Turing test is the way Parry works. "He"—as they call him—acts like a paranoid in that he gets abruptly defensive, veers away from undesirable topics in the conversation, and, in essence, maintains control so that no one can truly probe "him." In this way, a simulation of a paranoid is a lot easier than a simulation of a normal person.

PAT: No kidding! It reminds me of the joke about the easiest kind of human for a computer program to simulate.

CHRIS: What is that?   135

PAT: A catatonic patient—they just sit and do nothing at all for days on end. Even I could write a computer program to do that!

SANDY: An interesting thing about Parry is that it creates no sentences on its own—it merely selects from a huge repertoire of canned sentences the one that best responds to the input sentence.

PAT: Amazing! But that would probably be impossible on a larger scale, wouldn't it?

SANDY: Yes. The number of sentences you'd need to store to be able to respond in a normal way to all possible sentences in a conversation is astronomical, really unimaginable. And they would have to be so intricately indexed for retrieval. . . . Anybody who thinks that somehow a program could be rigged up just to pull sentences out of storage like records in a jukebox, and that this program could pass the Turing test, has not thought very hard about it. The funny part about it is that it is just this kind of unrealizable program that some enemies of artificial intelligence cite when arguing against the concept of the Turing test. Instead of a truly intelligent machine, they want you to imagine a gigantic, lumbering robot that intones canned sentences in a dull monotone. It's assumed that you could see through to its mechanical level with ease, even if it were simultaneously performing tasks that we think of as fluid, intelligent processes. Then the critics say, "You see! It would still be just a machine—a mechanical device, not intelligent at all!" I see things almost the opposite way. If I were shown a machine that can do things that I can do—I mean pass the Turing test—then, instead of feeling insulted or threatened, I'd chime in with the philosopher Raymond Smullyan and say, "How wonderful machines are!"

CHRIS: If you could ask a computer just one question in the Turing test,   140
what would it be?

SANDY: Uhmm. . . .

PAT: How about "If you could ask a computer just one question in the Turing test, what would it be?"?

EXPLORING THE TEXT

1. What does Pat mean by saying that the question of whether machines can "think" is just a matter of words (para. 17)? What words? Why might the definition of these terms be "fundamental to our concept of ourselves," as Sandy suggests (para. 18)? Would you agree?

2. How does the Turing test work? What does it seek to measure? What would be "proven" if a machine could pass it? To what extent would you agree that the ability to think intelligently is essentially equivalent to the ability to "discourse" intelligently? How else could the ability to think be measured or tested?

3. In what sense is the Turing test a "probe" for consciousness? Why is it necessary for us to use such probes to verify the consciousness of other human beings? Exactly how do we monitor the consciousness of others? How aware are we of this process?

4. Why is human thinking like a "simulated hurricane"? In what ways are human and machine thinking comparable, in Sandy's view? In what ways, if any, are they different? Would you be willing to recognize your own "machinehood"? Why or why not?

5. Why do you think Hofstadter chose to present this essay in the form of a dialogue? What does he gain as a writer by doing this? Why does he bother to identify his characters with specific academic disciplines? To what extent do their views seem to reflect particular academic perspectives or assumptions about machine intelligence?

FURTHER EXPLORATIONS

1. To what extent might it be possible to view the identity swapping that Sherry Turkle documents on the Internet (p. 675) as a kind of Turing test? What does the Turing test suggest about the relation between human identity and computing?

2. Given her analysis of the gender biases associated with electronic technology, how might Claudia Springer (p. 689) interpret the significance of the gender imitation game that Turing used to introduce the concept of the Turing test? Would you agree that a man who passed the imitation test would have to have "good insights into what it's like to be a woman"? Why or why not? What, incidentally, are the genders of the three characters Hofstadter employs in this "conversation"? Does it matter?

3. How does the Turing test compare with Koko the gorilla's acquisition of American Sign Language (p. 592)? To what extent does the evidence of Koko's intelligence and consciousness rely on interpretation or decoding of "indirect" discourse? Which would you be more likely to grant "personhood" to—a gorilla that can offer one- or two-word answers to specific questions or a machine that can do the same? Why?

4. How might Frans de Waal (p. 552) respond to the suggestion that the way we talk about computers shows that we are already beginning to see them as "intentional" beings—entities with their own interests and desires? Do you think it might be possible to achieve what de Waal terms "mature" anthropomorphism in relation to an intelligent machine? Why or why not?

5. Using your campus' or classroom's computer network, set up a trial run of the imitation game Turing proposed as a model of his test for computer intelligence. Working at remote terminals, have all-female and all-male groups of students

collaboratively answer questions put to them by small mixed groups of students, with the mixed groups charged to determine males from females. How easy is it to fool interrogators? What kinds of questions work best to reveal the differences between male and female respondents? What does this test reveal, if anything, about the reality of gender and gender identity?

ESSAY OPTIONS

1. At the end of "A Coffeehouse Conversation," Pat asks "'If you could ask a computer just one question in the Turing test, what would it be?'" (para. 142). Write a paper in which you present several possible questions that you think would help you distinguish between human and machine intelligence. What would the questions be? How would you expect a computer's answer to them to differ from a human's? Why do you think these questions would "stump" a computer? What do your questions suggest about the nature of human thinking, consciousness, or intelligence?

2. For many years, it was believed that machines would have surpassed humans in intelligence if a computer could defeat a grand master at chess. In 1997, IBM's "Deep Blue" did just that by defeating Gary Kasparov, then the top-ranked chess player in the world. Yet, few scientists today believe that Deep Blue did anything even remotely comparable to human thought. Using Internet and your library's resources, research what experts in artificial intelligence are doing today to create machines capable of simulating human intelligence. Is the field of artificial intelligence still aiming at the duplication of human thinking in computers? What new directions has AI research taken during the past fifteen years? How have scientists begun to rethink what it means to think like a human being? Synthesize your findings in the form of a standard text-based report or as a hypertext presentation.

Redefining the Measure of Mankind

MAUREEN CAUDILL

Remember Robbie the Robot? Chances are you do — even if you've never seen *Forbidden Planet*, the 1956 film that made him famous. The same is true for C3PO, R2D2, and HAL — the machine minds, friendly or homicidal, featured by George Lucas in *Star Wars* and Stanley Kubrick in *2001*. The idea of assembling an artificial human has haunted the dreams of prophets, poets, and mythmakers for centuries. It shows up in the ancient Jewish legend of the golem, in classic children's tales like *Pinocchio*, and in masterpieces of gothic horror like Mary Shelley's *Frankenstein*. Today, we appear to be on the verge of realizing the age-old dream of creating a conscious being in our own image. At least that's the reasoned opinion of Maureen Caudill. In this selection, Caudill argues that android consciousness is bound to arise sometime within the next generation and suggests that the birth of intelligent machinery will force us to confront some of the most challenging social and ethical issues, that we, as a species, have ever had to face. President of

NeuWorld Services and a neural networks consultant in San Diego, California, Maureen Caudill is the author of *In Our Own Image: Building an Artificial Person* (1992), and coauthor, with Charles Butler, of *Naturally Intelligent Systems* (1990), and *Understanding Neural Networks* (1992).

BEFORE READING

Do a brief freewrite on how you think computers and other forms of intelligent machinery will transform life over the next one hundred years. What kinds of jobs will computers do for us a century from now? How do you think computerization will affect the workplace? How will it affect society at large?

More than at any time in history mankind
faces a crossroads.
One path leads to despair and utter hopelessness,
the other to total extinction.
Let us pray that we have the wisdom
to choose correctly.
                                        — WOODY ALLEN

Someday in the not-so-distant future we will awaken to a world that is radically different from the one we know now. We will be sharing our world with the products of our own imagination, androids. What will life be like then? What will happen to our society when we share it with peoplelike machines? And how soon will all this happen?

To answer the last question first, I believe that the first working android will be built shortly after the turn of the century. Within twenty years, we will have the knowledge and ability to build androids that look and act in a way most people will consider "humanlike." Even within a single decade, before or shortly after the year 2000, androids will begin to be a part of everyday life in a way they are not now.

Today's robots are limited mostly to very specific assembly-line tasks or highly specialized environments few people ever encounter. By the year 2000 or shortly thereafter, I believe that most people will have had some interaction with a robot, and many will deal with them on a regular basis. The Japanese have already developed a working robot that can cook and serve microwaved meals; they plan to house it in a mannekin form and use it as a fast-food restaurant "employee." The manufacturer predicts that such robots — or improved versions that can also operate a grill — will be in widespread use in the fast-food industry before the turn of the century. So your future meals at McDonald's or Burger King or Wendy's may be filled by a robotic cook. It is even very possible that the mythic housemaid's robot will be commercially available by then, although it is likely to still be a luxury item beyond the means of most households. There will certainly be android space travelers exploring—or on their way to explore—Mars and the Moon by the turn of the century. If not built by the United States, the Japanese or the Europeans will ensure that humanity's mechanical delegates take the next steps into space.

This prediction may be shocking to many, particularly in light of the enormous distance we have yet to go in developing the necessary systems and subsystems involved in such an undertaking. [But] we have—or are about to have—excellent technologies that can provide memory, learning, training, speech, and vision systems. Each of these areas is either sufficiently advanced today to build the necessary systems for at least a primitive android, or we can expect them to be so within three to five years. Other areas are less well developed, but even these research areas are likely to see advances that will lift them to the minimum necessary levels within just a few years. While the first android systems may not be as smooth and debonair as we might like, it seems evident that they will be built, and quickly too.

This does not mean to imply that all the problems have been solved, nor   5
that all remaining problems are even close to a solution today. Many of these are going to be difficult to solve in the available time. Instead of glossing over these difficulties, my prediction is actually an assertion of faith in the ingenuity and talents of the researchers involved. Looking back at the progress that has been made over the last ten or twenty years is exceedingly instructive. The technology that is readily available today was practically unimaginable twenty years ago. I have enough faith in this current generation of researchers to believe that they too will make similar strides into the future.

Furthermore, just as the race to land on the Moon resulted in tremendous by-products that have carried over into nearly every aspect of the way we live—ranging from freeze-dried coffee, to improved ceramics and other materials, to better, smaller, and cheaper computers—so, too, will efforts to develop an android result in the development of products and technologies that will spill over into everyone's lives. Robotics technologies will improve everything from video games to artificial limbs that directly interact with a patient's nervous system so that they feel like natural limbs. Improved vision systems will permit far more sophisticated security systems to be developed, as well as cars and trucks that drive themselves—most likely much more safely than the average big-city cab driver. Development of language understanding systems will give us appliances and cars that talk to us, and dictation machines that truly take dictation and convert it directly to letter-perfect text. Improvements in robotic arm control will of course make factory automation more efficient, but also will make gasoline pumps that are more self-service than anything we have seen before. And once we can add common sense to computers, they will be able to perform tasks for us that we can only dream about now. . . .

The most common way in which future predictions err is that the predictor underestimates the rate of advance in the sciences. Practically no one, twenty years ago, could have predicted the power, flexibility, and ease of use of today's personal computers. The cars we drive now may have sophisticated computers built into them and "heads-up" displays that cast the instrument panel onto the windshield so the driver never has to look down. Only a few years ago the heads-up display technology was a hot new innovation in the most advanced fighter jets; yet today it is available in cars anyone can buy. We are manipulating genes and attacking illnesses that were considered hopeless only a few years ago. Practically none of this could have been predicted with assurance in the early 1970s.

Even more dramatic, however, are some new technological developments being made today. Researchers at NTT Labs (the Japanese equivalent of America's AT&T) have developed a neural network system that quite literally reads a person's mind. The system receives inputs from about a dozen sensors attached to the skull, just as an EEG recorder does. Then the user literally *thinks* the words "up," "down," "left," or "right" and the neural network translates the changes in EEG patterns into controlling commands for a joystick. A similar device in the form of a headband has been produced by other researchers at Stanford University. Interestingly, not only are users such as the U.S. Air Force interested in this technology for use in fighter plane controls — remember the movie *Firefox* in which Clint Eastwood controlled the weapons system of a new Soviet plane by thinking the appropriate commands in Russian? — but one of the most eager potential customers is a major video game manufacturer. Such "science-fiction" technology may end up in American homes by way of a special video game helmet or headband that reads the user's mind.

What will the development of such "telepathic controllers" do to our world? The obvious possibilities are in the control of complex systems, such as airplanes and other machinery. Video games are similarly obvious, as are systems to help the handicapped — imagine a system that could control a robot arm for a quadriplegic, merely by having the person think about what the arm should do. But more astounding possibilities are also likely, many of which we cannot even envision. What about a "telepathic" house, in which all the systems and appliances responded to the thought commands relayed by a simple headpiece, similar to a set of earphones? Or a nursing station that was similarly equipped? Or a car that responds only to the thoughts of its rightful owner? Or a telepathic "realie" that allows viewers to control the action in a virtual-reality environment so that experiences there are tailored to the individual's tastes and preferences? It would surprise me greatly if such "telepathic" controllers were not readily available before or soon after the year 2000.

Companies have already arisen that specialize in developing applications   10 in "virtual reality." These companies produce devices — headbands, gloves, even full bodysuits — that a user wears or otherwise manipulates. The natural gestures of the user are interpreted by high-powered supercomputers and translated into changes in a simulated environment. A simple version of this is used in aircraft flight simulators in which changes to the simulated plane's controls cause the pilot to see changes in the instrument readings and exterior views through the simulator's "windows." More complex versions are being developed for use for such varying applications as interactive games, walk-throughs of buildings that have not yet been built, and truly interactive tele-conferencing. Just as the cave paintings of our neolithic ancestors may have allowed hunters to anticipate and learn about the hunt, such virtual realities will provide each of us with a way to experience things that would otherwise be beyond our ken.

Yet another reason future predictions are often wrong is that social changes are nearly impossible to predict, and society determines which technologies are developed and which are ignored. In 1960 John Kennedy issued challenges to the young people of America, and the result was both humanity's first step on the Moon and an outpouring of aid to underdeveloped countries through the Peace Corps. If Richard Nixon had won that Presidential election, would there have been a U.S. Moon landing in 1969? I suspect not. A few thousand people, by voting for Kennedy in the extremely close presidential elections that year, literally changed the course of world history. Was that predictable? Probably not, and certainly not from a decade or more before. Could any prognosticator have predicted the AIDS epidemic and its resulting impact on social and sexual mores? Or the crumbling of the communist bloc in Eastern Europe in late 1989? Or the invention of the transistor? Or television's impact on the family and politics?

The point is that seemingly small events can cause dramatic changes in the history of the world. Yet it really is the desires of society as a whole that determine the direction of technological development. For example, in the 1970s there were a large number of grandiose and complex plans for public transportation systems in various cities in the United States. These largely fell into dust, mainly because the American people don't much like public transportation. We are a society that prefers private automobile transportation, so it is the technology of road-building that is most developed here. In Europe and Japan public transportation is far more acceptable, and therefore much more advanced. Society seems willing to pay any price for a technology that is deemed desirable and worthwhile—and little or nothing for one that is unpopular, or otherwise unwanted. In the 1960s the American people *wanted* to put a man on the Moon; it was a necessary achievement to maintain our image of ourselves as a people. As a result, and in spite of increasing grumblings, the price was paid and our egos soothed. Now, the race for space takes a backseat to other problems—but if it again became a national priority, we can be assured that the resources would be found to reach the desired goals.

The result of all this is that a predictor of technological advances must also be a predictor of sociological trends. He or she must try to anticipate what social pressures will be brought to bear on scientists, and, from that, determine where resources will be allocated. This is an undertaking that is fraught with the likelihood of error and inaccuracy. . . .

The next question, of course, concerns what social changes will result because of the development of robot technology. Scientists and engineers have a strong inclination to list vast amounts of benefits for society and mankind as a whole. Possibilities for these benefits include improved care for the aged and the very young, relief from household drudgery and other unpleasant or dangerous tasks, improved productivity, and many others. Certainly some of these benefits will come true. For example, I suspect that initially most of the impact of intelligent androids will occur in the workplace, rather than at home. Until a housemaid robot costs as little as, say, a quality automobile, not too many households will be able to afford one. Once the price gets down that low, however, the broad middle class will probably find that a robot to keep house, like today's VCR, portable telephone, and video game, is something that they simply cannot live without.

At work it is likely to be a very different story indeed. There are many 15 "drudgery" jobs that a competent android should be able to accomplish with ease. Possible "android jobs" include: waiters, store clerks, manufacturing assembly-line positions, security guards, farm workers, bank tellers, cab and bus drivers, house cleaners, maids, nursing aides, nannies, cooks, teacher's aides, and dozens of others, including the fast-food restaurant workers mentioned before. Notice that many (though not all) of these positions require few skills and/or earn relatively low pay. If, for a modest capital investment, a company can obtain an android worker that takes no breaks, never is sick or on vacation, never leaves for another company or position, needs no fringe benefits, and works honestly and reliably, then even a high initial purchase price could well make solid financial sense. On the other hand, this could result in real hardship for those humans who lack the technical skills to perform more demanding and creative jobs that androids cannot yet do. There may be far fewer positions available for those people who lack a high school diploma — or perhaps even a college degree — and as a result, unemployment may rise and social services could be strained.

There could be a bright side to such trends in this country, however. It is predicted that in the first half of the twenty-first century, the population of the United States will be growing significantly older. In fact, many fear that as the baby boom generation reaches and passes retirement age there will not be enough working adults to support them in their old age. The addition of androids to the workforce, particularly in the low-paying service industry, may help take up the slack from the demographic losses in the population at large.

The answer to the question of whether android workers will be a blessing or a curse to society will likely depend strongly on each individual's position in the workforce. Those on the upper end of the economic scale, and who hold positions that are not likely to be exposed to android competition, will probably consider them to be a boon; those whose jobs and livelihoods are directly threatened will certainly take a darker, more negative view. Which view will dominate is a question that only time can answer.

Given the possibility of (human) worker revolt as androids begin to compete directly with human workers, what incentive exists for us to build them at all? Why would we develop devices that may prove to be disruptive in the workplace and threaten the job security of human workers? There will be as many answers to this question as there are people who work on android development projects, but I can present a few of the more prevalent reasons here. First, some people will build androids because of the sheer intellectual challenge in creating a device so complex. This is the most difficult problem we have ever tried to solve — much more so than merely sending a man to the Moon — and simple intellectual curiosity and determination will drive many researchers. Others will build androids because they hope to improve the world by providing competent, low-cost (relatively) workers for difficult or dangerous jobs. Some will build them because they think money can be made by doing so — and undoubtedly they will be correct. A few will construct androids because they will be easier to manage than people, less independent and demanding of rights and privileges than a human being placed in the same circumstances. And some will build them just because it's their job to do so.

As time passes, and robot generation succeeds robot generation, their physical appearances will change dramatically. Depending on their individual destinies, each android type is likely to have a specialized form. Some may have multiple hands or legs; others may have eyes on all sides — nannies, like parents, really need eyes in the backs of their heads, for instance. Some will look more like a refrigerator than a person, and others may appear more like an insect. No matter what their physical form, however, the brightest of these, the ones that can truly be called androids, will be those that are destined for general operation in a wide variety of situations.

These general-purpose robots will have to be smarter than those devoted   20
to individual specific tasks in order to cope with a changing set of problems and environments; they are likely, in fact, to be the geniuses of the robot world. Such robots must have a general-purpose form as well, one that may not be optimal for each individual task, but one suitable for many different roles. In nature, the most adaptable animal on Earth is *Homo sapiens,* and our form has the general characteristics needed for such adaptability. We walk erect so we can see more of our environment; we have a couple of manipulating hands and arms; we have a head at the top of the body, with a well-protected braincase and most sensing organs located there as well.

There is a logic to why we are put together the way we are, and there is no reason not to take advantage of that logic when we construct a general-purpose robot. There would be little point in locating eyes in the feet, for example — we couldn't even see over a curb in that case. By locating sensory organs such as eyes and ears in the head at the top of the body, we achieve the maximum range of detection in these senses. Yes, we may give an android an extra hand or two, or improve the design in other ways, but the basic body shape will be a recognizable copy of a human being, and thus will merit the title "android."

There is little doubt in my mind that the smartest robots we build will look reasonably human—our egos, if nothing else, will assure that this is the case. But might they not look *too* human? Might they bear such a close resemblance that we cannot tell them apart from us? This is unlikely as long as we are talking only about mechanically constructed devices. But it is not necessarily true that androids must be constructed mechanically—we might grow them instead.

Biotechnology and genetics are growing as fast or faster even than computer technology. Already a massive, decades-long Human Genome Project is underway that has the goal of completely deciphering the entire genetic code of our species. We are learning how to clone animals, and already have developed microorganisms and even laboratory animals that carry a specific genetic heritage and can accomplish specific tasks, ranging from cleaning up after oil spills to manufacturing desirable drugs. The technology that today manufactures a specialized organism to produce interferon may tomorrow manufacture a device that looks utterly human—but carries an artificially crafted brain.

Legal precedents have been set in these cases: patents have already been issued on several genetically engineered organisms, including a laboratory mouse with a specific genetic heritage. Such precedents will certainly have tremendous long-range implications for ourselves and the beings we construct.

Biological androids, should they ever be built, would have many of the same frailties of a person, but might be manufactured to meet physical, emotional, or intellectual specifications that may be difficult to locate in the general human population. In addition, such beings may offer a "sure thing" in terms of the end result—something that no parent in the ordinary sense can ever be granted. Would you like your son to be an exceptional pianist? Just go down to the bio-android store and select the hair and eye color you'd prefer. Do you want little Susie to be gorgeous and a brilliant scientist? Make your selection and pay your money. The results are perfectly guaranteed, because the devices are built to your specifications, with none of the risk involved in letting your genes randomly merge with those of your partner.*

But even if androids are purely mechanical (as seems most likely to me), they will still take advantage of the general-purpose shape that has served us so well. Their mechanical forms, however, will make them stronger, more durable, and less susceptible to disease and injury than human beings. They may also be able to tolerate an even broader range of environments than

---

*The guarantee only applies to those characteristics that are determined solely or primarily by genetics. The dividing line between effects dictated by genetic heritage and those caused by environmental influence is fuzzy and highly disputed. The current trend is to assign greater and greater importance to genetic heritage, with the result that many people may soon find themselves discriminated against in insurance and the workplace for genes they carry that may someday make them susceptible to diseases or other problems. Genetically engineered offspring guaranteed to be free of such failings are likely to become much more attractive should this trend continue to grow.

people, such as the cosmic radiation found in space or on other planets. This is likely to give them a strong competitive advantage over similarly qualified (but less durable) humans for many jobs. And when combined with their other characteristics such as reliability, and low (or no) fringe benefits and salary, androids may well take over many positions in the workforce.

These issues do not strike at the heart of the impact of androids on society, or how they will change us as a people. The widespread use of intelligent androids is likely to be the most important development in history, and perhaps in the whole evolutionary development of our species. Their effect on us and on our society will be profound and, possibly, devastating. While many of the side effects may be beneficial — improved care for the aged and the very young, for example — the negative side effects from this technology may well outweigh the benefits.

I believe androids will (sooner or later) have the quality we describe as mind. Mind will emerge from the complex interaction of the independent subsystems that make up an intelligent android. We will not need to program it in; we will not have to explicitly build it. We probably won't be able to understand it any better than we understand our own minds — and maybe not as well. But when the android becomes sufficiently complex and intelligent, self-awareness and mind must inevitably follow. Mind is not likely to be present in the first android, but eventually it will come, and we may not know exactly when that fuzzy line between mind and not-mind is crossed.

On an individual basis, people may have a hard time adjusting to these ever-smarter androids, because while the first ones will certainly be "mere" machines, somewhere in the twenty to fifty years after their initial widespread introduction androids will take on the characteristics of mind and personality. The social rules and laws that will govern the first androids will not be adequate to govern these later, self-aware systems. And that is when the trouble will begin.

You may wonder why I am so sure that androids will eventually be self-aware. I can explain this belief best in the form of a simple thought experiment. Suppose that the first "intelligent" android is, at best, nothing more than a low-grade moron. In fact, suppose that it has an IQ-equivalent of 10, or even 1. This is clearly not a very bright device at all, and one that few people would have any trouble calling a "mere" machine. In fact, it is probably too dumb to even be considered intelligent.* Nevertheless, as I mentioned before, computer technology is racing ahead at the steady rate of a one thousand-fold increase in performance every twenty years, and shows no sign

30

*A strong argument could be made that existing robots have already exceeded IQs of 1; for example, WABOT, the Japanese keyboard-playing robot can be argued to be more capable than an IQ of 1 would indicate. Even Rodney Brooks's "spider" robots seem more capable than this simple criterion. On that basis, I could argue that the android "Adam" has already been built and the twenty-year countdown to an android of average human intelligence is well underway.

of slowing. It is inconceivable that improvements in computational technology will not quickly find their way into the design of current androids. Thus, a mere twenty or so years after that first moronic android, we should expect its successors to be one thousand times as fast, smart, and capable. So the android "Adam" with an IQ of 1 is likely to be succeeded within a single human generation by "Adam X" with an IQ of 1000. (The IQ of the "average" human being is 100 ± 10 or so IQ points.) Even if computer technology development shows drastically, to, say, a one hundred-fold improvement every twenty years, that still means that the android constructed a mere single human generation after the original one will have a measure of intelligence very comparable to that of the average human being.

If we truly build an intelligent android that can interact with people, experience pain and pleasure, make decisions, operate independently on the job — or at least as independently as a human being — then is this invention still a machine? Or is it really another being like ourselves, albeit with a different body chemistry, but still a being to be respected as having self-worth? Have we created a sophisticated machine, or have we invented a new species of being, one that can become our ally — or our enemy?

The questions and problems such a development raises are many and deeply disturbing to a species that has long considered itself the master of all it surveys. Society must consider carefully whether intelligent androids are property or independent beings. What is it that makes a machine a piece of property, and a person not? A mere trick of chemistry — in other words, being based on carbon molecules instead of silicon? It is certainly true that the computer systems we have today have no sense of self-awareness, no recognizable personality, no *mind.** But will that be true of an android?

At the moment American society cannot even decide when a fetus becomes a human being; it seems unlikely that a possible mechanical intelligence — and an artificial life — would be any less controversial. The legal system today struggles mightily — and sometimes violently — with the issue of what constitutes a human being, always running months, years, even decades behind the latest in scientific advances. When is it acceptable to "turn off" a human being on life support? When is it acceptable to abort a fetus? What constitutes human life? What quality must be present to make the physical being sacrosanct?

Now imagine, if you will, the possibilities for argument, counterargument, and violent dispute among people who are basically rational and well intentioned, when the concept of *android* life enters this arena. Will any two people

---

*A surprising number of people who work with advanced workstations — Macintoshes, Suns, and the like — may dispute the assertion that their current computers have no recognizable personalities. Fans of the Macintosh in particular frequently ascribe personalities to their systems, as can be seen by the popularity of software packages such as the "Talking Moose" (Baseline Software) and "At Your Service" (Bright Star Technology). Both offer users the chance to interact with "characters" who "live" inside the Macintosh and perform entertaining and useful functions.

agree on which kinds of androids are intelligent beings—and thus deserving of the respect due to any living, intelligent being—and which are not? Will those people who today call themselves "pro-life" take up similar cudgels on behalf of androids? If not, do they not betray themselves as hopelessly bigoted, displaying their (apparent) inability to honor or appreciate any form of life except their own? And those who are "pro-choice" in human affairs: Will they march and protest in favor of the right to choose whether or not to turn off an android?

Will androids become *too* humanlike? Will they become prey to the evils in mankind as well as our virtues? Is an android likely to develop prejudices, become selfish, or turn violent? We don't now know fully how such emotions work in people, but is it possible for an android to fall in love? To feel jealous? To learn to hate? If this is the case, surely there is little incentive for us to build them, for we are perfectly capable of generating beings with these flaws right in our own species. While androids are not likely to have deep emotions until long after the first one is built, I think it would be a mistake to brush these questions off as irrelevant.

Emotions in people and animals derive at least partially from the necessity of preparing the body for action. Adrenaline surges into the body, readying it for fight or flight responses in emergency situations. Feeling of rage and fear derive directly from such adrenal stimulation. Other feelings such as love and sorrow are less well understood now, but also seem to have a chemical basis, at least in part. In all these cases, however, it is difficult to see what subsystem in an android would provide a similar stimulus as the adrenal system in humans. It is likely that androids will be limited initially to the more sedate emotions: concern, liking, caring, satisfaction, perhaps even sorrow and enjoyment. They may eventually move past these feelings—or then again, they may not.

This emotional stolidity may also add to their reliability in the work place. Certainly it is extremely difficult to envision an android allowing its emotions to interfere with their work, as frequently happens with human beings. It is equally difficult to imagine an android pining away for love, or distraught and grief-stricken from the loss of a friend. Unless there is some evolutionary or performance advantage carried with these profound emotional responses, it seems unlikely that they will ever be part of an android's makeup—in fact, androids may never move past a strong sense of duty and responsibility. Nevertheless, some level of basic emotional response will almost certainly be present, and must be considered when determining how to deal with these beings.

When we construct an android with a built-in sense of pain (for self-protection and self-diagnosis), and at least some minimal collection of emotional responses as that described above, does that mean that we can feel free to ignore those emotions and feelings simply because it is a machine and not a person? If we have a dangerous task that will likely result in the destruction of the android, can we feel free to order the android to carry out the task,

35

dooming if forever? Or must we offer an intelligent android a choice — and what do we do if it refuses to comply?

If we decide that androids are independent beings, how much freedom does that imply? Are they eligible for citizenship? Can they vote? Can they run for office? Can they be managers and supervisors in a factory? (Won't *that* be an interesting tangle, when managers instead of factory workers have to worry about losing their jobs to androids?)

Should it be legal to have a sexual relationship with an android? Is it moral 40 to do so? In fact, should androids be built with any kind of sexual function at all? You may wonder why this would even be an issue, but consider this: Might it not be safer from a hygienic perspective to use androids as sexual surrogates and prostitutes than human beings? At least the possibility exists of disinfecting an android between clients, thus reducing the risk of spreading disease. Could this not be a more socially acceptable way of providing sexual services for hire? Certainly prostitution has existed as long as society — does it not make sense to control the medical consequences by applying some basic principles of hygiene? Humans have consistently manufactured sexual toys of increasing realism and talent; surely someone, somewhere will construct a sexually functional android if only for the titillation value.

But would you want your sister or daughter — or your brother or son — to marry a sexually functional android? Would *you* marry one? (And before you cast this notion aside as being too ridiculous to contemplate, just consider that many people accept same-sex gay marriages as reasonable; marriage today frequently has little to do with procreation. And might not an android stepparent prove to be superior to many human ones?)

And if we are the creators of this race of independent intelligent beings, does that mean that we are on a par with God? What's the difference between breathing life into a lump of clay to make a human being, and constructing an intelligent, self-aware android? Does an android that we create have a soul? Or is it, like Mary Shelley's Frankenstein monster, forever doomed to soullessness? If it has a soul, could an android become a Catholic priest? A Jewish rabbi? A nun? Could an android be a prophet?

If it has no soul that we humans recognize, might androids band together to form their own religion? And, if so, would their God be *Homo sapiens*? Is it not the height of arrogance to assume that we can usurp such a central role in any religion? Or would they even bother with religion at all?

Will the development of intelligent androids lead to riots in the streets as human beings begin to resent the fruits of their own labors? I suspect that such an event is all too probable once their true impact on society is realized. We humans are not noted for our tolerance of beings who are different, and I doubt that a few decades' worth of experience with intelligent androids will be enough to forestall such unrest. The social, legal, ethical, moral, and religious questions raised by the development of a new set of intelligent beings may touch off a social upheaval that makes the 1960s race riots seem mild.

Social upheavals, racism, and other forms of intolerance are usually at   45
least partially triggered by economic competition. How will humans react to
competition with the devices we ourselves created? It is difficult to believe that
those whose livelihoods and standards of living are threatened by the use of
android labor—whether as factory worker, gardener, or white-collar manager—will take such competition calmly. People in general and Americans in
particular are quite sensitive to "unfair" competition; an android that needs
no employee benefits, and against whose dedication and efforts a human's
performance may be compared, is likely to seem exceptionally unfair competition. This could have the dual result of either dehumanizing working conditions for human workers, or even of outlawing android labor altogether.

And what happens to us and our egos when our metallic children outstrip
their creators in intelligence? You may wonder why I seem so concerned with
the evolutionary forces acting on androids, when "clearly" android development is in our hands and will not be the result of evolutionary forces. The reason is that as androids become more capable than human beings, they are
likely to take over much of their own development and reproduction. After all,
would *you* willingly trust the reproduction of your kind to a species who was
your own intellectual and physical inferior? Certainly the first ten to fifty years
of android development are likely to be guided by humans, but eventually androids themselves will most likely be in charge of their own future. The first
android "Adam" may soon be joined by a metallic "Eve." And we may have
created our successor—a successor that may exceed our own capabilities in
many ways.

None of the questions and issues raised above can be answered today, nor is
the scenario of social upheaval I have sketched more than just a single possibility out of hundreds or thousands of other possibilities. But I would like to
pose just one more question.

Consider the point I mentioned above that the android worker will never
need breaks, never call in sick, never take vacations, never defect to another
company, and so on. These are not the attributes of a human worker; they are
the attributes of a slave.

A slave is a being that is bound in servitude to another. A slave can make
no decisions about his life, not even about his very existence; he is simply
bound to obey his master's orders. His life or death is a matter of the whim of
his master. A slave is not a person; a slave is a thing. From time immemorial,
we as a species have enslaved the animals around us and even others of our
own species by considering them as less than human, as mere property. Now
we may be preparing to do the same with our own creations.

Suppose we as a society decide that an intelligent android is nothing more   50
than a smarter computer, a machine that is property, with no rights or ability
to decide its own fate. In that case, have we not just created a collection of
slaves? And in doing so, have we not condemned ourselves? All civilized soci-

eties today consider slavery a barbaric, brutish practice that must not be tolerated. Would we not be reinstating an institution that civilized people abhor? Are we as a species so parochial and prejudiced that we cannot see the worth of another kind of being, beings that will be our children in a very real sense, but that differ from us in chemistry and (possibly) in form? And if we cannot cope with the minor differences in form of our own creations, how could we ever cope with the really significant physical differences that are likely should we ever encounter a society from another world or star system?

I believe that society will be placed under strong duress by the invention of an intelligent android. This opportunity presents a challenge to us as humans — presumably civilized humans — to decide whether we choose to react in a civilized fashion, or as slaveholders. Obviously, the human species does not have a very good record in this regard. In our thousands of years on this planet, it is only in the past handful of decades that we have cast aside slavery within our own species; we still abide by the practice with regard to the other species on this planet. We have not yet learned to respect those other biological species, and grant them the same autonomy we have reserved for ourselves. In large measure, I believe this is because of our overweening human ego, combined with other animals' inability to communicate with us on our own terms, in a human language. Androids from the very beginning will have human language as a communications tool, however, and they will be able to tell us what they think and feel and want. I suspect that this single characteristic will make it impossible for us to ignore an android's needs and wants and desires the way we often do with animals. Androids can just keep shouting their needs in our ears until we are forced to listen.

Whether or not we will be sufficiently civilized to take our intelligent creations in stride and deal with them graciously is difficult to predict. Certainly, there will be powerful economic, legal, political, and social pressures exerted to keep our creations as property rather than as partners who share our world. The patents granted for genetically engineered organisms already indicate that we have started down the path of considering them property and not independent beings. But doing so may prove, in the long run, to be disastrous for our society, and possibly for our species. Personally, I am not sure I want to participate in the forcible suppression of the rights of a group of beings who are likely to become my intellectual — and physical — superiors within a few decades. To me, this sounds like a highly dangerous stance to take over the long run.

This may be particularly true if the androids we create absorb more from us than just our intellect. In large part our species has become enormously successful by being, quite frankly, the toughest, meanest, most adaptable animals around. If our android children carry this same tendency, we may easily find ourselves usurped from the position of "King of the Hill." It might behoove us to treat such beings with considerably more care and respect while they are still under our control—the prospect of meaner, smarter, tougher androids coming after us with vengeance on their minds is not a comforting notion to contemplate.

There is one final point I would like to make. Some may think that the way to avoid the conflict and upheaval I have suggested here is merely to refrain from building androids at all. It is true that such a path might avoid the need for humanity to decide how humane we really are. Unfortunately, this is a highly unlikely solution to the dilemma that faces us. Never in our history has mankind *ever* refused to develop a technology that we knew we could exploit. We as a people have built every invention we ever thought of, developed it and tried to make it work. That does not mean that we have always used the invention to its fullest extent once it was complete—the hydrogen bomb and various biological warfare devices are cases in point. Nevertheless, we have always built things once we knew how. I cannot believe that the development of an android will be any different. From whatever variety of motives and methods, we are now standing at the very threshold of knowing how to build an artificial person; I find it extremely unlikely that, once possible, it will not be built by someone, somewhere.

Society as a whole is going to have to learn how to cope with this technology. It will be up to each of us to decide how we should react to it; what limits, if any, are appropriate to apply. The problems involved are knotty and difficult, and will not be solved in a few years or even decades. We must solve them somehow, however, and the way to start is for each of us to begin to consider the implications of such technology. We cannot turn back the clock; neither can we ignore the genesis of intelligent systems that we know—or even just believe—we can construct. To a large extent, humanity is a race of inventors and builders; asking us to not build something new is like asking a bird not to sing—it is counter to our whole nature. For this reason alone, we again must learn to cope with the fruits of our own labors—just as we always have.

The title of this selection says it all: Intelligent androids will in fact redefine the measure of mankind—but they will redefine the measure of the human species, not that of the beings we create. We will learn much about ourselves in the next decades as we see how we begin to cope with another group of intelligent beings sharing the world with us. It is not likely to be an entirely comfortable time for anyone—but it will certainly be interesting.

There is an ancient Chinese curse that goes, "May you live in interesting times." We have been cursed—and blessed—for we all do live in most interesting times, indeed—and even more interesting times are coming. Whether we are ready to cope or not, the revolution is just around the corner.

Selected Bibliography

"Behind Closed Doors: Unlocking the Mysteries of Human Intelligence," Robert J. Sternberg, in *Speculations: The Reality Club,* edited by John Brockman, Prentice Hall Press, New York, 1990.

"We Aren't Ready for the Robots," Noel Perrin, editorial page of *Wall Street Journal,* February 26, 1986.

Gödel, Escher, Bach: An Eternal Golden Braid, Douglas R. Hofstadter, Vintage Books, 1980.

EXPLORING THE TEXT

1. What is Caudill's vision of the future of computer technology? What does she base her predictions on? How plausible does this forecast seem to you? What flaws in logic or unforeseen problems might complicate her vision of the future?

2. What jobs, according to Caudill, will probably be replaced first by androids? What kinds of jobs might be more difficult to fill with intelligent machines? Why? What do you think will happen as more and more androids enter the workplace? What social questions will the widespread use of android workers raise?

3. What would you find more acceptable, a machine with human-level intelligence or a genetically engineered human being? Which would strike you as more unsettling from an ethical or moral perspective? Why?

4. How would you respond to the larger moral or ethical questions Caudill associates with the inevitable development of intelligent androids? What quality might define the difference between human and machine minds? What, if anything, makes human life sacrosanct? At what point will androids cease to be seen as mere "devices" that are owned by human beings? Would you condone sex with an android surrogate? Would you condone human/ android marriage? Could an android fulfill the role of rabbi, minister, or priest? Why or why not?

5. What questions does Caudill raise about human nature in this selection? To what extent would you agree with the assumptions she makes about human values, motives, and desires?

6. What solution, if any, does Caudill suggest to the problems posed by the development of machine minds? How do you interpret the Woody Allen epigraph she uses to introduce this selection? Do you think Caudill would favor banning the development of intelligent machines? Would you?

FURTHER QUESTIONS

1. Should a computer capable of passing the Turing test, as described by Douglas Hofstadter (p. 719), be recognized as an "independent being"? Why or why not? If not, what kind of test would it take to convince you that a machine might, in fact, be seen as an independent being?

2. How might the social questions involved with the development of intelligent machines help explain the "dark" tone of much recent science fiction, as documented by Claudia Springer (p. 689) and illustrated by William Gibson's "Johnny Mnemonic" (p. 703)? Is it possible to read Gibson's story itself as an act of resistance against the future domination of cyberminds?

3. How might Peter Singer (p. 607) respond to Caudill's claim that machines will become "persons," not property, in the future? What would Singer require of machines before he would be willing to extend to them the principle of equality?

4. How might Paul Shepard (p. 624) respond to Caudill's suggestion that androids may one day earn the right of citizenship with all the freedoms and legal protections that equal citizenship entails?

5. To what extent are the arguments for and against cloning advanced by Philip Kitcher (p. 350) and Jean Bethke Elshtain (p. 359) also applicable to the development of androids? What difference is there, if any, between the duplication of human beings through genetic engineering and the duplication of humanlike intelligence through computer simulation? If cloning is morally repugnant, why then shouldn't the development of androids be equally distasteful?

6. As a class, view the award-winning 1997 documentary *Fast, Cheap, and Out of Control* and discuss what it seems to be saying about human, animal, and machine minds. What does this film imply about the evolution of human intelligence in relation to ideas like domination, empathy, and beauty?

ESSAY OPTIONS

1. Research and write a report on the social costs of automation over the past twenty years. What kinds of jobs have been replaced by intelligent machines since the beginning of the computer era? What has happened to the workers who have lost their positions due to automation? What are the forecasts for the future automation of the workforce over the next twenty-five to fifty years? What might be the social, political, and economic consequences of these trends?

2. Research and write an essay or create a hypertext presentation/Web site on the current state of robot development. How far have we come toward the fulfillment of Caudill's predictions about the evolution of intelligent machines? How far do current roboticists believe we will be in twenty-five to fifty years? What challenges remain to be overcome in the quest to duplicate human intelligence?

3. View a postcomputer-era movie dealing with android characters, such as *A.I.: Artificial Intelligence, Bicentennial Man,* or *Blade Runner,* and write an essay about how the film depicts the conflict of human and machine minds. How do recent films portray androids? What issues do they raise about human/machine relationships and human and machine intelligence? What do they seem to be saying about current attitudes toward machine intelligence? About the ethical questions inherent in the quest to create life in our own image?

Grandfather Clause

HANS MORAVEC

The "brain in a vat" is a science-fiction cliché. It's the stuff of comic books and bad B movies, and deservedly so, because even as a fantasy it seems singularly unappealing. Who would want to purchase immortality at the price of losing their body? How excited can you get about the prospect of living forever if you have to spend the rest of your life dangling from a couple of electrodes in a fish tank full of bubbling chemicals? In this selection, computer scientist Hans Moravec puts a new twist on this cheesy sci-fi fantasy. Instead of consigning your brain to a vat, what if you could "download" your consciousness into the sleek new body of a cyborg? Moravec's bizarre predictions of human obsolescence may provoke you to tears, but they are just as sure to raise serious questions about what it means to be "you" in the first place. Founder and director of the center for Mobile Robotics at Carnegie Mellon University, Moravec (b. 1948) is a leader in the field of artificial intelligence theory and an outspoken proponent of cybernetics. His publications include *Mind Children, The Future of Robot and Human Intelligence* (1988), the source of this selection, and *Robot: Mere Machine to Transcendent Mind* (1999).

BEFORE READING

What parts of the human body are currently replaceable with mechanical prostheses? If it were technically feasible to fit a human being with multiple prostheses, how much of a person's body could be replaced before that person's humanity would be in doubt? Could you, for example, replace an arm and a leg? An arm, leg, eye, and hip? A heart? The left hemisphere of the cerebral cortex? At what point would our imaginary subject become a machine? Why?

W hat happens when ever-cheaper machines can replace humans in any situation? Indeed, what will I do when a computer can write this book, or do my research, better than I? These questions have already become crucial ones for many people in all kinds of occupations, and in a few decades they will matter to everybody. By design, machines are our obedient and able slaves. But intelligent machines, however benevolent, threaten our existence because they are alternative inhabitants of our ecological niche. Machines merely as clever as human beings will have enormous advantages in competitive situations. Their production and upkeep cost less, so more of them can be put to work with the resources at hand. They can be optimized for their jobs and programmed to work tirelessly.

As if these technological developments were not threatening enough, the very pace of innovation presents an even more serious challenge to our security. We evolved at a leisurely rate, with millions of years between significant changes. Machines are making similar strides in mere decades. When multitudes of economical machines are put to work as programmers and engineers, presented with the task of optimizing the software and hardware that makes them what they are, the pace will quicken. Successive generations of machines produced this way will become smarter and less costly. There is no reason to believe that human equivalence represents any sort of upper bound. When pocket calculators can outthink humans, what will a big computer be like? We will simply be outclassed.

So why rush headlong into an era of intelligent machines? The answer, I believe, is that we have very little choice, if our culture is to remain viable. Societies and economies are surely as subject to competitive evolutionary pressures as are biological organisms. Sooner or later the ones that can sustain the most rapid expansion and diversification will dominate. Cultures compete with one another for the resources of the accessible universe. If automation is more efficient than manual labor, organizations and societies that embrace it will be wealthier and better able to survive in difficult times and to expand in favorable ones. If the United States were to unilaterally halt technological development (an occasionally fashionable idea), it would soon succumb either to the military might of unfriendly nations or to the economic success of its trading partners. Either way, the social ideals that led to the decision would become unimportant on a world scale.

If, by some unlikely pact, the whole human race decided to eschew progress, the long-term result would be almost certain extinction. The universe is one random event after another. Sooner or later an unstoppable virus deadly to humans will evolve, or a major asteroid will collide with the earth, or the sun will expand, or we will be invaded from the stars, or a black hole with swallow the galaxy. The bigger, more diverse, and competent a culture is, the better it can detect and deal with external dangers. The larger events happen less frequently. By growing rapidly enough, a culture has a finite chance of surviving forever. . . .

Transmigration

Some of us humans have quite egocentric world views. We anticipate the discovery, within our lifetimes, of methods to extend human life, and we look forward to a few eons of exploring the universe. The thought of being grandly upstaged in this by our artificial progeny is disappointing. Long life loses much of its point if we are fated to spend it staring stupidly at our ultra-intelligent machines as they try to describe their ever more spectacular discoveries in baby-talk that we can understand. We want to become full, unfettered players in this new superintelligent game. What are the possibilities for doing that?

Genetic engineering may seem an easy option. Successive generations of human beings could be designed by mathematics, computer simulations, and experimentation, like airplanes, computers, and robots are now. They could have better brains and improved metabolisms that would allow them to live comfortably in space. But, presumably, they would still be made of protein, and their brains would be made of neurons. Away from earth, protein is not an ideal material. It is stable only in a narrow temperature and pressure range, is very sensitive to radiation, and rules out many construction techniques and components. And it is unlikely that neurons, which can now switch less than a thousand times per second, will ever be boosted to the billions-per-second speed of even today's computer components. Before long, conventional technologies, miniaturized down to the atomic scale, and biotechnology, its molecular interactions understood in detailed mechanical terms, will have merged into a seamless array of techniques encompassing all materials, sizes, and complexities. Robots will then be made of a mix of fabulous substances, including, where appropriate, living biological materials. At that time a genetically engineered superhuman would be just a second-rate kind of robot, designed under the handicap that its construction can only be by DNA-guided protein synthesis. Only in the eyes of human chauvinists would it have an advantage — because it retains more of the original human limitations than other robots.

Robots, first or second rate, leave our question unanswered. Is there any chance that we — you and I, personally — can fully share in the magical world to come? This would call for a process that endows an individual with all the advantages of the machines, without loss of personal identity. Many people today are alive because of a growing arsenal of artificial organs and other body parts. In time, especially as robotic techniques improve, such replacement parts will be better than any originals. So what about replacing everything, that is, transplanting a human brain into a specially designed robot body? Unfortunately, while this solution might overcome most of our physical limitations, it would leave untouched our biggest handicap, the limited and fixed intelligence of the human brain. This transplant scenario gets our brain out of our body. Is there a way to get our mind out of our brain?

You've just been wheeled into the operating room. A robot brain surgeon is in attendance. By your side is a computer waiting to become a human equivalent, lacking only a program to run. Your skull, but not your brain, is anesthetized. You are fully conscious. The robot surgeon opens your brain case and places a hand on the brain's surface. This unusual hand bristles with microscopic machinery, and a cable connects it to the mobile computer at your side. Instruments in the hand scan the first few millimeters of brain surface. High-resolution magnetic resonance measurements build a three-dimensional chemical map, while arrays of magnetic and electric antennas collect signals that are rapidly unraveled to reveal, moment to moment, the pulses flashing among the neurons. These measurements, added to a comprehensive understanding of human neural architecture, allow the surgeon to write a program that models the behavior of the uppermost layer of the scanned brain tissue. This program is installed in a small portion of the waiting computer and activated. Measurements from the hand provide it with copies of the inputs that the original tissue is receiving. You and the surgeon check the accuracy of the simulation by comparing the signals it produces with the corresponding original ones. They flash by very fast, but any discrepancies are highlighted on a display screen. The surgeon fine-tunes the simulation until the correspondence is nearly perfect.

To further assure you of the simulation's correctness, you are given a pushbutton that allows you to momentarily "test drive" the simulation, to compare it with the functioning of the original tissue. When you press it, arrays of electrodes in the surgeon's hand are activated. By precise injections of current and electromagnetic pulses, the electrodes can override the normal signaling activity of nearby neurons. They are programmed to inject the output of the simulation into those places where the simulated tissue signals other sites. As long as you press the button, a small part of your nervous system is being replaced by a computer simulation of itself. You press the button, release it, and press it again. You should experience no difference. As soon as you are satisfied, the simulation connection is established permanently. The brain tissue is now impotent—it receives inputs and reacts as before but its output is ignored. Microscopic manipulators on the hand's surface excise the cells in this superfluous tissue and pass them to an aspirator, where they are drawn away.

The surgeon's hand sinks a fraction of a millimeter deeper into your brain, instantly compensating its measurements and signals for the changed position. The process is repeated for the next layer, and soon a second simulation resides in the computer, communicating with the first and with the remaining original brain tissue. Layer after layer the brain is simulated, then excavated. Eventually your skull is empty, and the surgeon's hand rests deep in your brainstem. Though you have not lost consciousness, or even your train of thought, your mind has been removed from the brain and transferred to a machine. In a final, disorienting step the surgeon lifts out his hand. Your suddenly abandoned body goes into spasms and dies. For a moment you experience only quiet and dark. Then, once again, you can open your eyes. Your perspective has shifted. The computer simulation has been disconnected from the cable leading to the surgeon's hand and reconnected to a shiny new body of the style, color, and material of your choice. Your metamorphosis is complete. 10

For the squeamish, there are other ways to work the transfer of human mind to machine. A high-resolution brain scan could, in one fell swoop and without surgery, make a new you "While-U-Wait." If even the last technique is too invasive for you, imagine a more psychological approach. A kind of portable computer (perhaps worn like magic glasses) is programmed with the universals of human mentality, your genetic makeup, and whatever details of your life are conveniently available. It carries a program that makes it an excellent mimic. You carry this computer with you through the prime of your life; it diligently listens and watches; perhaps it monitors your brain and learns to anticipate your every move and response. Soon it can fool your friends on the phone with its convincing imitation of you. When you die, this program is installed in a mechanical body that then smoothly and seamlessly takes over your life and responsibilities. . . .

Many Changes

Whatever style of mind transfer you choose, as the process is completed many of your old limitations melt away. Your computer has a control labeled "speed." It had been set at "slow," to keep the simulations synchronized with the old brain, but now you change it to "fast," allowing you to communicate, react, and think a thousand times faster. The entire program can be copied into similar machines, resulting in two or more thinking, feeling versions of you. You may choose to move your mind from one computer to another that is more technically advanced or better suited to a new environment. The program can also be copied to a future equivalent of magnetic tape. Then, if the machine you inhabit is fatally clobbered, the tape can be read into a blank computer, resulting in another you minus your experiences since the copy. With enough widely dispersed copies, your permanent death would be highly unlikely.

As a computer program, your mind can travel over information channels, for instance encoded as a laser message beamed between planets. If you found life on a neutron star and wished to make a field trip, you might devise a way to build a robot there of neutron stuff, then transmit your mind to it. Since nuclear reactions are about a million times quicker than chemical ones, the neutron-you might be able to think a million times faster. You would explore, acquire new experiences and memories, and then beam your mind back home. Your original body could be kept dormant during the trip and reactivated with the new memories when the return message arrived—perhaps a minute later but with a subjective year's worth of experiences. Alternatively, the original could be kept active. Then there would be two separate versions of you, with different memories for the trip interval.

Your new abilities will dictate changes in your personality. Many of the changes will result from your own deliberate tinkerings with your own program. Having turned up your speed control a thousandfold, you notice that you now have hours (subjectively speaking) to respond to situations that previously required instant reactions. You have time, during the fall of a dropped object, to research the advantages and disadvantages of trying to catch it, perhaps to solve its differential equations of motion. You will have time to read and ponder an entire online etiquette book when you find yourself in an awkward social situation. Faced with a broken machine, you will have time, before touching it, to learn its theory of operation and to consider, in detail, the various things that may be wrong with it. In general, you will have time to undertake what would today count as major research efforts to solve trivial everyday problems.

You will have the time, but will you have the patience? Or will a thousandfold mental speedup simply incapacitate you with boredom? Boredom is a mental mechanism that keeps you from wasting your time in profitless activity, but if it acts too soon or too aggressively it limits your attention span, and thus your intelligence. One of the first changes you will want to make in your own program is to retard the onset of boredom beyond the range found today in even the most extreme intellectuals. Having done that, you will find yourself comfortably working on long problems with sidetracks upon sidetracks. In fact, your thoughts will routinely become so involved that they will call for an increase in your short-term memory. Your long-term memory also will have to be boosted, since a month's worth of events will occupy a subjective span of a century! These are but the first of many changes. 15

I have already mentioned the possibility of making copies of oneself, with each copy undergoing its own adventures. It should be possible to merge memories from disparate copies into a single one. To avoid confusion, memories of events would indicate in which body they happened, just as our memories today often have a context that establishes a time and place for the remembered event. Merging should be possible not only between two versions of the same individual but also between different persons. Selective mergings, involving some of another person's memories and not others, would be a superior form of communication, in which recollections, skills, attitudes, and personalities can be rapidly and effectively shared. Your new body will be able to carry more memories than your original biological one, but the accelerated information explosion will ensure the impossibility of lugging around all of civilization's knowledge. You will have to pick and choose what your mind contains at any one time. There will often be knowledge and skills available from others superior to your own, and the incentive to substitute those talents for yours will be overwhelming. In the long run you will remember mostly other people's experiences, while memories you originated will be incorporated into other minds. Concepts of life, death, and identity will lose their present meaning as your mental fragments and those of others are combined, shuffled, and recombined into temporary associations, sometimes large, sometimes small, sometimes long isolated and highly individual, at other times ephemeral, mere ripples on the rapids of civilization's torrent of knowledge. There are foretastes of this kind of fluidity around us. Culturally, individual humans acquire new skills and attitudes from others throughout life. Genetically, in sexual populations each individual organism is a temporary bundling of genes that are combined and recombined in different arrangements every generation.

Mind transferral need not be limited to human beings. Earth has other species with large brains, from dolphins, whose nervous systems are as large and complex as our own, to elephants, other whales, and perhaps giant squid, whose brains may range up to twenty times as big as ours. Just what kind of minds and cultures these animals possess is still a matter of controversy, but their evolutionary history is as long as ours, and there is surely much unique and hard-won information encoded genetically in their brain structures and their memories. The brain-to-computer transferral methods that work for humans should work as well for these large-brained animals, allowing their thoughts, skills, and motivations to be woven into our cultural tapestry. Slightly different methods, that focus more on genetics and physical makeup than on mental life, should allow the information contained in other living things with small or no nervous systems to be popped into the data banks. The simplest organisms might contribute little more than the information in their DNA. In this way our future selves will be able to benefit from and build on what the earth's biosphere has learned during its multibillion-year history. And this knowledge may be more secure if it is preserved in databanks spreading through the universe. In the present scheme of things, on our small and fragile earth, genes and ideas are often lost when the conditions that gave rise to them change.

Our speculation ends in a supercivilization, the synthesis of all solar-system life, constantly improving and extending itself, spreading outward from the sun, converting nonlife into mind. Just possibly there are other such bubbles expanding from elsewhere. What happens if we meet one? A negotiated merger is a possibility, requiring only a translation scheme between the memory representations. This process, possibly occurring now elsewhere, might convert the entire universe into an extended thinking entity, a prelude to even greater things.

What Am I?

The idea that a human mind can be transferred to a new body sometimes meets the following strong objection from people who do not dispute the theoretical possibility: "Regardless of how the copying is done, the end result will be a new person. If it is I who am being copied, the copy, though it may think of itself as me, is simply a self-deluded impostor. If the copying process destroys the original, then I have been killed. That the copy may then have a great time exploring the universe using my name and my skills is no comfort to my mortal remains."

This point of view, which I will call the *body-identity position*, makes life extension by duplication considerably less personally interesting. I believe the objection can be overcome by acceptance of an alternative position which I will call *pattern-identity*. Body-identity assumes that a person is defined by the stuff of which a human body is made. Only by maintaining continuity of body stuff can we preserve an individual person. Pattern-identity, conversely, defines the essence of a person, say myself, as the *pattern* and the *process* going on in my head and body, not the machinery supporting that process. If the process is preserved, I am preserved. The rest is mere jelly.

The body-identity position, I think, is based on a mistaken intuition about the nature of living things. In a subtle way, the preservation of pattern and loss of substance is a normal part of everyday life. As we humans eat and excrete, old cells within our bodies die, break up, and are expelled and replaced by copies made of fresh materials. Most of our body is renewed this way every few years. The few body components such as nerve cells that tend to be more static nevertheless have metabolisms that cause their inner parts to be replaced, bit by bit. Every atom present within us at birth is likely to have been replaced half way through our life. Only our pattern, and only some of it at that, stays with us until our death.

Let me explore some of the consequences of the pattern-identity position. Matter transmitters have appeared often in the science-fiction literature, at least since the invention of facsimile machines in the late 1800s. I raise the idea here only as a thought experiment, to simplify some of the issues in my mind-transfer proposal. A facsimile transmitter scans a photograph line by line with a light-sensitive photocell and produces an electric current that varies with the brightness of the scanned point in the picture. The varying electric current is transmitted over wires to a remote location, where it controls the brightness of a light bulb in a facsimile receiver. The receiver scans the bulb over photosensitive paper in the same pattern as the transmitter. When this paper is developed, a duplicate of the original photograph is obtained. This device was a boon to newspapers, who were able to get illustrations from remote parts of the country almost instantly, instead of waiting for a train to deliver photographic plates.

If pictures, why not solid objects? A *matter transmitter* might scan an object and identify its atoms or molecules one at a time, perhaps removing them in the process. The identity of the atoms would be transmitted to a receiver, where a duplicate of the original object would be assembled in the same order from a local supply of atoms. The technical problems are mind-boggling, but the principle is simple to grasp, as millions of devotees of *Star Trek* will attest.

If solid objects, why not a person? Just stick him in the transmitter, turn on the scan, and greet him when he walks from the receiver. But is he really the same person? If the system works well, the duplicate will be indistinguishable from the original in any substantial way. Yet, suppose that you fail to turn on the receiver during the transmission process. The transmitter will scan and disassemble the victim and send an unheard message to the inoperative receiver. The original person will be dead. Doesn't the process, in fact, kill the original person whether or not there is an active receiver? Isn't the duplicate just that, merely a copy? Or suppose that two receivers respond to the message from one transmitter. Which, if either, of the two duplicates is the real original?

The body-identity position on this question is clear. A matter transmitter   25 is an elaborate execution device that kills you and substitutes a clever impostor in your place. The pattern-identity position offers a different perspective. Suppose that I step into the transmission chamber. The transmitter scans and disassembles my jellylike body, but my pattern (me!) moves continuously from the dissolving jelly, through the transmitting beam, and ends up in other jelly at the destination. At no instant was the pattern (I) ever destroyed. But what about the question of duplicates? Suppose that the matter transmitter is connected to two receivers instead of one. After the transfer there will be a copy of me in each one. Surely at least one of them is a mere copy: they cannot both be me, right? *Wrong!*

Rooted in all our past experience is the assumption that one person corresponds to one body. In light of the possibility of separating mind from matter and storing and transmitting it, this simple, natural, and obvious identification becomes confusing and misleading. Consider the message, "I am not jelly." As I type it, it goes from my brain into the keyboard of my computer, through myriad electronic circuits, and over great amounts of wire. After countless adventures, the message shows up in bunches of books like the one you are holding. How many messages were there? I claim that it is most useful to think there is only one, despite its massive replication. If I repeat it here: "I am not jelly," there is still only one message. Only if I change it in a significant manner ("I am not peanut butter") do we have a second message. And the message is not destroyed until the last written version is lost and until it fades sufficiently in everybody's memory to be unreconstructable. The message is the information conveyed, not the medium on which it is encoded. The "pattern" that I claim is the real me has the same properties as this message. Making a momentary copy of my state, whether on tape or in another functional body, does not make two persons.

The "process" aspect is a little more complicated. At the instant that a "person message" is assembled, it is just another copy of the original. But if two copies are active, they will in time diverge and become two different people. Just how far this differentiation must proceed before society grants them unique identities is about as problematical as the questions "When does a fetus become a person?" or "When does an evolving species become a different species?" But if we wait zero time, then both copies are the same person—if we immediately destroy one, the person still exists in the other copy. All the deeds that that person might have done, and all the thoughts she might have thought, are still possible. If, instead, we allow both copies to live their separate lives for a year and then destroy one, we are the murderers of a unique human being. But if we wait just a short time before destroying one copy, then only a little unique information is lost.

This rationale might be a comfort if you were about to encounter danger but knew that a tape copy of you had been made recently. Should you die, an active copy made from the tape could resume your life. This copy would differ slightly from the version of you that died, in that it lacked the memories since the time of copy. But a small patch of amnesia is a trivial affair compared with the total loss of memory and function that results from death in the absence of a copy.

Intellectual acceptance that a secure and recent backup of you exists would not necessarily protect you from an extreme desire to preserve yourself if faced with imminent death, even in a worthwhile cause. Such feelings would be an evolutionary hangover from your one-copy past, no more in tune with reality than fear of flying is an appropriate response to present airline accident rates. Old instincts are not automatically erased when the rules of life are suddenly rewritten. . . .

Immortality of the type I have just described is only a temporary defense   30 against the wanton loss of knowledge and function that is the worst aspect of personal death. In the long run, our survival will require changes that are not of our own choosing. Parts of us will have to be discarded and replaced by new parts to keep in step with changing conditions and evolving competitors. Surviving means playing in a kind of cosmic Olympics, with each year bringing new events and escalated standards in old events. Though we are immortals, we must die bit by bit if we are to succeed in the qualifying event—continued survival. In time, each of us will be a completely changed being, shaped more by external challenges than by our own desires. Our present memories and interests, having lost their relevance, will at best end up in a dusty archive, perhaps to be consulted once in a long while by a historian. Personal death as we know it differs from this inevitability only in its relative abruptness. Viewed this way, personal immortality by mind transplant is a technique whose primary benefit is to temporarily coddle the sensibility and sentimentality of individual humans. It seems to me that our civilization will evolve in the same direction whether or not we transplant our minds and join the robots.

The ancestral individual is always doomed as its heritage is nibbled away to meet short-term environmental challenges. Yet this evolutionary process, seen in a more positive light, means that we are already immortal, as we have been since the dawn of life. Our genes and our culture pass continuously from one generation to the next, subject only to incremental alterations to meet the constant demand for new world records in the cosmic games. And even within our personal life, who among us would wish to remain static, possessing for a lifetime the same knowledge, memories, thoughts, and skills we had as children? Human beings value change and growth, and our artificial descendants will share this value with us—their survival, like ours, will depend on it.

Bibliography

Forward, Robert L. 1980. *Dragon's Egg.* New York: Ballantine Books.
——— 1984. *The Flight of the Dragonfly.* New York: Simon & Schuster.
Hofstadter, Douglas R., and Daniel C. Dennett, eds. 1981. *The Mind's I.* New York: Basic Books.
Rucker, Rudy. 1983. *Software.* Middlesex: Penguin Books.
Sperry, Roger. 1982. "Some effects of disconnecting the cerebral hemispheres." *Science* 217:1223–1226.
Vinge, Vernor. 1984. *True Names.* New York: Bluejay Books.

EXPLORING THE TEXT

1. Why does Moravec believe that machines will inevitably replace human beings? What assumptions underlie his view of technology, culture, and human history? To what extent would you agree with him? Why?

2. What would be the advantages of "transmigration," in Moravec's view? If it became technologically possible to carry out the kind of surgical procedure that Moravec describes, would you consider it? Why or why not?

3. How, according to Moravec, would the merger of mind and machine alter our view of personal identity, memory, and communication? What is his ultimate vision of the future of mind?

4. Why does Moravec believe that an individual human being is a "pattern" of information and not simply a mass of "mere jelly"? How persuasive do you find his contention that a human being is a "message" and not the "medium" that contains it? Why?

FURTHER EXPLORATIONS

1. How does Moravec's view of the technological future compare with that expressed by Maureen Caudill in "Redefining the Measure of Mankind" (p. 736)? Why do both of these writers view the development of intelligent machines as inevitable? Which of these views of the future do you find more plausible? Why?

2. How does Moravec's view of human identity compare with that expressed by Sherry Turkle in "Who Am We?" (p. 675)? What happens to personal identity, according to these authors, when the mind is freed from the limitations of the body? What does this suggest about the nature of selfhood?

3. What similarities can you find between Moravec's surgical transplant scenario and the simulation or imitation game involved in the Turing test, as described by Douglas Hofstadter (p. 719)? Is it possible to see Moravec's proposal as simply another version of the Turing test? What might this suggest about the effectiveness of Moravec's proposed surgical procedure?

4. Given his views on the values and attitudes associated with "white" society, how might John (Fire) Lame Deer (p. 512) interpret Moravec's fascination with the prospect of transmigration into a mechanical body? To what extent might the Native American belief in animal ancestors and totems help explain Moravec's desire to live on in machine form?

5. To what extent might Frans de Waal's discussion of the limits of anthropomorphism in reading animal minds (p. 552) also apply to Moravec's view of machine intelligence? Would de Waal be likely to agree with Moravec that we will one day be able to merge minds with other species? Would he be likely to view Moravec's understanding of machine minds as a case of naive or mature anthropomorphism? Why?

6. How might the discussions of "impersonal," "social," or "historical" memories offered in earlier selections by bell hooks (p. 237) and Eviatar Zerubavel (p. 217) complicate Moravec's vision of a time in the future when we will gladly download other people's memories and experiences into our minds? Why might Zerubavel and hooks view this as a less than attractive prospect?

ESSAY OPTIONS

1. Drawing on ideas presented by Moravec, Ullman (p. 656), Sherry Turkle (p. 675), and Douglas Hofstadter (p. 719), write an essay exploring the ways in which information technology is transforming our understanding of human identity. How is electronic technology changing the way we view the body, the mind, gender, and other aspects of what it means to be human?

2. Drawing on the ideas presented by Moravec, Hofstadter (p. 719), and Turkle (p. 675), and on additional library and Internet research, write a report or develop a hypertext presentation/Web site on the role that simulation plays in machine intelligence. What does simulation mean in the context of information technology? To what extent do all computer programs function according to the logic of simulation? Would it be accurate to say that we are entering into the era of simulation? Why or why not?

Cyber Soul-Space

MARGARET WERTHEIM

Most religions view the world from what philosophers term a "dualist" perspective. According to Christian theology, for example, all of creation exhibits a dual nature—the physical and the spiritual. Human beings, according to Christian dualism, live inside fleshy bodies, but they possess immortal souls independent of bodily existence. For Christian thinkers, the cosmos contains the material world of the senses—the world of atoms, planets, space, and time—but at the same time it is also a purely spiritual realm inhabited by angels, demons, and spiritual forces. Modern science rejected dualistic thinking early on in its development. From the perspective of science, all phenomena—no matter how mysterious—occur within the context of a material world and all can be accounted for in purely materialist terms. That's why the quest for artificial intelligence is unsettling for some people. The idea that human consciousness itself can be engineered from a pile of silicon chips threatens the fundamental assumptions of most religious thinking. Who needs a vague idea like the "soul" if you can account for the most profound and mysterious aspect of human experience in terms of good programming?

Yet, as Margaret Wertheim suggests in this selection, the entire AI enterprise may itself be motivated by the same spirit of dualism that it ostensibly challenges. Dreams of cyberintelligence, according to Wertheim, offer just one more example of the age-old desire to transcend the flesh and leave the body behind. A science writer and commentator whose articles have appeared in magazines and newspapers like the *New York Times*, *The Sciences*, and *The New Scientist*, Margaret Wertheim (b. 1960) is also the author of *Pythagoras' Trousers* (1995) and *The Pearly Gates of Cyberspace: A History of Space from Dante to the Internet* (1999), the source of this selection.

BEFORE READING

What is the "soul," in the context of Western Christian religious ideology? Where do souls come from and what happens to them after death? What does the concept of the soul imply about the mind and its relation to the body?

Let us begin with the object of desire. It exists, it has existed for all of time, and will continue eternally. It has held the attention of all mystics and witches and hackers for all time. It is the Graal. The mythology of the Sangraal—the Holy Grail°—is the archetype of the revealed illumination withdrawn. The revelation of the graal is always a personal and unique experience. . . . I know—because I have heard it countless times from many people across the world—that this moment of revelation is the common element in our experience as a community. The graal is our firm foundation.[1]

the Holy Grail: In medieval legend, the Holy Grail is a sacred object, often identified with the cup that Jesus Christ drank from during the Last Supper, which was lost after being transported to England. Tales surrounding the Grail often describe the adventures of knights, like Sir Galahad of the Arthurian legends, who set out on quests for its retrieval.

This statement would probably seem at first glance an expression of religious faith. With its focus on the Holy Grail, surely the "community" referred to must be Christian. The clue that it is not is in the second sentence. What is the word "hackers" doing there? In fact this is not an extract from a Christian revival meeting but from the capstone speech to a conference of cyberspace and virtual reality developers. The speech was given by Mark Pesce, codeveloper of VRML, Virtual Reality Modeling Language. With VRML, Pesce is a key force behind the technology that is enabling online worlds to be rendered graphically, thereby moving us closer to Gibson's original cyberspace vision.°

As one whose work contributes centrally to the visual realization of cyberspace, Pesce is a man of considerable influence within the community of cyberspace builders and technicians. His views here command attention. What, then, is the "moment of revelation" he declares as "the common element in our experience of a community"? Just what is the almost mystical experience these cyberarchitects apparently share?

According to Pesce, for each individual it takes a unique form. For him personally it took the form of a William Gibson short story—an early precursor to *Neuromancer*. True to the mythic archetype he outlines in his speech, Pesce told his cybercolleagues the experience occurred at a time of crisis: He had just been expelled from MIT, and was on his way home by bus to break the news to his parents. To while away those Greyhound hours he had purchased a copy of *OMNI* magazine, wherein he discovered Gibson's seminal foray into cyberpunk. As he recounted, the story "left me dazzled with its brilliance, drenched in sweat, entirely seduced. For here, spelled out in the first paragraph in the nonsense word 'cyberspace,' I had discovered numinous beauty; here in the visible architecture of reason, was truth."[2] Everything that comes after this, he continued, even "our appearance here today—is simply the methodical search to recover a vision of an object that declares its existence outside of time." . . .

In one form of another, a "religious" attitude has been voiced by almost all the leading champions of cyberspace. *Wired* magazine's Kevin Kelly is by no means alone in seeing "soul-data" in silicon. VR guru Jaron Lanier has remarked that "I see the Internet as a syncretic version of Christian ritual, I really do. There's this sensibility and transcendence that's applied to computers, regularly. Where did that come from? That's a Christian idea."[3] Speaking at another conference Pesce has said that it "seems reasonable to assume that people will want to worship" in cyberspace. Elsewhere he refers to "the divine parts of ourselves, that we invoke in that space."[4]

And let us not forget VR animator Nicole Stenger's claim that "on the other   5 side of our data gloves . . . we will all become angels." Like Pesce, Stenger too

Gibson's original . . . : American science-fiction writer William Gibson (b. 1948) created the term *cyberspace* in the 1994 novel *Neuromancer*. (See p. 151.)

experienced a moment of quasi-mystical revelation that precipitated her into the cyberspace profession. For her, this occurred while watching an early work of computer animation. Describing the experience, she writes that the animator "had revealed a state of grace to us, tapped a wavelength where image, music, language and love were pulsing in one harmony."[5] According to Stenger, those "who decided to follow the light" would "find a common thread running through cyberspace, dream, hallucination, and mysticism."[6] . . .

Throughout history, in cultures across the globe, religion has played a central role in people's lives, and as the current tsunami of religious and quasi-religious enthusiasm attests, the desire for a "spiritual life" continues in America today. Through prayer, meditation, retreats, home churching, spirit chanelling, and psychotropic drugs, people across the nation are seeking pearly gates of one sort or another. And the United States is far from alone in this trend: Around the world, from Iran to Japan, religious fervor is on the rise. In this climate, the timing for something like cyberspace could hardly have been better. It was perhaps inevitable that the appearance of a new immaterial space would precipitate a flood of techno-spiritual dreaming. That this site of religious expectation is being realized through the by-products of science—the force that so effectively annihilated the soul-space of the medieval world picture—is surely one of the greater ironies of our times.

Speaking of the dreams that people project onto science and technology, philosopher Mary Midgley° has written that "Attending to the workings of the scientific imagination is not a soft option. [This imagining] is not just harmless, licensed amusement. It plays a part in shaping the world-pictures that determine our standards of thought—the standards by which we judge what is possible and plausible."[7] As a subset of the scientific imagination, the cyber-imagination is becoming a powerful force in shaping our world, and we would do well to attend closely to its workings. What then are the particular forms of cyberreligiosity? What are the specific ideals these techno-spiritualists are beginning to judge as "possible and plausible"? Finally, what are we to make of all this? What does it all mean? These are the question we must ask.

Religious dreaming about cyberspace begins with the vision of the Heavenly city—that transcendent polis whose entrance is the legendary pearly gates. A connection between cyberspace and the New Jerusalem° has been spelled out explicitly by commentator Michael Benedikt. Benedikt explains that the New Jerusalem, like the Garden of Eden, is a place where man will walk in the fullness of God's grace, but "Where Eden (before the Fall) stands for our state of innocence, indeed ignorance, the Heavenly city stands for our state of wisdom and knowledge."[8] The New Jerusalem, then, is a place of *knowing*, a space that like cyberspace Benedikt says is rooted in *information*.

Mary Midgley: (b. 1919), English philosopher.

the Heavenly City . . . the New Jerusalem: Early Christians believed that after death they would be transported to this idealized heavenly metropolis.

In the Book of Revelation,° this key feature of the Heavenly City is signaled by its highly structured geometry, which is glimpsed in the repeated use of twelves and fours and sevens in its description. In this sense the Heavenly City suggests a glittering numerological puzzle, which in contrast to the wilderness of Eden is rigor and order incarnate. It is "laid out like a beautiful equation," Benedikt says. According to him, the Heavenly City is indeed nothing less than "a religious vision of cyberspace."[9] While Benedikt sees the New Jerusalem as a Christian prevision of cyberspace, reciprocally he suggests that cyberspace could be a digital version of the Heavenly City.[10]

On a purely visual level the most famous description of cyberspace—in Gibson's *Neuromancer*—does indeed bear an uncanny resemblance to the biblical Heavenly City. Here too we find a realm of geometry and light that is "sparkling, insubstantial," and "laid out like a beautiful equation." Here too is a glittering "city" adorned with "jewels"—the great corporate databases that decorate the "matrix" with a sparkling array of blue pyramids, green cubes, and pink rhomboids. Built from pure data, here is an idealized polis of crystalline order and mathematical rigor.

Most prominently, the Christian vision of the Heavenly City is a dream about transcendence. Transcendence over earthly squalor and chaos, and above all transcendence over the limitations of the body. For the elect in Heaven, Revelation 21:4 tells us, "God himself . . . will wipe away every tear from their eyes, and death shall be no more; neither shall there be mourning or crying nor pain any more, for the former things have passed away." In Heaven we are promised that the "sins of the flesh" will be erased and men shall be like angels. Among many champions of cyberspace we also find a yearning for transcendence over the limitations of the body. Here too we witness a longing for the annihilation of pain, restriction, and even death.

Throughout Gibson's cyberpunk novels the body is disparaged as "meat," its prison-like nature contrasted with the limitless freedom that console cowboys enjoy in the infinite space of the matrix. Like the biblical Adam, *Neuromancer*'s hero Case experiences his banishment from cyberspace and his subsequent "imprisonment" in his flesh, as "the Fall." From Lanier's claim that "this technology has the promise of transcending the body" to Moravec's hopes° for a future in which we will "be freed from bondage to a material body," the discourse about cyberspace thrums with what Arthur Kroker° has dubbed "the will to virtuality."

Dreaming of a day when we will be able to download ourselves into computers, Stenger has imagined that in cyberspace we will create virtual doppelgangers° who will remain youthful and gorgeous forever. Unlike our physical

the Book of Revelation: The final book of the New Testament, which offers apocalyptic visions of the end of the world and the last judgment.

Moravec's hopes: American roboticist Hans Moravec (b. 1948) is a leading proponent in the development of intelligent machines. (See p. 752.)

Arthur Kroker: American author, editor, and cybertheorist.

doppelgangers: Doubles.

bodies, these cyberspatial simulacra will not age, they will not get sick, they will not get wrinkled or tired. According to Stenger, the "eternal present [of cyberspace] will be seen as a Fountain of Youth, where you will bathe and re-fresh yourself into a sparkling juvenile."[11] As we are "re-sourced" in cyber-space, Stenger suggests, we will all acquire the "habit of perfection."[12]

Nothing epitomizes the cybernautic desire to transcend the body's limita-tions more than the fantasy of abandoning the flesh completely by download-ing oneself to *cyberimmortality*. At the end of *Neuromancer,* a virtual version of Case is fed into the matrix to live forever in a little cyberparadise. A similar fate awaits Gibson's next hero, Bobby Newmark, who at the end of *Mona Lisa Overdrive* is also downloaded to digital eternity. The dream of cyberimmortal-ity was presaged in what is now recognized as the first cyberfiction classic, Vernor Vinge's novella *True Names* (published in 1981, three years before Gibson coined the word "cyberspace"). At the end of Vinge's story, the phys-ical woman behind the cyber-heroine, known online as "the red witch Erythrina," is gradually transferring her personality into a cyberspace con-struct. "Every time I'm there," she explains, "I transfer a little more of myself. The kernel is growing into a true Erythrina, who is also truly me."[13] A "me" that will "live" on forever in cyberspace after the physical woman dies.

Yet there is a paradox at work behind these dreams. Even though many cyberspace enthusiasts long to escape the limitations of the body, most also cling to the glories of physical incarnation. They may not like bodily finitude, especially the part about death, but at the same time they desire the sensations and the thrills of the flesh. In Case's tropical cyberparadise, he relishes the warmth of the sun on his back and the feel of sand squishing beneath his feet. Above all, he delights in the ecstasy of sex with his cybergirlfriend Linda Lee. He might not take his flesh into cyberspace, but Gibson's hero is vouchsafed the full complement of bodily pleasures.

Cybernauts' ambivalent regard for the body is indicated by the very metaphor of "surfing" they have chosen. Who more than a surfer revels in the unique joy of bodily incarnation?

Commenting on this paradox, Steven Whittaker has described the typical cyberspace enthusiast° as "someone who desires embodiment and disembod-iment in the same instant. His ideal machine would address itself to his senses, yet free him from his body. His is a vision which loves sensorial possibility while hating bodily limits."[14] In other words, he wants his cake and to eat it too — to enjoy the pleasures of the physical body, but without any of its weak-nesses or restrictions.

Yet is this not also the promise of Christian eschatology?° Repackaged in digital garb, this is the dream of the "glorified body" that the heavenly elect can look forward to when Judgment Day comes. Christ's resurrection has al-

Christian eschatology: The branch of Christian theology concerned with the last judgment and the end of the world.

ways been interpreted by orthodox theologians to mean that when the last trumpet sounds the virtuous will be resurrected in *body* as well as soul. "The person is not the soul" alone, wrote Saint Bonaventure, "it is a composite. Thus it is established that [the person in Heaven] must be there as a composite, that is, of soul and body."[15] In the eternal bliss of the Empyrean the elect will be reunited with their material selves to experience again the joy of their incarnated form. But this heavenly body will be a "glorified body," free from the limitations of the mortal flesh. In the words of the medieval scholar Peter the Venerable, it will be a body that is "in every sense incorruptible."[16] Just what it meant to have a body in a place that was, strictly speaking, *outside* space and time was a question that much vexed medieval scholars, but that was indeed the position on which all the great theologians insisted.

Medieval scholar Jeffrey Fisher has noted the parallels between this Christian vision and that of many cyberspace enthusiasts. Just as the Christian body returns in glorified form, so Fisher explains that in contemporary cybernautic dreaming the "body returns in a hypercorporeal synthesis."[17] "Hypercorporeal" because like the glorified body of Christianity, this longed-for "cybernautic body" is not apparently bound by any physical limitations. Like the heavenly Christian body, it too is seen as incorruptible, and ultimately indestructible. Fisher cites, for example, the fact that in many hack-and-slash MUDs players who have been killed can simply reboot themselves. Get your head kicked off? No problem, just boot up another. Transcending the limits of the physical body, this cybernautic body has powers far beyond mortal means. "No longer restricted to what it could see with its bodily eyes or do with its bodily arms, the hypercorporeal simulacrum finds itself capable of amazing feats of knowledge and endurance."[18] . . .

Such cybernautic dreams of transcending bodily limitations have been fueled   20
by a fundamental philosophical shift of recent years: The growing view that man is defined not by the atoms of his body, but by an information code. This is the belief that our essence lies not in our matter, but in a *pattern of data*. The ease with which many cyberfiction writers shuttle their characters in and out of cyberspace is premised on a belief that at the core a human being is an array of data. While atoms can only construct the physical body, according to this new view *data* can construct both body and mind. Indeed, many cyberfantasies imply that in the end we will not need physical bodies at all, for we will be able to reconstruct ourselves totally in cyberspace. As long as these cyberconstructs are sufficiently detailed, Gibson et al. imply, the illusion of incarnation will be indistinguishable from the real material thing.

Look at Case's girlfriend Linda Lee. Halfway through the novel Lee is murdered, but just before she dies she is uploaded into the matrix for complete simulation in cyberspace. So perfect is this reconstruction, so "real" is her cyberpresence as both a mind and a body that she does not know she is only a digital simulation. Cyberfiction is full of stories of humans being downloaded, uploaded, and off-loaded into cyberspace. Like the medieval Christian

Heaven, cyberspace becomes in these tales a place *outside* space and time, a place where the body can somehow be reconstituted in all its glory. Again, it is not at all clear what it would mean to have a "body" in the immaterial domain of cyberspace, but that is the dream many cyberenthusiasts are beginning to envision. What is extraordinary here is that while the concept of transcending bodily limitation was once seen as *theologically possible,* now it is increasingly conceived as *technologically feasible.* To quote N. Katherine Hayles, "perhaps not since the Middle Ages has the fantasy of leaving the body behind been so widely dispersed through the population, and never has it been so strongly linked with existing technologies."[19]

Lest one imagine that fantasies of cyberimmortality are just in the minds of science-fiction writers, we should note that much of the underlying philosophy guiding this fiction is emerging from the realm of science, from fields such as cognitive science, robotics, and information theory. It's all part of the same imaginative flux that produces the dream of "artificial intelligence." What is human mental activity, these believers say, but a pattern of electrical signals in a network of neurons? Why should such a pattern not also be constructed in silicon? AI advocates insist that if computers can be "taught" to do such tasks as parsing sentences and playing grandmaster chess, it should only be a matter of time before they will be able to simulate the full complement of human mental activity.

In the futuristic worlds of many cyberpunk novels this goal has of course been realized. Gibson's matrix, for example, is inhabited by a slew of superhuman AIs; the eponymous *Neuromancer* is one of them. Far more than mere calculators, these computer constructs are personalities with their own emotions, desires, and egomaniacal goals. From the vision of creating an *artificial mind* inside a computer it is but a short step to imagining that a *human mind* also might be made to function inside a machine. If both types of "mind" are ultimately just patterns of data encoded in electrical signals, then why should we not be able to transfer one from *wetware* to *hardware?* So goes the argument.

This is precisely the fantasy touted by Carnegie Mellon's Hans Moravec, a world-renowned robotics expert. Moravec, whose lab develops sophisticated robots with three-dimensional vision and mapping capabilities, has seriously suggested that digital mind-downloading will one day be possible. In an extraordinary passage in his book *Mind Children,* he imagines a scenario in which "a robot brain surgeon" gradually transfers a human mind into a waiting computer.[20] As you lie there fully conscious, Moravec describes how a robot surgeon would "open your brain case" and begin downloading your mind layer by layer using "high-resolution magnetic resonance measurements" and "arrays of magnetic and electric antennas." Gradually, as your brain is destroyed, your "real" self—that is, your mind—would be transformed into a digital construct. Just how this is all supposed to happen is never really explained; but it is not the details that concern us, it is the overall fantasy. . . .

Immortality, transcendence, omniscience—these are dreams beginning to 25
awaken in the cyberreligious imagination. To paraphrase Midgley, these are
the things some cyberspace enthusiasts are beginning to think of as "possible
and plausible." Myself, I cannot imagine a worse fate than being downloaded
into immortality in cyberspace. In Christianity, the elect are promised an eternity of bliss in the presence of ultimate Grace, but what would be the fate of
an immortal cyberelect? What would one *do* in cybereternity? There are only
so many times you can read the complete works of Dante or Shakespeare or
Einstein, there are only a finite number of languages to learn; and after that
eternity is *still* forever.

But even for those who desire cyber-immortality there is a fundamental
problem: Is the human mind something that could, even in principle, be
downloaded into a computer? Is it something that could *ever* be reconstructed
in cyberspace? Most cyberfiction writers and scientists like Moravec assume a
priori° that since the human mind is an emergent property of the human
brain, then it must be just a pattern of electrical data—hence it must
ultimately be possible to transfer the files, as it were, from a brain to a computer. . . . But is the human mind really just a pattern of data, a collection of
"files" that could be transferred from one physical platform to another?

One reason such a vision is problematic is that a human mind has *faulty*
memories, and even entirely *false* ones. Memory researchers have shown that
by the time we reach adulthood most of us "remember" things that never actually happened; our brains have somehow "created" events that to us seem
entirely real. How would such false memories be programmed into a computer? How, in effect, would a machine be taught self-delusion? Moreover, in
a human mind many memories are buried well below conscious awareness, yet
if they are properly triggered, these memories come flooding back. How would
a computer know which memories were supposed to be the conscious ones,
and which were to remain unconscious? How would it know at what level of
activation the unconscious memories should be triggered into consciousness?
How would it have an "unconscious" at all?

In Moravec's scenario, a human mind would supposedly be downloaded
in situ. Here, each "layer" of the physical brain would be recorded in sequence
into a computer in one continuous sitting. According to him, such a process
could capture the *whole mind* in one go. But again we have the problem of un-
consciousness. Let us imagine, for argument's sake, that Moravec's setup was
possible, and that you could completely record the set of electrical signals
going on in someone's mind at some particular time. Now at any moment a
human mind can only be recalling a finite range of thoughts and memories. It
cannot be thinking about *everything* it has ever known. How could Moravec's
process possibly capture the complete range of memories and knowledge that
were not remotely within conscious awareness at the time of the recording?

a priori: Assumed true by deductive reasoning on the basis of obvious self-evidence.

For Moravec's process to work you would have to argue that *every* memory and *every* piece of knowledge that someone possessed were somehow electrically present at every waking moment. But in that case every moment would be one of *omniscience*. I find such a notion untenable. One of our most fundamental experiences as conscious beings is of time passing, precisely because every moment is *different*. The human mind is quintessentially a *dynamic* phenomena, and it seems absurd to suggest that you could capture it "all" at any one moment. I do not raise these objections to be churlish, but only to point out the degree to which mind-download fantasies elide over very real difficulties, not merely with respect to the technology, but more importantly with respect to the perplexing question of just what is a human mind. . . .

What we have here, with these visions of cyberimmortality and cyberresurrection, is an attempt to reenvision a *soul* in digital form. The idea that the "essence" of a person can be separated from his or her body and transformed into the ephemeral media of computer code is a clear repudiation of the materialist view that man is made of matter alone. When the further claim is made that this immaterial self can survive the death of the body and "live on" forever beyond physical space and time, we are back in the realm of medieval Christian dualism. Once again, then, we see in the discourse about cyberspace a return to dualism, a return to a belief that man is a bipolar being consisting of a mortal material body and an immaterial "essence" that is potentially immortal. This posited immortal self, this thing that can supposedly live on in the digital domain after our bodies die, this I dub the "cybersoul."

It is an astonishing concept to find emerging from the realm of science and technology, but again I suggest this is not wholly an unexpected development. This posited cybersoul may indeed be seen as the culmination of a tradition that has been informing Western science for over two thousand years. I refer to that curious admixture of mathematics and mysticism that traces its origins to the sixth century B.C. and the enigmatic Greek philosopher Pythagoras of Samos. Whether they realize it or not, today's champions of mind-download not only follow in a Christian tradition, they are also heirs of the Samian master.

As the man who is credited with introducing the Greeks to mathematics, Pythagoras was one of the founders of the Western scientific enterprise. At the same time he was a religious fanatic who managed to fuse mathematics and mysticism into one of the most intriguing syntheses in intellectual history. A contemporary of the Buddha in India, of Zoroaster in Persia, of Confucius and Lao-tzu° in China, Pythagoras was a mystic of a uniquely Western stripe. Half a millennia before the birth of Christ, he formulated a radically dualistic philosophy of nature that continues to echo in cybernautic visions today. According to the Samian sage, the essence of reality lay not in matter—in the four elements of earth, air, fire, and water—but in the immaterial magic of *numbers*. For Pythagoras, the numbers were literally gods, and he associated

Buddha . . . Zoroaster . . . Confucius . . . Lao-tzu: Four founders of great world religions.

them with the gods of the Greek pantheon. True reality, according to him, was not the plane of matter, but the transcendent realm of these number-gods.

For Pythagoras, the soul too was essentially mathematical. To him it was the soul's ability to express things rationally—literally in terms of *ratios*—that was its primary characteristic. In Pythagorean cosmology, the true home of the soul was the transcendent realm of the number-gods, and after death this is where all souls would return. Unfortunately, during our mortal lives this immortal spark is trapped within the prison of the body, from which it longs to be freed. For the Pythagorean, the aim of religious practice—which necessarily included the study of mathematics—was to free the soul from the shackles of the flesh that it might ascend as often as possible into the divine mathematical realm beyond the material plane.

Even from this cursory description, we see immediately the Pythagorean undertones in contemporary cybernautic dreams. Whatever is downloaded into computers must necessarily be expressed in terms of numbers—to be precise, in terms of the numbers "zero" and "one." The sublimely simple yet infinitely malleable code of zeros and ones is the erector set from which all cyberspace constructs are built. Behind dreams of mind-download is thus a profoundly Pythagorean attitude. Like the ancient Pythagoreans, today's mind-download champions see the "essence" of man as something that is numerically reducible; like the Pythagorean soul their "cybersoul" is ultimately mathematical. This cybersoul's "true" home is not the realm of the "meat," but the "eternal" domain of digital data. We have here, then, what Eliade would call a "crypto-religion," a quasi-religious system in which cyberspace reprises the role once accorded the divine space of the ancient Pythagorean number-gods. . . .

But is there not something missing from this technological reincarnation? 35 What about a moral or ethical context? In Hinduism, the form in which one is reincarnated in the next life depends on one's moral choices in past lives. For Hindus, *metempsychosis°* is also a moral process. Eventually, in the Hindu scheme, there is supposed to be an end to the process, when one finally attains "enlightenment" and the rounds of reincarnation cease. (In Christianity, where the soul is granted but a single incarnation, there is a much more draconian moral context because it has but *one* chance to make the "right" choices—or pay the price forevermore.)

For ancient Pythagoreans, also, the soul was quintessentially a moral entity. In particular, they believed the soul needed constant cleansing, and they adhered to strict codes of behavior as well as strict regimens of fasting and bodily purification. The cybersoul, however, has *no* moral context. In cyberspatial fantasies of reincarnation and immortality, the soul's eternity entails no ethical demands, no moral responsibilities. One gets the immortality payoff of a religion, but without any of the obligations. . . .

---

metempsychosis: The passing of a soul after death into another body.

As historian David Noble has shown, in the Christian West champions of technology have been reading religious dreams into technological enterprises ever since the late Middle Ages. *If* "the technological enterprise . . . remains suffused with religious belief" Noble writes, that is hardly surprising, for "modern technology and religion have evolved together."[21] The pattern of seeing new technology as a means to spiritual transcendence has been repeated so many times that Erik Davis has coined the term "techgnosis" as a generic description of the phenomena.[22] As the latest incarnation of techgnosis, cybergnosis reflects a deep and recurring theme in Western culture.

In the glorious futures imagined by cyberreligionists like . . . Moravec, god-like omniscience and immortality will be vouchsafed to everyone. *This*, then, is the promise of the "religion" of cyberspace: Through the networked power of silicon we can all become as one with the All. . . . Freed from the "prisons" of our bodies by the liberating power of the modem, we too are promised that our "cybersouls" will soar into the infinite space of the digital ether. There, like Dante° in the *Paradiso*, we will supposedly find our way "home" to "Heaven."

We would do well to approach such dreams with our skeptical antennae well tuned, for again there is all too often here an element of moral evasion. Even in its nonelectronic forms Gnosticism° has long been problematic. With their focus on transcendence, Gnostics through the ages have often inclined toward a Manichaean° repudiation of the body, and along with that has been a tendency to disregard the concerns of the earthly world and earthly communities. Orthodox Christian theologians have long stressed that an essential reason for valuing life in the flesh is that on the physical plane we are bound into physical *communities* to whom we have obligations and responsibilities. Someone who does not value life in the body is less likely to feel obligated to contribute to their physical community: Why bother helping a sick friend if you believe he would be better off dead? Why bother trying to extend life in the flesh if you think it is an evil to be transcended as quickly as possible?

Orthodox Christianity has always affirmed the *value* of the flesh. Humanity was created in body as well as soul, the great medieval theologians asserted, and the duty of the Christian is to live life well in body as well as in spirit. Visions of cybergnosis and cyberimmortality are often at heart Manichaean, for we see here as well a strong tendency to devalue life in the flesh. Michael Heim° is right when he notes that Gibson's vision of cyberspace evokes   40

Dante: Dante Alighieri (1265–1321), Italian poet and author of *Paradiso*, or *The Paradise*, the final segment of *The Divine Comedy*, a three-part account of his allegorical journey through hell and purgatory to heaven.

Gnosticism: The thought and practice of various early Christian cults, distinguished by the belief that matter is evil and that spiritual freedom comes only through "gnosis" or secret knowledge.

Manichaean: Related to Manichaeanism, a dualistic religion originating in Persia in the third century A.C.E., holding that the spirit can be released from the body only through extreme self-discipline and self-denial.

Michael Heim: American cyberspace philosopher and author.

a "Gnostic-Platonic-Manichaean contempt for earthy, earthly existence."[23] Too often, cyberreligious dreaming suggests a tendency to abandon responsibility on the earthly plane. Why bother fighting for equal access to education in the physical world if you believe that in cyberspace we can all know everything? Why bother fighting for earthly social justice if you believe that in cyberspace we can all be as gods? What would be the point? Commentator Paulina Borsook has noted that the culture of the Silicon Valley cyberelite is indeed imbued with a deeply self-serving libertarianism that shuns responsibility toward physical communities. It is a tendency she terms "cyberselfishness."[24]

Behind the desire for cyberimmortality and cybergnosis, there is too often a not insignificant component of cyberselfishness. Unlike genuine religions that make ethical demands on their followers, cyberreligiosity has no moral precepts. Here, as we have noted, one gets the payoffs of a religion without getting bogged down in reciprocal responsibilities. It is this desire for the personal payoff of a religious system without any of the social demands that I find so troubling. In its quest for bodily transcendence, for immortality, and for union with some posited mystical cyberspatial All, the emerging "religion" of cyberspace rehashes many of the most problematic aspects of Gnostic-Manichaean-Platonist dualism. What is left out here is the element of *community* and one's obligations to the wider *social whole*. Ironically, it is in just this communal aspect that cyberspace may ultimately prove to be of the greatest value.

Notes

1. Mark Pesce, "Ignition." Address to "World Movers" conference, January 1997, San Francisco. This speech is available online at www.hyperreal.com/~mpesce/.

2. Pesce, ibid.

3. Quoted in Jeff Zaleski, *The Soul of Cyberspace*. San Francisco: HarperEdge, 1997, p. 156.

4. Quoted in by Erik Davis, "Technopagans." *Wired*, July 1995, vol. 3.07.

5. Nicole Stenger, "Mind Is a Leaking Rainbow." In *Cyberspace: First Steps*. Ed. Michael Benedikt. Cambridge, Ma.: MIT Press, 1991, p. 52.

6. Nicole Stenger, ibid., p. 50.

7. Mary Midgley, *Science as Salvation: A Modern Myth and Its Meaning*. London: Routledge, 1992, p. 15.

8. Michael Benedikt, "Introduction." In *Cyberspace: First Steps*, p. 15.

9. Benedikt, ibid., pp. 15–16.

10. Benedikt, ibid., p. 18.

11. Stenger, "Mind Is a Leaking Rainbow," p. 56.

12. Stenger, ibid., p. 57.

13. Vernor Vinge. *True Names*. New York: Baen Books, 1987, p. 142.

14. Steven Whittaker, "The Safe Abyss: What's Wrong with Virtual Reality?" In *Border/Lines* 33, 1994, p. 45.

15. Caroline Walker Bynam, *Fragmentation and Redemption*. New York: Zone Books, 1992, p. 256.

16. Bynam, ibid., p. 264.

17. Jeffrey Fisher, "The Postmodern Paradiso: Dante, Cyberpunk, and the Technosophy of Cyberspace." In *Internet Culture*. Ed. David Porter. New York: Routledge, 1997, p. 120.

18. Fisher, ibid., p. 121.

19. N. Katherine Hayles, "The Seduction of Cyberspace." In *Rethinking Technologies*. Ed. Verena Andermatt Conley. Minneapolis: University of Minnesota Press, 1993, p. 173.

20. Hans Moravec, *Mind Children: The Future of Robot and Human Intelligence.* Cambridge, Ma.: Harvard University Press, 1988, pp. 109–110.

21. David F. Noble, *The Religion of Technology: The Divinity of Man and the Spirit of Invention.* New York: Alfred A. Knopf, 1997, p. 5.

22. Erik Davis, see *Techgnosis: Myth, Magic and Mysticism in the Age of Information.* New York: Harmony Books, 1998.

23. Michael Heim, "The Erotic Ontology of Cyberspace." In *Cyberspace: First Steps,* p. 75.

24. Paulina Borsook, "Cyberselfish." *Mother Jones,* July/August 1996.

EXPLORING THE TEXT

1. What similarities does Wertheim see between Christian ideology and the ideology of cyberspace? Why does she find the concept of cyberreligiosity particularly ironic? Would you agree that a tone of religious faith or conviction colors the thinking of many advocates of cyberculture? What examples, if any, of this cyber-religiosity can you think of?

2. How does the "cybernautic body" differ from the body in Christian teaching, according to Wertheim? Why does she find attitudes toward transcendence and the body in cyberspace "paradoxical"? What assumptions underlie this view of the body and its relation to the mind?

3. Why, according to Wertheim, does the cybernautic view of the mind involve what she refers to as a return to "the realm of medieval Christian dualism" (para. 30)? What role does Pythagorean philosophy play in the thinking that dominates cyberculture?

4. What's wrong with the mind/body dualism that informs the philosophy of cyberspace, in Wertheim's view? To what extent would you agree that the cultures associated with computing and the Internet are "cyberselfish"? Why?

FURTHER EXPLORATIONS

1. What problems does Wertheim see associated with Hans Moravec's idea of downloading a human mind into a computer (p. 752)? To what extent does Moravec's "Grandfather Clause" illustrate the kind of pseudoreligious thinking that Wertheim describes in this selection?

2. What similarities can you find between the pseudoreligious culture of cyberspace, as detailed by Wertheim in this selection, and the culture of "the boy engineer" discussed by Ellen Ullman in "Out of Time: Reflections on the Programming

Life" (p. 656)? How might Ullman explain cyberculture's contempt for bodies made of "meat"?

3. To what extent is the kind of identity swapping that Sherry Turkle (p. 675) notes among online "MUDders" an example of the lack of moral commitment that Wertheim associates with the "flesh"? Would Turkle be likely to agree that minds without bodies have little sense of responsibility to real communities? Are the MUDders she describes "cyberselfish"?

4. Compare Claudia Springer's analysis of the hypermasculine body images of cyborg heroes in "Muscular Circuitry" (p. 689) with the spiritual vision of cyberspace offered by Wertheim. How might you account for these different interpretations of the role of the body in cyberculture?

5. How might the personal experiences of Barry Lopez (p. 27), Bill McKibben (p. 109), and Scott Russell Sanders (p. 142) challenge the idea that it is possible to separate mind and identity from the physical body? In what ways are the identities of these three authors dependent on their physical sense of self?

ESSAY OPTIONS

1. Do additional research on the topic of artificial intelligence to determine the validity of Wertheim's central claim about the crypto-religiosity of cyber culture. To what extent do proponents of the development of intelligent machines — people like Hans Moravec, Rodney Brooks, Ray Kurzweil, Kevin Kelly, or Neil Gershenfeld — reflect the pseudo-Christian values and attitudes that Wertheim associates with the study of AI?

2. Research and compose a conventional essay or hypertext "collage" on the concept of cyberspace. How has the concept of cyberspace been depicted in cyberpunk fiction by authors like William Gibson (p. 703) and Vernor Vinge? How has cyberspace or "the matrix" been conceptualized in popular articles on computing and the Internet and in science-fiction films and television shows? What features or techniques are used to convey this imaginary "space"? What cultural meanings, desires, or dreams does it appear to embody?

3. Drawing on ideas presented by Wertheim, Ellen Ullman (p. 656), Clifford Stoll (p. 648), Sherry Turkle (p. 675), and Maureen Caudill (p. 736), write an essay exploring the ethics of electronic technology. What ethical challenges are presented by the widespread use of electronic communication and information technologies? What ethical questions are raised by the culture of computing? How serious, in your view, are these issues?

ACKNOWLEDGMENTS (continued)

Deborah Blum, "Heart to Heart: Sex Differences in Emotion." From *Sex on the Brain* by Deborah Blum. Copyright © 1997 by Deborah Blum. Used by permission of Viking Penguin, a division of Penguin Putnam, Inc.

Maureen Caudill, "Redefining the Measure of Mankind" from *In Our Own Image* by Maureen Caudill. Copyright © 1992 by Maureen Caudill. Used by permission of Oxford University Press, Inc.

Constance Classen, David Howes, and Anthony Synnott, "The Olfactory Revolution" from *Aroma: The Cultural History of Smell*. Copyright © 1994. Reproduced by permission of Taylor & Francis, Inc./Routledge, Inc., http://routledge-ny.com.

K.C. Cole, "Seeing Things" from *First You Build a Cloud and Other Reflections on Physics as a Way of Life*. Copyright © 1999, 1985 by K.C. Cole. Reprinted by permission of Harcourt, Inc.

Mihaly Csikszentmihalyi, "What Is the Self?" from *The Evolving Self* by Mihaly Csikszentmihalyi. Copyright © 1993 by Mihaly Csikszentmihalyi. Reprinted by permission of HarperCollins Publishers, Inc.

John (Fire) Lame Deer and Richard Erdoes, "Talking to the Owls and Butterflies" from *Lame Deer, Seeker of Visions* by John (Fire) Lame Deer and Richard Erdoes. Copyright © 1972 by John (Fire) Lame Deer and Richard Erdoes. Reprinted by permission of Pocket Books, a division of Simon & Schuster, Inc.

Loren Eiseley, "The Brown Wasps" from *The Brown Wasps: A Collection of Three Essays in Autobiography*. Copyright © 1971. Mount Horeb: Perishable Press, 1969.

Jean Bethke Elshtain, "To Clone or Not to Clone." Copyright © 1998 by Jean Bethke Elshtain, from *Clones and Clones: Facts and Fantasies About Human Cloning* by Martha C. Nussbaum and Cass R. Sunstein. Used by permission of W.W. Norton & Company, Inc.

Susan Engel, "Then and Now: Creating a Self Through the Past" from *Context is Everything*. Copyright © 1999 by W.H. Freeman. Reprinted by permission of Henry Holt & Co., Inc.

Mick Fedullo, "Mrs. Cassadore" from *Light of the Feather: Pathways Through Contemporary Indian America* by Mick Fedullo. Copyright © 1992 by Mick Fedullo. Reprinted by permission of Mick Fedullo.

Ian Frazier, "Take the F." Copyright © 1996 by Ian Frazier. Reprinted with the permission of The Wylie Agency, Inc.

James Garbarino, "Rejected and Neglected, Ashamed and Depressed." Reprinted and abridged with the permission of The Free Press, a division of Simon & Schuster, Inc., from *Lost Boys: Why Our Sons Turn Violent and How We Can Save Them* by James Garbarino, Ph.D. Copyright © 1999 by James Garbarino.

William Gibson, "Johnny Mnemonic" from *Burning Chrome*. Copyright © 1986 by William Gibson. Reprinted by permission of HarperCollins Publishers, Inc.

Guillermo Gómez-Peña, "The Virtual Barrio @ the Other Frontier (or the Chicano Interneta)" from *Clicking In: Hot Links to a Digital Culture*, edited by Lynn Jurschmann-Leeson. Copyright © 1996 by Guillermo Gómez-Peña. Reprinted by permission of New York University Press.

Edward T. Hall, "Hidden Culture" from *Beyond Culture* by Edward T. Hall. Copyright © 1976, 1981 by Edward T. Hall. Used by permission of Doubleday, a division of Random House, Inc.

Patricia Hampl, "Memory and Imagination" from *The Anatomy of Memory: An Anthology*, edited by James McConkey. Copyright © 1996 by Oxford University Press. Reprinted by permission of Oxford University Press.

Douglas R. Hofstadter, "The Turing Test: A Coffeehouse Conversation" from *The Mind's I* by Douglas R. Hofstadter and Daniel C. Dennett. This selection appeared in *Scientific American*, May 1981, pp. 15–36. Copyright © 1981 by Douglas Hofstadter. Reprinted by permission of the author.

bell hooks, "Columbus: Gone But Not Forgotten." Copyright © 1994 from *Outlaw Culture* by bell hooks. Reproduced by permission of Routledge, Inc., part of The Taylor & Francis Group.

Maxine Hong Kingston, "Memories of a Girlhood Among Ghosts" from *The Woman Warrior* by Maxine Hong Kingston. Copyright © 1975, 1976 by Maxine Hong Kingston. Used by permission of Alfred A. Knopf, a division of Random House, Inc.

Philip Kitcher, "Whose Self Is It, Anyway?" This article is reprinted by permission of *The Sciences* and the author from the September/October 1997 issue. Individual subscriptions are $21 per year. Write to: The Sciences, 2 East 63rd Street, New York, NY 10021.

Georgina Kleege, "The Mind's Eye" from *Sight Unseen* by Georgina Kleege. Copyright © 1999 by Georgina Kleege. Reprinted by permission of Yale University Press.

Richard Leakey, "Murder in a Zoo" from *Origins Reconsidered: In Search of What Makes Us Human* by Richard Leakey. Copyright © 1992 by B.V. Sherma. Used by permission of Doubleday, a division of Random House, Inc.

Barry Lopez, "A Passage of the Hands" from *About This Life* by Barry Lopez. Copyright © 1998 by Barry Holstun Lopez. Used by permission of Alfred A. Knopf, a division of Random House, Inc., and Sterling Lord Literistic, Inc.

Arnold Ludwig, "Living Backwards" from *How Do We Know Who We Are?: A Biography of the Self* by Arnold Ludwig. Copyright © 1997 by Oxford University Press, Inc. Used by permission of Oxford University Press, Inc.

Rubén Martínez, "Technicolor" from *Half and Half* by Claudine Chiawei O'Hearn. Copyright © 1998 by Claudine Chiawei O'Hearn. "Technicolor" copyright © 1998 by Rubén Martínez. Used by permission of Pantheon Books, a division of Random House, Inc.

Bill McKibben, "Television and the Twilight of the Senses" from *The Age of Missing Information* by Bill McKibben. Copyright © 1992 by Bill McKibben. Used by permission of Random House, Inc.

Faith McNulty, "Mouse" from *Living With Animals*, edited by Gary Indiana. Copyright © 1994 by Faith McNulty. Reprinted by permission of Faber and Faber, Ltd.

Hans Moravec, "Grandfather Clause." Reprinted by permission from the publisher from *Mind Children: The Future of Robot and Human Intelligence* by Hans Moravec, pp. 100–122, Cambridge, Mass.: Harvard University Press. Copyright © 1997 by the President and Fellows of Harvard College.

778

Martha C. Nussbaum, "The Narrative Imagination." Reprinted by permission of the publisher from *Cultivating Humanity: A Classical Defense of Reform in Liberal Education* by Martha C. Nussbaum, pp. 85–97, Cambridge, Mass.: Harvard University Press. Copyright © 1997 by the President and Fellows of Harvard College.

Francine Patterson and Wendy Gordon, "The Case for the Personhood of Gorillas" (edited) from *The Great Ape Project*, ed. by Paola Cavalieri and Peter Singer. Copyright © by St. Martin's Press. Reprinted by permission of St. Martin's Press.

Walker Percy, "The Loss of the Creature" from *The Message in the Bottle* by Walker Percy. Copyright © 1975 by Walker Percy. Reprinted by permission of Farrar, Straus and Giroux, L.L.C.

Scott Russell Sanders, "The Inheritance of Tools." Copyright © 1986 by Scott Russell Sanders. First appeared in *The North American Review*. From *The Paradise of Bombs*. Reprinted by permission of the author and The Virginia Kidd Literary Agency, Inc.

Robert Sapolsky, "Ego Boundaries, or the Fit of My Father's Shirt" from *Discover*, November 1995, pp. 62–67. Copyright © 1995 by Robert Sapolsky. Reprinted with permission of *Discover Magazine*.

Daniel L. Schachter, "Building Memories: Encoding and Retrieving in the Past and the Present" from *Searching for Memory: the Brain, the Mind and the Past* by Daniel L. Schachter. Copyright © 1996 by Daniel L. Schachter. Reprinted by permission of BasicBooks, a member of Perseus Books, L.L.C.

Roger C. Schank, "Understanding Other People's Stories" from *Tell Me A Story: Narrative and Intelligence*. Evanston: Northwestern University Press, 1990, pp. 56–59, 63–79, 83. Copyright © 1990 by Northwestern University Press. Reprinted by permission of Northwestern University Press.

Paul Shepard, "Rights and Kindness: A Can of Worms" from the work *The Others: How Animals Made Us Human*. Copyright © 1997. Granted with permission from the publisher, Island Press, Washington, D.C. & Covelo, California.

Charles Siebert, "The Artifice of the Natural." Copyright © 1993 by *Harper's Magazine*. All rights reserved. Reproduced by special permission.

Peter Singer, "Equality for Animals?" Excerpt from *Practical Ethics*, 2nd edition, pp. 55–77, by Peter Singer. Copyright 1993. Reprinted by permission of Cambridge University Press.

Mark Slouka, "Listening for Silence." Copyright © 1998 by Harper's Magazine. All rights reserved. Reproduced from the May 1998 issue by special permission.

Claudia Springer, "Muscular Circuitry" from *Electronic Eros: Bodies and Desire in the Postindustrial Age* by Claudia Springer. Originally appeared in *Genders*, Vol 18, 1993. Copyright © 1993 by Claudia Springer. Reprinted by permission of the University of Texas Press.

Clifford Stoll, "Isolated by the Internet" from *High-Tech Heretic* by Clifford Stoll. Copyright © 1999 by Clifford Stoll. Used by permission of Doubleday, a division of Random House, Inc.

Andrew Sullivan, "What's So Bad About Hate?" from *New York Times*, September 26, 1999. Copyright © 1999 by Andrew Sullivan. Reprinted by permission of The Wylie Agency, Inc.

Sherry Turkle, "Who Am We?" Reprinted with the permission of Simon & Schuster from *Life on the Screen* by Sherry Turkle. Copyright © 1995 by Sherry Turkle. Originally appeared in *Wired* 4.01 (Jan. 1996).

Ellen Ullman, "Out of Time: Reflections on the Programming Life" from *Resisting the Virtual Life*, edited by James Brook and Iain A. Boal. Copyright © 1995 by City Lights Books. Reprinted by permission of the publisher.

Frans de Waal, "The Whole Animal" from *The Ape and the Sushi Master* by Frans de Waal. Copyright © 2001 by Frans de Waal. Reprinted by permission of BasicBooks, a member of Perseus Books, L.L.C.

Alice Walker, "Everyday Use" from *In Love & Trouble: Stories of Black Women*. Copyright © 1973 by Alice Walker. Reprinted by permission of Harcourt, Inc.

Margaret Wertheim, "Cyber Soul-Space" from *The Pearly Gates of Cyberspace* by Margaret Wertheim. Copyright © 1999 by Margaret Wertheim. Used by permission of W.W. Norton & Company, Inc.

Eviatar Zerubavel, "Social Memories." Reprinted by permission of the publisher from "Social Memories" in *Social Mindscapes* by Eviatar Zerubavel, pp. 81–99, Cambridge, Mass.: Harvard University Press. Copyright © 1997 by the President and Fellows of Harvard College.

ART ACKNOWLEDGMENTS

Brigitte Helm as the Robot Maria in *Metropolis*. Bettmann/Corbis.

Chimpanzee Plays Chess. Hulton-Deutsch Collection/Corbis

"How Rutherford 'saw' the nucleus," "Wavelength of Radiation in Meters," "Rotating shadow of a spring" and "The Impossible Triangle" from K.C. Cole's "Seeing Things" from *First You Build a Cloud and Other Reflections on Physics as a Way of Life* by K.C. Cole. Copyright © 1999, 1985 by K.C. Cole. Reprinted by permission of Harcourt, Inc.

M.C. Escher's "Hand with Reflecting Sphere" © 2001 Cordon Art B. V. — Baarn — Holland. All rights reserved.

"Hand and Ear." Used by permission of the photographer, Susan Segal Photography & Digital Image, Napa, CA.

Photographs from Chimpanzee Politics. Courtesy of Frans de Waal.

René Magritte, "The Schoolmaster." Copyright © 2001 C. Herscovici, Brussels/Artists Rights Society (ARS), New York.

"Michael Stokes at Wellness Center." Photo credit by Joe McNally/Timepix.

René Magritte, "The Menaced Assassin {L'Assassin menacé}." (1926) Oil on canvas, 59¼″ × 6′4⅞″. The Museum of Modern Art, New York. Kay Sage Tanguy Fund. Photograph © 2001 The Museum of Modern Art, New York.

Jerry Coker, "The Memory Tree Man," 1993. Used by permission of Marion Harris, Simsbury, CT and New York, NY.

Index of Authors and Titles

Research and Writing Online

Whether you want to investigate ideas behind a thought-provoking essay or conduct in-depth research for a paper, the Web resources for *Mind Readings* can help you find what you need on the Web — and then use it once you find it.

The English Research Room for Navigating the Web

www.bedfordstmartins.com/english_research

The Web brings a flood of information to your screen, but it still takes skill to track down the best sources. Not only does *The English Research Room* point you to some reliable starting places for Web investigations, it also lets you tune up your skills with interactive tutorials.

- Want to improve your skill at searching electronic databases, online catalogs, and the Web? Try the *Interactive Tutorials* for some hands-on practice.

- Need quick access to online search engines, reference sources, and research sites? Explore *Research Links* for some good starting places.

- Have questions on evaluating the sources you find, navigating the Web, or conducting research in general? Consult one of our *Reference Units* for authoritative advice.

Research and Documentation Online for Including Sources in Your Writing

www.bedfordstmartins.com/resdoc

Including sources correctly in a paper is often a challenge, and the Web has made it even more complex. This online version of the popular booklet *Research and Documentation in the Electronic Age,* by Diana Hacker, provides clear advice for the humanities, social sciences, history, and the sciences on —

- Which Web and library sources are relevant to your topic (with links to Web sources)

- How to integrate outside material into your paper

- How to cite sources correctly, using the appropriate documentation style

- What the format for the final paper should be

Gary Colombo

Resources for
Teaching

AN

ANTHOLOGY

FOR

WRITERS

MIND
READINGS

Resources for Teaching
Mind Readings
AN ANTHOLOGY FOR WRITERS

Resources for Teaching
Mind Readings
AN ANTHOLOGY FOR WRITERS

Gary Colombo
Los Angeles City College

Bedford / St. Martin's
Boston ◆ New York

Preface

I've always thought of *Mind Readings* as an experiment in long-distance collaboration. The best teaching experiences I've ever had — and the best learning experiences as well — have always involved collaborative effort. It just makes sense that two minds work better than one. So, you may find it helpful to approach this instructor's manual as a resource for team teaching. Up to this point, my part in this asynchronous partnership of ours has been to offer you a rich selection of readings and to generate as many thought-provoking follow-up questions and essay topics as possible. As I collected materials and created the apparatus for *Mind Readings,* I worked hard to provide you with a wealth options, and if you've already spent some time browsing through the book, you'll know what I mean. *Mind Readings* offers fifty-three reading selections representing a broad range of voices, modes, and academic disciplines. The apparatus that accompanies these readings features nearly 500 follow-up discussion questions and contains particular suggestions for more than 125 writing assignments. Now it's your turn to tap these resources as you design a course that's uniquely yours and that meets the particular needs of your students. Early on in planning the book, I decided against an approach that would lock-step you into an inflexible sequence of assignments. You're the only person who understands where your students stand in their development as readers and writers, and you're the only one who can appreciate their individual strengths and interests. I've done a lot of the background research and curriculum development. Now it's your turn to shape the raw materials that *Mind Readings* provides into a course that works for you. This instructor's manual is your curriculum construction kit. It provides you with a rich menu of options for thematic course design, creative assignment sequences, and productive classroom activities. It also offers you the tools you'll need to sift through all of the possibilities contained in *Mind Readings* as you design your course. Here's a synopsis of the kinds of help you'll find in these pages:

Sample Syllabi: Nine individual sample syllabi are provided featuring different thematic approaches. Ranging from the general theme of "Mind Reading" to more specific topics such as "Gendered Minds," "The Ethical Mind," and "Minds and Media," these outlines offer you suggestions for ways to focus your course. They also help to narrow down your search for the right reading selections and writing assignments.

Essay Option Bank: The 126 Essay Options that accompany the reading selections in the text are summarized here in two ways: first, in chapter order and, second, by assignment type. This system is meant to provide you with a quick guide to the challenges associated with each chapter as well as an overview of possible assignment sequences.

Media Connections: All of the follow-up questions, activities, and Essay Options in *Mind Readings* that involve media connections are noted by chapter in this section. Brief thematic descriptions of each activity are also provided for quick reference.

IM Chapter Introductions: The introduction provided here for each chapter of *Mind Readings* offers additional context for the chapter focus, practical hints for how to approach chapter themes, and suggestions for in-class pre-reading activities to help you get started. In addition, these sections offer you suggestions for assignment sequences within chapters, as well as suggestions for stand-alone readings, productive pairings, and thematic reading clusters. Separate Essay Options and Media Readings summaries are also provided for each chapter.

IM Selection Notes: The notes provided for each reading offer additional suggestions for making productive connections with other selections throughout the book. They also offer in-depth discussions of responses to each of the Exploring the Text and Further Explorations questions included in the book. Specific approaches to the Essay Options for each selection are also discussed.

As you can see, I've tried to provide you with a rich collection of materials and options for teaching. Now it's time for you to take over and to shape these resources into an effective course. If *Mind Readings* works and our collaboration is a success, you should have more time and energy to devote to your students — and you should find that you yourself keep making new discoveries about how to use the materials the book contains. As you experiment with different selections, sequences, and assignments, I'd appreciate it if you'd take the time now and then to give me some feedback. I'd particularly like to hear about your experiences using specific selections from *Mind Readings* in class as well as your ideas about other selections that might be included in future editions. So, whenever you can spare a moment, please send me your thoughts and suggestions about selections, questions, and essay assignments. You can reach me at english@bedfordstmartins.com. I promise to check in regularly and to get back to you throughout the year.

Contents

2

Reading Memory: Rebuilding the Past   71

3

Reading The Self: Ghosts in the Machine?   107

4

Reading Other Minds: Inside the Black Box   143

5

Reading Animal Minds: Objects or Equals?   174

6

Reading Cyberminds: The Internet to Artificial Intelligence   212

Resources for Teaching
Mind Readings
AN ANTHOLOGY FOR WRITERS

Introduction

A Note on "Mind Reading" for Instructors New and Old

Some instructors might have misgivings about focusing their composition classes on the theme of the mind. After all, the cognitive sciences comprise a formidable collection of academic disciplines — including not a few representatives from the so-called hard sciences. Doesn't it require special preparation to deal with topics such as the senses, memory, animal minds, and artificial intelligence? Questions like this may be particularly troubling for new instructors fresh from their work in English and other literary fields *and* for those of us who have devoted the last few decades to comp classes focused on broad social issues. For some reason, we feel right at home weaving materials into our classes from disciplines such as anthropology, history, political science, ethnography, psychology, and even economics, but we balk when it comes to subjects that touch on biology, animal ethology, and computer science. Part of the reason for these doubts, of course, lies in the fact that the thematic focus of *Mind Readings* is genuinely new. Thirty years ago, composition classes dealt primarily with personal experiences and broad social questions such as those involved in capital punishment. Back then, the idea of addressing issues such as race, gender, and class differences in a first-year composition curriculum would have seemed as radical as discussing the issue of artificial intelligence does today. But the rapid rise of cognitive science as a field of intellectual inquiry and the increasing pace of technological developments over the past two decades have changed all of that. Today, issues related to the nature of mind and consciousness have moved to the forefront of a number of public and academic debates. As we learn more about the mind — and as "machinery" become increasingly intelligent and capable of reproducing human activity — we are being challenged to redefine what it means to be human and to reassess age-old assumptions about human superiority and the centrality of human experience. Today, it's no longer safe to assume that *anything* separates us from other species or that any particular ability or skill falls beyond the ken of our own mechanical creations. It's also no longer given that the mind itself works as independently or as simply as we once assumed. In these "postmodern" times, it's becoming clear that even our senses are filled with interpretive biases, that memory is both selective and highly imaginative, and that the self has more in common with a chorus of voices or a dynamic organization than it does with a unique and unchanging identity or spirit. *Mind Readings* brings these issues into your class and gives students the chance to address ideas that are already moving to the fore in popular culture and the popular imagination.

Another reason to feel comfortable with the theme of mind reading is that it's what we composition instructors have been doing all along. The art of interpretation is central to the study of rhetoric. In order to learn how to write, you have to learn how to *read* the expectations of your audience and to interpret the ideas available to you in the cultures in which you participate. The act of mind reading, as it's presented in this book, has to do with mastering the art of interpretation — and not with brain scans, electroencephalography, and neurosurgery. It also has a lot to do with the development of the skills that composition students need. Thus, you can rest assured that using *Mind Readings* won't require you to help students translate technical journal articles on subjects like "parallel processing systems in relation to genetic programming." Indeed, most of the science writing you'll find in the book's six chapters was originally penned for a lay audience. You'll also find that the topics covered in *Mind Readings* have direct application to the composition classroom — topics such as the sensual life of language, the role of memory in the writing process, the function of mind reading in argumentation, and the impact of electronic technology on the "technology" of writing. So, I encourage you to go ahead and get comfortable. Neuroscientists may know a lot about the brain and its structure, but humanists know as much or more about the mind and the arts of interpretation.

Getting Started

There's no right place to begin exploring the topic of the mind, and there's no particular place where you need to begin your exploration of *Mind Readings.* In fact, you can begin at any point, and you should feel free to experiment with combinations of readings across all of the chapters. The book divides neatly into two halves. Looking "inward," the first three chapters focus on themes related to the senses, memory, and the self. The last three chapters, looking "outward," focus on ideas related to reading "other," animal, and machine minds. While you'll find a healthy mix of personal essays, fiction, and theoretical selections throughout the book, earlier chapters tend to offer more personal narratives and later chapters tend to highlight reading selections that are more conceptually and academically challenging. Thus, the book begins with Ian Frazier's personal essay on his experience of life in Brooklyn and ends with Margaret Wertheim's philosophical analysis of the theological assumptions underlying recent thinking about the future of cyberspace. The same movement, from more accessible to more conceptually challenging pieces, is recapitulated within each chapter, so that you can tailor your approach to each of the book's six themes according to the ability of your class. Thus, while the first chapter leads off with personal essays by Frazier and Barry Lopez, it ends with Walker Percy's highly conceptual "The Loss of the Creature," and while the final chapter ends with conceptual selections on the nature of artificial intelligence, it begins with relatively more accessible pieces by Clifford Stoll and Ellen Ullman on the nature of life online. The Essay Options offered throughout the book reflect this pattern as well. The first three chapters offer opportunities for informal papers and personal essays, while the later chapters focus more heavily on topics calling for a more traditionally academic approach and additional research.

If your college offers a two-term sequence in composition, you might want to consider using *Mind Readings* for both sessions, covering the first three chapters in a course on the theme of "Exploring the Self" and the last three chapters in a follow-up course on the theme of "Reading Other Minds." If you're planning for a single term, you'll have to whittle down your options. To get started, I recommend that you take the time to browse through the draft syllabi offered below, if for no other reason than to arm yourself with alternative visions of how the book might be used. The nine sample syllabi should serve as a "rough guide" as you begin to select the readings and assignments that will work best for you and your students. If one of these themes interests you, take a little more time to scan the Essay Option Bank and Media Connections listed in the following pages. I've included a few suggestions for essay topics in the sample syllabi below, but you'll find a great many more throughout the text. After browsing through the Essay Options, spend some time examining the discussion questions after the readings that you might include in your course plan. You'll find that the Essay Options and the Further Extensions questions associated with each selection will help you discover even more ways to approach readings in your class. You'll also find additional suggestions for pairing and clustering selections at the beginning of each chapter introduction in this manual. These provide a closer look at the natural thematic connections between readings within a particular chapter. Spending a couple of hours with these resources should prepare you to draft an outline for your course, complete with a sketch of the readings you'll cover, the major and minor writing assignments they'll involve, and the media resources you'll need to make your class a success.

Sample Syllabi

Below, you'll find outlines for nine courses on themes ranging from the general topic of "Mind Reading" to more specialized themes such as "Gendered Minds," "The Ethical Mind," "The Mind and Imagination," and "Minds and Media." These sample syllabi are offered as rough drafts of possible courses and not as detailed calendars of daily class activities and assignments. They're meant to help you appreciate some of the different thematic approaches you might want to adopt in your class. They also should help you narrow the number of potential reading selections. Most of these sample syllabi trim the book's total content at least by half. Of course, you'll probably have to trim these recommendations a bit more to fit your course calendar. I've tried to make them as inclusive as possible, so that they provide you with a quick index to a particular theme rather than a strict prescription of what I think you should do day by day. I've also included possible Film Options and essay assignments. You'll find many more in the apparatus following individual selections in the text and in the individual Selection Notes included in the chapter units that follow this introduction.

An Entry-Level Course on the General Theme of "Mind Reading"

Unit 1: Reading the Senses (2 weeks)

Selections:	*Take the F* (Frazier)
	A Passage of the Hands (Lopez)
	Taste: The Social Sense (Ackerman)
	Listening for Silence (Slouka)
	The Mind's Eye (Kleege)
Film Options:	*Babbette's Feast, Tampopo, Big Night,* or *Hannibal*
Assignment:	Personal essays on "Sense in the City" and "The Education of a Sense"

Unit 2: Reading Memory (2 weeks)

Selections:	*The Inheritance of Tools* (Sanders)
	The Brown Wasps (Eiseley)
	Building Memories (Schacter)
	Memory and Imagination (Hampl)
	Social Memories (Zerubavel)
	No-Name Woman (Kingston)
Film Option:	*Memento*
Assignment:	Personal essay on "Building Memories" and/or academic essay on "Impersonal Memories"

Unit 3: Reading the Self (2–3 weeks)

Selections:	*Ego Boundaries, or the Fit of My Father's Shirt* (Sapolsky)
	What Is the Self? (Csikszentmihalyi)
	Everyday Use (Walker)
	Living Backwards (Ludwig)
	Technicolor (Martínez)
	The Self and Society (Baumeister)
Assignment:	Personal essay on "Elements of Identity" and/or academic essay on "Emerging Images of Selfhood"

Unit 4: Reading Other Minds (2–3 weeks)

Selections:
Sonny's Blues (Baldwin)
Understanding Other People's Stories (Schank)
Hidden Culture (Hall)
Mrs. Cassadore (Fedullo)
Heart to Heart: Sex Differences in Emotion (Blum)

Assignment:
Personal essay on "Cross-Cultural Conflict" and/or academic essay on "Reading Male and Female Minds"

Unit 5: Reading Animal Minds (2–3 weeks)

Selections:
Talking to the Owls and Butterflies (Lame Deer and Erdoes)
Why Look at Animals? (Berger)
Mouse (McNulty)
The Whole Animal (de Waal)
Murder in a Zoo (Leakey and Lewin)
The Case for the Personhood of Gorillas (Patterson and Gordon)

Assignment:
Academic essay on "The Disappearance of Animals" and/or "Anthropomorphism and the Case for Primate Intelligence"

OR

Unit 5: Reading Cyber Minds (2–3 weeks)

Selections:
Isolated by the Internet (Stoll)
Out of Time (Ullman)
Who Am We? (Turkle) or *The Virtual Barrio* (Gómez-Peña)
Muscular Circuitry (Springer)
Johnny Mnemonic (Gibson)

Film Options:
Terminator, Bladerunner, Robocop

Assignment:
Academic Essay on "The Impact of the Internet," "Access to the Internet," or "The Cyborg in Pop Culture"

A More Challenging Course on the General Theme of "Mind Reading"

Unit 1: Reading the Senses (2–3 weeks)

Selections:
Take the F (Frazier) or *A Passage of the Hands* (Lopez)
Taste: The Social Sense (Ackerman)
The Olfactory Revolution (Classen, Howes, and Synnott)
Seeing Things (Cole)
The Mind's Eye (Kleege)
The Loss of the Creature (Percy) or
Listening for Silence (Slouka) and
Television and the Twilight of the Senses (McKibben)

Film Option:
Koyannisquatsi

Assignment: Personal essay on "Sense in the City" and academic essay on "The Social Construction of the Senses," "The Impact of Technology on the Senses," or "The Dominance of Vision"

Unit 2: Reading Memory (2–3 weeks)

Selections: *The Brown Wasps* (Eiseley)
Building Memories (Schacter)
Memory and Imagination (Hampl)
Social Memories (Zerubavel)
No-Name Woman (Kingston)
Columbus: Gone But Not Forgotten
   (hooks)

Film Options: *Rashomon* or *Memento*

Assignment: Personal essay on "Building Memories" and/or academic essay on "The Politics of Memory"

Unit 3: Reading the Self (2–3 weeks)

Selections: *Ego Boundaries, or the Fit of My Father's*
   Shirt (Sapolsky)
Everyday Use (Walker)
Living Backwards (Ludwig)
Technicolor (Martínez)
The Self and Society (Baumeister)
A Mutable Self (Bateson)

Assignment: Academic essay on "Cultures of Identity"

Unit 4: Reading Animal Minds (2–3 weeks)

Selections: *Why Look at Animals?* (Berger)
The Whole Animal (de Waal)
Murder in a Zoo (Leakey and Lewin)
The Case for the Personhood of Gorillas
   (Patterson and Gordon)
Equality for Animals? (Singer)
Rights and Kindness: A Can of Worms
   (Shepard)

Assignment: Academic essay on "The Case for Animal Equality" or "The Debate over Animal Rights"

Unit 5: Reading Machine Minds (2–3 weeks)

Selections: *Isolated by the Internet* (Stoll)
Out of Time (Ullman)
Who Am We? (Turkle) or *The Virtual*
   Barrio (Gómez-Peña)
Redefining the Measure of Mankind
   (Caudill)
Grandfather Clause (Moravec)
Cyber Soul-Space (Wertheim)

Film Options: *Fast, Cheap, and Out of Control, A.I.,*
   Millennium Man

Assignment: Academic essay on "The Culture of the
                                Internet," "The Ethics of High Technology,"
                                or "The Future of Human and Machine
                                Minds"

A Course on the Theme of "The Social Construction of Mind"

Unit 1: Society and the Senses (2–3 weeks)

Selections: *A Passage of the Hands* (Lopez)
                                Taste: The Social Sense (Ackerman)
                                The Olfactory Revolution (Classen,
                                    Howe, and Synnott)
                                Seeing Things (Cole)
                                The Mind's Eye (Kleege)
                                The Loss of the Creature (Percy)
Film Options: *Babbette's Feast, Tampopo,* or *Big Night*
Assignment: Personal essay on "The Education of a
                                Sense" and academic essay on "The Role of
                                Society in Sense Perception"

Unit 2: Building Memories (2 weeks)

Selections: *The Brown Wasps* (Eiseley)
                                Building Memories (Schacter)
                                Memory and Imagination (Hampl)
                                *Then and Now: Creating a Self Through
                                    the Past* (Engel)
                                Social Memories (Zerubavel)
                                No-Name Woman (Kingston)
Film Option: *Rashomon*
Assignment: Academic essay on "Memory as Revision
                                and Resistance"

Unit 3: Composing a Self (2–3 weeks)

Selections: *What Is the Self?* (Csikszentmihalyi)
                                Everyday Use (Walker)
                                Living Backwards (Ludwig)
                                Technicolor (Martínez)
                                The Self and Society (Baumeister)
Assignment: Academic essay on "Adopting a Self"

Unit 4: Defining Animal Intelligence (3 weeks)

Selections: *Talking to the Owls and Butterflies* (Lame
                                    Deer and Erdoes)
                                Why Look at Animals? (Berger)
                                Mouse (McNulty)
                                The Whole Animal (de Waal)
                                Murder in a Zoo (Leakey and Lewin)
                                The Case for the Personhood of Gorillas
                                    (Patterson and Gordon)
                                Equality for Animals? (Singer)
Assignment: Academic essay on "Naïve and Mature
                                Anthropomorphism"

Unit 5: Constructing Machine Minds (2 weeks)

Selections:	*Isolated by the Internet* (Stoll)
	Out of Time (Ullman)
	Muscular Circuitry (Springer)
	Johnny Mnemonic (Gibson)
	Grandfather Clause (Moravec)
	Cyber Soul-Space (Wertheim)
Film Options:	*Bladerunner, Terminator, A.I.*
Assignment:	Academic essay on "The Construction of Cyberspace in Pop Culture"

A Course on the Theme of "Gendered Minds"

Unit 1: The Senses, Sex, and Gender (2 weeks)

Selections:	*A Passage of the Hands* (Lopez)
	Taste: The Social Sense (Ackerman)
	The Olfactory Revolution (Classen, Howe, and Synnott)
	The Mind's Eye (Kleege)
	The Loss of the Creature (Percy)
Film Options:	*Babbette's Feast, Tampopo, Big Night*
Assignment:	Academic essay on "Sexed Senses?"

Unit 2: Gendered Selves (3–4 weeks)

Selections:	*Ego Boundaries, or the Fit of My Father's Shirt* (Sapolsky)
	Everyday Use (Walker)
	Living Backwards (Ludwig)
	Technicolor (Martínez)
	The Self and Society (Baumeister)
	A Mutable Self (Bateson)
	No-Name Woman (Kingston)
	Social Memories (Zerubavel)
	Columbus: Gone But Not Forgotten (hooks)
Assignment:	Academic essay on "Bounded Egos and Mutable Selves"

Unit 3: Reading Minds Across Genders (2 weeks)

Selections:	*Heart to Heart: Sex Differences in Emotion* (Blum)
	Mrs. Cassadore (Fedullo)
	Rejected and Neglected, Ashamed and Depressed (Garbarino)
	Murder in a Zoo (Leakey and Lewin)
Assignment:	Academic essay on "Violence and Empathy: Reading Male and Female Minds"

Unit 4: Gender and the Net (2 weeks)

Selections:	*Isolated by the Internet* (Stoll)
	Out of Time (Ullman)
	Who Am We? (Turkle)

	The Turing Test: A Coffeehouse Conversation (Hofstadter)
Film Option:	*Dot-Com*
Assignment:	Academic essay on "The Cult of the Boy Engineer"

Unit 5: Sexing Machine Minds (2 weeks)

Selections:	*Muscular Circuitry* (Springer)
	Johnny Mnemonic (Gibson)
	Grandfather Clause (Moravec)
	Cyber Soul-Space (Wertheim)
Film Options:	*Bladerunner, Johnny Mnemonic, Metropolis, Terminator, Robocop*
Assignment:	Academic essay on "Cyborg Bodies in Pop Culture"

A Course on the Theme of "Minds and Difference"

Unit 1: Points of View (2–3 weeks)

Selections:	*Take the F* (Frazier)
	Taste: The Social Sense (Ackerman)
	The Olfactory Revolution (Classen, Howe, and Synnott)
	Seeing Things (Cole)
	The Mind's Eye (Kleege)
	Listening for Silence (Slouka)
	The Loss of the Creature (Percy)
Film Options:	*Babbette's Feast; Eat, Drink, Man Woman*
Assignment:	Personal essay on "Senses of the City" and academic essay on "The Senses Across Cultures" or "Different Ways of Seeing"

Unit 2: Remembering Differently (2 weeks)

Selections:	*Memory and Imagination* (Hampl)
	Building Memories (Schacter)
	Then and Now: Creating a Self Through the Past (Engel)
	Social Memories (Zerubavel)
	No-Name Woman (Kingston)
Film Options:	*Rashomon* or *Memento*
Assignment:	Personal essay on "Multiple Drafts of an Experience" or academic essay on "The Multiple Drafts of Memory"

Unit 3: How Many Selves? (3 weeks)

Selections:	*Ego Boundaries, or the Fit of My Father's Shirt* (Sapolsky)
	Technicolor (Martínez)
	Living Backwards (Ludwig)
	The Self and Society (Baumeister)
	A Mutable Self (Bateson)
	Who Am We? (Turkle)
	Whose Self Is It, Anyway? (Kitcher)

Assignment:	Academic essay on "Multiplicity and Identity"

Unit 4: Mind Reading Across Cultures (2–3 weeks)

Selections:	*Sonny's Blues* (Baldwin)
	Understanding Other People's Stories (Schank)
	The Narrative Imagination (Nussbaum)
	Hidden Culture (Hall)
	Mrs. Cassadore (Fedullo)
Assignment:	Personal essay on "Cross-Cultural Conflict" and/or academic essay on "Reading Male and Female Minds"

Unit 5: Reading Violent Minds (2 weeks)

Selections:	*Heart to Heart: Sex Differences in Emotion* (Blum)
	Rejected and Neglected, Ashamed and Depressed (Garbarino)
	Murder in a Zoo (Leakey and Lewin)
	Muscular Circuitry (Springer)
	What's So Bad About Hate? (Sullivan)
Film Option:	*Dead Man Walking*
Assignment:	Academic essay on "Explaining Violence" or "Debating Hate Crime Legislation"

A Course on the Theme of "The Ethical Mind"

Unit 1: The Ethics of Creative Memory (3 weeks)

Selections:	*The Brown Wasps* (Eiseley)
	Building Memories (Schacter)
	Memory and Imagination (Hampl)
	Then and Now: Creating a Self Through the Past (Engel)
Film Options:	*Rashomon* or *Memento*
Assignment:	Personal essay on "Multiple Memories of the Same Experience" and/or academic essay on "The Reliability of Memory"

Unit 2: Impersonal Memory, Revisionism, and History (2 weeks)

Selections:	*Social Memories* (Zerubavel)
	No-Name Woman (Kingston)
	Columbus: Gone But Not Forgotten (hooks)
Film Options:	*Rashomon* or *Memento*
Assignment:	Personal essay on "The Personal Costs of Impersonal Memories" or academic essay on "What Is History?"

Unit 3: Selfishness and the Ethics of Cloning (2 weeks)

Selections:	*The Self and Society* (Baumeister)
	Whose Self Is It, Anyway? (Kitcher)
	To Clone or Not to Clone (Elshtain)

Assignment:	Academic essay on "The Ethics of Human Cloning"

Unit 4: My Brother's Keeper (2–3 weeks)

Selections:	*Sonny's Blues* (Baldwin)
	The Narrative Imagination (Nussbaum)
	Heart to Heart: Sex Differences in Emotion (Blum)
	Rejected and Neglected, Ashamed and Depressed (Garbarino)
	What's So Bad About Hate? (Sullivan)
Film Options:	*Count on Me* or *Dead Man Walking*
Assignment:	Academic essay on "The Role of Empathy in an Ethical Society" or "The Ethics of Hate Crime Legislation"

Unit 5: Cyberselfish? (3 weeks)

Selections:	*Isolated by the Internet* (Stoll)
	Out of Time (Ullman)
	Who Am We? (Turkle)
	Redefining the Measure of Mankind (Caudill)
	Grandfather Clause (Moravec)
	Cyber Soul-Space (Wertheim)
Film Option:	*Dot-Com*
Assignment:	Academic essay on "Cyberselfishness" or "The Ethical Implications of High Technology"

A Course on the Theme of "The Mind and Imagination"

Unit 1: "Making" Sense (2 weeks)

Selections:	*Take the F* (Frazier)
	A Passage of the Hands (Lopez)
	Seeing Things (Cole)
	The Mind's Eye (Kleege)
	The Loss of the Creature (Percy)
Assignment:	Personal essay on "Sense in the City" and academic essay on "The Social Construction of the Senses," "The Impact of Technology on the Senses," or "The Dominance of Vision"

Unit 2: Creative Remembering (2–3 weeks)

Selections:	*The Brown Wasps* (Eiseley)
	Memory and Imagination (Hampl)
	Building Memories (Schacter)
	Then and Now: Creating a Self Through the Past (Engel)
	No-Name Woman (Kingston)
Film Options:	*Rashomon* or *Memento*
Assignment:	Personal essay on "Multiple Drafts of an Experience" or academic essay on "The Role of Imagination in Memory"

Unit 3: Spinning a Self (3 weeks)

Selections:	*The Inheritance of Tools* (Sanders)
	What Is the Self? (Csikszentmihalyi)
	Everyday Use (Walker)
	Living Backwards (Ludwig)
	Technicolor (Martínez)
	The Self and Society (Baumeister)
	A Mutable Self (Bateson)
Assignment:	Personal essay on "Self as Collage" and/or academic essay on "The Self as Inheritance or Work of Art?"

Unit 4: Imagining Others (2–3 weeks)

Selections:	*Sonny's Blues* (Baldwin)
	Understanding Other People's Stories (Schank)
	The Narrative Imagination (Nussbaum)
	Hidden Culture (Hall)
	Mrs. Cassadore (Fedullo)
	What's So Bad About Hate? (Sullivan)
Assignment:	Academic essay on "Storytelling and Understanding" or "The Limits of Empathy"

Unit 5: Cyberspace Fantasies (2–3 weeks)

Selections:	*Who Am We?* (Turkle)
	Muscular Circuitry (Springer)
	Johnny Mnemonic (Gibson)
	Grandfather Clause (Moravec)
	Cyber Soul-Space (Wertheim)
Film Options:	*Terminator, Bladerunner, Johnny Mnemonic, Robocop, A. I.*
Assignment:	Academic essay on "Cyborgs in the Popular Imagination" or "Images of Cyberspace"

A Course on the Theme of "Minds and Media"

Unit 1: Mediating the Senses (2–3 weeks)

Selections:	*Taste: The Social Sense* (Ackerman)
	Seeing Things (Cole)
	The Mind's Eye (Kleege)
	Listening for Silence (Slouka)
	Television and the Twilight of the Senses (McKibben)
	The Loss of the Creature (Percy)
Film Options:	*Babbette's Feast, Tampopo, Big Night, Hannibal,* or *Koyannisquatsi*
Assignment:	Academic essay on "A Filmography of Taste" and "The Media and Their Relation to Perception"

Unit 2: Memoirs and "Mementos" (2–3 weeks)

Selections:	*Memory and Imagination* (Hampl)
	Building Memories (Schacter)
	Social Memories (Zerubavel)
	Columbus: Gone But Not Forgotten (hooks)
Film Options:	*Memento, Rashomon,* or any treatment of a famous historical subject
Assignment:	Academic essay on "The Nature of Memory in *Memento* (or *Rashomon)*" and/or "Film and Impersonal Memories"

Unit 3: Celluloid Selves (1–2 weeks)

Selections:	*Technicolor* (Martínez)
	What Is the Self? (Csikszentmihalyi)
	Everyday Use (Walker)
	Living Backwards (Ludwig)
Film Options:	Recent films featuring what students agree are "ideal" selves or exemplary "roles"
Assignment:	Personal essay on "Media Influences on Personal Identity" and/or academic essay on "Ideal Selves in Popular Culture"

Unit 4: "Disneyfication" (2–3 weeks)

Selections:	*Talking to the Owls and Butterflies* (Lame Deer and Erdoes)
	Why Look at Animals? (Berger)
	Mouse (McNulty)
	The Artifice of the Natural (Siebert)
	The Whole Animal (de Waal)
Film Options:	*Dr. Doolittle* or any film or television show featuring anthropomorphized animal "actors"
Assignment:	Academic essay on "The Disneyfication of Animals in Mass Media"

Unit 5: Cybermedia/Cyberminds (2–4 weeks)

Selections:	*Isolated by the Internet* (Stoll)
	Out of Time (Ullman)
	Who Am We? (Turkle)
	Muscular Circuitry (Springer)
	Johnny Mnemonic (Gibson)
	Grandfather Clause (Moravec)
	Cyber Soul-Space (Wertheim)
Film Options:	*Terminator, Bladerunner, Johnny Mnemonic, Robocop, A.I., Metropolis*
Assignment:	Academic essay on "The Impact of Electronic Media on Human Identity and Relationships" and/or "Cyborgs in the Popular Imagination"

A Course on the Theme of "The Mind and Technology"

Unit 1: Making "Sense" of Technology (3–4 weeks)

Selections:	*Listening for Silence* (Slouka)
	Take the F (Frazier)
	The Olfactory Revolution (Classen, Howes, and Synnott)
	Seeing Things (Cole)
	The Mind's Eye (Kleege)
	Television and the Twilight of the Senses (McKibben)
	The Loss of the Creature (Percy)
Film Option:	*Koyannisquatsi*
Assignment:	Academic essay on "Sounds in the City," "The Impact of Technology on Sense Experience," or "Technology and the Dominance of Vision"

Unit 2: Selfhood in a High-Tech Culture (3–4 weeks)

Selections:	*Ego Boundaries, or the Fit of My Father's Shirt* (Sapolsky)
	Technicolor (Martínez)
	What Is the Self? (Csikszentmihalyi)
	Everyday Use (Walker)
	The Self and Society (Baumeister)
	A Mutable Self (Bateson)
	Isolated by the Internet (Stoll)
	Out of Time (Ullman)
	Who Am We? (Turkle)
Assignment:	Academic Essay on "Western Concepts of the Self" " and/or "The Impact of Electronic Media on Identity"

Unit 3: Technology and the Domestication of Nature (2–3 weeks)

Selections:	*Talking to the Owls and Butterflies* (Lame Deer and Erdoes)
	Why Look at Animals? (Berger)
	Mouse (McNulty)
	The Artifice of the Natural (Siebert)
	The Whole Animal (de Waal)
	The Case for the Personhood of Gorillas (Patterson and Gordon)
Assignment:	Academic essay on "The Domestication of Nature in Contemporary American Culture"

Unit 4: Machine Intelligence? (1–2 weeks)

Selection:	*The Turing Test: A Coffeehouse Conversation* (Hofstadter)
Assignment:	Academic essay on "Designing Your Own Turing Test"

Unit 5: The Future of Meat and Machine Minds (2–3 weeks)

Selections:	*Muscular Circuitry* (Springer)
	Johnny Mnemonic (Gibson)
	Redefining the Measure of Mankind (Caudill)
	Grandfather Clause (Moravec)
	Cyber Soul-Space (Wertheim)
Film Options:	*Fast, Cheap, and Out of Control; A.I.;* *Metropolis; Blade Runner*
Assignment:	Academic essay on any of the following topics: "The Cyborg in Pop Culture," "Robot History," "The Current State of A.I. Research," or "The Ethics of High Technology"

Essay Option Bank

All 126 Essay Options included in *Mind Readings* are listed below in two different ways. First, they are listed by chapter and reading selection. These chapter overviews allow you to see the progression of assignments within a given unit of the book, and they help you appreciate how readings connect. Topics for academic papers that ask students to synthesize and respond to information in several readings are followed here by parenthetical notations of the other authors they involve. Thus, Essay Option #2 for Mark Slouka's "Listening for Silence" in Chapter 1 also recommends that students draw information or ideas from "The Olfactory Revolution" by Constance Classen et al., "Television and the Twilight of the Senses" by Bill McKibben, and "The Loss of the Creature" by Walker Percy. All of the authors included in parentheses are mentioned in the Essay Options assignments as they appear in the text of *Mind Readings*. However, as you look them over, keep in mind that it's not always necessary to cover all of these selections in order to respond effectively to the topic with which they're associated. The recommendations here are meant to be as inclusive as possible on a particular topic, but it's not always necessary to cover them all. So don't be daunted if a given Option is tied to more selections than you think you'll be able to handle. Before ruling out an attractive assignment, take a closer look at the way it's presented in the text to see if you can make it work with fewer connections. Browsing through the chapter-by-chapter summaries provided below should give you a good idea of the sequences of readings and assignments that will work best for your class. For your convenience, appropriate sections of these summaries will be repeated along with the introductory material for each chapter in this manual.

Essay Options are also categorized by general assignment type. I know it's often devilishly hard to distinguish between generic types of writing assignments. And I also appreciate the fact that it's tough to generalize about the difficulty involved in different categories of writing. Still, I think this summary might serve as a rough guide to the level of difficulty you'll encounter as you work your way through the text. Essay Options are broken down into four categories: "Personal Essays," "Single-Text Academic Essays," "Multi-Text Academic Essays," and "Research/Hypertext Projects." Personal essays call for students to write papers based on personal experiences or involving personal responses to ideas in reading selections. Single-text academic essays require students to respond critically to ideas and theories encountered in a text or to apply them in the analysis of some other object — whether it's a film, a work of art, or a collage of ads from popular magazines. These relatively limited assignments offer students the chance to learn essential academic writing skills, such as those involved in defining key terms, summarizing information and arguments, citing authors, and applying academic concepts analytically. Multi-text academic essays draw on ideas, theories, or perspectives presented in two or more reading selections. These assignments challenge students to cope with multiple references, voices, and points of view in a single paper. Assignments in both of these "academic" categories also typically require students to think critically about academic concepts, theories, and arguments and to tap into their own general knowledge in the process. Research/hypertext essays may involve gathering information from "informal" sources such as film and popular magazines, or they may require more formal, in-depth library and online research projects. The hypertext options associated with readings in Chapter 6 may be used as the occasion for the development of genuine online hypertext essays or as the basis for non-electronic multimedia projects, including collages, mixed media presentations, and art installations — or, if you choose, they may take the form of traditional research reports. More specific guidance on these projects is presented below in the introduction to Chapter 6.

Finally, keep in mind that you can easily translate many of the follow-up discussion questions in *Mind Readings* into productive topics for personal or academic essay assignments, so don't let yourself be limited by the suggestions that appear as formal Essay Options.

Essay Options by Chapter

Chapter 1: Reading the Senses

Take the F, Ian Frazier

Option #1. Describe your cross-town commute/neighborhood.
Option #2. Compare Frazier's descriptive techniques with those of Lopez. (Lopez)

A Passage of the Hands, Barry Lopez

Option #1. Write about the education of your own sense of touch.
Option #2. Compare the species functions of touch and taste. (Ackerman)

Taste: The Social Sense, Diane Ackerman

Option #1. Write about the tastes of your home cultures.
Option #2. Write about the education of your own sense of taste.
Option #3. Write about a memorable cross-cultural experience of taste.

Listening for Silence, Mark Slouka

Option #1. Rewrite the cross-town commute essay done for Frazier to focus on aural experience.
Option #2. Examine the erosion of sense experience in contemporary society. (Classen et al., McKibben, and Percy)
Option #3. Explore the relation between sensory deprivation and creativity. (Kleege, McKibben, and Percy)

The Olfactory Revolution, Constance Classen, David Howes, and Anthony Synnott

Option #1. Write an olfactory history of your education.
Option #2. Write an olfactory geography of your community or campus.

Seeing Things, K. C. Cole

Option #1. Write about a time when you learned to see something in a new way.
Option #2. Explore the role that education and acculturation play in sense perception. (Lopez, Ackerman, Classen et al., and Kleege)

The Mind's Eye, Georgina Kleege

Option #1. Compare two visual perspectives on the same work of art.
Option #2. Offer your own analysis of an abstract work of art.

Television and the Twilight of the Senses, Bill McKibben

Option #1. Write a multisensory description of an experience modeled on McKibben's.
Option #2. Evaluate McKibben's claim that TV "tranquilizes" its audience.
Option #3. Examine the notion of the education of the senses. (Lopez, Ackerman, Classen et al., Cole, Kleege, and Percy)
Option #4. Explore the visual bias of contemporary technological society. (Classen et al., Kleege, Cole, and Lame Deer and Erdoes)

The Loss of the Creature, Walker Percy

Option #1. Write about an experience of the "sovereign" reality of an object or place.
Option #2. Examine the role of the mind in visual experience. (Cole and Kleege)
Option #3. Assess the idea that modern society has lost contact with real perception. (Slouka, Classen et al., Cole, and McKibben)

Chapter 2: Reading Memory

The Inheritance of Tools, Scott Russell Sanders

Option #1. Write about an object that holds special meaning and memories for you.
Option #2. Write a dialogue between Sanders and Walker Percy on the influence of the past on the present. (Percy)

The Brown Wasps, Loren Eiseley

Option #1. Compare the use of symbols in Sanders and in Eiseley. (Sanders)
Option #2. Explore the notion of "stereoscopic memory" in Eiseley. (Schacter)
Option #3. Compare Sanders's and Eiseley's approaches to writing from memory. (Sanders)

Building Memories: Encoding and Retrieving the Present and the Past, Daniel L. Schacter

Option #1. Compare and analyze different recollections of a work of art or image.
Option #2. Explore the "stereoscopic" quality of memory in memoirs. (Sanders and Eiseley)

Memory and Imagination, Patricia Hampl

Option #1. Write about a childhood experience in the "elaborated" mode of Hampl.

Option #2. Write about a memory triggered by a childhood photograph.

Option #3. Explore Hampl's claim that "True memoir is written in an attempt to find not only a self but a world." (Sanders, Eiseley, and Lopez)

Option #4. Analyze your own writing process in light of Hampl's.

Then and Now: Creating a Self Through the Past, Susan Engel

Option #1. Analyze the relation of past and present "selves" in a personal essay written earlier in the term.

Option #2. Discuss "template memories" in Eiseley, Hampl, and Kingston. (Eiseley, Hampl, and Kingston)

No-Name Woman, Maxine Hong Kingston

Option #1. Offer your own retelling and evaluation of an important "family" story.

Option #2. Examine the idea of the politics of memory, as discussed in readings in this chapter. (Eiseley, Hampl, Zerubavel, and hooks)

Social Memories, Eviatar Zerubavel

Option #1. Write about how memories are preserved in a culture of which you are part.

Option #2. Compare the role that memory plays in two cultures with which you're familiar.

Option #3. Research and discuss a recent "mnemonic battle" in the United States.

Option #4. Assess the notion of memory as an accurate "transcript" of experience. (Eiseley, Schacter, Hampl, Engel, Kingston, and hooks)

Columbus: Gone But Not Forgotten, bell hooks

Option #1. Examine how writers in this chapter transform historical memories. (Hampl, Kingston, and Zerubavel)

Option #2. Research portrayals of Columbus and compare them with that presented by hooks.

Option #3. Read descriptions of the "discovery" of the Americas by Ivan Van Septima, Howard Zinn, and/or Ward Churchill and compare them with the "traditional" version.

Chapter 3: Reading the Self

Ego Boundaries, or the Fit of My Father's Shirt, Robert Sapolsky

Option #1. Write about a time you felt yourself adopting or emulating some of the characteristics of another person.

Option #2. Examine the role of parents and family in the construction of the self. (Sanders, Kingston, Walker, and Martínez)

What Is the Self?, Mihaly Csikszentmihalyi

Option #1. Assemble and analyze a collection of images of "ideal selves" from pop culture.

Option #2. Inventory the ingredients of your sense of self.

Everyday Use, Alice Walker

Option #1. Write about an object with special meaning or cultural significance in your family.

Option #2. Assess the role of memories in the construction of the self. (Lopez, Sanders, Hampl, Engel, and Zerubavel)

Living Backwards, Arnold M. Ludwig

Option #1. Write about the "roles" that you see guiding your life story.

Option #2. Discuss how the self lends coherence and continuity to our lives. (Sapolsky and Engel)

Option #3. Examine some of the challenges to living in the present. (Cole, Percy, and Schacter)

Technicolor, Rubén Martínez

Option #1. Explore the impact of the media on your sense of self.

Option #2. Respond to the claim that America is becoming a "mestizo" nation.

Option #3. Explore the thesis that the self is something we create, like a work of art. (Sapolsky, Walker, Ludwig, Hampl, Kingston, and Zerubavel)

The Self and Society: Changes, Problems, and Opportunities, Roy F. Baumeister

Option #1. Survey media images to assess the dominance of the modern self.

Option #2. Respond to the claim that the self has become a "burden."

Option #3. Survey magazine images to test Baumeister's claims about female selves.

A Mutable Self, Mary Catherine Bateson

Option #1. Write about a time when you had to adapt to a new culture or community.

Option #2. Write about a time when you felt silenced in school.

Option #3. Inventory the relationships that contribute to your sense of self.

Option #4. Evaluate the status of the self in contemporary American culture. (Sapolsky, Baumeister, and Martínez)

Whose Self Is It, Anyway?, Philip Kitcher

Option #1. Examine the ethics of pre-determining a child's attributes.

Option #2. Research and analyze depictions of cloning in popular culture.

To Clone or Not to Clone, Jean Bethke Elshtain

Option #1. Research and debate the pros and cons of human cloning.

Chapter 4: Reading Other Minds

Understanding Other People's Stories, Roger C. Schank

Option #1. Compare multiple interpretations of a story.

Option #2. Compare theories of learning in Schank and Bateson. (Bateson)

Sonny's Blues, James Baldwin

Option #1. Write about a person who is a mystery to you.
Option #2. Discuss the problems of mutual understanding within families.
(Walker, Hampl, Zerubavel, and Kingston)

The Narrative Imagination, Martha C. Nussbaum

Option #1. Apply Nussbaum's theory of the "democratizing" function of narrative to stories from popular media.
Option #2. Apply Nussbaum's theory to examples of children's literature.

Hidden Culture, Edward T. Hall

Option #1. Analyze a personal experience of cross-cultural misunderstanding.
Option #2. Examine the concept of the "cultural unconscious." (Ackerman, Classen et al., Cole, Kleege, Percy, and Zerubavel)

Mrs. Cassadore, Mick Fedullo

Option #1. Apply Schank's and Bateson's notions of cross-cultural learning to Fedullo. (Schank and Bateson)
Option #2. Examine the challenges involved in learning to listen to others. (Schank, Baldwin, Nussbaum, and Hall)

Heart to Heart: Sex Differences in Emotion, Deborah Blum

Option #1. Analyze a personal experience of cross-gender conflict.
Option #2. Explore the challenges women face in the electronic workplace. (Ullman)

What's So Bad About Hate?, Andrew Sullivan

Option #1. Research and analyze a category of hate crimes.
Option #2. Research and debate the pros and cons of hate crime legislation.

Rejected and Neglected, Ashamed and Depressed, James Garbarino

Option #1. Research and report on the causes of teen violence.
Option #2. Discuss the role of empathy in the creation of a civil society. (Nussbaum and Blum)

Chapter 5: Reading Animal Minds

Talking to the Owls and Butterflies, John (Fire) Lame Deer and Richard Erdoes

Option #1. Respond to the authors' charges against "white society."
Option #2. Analyze the authors' sense of self, using theories from Chapter 3. (Sapolsky, Baumeister, and Bateson)

Why Look at Animals?, John Berger

Option #1. Discuss the social functions of zoos.
Option #2. Explore the notion of "animals of the mind" in popular culture.
Option #3. Evaluate attitudes toward animals and "wildness" in contemporary American culture. (McKibben, Percy, and Lame Deer and Erdoes)

Mouse, Faith McNulty

Option #1. Write a profile of an animal you've known well.
Option #2. Debate the pros and cons of pet ownership. (Lame Deer and Erdoes, and Berger)

The Artifice of the Natural, Charles Siebert

Option #1. Survey and analyze media portrayals of animals.
Option #2. Assess Siebert's claim that we are losing contact with nature. (Lame Deer and Erdoes, Slouka, and McKibben)

The Whole Animal, Frans de Waal

Option #1. Examine and assess the role of TV in the "Bambification" of animals. (Berger and Siebert)
Option #2. Assess the current state of "anthropodenial" in American culture.
Option #3. Research and report on a book or article on animal ethology.
Option #4. Assess the presentation of animal minds in an ethological documentary.

Murder in a Zoo, Richard Leakey and Roger Lewin

Option #1. Research and assess the controversy associated with sociobiological theories of human behavior.

The Case for the Personhood of Gorillas, Francine Patterson and Wendy Gordon

Option #1. Evaluate the case for the personhood of higher primates. (Leakey and Lewin)
Option #2. Research and report on the issue of animal languages.

Equality for Animals?, Peter Singer

Option #1. Research and compare the views of animal rights organizations with those of Singer.
Option #2. Research and report on the state of animal experimentation on your campus.

Rights and Kindness: A Can of Worms, Paul Shepard

Option #1. Contrast Singer and Shepard on animal rights. (Singer)
Option #2. Research and debate the pros and cons of animal liberation and rights.
Option #3. Research and report on the use of animals in the food, entertainment, fashion, or medical industries.

Chapter 6: Reading Cyberminds

Isolated by the Internet, Clifford Stoll

Option #1. Respond to Stoll's claim that the Internet "dehumanizes" its users.
Option #2. Discuss the impact of electronic technology on solitude and the self. (Slouka and McKibben)

Out of Time: Reflections on the Programming Life, Ellen Ullman

Option #1. Compose a hypertext, multimedia, or formal essay on what it means to live "close to the machine" (Stoll and Turkle)

Option #2. Examine the "gender" of computer technology. (Turkle and Springer)

The Virtual Barrio @ the Other Frontier, Guillermo Gómez-Peña

Option #1. Research and report on the issue of equal access to the Internet.

Option #2. Compose a hypertext, multimedia, or formal essay on the culture of the Internet.

Who Am We?, Sherry Turkle

Option #1. Assess the impact of electronic media on human relationships. (Stoll and Ullman)

Option #2. Research and analyze the implications of online fantasy games (MUDS).

Muscular Circuitry, Claudia Springer

Option #1. Compose a hypertext, multimedia, or formal essay on the history of the robot.

Option #2. Analyze the changing role of women in recent science fiction films, TV shows, books, and so on.

Johnny Mnemonic, William Gibson

Option #1. Write your own gender analysis of "Johnny Mnemonic."

Option #2. Analyze the gendering of current depictions of machine minds in pop culture.

The Turing Test: A Coffeehouse Conversation, Douglas R. Hofstadter

Option #1. Create and evaluate your own version of the Turing test.

Option #2. Research and report on recent developments in the field of artificial intelligence.

Redefining the Measure of Mankind, Maureen Caudill

Option #1. Research and report on the social costs of automation over the past twenty years.

Option #2. Compose a hypertext, multimedia, or formal essay on the current state of robot development.

Option #3. Analyze images of human-android interactions in films such as A.I. and Bladerunner.

Grandfather Clause, Hans Moravec

Option #1. Assess how computing is changing our view of human identity. (Stoll, Ullman, Turkle, and Hofstadter)

Option #2. Compose a hypertext, multimedia, or formal essay on the role of simulation in smart machines. (Hofstadter and Turkle)

Cyber Soul-Space, Margaret Wertheim

Option #1. Research the issue of the "crypto-religiosity" of A.I. enthusiasts.

Option #2. Compose a hypertext, multimedia, or formal essay on the concept of cyberspace.

Option #3. Assess the ethical implications of electronic technology. (Stoll, Ullman, Turkle, and Caudill)

Essay Options by Assignment Type

PERSONAL ESSAYS

Chapter, Author, and Essay Option	*Topic*
1. Frazier #1	A multisensory description of your cross-town commute or neighborhood
1. Lopez #1	The education of your sense of touch
1. Ackerman #1	The tastes of your home cultures
1. Ackerman #2	The education of your sense of taste
1. Ackerman #3	A memorable cross-cultural experience of taste
1. Slouka #1	An auditory revision of cross-town commute/neighborhood essay
1. Classen et al. #1	An olfactory history of your education
1. Classen et al. #2	An olfactory geography of your community/college
1. Cole #1	The experience of seeing something in a new way for the first time
1. McKibben #1	A multisensory experience modeled on McKibben
1. Percy #1	The "sovereign" experience of an object or place
2. Sanders #1	An object that holds special memories for you
2. Hampl #1	An "elaborated" memory of a childhood experience
2. Hampl #2	A memory triggered by a childhood photograph
2. Kingston #1	A retelling of an important family story
3. Sapolsky #1	The experience of blurring ego-boundaries
3. Csikszentmihalyi #2	An innventory of the components of your own sense of self
3. Walker #1	An object with special meaning or cultural significance
3. Ludwig #1	The roles that guide your life story
3. Martínez #1	The impact of the media on your sense of self
3. Bateson #1	A time when you adapted to a new culure or social context
3. Bateson #2	A time when you felt silenced in school
3. Bateson #3	An inventory of relationships that contribute to your sense of self
4. Baldwin #1	A profile of a person who is a mystery to you

4. Hall #1	A personal experience of cross-cultural misunderstanding
4. Blum #1	A personal experience of cross-gender conflict
5. McNulty #1	Profile of an animal you've known well

SINGLE-TEXT ACADEMIC ESSAYS

Chapter, Author, and Essay Option	*Topic*
1. Kleege #1	Compare two visual perspectives on a single work of art
1. Kleege #2	Your own analysis of an abstract work of art
1. McKibben #2	Evaluate the claim that TV "tranquilizes" its audience
2. Schacter #1	Compare different recollections of the same work of art
2. Hampl #4	Analyze your own writing process in light of Hampl's
2. Engel #1	Analyze the relation of past and present selves in an earlier essay
2. Zerubavel #1	Analyze how memories are preserved in a culture to which you belong
2. Zerubavel #2	Compare the role of memory in two cultures you are familiar with
3. Csikszentmihalyi #1	Analyze a collection of pop cultural images of "ideal selves"
3. Martínez #2	Debate whether America is becoming a "mestizo" nation
3. Baumeister #1	Assess the dominance of the modern concept of self in media images
3. Baumeister #2	Debate the claim that the modern self has become a burden
3. Kitcher #1	Debate the ethics of pre-determining a child's attributes
4. Schank #1	Compare multiple interpretations of the same story
4. Nussbaum #1	Apply Nussbaum's theory of the "democratizing" nature of narrative to pop culture
4. Nussbaum #2	Apply Nussbaum's theory of the democratizing influence of story to children's literature
5. Lame Deer and Erdoes #1	Respond to the authors' charges against "white society"
5. Berger #1	Discuss the social functions of zoos
5. Berger #2	Explore the notion of "animals of the mind" in popular culture
5. de Waal #2	Assess the current state of "anthropodenial" in American culture
5. de Waal #4	Assess the presenation of animal minds in an ethological documentary
6. Stoll #1	Debate the claim that the Internet "dehumanizes" its users

6. Gibson #1	Write a gender analysis of "Johnny Mnemonic"
6. Hofstadter #1	Create your own Turing test for machine intelligence
6. Caudill #3	Analyze images of human/android interactions in films such as *Bladerunner, and A.I.*

MULTI-TEXT ACADEMIC ESSAYS

Chapter, Author, and Essay Option	*Topic*
1. Frazier #2	Compare Frazier's descriptive techniques with those of Lopez
1. Lopez #2	Compare the species functions of touch and taste
1. Slouka #2	Examine the erosion of sense experience in contemporary society
1. Slouka #3	Explore the relation between sense deprivation and creativity
1. Cole #2	Explore the role of education and acculturation in sense perception
1. McKibben #2	Examine the notion of the education of the senses
1. McKibben #3	Explore the visual bias of contemporary technological society
1. Percy #2	Examine the role of the mind in visual experience
1. Percy #3	Assess the claim that authentic perception is impossible in modern society
2. Sanders #2	Write a dialogue between Sanders and Percy on the influence of the past
2. Eiseley #1	Compare Eiseley's and Sanders's use of symbols
2. Eiseley #2	Explore the use of stereoscopic memory in Eiseley
2. Eiseley #3	Compare how memory works in Sanders and in Eiseley
2. Schacter #2	Explore the notion of stereoscopic memory in memoirs
2. Hampl #3	Examine Hampl's claim that "True memoir is written in an attempt to find. . . a world"
2. Engel #2	Discuss "template memories" in Eiseley, Hampl, and Kingston
2. Kingston #2	Examine the notion of the "politics of memory"
2. Zerubavel #4	Assess the idea of memory as an accurate "transcript" of experience
2. hooks #1	Examine how writers transform historical memories for individual purposes
3. Sapolsky #2	Examine the role of parents and family in the construction of the self

3. Walker #2	Assess the role of memory in the construction of the self
3. Ludwig #2	Discuss how the self lends coherence and continuity to our lives
3. Ludwig #3	Examine the challenges to living in the present
3. Martínez #3	Explore the thesis that the self is something we create, like a work of art
3. Bateson #4	Evaluate the status of the self in contemporary American culture
4. Schank #2	Compare theories of learning in Schank and in Bateson
4. Baldwin #2	Discuss the obstacles to mutual understanding in families
4. Hall #2	Examine the concept of the "cultural unconscious"
4. Fedullo #1	Apply Schank's and Bateson's notions of learning to Fedullo
4. Fedullo #2	Examine the challenges involved in learning to listen to others
4. Blum #2	Explore the challenges women face in the electronic workplace
4. Garbarino #2	Discuss the role of empathy in the creation of a civil society
5. Lame Deer and Erdoes #2	Analyze the authors' sense of self using theories from Chapter 3
5. Berger #3	Evaluate attitudes toward animals and "wildness" in contemporary American culture
5. McNulty #2	Debate the pros and cons of pet ownership
5. Siebert #2	Assess Siebert's claim that we are losing contact with nature
5. de Waal #1	Assess the role of TV in the "Bambification" of animals
5. Patterson and Gordon #1	Evaluate the case for the "personhood" of higher primates
5. Shepard #1	Contrast Singer and Shepard on the issue of animal rights
6. Stoll #1	Discuss the impact of electronic technology on solitude and the self
6. Ullman #2	Examine the "gender" of computer technology
6. Turkle #1	Assess the impact of electronic media on human relationships
6. Moravec #1	Assess how information technology is changing our view of human identity
6. Wertheim #3	Assess the ethical implications of electronic technology

RESEARCH AND HYPERTEXT PROJECTS

Chapter, Author, and Essay Option	*Topic*
2. Zerubavel #3	Research and report on a recent "mnemonic battle" in the United States

2. hooks #2	Research portrayals of Columbus and compare with that of hooks
2. hooks #3	Read and compare alternative versions of the "discovery" of the Americas
3. Baumeister #3	Survey magazine images to test claims about the modern American female self
3. Kitcher #2	Research and analyze depictions of clones and cloning in popular culture
3. Elshtain #1	Research and debate the pros and cons of human cloning
4. Sullivan #1	Research and analyze a specific category of hate crimes
4. Sullivan #2	Research and debate the pros and cons of hate crime legislation
4. Garbarino #1	Research and report on the causes of teen violence
5. Siebert #1	Survey and analyze media portrayals of animals
5. de Waal #3	Locate, read, and report on a book or article on ethology
5. Leakey and Lewin #1	Research the controversy over sociobiological interpretations of human behavior
5. Patterson and Gordon #2	Research other animal languages
5. Singer #1	Research and compare the views of animal rights organizations with Singer's
5. Singer #2	Research the state of animal experimentation on your campus
5. Shepard #2	Research and debate the pros and cons of animal liberation and rights
5. Shepard #3	Research the use of animals in the food, entertainment, fashion, and medical industries
6. Ullman #1	Compose a hypertext, multimedia, or formal essay on what it means to live "close to the machine"
6. Gómez-Peña #1	Research and report on the issue of equal access to the Internet
6. Gómez-Peña #2	Compose a hypertext, multimedia, or formal essay on the culture of the Internet
6. Turkle #2	Research and analyze the implications of online fantasy games (MUDS)
6. Springer #1	Compose a hypertext, multimedia, or formal essay on the history of the robot
6. Springer #2	Analyze the changing role of women in recent science fiction films, books, and TV shows
6. Gibson #2	Research and analyze the gender imagery of android portrayals in pop culture
6. Hofstadter #2	Research and report on recent developments in the field of artificial intelligence

6. Caudill #1	Research and report on the social costs of automation over the past twenty years
6. Caudill #2	Compose a hypertext, multimedia, or formal essay on the current state of robot research
6. Moravec #2	Compose a hypertext, multimedia, or formal essay on the role of simulation in machine intelligence
6. Wertheim #1	Research the issue of the "crypto-religiosity" of A.I. enthusiasts
6. Wertheim #2	Compose a hypertext, multimedia, or formal essay on the concept of cyberspace

Media Connections

You'll also find a wealth of media connections woven throughout *Mind Readings*. Some selections, like Bill McKibben's "Television and the Twilight of the Senses" or Claudia Springer's "Muscular Circuitry," focus squarely on the impact that various forms of media have on the mind. Others connect with media-related issues more indirectly. Thus, you can use Diane Ackerman's "Taste: The Social Sense" as a springboard for analyzing representations of taste and the social functions of food in films such as *Like Water for Chocolate* and *Babbette's Feast* — or you can use Ackerman as a point of departure for exploring the role of "taste" in horror in films such as *Silence of the Lambs* and *Hannibal*. You'll also find suggestions throughout the text for activities that promote visual literacy, including assignments that ask students to analyze ads and images in popular magazines as well as works of ancient and abstract art. Additional notes on media connections are included in the chapter introductions and in the notes associated with specific reading selections throughout this manual.

Chapter 1: Reading the Senses

Media images of life in urban America	Frazier, FE #1
Taste in *Like Water for Chocolate*, *Babbette's Feast, Tampopo,* and *Big Night*	Ackerman, FE #3
Silence of the Lambs and *Hannibal* as examples of "taste" in horror	Ackerman, FE #4
Representations of silence in visual art	Slouka, FE #4
Analyzing the visual experience of a painting	Kleege, FE #3
Shifting your perspective on art	Kleege, FE #4
Contrasting perspectives on a painting	Kleege, EO #1
Analyzing a work of abstract art	Kleege, EO #2
Analyzing the plot structure of TV programs	McKibben, FE #3
TV as tranquilizer	McKibben, EO #2
Analyzing photo and ad images of a famous natural object	Percy, FE #1

Chapter 2: Reading Memory

Differing interpretations of Rene Magritte's *The Menaced Assassin*	Schacter, ET #4
Different recollections/interpretations of a work of art	Schacter, EO #1
Public and private memories in *Rashomon* and *Death and the Maiden*	Zerubavel, ET #5
Researching and comparing textbook portrayals of Columbus	hooks, EO #2

Chapter 3: Reading the Self

Ego-boundaries, selfhood, and aging in *American Beauty* and *Magnolia*	Sapolsky, FE #5
Making a collage of ad images of objects that define the self	Csikszentmihalyi, FE #5
Collecting images documenting the "ideal selves" of ancient cultures	Csikszentmihalyi, FE #6
Collecting and analyzing pop cultural images of the "ideal self"	Csikszentmihalyi, EO #1
Images of "ideal selves" offered by Hollywood films	Martínez, FE #2
The impact of the media on your sense of self	Martínez, EO #1
Surveying media imagery to assess the dominance of the modern self	Baumeister, EO #1
Surveying magazine images to assess claims about the modern female self	Baumeister, EO #3
Cloning as a source of horror in Hollywood films such as *Gattaca*	Kitcher, FE #5
Portrayals of cloning in popular culture	Kitcher, EO #2

Chapter 4: Reading Other Minds

The role of stories in *Diner* and *The Breakfast Club*	Schank, ET #3
The imagination as a source of "civic culture" in popular media	Nussbaum, EO #1
Reflections of Japanese culture in films such as *Shower* and *Dance with Me*	Hall, FE #5
A collage of "male" and "female" images in contemporary popular culture	Blum, FE #1
Understanding violent minds in *Dead Man Walking*	Garbarino, FE #5
Youth violence in *Boyz in the Hood* and *Once upon a Time in America*	Garbarino, FE #6

Chapter 5: Reading Animal Minds

Koyannisquatsi as a critique of "white society"	Lame Deer and Erdoes, FE #4
A collage of "animals of the mind" images from pop culture	Berger, FE #4
An essay on "animals of the mind" in popular media	Berger, EO #2
An analysis of animal representations in TV nature shows	Siebert, ETs #1–4
A survey of TV show portrayals of animals	Siebert, EO #1
The role of TV in the "Bambification" of animals	de Waal, FE #3
An essay on the "Bambification" of animals in popular culture	de Waal, EO #1
Reflections of animal minds in ethological documentary films	de Waal, EO #4

Chapter 6: Reading Cyberminds

1

Reading the Senses:
From Sight to Insight (p. 11)

Getting Started

Students like this chapter, perhaps because they're so used to reading social issues topics in composition classes that the selections they find here strike them as refreshingly different. The topic of the senses may come up in their science classes, but it usually arises only in the context of the physiology of sense perception. You know the routine — the eye is a little camera with rods and cones and the ear has got those three little bones that everyone learns about and a couple of other pieces of bio-architecture that look like something out of a '50s science fiction film. But what students rarely if ever get the chance to explore in school nowadays is the "felt experience" of perception — unless, of course, they're highly trained artists or performers. The study of how we actually make contact with the world around us is only occasionally addressed in academic contexts. Yet, if you think back on it, the teachers who had the most impact on you as a student — the ones who really made a topic come alive — were probably the ones who knew how to engage all of your senses in the act of learning. Maybe it was a biology class where you learned how to look at a worm or a fetal pig not merely as a creepy dead thing but as an elegantly and intricately designed piece of bio-engineering. Or it might have been an English class where you learned how a few well-chosen words by a poet long dead could conjure up vivid recollections of a particular smell, taste, or touch. I also think students enjoy this chapter because they — being human — have all the apparatus and expertise they need to test and appreciate the ideas they find in these selections. Who hasn't experienced a neighborhood like Ian Frazier's Brooklyn as a cacophony of sights, sounds, and smells? Who hasn't made the age-old connection between food, appetite, sex, and death that Diane Ackerman so skillfully explores in "Taste: The Social Sense"? Who among us has never been appalled at the incessant din of a modern city or transfixed by the purity of bodily sensation when left alone in nature?

Reading the senses is also a good place to begin exploring the mind and its relation to reading and writing, because sense perception is itself closely allied to interpretation. Most of the time people take a "what you see is what you get" attitude toward the senses — just as they often take a "what you see is what it means" approach to reading. From this passive perspective, the mind simply reflects the world around it, just as the reader simply "decodes" the meanings that inhere in texts, and thinking thus becomes little more than the mechanical transcription of input and its eventual expression as output. As the selections in this chapter demonstrate, however, even the most fundamental levels of sense perception depend on sophisticated acts of selection, analysis, editing, and interpretation. Our senses don't simply reflect what we see, hear, feel, smell, and touch: they transform the world; they translate it into terms that "make sense." They shape our experiences in response to the preconceptions and biases we absorb from the cultures in which we live and hammer them into something we can recognize, evaluate, and appreciate. Exploring the senses, then, encourages students to reflect on the nature of interpretation and on the mind's transformative powers. It challenges students to grapple with the fact that the cultures in which we participate both facilitate *and* limit our perceptions, and it invites students to assess and hone their interpretive abilities. Reading the senses encourages students to recognize that even the most casual sensation is a kind of "text," a culturally constructed document that they can critique, interpret, and revise.

Another reason this chapter may resonate with students is that it reveals so much about the craft of writing. Many first-year students enter college without having thought very deeply about the relation between language and experience. At this point in their education, students often think of language as something that's both completely transparent and 100% efficient: when you want to express an idea or feeling you simply think the thought and then match it with the right words. The words contain the thought and convey it to the mind of your reader. Exploring the relation between language and the senses raises serious questions about this simplistic view of linguistic self-expression. As noted in the section on "Writing the Senses" included in the introduction to this chapter, language is biased toward the communication of concrete objects or abstract ideas: it's easier to describe the objects in a room or to discuss an idea such as freedom than it is to convey the way something feels, sounds, or looks. Trying to discuss the issue of sense experience thus puts students in the position of having to confront the limitations of verbal discourse. It also encourages them to think critically about some of the ways writers cope with such linguistic challenges. To convey what a moment of solitude in nature felt like to you, you can fall back on a few well-worn adjectives such as "peaceful" and "refreshing" — or, like Bill McKibben, Henry David Thoreau, or Louise Erdrich, you can draw on the evocative power of concrete detail, sense imagery, and figurative language. The point is not to have students writing lyric poetry in the first few weeks of freshman comp but to help them begin exploring some of language's most powerfully expressive resources.

Reading about the senses also gives students the chance to see how a number of expert writers tackle a particularly challenging topic. How do you approach the theme of taste in an essay? How do you discuss vision without collapsing into clichéd camera's-eye analogies? How do you make something as apparently self-evident as hearing or smell interesting? The answer, of course, is that you do what talented writers always do: you don't attack the subject "head on" in a manner that almost guarantees you'll end up on hackneyed ground; you approach it more subtly and creatively. In her essay on taste, Diane Ackerman only occasionally tries to capture the specific flavor of a thing in words; more often, she comes at the importance of taste from a number of different angles, exploring the social functions of the human palate, cultural preferences in relation to foods, the link between eating and sexuality, the ethical implications of being an omnivore, and so forth. To help us understand the phenomenon of sight, K. C. Cole examines the kind of indirect observation that physicists engage in to "see" subatomic particles, and Georgina Kleege explains the painstaking process that she uses to appreciate a Matisse painting with her seriously damaged retinas. The selections in this chapter model the kind of creative strategies that experienced writers employ to promote critical thinking and the opportunity for discovery. The topic of the senses thus offers an ideal way to help students appreciate the kind of "indirect," divergent, or associative thinking expert writers use to move from sight to insight.

If you want to start the first day of class off with some freewriting, here are a few topics you might consider:

- Have students freewrite and compare notes about the most memorable educational experience they can remember and about the role that the senses played in it.
- Have students freewrite and compare notes about the sense that's most important to them — and about the sense they think they could live without.
- Have students freewrite and compare notes about the most dramatic early childhood sense experience they can remember.

Sequences and Pairings

The structure of the chapter suggests a two-part approach. Readings in the first half offer a survey of the senses, with individual selections devoted to touch, taste, and smell and a pair of selections focusing on vision. The last section of the chapter offers three readings addressing the impact of electronic media and contemporary culture on the senses. You can easily build two essay assignments around these groupings. You might begin with Frazier's "Take the F" as an illustration of how to capture the felt experience of a place in words. Then sample a couple of selections on the senses before settling down to your first assignment. For this one draw on any of the Essay Options that follow Lopez, Ackerman, Classen et al., Cole, or Kleege — or return to Frazier and have students write their own version of "Take the F" based on their cross-town commute or a neighborhood with which they're intimately familiar. For a more academic paper, focus on the last three selections and have students write an essay on the fate of the senses in contemporary culture. You'll find many other possibilities to choose from among the many Essay Options included in this chapter, but this two-part approach moves students rapidly from personal to academic writing within the space of a few weeks.

Recommended Stand-Alone Readings

Just about all of the readings in this chapter can be used as the basis for stand-alone personal response essays. The only two that might require pairing are K. C. Cole's "Seeing Things" and Georgina Kleege's "The Mind's Eye." The three selections on the erosion of sense experience in contemporary society can also be used independently. Here's a list of some productive topics you may want to consider in approaching stand-alone assignments:

The felt experience of a specific environment	*Take the F* (Frazier)
The "education" of a particular sense	*A Passage of the Hands* (Lopez)
Tastes across cultures	*Taste: The Social Sense* (Ackerman)
The importance of silence in modern society	*Listening for Silence* (Slouka)
The impact of TV on the senses	*Television and the Twilight of the Senses* (McKibben)
Education, theory, and the senses	*The Loss of the Creature* (Percy)

Recommended Pairings

Silence in the city	*Take the F* (Frazier) and *Listening for Silence* (Slouka)
Senses and the self	*A Passage of the Hands* (Lopez) and *The Mind's Eye* (Kleege)
Sense and culture	*Taste: The Social Sense* (Ackerman) and *The Olfactory Revolution* (Classen et al.)
Vision and interpretation	*Seeing Things* (Cole) and *The Mind's Eye* (Kleege)
The impact of technology	*Listening for Silence* (Slouka) and *Television and the Twilight of the Senses* (McKibben)

Suggested Thematic Clusters

A survey of the senses	*A Passage of the Hands* (Lopez), *Taste: The Social Sense* (Ackerman), *Listening for Silence* (Slouka), *The Olfactory Revolution* (Classen et al.), *Seeing Things* (Cole), and *The Mind's Eye* (Kleege)

The social construction of sense experience	*Taste: The Social Sense* (Ackerman), *The Olfactory Revolution* (Classen et al.), *Seeing Things* (Cole), *The Loss of the Creature* (Percy)
The dominance of vision	*The Olfactory Revolution* (Classen et al.), *Listening for Silence* (Slouka), *Seeing Things* (Cole), *The Mind's Eye* (Kleege), *Television and the Twilight of the Senses* (McKibben)
The erosion of the senses	*Listening for Silence* (Slouka), *Television and the Twilight of the Senses* (McKibben), *The Loss of the Creature* (Percy)

Essay Options

Take the F, Ian Frazier

Option #1. Describe your cross-town commute/neighborhood.
Option #2. Compare Frazier's descriptive techniques with those of Lopez. (Lopez)

A Passage of the Hands, Barry Lopez

Option #1. Write about the education of your own sense of touch.
Option #2. Compare the species functions of touch and taste. (Ackerman)

Taste: The Social Sense, Diane Ackerman

Option #1. Write about the tastes of your home cultures.
Option #2. Write about the education of your own sense of taste.
Option #3. Write about a memorable cross-cultural experience of taste.

Listening for Silence, Mark Slouka

Option #1. Rewrite the cross-town commute essay done for Frazier to focus on aural experience.
Option #2. Examine the erosion of sense experience in contemporary society. (Classen et al., McKibben, and Percy)
Option #3. Explore the relation between sensory deprivation and creativity. (Kleege, McKibben, and Percy)

The Olfactory Revolution, Constance Classen, David Howes, and Anthony Synnott

Option #1. Write an olfactory history of your education.
Option #2. Write an olfactory geography of your community or campus.

Seeing Things, K. C. Cole

Option #1. Write about a time when you learned to see something in a new way.
Option #2. Explore the role that education and acculturation play in sense perception. (Lopez, Ackerman, Classen et al., and Kleege)

The Mind's Eye, Georgina Kleege

Option #1. Compare two visual perspectives on the same work of art.
Option #2. Offer your own analysis of an abstract work of art.

Television and the Twilight of the Senses, Bill McKibben

Option #1. Write a multisensory description of an experience modeled on McKibben.
Option #2. Evaluate McKibben's claim that TV "tranquilizes" its audience.
Option #3. Examine the notion of the education of the senses. (Lopez, Ackerman, Classen et al., Cole, Kleege, and Percy)
Option #4. Explore the visual bias of contemporary technological society. (Classen et al., Kleege, Cole, and Lame Deer and Erdoes)

The Loss of the Creature, Walker Percy

Option #1. Write about an experience of the "sovereign" reality of an object or place.
Option #2. Examine the role of the mind in visual experience. (Cole and Kleege)
Option #3. Assess the idea that modern society has lost contact with real perception. (Slouka, Classen et al., Cole, and McKibben)

Media Connections

Media images of life in urban America	Frazier, FE #1
Like Water for Chocolate, Babbette's Feast, Tampopo, and *Big Night*	Ackerman, FE #3
Silence of the Lambs and *Hannibal*	Ackerman, FE #4
Representations of silence in visual art	Slouka, FE #4
Analyzing the visual experience of a painting	Kleege, FE #3
Shifting your perspective on art	Kleege, FE #4
Contrasting perspectives on a painting	Kleege, EO #1
Analysis of a work of abstract art	Kleege, EO #2
Analyzing the plot structure of television programs	McKibben, FE #3
TV as tranquilizer	McKibben, EO #2
Analyzing images of a famous natural object	Percy, FE #1

IAN FRAZIER, *Take the F* (p. 18)

This essay isn't actually about the senses. But it does offer a sense-drenched example of personal writing at its best. Frazier's account of his cross-town commute on the Manhattan Transit Authority's F train brims with the sights, sounds, and smells of life in Brooklyn, New York. You can use this selection productively in a couple of different ways. Assign it on the first day of class as a quick introduction to the topic of the senses. Most students enjoy reading Frazier. Many of my first-year students at Los Angeles City College take the bus themselves for miles every day to get to campus and go to work, so it's easy for them to relate to the daily sensory cross-town trek that Frazier describes here. "Take the F" also offers you the chance to begin discussing the challenges involved in expressing personal experience in words as well as the opportunity to introduce several key composition concepts. Students can explore the verbal techniques Frazier uses to create this multisensory portrait of daily life in Brooklyn and see first-hand how he blends sense images and illustrative stories to create the illusion of actual sense experience. Reading Frazier also demands that students go beyond the words on the page to grasp the import of what he's saying about his experience of the city. Frazier doesn't clobber the reader with a thesis in this personal reflection: he never does more than suggest what he feels and thinks through his skillful use of language. Reading Frazier requires that students work selfconsciously to interpret his underlying intentions as an author, and thus it offers an immediate context for discussing issues such as active reading and composition concepts such as "thesis" and "focus." Finally, you should consider using Frazier as the point of departure for a personal essay documenting your students' sense impression of the city or town where they live (EO #1). You can assign this paper immediately after reading Frazier as a way of getting your class off to a fast start with formal writing, or you may want to postpone it until after you've sampled a number of other selections on the senses from the chapter's first half. Frazier connects well with Lopez, Ackerman, Slouka, and Classen et al., so you may want to follow up with several of these readings and then have students write their own version of "Take the F" as a capstone assignment for the first half of the chapter. The Before Reading activity works best if you ask small groups of students to brainstorm or "free associate" a list of words they associate with life in the city. Chances are that this will elicit some of the expected negative stereotypes — "dirty," "crowded," "smelly," and "dangerous." But then, you may get some more positive images as well. The point is to get students thinking about the preconceptions they may have about places like Brooklyn so that they can appreciate how thoroughly Frazier challenges such stereotypes.

Exploring the Text

1. So what *is* Frazier saying here about life in Brooklyn? "Everything and nothing" might be one answer. The essay begins inauspiciously enough by comparing Brooklyn to the "hard-to-remember shape of a stain." In a single phrase, Frazier reminds us about the bad rep of his neighborhood: Brooklyn is famous for being nowhere in relation to the Big Apple and for being notoriously poor and run-down. Hollywood back lots are filled with streets that are supposed to look just like Brooklyn — dingy streets of anonymous brownstone tenements with bared windows and heavy-duty security doors, all smeared with a decorative haze of graffiti. But even though he was once a country boy, Frazier is clearly smitten with this place that refuses to "conform neatly to the points of the compass." This is where active, interpretive reading comes in. The initial impression that students are likely to come away with is that, overall, Frazier likes Brooklyn. The challenge is to get them to unearth the clues that lead them to this reading of his authorial intentions. What, specifically, is it that he seems to like about the city? What particular lines or passages offer clues that help us read his mind? Frazier does find much to admire in his adopted hometown: there's the beauty he finds in the "disheveled" urban landscape, the smells of innumerable cooking suppers, the sounds of city accents, even the very fact that, by being where it is, Brooklyn is helping to "preserve" nature somewhere else. But, clearly, it's the people that Frazier is most in love with. "Everybody, it seems, is here," he notes in awe. If there is a central message or focal idea in Frazier's essay, it seems to center on the notion of diversity. Brooklyn is a kind of dingy crazy-quilt of world cultures; in his trips on the F and his walks through city parks, Frazier introduces us to Jews, African Americans, Italians, Russians, Latinos, and the homeless. Still, it isn't diversity alone that Frazier celebrates. Underlying the essay is the conviction that, despite its size and lack of "shape," Brooklyn is a real community — a whole that's more than the sum of its parts. Exactly like Frazier's essay itself, Brooklyn is a collection of fragments, a riot of sense impressions that adds up to a coherent whole. This would seem to be the point of the last story Frazier tells about his neighbor (ET #4). Chris is the

person who makes contact with everyone in Frazier's building; she's the building's memory and conscience. The story of Chris's hospitalization illustrates the kind of human connection that Frazier sees everywhere he looks in Brooklyn, whether it be in the exchange he overhears about a wayward crab on the subway, in the casual wisdom offered by a man on a park bench, or in a stranger's defense of the homeless in a local copy shop. Frazier's Brooklyn isn't the kind of angry, anonymous place we've come to think of when we think of urban America. Despite its size and diversity, it's a place with an identity and a heart — more like an extended family than an alienated city. The faces of the people who get off the subway after the mishap he tells about at the beginning of the essay may be "varied as usual," but their typically Brooklyn expressions of "indignant surprise" are "all about the same." Thus, Frazier offers you an excellent opportunity for working with students on the art of interpretation and active reading. Not all will see this message of unity in diversity in his description of Brooklyn. Some will get sidetracked by their own associations with city life; others will have their own individual views of Frazier's message. The point is that Frazier gives you the chance to engage your class in the process of close interpretation.

2. One way to encourage this kind of intense engagement with the text is to have students keep track of passages that strike them as particularly effective in terms of their descriptive power. They shouldn't have too much trouble coming up with some good candidates. The essay's very first paragraph offers the image of "detailed airplane shadows" sliding down the side of Frazier's apartment building and up the building across the street. A few paragraphs in, he describes the people he sees on the F train as if they were themselves linked together like subway cars:

> On the F, I sometimes see large women in straw hats reading a newspaper called the *Caribbean Sunrise,* and Orthodox Jews bent over Talmudic texts in which the footnotes have footnotes, and groups of teenagers wearing identical red bandannas with identical red plastic baby pacifiers in the corners of their mouths, and female couples in porkpie hats, and young men with the silhouettes of the Manhattan skyline razored into their short side hair from one temple around to the other, and Russian-speaking men with thick wrists and big wristwatches, and a hefty, tall woman with long, straight blond hair who hums and closes her eyes and absently practices cello fingerings on the metal subway pole. (para. 3)

Like Whitman, the great nineteenth-century bard of Manhattan, Frazier builds descriptive passages through the addition of concrete detail. He doesn't bother with abstractions like "There's a lot of diversity in New York" or "People come here from all over the world." Instead, he presents image after image of people and things — Orthodox Jews bent over Talmudic texts, female couples in porkpie hats, Russian-speaking men with thick wrists and big wristwatches — piling them up until they become an unstated argument for his experience. Frazier also layers his sense impressions of the city. He peppers the reader with visual impressions throughout the essay, but he also makes room for the smells, sound, and even the "feel" of his daily commute. He captures the onslaught of the city's smells in a few carefully chosen details: "The smells in Brooklyn: coffee, fingernail polish, eucalyptus, the breath from laundry rooms, pot roast, Tater Tots. A woman I know who grew up here says she moved away because she could not stand the smell of cooking food in the hallway of her parents' building" (para. 6). Passages such as this offer you the chance to talk about the way sense imagery works. Students often don't take the time to breathe life into sensory images by re-experiencing them in memory. Ask them to pause here and actually smell the coffee, fingernail polish, pot roast, and Tater Tots. Do they remember a moment from their own past when they smelled dinner floating down a hallway or out of the window of a house in their neighborhood? What was being served? What was that particular experience of smell like? Did it repulse them the way it does the woman Frazier mentions, or did it make them wonder about the scene inside? Learning to appreciate sense-based writing, like any kind of critical reading, requires the active engagement of the reader. You have to engage the concrete sense images that Frazier provides here and bring them to life in your imagination to fully understand the experience he's trying to convey. That's why he works so hard, for example, to help the reader literally "hear" the sound of the voices that fill Brooklyn streets:

> And I like the way the people talk; some really do have Brooklyn accents, really do say "dese" and "dose." A week or two ago, a group of neighbors stood on a street corner watching a peregrine falcon on a building cornice contentedly eating a pigeon it had caught, and the sunlight came through its tail feathers, and a woman said to a man, "Look at the tail, it's so ah-range," and the man replied, "Yeah, I soar it." (para. 6)

Frazier scatters linguistic nuggets like this throughout the piece. Seeing a beach-comber chopping driftwood, a Russian passerby says, "He's working hard, that guy!" Two women talking about getting revenge on a third shout, "Her butt be in the *hospital!*" and "Bring out the ar-*tillery!*" Another woman who catches him reading says, "From a distance, I t'ought you were watchin' ants." The ducks in the park by his apartment building quack, "Yeah, yeah, yeah" in their own jaded Brooklynese. Frazier doesn't want us just to read these words; he wants us to hear the voices that speak them. It's a subtle difference, but one that's crucial if students are to begin thinking seriously about the expressive power of language. Frazier also offers a clear illustration of the way writers use appeals to multiple senses in order to bring an experience to life. He doesn't settle for simply describing what Brooklyn looks like; he takes the time to tell us how it smells, how it sounds, even how it feels. Here he is trying to convey the speed of the subway cars as they race through the cityscape:

> To the south you can see the Verrazano-Narrows Bridge, to the north the World Trade towers. For just a few moments, the Statue of Liberty appears between passing buildings. Pieces of a neighborhood — laundry on clothes lines, a standup swimming pool, a plaster saint, a satellite dish, a rectangle of lawn — slide by like quickly dealt cards. Then the train descends again. (para. 4)

Speed fractures his view; it fragments the passing neighborhoods, transforming them into a kind of suburban cubist collage — or, in a rare use of simile — into a hand of rapidly dealt cards.

3. Frazier also calls on the power of storytelling to bring his impressions of Brooklyn to life. Students shouldn't have any trouble finding at least a dozen anecdotes in this essay. He starts with the story about his daughter and her discriminating palate for pizza. Then there's the story about the day the F train broke down and firemen had to evacuate its passengers. Then the one about the two men who jumped into the toxic canal while trying to escape from the police. Some of these are genuine anecdotes — like the story of the itinerant crab — complete with characters, complications, and resolutions. Others flash by in an instant, serving only to vivify a specific sense impression. Before we get to the tale of the crab that concludes the essay's fifth paragraph, Frazier offers one-liners about the woman who pulled a knife, the man who sang the Lord's prayer, the violent white bully who hit the window, and the two women who wanted to slap someone silly. Frazier tells stories about the students he teaches as a volunteer at the public elementary school, about barbecue conflicts at Prospect Park, and about the homeless woman who couldn't remember her own last name. He tells one particularly poignant anecdote about finding and reading a lone page from Tolstoy's *Anna Karenina* on a busy city street. You'll want to spend some time analyzing what these anecdotes add to Frazier's description of New York and why he lingers over some and scatters others in handfuls. You'll also want to devote some time in class to analyzing the purpose of some of the more extended stories that Frazier offers. Does each of these brief stories have a specific point? When he tells how a man canvassing for a petition to close a homeless shelter is shouted down by the customers in a copy shop, it's safe to say that Frazier is

suggesting something about the values of his fellow Brooklynites. But what is he saying when he offers the image of a man leaving behind a trail of holes as he sweeps the beach with his metal detector? Or, for that matter, what is he suggesting when he pauses to read the page of Tolstoy?

4. The key story in the essay, of course, is the final one about Chris and her pregnancy. This anecdote changes the focus of "Take the F" by making it more personal. Frazier plays a more active role in this vignette: his feelings about Chris and the people in his building are central to the story's point. The last action he describes — walking into the Rose Garden and breathing in a Betsy McCall rose "as if it were an oxygen mask" — underscores several of the unstated themes he's been developing: the hidden beauty of the city, the value of real community, and the notion that dissonance and contradiction — things like roses and oxygen masks — give life.

Further Explorations

1. You may want to have students do the urban collage activity as an "ice-breaker" during the first couple of days of class. This gives them the chance to work together in a productive, collaborative way and sets the stage for more open in-class exchanges and collaborations. But don't expect students to come up with images that reproduce the grimmer stereotypes that you might expect to see associated with urban life. Popular magazines shy away from anything that might be construed as depressingly "realistic." It's likely that students will find a mix of images — some portraying the seedier side of urban America, but a great many projecting cityscapes that are shiny, progressive, and evocative of power and success. If that's what they do come up with, use this as an opportunity to discuss and analyze their own impressions of America's cities. You may also want to transform this activity into a pre-writing assignment for Essay Option #1 by having students make a photo collage about their own neighborhood or cross-town commute.

2. You can also help them warm up for this paper by asking them to experiment in their journals with some of the expressive verbal techniques that Frazier uses in "Take the F."

3. Even if you're pausing here for an early paper, you'll probably want to have students read Barry Lopez's "A Passage of the Hands" so that they can compare the descriptive strategies of these two authors. Lopez doesn't project us into specific dramatic situations as frequently as Frazier does. Owing to the nature of his topic — his hands and the education of his sense of touch — he relies much more heavily on sense impressions: the "pressure and friction" of a pencil lodged between his fingers, the "velvet rub" of a horse's nose, the "texture and weave" of a piece of fabric. Even when he does relate stories from the past about his hands, Lopez tends to present them more generally than does Frazier. Lopez tells us about the way he and his boyhood friends pelted each other with fruit, but he doesn't settle on a specific incident on a particular day. Instead, he reserves this kind of detailed and dramatic narration for what might be seen as the essay's climax — the story about the day his hands "lost innocence" and almost killed a friend with a careless toss of a stone. Spend some time debating which style students like better and deem more effective. To help your class appreciate what stories and concrete images do for Frazier and Lopez, you might also want to have them write a brief general summary of each essay. It may be possible to reduce "Take the F" to: "Life in Brooklyn may seem like a chaos of voices, nationalities, sights, and sounds, but behind all of this diversity you'll find the spirit of a true community." It's just that this nutshell treatment skips over everything that's interesting and valuable about Frazier's essay.

4. You may also want to give students the chance to contrast Frazier's impressions of the city with Bill McKibben's experince of swimming alone on Crow Mountain. At first blush, these two very different essays might not seem to have much to say to one another. But Frazier and McKibben actually have quite a bit in common. McKibben believes that real sensual pleasure is never a matter of comfort but a matter of contrast:

you can't savor real pleasure unless you've experienced some pain; real comfort can come only after serious deprivation. Frazier also sees beauty in contrasts: he loves Brooklyn because it's a kaleidoscope of contrasting sights and sounds — even the essay's final flower/oxygen mask image underscores this point. Then, too, we also get the impression that Frazier is, in some sense, just as isolated in the city as McKibben is in the country. He may be speeding through an underground tunnel on a subway car that has more in common with a Ship of Fools than an isolated mountain pond, but Frazier always seems deeply reflective. We sense his mind at work behind every image and anecdote. Even at the end of the essay when Frazier hugs Chris for the "whole building," he maintains his reflective distance. He celebrates Chris's return to the neighborhood — and his solidarity with her and the city as whole — by retreating, alone, we presume, to the Rose Garden and his private experience of a Betsy McCall in full bloom. So, even in the heart of Brooklyn, he's not that far removed in spirit from McKibben posed for his dive into Crow Pond.

5. He is miles apart, however, from Walker Percy when it comes to the impact of familiarity on perception. Percy argues that repeated experience dulls the senses and makes it impossible to "see" things that are there right in front of us. Our "preformed" ideas blind us to the "sovereign" experience of the most magnificent natural wonders — even to things like the Grand Canyon. The whole point of Frazier's essay, by contrast, seems to be that you can't possibly appreciate a place like Brooklyn unless you've spent many a morning and afternoon riding the F. The power and authenticity of Frazier's writing derives from the authority he has because of his intensely personal relationship with the city. Even a relatively casual observation like the one about the airplane shadows going down and up the buildings that line his street bears witness to this intense familiarity. Brooklyn fits Frazier like a well-worn glove or a favorite shirt, and I suspect he'd argue that you can't really appreciate any place, including the Grand Canyon, until you've spent a healthy chunk of your life living there. Familiarity seems to deepen perception for Frazier: returning again and again along the same path allows you literally to see more.

Essay Options

1. Students learn a lot about observation and writing from this essay, and they usually enjoy trying their own hand at a "Frazier-eque" essay on their own neighborhood. Approach this assignment as a chance for students to experiment with language and writing style. Use it to encourage them to take a few risks — to try at least a few moves with words that they've never tried before.

2. Essay Option #2 offers a more typically academic assignment. Try analyzing a couple of select passages from Lopez and Frazier together in class to get them started with this one. Since you're probably assigning it early in the term, you'll want to keep the scope of this comparison relatively limited, but do encourage students to offer their own assessments of the two essays. Figuring out what they like about Lopez and Frazier will help them begin to see their own writing and that of their peers from a more constructively critical perspective.

BARRY LOPEZ, *A Passage of the Hands* (p. 27)

This personal essay on the theme of touch pairs well with Frazier and complements several other selections in this and other chapters. It also provides the basis of a solid single-reading personal essay on the theme of the "education" of the senses (EO #1). Writing — and even talking — about touch can be a challenge in class. Being good products of the Enlightenment, schools are generally hostile to the senses of touch and smell: we tend to teach and learn through the eye and ear — vision and hearing being the senses most closely identified with modern science. So, there's a historical bias built into the classroom against what are commonly seen as the "secondary" or "lower" senses. The point of Lopez's essay, of course, is that touch is in many respects the most intimate sense. Touch represents our first and most personally direct form of contact with the world, and, thus, it is central to the development of our sense of self. Still, this very intimacy can present problems in class. Students may shy away from the topic as being "too personal" — or simply not have a clue about how to approach it in public. Touch is also hard to talk about because, like the sense of smell, it lacks a well-developed vocabulary. As stated in the headnote to this selection, relatively few words are dedicated to the experience of touch. Lopez copes with these cultural and linguistic challenges by approaching his topic through the trope of education. Skilled essayist that he is, Lopez knows it's difficult to talk about the experience of touch head-on, so he focuses instead on the education of his hands: doing so is both less personal and more concrete than focusing exclusively on his lifetime relationship with the sense of touch. He also dignifies his topic and adds a dose of intellectual rigor by viewing it as a kind of "Bildungsroman" — by focusing on the story of the education or development of his hands since their birth. This self-consciously developmental approach links "A Passage of the Hands" with several selections in Chapter 2. You'll want to give it special consideration, then, if you plan to cover some of the book's later readings on memory. The pre-reading activity asks students to return to an early childhood memory of touch. The emphasis here should be on touching something remarkable — some object in the world that has stuck in memory ever since.

Exploring the Text

1. When Lopez says that his hands have had their own education, he means that he has learned about the world through his hands since his birth. This conceit, the "illusion" that his hands "have a history independent of the mind's perception," allows Lopez to chart the development of his own sense of touch, and through it, to tell his own life story. Some of the formative experiences of Lopez's hands include feeling the "bend of a horse's short-haired belly," the coarse sheeves of unshucked ears of corn, the "bony crest" of a dog's head, and the "raised oak grain" of a schoolroom desk. He recalls the texture of the fabrics his mother sewed, the squish of the ripe fruit that he and his childhood friends used as weapons, and the heft of a baseball as it's fielded at third base and thrown for an out to first. He also recalls the tactile sensation of more mature experiences: the intricacies of a full Windsor knot, the touch of a girl's skin, the strain of a fishing line, and the dance of a pencil as he mastered the craft of writing. Through his hands, he remembers the time he nearly killed a friend as well as his first experience of physical intimacy. The story of Lopez's hands offers us a tremendous amount of information about him as a person. He comes across through this autobiography as an active, outgoing man who is proud of his achievements and still sensitive to the feelings and needs of others. The story of his hands tells us that he's a Westerner, a man who's comfortable in the wilds of nature, and an intellectual. Perhaps most of all, this essay suggests that Lopez understands that his self is bigger than his mind — and that the very best and most thoughtful aspect of his personality lives in the strength and tenderness of his touch. This essay gives the impression of Lopez as a person who is not too proud to listen attentively to the stories that his own hands have to tell him — an act of authorial humility that says much about his attitude toward himself and the world at large.

2. Early on in the essay, Lopez appeals directly to the reader's sense of touch through the use of tactile imagery. Here he describes some of the earliest lessons learned through his hands:

> It is from these first years, five and six and seven, that I am able to remember
> so well, or perhaps the hands remember, a great range of texture —
> the subtle corrugation of cardboard boxes, the slickness of the oilcloth on the
> kitchen table, the shuddering bend of a horse's short-haired belly, the even give
> in warm wax, the raised oak grain in my school-desk top, the fuzziness of dead
> bumblebees, the coarseness of sheaves immediate to the polished silk of
> unhusked corn, the burnish of rake handles and bucket bails, the rigidity of

the bony crest rising beneath the skin of a dog's head, the tackiness of flypaper, the sharpness of saws and ice picks. (para. 3)

We feel along with him here as he runs his hands in memory over the corrugations of a piece of cardboard, the slickness of a piece of oilcloth, or even the simple sharpness of tools around the farm. But Lopez has other verbal strategies for conveying the tactile richness of the sense of touch as well. In the following passage, for example, he depends on the sounds of words to convey the tactile richness of the sense of touch:

> Growing on farms and in orchards and truck gardens around our home in rural California was a chaos of fruit: navel and Valencia oranges, tangerines, red and yellow grapefruit, pomegranates, lemons, pomelos, greengage and damson plums, freestone and cling peaches, apricots, figs, tangelos, Concord and muscadine grapes. Nectarines, Crenshaw, casaba, and honeydew melons, watermelons, and cantaloupes. My boyish hands knew the planting, the pruning, the picking, and the packing of some of these fruits, the force and the touch required. I sought them all out for the resilience of their ripeness and knew the different sensation of each — pips, radius, cleavage. I ate even tart pomegranates with ardor, from melons I dug gobs of succulent meat with mouth and fingers. (para. 7)

Lopez knows that in the verbal economy of the senses, it's acceptable to mix and mingle — that you can convey the experience of one sense through the language of another. Thus, he uses the aural lushness of the names of fruits in this passage to express the tactile experience of handling the fresh home-grown fruit of his family farm. He relies on the alliterative excess of "planting," "pruning," "picking," and "packing" to convey the bounty of this childhood experience. In a later passage, he returns to the same topic, this time drawing on the power of active verbs to express the sensation of touch:

> We pelted one another with rotten plums and the green husks of walnuts. We flipped gourds and rolled melons into the paths of oncoming, unsuspecting cars. This prank of the hand — throwing, rolling, flipping — meant nothing without the close companionship of the eye. The eye measured the distance, the crossing or closing speed of the object, and then the hand — the wrist snapping, the fingers' tips guiding to the last — decided upon a single trajectory, measured force, and then a rotten plum hit someone square in the back or sailed wide, or the melon exploded beneath a tire or rolled cleanly to the far side of the road. And we clapped in glee and wiped our hands on our pants. (para. 10)

Here, the verbs do most of the work. Vigorous active verbs such as "pelt," "flip," and "snap" help us appreciate the sensations of touch that Lopez experienced as a boy. Lopez's hands always seem to be in motion, always seem engaged in doing something — whether it's "collecting chicken's eggs" or writing out a story "longhand in pencil." These are the techniques he returns to again and again — the active verb, the sonorous name, the doubling of tactile experience with the experience of sound or sight — to awaken in his reader the dormant experience of touch.

3. But stories also play a part here. The anecdote about targeting passing cars with ripe watermelons is a case in point. Lopez uses these brief illustrative stories sparingly. He tells us in passing about recognizing a type of fabric while reading a page in *Parzival*, about a "furious nun" who corrected the way he folded his hands in prayer, and about how he learned to butcher a whale. He tells about a couple of summer jobs, but never in great detail. He relates the story about how his mother's oldest friend sees his mother's hands in his. But he reserves the full power of anecdote for one particular occasion — when he offers the story of how his hands cost him the innocence of his youth. In the essay's one clear dramatic scene, he tells how he nearly killed a boyhood friend while casually "firing" stones out over an ocean breakwater. He follows this scene with the outline of a few other near-tragic incidents involving his hands, but none as detailed or dramatic as the story of this moment of carelessness.

4. Indeed, despite the quiet sensitivity in Lopez's writing, there's a kind of reticence in this essay that might be seen as distinctly male. He tells us a good deal about what he does and learns, and he does mention his connection to other people and creatures, but he shies away from dwelling on his feelings — or even on the specific details of his life experiences. Much of this essay is presented very generally. Lopez tells us about the skills or knowledge he's acquired with his hands over the years and about what he's done, but he seems to veer away from discussion of more personal situations and relationships. The very idea of offering an autobiography of yourself through your manual experiences might be seen as reflecting a particularly "male" way of thinking. Lopez comes across here as an active, tough, and straightforward kind of guy. He may be a writer, but he's also an outdoorsman and a naturalist — a man who has spent his life relating to the world through his hands. This emphasis on things manual perhaps inevitably distances him from the details of his own biography: we hear precious little in this essay about specific people and places. The only person who draws his attention for more than a few lines is his mother, and all we learn about her is that she sewed and — interestingly enough — that she slept in her sewing room in the small house where he grew up. Would this history be different if told from a woman's point of view? It might if it were told from the perspective of a woman growing up in a relatively traditional household where women were expected to clean, cook, sew, and play the role of primary caregiver for others. Less traditionally oriented women, however, may not feel very far removed from Lopez's experiences. In fact, many contemporary female students take just as much pride as Lopez does in the strength and sense of mastery they've gained through their sense of touch.

Further Explorations

1. Touch also shows up in Ian Frazier's "Take the F," but it clearly plays a small role compared to vision, smell, and hearing (FE #1). The question here is whether it's possible to relate to something as big, as public, and as potentially impersonal as a city through the sense of touch. The most notable tactile moment in Frazier's essay comes when he embraces Chris to welcome her home from the hospital — but even this isn't offered as a tactile experience per se. Clearly, Frazier could have dwelt on the feel of the molded plastic chairs of the F-train cars or the warmth of the sand along the beach where he saw people combing the shore with their metal detectors, but he isn't really interested in conveying an intimate portrait of the city or in anatomizing his sense of self: he's focused on the chaotic and colorful diversity of life he finds in Brooklyn's neighborhoods, and this topic lends itself more readily to the public senses of vision, hearing, and smell than it does to the more intimate sense of touch.

2. The story of Lopez's hands finds a much closer comparison in Scott Russell Sanders's "The Inheritance of Tools." In fact, if you don't plan to read much in Chapter 2, you may want to pair these two readings at this point in the term. Sanders covers much of the same ground that Lopez does in his essay. The tools he inherits from his father and grandfather are "wrapped in a cloud of knowing": they contain innumerable lessons about how they should be used to build furniture, repair broken toys, or add a room onto a house. But more important, they convey lessons about what it means to be a responsible person, lessons about integrity, honesty, diligence, and love. And that's perhaps the most interesting difference between these two "manual" memoirs. Although Lopez comes across in his essay as a sensitive and sympathetic person, he emerges from it literally alone with his hands. In fact, it's interesting how much he focuses on sharp objects, cutting, hitting, and scaring in his memoir; the idea of separation or disconnection seems to loom large for him. Sanders, by contrast, is linked by his tools with not only the men of his family but with his wife and children as well. He uses his hammer to mend things, to build relationships that are just as plumb and as firmly founded as the walls of his daughter's new bedroom. Indeed, the one scar that Sanders notes in this essay, the result of a wound he inflicts on himself the moment he hears about his father's death, eventually heals and leaves him sound.

3. Susan Engel's notion of remembered and remembering selves may help to explain the apparent solipsism of "A Passage of the Hands." Lopez does not dwell much on his relationships with others in this essay because he is primarily interested in exploring the relation between his present and past selves. The entire selection can be read as an effort to integrate the various people that Lopez has been at different moments in his life, to harmonize the prank-loving child with the careless adolescent, the earnest young naturalist with the mature and reflective writer and thinker. Lopez's hands play out all of these roles as the "remembered" selves of his "remembering" present. In the present moment of writing, he offers us the image of himself as a thoughtful, caring, and mature adult in relation to his own hands. Looking down at them in his lap "as if asleep like two old dogs," he seems both gently affectionate and bemused — perhaps an apt pose for someone whose hands contain stories that he himself can no longer recall.

4. Arnold M. Ludwig's discussion of storytelling in relation to identity formation might further suggest specific roles or scripts that Lopez assigns to himself during the various stages of this brief autobiography. From Ludwig's perspective, Lopez might be seen as casting himself as a kind of Huck Finn — or less literarily as a Bart Simpson figure in his youth — while as a young man he comes across as the kind of free-living Wyoming cowboy that he aspired to become. What makes Lopez interesting, of course, is the fact that his identity in this piece is never reducible to any one role: he is the aspiring writer at the same time that he plays the part of the outdoorsman and adventurer.

Essay Options

1. Once students spend some time discussing Lopez, they'll be better prepared for the challenge of writing the story of their own hands. The key to this assignment lies in thoughtful pre-writing and brainstorming activities. It helps to have students focus on specific "lessons" or skills they recall learning through their sense of touch. It also helps if they think about their hands in relation to specific periods of their lives — the way that Lopez distinguishes between his early childhood, adolescence, and early adulthood, for example.

2. Essay Option #2 offers a very challenging academic topic. While Lopez explores touch from a purely personal point of view, this assignment asks students to take a broader approach and view it from a "species perspective." This will become clear after students read Ackerman's analysis of the functions of taste. What does touch do for us as a species? Well, it allows us to manipulate the physical objects that constitute our worlds. Like taste, touch is intensely intimate and directly associated with sex. But unlike taste, touch has little "aesthetic" or social function. We do make a point of touching fabrics and sculptures, but the aesthetic enjoyment of touch is relatively limited in scope compared to that of taste. Ackerman suggests that while taste is a source of delight, it also has a darker aspect in that it provides the motive that lures us to consume other creatures for our own survival. Taste is thus always somehow associated, for her, with death and horror. And the same might be said for touch. Through our sense of touch we reach out and manipulate the world around us. We use touch to dominate as well as to connect with others, to break things apart as well as to bring them together. Taste gives us the motive to consume; touch gives us the power and ability to fulfill our appetites.

DIANE ACKERMAN, *Taste: The Social Sense* (p. 36)

This selection offers a bridge between the two personal essays that begin the chapter and the more academic selections that follow. Ackerman's style is casual in this selection, as you might expect it to be given her topic, but her ideas range everywhere from culinary history to the role of food in pop culture and even the evolutionary implications of the phenomenon of taste. Because Ackerman stresses the social nature of taste, this piece connects well with several others in this and other chapters that deal with the relation of the mind and society. It pairs productively, for example, with Constance Classen et al., on the relation of culture and the senses, and it can be assigned with Classen et al., K. C. Cole, and Walker Percy as a unit on the social construction of perception. It also connects with selections in Chapter 4 that deal with mind reading across cultures. You can use Ackerman as the point of departure for at least three very productive personal essays that explore the role of culture in the formation of the sense of taste (Essay Options #1–3). If time permits, you may also want to consider screening any one of a number of fine films that deal with the social functions of food and taste, such as *Babbette's Feast, Big Night,* or *Like Water for Chocolate* (FE #3). There's even a chance to link Ackerman with the peculiar culinary habits of Hannibal Lecter (FE #4). Since taste is perhaps the most social of the senses, as Ackerman proclaims, students generally have little trouble engaging with the topic. Every student comes to class with a menu of tastes that represents home and the cultures associated with it, and, in general, students enjoy writing about these home flavors and foods. The suggested Before Reading activity asks them to freewrite about the foods they connect with their home cultures, or as an alternative, to write about the most exotic cross-cultural taste experience they've ever encountered. Most classes enjoy these practical exercises in cross-cultural awareness, so you may want to allow time for some small group discussion of the activity before you begin reading.

Exploring the Text

1. Ackerman associates taste with a number of functions in this essay. Love of food brings cultures and families together. We use food to mark special occasions, to indicate approval, and even to evoke supernatural powers. Food plays a role in almost all religious traditions; indeed, in Christianity the central act of worship involves the ritual consumption of the body and blood of Jesus, symbolized by the ingestion of bread wafers and wine. In many cultures, such as those of many Native American tribes, food itself is worshiped as a deity: the corn god Mais is a figure of veneration in the Hopi and in other American Indian traditions. As Ackerman notes, taste is such a dominant experience that it has assumed aesthetic implications that range far beyond the domain of nourishment. The idea of taste demarcates a whole spectrum of cultural activities and is used to distinguish those who have achieved a certain level of cultural sophistication from those who lack such development. The sense of taste and the enjoyment of food are also closely linked with sex and sexual pleasure. When we eat, we consume the offspring of beasts and the reproductive organs of plants and fruits. Taste helps us to be good omnivores by tempting us to try unusual foodstuffs. It leads us, via craving, to the basic substances our bodies need for health in certain environmental conditions and at particular times of our lives. It tempts us so that we won't allow our natural animal laziness to keep us from the task of seeking our supper.

2. Ackerman dubs taste the "social sense" because it unites us with others and because it is itself socially conditioned. In most cultures it's rare for people to eat alone: food is generally part and parcel of social life. Indeed, that's why food in general and even some specific dishes and flavors can easily assume symbolic importance in certain cultural contexts. At the same time, the perception of taste is also intensely intimate. Tasting requires that we literally place bits and pieces of the world inside our bodies' boundaries — something that vision and hearing, for example, don't require. The intimacy of taste shows up in our attitudes toward sharing food: when we "break bread" with people, we establish a bond of intimacy with them. When we savor oysters on the half shell with a date over a glass of champagne, dinner becomes part of the ritual of courtship. Most students can come up with a number of dishes or flavors that have relatively clear social meanings in the contexts of their home cultures. Some foods bring families together. Some are powerful sources of cultural identity. Some are reserved for special occasions such as weddings, birthdays, or New Year celebrations.

3. Chances are, however, that students will have a little more trouble pinning down Ackerman's attitude toward her subject. She begins this selection in a chatty, informative way: as she ranges from kachina dolls to leaf cutter ants and roasted turtle, she seems

to celebrate the variety of the human palate — much as we might expect her to, given that for a great many of us, food is a favorite subject. Yet, Ackerman's tone darkens considerably toward the end of the selection. From the glories of food as a source of intimacy and cultural connection, Ackerman moves on to highlight some of gastronomy's weirder aspects. She focuses on the odd things that are eaten in different cultures, on the way that cravings work as chemical delivery systems, and on the fact that people in almost all societies regularly consume things that are potentially dangerous, such as fugu and caffeine. The point is that taste links us, in Ackerman's view, to death. Every bite we eat reminds us at some level that we exist at the price of other lives, that we must kill something else if we're to avoid starvation. "We kill to live," she reminds us: "Every one of us performs or tacitly approves of small transactions with torture, death, and butchery each day."

4. It's clear that Ackerman structures her essay deliberately to ease us toward this moral interrogation of our own humanity. She begins cheerfully enough with the familiar celebration of food as a source of warmth and meaning and slowly draws us toward the apparently inescapable conclusion that taste links us to the drooling ghouls we love to be tormented by in horror movies. Of course, all along the way, she's dropped hints about the selection's final destination: she tells us early on that finding food is not involuntary like breathing and that taste acts to "decoy us out of bed" to get our dinner. She also undermines the trappings of culture that allow us to conflate the taste with the notion of an aesthetic ideal. Civilization, she reminds us again and again, is only a recent stage in human development: strip away all the pretense, and toss out the *Gourmet* magazines, and we're still hunter-gatherers at heart. As she moves through her analysis of taste, Ackerman de-centers us. She invites us to look at ourselves from a distanced point of view, from what amounts to a "species" perspective. She invites us to step outside the kind of cultural perspective we usually take on taste — a perspective that surrounds foods and flavors with warm associations — and to adopt, instead, an evolutionary or ecological point of view. Clearly, Ackerman wants to shock us, to make us see something familiar in a new, and perhaps even an upsetting, way. Does she want to move us to action, to literally "put us off our feed"? Probably not. Her evolutionary perspective — as well as the joy she so obviously discovers in food and the act of eating — suggest that she takes a balanced view of her topic. Ultimately, she wants only to make us think about who and what we are as a species. And she wants to show us how critical thinking can reveal something startling and new even when applied to the most time-worn subject.

5. As she moves us toward this unsettling view of ourselves, Ackerman employs several strategies to keep us engaged. At times she regales us with dramatic scenarios — the vignette of the diner-lovers who linger over a "delicious prelude," the story of her experience dining with cattle hands on a ranch in Mexico, or the anecdote about a "perfect picnic" shared with Turkish friends. These scenarios illustrate her point and add to her credibility as an authority on the subject of taste. The layers of historical and scientific fact that Ackerman includes here serve much the same function. When she pauses to explain the physiological connection between lips, tongue, and genitals, she's doing more than simply giving us information about taste: she's claiming authority to speak on this subject. Ackerman uses illustrations and facts so well to develop her ideas that it's tough to decide which of these strategies serves her better. You might want to reserve this question for classroom debate.

Further Explorations

1. Barry Lopez might well object to the suggestion that taste is the "social sense" par excellence. Touch links Lopez to the childhood culture of boys that played such a large role in his life. It also links him to the craft of writing and the skills of the naturalist. Touch, as he reminds us, is the root of human intimacy: it brings us together as lovers and as parents and children. But it's hard to think of touch as being more social than taste. Taste is more culturally determined than touch, and it's woven more tightly into

public celebrations and rituals. Indeed, taste might be seen as touch with greater "bandwidth": celebrants at a banquet can share a collective experience of taste during a ritual toast, while it might prove inconvenient or even unsavory for everyone to embrace the guest of honor. Because it's grounded in traditions of cooking and links us to our cultural heritage, taste also allows individuals to participate in cultural experiences even when alone. That's why Americans sometimes seek out peanut butter sandwiches in Paris when they could be eating coq au vin. Touch, by contrast, offers no remote connection to others. To get in touch, you have to be face-to-face.

2. In some respects, taste may actually have more in common with vision than it does with touch. As K. C. Cole indicates in "Seeing Things," visual perceptions are always culturally mediated: when we view something, we see it through a lens of expectations produced by personal experience and cultural biases. All perception, according to Cole, is "theory laden"; all perception depends on interpretation. Thus, it's possible to look directly at something new and not see it at all — or at least to misunderstand it. To see something clearly, you have to be prepared to see it. We see things in the present because they are familiar — because we already have interpretive frameworks based on past experience and learning that allow us to see them. What we are able to appreciate with our eyes, like what we are able to taste, thus depends on cultural construction: our palates, like our eyes, are predisposed by prior cultural experiences to react positively to certain stimuli. Learning to appreciate the flavors of a different culture, like learning to appreciate a new form of art or to "see" a new kind of subatomic particle, requires patience, education, and the willingness to take a risk.

3. Interestingly, several relatively recent films are available that feature the sense of taste and the social function of food. You may want to schedule a screening of a film such as *Babette's Feast, Like Water for Chocolate, Big Night,* or *Tampopo* to complement Ackerman and your class's exploration of the sense of taste. Set in nineteenth-century France during the reaction that set in after the French Revolution, *Babette's Feast* portrays food and the cultivation of taste as a form of personal liberation and collective resistance. Based on Isabell Allende's popular novel, *Like Water for Chocolate* explores the erotic and cultural meanings inscribed in culinary and gastronomic cultural traditions. In this film, cooking is allied with alchemy and eating itself is portrayed as a kind of magic. *Tampopo* explores the economics and erotics of food in contemporary Japanese society, while *Big Night* is a period film set in 1950s New York that presents food as a form of resistance against the predations of modern American capitalism.

4. For something a bit more hair-raising, you might also consider viewing either *The Silence of the Lambs* or *Hannibal* as an illustration of Ackerman's claim that the idea of eating and being eaten plays a central role in the creation of cinematic horror. Both of these films play with the distinction between taste as the perception of flavor and taste as a matter of connoisseurship. Hannibal Lecter is, first and foremost, a connoisseur — someone who has self-consciously cultivated his aesthetic sensibilities and thus become the ultimate consumer. The irony, of course, is that Lecter has refined his palate to the point where he's content only when consuming the flesh of his own species. In many ways Lecter is the perfect embodiment of the gustatory terror and guilt that Ackerman associates with the horror movie genre. He is the top omnivore, a monster who has carried the cultural imperatives of civilization to their most bone-chillingly logical conclusion. He lives to satisfy his cravings, and his cravings all lead — as Ackerman suggests all cravings inevitably must — to death.

Essay Options

All three of the Essay Options associated with this reading offer excellent opportunities for papers based on personal experience.

1. Essay Option #1 invites students to explore the meaning of specific foods and flavors within the context of their home cultures. Students who come from homes with

strong cultural backgrounds will have a lot to contribute on this topic, and even students from backgrounds that seem culturally "neutral" usually are able to find something here to write about — even if it's about Shake 'n Bake pork chops, macaroni and cheese, and apple sauce.

2. Before assigning Essay Option #2, you'll want to be sure to read and discuss Lopez's "A Passage of the Hands." Lopez is the model for this assignment: all students have to do is adapt the conceit of the education of a particular sense to their experiences with the sense of taste.

3. The Before Reading activity for this selection may also be expanded, after some diligent pre-writing and group discussion, into a more fully developed personal essay on the topic of a memorable cross-cultural culinary experience. You might want to consider this option if you'd like to assign a two-to-four page personal essay at this point in your class or if you plan to move on to readings on cross-cultural understanding in Chapter 4.

MARK SLOUKA, *Listening for Silence* (p. 50)

The topic of silence presents students with some special challenges. For one thing, silence is the absence of sound, and, thus, to write about silence is to struggle with the challenge of writing about something that's not right there in front of you — a pure abstraction. Yet, as Slouka argues in this essay, our need for silence is anything but abstract. Silence is the foundation of the self and the source of just about everything that Slouka sees as genuinely valuable in human existence. This selection will challenge students conceptually and stylistically; Slouka's prose is complex and chock full of allusions to art, intellectual history, and philosophical concepts. But it's also extremely productive. It continues the chapter's discussion of the relation between sense and society, and it provides the basis for several key assignments. Use it alone as the foundation for a paper on the fate of silence in a high-tech age — or pair it with Frazier in preparation for an essay on silence in the city, or with McKibben for a paper on the relation between electronic technology and solitude. Or you can use it as a key selection in three of the four thematic clusters suggested above (manual pp. 33–34). Slouka even offers the chance for an interesting assignment involving the representation of silence in famous paintings (FE #4) — a topic that's bound to test the interpretive abilities of even your most able students. To help prepare your class for Slouka, the Before Reading activity asks students to think back to their last self-conscious experience of pure silence. For many, this won't be an easy experience to summon up. Nature used to offer a refuge from sound, but in the era of cell phones, FM radio, and GPS, you can't even count on the wilds to insulate you from the incessant chatter of civilization. This activity actually works best if a few students can't recall a self-consciously silent moment in the recent past, because that allows you to explore why silence is so rare today and whether they miss the experience. And, of course, you shouldn't expect students to embrace Slouka's crusade against electronic communications technology and capitalist culture. For some, silence isn't a source of inspiration or a keystone of the self, it's just a way to tell when you are bored.

Exploring the Text

1. Anyone who's spent even a few minutes at a busy intersection in a major American city will be able to grasp Slouka's central claim — that silence is disappearing from the modern world. As Slouka sees it, we in the industrialized West live "[e]nsnared in webs of sound" generated by commercial traffic, airplanes, bulldozers, and electronic gadgets of all sorts. The "aural universe" that we inhabit has been completely "colonized" by the forces of modern commercial culture. Slouka sees this as potentially even more dangerous than the impact of visual technology, because the ear, unlike the eye, can't block sounds out: "There is no aural equivalent for the eyelid." The eye must be aimed at what it's meant to see: vision requires intention and focus. Hearing, by contrast, is involuntary: the ear puts the mind into contact with the world whether we want it to or not.

2. This is important to Slouka, because he believes that silence is essential for the creation of individual identity. Developing character requires serious work, in Slouka's view. It requires contemplation and self-reflection — types of mental activity that don't mix with the blare of Top-40 radio and the aural onslaught of city streets. A direct intellectual descendent of Henry David Thoreau, Slouka believes you have to isolate yourself to have a self — you have to "court" silence in order to hear your own voice. Silence also plays an essential role in the development of creativity. Slouka offers us the image of Edison, who was freed from the world's distractions by early deafness so that he could think independently and creatively. And because silence promotes the cultivation of individual differences, it plays a central role in the life of democratic culture. Take away silence and you take away our ability to differentiate ourselves from one another as well as our ability to tolerate differences in others. Of course, Slouka isn't insensitive to the negative dimensions of silence. The ultimate silence, as he points out, is found in the grave, and this kind of life-ending silence is the very thing that great art seeks to subvert when it "attempts to force a wedge beneath the closed lid of the world." Slouka respects the dangers that silence represents — voicelessness and death.

3. The KGB photo that hangs in his office reminds him about the relation between silence and political oppression. Totalitarian states, such as those established by Pinochet, Milosevic, and Himmler, use silence as "a tool of repression." Slouka makes it clear that he understands such dangers: it's one thing to sing the praises of silence and solitude when you're living in the woods next to Walden Pond, and another when you're part of the era of electronic surveillance and the "panopticon" of state power. Slouka is not naïve about the dangers of silence, but he also understands that it takes the danger of silence to give our lives deeper meaning.

4. Ultimately, capitalism shoulders most of the blame for the loss of silence, in Slouka's opinion. The noise that fills the world today is the noise of people "buying and selling." Indeed, as he indicates, communication itself has become the latest commodity, and this has driven us to fill our lives with phones, faxes, TVs, and pagers. (Ideally, a cell phone will ring at just this point in your class.) The tragic aspect of all this for Slouka is that the commodification of communications technology drives us into a vicious cycle: technology impoverishes our relationships and surrounds us with a chaos of essentially meaningless sounds, and we respond by buying more technology to block the chaos out. We've become adept at using technology as a means of "forcing a privacy where none exists." We plug ourselves into the 24/7 programming of pop radio; we don our Walkman earphones to blot out the barrage of sounds on city streets; we surround ourselves with Muzak; we discuss private affairs in public over our cell phones. The irony in all this, from Slouka's perspective, is that we now even try to buy back the silence we've lost. After filling the world with sound by commodifying and marketing mass communications, capitalism is attempting to respond to our need for silence — a need that it itself created. Thus, the rich have the option of purchasing homes in the country that isolate them from the sounds of civilization or expensive vacations at "spas advertising the promise of silence." Students might recognize other ways in which money can be used to purchase the right to silence. Movie stars and dot-com billionaires move to places like Montana to escape the chaos of city life. Sport-utility vehicles serve much the same purpose — acting like large sound-proof rooms that insulate their owners from urban soundscapes. Electronic specialty shops now regularly stock earphones that actively block ambient sounds. Even the phenomenon of techno music — the trance-inducing ultra-repetitive electronically synthesized disco that's become popular at rave scenes over the past decade — might be seen as a form of sound-blocking "white noise."

Further Explorations

1. According to Classen et al., after the Enlightenment smell was displaced by sight as the primary sense for the gathering and communication of information. Before the birth of modern science, smell was widely regarded as an important source of intelli-

gence. In church doctrine, for example, the "odor of sanctity" was regarded as a sign of sainthood, and odors, in general, were deemed a common form of communication with higher spiritual realms by means of olfactory hallucinations and dreams. Modern science relegated aroma to a secondary position, placing greater weight on vision as a source of scientifically reliable data. Thus, while vision and hearing are widely promoted in contemporary Western cultures, the sense of smell is actively discouraged. This bias in favor of hearing and vision goes back to at least to the eighteenth century, when the connection was first made between refuse and the spread of disease in urban Europe. Indeed, there's a striking parallel between the "smell pollution" that plagued cities during the Middle Ages and the "noise pollution" that Slouka hears everywhere in contemporary urban America. We even respond to noise pollution in the same way that our European forerunners responded to the stench of medieval city streets: we either cover it up with more pleasing noises, just as the sixteenth-century courtier doused himself with cologne to mask unpleasant odors, or, if we have the means, we escape to our country estates.

2. In "Seeing Things," K. C. Cole suggests that perception is always a two-stage process: first you gather and sort information and then you figure out what it means. Interpretation is central to the act of sensation: things that don't "make sense" are ignored or not seen at all. Scientific technologies extend the senses; machines such as microscopes, telescopes, and atom smashers give us access to sense impressions about things that our natural sensory systems aren't built to address. Electronic communications technologies, by contrast, amplify the reach of our expressive capacities: satellite TV dishes, microwave transmissions, cell phones, radios, and beepers make it possible for us to reproduce and transmit information beyond normal human limits. The danger here, from Cole's perspective, is that information can both promote and hinder real perception. You need background information to appreciate what you see and hear around you: chances are you won't be able to comprehend a symphony or a meteorite if you are utterly unfamiliar with Western classical music and the study of astronomy. But too much information — or too much information dogmatically trusted — can lead to perceptual paralysis. If you flood a sensory channel with constant information, "sensory atrophy" sets in and you lose the ability to make sense of the data you receive. Too much information leaves you with nothing but noise. And this is exactly what Slouka fears most — that by immersing us in sound, modern capitalist culture is depriving us of the ability, quite literally, to hear our own voices and to make sense of our selves.

3. Like Frazier (manual p. 35) and Lopez (manual p. 40), Slouka also uses anecdotes and examples to develop the theme of this essay. He tells us about the middle-aged man who calls someone a "bitch" over his cell phone while shopping, about Edison's technique for "hearing" music by sinking his teeth into a piano, about the Russians pictured in the KBG photo that hangs over his desk, and about the performance of John Cage's 4' 33". To some extent, all of these stories serve similar functions: they offer dramatic illustrations of the various points he's trying to make and they provide an expository change of pace. For Slouka, this second function is critical, because his densely allusive prose style can be tough going even for experienced readers. Brief narrative passages — even if only a couple of lines long — give us the chance to take a deep breath and reflect on the ideas he's been presenting. This, in itself, is somewhat different from the way narrative passages work in Frazier and Lopez, where they either convey the substance of the essay or are used for emphasis.

4. Great writing, like great art, in Slouka's view, exploits the resources of silence as much as it denies its dominion. Great poems, paintings, and songs make silences stand out; they help us appreciate the purifying and revivifying influence of absence. Having students actually examine a good reproduction of one of Edward Hopper's paintings — like the famous diner scene in his *Nighthawks* — might help them better understand what Slouka is getting at. Matisse's "Three Dancers," mentioned by Georgina Kleege later in this chapter, and Magritte's "The Menaced Assassin," mentioned by Daniel L.

Schacter in Chapter 2, also offer examples of paintings that give visual expression to silence. Of course, you may have your own examples of silence in art that you want to explore in class, or you may want to invite students to bring in reproductions of works they're familiar with that capture silence in some dramatic fashion. Hopper conveys a sense of silence through his themes and his use of open, utterly vacant spaces. The city at night and the nearly abandoned diner in *Nighthawks* force us to hear the sounds that are *not there* in Hopper's painting. Color also plays a role here, as does scale. The human forms in Hopper's works are dwarfed and isolated by their surroundings; there's nothing to suggest even the possibility of voice. The colors — gray-greens, blues, and black — make even the light that comes from the diner seem muted. Because there's some truth to Slouka's claims about art and silence, there are many paintings you can use in class as the basis for this type of analysis.

Essay Options

1. It's actually quite easy for students to do an "auditory" revision of the cityscape or neighborhood essay that they wrote originally in response to Frazier (Frazier, EO #1). As Slouka asserts, modern American society is awash in sound, so the notion of writing an aural description of the area one lives in shouldn't really be all that daunting. Generally, what students feel they lose through this experiment is the security of sight; what they gain is a new appreciation for the richness of their auditory environment — and, perhaps, at least a measure of appreciation for what it means to live without vision.

2. Essay Option #2 offers the chance for a major academic paper. Think of this assignment as a kind of self-contained mini-research assignment that requires students to synthesize information from four different sources. All four selections — Classen et al., McKibben, Percy, and Slouka — approach the topic of technology's impact on the senses from different perspectives. Classen et al. see the rise of modern science as having sanitized the senses by minimizing the importance of smell in favor of vision. McKibben argues that television narrows our perceptual range by restricting us to sight and sound and that TV generally has a narcotic effect because of the predictability of commercial programming. Percy holds that technology cuts us off from the "sovereign" experience of perception by mediating between us and the realities we encounter. Technology, for Slouka, disrupts perception because it surrounds us with so much input that we lose our ability to make sense of any of it: in a world filled with commodified sound, no sound retains its significance. All four, however, agree that technology has done damage to our ability to perceive the world around us and, as a result, to our sense of self. Students should be sure to offer and explain their own perspective on the topic in this paper.

3. Essay Option #3 resembles #2 but focuses more narrowly on the relation between sense deprivation and creativity. Again, in order to respond to this academic topic, students will have to explore the views of Slouka, Kleege, McKibben, and Percy and follow up with their own ideas on the topic. Slouka believes that silence stimulates creative thinking: Edison's deafness swaddled him in a layer of silence that in some sense also freed him to think about sound in new and creative ways. All art, in Slouka's view, is a response to the cosmic silence of death: lose touch with this powerful motive and you lose touch with the impetus to create. Cole is also instructive in this context. According to Cole, too much sensation can lead to sensory fatigue, and too much dependence on commonplace ways of perceiving can stifle creative insight. Brilliant thinkers, in Cole's view, have the habit of seeing things in socially unacceptable ways — in today's jargon, they have a predisposition for thinking "outside the box." Kleege seems to support the notion that an abundance of sensory input can actually dull perception and make people passive or lazy thinkers. Certainly, her encounter with the fully sighted man at the Matisse exhibit illustrates this basic idea: engrossed in the museum's audio tour, he breezes through the gallery apparently paying more attention to the experts he's listening to on tape than to the paintings themselves. Kleege, by contrast, must struggle

to gather even fragmentary sense data from each canvas, yet her observations about Matisse seem genuinely insightful. All real perception, for Percy, is in some sense both an act of discovery and an act of creation. The problem is that most perception, in Percy's view, is simply a matter of reproduction. Instead of actually "confronting" the world around us without bias, preconception, or phony expectations — the way an explorer might encounter a new continent — we see things through the mediating perspectives of theory, education, and technological reproduction. Instead of actually seeing something like the Grand Canyon head-on, we tend to see only its culturally mediated image. For Percy, every act of genuine perception is always an act of creation, and every real confrontation with reality requires that we be intellectually alone. The point, of course, is highly debatable. The idea of the isolated artist or inventor is itself a cultural cliché, and, certainly, there's plenty of evidence that many creative types do, in fact, enjoy immersing themselves in their art, the society of other artists, and the world of the senses. Encourage students to take a critical view of this topic and to consider people they've known whom they might regard as particularly creative thinkers.

CONSTANCE CLASSEN, DAVID HOWES, and ANTHONY SYNNOTT, *The Olfactory Revolution* (p. 59)

A history of the sense of smell might seem out of place in a composition class, but don't be tempted to dismiss this selection out of hand. In this reading, Classen, Howes, and Synnott make a startlingly effective case for the social construction of sensory experience and touch on important issues such as the development of science and the formation of modern gender identities. The only real difficulty this selection might present is associated with the fact that we have deodorized education and the mind so thoroughly in the West that it may be hard for students to see how smell could be viewed as a serious academic subject. You probably wouldn't want to assign "The Olfactory Revolution" if you plan to cover just one reading in this chapter, but Classen et al. does pair well with Ackerman on the theme of the social construction of sense experience, and it figures in three of the chapter's four thematic clusters (see manual pp. 33–34). In addition, it offers the chance for two unusual Essay Options — one featuring olfactory memories of early educational experiences and one inviting students to write an "olfactory geography" of a familiar area or institution. The Before Reading activity appears to call for an exercise in pure imagination, but it's meant to get students thinking historically. What odors, fragrances, and aromas might they imagine wafting on the breezes of eighteenth-century Paris? Well, some possibilities might include the aroma of baking foods, the cloying scent of a hundred thousand unbathed but heavily perfumed bodies, the reek of rotting fish and meat, the stench of raw sewage flowing into the Seine, and the omnipresent background aroma of a hundred stables full of horses, cows, pigs, and sheep. If students are stumped by this one, ask them instead to think back to a place that they associate with a particularly strong smell or aroma. Owing to the Proustian nature of smell — the peculiar way that olfactory memories remain accessible in the mind — most students have little trouble remembering a classroom, a friend's house, a place of worship, a summer camp, or a workplace that still evokes a particular experience of smell.

Exploring the Text

1. The central point of this reading is that Western attitudes toward aroma, fragrance, and the sense of smell have changed radically over the past few hundred years. Prior to the eighteenth century, Europeans viewed bathing as a form of exotic recreation, not as a daily necessity. Since water was seen as a potential source of spiritual and physical corruption, bathing was commonly thought to be a risky undertaking. As Classen, Howes, and Synnott point out, medieval Europeans often chose to wash their clothes instead of their bodies. Perfumes were thus used to camouflage bodily odors; in fact, scents of all kinds played an important economic and cultural role in pre-modern European societies. It was even commonly believed that perfumes had medicinal pow-

ers that could protect those who used them from the plague. Because of rapid urbanization in the early Renaissance, local sanitation and garbage disposal systems of European cities frequently broke down, and this, combined with the fact that every city also housed slaughter yards, stables, sugar refineries, and manure manufactories, made the stench of the average European town "perfectly unendurable." Of course, little of this shows up in cinematic depictions of the pre-Enlightenment West. Hollywood movies visually deodorize the past; they eliminate even the slightest visual or aural reference to smell. Thus, there may have been horses in Elizabethan London, but chances are you won't see piles of dung and garbage on street corners in *Shakespeare in Love* — or, for that matter, streets flooded with raw sewage, greasy waistcoats, or hair that's matted from lack of washing.

2. European attitudes toward sewage and smell began to change, according to the authors, with the birth of modern science and the rise of the modern middle class. After watching animals die in vacuums created in bell jars, early scientists became convinced that fresh air was essential for health; thus, after the London cholera epidemics of 1858, cities began to design modern sanitation systems. The cult of personal hygiene followed, with physical cleanliness eventually becoming a matter of moral reform. Personal hygiene was a sign of enlightenment and education and was thus associated with the lifestyle of the rising middle class. People who smelled — that is, laborers and farmers — came to be seen as hygienically and morally inferior to their deodorized social betters. And, clearly, the cult of personal hygiene still plays a significant role in contemporary American society. Students should have little trouble coming up with examples of how the ideal of the deodorized body is packaged and sold through the mass media. In contemporary America, dirt is not a mark of holiness as it was in the era of St. Francis of Assisi. In fact, it would be interesting to calculate how much the average American spends on personal hygiene and household cleanliness every year — probably more than the average family income in most developing nations. Students might also note that the new fitness craze that's emerged over the past twenty years might be seen as a modern extension of the "new olfactory order." For while it might, in fact, be deemed healthy and even socially desirable to work up a good sweat nowadays, it has got to be done in the right clothes, with the right shoes, and ideally either in a private gym or with a substantial amount of specialized equipment. In other words, it's good to perspire if it shows you're not poor.

3. Classen et al. point out that odor also became gendered after the eighteenth century. Prior to this time, men and women used the same perfumes; during the 1800s, however, sweet, flowery scents became identified with women while sharper, more "outdoorsy" scents were typically worn by men. This olfactory division of the sexes came about as gender roles were segregated during the nineteenth century. Women, at this time, became identified with domestic pursuits and sensuality — with flower gardens, pabulum, and potpourris; men were identified with the world of nature, with "maps, microscopes, and money." Today, the basic outlines of these olfactory gender prejudices still exist, although they were challenged somewhat during the '60s, when scent made a comeback as a countercultural force: the smell of patchouli and strawberry incense still conveys a hint of resistance to dominant culture values and attitudes. And the notion of unisex colognes, like cross-gendered fashion, has also reemerged in recent years.

4. According to the authors, the widespread deodorization of modern society also reflects deeper changes of attitude about the senses as sources of information. After the rise of modern science, vision emerged as the dominant source of information: the "keen gaze" of the explorer and scientist became the standard by which the truth was judged. Smell was too hard to measure to provide an accurate objective standard for science; indeed, smell was viewed by philosophers such as Descartes, Kant, and Condillac as a useless mental function. After Darwin, scientists often cited *Homo sapiens'* poor sense of smell as evidence of evolutionary progress and assumed that the distinctive scents and flavors associated with newly discovered tribal peoples marked them as "uncivilized."

Such attitudes suggest that, following the eighteenth century, the West placed high value on relatively abstract mental functions and correspondingly denigrated all things associated with the material existence of the body. Civilization, seen from this perspective, is founded on the "distanced" sense of sight: it is the culture of the observer, the explorer, the student, and the administrator, and it is closely allied to the technologies of modern science — to the world of microscopes, telescopes, the surveyor's sextant, and the compass.

Further Explorations

1. As suggested above, current American attitudes toward smell still favor deodorization, but may be seen as less antiphysical and less moralistic than nineteenth-century attitudes. The scent industry appears to have grown over the past twenty years, with perfumes and colognes being marketed aggressively once again to men as well as women. A resurgent interest in cooking and in cross-cultural experiences has opened American homes to aromas that might well have been seen as "uncivilized" just a few generations ago — aromas such as those produced by garlic, curry, salsa, and cilantro. Still, a strong case can be made that we continue to live in a deodorized world. Corporations still market hundreds of products for the elimination of mouth, underarm, body, home, car, garbage, and pet odors, and American homes and places of business are still relatively odor-free. It might also be argued that smell is still tied closely to class differences in America: when you think of the pungent smells of cooking wafting from an open window, chances are you're picturing a working-class or immigrant neighborhood and not a mansion with servants and rolling lawns.

2. As both Ackerman and the authors of this selection suggest, our senses of taste and smell are highly conditioned by the cultures in which we participate. Western culture has done its best over the past two hundred years to denigrate the sense of smell and limit its scope. This means that Westerners typically have a fairly narrow range of tolerance for olfactory stimulation: most urban Americans, for example, have trouble tolerating the kind of pungent odors that are associated with agricultural life, and many even find it increasingly difficult to tolerate the scent of tobacco. In other parts of the world, however, the "earthy" smells of farming are associated with health, tobacco smells like fathers, and sweet flowery scents are more commonly involved in cooking than in the boudoir. Ackerman notes the same cultural variability in relation to taste: what tastes good in Africa or Japan is often very different from what is savored in Oklahoma or Ohio. Americans might eat snack foods that look like fried radioactive roundworms, but most of us shudder to think of munching a tastily prepared cricket or a nice slice of fugu.

3. Given the cultural diversity of Brooklyn, you might expect Frazier to highlight the smells he encounters as he wanders through its neighborhoods, and, in fact, he does pay homage to the smells of Brooklyn, which he ticks off as "coffee, fingernail polish, eucalyptus, the breath of laundry rooms, pot roast, [and] Tater Tots." Frazier goes on to talk about the smell of cooking food and toast, but within the space of a couple of lines he's got us out in the country, thinking about all the "pine-timbered canyons" that New Yorkers are preserving by "not living there." The olfactory barrage that is New York seems to drive him out to the countryside; in fact, he doesn't return to the sense of smell until the last line of the essay, when he inhales the fragrance of a Betsy McCall rose "as if it were an oxygen mask." Frazier also mentions his daughter's love of pizza, but given the variety and availability of ethnic foods in New York, it's surprising that he doesn't exploit smell and food imagery more than he does. It would be easy to celebrate the diversity of Brooklyn through its food — perhaps even easier than it is to describe its diversity through its voices. Yet, for the most part, Frazier's portrait of Brooklyn appeals to the eye and ear — and not the nose or palate.

4. In fact, McKibben might be tempted to observe that, despite the gorgeous detail he includes, Frazier takes what might be described as a videophile's perspective on life in New York. According to McKibben, television impoverishes perception by limiting us to visual and aural stimulation: as McKibben sees it, TV restricts our connection to the

world by forcing us to experience it through the relatively narrow porthole of the cathode-ray tube. Thus, television itself might be viewed as a logical extension of the deodorization that modern science began back in the eighteenth century. Like science, TV favors the "intellectual" senses of sight and hearing over smell and touch. McKibben, however, would not agree that what we see and hear on television is particularly informative or edifying. He'd be more likely to find the tactile and olfactory experiences associated with live contact with nature to be more intellectually stimulating. Taste, smell, and touch require face-to-face contact with the world; they can't be sustained without direct connection, participation, and relationship — things that McKibben values over abstract information.

Essay Options

1. You may want to take a broader approach to Essay Option #1 by allowing students to write about any setting in the past that they associate with a particularly olfactory impression. Summer camps, churches, vacation sites, the homes of friends, the kitchen of a favorite relative, a neighborhood garage, club houses, secret hideouts — any and all of these places might be linked to a particularly strong memory of smell. Of course, schools are famous for their aromas — perhaps because the smells that fill school buildings always remind us of things extracurricular: education comes to us through the eyes and ears, so the senses of touch, smell, and taste are always to some extent interlopers in school, distractions that remind us of life beyond our textbooks. Whole generations of Americans are united by the remembered fragrance of mimeos fresh from the copying machine or the jars of white paste with wooden applicators that used to adorn elementary school classrooms. Then there's that peculiar blend of brown gravy, wet clay, and locker room that distinguishes American middle schools. Things really haven't changed much over the years. Students still often recall the whiff of acids and bases in a chemistry class better than they do the periodic table of the elements. This assignment allows them to explore how their sense of smell worked as a form of resistance against the abstract regimen of modern Western education.

2. Essay Option #2 offers the chance to map in words the "olfactory geography" of a particular area — be it a city, a town, or a college campus. For this assignment to work well, students have to be intimately familiar with the place they're mapping, and the area itself must offer enough olfactory diversity to actually have a "geography." A place like Brooklyn, for example, would offer students plenty of material to work with. A village of a few hundred homes clustered around a single main street might not. Be sure to encourage students to analyze the information they gather from the smells they associate with certain places. What does the smell of a seaport suggest? What do they think of when they encounter it? What memories or moods does it evoke?

K. C. COLE, *Seeing Things* (p. 75)

This selection offers a science-based introduction to the nature of visual perception. A professional science writer who specializes in issues related to math, physics, and astronomy, Cole does an effective job of debunking the myth of direct perception — her primary goal in this reading. As she reminds us, perception is never simply a matter of "what you see is what you get." All perception, in Cole's view, is shaped by culture, education, and prior knowledge; every act of vision takes place within a specific social, cultural, and historical context. It's this idea of the interplay between individual mind, intellectual context, and raw fact that makes Cole worth reading. Cole is also valuable because of her ability to discover connections between different realms of knowledge. In this piece, she discusses the way physicists "observe" subatomic particles, Galileo's discovery of relative motion, the concept of sensory atrophy, the use of technology to extend the senses, the interpretive nature of perception, the logic behind optical illusions, and the nature of scientific inquiry — not a bad range for fewer than twenty pages. In addition, Cole expands on several of the chapter's major themes, including the social construction of knowledge and the relation between perception and creativity. As a result, you'll find it easy to connect this reading with three of the chapter's four thematic clusters. It also pairs nicely with Georgina Kleege's personal account of what it's like to see with seriously damaged retinas in "The Mind's Eye." Assigned for a single class, these two readings provide background for an academic essay assignment on the interpretive nature of vision. The Before Reading activity invites students to begin thinking about the relative nature of vision. The folks mentioned here would be likely to see the stars in dramatically different ways. While an astronomer would probably see the night sky filled with huge clouds of super-heated gas and mind-boggling galaxies, a meteorologist might see it as a celestial barometer predicting the next day's weather. A filmmaker might look up and see a setting for romance or horror, while an astrologer might see impending doom or the chance to make millions. Philosophers might discover unending questions in the darkness; theologians, the assurance of cosmic answers. The point is *not* that we see what we want to see but that we tend to see what experience and expectation prepare us to see.

Exploring the Text

1. Cole points out that our senses are inherently limited by the scope of our own existence. We are, in her words, "narrow minded" because we are "narrow sensed." This is really Cole's central point. The nature of our bodies, for example, restricts our ability to comprehend numbers beyond ten or twenty, just as the length of our life span makes it difficult for us to grasp periods of time longer than a century. Cole uses a number of metaphorical illustrations to convey this idea. We are like spiders living within the perceptual frameworks of the webs we weave: we perceive what happens in our essentially two-dimensional world and miss the rest. Or, as Galileo noted centuries ago, we're like people below deck on a moving ship: we don't perceive that we're moving, because our environment is moving with us. The result is that we miss a lot. We can't, for example, see the rotation of the earth or the earth's movement around the sun. Moreover, it turns out that much of what we might be able to see, we simply ignore. The senses "edit out" data that seem unimportant — the "noise" that clutters up our perceptual fields. Our eyes automatically erase the things we get used to, so, for example, we tend not to see the tips of our noses or the bottom rims of our eyeglasses. Of course, we also tend to skip things like sunsets and the voices of our own children. "Sensory atrophy," as Cole demonstrates throughout this selection, is something we have to fight in order to see clearly and think creatively.

2. Technology augments perception by helping us overcome the problem of proportion or scope. Devices such as telescopes literally extend our senses, "opening up untapped realms of time, space, and temperature." Today, our knowledge about the universe is changing rapidly because we can see more than we could in the past. Microscopes make it possible to see minute things; computers make it possible to count and analyze gigantic numbers; magnetic resonance scanners allow us to see inside bodies; sonar allows us to hear things miles away under water. Television, radio, and cell phones do much the same thing.

3. Technology provides us with new ways of perceiving things, but technologically enhanced perceptions are, in fact, no different from apparently "natural" perceptions, because all perception relies on the active interpretation of indirect evidence. The mind is wired to go out and get certain kinds of information: we find what we tend to look for. But once we find it, we have to interpret it. Cole devotes the last half of the selection to the role of active interpretation in perception and thinking. Here she reminds us that we tend to perceive what we're familiar with or prepared to see: show us something unique or wildly out of context, and we're likely to ignore it or explain it away. Thus, the myth of the "objective" scientist who dispassionately waits for nature to reveal "the truth" is just that: scientists such as Pasteur and Fontenelle made discoveries by pursuing their hunches — the preconceptions they had about how things work. Preconceptions, thus,

both enable and hinder our ability to gain information through the senses: without them, we tend to ignore the obvious, but if they are too strong, they can get in the way of what's there in front of us. "All perception is theory laden," as the author Richard Gregory says. We see the things our cultures have prepared us to see — the familiar things that we've come to expect. People have to be taught to see things through a microscope, just as they have to be taught racial prejudice. Of course, Cole might also have noted that people have to be taught how to see beyond prejudice, as well. How then do we see something new — something we have never encountered before? Sometimes we do it by shifting our perspective, the way a child looks at the moon upside down. But perhaps the best way to do this is by being aware of our own perceptual limitations.

4. To see better, according to Cole, we have to "get to know our perceptual selves," which means that we have to keep the factors that limit perception constantly in mind — factors such as the relativity of our perceptions, their dependence on familiarity and active interpretation, and their susceptibility to prejudice. Without taking "the workings of our inborn instrumentation into account," we can never be sure about the validity of what we see — whether we see it with an atom smasher or with our own eyes.

Further Explorations

1. Ian Frazier's "Take the F" illustrates the role of familiarity in everyday observation. Frazier's commute on the subway takes him past the same places and people every day. And, clearly, it's this familiar world that he wants to celebrate — a world made up of commonplace observations — such as Frazier's notation about the airplane shadows that course up and down the buildings on his street, probably a hundred times in a single afternoon. Frazier conveys the familiarity of such experiences by offering "Whitmaneque" lists of details and observations. He catalogues fragments of perceptions that add up to an impression of "the cityscape" or of "ethnic diversity." At the same time, he also offers us highlighted or unique experiences that break through the everyday — things such as the anecdote about the crab on the subway and the story of Chris and her trip to the hospital. Still, even these exceptional experiences serve to underscore the essential familiarity of the scene Frazier describes. Nothing violates the spell of expectation during Frazier's account of his daily trip on the F. The itinerant crab is a diversion, but the little man eventually restores order by slipping it safely into his pocket. Even the story of Chris is presented as a "return" to the order of daily life. It's this underlying security and order amid the chaos of Brooklyn that Frazier seems determined to express. Of course, at this point, Cole might ask what this interpretation says about Frazier's own preconceptions and prejudices. (Or she might ask what my view of Frazier's essay suggests about *my* personal and cultural assumptions and biases.)

2. Walker Percy's "The Loss of the Creature" offers an interesting contrast with Cole. Percy argues that we've lost touch with what he terms "sovereign" experience because most of our contacts with the world are culturally mediated. When we visit the Grand Canyon, we don't actually see what's there in front of us, we see the residue of all of the stories and imagery that have been associated with the canyon in our minds. We see only the "preformulated complex," not the *ding an sich*. Familiarity is, thus, for Percy, a source of illusion: thanks to education and technology, we've become so familiar with the world that we can't see it clearly any more. Cole would likely agree with Percy about the potential dangers of familiarity. She does say that cultural expectations can obstruct our ability to perceive things clearly. But Cole, unlike Percy, also acknowledges the fact that our ability to see things depends on our familiarity with them. That's why, in her view, it's hard to grasp something that is completely unique: we have trouble seeing things that we don't expect to see. Cole, then, might easily disagree with Percy about the young Falkland Islander who discovers a dead dogfish on the beach. She'd probably note that to this perceptual Robinson Crusoe, free from all the distorting theory of modern education and science, the fish would probably be just "a fish" — just something to eat if it isn't too rotten — because that's all he's prepared to see it as. She

might also argue that the zoology student at Sarah Lawrence College would be much better positioned to encounter this creature, because the ideas she's learning in class force her to shift her perspective on marine life. Indeed, she may now for the first time see the fish not as an unappetizing main course but as a biological precursor to her own species — or as a representative of a threatened ecosystem. Percy likes the way the Falkland Islander sees things, because he believes there is a reality out there for us to come into contact with. The problem, in Percy's view, is that things such as culture, education, and theory keep us from grasping reality in all of its raw truth. Strip those things away by escaping from the influence of the past, and that Ur-reality can be "recovered." Like Percy, Cole also believes that clear perception requires work: to see clearly, you have to question your own limitations and compensate for the biases and prejudices of your culture, etc. But perception for Cole isn't as lonely a process as it is for Percy. For Percy, the observer must confront reality alone. For Cole, the challenge is to discover what is "invariant" in the phenomena we see — to focus on the things we can, in fact, share with and have confirmed by others despite the "subjective" differences that separate us. Thus, Cole, like Percy, does believe that there's a reality out there; she just isn't convinced that any one person can have immediate access to it.

3. As someone who is legally blind, Georgina Kleege experiences vision in a way that generally confirms much of what Cole says about the active, interpretive nature of perception. Kleege disparages some sighted people, like the man she encounters in the museum, because of their naïve understanding of how vision works. Sight, according to Kleege, is never just a matter of automatically capturing visual phenomena the way a camera captures images on film. In Kleege's view, vision always involves "revision": it's always a laborious process involving the active interpretation of fragmented sense data. Kleege's impaired vision puts her into essentially the same position as the subatomic physicist: in order to "see" things at all, she has to actively reconstruct them from a mix of indirect observations and good hunches. Kleege recognizes that her vision involves active interpretation and that it is based on the expectations she brings to the things she sees. And that's why she takes such pleasure in the act of seeing. Sight, for Kleege, is a creative process: every time she enters an art gallery or even walks down a street, she's aware that she's on the brink of making a discovery. Oddly enough, her impaired retinas place Kleege in the position of someone who has permanently shifted her perspective on things and is thus always acutely aware of the limitations of her "perceptual self."

Essay Options

1. The challenge in Essay Option #1 lies in hitting on the right subject. No amount of effort will help students cope with this topic if they can't recall a time when their view of something changed dramatically or when they learned to see in a radically new way. As suggested, they may want to focus on an educational experience: most memorable teachers have helped students to see a book, a subject, a mathematical concept, or a natural object in new ways. It might be a teacher who helped them first understand the concept of social inequity or the basic principles of feminism or the internal structure of a computer. It might be a coach who showed a student a new way of thinking about competition or a librarian who opened her eyes to the power of books. Or, for that matter, it might revolve around a lesson learned outside of school. The important thing is for students to focus on the process that led up to this change of perspective. Encourage them to explore the biases or assumptions that influenced their original view of their subject and to analyze how their view of things was altered as a result of this experience.

2. Essay Option #2 offers the chance for an ambitious academic essay on the relation between education and perception. Think of this one as a miniature, self-contained research paper involving as many as five sources — Cole, Lopez, Ackerman, Classen et al., and Kleege. Lopez offers a dramatic illustration of how our senses are educated: he views his sense of touch in terms of the things he has learned to do with his hands, in and out of school. This is something he acquires through experience and acculturation;

thus, the experience of touch for Lopez reflects the rather traditional masculine universe in which he grew up. Kleege also depends heavily on education to help her make sense of the jigsaw puzzle of sensations offered by her impaired vision. She relies on what she knows Matisse is "supposed" to look like in order to make sense of the visual sensations she collects while scanning a Matisse on display. She has no illusions about sensation being a passive or reflective mechanical process: she knows that to see means using all of the knowledge she possesses — whether it be about modern art or raccoons — to build an interpretation of what's happening in the world around her. The role of acculturation in relation to perception also stands out clearly in Ackerman, because flavors are so closely associated with cultural culinary traditions. Of course, you can overcome your culinary biases, but you have to work at it — just as scientists have to work at combating the intellectual biases of the cultures in which they grow up. Classen, Howe, and Synnott demonstrate how culture can literally change our orientation to sense experience. In a little more than two centuries, the sense of smell underwent a revolution in the West that altered even the most basic olfactory biases and attitudes. As the result of scientific developments during the eighteenth century, odors that had once been tolerated in urban contexts — or masked by perfumes — came to be viewed as intolerable and even linked to moral decay.

GEORGINA KLEEGE, *The Mind's Eye* (p. 93)

"The Mind's Eye" offers a perfect complement to the theoretical analysis of vision offered by K. C. Cole. Kleege's account of how she sees the world despite her severely damaged retinas illustrates many of Cole's assertions about the nature of visual perception. It also gives you the chance to weave a wonderful voice into your syllabus. Kleege is an amazing person: the daughter of sculptor and an illustrator, she's a lifelong fan of the visual arts and a dancer by training, despite the fact that she's been legally blind since the age of eight. She's also utterly unapologetic about her views on what it means to be visually challenged and the prejudices of the sighted world. You may want to consider assigning Kleege and Cole as a self-contained unit on the role of interpretation in vision. Or consider pairing it with Lopez on the theme of the relationship between the senses and the self. Kleege also works well with a cluster of selections centered on the theme of the dominance of vision. Kleege begins her essay by reflecting on the way she "sees" a painting by Matisse at New York's Museum of Modern Art, so you may want to begin in class by having students think back to the last time they can recall visiting a museum to look at a work of art (Before Reading). Many will probably recall "just looking" at the paintings they encountered there — although you may find some who can remember sitting in front of a particularly meaningful canvas for long periods of time. The question of what they actually saw is usually revealing. Most will report seeing what the painting was about. Others may focus on the style of the painting, the artist's technique, or the artistic period the painting represents. A few may recall seeing something in the work that touched them or an allusion to some contemporary issue. And, of course, there may be a few who report having seen nothing — either because they weren't interested or because they were distracted. Any and all of these responses will help prepare students to appreciate the special perspective Kleege offers on visual perception.

Exploring the Text

1. According to Kleege, most sighted people have a rather naïve, unreflective understanding of vision. Like the impatient man she encounters at the Museum of Modern Art, most of the sighted assume that seeing is an automatic process — something like the process of pointing a camera and pushing a button. They assume that "[s]ight provides instantaneous access to reality" and that the eye offers a transparent "window on the world." Thus, from the perspective of a fully sighted person, looking at a work of art is a relatively straightforward proposition: you just position yourself at a comfortable dis-

tance from the wall and stare. You take in all the detail you can see and move on to the next canvas. For Kleege, however, seeing isn't so simple. To "see" a painting such as Matisse's *Waterlilies,* she has to scan it systematically to grasp its general outline. As her brain begins to recognize the basic forms the painting contains, she goes over the whole thing again, scanning one small section of the work at a time to build up detail. She inches forward as she does this to get a better view, and eventually she finds herself paying more attention to the stylistic features of the work — the way a brushstroke was applied to represent a shadow or how a daub of paint was allowed to harden into a crust. Clearly, Kleege feels that her unorthodox mode of seeing is superior to that of arrogantly sighted types like the man who corrects her at the Matisse exhibit. Her approach makes it possible for her to appreciate the technical skill and ingenuity of the works she views and to make her own discoveries about them. Appreciating art for the sighted, by contrast, amounts to little more than reading about what they're "supposed" to see and then hurrying on "to the next correct vantage point, the next preordained point of view," as suggested by the audio tour.

2. The sighted are naïve, according to Kleege, because they don't recognize that vision always is a matter of "revision" — that, seeing is always an active, constructive process of interpretation. Whenever Kleege looks at anything with her damaged eyes — whether it's a work of art or her desktop at home — she has to use all the information at her disposal, including all that she can glean from her general knowledge base and her past personal experiences. A blob of color shimmers on her desk: it might be a note card she left there or something else. Another blob pulses iridescently: she touches it and realizes it's her cat. Sometimes she uses "a process of elimination," piecing together clues about the object until she can finally feel confident that she recognizes what it is. Expectations play a big part in this process. If she's walking down the street, and she sees an indistinct "grayish mass" ahead of her, she might first surmise that it's a local cat. But when it ambles away with an awkward gait, she knows something's up, and she looks more closely, trying to fit the clues of its appearance to the animal patterns she has stored in her memory. In this particular instance, Kleege fails to make a match, because the animal on the sidewalk — a rabid racoon — doesn't look like any she's ever encountered before. Kleege's point, however, is that the mind privileges certain signals coming from the outside world; it selects what it sees in advance by highlighting the things it expects to encounter. It operates on the least amount of visual information. If it didn't, we'd be overwhelmed by the visual detail the world offers. Seeing is, thus, always a constructive process. It's always a matter of stitching together fragments of experience and always depends on the interpretive skill of the viewer. Seeing is not something that simply "happens." It's not a "God-given gift" that you either have or don't have; it's a talent you can develop, something you can cultivate.

3. Kleege offers several illustrations of what this constructive process of seeing is like for her. She begins by describing how she decodes the paintings in the Matisse exhibit. Later she describes how she makes sense of the mess on her desk and her mistaken encounter with a rabid raccoon. It's worth paying attention to the way she does this, because she offers a wonderful example of what it takes to convey the uniqueness of an individual sensory experience in words. Here she is detailing her view of her desk:

> When I look at a simple object — a white 3-by-5-inch index card on my desk, for example — it disappears. More accurately, the beige wood color of the desktop flows into the central blurry region of vision, while flecks of white pulsate above. The card seems to disintegrate into tiny, quivering particles, to dissolve into the desktop and the air. If I shift my eyes slightly in any direction, the card reappears. It seems to emerge from the desk's surface, to differentiate itself from the pale wood grain. I shift my gaze back and it's gone. When the object is larger and there's a higher degree of contrast between it and the background — a 5-by-8-inch paperback book — its disappearance is less complete. . . . It's something like what they do on the TV news to protect the identity of a court-

room witness or accused criminal. The person's face is blotted out by a moving pattern of tiny squares. But for me the pattern is less regular and moves faster. (para. 17)

Kleege uses strong verbs here to convey the ever-moving chaos that her visual field presents to her mind — "flow," "pulsate," and "disintegrate." Every sentence conveys a sense of movement and change, and everywhere the unclear scenario she presents is flooded with images of color and light. This conveys both the beauty of the world as she sees it and its inherent confusion. Kleege also uses figurative language to convey the effect of her blind spot. Like the smudge on a TV news camera, her blind spot obliterates the "face" of everything she sees, the comparison itself conveying some of the eeriness of this phenomenon.

4. If the man on the audio tour of the Matisse exhibit is any indication, it's clear that Kleege sees the sighted as a bunch of insensitive, ignorant louts. The sighted, in Kleege's view, don't appreciate the true nature of vision: they're blinded by their self-satisfied arrogance. To add insult to injury, the sighted world is filled with animosity — or fear — in relation to the blind. As Kleege observes, to be "clear-sighted" in most cultures is to be level-headed, trustworthy, and intelligent; to be unable to "see" is synonymous with ignorance. To test this assumption in class, take a few moments to have students brainstorm a list of other common phrases that link positive characteristics with sight and negative ones with blindness. There are plenty to choose among — from the idea of being "far-sighted" or having "vision" to the old adage about "the blind leading the blind." According to Kleege, the sighted world thinks of blindness — and to some extent of the blind — as the "enemy." Kleege herself seems fond of her blindness. She notes that she already has access to several aids to improve her vision and that in the future other more powerful devices might become available. But she doubts that she would ever use them. Being visually impaired doesn't decrease or limit Kleege's involvement with the world around her. In fact, she seems to suggest that she might lose something if she were able to see as a fully sighted person does — that, perhaps, she would sacrifice the active relationship she has with the world around her and the beauty of her own particular point of view.

Further Explorations

1. Oddly enough, there's a lot of overlap between the way that physicists view subatomic particles and the way that Kleege views Matisse. Like a scientist, Kleege gathers data about the world and then patches it together by theorizing about what the data suggest. She "sees" inferentially, not directly. She also uses "probes" the way a scientist would: in order to be sure the smudge in front of her is her cat, she reaches out and touches it. She builds on her past knowledge base and formulates expectations that she tests against the things she encounters. Finally, like a scientist, Kleege looks outside herself to confirm her visual impressions. She understands the limits of her "perceptual self" too well to rely solely on her first impressions; thus, she talks to a neighbor to find out what that creature was on the sidewalk, and she wants to compare notes with someone about the "red" that she sees in *The Dance.* Kleege collaborates with others, the way a scientist would, to determine the outlines of the "objective" world, and she offers a clear example of just how we can hone our perceptual skills simply by recognizing our inherent limitations.

2. Given Kleege's insistence on the role that expectation and interpretation play in perception, you might expect her views to be totally incompatible with those of Walker Percy. Percy seems to epitomize the ideal of perception as "God-given gift." Genuine perception, according to Percy, is possible only when the perceiver is free from the biases of all "preformed" ideas — including those associated with education, theory, mass media, and even personal memory. True perception for Percy is a "sovereign" experience: it's something that happens *to you,* not something you make happen or develop

a knack for. That's why he believes that the harder you try to see the Grand Canyon, the less likely you are to see it at all. That's also why he thinks the untutored Falkland Islander would make more discoveries in a fish he finds washed up on the beach than would a student in a biology lab at a contemporary American university. Thus, while perception for Kleege is a skill whose development depends on effort, education, and self-examination, for Percy it is a mystery — something beyond individual understanding and absolutely opposed to collective intelligence. Yet, it's possible that Percy would approve of Kleege's way of viewing Matisse and of the "discoveries" she makes when she looks at art. The peculiar manner Kleege uses for viewing a work of art might well strike Percy as a technique for "recovering" the sovereign experience the work conveys. By immersing herself in the details of technique, Kleege takes a quintessentially indirect approach to observation and thus becomes more than simply a "consumer" of preformulated imagery. In fact, it's likely that Percy would join Kleege in her disdain for the sighted man who takes the time to "correct" her in the Matisse exhibit. Percy would probably view this earphone drone as a prime example of the disinherited consumer of perceptions — the kind of person who is literally programmed by curators, educators, and theorists to "see" what they want him to see and not what's actually there before his own eyes.

3. Further Explorations #3 and 4 invite students to do some experimentation of their own with the way they look at art. By taking the time to visit a local museum, you can give your class the chance to test some of Kleege's ideas about perception. Have them make detailed observations about how they tend to look at individual works of art and then compare them later in class. As a variation, have them disperse throughout the museum to collect "field notes" on how other museum patrons look at art. They might even want to interview a few to find out more about the process they use. Do they scan a painting before viewing it? Do they read the title and catalogue notes or listen to a tape before actually looking at a painting or sculpture? Do they view paintings from different perspectives and distances? What do they look for? What do they tend to like or dislike in a painting?

4. Ask students to re-create Kleege's approach to viewing a painting and to take notes about what they discover through this experience. Or ask them to develop their own detailed interpretation about what they "see" in a particular painting. Have students write these interpretations out and later compare them in class. How do students explain the differences in "vision" that distinguish their interpretations? How would they explain why some people seem to see more in a given painting than do others? What perceptual skills did students employ as they carried out these observations? What did they look for? What role did prior knowledge or expectations play? Students will draw on these observations in their responses to both of the Essay Options that follow Kleege.

Essay Options

1. Essay Option #1 asks for a paper summarizing the experiment in observation linked to Further Explorations #4. Here, students simply compare the experience of viewing a painting from several different perspectives. As a variation, have them compare their own interpretation or experience of a painting with those of two of their classmates. If your students made live field observations of museum patrons looking at art, you might also have them summarize the results of their efforts and present their conclusions in a brief report.

2. Essay Option #2 invites students to explore the relation between perception, prior knowledge, and interpretation through another practical exercise at the museum — this one involving the "reading" of a single abstract painting. In this case, students try to convey the experience in much the same way that Kleege tries to convey her own sense impressions of Matisse. You may find that more abstract canvases work better for the purposes of this assignment than even vaguely figurative ones.

BILL McKIBBEN, *Television and the Twilight of the Senses*
(p. 109)

Students enjoy thinking and writing about mass media, but they're often put off by the kind of clichéd diatribes against the media that they sometimes encounter in school. By this point, most students can recite the "TV-is-a-drug-that-hooks-its-users-and-dumbs-them-down" mantra by heart, having learned it well either from their parents or from television itself. Mercifully, McKibben offers them more than that in this selection. This excerpt from McKibben's popular *The Age of Missing Information* (1992) is the first in a pair of readings in this chapter on the topic of technology and its relation to perception. One of the best parts of McKibben is his refreshingly direct and personal style: this is a diatribe against TV, but it's also a thoughtfully written personal essay. McKibben can be read alone as the basis for a paper on the impact of television on the senses. By pairing it with Mark Slouka's "Listening for Silence," you can broaden the scope of this assignment to include the impact of other electronic technologies and corporate capitalism. Slouka's emphasis on the economics of sense experience also adds a dimension that McKibben overlooks. Combine McKibben, Slouka, and Walker Percy for a comprehensive unit on the fate of the senses in contemporary society. Percy is a challenge (see manual p. 67), but well worth the effort if your class is prepared for it. McKibben also looks forward to selections in future chapters of *Mind Readings*. His exploration of media and the senses connects well with several selections on the nature of the self in Chapter 3 and on the impact of electronic technology in Chapter 6. In addition, McKibben offers at least four possible assignments on issues related to television and mass media, including a content analysis of TV programming and a debate on the "tranquilizing" effect of the television habit. The Before Reading activity is meant to get students thinking about the arguments commonly advanced against TV so that they can appreciate the subtlety of McKibben's case. In his view, television isn't just boring or a waste of time or simply vulgar — it's a technology that threatens to undermine the way we sense the world around us. Television is changing what it means to be human, according to McKibben, and not at all for the better.

Exploring the Text

1. McKibben's complaint against television is that it restricts the senses. Watching TV straightjackets our perceptions, forcing us to relate to the world only through sight and hearing. Worse, TV impoverishes even these two primary senses by "narrowing" our perspective to that offered by the television screen. When we watch TV, according to McKibben, we lose consciousness of our bodies and an "achy torpor" sets in that we try to deflect with snacks and soda. Other forms of mass communication, such as theater and writing, don't have this effect because they invite sensory participation: a play allows you to make choices about what you watch; a book offers images that "trigger sense memory." At a live event such as a baseball game, you have an "enormous perspective" of visual and aural stimuli to chose from. Television, by contrast, limits you to the choices made by a director and camera crew. Of course, students may well debate much of this. Television may limit sensory contact, but students may find value in the fact that it puts us in touch with people, places, and events we might never have the chance to encounter without it. Besides, even the experience of swimming on Crow Mountain might become dull after the first few dozen morning dips in the pond. It can also be argued that we often subject ourselves to situations that limit the senses in order to gain different sorts of information: the average college classroom isn't exactly a sensory feast for most students, yet the information and experiences students gain there can be stimulating in their own right.

2. In fact, McKibben admits that, paradoxically enough, while TV "amputates your senses," the events it covers seem "more real." McKibben is convinced that things seen on television gain a sense of "immediacy," that they come across as more "live" than life

itself. You'll probably want to spend some time exploring this claim in class. Events on TV do take on a heightened sense of importance, perhaps because we associate television with authority and we assume that things shown on TV have to be true. Television also tells us what's important, what's valuable enough to focus our mental energies on. The problem here from McKibben's perspective is twofold: when we watch TV we relinquish authority for making our own choices about what's important or worthy of attention, and we lose contact with the felt experience of what we see. On TV, the bombing of a city looks "miniaturized": conveyed through a piece of furniture sitting in the living room, war is dissociated from the "concussion, the dust, the smell" — the things that make it real and terrifying.

3. This loss of felt experience in our daily lives has even changed the way we think about pleasure. McKibben quotes Abert Borgmann as saying that, "pleasure can only be had at the price of discomfort"; real pleasure, like all real sensation, depends on contrast. To experience the pleasure of rest, you have to exhaust yourself; to experience the pleasure of something as simple as a milk shake, you have to spend a couple of days tramping with spare rations in the outback. Comfort, by comparison, is like a tepid bath: it requires only the moderation of all intense feelings. In the era of television, we've all become hooked on the ideal of comfort, and as a result, we've lost an important source of "information about our bodies" and about "what it is like for others to be cold and hungry and dirty." This is really the crux of McKibben's argument. As he sees it, television cuts us off from information about the extremes of the human condition and thus deprives us of the ability to be empathetic. It keeps us from appreciating our own experiences and from feeling for the lives of others.

4. Television's tendency to "flatten" our experiences also accounts for its powerful attraction. As McKibben sees it, people use TV as a kind of tranquilizer: we watch TV out of habit as a way of blotting out the unpleasantness of our lives. People who are happy tend to do other things; those who are depressed, irritable, sad, or lonely watch TV. Television works like this because it is so utterly predictable. In a world that's becoming increasingly complicated and chaotic, TV offers us a refuge where everything seems familiar and we feel in control. Unlike real, mind-altering drugs such as LSD or crack, TV doesn't threaten us with the danger of the unexpected; it lulls us like a sedative and "insulates" us against reality.

5. Before you leave McKibben, you'll probably also want to spend some time exploring the way he captures and conveys sense experience in language. For additional help with this, see the introductory essay to this chapter in *Mind Readings*.

Further Explorations

1. McKibben would probably find much to agree with in Georgina Kleege's "The Mind's Eye." Both Kleege and McKibben feel that vision is overrated in contemporary society. Still, McKibben's argument isn't with vision per se. He celebrates the power of sight — its ability to deliver whole vistas and landscapes to the mind in a single glance — as long as it's not limited to the scope of a television set. Kleege, by contrast, feels that vision is too easy and unreflective a sense; the sighted aren't self-aware enough, from her point of view, about the mind's involvement in perception. Both Kleege and McKibben would also agree that the senses are being impoverished in contemporary society. McKibben places the blame for this on technology; Kleege, on the arrogance of the sighted and the power they wield in our vision-dominated culture. Clearly, both would advocate a return to a more balanced use of the senses. McKibben challenges us to join him outdoors where we can feel the world of sense experience at first hand — and where we can get back in contact with our bodies. Kleege suggests that we take a hard look at the way we look at things. She doesn't urge any particular course of action, but it's clear she'd like all of us to begin questioning the "unwavering faith" we place in our powers of vision. She knows we can't begin to see the world as she does through all of her senses, but she would like to jar us at least partially out of our unreflective visual complacency.

2. McKibben is even closer in some ways to Percy than he is to Kleege. Both McKibben and Percy would probably agree that television anesthetizes its users; but though McKibben sees this dulling in perceptual terms, Percy is more interested in the way that modern media work on us conceptually. In McKibben's opinion, television restricts and "flattens" our sense impressions; it undermines our connection to reality by undermining our ability to feel. For Percy, the media limit our understanding of the natural world — our comprehension of what he terms the "creature" — by forcing us to see things in certain culturally and theoretically acceptable ways. In Percy's view, all forms of collective consciousness, from education to mass communication, blind us to the real world by imposing the "symbolic machinery" of mass thinking on our perceptions. Both McKibben and Percy would agree that we are being transformed by modern life into consumers who prefer to have their experiences pre-digested or mediated for us by "experts." They would agree that modern technological society is turning us all into "sightseers" who are content to view our experiences as a series of "consumer items" — as things we acquire casually and without much effort — instead of as the result of adventure, struggle, and hardship.

3. It's fairly easy for students to sketch the plots of drama/action shows like *ER*. A typical episode goes something like this: a clash between two of the hospital staffers is interrupted when a school bus collides with an SUV and the mother-driver is delivered to the ER in full cardiac arrest and the doctors struggle unsuccessfully to revive her as her child watches amidst the chaos created by dozens of injured children and their hysterical parents and the conflict that began the show is somehow resolved. Students have little trouble dissecting the plots of dramas, cop shows, sitcoms, and other types of TV formula fiction. So, for an extra challenge, have them turn their attention to less plot-driven types of programming. What plots do they discover in TV news shows? In sporting events? In so-called "reality" programming? The case could be made, for example, that even local evening news broadcasts follow a relatively predictable format: they open with the disaster of the day and follow up with a minute or two on the top national story or scandal, coverage of the area's most lurid daily crimes, a minute of "breaking news," and then close with a human interest or animal piece. The question is whether the representative plots students come up with actually do have the calming effect that McKibben claims. Although *ER* moves at a frenzied pace, and it regularly portrays the most horrific medical procedures, the very consistency and familiarity of the world it portrays might be seen as offering a kind of comfort to viewers. After all, even in the chaos of the *ER*, surrounded by all that tragic gore, you still can count on meeting that nice eastern European doctor with the sympathetic eyes and the charming English surgeon with the mane of curly hair. They survive it, why shouldn't you? And the same kind of logic might also be applied to the smiling faces you see spinning tales of disaster on the evening news.

4. Sioux medicine man John "Fire" Lame Deer would likely see this overwhelming need for comfort as the result of white society's innate fear of death. According to Lame Deer, white civilization has attempted to domesticate both the natural world and human nature in its attempt to deny its mortality. The white world cuts itself off from nature — and from real pleasure — by surrounding itself with comfort. Whites overheat their houses, place too much importance on material things, and even deprive themselves of the pleasures of midnight trips to the privy. Whites do this in the name of comfort, but the result is that they divorce themselves from the power of life and the natural world. The Indian, by contrast, recognizes death as a natural part of existence and embraces it as just one more experience. As a result, Indians have no stake in denying hardships and the peak moments associated with an undomesticated life. They have no need for the kind of narcotic comfort that modern white society so apparently craves. Lame Deer would, then, understand and approve McKibben's trek to Crow Mountain and the pleasure he takes in an icy early morning swim. He would appreciate the kind of "information" about the body and its relation to nature that McKibben claims to gain from this sort of unmediated physical experience.

Essay Options

The Essay Options associated with this selection offer a range of possible assignments.

1. Essay Option #1 invites students to write a personal essay describing a single experience of real pleasure as the notion is defined by McKibben. You may want to have your class tackle this one if they haven't already written a personal essay in response to Frazier or any of the other readings earlier in this chapter. If you have already taken time for a personal essay, you may want to consider one of the three more academic assignments that follow.

2. Essay Option #2 asks students to assess McKibben's central claim — that TV dulls the senses. This one gives students the chance to draw on their own personal experience to critique McKibben's thinking. And clearly there's plenty of room for debate on the issue of television's impact. Students may argue that, far from dulling the senses, television offers us access to ideas and sense impressions we would have never experienced without it. It might not reproduce the actual experience of walking along the Great Wall of China, but isn't seeing this famous sight on TV an acceptable alternative to never seeing it at all? And, for that matter, isn't McKibben exaggerating the freedom that we have over direct sensory experience? How different, really, is a ball game on TV from one witnessed at the ballpark? How much more freedom does a playgoer really have in comparison to a viewer who watches the same play on TV? And are we to believe that human beings suddenly became addicted to comfort with the dawn of the video age? Isn't there plenty of indication that we've been pursuing the drug of comfort for centuries?

3. Essay Options #3 and 4 offer opportunities for challenging text-based papers. Kleege and Cole both agree that the senses depend on prior knowledge and that we can develop or "educate" our perceptual skills. Ackerman and Classen et al. would seem to support this position by demonstrating that sense perceptions are associated with particular cultural and historical contexts. We learn to eat sushi just as we have learned to be intolerant of certain organic smells. McKibben suggests that electronic media can actually lead to the atrophy of our inborn perceptual abilities; in a sense, he argues that we all need perceptual remediation. Percy, by contrast, would reject any association of education and perception. In his view, education subverts original perception by imposing the "symbolic machinery" and theory of the past on minds in the present. You'll want to encourage students to do more than summarize these perspectives in their papers. Ask them to evaluate the views of each author and to explain their own thinking about the impact of education on taste, touch, smell, sight, and hearing.

4. Essay Option #4 sets the stage for a major text-based paper on the dominance of vision. The notion of a hierarchy of the senses runs throughout this chapter. Classen et al. argue that sight and hearing displaced smell and the other direct senses during the scientific revolution and thus suggest that the modern era is predisposed to favor vision over other modes of perception. Kleege's experience as someone who is visually challenged would seem to support the idea of a visual bias in contemporary society, as would McKibbben's analysis of the impact of television. The question of what's lost as the result of visual dominance is a thorny one. No one is likely to argue that we should return to the days when raw sewage coursed down the streets of European capitals, and it's quite possible that students will have some trouble imagining what the alternative to a visual culture might be. Kleege offers the most help here. She obviously isn't arguing that the man who corrects her at the Matisse exhibition would be better off visually impaired; she's simply noting that the dominance of vision has resulted in a kind of cultural arrogance that makes us insensitive to other ways of perceiving things. Living in a visual culture has also made us rather naïve, in the sense that we assume that the world is just a matter of appearances and that these are simply "given" to sight automatically. And this is where students may find a lot to say. What evidence do they see in their daily lives that superficial visual appearances dominate contemporary American culture? Surely, most will find some evidence — owing to the dominance of visual mass media

such as television, cinema, and photo journalism — that the eye has skewed the way we think about gender, beauty, health, and even success.

WALKER PERCY, *The Loss of the Creature* (p. 118)

A word of caution before you tackle this selection: Percy's analysis of the impact of culture on perception is a wonderful example of sophisticated thinking and literate argumentation, but it's not for every class. In fact, you might consider reserving it for groups that are particularly well prepared for a serious academic challenge. Percy's argument is conceptually difficult, and it assumes more than a casual acquaintance with topics such as world tourism, existentialism, and the problems of theory — not to mention passing knowledge of authors such as Aldous Huxley, Arnold Toynbee, and Søren Kierkegaard. That said, you still may want to plan it into your syllabus, because Percy offers an intellectual counterpoint to the "social constructivist" bias of several readings in this chapter and because he pairs so well with so many pieces in later chapters of *Mind Readings*. Percy can be used as the basis of a stand-alone assignment on the topic of the relation between education, theory, and sensory experience. Or it can be read as part of a cluster of selections on the themes of the social construction of experience and the erosion of the senses in contemporary society. In addition, because of the emphasis Percy places on received ideas and education, he connects with several selections in Chapter 2, particularly with Zerubavel and hooks. Percy also links productively with readings in Chapter 5, especially with selections by Lame Deer and Erdoes, Berger, and Siebert that have to do with our inability to see the natural world around us. Finally, you'll also find connections between Percy and readings in Chapter 6 centering on the notion of technology and the "symbolic machinery" that dominates minds in contemporary postelectronic society. Since Percy begins by discussing how difficult it is to actually see for ourselves something that we've already seen hundreds of times in books, on TV, and in school — something like the Grand Canyon — the best way to prepare to read him might be to think back to equally famous places that students have visited. The Before Reading activity asks them to reflect on what they actually saw when visiting a world-famous landmark such as the Eiffel Tower, the Hoover Dam, or the Grand Canyon. It also challenges them to explore how the experience of visiting such a sight might differ from seeing it reproduced in mass media such as a textbook or a television documentary.

Exploring the Text

1. Percy deliberately overstates the argument of this essay. He claims that the only person who actually sees something like the Grand Canyon is its discoverer — the one who sets eyes on it for the very first time. Only this person enjoys the sovereign experience of a place or object. The rest of us merely "consume" and thus attenuate this original impression again and again. Such a sovereign perceiver may see his discovery as "beautiful," and to him it may truly be so, but we're wrong, according to Percy, if we assume that it will be for others what it once was for him. In the weird economy of vision that Percy presents in this selection, an object relinquishes part of its meaning every time it is seen, so that by the time we drive up to the rim of the Grand Canyon there's nothing left to see. Instead, what we see in place of the actual Grand Canyon is the "preformed complex" of images and ideas that has been provided by the "symbolic machinery" of our culture. Percy himself deliberately avoids spelling out what he means by these terms, and this is part of what makes his essay both so challenging and thought-provoking. He tells us that such preformed images can be conveyed by "picture postcard, geography book, tourist folders, and the words *Grand Canyon*," suggesting that any form of communication or symbolic reproduction — even the verbal — is capable of removing us from the thing itself. Photographs, thus, condemn us to the past; they encode what we've learned about something and freeze it in time, and do not even come near the experience of the thing as it exists in the present on its own. Looking, according to Percy, is like "sucking": "the more lookers, the less there is to see."

2. Percy is equally elusive when it comes to how we might "recover" or recapture the original sovereign experience of something like the Grand Canyon. You can't simply ignore the influence of the preformed complex or wish it away. You can only get back to authentic perception when the symbolic machinery breaks down. Sightseers do this when they wander away from the guided tour that is meant to acquaint them with the "approved" view of the canyon or when a disaster such as an outbreak of typhus closes the park and forces them to "confront" the reality of the object in a new and unforeseen way. They can also recover the object by doing what Percy himself does in this essay, by self-consciously viewing the canyon through the perspective of the common viewer. By taking a "dialectical" view of the object — by observing it side-by-side with its culturally approved image — the observer gains a certain critical perspective and thus frees himself from the preformed complex of associations that surrounds it.

3. Oddly enough, while Percy freely condemns photography and all of the other forms of symbolic machinery associated with consumer culture, he exempts the cinema. Movie makers, in Percy's view, know that they can recapture the essence of a place only by coming at it obliquely; they instinctively employ one of the strategies that Percy has outlined for recovering sovereign experience. Of course, students may find fault with Percy's reasoning here. First, it's not particularly clear that filmmakers are even vaguely interested in how the audience experiences any particular place — as long as they stay absorbed in the film itself. It might well be argued that the romances, disasters, and mysteries that directors include in their films are there to keep us enthralled in the action and not to make the background scenery "more accessible." What does become clear through Percy's preference for film over other forms of mechanical reproduction, however, is his own aesthetic bias: essentially a romantic, Percy is arguing that we can see things truly only when they are refracted through the transforming prism of art. Thus, movies — because they are art forms and not simply modes of communication — jar us out of consumer complacency; they force us to see in new and revealing ways places and types of people we might otherwise take for granted.

4. A true child of the Romantic Revolution, Percy is also a vehement critic of formal education. Schools exist, in Percy's view, to pass along received ideas and "approved" ways of thinking from one generation to another; schools are devoted to teaching us what to expect when we go to Paris or when we encounter nature on the beach. For Percy, education transforms sovereign beings into passive consumers — a particularly lazy breed that accepts the world as it is presented by "theorists and planners." Thus, Percy feels that an untutored Falkland Islander would get more out of his encounter with a dogfish on the beach than would a student in a biology lab at Sarah Lawrence College, who will see in her dissecting tray only what her instructor tells her to see. This poor freshman is "twice removed" from the creature she encounters in class — once by the symbolic machinery that surrounds the dogfish and once by the theory that she is "imbibing" along with her education. As you might expect, discussion of student reactions to Percy's critique of education are always revealing. Some students will warm to Percy's overt anti-intellectualism and may even be amazed to encounter a writer who is critical of formal schooling. Some will echo the idea that genuine learning is always a matter of self-education and that the idea of "teaching" anyone anything is inherently flawed. Others may object to Percy's dismissal of formal instruction as a way of knowing and may even point out that the purpose of dissecting a dogfish at Sarah Lawrence College isn't to embark on the sovereign experience of "fishness" but to learn valuable lessons about anatomy and physiology — things that might never occur to Percy's Falkland Islander.

5. Some students might, in fact, be tempted to turn Percy's own arguments against him. After all, isn't Percy himself theorizing about the nature of perception in this essay? Isn't every claim made in writing a theory and thus a piece of cultural machinery that imposes itself on its reader-consumers? Interestingly enough, even the images that Percy presents of others throughout this essay might be seen as falling into the category of

"preformulated" perceptions. The naïve sightseer in search of exoticism, the dutiful student at Sarah Lawrence College, the "genuine research man" who's slightly befuddled but "always humble" before the mystery of the real — don't all of these echo the hoariest of stereotypes? Don't they suggest that Percy is himself a victim of the imagery of his own cultural context and historical era? But, then, might that not be still more evidence in support of Percy's central point — that none of us can easily escape the symbolic machinery associated with the cultures in which we live?

Further Explorations

1. In order to add some specificity to Percy's argument, you may want to take the time to have students make collages of images suggestive of the "preformed complex" of ideas surrounding famous places such as the Grand Canyon, the American West, New York City, New England, Mexico City, Paris, the Pacific Northwest, Texas, the Caribbean, the Far East — or just about any easily identifiable region or destination. It isn't very difficult for students to find images in ads, textbooks, and Web sites that convey an impression of such places, although you'll find that more obviously "mythic" places such as the American West are generally easier to deal with. It should also be fairly obvious that such images do, in fact, tend to convey a recognizable "preformed complex" of ideas. Most images of the West, for example, tend to convey the impression of a kind of desolate or rugged independence, while images of Paris tend to convey images associated with glamour or fashion. Yet, the real experience of both places may, in fact, have little to do with either of these cultural impressions.

2. You can also use Ian Frazier's "Take the F" as a test case for Percy's theory of perception. Frazier's essay might be seen as promoting the idea of the New York area as a kind of cultural carnival — a celebration of ethnic diversity that fits in nicely with at least one aspect of the city's worldwide identity. Or it might be possible to view Frazier's presentation of life in Brooklyn as an example of authentic perception: while the city is commonly portrayed as a threatening environment full of alienated strangers, Frazier presents it as a community — a place where people support one another and tolerate differences. In either case, students may react strongly to the notion that reading Frazier will have an indelible impact on their own ability to confront the reality of life in New York. It's one thing to consider Percy's argument in the abstract and quite another to agree that you yourself are a passive consumer of the images generated by your culture.

3. Those who are most critical of Percy will find solace in the positions of K. C. Cole and Georgina Kleege on the nature of perception. Our ability to see, according to Cole and Kleege, depends on our expectations: we can't see things we aren't prepared to see. This idea runs counter to Percy's essentially romantic understanding of perception. While Percy believes that the more something is observed, the less it is actually "seen," Cole and Kleege believe that prior experience actually facilitates future discoveries. Kleege's approach to seeing is broadly comparative. She "sees" by actively comparing current visual sensations with expectations based on experience. She even appeals to experience when she tries to evaluate the impact of "red" in a new version of Matisse's *The Dance* toward the end of her essay. For Cole, all vision is indirect; thus, it makes little sense to bother thinking about "sovereign" perception: no one, in Cole's view, ever directly confronts reality head-on. Furthermore, Cole assumes that every perception depends directly on prior knowledge. If the brain weren't busily engaged in the art of interpretation even before the level of conscious perception, according to Cole, we would be overwhelmed by visual input. Seeing everything, we would see nothing.

4. Like Cole, Percy and Mark Slouka both address the issue of consumerism, but from entirely different perspectives. By marketing sensation, capitalism drains hearing of its significance, according to Slouka. Sound reduced to the level of a commodity results in chaos — pure noise — not something that means anything in particular. In Percy's view, by contrast, it's exactly the meanings produced by mass culture that are particularly crippling. The received ideas generated by the machinery of mass culture stifle indi-

vidual perceptions and make it all but impossible to confront the world as a sovereign person. Percy faults technological society for overwhelming us with theories and ideas; Slouka thinks that technology has emptied sounds of the meanings they once contained.

5. Both Percy and John Berger believe that capitalism has robbed us of the ability to confront the world of nature of which we were once a part. Berger sees this loss in the fact that animals are literally fading from view in the modern world. As real animals move to the margins of reality, according to Berger, we become increasingly engrossed with the "animals of the mind" provided by mass culture; thus, the moment of confrontation — the exchange of look between human and animal that once defined who we were as a species — has ceased to exist. Percy would agree with most of this and with the notion that animals have been reduced to consumer commodities in the capitalist culture of the West. Animals have "disappeared," according to Berger, because they have been thoroughly domesticated or marginalized, just as the world of the "creature" has been lost, according to Percy, because it has become something we consume rather than something we confront.

Essay Options

1. Essay Option #1 offers students the chance to apply the ideas in this selection to their own personal experience. At one time or another, most of us have felt the jolt of encountering something unexpected and "authentic." It may have been an idea we met in a book, an experience we encountered in nature, or a lesson we learned at work. Part of the challenge of this assignment lies in defining what the experience of confronting a sovereign reality amounts to. This should be more than simply "a lesson learned" — or something that Percy would probably dismiss as approved knowledge. Clearly, a sovereign experience should be something that changes you and forces you to question the values and attitudes that you've derived from your surroundings. It should, at bottom, be a liberating experience that challenges your entire worldview. The relation of education to this kind of experience may be a matter of perspective. For someone like Percy, education may be a domesticating force that works against sovereign experience. For a student new to the world of higher education, however, the schoolroom may itself represent a sovereign experience in its own right — a new way of seeing the world and the student's relationship with it.

2. Essay Option #2, focusing on the role that the mind plays in perception, might be seen as the capstone assignment for this chapter. Cole and Kleege argue that the mind makes sense of the objects we meet in the world around us by comparing them with our expectations and that we derive these expectations from education and experience. Percy seems to suggest, by contrast, that the mind can only engage the outer world when the influences of culture and education are minimized. Thus, Cole and Kleege would probably agree that memory, expectation, and learning play a vital role in perception, while Percy would certainly argue that anything that connects us to the past subverts genuine perception.

3. Essay Option #3 offers the chance for another academic paper, this one focusing on Percy's claim that experts and theorists in technologically advanced societies have usurped the authority of individuals in relation to their own sense experiences. In preparing for this paper, students might want to consider the implications of recent media developments, such as the emergence of "reality" programming on TV and the growing popularity of "virtual" experiences like those provided by video games and amusement parks. How would Percy view a day at Disneyland, for example? Or an afternoon spent tracking evildoers through the canals of Venice during a three-hour session of *Tomb Raider?* Slouka, McKibben, and Classen et al. might argue that we are losing contact with the sovereign experience of our bodies owing, in part, to technological advances. Cole, however, would be likely to argue the opposite — that the illusion of sovereign experience is just that — an illusion — because all sense experience results from the complex interaction of mind, body, and culture.

Reading Memory:
Rebuilding the Past (p. 135)

Getting Started

The topic of memory holds special importance for writers, and not just because the memoir is such a literary favorite. All writers depend on the sharpness of their memories. Without memory, we have no words to write with and nothing to write about. Memory provides novelists with plots and characters, just as it provides scholars with dates, data, and theories. With the aid of memory, we compose books and we compose our own identities. That's why the topic of memory works so well at this point in *Mind Readings*. Memory is the foundation of the self; it mediates between our moment-to-moment perceptions and experiences of the world and the person those perceptions and experiences add up to. Memory also works well at this point in the text because the readings in this chapter continue to highlight the role of active interpretation. It's common to think of the senses as simply "copying" what they encounter in the world, and it's even easier to think of memory as simply reproducing the past the way a CD player reproduces a musical performance. In an era of mechanized memory, we tend to ignore the more creative aspects of recollection. As noted in the chapter introduction, we tend to think of memory as something that happens to us — or in us — and not as something that we make happen or as something that's open to external influence. Yet, as any preindustrial oral poet — or any present-day police detective — might attest, human memory often depends heavily on creativity and imagination. Memories, like ideas, don't simply "pop" into consciousness without art and effort. Most often, memories are made: they are built, either consciously or unconsciously, for specific reasons and to serve specific purposes.

Thus, the idea of "reading" memory enters this chapter in two different ways. Since past experiences present themselves to us not ready-made but in fragments, we have to "read" these bits and pieces in order to re-"collect" the past. The very act of remembering, seen in this light, is deeply interpretive in nature. In addition, because memories, like artifacts, are constructed for particular audiences and in particular social, historical, and cultural contexts, to understand them critically means we have to "read" the motives that guided their reconstruction. Understanding a memory requires us to read the intentions that inspired its creation — whether it be the recollection of a childhood educational experience or the memory of a public event such as the Vietnam War. Indeed, once students recognize that all memories — personal and collective — are, in fact, assembled for specific present purposes, it's possible to question and critically examine the motives that lead to their formation, and it's equally possible to explore topics such as the way that cultures, families, and other social groups enforce the memory of certain events and edit the memories of others — or the way that individuals resist such forms of collective recollection.

These themes — the constructing, editing, and revising of memories — connect naturally with issues involved in the writing process. The subsection of the chapter introduction devoted to composition, "Writing and Memory: The Writing Process," offers you the opportunity to make this connection explicit. Peter Elbow's notion of "cooking" is introduced here, as is the basic multistage approach to the writing process. This is a section you'll want to go over with students, even if you've already discussed writing and revision in class. "Cooking" is that stage in the writing process when you discover what you want to say. It almost always involves a span of relaxation and inattention — or indirect attention — after a period of intense intellectual activity. Thus, experienced writers will spend hours taking notes, talking, and brainstorming — and then will break for a jog or go to sleep in order to stimulate the cooking that leads to discovery. Elbow himself is always rather mysterious about this most creative step in the writing process. But it's clear that cooking has a lot in common with remembering. In fact, the most obvious explanation behind cooking and all other strategies for the promotion of creative thought is that they all involve the stimulation of memory. Unless you are a classical Greek who literally believes in the existence of the muses, creative ideas have to come from somewhere, and the most likely source of insight is the knowledge you already possess — the knowledge stored in memory. All of the techniques associated with cooking are really techniques for stimulating the recollection of what you already know about a given topic. Thus, when you brainstorm, you're activating "indices" associated with the topic you're trying to write about. Based on past knowledge, your ideas about the topic may not "bubble up" right away as you sit there in class, but if you take the pressure off and go and do something else, it's likely that the "muse of memory" will begin to speak to you and remind you about the ideas you already have. Seen from this point of view, composition always involves recollecting what you want to say about a topic, and, clearly, understanding how recollections are actively constructed and interpreted can only aid in this process of discovery. Reading Hampl offers you an extra opportunity for extending this discussion of the discovery process, because Hampl's analysis of her own writing process can be used in class as the occasion for your students' self assessment (EO #3). The emphasis that Hampl places on revision and elaboration also should help your students to take more chances and to be more creative when they compose.

One way to get this chapter going is to screen a film about memory in class. There are a couple of fine possibilities to choose from, several of which are already included in follow-up activities associated with reading selections. You might, for example, watch Akira Kurosawa's *Rashomon,* if you have the time, or *Memento,* the recent cinematic treatment of short-term memory loss. Another easy way into the topic is to conduct a simple memory experiment in class. Have students write about what happened during a recent class meeting or have them try to recall verbatim what was said and who said it during the first fifteen minutes of class, and then compare results. Or have them try to recall what they were doing exactly one month or one year ago. As an alternative, if you plan to cover Daniel L. Schacter's analysis of the mechanics of constructive memory, give them ten minutes to look at a painting that you bring into class, and then ask them to describe it in as much detail as possible. You can then have students compare their recollections in small groups or put these descriptions away and re-test their memories of the painting a week later to see how their recollections change over time. This experiment can also be used as preparation for a follow-up activity and possible Essay Option associated with Schacter's notion of selective memory (see Schacter, EO #1, pp. 87–88 below). All of these exercises underscore the variability of memory and the fact that memory is heavily dependent on point of view.

Sequences and Pairings

This chapter is particularly rich in terms of productive pairings and thematic clusters. If you don't plan to spend much time on the topic of memory, you may want to assign only one or two of the memoirs included here as the basis of a personal essay. But the real value of the chapter lies in the way that these selections support each other. To start, try reading Sanders against Eiseley. These two personal memoirs might seem unrelated at first, but the more you work with them, the more productive connections and contrasts you'll discover. If you want to emphasize gender, pair Sanders with Hampl. Sanders's attachment to his hammer — and through it to his father — seems self-assured and distinctly "male," particularly when compared with Hampl's self-consciously exploratory treatment of her early educational experiences. These personal selections should help you get the chapter off to a fast start. They'll also provide students with some concrete examples to reflect back on if and when you assign Schacter's scientific overview of the mechanics of memory. This piece can be challenging because of its length, but it's necessary if you plan to address some of the academic issues raised later. Hampl pairs well with Engel concerning the idea of past and present selves. Engel also reinforces the concept of the active construction of memories that's introduced in Schacter and amplified in Hampl. Finally, the last three selections form a logical grouping around the idea of the social construction of memory. The key selection here is Zerubavel's, because he offers an overview and a conceptual context for the discussion of historical or impersonal memories. You may want to assign Zerubavel along with either or both Kingston and hooks depending on the tack you'll take in the follow-up assignment. Use Kingston if you're particularly interested in the idea of the accuracy of personal memories; use hooks if you want to focus on historical memories and the notion of public "mnemonic battles."

Some terrifically productive themes emerge from the readings in this chapter. The central idea of almost every selection is the notion of the constructedness of memory. The idea that memories are tailored to specific situations and audiences for specific purposes contradicts most of our assumptions about how memory works. It also introduces the possibility of reading the intentions that underlie various acts of remembering — whether they be acts of personal recollection like Hampl's memoir of her first piano lesson with Sister Olive or cultural acts of remembrance like the Vietnam War Memorial. Almost every selection in this chapter connects with this basic theme. Once the premise that memories are built is accepted, other issues such as the politics of memory and the question of the individual's ability to resist impersonal memories immediately arise. You'll find productive clusters of readings centered around both of these topics. In addition, you can take a more technical approach to the chapter by focusing on one or more of the key academic concepts that are introduced here. Thus, you'll find clusters below on the notion of "template" memories — Engel's term for memories that represent a complex of emotions associated with a stage of life that may not as yet be clearly understood — and on the "stereoscopic" nature of memory — Schacter's term for the way that memory juxtaposes different experiences and time periods in the mind. If you plan to spend a lot of time on this chapter, consider beginning with a unit on the constructed nature of memory that includes Sanders, Eiseley, Schacter, Hampl, and, if time permits, Engel. Then follow up with Zerubavel and one or both of the last two selections as the basis of a second paper on the concept of social or impersonal memory.

Recommended Stand-Alone Readings

You'll find that several of the memoirs offered in this chapter make excellent points of departure for personal essays. Sanders and Hampl work best in this regard, because both deal with experiences to which students relate easily. Eiseley poses more of a challenge for many students, so you probably wouldn't want to use this essay on its own. Schacter's essay can be assigned independently as the basis for a piece on the recollection of a specific work of art; however, this selection is one of the longest in the book and also one of the most technical. Hampl's essay is wonderful for use independently or in association with other selections. Assign the Hampl as a one-reading introduction to the concept of constructed memory and/or as a point of departure for exploring the complexity of the writing process. Like much scholarly writing, Zerubavel's is a bit dry, but he does introduce concepts (such as "impersonal memory" and "mnemonic battles"), that can lead directly to effective writing assignments. Finally, you're probably already familiar with Kingston's "No-Name Woman," a composition classic that is worth reading on its own as a stunning example of how a writer uses cultural and family identity to forge an authentic sense of self. Here's a list of some topics you may want to consider in approaching stand-alone assignments:

An object that has special memories for you	*The Inheritance of Tools* (Sanders)
Differing memories of a work of art	*Building Memories* (Schacter)

Retelling an educational experience	*Memory and Imagination* (Hampl)
Historical and cultural memories	*Social Memories* (Zerubavel)
Family memories	*No-Name Woman* (Kingston)

Recommended Pairings

Contrasting memoirs	*The Inheritance of Tools* (Sanders) and *The Brown Wasps* (Eiseley)
Gendered memories	*The Inheritance of Tools* (Sanders) and *Memory and Imagination* (Hampl)
Creative memories	*Building Memories* (Schacter) and *Memory and Imagination* (Hampl)
Past and present selves	*Memory and Imagination* (Hampl) and *Then and Now* (Engel)
The influence of historical memory	*Social Memories* (Zerubavel) and *Columbus* (hooks)
Resisting impersonal memories	*Social Memories* (Zerubavel) and *No-Name Woman* (Kingston)

Suggested Thematic Clusters

Memory as "construction"	*The Brown Wasps* (Eiseley), *Building Memories* (Schacter), *Memory and Imagination* (Hampl), *No-Name Woman* (Kingston), *Social Memories* (Zerubavel)
The "stereoscopic" nature of memory	*The Inheritance of Tools* (Sanders), *Building Memories* (Schacter), *The Brown Wasps* (Eiseley)
"Template" memories	*The Brown Wasps* (Eiseley), *Memory and Imagination* (Hampl), *Then and Now* (Engel), *No-Name Woman* (Kingston)
The politics of memory	*The Brown Wasps* (Eiseley), *Memory and Imagination* (Hampl), *No-Name Woman* (Kingston), *Social Memories* (Zerubavel), *Columbus* (hooks)
Memory as accurate transcript	*The Brown Wasps* (Eiseley), *Building Memories* (Schacter), *Memory and Imagination* (Hampl), *Then and Now* (Engel), *No-Name Woman* (Kingston), *Social Memories* (Zerubavel)
Past and present selves	*Memory and Imagination* (Hampl), *Then and Now* (Engel), *No-Name Woman* (Kingston), *A Passage of the Hands* (Lopez, Ch. 1)

Essay Options

The Inheritance of Tools, Scott Russell Sanders

Option #1. Write about an object that holds special meaning and memories for you.

Option #2. Write a dialogue between Sanders and Walker Percy on the influence of the past on the present. (Percy)

The Brown Wasps, Loren Eiseley

Option #1. Compare the use of symbols in Sanders and in Eiseley. (Sanders)
Option #2. Explore the notion of "stereoscopic memory" in Eiseley. (Schacter)
Option #3. Compare Sanders's and Eiseley's approaches to writing from memory. (Sanders)

Building Memories: Encoding and Retrieving the Present and the Past, Daniel L. Schacter

Option #1. Compare and analyze different recollections of a work of art or image.
Option #2. Explore the "stereoscopic" quality of memory in memoirs. (Sanders and Eiseley)

Memory and Imagination, Patricia Hampl

Option #1. Write about a childhood experience in the "elaborated" mode of Hampl.
Option #2. Write about a memory triggered by a childhood photograph.
Option #3. Explore Hampl's claim that "true memoir is written in an attempt to find not only a self but a world." (Sanders, Eiseley, and Lopez)
Option #4. Analyze your own writing process in light of Hampl's.

Then and Now: Creating a Self Through the Past, Susan Engel

Option #1. Analyze the relation of past and present "selves" in a personal essay written earlier in the term.
Option #2. Discuss "template memories" in Eiseley, Hampl, and Kingston. (Eiseley, Hampl, and Kingston)

No-Name Woman, Maxine Hong Kingston

Option #1. Offer your own retelling and evaluation of an important family story.
Option #2. Examine the idea of the politics of memory, as discussed in readings in this chapter. (Eiseley, Hampl, Zerubavel, and hooks)

Social Memories, Eviatar Zerubavel

Option #1. Write about how memories are preserved in a culture of which you are part.
Option #2. Compare the role that memory plays in two cultures with which you're familiar.
Option #3. Research and discuss a recent "mnemonic battle" in the United States.
Option #4. Assess the notion of memory as an accurate transcript of experience. (Eiseley, Schacter, Hampl, Engel, Kingston, and hooks)

Columbus: Gone But Not Forgotten, bell hooks

Option #1. Examine how writers in this chapter transform historical memories. (Hampl, Kingston, and Zerubavel)
Option #2. Research portrayals of Columbus and compare them with that presented by hooks.
Option #3. Read descriptions of the "discovery" of the Americas by Ivan Van Septima, Howard Zinn, and/or Ward Churchill and compare them with the "traditional" version.

Media Connections

Compare differing interpretations of   Schacter, ET #4
Rene Magritte's *The Menaced Assassin*

Compare different recollections or   Schacter, EO #1
interpretations of a work of art

Compare public and private memories   Zerubavel, ET #5
in *Rashomon* and *Death and the
Maiden*

Research and compare textbook   hooks, EO #2
portrayals of Columbus

SCOTT RUSSELL SANDERS, *The Inheritance of Tools* (p. 142)

The idea of recollection as a kind of "construction" is built into Scott Russell Sanders's moving account of the memories he associates with a hammer that's been passed down in his family from father to son for generations. It's not that Sanders explicitly discusses the way individual memories are built up from fragments of experience in the way that Schacter and Hampl do. In fact, Sanders gives no indication that the memories he discovers in his toolbox are "invented" in any way. Indeed, the stories he sees in an heirloom hammer or a carpenter's square seem just as solid and as durable as the objects that contain them. For Sanders, memories are "constructed" in the sense that they accumulate over time in much the same way that a fine patina builds up on the surface of his tools during decades of use. Sanders offers students an attractive introduction to the topic of memory and its relation to the mind. They generally appreciate the way he "concretizes" the act of memory in a physical object, and they find it relatively easy to use Sanders as a model for writing about an object of their own that has similar associations (EO #1). You can thus use Sanders to get your students off to a fast start in this chapter. You may also want to consider pairing this essay with Eiseley's "The Brown Wasps." Side-by-side, these two personal reflections on the past are different enough to generate some interesting class discussion — and challenging enough to get students engaged with the topic. As you consider whether to include Sanders in your course, you may also want to keep in mind the fact that his piece connects particularly well with issues and individual selections related to the notion of the self in Chapter 3, in particular Sapolsky, Csikszentmihalyi, and Walker. The Before Reading activity invites students to begin thinking about a concrete object that contains important memories for them. It doesn't hurt to start brainstorming this idea early on if you plan to do even a brief essay on the topic, because students' first responses to this question aren't always the most productive. It may take some time in class to get them to look beyond obvious choices like the souvenirs they brought back from summer vacation or the stuffed animal or watch they got when they graduated from high school. The best objects for this exercise are often those that belong more generally to a student's family. They tend, like Sanders's hammer, to be objects that have been passed down over time and that have been around long enough to have acquired the "patina" of history.

Exploring the Text

1. From the beginning of this essay, it's clear that Sanders's tools are more than things he works with. Passed down from his grandfather to his father and eventually to him, his hammer connects him directly with the men in his family. It thus represents his identity as a male and as an adult. The tools in his toolbox are more than things that help him in his work around the house. They are "wrapped in a cloud of knowing." They represent the accumulated knowledge of innumerable past generations of men, of active "makers," who have used all sorts of tools to shape the world to fit their own purposes. Thus, Sanders's hammer links him to "hundreds of carpenters" from the beginning of civilization to the present, and it conjures up associations with other great cultural achievements, such as "Greek vases, Gregorian chants, [and] *Don Quixote*." As an emissary of the past, Sanders's

hammer is an extension of the mind: it's an expression of human ingenuity and a symbol of humankind's determination to transform the world we inhabit.

2. As Sanders explores the meanings that surround his tools, he tells us a great deal about their previous owners — his father and grandfather. We learn that his grandfather was an independent Mississippi farmer who had enough work to keep him busy putting up a house on the afternoon of the day he was married. We learn that the men in his family are active, industrious, competent, and thoroughly domestic types, who know their way around a building site and seem to like nothing better than tacking new rooms onto the family home whenever they have the chance. As you read, you get the impression that these men are as resilient as the hand-carved hickory handles they fashion for their tools. Yet, they're also clearly loving husbands and fathers. Sanders recalls the hours he spent in his father's and grandfather's company as a child, and he fondly remembers how they taught him lessons in patience and respect for others. His father was a "colossus" of a man, but he wasn't too big to help him finish sawing a board in half by placing his hand firmly over Sanders's. Nor was he too busy to stoop down to appreciate his young son's handiwork. These are lessons that Sanders passes along to his own children — male and female. This "apprenticeship to wood" is a family tradition of which he's clearly proud. Tools such as saws, hammers, and squares contain traditional values in which Sanders takes great pleasure — values such as diligence, ingenuity, responsibility, carefulness, honesty, balance, hard work, and pride in a job well done. They are the forces that "hold the universe together." And at bottom, that's perhaps the most important thing that Sanders sees in his hammer — the idea of connection and commitment. Hammers make connections; they mend things and keep them strong, just as Sanders's hammer connects him with the past and future generations of his family. Still, it's interesting that Sanders approaches the topic of love and relationship through an object that's also commonly associated with controlled violence. Some students may feel that despite his obvious sensitivity and devotion to his family, Sanders is still typically male in the way he deals with emotion. He expresses himself in this eulogy of his father by talking about his tools. That's about as indirect as you can get. But, then, would the essay have been better if Sanders had simply told us directly about how much he loved and missed his father? Or would it have simply become an exercise in sentiment?

3. The conceit Sanders offers about hitting his thumb is a case in point. The self-inflicted wound he describes at the start of the essay obviously symbolizes the pain he feels at the moment of his father's death, as well as the emotional scar that his father's passing leaves on his life. Interestingly, his first response after hitting his thumb, as we learn at the end of the essay, was to get so angry that he wanted to cut this thumb off and bury it in the snow. But the remembered voice of his father distracts him from this fantasy of self-mutilation and separation, and soon he's back to doing what he does best — making "connections" by nailing boards together "square and true" for the benefit of his family. There is no "door" or way out of the grief he feels at his father's loss, only the memory of his father's love, which he can use to build another strong wall against grief and forgetfulness.

4. Indeed, Sanders is so devoted to his family that students may well begin to wonder about the quality of his commitment to the rest of us. He notes the "headlines" in the news on the day his daughter's gerbils get stuck behind the bedroom wall, and thus acknowledges the existence of such tragedies as the poisoning of thousands of people outside a Union Carbide plant in Bhopal, India, the calamity of apartheid in South Africa, and the fact of widespread homelessness in the United States. But he admits that these are things he can't cope with. Sanders suggests here that the only things that really matter for him are those that fall within his immediate experience — the things and relationships that are part of his daily life and that he can do something about. He may be a loving father and a devoted son, but he's also a pragmatist who is only willing to handle problems that are immediate enough for him to handle personally. The news, Sanders seems to be suggesting, is only something that distracts you from the real "calamities" of your own life: the wider world is meaningless if it's not something you can reach and make right with a hammer or a chisel.

5. The tool that Sanders uses as a writer to bring his memories to life is storytelling. The essay is structured around the story of how he hits his thumb while building a wall for his daughter's bedroom on the day his father dies. This story then opens up into a corridor of recollections connected with his hammer: the story of his grandfather's wedding day, the story of how Sanders learned about the relationship of space, sound, and time while watching his grandfather pound nails on a distant roof, the story about his "apprenticeship to wood" under the tutelage of his father, the story about the day his daughter's gerbils escaped into the "drum tight" wall he'd just completed in her bedroom. Sanders fills these anecdotes with enough sensuous detail to bring the past alive for us. He invites us to smell the fragrance of the sawdust that filled his father's garage — the aroma of "oak or walnut or cherry or pine" — that, he recalls, smelled like "something freshly baked." Through the use of such concrete details, he helps us "see" the level his grandfather used to carry on the gun rack of his pickup truck, with the bubbles that would "dance" when you turned it round — or the "flat steel elbow" of the framing square, with numbers so faded you can barely make them out. Sanders uses visual, olfactory, and tactile images to convey the experience of these memories to his readers. An experienced writer and an expert memoirist, he isn't content to speak in general terms: "As a child, I remember spending long days building toy guitars and boats in my father's garage." With luck, students will see the weakness in this kind of purely conceptual approach to writing from memory when they try to reduce Sanders's essay to a paragraph-long summary. Squeezing all the stories and concrete details out of Sanders does make reading his essay a lot faster, but it also leaves out everything that makes it distinctly his. Paraphrase omits the lived memories and feeling that distinguish Sanders's essay; it reduces his experiences to the point where they could be anyone's and, thus, no one's.

6. One of the things that gives Sanders's memories their concreteness is his use of direct quotation. Throughout the essay, we hear the voices of Sanders's family. There's the echoing voice of his father, offering a judicious piece of advice or a bit of constructive wisdom: "Don't force it," he would say, "just drag it easy and give the teeth a chance to bite." There's the plaintive voice of his daughter: "'What can we do?' my daughter wailed. 'They'll starve to death, they'll die of thirst, they'll suffocate.'" There's the "stillness" he reports in his wife's voice that makes him drop a "framed wall" and hurry downstairs to hear the details of his father's death. Sanders knows that the past is full of voices and that voices, judiciously evoked, can bring the past to life.

Further Explorations

1. The comparisons between Sanders and Lopez are obvious. Both writers reflect on lessons they learned in the past through manual means — Lopez through the education of his hands, Sanders through the education he received as a child in the use of tools. Students may find, however, that Lopez's style is generally more sensual than that of Sanders: Lopez relies more on sense imagery and the sonorous effects of language to convey the tactile experiences of his youth (see p. 27). And this shouldn't be particularly surprising, because the aims of these writers differ. Lopez is trying to convey the texture of a lifetime of physical experience, whereas Sanders is describing the intellectual and ethical knowledge that are part of the "inheritance" he received from his father. Lopez wants the reader to re-experience the sensations he felt through his hands in his youth, whereas Sanders seems less aware of the reader and more determined to use the essay as an opportunity for sorting out his own thoughts and feelings about the meaning of life and death. It may be interesting to see how the women in your class respond to these two distinctly "male" and "manual" selections, and to see which they prefer. If female students need something they can relate to, you may want to move from here directly to Patricia Hampl's "Memory and Imagination."

2. Eiseley offers an interesting contrast to Sanders, and one that leads directly into some of the issues that Daniel L. Schacter raises in his scientific analysis of memory cues and retrieval later in the chapter. Memory, in Eiseley's essay, is a river in time — a fluid,

flowing path that leads him on a reflective adventure. Unlike Sanders, who focuses on the skein of memories wrapped around a particular object, Eiseley follows the thread of an apparently accidental encounter — the sight of some homeless people in a railway station — as it leads him from memory to memory, until it stops outside his boyhood home. Both experiences involve recollection, but they couldn't differ more in the way they represent the experience. Sanders tells us what he knows and is sure of: he is a dutiful son reciting the lessons he's learned at the hands of a loving father. Eiseley leads us on a journey that seems to be a mystery even to himself: once he teases out the meaning behind the scene he sees in the railway station, he seems genuinely surprised to find that, in some sense, he's been "homeless" himself his whole life. Reflection on the past centers Sanders; it bears him inward toward the core of his identity and character, and in so doing it links him to his family. Reflection, for Eiseley, might be seen as de-centering: it does carry him back to the site of his childhood, but when he arrives at the family homestead, he doesn't find a solid core of values; in fact, what he does find is the emptiness left by a tree that never really existed. The act of reflection, then, seems to bear Eiseley out of himself; it connects him with others who might at first seem unlike himself — the homeless, some wasps, a mouse, a flock of pigeons, the man who waits for the train that never comes. It challenges rather than confirms Eiseley's understanding of his own identity.

3. The issue of memory in relation to identity is the central concern of Susan Engel's "Then and Now: Creating a Self Through the Past" later in this chapter. The most obvious "past self" projected by Sanders in this essay is that of the inquisitive, industrious son who spends his days hammering away at toy guitars in his father's garage. But he also projects a number of other self-images — only these aren't quite so far removed into the past. There's the image of himself as the loving and dutiful father who builds walls for his family home and would even sacrifice his perfectly built wall for the sake of his daughter's gerbils. And there's the image of the young man who's impatient with himself for hitting his thumb with a hammer and angry at life because of the inevitability of death. But, in fact, the range of these images of past selves is pretty limited. Sanders's focus, in this essay, isn't so much on himself but on his father. Indeed, the essay might be read as an affirmation that the "self" of this plain, kind, hardworking man is enough for Sanders to aspire to.

Essay Options

1. You can use Essay Option #1 as a way to get students writing fast in this unit. The topic presents no particular conceptual difficulty, and students often do a good job with it in three to four pages. As suggested above, the only special guidance you might want to offer involves helping students look beyond objects connected with very recent memories — souvenirs of recent trips and so forth.

2. The dialogue between Sanders and Walker Percy would obviously hinge on the relation between past and present knowledge. Percy might argue that all "inherited" knowledge limits our ability to see the world around us. Thus, a contemporary visitor to the Grand Canyon can't really "see" it at all, because the actual canyon itself has been hidden by the "preformed complex" of ideas and associations that have congealed around it over the past two hundred years. Sanders, by contrast, takes delight in the "cloud of knowing" that envelops his tools. From his perspective, objects become precious precisely because of the memories and skills that collect around them. Exactly opposed to the ideal of the radically free thinker that Percy finds so attractive, Sanders has the heart and soul of a craftsman. He believes that we can appreciate the present only through the connections that bind us to the past.

LOREN EISELEY, *The Brown Wasps* (p. 150)

This is a wonderful essay on the nature of memory and our ambiguous relation to the past. It's short and it pairs well with both Sanders and Schacter. It also raises some wonderful questions about the role that memory plays in helping us to discover our relatedness to others. Part of what makes Eiseley's essay so attractive is the mystery that lurks at its core. Eiseley bears us back in time from the moment he sees a group of elderly homeless people in an anonymous urban train station, and we get the impression that he himself is unsure where this chain of recollection is taking him. Eiseley also illustrates some of the key theoretical concepts that Schacter discusses in his scientific treatment of memory retrieval in the next selection. The way Eiseley juxtaposes past experiences offers a good example of the concepts of "stereoscopic memory" and "memory cues" that Schacter discusses. In addition, you'll find that Eiseley connects productively with Patricia Hampl's "Memory and Imagination." Eiseley's haunting recollection of a tree that never existed outside his childhood home raises serious questions about the reliability of personal memory and the role that imagination plays in the process of mentally resurrecting past events. Begin with the Before Reading activity, which invites students to freewrite about their own earliest childhood recollections. The follow-up question about the reliability of personal memory touches on a theme that runs throughout the chapter and that culminates in a comprehesive academic essay associated with Zerubavel's "Social Memories."

Exploring the Text

1. Eiseley begins his archeological exploration of memory with a scene in a "great Eastern station" where he sees "the abandoned poor" seeking refuge from the cold. The elderly homeless people that Eiseley describes in this opening passage strike him as tenaciously clinging to the life of the city — almost as if they were unwilling to give in to the inevitability of death. This idea leads him back to the recollection of a doomed hive of wasps in midwinter, clinging to their nest before dying in the snow. Later, when the homeless people he sees are rousted by a police officer, he thinks of them as birds frightened by a farmer walking through a field. At first, these connections might seem inappropriate or bizarre. What do the homeless in a train station have to do with a hive of wasps out in some field? And isn't it odd — or even insensitive — to think of these people in terms of animals and insects? What underlies this association for Eiseley are the ideas of tenacity and relatedness — the desire to stay connected to "the great droning center of the hive." Every creature, human and beast, holds on to its place in the world, the "place at the heart of things."

2. The problem that Eiseley confronts in this essay is the problem of time and its relation to memory — the problem of how to get back to, or how to hold on to, one's original "place." From the scene he witnesses in the train station, Eiseley moves consistently backward in time. He bears us from the train station in his "present" to the memory of the brown wasps, and then to the recollection of the mouse that lived in a "remembered field," and then to a flock of pigeons and an old blind man he once saw haunting an abandoned subway station. As he moves along this chain of associations, he recognizes the power of the past and the insubstantiality of what we call the "present." From the archeological perspective he adopts in this essay, time dissolves the apparent solidity of the world and the present moment begins to fade and flow into the past. "Everything," as he says, "takes on an aspect of illusion." All creatures, he seems to suggest, cling to what they've known, as do the homeless people he originally observed. But as we move backward with him in time, this anachronistic instinct seems both more defiant and more ennobled. The wasps, the elderly poor, the field mouse, the blind man aren't just stuck or lost in the past: they seem to be rebelling against impermanence, change, and death.

3. At the end of the essay, Eiseley finally unearths the import of the scene he saw in that "great Eastern station." Returning to his boyhood home, he confronts the fact that the cottonwood tree that he remembers planting with his father — and that had "grown" in his memory for sixty years — had never really existed. Eiseley doesn't give us many details about his early family life, probably because the details themselves aren't important. He tells us straight off that his memory of the tree stuck in his mind because

it symbolized his love for his father. Otherwise, all we learn is that in the intervening years "everyone died or moved away who was supposed to wait and grow old under its shade." It's a telling remark — one that suggests a terrific longing on Eiselely's part for the permanency of home. Indeed, the only sense of permanency and place he has is provided by the mistaken memory of a sheltering cottonwood tree that apparently died sixty years earlier. This illusion has been the "hive" to which he's clung, the railway station that's offered him shelter.

4. Thus, it's possible to read "The Brown Wasps" as a kind of personal archeological exploration of the past. It begins when Eiseley sees the elderly homeless people and recognizes something in them that he can't let go of. They become a symbol of an experience and an idea that links them to other recollections — and other creatures — he's seen during his life. As he digs through the strata of memory, he unearths secrets about himself and his own identity. At bottom, he sees himself — and probably all of us — in the destitute elderly who haunt that railway station. All of us are clinging to life and our place in it, and all of us, in some sense, spend our days under the shadow of an imaginary past that we've fabricated in order to endure the present. We all, to some extent, inhabit "an elusive world" of our own making, a world that has more to do with past dreams than with present realities. This is a part, at least, of what Eiseley hints at in this evocative essay.

5. Chances are that students may find other ideas and themes here as well. One of the most interesting ideas that Eiseley himself touches on is the notion that attachment to the past is "part of our morality." It would be possible to argue that this essay itself is an exercise in moral reflection, in that it forces Eiseley to step outside the limitations of his own life and to attend to the lives of others — whether they be people less fortunate than himself, animals, or insects. Eiseley seems to be suggesting that the act of reflection is itself a fundamentally moral act because it always connects us with something or someone else — even if the other is an earlier version of ourselves.

Further Explorations

1. As noted above in the discussion of "The Inheritance of Tools" (see Sanders, FE #3), some interesting connections and contrasts can be found between Sanders and Eiseley. Reading Sanders is about as direct and uncomplicated an experience as you could want. Sanders unpacks the memories that his tools contain much as he might unpack his toolbox before framing a wall. The past is "right there" for him, encoded in these concrete objects; all he has to do is relate the stories that each contains. For Eiseley, by constrast, things aren't so simple, and, as a result, the process of reading him is a bit more complicated. To understand what he's getting at, we have to follow him as he moves along the chain of recollection that carries him from the Eastern urban train station where the essay begins to his childhood home in Nebraska sixty years earlier. And even then, the meaning of Eiseley's essay isn't neatly delivered to us. We have to infer much of what he's saying about memory, time, identity, imagination, and morality by making our own connections between the different memories he presents. Whereas Sanders unpacks the toolbox of memory for us, Eiseley throws us into the river of time and invites us to paddle along with him. Thus, even when Sanders becomes serious toward the end of the essay as he thinks back to his reaction after learning about his father's death, the tone of the piece never really falters. Within a page he's back at work with the kind of clear-headed determination and indefatigable spirit that he inherited along with his father's hammer. The past and his memory of it are things he's sure of, things that are completely "nailed down," straight and true. The past and memory for Eiseley, however, disrupt the present; in fact, it's hard to come away from Eiseley confident that what we optimistically call the "present" actually exists. All the places that we cling to, all the things we value, commemorate, and hold dear, Eiseley seems to hint, are illusions, and memory itself relies more on imagination than it does on reality. The only thing that's nailed down for Eiseley is that we all need our illusions and that we can achieve something like moral vision by

recognizing our own essential connectedness with others. Sanders's essay celebrates his identity: although he's shaken by his father's death, he knows he really hasn't lost anything. Indeed, his identity is so intertwined with that of his family that he admits to having trouble connecting with the fates of those who suffer at a distance. Eiseley's essay lacks this sense of centeredness. Nothing is certain — not even memory — in a world that's constantly being undermined by the river of time. The only thing that ennobles life and gives it moral value, Eiseley suggests, is our ability to make connections in memory between other people, other creatures, other times, and other places. And it's exactly this moral action of memory that he demonstrates in "The Brown Wasps."

2. Eisley's idea of juxtaposing different moments clearly illustrates what Daniel L. Schacter refers to as the "stereoscopic" relation of "cue" and "engram." According to Schacter, every experience of memory unites a cue — the stimulus that triggers a recollection — with an engram — the residue of experience that remains encoded in the brain. It's possible, then, to think of the scene of the homeless that begins Eiseley's essay as a cue that triggers his recollection of the brown wasps. It's even possible to imagine that this recollection of the wasps clinging to their hive itself becomes a cue that triggers the subsequent memory of the mouse re-creating its home in a potted plant in Eiseley's living room — and that this engram then becomes a cue that triggers his former experience with the pigeons and the blind man outside the subway station. This chaining of memories, cue to engram, isn't reflected in Sanders's essay. Sanders's tools are wrapped in layers of memory: each one is a cue that triggers multiple engrams and multiple recollections. Schacter, however, does help to explain why Eiseley "remembered" so vividly the tree that never actually existed in his family's front yard. Memory, according to Schacter, has little to do with the verbatim transcription and reproduction of past experiences. We don't reproduce the past, we "assemble" it from the fragments of experience associated with engrams, and this process of assembly is often influenced by our present needs and context. In Schacter's view, then, cue and engram merge to create something totally new — something he calls the "recollective experience." Thus, Eiseley's misremembered tree may not be an anomaly at all. It may, in fact, be a fairly accurate model of the way that memory works.

3. "The Brown Wasps" may also serve to illustrate Susan Engel's concept of "template memories." A template memory is one that has taken on special meaning because it crystallizes an important moment or event in our lives: it serves as a template in that it "stands for a larger, more diffuse meaning or theme" that we use to make sense of our actions, motives, and identities. Eiseley's childhood recollection of planting the cottonwood tree with his father clearly illustrates this kind of important memory. It expresses a whole constellation of yearnings and desires that have obviously haunted him all of his life, and you also get the feeling that he himself doesn't completely grasp all of its ramifications. This "mistaken" recollection expresses his desire for permanency and a place to belong to — two wishes that may have affected Eiseley's choice of a career as a student of human ecology.

4. The fantasy of place and permanence that underlies this mistaken memory would not, however, trouble Patricia Hampl in the least. In her own excursion into the personal past, Hampl freely admits to imagining not only details but whole episodes and characters. Memory is allied to imagination, according to Hampl, not opposed to it. In her view, we call on the imagination to help build our memories, and every act of remembering is thus both highly creative and highly political. If Hampl herself had written "The Brown Wasps," we might even expect her to return to it in yet another draft to further probe the feelings that cling to the image of the cottonwood tree. Of course, we can't tell how many times Eiseley himself returned to rewrite "The Brown Wasps." It's possible that there were, in fact, no elderly poor in a great Eastern station or that he never actually entertained a homeless field mouse in his living room. What Eiseley gives us might already be the result of several bouts of imaginative elaboration and accretion.

Essay Options

1. Both Sanders and Eiseley rely on the use of symbols. Concrete objects take on all sorts of thematic importance in these two memoirs. Both exist, in some sense, to convey the meanings that surround significant objects in the past such as Sanders's tools or Eiseley's wasp hive or cottonwood tree. Sanders's hammer can be read as embodying all the virtues he feels he's learned from the men in his family. Its hickory handle is coarsely grained and resilient, just as his father and grandfather were simple, hard-working men who tempered labor with affection. His hammer is better for building things — for making connections — than it is as a tool for demolition. His level helps him stay in balance. It makes sense that memories cluster around such symbols because we only recall the most meaningful experiences in our lives, and these experiences often become associated with specific objects or events that then assume the aura of special significance.

2. Essay Option #2 offers a chance for students to extend the thinking that they did if you assigned Further Exploration #2. Every one of the recollections that Eiseley offers in "The Brown Wasps" can be seen as a "stereoscopic" doubling of his initial encounter with the homeless poor. A number of themes emerge when these recollections are compared. All of the protagonists in Eiseley's memories are exiles; they've all lost their sense of place in the world, and they're all balanced precariously on the brink of death. All have literally lost their homes. Most are in some sense destitute. All are also remarkably resilient — perhaps even heroic. If Eiseley's memory of the cottonwood tree were doubled with the scene he sees of the homeless, there's no doubt that he would stand in their place. This is, in fact, the specifically "moral" lesson that Eiseley's essay offers us. Eiseley values memory not because it directly ties us to anything in particular, but because it makes it possible for us to "double" our vision — to connect the present with the past and to see ourselves in the others with whom we share our existence.

3. The last Essay Option offers students the chance to extend the comparison that they've already done of Sanders and Eiseley into a formal academic essay. You may want to assign either of these last two academic writing options at this point if you plan to end your exploration of memory with Eiseley. But if you plan to go on to Schacter and other topics related to memory, I'd recommend that you postpone academic writing until more developed opportunities are available later in the chapter.

DANIEL L. SCHACTER, *Building Memories: Encoding and Retrieving the Present and the Past* (p. 157)

This is one of three analytic selections in this chapter. Schacter's examination of the mechanics of memory introduces concepts that your class will need as it explores the "constructed" nature of recollection. Schacter also brings to your class the perspective of a practicing scientist. A professor of psychology at Harvard with a lengthy list of professional and popular publications, Schacter will help to make it clear that writers such as Eiseley and Hampl aren't simply suffering from poor memories or a weakness for confabulation. When Schacter notes that memories are "built" from trace recollections the way that dinosaurs are reassembled from sets of bone fragments, he speaks with the authority of modern science. What's particularly nice about Schacter is that he's not only an expert scientist but an accomplished writer with a love of the arts and a knack for popularlizing technical concepts. Thus, when Schacter introduces a technical term or a theory, he isn't content to just let it lie there: he always finds the time to present a thought-provoking anecdote or a particularly powerful illustration to help us think through all of its implications. This is how we meet "Bubbles P.," the bookie with a prodigious memory, and Richard Semon, the tragic nineteenth-century memory researcher who suffered the ironic fate of having been forgotten by practitioners in his own field. The downside to Schacter's essay is its length. I've tried to prune back this selection as much as possible, but I didn't want to sacrifice too much of Schacter's storytelling. So, I recommend that you use the length of this piece as an occasion for an effective in-class learning experiment (see ET #1 below). I also suggest that you begin by spending some time collectively reviewing what students already know about the mechanics of memory. The Before Reading exercise asks students to compare notes on the process of how memory works. The point of this discussion is to elicit the metaphors that shape our commonplace understandings of memory — metaphors such as the wax tablet, the photographic plate, and the computer disk. Most people imagine memory to involve a rather mechanical, verbatim transcription of experience. Thanks to some famous misinformation that was widely circulated during the early years of neuro-surgery, many believe that we literally remember every event that's ever happened to us and every word we've ever heard. Schacter will debunk most of these reassuringly mechanistic models of memory and challenge students to take a more creative view of recollection. If you're looking for models of how human memory actually works, Schacter suggests, you should look to Marcel Proust and the way he thought about the past, and not to things such as videotape and twenty-gigabyte hard drives.

Exploring the Text

1. I recommend that you take the time to try the activity in this question. It's not often that students can learn something about the mind in school that will help them excel in every academic situation — but here it is. Have your class test their memories of Schacter's essay by writing in-class summaries. The point is not simply to summarize the gist of what Schacter says in this selection about memory but to "reproduce" his essay in as much detail as possible. Students should try to recall all of the topics and concepts he addresses, the exact order he follows, and all the details of the illustrations and anecdotes that he offers to explain them. The real purpose of this exercise is to get students to explore why some of them may recall more about Schacter than others. Some may find that they recall more because they took notes or highlighted the text or wrote comments in response to Schacter's ideas in the margins of their book as they read. Some may have outlined the chapter as the result of study habits they practiced in high school. Others may have remembered more of what they read simply because they're interested in the topic of memory and already know something about it — or because they scanned the Exploring the Text questions before they began reading and thus were aware of the need to remember what they read. Any and all of these are possibilities — and all offer productive lessons about how memory works and what students can do to sharpen their recall when they read in academic situations.

2. When most people think of how memory works, according to Schacter, they evoke such metaphors as the classic wax tablet or Freud's image of a house composed of rooms filled with objects. Memory has even been likened to a "garbage can" loaded with random types of mental "refuse." Your students may come up with creative analogies of their own to convey how memory works. Human memory can be compared with a video- or audiotape, with a photograph, or even with a computer hard drive or a copying machine. It has, in the past, often been compared with a book, a set of accounting ledgers, and even a filing cabinet. Interestingly, most of these metaphors involve likening memory to inscription — to the act of writing. Thus, you write on a wax tablet, on a page in a filing cabinet, and on a ledger. You even "write" electronically on a hard drive or on videotape. When you remember, according to these analogies, you simply open the right mental file and "read" what's been deliberately written in the past. But Schacter suggests that memory isn't as simple or as mechanical as this. He offers an alternative to the commonplace metaphor of memory as inscription. Evoking an image first used by the psychologist Eric Neisser, he claims that the process of recollection resembles the process a paleontologist goes through as he reconstructs a dinosaur from relatively small bone fragments.

3. Memory, as Schacter sees it, is a fragile and creative process — one that depends from start to finish on the point of view of the "encoder." We possess two independent memory systems. "Working memory" holds discrete amounts of information for rela-

tively brief periods — typically no more than a few seconds. After that, if a memory is to be durable, it must be "encoded" through deliberate effort. Deep encoding generally requires that new information be integrated with something you already know; thus, we tend to recall information that's already to some extent familiar to us, just as the book-ie Bubbles P. found it easy to recall numbers because he worked with long lists of them on a daily basis. "Elaborative encoding" allows us to recall information by deliberately and self-consciously linking it to information that is already familiar. Things that are not linked with existing knowledge are soon forgotten, no matter how often we're exposed to them. Thus, we've all handled and looked directly at pennies or dollar bills hundreds of times, yet most of us would be hard pressed to draw the reverse of either in detail. Formal mnemonic training always involves specialized devices that promote deliberate elaborative encoding. Thus, the "memory theaters" that were popular during the Middle Ages required learners to link new information to pre-existing locations in a picture of a building. Visual diagrams of the information presented in a science textbook serve much the same function.

4. Because we tend to recall things that connect with what we already know, we all remember things differently: we all encode our own point of view in the memories we store for the long term. As a result, Schacter has little difficulty guessing the occupation of the participants in Sophie Calle's memory experiment. He links the comment about Magritte's painting being a "murder scene" to the museum guard, while he guesses that the comment that highlights the dimensions of the painting belongs to someone from the maintenance staff. What we remember is a function of who we are, Schacter asserts, and who we are depends in no small part on the sum of what we remember.

5. Schacter himself engages in several bouts of verbal reminiscence in this selection. He devotes considerable stretches of writing to relating the stories of Bubbles P., Richard Semon, Neil (the boy with impaired memory retrieval), and Marcel Proust. In general, we can assume that Schacter includes these anecdotes because stories are always more interesting than exposition and because we're more likely to remember information that's presented in a context that's familiar to us. Still, there are differences in the ways that sto-ries work for Schacter. The story of Bubbles P. is offered simply to introduce and debunk a commonplace misconception about how memory works; it's purely an illustration. The story of Richard Semon, by contrast, is offered as a mini-tragedy that we can all relate to and thus will probably remember. The question is whether Schacter wants us to recall Semon in order to correct one of history's ironies or whether he simply wants to use the story of Semon as a vehicle for the "deep elaboration" of his theory of memory.

6. In any case, what emerges from this account of memory is the proposition that recollections are, at best, only fragmentary reconstructions and not verbatim transcripts of experiences. Indeed, what we recall, according to Schacter, depends more heavily on the retrieval cue than it does on the original information we encode. We construct our personal memories the same way a fossilized dinosaur is built, based on a few original fragments and a lot of general knowledge. The cue — the "ecphoric stimulus" in the present — combines with the engram — the traces of actual memory encoded during deep elaboration — to produce a third mental phenomenon: "the recollective experi-ence." This "subjective experience" that we call memory emerges from the interplay of the present situation with the past and thus gives us a "double" or "stereoscopic" per-spective on our lives. As Proust suggests in his novels, our minds "see time" by doubling our experiences, by layering the past with the present.

Further Explorations

1. You'd be right to expect a direct link between the idea of the construction of sense perception and the construction of memory. That link is provided by prior experience. According to K. C. Cole, we see the things we expect to see: our prior experiences estab-lish expectations that help us select the sense data that are important to us. Without the ability to screen sense data in this way, we'd be overwhelmed by all the available infor-

mation that surrounds us. Conversely, we tend to ignore sensory input that doesn't make sense to us; thus, we edit out things that we're not familiar with, things that don't connect in some way with the knowledge we already have. That's why it's often difficult to comprehend a totally fresh thought or to see the world from a radically new or different perspective. Our perceptions, like our memories, are also constructed in the sense that both involve active interpretation. Not only do we sort our perceptions, giving preference to those that connect with our established expectations, we also must interpret them and decide what they mean. And again, familiarity plays a key role in this interpretive process. We understand the sense data we gather from the world around us in the context of what we already believe. Our theories about the way the world works shape our understanding of what we perceive, and many of these theories derive from the cultures in which we live. Thus, just as the prior knowledge, expectations, and interests of the museum workers shaped their recollections of Magritte's *The Menaced Assassin* in Sophie Calle's experiment, so do our expectations shape our basic sense perceptions of the world around us. Given the biases that are built into both perception and memory against things that are new, it's no wonder that learning can often be such a challenge. When we encounter a new idea or a new phenomenon, we tend to ignore it, to rationalize it away, or to forget it in short order. Given the built-in limitations of both perception and memory, the best and perhaps the only way to learn something new is by connecting it with prior experience. That's probably why analogies play such an important role in learning: a good analogy helps us comprehend a new idea by mapping it onto an idea, object, experience, or event with which we're already familiar.

2. The relation of memory and belief would play an important role in a Schacterian analysis of Sanders and Eiseley. The moment before Sanders hears about his father's death, his hammer is just a hammer, something he uses to build walls. But the news of his father's passing becomes a cue that triggers a series of engrams connected with this household implement. The hammer itself, then, might be seen as emerging as a cue in the present that conjures up a whole host of past associations. For Eiseley, there seems to be more of a serial relationship between cues and engrams. The scene of homeless elderly people in a train station triggers the engram that leads to the "recollective experience" of a hive of brown wasps dying in midwinter. Then, perhaps, this recollection itself becomes a cue that connects with another engram — this one leading to the reconstruction of the memory of the mouse that once took up residence in Eiseley's living room. This reconstructed memory might then also become a cue that leads back to engrams connected with the pigeons that "return" to the subway they once frequented, and so forth until we arrive with Eiseley at the memory of the cottonwood tree. As Schacter would point out, engrams themselves provide incomplete clues to experiences that we then build into full-blown memories in response to the cues that evoked them. Once they emerge as memories, they can themselves become cues for other engrams. Eiseley never explicitly states that one memory triggers another in this way, but he does represent the process of memory as a river of time in his essay, and he does give the reader the impression that his movement along this river is a kind of journey of discovery — a movement back toward some indistinctly perceived meaning or significance. Indeed, that may be why the memories that Eiseley explores never seem gratuitous or repetitive. As we move with him from past scene to past scene, our sense of what he first perceived in those people in the train station becomes deeper and richer, until at last we realize that he has seen himself — and all of us — in them. Of course, it's important to remember that we never actually see the engrams that Sanders and Eiseley "build" into memories. As Schacter would remind us, such anecdotes are fabrications — recollective experiences — that reflect the present motives and aims of each author more than they do the actual details of the past. Thus, it makes sense that Sanders discovers memories connected with themes of strength, integrity, continuity, and affection in this heirloom hammer — virtues that he can use to "build" a wall of relationships that will both protect him from the cosmic injustice of death and keep him connected to the spirit of his deceased father. It also makes sense that Eiseley's chain of recollections links the elder-

ly poor he sees initially with the tree that always offered him protection in memory. In his sixties at the time of writing, Eiseley had ample motive in the present to see himself in fellow beings who were poised on the brink of their own mortality. His present reality clearly influenced the recollections that emerged from his past.

3. Because our preoccupations in the present shape our recollections, it's also relatively easy to read the values and attitudes of Eiseley, Sanders, Frazier, and Lopez from the memories they share with us. Thus, for example, Eiseley's memories tell us that he's intensely interested in nature, a close observer, a compassionate type who doesn't turn his back on suffering, a man who respects even the smallest forms of life, a basically open person who isn't too concerned about sharing his home with local wildlife, a dreamer, and someone who might even be a bit insecure — someone who would cling to the childhood memory of a tree for the comfort and strength it offers. You might want to have students work in small groups as they brainstorm lists of qualities, values, and attitudes that emerge from the essays by Sanders, Lopez, and Frazier. This shouldn't be too hard, given that they've already spent some time dissecting the character of Lopez and Sanders. Still, you'll want to encourage them to go beyond the kinds of conclusions they may have reached earlier while doing thematic analysis of these selections. What does it suggest about Sanders, as a person, that he thinks of his tools when he hears about his father's death? What images arise of Sanders, Lopez, and Frazier as students read these selections? What do the things that Frazier pays attention to on a daily basis tell us about him as a person?

4. If you want to include a female voice in this discussion, you may want to read ahead at this point to Maxine Hong Kingston's "No-Name Woman." Kingston offers several contrasting versions of her aunt's tragic story in her memoir, including the original version that she hears from her mother and a number of imaginative re-creations that she elaborates herself. Given Schacter's belief that memory always reflects the knowledge, experiences, and needs of the rememberer, it should be possible to speculate about what these different versions reveal about Kingston and her mother. Her mother's version of the story is brutally direct: her sister-in-law was a source of humiliation for her family. From her mother's perspective, Kingston's aunt broke the laws of her community and her community retaliated. The very fact that Kingston's mother spends more time detailing the destruction of the family's house than she does addressing the situation or feelings of her aunt is revealing. Her mother is very much like the villagers themselves: she's a practical person, a "traditional" Chinese woman, who sees danger in rebellion and safety in group solidarity. The multiple versions that Kingston offers reveal a different sort of person. The very fact that Kingston explores various retellings of her aunt's story suggests a kind of openness and willingness to experiment that her mother probably wouldn't understand or appreciate. Through most of these versions, Kingston comes across as more romantic and individualistic than her mother. She "remembers" her aunt as a pathetic, suffering figure, as an independent woman rebelling against the narrowness of a backward culture, and as a hero who defies tradition and takes her own life and the life of her child to spare it further punishment. Kingston's reconstruction of this inherited memory suggests that she's a young, rebellious woman herself, a woman who feels constrained by and impatient with the traditional values and attitudes of the culture in which she's grown up.

Essay Options

1. Essay Option #1 is refreshing because it invites you to escape the classroom — or at least the restrictions of traditional text-based academic analysis. You may want to lay the groundwork for this assignment by asking students to study a painting you bring with you to class when you first begin your discussion of memory. Have them study the work individually and then ask them to write a one-page summary of what they see in it. Collect these and keep them while you work on other assignments. After they've finished Schacter, have them write descriptions of what they recall of the painting in as

much detail as possible. Then have them compare these recollections among themselves in class and compare them with their earlier efforts as well. This should give them ample "data" to work with in their papers. Ask them to consider not only the ways in which their memories differ from those of other students, but also how their later recollections differ from their initial impressions. And be sure to ask them to probe the reasons that might account for the differences they note.

2. Essay Option #2 offers the chance for a more extensive text-based academic essay on the topic of the stereoscopic effect of memory. Students may have some trouble here with the rather abstract notion of experiences interpreting or commenting on one another. To help them with this, ask them to think about the connections they can find between Eiseley's and Sanders's present and past experiences and to speculate about what led these writers to make such connections in the first place. How does Eiseley's memory of the wasps comment on the situation of the elderly poor he sees in the train station? What is suggested by his mental doubling of wasps and people? What meaning emerges from the overlay, in memory, of the image of a hive with that of a train station, a mouse hole, and Eiseley's family home in Nebraska? What links Sanders's experience of building a wall with his father's death? How might the fact of his father's death transform the meaning he sees in childhood recollections he associates with tools and woodworking? This isn't a particularly easy topic, but if students stay with it and spend enough time brainstorming it in groups, it can teach them a lot about close analysis and the subtleties of memory.

PATRICIA HAMPL, *Memory and Imagination* (p. 180)

I strongly recommend you assign this entertaining and instructive personal essay on the nature of memory and the art of writing. It's wonderfully readable, it offers a striking illustration of the interpretive nature of memory, and it invites students to think critically about writing as a process of discovery. It also provides the basis for several attractive personal and academic writing assignments. Hampl is central to almost every theme taken up in this chapter. This account of her first piano lesson with Sister Olive Marie is indispensable if you're addressing the construction of memory, the notion of template memories, the politics of memory, or issues involved with memory as a reliable record of past events. You'll find that it also connects productively with selections in other chapters. It's particularly useful as a bridge reading between Chapter 2 and the idea of reading the self taken up in Chapter 3. Hampl is also important because her memoir offers a woman's perspective that helps to balance earlier contributions by Sanders and Eiseley. Hampl's experiences, along with those of Maxine Hong Kingston later in the chapter, offer your class a different view of memory and what it means to be connected to the past. One reason why students take to Hampl is that she's thinking back to a source of memory that everyone can relate to — an early educational experience. The Before Reading activity directs students to freewrite about their earliest educational experience. This can later be used as a preliminary draft of a personal essay in response to Essay Option #1. Having students return to elaborate on this freewriting gives them the chance to test some of Hampl's ideas about the relation between memory and imagination as well as the opportunity to observe, reflect on, and experiment with their own writing processes.

Exploring the Text

1. One of the things that students appreciate about Hampl is her honesty. Writers go to such lengths to hide the mechanics of their creative process that it's refreshing to meet one who admits that a lot of the "memoir" she just presented as the truth is actually made up of lies. In fact, Hampl's not really sure that her father took her to her first piano lesson or that he played the violin at that time or that Sister Olive actually existed. All she recalls of her first music teacher is "a sneeze in the sun and a finger touching middle C." There was no "Thompson book." Mary Katherine Reilly was a girl she met

later when she was in the Girl Scouts. And when she did finally get to know her, it was Hampl who played the dominant role in their relationship. In Hampl's view, these "embellishments" aren't actually lies: they're inventions she cooks up to help her discover the meaning of past events. She does, in fact, view herself as someone who's trying to capture and convey the truth of her experiences. It's just that, as she sees it, the truth about the past isn't something that can be easily recaptured. It's not simply "a matter of transcription," and the past isn't like a "warehouse" full of stories or a "gallery" of ready-made memories. The past, for Hampl, has to be reconstructed. What she actually recalls are merely fragments or traces of past events and actions. She literally remembers a slant of light, a finger poised above middle C, a sneeze — that's all. Then she elaborates on these fragments by allowing her imagination to fill in details that somehow just "seem right" — things like Sister Olive's name, her wimple, or the dominating Mary Katherine Reilly and her famous grandfather. Of course, your students may have some trouble buying this line of thought. Hampl challenges two of our most cherished beliefs: that writers always know precisely what they're talking about and that our minds have immediate access to the events of our past lives. Thus, it's possible to understand what Hampl is getting at in this essay and still feel cheated by her admission. The point is that Hampl is holding truth to a higher standard. It's not enough for her to offer a factually accurate picture of what happened: she wants to discover the meaning of her experiences; she wants to understand why a particular person, event, or experience lingered in her memory.

2. Hampl's ally in this quest is the writing process. The story of Sister Olive is, by Hampl's admission, only a "first draft." In putting it together, she gives her imagination free rein. She doesn't censor or correct anything, because she doesn't want to impose any "preconceived notions" on her experience. When drafting, her aim is to keep "moving" so she can begin to discover what the memory wants to say — not what she thinks it ought to say. The first draft exists, according to Hampl, in order to help her "discover" her real purpose as a writer. It allows her to explore "the mysterious relationship between all the images" that lurk in her memory and to probe the "impacted feelings" associated with them. Her job as a writer is "Stalking the relationship, seeking the congruence between stored image and hidden emotion." Once she begins to see the pattern of significance that emerges from this first draft, she can begin to plan a revision of her essay. The rough draft helps her frame questions about the experience that she will then explore in future drafts, and as she continues to write, she may add, delete, or refocus details as she sees fit. There is, thus, no clear distinction between memory and imagination, in Hampl's opinion. Memory relies on imagination as a way of communicating from the past to the present: the mind relies on imagination to grasp the real significance of past events.

3. As she rereads her first draft, Hampl realizes that Sister Olive and the piano lesson may not, in fact, be its most central ideas or images. Reflecting back through this imaginative re-creation of the experience, she begins to suspect that her father is the real focus of this memory, and she hints that the feeling of being buried under all the images of red books, opera hats, and competitive classmates is inadequacy — or, perhaps, envy. The next draft, she suggests, might thus involve a total "re-vision," a completely different retelling of this experience, focusing, we assume, more directly on her father and why she, as a child, may have grown up feeling that her life wasn't sufficiently "remarkable."

4. Each draft offers Hampl the chance to establish a new relationship between her present self and a past self, between what she terms her "narrative self" and her "reflective self." Hampl sees writing as a means of entering into an intimate relationship with such past selves. That's why it requires time, attention, and effort. Your present self can't simply speak for the selves of your past; you have to explore them until they reveal the truth that they contain. The key to our past selves lurks, for Hampl, in the concrete details we remember and in the ones we invent. She sees such "touchstones" — such things as the red music book and her fascination with Sister Olive's name and "gleaming face" — as symbols that have the power to transport her back to the past. Memory

uses these symbols as a way of encoding the feelings we experience in relation to past events. To interpret these symbols is thus to recapture the feeling associated with it, and this gives us insight into the person we once were. The lessons that Hampl offers here about writing, thus, might include the idea that composition always involves discovery, in that the writer's present reflective self never has immediate access to the thoughts and feelings of past selves, that this process must be as free, unconstrained, and unjudgmental as possible to promote the emergence of new meanings and ideas, and that all writing — even writing about the factual past — is inherently creative.

5. Hampl also believes that writing from memory is inherently political. When we write about experiences, we create alternative visions of the past, in Hampl's view. We make the past plural and "accept the humble position of writing a version rather than the whole truth." This is liberating for Hampl, because when the past is seen as a series of potential versions, no one version can be true and no one person can "own" the past and control it for political purposes. Hampl also believes that writing a memoir is important because the act of remembering creates not merely a self but a world. We invent the world when we remember it. If we stop writing down our memories — if we cease being "pilgrims" in search of our own personal truths — then we will "have no life." All of our experiences and all the feelings and ideas associated with them will be lost.

Further Explorations

1. Schacter would likely agree with Hampl's general perspective on memory. He would probably identify the symbolic "touchstone" details that play such a key role in Hampl's writing process with "engrams" — the traces of experience left behind in memory. Hampl expands on these memory traces by elaborating and interpreting them with the help of her imagination, much as Schacter's paleontologist assembles a whole dinosaur from a small collection of the bone fragments. Schacter would also likely agree that although personal memories aren't exactly fictions, they aren't verbatim transcripts of experience. What we remember, as Schacter notes again and again, depends on who we are and what we know. Thus, no one version of a past event could possibly capture the richness of experience of all those who participated in it. Hampl's writing process also finds support in Schacter's analysis of the mechanics of memory. When Hampl elaborates on the key details she recalls from an experience, she isn't fabricating lies, she's actually elaborating on a cue that will lead her to further discoveries about the past. According to Schacter, the subjective experience of memory unites a present cue with the traces of a past experience to form something that's wholly new — what he calls the "recollective experience." This seems to be precisely what Hampl does when she journeys through her elaborated memories in search of the truth that they contain.

2. The kind of symbol or "touchstone" that plays such an important role in writing from memory for Hampl also shows up prominently in Sanders and Eiseley. The obvious touchstone in Sanders is his hammer, although other things might be seen as fulfilling this function as well in this selection. Indeed, one touchstone detail that Sanders mentions but perhaps could explore more thoroughly is contained in the early recollection of seeing and listening to his grandfather hammering nails on a distant roof. There's something haunting about this passage, suggesting that there's more to it than simply the memory of having learned about the relative speed of sound and light. The touchstones in Eiseley are equally obvious — the most significant being the "non-existent tree." The entire purpose of "The Brown Wasps" is to unearth the meaning of this emblematic memory. In fact, Eiseley seems perfectly aware of the exploratory or archeological nature of writing about the past. Since neither Sanders nor Eiseley is about to confide in us concerning their own creative processes, as does Hampl, we can only speculate about which details they may have invented in these selections. It's possible, for instance, that Sanders made up the story about hitting his thumb to provide a framework for his essay and to give concrete expression to the pain he felt when his father died. This detail seems almost too perfectly suited to his purpose as a writer to be an accurate reflection of real-

ity. There's no doubt, though, about the hammer itself: it seems too central to Sanders's identity to have been made up from whole cloth. In the same way, the cottonwood tree strikes us as absolutely real in Eiseley — even if it hardly ever existed in reality. But other details that Eiseley mentions might well be "lies" in Hampl's sense of the term. Was there really a little kid on a bicycle outside Eiseley's childhood home when he returned to it? Or is this an invention, a reflection of the child he was sixty years earlier when he planted the tree with his father? Similar questions might be raised about other details in Eiseley's memoir. It might even be wondered if he actually ever saw a specific group of elderly homeless people spending the night in one of the great Eastern stations, as he claims, or whether he constructed this memory from his general knowledge of urban train stations because it fit his touchstone memory of the tree so well.

3. Eiseley's essay invites this kind of speculation, because it was clearly conceived as a kind of journey or pilgrimage toward a truth hidden in the past. Eiseley doesn't simply explain the meaning of the nonexistent tree to us or tell us what he felt about it; he carries us back, from memory to memory, uncovering different layers of significance and emotion as he moves down the "river" of time. Indeed, we get the feeling that each individual memory Eiseley explores in this piece is a kind of "draft" — one more attempt to capture and come to terms with the emotions he felt when he first saw the homeless people featured in the essay's introduction.

4. There are also strong connections between Hampl's notion of narrative and reflective selves and Susan Engel's concepts of remembered and remembering selves. Like Hampl, Engel believes that memory isn't simply a matter of transcription. Even the casual memories that we entertain in our daily lives are constructed, in Engel's view. Indeed, as she sees it, we function as writers in relation to our past selves: "We dig out, amplify, and create autobiographical material as a way to know and communicate who we are now."

5. Memory, for Engel, is thus also an imaginative or creative process. In fact, in Engel's view, not only do we elaborate on the details of our lives in pursuit of self-understanding, we shape our recollections to meet the needs of our present social context. We are constantly involved in adjusting and detailing our memories to fit the notion of who we ought to be. It's here that Hampl might part ways with Engel. Hampl sees the present "reflective" self as trying, through the art of memoir, to establish a relationship of intimacy with past selves. Imagination, for Hampl, comes into play as a tool that helps to facilitate the process of self-discovery. Engel, by contrast, believes that the present self selects, edits, and creates past selves for present purposes. Imagination, in her view, acts as a kind of mental "spin doctor" who is constantly trying to revise the image of our past selves so that they will conform with our current sense of who we should be.

Essay Options

Essay Options #1 and 2 give students the chance to experiment with the kind of constructive recollection and recursive writing process that Hampl discusses in her essay.

1. Have students return to the freewriting that they did for the Before Reading activity and ask them to analyze it the way she does her own first draft. What "touchstone" details do they note in this memory of an early childhood educational experience? What additional details might they include in a subsequent draft? What themes or feelings begin to emerge from this experience as they reflect on their initial recollections?

2. Essay Option #2 uses a childhood photo as a cue, but it can be approached in much the same way as Option #1. The purpose behind both assignments is to encourage students to be both experimental and exploratory in their writing, as well as to help them begin to see revision as a process of discovery and not simply as a matter of simple correction.

3. The idea that memoir is an attempt to create a world as well as a self should resonate for students who have read Sanders, Eiseley, and Lopez. Sanders clearly wants to recreate the safe, straightforward boyhood world of his family — a world where every

wall is plumb, every corner square, and every man on the level. The world evoked by Lopez's memoir of his hands is also a man's domain, but it's one marked by adventure rather than by domesticity. His emphasis is on skill and its application in the world of nature and in the world of art. The question of the world that Eiseley creates is more problematic. It might, in fact, be argued that Eiseley doesn't create a particular place so much as he undermines all sense of place and permanency in his essay. By the end of "The Brown Wasps," the reader must feel that all memories may be founded on "illusion" and that our attempts to cling to the past are as doomed as the blind man's effort to rediscover the entrance of the subway that lives in his memory. Yet, perhaps this is world enough for Eiseley. By inviting us to share his perspective on things, Eiseley also helps us to see how equal and essentially related we all really are. Viewed from the ever-moving vantage of time, we are connected to one another by our desire to cling to what we know and what makes us feel safe.

4. Essay Option #4 may be assigned as a brief informal assignment or as a journal entry. This topic gives students the chance to think about and compare notes on their own writing processes. It also invites them to think about how their approach to writing differs according to the nature of the writing task. You'll probably return to this theme throughout your course, but Hampl's discussion of her own creative process makes this a logical time for students to engage in some serious self-analysis. Do your students spend much time pre-writing their essays? Do they see writing, as Hampl does, as a process of discovery? As a journey? Or do they see it as a matter of transcribing what they already know? What specific problems have they encountered in preparing to write in academic situations? Who in the class has the most elaborate writing process? How did it develop? Once you begin exploring this topic in class, you'll probably want to return to it after every future assignment to chart how students experiment with or develop their own approaches to composing.

SUSAN ENGEL, *Then and Now: Creating a Self Through the Past* (p. 192)

Susan Engel is a psychologist with a writer's eye for the role that imagination plays in everyday life. Engel's analysis of how we creatively shape and reshape our memories to accommodate our changing self-image carries this chapter's discussion of the construction of the past one very significant step farther. It is one thing, after all, to say that we build up the present experience of memory by combining elements of the present with traces of the past, as does Schacter, or to say that we elaborate on our memories of the past in order to discover our true past selves, as does Hampl, but it's entirely another to suggest that we literally re-create who we are in response to the exigencies of the present moment. Reading Engel is a must, then, if you are planning to have students pursue themes related to the social construction of the past or the accuracy of personal memory. Think about pairing this selection with Hampl. Engel provides plenty of analytic concepts that can be applied to Hampl and to other readings earlier in the text. Or, if you choose, pair it with Kingston. Engel also links in critical ways with selections in Chapter 3 on the theme of multiple selves. You may find that some students will balk at the dialogue suggested in the Before Reading assignment. Some, of course, will have no trouble at all with this idea. Students who've gone through a major personal crisis of some sort — like that involved in changing peer group affiliation — won't have too much trouble with it. But a few may insist that they're the "same person" they've always been. The idea of having a clear identity — of knowing who you are — is so strong in contemporary American culture that some students may find it difficult to think of having had any other self than the one they obviously have in the present. To help them out, you might want to suggest that the difference between past and present selves might be as simple as the difference between who they are today and who they were at the age of five. Even those who are most committed to the ideology of authenticity will agree that they've changed in fundamental ways since childhood. The best responses to this exercise, however, usually involve present and past selves that conflict in some significant way. Ask students to explore the circumstances that led to this change in their lives, and have them reflect on what external forces or expectations may have influenced or led to this transformation.

Exploring the Text

1. According to Engel, our present identity results from the complex interaction of our present situation and our memories of the past. We all serve as "personal historian" to ourselves. We create autobiographies that provide our lives with a sense of meaning and coherence and that also help to justify who we currently are. As children, we hear and repeat stories told about us by parents, siblings, and friends, and in so doing we create a self "in collaboration" with others. We adopt these stories, repeat them, and embellish them, but we don't actively reflect on them or understand how they relate to who we are in the present — at least not until the age of roughly twelve, when children begin to become aware of their own memory processes. It's at about this time that we develop what the psychologist Ulric Neisser terms an "extended self." This is the consciously held concept of a self that exists over time — the subjective experience of being an "I."

2. When we look back at past selves from the perspective of the "I," we take what Engel calls a "bifocal view" of the past. We see ourselves in the present as a "remembering self" and simultaneously we see ourselves represented in memory as a "remembered self." Our remembering self is an expression of our extended self, or of what Engel calls our "self for self." It is the result of the life story that we've settled on to make sense of who we are in the world and to provide us with a stable or continuous identity. For Engel, this "self for self" is itself a construct, yet it is as close as we get to having an authentic identity. This is the self we actually believe ourselves to be. We also present a particular version of our self to others in the present. We create this "face" or "persona" in response to the expectations of others or to achieve some particular end. Thus, one might act the part of the dutiful child in the presence of one's parents in order to win their approval and still assume the role of rebel in the presence of friends to come across as an exciting peer. Remembered selves are always "selves for others" because they are shaped by our desire to project a particular identity. The remembered self is always conditioned by the present situation of remembering — by the social context we remember in, the audience we remember for, and the motives that underlie our reason for remembering. "We are," as Engel says, "always remembering in the company of others."

3. When our actions threaten to contradict our extended self-concept, we engage in what is known as "cognitive dissonance reduction." That is, we actively reshape past events in our minds so that they will support our positive self-concept. Thus, a smoker who sees himself as "smart" rationalizes his self-destructive habit either by rejecting anti-smoking research or by seeing himself as someone who lives his life on his own terms. According to Engel, two opposing forces shape our recollections of the self in the past: on one hand, we reshape the selves we recall in order to make them conform to our dominant self-concept and thereby reduce cognitive dissonance; on the other, we reshape our past selves in response to different social situations. The past selves we recall result from the interplay of these two powerful motives. Of course, the distinction that underlies this supposed paradox — the difference between self for self and self for others — may in fact be only a matter of semantics. Isn't our present self-concept often constructed in response to external pressures and expectations? In what substantial way, then, does it differ from the self we present to others? And when we attempt to reduce cognitive dissonance, aren't we also trying to "save face" with those who surround us?

4. A "template memory," according to Engel, is one that stands for "a whole strand of feeling or events in one's life." Often, such template memories represent a whole host of unresolved feelings that we have trouble confronting directly. In this respect, a template memory resembles a "screen memory" — a relatively bland memory that conceals some deeper feeling or emotion. Such memories — often conveying a sense of distur-

bance or something unexplained — represent conflicts or unresolved themes that run throughout a person's life. Owing to the sense of "irresolution" they contain, they may force themselves repeatedly into consciousness. Engel's memory of being miserable after having her tonsils out at the age of five illustrates this kind of template or screen memory. It troubled her for years, but it was only after she had to make a difficult job decision as an adult that she realized it really represented having to choose between her mother and her father. Unlocking the meaning of such template memories is, thus, an important tool for learning more about past and present selves.

Further Explorations

1. Since students may have trouble discussing their own "screen memories" and such in class, you'll probably want to mine some of the personal memoirs you've already covered in class for illustrations of the concepts that Engel examines in this essay. Lopez, Sanders, Eiseley, and Hampl all present relatively clearly identifiable images of their past or remembered selves. Lopez portrays himself as an intellectual man of action. The past image he projects of himself is that of a man who has worked hard, lived close to nature, and reflected deeply on the meanings of his experiences. It's the way you might expect one of the country's premier nature writers to portray himself. Sanders also comes across as a relatively physical type, but he places more emphasis on the domestic side of his nature and less on the intellectual than does Lopez. Indeed, there seems to be less distance between the remembering and remembered selves of Sanders than there is for Lopez. Lopez's identity seems split, as if the intellectual side of him were looking back on a rough-and-tumble kid in the past. It's almost as if he were describing his younger brother. Sanders's remembering self, by contrast, seems very close if not identical to the self he presents in the past. Interestingly enough, Eiseley offers little direct self-portrayal in "The Brown Wasps." A scientist by training, he seems more comfortable observing from a distance. Still, the essay does convey a strong image of its author, at least by implication. From the things that attract his attention, his observations about them, and the kinds of connections he makes, you might get the impression that Eiseley's a thoughtful person, a keen observer, and a lover of nature with a philosophical bent. Whether this is the "real" Loren Eiseley or a persona constructed for professional purposes, however, is another matter. Hampl's remembered self comes across clearly: she's a reluctant musician with an eye for telling details, who willingly and rather pathetically accepts her fate as "second fiddle" to her domineering best friend. But this remembered self is not at all like Hampl's remembering self, which comes across as straightforward, sharp-minded, and self-confident enough to take on topics such as the truth and the politics of memory without the slightest qualm. In fact, Mary Katherine Reilly never really did dominate her, and once we've met her in the second half of the essay, we can easily see why. She wants us to pity — and perhaps even to chuckle at — the pathetic schoolgirl she shows us in her original memoir. She casts herself as a forlorn figure — a girl consumed by desire for something that's out of her grasp — yet she herself is clearly a woman who knows how to get what she wants — particularly if it's the truth that lies buried deep in her own experience.

2. There are also clear connections between Engel's basically psychoanalytic understanding of memory and Schacter's cognitive approach. Both believe that memory "doubles" our view of life by overlaying past and present perspectives. For Schacter, however, the stereoscopic effect of memory involves a true fusion of past and present. When the cue, or present stimulus, connects with the engram or fragment of memory that remains in the mind, the result is something entirely different — a recollective experience that is neither wholly of the present nor of the past. For Engel, our recollection of the past is always shaped by immediate concerns. Although Engel does acknowledge the role of our past selves in helping to determine the outlines of our "extended self," she ultimately looks to the present as the force that shapes the past. Memory is, thus, not so much a matter of the fusion of past and present as it is a revision of the past through the perspective of the self's present social context.

3. The concept of the "template memory" does find clear support, however, in both Eiseley and Hampl. Eiseley's cottonwood tree and Hampl's unsatisfying first musical experience with Sister Olive both perfectly fulfill the definition of a memory that haunts the rememberer because it embodies a set of unresolved issues or themes. Eiseley's cottonwood grows in memory throughout his life, yet he admits that returning home to see it after sixty years is an "act of madness." In some sense, all of the memories that Eiseley offers are screen memories. The memory of the nonexistent tree, however, is clearly a template experience. For Eiseley, the theme is the need for a sense of place — the need for security — in a world constantly threatened by change. For Hampl, the theme is finally getting what she always wanted. It may be the red book or a famous grandfather, but, as she suggests, it probably has to do with her violin-playing father. Was there something in him that she found wanting? Some spark of the "remarkable" that never surfaced in his life or in his relationship with her? Again, Hampl's experience with Sister Olive might be seen as a screen memory in that it may indirectly represent an experience or feeling that is too potentially painful or unacceptable for her to confront more directly. Both concepts, however, would seem less applicable to Sanders and Lopez. Neither of these authors fixates on a single moment in the way that Hampl and Eiseley do, and neither associates any particular mystery or unresolved feeling with any of the their memories.

4. It is far easier, in fact, to apply Engel's thinking to the multiple personae that Maxine Hong Kingston fashions for her aunt in "No-Name Woman." Kingston offers several different portrayals of her aunt in this family memoir. She sees her as an innocent raped by a fellow villager, as a girl who gives in to a moment of temptation, as a "wild woman" who indulges her own desires freely, as an individualist trapped in a traditional society, as a secret conspirer, as a spoiled daughter, and as a heroine who turns an ignominious death into a protest. All of these personae seem to attract her, probably because they each express some aspect of her own present self-image. She seems particularly drawn, however, to the image of her aunt as social rebel and feminist hero — again most likely because these are roles that set her against the role of women as taught within her family.

5. Given Eviatar Zerubavel's theory of "impersonal memory," it may even be possible to apply personal concepts such as cognitive dissonance and the extended self to issues of national identity. A nation, like a person, develops a coherent sense of self over time by selectively listening to the stories that are told about it, rehearsing some and censoring or forgetting others. This "extended identity" gives the nation a sense of coherence and continuity — even if it relies primarily on a series of historical fictions. Thus, the United States, like most nations, has a long history of selective self-presentation. For decades, the United States saw itself as a nation set apart by destiny, as the home of equality, justice, and opportunity for all, with a heavenly mandate to pursue its "manifest destiny." Events such as World War II, the Vietnam War, and the civil rights movement, however, might be seen as generating a nationwide case of cognitive dissonance by contradicting many of the beliefs associated with America's dominant national self-image. The result, as Engel would predict, has at times been a massive effort of historical revision. Today, despite the horrors that all sides engaged in during World War II, the tendency in the United States is again to see ourselves as relatively innocent victims of foreign powers — particularly in recent mass-market films such as *Saving Private Ryan* and *Pearl Harbor.* In the same way, the civil rights movement has been revised today to erase much of the nationwide racism that was a fact of life during the century after the Civil War. Indeed, it's possible to watch any number of popular films or television specials on the civil rights movement and come away with the impression that whites played an important role in places such as Selma and Montgomery and that the opposition was limited to a few dozen badly behaved Klansmen. Such historical revisionism makes it possible for America to reduce cognitive dissonance and maintain its extended identity.

Essay Options

1. Essay Option #1 gives students the chance to apply Engel's distinction between remembering and remembered selves to a paper they've already written in response to an assignment in this chapter. Students may find that it's actually easier to apply these ideas to their own work than it is for them to speculate about the motives of the essayists they've been reading, since they may have a better grasp of the motives that underlay their own self-portrayals. Of course, the question of audience has special meaning here: students should consider how their self-portrayals may have been influenced by the fact that they were writing for you, their English instructor. To extend this assignment, you may want to ask them to revise the same memory, this time directing it to a different audience with different values and expectations.

2. Essay Option #2 sets up a traditional text-based paper on the topic of template memories. Students can draw material for this paper from their class discussion of Further Explorations #3 and 4. The only real challenge here is the extension of the idea of template memories to Kingston. The story of Kingston's aunt haunts her in much the same way that the memory of a nonexistent tree lingers in Eiseley's mind or the recollection of that spectacular opera-hat-inventing grandfather sticks with Hampl. Thus, it might be seen as a kind of "impersonal" template memory — one that is inherited with the other family memories that Kingston learns from her mother. It also functions in much the same way as a personal template memory in that it represents a complex of unresolved themes for Kingston (the conflict between her family's traditional cultural values and her own independent American values, for instance), and it establishes a theme that may shape her own self-image. Thus, we see traces of what may be her own emerging identity in the multiple versions that she offers of her aunt's story.

MAXINE HONG KINGSTON, *No-Name Woman* (p. 206)

Selections from Maxine Hong Kingston's *The Woman Warrior: Memoirs of a Girlhood Among Ghosts* have been a staple in composition classrooms since the book first appeared in 1975. Most often, the selection that's featured involves Kingston's own early educational experiences. This selection usually enters composition texts in relation to themes of traditional women's roles and male domination. I think it takes on new significance, however, when considered in connection with the theme of memory — and particularly in connection with the notions of past and present selves, as presented by Patricial Hampl and Susan Engel, in the two previous selections. Kingston can be assigned as a paired reading with Engel, or, if your class is up to the workload, Hampl, Engel, and Kingston can be assigned and discussed productively in a single extended class session on the topic of "remembering and remembered selves." If you plan to stress the theme of "impersonal memories," you may want to group Kingston, instead, with Zerubavel and/or hooks, the two selections that follow. This selection also offers the chance for an excellent personal writing assignment focused on re-telling a family story (EO #1). This bit of creative revision of a family legend is often a hit with students. The Before Reading activity encourages students to begin thinking about specific stories that have been told and retold in their own families. Most families have at least one great family story about an aunt, a grandfather, or a past family friend who did something either remarkably bad or good — something that either was the occasion of stunning success or terrible misfortune. Have students freewrite about these family legends in their journals and perhaps even share a few in small groups before you begin reading Kingston's radical revision of the story of her aunt.

Exploring the Text

1. Kingston's mother tells her the short version of her aunt's story. It might be summarized as follows:

In 1924, Kingston's father's sister stayed behind in China while her new husband went off to seek his fortune in the United States. One day after he left, her mother noticed that her aunt was pregnant. No one said anything at the time. When her aunt was about to deliver the child, everyone in the village realized that it could not be her husband's, so on the night the baby was born, the villagers came to her family's house in white masks and attacked them. The villagers threw mud and rocks, killed their animals, broke down their doors, and destroyed or carried away their belongings and clothes. Later, Kingston's aunt gave birth in a pigsty. The next morning, her mother found her aunt's body and the baby plugging the well. No one ever spoke of her again, and she was forgotten.

This grim tale, told almost this succinctly, was meant as a warning to the adolescent Kingston about the dangers of premarital sex and the risks of humiliating her parents. It was offered as a way of strengthening her and protecting her against the evils that her mother associated with life in America. But for Kingston, her mother's cautionary tales are only a source of confusion. They serve only to make her question her own relation to traditional Chinese culture. She resists this particular story by retelling it in her own distinctive way.

2. As she begins to tell her own version of her aunt's story, Kingston reflects on the realities of village life in early-twentieth-century China. In the social context in which her aunt grew up, "adultery is extravagance." The subsistence economics of village life argue against the idea that her aunt was a "romantic." Instead, Kingston assumes that her pregnancy was the result of rape, because "[w]omen in old China did not choose." Kingston underscores the subservience of women by noting that her assailant may not have bothered to mask himself when he joined the other villagers in their raid against her family. Furthermore, although his demand for sex would have shocked her, she would have obeyed him, because she had been trained to submit to men. Indeed, marriage itself in those days wasn't much different from rape, in Kingston's eyes: "The other man was not, after all, much different from her husband." Still, Kingston herself seems divided in her judgments about these villagers. She is clearly repulsed by their backwardness, particularly in relation to the unjust and sexist treatment of her aunt. But she also seems to comprehend their motivation. In the "commensal tradition" that ruled village life, no departure from the norm could be tolerated. Kingston, thus, understands why her aunt's example frightened her fellow villagers, even if she condemns their response. Indeed, at times Kingston even seems to take pride in the toughness of these simple village ancestors of hers. These were people who had to cope with "ghost plagues, bandit plagues, wars with the Japanese, [and] floods." They had no time to sympathize with rebelliousness.

3. In trying to explain her aunt's behavior to herself, Kingston spins out several different versions of her story. Initially, she thinks that it must have been rape and that her aunt had simply submitted to the desire of a dominant male, because her aunt's backward village culture left her no other choice. However, Kingston soon moves beyond this passive portrayal of her aunt and re-envisions her "forerunner" as a romantic dreamer rebelling against the killing routine of village life. This aunt sacrifices home and security for "a charm that vanished with tiredness." Then, she sees her aunt as "a wild woman" who lives free and keeps "rollicking company." But Kingston rejects this image, because she can't imagine any woman being so free with sex. The next image of her aunt that she entertains is that of an independent individualist. In this embodiment, Kingston's aunt spends hours peering into her mirror, tending to her appearance and thinking about how she could attract her lover. Absorbed by her own self-image, her aunt refuses to resemble other Chinese women, who "looked like great sea snails" carrying loads of wood, babies, and laundry on their backs. She rebels against collectivity and curses "the family, the village, and herself." In Kingston's imagination, her aunt is next transformed into a temptress who drives her kinsmen out of the house because they feared "that their glances, like a field of nesting birds, might be startled and caught" by her beauty. Then she becomes the favorite daughter and an honored child — a girl so beloved by her family that she actually displaces her brother at the family table.

4. After the attack of the villagers, she changes once again. Now she becomes a heroic figure. Cast out of village life and excluded from tradition, tribe, and culture, she "got on her feet to fight better and remembered that old-fashioned women gave birth in

their pigsties to fool the jealous, pain-dealing gods." Kingston's aunt emerges from her niece's retelling of her story as a defiant loner, a woman who stands up against her family, community, culture — even her gods. Going to the pigsty is "a last act of responsibility." Heroically, she takes the name of her baby's father to the grave and she takes her child with her — not out of shame, as in her mother's version of the story, but to spare it further suffering. Carrying her baby into death with her also becomes an act of feminine solidarity for Kingston, since the child "must have been" a girl, considering that there is always "some hope of forgiveness for boys." This final version of her aunt's story may be the most satisfying for Kingston and her readers, but students may well wonder if it's the most plausible. Kingston's first conjecture is probably still the most realistic. Her aunt was, more likely than not, a typical Chinese village girl who had the misfortune of attracting the attention of a village male and was forced to submit to his superior social power. Certainly, if told from the perspective of the village, the story of Kingston's aunt would be quite different. Most likely it would resemble the cautionary tale that her mother originally tells. Or it's possible that Kingston's aunt would have been portrayed as a degenerate who seduced some young man and wasn't intelligent enough to realize that she would have to pay the consequences. The villagers probably would have viewed her suicide as an admission of guilt and a sign that she could not live with the shame of her actions.

5. Interestingly enough, the only shame that Kingston sees in the whole episode seems to be attached to her family's deliberate "forgetting" of her aunt. This, she suggests, inflicted a kind of suffering that pursued her aunt even after death. And it's the threat of such ostracism that Kingston herself clearly fears when she considers her own ambivalent attitude toward her Chinese background. Kingston's aunt haunts her. The story of her rebellion and punishment pursues her as she tries to navigate her path between American independence and traditional Chinese values. Indeed, memory and the past are not neutral concepts for Kingston: the past constantly threatens to overwhelm the reality of the present. Memory and past are like the ghosts of the drowned who wait, according to Chinese legend, to pull an unsuspecting substitute down to a watery grave.

Further Explorations

1. It's relatively easy to speculate about which of the details that Kingston includes in her revision of her aunt's story are based on fact and which are probably "lies" invented à la Hampl. Her mother's initial telling of the story is the closest thing we have to a "fact-based" version. Almost every detail that Kingston adds is based either on her general knowledge of Chinese family culture or on her own understanding of what it's like to be a young woman stuck in a traditional society. Thus, she goes into considerable detail about her aunt's toilet and her depilatory techniques, but these are borrowed from the practices she's seen in her own family. Her insights into her aunt's thoughts and motives come, we assume, from reading her own thoughts and feelings — although some aspects might also derive from other depictions of heroic young women. It's hard not to think of figures such as Antigone and Medea during Kingston's account of her aunt's final moments.

2. The heroic nature of this final image of Kingston's aunt clearly reflects the way she thinks of herself in relation to traditional Chinese culture. As a kind of remembered self, this final version might be seen as a model of resistance and as a warning to Kingston's remembering self. Kingston explores a number of personae for her aunt in her multiple revisions of this story. Initially she portrays her aunt as a passive victim of male oppression, but even though this may present the most probable scenario, given the historical and cultural context, Kingston rejects it and experiments with other possibilities. Each of these personae, we assume, reflects some aspect of Kingston's own present identity. Thus, she can accept the notion of her aunt as a bored romantic or as an individualist, but she rejects the possibility of seeing her as a sexual adventurer. The final image of her aunt as heroic outsider seems to express the anxiety and ambivalence that she herself feels about being

Chinese. Kingston herself may want to curse family, culture, and tradition, but she can do so only by risking significant aspects of her own identity. This is why Kingston can also sympathize to a certain extent with the villagers who destroy her aunt. Looking back on the past, she sees herself allied to both positions: she is both part of the village and at one with her rebellious aunt. Thus, she suffers from her own brand of cognitive dissonance. She craves independence, but at the same time she's aware that being too American is an occasion for guilt and perhaps even for cultural ostracism. That's why she comes away from the heroic retelling of her aunt's story not inspired but frightened.

3. According to Eviatar Zerubavel, the social and cultural environment in which we grow up helps to determine what we remember and what we forget. Our "mnemonic socialization" inculcates a particular "tradition" of remembering in each of us, and our families play a critical part in this socialization process. Because of this fact, we each must expend considerable mental effort, in Zerubavel's view, "trying to 'reclaim' our own personal recollections from our parents or older siblings." Kingston's retelling of her aunt's story might, then, be seen as exactly this kind of personal reclamation project. Kingston offers a countermemory against the official story of her aunt's death. By recasting her aunt as a tragic figure, she engages in a one-woman "mnemonic battle" and rewrites the collective memory of her family. Of course, the very act of retelling also binds her to her cultural heritage. The ultimate act of individual liberation would, perhaps, have been simply to have forgotten her aunt as her family did — not out of shame but out of the kind of forced cultural amnesia that sometimes afflicts second-generation immigrants.

Essay Options

1. If you haven't already assigned a personal essay at this point in your work on memory — or if you want to follow up with another solid personal topic — you should consider Essay Option #1. This assignment is more challenging than it might appear to be at first glance. Most students will be able to come up with a few serviceable family stories, but exploring them in the kind of creative way that the assignment calls for poses a challenge. The best papers written in response to this assignment always involve stories that do, in fact, haunt students at some level. It may be a cautionary tale about an aunt or uncle or the story of a rebellious older brother or sister — but it should be one that students connect with at a visceral level.

2. Essay Option #2 offers the foundation for a comprehensive academic essay on the topic of the politics of memory. You'll probably want to finish Zerubavel and perhaps even hooks before attempting — or completing — this assignment. The notion of the politics of memory suggests that every act of memory involves struggle or resistance against some dominant cultural force. It also suggests that forgetting itself is a political act that works to the advantage of the dominant social order. Nearly every selection in this chapter connects with these ideas at some level. Hampl lays out the argument for a politics of memory. Eiseley's meditation on homelessness and the dispossessed has obvious political implications. Kingston's revision of her aunt's story can be read as an individual act of resistance against cultural traditions that stifle individuality and limit women's aspirations. Zerubavel and hooks both address the struggles that surround our collective representations of the past. Both also address the way that given "thought traditions" silence those who lose "mnemonic battles." Before you begin work on this topic, you may also want to screen either Akira Kurosawa's *Rashomon* or the film version of Ariel Dorfman's *Death and the Maiden,* as suggested in FE #5 associated with Zerubavel. *Death and the Maiden* is particularly interesting in relation to the issue of politics, in that it raises questions about how we should remember past acts of political injustice and state terror.

EVIATAR ZERUBAVEL, *Social Memories* (p. 217)

This isn't the most inspired piece of prose in *Mind Readings,* but it does raise issues that are well worth covering in class. Zerubavel is a cognitive sociologist working in the tradition of George Herbert Meade and Erving Goffman, and his style is classically academic. So, don't expect to find much in the way of poetry in these pages. But the ideas he introduces — such as the concepts of "thought communities," "mnemonic socialization," "mnemonic battles," and "impersonal memory" — are extremely valuable if you are exploring the social construction or the politics of memory in your class. You'll want to use Zerubavel as a key selection in the clusters of readings associated with these two themes. If, however, you have only a limited amount of time, you may want to pair him with either Kingston or hooks on the theme of resisting historical memory. Like Engel, this selection connects well with several readings in Chapter 3 on the theme of reading the self, and you'll also find that it shows up as well in Chapter 4 in relation to the notion of reading other minds. The Before Reading activity associated with Zerubavel, broadly inspired by E. D. Hirsch, asks students to create an inventory of historical facts that every American ought to know as part of our nation's "collective memory." Obviously, you can't expect students to offer exhaustive lists of famous people, places, events, facts, and dates. But they should be able to generate at least some examples of the kinds of information every American should know. The purpose, naturally, is to begin questioning why we would include particular bits of information in this list and why other bits would be excluded. Who is to say what every American should know? Should we remember the Pilgrims, the Boston Tea Party, 1776, the Alamo, Pearl Harbor, the *Maine,* the Marne, Mai Lai, Hiroshima, the Trail of Tears, Wounded Knee, Selma, John Brown, the Thirteenth Amendment to the Constitution, Manzanar, AZTLAN, Washington, Lincoln, Edison, Reagan, Marshall, Twain, Hemingway, Hughes, Ellington, Morrison, Elvis, and Michael Jackson? Is it really so important that we, as citizens of the same country, all share a particular set of memories?

Exploring the Text

1. Although we tend to think of ourselves as "mnemonic Robinson Curusoes," as Zerubavel reminds us in this essay, even our most personal memories take place within a social context. Memories aren't formed in a "social vacuum," according to Zerubavel. On the contrary, we tend to remember the public events along with others. Most adults, for example, remember events like the death of Princess Diana or the impeachment of Bill Clinton. A large part of our memory is devoted to such commonly held public recollections. Yet, even our private memories are social in nature. As children we "learn" some of our most fundamental personal memories from our parents, siblings, and other family members. We frequently depend on others to corroborate our own accounts of the past — or literally to remember for us, as when a wife reminds a husband about a forgotten acquaintance. As Zerubavel notes, the "mnemonic others" who populate the "remembrance environments" to which we belong would include all the people who are close to us — spouses, relatives, friends, teachers, coaches, clergy, and counselors whose opinions we trust and rely on. Clearly, just about anyone who occupies a position of authority or respect can play the part of mnemonic other. In fact, nowadays, it might be possible to think of certain mass media personalities in this light. Celebrity opinion makers and news media commentators, such as Oprah, Don Imus, and Rush Limbaugh may serve this mnemonic function by virtue of their ability to communicate their views of recent past events to a mass audience.

2. We also inhabit various "thought communities," according to Zerubavel, each with its own "rules of remembrance." Each thought community establishes its own "historical horizons" that tell its members what's included in its history and also tells them what to forget. Thus, in Israel, the Arab names of certain towns and locations are never mentioned in the media and are consequently excluded from memory, and in Islamic nations, A.D. 622 marks the beginning of "real" historical time. In much the same way, within the thought community of U.S. culture, for many years the "discovery" of America was believed to be 1492, thus "suppressing the memory of millions of Native Americans." Moreover, almost any social group with a sense of its own past or its own interpretive traditions might be seen as a thought community. Organizations such as the

Boy Scouts, the NAACP, the Daughters of the American Revolution, and the Catholic Church all have their own rules of remembrance. All nations obviously qualify as thought communities, as do well-defined geographical regions with strong cultural identities. For at least a century after the American Civil War, for example, the South promoted rules of remembrance that contradicted many of the traditions and beliefs commonly held in the North. Even major league sports associations might be seen as thought communities with their own history and mnemonic traditions. Most baseball fans, for example, can rattle off the dates of famous World Series match-ups — and even the years associated with some specific hits and plays. Every avid baseball fan "knows," for example, that the sport was invented by Abner Doubleday in Cooperstown, N.Y., despite the fact that the myth of Doubleday's creation of the game has been thoroughly discredited. Of course, Zerubavel's affection for concepts sometimes gets in the way of the fairly good points he's trying to make. Many of the "rules" of memory that he offers here are not really rules at all, in the sense of generalized formal procedures. Often, his examples are really beliefs or biases and not rules at all. Still, this doesn't seem to undermine his overall point — that every culture and subculture has its own way of interpreting the past and its own distinct set of memories.

3. The process by which we are educated into a specific mnemonic group or culture is "mnemonic socialization." We undergo mnemonic socialization whenever we join a new social environment, whether it's a new family, school, church, club, corporation, or country. Clearly, families and formal education play an important role in equipping us with the key memories we need as members of particular national, cultural, and religious groups. They — along with the media today — provide us with certain "script-like plot structures" that help us make sense of the events that fill our lives. Thus, the Zionist "script" of the "persecuted Jew" shapes the experiences of many Israelis, according to Zerubavel. These prefabricated scripts and roles promote a kind of "cognitive bias" because they prompt us to remember things selectively. We tend to remember what we are familiar with, and thus, these scripts prejudice us in favor of remembering things that conform to our expectations. When members of a liberal family reminisce about the 1960s, they might draw on the "script" of the radical, revolutionary free-thinker, who opposes the established, oppressive social order to promote social justice and other antiestablishment ideals. When members of a conservative family think back on the 1960s, they most likely resort to a script that features self-indulgent, drug-abusing, law-breaking hippies who did their best to undermine law and order and promote the cause of anarchy. Zerubavel thinks that all such formulaic approaches to the past are illogical and unnatural because they reflect the biases we inherit from our cultural contexts.

4. "Impersonal memories" include every recollection we have that is not the result of direct personal experience. We all, for example, remember events such as the Crucifixion, Pearl Harbor, and Columbus's voyage to the Americas, but none of us actually experienced them. As Zerubavel indicates, most of the historical events that occur during our own lifetimes also fall into this category. We may have lived during Operation Desert Storm or the Clinton-Lewinsky scandal, but few of us played a personal role in either event. The odd thing is that much of what we "remember" involves such impersonal experiences. And much of our personal identity depends on exactly this kind of impersonal recollection. Thus, if you're gay, the Stonewall riots may be an important part of your identity, even if you were only a few years old when they occurred, just as the music of Charlie Parker might spark specific memories if you're a jazz fan, despite the fact that he died before your birth. As Zerubavel suggests, being part of a social or cultural group involves the ability to experience that group's past as if it were part of your own. It is the "existential fusion" of one's personal past with the collective history of a group that makes the notion of cultural or group identity possible. Without this kind of "sociobiological memory," present-day Greeks would not feel pride in the accomplishments of their ancient forebears and African Americans would not feel solidarity with the suffering of their ancestors. Formal education obviously plays an important part in establishing this kind of cultural identity. Every time a child in elementary school

enacts the voyage of the Pilgrims on the *Mayflower* — or Rosa Parks's protest against moving to the back of the bus — she learns to "remember" this aspect of her cultural inheritance.

5. It's important also to note that "impersonal memories" are genuinely "collective" in the sense that they represent an "integration of various different personal pasts into a single common past that all members of a community come together to remember collectively." We "commemorate" the shared past cultural experiences that bind us into a single community. We remember such events together in ways that guarantee "synchronized access to [the] collective past." And because the way we remember the collective past is so important to personal and cultural identity, we often engage in what Zerubavel terms "mnemonic battles" over what we include in our mnemonic traditions. Thus, the inclusion of a national holiday commemorating the birth of Martin Luther King Jr. was a matter of debate during the 1980s and 1990s, and today we are still debating how to interpret collective events such as Watergate and the Vietnam War.

Further Explorations

1. College campuses are often rich in "mnemonic geography" — places that are filled with a sense of shared history and collective experience. This activity invites students to explore the mnemonic topography of your campus as a living illustration of how "thought communities" exploit the past as a source of collective identity. What monuments and statues on your campus commemorate past events and traditions? What collectively recalled stories are associated with particular locations, building, and sites?

2. Of course, it's quite possible to argue with Zerubavel's notion of "impersonal memory." After all, one might read Ian Frazier's description of what it's like to take the F train and to live in Brooklyn, but is that the same as having Frazier's memories of this experience? Isn't Zerubavel overlooking the difference between remembering an experience and merely knowing about it? It could be argued that the experience of actually living in Brooklyn on a daily basis can't be duplicated by reading or by any other form of learning because learning fails to reproduce the richness of lived experience in all of its sensory variety and depth. But, then, isn't it possible that Frazier's essay conveys a truer and more meaningful impression of life in Brooklyn than many people achieve even after a lifetime of F train commutes? Yet, wouldn't a Brooklyn native gain more from reading Frazier's essay than would a person who'd never been east of the Mississippi? The point, as you can see, is open to debate. It touches on fundamental issues of identity, experience, art, and cultural membership and can lead to some excellent opportunities for critical and creative thinking in class.

3. Sanders's "The Inheritance of Tools" also can be given a "Zerubavelian" treatment. Sanders's memories are divided between actual personal experiences (like that of hoarding sawdust in his father's garage) and experiences that he probably learned about through family stories (like the story about his grandfather's wedding). Overall, however, Sanders makes it clear that he places greater value on personal and family memory than he does on the kind of abstract cultural learning that you might acquire by watching television or even by going to college. He respects the layers of knowing that envelop his tools because they put him in direct contact with other human beings, and he dismisses news about tragedies in foreign lands because they don't really touch him and he can't do much about them.

4. But while Sanders might dispute the importance of "impersonal memory" for individual identity, Walker Percy would probably reject it out of hand. Formal education, cultural training, and indoctrination of all kinds are abhorrent to Percy, who believes that we can actually "see" the world around us only by confronting it directly without the aid of cultural mediation. In fact, all memory is suspect, in Percy's view. Even Percy's young Falkland Islander might lose his ability to "see" "the dogfish he encounters on the beach after the fourth or fifth time he happened to stumble on one." Every memory, personal or impersonal, represents a distraction from the thing in itself, for Percy, whereas

Zerubavel believes that we each rely on our "mnemonic communities" to make sense of our experiences.

5. For a break from Zerubavel and all of his sociological conceptualization, you might want to take the time to view either Akira Kurosawa's classic study of selective memory in *Rashomon* or the film adaptation of Ariel Dorfman's *Death and the Maiden*. Both of these films raise intriguing questions about the relation of personal and collective memories and about the kind of "mnemonic battles" that we engage in as we collectively try to interpret the past.

Essay Options

1. and 2. The first two Essay Options offer the chance for personal explorations of the notion of impersonal memories and their relation to various cultural communities to which students belong. The first is more limited and more easily managed than the second, which calls for a comparison between two different cultural groups. If you decide to have students write on a personal topic at this point, you may want to offer them the chance to choose either of these options. You certainly don't want to force them to analyze cultural groups with which they are not intimately familiar.

3. This topic can be approached as a kind of informal research assignment. Recent "mnemonic battles" have included the controversy over the use of Confederate flag imagery on official state symbols in Mississippi and South Carolina as well as the ongoing debate about the World War II memorial in Washington, D.C. You might also consider asking students to explore how our collective memory of events such as World War II and the Vietnam War appear to be changing in light of recent mass media representations of these events. Vietnam is particularly interesting in this regard, given the differences of tone and subject that distinguish films such as *Apocalypse Now, Platoon, Full Metal Jacket, Born on the Fourth of July,* and *Forrest Gump.*

4. This assignment offers another opportunity for a major academic assignment, this one synthesizing information from at least six selections on the theme of the reliability of memory. Most of the selections here present some reason to question or at least qualify the idea that memory offers an objective "transcript" of past events. You may want to have students do additional outside library or newspaper research on this topic, because the issue is regularly explored by the press in relation to the accuracy of eyewitness testimony in court cases.

BELL HOOKS, *Columbus: Gone But Not Forgotten* (p. 237)

This examination of the personal impact of the Columbus legend complements Zerubavel's discussion of the importance of historical memory. Bell hooks wrote this essay on the eve of the 500th anniversary of Columbus's "discovery" of the Americas. But while she focuses on the Columbus legend, her general point has to do with the way historical memories "haunt" and sometimes harm individuals who struggle with the legacy of oppression. Hooks is not easy for students to read. Her language is steeped in the tradition of radical feminist discourse, and students may have some trouble dealing with concepts that she takes for granted — the notion of "cultural capital," the "misogynistic masculine ideal," or "the institutionalized system of male gender domination." Generally, however, students who've read Zerubavel will have little trouble grasping the central outlines of hooks's argument. Her language may seem a bit odd, but her meaning and the feelings underlying it come across loud and clear. You'll probably want to pair this selection with Zerubavel as the basis for an assignment on the impact of historical memory. Alternatively, you can approach hooks as part of a cluster of selections leading to an essay on the way individuals resist and transform historical memories (EO #1) or as the point of departure for an informal research paper on the current state of the Columbus myth (EO #2 and 3). Have students begin, as suggested in the Before Reading activity, by collectively reflecting on how they were taught the story of

Columbus and the "discovery" of the Americas. Hooks acknowledges that some changes have already been made in the way schools portray Columbus and colonization, but it may be interesting to see if these pedagogical revisions have had much impact on student consciousness. It may also be interesting to see how students' experiences with the Columbus story compare. Does the version of the discovery story change depending on the school that students attended? How might they account for differences that they note between the various versions of the story?

Exploring the Text

1. Hooks begins her essay with a personal memory of her own — the story of how she felt one night after her doorbell rang and she met a "strange white man" standing outside her house. This little anecdote serves at least two functions. It illustrates the way in which the myth of Columbus literally "haunts" hooks, even to the present day. The legacy of Columbus is such that she still can't open the door to a white man without wondering what his intentions are or where this chance encounter might lead. This opening strategy also allows hooks to introduce what might be seen as a representation of her target audience. The white messenger is sympathetic enough to have read her books, but he still balks at her condemnation of "white supremacist capitalist patriarchy." This essay is, in some sense, directed at people just like him. It is meant to explain why hooks can't just "forgive and forget" even after all these years.

2. One of the primary reasons why hooks can't forget the past is that key elements of the "cultural capital" of the West — such as the Columbus myth — won't let her. The legend of Columbus's "discovery" of the "New World" perpetuates the oppressive ideologies of imperialism, white supremacy, and male domination, according to hooks. As the story is traditionally taught in school, Columbus and the other European explorers who followed him are portrayed as triumphing over the native inhabitants of the Americas because of the superiority of their "civilization." The Indians, in the dominant versions of the story of colonization, would have enslaved each other or subjugated the Europeans if it had been in their power to do so. The legend of discovery, thus, legitimizes the idea that civilization is founded on domination and that "the will to conquer is innate [and] natural." It also reinforces the notion that those who were conquered participated in their own domination because they were culturally and genetically "inferior" to their conquerors. Finally, hooks sees the story of discovery as perpetuating "patriarchal romanticization" of the idea of conquest: she sees it as a story that transforms "rape" into a cultural good and that equates women with passive "territory" free for the taking.

3. At this point, you'll probably want to spend some time discussing the accuracy of hooks's depiction of the way the Columbus myth is taught in school. Students can return now to the discussions they had in response to the Before Reading activity and assess whether they noted any "progressive interventions" in the way the legend of discovery was originally presented to them.

4. They may also want to compare the lessons they learned about Columbus with the alternative versions of the discovery story that hooks explores in this essay. According to Ivan Van Septima and Howard Zinn — the two progressive historians on whom hooks relies here — there are alternative ways to imagine the meeting of different peoples, ways that "do not privilege domination" in any of its many forms. Thus, the Africans who journeyed west before Columbus did not attempt to exploit the native peoples they encountered. Instead, they greeted one another and shared resources openly. Columbus himself noted how open and friendly the tribal groups were that he encountered — evidence, hooks suggests, that this had been their approach with early non-European visitors. Thus, hooks would have us replace celebrations of Columbus Day with events that would "challenge patriarchy" and serve as "a catalyst for resistance." Although she doesn't specify a particular alternative, she desires that we begin to commemorate the events of 1492 in a way that rejects the mythology of domination and promotes in its place the values of interracial solidarity, "human bonding," and "the increased capacity of folks to

care for the earth and for one another." Of course, you might want to spend some time in class thinking about the specific form such a countercelebration might take. Should we just erase the memory of Columbus Day from our calendars? Or should we change the way the day is currently remembered?

5. You may also want to spend a few moments thinking out loud about other moments or images in American history that might still haunt students today. These might include scenes from the slave trade, the forced "civilization" of Native Americans through resettlement on reservations, the "land rushes" of the mid-1800s, the Jim Crow era and the history of lynching, the detention of Japanese citizens during World War II, the dropping of the atomic bomb at Hiroshima, the Vietnam War and the Mai Lai massacre, or even the Watergate scandal. Such images might come from history textbooks or from popular movies, songs, or television shows. Almost any form of media might be involved in perpetuating these impersonal memories of the American past.

Further Explorations

1. Maxine Hong Kingston's revision of her aunt's story in "No-Name Woman" might be seen as a clear example of the kind of "cultural retelling" that hooks calls for in this essay. The story of Kingston's aunt is meant to demonstrate the danger of sexual activity, but she sees more in it than simply a cautionary tale about a loose woman. From her perspective as a second-generation Chinese immigrant, this story conveys lessons about what it means to be both a woman and an individual within the context of traditional Chinese culture. It suggests, among other things, that a Chinese woman exists solely as part of larger family and village groups and that her group identity outweighs her own desires and needs. It also suggests that a woman has little "voice" in this context and that she lives at the mercy of men. Kingston's revision of her aunt's story changes all of this. She recasts her aunt as a woman who follows her own desires and is independent enough to want something more than the routine existence the village offers her. She also endows her aunt with a hero's resolve and purpose. As Kingston sees it, her aunt's suicide is motivated by pride and love for her child — not out of shame for what she's done or who she is. Thus, in Kingston's retelling, her aunt's death becomes an act of resistance and not an act of self-censorship.

2. Hooks's reaction to the Columbus legend also offers a good illustration of Zerubavel's concept of "impersonal memory." Hooks lives half a millennium distant from the era of "discovery," yet she still suffers from what might be seen as haunting "flashbacks" that return her to the violence of colonization. It's as if she were experiencing post-traumatic stress syndrome as the direct result of events that transpired five hundred years ago. In fact, hooks makes it clear that the memory of Columbus and the history of colonization is far from being impersonal to her. She is very personally involved in what this cultural story means and what it does to people in the present.

3. Given her alternative reading of pre-Columbian history, you might also expect that hooks would have little patience with Percy's claim that only de Cárdenas was ever really able to "see" the Grand Canyon for what it truly is. Hooks surely would respond by pointing out that de Cárdenas was obviously not the first person to ever set eyes on this natural wonder — he was just the first European. De Cárdenas didn't really discover the canyon at all; he merely claimed it, the way that all European explorers extended their power over the "virgin" land they encountered. Indeed, hooks would probably also detect a whiff of imperialism in Percy's insistence that real perception always involves "confrontation." She might well critique this as a stereotypically male way of conceptualizing the act of perception. Once students begin to view Percy from this perspective, they may begin to pick up other hints of sexist ideology in Percy's thinking. Certainly, his disdain for overeducated coeds at Sarah Lawrence College — or, for that matter, his lionizing of the "research man" and the untutored boy on the beach — might seem to express a rather phallocentric point of view.

4. Whether or not Engel's concepts of "remembering" and "remembered" selves can be stretched to cover the case of historical memory that hooks discusses is itself open for debate. In traditional versions of the Columbus legend, Native peoples come across as "uncivilized," submissive, and inferior. This "persona" or collective "remembered self" differs radically from the image that hooks offers in her depiction of pre-Columbian Native peoples. In her revision, tribal peoples respect the past and each other. They coexist peacefully with one another and approach cross-cultural contact as a matter of mutual recognition and affirmation. They come across as cultural explorers who are interested in sharing resources, probing differences, and celebrating their similarities. Of course, it might be objected that what hooks is doing here is simply projecting current attitudes on people in the past — that she, along with Zinn and Van Septima, is revising the past to fit the values and attitudes of a contemporary multicultural audience. But, in hooks's defense, Engel might note that this is exactly what we all do with even our most precious personal memories. We constantly update our remembered selves in response to our current social and cultural context. Our remembering selves constantly reshape our remembered selves to reduce the dissonance between our past and present self images.

5. Finally, it's likely that hooks would approve Lame Deer and Erdoes's critique of white society as a form of political resistance. Lame Deer and Erdoes present a radical revision of white society's view of itself and its past. From their perspective, whites are not "civilized" so much as they are house-broken, or "domesticated." White society has transformed wild creatures into domestic species that have no power left in them — except the power of turning a profit. This has happened, according to the authors, because white society has lost touch with other species, nature, and the earth. By contrast, the Indian stays connected with nature. Like the pre-Columbian tribal peoples that Zinn and Van Septima describe, Indians approach others not to exploit, dominate, or colonize them, but to enjoy them and celebrate their spirit.

Essay Options

1. This assignment offers an academic essay that draws on key ideas in hooks, Hampl, Zerubavel, and Kingston. On the general topic of impersonal memory, this paper invites students to explore how the writers in this unit transform or challenge historical memories in order to make them more palatable. Zerubavel lays the conceptual groundwork for this assignment, and you should expect students to spend some time discussing his analysis of thought communities, collective memories, and the idea of "comemoration." The ways in which Kingston and hooks transform or revise cultural and family memories has been discussed above and should also receive serious attention in this assignment. Although Hampl doesn't address obviously political themes in the memoir she offers, she does address the politics of memory at length and the need for individuals to narrate their own versions of the events that affect their lives.

2. The last two Essay Options suggest possible research topics. Essay Option #2 invites students to do additional research on recent depictions of Columbus and the story of discovery. The aim here is to test hooks's assertion that "progressive interventions" have already changed the way we recall the "Great Navigator." This topic also allows for students to debate the propriety of historical revisionism.

3.   You'll need some extra time to attempt Essay Option #3. If your students are particularly interested in alternative versions of the past, you may want to give them the chance to read at least a chapter on Columbus from Zinn, Churchill, Van Septima, or any other radical historian. Churchill's comparison of Columbus and Himmler is particularly instructive in this regard. You may also want to have students report their findings back to the class after they've completed their research.

3

Reading the Self:
Ghosts in the Machine? (p. 247)

Getting Started

Perhaps the first thing you'll note about this chapter is the way it links with the chapters surrounding it. Clearly, the idea of the self isn't something that can be easily contained. Our self-concept connects with just about every other aspect of the mind. Thus, it's hard, if not impossible, to separate issues of "memory" and "other minds" from examination of the self. Who we are is, to a large extent, determined by the memory of what's happened to us and who we've been in the past. Similarly, the way we interpret the minds of others depends, in large part, on our own values, beliefs, and attitudes. Thus, you'll probably want to devote some time to this chapter — particularly if you're planning to work heavily in Chapter 2 or Chapter 4 — if only for the synergy that develops between the selections you'll cover here and those you've covered earlier in the term or plan to cover in future weeks.

The topic of the mind's relation to the self, as you might expect, can also present some unusual challenges in class. One reason it's useful to address the nature of the self in a composition course is that it's both something we are all deeply familiar with *and* something that exists only as an abstract idea. As the chapter introduction in *Mind Readings* suggests, the self is a pure concept: while it's possible to look at a face or touch a body, no one has ever come into direct contact with a "self." Selfhood is a state of mind, a fiction we create and use to organize our experiences, govern our relationships, and make sense of the things we encounter in life. And because the self is both so intimate and so abstract, some students are bound to have trouble dealing with it analytically in class. The chapter introduction may help in this regard, because it addresses the notion head-on. It also offers a thumbnail sketch of the historical development of the self, from the ancients to Emerson. With luck, the idea that the concept of the self has changed over time will help students see selfhood as a topic they can examine critically — as a theme or idea that isn't just a given or a matter of faith.

The idea of the self also works well as a theme for composition instruction, because it fits in snugly with several key writing concepts. Every time we meet a writer in print, we set ourselves a double task: we try to decipher the information, theories, and arguments she wants to convey, *and* we try to figure out who she is as a person. Until we grasp the self that lingers behind the words, we haven't understood a piece of writing in any real depth. This sense of the writer's self, as noted in the chapter introduction, can be read from the decisions a writer makes. It inheres in the writer's choice of topic, the arguments she selects to support her point, and even in the attitude she adopts toward her intended audience. But most directly, a writer's self is revealed in her words. The chapter introduction invites students to begin thinking about how voice and style work to shape the self of a writer. Certainly, students shouldn't have any trouble "hearing" the difference between the stylistic selves of Emerson and Rubén Martínez. To continue this exploration of self and language, you may want to ask students to reflect on other selections they've read in *Mind Readings* that have left the impression of a distinctive voice or style. Some of the obvious possibilities might include Frazier, Ackerman, Lopez, Slouka, Kleege, McKibben, Percy, Sanders, Eiseley, Hampl, Kingston, and hooks. If time permits, you may even want to re-examine a few paragraphs from these authors to see exactly what they do to convey a sense of voice or self to their reader. In fact, it might be worthwhile to look at a few more traditionally academic styles, as well. Some students come to college with vague impressions of how academic writing is supposed to sound — impressions that can often hobble their ability to develop their own voices as writers and to convey their ideas clearly and effectively. This, then, might be an ideal time to examine what it means to "sound" academic and to begin discussing the way effective writers adjust their tone and style in relation to changing writing tasks and situations.

You may want to begin your exploration of the self by asking students to divide into small groups and engage in one or more of the following activities:

- Discuss the Escher "self-portrait" that serves as the frontispiece for this chapter and what it suggests about the concept of selfhood. What is Escher saying about the way we tend to see the self and its relation to the rest of the world? What significance might there be in his use of a mirrored sphere as the center of this image of the self? What does this self-portrait tell us about Escher's own self-image or identity?

- Draw a visual representation of a person and his or her self. Share these drawings in groups and discuss the ideas of selfhood that emerge from them.

- Freewrite a page about what the experience of having a self is like. What does it feel like to have a self? Compare the results in small groups and see what conclusions can be drawn from them about the experience of selfhood.

- Working in small groups, write a collective paragraph defining what a self is. To help in this effort, consider the following questions: What is the self made of? Where is it located? What does it do? How can you be sure that you have one? What might it be like *not* to have a self, yet still exist? What happens to the self when someone sleeps, or loses consciousness, or dies?

Sequences and Pairings

The readings in this chapter divide easily into manageable assignments. If you plan to cover most of the topics here, I suggest that you begin by pairing Sapolsky's exploration of the idea of "ego boundaries" with Csikszentmihalyi's analysis of the external things that contribute to our sense of self. These two engaging readings set the tone for the rest of the chapter and connect with other selections in relation to a number of key essay assignments. If you want, you might even pause at this point to assign one of the personal essays associated with either Sapolsky or Csikszentmihalyi. For your next class, have students read Walker, Ludwig, and Martínez. Ludwig can be difficult at first, primarily because of the emphasis he places on Stephen Crane's life story, but once students work their way past the opening pages, they usually connect well with what he says about social roles, scripts, and identity. Martínez and Walker are both enjoyable and can be used to illustrate key ideas in Csikszentmihalyi and Ludwig. Again, you may want to pause here to assign a paper on the social construction of the self — or wait until after you've covered the next two selections. Baumeister and Bateson can also be assigned as a pair on the theme of cultural attitudes toward the self. In addition, they both address the nature of male and female concepts of selfhood. To complete the chapter, assign Kitcher and Elshtain together as a self-contained unit on the topic of cloning and the self.

This chapter may not be quite as thematically rich as are other sections of *Mind Readings,* but it does link well with key concepts and themes in neighboring units. As noted above, you'll find plenty of connections between selections you covered in Chapter 2 on the topic of memory and themes of the self and selfhood. As a result, you may want to devote some time in class to exploring memory's contribution to the self or to examining the influence that families have on personal identity. Together, these two themes link readings in this chapter with selections by Sanders, Lopez, Kingston, Hampl, Engel, and Zerubavel. The chapter itself divides thematically into two parts. The first half focuses on the elements that make up our sense of self, including our family relations, the objects we own, and our cultural role models. This section culminates in an assignment on the notion of the self as a consciously created object or artifact (Martínez, EO #3). Baumeister and Bateson introduce the chapter's second major thematic focus: the notion that there is a dominant cultural pattern or definition of selfhood that has developed in the West over the past few centuries. This theme culminates in a paper examining the status of the self in contemporary American culture (Bateson, EO #4), and offers the chance for students to compare notions of selfhood across cultures. The last thematic cluster focuses on the notion of ego boundaries and the ethics of cloning.

Recommended Stand-Alone Readings

If time doesn't permit you to work your way through the chapter, you may want to consider touching on the notion of the mind and its self in relation to a few individual selections. Csikszentmihalyi's "What Is the Self?" asks the chapter's central question and can be used as the point of departure for a personal essay that inventories the "ingredients" of the self, or it can be used as the basis of an informal media research project on the topic of "ideal selves" in pop culture. If you're looking for less academic selections, consider assigning Alice Walker or Rubén Martínez. Walker's "Everyday Use" can be read alone as the occasion for a personal essay on a family heirloom that holds special meaning for students, while Martínez's "Technicolor" can lead to a good personal essay on the way movie heroes influence students' self-concepts. Bateson can be read as the basis of a paper on cross-cultural experiences of selfhood, but this selection presents more of a challenge in terms of accessibility. For a one-reading approach to the issue of cloning, offer students Kitcher, not Elshtain, primarily because Kitcher presents logical arguments in favor of cloning that students may not have encountered in news coverage of the subject. The related paper topic on the ethics of "engineering" a child is terrific for critical thinking since, as Kitcher indicates, parents have always tried to "engineer" their children. Here's a list of some possible topics for stand-alone assignments:

"Ideal selves" in contemporary culture	*What Is the Self?* (Csikszentmihalyi)
Objects that contribute to the self	*Everyday Use* (Walker)
The impact of the media on the self	*Technicolor* (Martínez)
Accommodating the self to a new culture	*A Mutable Self* (Bateson)
The ethics of "engineering" a child	*Whose Self Is It, Anyway?* (Kitcher)

Recommended Pairings

Ideals of selfhood	*What Is the Self?* (Csikszentmihalyi) and *Everyday Use* (Walker)
Social roles and scripts and the self	*Living Backwards* (Ludwig) and *Technicolor* (Martínez)
Women's selves and selfhood in the West	*The Self and Society* (Baumeister) and *A Mutable Self* (Bateson)
The ethics of cloning	*Whose Self Is It, Anyway?* (Kitcher) and *To Clone or Not to Clone* (Elshtain)

Suggested Thematic Clusters

The role of families in the construction of the self	*Ego Boundaries* (Sapolsky), *Everyday Use* (Walker), *Technicolor* (Martínez), *The Inheritance of Tools* (Sanders, Ch. 2), *No-Name Woman* (Kingston, Ch. 2)

Memory and the construction of self	*Ego Boundaries* (Sapolsky), *Everyday Use* (Walker), *The Inheritance of Tools* (Sanders, Ch. 2), *Memory and Imagination* (Hampl, Ch. 2), *Then and Now* (Engel, Ch. 2), *No-Name Woman* (Kingston, Ch. 2), *Social Memories* (Zerubavel, Ch. 2)
The self as artifact	*Ego Boundaries* (Sapolsky), *What Is the Self?* (Csikszentmihalyi), *Everyday Use* (Walker) *Living Backwards* (Ludwig), *Technicolor* (Martínez)
The status of the self in American culture	*Ego Boundaries* (Sapolsky), *Technicolor* (Martínez), *The Self and Society* (Baumeister), *A Mutable Self* (Bateson)
Ego boundaries and the ethics of cloning	*Ego Boundaries* (Sapolsky), *The Self and Society* (Baumeister), *A Mutable Self* (Bateson), *Whose Self Is It, Anyway?* (Kitcher), *To Clone or Not to Clone* (Elshtain)

Essay Options

Ego Boundaries, or the Fit of My Father's Shirt, Robert Sapolsky

Option #1. Write about a time you felt yourself adopting or emulating some of the characteristics of another person.

Option #2. Examine the role of parents and family in the construction of the self. (Sanders, Kingston, Walker, and Martínez)

What Is the Self?, Mihaly Csikszentmihalyi

Option #1. Assemble and analyze a collection of images of "ideal selves" from pop culture.

Option #2. Inventory the ingredients of your sense of self.

Everyday Use, Alice Walker

Option #1. Write about an object with special meaning or cultural significance in your family.

Option #2. Assess the role of memories in the construction of the self. (Lopez, Sanders, Hampl, Engel, and Zerubavel)

Living Backwards, Arnold M. Ludwig

Option #1. Write about the "roles" that you see guiding your life story.

Option #2. Discuss how the self lends coherence and continuity to our lives. (Sapolsky and Engel)

Option #3. Examine some of the challenges to living in the present. (Cole, Percy, and Schacter)

Technicolor, Rubén Martínez

Option #1. Explore the impact of the media on your sense of self.

Option #2. Respond to the claim that America is becoming a "mestizo" nation.

Option #3. Explore the thesis that the self is something we create like a work of art. (Sapolsky, Walker, Ludwig, Hampl, Kingston, and Zerubavel)

The Self and Society: Changes, Problems, and Opportunities, Roy F. Baumeister

Option #1. Survey media images to assess the dominance of the modern self.
Option #2. Respond to the claim that the self has become a burden.
Option #3. Survey magazine images to test Baumeister's claims about female selves.

A Mutable Self, Mary Catherine Bateson

Option #1. Write about a time when you had to adapt to a new culture or community.
Option #2. Write about a time when you felt silenced in school.
Option #3. Inventory the relationships that contribute to your sense of self.
Option #4. Evaluate the status of the self in contemporary American culture. (Sapolsky, Baumeister, and Martínez)

Whose Self Is It, Anyway?, Philip Kitcher

Option #1. Examine the ethics of predetermining a child's attributes.
Option #2. Research and analyze depictions of cloning in popular culture.

To Clone or Not to Clone, Jean Bethke Elshtain

Option #1. Research and debate the pros and cons of human cloning.

Media Connections

Discuss ego boundaries, selfhood, and aging in *American Beauty* and *Magnolia*	Sapolsky, FE #5
Make a collage of ad images of objects that define the self	Csikszentmihalyi, FE #5
Collect images documenting the "ideal selves" of ancient cultures	Csikszentmihalyi, FE #5
Collect and analyze pop cultural images of the "ideal self"	Csikszentmihalyi, EO #1
Discuss images of "ideal selves" offered by Hollywood films	Martínez, FE #2
Write about the impact of the media on your sense of self	Martínez, EO #1
Survey media imagery to assess the dominance of the modern self	Baumeister, EO #1
Survey magazine images to assess claims about the modern female self	Baumeister, EO #3
Discuss cloning as a source of horror in Hollywood films such as *Gattaca*	Kitcher, FE #4
Write an essay on portrayals of cloning in popular culture	Kitcher, EO #2

ROBERT SAPOLSKY, *Ego Boundaries, or the Fit of My Father's Shirt* (p. 254)

Sapolsky's personal reflection on the concept of ego boundaries is a good place to begin your exploration of the theme of selfhood. This relatively brief selection challenges students to think critically about two of the most central features of the self. As Sapolsky reminds us, we tend to assume that the self has relatively well-defined boundaries — that there's a difference between what's inside and what's outside the self. We also assume that the self is indivisible — that, unless there's a problem, selves come one to a customer. The confusion Sapolsky experiences after his father's death raises questions about both of these central assumptions. Although you probably wouldn't want to assign this as your class's only reading on the self, Sapolsky does connect with every thematic cluster in this chapter. Sapolsky's meditation on ego boundaries and aging raises questions about the construction of the self and cross-cultural concepts of selfhood. You might also want to consider showing a recent film on related topics to accompany this selection. *Amercian Beauty* and *Magnolia,* for example, both deal with characters who suffer identity crises as they age. The Before Reading activity gives you the chance to discuss commonplace ideas about the self and multiple personalities. Most students have at least a passing acquaintance with the folklore surrounding the idea of multiple personalities. Having too many selves or selves that are out of control is seen as a sign of mental illness in the contemporary West. In other historical and cultural contexts, however, the ability to access different personalities and voices has often been seen as a mark of spiritual power and personal distinction. Sapolsky's essay encourages us to begin questioning these and other cultural biases about the self.

Exploring the Text

1. Sapolsky begins by describing the experience of "hearing" a lecture by the famed astrophysicist Stephen Hawking. His initial attitude toward Hawking is reverential. He is "paralyzed by awe" as Hawking, "this mummy brain from the crypt," is carried onto the stage. Although Sapolksy doesn't come out and say it, Hawking symbolizes one of the most enduring assumptions about the nature of selfhood and a central enigma in what's known as the "mind/body" problem in philosophy. Hawking is a classic, if tragic, embodiment of the belief that the seat of consciousness lies in the brain and that the mind inside this brain exists independent of the body that houses it. The problem is that the person Hawking has chosen to convey his ideas to the world is so annoying. Sapolsky can't stand the self-assured arrogance of Hawking's young interpreter. The point, of course, is that bodies give no clue about the minds they harbor: you can't tell from looking at Hawking's wasted form that the self inside still has the cocky arrogance of a Cambridge don. Nor can you even be sure exactly how many "selves" Hawking's body contains.

2. Sapolsky goes on to elaborate the case for the actual existence of multiple selves. He notes that while substantial evidence suggests that the mind was once the home of different personalities and voices, modern science takes a dim view of multiple selves in a single body. Freud, for example, saw the tendency for mourners to assume characteristics of the dead as a sign of mental illness. According to Freud, the melancholic who is wracked with guilt over the loss of a loved one is actually angry because he will not be able to resolve past conflicts. As a result, he "makes room within himself for aspects of the dead." As Freud saw it, the depressed survivor becomes self-accusing, because he has taken on the very features of the dearly departed that he himself most hated. Punishing the self then becomes a way to punish the dead. Science since Freud has steadfastly categorized the experience of multiple selves as "dissociative identity disorder" — a mental anomaly that, from the perspective of Western notions of individual identity, should be treated as a disease. For modern science, the self is inviolate. If two personalities seem to speak through a single person, this is only a sign that the person's real self has "fragmented" and certainly not a sign that two distinct selves actually occupy the same mind. Sapolsky's own experiences with his father force him to question these assumptions about what constitutes the self. As his father sinks deeper into dementia toward the end of his life, Sapolsky observes the loosening of his ego boundaries. Sapolsky begins to feel "intruded upon" as his father assimilates aspects of his own biography and personality. After his father's death, Sapolsky himself experiences this kind of problem with ego

boundaries. He finds himself humming his father's favorite songs, wearing his clothing, developing a sudden interest in architecture (his father's profession), feeling insecure if he doesn't have his father's heart medication with him, and even speaking in his father's voice. As a scientist, Sapolsky's instinct is to diagnose and seek a cure for this "disorder." But he resists this tendency to "overpathologize" what may be a healthy expression of loss, love, and community.

3. Sapolsky's experience working with tribal groups in Africa offers him another perspective on the nature of the self. In the East African homes he has visited, he has encountered a culture in which individuation is not as important as it is in the West — a culture in which people adopt and play out the parts assigned to them by their societies. In such traditional, noncompetitive cultures, people turn into their parents and become their elders. The self in a tribal society is "opened at the back" to the archetypes of the past. In a traditional community, the servant Eliezer assumes the identity of his father and an Abraham lives for nine hundred years. Identity does exist in such cultures, according to Sapolsky, but it transcends individual bodies. The self of a tribal member is open to the collectively defined identity that inhabits it.

4. Whether students accept the suggestion that Sapolsky himself experienced something like this kind of openness depends on their own views of identity and individuality. Some may argue that, despite his rationalizations, Sapolsky's behavior indicates that he really was at least temporarily mentally ill. It's one thing to follow in your father's footsteps and another thing entirely to contemplate taking his heart medication. Yet, others may be convinced that Sapolsky is onto something here: the notion of community that he offers in this essay as a spiritual or psychological phenomenon, and not simply as a place where you live, may ring true for many. The idea that our selves can open and overlap may be attractive in an era that's beginning to explore concepts such as the ecological interdependence of all living creatures and the "fuzzy" distinctions between even hard and fast scientific and mathematical concepts. Still, what if Sapolsky hadn't found his way back to "the battlefield of individuation"? What if he had written this essay as a dialogue in two different voices and signed it with his father's name as well as his own? Would that have been acceptable?

5. Sapolsky recognizes that we can't "re-attain" the mindset of a tribal culture, and he's not arguing that we should change our views of those who think they're different people in different situations. His aim in this essay is less ambitious. He wants us to acknowledge that the mind is not the same as the self; that we are bigger, in a way, than any one identity or role that we inhabit; and that to embody aspects of another self may, in fact, be not a sign of mental illness but the truest expression of love and community connection.

Further Explorations

1. It might be argued that Scott Russell Sanders and Maxine Hong Kingston both experience something like the loosening of ego boundaries that Sapolsky describes in this selection. The tools that Sanders inherits are clearly more than mere souvenirs of his father and grandfather. They are vehicles for a set of values, skills, and attitudes that link Sanders with past generations. The honesty, integrity, and pride in accomplishment that they represent are fundamental aspects of Sanders's identity, and, thus, these tools link him directly to men from past generations of his family. The same might also be said for Kingston in relation to the memory of her aunt. Once she hears her aunt's story, she becomes haunted by it. It isn't just a family anecdote or a cautionary lesson to her, but something that connects deeply with her own sense of self. Her revision of her aunt's story enacts this blurring of intergenerational identities in that Kingston obviously draws on her own values, beliefs, and motives as she reshapes the story of her doomed predecessor. It might also be observed that while they're contemporary Americans, both Sanders and Kingston have what could be seen as a "traditional" or even a tribal view of relationships. Both see themselves as enmeshed in organic communities where rela-

tionships and roles are more important than individual identities. Thus, Sanders has learned that being a father takes precedence over more self-interested pursuits and that family issues outweigh the concerns of the wider world. Kingston is similarly focused on the traditional world of Chinese culture and its impact on her own fledgling sense of self. It might be argued that all she needs to do is to forget the past, but this only suggests a lack of understanding about the individual's position in relation to a traditional cultural system. Kingston knows the past is part of her and not something she can easily put aside. The story of her aunt is more like a malevolent ghost than a simple recollection: it is capable of ambushing her and forcing her to take her aunt's place in the past.

2. Zerubavel's discussion of impersonal memories helps to clarify how ego boundaries might, in fact, be loosened or opened to the past. The idea of impersonal memory itself blurs the distinction between personal identity and other, self and society. How can a memory be impersonal? Zerubavel suggests that the historical facts we learn as part of our socialization into any group are actually more than mere bits of information: they become personal memories that fuse our identities with the identity of the larger group. The self, seen from the perspective of "mnemonic socialization," is thus never really free. The self of every individual represents a mix of personal and impersonal experiences and is both individual and collective. Indeed, when you try to separate what's cultural and collective from what's purely personal in our experiences, the question of the independent self becomes even more problematic. Is the experience of love unique for every individual? Or do our experiences of falling in love reflect predictable patterns established by cultural memories?

3. The tension between traditional cultures and individual selves also emerges in Alice Walker's "Everyday Use." The idea of ego boundaries can easily be applied to explain the motives and reactions of Walker's characters. Dee, the most contemporary figure in this story, has re-created herself while away at college. She returns home having adopted an African name, a Muslim boyfriend, and a way of dress that suggests she has self-consciously decided to reclaim her cultural heritage as an African American. The irony is that she is herself too ego-bounded to connect with her own family, let alone with the anonymous generations that link her to her African past. Walker's narrator and her daughter Maggie, by contrast, still inhabit what might be seen as a traditional cultural context. Maggie, for example, isn't the "individual" that Dee is, but she has a firm sense of self nonetheless that draws its strength from direct connection with an uninterrupted line of women going back beyond memory. Indeed, Walker's story could be interpreted as saying that the self isn't something you create *for yourself* but something you inherit from generations of selves that have gone before.

4. The perspective offered by Arnold M. Ludwig, however, complicates this picture of the self even further. Ludwig's theory of social roles and scripts might be seen as offering a middle ground between the notion of the unique individual self and its "open" or collectively defined counterpart. In Ludwig's view, we each choose the self we want to be, but we choose from the pre-established set of plots or roles that our cultural context makes available to us. Thus, in Ludwig's view, you might be the son of the village chief but still elect to become the village drunkard. Moreover, Ludwig's analysis seems to avoid making a potentially stereotypical distinction between "modern" and "traditional" cultures. In Ludwig's view, the modern self would be just as open to influence as the self in a tribal context. The only difference might be that today we have more roles to choose from, while in village societies choices were relatively restricted. Thus, we don't have to "re-attain" a tribal mindset to expand our ego boundaries in Ludwig's view. In fact, Ludwig might point out that Sapolsky isn't actually *becoming* his father now that his father has died. As Ludwig would likely see it, Sapolsky decided long ago to become a scholar — and thus to assume a role that strongly resembled the role his father played throughout his life. Growing stooped, wearing old clothes, and lecturing students until they become bored are part and parcel of the standard "plot" that Sapolsky chose to follow and not evidence that Sapolsky's self is being invaded by his father's ghost.

5. Themes of ego boundaries and aging also play a large part in the movies *American Beauty* and *Magnolia*. Both films feature male characters who suffer from rather rigidly defined senses of self, and both suggest that coping with aging and death requires more flexibility and openness to other potential identities. Both are clearly meant as critiques of contemporary American notions about individual identity and of the lack of any authentic sense community in American society.

Essay Options

1. Students may have some difficulty with Essay Option #1 for the simple reason that most of us don't like to acknowledge the influence of others. Yet, almost everyone has had the experience of feeling aspects of another person's identity subtly infiltrate our own behavior and consciousness. The point is not to challenge the integrity of your students' sense of identity but to invite students to explore how our selves open to accommodate selected aspects of those we feel close to or admire. If this topic strikes you as too sensitive for students to be comfortable with, you may want to wait until after reading Csikszentmihalyi before assigning a personal essay in this chapter.

2. Or you can consider Essay Option #2, which offers a text-based assignment on the role of families in the construction of the self. You may want to read ahead to both Walker and Martínez as you prepare for this topic, since both of these selections speak to the influence that families have on our personal notions of identity. Zerubavel's concepts of impersonal memories may also help to explain the impact that families have on personal identity.

MIHALY CSIKSZENTMIHALYI, *What Is the Self?* (p. 264)

This selection complements Sapolsky and segues directly into Alice Walker's short story "Everyday Use." Csikszentmihalyi's essay is a key reading in this chapter because it introduces the notion that the self is a kind of artifact — a product of the mind that is composed or constructed of elements that can be taken apart and analyzed. Once this conceptual groundwork is laid, it's possible to climb outside the self and to see it from a certain analytical distance. Once you accept the idea that your self is, in some sense, "composed of" things you own or the clothes that you wear, you can start to inventory the ingredients that make up your identity. The best part about this selection is the concreteness of Csikszentmihalyi's approach. Despite his academic tone and his use of academic concepts such as reification, Csikszentmihalyi offers your class ideas it can hold on to. Students readily understand that the way we decorate our bodies and our homes says much about our self-concept. Nor is it particularly hard for them to affirm the notion that every culture promotes certain "ideal" models of the self. The ideas Csikszentmihalyi presents here can also be used as the basis for some interesting practical research involving media collages of the "collective representations" of the self that dominates modern American culture. Csikszentmihalyi can be assigned alone as preparation for a paper on selfhood, but it's better to combine him with Sapolsky, Walker, Ludwig, and Martínez as a thematic unit on the "construction" of selves. You'd do well to pair Csikszentmihalyi with Sapolsky and then follow up by assigning the three remaining readings for another class. The Before Reading activity prompts students to begin thinking about the self in terms of the "ingredients" it contains. Have students brainstorm their recipes for the self in groups and then report back to the whole class as you summarize their ideas on the board. This exercise is bound to raise the question of whether there's anything that *can't* be thought of as an ingredient of the self.

Exploring the Text

1. The self, according to Csikszentmihalyi, is a "reification" — the projection onto reality of a "mental construction." In short, it's a fiction created by the mind. Csikszentmihalyi's approach to the self is functionalist and materialist. He acknowledges

that we typically think of the self as a kind of "force, spark, or inner flame" — something magical with "an indivisible integrity." But he sweeps these ideas aside and suggests, instead, that the self is simply a "figment of the imagination" — an idea we create "to account for the multiplicity of impressions, emotions, thoughts, and feelings that the brain records in consciousness." This may sound harsher than it is: in reality, Csikszentmihalyi sees the self as an amazing solution to a number of serious mental problems. The self serves several important functions: it is a "centralized director" that brings order to the sensory chaos of experience, it helps us monitor our goals, and it gives us a motive for survival. Of course, you should expect some students to react strongly to this portrayal of what many see as the most central and, perhaps, most self-evident "fact" of life. Can we really accept the idea that the felt experience of consciousness is a convenient fiction — or that we "create" a self to "rule" over our existence? Most of us take a more spiritual and deterministic approach to selfhood. We view the self as something we're born with, as something that can't be separated from our being. We might accept the self as the product of nature or nurture — genes or our environment — but it's not something that we deliberately create.

2. In addition to the traditional view of the self as spark and flame, Csikszentmihalyi evokes the image of the self as a "traffic cop" or executive director — a central authority in the mind that screens input and makes decisions. He also mentions the famous concept of the "homunculus" — the image of the self as a "little man" in the mind who looks through our eyes and directs our activities. Students may want to come up with metaphors of their own that capture the experience of the self. Is the self like the central processing unit in a computer, the CEO of a Fortune 500 corporation, the minister of a church, a colony of ants, or a mental "desktop" that translates the machine code of the brain into usable form? Each metaphor suggests a different set of powers and a different relation to the other mental functions that are involved in consciousness.

3. No Cartesian idealist, Csikszentmihalyi defines the self in what might strike some as refreshingly materialist terms. In his view, our selves are determined, in part, by the things we pay attention to. Thus, the self of an East African Nuer tribe member is "made up, in part, by the cows and the bulls he spends his life caring for, while the self of an average American might be defined in part by his car." Personal objects, possessions, body decorations, and clothing also contribute to our "images of the ideal self." In tribal societies, face painting and tattoos connect individuals to important cultural ideals and groups and convey important information about personal status and position in kinship networks. In so-called technologically developed nations, the same functions are served by particular styles of clothing, cosmetics, plastic surgery, and personal possessions such as sports cars, computers, and jewelry. Most students can generate an exhaustive list of such "power possessions" in a matter of minutes, so this shouldn't come as a surprise to your class. In fact, you might want to pause at this point to have students brainstorm lists of such objects and then discuss the messages that they convey about the selves of their owners.

4. But Csikszentmihalyi isn't content to equate the self with only its physical manifestations. He also notes the way that our selves are intimately connected to what he calls "collective representations." These are cultural symbols that link us to larger group or ideological identities. Collective representations can take the form of tribal dances, ceremonial masks, or the music at rock concerts. During World War II, the collective identity of Mussolini's Fascist Party was represented by the image of the fasces — bundles of elm rods bound together to symbolize the strength of group unity. Medieval cathedrals, nuclear reactors, and space centers all have served to represent the collective power of various cultures. Other examples today might include the White House and other governmental buildings, museums, sports stadia, colleges, research centers, airports, and even certain urban cityscapes — just about any place, environment, object, tradition, ritual, or symbol that links people to the collective power of their cultures.

5. In addition to such overt symbols of collective identity, the self also draws meaning from what Csikszentmihalyi terms "images of the ideal self." According to the
author, every culture in history has depicted ideal images of the self that it aspires to create. In ancient Greece, such cultural ideals of selfhood took the form of *kouroi* — the
highly stylized figures of youthful nobility that dominated early Grecian art. In the East,
the figures of the Bodhisattvas, "the enlightened ones," performed much the same self-
shaping function. In Csikszentmihalyi's view, all of these images expressed roughly the
same constellation of qualities: "a calm power, a restrained energy at peace with itself
and the world." During the Renaissance and in modern times, this ideal conception of
the self began to change in the West. Obedience to authority and self-control gave way
to the possibility of unlimited individual achievement. By the twentieth century, Western
artists gave up the project of expressing cultural images of the ideal self and resorted,
instead, to "the scribbles of children and the art of the insane" to express the desperate
state of the human condition in modern times. Today, Csikszentmihalyi suggests, collective representations of the ideal self have become suspect. In tyrannies such images
are used as a form of propaganda to promote social control; in capitalist democracies,
they are used by corporations to market cosmetics or cigarettes. In Csikszentmihalyi's
view, the images of the self that are marketed to consumers today no longer have the
"balanced self-discipline" of earlier heroic figures associated with ancient civilizations.
Instead, they convey only a general impression of "good animal health, sensual contentment, and a lack of worries or responsibilities that could interfere with enjoying the latest fashion in consumption or sensory stimulation." Contemporary ideals of the self
project a world "obsessed by narcissism and the fetishism of commodities." The ideal
selves we see projected in ads and on television are evidence of a culture whose highest
goal is "to live a life of carefree pleasure." Interestingly, then, it might be noted that while
Csikszentmihalyi begins his analysis of the self from what appears to be an exclusively
materialist perspective, he ends sounding like a disappointed moralist. The self may be
an illusion the mind creates as a kind of mental traffic cop, but clearly he believes it can
— and should — amount to much more than the sum of its parts.

Further Explorations

1. Students shouldn't have much difficulty seeing the connection between attention
and self in relation to Frazier, Lopez, Sanders, and Eiseley. Frazier, for example, is someone who attends to the small adventures that life offers — things such as the crab that
appears on the F train one afternoon or the random page of Tolstoy that he finds on a
street corner. He is a "collector" of such incidents, and of other things, such as the voices he hears everywhere in the city. This attention to voices also marks him as a writer
and as a lover of diversity. Frazier attends primarily to people rather than to things: his
tour of Brooklyn introduces us to people of all kinds, conditions, and stages of life, but
it offers little information about the physical environment in which he lives. It also brims
with stories, and this tells us something about Frazier, too. He the kind of person who
is interested in the stories that shape other people's lives — stories like that of his neighbor who — a people-person herself — has just returned from surgery. As you can see,
you can do a lot in class with this simple analytical tool. Have students return to Frazier,
Lopez, Sanders, and Eiseley, and ask them to examine several pages to see exactly what
each writer pays attention to and what this reveals about each author's own sense of self.

2. Of course, if you are what you attend to, you'd better be able to attend to it in
the first place. Slouka, McKibben, and Percy all suggest that our ability to attend to the
world around us has already been seriously compromised by the high-tech society in
which we live. Slouka makes the case that the deluge of sound we live with in so-called
advanced societies is making it literally impossible to shape a coherent sense of self. We
are so distracted, it would seem, that we can't attend to anything — even ourselves.
McKibben argues that video technology is robbing us of the acuity of our senses and
leading us to confuse mere comfort, which he sees as the lack of negative sensation, with

genuine sensual pleasure, which depends on the contrast of sensual deprivation and gratification. Television thus "drugs" us by dulling our sense responses and, as Csikszentmihalyi might see it, by making it more difficult to attend to the real world at all. According to Percy, the situation is even grimmer. We can't attend to the world around us because the "preformed complex" of education, theory, expert opinion, and other forms of cultural mediation insulate us from direct contact with reality. The only thing most of us pay attention to, in Percy's view, is the opinion of those who would control, educate, or otherwise abuse us. Thus, all three of these authors might note that the breakdown of ideal selves that Csikszentmihalyi describes in the twentieth century isn't really so surprising after all. Without the ability to attend to anything in an authentic way, we are deprived of one of the most fundamental sources of selfhood and are thus forced to depend even more heavily on collective representations and ideal images of the self that are subject to social and corporate control.

3. It would seem particularly difficult to square Csikszentmihalyi's notion of the "extrasomatic" sources of the self with the concept of ego boundaries that Sapolsky discusses. From the beginning of his analysis, Csikszentmihalyi seems to reject the notion of a rigidly defined, clearly bounded, or unitary self. In his view, the self is not an indivisible and inviolable "spark" or "flame" but an assemblage of elements that is endowed with the *appearance* of unity by a trick of the mind. No one thing determines the essence of the self, according to this perspective. Instead, the self emerges from the things we own, wear, and live with, the goals we seek to achieve, the objects we attend to, the collective representations we identify with, and the ideal selves we aspire to become.

4. This activity invites students to interpret advertising imagery within a relatively sophisticated academic context. Have students collect ad images as well as images from popular magazines and then work in small groups to select the best and assemble them in collages. Once they're done, have them reflect on what their group's collage suggests about current American images of the self and report this analysis back to the class as a whole.

5. If your class is ready for a more challenging research project, you may want to have them find and make copies of images documenting the "ideal selves" of other cultures. This will allow them to test Csikszentmihalyi's rather sweeping claim that all ancient cultures seem to have promoted the same basic ideal of the noble, disciplined, and contemplative self.

Essay Options

1. Essay Option #1 extends the informal ad research that students began in response to Further Exploration #4. This assignment presents a two-part challenge: the imagery that students assemble needs to be rich enough to lead to some productive conclusions about "ideal selves" in American culture, and students have to spend a lot of time and effort analyzing it in light of Csikszentmihalyi's claims. You may choose to limit the scope of the assignment or give it a particular emphasis that suits the focus of your class. For example, you may want to direct students to focus on distinctions between male and female images of the ideal self and what they convey. Or you may want to stress the idea of debating Csikszentmihalyi's claims about the ideal self in a consumer culture. Or ask them to debate whether they feel such images actually do have the kind of impact that Csikszentmihalyi suggests.

2. Essay Option #2 offers the chance for students to write a comprehensive "recipe" or "inventory" for their own sense of self. Csikszentmihalyi touches on so many different "extrasomatic" sources of selfhood in this selection that students usually have little trouble generating responses to this rather unusual topic.

ALICE WALKER, *Everyday Use* (p. 283)

This short story usually enters the classroom as a celebration of heritage and the meaning of family history. But I think you'll find that it takes on new significance when you view it as a story about conflicting sources and definitions of the self. "Everyday Use" complements Csikszentmihalyi by illustrating the way that "extrasomatic" objects contribute to the construction of individual identity. It also complicates Csikszentmihalyi's approach to the self by raising questions about whether the self is, in fact, something that can be deliberately created without becoming inauthentic. In addition, you'll find that Walker connects well with Sapolsky and Ludwig on the theme of the various culturally approved roles that we play and the way such roles influence our sense of self. If you plan to do some work "reading other minds" in Chapter 4, you may also want to take this opportunity to read Walker, because "Everyday Use" is involved in follow-up discussions relating to key theoretical selections by Schank and Nussbaum. As you assign this story, ask students to freewrite for a few minutes about a particular object that has special importance in their family or that connects their family to their culture. This Before Reading activity will get them thinking about the symbolism that's associated with heirloom objects, and it can also be used as pre-writing for Essay Option #1.

Exploring the Text

1. Walker's famous narrator is a simple woman with a wonderfully rich sense of self. In the story's opening pages, we learn that she's a hard-working, "big-boned" southern farm woman, "with rough, man-working hands." She lives on her family's land in what was probably a sharecropper's house, without windows, doors, or the luxury of a grassy suburban front yard. She's proud of her toughness and physical strength: she boasts that she can "kill and clean a hog as mercilessly as a man" and that she once killed a bull calf with a sledgehammer blow and "had the meat hung up to chill before nightfall." She's a big woman who sees her size as an asset, because her fat keeps her "hot in zero weather." But she's also insecure. She knows she's uneducated and unsophisticated, and she easily slips into daydreams about how she'd like to be. She sees herself on a fantasy TV show "a hundred pounds lighter" with "skin like an uncooked barley pancake," chatting wittily with a "sporty" white man who looks like Johnny Carson. In fact, this is the self she'd have to be to live up to her daughter Dee's expectations. Walker's narrator is a complex character because she's both proud and insecure. She's content with who she is, yet her television daydream suggests that she wishes she could please her demanding older daughter by being the kind of parent she knows Dee would like to have. But she also knows that she will never live up to Dee's expectations. She even confesses that she never watches the kind of TV shows that appear in her daydreams. Her sense of self derives, instead, from the place where she lives, the work she does, and the part she plays as the loving mother of two very different daughters.

2. We learn a great deal about Dee from her mother. From the story's second paragraph, we learn that Dee inspires "envy and awe" in her younger sister Maggie and that she has "held life always in the palm of one hand." She is a person who's used to getting her way in the world. Dee has been off to college and is coming home to visit and bringing with her a new identity. Before leaving, Dee had always been a demanding, headstrong, and difficult child. She was the family intellectual, who "burned" her mother and sister "with a lot of knowledge." Dee was born a social climber who was so ashamed of the house she grew up in that she was gleeful when it burned down, who always "wanted nice things," and who "had a style of her own, and knew what style was." When she arrives home, it's clear that Dee has changed her style — and with it her identity. The new Dee has learned about her African roots, changed her name, adopted African-style dress, and even found a Muslim boyfriend. She arrives taking snapshots of the house she once hated and coveting old churn tops, wooden benches, and quilts that she had been glad to be rid of just months earlier. Dee's sense of self, unlike the identities of her mother and sister, has little to do with her physical environment, personal relationships, or even her family's past. She doesn't inherit a self the way her mother does; she "chooses" her identity. Indeed, while the narrator seems relatively fatalistic about where she lives and who she is, Dee faults her mother because she "chooses" to live in a dilapi-

dated house, and, later in the story, because she doesn't choose to "make something" of herself. For Dee, self is a matter of choice, a matter of personal style: it's a fashion that's assumed, displayed, and then, we assume, discarded when a new fashion comes along.

3. Within the symbolic context of the Afrocentric self she's acquired, the household objects that Dee now covets represent her "heritage" — her symbolic link to the past of her African American ancestors. As such, they certify the "authenticity" of her newly acknowledged identity.   She will display these things in her college apartment like objects in an art gallery, and like emblems they will function to convey messages about who she is. By refusing Dee the quilts and giving them instead to Maggie, the narrator resolves the story's central conflict. She sides with her downtrodden younger daughter — the one who doesn't see life in terms of options and choices but draws her strength and sense of self directly from her lived relationship to the past. Of course, students may not necessarily see this as the best decision. Many students are strongly attracted to Dee, perhaps because she embodies so many current cultural values — self-confidence, determination, the will to succeed, and even the idea that you can choose your own identity and be who you want to be. Dee represents freedom and many students have trouble understanding why freedom doesn't come off better in this story.

4. Seen from Dee's point of view, this story would be a tragedy and not the tale of a heroic decision. Dee would probably portray her mother and sister as two relics of a past age, when African Americans were content to submit to poverty and ignorance and didn't even have the courage to recognize their cultural heritage and claim their true identities. Walker, however, makes it pretty clear that the narrator, not Dee, represents the story's moral voice. While Walker probably sympathizes with Dee's determination and courage, she builds the story around her narrator, and, through it, confirms her point of view.

5. It's easy to interpret — and perhaps to dismiss — "Everyday Use" as a critique of the early advocates of black consciousness and Afrocentrism who may have lost touch with the real meaning of heritage as they worked to recover their African roots. Seen from this perspective, the story is a kind of historical curiosity, tied to a specific moment that has passed. But it's also possible to see the story as a commentary on contemporary attitudes toward the self. From this perspective, Dee is a forerunner of an era when the self is seen as a choice we make from a menu of options and personal styles. And that's another reason why Dee may seem more familiar to students than either her mother or Maggie. Dee may resonate better in an era when the self is more a matter of image than inheritance — a world where identities are adopted and discarded as fashions come and go.

Further Explorations

1. Sanders's attitude toward his tools is remarkably similar to the attitude that Maggie and her mother take toward the quilts in this story. In both stories the objects connect their owners to their family history and link them to stories and values that are intimately tied up with their gender and sense of self. The quilts, like Sanders's tools, are wrapped in a "cloud of knowing." They require skill and education to make, and the knowledge associated with them connects their makers with a line of women extending back into the past beyond memory. In similar fashion, Sanders's hammer links him not only to the men of his immediate family but to generations of men who used hammers to build things and give shape to their dreams. In addition, Sanders, like Maggie and her mother, puts his heirloom tools to "everyday use." No Dee in this regard, he wouldn't consider displaying them in his home workshop as priceless artifacts. Instead, exactly as Maggie does, he connects to his family's past through these tools by using them as his father and grandfather used them — to build a home for his family and to construct an authentic personal identity for himself.

2. From Zerubavel's perspective, Dee's desire to preserve and display her family's heirloom quilts makes perfect sense. Zerubavel would probably see these quilts as tokens of important "impersonal memories" that link Dee with her racial and family identities.

Indeed, Zerubavel might suggest that when Dee went to college, she joined a new "thought community" and underwent a process of "mnemonic socialization" that helped her associate these artifacts with historical memories that her mother and sister only partially appreciate. That's why she suddenly feels these objects are priceless. When Dee looks at the quilts, she may see them not only as objects that link her to her family's past but as sites of historical memory that link her with the entire African American experience. Thus, from Zerubavel's perspective, Dee might seem less arrogant and self-aggrandizing than she initially appears.

3. "Everday Use" also raises some serious questions about the idea of ego boundaries that Sapolsky introduces. At first it's tempting to think of the narrator and Maggie as representatives of a relatively "traditional" society like the East African villagers Sapolsky visits, who merely adopt cultural identities that have been passed down from generation to generation. Thus, Maggie will eventually herself be stitched into the quilt of identity that makes up her family heritage. She will become a woman and probably a mother who closely resembles the other women and mothers who have come before her in her family line. Dee, by contrast, would seem to represent the ego-bounded hyper-individuality that Sapolsky identifies with contemporary American cuture — the aggressively self-assured culture of the students he meets in his classes. Yet, it's difficult to see Dee as being quite so self-contained, particularly since she arrives home having just adopted a whole new persona. The case could be made that, despite her self-assuredness, Dee is perhaps even more "open" than either her sister or mother. After all, she's the one who almost literally becomes someone else in this story. And the impression she leaves us with is that this won't be the last "self" she adopts. Thus, we're left wondering about which type of culture does, in fact, promote the most fluid or permeable sense of self. Are ego boundaries more closed in so-called traditional cultures, where people evolve into pre-established identities, or in contemporary Western cultures, where they may exchange identities rather easily for their own egotistical purposes?

4. Csikszentmihalyi offers yet another way of conceptualizing the conflict between Dee, Maggie, and her mother. As he sees it, "extrasomatic" objects have always served as tokens of the self: the tattoos and ritual objects of a member of a tribal society convey important information about social status and kinship group membership, just as a Rolex and an uptown address convey information about someone living in contemporary urban America. Csikszentmihalyi would probably deny the difference between the identity-building functions of these objects, based solely on cultural context. Yet, he might still be able to explain the story's conflict in terms of clashing "ideal selves." The ideal self for Maggie and her mother is defined by the women they recall from their family's past — women such as Big Dee and Grandma Dee before her — who made the quilts, churned the butter, and left their "rump prints" in the wooden benches that Dee's father made by hand. These were women who measured themselves in terms of what they could do in the roles they played in their families. And they were, more likely than not, all tough "man-working" women, exactly like the narrator. Dee, by contrast, finds her ideal self not at home but in the images surrounding the black pride movement of the 1960s and 1970s. She arrives home bedecked in jewelry and clothes that express her connection to her newly acknowledged African identity. Is one of these ideal selves more authentic or valuable than the other? Csikszentmihalyi himself seems to feel that the ideal selves of the present are relatively empty and superficial when compared to ideals of identity in the past. Perhaps he would, then, also see Dee as having adopted a kind of "consumer cuture" version of the self — a self that relies primarily on style and display instead of on achievement and personal virtue.

5. This question invites you to connect Walker with Baumeister's historical overview of the self later in this chapter. Baumeister might see Maggie and her mother as throwbacks to earlier concepts of selfhood in which identity emerges from "the local clan and small society where it has lived for centuries." He might easily view Dee, however, as reflecting the realities — and perhaps the problems — of the modern self. In the modern era, according to Baumeister, the self becomes more independent of its social and

cultural environments. The modern self is both more inward and more aware of its separateness, and it also begins to displace traditional cultural systems as a source of value. Dee might be seen as having just such a self. She is economically and intellectually independent of the smaller social world of her family. And she clearly feels her separateness, symbolized in the story, perhaps, by the sunglasses that she uses to conceal her eyes. The irony, of course, is that she now finds a source of cultural pride in the very things that she has defined herself against, and she is losing contact with traditional family ties that might have once provided her with an authentic source of value and identity. As Baumeister might note, she will now have to struggle with the task of replacing her original "value base" with values she herself creates.

Essay Options

1. Essay Option #1 expands the journal entry students made for the Before Reading activity into a personal essay. To do a good job with this assignment, students should describe the object they've chosen in detail, comment on its cultural significance, and relate the stories or memories that they and other members of their family associate with it. Dee, for example, would probably have to go into some detail about slavery, the Civil War, and Reconstruction in order to fully explain the meaning encoded in the family heirlooms she wants to take back with her to college. She might also have to relate a number of family stories associated with the making and use of these objects in order to convey their meaning.

2. Essay Option #2 calls for a wide-ranging academic essay on the general topic of how memories contribute to the construction of the self. Engel and Zerubavel offer the conceptual framework for this assignment. Engel's notions of the remembering and remembered selves suggest that there's a dynamic relationship between our past and present identities and that we shape our past self-conception to accommodate our immediate social situation. The self emerges, in Engel's view, from the tension between past memories and the exigencies of our present situations. Zerubavel's theory of impersonal recollection suggests that the self is founded on a broad base of historical and cultural memories that are only personal to the extent that they become woven into our identities. According to Hampl's theory of memoir, we employ imagination to construct memories that help us discover what we felt and who we were in the past. Memory doesn't create the self so much as it offers a way of unearthing truths about the past selves that lie hidden within us. Walker, Lopez, and Sanders provide illustrations for all of these views.

ARNOLD M. LUDWIG, *Living Backwards* (p. 292)

Ludwig's theory that we live out "pre-written" plots, roles, and scripts from the cultures to which we belong resonates deeply with ideas about the self in Sapolsky, Csikszentmihalyi, and Walker, so you'll want to give some serious consideration to this selection. Don't be put off by the extended illustration Ludwig offers from the life of Stephen Crane to open his discussion of "living backwards." The theoretical perspective he offers is well worth the initial effort. Ludwig adds a further twist to the notions of selfhood presented by Sapolsky and Csikszentmihalyi. As he sees it, the self is neither a fortress walled off from the world of others by ego boundaries, nor something we create. For Ludwig, the self grows around a "life story," a personal narrative we choose from the pre-fabricated plots our culture provides in order to make sense of our experiences. This is a very useful idea if you're emphasizing the theme of the social construction of the self in class. It's also useful because it raises important questions about the limits of what Ludwig calls "biographical freedom" and opens up the possibility of several productive in-class projects and activities. With Ludwig as your point of departure, you can have students brainstorm the "plots" that dominate contemporary American culture (FE #4) or think about the "scripts" that guide us in everyday actions, like meeting a friend at the college cafeteria or calling home to touch base with parents (ET #5). Ludwig's narrative analysis of the self also connects well with all the fictional selections you'll find in *Mind Readings*. The Before Reading activity challenges students to acknowledge the narratives that already shape their views of themselves — the stories they draw on when they speculate about their future lives. As students begin to compare their future stories and question where these stories come from, they'll be asking questions that Ludwig explores in this narrative analysis of selfhood.

Exploring the Text

1. As Ludwig sees it, Stephen Crane lived his life backwards in the sense that the events in his life closely followed situations and plots he had already sketched in his novels. A good nineteenth century American steeped in the traditions of a Christian culture that urged people to pattern their actions on the stories in the "Good Book," Crane was predisposed to the idea that one's life should conform to a pre-established script. Ludwig also speculates that, as a journalist, Crane would have expected to "frame" the events of his life in terms of a story. Ludwig believes that we all act out events we've imagined beforehand and thus experience the kind of "lived doubleness" that the literary critic Christopher Benfey discovers in Crane's biography. Instead of seeing the self emerge retrospectively from a series of experiences and memories, Ludwig suggests, we do just the opposite: we choose a life story and then act out the events and experiences of our lives according to the expectations it provides. The self, in this view, develops prospectively, not retrospectively.

2. To illustrate this idea, Ludwig offers the story of the Garden of Eden. Before the creation of Eve, Adam has no self and no story. He inhabits an "undifferentiated, mindless, care-free, womb-like existence." But after the advent of Eve, temptation, and the Fall, he enters into the flow of experience we call "time" and, as a result, acquires both a self and a life story. The point of Ludwig's biblical digression is that "[w]ithout new experiences, you can't live out a personal life story. Without having a personal life story, you can have no sense of self." This may seem like a fairly extreme claim to many students. Do you really have to script the future events of your life in order to have a self? Some will argue that you do and that even if you think you don't, you are only living according to someone else's script.

3. Of course, Ludwig himself doesn't mean to suggest that we all self-consciously engage in creative acts of prospective autobiography. We don't actually draft our own life stories for ourselves; we adopt them ready-made from our cultural contexts. Every culture, in Ludwig's view, offers a "vast reservoir" of collective myths, dreams, and story plots that we use to give shape and coherence to our personal experiences. Among the plots offered by contemporary American culture, for example, you'll find the "typical middle-class story of professional success," the story of the "frenetic, driven life" of rock musicians, the story of the "typical life of a daughter of an alcoholic father and long-suffering mother," the story of the "unhappy housewife," and the story of the "unconventional" artist. You may want to pause at this point to have students reflect on the storylines that are common in their own home cultures. Are there mythic stories that seem to pattern the lives of the people they've known? Are any of these stories specific to their cultural backgrounds — or are they all available within the context of the dominant culture?

4. We tend to adopt our life stories ready-made from the conventional stories available to us in our cultures, according to Ludwig, because we are "trained" to prefer them by parents, teachers, and other cultural authorities. These pre-written stories also provide a measure of security and comfort, because they are already "spelled out" for us in advance. The roles and plots associated with these life stories help us determine what's expected of us and what to expect of others. Bankers, for example, are supposed to be sober, businesslike types who lead well-regulated and carefully planned lives. They are not supposed to dye their hair fluorescent colors, dress in studded outfits, and show up for work when it pleases them. The roles we adopt "provide the blueprints" for our thoughts and actions and keep us from "responding haphazardly" in the situations we encounter.

5. Roles control our moment-by-moment behaviors through the "scripts" that they provide for us. Every role includes a number of "ready-made, prepackaged scripts" that specify various aspects of our behavior, from our fashion choices to the way we greet people on the street. According to Ludwig, conventional scripts even exist for people who appear to be rebelling against conventional behavior. Scripts signal others about the roles we've adopted and help them adjust their expectations about us. When we violate the scripts attached to our roles, we evoke suspicion and invite censure. Students can work together in groups to test some of these assertions about roles and scripts. It is relatively easy to write out scripts for familiar social situations such as ordering food at a fast food or a four-star restaurant. To enrich their analysis of Ludwig's thinking, students try to imagine a situation that would fall outside such scripted expectations. Is there any situation when we don't have some notion of the appropriate way to act or respond? What would such a situation be like?

6. Ludwig's theory about the way culturally scripted roles shape our daily lives poses a serious challenge to the existence of individual autonomy. If the roles we play exist before we're born and come complete with scripts that specify how we talk, dress, act, and respond in particular situations, then how much real freedom could we possibly have? Are we simply actors speaking lines that have already been written for us by our cultures, or are we playwrights who get to create our own original thoughts and shape our own destinies? Ludwig claims that we all enjoy a certain amount of "authorial freedom" with respect to our individual life stories. We each get the chance to "improvise" our own lines from time to time, and we are free to interpret the meaning of our stories in our own way. Whether this will seem like poor consolation will be up to your class to debate for themselves. It might well be argued, for example, that we have even less real freedom than Ludwig suggests, because for many of us a large number of potentially available social roles and life stories are ruled out in advance by limitations imposed by gender, income, educational background, and other extrinsic factors.

Further Explorations

1. Given her belief that we shape our past selves in response to social forces in the present, it might seem that Engel would agree with much of what Ludwig says on the topic of stories, roles, and personal identity. Engel herself says that we are like writers who shape life stories to achieve particular purposes or to impress an audience in a particular way. But Engel sees us *retrospectively* drafting and editing our presentations of self for others, not *prospectively* tailoring our actions to fit a pre-written story that we've borrowed from our cultural context. And, as she sees it, even if we do shape our presentations of self to meet the expectations of the present social context, we play an active, not a passive, role in the process of self-creation. Far from being something we know in advance, the self, as Engel sees it, remains a mystery — even to its own possessor. That's why it's possible to engage in self-deception and to experience phenomena such as screen memories that are meant to keep our present selves from understanding the motives and feelings of past selves. Ludwig, by contrast, allows us less freedom. In his view, the life stories and roles we can choose from are drummed into us by our cultures, and the only real freedom we have comes through our choice of role and the occasional chance to improvise.

2. Certainly, Maggie and the narrator in Walker's "Everyday Use" would understand the idea that we are destined to play certain preordained cultural roles. Walker's narrator may fantasize about the alternative roles she could play or the scripts she might enact — as she does when she imagines herself as a witty, slim, light-skinned woman conversing comfortably on TV with a jaunty Johnny Carson–like talk-show host. But she knows this role is out of her reach. Dee, by contrast, has "chosen" differently. She comes home in the role of the liberated, young, upwardly mobile African American who has just had her consciousness raised and discovered the meaning of black pride. And with this new role, she has adopted a new way of dressing, a new language, new tastes, even

a new male companion — all, as Ludwig would point out, in accordance with the scripts associated with her new life story. The script that the narrator would write for Dee already exists in her television fantasy: Dee, as a good daughter in her mother's eyes, would embrace her mother and tell her how much she loves her. The script that Dee would have her mother enact would probably involve her mother taking her aside and telling her stories passed down in the family about suffering, discrimination, and injustice — and then giving her the quilts as tokens of what these stories represent. Walker's story also serves, however, to raise questions about how free many of us really are to choose a particular life story in the first place. Many of us, like Walker's narrator and Maggie, may not have the economic, educational, and emotional resources required to adopt any role we wish. The idea of choice itself reflects a privileged cultural position that is not equally available to everyone.

3. This question invites students to connect Ludwig with Rubén Martínez's experience of growing up Chicano in a world dominated by Hollywood role models. Martínez's experience confirms much of Ludwig's thinking about how such roles shape the self. Martínez initially rejects the role of "cholo" that is available to him through the culture of his immediate neighborhood and elects instead to identify with the white cowboy heroes he sees in the movies. When he fails to carry off the scripts associated with these parts because of his ethnicity, he opts for a new role — the part of the "ethnic rebel" — which, he suggests, is also modeled on Hollywood stereotypes. But Martínez also challenges Ludwig in that he seems to enjoy a greater freedom in relation to these self-images than Ludwig might predict. Martinez isn't committed from youth to a particular life story that then guides his every thought and action. He adopts roles and plays out the scripts associated with them, but he also reserves to himself the power to choose. His ability to be who he wants to be from moment to moment suggests a kind of personal freedom that goes far beyond the occasional improvisation that Ludwig allows us.

4. Students can test Ludwig's ideas by developing plot lines for a number of common cultural roles in small groups and then comparing the outcomes. If Ludwig's theory is accurate, then you'd expect that the plots generated for these conventional roles would be relatively similar. If notable differences crop up, you'll want to explore their sources as well as question whether they weaken Ludwig's argument.

5. Baldwin's story "Sonny's Blues" also works well in relation to Ludwig, so you might consider assigning it along with Martínez. In this story of interfamily conflict, Sonny has opted for the life story of the jazz musician, while his brother has chosen the straight-and-narrow path of teaching algebra at the local middle school. The scripts associated with these choices — as different as equations are from jazz improvisation — make it understandably difficult for Balwin's characters to communicate. Drug use, for example, falls within the realm of possibility according to the scripts associated with Sonny's role, while his straight-arrow brother gets uneasy when Sonny drinks a can of beer in his presence. When Baldwin's algebra teacher narrator finally learns to listen to Sonny, he does so by seeing both himself and his brother in a larger narrative framework. At the end of the story, the narrator sees himself together with Sonny and his other family members reflected in the story of suffering and redemption told through Sonny's music. Thus he is able to transcend, at least momentarily, the limitations of the role he has opted to play in life.

Essay Options

1. You may want to postpone Essay Option #1 until after reading and discussing "Technicolor" by Rubén Martínez. The discussion of Hollywood role models that Martínez offers will help students appreciate the kinds of roles that Ludwig alludes to in his analysis of the self. Once students grasp this idea, they typically have little trouble outlining two or three role models that they've been or currently are attracted to. What makes this assignment particularly interesting is its emphasis on self-analysis. It's one thing to admit that you've always wanted to be a cowboy, and another thing to think about the motives that underlie this desire.

2. This assignment calls for an academic paper exploring the claim that the self exists to provide coherence and continuity in our lives. Engel and Ludwig both directly address this idea, and Sapolsky might be seen as offering an illustration of why this sense of coherence is necessary — even if it is founded on an illusion. You might want to include Csikszentmihalyi in this assignment, since he also comments on this function of the self. And if you plan to make this paper the focus of your work in this unit, you might include Martínez and Baldwin, as well. Both of these selections suggest that although self-definition is a necessity, too much internal coherence may lead to a kind of paralysis that undermines the ability to learn and communicate.

3. Essay Option #3 offers another rather academic paper on the challenges of living in the present. Cole, Percy, Schacter, and Ludwig all suggest that the past structures our sense of the present to a certain extent. Indeed, according to Percy, the preconceived ideas we bring with us from the past can blind us to the physical realities of the present world. As a species, we rely on our memories to help us control the present and predict the future, but our tendency to hold on to the past may also make it difficult to think creatively, to appreciate things that are radically new, and to adapt ourselves to changing circumstances and conditions.

RUBÉN MARTÍNEZ, *Technicolor* (p. 306)

I hope you'll consider working this selection into your course. Martínez's reflection on the role that Hollywood has played in the development of his sense of self is as entertaining as it is thought-provoking. What's particularly nice about this essay is the way that Martínez uses it to challenge "politically correct" conceptions of ethnic identity. The role models that Martínez inherits from the movies include cowboys and Indians, mainstream heroes and ethnic rebels. You can use Martínez to illustrate Ludwig's ideas about how we adopt ready-made life stories from the cultures we're exposed to as children or to complicate Sapolsky's views on ego boundaries. In addition, since Martínez discovers his role models in Hollywood films, you can use this selection to introduce the mass media into your exploration of the self. Martínez also connects with two of the chapter's dominant themes — the role of family in the construction of the self and the notion of the self as a self-consciously created artifact. The Before Reading activity invites students to reflect back on film or television characters that they may have identified with during their adolescence. If students want to, let them go beyond the limitations of this prompt to consider other forms of mass media and mass entertainment. For many students today, particularly in the era of MTV, musicians serve as role models and taste-makers more often than do film heroes.

Exploring the Text

1. As a kid growing up in Los Angeles during the 1950s, Martínez had few role models. One obvious choice was to become a "cholo" — a gang member who "wore the uniform of the ethnic rebel" and "lived at odds with white society." But Martínez chose to "acculturate" by identifying with the cowboys who dominated the film industry where his father worked. The John Waynes and Audie Murphys that Martínez met during Saturday afternoon matinees taught him what it meant to be an American. It may, however, be a challenge to think of contemporary film heroes who might serve the same function for kids today. Do modern teens really model themselves on Adam Sandler or Tom Green? Oddly enough, you may find more agreement about the heroes who serve as role models for young girls — although, again, many of these characters actually come from the world of pop and rap music rather than from Hollywood.

2. The problem with Martínez's obsession with Hollywood heroes was that he wasn't white. Because he didn't physically fit the type of the Anglo cowboy hero of his fantasies, he repeatedly encountered trouble in the world of reality. Thus, when he imagined himself as a member of the Jets in his *West Side Story* fantasies, his classmates insisted that he was a Shark. The tension between the "reel world" of Hollywood and the "real

world" of school and neighborhood induce a "schizophrenic consciousness" in Martínez. He tended to view himself and the things around him from the white perspective he had adopted from the movies, yet at the same time he had to deal with the reality of racism in American culture.

3. This conflict shows up in the Mexican stereotypes he encounters in Hollywood films and in his experiences trying to date white girls in school. While Martínez may have been convinced that he was a bluegrass-loving Jack Lemmon–style Anglo hero at heart, the girls he encounters keep reminding him that he can't wash away the "chocolate" hue from his skin no matter how much Irish Spring he uses. Eventually, Martínez adopts a new identity — that of the "ethnic rebel." He goes from cowboy to Indian. Yet, as he notes with considerable good humor, Hollywood is "right there" to help with the construction of this new identity as well. As he says, both identities "were fantasies, beautiful lies, Hollywood constructs."

4. Perhaps as a result of this experience, Martínez is leery of all simplistic attempts at self-definition. He rejects what he terms "the binary notion of cultural identity," because he knows that he has never belonged to just one ethnic group — even if he is "officially" Mexican by descent. He even rejects the images commonly associated with the "melting pot" and more pluralistic notions of racial diversity. He didn't stop being a "cowboy" when he became an "Indian"; he just became both at once. As he puts it, he is a "cultural chameleon," someone who, in Whitmanesque fashion, "contains multitudes" and is, therefore, not limited to a single narrowly defined identity. Indeed, the real aim of Martínez in this essay is to critique America's fear of cultural complexity.

5. In his view, America is fast becoming a "mestizo nation" — a place where cultures and identities merge and mix — in spite of its segregationist tendencies. Today, more than ever, it's a place where kids can grow up watching the *Brady Bunch* and venerating the Virgin of Guadalupe without any real sense of contradiction. Yet, in all fairness, Martínez also recognizes the tensions that are involved in living with multiple and often conflicting identities. He recognizes that African Americans can be celebrated publicly but discriminated against off-camera, and he knows first-hand that he still feels safer playing "white" when traveling through certain parts of the South. Again, whether the United States is really becoming mestizo because salsa has replaced ketchup as the top condiment nationwide or because "J-Lo" is big box office is debatable, and your students' judgments on this issue will vary depending on the area they live in, the extent of their exposure to so-called nontraditional cultural groups, and the extent to which they agree that we are all becoming "exiles" who are at home wherever we happen to be.

6. Students may also have some strong reactions to the way Martínez ends his essay. What *is* he saying by having John Wayne kiss Pedro Armendáriz? He might simply be taking a potshot at the mythic masculinity of Wayne's Hollywood image, or he might, in fact, be challenging the reader to extend his comments about embracing multiple identities beyond ethnicity into the realm of sexual orientation. If we can be all ethnicities, can we also be all genders? Finally, you'll probably want to debate whether the idea of being "between, and beyond, all colors" isn't just a way of avoiding the very real and often painful consequences of racism. Movies may "fade to black," but Martínez will personally never become black and suffer the consequences of anti-black racism no matter how much he identifies with black culture or black role models.

Further Explorations

1. According to Sapolsky, contemporary Americans live with relatively rigid ego boundaries. The average American is remarkably sure of his own sense of self and rarely questions the coherence or continuity of his identity. Martínez's ego seems absolutely porous by these standards. He not only admits to falling under all kinds of external influences, he sees this impressionability as a mark of distinction. He glories in his capacity to "embrace" cowboys and Indians in one body. This might have to do with the fact that Martínez is, in a sense, an "exile" in his own country — a person who must learn to cope

with another, more dominant culture. Or it may be that Sapolsky is simply wrong and that America is, in fact, becoming a mestizo nation that accepts the idea of external and internal diversity as a positive value. Still, it may also be possible that Martínez is an exception and that most Americans maintain relatively rigid ego boundaries — even as intermarrage and other forms of cultural mixing occur — by continuing to cling to simplistic, "binary notions" of ethnic identity. Thus, even though American culture itself is opening to and embracing many different cultural influences — and while a few individual Americans such as Martínez may welcome this change — many simply enjoy the fruits of these developments without questioning the integrity of their own ethnic identity. Indeed, it might even be argued that ethnic identities have become more exclusionary and rigid — more ego-bounded — since American culture began diversifying in the wake of the civil rights movement.

2. There's no doubt, however, that Csikszentmihalyi would recognize "ideal selves" in the cowboys and Indians that Martínez encountered in Hollywood films he saw while growing up. These heroic cinematic figures did for the 1940s, 1950s, and 1960s the same thing that the *Kouroi* did for ancient Greeks: they conveyed important lessons about how to act, what to value, and what to expect of others. The question of what "ideal selves" Hollywood currently offers is open to debate. Students might even want to speculate about whether Hollywood films still fulfill this cultural function, or whether, like high art, the cinema has given up portraying cultural ideals and, instead, is content to feature characters who more nearly resemble "the stick figure of a child" or "the scrawls of a schizophrenic." Certainly, it might be possible to view the protagonists of many films aimed specifically at teen audiences in this light.

3. Ludwig would probably view the cinematic cowboys and Indians after whom Martínez patterns himself as illustrations of the kinds of cultural roles that he believes shape personal identity. These cultural stereotypes do everything that Ludwig associates with such roles: they provide ready-made structures of values, expectation, attitudes, and behaviors; they are readily available within the culture; and they are easily recognizable by others. But Martínez's experiences with these adopted identities also challenge some of Ludwig's assumptions. Martínez may, indeed, adopt the roles that he plays ready-made from the media-dominated culture in which he lives, but he isn't content to live out just one life story. He changes roles as he develops, and he even insists that he sees himself playing out several conflicting roles at once. The freedom he thus claims in relation to the roles he plays goes far beyond the limited ability to "improvise" that Ludwig offers us. Martínez's experiences also suggest that choosing a life story may be more complicated in reality than it is in Ludwig's analysis. According to Ludwig, we adopt ready-made roles because they organize our experiences and facilitate social interaction by letting others know what to expect from us. For Martínez, however, the roles he adopts often do the opposite: they generate inner conflicts and tensions and complicate his interactions with others. Ludwig's theory may explain how Martínez exploits cultural patterns to create a self, but it does little to help us appreciate the difficulties Martínez encounters, because it does not address racism, class differences, sexism, and homophobia — factors that limit our freedom to choose who we become.

4. Clearly, however, these are issues that bell hooks would be well aware of. Because historical memories are also deeply personal, hooks might look doubtfully on Martínez's attempt to embrace multiple and conflicting identities and on his claim that America is becoming a mestizo nation. As hooks recognizes, it's one thing to proclaim your freedom and equality and another to escape the oppression and indignities of the past. Far from agreeing with Martínez's assertion that we are moving beyond race and color, hooks would likely note that we, as a culture, still perpetuate many of the oppressive practices and attitudes of past "role models" such as Christopher Columbus. Indeed, she would probably point to Martínez's own childhood love of the cowboy as an example of how a potentially oppressive memory of the past can "haunt" us even in the present. Hooks does suggest that America is changing: white delivery men now bring her packages in the mid-

dle of the night and take the time to read the ideas of black female authors. But, as the introduction to her essay suggests, she still can't forget the legacy of white oppression.

Essay Options

1. This assignment offers a personal essay topic that students find interesting and enjoyable. Return to the freewriting that students did for the Before Reading activity and have them discuss these original responses in small groups. Then, after they've read Martínez, ask them to do at least one more piece of exploratory freewriting in which they consider the subject in greater depth. Again, as they approach the final draft, they should reserve at least a third of the paper for serious analysis — in the manner of Martínez — regarding the meaning and the "costs" of these role models.

2. This option gives students the chance to debate Martínez's claim that America is becoming a mestizo or mixed nation. You'll want to complicate this assertion by reading Martínez against hooks, as suggested by Further Exploration #4. Martínez himself suggests that much of our interest in other racial groups may only reflect cross-cultural interest in the "exotic" and not really involve "a negotiation of any power beyond the aesthetic realm." Can a nation become mestizo if it means only sharing foods and musical styles but not political and economic power? You may also want to look ahead to other readings that connect with this topic, including Mick Fedullo's "Mrs. Cassadore" (*Mind Readings*, p. 441) and Guillermo Gómez-Peña's "The Virtual Barrio @ the Other Frontier" (*Mind Readings*, p. 667).

3. Essay Option #3 sets the stage for a major text-based essay on a theme that is central to nearly all the readings in this chapter — the notion that we actively and self-consciously shape the self we become. This theme raises important questions about the nature of consciousness and free will, and it also addresses many of our most deeply held assumptions about the self. We live in a culture that bombards us with the message that we can be anything we want — that we are the masters of our own destiny. Yet, it's equally clear that we live in an age when the models of what we might become are themselves mass-produced and controlled more than ever by specific individual or corporate interests. This topic invites students to evaluate our cultural sources of personal identity and to assess the degrees of freedom that we as individuals have in relation to the project of constructing our "selves." As you prepare for this assignment, keep in mind readings in earlier chapters that also relate to the notion of self-creation, including selections by Sanders, Hampl, Engel, Kingston, and Zerubavel.

ROY F. BAUMEISTER, *The Self and Society: Changes, Problems, and Opportunities* (p. 320)

This selection offers an overview of the historical development of attitudes toward the self in Western civilization. It's fairly dry going, because Baumeister is a serious academician, writing for a professional audience, but it does introduce a new perspective on issues related to the self. If your class is up to the challenge, you may want to assign it together with Bateson as a self-contained unit on the topic of cross-cultural understandings of selfhood. Baumeister offers the historical framework for this topic and introduces ideas such as the Western concept of the "inner self" as well as the idea of radical individualism. The self has become so important in the modern West, according to Baumeister, that it has displaced all other traditional sources of value and is in danger of becoming "a burden" instead of an asset. You'll find plenty of connections between Baumeister and earlier readings in this chapter. The idea of the "inner self" links with Sapolsky and Csikszentmihalyi, and the concept of the self as the center of all value has obvious application to Walker. Baumeister also connects with readings later on in the book, particularly those in relation to the theme of reading animal and machine minds in the last two chapters. To begin, take advantage of the Before Reading activity to get students thinking historically about the idea of selfhood. If your class has trouble imagining what the self was like in the Middle Ages, ask students if they think people today are more or less self-centered than they were in past times. Then ask them to explain why they think so. Most students have an intuition that our forerunners were less fixated on the self than we are today, but they may have a hard time articulating where this impression comes from. For some, it may stem from what they've learned in school about the Renaissance, the rise of humanism, or the birth of modern democracy. For others it may derive from the general image of the past as a period more devoted to the collective values associated with community and religion than is the present. If you want to push them a bit further, ask them to offer specific stories or historical facts that support their impressions of past concepts of selfhood.

Exploring the Text

1. Baumeister begins his historical analysis of personal identity by noting that three universal experiences transform bodies into selves: reflexive consciousness, interpersonal being, and the executive function. The foundation of the self, reflexive consciousness arises when we meditate on our actions, motives, values, beliefs, and so forth. Interpersonal being is that aspect of the self that's involved in our relationships with others. The executive function of the self refers to the mind's ability to make decisions and exercise self-control on its own behalf. This is what makes the self a true subject or agent and not simply a "passive spectator of events."

2. The central point of Baumeister's analysis is that the self, as we know it, is a relatively recent development. You may want to have students work in groups to construct timelines summarizing the evolutionary story of the self that Baumeister details in the first half of this selection. During the Middle Ages, people lived in collective societies, where the clan formed the power base of local officials and nobles. As the feudal system gave way to the rise of the nation-state, individuals gained the ability to move, make decisions, and choose their own spouses and occupations. The feudal system tied people to the land as "serf farmers," froze them into specific social roles, and channeled their labor to support the status quo. The plagues that swept Europe during the late Middle Ages may have contributed to the end of the feudal era by decimating the population and by creating labor shortages and land surpluses that made it possible for individuals to move and improve their life chances. Plague also concentrated wealth by decreasing the overall population, and this promoted the rise of the middle class, which undermined the control of local barons. These political and economic changes made it possible for people to expand the executive function of the self and liberated it from the rigid interpersonal ties associated with feudal collectivism. With more choices about what to be and where to live, and with fewer social ties, the stage was set for the rise of the modern notion of the independent self. These changes were accompanied by a major ideological shift — the rise of the notion of the "inner self." This idea is implied in the Christian doctrine of the soul. By the end of the Middle Ages, Christians came to believe that people would be held accountable in the afterlife for their own individual actions: the soul thus was seen as bearing "a personal record" of one's actions. During the sixteenth century the idea of duplicity also emerged as a major theme in theater and human affairs: as society became more mobile and more anonymous, it also became possible for individuals to assume false identities or to "imitate" the manners and attitudes of people from different social classes. Upwardly mobile families sent children to "finishing schools" at this time so that their outward manners might match their inner aspirations and qualify them for aristocratic marriages. At about this time, sincerity also arose as an important social virtue, and this, in turn, indicates how widespread were fears about the disjunction between inner selves and outward appearances in this era. Correspondingly, the Puritanical suspicion that, in order to appear pious, a person might even deceive himself about the truth of his inner motives, desires, and impulses suggests how powerful this new notion of selfhood had become. The Romantics and the Victorians furthered this idea of a potentially mysterious and perhaps even duplicitous inner self. The

Romantics promoted the idea that the self must be examined and nurtured in order to bring its true potential to fruition, and the Victorians expanded on the notion of a "hidden" self by adopting the view that an individual's outward actions are no more than signs or "small clues" about the "vast and inner realms of selfhood." The self emerges in the twentieth century, then, as an immense but potentially unfathomable aspect of the individual, a "secret entity" whose nature may be concealed from "the very person whose self it is." As Baumeister indicates, the modern hidden self, thus, presents special problems in that it greatly complicates the task of acquiring self-knowledge. Indeed, when you embark on the "treasure hunt" of self-knowledge, how can you ever be sure you've discovered the truth if the self is hidden and can always engage in self-deception?

3. Baumeister also points out that the modern inner self has assumed a new role in relation to morality. As the "value bases" of Western culture began to weaken in response to the declining political power of organized religion, the self emerged as a new source of moral authority. In Baumeister's view, the "value gap" created by the erosion of traditional sources of morality and meaning has been partially filled by the "work ethic" and the family. But for the most part, "Americans believe that they have a certain right and even a duty to do what is best for their individual, unique, esteemed selves." Baumeister notes that even religion has bowed to the power of the self, in that the most successful churches today "evoke the value of selfhood" by appealing to the self-interests of their followers. But Baumeister also notes that the new moral stature of the self is, in some sense, paradoxical, because it "inverts" traditional thinking, which often portrays sheer self-interest as the antithesis of morality. Traditional moral authorities, Baumeister suggests, have always tried to curb self-interest, not glorify it.

4. Baumeister also believes that the new central self is currently creating a host of problems for individuals in Western societies. Because such high value is placed on the self, people have become suspicious of all forms of self-control, and this may lead to increases in crime and other types of violent behavior. People today also face the increasingly daunting task of creating a "unique and autonomous" sense of self that can establish valid standards of moral action and be "socially validated through a constantly changing series of interpersonal relationships." These extra "burdens" placed on the modern self have transformed adolescence into "an age of identity crisis" and have generated stress because people feel they must "maintain a highly positive image of the self that requires constant vigilance against dangers and threats."

5. Before you leave Baumeister, you may also want to challenge students to think about how the notion of the radically independent self might still function as a source of social control. As Baumeister states in the opening paragraph of his analysis, "the broader society assigns roles to the individual and shapes the values the person holds, so that identity is also an important means by which society can influence and control his or her behavior." The modern independent self might seem to resist this idea, but students may also be able to think of ways in which it actually enhances society's control over individuals. For example, the imperative to "be all that you can be" can be used as a tool for enforcing conformity and controlling behavior, as it is in innumerable advertising campaigns. Students shouldn't have difficulty grasping the irony implied in the notion of becoming all that you can be by joining the army. Today, people may have been liberated from traditional systems of social control — religion, gender roles, and family structures — but they seem even more vulnerable to forms of media and commercial manipulation. Now, instead of getting our moral values from reading the Bible, the Koran, or the Analects, we get them from radio talk shows, self-help magazines, and television docu-dramas. And the fact that we don't have ready-made systems of belief and value to fall back on might be seen as making us even more dependent on these commercial sources of identity and value. Correspondingly, as traditional value systems erode, we become even more dependent on outward signs of social status to measure our worth. Thus, while it was possible to be deemed "successful" in the past because of carrying out certain prescribed social roles and functions — such as being a good parent, holding a

steady job, or being a good citizen — today, success is measured in terms of the things you can buy — luxury sports cars, vacation houses, expensive ivy-league educations — all of which require an enormous personal investment of time and energy to acquire.

Further Explorations

1. Hampl offers a clear illustration of the Romantic notion of the hidden self. In Hampl's view, the self is a mystery that we can only know through serious reflection and exploration. When we think back to past events in our lives, our true feelings about these experiences often remain hidden to us. We have to tease out details from the past by imaginatively elaborating on what we can remember, and, if we're lucky, we'll eventually be able to grasp what we actually felt and who we actually once were. As Hampl says, every memoir is a journey, a "pilgrimage" into the past — a kind of exploration into the mysteries of selfhood. Hampl also seems to suggest that the self is even larger than history. In her view, there is no one true version of the past; there are only different versions. As individuals, she suggests, we all construct the past in our own unique way, and only this version is valid for any one of us. As Baumeister might observe, Hampl places the self at the center of her view of history: traditional interpretations of the past, like those offered by the state or educational authorities, are no more authoritative than the versions we each construct. In fact, they are less authoritative because they omit the individual's point of view.

2. We might well expect Sapolsky to dispute Baumeister's initial claim that "the number of selves in a given room is equal to the number of bodies," because after his father's death, Sapolsky sensed that his own personal identity opened to embrace aspects of his father's sense of self. Sapolsky saw this happening as he began, unconsciously, to dress like his father, to talk like him, and even to feel more secure when he carried his father's heart medication around with him. Sapolsky also suggests a view of the self in traditional cultures that might offer an alternative to Baumeister's. Whereas Baumeister presents the self in traditional societies as something that's limited or bound by local control, Sapolsky sees the self in tribal cultures as something "open" and fluid, while the individual self of the modern West strikes him as relatively "bounded." However, this may only amount to a difference of semantics, for both Sapolsky and Baumeister would probably agree that although we are relatively freer than those who live in traditional societies, our sense of personal integrity is more jealously defended against outside intrusion.

3. Unlike Baumeister, Csikszentmihalyi doesn't take a historical view of the self. In fact, for the latter, there is no such thing as the self, per se, with its own history or evolution. The self is only "an illusion" that the mind creates with the help of our society. Both would probably agree, however, that the self can provide a source of social control. The "ideal images" that Csikszentmihalyi describes in relation to ancient civilization clearly function to convey the need for virtues associated with moderation and self-discipline. Yet, overall, it's hard to square his ahistorical, materialistic analysis of the self with Baumister's developmental view. Indeed, while Csikszentmihalyi might put the tattoos of a tribesman in the same category as the Rolex or power tie worn by a modern executive, Baumeister would probably see very different meanings and functions in these objects. For Csikszentmihalyi, the tattoo and the tie *both* communicate information about the self of their owners. For Baumeister, the tattoo is a token of clan membership that specifies the self of its owner, while the executive's tie is simply a matter of "choice" — regardless of the particular message that its owner chooses to convey. In terms of Baumeister's historical understanding of the self, a silk tie or a Rolex wristwatch is evidence of "executive function" and not a matter of group identification.

4. The distinction that Baumeister draws between modern and traditional selves in this selection might also be used to explain the conflict between Dee and her mother in Alice Walker's "Everyday Use." Baumeister might easily view Walker's narrator as someone who is still part of a clan culture, someone whose sense of self is tied to a specific

location and a particular network of relationships. By contrast, he would surely see Dee as representing the modern autonomous sense of self, in that Dee is both highly mobile — geographically, socially, and, we assume, economically — and also extremely self-directed. Despite her protests to the contrary about the importance of her heritage, Dee is a thoroughly modern type who creates or adopts her own values and stands free from the past. In fact, Baumeister might note that it's the very hiddenness of Dee's self that's so disconcerting in this story — and that Walker deliberately underscores this hidden-ness by having Dee conceal her eyes behind a very modern pair of sunglasses that clearly conflict with the traditional mode of dress she's recently chosen to wear. Such choices and acts of deliberate self-concealment, as Baumeister might indicate, are not an option for those who live in a traditional social context.

5. Interestingly enough, Baumeister's view of women in relation to the modern self contrasts strongly with that expressed by Mary Catherine Bateson in the next selection. Baumeister indicates that traditional values such as those associated with marriage and family have been eclipsed by the self for women in the West over the past few decades. As a result, while women in the past may have remained in an unfulfilling marriage out of a sense of obligation, today women feel it's almost a duty to end bad marriages in order to pursue their own self-development. Bateson, however, paints an entirely different picture of the female self. In her view, men in Western cultures are particularly wedded to the idea of independence, while women, East and West, still derive their sense of self from the network of family and community relationships in which they participate. Students may find support for this view in their own experience and their knowledge of women they've known in family and neighborhood contexts. But they may also see ample evidence supporting Baumeister's claims about female selves in popular culture. Certainly, many contemporary women's magazines, for example, continue to convey messages about the importance of the self as a source of value in women's lives.

6. One way to test Baumeister's notions about the new role of selfhood is to examine the mission statements of secondary schools or colleges to see how they portray their function in relation to the students they serve. Most educational institutions include language in their philosophy statements about helping students to "empower themselves," "realize their true potential," or "achieve their individual dreams." Such goals clearly reflect the dominance of the independent self in modern society.

Essay Options

1. You might want to have students make a collage of images drawn from popular magazines, television shows, and Web sites in preparation for Essay Option #1. Or have your class keep a running journal in which they collect evidence of the "modern self" from their own daily interactions with others, as well as from images and models available in mass media. The focus of this assignment is the question of whether students agree with Baumeister's claims about the centrality of the contemporary self.

2. Closely related to the first assigment, Essay Option #2 focuses on the idea the self has become a burden in today's society. Again, students will probably have plenty to say on their own about this topic. Nearly everyone has an opinion about how self-centered we're becoming as a culture nowadays. The real challenge here is being able to support these personal opinions with examples and illustrations that are clear and convincing.

3. This assignment invites students to test Baumeister's claims about the way the topic of the self has changed in popular publications for women since the 1940s. Clearly, results of this survey depend on the type of media consulted. The self may loom larger in publications aimed at young working women than it does in magazines directed at an older, family-centered audience. But even magazines such as *Cosmopolitan* and *Elle,* which obviously celebrate individual autonomy, may still harbor vestiges of more traditional, "relational" notions of the female self. Although many of the articles and features in these publications address ways to enhance personal power, attraction, and so on, they often also raise concerns about the impact of the self on immediate interpersonal relationships.

MARY CATHERINE BATESON, *A Mutable Self* (p. 337)

Bateson offers a cross-cultural counterpoint to Baumeister's historical analysis of the development of the self. As Bateson sees it, different cultures have different notions of the self, and women, in particular, draw their sense of selfhood from different sources than do men. Bateson's account of what she learned about "mutable" selves in places such as Iran, Israel, and the Philippines offers a sharp contrast to Baumeister's notion of the self as the mysterious hidden center of individual existence. You can assign this selection in connection with Baumeister as a pair of readings on the theme of cultural perspectives on the self. Or assign it as a one-reading preparation for an essay about a personal experience of accommodating oneself to a different culture (EO #1). Bateson also connects with several important thematic clusters in this chapter, most directly with readings addressing the status of the self in American culture and those touching on individual identity and the ethics of cloning. You'll also find that reading Bateson now will come in handy if you plan to address issues of gendered minds that arise in Chapter 4 in relation to Deborah Blum and Chapter 6 in relation to Ellen Ullman and Claudia Springer. When you assign this selection, be sure to have students read the headnote, because it provides information they'll need to make sense of the first few paragraphs. Bateson begins this selection rather obliquely by referring to the old adage about gifts for a wedding — the one about "something old, something new, something borrowed, something blue." She notes that in one variant, the last term was "and a silver sixpence in her shoe" and goes on to compare this coin with the "hard," "stable," and well-defined notion of the self in Western culture. Once students get past this rather elusive opening, they should have little trouble following Bateson's observations about mutable selves in other cultures. To help get them started, use the Before Reading activity as a chance for students to reflect on a time when they felt they had to accommodate themselves to a new culture. After they freewrite on this topic, have them compare notes on the experience in small groups or put their ideas aside as preparation for a possible follow-up essay assignment.

Exploring the Text

1. This selection offers a wide-ranging critique of the Western concept of the autonomous self. According to Bateson, American culture promotes a concept of the self that emphasizes independence, competition, and rigidity. American mothers are counseled to separate early from their children and to force them to sleep alone. American boys are taught to compete rather than to cooperate with one another.

2. By contrast, children in other cultures rarely are taught to value independence at such an early age. In Iran and on the kibbutz in Israel, mothers keep their children with them longer and allow them to share their parents' beds. Personhood, in such contexts, means connection, not independence, according to Bateson. Rather than enforcing an illusory sense of independence on a child, such non-Western cultures foster what Bateson sees as a healthy sense of interdependence. Of course, students may note that attitudes about childrearing certainly are not consistent even within the United States and that in the past ten years American parents have, in fact, been encouraged to maintain closer contact with their children by some child care experts. Still, there is something to Bateson's claim that the American self is founded on competition and conflict rather than on community and relationship.

3. Because the Western notion of the self is relatively inflexible, Bateson feels that selfhood can become an obstacle to learning. Despite the fact that the self changes and develops over time in response to its social and cultural environment, we in the West tend to view it as something continuous, as something that resists change. Thus, formal education can be a traumatic experience in Western cultures. According to Bateson, students are forced to leave their self-esteem "at the door" when they enter school. Their confidence and self-worth are undermined by the process of being forced to recognize themselves as "ignorant" so that they can subject themselves to "some number of years of submission and deference" and thus emerge as "somebody." The self is forcibly

"silenced" in the context of formal education. Teachers discourage students from using the word "I" and instead teach them how society is organized and "where they fit into that organization." They also use competition as a way of enhancing performance, but only at the price of "stripping away dreams and undermining confidence." The irony in all this, as Bateson suggests, is that by the time we finish school we've become resistant to further learning. The more successful and the more powerful we are, the more ignorant we become, because we are more able to resist the need to change that all real learning requires. Again, you'll probably find that students divide fairly equally over Bateson's view of schooling. Some will resonate with her charges about the way that schools stifle self-esteem and creativity, while others will never have experienced this kind of "insult" in school. Others yet may wonder why Bateson is so critical of schools in the West. American schools are not particularly harsh in comparison with schools in the Middle East or the Far East, in terms both of discipline and educational styles. And it may also strike some students as strange that Bateson criticizes American culture for the emphasis it places on individual autonomy and still worries so much herself about how Western schools force children to "fit in" with a particular social system. Aren't children who are raised on the kibbutz also expected to fit in?

4. Because learning is related to power and concepts of self, Bateson feels that men are less able to learn from new experiences than are women. This is particularly true of highly successful men raised in the West, who have the power and the resources required to insulate themselves from the requirements of new cultural contexts. Women, however, often must learn how to accommodate themselves to new situations, even if this learning entails a loss of status. Indeed, the fact that women have been forced to adapt more than men to change in the past enables them to be more "responsive" to change in the present. The concept of the autonomous self makes such change painfully difficult. Indeed, in order to make real personal change palatable for most Westerners today, it has to be packaged as "therapy" and undertaken only when people reach the point of desperation. The alternative, Bateson suggests, would be to conserve the native "openness" of the child and to be, like Einstein in the example that she offers, willing to learn from new experiences.

5. Bateson insists that the self emerges from personal interaction and that holding onto one point of view or perspective can hinder personal growth. Thus, it makes sense that her own writing reflects this trust in fluidity and openness. Although it's fairly easy to paraphrase Bateson's message in this essay, it's not particularly easy to sketch the essay's overall organization. Instead of building her case against the autonomous self logically by noting one drawback after another — the way a more traditional or legalistic academic essayist might — Bateson takes a less rigidly organized approach to her topic. She begins with a relatively straightforward statement of what she sees wrong with the American notion of the self and illustrates it with several examples relating to American childrearing practices. Then she offers an alternative view of the self as something that grows out of a network of interrelationships — as a pattern we weave "across a gap of mutual incomprehension" — and follows up with the story of her experiences during the Iranian revolution. At this point, her writing seems to be following chains of association rather than pre-set logical patterns. She touches on the idea of learning in general, then discusses the experience of education in Iran, then moves on to Israeli teens learning about mutual support, and then raises questions about the self as a barrier to learning. Eventually, she critiques Western educational methods, examines the differences between the way men and women negotiate different cultures, and even compares different learning styles. All of these subtopics relate to the central opposition between the inflexible autonomous self and the "mutable" interdependent self. Yet, there is little sense of clear logical structure here, little hint of a necessary order or pattern in the presentation of her ideas. Indeed, rather than imposing an extrinsic structure on her ideas, Bateson seems content to allow her ideas to "discover" their own interconnections and their own most effective manner of presentation. In the same way, Bateson's tone is consistently and self-consciously personal throughout this selection. Indeed, she takes pride in deliberately "personalizing" her topic and the tone of her voice.

Further Explorations

1. Bateson seconds Baumeister's view that within the context of Western civilization, the modern self is more central, autonomous, and inflexible than it is in other more traditional cultural contexts. Bateson, however, places less emphasis on the spiritual origins of this Western concept of self. For Baumeister, the Western notion of the self grows out of the Christian concept of the soul, and, thus, the "hiddenness" of the self — its distinction from the outward appearance of the person — is what's crucial. Bateson is critical of the notion of the inflexible, autonomous self, but she seems to accept and perhaps even to approve of the notion of a mysterious or hidden inner self. That's why she's so caustically critical of formal education. Like a good Romantic, she worries that education will deform or extinguish the naturally curious self that every child is born with. And this may explain the fact that while Bateson begins by attacking the idea of the autonomous individual self, she ends by celebrating the power of personalized writing and thinking. Bateson also adds a new dimension to Baumeister by reminding us that not all modern selves fit the pattern he describes. In fact, most cultures in the world — and perhaps at least half the people on the planet — may have selves that are more open, mutable, and self-consciously interdependent than the typical self he associates with the West.

2. Students should have little trouble tracing the role that relationships play in the construction of personal identity as reflected in Frazier, Sanders, Eiseley, Kingston, Sapolsky, Walker, and Martínez. We get the feeling, for example, that Frazier's own identity is tied up with a rich network of relationships that he sees wherever he looks in Brooklyn. Similarly, Sanders's sense of self is colored by memories of his father and grandfather. And although we hear very little about his personal life, there's no doubt that Eiseley long remembered the "non-existent" tree outside his childhood home because of the sense of connection it provided to his family. All of these selections suggest that the self is, to a certain extent, both open to the influence of others and something that is made or developed over time. Several might also be seen as supporting Bateson's reflections on the relation between the self, power, and education. Thus, Sapolsky notes that modern science promotes the notion of closed ego boundaries, but he suggests that the experience of death challenges him to become a learner again and to open himself up to new ways of thinking. Similarly, Kingston refuses to learn from the "pedagogical" lesson delivered by her mother, but she does learn something valuable and frightening from her own creative exploration of her aunt's tragic story. Likewise, Dee is the best "educated" character in Walker's story, but she has learned relatively little because she's handicapped by her own natural intelligence and self-assuredness. Her mother, by contrast, does learn something valuable, but only because she is forced to deal with her headstrong daughter.

Essay Options

1. The first three Essay Options present opportunities for productive personal essays based on some of the themes that Bateson stresses in this selection. Building on the Before Reading activity associated with this selection, Essay Option #1 invites students to reflect on a time when they, like Bateson, had to accommodate themselves to a new culture, community, or institution.

2. Essay Option #2 offers the chance for students to consider how their own sense of self may have been put at risk during their prior educational experiences.

3. And Essay Option #3 focuses on a topic that's crucial to any discussion of identity but that has only been touched on in other readings in this chapter: the role that interpersonal relationships play in the construction of the self. You might offer students the chance to respond to any one of these three options if you want to assign a personal paper at this point in your course.

4. If you want to assign a comprehensive academic essay, you might consider Essay Option #4, which invites students to synthesize ideas from at least four selections in this

chapter on the theme of the status of the self in contemporary American culture. Sapolsky, Baumeister, and Bateson all deal with the notion of American individualism and autonomy. Sapolsky and Baumeister provide important background information on the history of the autonomous self, while Martínez and Bateson offer cross-cultural perspectives on the concept of the American self. In addition, you might also invite students to include consideration of other selections in this assignment if they wish. Hampl, Kingston, and Walker, for example, could all easily be used to illustrate contemporary American attitudes toward the self.

PHILIP KITCHER, *Whose Self Is It, Anyway?* (p. 350)

You may want to assign this selection even if you don't plan to debate human cloning in your class. In this thoughtful exploration of issues related to cloning, Kitcher raises important questions about the nature of the self and the puzzle of individual identity — questions that touch on issues like the genetic bias in contemporary American thinking and the ethics of trying to control the development of a human self. During recent months, the international debate over cloning has taken on new urgency. As officials in the United States make it clear that they will not support further research on human cloning, scientists in other countries have redoubled their efforts to produce embryos from the process officially known as "somatic cell nuclear transfer." Thus, it appears that regardless of the position of any particular U.S. administration, the debate over cloning and its implications for our notions of human selfhood will continue well into the future. If you want a one-reading introduction to the subject, this is your selection. If, however, you want to explore the issue of cloning in greater depth, combine Kitcher with the following selection by the ethicist Jean Bethke Elshtain. You'll also find that the issue of cloning overlaps with readings in Chapter 6 related to the differences between human and machine minds. Most students already have some preconceptions about the notion of cloning human beings, so to prepare for Kitcher, ask them to get into small groups to share their views about when it might be appropriate to resort to this new technology, as suggested in the Before Reading activity. This will help them focus on some of the ethical considerations that Kitcher will eventually raise.

Exploring the Text

1. The case of Abe and Mary Ayala offers a good illustration of some of the ethical issues involved in the cloning debate. Many people feel that the Ayalas were justified in giving birth to a second child in order to save the life of their sixteen-year-old daughter. In fact, the press portrayed this story as a tale of heroism when it appeared in the early 1990s. Still, some students may object to the comparison between the situation of the Ayalas and the issue of cloning. It might have been noble to bring a child into the world to save another child, but that was because a human life was at stake. This example doesn't correspond to the situation of creating a person "to fulfill their parents' preordained intentions." The Ayalas didn't give birth to their second daughter in order to control who she'd become; they merely wanted to borrow some of her bone marrow for her sister. But, then, is this in itself a justifiable purpose for conceiving a human life? Kitcher seems to think so. The crux of the debate over cloning, in his view, lies in the notion of intentionality. As he sees it, what people fear most about cloning is the nightmare scenario of someone intentionally mass producing humans for some demented purpose.

2. But as Kitcher points out, it's doubtful that cloning will ever enable anyone to "duplicate people like so many cookie-cutter gingerbread men." First of all, cloning is far from being an exact science. Of the 277 adult lamb nuclei produced at the Roslin Institute outside Edinburgh, Scotland, only one resulted in a healthy birth. What's more, no clone is an absolutely exact duplicate, in that every cloned nucleus must be combined with an egg and, thus, the mitochondrial DNA of another individual. As a result, the offspring produced in this manner is "shaped by the interaction between the DNA in the nucleus and the contents of the egg cytoplasm." But Kitcher rejects the idea that cloning

equals replication primarily because he's convinced that the self depends more on individual life experience than it does on genetics. As he points out, identical twins are genetic duplicates, yet twins often display very significant differences in their attitudes, values, and behaviors. Even if you set out to engineer another you, you'd be "doomed to disappointment," according to Kitcher, because the traits we most value in others result from "complex interactions between genotypes and environments." And even though parents might still resort to cloning to create children with a propensity for certain abilities and talents, Kitcher points out that this is really no different from what parents have tried to do with their offspring throughout history. In fact, he offers the case of John Stuart Mill as evidence that, no matter how hard a parent tries to control a child's development, he's doomed to failure.

3. Thus, the question for Kitcher then becomes: Under which circumstances might cloning be deemed morally acceptable? Kitcher offers three test cases: the case of the dying child, the case of the grieving widow, and the case of the loving lesbians. Kitcher critiques the first two cases because he feels that in both the child involved is subordinated to "the special purposes or projects of the adults." The parents who want to replace a dying child and the widow who wishes to reproduce a deceased husband are motivated by nostalgia for what they've lost — not by the desire to bring a new life into the world. The case of the loving lesbians, however, is different. Kitcher argues that they want to use cloning in a way that is "completely natural and justifiable." They want to clone a child to express their mutual love, not to produce a specific kind of child. Overall, Kitcher is against the outright banning of human cloning. He believes it should be permissible "in a small range of cases" if they involve no attempt to engineer a child with certain outcomes and if there is no other way to provide a biological connection between parent and child.

4. But Kitcher is clearly troubled by the implications of cloning. He wonders why the U.S. government is suddenly so troubled about the sanctity of the self while it "institutes policies that permit existing children to live without proper health care and that endanger children's access to food and shelter." If you're worried about the sanctity of human life, he suggests, there are more pressing issues than cloning to address.

Further Explorations

1. As Baumeister might indicate, the notion of cloning should be expected to be explosive in the context of Western civilization because of the spiritual origin of the West's conception of selfhood. Since we glorify the self as a hidden, potentially mysterious essence that is unique in every individual, it is natural that people and governments in the West find the idea of genetic engineering by means of cloning morally repugnant. But, paradoxically enough, the same attitudes toward the self may explain why the West is particularly attracted to the idea of cloning. If the self is perceived as sacred and essentially unique, the loss of an individual is a terrible blow. It would make sense, then, that a grieving widow might not want simply to find a new husband or that the parents of a dying child might not want merely to have another child, but that they would seek to create exact duplicates of the precious "selves" they had lost.

2. In addition, the perspectives on identity offered by Sapolsky, Ludwig, and Bateson all further complicate the notion of individual ownership of the self as expressed in Kitcher's title. Sapolsky suggests that the self may actually be much more "open" than the Western notion of ego boundaries might suggest. Within the context of a tribal society, for example, where identities are passed down from generation to generation, the idea of cloning might not seem as "unnatural" or "immoral" as it does in a Western social context. Ludwig's theory of life stories and social roles also challenges the notion of the autonomous self. From Ludwig's perspective, selves are never "born," they're "adopted" from the stock of roles and plots that cultures make available to their members. Similarly, Bateson might argue that the notion that a self can be cloned is itself a manifestation of the Western belief in absolute individual autonomy. In non-Western cultures,

the self emerges from a network of lived relationships and cannot exist as a self-contained independent entity.

3. Zerubavel's theory of social memory might also be seen as arguing against the idea of the free, autonomous self. Zerubavel challenges the ideal of individual autonomy by blurring the distinction between personal and impersonal memory. Once we accept that the memories we acquire through socialization can become an intimate part of the self, we have given up on the idea of absolutely individual autonomy. In Zerubavel's view, the self is, to a large extent, the product of its cultural environment. Every individual's identity is founded on the memory of important personal and impersonal experiences. Thus, no one is absolutely unique or completely autonomous.

4. Despite all of these arguments to the contrary, the idea of cloning has long been a horror-inspiring topic in America's popular culture. To open up this topic, try viewing a representative sci-fi or horror film about cloning in your class. In Hollywood, clones are always unconscious, selfless zombies who are inevitably under the control of their collectivist masters. Most of these fantasies might be dismissed as reflecting Cold War anti-Communist fears, and, indeed, it's possible that much of our national reaction against cloning can be traced back to the role that the concept of individualism has played in the "war against Communism." But there's also no question that these films also speak to deeply held beliefs about the nature of the self in American culture.

Essay Options

1. This assignment picks up on what seems to be the central ethical question in Kitcher's analysis of cloning: the question of why it seems unethical to "create a child with specific attributes." This is a good topic for debate because it's clear that parents have always tried to shape the skills, behaviors, and attitudes of their offspring. Why, for example, might it be acceptable for parents to subject their children to punishment — or long hours of tutoring or practice — in order to turn them into future doctors or athletes while it's unacceptable to alter their DNA to enhance their ability to do advanced mathematics or to run the mile in less than four minutes? Why are strict religious training, plastic surgery, and hormone therapy more morally defensible than a little genetic tinkering?

2. This topic expands on your class's discussion of cloning in popular culture. Students will have to do some significant informal research to respond well to this assignment. At the least, they should survey online resources on the topic and explore how it's been portrayed in several different popular venues.

JEAN BETHKE ELSHTAIN, *To Clone or Not to Clone* (p. 359)

Jean Bethke Elshtain's critique of the motives underlying the notion of human cloning complements Kitcher and raises additional questions about American beliefs about genetics and issues of identity and individuality. Read it together with Kitcher as preparation for a major research project on the issue of cloning (EO #1) or as part of a suite of readings on the subject of ego boundaries and the ethics of cloning technology. The Before Reading activity encourages students to speculate about what life might be like if human cloning were to become an acceptable practice in the future. Would students imagine scenarios like Elshtain's nightmare of a whole NBA team made up of Michael Jordans or the traditional army of look-alike storm troopers? What difference is there between reproducing a society of genetically identical people and creating a society in which everyone aspires to become a particular type?

Exploring the Text

1. Elshtain's cloning nightmares include the standard scenarios: the basketball team composed of identical Michael Jordans, the orchestra of forty Mozarts, an army of Hitlers, and even a phalanx of Mother Theresas. In addition, and perhaps more to the point, she also fears the prospect of a society that clones anencephalic babies as a source

of spare parts — a society that resembles the dystopic future world of Stanislaw Lem's novel *The Star Diaries,* in which there are no separate individuals and people are punished for the "crime of personal differentiation." Elshtain is particularly revolted by the idea of human cloning because it strikes her as "obscene" that someone would think of literally replacing a dying human or a lost child through technological means. The dead, in her view, deserve to retain their uniqueness, just as much as the living; thus, it's doubly immoral to make "Tommy 2" so that you can get over the loss of his original.

2. But Elshtain objects to more than just cloning. She's dead set against all forms of human reproductive techology. Medical procedures such as in vitro fertilization, embryo flushing, surrogate embryo transfer, and sex preselection all lead us, she implies, down the slippery slope towards human cloning. In her view, all of these techniques involve the creation of multiple duplicate embryos, and thus all already make cloning a real possibility. Elshtain objects to the fertility doctor Mark Sauer's dream of "cloning" siblings from a single embryo because of the "potentially shattering questions it presents to the identity and integrity of the children involved." However, it's not clear why she feels this way. You may want to have students speculate about what she's getting at. Why might the deliberate cloning of an embryo into two or more identical beings born several years apart present "potentially shattering questions" about their identities and integrity? One possible response might be that the older member of a pair of asynchronous "twins" might exercise an unusual influence or impact on his younger sibling — or that parents might view their experiences with older "twins" as "practice" for the way they might handle younger ones. But then neither of these cases seems egregiously unethical or immoral. Older siblings often have unusual influence over younger ones, and there's no particular reason to expect that resemblance would increase this effect. Moreover, parents have long treated children differentially and learned from their mistakes in parenting, so why would it matter if one clone gets better treatment than another?

3. Perhaps the reason why Elshtain skips over this issue is that her real interest lies elsewhere. She is repulsed by the potential immorality of cloning, but what really puzzles her is why so many women are resorting to these elaborate reproductive technologies in the first place and why these technologies have been "surrounded by the halo of 'rights.'" Contemporary women, she fears, no longer accept the idea of "embodied limits." If a woman can't have a child, she no longer adopts or finds another socially useful avenue into which to direct her energies. Instead, she contacts a medical expert and explores her fertility options. To Elshtain this suggests that, ironically enough, individual identity has become such an overriding value in contemporary society that we are not content unless we reproduce ourselves in our children. Raising a child isn't enough: we don't feel complete unless we raise a child who is our own — a child who reflects our own genetic inheritance.

4. This deeper biological selfishness is what really troubles Elshtain. As she sees it, we live in an era obsessed with the notion of individual identity. We want, as she says, "to be all we can be, to achieve, to produce, to succeed, to define our own projects, to be the sole creators of our own destinies." Given this inflated view of the self, we understandably have trouble accepting our natural limits. And when all else fails, we turn to "the bedrock of biology" as the ultimate source of our identity. Thus, it's no longer enough to pass a part of ourselves along to future generations through good works or even through the way we nurture the children with whom we share our homes. In our present self-obsessed culture, we have to pass along our genes. And, in fact, this idea may not strike students as being all that shocking, since genetic explanations of human behavior and talents are becoming increasingly common in popular culture. Indeed, many students may find the notion that we are what our genes make of us quite acceptable. The problem, of course, is that all such genetic analyses lead us back into sheer determinism and, thus, to the disappearance of the self.

Further Explorations

1. We might well assume that Elshtain would balk at the notion of having a child in order to save an older sibling. After all, wouldn't the situation of the Ayalas, as described by Kitcher, raise the same sort of "potentially shattering" questions about the identity and integrity of a child that she associates with all forms of fertility science? Yet Elshtain is particularly concerned about the idea of what we might call genetic or biological self-ishness in this essay. What she objects to is the fact that parents, and particularly women, seem to feel they have failed unless they pass their genes along to the next generation. Kitcher, by contrast, is more concerned about the general issue of engineering or con-trolling children. Thus, whereas Elshtain might worry about the possibility of cloning whole basketball teams made up of Michael Jordans, Kitcher would likely point out that simply reproducing Jordan's genes would not guarantee that all the resultant "Michaels" would become NBA scoring champions. In any case, the situation of the Ayalas seems to avoid the objections of both Kitcher and Elshtain. The Ayalas didn't conceive their second daughter specifically to duplicate their genes, nor did they do it to control her identity. So, it's possible that even Elshtain might see their motives as fundamentally sound, since the extreme measures they took were for the sake of their child and not specifically for themselves. It's also clear that Kitcher and Elshtain might agree on at least one thing: they're both concerned about the self-absorption of modern society and the fact that we seem relatively willing to turn our backs on others as we pursue the pos-sibility of duplicating ourselves.

2. Baumeister, by contrast, would probably see the idea of biological selfishness as a logical extension of the evolution of selfhood in Western civilization. Once the self has displaced all extrinsic institutions as a source of value, there's little reason to think that people who can't have children of their own — or that people who suffer a painful loss of a beloved child or spouse — will hesitate to resort to cloning. The kind of altruistic devotion that's involved in adoption or in the public service that Elshtain suggests as an alternative to genetic parenting might seem like a poor substitute to someone who has been raised in a culture where the self is the source of all value. Given the fact that, as Baumeister believes, this concept of the central self has taken hold among women, it's also unlikely that many families will accept the "embodied limits" they encounter in life and opt against the use of reproductive technologies to aid in conception. Baumeister might thus note that although cloning appears to threaten the concept of the central self, it actually represents the ultimate manifestation of selfhood in Western culture, for what could be a greater tribute to the self than self-perpetuation?

3. Both Sapolsky and Bateson suggest that the rigid, immutable, ego-bounded self is sustained by arrogance and power in modern society. Sapolsky himself only began to ques-tion the permeability of his sense of self after the death of his father and the onset of aging. It became easier for him to see alternatives to the closed self once he was on the brink of losing power. Bateson suggests that women are inherently more open to new experience and learning because, lacking the power of men, they must be ready to accommodate themselves to new situations. Elshtain also sees a connection between power and identity and hints at it when she suggests that cloning is associated with "our arrogant search for dominion." For Elshtain, cloning represents our defiance of natural limitations. It also rep-resents a radical extension of the self. Cloning might give us power over nature, but it is meant primarily to extend our control over the others with whom we share our immediate environment. Seen in this way, the prospect of cloning represents a kind of misdirected flight from difference and an open admission of our fear of real connection.

4. Lame Deer would surely see cloning as just one more example of white society's obsessive fear of death. Fear of death, according to Lame Deer, is what makes white society destroy nature, domesticate animals, and sanitize life to the point where it's hard-ly worth living. By controlling the world, Lame Deer hints, whites seem to think they can avoid the inevitable. Of course, much the same notion lies just below the surface of Elshtain's own thinking in this essay.

Essay Option

The sole assignment associated with Elshtain offers the possibility of an in-depth research paper on the topic of cloning. A large number of books and Web sites have been dedicated to this issue since the announcement of Dolly's birth, so students shouldn't have much trouble locating resources on this topic. Contrary to expectation, some of the most interesting arguments about cloning come from evolutionary biologists and not from ethicists or politicians. You may, thus, want to steer students toward essays by writers such as Stephen J. Gould or Richard Dawkins, both of whom believe that the real danger in cloning stems from the threat it poses to natural selection.

4

Reading Other Minds:
Inside the Black Box (p. 367)

Getting Started

Chapter 4 might easily be seen as the central chapter in *Mind Readings*. The idea of interpreting other minds underlies much of what the book is about, and it certainly plays a major role in the development of critical thinking and writing skills. This chapter introduces the central theme of the book's second half. Whereas the first three chapters focus inwardly on topics that relate to the self — sense, memory, and personal identity — the last three chapters look outward to the challenges involved in understanding the motives and intentions of other minds — including those of other humans, animals, and machines. This chapter also serves as a bridge between the book's two halves. The idea of reading other minds inevitably leads back to the task of dealing with your own expectations, preconceptions, and biases. Thus, you'll find plenty of resonance here with ideas you encountered in the first three chapters. Readings by Bateson, Ludwig, Baumeister, and Csikszentmihalyi in Chapter 3, for example, tell us a great deal about how the cultures to which we belong shape our expectations of and reactions to other people, just as selections by Zerubavel, hooks, Engel, Percy, Cole, Kleege, and Ackerman in Chapters 1 and 2 help explain why our perceptions and memories differ from those of the people around us.

This chapter might also seem like the most familiar in *Mind Readings*, because its themes, such as cross-cultural and cross-gender differences, are standard fare in many composition classrooms. What may be new here, however, is the idea that it's not enough simply to acknowledge differences between people of different backgrounds, sexual orientations, or cultural groups. Indeed, as explained in the chapter introduction, we can't really assume that we ever understand anything others are thinking — no matter how much we have in common with them. Despite ties of family, culture, gender, class, and nationality, the mind of every other person is a "black box" — a mystery whose contents we can only guess at. The challenge is to move beyond the recognition of "otherness" and to address the difficulties of interpreting other minds despite the obvious differences from our own. The chapter introduction gets you started on this task by discussing the concept of "theory of mind" and by reinforcing the idea that although all other minds are essentially closed to direct inspection, we do manage to "read" them quite effectively by modeling them on what goes on in our own. Theory of mind explains how we bridge the existential gap that separates us from one another through the use of imaginative analogy. Thus, we understand the feelings of a friend when he tells us about something terrible that's happened to him, because we associate his situation with something roughly equivalent that's happened to us. In addition, theory of mind builds on the knowledge that we inherit from our cultural groups. By the time they get to college, most students understand that their English teacher expects them to be attentive in class and to get their work in on time, because they're steeped in an educational culture that models these expectations for them.

The ability to read other minds also plays a crucial role in composing. As explained in the "Readers as 'Others'" section of the chapter introduction, in order to become effective writers, students have to learn how to read the minds of the audiences for whom they write. They must learn how to anticipate their reader's reactions to the ideas they present and how to use these expectations to guide the decisions they make about the content, structure, and tone of their essays. The paragraphs from Andrew Sullivan's

"What's So Bad About Hate?" quoted in this section illustrate this kind of rhetorical sensitivity at work. As a follow-up exercise in audience analysis, you might want to have students revisit a selection read earlier in the term in order to explore how its author seems to have taken audience expectations and reactions into account. Even a quick glance at Ian Frazier's "Take the F," for example, shows this kind of rhetorical awareness. In his introduction, Frazier is careful to address our commonplace expectations about Brooklyn. He notes that when you see Brooklyn on a map, it takes the "hard-to-remember shape of a stain." Frazier begins by acknowledging the negative associations that we, his readers, have about his topic so that he can move us beyond them: Brooklyn, he reminds us, is a forgettable place associated with the "stain" of urban blight in the popular imagination. Having mentioned and dismissed this bias, he can move on to offer his own affectionate portrayal of life in his hometown. Other good bets for this kind of audience analysis include Barry Lopez's "A Passage of the Hands," Mark Slouka's "Listening for Silence," Patricia Hampl's "Memory and Imagination," bell hooks's "Columbus: Gone But Not Forgotten," Robert Sapolsky's "Ego Boudaries, or the Fit of My Father's Shirt," Rubén Martínez's "Technicolor," and Jean Bethke Elshtain's "To Clone or Not to Clone." For yet another activity on this topic, ask students to return to a paper they've already written and consider how they might revise it for another type of audience. If time doesn't permit a complete revision, have them write a page or two describing their alternative audience and outlining how they might modify the content, structure, and tone of the original essay in response to the expectations of this new readership.

To get started with your exploration of this chapter, you might try one of these activities in class:

- Have students discuss their responses to the Magritte painting that serves as the frontispiece to this chapter. What does this unusual "portrait" say to them about understanding other minds? About the idea of capturing the life of another person through a painting?

- Ask students to freewrite about a recent experience they've had that involved a misunderstanding. What was the situation? Looking back on it, how would they explain why this misunderstanding occurred? Have them compare these experiences in small groups to see if they can reach any conclusions about the factors that block understanding between minds.

- Ask students to freewrite about someone they feel they understand deeply. On what factors do they base this conclusion? How do they account for the fact that some people seem easier to understand than others?

Sequences and Pairings

Because this chapter touches on so many different issues — interpreting other minds in general, reading minds across cultures and genders, and the problem of violent minds — you'll find it doesn't divide into broader thematic units as neatly as do the other chapters in *Mind Readings*. The first trio of selections can be approached as a unit, although, given their length, you won't want to assign them for a single class. For a good general introduction to the difficulty of reading other minds, have students cover Schank and Baldwin over a two-day period. Schank's analysis of student reactions to stories told in the context of popular films raises questions about whether we ever really understand what others are saying. Baldwin's "Sonny's Blues" further complicates the project of reading other minds by dramatizing how hard it can be to understand the motives and intentions of others even within a family. Follow up with Nussbaum on the third day of class, because the story-based theory of empathy she offers resonates with issues raised in both Schank and Baldwin. Nussbaum can also be used as the occasion for two interesting informal research projects focusing on the way that stories told in children's books and the popular media shape our "civic" values. These three selections lay the groundwork for your investigation of the issue of reading other minds.

At this point, you have to make some decisions about the themes you'll focus on during the rest of the unit. If you want to emphasize cross-cultural understanding, you should move directly to Hall and Fedullo. These selections can be assigned together for a single day's discussion if you're working with relatively strong readers. If you want to address the challenges of reading minds across genders, move directly to Blum. Blum, Hall, and Fedullo set up effective topics for personal essay assignments. Sullivan and Garbarino introduce the theme of reading violent minds. Sullivan can also be assigned alone as the basis for a paper on hate crimes. If you want to examine the issue of violent minds further, follow Sullivan with Garbarino's theory about the causes of teen violence.

You can also approach the chapter in terms of the broader thematic units suggested below. Note that more than half of these thematic clusters require connections with other chapters. The major thematic clusters that arise directly from this chapter focus on learning how to listen to others and the role of empathy in the creation of a civil society. Blum, Sullivan, and Garbarino all address the notion of male minds and violence, but they also link to selections on the same topic in later chapters. Two other thematic groupings around the idea of reading minds within families and the "cultural unconscious" draw heavily on selections from earlier chapters.

Recommended Stand-Alone Readings

Should you have time for only a few days on this topic, you might want to consider focusing on one or two individual selections that lead to productive assignments. Baldwin's "Sonny's Blues" dramatizes the central idea in this chapter — the challenge of reading another person's mind, no matter how close you are in terms of family background, culture, gender, experience, and so forth. It also presents the opportunity for a personal essay in which students profile someone who has always remained a mystery to them. For a more analytic project based on a single reading, you want to assign Nussbaum and follow up with a paper exploring the function of stories in either children's literature or popular media. Other options might include Hall and Blum, which can be assigned individually as points of departure for personal essays on cross-cultural and cross-gender misunderstanding. If you'd prefer to have students debate a current social issue, have them read Sullivan as preparation for a paper on the question of hate crime legislation. Here's a list of possible topics for stand-alone assignments.

Portrait of a person who's a "mystery"	*Sonny's Blues* (Baldwin)
Imagination and civic culture in popular media	*The Narrative Imagination* (Nussbaum)
A cross-cultural misunderstanding	*Hidden Culture* (Hall)
A cross-gender misunderstanding	*Heart to Heart* (Blum)
Debating "hate crime" legislation	*What's So Bad About Hate?* (Sullivan)

Recommended Pairings

Other people's stories	*Understanding Other People's Stories* (Schank) and *Sonny's Blues* (Baldwin)
Reading minds across cultures	*Hidden Culture* (Hall) and *Mrs. Cassadore* (Fedullo)
Violent minds	*What's So Bad About Hate?* (Sullivan) and *Rejected and Neglected* (Garbarino)

Suggested Thematic Clusters

Empathy and civil society	*The Narrative Imagination* (Nussbaum), *Heart to Heart* (Blum), *Rejected and Neglected* (Garbarino)

Learning how to listen to others	*Understanding Other People's Stories* (Schank), *Sonny's Blues* (Baldwin), *The Narrative Imagination* (Nussbaum), *Hidden Culture* (Hall), *Mrs. Cassadore* (Fedullo)
Mind reading within families	*Sonny's Blues* (Baldwin), *Everyday Use* (Walker, Ch. 3), *Memory and Imagination* (Hampl, Ch. 2), *Social Memories* (Zerubavel, Ch. 2), *No-Name Woman* (Kingston, Ch. 2)
The cultural unconscious	*Hidden Culture* (Hall), *Taste: The Social Sense* (Ackerman, Ch. 1), *The Olfactory Revolution* (Classen et al., Ch. 1), *Seeing Things* (Cole, Ch. 1), *The Mind's Eye* (Kleege, Ch. 1), *Social Memories* (Zerubavel, Ch. 2), *Living Backwards* (Ludwig, Ch. 3)
Reading violent minds	*Heart to Heart* (Blum), *What's So Bad About Hate?* (Sullivan), *Rejected and Neglected* (Garbarino), *Murder in a Zoo* (Leakey and Lewin, Ch. 5), *Muscular Circuitry* (Springer, Ch. 6)

Essay Options

Understanding Other People's Stories, Roger C. Schank

Option #1. Compare multiple interpretations of a story.
Option #2. Compare theories of learning in Schank and in Bateson. (Bateson)

Sonny's Blues, James Baldwin

Option #1. Write about a person who is a mystery to you.
Option #2. Discuss the problems of mutual understanding within families. (Walker, Hampl, Zerubavel, and Kingston)

The Narrative Imagination, Martha C. Nussbaum

Option #1. Apply Nussbaum's theory of the "democratizing" function of narrative to stories from popular media.
Option #2. Apply Nussbaum's theory to examples of children's literature.

Hidden Culture, Edward T. Hall

Option #1. Analyze a personal experience of cross-cultural misunderstanding.
Option #2. Examine the concept of the "cultural unconscious." (Ackerman, Classen et al., Cole, Kleege, Percy, and Zerubavel)

Mrs. Cassadore, Mick Fedullo

Option #1. Apply Schank's and Bateson's notions of cross-cultural learning to Fedullo. (Schank and Bateson)
Option #2. Examine the challenges involved in learning to listen to others. (Schank, Baldwin, Nussbaum, and Hall)

Heart to Heart: Sex Differences in Emotion, Deborah Blum

> Option #1. Analyze a personal experience of cross-gender conflict.
> Option #2. Explore the challenges women face in the electronic workplace.
(Ullman)

What's So Bad About Hate?, Andrew Sullivan

> Option #1. Research and analyze a category of hate crimes.
> Option #2. Research and debate the pros and cons of hate crime legislation.

Rejected and Neglected, Ashamed and Depressed, James Garbarino

> Option #1. Research and report on the causes of teen violence.
> Option #2. Discuss the role of empathy in the creation of a civil society.
(Nussbaum and Blum)

Media Connections

The role of stories in *Diner* and *The Breakfast Club*	Schank, ET #3
The imagination as source of "civic culture" in popular media	Nussbaum, EO #1
Reflections of Japanese culture in such films as *Shower* and *Dance with Me*	Hall, FE #5
Collage of "male" and "female" images in contemporary popular culture	Blum, FE #1
Understanding violent minds in *Dead Man Walking*	Garbarino, FE #5
Youth violence in *Boyz 'n the Hood* and *Once Upon a Time in America*	Garbarino, FE #4

ROGER C. SCHANK, *Understanding Other People's Stories*
(p. 373)

A computer scientist who has devoted his career to exploring how human understanding works, Schank offers an interesting point of departure for your class's examination of the challenges involved in reading other minds. In this selection, Schank confronts us with a startlingly simple question: How do we know when we understand the stories that other people tell us? From Schank's own mechanistic perspective, the same question might be rephrased as follows: What do we do to demonstrate that we understand the stories of others? Schank's answer is sobering, but the approach he takes to arrive at it isn't. The cinematic experiment that he conducts with his students at Northwestern University is entertaining in itself, and it suggests a series of similar practical classroom activities that you can use to explore interpersonal understanding and storytelling. Schank is particularly useful as an introductory selection, because he underscores the role of interpretation in the way we understand one another and because he isn't focusing on "exotic" situations that might make misinterpretation more acceptable. This selection pairs well with Baldwin's "Sonny's Blues," which relates the story of a Harlem teacher who has trouble understanding the needs and desires of his younger brother. But given the length of both selections, you'll want to assign them for separate class meetings. Schank also works well in a cluster of readings on the theme of the challenges involved in listening to others. To prepare for Schank, you may want to locate videotapes of *Diner* and *The Breakfast Club* so that you can preview the scenes that Schank uses in his experiment. As suggested by the Before Reading activity, you may also want to have students think back to the last story they can recall hearing from a friend or relative to consider its point and to think about how they might "prove" they had understood it.

Exploring the Text

1. The point of Schank's experiment is that words never settle anything. When you hear a story, the only way you can "prove" you understand it is by sharing a story of your own. Words don't really clarify what we mean; they just multiply possible responses and interpretations. The only way we can tell if a person understands us is by comparing the story with which they respond to the story we originally told them. But this too relies on our interpretation of their interpretation, and so forth. Our memories and expectations shape the way we hear the stories other people tell us because we tend to hear what we're expecting to hear. We respond most effectively to stories that resonate with our own prior experiences. Stories that are too novel cannot be "mapped" onto stories we already have and, thus, can't be deeply understood. As a result, the "shallowest" form of understanding, according to Schank, occurs when a hearer has just one story that he can respond with. Every story he hears will trigger this story as a response and will probably leave the teller feeling poorly understood. Less shallow understanding occurs when listeners have several stories they can use to match with the stories they hear. The process of story selection, in this case, becomes an argument for deeper understanding of the original story. Deep understanding from Schank's point of view, then, isn't a qualitative but a quantitative matter. If you have a hundred thousand stories in your mental repertoire, the process of story matching will indicate exceptionally fine discrimination and deep comprehension; if, however, you have only a few stories to tell, your selection of a particular story shows less comprehension. Students may well question this mechanical approach to interpersonal understanding — or the apparently pessimistic conclusion Schank reaches about our inability to ever understand things in the same way — so you'll want to take the time to challenge his thinking. Still, it's not easy to imagine what might be actually happening when we feel we understand a story that someone tells us, if it isn't something like the process that Schank describes.

2. According to Schank, our memories are stocked with thousands of stories, each one "indexed" in different ways. Thus, the first subject in his experiment responds to Shrevie's story by telling a story that Schank believes bears the index "Marrying too early can lead to a dull life." It's clear from this example that, in Schank's view, an index is something like a general "belief" or a "question" that triggers the recall of particular story. When Schank's first subject heard Shrevie's story, he connected it with this particular belief about early marriage, and this belief led him back to the story of his friend Larry. (The idea of memory indices is similar to the concept of "memory cue" that Daniel L. Schacter discusses in "Building Memories: Encoding and Retriving the Past and the Present" [*Mind Readings,* p. 157].) Understanding, in Schank's view, thus becomes the attempt to comprehend "the beliefs of another in terms of one's own beliefs." Shallow understanding involves little more than matching our interpretation of the belief we find in a given story to a belief of our own and then telling that story as an illustration of it. Deeper understanding involves the creation of a new belief that must then be captured in a story we create to illustrate or express it.

3. Schank himself is wonderfully judgmental about the stories his subjects come up with in response to the film sequences he shows them. Many of the responses he records here stop short of deep understanding because they do no more than offer a belief in response to a belief — a remembered story in response to the original story told. Thus, in response to Andy the athlete's story about his overbearing father in *The Breakfast Club*, Subject 4 recalls his own experience of getting beaten up in school, offers it, and can think of nothing else to say. His thinking and his comprehension stop, because he has matched this new story with an old one, which, in his mind, interprets or explains it.

4. Deeper understanding requires that we learn from the stories we hear. According to Schank, Subjects 3 and 6 attain this deeper level because they reevaluate their own stories in light of the anecdote about Andy. They learn or discover something about themselves as they actively reflect on how their story compares with the one they've just heard. They also ask questions of themselves that they then seek to answer. This process of reflection and self-interrogation, Schank feels, is what we really mean by understanding. Unfortunately, as he points out, we tend to engage in this kind of deeper understanding only when we are open to questioning our own beliefs or when we are "flirting" with new ways of seeing things. Most of the time, we remain entranced by our own stories, which are richer in detail and emotional force than the stories we hear from others.

5. Thus, Schank's conclusion seems rather grim: "Real communication is rather difficult to achieve." The stories we hear send us back to the stories we already know, and even when we do "learn" something, we learn it by revising or rethinking our own prior experience. Thus, it is impossible for two people to understand a story in the same way. Every act of understanding locks us within ourselves and our experiences. In a sense, Schank is saying that every act of communication simply drives us deeper into ourselves.

Further Explorations

1. From a "Schankian" point of view, Baldwin's narrator in "Sonny's Blues" has trouble listening to and understanding the motives and dreams of his younger brother, because he can't get beyond the "stories" he already knows about jazz music and drug addiction. Baldwin's narrator is a relatively rigid type: he's an algebra-teaching ex-military man, who is trying desperately to live an exemplary middle-class life in the middle of Harlem in the 1960s. When he first learns about his brother Sonny's arrest for drug possession, he runs into a childhood friend of Sonny's who's living on the street and once supplied Sonny with drugs. This chance encounter might be seen as illustrating the narrator's thought processes. The "boy" the narrator encounters in the "shadow of a doorway" doesn't just resemble Sonny; he represents the "story" that comes to mind when the narrator learns of Sonny's difficulties with the law. The deadened skin, yellow eyes, and listless manner of this erstwhile friend, whom the narrator "never liked," tell the all-too-familiar tale of life on the "killing streets" of Harlem, a story of suffering that the narrator has worked assiduously to avoid. The narrator's expectations get the best of him in relation to Sonny's future profession, as well. When he hears that Sonny wants to become a musician, he wonders if he means a "concert pianist" and reacts angrily when he learns that Sonny wants to devote his life to jazz. As he says, "I had always put jazz musicians in a class with what Daddy called 'good-time people.'" For Baldwin's narrator the world of jazz conjures up stories about sex, drunkenness, drugs, and dissipation, and this internal story makes it nearly impossible for him to understand the kind of man his brother really is. As Schank might predict, stories and storytelling also work to change his original views. After he receives Sonny's letter, he begins to reflect on the past, and the stories he remembers force him to revise his original attitudes toward Sonny and the art of jazz. He remembers the story of his family sitting around after dinner and feeling safe inside the house as darkness — and death — approached inevitably from outside. He recalls the story of his father's suffering and his uncle's senseless death. And he reflects on the story of his own daughter Grace and how she was struck down by disease in the living room of his apartment. Every one of these stories forces him to rewrite his understanding of his life. Every one compels him to recognize that, as his father says, "Ain't no place safe for kids, nor nobody!"

2. This analysis of "Sonny's Blues" reminds us that not all the stories we recall are strictly personal. In fact, as Zerubavel might point out, the majority of the stories we know are, in all likelihood, stories that we learned as part of our socialization into the cultures to which we belong. Thus, when an American hears about a great tragedy, it might connect with any number of "indices" connected to historical stories she learned

in school — anything from the history of slavery to the story of the bombing of Pearl Harbor. The interesting thing about such impersonal stories is that, as Schank might point out, they may serve to *stop* real learning or deep understanding just effectively as personal ones do. Thus, Schank might question whether we ever engage in real understanding when we simply "exchange" stories that we've learned as part of our cultural inheritance. Real understanding would, in Schank's view, probably involve revision of these impersonal stories.

3. Interestingly, Kingston's retelling of her aunt's story might be seen as demonstrating exactly this kind of deep understanding. Kingston's multiple revisions ares clearly meant as responses to the version her mother offers her as a cautionary tale against sexual adventurism. But it's equally clear that Kingston discovers things about herself in the act of revision that she didn't originally know — things like her appreciation for the motives of the villagers who collectively punish her aunt and, perhaps, the strength of her own rebellious spirit. Kingston fears being trapped by the story of her aunt, but she also appears able to move beyond it through her determination to rewrite it to fit her own motives and aspirations.

Essay Options

1. This assignment offers students the chance to test Schank's theory of story-based understanding by asking three or more people to read and respond to Frazier's "Take the F." If you want, you can substitute a short story of your own choice for Frazier or have students use a personal story about an important personal experience. Frazier works relatively well here because he doesn't clearly underscore the point he's making about Brooklyn, and thus, his essay often elicits a range of different stories and reactions. Once students have collected at least three different interesting responses, they will need to summarize them in essay form and evaluate the depth of understanding shown by their subjects, much in the way that Schank does in this selection. They should also ask themselves if their findings bear out Schank's general conclusions that we usually remain trapped inside our own stories and that "real communication" is a relatively rare phenomenon.

2. Essay Option #2 invites students to write an academic paper comparing the theories of learning that are implied in Schank and in Bateson. These authors agree about the general nature of what it means to learn something new. Both believe that prior learning can be a great obstacle to the assimilation of new ideas and new ways of doing things. Both are also convinced that learning occurs best when you are open to the possibility of questioning your beliefs. This is why Bateson believes that the poor and the oppressed are inherently better learners than those in power and why Schank feels that real learning is such a rare phenomenon.

JAMES BALDWIN, *Sonny's Blues* (p. 390)

"Sonny's Blues" is a salute to the power of music and a celebration of the mystery of art. It's also a poignant story of miscommunication between two brothers. As such, it's does a wonderful job of illustrating the difficulties involved in reading other minds. Baldwin's story is unusually long, but it's well worth the effort, because it doesn't just illustrate the tragedy of miscommunication, it also suggests how we can surmount the obstacles to genuine understanding. You can use it to illustrate Schank's story-based theory of understanding and to anticipate Nussbaum's analysis of the way that great works of narrative art prepare us to read other minds. Since "Sonny's Blues" deals with the issue of drug addiction, you may want to begin by asking students to speculate about what leads some young people to a life of drug dependency while others are able to resist drug use, even though they may grow up in the same social, cultural, and economic environment. How do students explain why one person becomes hooked on drugs while someone raised in the same household never shows the slightest interest in them?

Exploring the Text

1. Baldwin's story clearly focuses on its narrator. From the outset, we learn about the conditions of his life and the outline of his character. He's the "good" older brother — or at least that's the way he comes across. He's a college graduate, a teacher, and a veteran. He's married, has a steady job as an algebra teacher in a public high school, and is raising a family. He is, thus, the straightest of straight arrows, and his values seem even more traditional in comparison with his heroin-addicted, piano-playing, jazz-loving younger brother. Baldwin's narrator is a man who is full of terror: from the moment he learns about his brother's arrest, he's gripped by the icy fear of what his brother represents. This is a man who has spent his entire life fleeing the "killing streets" of Harlem, only to find that the streets have come back to claim his brother. Sonny, by contrast, is far less rigid and less closed or protected than his brother. Beyond the fact that he loves jazz, we actually learn very little about him. The only other real detail that Baldwin gives us about Sonny is that he dreams of going to India — an appropriate destination for a young man who is both open to experience and fundamentally "spiritual" in the way he sees life. The narrator can't appreciate Sonny and his life choices because, despite the fact that they are brothers, they are essentially different. Jazz is founded on the idea of risk and improvisation. It is diametrically opposed to the rigid mathematical logic that rules his brother's life. This makes it difficult for Baldwin's narrator to comprehend Sonny. His preconceptions about drugs, the streets, and the world of jazz blind him to the reality of his own brother's being.

2. During the course of the story the narrator learns to open himself up to his brother and to "listen" to him for the first time in his life. This transformation comes about as the result of the stories the narrator recalls following Sonny's arrest for drug possession. The first is the memory of sitting around his family home as a child after Sunday dinner and feeling the approach of night — and with it the inevitable approach of death. He also remembers the story of how his uncle was murdered by a carload of drunken whites years before — and the story of his own daughter, who collapses one afternoon at home. All of these stories work to undermine the rationale on which the narrator has constructed his existence — the idea that you can somehow make yourself "safe" from the senseless tragedies of human existence. When Sonny returns home, the narrator is nearly paralyzed by the fear that Sonny will do something to hurt himself. But eventually he realizes that, as his father used to say before he died, "Ain't no place safe for kids, nor nobody!" Life, by definition, is fraught with danger, and an innocent can die as easily in the front room of her family's apartment as a junkie can in the shadows of a Harlem street.

3. By the time he enters the club, the narrator has learned what it means to listen. During the first part of the story, he can't hear Sonny because he's deafened by his own fears. The preconceptions he carries around with him about drugs, jazz, and life on the streets make it impossible for him to comprehend the complexity of Sonny's feelings and experiences. By the story's final pages, however, all of this has changed. When the narrator hears Sonny play at the club, he listens with his heart, and instead of hearing the drumbeat of his worst fears, he hears an echo of his own deepest feelings. In the music that Sonny plays, the narrator relives all the suffering that he had once tried so hard to hide from. He says, "I saw my mother's face again, and felt, for the first time, how the stones of the road she had walked on must have bruised her feet. I saw the moonlit road where my father's brother died. And I brought something else back to me, and carried me past it, I saw my little girl again and felt Isabel's tears again, and I felt my own tears begin to rise." Real listening, Baldwin suggests, requires that we put aside our immediate preoccupations, hopes, and fears and begin to listen with our hearts. We have to hear the words and stories of others as they resonate with our own deepest memories and experiences. Unless we listen this way with our whole being, we don't really hear others at all.

4. Of course, what students think will happen to Sonny and his brother in the future will say more about their own preconceptions than it does about Baldwin's characters. Sonny might succumb to his drug habit within a few years, and the narrator might die

of a heart attack two weeks after hearing him play at the club. The point of Baldwin's story, however, is that all such speculation is beside the point. We are all going to die, and death is always going to be tragic. But as long as we're alive, we can share our stories and our suffering through music and literature and take some consolation in the understanding we can offer one another.

5. The question of which character to sympathize with may be difficult for some students to answer. It might seem easy to sympathize with Sonny because he's a relatively attractive type — the struggling young artist — and he isn't the source of the story's conflict. Yet he is a drug user, and some students won't be able to accept this weakness. The narrator, by contrast, embodies most of the values we're taught to admire. But his rigidity, critical attitude, and initial unwillingness to help Sonny might make him less than sympathetic. The question of which character students understand better raises, once again, the role of familiarity in relation to the way we read other minds. Is it, in fact, always more difficult to comprehend the motives and feelings of someone who is different from us? Isn't it possible to understand someone who has different attitudes, values, and beliefs? (Both of these questions connect directly to ideas raised in Nussbaum's exploration of the role that empathy plays in the creation of civic culture.)

6. The final scene of the story dramatizes the narrator's reconciliation with Sonny and illustrates the kind of critical attention that it takes to really listen to someone who is different from ourselves. It also says much about the power of art as a form of expression that can help us transcend the personal differences that separate us. In this climactic scene, Baldwin casts Sonny in the role of the fledgling artist-seer who is supported by his fellow musicians as he heads out into the "deep water" of his craft. During this rite of passage, enacted as a kind of musical baptism of Sonny, Creole offers "the immense suggestion that Sonny speak for himself." Sonny's music does what great art has always done: it reaches beyond the merely personal and moves us by addressing our collective joys and woes. When Sonny plays, his brother hears the stories of his mother, his father, his uncle, and his daughter, he hears their experience and suffering — and his own — echoed in Sonny's music. The creation of art, Baldwin seems to say here, is a sacred act, in the sense that, like all things sacred, it bridges the differences between us and unites us in a higher truth. And the artist, thus, is a kind of saint, as Baldwin indicates through the biblical allusion in the last line of the story and the lingering image of a halo, reflected upward from a glass of scotch sitting on Sonny's piano.

Further Explorations

1. Schank might easily view "Sonny's Blues" as a tale about conflicting personal stories. As noted above, the inability of Baldwin's narrator to understand his brother can be seen as a reflection of the stories he tells himself about topics such as drug addiction, the lifestyle of jazz musicians, and the dangers of street life. When the narrator first learns about Sonny's arrest, he's haunted by the fears he attaches to these stories. When he hears the laughter of the high school students he teaches, he hears nothing but the disenchanted, mocking insolence of kids who grow up in a world that dooms them to failure. Later, as he leaves school, he runs into a living embodiment of the story he most fears about the "killing streets" of Harlem: the junkie who once was Sonny's boyhood friend. This "boy" lurking in the shadows of a street corner symbolizes the narrator's worst nightmare: he sees in this wasted life a foreshadowing of Sonny's future. Baldwin's narrator is a man who has tried to ward off the dangers of his environment by surrounding himself with a wall of middle-class respectability. He serves in the military, goes to college, works hard, becomes a teacher, marries, has a family, and moves into a housing project that "looks like a parody of the good, clean, faceless life" — all in the effort to escape from the "menace" he sees everywhere on the streets. The old boyhood friend of Sonny's embodies the story of hopeless despair and personal destruction that he's been fleeing. And it's this story of menace that makes it impossible for him to understand his brother. When he learns that Sonny wants to

become a musician, his personal stories about the jazz lifestyle also get in the way: "I had always put jazz musicians in a class with what Daddy called 'good-time people.'" For Baldwin's respectable, algebra-teaching narrator, the idea of jazz conjures up stories about sex, drunkenness, drugs, and dissipation. Perhaps even worse, jazz represents a world of freedom and play to him — a world that isn't "serious." Baldwin's narrator remains imprisoned by the stories he tells himself about jazz, drugs, and Harlem until he recalls other stories that force him to reconsider some of his primary beliefs. He remembers the story of his family sitting around after dinner and feeling safe inside the house as darkness — and death — approached inevitably and ineluctably from outside. He recalls the story of his father and his uncle's senseless death at the hands of some drunken whites. And he reflects on the story of his daughter Grace and how she was struck down by disease in the living room of his apartment. As Schank might stress, all of these remembered stories encourage him to reconsider and revise his beliefs about the possibility of escaping from life's dangers.

2. Ludwig might interpret the conflict between Sonny and his brother as a clash of cultural roles or life stories. Seen from the perspective of Ludwig's theory of story-based identity, Sonny has chosen to live out the life story of the jazz artist. He's opted for the life of the open, free-spirited musician, who hangs out partying with friends until all hours of the morning and even experiments with drugs as a way of escaping the banality — or the danger — of daily existence. The narrator, by contrast, has chosen a conflicting life story. His is the life of the solid and steady middle-class family man — the college-educated algebra teacher who has tried to make his life as orderly and as unassailable as a well-constructed equation. These roles are so clearly opposed that it's little wonder the narrator fails to understand the motives of his brother. Eventually, however, the narrator succeeds in questioning his own assumptions and biases and begins to see Sonny in a different light. In the story's final scene, the narrator revises his own understanding of the role of the jazz musician. He realizes that jazz isn't simply a dangerously irresponsible pastime; it's a form of sacred self-expression in which the musician plays the part of self-sacrificing spiritual leader who risks his own being for the good of the community he creates through his music.

3. Bateson, likewise, might view Baldwin's story as dramatizing the difference between the rigid Western concept of the self and the more fluid and relational notion of selfhood that she discovers in many non-Western cultures. There's no doubt that the narrator has tried to emulate traditionally Western notions of selfhood. All of his life choices and personal characteristics mark him as a person with particularly impenetrable ego boundaries. By the time we meet him in the opening pages of the story, his sense of self has become so guarded that he can't even bring himself to help his own brother. Sonny's sense of self, by contrast, is more relational and, perhaps, less traditionally Western. This is clear from his interest in things spiritual, his love of jazz, with its emphasis on improvisation, and the role that community plays in his music. Indeed, in the final scene of the story, Baldwin portrays Sonny's jazz quartet more like an extended family than a group of pros sitting in for a set at a local nightclub.

Essay Options

1. The first option presents a formidable challenge: it asks students to write about something they *don't* understand. Most of the time we dismiss or denigrate people whom we fail to comprehend. Obviously, that's not the purpose of this assignment. The real task here is to tease out the differences in background, attitude, values, and beliefs that might explain why this person is so hard to fathom. You'll want to be sure that students engage in some serious self-analysis, as well, since their failure to understand this other mind clearly originates in their own attitudes, values, and beliefs. In a sense, this assignment asks students to do what Baldwin's narrator does — to practice the art of "listening" by looking inward and examining the biases and preconceptions that hinder real understanding.

2. As an alternative, Essay Option #2 calls for a text-based essay on the topic of understanding within families. Clearly, the characters in Walker's "Everyday Use" have just as much trouble understanding each other's motives and desires as do those in "Sonny's Blues."

MARTHA C. NUSSBAUM, *The Narrative Imagination* (p. 416)

If your class is up for a challenge, you'll want to assign this reading. Nussbaum's theory is elegantly concise: she hypothesizes that narratives teach us how to empathize with other minds and that this fellow feeling is the basis of the tolerance that holds society together. Clearly, this is a wonderful notion if you're an English teacher, because it means that stories are more than mere entertainment. Every narrative we read, in Nussbaum's view, plays a vital role in the creation of our common civic culture. It's also a good companion piece for Baldwin's exploration of intolerance and empathy in "Sonny's Blues." In addition, you'll find that Nussbaum connects with other selections related to themes of empathy and animal minds in Chapters 5. When you assign this selection, you may want to ask students to freewrite about memorable characters they've encountered in works of fiction they've read or in plays or movies that they've seen, as suggested by the Before Reading activity. You should direct them specifically to reflect on characters from books *and* from television shows and film. This will allow them to compare the kinds of characters they've encountered in these two forms of media, and it will also help prepare them for follow-up discussion questions associated with Nussbaum.

Exploring the Text

1. According to Nussbaum, civil society requires that we cultivate "powers of imagination that are essential for citizenship." In order to survive in a democratic society, we must develop what she calls "the civic imagination." This involves the ability to recognize "how different circumstances shape the lives of those who share with us some general goals and projects" and how these circumstances "shape not only people's possibilities for action, but also their aspirations and desires, hopes, and fears." Reading works of literature such as Ralph Ellison's *Invisible Man* or Sophocles' *Philoctetes* allows us to empathize with people whose life circumstances may differ dramatically from our own. Reading such works invites us, for example, to "imagine the sort of needy, homeless life" of Sophocles' hero or to experience through the phenomenon of "sympathetic vision" the insults of invisibility that Ellison documents in his novel. Narrative art, thus, has the ability to expand our own limited perceptions of life and to make us more open and responsive to the situations of our fellow citizens. Of course, you may want to question whether all works of narrative art produce this kind of positive empathetic effect. It could easily be argued that many historical works have done exactly the opposite by reinforcing pernicious stereotypes and narrowly defined notions of citizenship and public virtue. Does reading *Huckleberry Finn* make you more tolerant of racial differences? Does watching *The Birth of a Nation?* It might also be suggested that a great many novels and stories are simply commercial products designed to offer momentary diversion. Does a Stephen King mystery or a grocery-store romance cultivate "powers of imagination that are essential for citizenship"?

2. Still, Nussbaum does make a persuasive case for the way children's literature helps us develop our capacity for wonder and curiosity about other minds. Nussbaum reminds us that children have to learn that people have "insides" that must be wondered about. Narrative play and children's stories teach children about the mental states that exist in other minds and dramatize the limits of our access to them. In this way, children develop the "habits of empathy and conjecture" that are necessary to understand the needs and feelings of others and that serve as the basis of "a certain type of citizenship and a certain type of community." Moreover, not only do stories teach children about the inner lives of others, they also help them recognize the rich variety of their own

thoughts and feelings. Through reading tales of heroism and tragedy, children learn to recognize in themselves complex traits such as "courage, self-restraint, dignity, perseverance, and fairness." Stories also help children understand their own "vulnerability to misfortune" and thus promote the development of compassion. Such compassion makes it possible for us to "transcend" the boundaries of race, class, gender, and nationality that separate us, in Nussbaum's view, and this makes it possible for us to identify with others and to appreciate the difficulties of their lives. Again, of course, you may want to challenge students to think critically about these claims. Does reading about people in other circumstances really change our view of them or help us actually feel what it's like to walk in their shoes? Or do we enjoy reading about others because it's a way of diverting ourselves from the realities of our own daily lives? Isn't it possible that instead of filling us with badly needed civic virtue, narrative art just panders to our voyeuristic tendencies?

3. Nussbaum also believes that tragedy does the best job of promoting this kind of empathetic identification with others. She argues that Sophocles' plays encouraged the young, wealthy, and free Athenian males who watched them to identify with all kinds of "others" — beggars, exiles, generals, slaves, Trojans, Africans, mothers, wives, and daughters. Tragedy thus invites the privileged spectator to recognize that "people as articulate and able as he face disaster and shame in some ways that males do not." And this recognition, in turn, makes him reflect on his own lot and "perceive, for a time, the invisible people of his world." As a result, Nussbaum asserts, all great books contain a "political agenda" that promotes "at least the beginning of social justice." Reading or viewing such works helps us recognize our connection to the others around us and "promotes a respect for the voices and rights of others." To test these assertions, students should think back to some of the classics they've encountered in school. What specific lessons did these great books teach about other lives and other minds?

Further Explorations

1. It's easy to see how "Sonny's Blues" might be interpreted as illustrating Nussbaum's belief that literature promotes the development of empathy and compassion. Baldwin's story gives readers some sense of the challenges faced by young men living in America's inner cities. It also conveys some of the psychological costs that growing up in places like Harlem exact from the individual. Presumably, the reader comes away from the story with a deeper appreciation for why a young man living in urban America might be tempted to use drugs — or feel hatred for those who stand clear of the difficulties he's had to deal with since childhood. Like classical tragedy, "Sonny's Blues" testifies to the fact that suffering is inevitable and that our inability to avoid suffering unites us as equals. Like tragic heroes, Baldwin's characters face a destiny they didn't create or deserve, yet they embrace it with courage and fortitude. In fact, Sonny might even be seen as fulfilling the tragic hero's traditional role as sacrificial victim, as he willingly submits himself to the experience of suffering in order to create the blues that provide some solace for people like his brother.

2. Walker's "Everyday Use" and Eiseley's "The Brown Wasps" might also be seen as fulfilling the distinctly political function that Nussbaum associates with great works of narrative art. Walker's story "makes visible" the lives of Maggie and her mother, two characters who clearly might be seen as representing "the invisible people of the world." Similarly, Eiseley's essay focuses our attention on the homeless, elderly poor he encounters in an urban train station. By having the mother narrate her own story in "Everyday Use," Walker gives her a voice and invites us to sympathize with the conflicts she feels about her lack of education and worldliness. At the same time, however, she encourages us to appreciate this simple woman's strength, integrity, loving nature, and sense of justice. Eiselely also invites us to explore the thoughts and feelings of the homeless people he observes. But since "The Brown Wasps" is an essay and he is narrating his own experience, we watch as he exercises his "civic imagination" to understand their feelings and desires. As he probes the motives that lead them to congregate in the train station,

Eiseley eventually connects them, through an act of pure empathetic imagination, with a memory of his own childhood — and, through it, with his own yearning to hold on to the past. This act of imaginative solidarity with those more unfortunate than himself would, in Nussbaum's eyes, probably qualify Eiseley's essay as a great work of art. Thus, it's possible to view both of these selections as essentially political documents, because both offer us views of people who have been silenced or marginalized by the dominant culture and who, in at least some limited way, resist oppression.

3. It's hard to imagine that Schank wouldn't question Nussbaum's rather optimistic view of interpersonal communication. As Schank might note, Nussbaum assumes that when a young Athenian male sees a tragic heroine suffering on stage, he immediately empathizes with her and contemplates the differences between her situation and his own. Schank's own experiment in story-based understanding suggests that real empathy is much harder to come by. It's true, for example, that many of Schank's subjects express sympathy for the situation of Andy the athlete, but, as Schank might note, many express sympathy for purely personal reasons. His first subject comes away from Andy's story feeling oddly relieved that the "assholes" who beat up on him in high school were really human after all. Subject 4 associates Andy's story with the time he learned how to stand up for himself against locker room bullies. Subject 7 hears in it the echo of a story he knows about a guy who grows up in an artistic family but decides to become "just a regular guy." Thus, as Schank might suggest, you can't assume that people will respond to the stories they encounter in the same way — even if the stories deal with human suffering and are told on stage by Sophocles. In Schank's view, we are all too focused on our own stories to empathize deeply with the events and characters in the stories we hear. Of course, it might be observed that Nussbaum isn't talking about just any type of story here but about Greek tragedy. The anecdotes Schank borrows from the movies for his experiment certainly aren't as vividly detailed or as powerful as the story of *Oedipus the King* or Ellison's *Invisible Man*, for example. It may be that narrative performs the kind of political function that Nussbaum describes only when it achieves the level of intensity and impact that we associate with great art.

Essay Options

1. Nussbaum's claims for the democratizing influence of narrative might seem relatively well founded in relation to great works of literature, but it's not at all clear that pop cultural narratives have the same effect. This assignment invites students to survey stories in popular films and television shows to determine how they influence our view of other minds.

2. Essay Option #2 offers another opportunity for an informal research assignment, this one focusing on Nussbaum's claims about children's literature. The assignment directs students to compare several recent popular children's books with stories they recall from their own childhood and to use the results to test the notion that children's stories teach invaluable lessons about other minds. You may want to tailor this assignment in different ways for your class. For example, you may want to have students divide into groups and then have each group survey children's books from different decades over the past century. Or you may want to include other forms of children's media in this project, such as television shows and films. Or you may want to divide the class into groups to address books by gender, topic, or genre.

EDWARD T. HALL, *Hidden Culture* (p. 428)

This is the first of two selections focusing on the theme of reading minds across cultures. Hall offers a theoretical context for examining cross-cultural interactions and misunderstandings. The central idea here is the concept of the "cultural unconscious" — a notion that connects neatly with themes raised in earlier chapters on sense, memory, and the self. Hall's theory is a natural for critical thinking. Once you agree that our cultures operate automatically to interpret our experiences, the only way to deal with intercultural conflict is to become aware of how your own culture influences your ideas, judgments, and perceptions. Hall is also refreshingly easy to read. Although he discusses theoretical concepts such as "high-" and "low-context" cultures, he presents his analysis of the problems of intercultural communication through his own personal experiences of traveling in Japan. You can use Hall as the occasion for a one-reading paper describing a personal experience of cultural conflict or pair this selection with Fedullo's "Mrs. Cassadore" for more a more in-depth look at the issue of learning to listen to others across cultural divides. The Before Reading activity invites students to prepare for Hall by freewriting about a cross-cultural conflict they've witnessed or about one they've been personally involved in. This can later be used as a pre-writing exercise for an expanded personal essay on the same topic (EO #1).

Exploring the Text

1. As Hall sees it, cultures exist to provide "stability and predictability" in human affairs. They do this by establishing clear expectations about other people's behaviors, attitudes, and values. A culture offers each individual within it "a total communication framework" that assigns meanings to "words, actions, postures, gestures, tones of voice, facial expressions, the way he handles time, space, and materials, and the way he works, plays, makes love, and defends himself." Once such cultural meanings are learned, they "sink below the surface of the mind" and control our thoughts and feelings unconsciously "from the depths." Taking a cue from Freud, Hall sees the "cultural unconscious" as a "hidden" mind within the mind that automatically conditions individual behavior and shapes expectations. The problem, according to Hall, is that although the cultural unconscious works to ease social relations within the context of a closed society, it actually creates problems once we cross cultural boundaries. This is because we can't control the expectations and assumptions that are assimilated into the cultural unconscious; in fact, they control us. It's also true because we tend to see our own cultural values as innate and universally applicable "truths" and not as conventions that are relevant only within a particular cultural framework. Hall sees value in intercultural contact because he believes that we can learn how cultural patterns shape our lives only if we are forced to become aware of them through cross-cultural encounters.

2. To illustrate this idea, Hall examines his own reactions after having been unceremoniously moved to a new room while staying at a Japanese hotel. When he finds his personal belongings moved without his knowledge, Hall first reacts with shock because he feels his personal space has been violated. Later, when he's moved to another hotel, he assumes that he's being deliberately mistreated because the management thinks he is a "low-status" guest. Eventually, Hall realizes that his reactions say more about his own cultural conditioning than they do about the motives of his Japanese hosts. In the United States, moving someone without telling them would be an insulting violation of personal autonomy, indicating a total lack of respect. That's because in a highly mobile society people place great importance on symbols of individual status — things like the size of an office or the place where your name appears on a corporate masthead. Such "externalized" tokens of status mean much to an American. Thus, when Hall is moved, he takes it personally and feels it as a blow to his ego. As a trained anthropologist, he understands that his reactions are colored by his cultural expectations, but that doesn't stop his primitive "mammalian brain" from feeling resentful.

3. The real source of this conflict, according to Hall, lies in two clashing sets of cultural attitudes and values — and two different ways of looking at human relationships. Whereas Hall sees himself, from an American point of view, as an individual with his own sense of autonomy, status, and rights, his Japanese hosts see him as part of a larger "family" once he checks into their hotel. Hall thus assumes that the management of his hotel is treating him opportunistically when, in fact, they see him "as a member of a family." This is difficult for an American to understand, in Hall's view, because Americans live in a culture where personal relationships are slow to form and where we are often only

"peripherally tied to the lives of others." In Japan, by contrast, the need for intimacy extends beyond the home. The average Japanese, in Hall's view, wants to feel part of a comfortable, intimate family group. Thus, being moved from room to room or place to place is interpreted as a sign of group membership and not as a personal slight.

4. Hall explains the apparent contradictions that Westerners see in Japanese society in terms of what he calls "high-" and "low-context" cultures. These rather slippery concepts may prove difficult for some students to grasp. In a high-context culture, individuals rely heavily on collective cultural assumptions to interpret each other's words and actions. Such cultures might appear casual or "relaxed" because interpersonal interactions within them seem not to follow prescribed patterns or rules. Low-context cultures, by contrast, rely on well-established sets of external rules, ceremonies, and rituals to regulate behaviors and expectations. When Westerners complain about the "contradictions" they see in Japanese society, they, in Hall's view, are simply failing to recognize that Japanese culture embraces both of these modes of cultural interaction. In the high-context mode associated with intimate situations, Japanese appear to be open, friendly, warm, and informal. In the low-context mode — the one most often seen by Westerners — Japanese appear to be extremely formal and obsessed with status and ceremony. According to Hall, the "principle drive" of the Japanese is to move from the low-context mode of interaction to the high-context mode — to move from public ceremony to communal intimacy. By contrast, Americans are less focused on "close human relations" and more interested in achieving individual goals. Students may want to try applying these analytic concepts to cultural groups they're intimately familiar with themselves. Ask them to think about how they would describe the "context" of their cultures. Are the members of their cultural groups "driven" toward collective intimacy, or do they tend to maintain their distance and prize their individual space? Do they find Hall's claim that Americans are more interested in achievement than relationship to be accurate?

5. In Hall's view, it does no good to talk about "respecting cultural differences." Since culture is built into the brain, trying to explain cultural interactions and interpret cultural differences requires serious intellectual analysis. Our culturally conditioned values and preconceptions color our reactions and opinions even when we're aware of and claim to respect the differences that separate us. Thus, the only way to begin to understand another culture is to start, as Hall demonstrates in this selection, by trying to understand how culture shapes one's own values, expectations, and reactions. To understand the incident that happened to him during his stay in Japan, Hall had first to explore the unconsciously held cultural assumptions that shaped his response.

Further Explorations

1. Although it might seem odd, it may be possible to view the conflict between the brothers in Baldwin's "Sonny's Blues" as a matter of clashing cultural values. Certainly, Baldwin's narrator is as perplexed by Sonny as Hall is by his experiences in Japan. And it's equally clear that although Baldwin's narrator realizes he *should* feel protective of and compassionate toward his younger brother, he can't get beyond the feeling of fear that his brother inspires in him. Like Hall, Baldwin's narrator experiences a split between his conscious mind and his "mammalian brain." But is this the result of culture? The case could be made that Sonny and the narrator represent two different subcultural perspectives, even though they grew up within the same family and social milieu. Sonny reflects the attitudes and values associated with the free, creative, and essentially "open" cultural world of the jazz musician. Although we don't get much information about Sonny in Baldwin's story, we do know that he dreams of traveling to India, that he's open to new people and new experiences, and that he's established his own identity within the context of the "family" of musicians who make up his group. The narrator, by contrast, has adopted values and attitudes that Hall might identify more closely with "dominant" American culture. He is more "closed" to others than Sonny is, he associates intimacy with only his immediate family, and he measures his worth in terms of symbols of success

and status such as the "middle-class" apartment he lives in with his family. From this perspective, life on the streets is full of "menace" and the life of a jazz musician appears to be a dangerous waste of time. From Sonny's perspective, life on the streets can be a source of inspiration and the life of a jazz musician is a sacred calling. The key question is whether these attitudes result solely from personal experience or if they reflect more generally held cultural values. It might be argued that given the similarity of their personal lives, the very fact that Sonny and his brother have turned out so differently indicates that they've fallen under the influence of competing cultural systems.

2. Similarly, the connection between Hall and Nussbaum might not be immediately apparent. Nussbam claims that great narrative works of literature can help us transcend the differences that separate us — including those of gender, class, and culture. Hall's view of the difficulties involved in cross-cultural understanding might be seen as seriously challenging this notion. How can we transcend cultural differences by reading a novel or watching a play for a couple of hours if it's true that genuine cross-cultural understanding requires such extraordinary effort in real life? Hall might well dismiss our empathetic identification with cultural "others" in literature as just another way of glossing over the real problems of cross-cultural communication. We might think we've learned something about what it's like to be "invisible" by reading Ralph Ellison, but in reality we've only come away feeling comforted while our cultural ignorance remains intact. It might also be argued, however, that Nussbaum never claims that we actually learn much about other cultures through literature — only that we become aware of what it's like to suffer from the differences established by cultural systems. In fact, Nussbaum's central point is that great works of literature force us to do exactly what Hall finds most valuable in cross-cultural encounters: they force us to acknowledge the existence of "other" minds and thus to question the innateness of our own most cherished values and beliefs.

3. According to Bateson, Americans have trouble learning from other cultures because of the importance they place on individualism and because they have power. American men are particularly closed to cross-cultural experiences, in Bateson's view, because they have been raised in a competitive society that places a high value on personal autonomy. Men are also closed off to real intercultural contact simply because they wield power. The more important and powerful you are, the less you have to accommodate yourself to the changes and differences you encounter, no matter where you live or travel. Bateson suggests that women are generally more open to cross-cultural learning and more skilled at negotiating cultural differences because they have relatively less power than do men. She also appears to suggest that people raised in more open, flexible, and collective societies may be more skilled in cross-cultural exchanges. Hall would likely agree with much of what Bateson says about American culture and American identity, but he would certainly object to the notion that any one group is more adept at intercultural communication than another. All individuals are victims of the cultures they participate in, according to Hall. The cultural unconscious works against intergroup communication regardless of the specific values or attitudes of any given culture.

4. You may want to have students apply Hall's perspective on intercultural communication to Fedullo's experience with Mrs. Cassadore in the following selection. Fedullo's conflict with Mrs. Cassadore and the way he copes with it illustrate much of what Hall suggests about intercultural communication. Fedullo's overtures of friendship are initially rejected by Cassadore because the idea of openness and friendliness that he has learned in white society do not correspond to her Native American attitudes toward strangers. To overcome this rejection, Fedullo does what Hall recommends: he analyzes his own attitudes, values, expectations, and beliefs and tries to modify them. Of course, it's also possible to argue that Fedullo's conflict with Mrs. Cassadore involves other factors. She may be cool to his initial advances simply because he's a strange man whom she's only recently met. And, of course, the fact that he reminds her of the white doctor who once separated her from her family suggests that there are emotional and perhaps even political factors that may make it difficult for her to embrace his initial gesture of friendship.

5. As a way of testing Hall's assertions about Japanese culture without relying solely on your class's general knowledge, you may want to screen any one of several recent
movies by Japanese filmmakers. One question you may want to explore is whether the
film illustrates or challenges the distinction Hall makes between the high- and low-context modes of Japanese culture. Do the Japanese portrayed in this film move from highly structured, formal relationships to a more relaxed collective intimacy, as Hall suggests? Or do their relationships and behaviors seem relatively consistent throughout the
film, regardless of context? How does the film's portrayal of Japanese customs, values,
and attitudes compare with your students' assumptions about Japanese culture?

Essay Options

1. The Before Reading activity associated with Hall can be used as a point of departure for a personal essay in which students document and analyze an experience of
cross-cultural misunderstanding or conflict. If students can't think of or are uncomfortable about discussing a personal experience, offer the option of focusing on a particular
instance of cultural conflict that they've witnessed. They should, of course, do more than
simply describe what happened. Encourage them to explore the contrasting systems of
values and beliefs that caused the conflict. The idea of asking someone from the cultural group involved to offer an analysis of the situation may help students appreciate the
role that their own cultural values may have played in the situation.

2. This assignment offers the chance for a wide-ranging academic exploration of the
notion of the "cultural unconscious" — a topic that brings together selections from the
first four chapters of *Mind Readings*. You may want to include even more options than
are mentioned in the text. For example, Sapolsky's discussion of ego boundaries,
Ludwig's theory of life stories, and Bateson's analysis of American identity in a cross-
cultural context all suggest that personal identity is shaped by unconsciously held cultural values and beliefs.

MICK FEDULLO, *Mrs. Cassadore* (p. 441)

This selection offers a concrete illustration of the difficulties involved in reading
minds across cultures. It also offers an example of how these difficulties may be overcome. As a result, it works well when read against Hall's analysis of "hidden culture" and
the way it obstructs intergroup communication. You can also use it to raise critical questions about some of Hall's assertions — and about some of our own commonplace ideas
about the nature of cross-cultural misunderstandings. The conflict between Mrs.
Cassadore and Fedullo can be seen as arising from contrasting cultural values and
beliefs, but it might also be seen as reflecting personal or political issues that are not
specifically cultural in nature. In addition, Fedullo may be read as part of a thematic
suite of selections on the topic of learning how to listen to others. When you assign
Fedullo, have students reflect for a few moments on the stereotypes that are associated
with Native Americans and other cultural groups, as suggested by the Before Reading
activity. We usually assume that stereotypes are mistaken ideas that should be avoided at
all costs. Unfortunately, this keeps us from considering why stereotypes seem to be so
difficult to overcome. The fact is that some stereotypes may actually reflect at least partial truths: it is possible that Latinos are, in fact, more family oriented than other ethnic
groups or that Asian American families do place a heavy emphasis on academic achievement. It's also true that, to a certain extent, all thought relies on stereotypical patterns
of expectation and belief. If we were to confront every person and event in our lives as
a genuinely unique experience, we'd probably never be able to reach a conclusion or
frame an expectation about anything. The only honest approach to dealing with cultural stereotypes is to admit that we all have them and then to consider their inherent limitations and inaccuracies.

Exploring the Text

1. Fedullo makes several key mistakes in his initial approach to Mrs. Cassadore. After she rejects his invitation to dinner, he realizes that he has been too "abrupt" and allowed his "Anglo forwardness" to get the best of him. Led by the values of his own culture, he assumes that this unknown Indian woman will welcome his straightforward offer of friendship. To overcome this mistake, Fedullo decides to try "to see things from Mrs. Cassadore's point of view, from an Indian point of view." Seeing himself through Mrs. Cassadore's eyes, he realizes that he must have come across as an "intimidating" and "unnatural" stranger whose unconventional mode of dress sent mixed messages about his identity. He realizes that he must have seemed overly aggressive and perhaps even exploitative. He also recognizes that he broke several fundamental "rules of Indian friendship" — rules about avoiding direct eye contact and allowing time for trust to mature and develop. Eventually, he takes all this self-criticism to heart and decides to approach Mrs. Cassadore only after he has established himself further at the reservation school.

2. In the survival skills classes that he teaches, Fedullo tries to prepare young Native Americans for the challenges of life in Anglo society. In order to survive in the Anglo world, Fedullo's Apache students have to develop whole new sets of concepts and behaviors. But he personally opposes the idea of their "assimilating" with Anglo culture, because he feels that Native Americans have to maintain their own cultural heritage and with it their own identities. You may want to pursue this idea further in class by asking students if and why they think this might be a good idea. Do students generally believe that members of an ethnic group should maintain their cultural identity and traditions? What reasons can students offer in support of this idea? What costs, if any, might individuals incur who hold too closely to traditional customs, values, and beliefs?

3. Interestingly, much of what Fedullo seems to do in his classes involves getting his students to question their own assumptions and beliefs about white society. The Apache kids often encounter suspicion when they venture into Anglo society. That, at least, is what they feel. When Anglos "stare" at them in public, they assume it's because they might be angry with them or because they suspect them of stealing or simply because they're prejudiced. Fedullo offers them other possible interpretations of the motives for this apparently rude behavior. He suggests that some people "just like to stare" and that they might be taking a long look because they like what they see. Still, it's quite possible that Fedullo's students aren't very far off the mark in some of their interpretations of Anglo minds. The store proprietor who zeroes in on every Indian who enters his place of business might well be a racist. But the couple in the restaurant might just as easily be tourists who are thrilled to see an Indian. The point of this lesson is not that you can interpret Anglos' stares in any one particular way but that every individual has to evaluate and assess the meaning of each cross-cultural encounter on its own terms and then react to it in a way that's best for him. Fedullo is less interested in telling his students what to think about the Anglo world than he is in helping them to acquire the kinds of interpretive skills — and the self-respect — that they'll need to survive in it.

4. At dinner with Mrs. Cassadore, Fedullo continues to learn lessons about Native Americans and the woman he wanted to befriend. Mrs. Cassadore blows away stereotypes by reminding him about how open Indians are with their friends and about how much they love to laugh and share stories. She also explains to him that his assumptions about the importance of literacy aren't widely shared by many Native Americans — primarily because of the government's past attempts to force assimilation through education. He also learns that even after he tried to see things from Mrs. Cassadore's point of view, he still misunderstood her. She wasn't actually "intimidated" by his approach or confused by his manner of dress; she actively "disliked" him because he resembled a white doctor who almost killed her through misdiagnosis when she was a young woman. Thus, it might be argued that her original hesitation about going out with him was not culturally motivated at all but was the unfortunate result of her associating him with a past traumatic experience.

Further Explorations

1. Fedullo's experince with Mrs. Cassadore can be seen as clearly illustrating Hall's concept of the "cultural unconscious." Fedullo initially approaches Mrs. Cassadore too "abruptly," because he acts from "instinct," and the instincts he's learned within his own culture make him seem too forward and aggressive. To rectify this situation, he does exactly what Hall suggests: he stops reacting and tries, instead, to analyze both Mrs. Cassadore's and his own culturally conditioned assumptions and expectations. This leads him to think through what friendship means and how friendships are formed in both Anglo and Indian cultures and, as a result, he alters his approach in his future dealings with Mrs. Cassadore. Hall might well applaud Fedullo's response in this situation, because it acknowledges the fact that culture shapes our behaviors and expectations at an unconscious level and the fact that cross-cultural conflicts can be rectified only if we are able to grasp the underlying pattern of meanings and behaviors associated with the cultures involved.

2. Given his theory of story-based understanding, Schank might suggest that Mrs. Cassadore's initial reaction to Fedullo reveals more about the power of personal stories than it does about cultural influences. Schank's claim that we understand the stories we encounter in the present by matching them with the stories we already know from the past might be seen as accounting for Mrs. Cassadore's initial rejection of Fedullo. When she first meets him, she doesn't see an Anglo per se or even the intimidating, bearded, oddly dressed Anglo businessman-hippie he thinks she sees. Instead, she's reminded of a story from her own past: that of a negligent doctor who nearly killed her in her youth. Schank might also question whether this case of misunderstanding is necessarily cleared up even after Mrs. Cassadore tells Fedullo the story that interfered with her initial reaction to him. We don't know, for example, how Fedullo himself "understands" her story. Does he see it as confirmation of the power of white racism or as a dramatization of how stereotypes distort perception or simply as an example of a traumatic memory? From a Schankian perspective, "communication" is never something that we can be sure of.

3. By contrast, Zerubavel might note that Mrs. Cassadore's reaction to Fedullo is, in fact, deeply tied up with cultural memory. The Anglo doctor who misdiagnosed her cough as tuberculosis was provided to the reservation by the government and thus must be associated in her mind with any number of historical interventions that the United States has undertaken ostensibly for the "good" of Native Americans and that have, in fact, often resulted in additional suffering. As Fedullo notes, the moment before Cassadore told him this story she had been explaining why Indians hated the BIA schools that had separated them from their families in the hopes of "bettering" them, much in the same way that the white doctor separated her from her family. Thus, as Zerubavel might suggest, this personal memory may gain special power and poignancy owing to the way it echoes the historical experiences of Native Americans within the reservation system. From this perspective, when Cassadore sees Fedullo for the first time, she doesn't just recall the white doctor who nearly killed her but remembers the whole history of white oppression of native peoples.

4. The connection between Fedullo and Nussbaum certainly isn't this clear. It arises only in relation to Cassadore's opinions about books. Fedullo, like Nussbaum, seems to assume that literacy is, in and of itself, a cultural good. Cassadore, however, explains that from the Native American perspective, education and literacy — and, we assume, even so-called great books — may be perceived as tools of oppression. Standing outside the culture of Sophocles and Ellison, Cassadore doesn't share Nussbaum's reverence for books or reading. Still, Nussbaum might counter by indicating that Fedullo's essay itself offers an example of how stories work to stimulate empathy and lay the groundwork for life in a diverse, democratic society. The stories that Fedullo and Cassadore relate here give us insights into minds that are wrestling with the problems of "otherness." Both also give us examples of people who are struggling to overcome the limitations of the worlds into which they were born — people who are trying to empathize with the others they encounter around them.

Essay Options

1. Both of the Essay Options associated with Fedullo set up academic papers on major themes in this chapter. Essay Option #1 asks students to draw on ideas in Schank and Bateson to discuss the topic of learning in "Mrs. Cassadore." Bateson's ideas about openness and flexibility are clearly relevant to the way that Fedullo reacts to Cassadore's initial rejection. He responds with curiosity and a willingness to question his own assumptions — characteristics that Bateson would probably find unusual in an American man. Schank might also see some real learning in this essay, particularly in the sense that Fedullo is repeatedly forced by his encounter with Cassadore to revise details in the stories he tells himself about her. Even during their final encounter, Fedullo discovers that at least two of his assumptions about her have been mistaken. His ability to assimilate her perspective might, from a Schankian point of view, be seen as evidence of genuine learning or understanding.

2. This assignment calls for a more comprehensive essay on the theme of the challenges involved in learning to listen to others. All four of the readings already covered in this unit offer something valuable on this topic. In addition to readings included in this chapter, you might want to encourage students to consider how selections in other chapters might also be worked into this assignment. Slouka, Zerubavel, Kingston, Baumeister, and Bateson all may be seen as addressing the issue of what's involved in the ability to listen to others.

DEBORAH BLUM, *Heart to Heart: Sex Differences in Emotion*
(p. 453)

Any exploration of what it means to read other minds wouldn't be complete without addressing transgender differences. Blum introduces the issue of the differences between male and female minds and offers you some terrific material for in-class discussions and debates. As a science writer, she acknowledges but doesn't dwell on the controversies that rage over whether women are inherently more nurturing than men and related questions of gender difference. Instead, she summarizes research that documents essential differences in the ways that women and men relate to their worlds. You'll find that this selection connects well with issues relating to male minds and violence in the next two selections. You'll also find that Blum resonates with Fedullo in that the misunderstanding he experiences with Mrs. Cassadore may be seen as involving gender as well as cultural differences. You'll also want to read Blum if you're planning to work extensively in the next two chapters, because she connects solidly with issues raised in relation to primate minds and with the idea of gendered cyborgs. You won't find any revolutionary insights here about the differences between male and female minds, but Blum does offer a thoughtful introduction to the topic, and she provides the foundation for a good personal essay on an experience of cross-gender miscommunication. When you assign Blum, have students brainstorm the differences that are commonly associated with male and female behavior patterns, as suggested by the Before Reading activity. Students may be surprised at how many of the claims that Blum advances appear to support traditional stereotypes about male-female differences.

Exploring the Text

1. According to the research that Blum summarizes, women are generally more sensitive and empathetic than men. Throughout the history of the species, females have been more directly involved in nurturing than have males. Research indicates that female babies respond more immediately to cries of distress from others; females have more sharply attuned senses of smell and touch; and females hear the kinds of high-pitched sounds that infants make more readily than do males. Females are particularly attuned to others because they have developed in relation to the task of nurturing infants and children. Men, by contrast, tend to be more competitive and hierarchical than women.

Men commonly bond through conflict and avoid direct displays of emotion. As boys mature, they spend increasing amounts of time vying for status, while girls "seem less determined to be number one." Girls tend to negotiate or minimize differences, while boys appear to enjoy games with clear-cut winners and losers. Because girls have a stronger emotional response to conflict, they tend to hold on to resentment longer than boys, who frequently view fighting as a relatively normal interaction. Obviously, there's nothing particularly challenging in any of this. The real question is whether students agree with the rather traditional distinction Blum draws between male and female minds. Three decades after the beginning of the modern feminist movement, do students believe that women are, in some sense, born to be nurturers and that men are born to compete? What evidence do they offer to support or challenge these conclusions?

2. The point that Blum really wants to make here is that women are naturally more empathetic than men. To support this distinction, she cites the research of the psychologist Michael Milburn, who conducted experiments exploring the connection between the punishment that children received, gender, and their eventual political attitudes. Milburn found that men who were raised by "high-punishment" parents tended to be more politically conservative as adults; that is, they tended to assimilate the stern views with which they were raised. Women raised by such high-punishment types, by contrast, tended to be more politically liberal. Milburn saw this difference as the result of greater natural empathy among women. Females tend, according to Blum, to place themselves in the position of others more readily than do men, and this gives women a "powerful emotional advantage." Women are more skilled at reading other people's facial expressions and can predict the moods of others more accurately than can men. Women also show more sophistication than men in the way they use language and control emotional responses. Again, however, the interesting question is whether students tend to agree that women are inherently more adept at mind reading than are men. What evidence do students see in their own experience that suggests that women may, in fact, be more empathetic and better judges of other's emotional and mental states?

3. As you discuss this distinction, you may also want to consider how male and female roles are changing. Some students may well agree that it has become "politically incorrect" nowadays to be male. Of course, female virtues such as empathy and community building may be hot in traditionally progressive venues such as college campuses, but it may be difficult to make the case that women's values and interests have displaced men's across the board in American culture. Some men may be living in ways that seem more connected with the values of nurturing and community building, but year after year it remains relatively clear that traditional, hierarchical, aggressive male values still dominate popular culture and the daily lives of millions of Americans.

4. The distinction that Blum notes between male and female minds also shows up in differences in male and female health issues. Women may live longer, more vigorous lives because of their skills at forming supportive relationships. Men, by contrast, may suffer more stress due to their competitive instincts. Blum is especially concerned that stereotypical attitudes about males may lead caregivers to consistently underestimate the emotional needs of young boys. Baby girls, the research suggests, are generally more resilient than boys and may also need less personal attention. Yet our cultural attitudes toward boys and girls may work against these natural needs. Girls, Blum suggests, may need more independence at a younger age, boys, more nurturing. Blum herself offers little help with how to address this problem. She notes that the stresses of modern life may be worsening things, particularly for males, whom she sees as more vulnerable to stress because they lack the support network that women create for themselves. Still, even this idea may deserve to be challenged in class. Are men the isolated loners that Blum and her researchers make them out to be? Haven't men always found ways to bond publicly and privately despite their competitive interests? Indeed, isn't the most common stereotype associated with male "competition" the image of a houseful of guys sitting around a bowl of potato chips, watching the Super Bowl?

Further Explorations

1. Obviously, you'll want to test almost every assertion Blum makes in this selection. You can begin by having students collect images from popular magazines that express current concepts of masculinity and femininity. Have students form small groups to assemble them and then discuss the conclusions they can draw from them. Follow up by asking each group to present their interpretations of their gender collages in class and discuss the extent to which these image collections confirm or challenge the research that Blum presents. You may also want to divide groups by gender for this activity or assign groups to particular types of publications to guarantee that your class's informal research doesn't just cover the four or five most common magazines.

2. You can also apply Blum's work to any number of selections you may have already covered in *Mind Readings*. Kleege's analysis of how the mind functions in vision, for example, seems relatively "ungendered," unless you consider the way she knits together her perception of the world with a particularly "female" way of seeing, as opposed to the "what-you-see-is-what-you-get" arrogance of "male" vision. Kingston's revision of her aunt's story, however, is remarkably empathetic. Indeed, the point of Kingston's memoir is that while she is trying to distance herself from her aunt's fate, she places herself in a relationship with her. Bateson self-consciously recognizes the "femaleness" of her ability to open herself to new experiences, and McNulty demonstrates remarkable empathy in her ability to read the moods and aptitudes of her pet field mouse.

3. Selections by Lopez, Sanders, Sapolsky, and Martínez might all be seen as at least acknowledging the male's fascination with achievement, conflict, and competition. The crucial moment in the education of Lopez's hands, for example, is when he nearly kills a friend with the toss of a stone, and Sanders prides himself on the skill and ability that he's inherited along with his father's tools. Other selections by men suggest, perhaps, a greater capacity for empathy. Think of the interest in community that Frazier demonstrates, or Sapolsky's identification with his father, or the effort Fedullo expends on trying to read Mrs. Cassadore's expectations and reactions. You'll find that most of these selections resist simple categorization as "male" or "female," although it does seem that female authors are more acutely attuned to issues of gender than are males.

4. Baldwin's "Sonny Blues," however, does offer a rather dramatic example of the male mind at work. Baldwin's narrator initially comes across as a particularly rigid, closed, cold, and unsympathetic character. He complains constantly of feeling an "icy" chill in his guts — evidence of the stress he lives with in his daily life. He also seems particularly alone. The only person we see him relate to in this story is Sonny, and he has assiduously avoided him for the past ten years. He even avoids him when he hears about Sonny's problems with drugs. Thus, it could easily be argued that Baldwin's narrator represents a classic male type — the sensitive man who withdraws into self-imposed isolation in order to keep the disintegration he sees in the world around him at bay. From this perspective, he might even be seen as resembling the vulnerable male children pushed too soon toward independence whom Blum discusses toward the conclusion of her selection.

5. Walker's "Everyday Use" offers a different picture of what it means to be a woman. The women in Walker's story are remarkably strong and resilient. All three are clearly survivors. Maggie and her mother gain their strength from the organic connection they've maintained with each other, their community, and the past. Dee, by contrast, seems more self-contained and even more competitive in her orientation. You can't help suspecting that she'd like to take the family quilts back to college with her just so that she can gain status among the other women on campus. Walker's story, then, suggests that emotional differences between males and females may be declining as women move out of traditional communities, relationships, and family roles. As women like Dee move away from home and up the ladder of success, they may also be leaving behind some of the traits that Blum associates with female mental health.

6. In fact, when Baumeister considers the emergence of modern definitions of the self, he makes no distinction between male and female identities. According to Baumeister, women's magazines have downplayed the importance of family and relationships in women's lives, suggesting, instead, that the primary value in a modern woman's life should be self-fulfillment. The difference between Baumeister and Blum on female minds might be explained as a difference of focus. Baumeister is addressing the images that commercial culture conveys to women about the female self; Blum, by contrast, is addressing behavioral and biological differences between male and female minds. Althought the images of modern women portrayed in magazines may reflect contemporary attitudes toward the self, they may be out of line with enduring biological predispositions that women bring with them from birth.

7. The distinctions Blum advances in relation to male and female minds also calls into question Nussbaum's claims about the democratizing function of great works of literary art. Given Blum's depiction of the dominant features of male minds, it's hard to imagine that theaters full of privileged Athenian males once empathized deeply with the women featured in Greek tragedies. Indeed, Blum's portrait of male and female predispositions suggests that Nussbaum's view of art as a source of empathy may itself represent a particularly "female" perspective. As a woman, Nussbaum may be particularly sensitive to the opportunities for sympathetic identification that literature provides. Thus, although it is possible that art promotes the development of civility in a great many women and some men by encouraging empathy with others, it is also likely that it fails to do so for some women and a great many men who are more attuned to competition or status than they are to habits of sympathetic identification.

Essay Options

1. Parallel to the cross-cultural assignment that follows Hall, this assignment invites students to reflect on a time when they were involved in a cross-gender conflict. This paper requires that students apply the distinctions that Blum presents between male and female minds in order to explain how this conflict arose. As in the prior assignment, you'll want to encourage students to spend some time examining their own part in this conflict and exploring the assumptions, "male" or "female," that may have led up to it.

2. Essay Option #2 looks ahead to Ellen Ullman's account of the "cult of the boy engineer" and the way that it is shaping life in the emerging information technology industry. You may want to pursue this topic if you plan to spend some time later on the issue of machine minds — or if your students already have some experience in the modern workplace. Ullman's account of the high-competition, low-human-interaction world of information technology suggests that women will encounter serious trouble in the electronic workplace if they are, in fact, as naturally empathetic and relationship-oriented as Blum suggests.

ANDREW SULLIVAN, *What's So Bad About Hate?* (p. 469)

The title of this selection alone may be reason enough to assign it. Sullivan is a firebrand intellectual who's built a reputation by stirring up controversy among his fellow gay Americans. The argument he advances here challenges the central assumption behind *Mind Readings* — the idea that we can ever speculate with any degree of certainty about the motives, feelings, or beliefs that underlie any overt action. You can read Sullivan as preparation for a one-selection essay on the issue of hate crime legislation or as part of a thematic cluster of readings on interpreting violent minds. Sullivan also offers you a good example of the art of crafting argumentative essays. You'll find that his reasoning and use of supporting evidence are just questionable enough to invite critical analysis and response. If you have more than a couple of days between classes, you may want to consider pairing this selection with Garbarino as a single reading assignment, but you'll find that each of these selections gives you enough material to cover for a full class meeting, particularly if you give students the chance to work in small groups as they explore the issues Sullivan and Garbarino raise. Sullivan also looks backward to Blum, in the sense that Blum's comments on female and male differences might be seen as support for special protections against male aggression. The Before Reading activity seeks to pool students' current knowledge about the issue of hate crime legislation. It also challenges them to think about the central question that Sullivan raises — that of how we can ever be sure about what's going on in another person's mind.

Exploring the Text

1. The central problem with hate crime legislation, according to Sullivan, is that it assumes that we understand what hate is and that we can read it in the intentions of criminal minds. Hate can stand for just about anything, in Sullivan's view. It is a broader idea than "prejudice, or bigotry, or bias, or anger, or even mere aversion to others." As he suggests, "Hate is everywhere." He argues that it's natural for humans to "dissociate," just as it's natural for us to "associate." Hate is an automatic impulse that gets the better of us for a moment and that most of us are usually able to control. Thus, we all hate at times; we just don't bother to pathologize our negative feelings. Sullivan follows up with two examples that are meant to raise questions about the nature of hate — one involving a dispute between a gay man and his straight neighbor over grass clippings, the other involving the display of a parade float titled "Black to the Future" by a group of white firefighters in Queens, New York. Sullivan suggests that the first conflict may have been nothing more than a neighborly scuffle and that the second might be seen simply as a matter of "poor taste." Students may agree that the first case presents an unclear situation, unless the antigay insult that the straight neighbor used can be seen as expressing the entire motivation for his assault. The second example, however, might seem less "murky" than Sullivan would claim it to be. Can there be any doubt that the firefighters were expressing hatred when they mocked the dragging death of James Byrd?

2. In the past, hate was easier to understand, in Sullivan's view, because it was better organized. Hate "made sense," Sullivan seems to say, when it involved specific criminal actions undertaken in the name of "a very specific array of firmly held prejudices, with a history, an ideology, and even a pseudoscience to back them up." The Holocaust demonstrated this kind of hate in the sense that it was a widespread, systematic assault on an entire population. Random, individual acts of violence, like Buford Furrow's attack on a Jewish daycare center, don't meet the same standard; they're just manifestations of a deranged mind. Sullivan argues that most recent hate crimes in America express individual neuroses, not systematic programs of extermination, and thus do not justify association with a particular ideology or power structure. That's why he thinks terms such as "sexism," "racism," "anti-Semitism," and "homophobia" are wrong: they imply impersonal institutional structures and overlook the personal motives that underlie individual criminal acts.

3. In addition, Sullivan believes that there are distinctly different kinds of hate. Some hatreds are "unreasonable," but some, like the Tutsis' hatred of the Hutus, is "reasonable." The victims of hate who retaliate against their victimizers "are not as culpable as the perpetrators." Hate can also be grounded in fact and experience. Sullivan goes on to discuss three categories of hate: "obsessive hate," which leads to the desire to eradicate a scapegoated minority group; "hysterical hate," which associates a hated group with projected sexual desires; and "narcissistic hate," which involves men's lack of empathy for women. Sullivan's point is that any individual act of hate may blend these and other forms of hatred, and it is thus impossible and unjust to lump all of these complex "human impulses" together under a few "crude" conceptual labels. Indeed, Sullivan suggests that the impulse to label hatred is itself a bias or prejudice on the part of those who want to divide society into camps of "oppressors" and "victims." Hate crime legislation, then, is wrong because, like the hatred it is meant to address, it "hammers the uniqueness of each individual into the anvil of group identity. And it postures morally

over the result." The problem with such politically motivated oversimplifications, Sullivan suggests, is that they ignore the fact that some of the most vicious haters have also been the victims of hate — people like the Columbine shooters, anti-Semitic blacks, and anti-Catholic gays.

4. Sullivan counters several of the main arguments for hate crime legislation in this essay. Whereas advocates of hate crime bills argue that hate crimes terrorize entire populations and not just individuals, he notes that *all* crimes spread terror and that some non-hate crimes inspire more fear than crimes aimed at a particular group. He also notes that the thinking behind hate crime laws is condescending to protected groups because it assumes that they are somehow more susceptible to terror. The distinctions fostered by hate crime legislation also perpetuate the kind of group "profiling" that they are meant to combat. They thus reinforce the collective identities that lead to hate-motivated violence in the first place. In addition, Sullivan counters the claim that such laws are needed because of a recent upsurge in hate crime activity. To refute this notion, he presents statistics showing that the incidence and violence of hate-motivated attacks have held constant or declined over the past ten years. Of course, it could be noted that hate crime statistics may have dropped precisely because of the message that hate crime legislation communicates. It might also be observed that groups that have historically suffered from prejudice have a right to live without the constant threat of terror in a democracy, or that the terror they experience is qualitatively different from the anonymous terror that's inspired by random acts of violence, or that blaming such groups for perpetuating prejudice is a lot like blaming the victim.

5. Sullivan's central point, however, is that it just isn't the government's business to read the minds of its citizens. Governments should prosecute criminals and stop crimes, but they should not be concerned with who hates whom — at least not in a free society. Human beings, in Sullivan's view, are predisposed to hate: thus, as he says, "A free country will always mean a hateful country." Hate crime legislation is, in his view, a type of social engineering that aims at increasing "tolerance" by taking away our freedom to be what we are. Instead, the government should promote "toleration" — peaceful coexistence despite the reality of hate. If this were government policy, Sullivan suggests, then the "hated" would have the chance to "rise above" the bigot's power and would be able to face prejudice with "equanimity."

6. Before leaving your examination of Sullivan, you may want to pause to consider why he mentions his own sexual orientation in this essay. Clearly, he expects that this revelation strengthens his arguments and adds to his credibility. Yet it does seem odd that he makes this appeal, particularly given his impassioned stand against special consideration for any particular group. Why should his experience as a gay man influence our consideration of the arguments he advances, unless that experience gives him some special perspective? How does this claim for special consideration differ from claims for special protection because of group identity forwarded by supporters of hate crime laws?

Further Explorations

1. Sullivan and Nussbaum have strongly contrasting views of democracy and the nature of civil society. For Sullivan, a free, democratic society is a collection of utterly autonomous individuals who "get along" despite the fact that they may despise one another. In a sense, the statement "democracy is as democracy does" might be seen as summarizing Sullivan's view. It doesn't really matter what the members of a free society think about each other; the only thing that matters is that we don't commit crimes against one another. Nussbaum's standards for civil society are more ambitious. She believes that an open society must be based on "tolerance" and not simply on "toleration." For civil society to cohere, the individuals who compose it must be joined in bonds of empathy. They must not merely "put up with" one another; they must actively understand something about each other's feelings and experiences. That's why she sees the arts as so important in a democracy. Great works of narrative art help people learn about the

others with whom they share their civic world. Democracy for Nussbaum requires culture, education, and hard work — not simply impulse control. In fact, Nussbaum might note that without the development of such inner bonds of empathy and understanding, individuals in a free society could never be free of the threat of terror. A "hateful country," from her perspective, might never really be free. Of course, Sullivan might scoff at the idea that reading a classic is a good way to combat racism or anti-Semitism, and he might also point out that we have no clearer conception about what went on in the mind of a young Athenian watching Sophocles than we do about what motivated the killers of James Byrd Jr. or Matthew Shepard. From his perspective, all such speculation is just a pointless intellectual exercise.

2. Fedullo's experience with Mrs. Cassadore might be seen as a direct challenge to Sulllivan's claim that familiarity doesn't mitigate the differences between individuals. Fedullo does succeed in overcoming the cultural distance that separates him from Mrs. Cassadore, and he achieves this feat because he has spent considerable time living and working in bi-cultural contexts. Fedullo might, thus, be seen as proof that you can bridge cultural divides through familiarity. Yet, as Sullivan would be sure to point out, Fedullo was predisposed to like Mrs. Cassadore and the Apaches he worked with from the outset. He didn't *overcome* racism through familiarity; he merely overcame a momentary misunderstanding. In fact, Sullivan might use Fedullo's experience as evidence of just how difficult it is to promote "tolerance" instead of "toleration" in a free society. Clearly, not everyone has the motive, interpersonal skills, or energy that Fedullo needed to get to know Mrs. Cassadore.

3. Blum's account of the differences between male and female minds might be seen as a significant challenge to Sullivan's stand against special protections for women against sexism. The picture that Blum offers of men's and women's aptitudes and interests suggests that women have had to accommodate themselves to male power, insensitivity, and violence throughout history. It also suggests that living around women might not be enough to make men particularly sensitive to women's rights as individuals. Despite the fact that individual "sexist women" do exist and that every sexist man "was born of a woman," Blum's account of the differences between males and females might be seen as supporting the idea that women constitute a biologically defined group and not one defined solely by narrow political interests, as Sullivan suggests. And because their inborn attributes make them especially vulnerable to domination by males, women may, thus, be seen as requiring special consideration under the law.

4. In similar fashion, bell hooks might be expected to reject Sullivan's claims about the nature of hate and the resilience of the oppressed. We might expect hooks to be mystified by Sullivan's suggestion that hate can't be categorized or read in the minds of others — or by his idea that it's up to the victims of hate to "achieve equanimity in the face of prejudice." After all, haven't those in power always felt free to categorize the behaviors of the "inferior" peoples they've subjugated or to interpret their actions and motives as justifying their extermination or exploitation? Two wrongs may not make a right, but shouldn't hooks be free to judge a Columbus — or a John William King — for the crimes they perpetrated against all people of color and not simply view them as a couple of commonplace murderers? Given the toll that the historical memory of Columbus continues to take on her life, hooks might argue that "equanimity" and indifference aren't postures she's willing to assume in relation to racists. Racism isn't simply a "variety" of hatred or a matter of individual psychology, according to hooks. It's the root of five centuries of sustained violence directed against people of color, and, as such, it must be combatted directly and never merely treated with "toleration."

Essay Options

1. This assignment requires students to do informal research in newspapers and popular magazines about a particular form of hate such as sexism, homophobia, or racism. You'll want to let students choose their own specific focus for this topic. In addi-

tion to documenting specific hate crimes related to their choice of prejudice, you'll also want students to explore the motives that might explain them and to weigh the pros and cons associated with reading criminal minds.

2. This paper calls for a more direct debate of the issues related to hate crime legislation and is, thus, more directly focused on argumentation than is Option #1. In their response to this assignment, students should assess the key arguments for and against hate crime laws, comment on their relative strengths and weaknesses, and explore the counterarguments advanced in support of both positions. They should also take time to present their own thinking on the issue and be willing to support their opinions with additional arguments and evidence.

JAMES GARBARINO, *Rejected and Neglected, Ashamed and Depressed* (p. 485)

This selection offers a dramatic counterpoint to Sullivan. Not only does Garbarino believe that we can read the minds of the thousands of young men who fill state and federal prisons, he believes that their inability to read the minds of others is what put them there in the first place. This selection carries the focus of the chapter to its logical conclusion by asking how we might assess the motives, values, and beliefs of minds that we do our best to exclude from society — the minds of the violent. It also allows you to raise issues in class related to recent outbreaks of apparently unmotivated teen violence across the United States such as Dylan Klebold's and Eric Harris's 1999 attack on their fellow students at Columbine High School. You can pair it with Sullivan as part of a unit on reading violent minds, combine it with Nussbaum and Blum for a paper on empathy and its role in the creation of a civil society (EO #2), or use it as a point of departure for analyzing representations of violent minds in movies such as *Dead Man Walking, Boyz 'n the Hood, Do the Right Thing,* or *Once upon a Time in America* (FE #4 and 5). To get started, have students work in small groups to brainstorm theories that are commonly offered to explain why children resort to violence, as suggested in the Before Reading activity. This may help students recall that there are, in fact, a number of alternatives to the humanistic approach that Garbarino advocates in this selection.

Exploring the Text

1. Students may be surprised by the emphasis that Garbarino places on spiritual ideas like that of the soul. Following the lead of Leonard Shengold, Garbarino assumes that every child is born with a "spark of divinity" that can either be nurtured or crushed by its environment. Some children, in Garbarino's view, can be so abused or degraded by their initial encounters in life that their "soul departs," leaving behind either hatred or "an unfilled void." Others respond to degradation by withdrawing or "hardening" to the point of dormancy. The idea of "soul murder" may be attractive to Garbarino for several reasons. It reinforces the Romantic notion that all individuals are born essentially "good" and then are made "bad" by their environments. It also places the task of rehabilitating "lost boys" in a religious context. Seen this way, rehabilitation isn't just a matter of justice, it's a deeply moral undertaking that involves the reclamation of lost souls. Garbarino may also be drawn to the idea of soul murder because the notion of having a "sacred self" implies the possibility of its restoration. A mind that's been twisted through abuse might be seen as permanently lost or damaged beyond repair. The developmental philosophy of modern psychology, for example, argues against the idea that deep psychological damage can ever be fully "reversed." But the soul, as a concept, is more durable than the mind. A soul can be recovered and revived. Thus, the idea of soul murder may sound bleak, but it actually contains a ray of hope — and it's exactly this hope that Garbarino wants to emphasize.

2. Soul murder, in Garbarino's view, involves a complex interaction between character and environment. Some boys survive difficult circumstances because they resist

depression. Others survive because they are particularly resilient: they "bounce back" from adversity unscathed. Still others survive because they've been able to connect with at least one source of unconditional love. Finally, Garbarino notes that some children survive because of what seems to be "divine intervention" or because they have a special "vision" of a better world or a talent that helps them endure. Thus, Garbarino can still see a spark of life in the eyes of Byron, despite the history of childhood abuse and violence that brought him to prison. The greatest danger for young men, in Garbarino's view, lies in abandonment. If a boy cannot make a loving connection with anyone as he develops, he may not be able to cope with the stresses of his environment and may succumb to depression. This, in turn, may lead him to withdraw from the world, to lose the ability to feel, or to begin to view himself as a victim of others. Eventually a form of "emotional amnesia" may set in that serves to cut him off from the "shame" of abandonment. Disconnected from the past and the present, such a boy loses the ability to empathize with others and succumbs to a kind of "emotional retardation" that allows him to strike out at the world without scruple or regret. As Garbarino summarizes the process: "Shame at abandonment begets covert depression, which begets rage, which begets violence."

3. Gender role socialization also plays an important part in this process, according to Garbarino. The cultural lessons a boy learns about masculinity can reinforce the tendency to dissociate from others and become depressed. Thus, if a boy is taught that men should refrain from expressing their feelings and hide emotions linked to "connection, vulnerability, and softness," it will be that much more difficult to sustain contact with those who might offer him support. Fathers play a key role in conveying such lessons, particularly by modeling domination and brutal treatment of others, as does the father of Terrel. Indeed, Garbarino notes that it's often preferable to have no father at all than to have one who is neglectful, abusive, or domineering. What children in these circumstances need is "unconditional love," regardless of who supplies it. Thus, a relative, family friend, sibling, teacher, or just about anyone can step in and begin to "repair" the damage such boys incur simply by being there for them. Responsible adults can also provide support for parents with boys who have "attachment problems," can engage such children in "therapeutic relationships," can provide them with continuing forms of emotional support, and can provide services and stable homes to children who have lost their natural parents.

4. The evidence that Garbarino offers to support his theory of the development of violent minds is almost exclusively anecdotal. Most is based on interviews he conducted with young men imprisoned for serious crimes at juvenile detention centers between 1996 and 1998. Thus, he gives us his impressions of Byron, Terrel, Malcolm, Matt, Tyrone, and Shareef in support of his claims. He also cites well-known cases of childhood and teen violence such as those involving Kip Kinkel, Mitchell Johnson, Luke Woodham, and Andrew Golden. It might seem odd that Garbarino relies so little on statistical evidence in support of his theory. You might, for example, expect him to provide data on the total number of young offenders who come from broken homes or who have a history of child abuse. But Garbarino's anecdotal approach might make sense given his fundamentally religious orientation to his subject. It's hard to see a glimmer of hope in a pile of statistics, and it's also possible that Garbarino is more interested in inspiring us to do something than he is in convincing us about the correctness of his theory.

5. Garbarino's preference for anecdotal evidence also suggests something about the way he reads his prospective audience. A professor at Cornell University, Garbarino knows that the evidence he presents here would not be enough to sway an audience of professional psychologists or law-enforcement experts. This selection is clearly aimed, instead, at a more general readership. His ideal reader might not even be a typical intellectual, because we wouldn't expect intellectuals to respond positively to the kind of religious concepts he relies on here. It would seem more plausible that Garbarino is taking aim at a mid-level readership — one that is moved by personal stories and that places high value on religious practices and principles.

Further Explorations

1. Blum's theory of the differences between male and female minds connects remarkably well with Garbarino. According to Blum, males are predisposed to be competitive with others and to lack the kind of empathetic sensitivity to other minds that women enjoy. As a result, Blum worries that boys may be more vulnerable to depression and stress than are girls, because girls are able to create networks of supportive friendships that help them survive the difficulties they encounter in their environments. Blum, like Garbarino, is also concerned that gender role stereotypes may exacerbate the tendency of boys to become vulnerable to environmental stress, since the lessons such stereotypes convey reinforce male reticence and isolation. Your students, however, may want to challenge the assumption that boys are somehow more vulnerable or "at risk" than girls. To what extent does their own experience suggest that boys fall prey to alienation and depression more readily than do girls? Isn't it possible that girls suffer just as much as boys do from these factors but are trained to hide their suffering — or simply aren't as able as boys are to express their rage in acts of violence? What evidence, if any, do students see that girls may, indeed, be "catching up" with boys in this regard?

2. Garbarino would probably note that both Sonny and his brother survive Harlem's "killing streets" because of the unconditional love they received from their mother, father, and extended family. Family plays an important role in Baldwin's story. It's the backdrop against which the struggle between Sonny and his brother plays itself out. The story of the boy junkie in Baldwin would, by contrast, probably echo details that Garbarino associates with the development of the violent boys he documents in this selection: an absentee or brutal father, a victimized mother, a culture filled with images of male domination and violence, and a society that offers little in the way of hope or opportunity.

3. Despite their obvious differences, Garbarino and Sullivan might seem to agree on the idea that certain forms of hatred or violence are "reasonable" or at least comprehensible. Every instance of violent behavior that Garbarino cites is motivated by some constellation of environmental factors that were clearly beyond the control of the individual in question. Thus, Kip Kinkel suffered from depression that, Garbarino speculates, was occasioned by feelings of rejection due to competition with his "perfect" older sister, and Rasheen committed armed robbery at the age of fifteen as a result of having been abandoned by his father and left by his mother for a life of addiction. In every case, the rage and violence these boys feel can be accounted for — and in some sense understood or even forgiven — according to Garbarino. In much the same way, Columbine shooters Dylan Klebold and Eric Harris were themselves victims of abuse at the hands of their classmates, according to Sullivan. Given his belief in the possibility of soul murder and his views on the development of childhood violence, it's quite possible that Garbarino might oppose special sanctions for hate crimes. Hate, in Garbarino's view, is spawned by hate. It isn't a choice or something inborn in a criminal's mind. Thus, he might believe that the law should not seek to punish particular types of hatred more severely than others. It should seek to restore the souls of those who hate and are the victims of hatred.

4. and 5. The next two questions invite you to continue your exploration of violent minds as they are depicted in a number of well-known films. All of these movies suggest that violence is rooted in factors such as abandonment, shame, and cultural attitudes toward masculinity. However, other factors, including racism, poverty, and police brutality, are stressed as well. Thus, viewing these films opens up discussion of issues that Garbarino may only casually acknowledge in his analysis of the origin of violent minds.

Essay Options

1. This Option invites students to do informal research on a particular instance of teen violence in order to test Garbarino's theory of soul murder. Students can use any of the well-known cases mentioned by Garbarino or any additional cases that have come

to public attention since this selection first appeared in 1999. Students should use this assignment as an opportunity for considering competing theories offered to explain these incidents — including theories relating to the influence of media violence, America's gun culture, and the breakdown of traditional cultural values.

2. This assignment sets up an academic paper on the role of empathy in the creation of a civil society. Nussbaum, Blum, and Garbarino all comment on the need for empathy and the role that empathetic mind reading plays in mediating social and cultural differences in a diverse society. You may want to invite students to consider using ideas and examples from other readings as they prepare for this paper. Baldwin and Walker, for example, can be read as commentaries on some of the barriers to empathy in contemporary American life. As students explore this topic, you'll also want to encourage them to look beyond the readings they've done in this chapter and to consider how empathetic Americans appear to be today. What factors complicate the task of creating an empathetic society in today's world — the modern corporate work ethic, large-scale immigration, the rapid rate of technological change, the relative isolation of the modern family, the breakdown of collective forms of community, and so forth?

Reading Animal Minds:
Objects or Equals? (p. 504)

Getting Started

This chapter is one of my favorites. We often spend a lot of time in composition classes discussing how we relate to other human beings while we neglect our relationships with the rest of the universe. Yet you might expect we'd learn some interesting lessons about what it means to be human by looking at ourselves from the perspective of other species. This chapter invites you to explore animal minds from two different angles. The first half of the chapter focuses on human-animal relationships. Perhaps the most striking aspect of our current relationship with the animal world is that it has nearly ceased to exist. As John Berger insists in his "Why Look at Animals?" animals have become utterly "marginalized" in the modern world. They teeter on the brink of *mental extinction* — even if they haven't yet made it onto an "endangered species" list. The change between this state and the relation we enjoyed with other species for millennia speaks volumes about the kinds of creatures we're becoming. The second half of the chapter addresses recent changes in the way we think about animal minds. This section is anchored by ethnologist Frans de Waal's exploration of anthropocentrism and two arguments for the intelligence of primates. The second half of this section focuses on the case for and against animal rights.

Given student interest in animal rights and environmental issues today, you can expect your class to respond strongly to the readings you'll find here. The chapter introduction in *Mind Readings* offers an overview of how human attitudes toward animals have changed since ancient Greece, culminating in the revolution in consciousness that was set in motion by Darwin's theory of evolution. With humanists and sociobiologists still arguing more than a century after the appearance of the *Origin of Species*, there's little doubt that Darwin challenged us to rethink the boundary between human and animal minds. For at least three thousand years we've tried to convince ourselves of our uniqueness as a species and highlighted the differences separating us from lower "bestial" forms of existence. Today, however, we're rediscovering just how much we have in common with animals. None of the issues raised in this chapter require that you do any special preparation. But if you do want to read further on the topics of animal minds and animal rights before your class meets, I'd recommend Frans de Waal's *The Ape and the Sushi Master* (2001) or Gary L. Francione's *Introduction to Animal Rights: Your Child or the Dog?* (2000). De Waal offers a good overview of some of the ways thinking about animals has changed over the past century, and Francione complements de Waal by addressing all the important moral issues that have been raised lately about the way we relate to other species. For a more detailed study of issues related to animal intelligence, you might want to consult Donald R. Griffin's *Animal Minds* (1992).

The topic of reading animal minds intersects with issues of composition in the realm of argumentation. This really isn't as odd as it might sound. Since the time of the ancient Greeks, philosophers and theologians in the West have always offered reason as the feature that most clearly distinguishes man from beast. It was humankind's ability to frame logical arguments, weigh evidence, and reflect critically on important issues that separated us from "them" — even though it was quite clear that animals could feel, remember, dream, and even make rudimentary plans. The introductory section on writing, subtitled "Arguing Animals: Mind Reading and Reasoning," offers you the chance to explore the dialogical nature of argument with your class. This section picks up where the discussion of audience analysis left off in the previous chapter. The central point here is that argumentation is a dialectical, or discursive, process. Even when you're alone at your desk, the process of argumentation involves you in an ongoing exchange of ideas with one or more imaginary opponents. You build your own case and shape your supporting arguments for it in response to the ideas and objections you anticipate from these imaginary others. Students shouldn't have too much trouble seeing this process at work in Patterson and Gordon's argument for the "personhood" of Koko the gorilla. They'll also see clear examples of dialogical reasoning in Singer's and Shepard's debate on the issue of animal equality. This chapter offers you a perfect opportunity, then, to focus on the kind of argumentative and persuasive writing assignments that are often required in first-year composition.

To begin your exploration of human-animal relationships, you may want to have students work in small groups on one of the following activities:

- Discuss what the photograph that serves as the frontispiece to this chapter suggests about intelligence and animal-human relationships.
- Brainstorm the things that distinguish human and animal minds.
- Discuss their impression of how animal-human relationships have changed over the past century.

Sequences and Pairings

The chapter divides into two thematic units. If you want to focus primarily on human-animal relationships, concentrate on the first four readings. If you plan to focus on animal minds, read the last five. The final four selections also divide in two, with Leakey and Lewin and Patterson and Gordon addressing the issue of primate intelligence and Singer and Shepard debating the case for animal equality. If you plan to work your way through the chapter, you can begin by assigning Lame Deer and Erdoes paired with Berger and then follow up with McNulty paired with Siebert. Lame Deer and Erdoes provides a historical context for examining current attitudes toward nature and the world of animals. They also offer you a strong voice to begin your exploration of animal-human relationships. Berger is more challenging, but he's worth the effort, because he presents a good historical overview of attitudes toward animals and raises questions about human-animal interactions that resonate throughout the chapter. McNulty's reminiscence about the wild mouse that becomes her pet links back to Lame Deer and Erdoes as well as Berger and looks forward to both Siebert and de Waal. In fact, pairing Siebert and McNulty makes sense in that McNulty's personal experience of human-animal interaction contrasts sharply with Siebert's view of the way animals are portrayed on TV. Pairing these first four selections also offers you the possibility of several appealing personal and academic essay assignments, including one that involves analyzing the function of zoos (Berger, EO #1), one debating the pros and cons of pet ownership (McNulty, EO #1), and two exploring media representations of animals (Berger, EO #2 and Siebert, EO #1).

Frans de Waal's "The Whole Animal" bridges the chapter's two thematic halves and offers a useful discussion of concepts such as anthropocentrism, "anthropodenial," and "Bambification." De Waal is a must if you'll be reading any of the last four selections. However, I'd advise you to assign him for a separate class so you can spend some time discussing how scientific and lay attitudes towards animal minds are changing. You might also want to use this class to prepare for the next two selections by previewing fifteen or twenty minutes of a documentary film featuring Francine Patterson's work with Koko or Jane Goodall's research on chimpanzees. Leakey and Lewin and Patterson and Gordon can be assigned as a pair of readings leading to a paper on the "personhood" of primates. Singer and Shepard also offer a natural pairing, as well as excellent preparation for an essay debating animal equality, but, given the analytic challenge they present, you may want to devote a full class period to each.

A number of themes emerge from the readings in this chapter. You can combine Lame Deer and Erdoes with Berger, McKibben, and Percy to set up a unit on the topic of American attitudes toward the natural world. Or you can explore questions related to the ethics and functions of pet ownership through Lame Deer and Erdoes, Berger, McNulty, de Waal, and Shepard. If you want to focus on media issues, Berger, Siebert, and de Waal offer a unit on the "Bambification" of animals in the popular imagination. De Waal's discussion of anthropocentrism and anthropodenial connects with McNulty, Leakey and Lewin, Patterson and Gordon, and Shepard to offer one of the chapter's most challenging academic topics. The central theme of this unit, the notion of animal intelligence, brings together Lame Deer and Erdoes, Berger, McNulty, Leakey and Lewin, and Patterson and Gordon.

Recommended Stand-Alone Readings

This chapter presents many possibilities for stand-alone reading and writing assignments. Berger is conceptually challenging, but he sets up an interesting practical field research assignment, which sends students to a local zoo to document the various social and cultural functions that zoos perform. For a more accessible one-reading assignment, use McNulty's "Mouse" as the point of departure for a personal essay profiling an important animal-human relationship. Siebert can be used alone as the basis for a paper on media portrayals of animals in the wild, and Patterson and Gordon can be used as the basis of a project that asks students to explore recent research on animal language. The last two selections in the chapter can also be split and used individually in preparation for writing assignments. Even when read alone, Singer provides a good point of departure for a paper on animal liberation, while Shepard can be read independently as the foundation for a research paper exploring particular ways in which animals are exploited in modern society, including their use as sources of food, clothing, and entertainment.

Here's a list of some possible topics for stand-alone assignments.

Examining the function of zoos	*Why Look at Animals?* (Berger)
Profile of an animal-human relationship	*Mouse* (McNulty)
Mass media portrayals of animals	*The Artifice of the Natural* (Siebert)
Research on animal language	*The Case for the Personhood of Gorillas* (Patterson and Gordon)
Debating animal liberation	*Equality for Animals?* (Singer)
Using animals for food, fur, and entertainment	*Rights and Kindness* (Shepard)

Recommended Pairings

The marginalization of animals	*Talking to the Owls and Butterflies* (Lame Deer and Erdoes) and *Why Look at Animals?* (Berger)
The "personhood" of higher primates	*Murder in a Zoo* (Leakey and Lewin) and *The Case for the Personhood of Gorillas* (Patterson and Gordon)
Debating animal equality	*Equality for Animals?* (Singer) and *Rights and Kindness* (Shepard)

Suggested Thematic Clusters

American views of nature and animals	*Talking to the Owls and Butterflies* (Lame Deer and Erdoes) *Why Look at Animals?* (Berger)

	The Artifice of the Natural (Siebert) *Television and the Twilight of the Senses* (McKibben, Ch. 1) *The Loss of the Creature* (Percy, Ch. 1)
The pros and cons of pet ownership	*Talking to the Owls and Butterflies* (Lame Deer and Erdoes) *Why Look at Animals?* (Berger) *Mouse* (McNulty) *The Whole Animal* (de Waal) *Rights and Kindness* (Shepard)
"Bambification" and popular culture	*Why Look at Animals?* (Berger) *The Artifice of the Natural* (Siebert) *The Whole Animal* (de Waal) *Rights and Kindness* (Shepard)
Anthropomorphism and anthropodenial	*The Whole Animal* (de Waal) *Mouse* (McNulty) *Murder in a Zoo* (Leakey and Lewin) *The Case for the Personhood of* *Gorillas*(Patterson and Gordon), *Rights and Kindness*(Shepard)
Animal intelligence	*Talking to the Owls and Butterflies* (Lame Deer and Erdoes), *Why Look at Animals?* (Berger) *Mouse* (McNulty), *Murder in a Zoo* (Leakey and Lewin) *The Case for the Personhood of Gorillas* (Patterson and Gordon)

Essay Options

Talking to the Owls and Butterflies, John (Fire) Lame Deer and Richard Erdoes

Option #1. Respond to Lame Deer and Erdoes's charges against "white society."
Option #2. Analyze Lame Deer and Erdoes's sense of self using theories from Chapter 3. (Sapolsky, Baumeister, and Bateson)

Why Look at Animals?, John Berger

Option #1. Discuss the social functions of zoos.
Option #2. Explore the notion of "animals of the mind" in popular culture.
Option #3. Evaluate attitudes toward animals and "wildness" in contemporary American culture. (McKibben, Percy, and Lame Deer and Erdoes)

Mouse, Faith McNulty

Option #1. Write a profile of an animal you've known well.
Option #2. Debate the pros and cons of pet ownership. (Lame Deer and Erdoes and Berger)

The Artifice of the Natural, Charles Siebert

Option #1. Survey and analyze media portrayals of animals.
Option #2. Assess Siebert's claim that we are losing contact with nature. (Lame Deer and Erdoes, Slouka, and McKibben)

The Whole Animal, Frans de Waal

Option #1. Examine and assess the role of TV in the "Bambification" of animals. (Berger and Siebert)

Option #2. Assess the current state of "anthropodenial" in American culture.

Option #3. Research and report on a book or article on animal ethology.

Option #4. Assess the presentation of animal minds in an ethological documentary.

Murder in a Zoo, Richard Leakey and Roger Lewin

Option #1. Research and assess the controversy associated with sociobiological theories of human behavior.

The Case for the Personhood of Gorillas, Francine Patterson and Wendy Gordon

Option #1. Evaluate the case for the personhood of higher primates. (Leakey and Lewin)

Option #2. Research and report on the study of animal languages.

Equality for Animals?, Peter Singer

Option #1. Research and compare the views of animal rights organizations with those of Singer.

Option #2. Research and report on the state of animal experimentation on your campus.

Rights and Kindness: A Can of Worms, Paul Shepard

Option #1. Contrast Singer and Shepard on animal rights. (Singer)

Option #2. Research and debate the pros and cons of animal liberation and rights.

Option #3. Research and report on the use of animals in the food, entertainment, fashion, or medical industry.

Media Connections

Koyaannisqatsi as a critique of white society	Lame Deer and Erdoes, FE #4
Collage of "animals of the mind" images from pop culture	Berger, FE #4
Essay on "animals of the mind" in popular media	Berger, EO #2
Analysis of animal representations in TV nature shows	Siebert, ET #1–4
Survey of TV portrayals of animals	Siebert, EO #1
Role of TV in the "Bambification" of animals	de Waal, FE #3
Essay on the "Bambification" of animals in popular culture	de Waal, EO #1
Reflections of animal minds in ethnological documentary films	de Waal, EO #4
Evidence of "personhood" in the Koko documentary	Patterson and Gordon, FE #5
Role of TV in promoting notion of human-animal "friendship"	Shepard, FE #5

JOHN (FIRE) LAME DEER and RICHARD ERDOES, *Talking to the Owls and Butterflies* (p. 512)

Lame Deer's critique of white society and its relation to the natural world offers a strong voice to get your exploration of animal minds going. It also provides a historical context for your class's discussion of animal minds. One of the challenges of this chapter is the fact that, aside from pets and pests, animals have all but disappeared from the daily lives of most of us, a notion that John Berger emphasizes in the next selection. Lame Deer, however, recalls a different time and cultural context — an era when individual animals had real power and when humans and animals exercised direct influence on each others' lives. Lame Deer's central point is that humans have changed: over the past two hundred years, white society has tried to deny its connection with animals and the natural world. Lame Deer pairs well with Berger, whose analysis of the "marginalization" of animals in modern society echoes many of Lame Deer's opinions. You'll also find that this reading connects well with other selections in this and other chapters. Lame Deer's critique of Western civilization looks backward to bell hooks's reflections on the legacy of the "age of discovery" in the second chapter, and it anticipates Margaret Wertheim's analysis of the otherworldly yearnings of the cult of cyberspace in the last. The Before Reading activity asks students to examine their own preconceptions about the way Native Americans view the animal world. Unless they're Native Americans themselves, most students come to class with at least a few preconceived notions about how Indians relate to nature and their animal "ancestors." Some of these derive from popular films such as *Dances with Wolves,* from ecologically correct advertising campaigns, or from children's books. Lame Deer reminds us that, contrary to mass media idealizations of Indians as ecological guardians and animal protectors, Native Americans once lived in a complex relationship with the world of animals. It's true that Indians celebrated animals as companions and counselors, but it's also true that they delighted in "the taste, the smell, [and] the roughness" of buffalo steak and that they didn't lack "the courage to kill honestly."

Exploring the Text

1. Lame's Deer's point in this selection is that the white world is determined to tame or domesticate the wildness it finds in nature and itself. Whites, in Lame Deer's view, have transformed animals into freaks, meant either for entertainment or as sources of profit as food. "Man-made animals," as Lame Deer derisively refers to them, are so stupid they hold still while you butcher them or "go haywire" at the slightest sound because of bad treatment and overbreeding. Ironically, Lame Deer notes that most white Americans have also domesticated themselves by trying to deny their real nature. From Lame Deer's perspective, most Americans live in houses that are more like "prisons" than real homes. Our houses are little "boxes" that insulate us so completely from the real world that we've lost the ability to appreciate it. We've also lost our natural appetites and the "courage to kill." Being human, Lame Deer suggests, means acknowledging our connection to the animal world — not denying it. Real humans eat "real food" — "buffalo guts, full of half-fermented, half-digested grass and herbs" or "Wasna," a mixture of "meat, kidney fat, and berries all pounded together." The difference between Native Americans and whites, in Lame Deer's view, is that whites are driven by greed and the desire to deny their own animal nature, while to Native Americans "all life is sacred." Thus, the white world tries to exterminate nonprofitable animal species in order to increase the value of animals destined for slaughter.

2. The paradox that Lame Deer sees in white society is that it spreads death but at the same time does its best to deny death's reality. The white world's program of sanitation and domestication is meant to deny the fact that we, like all living creatures, will die. The Indian, by contrast, doesn't fear death and, thus, is free to appreciate the sacredness of life as it is. Instead of insulating himself against the world of real experience, the Indian embraces it, and with it he embraces death as just one more natural event. Every

day, the Indian accepts the fact that "today would be a perfect day to die." Students may be able to see some truth in Lame Deer's assessment of white attitudes. There's little doubt that most Americans now have little direct contact with either animals or killing. We've even done a good job of distancing ourselves from the fact of human mortality. In fact, Lame Deer would probably laugh at recent "reality" shows on television that simulate danger and death — in the form of stunts and "getting thrown off the island" — for an audience that's lost touch with real experience. Of course, some will be likely to disagree with Lame Deer's view of things. One of the strengths of this reading is that Lame Deer forces us to confront our own myths about nature and Native Americans. We like to imagine that we share the Indian's love of nature and respect for the animal world — but few of us would give up the comforts of civilization to return to these values.

3. Lame Deer's own relationship with the animal world is intensely intimate and predictably spiritual. As a Sioux medicine man, Lame Deer grew up consulting the natural world for advice about human affairs. Thus, when his mother dies, he goes up on a "vision hill" and surrenders himself to nature. Eventually, an eagle strikes him on the back and invites him to embrace all of nature in compensation for the loss of his mother. The natural world becomes for Lame Deer a second "self." Thus, Lame Deer sees himself living in and with nature, and he sees animals as part of his own family. In his vision, he hears animal voices calling him: "Brother, brother, brother." Of course, this doesn't mean that Lame Deer shares the kind of romantic ideas that many whites have about animals or the natural world. Lame Deer isn't above consulting the entrails of a dead badger to see the future or using the badger's "pizzle" as an awl or as something to barter with to get a good horse.

Further Explorations

1. Lame Deer would probably have no trouble understanding why the sense of smell declined in importance in Western civilization after the Renaissance, as explained in "The Olfactory Revolution." As Classen, Howes, and Synnott indicate, after the connection was made between disease and waste disposal, Europeans became increasingly intolerant of strong odors. Strong organic smells that were once accepted as part of daily life — including the smell of decaying animal and vegetable matter — became associated in the European mind with pestilence after the scientific discoveries of the eighteenth century. Lame Deer, thus, would likely see the subsequent "deodorization" of life in the West as a symptom of the white world's fear of death. It would probably strike Lame Deer as completely logical that Western science grew out of Europe's reaction against plague. Much of what Lame Deer dislikes most about the white world is associated with scientific and technological progress — things such as industrial animal breeding and farming methods, modern housing, electricity, and war technology. Lame Deer would probably view the scientific revolution as the moment when the white world turned against nature and began to deny its relationship with the animal world. In his view, we Americans won't be happy until we eradicate all smells — "even the good, natural man and woman smell" — or until we breed a race of people "without body openings." As he suggests, we want to seal ourselves off from the world around us and deny that we're a part of natural processes linked to death.

2. The picture of white society that Lame Deer paints in this selection isn't a very attractive one. The white world, according to Lame Deer, has cut itself off from all natural pleasures and sensations. We no longer appreciate what it means to be hungry, cold, or quiet. We've lost our ability to appreciate the charms of an outdoor privy on a snowy winter night as well as our ability to recognize the sacred when we see it. The modern world, in Lame Deer's view, is determined to tame itself the way it's tamed the animals it continues to put up with. Thus, we live regimented lives as office workers and housewives, we surround ourselves with "noise" instead of listening to nature, and we "rush, rush, rush" instead of taking the time for contemplation. Slouka's analysis of the role of

noise in the context of corporate capitalist culture would support Lame Deer's view. According to Slouka, we've commodified sounds the same way we've commodified chickens, and the resulting din that surrounds us day and night has made it impossible to reflect on our own lives. The supreme irony, as Slouka and Lame Deer might agree, is that the rich nowadays pay high prices to visit resorts or purchase property in out-of-the-way places where they can get away from the din of civilization — places such as Montana, Wyoming, and New Mexico that have long been home to large numbers of Native Americans. McKibben's analysis of the impact of television on the senses also supports Lame Deer's critique of white society. According to McKibben, TV restricts our senses and makes it increasingly difficult for us to appreciate the full sensory experience of nature. Television, in McKibben's view, also addicts us to "comfort" — which he defines negatively as the avoidance of strong physical experiences. Thus, McKibben would appreciate the charm that Lame Deer finds in watching the stars through the open door of an outdoor privy on a cold winter night. He would also likely understand Lame Deer's dream of the day when "nature will stop the electricity." Lame Deer might also find support for his view of the white world in Ullman's examination of the "cult of the boy engineer" and the way that it's shaping attitudes in the modern electronic workplace. The picture of the information age ethic that Ullman paints is every bit as bleak as Lame Deer's portrait of self-domestication in white culture. The men that Ullman encounters in the world of high technology are self-absorbed and unsympathetic. They are people who have lived so "close to the machine" and at such a fast pace for so long that they, as Lame Deer might phrase it, have become "crazy, no-good" humans.

3. There's little doubt that Lame Deer presents his views of white society as an act of political resistance. Lame Deer's recollections of what animals meant in past times and his memory of the way humans once lived are clearly intended as challenges to white dominance. In fact, like hooks, Lame Deer isn't content merely to offer an alternative perspective on the way things are. As you read this selection, it becomes clear that he sees his reminiscence as a revolutionary act and looks forward to a time when white cultural attitudes will be replaced by something better, something closer to nature.

4. As you begin your exploration of animal minds and modern society, you might want to view a few minutes of the documentary film *Koyaanisqatsi* in class. This frenetic depiction of life inside the "machine" of contemporary urban America illustrates much of what Lame Deer feels is wrong with white society. It also underscores how far from nature we've ventured during the past century. The question of what can be done to make American culture less machinelike challenges students to envision alternative futures of their own. Some may focus on measures aimed at mitigating the dehumanizing effects of technology and the modern workplace — things like shorter work weeks and better balanced lifestyles. Others may argue for more sweeping social changes, including the kinds of ecological and anarchist platforms that have been advanced by protesters at gatherings of the World Trade Organization.

Essay Option

This assignment, suitable for a two- to three-page academic paper, focuses on the idea of Lame Deer's sense of self and how it differs from the notion of selfhood that has dominated Western cultures for the past several centuries. Unlike the closed central or "inner" self that Baumeister associates with Western civilization, Lame Deer's self is more open. Indeed, the vision that Lame Deer offers at the end of this selection suggests that he sees little or no boundary between his inner self and the outer world of nature. In this sense, Lame Deer resembles the tribal peoples whom Sapolsky meets in East Africa. Like them, his self appears to be "open at the back." He has little of the rigidity or inflexibility that Bateson associates with Americans and in particular with American men. In fact, it's interesting that at a moment of great personal vulnerability — during the "transition" represented by his mother's death — Lame Deer deliberately "opens" or exposes himself to the world around him and seeks out something to learn.

JOHN BERGER, *Why Look at Animals?* (p. 521)

If you're going to spend some time discussing human-animal relationships, you'll want to assign this selection. Berger offers an illuminating history of how human views of animals have changed over the past few thousand years and challenges us to consider how invisible animals have become since the beginning of the industrial age — ever since the time we stopped exchanging looks with animals and started looking *at* them instead. In addition to making us think about topics we tend to take for granted, Berger also offers the opportunity for several interesting projects and assignments, including an analysis of the function of zoos and an exploration of what he calls "animals of the mind." Berger can also be used as the point of departure for a paper exploring current American attitudes toward animals and nature. To prepare students for this selection, ask them to freewrite about their own experiences of going to the zoo, as suggested in the Before Reading activity. If some of your students have never visited a zoo, ask them to speculate about how and why zoos were first created. Berger touches on the history of zoos in this selection and offers a political perspective on the topic that will probably come as a surprise to most students.

Exploring the Text

1. Animals, according to Berger, once occupied the center of human affairs. They "constituted the first circle of what surrounded man." When we first began keeping animals several millennia ago, they were central figures in our religions and magical rites. Humans once viewed animals as equals joined by the shared experiences of birth, life, and death. Animals confirmed our existence as a species and defined us with the "look" that we exchanged with them. In the past, Berger suggests, we didn't just look at animals; they also looked at us, and this act of objectification, Berger implies, was both frightening and healthy. Berger himself refuses to specify what this look meant, but it is clear that, as he sees it, our original relation with the animal world reminded us of the ways we resembled and differed from the animals we kept and encountered. In the regard of the animal others that we once lived among, we saw ourselves reflected as a species, and we could grasp our own otherness. Animals, thus, offered us a form of equal "companionship." They reassured us that we were not alone in the world, and they also reminded us that the world was something we shared with other beings that had "secrets" we would never decipher. As a result, we tended to treat animals as if they had mysterious powers. They offered "explanations" for the mysteries of nature and gave us the shape of our first alphabets. Animals also offered themselves as our first metaphors and as the subjects of our first works of art. Originally, then, humans saw animals from a perspective that Berger describes as "existential dualism." Because they lived among animals and experienced their mysterious difference with them, our ancestors saw animals as slaves *and* as gods; they both subjected them *and* worshipped them, and saw no contradiction in these attitudes.

2. Human beings also freely engaged in what Berger calls "anthropomorphism" prior to the nineteenth century. Anthropomorphism is the ascription of human emotions, mental states, and moral values to other species. Ancient literary works such as the *Iliad* show signs of anthropomorphic thinking when they compare the suffering of soldiers dying in battle with the suffering of the horses who die carrying them. Berger detects this kind of cross-species thinking in Aristotle, as well, and observes that it wasn't questioned in the West until the era of René Descartes and the dawn of modern science. Descartes did two things: he drew a firm boundary between humans and animals and he divided human existence into two mutually exclusive components. As Berger notes, Descartes "internalized" the dualism that had always colored humanity's view of animals *"within man."* By dividing human existence between the soul and the body and by linking consciousness with the soul, Descartes reduced the body to the level of a mere "machine." Denied souls within Descartes's philosophy, animals were thus nothing more than unconscious automatons. This radically changed humanity's view of

animals. From this point on, animals were "emptied of experience and secrets" and became part of a "receding past." As Berger repeats throughout this selection, after the era of Descartes, animals began to "disappear." They were "conquered and turned into slaves" and a "nostalgia" began to replace our original view of them. Indeed, during the earliest phases of the industrial revolution, animals were seen simply as motors that could provide useful sources of energy. In later phases, they became "sources of raw material." Throughout this process, Berger suggests, what we might see as the "de-spiritualization" of animals has preceded and set the stage for the dehumanization that reduces people to the level of "productive units." Indeed, Berger implies that our acceptance of animals as *things* rather than *others* prefigures future attitudes toward workers and other expendable or superfluous classes of human beings.

3. Today, in the place of the animals we once lived among on relatively equal terms, we have pets. Animals in the past served purposes in a household. They were "guard dogs, hunting dogs, mice-killing cats." The habit of pet-keeping arose with the development of "the private small family unit," a "distinguishing feature of consumer societies." In Berger's view, pets are rather pathetic. They are de-sexed, de-clawed, and deprived of contact with their kind. Indeed, they are meant to be reflections of their masters. The pet "completes" its owner by offering him "responses to aspects of his character which would otherwise remain unconfirmed." What Berger seems to be suggesting here is that the relation between pet and master represents a new kind of animal-human bond. But he stresses that because it is founded on utter dependency, the equality (or "parallelism," as he terms it) that once existed between animals and humans has been lost.

4. As real animals have disappeared from our daily lives or been marginalized, they have been replaced by what Berger calls "animals of the mind." Actually, animals of the mind have long existed. The animals in tribal myths, for example, exist only in human dreams and religions. But in the modern era, a new kind of mental animal emerges. In the twentieth century, "animals of the mind" began to appear that are patterned on pets and meant for "spectacle." These are the kind of "human puppets" that we've become familiar with through childrens' books, Disney movies, and contemporary television shows. According to Berger, such mass media animal portrayals "universalize" the "current social practices" of human beings by projecting them on humanized animal characters. Thus, Donald Duck wants to have some fun fishing or boating, but he can't because he's broke and the mailman hasn't brought his next paycheck. Such humanized imaginary creatures are to be found in the shape of stuffed animals, toys, comic books, cartoons, pictures, and "decorations of every sort." They are meant to remind us of the animals that have disappeared from our lives, yet at the same time they reinforce the "cultural marginalization" they are meant to deny, because they obscure the inherent difference that once was the hallmark of animal-human relationships. This is even true in relation to photographs of "real animals" in the wild, in that the animal as photographed is an artificial phenomenon — a staged, "normally invisible" spectacle that exists due to technological intervention. Berger implies that professionally photographed animals are just as much "animals of the mind" as is Donald Duck, because they exist solely to be observed. They are "objects" that we create and not "subjects" that have an independent existence and a will of their own. When we look at them, we do not, then, encounter an alien "look" that responds to our own with its own mysteries; we see only a reflection of ourselves or, as Berger puts it, the "index of our power." In this sense, the more we look at animals — animals, that is, that have been transformed into objects meant to be seen and understood — the less we actually see them and "the further away they are."

5. Zoos exist, in Berger's view, as testimony to the disappearance of animals and our transformation of animal life into a spectacle for human consumption. Zoos, as Berger reminds us, were created in the eighteenth century to celebrate colonial power. They were originally conceived as living "museums" where kings could display exotic species that confirmed the reach of their imperial might. In the nineteenth century, zoos were

rationalized as performing a civic function as a source of "knowledge and public enlightenment." But animals in zoos, for Berger, are no different from other "animals of the mind." They are meant to remind us not about the real animals we have lost contact with — animals filled with "experience and secrets" — but of the "innocence" we've come to associate with animal life. Adults take children to the zoo, according to Berger, "to show them the originals of their reproductions." But since the animals we seek really live only in our imaginations, the ones we see in the zoo are always a disappointment. As zoo visitors move "from cage to cage, not unlike visitors in an art gallery," they see animals that have been rendered utterly "dependent" and "marginal." Zoos attempt to surround them with "props" that are meant to re-create the spectacle that visitors expect, but even these efforts fail to bring animals to life, primarily because such features only underscore the fact that everything in the zoo is an "illusion." Indeed, as Berger stresses, it might even be tempting to think that zoos, stuffed animals, and other animal substitutes are meant to "compensate" for the loss of animal others, but, in fact, all of these "innovations" themselves are part of the very process that has systematically pushed animals to the margins of human affairs. Zoos, Berger suggests, make animals harder to see and more remote by making them seem both more familiar *and* more exotic than they actually are.

6. Overall, Berger seems to be suggesting that we humans are becoming an increasingly solipsistic and "lonely" breed of creatures. In the past, we shared the world with animals that were more than simply a source of spectacle or a screen upon which we could project our fantasies. We once lived our lives in parallel with the animals that worked alongside us and shared in our most fundamental experiences. The very fact that we couldn't comprehend the look that they exchanged with us was evidence of their integrity and independence — their similarity and difference. This look, which, as Berger suggests, played "a crucial role in the development of human society," has been replaced by the vacant stare of animals in the zoo and the imposed innocence of animals of the mind. Today, when we look *at* animals, we no longer see them seeing us, we see only reflections of ourselves, or we see evidence of their "disappearance." At the end of the essay, Berger refuses to do more than hint at what this change might mean. He does, however, suggest that there's a connection between zoos and "all sites of enforced marginalization," including "ghettos, shanty towns, prisons, madhouses, [and] concentration camps." The logic of modern capitalism, he seems to suggest, excludes or marginalizes "others." It locks us into a world of narcissistic fantasy — a world populated by pets and animals of the mind — where the "mystery" of difference or "distinctness" can no longer exist.

Further Explorations

1. If you have the time — and a nearby zoo — you may want to make a visit to test some of Berger's claims. Since this essay was originally published, most zoos have redefined themselves in response to modern ecological theory. So, chances are you'll find more simulated animal "habitats" and open exhibits than the kinds of cages that Berger describes. Of course, the question now is whether these more "natural" exhibits aren't themselves related to what Berger calls "animals of the mind." Perhaps more than ever, zoos are in the business of marketing illusions — illusions about our relation to nature, animal intelligence, and the future of animal life. They also, as Berger suggests, might be peddling the primary illusion of innocence. You shouldn't have too much trouble finding evidence of this, particularly since today's zoos often self-consciously borrow marketing strategies and display elements originally pioneered by their capitalist cousin, the modern theme park.

2. It's possible to read Berger as a theoretical gloss of Lame Deer's more personal remarks. Lame Deer recalls a time when animals had "power" — exactly the kind of power that Berger associates with human-animal relationships prior to the seventeenth century. Animals, for Lame Deer, are still "subjects." They still have the power to act on

the world and even on the men who hunt them. They are not like the "no-good" domesticated animals that the white world breeds. Lame Deer also illustrates the "existential dualism" that Berger associates with pre-modern views of animals. As Lame Deer sees them, animals are vital sources of human energy — food — and also sources of mystery and truth. Thus, he sees no contradiction in searching for his future in a pool of badger blood and then using its pizzle as a tool for working leather. In Lame Deer's view, white society has tried to domesticate animals and control nature because it fears death. Berger, however, links the marginalization of animals to the rise of industrial society. Yet there is clearly a connection between these views. As Berger suggests, the goal of seventeenth-century philosophers such as Descartes and Buffon was to separate humanity from the material world that was becoming associated with the laws of physics — the world of the body — and, thus, with the world of death. As Berger himself notes, animals once were seen as sharing with us the great mysteries of birth, life, and death. By denying our relationship to these realities — and by distancing ourselves from animals — we assert our own "innocence." "Animals of the mind," stuffed animals, animals in zoos, and even animals that live on factory farms are, in an odd sense, beyond mortality. They live outside of time and in no real place — a state that Lame Deer would clearly associate with the deepest fantasies of white culture.

3. This question directs you forward to McNulty's essay on her experience with her pet mouse. McNulty may be seen as either challenging or confirming several key ideas in Berger. She clearly anthropomorphizes her pet by ascribing motivations and reactions to him that seem all too human. Yet the wonder she expresses at her mouse's behavior and aptitudes and the fine-grained detail of her observations suggest a relationship that goes beyond the kind of narcissistic human-animal interaction Berger associates with masters and their pets. Clearly, McNulty is *not* the master of Mouse. Mouse may occupy a box in her kitchen, but she retains her independence. Indeed, even though Mouse appears to accept McNulty more readily than she does other humans, this seems a matter of choice, not a matter of dependency. McNulty also seems to appreciate the "parallel" nature of Mouse's life. She seems to respect and appreciate the differences between her and her tiny cohabitor, and she also seems to learn, through her, about the "arrogance" of fellow humans who find it difficult to take the life and feelings of a mouse seriously. Of course, it might also be argued that McNulty does little more than project her own feelings and emotions on her pet and that her relationship with Mouse never rises beyond the level of human fantasy. From this perspective, McNulty's mouse is just another spectacle, another caged animal like the specimens at the zoo, which exist not for themselves but for a human's gaze.

4. To test Berger's claims about "animals of the mind," students can assemble collages of animal imagery from comic books, magazines, ads, and so forth. To complicate this assignment, have some groups concentrate on images that are self-consciously imaginative — images from comics, films, television shows, and cartoons — and have others concentrate on photo images of "real" animals. Later, analyze the way animals are depicted in these two groups of images to see how they compare. Berger, of course, would predict that both sets of images convey human fantasies that actually tell us little about the animals themselves.

Essay Options

1. Further Exploration #1 above should provide sufficient preparation for this assignment. However, you may also want to have students do some additional encyclopedia research on the history of zoos before they sit down to write. This topic also allows students the chance to debate whether the zoo hasn't itself become an outmoded relic in the age of videotape and ecological consciousness.

2. This topic builds on work students have done in relation to #4. The interesting question here centers on the purpose of such mass media portrayals of animals. Berger suggests that they are meant to reflect aspects of our daily lives or to capture a kind of

"innocence." But students may be able to come up with examples of comic and cartoon animals that don't seem to fit either of these descriptions. Clearly some, like Mickey Mouse, are both innocent and anthropomorphic. But other figures may not fit easily into this mold. In fact, it might be noted that "animals of the mind" are themselves becoming rarer and rarer as we move further away from the twentieth century. Today, most cartoons and comics focus on fantasy humans more often than they do on fantasy animals, and when animals do appear in these entertainments, they often do so in the role of pet.

3. Essay Option #3 draws on Berger, McKibben, and Lame Deer for an academic paper on American attitudes toward nature and animal life. Once students have read Berger, they often begin to realize how absent animals are from urban America. Including McKibben here allows students to move beyond human-animal relations and to think about our increasing distance from nature in general. If you read Slouka and Percy in the first chapter, you might also want to include them as possible sources of material for this assignment.

FAITH McNULTY, *Mouse* (p. 535)

This selection provides a counterpoint to the relatively pessimistic view of animal-human interaction offered by Lame Deer and Berger. It also offers a bit of narrative relief after Berger's challenging analysis of the marginalization of animal life. The story of McNulty's relationship with a wild field mouse suggests that it is possible for humans to connect with animals in a way that respects their integrity and independence. It also offers a good example of the power of close observation in the service of reading other minds. You'll find, too, that McNulty looks forward to de Waal in that her relationship with Mouse can be seen as illustrating the kind of "mature anthropomorphism" that de Waal values in science. You can use McNulty as the point of departure for an essay that profiles an animal-human relationship or as the basis, with Lame Deer and Berger, of an academic paper debating the issue of pet ownership. Focusing as it does on the issue of pets, the Before Reading activity can be used as a pre-writing exercise for Essay Option #2.

Exploring the Text

1. McNulty begins her essay by confiding in us that she had "no idea there were so many things to notice about a mouse." By her own admission, McNulty spent hours watching her companion as Mouse groomed herself, fed, and slept. She tells us about Mouse's oddly "cat-like" way of cleaning herself with her "simian hands." She also lovingly describes her "gunmetal gray" coat and the way it eventually changed into a "bright reddish brown." She notes that Mouse loved to eat chicken, fruit, and vegetables and that she had a special weakness for melon seeds. She also tells us about the way she interacted physically with humans and could discriminate between individual people. Overall, McNulty thinks highly of her pet's intellectual abilities. Mouse, she tells us, "was full of curiosity and eager to explore." She had excellent spacial sense and manual dexterity. Mouse also showed signs of creativity — as when she fooled "Stinky" by banking her food supply — as well as evidence of real affection, possessiveness, loneliness, and joy.

2. There's no doubt that McNulty anthropomorphizes Mouse. The terms she uses to describe her pet's mental states all echo human emotions, motives, and desires. The real question is whether it's conceivable that Mouse actually experienced something akin to any of these human emotions or motives. It's relatively plausible, for example, that Mouse did feel love, loneliness, and even joy in relation to Stinky. And it's equally believable that Mouse had and expressed preferences for different individual human beings. But whether Mouse actually self-consciously felt "consternation" when Stinky raided her food supply is another matter. And it may be even harder for students to accept that a tiny field mouse could self-consciously understand the problem she faced in relation

to Stinky and then reach a deliberate "decision" about how to resolve it through a relatively "brilliant" strategy.

3. Of course, the story that McNulty ends her essay with is meant, to a certain extent, to anticipate our doubts about Mouse. The doctors she consults about Mouse's swollen leg all patronize her and dismiss her pet because of any number of possible biases. It may be that they find it hard to take Mouse seriously because of her size, or because she's an animal, or because she's a "pest." In any case, McNulty offers these examples of human arrogance to illustrate how quick we are to dismiss animal life and to overlook the marvel of animal minds. By contrast, the image we get of McNulty from this mouse-memoir is a lot like Mouse herself: she comes across as a remarkably sensitive, observant, and compassionate person — a person who is humble and perceptive enough to learn from and be changed by such a tiny being.

Further Explorations

1. It could easily be argued that McNulty's relationship with Mouse offers a clear example of the kind of reflective interaction that Berger sees between pet owners and their animal dependents. McNulty, it might be observed, reduces this poor wild creature to a dependent state and cuts it off from its natural habitat, much in the same way that zoos divorce wild creatures from the natural context that gives meaning to their lives. She also might be seen as projecting her own feelings, motives, and desires on her pet mouse. Indeed, there does seem to be a kind of "family resemblance" between Mouse and her mistress. Both are equally curious, detail-oriented, and affectionate, and both are skilled problem solvers. It's also clear that McNulty feels she enjoys a special bond with Mouse and takes some pride in the fact that her pet prefers her to other humans. From this perspective, Mouse does seem like a "mirror" in which McNulty sees aspects of herself that she can find in no other relationship. But it might also be argued that McNulty's relationship with Mouse actually harkens back to earlier forms of human-animal interaction. McNulty may anthropomorphize Mouse, but she never loses sight of the distance that separates her from her pet. As she notes at the end of her essay, when Mouse interacted with her, she felt "as though an affectionate message" were being communicated between them, but she never forgets the "enormous distance" that separates their minds and their worlds. In fact, reading this essay, you get the impression that what draws McNulty to her pet is precisely this sense of difference — the sense of "distinctness" that Berger claims always typified human-animal relationships before the industrial revolution. You also get the feeling that by watching Mouse, McNulty learns things about herself. She certainly learns things about the arrogance of her fellow human beings. When McNulty looks at Mouse, she doesn't see simple animal "innocence." She sees a complex intelligence with motives, desires, skills, likes, and dislikes. Thus, it could be argued that she sees Mouse as a "subject" and not simply as an "object" or a kind of "animal of the mind."

2. McNulty complicates Lame Deer's assessment of the white world's impact on the world of animals only to the extent that she herself is white and is yet remarkably open to the "power" that exists in even a creature as apparently insignificant as a wild field mouse. Otherwise, she might be seen as actually confirming much of what Lame Deer says about white society. It might be argued that McNulty "tames" this wild creature and deprives it of its rightful place in nature, just as Lame Deer says is typical of white-animal relationships. Yet, McNulty herself seems remarkably open to her tiny four-footed companion. Unlike the doctors she consults, who embody the "arrogance" that Lame Deer sees in the white world, McNulty sees value in her pet. In fact, it's not that she "loves" Mouse the way a pet owner might "love" an overbred and "freakish" toy poodle or Pekingese; she admires and respects her, much in the same way Lame Deer admires and respects the animals he comes into contact with. She acknowledges that her relationship with Mouse changes her — that Mouse contains a mystery that she's able to connect with — much as Lame Deer connects to all of nature through the birds that visit him

during his vision quest. McNulty also makes it clear that Mouse brings her face-to-face with the mystery of death. When Mouse's life runs out, McNulty reflects on the lessons Mouse had taught her and on the way she had "stirred" her imagination and expanded the borders of her life. Chances are that Lame Deer would even appreciate the fact that McNulty doesn't bother to bury Mouse but returns her, instead, to the grass where she was born — thus acknowledging the continuous cycles of birth, life, and death of which both she and Mouse are a part.

3. Nussbaum might see McNulty's relationship with Mouse as yet another way of deepening our understanding of other minds. Nussbaum discusses the ways that children's books, games, and even stuffed animals expand our understanding of other people's mental states. All these forms of imaginative "play" invite us to speculate about the thoughts and feelings of others and thus begin to appreciate the "hidden" mental life of other minds. Pets like Mouse might be seen as fulfilling much the same function. When McNulty speculates about why Mouse reacts in a particular way to other humans or to Stinky, she's expanding her own ability to empathize and, thus, from Nussbaum's perspective, deepening the mental capacity that underlies her own humanity. Nussbaum might also point out that McNulty's relationship with Mouse heightens her appreciation for the "invisible" beings who live in the world and, thus, fulfills a kind of political agenda, as well. Of course, McNulty might object to taking such an exclusively "functional" view of her relationship with Mouse. Viewing Mouse in this way reduces her to a kind of mental exercise and makes her relationship with McNulty seem less mutual or dynamic.

4. Chances are that Blum wouldn't be surprised by McNulty's attachment to Mouse or by the reactions of the male doctors McNulty turns to for help with Mouse's swollen leg. Women, according to Blum, are inherently more empathetic than men, and thus she might expect that McNulty would be able to see herself in the place of her tiny pet. Men, in Blum's view, are more interested in conflict and competition and are generally less sensitive to the feelings of others and thus might easily see a field mouse as something expendable.

Essay Options

1. This assignment invites students to write a personal essay, based roughly on McNulty's memoir of her relationship with Mouse, in which they explore their own association with an animal. Beyond simply documenting experiences that illustrate the animal's "level of intelligence," you may also want to direct students to try to convey, as McNulty does here, what this relationship meant to them or what they learned about themselves or their animal companion as a result of it.

2. Lame Deer, Berger, and McNulty provide a firm point of departure for an academic paper debating the pros and cons of pet ownership. To expand on this topic, you may also want to ask students to read de Waal and Shepard, since they both touch on issues related to anthropomorphizing animal minds. De Waal's concept of "mature anthropomorphism" can be applied to McNulty's experience and lays the foundation for a positive view of human-pet interaction. Shepard, by contrast, offers a scathing assessment of our fantasies about "bonding" with animals. If you want to assign additional reading on the topic, consider James Serpell's classic *In the Company of Animals* (1986).

CHARLES SIEBERT, *The Artifice of the Natural* (p. 542)

Siebert continues the discussion of the domestication of animal minds that runs throughout the first half of the chapter by examining how animals are portrayed on television nature shows. The issue of media portrayals of animals is important because, as both Lame Deer and Berger suggest, most Americans have lost daily contact with wild animal life. Thus, most of our information about animal minds comes to us from mass media sources such as books, television programming, and films. And today, with entire cable networks dedicated to documenting animal lives dawn to dusk, the media's influence on our ideas about animal others is greater than ever. Siebert links with Berger and de Waal to form a thematic unit on the issue of mass media animal imagery. This essay can also be used as a one-reading assignment for a paper on the same topic. As you might expect, you'll also find connections between Siebert and some of the other media-related pieces throughout the text. To prepare for Siebert, have students think back to specific nature shows they can recall seeing on television, as suggested in the Before Reading activity. Even if they can't recall individual episodes, you can have them think about the general impression such shows convey about animal behavior, nature, and life in the wilderness.

Exploring the Text

1. Television nature programming is "operatic," according to Siebert, in the sense that it tends to focus on unusually dramatic scenarios. Typically, TV animal shows highlight "fast-paced" situations that center on conflict and the struggle for survival. The world of televised animals is thus a "Sisyphean nightmare" full of tragedy, violence, and "arcane wonder" — a world that always has a "protagonist," a sense of impending fate, and a well-developed narrative structure that unfolds to the tones of a suitably "natural" soundtrack. Siebert's point is that we have always portrayed animals on television in completely human terms. We picture animals in the wild as if they were living in a prolonged soap opera, populated with villains, victims, and heroes. Indeed, the point of programs like the one Siebert watches on elephant seals is to stir up our sympathies in response to the "suffering" and struggle that we see onscreen.

2. The irony is that real nature just isn't like this, according to Siebert. Real nature and televised nature "have little to do with each other." Real nature is indifferent to human and animal concerns. It is "slow" by comparison with the fast-paced world of nature as seen on TV. In fact, as Siebert notes, televised nature actually has more to do with the pace and look of life in urban America. It is not "inscrutable," "spiritual," or "gradual," as Romantics and Transcendentalists once saw it. It's a world of "sexual mayhem" and random violence. In reality, however, as Siebert indicates, most of the time there's remarkably little to see in nature. In a jungle, life is "hidden" and full of "thriving indifference." Certainly, anyone who has ever been totally alone in a relatively remote natural setting might easily agree with this. Without the editing, music, lighting, and script that accompany televised animal soap operas, nature might be seen as the very opposite of what's shown on TV.

3. By constantly drawing us back to the situation he's in as he watches nature shows, Siebert shows us how far removed he is from the supposed natural world that's he watching on TV. While elephant seals fight for life on a wind-swept beach, he sits six floors above midtown Manhattan, in a world where jets whisk people through space and trees are "chained" with Christmas lights. We watch Darwinian dramas on television, Siebert suggests, in a world that has been completely transformed and tamed by technology.

4. The odd thing is that being alone in real nature is actually more like sitting at home in front of your TV than it is like being on a nature program. In fact, throughout this essay, Siebert hints that being alone with nature is a lot like being at home with the TV turned off — even in the middle of Manhattan. When you're alone in a jungle or forest, according to Siebert, you are "divested of your ego and ideas." The sheer vastness of what we call nature leads to the "unraveling" of our thoughts and our egos. This "belittling" is an experience that we've grown unaccustomed to and that we now flee, in Siebert's view. In fact, watching a nature show might be seen as the opposite of being alone with nature. Nature shows don't expose us to the unfocused, disorienting experience of nature's vastness and gradualness. Nor do they de-center us and make us question our place in the universe. Instead they "shamelessly" feed our egos by reflecting back to us images of ourselves and of the hyperactive world we've created for ourselves. That's why Siebert senses something "vaguely illicit" about watching these shows. Not

only does it seem wrong to watch all this struggle from the comfort of our snug urban dwellings, it seems wrong to watch something that claims to represent the truth and that's so obviously full of falsehood.

5. The last two anecdotes that Siebert offers might be seen as summarizing his view of TV nature programming. In Siebert's opinion, we've lost the ability to reconnect with real nature. We go out to nature as if we were going to a theme park, because that's essentially how we imagine real nature to be. Like the La Quinta doctor who travels unflappably through the jungles of Nepal as if he were going to the local country club, we've lost the ability to be alone with the vastness and gradualness of real nature. We keep looking for the highlights we've come to expect from the "Disneyfied" versions of wilderness we've seen on TV. Siebert's cabin in northern Canada represents the kind of wild nature that we've lost touch with. It's an ancient, run-down shack with none of the modern amenities, inhabited by critters that he visits once a year in the summer. When he's there, he feels disappointed that nature isn't more exciting — that it's not more like the shows he sees on television. For him, the experience of being there is less like "opera" and more like what happens to Alice when she wanders into a wood and forgets her own name. Nature, like Alice's world through the looking-glass, reacquaints us with our own insignificance; it puts us back into contact with what the world was like before humans began to transform it into a place with dramas, meanings, protagonists, and plots. Thus, when Siebert calls his cabin in the closing paragraph, he's reassured by the very fact that it's still there, empty and alone. It's as if that call puts him in touch with the vast inhuman "otherness" that real nature represents to him.

Further Explorations

1. It's possible that Lame Deer would agree with much of what Siebert says about the way we've "Disneyfied" nature on TV. Indeed, unlike Siebert in his midtown Manhattan apartment, Lame Deer has never lost contact with the lived experience of nature. When he sits down on the open prairie to tell his story without a blanket, he enjoys feeling the earth beneath him. When he walks to the outhouse on a cold winter night or sits there in summer with the door open listening to "the humming of the insects," he feels connected to nature and to its wildness. The telling difference between Lame Deer and Siebert is that while the natural world is an inhuman, "otherly" place for Siebert — a place of overwhelming "anonymity" and "indifference" that extinguishes the ego and "belittles" the self — for Lame Deer it is deeply personal and loving. Animals may not be operatic actors to Lame Deer, but they are his friends. Nature, for Lame Deer, may be vast and powerful, but it's also a realm that is filled with "brothers." As Lame Deer sees it, nature is the true home of mankind; it's a distant mystery for Siebert — and one that is becoming more distant and harder to tolerate as we become more "civilized."

2. As Berger notes, zoos tend to be "boring" places for most visitors, because the animals in them always seem lethargic and dull. Berger feels this is because zoo animals have been torn from their natural settings and thus have lost all connection to the world around them. They either stare off into space or carry out meaningless repetitive activities like pacing in their cages, because there is literally nothing there for them to react to. Siebert's theory of television nature programming offers a different explanation of why zoo animals might strike us as less than exciting. Animals in the zoo are bound to be disappointing because they can't possibly live up to the expectations that we bring to the zoo after watching animal "opera" on TV. Today, many zoos try to cope with this problem by building more imposing and "realistic" habitats for their exhibits or by enriching them with "interactive" displays and videos. As Siebert might observe, however, such embellishments make zoos even less like real nature and serve, instead, only to make them more like television.

3. To Percy, the blasé attitude of the La Quinta doctor who accompanies Siebert to the jungles of Nepal would make perfect sense. This laid-back tourist would embody

everything that Percy finds fault with in modern consumer culture. From this doctor's privileged theme-park perspective, there's no real wilderness left — only a series of sights or vistas that he moves between like prearranged stops on a group tour. He really isn't there to encounter, confront, or discover anything: instead, he moves from place to place as if he were "clicking off items on a checklist." For Percy, and we assume for Siebert, this overcivilized fellow would represent the nadir of human development. He has lost the ability to see himself in relation to the natural world around him; indeed, he has lost the ability to see anything that hasn't already been programmed, taped, and edited for him by the experts. Interestingly enough, while he's with this fellow, Siebert does exactly what Percy suggests one do to "recover" the authentic experience in nature: Siebert watches the La Quinta doctor as *he* watches nature, and thus, from this ironic perspective, gains some appreciation for what we've lost.

4. Baumeister would also probably find it quite easy to understand why television nature shows have come to favor an "operatic" format. It would make sense that as the self becomes more central in human affairs, it begins to obscure our ability to perceive and appreciate things that stand outside of us. Thus, what we see in nature shows on television are really just human dramas translated into animal terms. When we watch mother seals fighting for the lives of their babies, we see a moving, deeply human story played out in front of us — not a reflection of the way things really are in nature. That's why, as Siebert notes, "to sit here in front of a nature show is to have one's ego fed shamelessly." Nature shows exist, in Siebert's view, to show us pictures of ourselves refracted through the medium of creatures that were once genuine others to us. Seen in this way, nature programming on television is the highest tribute to the dominance of the central concept of self.

Essay Options

1. There are certainly enough animal shows on television today to test Siebert's claims. Ask students to compare their observations of recent animal shows with Siebert's observations of the way animals were depicted in 1993. If possible, it would also be interesting to screen a few earlier animal TV classics by either Marlon Perkins or Jacques Cousteau as points of comparison. The difficult part of this assignment is trying to get at the unconscious lessons that such shows convey. As Siebert indicates, animal documentaries are always earnestly pedagogical (perhaps, as Berger might note, because they are associated with the "educational function" attributed to zoos in the nineteenth century). Thus, they always try to teach something. But, as Siebert indicates, the most important lessons they convey are usually unintended. Of course, students will also want to explore new developments in nature programming. Shows such as *Animal Planet* and even "reality shows" such as the *Survivor* series offer a new vision of what the wilderness means — a vision that even Siebert, perhaps, didn't clearly foresee in his essay.

2. This assignment allows students to explore Siebert's claim that we, as a species, are losing contact with nature and with what he terms "gradualness." Lame Deer documents this loss when he feels nostalgia for the time when people could take pleasure in the simple, sensual details of life. McKibben and Slouka also offer evidence of how far we've come from the concept of living "gradually." For Slouka modern life is a disorienting chaos of random sounds and stimulations; for McKibben it's a barrage of numbingly predictable storylines and sensations. Students may be able to find support for these ideas in other readings, as well. McNulty's relationship with Mouse, for example, developed only through long hours of close observation, and even then it didn't result in any one particularly dramatic or "operatic" episode. However, you'll also want to encourage students to draw on their own experiences as they think about this topic. What evidence do they see in their own daily lives and in the lives of those around them that we humans are speeding up and losing our appreciation for "gradualness"?

FRANS DE WAAL, *The Whole Animal* (p. 552)

De Waal's detailed discussion of anthropomorphism bridges the two halves of this chapter. His presentation of concepts such as naïve and mature anthropomorphism, anthropodenial, and animal-centric thinking echoes concerns raised in the first four selections in relation to the history of human attitudes toward animal others. Interestingly, de Waal's scientific perspective contrasts sharply with much of what is said about animal-human relationships in Lame Deer and Erdoes, Berger, and Siebert. So you can use de Waal to round off your discussion of how we view other species and as the occasion for a major academic essay on this topic. However, because he addresses issues related to how we read signs of intelligence in animals, de Waal also looks forward to the second half of the chapter and in particular to the next two selections on primate minds. De Waal's notion of mature anthropomorphism connects well with ideas in Leakey and Lewin and Patterson and Gordon; it also connects with readings in Chapter 6. In addition, de Waal offers yet another paper topic: the "Bambification" of animals in popular culture. The Before Reading activity invites students to think in advance about the scenario that de Waal discusses at the end of this selection. At this point, students may not be able to take a stand on whether Binti's behavior was intelligent or whether it was just a matter of "instinct," but they should be able to speculate about the difficulties involved in trying to address such questions. Chances are they'll also have an opinion about whether it's important to bother reading animal intentions in cases like this.

Exploring the Text

1. According to de Waal, most people think of scientists as totally objective, utterly "unfeeling" researchers who approach animals the way you might "inspect a rock or measure the circumference of a tree trunk." This image of the compassionless scientist is a "caricature," in de Waal's view. On the contrary, he claims, most scientists who study nature and animal behavior "take great pleasure in animals." How else could they devote themselves to a lifetime of close encounters with other species in terrible conditions? To support his point, de Waal offers example after example of scientists such as E. O. Wilson and Konrad Lorenz — people whose passion for animals led them to risk their own safety at times to learn more about their favorite species. Students, however, may have some trouble accepting this portrayal of the compassionate scientist. Of course, thanks to Jane Goodall and a few other popular figures, there is some precedent for the image of the scientist as animal lover. But students may rightly question whether de Waal's claims for the compassionate scientist hold true for the majority of researchers and point out that modern science has itself to blame for the image of the cold, dispassionately objective researcher. Still, there's no doubt that Hollywood also bears some of the blame for promoting the stereotype. Since Dr. Frankenstein first ran amok back in the 1930s, the image of the heartless scientist has been a fixture in pop culture.

2. De Waal feels that animals present us with an "embarrassing problem" because they resemble us in so many ways — despite the fact that we have long taken pride in our distinctness from them. This leads us to resort to what de Waal terms "anthropodenial." We refuse to acknowledge our relatedness to animals, despite abundant evidence to the contrary, because it embarrasses us to do so. De Waal traces this prejudice against animals back to the philosophy of René Descartes and the Judeo-Christian tradition, both of which deny our relatedness to other animal species. De Waal also links anthropodenial with the British psychologist Lloyd Morgan, who once postulated that actions should always be interpreted as the result of lower rather than higher mental processes. As a result of "Morgan's Canon," generations of scientists eschewed any interpretation of animal behavior that hinted at human-like intelligence. De Waal, however, points out that it makes sense and is "far more economicial" to assume that similar intentions underlie similar actions in similar species. Thus, when Georgia the chimpanzee hides water in her mouth to spray on visitors at the compound, it makes sense to assume that

she is deliberately being deceitful and trying to trick them, much as would a mischievous child. Although anthropomorphic thinking is rampant in popular culture, students may well wonder if most people today have risen above anthropodenial. As renewed opposition to the teaching of evolution suggests, it's one thing to project human emotions onto animals in a playful way and quite another to see ourselves as physically and mentally related to other species.

3. De Waal tells the story of Thorleif Schjelderup-Ebbe to demonstrate the way that a childhood fascination with animals can lead to genuine scientific insight into animal behavior. This anecdote also dramatizes de Waal's point about the personal nature of science. Schjelderup-Ebbe was led to his discovery of pecking orders in chickens because he was painfully aware of the consequences of domination in human relationships. Thus, this story illustrates how anthropomorphism can pay off in valid scientific insight. De Waal suggests here that the kind of imaginative identification children regularly engage in is a powerful tool for scientific thinking and that it is only our adult prejudice against animals that keeps us from overcoming anthropodenial.

4. Simple-minded anthropomorphism is destructive, according to de Waal, because it denies the real differences that exist between human and animal minds. When we engage in the kind of "naive anthropomorphism" that de Waal associates with Bambification, we inappropriately project our intentions and values on animals. When, for example, we portray bears with their arms around one another or talk about female dogs saving themselves for their future "husbands," we deny the realities of animal minds. This kind of thinking actually keeps us from recognizing the "nasty side" of animal existence and keeps us out of touch with "the full picture of nature in all its glory and horror." Naïve anthropomorphism thus reinforces anthropodenial. Bambification itself, de Waal suggests, involves the "pedamorphic" depiction of animals — the transformation of animals into human-like creatures by endowing them with the kinds of features (enlarged eyes and rounded heads) we associate with human infants.

5. As a response to Bambification, de Waal offers "mature anthropomorphism." This is a kind of empathetic identification with animal minds that assumes the animal's point of view. It is "animalcentric" as opposed to humancentric anthropomorphism. In order to engage in this kind of empathetic identification with another species, you have to understand the details of an animal's behavior and take its "Umwelt, intelligence, and natural tendencies" into account. The "Umwelt" of an animal is the particular way it lives in the world. To grasp an animal's Umwelt is to understand its tendencies, expectations, actions, and reactions. Thus, when de Waal's cat approaches him aggressively, he understands that she is just being playful from a feline point of view, or when an animal keeper says "Yummy!" as she feeds mealworms to a squirrel monkey, she is expressing the chimp's natural reaction, not her own. In like manner, when horse trainer Monty Roberts reads the chewing movements of a mare as a sign of fear, he relies on his own deep knowledge of horse behavior to guide his intuitions. According to de Waal, such "animalcentric" thinking differs from the kind of "cheap projection" that he sees in Bambification in that it is undertaken not for human purposes of entertainment, education, and so forth, but for "heuristic" purposes. We engage in mature anthropomorphism not for our own gratification but to gain insight into the motives that underlie animal behaviors. It thus differs from naïve anthropomorphism in that it *highlights* rather than minimizes the differences between species.

6. The example of Binti offers a case in point. Most people were amazed by Binti's act of sympathy toward a human being. De Waal, however, interprets their surprise as evidence of their own anthropocentric thinking. To someone who works closely with primates, it's not at all amazing that a female takes care of a wounded infant — regardless of the species involved. Thus, anthropocentrism kept most people from understanding how utterly natural Binti's behavior really was. Many scientists, however, tried to avoid this trap by assuming that Binti's behavior was merely a conditioned response or a matter of instinct. But again, de Waal notes that such thinking is itself a form of anthro-

pocentrism. In his view, these scientists went to absurd lengths to explain a behavior that simply makes sense within the Umwelt of the average gorilla. Both of these responses suggest that we humans continue to resist an animal-centric approach to animal thinking and that we continue to see human beings as the only species capable of intentional action. Yet, de Waal argues, Binti's actions do make sense if only we view them from the perspective of mature anthropomorphism, recognizing the common ground between animal and human minds.

Further Explorations

1. De Waal challenges Lame Deer to the extent that the latter assumes unanimity of opinion within the white world. Lame Deer condemns white society for its heartless, death-dealing approach to nature. The white world exists, in his view, to dominate others and to exploit nature for its own ends. De Waal suggests, however, that there are differences of opinion about our relation to the natural world even within scientific circles. Thus, there are scientists who refuse to acknowledge the similarities between animal and human minds, but there are also those who live close to nature and who would clearly appreciate the kinds of extreme natural experiences that Lame Deer himself enjoys. Naturalists such as Wilson and Goodall, for example, have no desire to domesticate the species that they study and have not lived particularly domesticated lives themselves. Lame Deer would likely approve of the kind of mature anthropocentrism that de Waal promotes in this selection. Indeed, he might view it as a token of the change that he sees coming in the way that young whites view the natural world.

2. The question of whether McNulty engages in naïve or mature anthropomorphism gives students the chance to think through some of the difficulties involved in this conceptual contrast. Did Mouse actually "distinguish people," as McNulty suggests? Isn't it possible that Mouse always bit McNulty's husband because of some residue on his hands that may have irritated her? Did Mouse actually feel something like "consternation" when McNulty exposed her food to Stinky, and did she, in fact, make a "decision" to keep Stinky out of her food bank with a piece of bedding? Did Mouse really feel something like joy when she was reunited with Stinky after several days' absence? All of these behaviors might be explained away as mechanical responses or instinct. It may be hard to believe that Mouse actually engaged in all the relatively sophisticated mental processes that would be required to recognized that her food supply was placed in danger, that Stinky intended to raid it, and that she could stop him by plugging it up with some handy bedding. It may, however, make sense to see a kind of "affection" in Mouse's relationship with Stinky and even the possibility that she felt joy on Stinky's return, particularly since McNulty didn't care much for Mouse's companion herself and thus probably wasn't predisposed to see attachment in her behavior toward him. The fact that McNulty doesn't bother to bury Mouse after she dies might also be seen as evidence that she anthropomorphized Mouse in a mature rather than a naïve way. Indeed, McNulty seems to appreciate Mouse primarily for her "otherness." She never seems to lose sight of the fact that Mouse is something different and hence something special.

3. Television, as Siebert presents it, might be seen as a driving force in the Bambification of animals. When we watch an animal "opera" unfold on TV, according to Siebert, we don't see animals as they actually exist, alone in nature; we see them playing parts in a scripted melodrama calculated to appeal to our emotions. Animals on TV, thus, are not really animals at all but reflections of ourselves. Combined with television cartoon shows and children's programming, such animal operas might be thought of as promoting the kind of naïve anthropomorphism that de Waal disparages in this selection. Television thus might be seen as actually narrowing our view of the world around us by constantly feeding us reflections of our own human preoccupations and Umwelt.

4. There are obvious similarities between Nussbaum's theory of empathy and de Waal's notion of mature anthropomorphism. Both authors believe that our ability to identify with the thoughts, intentions, and feelings of other minds must be disciplined

by the recognition of difference. When a young Greek male views a tragic heroine suffering on stage, he isn't, in Nussbaum's view, supposed to think that he actually experiences what a real woman would experience; he is only supposed to recognize that another being as intelligent as himself is being made to suffer as the result of the situation into which she has been born. He comes away from the play not with the conviction that he knows what she feels but with compassion for what she must have felt. Similarly, a highly skilled animal trainer or ethologist doesn't presume to know precisely what it feels like to be a horse or a bat; she only know that horses and bats react to things in their environment in certain ways and that these reactions are vaguely similar to certain human mental states. Mature anthropomorphism, like real empathy, is thus always "heuristic." It offers us a kind of mental shortcut to understanding other minds, but it never means that we can assume that other minds are "transparent" to us. Interestingly, Nussbaum and de Waal also agree on the role that childhood plays in the development of our powers of imaginative identification. According to Nussbaum, children have to be taught that other people have minds and mental states. They also have to be taught how to reflect on their own feelings, thoughts, and identities. Children's literature fulfills this function, in Nussbaum's view, by constantly underscoring the thoughts, feelings, and intentions of others. Along with Freud, de Waal feels that children are less predisposed than adults to draw sharp distinctions between humans and animals. Children tend to see animals as their equals. In their innocence, children feel an intuitive connection to animals and sense a natural "cohesion" with all living things. This vivid sense of connection with animals is denied only later in life as children grow into adolescence and when, in the words of Paul Shepard, "we begin a lifelong work of differentiating ourselves from animals." De Waal clearly believes that many scientists, such as E. O. Wilson and Jane Goodall, who work closely with animals, never lose this sense of relatedness to other life forms.

5. This question directs your class forward to the way the authors of the next two selections read primate minds. The act of interprimate violence that Leakey and Lewin describe actually occured at de Waal's chimpanzee colony in the Netherlands, and de Waal himself is the one who describes it as an act of premeditated "murder." Thus, there can be no doubt that de Waal would find Leakey's and Lewin's interpretations of chimp behavior as falling within the bounds of mature anthropomorphism. The only question here is how far we can go in extending the idea of premeditation to the chimps involved. It may be plausible to label Yeroen a "murderer" in the sense that he was completely aware of what he was doing and why he was doing it when he attacked Luit. But it may be going too far to suggest that the plot that Yeroen hatched against Luit was similar to a "game of chess" or a political "alliance." Similarly, many of the conclusions that Patterson and Gordon reach about Koko's linguistic abilities might be seen as involving naïve anthropomorphism — if, that is, they were not supported by literally thousands of hours of repetition. For example, when Patterson and Gordon claim that Koko shows real "creativity" by using the word "rotten" in a new way to refer to a companion who has just called her a "stinker," it might be argued that they are naïvely anthropomorphizing what may be simply a kind of automatic reaction on Koko's part. Koko might respond with the sign "rotten" when she sees the sign for "stink" without actually intending to apply it to her companion. However, the bulk of the evidence that Patterson and Gordon provide suggests that Koko is, in fact, capable of such creative and playful thinking.

Essay Options

1. This assignment offers another opportunity for exploring pop cultural representations of nature and animal life. In approaching it, you should encourage students to examine specific examples of the way animals and nature are portrayed in television shows, movies, and advertising. You should also challenge students to explain why they feel certain representations of animals are either maturely or naïvely anthropomorphic.

2. Essay Option #2 offers the chance for students to explore the topic of anthropo-denial. Over the past twenty years, animal ethology has challenged us to rethink many of our preconceptions about nature and animal minds. Figures such as Jane Goodall and Dian Fossey, for example, have become household names and have popularized the idea that animal minds are accessible to human understanding. In fact, as even a few minutes in a bookstore will prove, popular interest in animal minds is at a new high. It might well be argued, then, that instead of actively denying our connection with other species, today we are bent on discovering new ways in which we relate to our animal friends and ancestors.

3. A number of excellent books and articles have appeared over the past twenty years documenting the work of ethologists such as de Waal. This paper topic sends students to the library in search of an example of this relatively new way of looking at animal minds.

4. As a variation, you may want to have students screen a documentary film on the topic of animal behavior or ethology. Over the past few years, for example, the Public Broadcasting Service has featured a number of television documentaries focusing on the behaviors of domesticated animals such as dogs and cats. This assignment may offer students the chance to consult another "text" without the time required to read a book or professional article on the topic of ethology.

RICHARD LEAKEY and ROGER LEWIN, *Murder in a Zoo* (p. 580)

This account of an animal-instigated "crime" introduces a pair of selections on the topic of primate minds. Leakey and Lewin focus on the seamier side of animal behavior. The story they relate here about the "murder" of a chimp as the result of a conspiracy by other chimps raises plenty of questions about the nature of intelligent behavior, the issue of anthropomorphism, and the moral implications of "keeping" self-conscious creatures. Leakey and Lewin pair well with the more sympathetic version of primate minds that Patterson and Gordon offer in their account of Koko in the next selection. They also connect with readings in the previous chapter on the nature of violent minds. To get students ready for this selection, the Before Reading activity asks them to think about how they might devise a test for animal intelligence. (In the next chapter, a similar prompt connected with Hofstadter will ask them to devise a test for machine intelligence.) This task encourages students to clarify their own ideas about intelligent behavior. Some, for example, might associate intelligence with the ability to play complex games such as chess; others may view intelligence as a matter of language use or problem solving. With any luck, at least a few will connect intelligence with imagination and empathy. Chances are, however, that few will see intelligence in the way that Leakey and Lewin view it here — as an aptitude associated with the ability to manipulate and triumph over others.

Exploring the Text

1. According to Leakey and Lewin, Luit's death is a matter of "politics" in that it is the result of a self-conscious and prolonged power struggle between Luit, Yeroen, and Nikkie. The idea of politics implies the existence of well-defined interest groups involved in a process that culminates in domination or rule by mutual consent. The situation of Luit, Yeroen, and Nikkie fits this definition to the extent that the struggle for power in the Arnhem colony existed over a prolonged period of time, involved shifting group alliances, and ended in the emergence of a new leader. The one element that seems to be lacking in this instance of primate politics is the notion of ideology. We generally assume that politics involves a particular theory or program of government, and obviously Yeroen and Nikkie acted solely on their own behalf and not in the name of any theory, agenda, or belief. (Of course, some students may want to point out that human

political agendas often seem like only flimsy rationalizations meant to justify the quest for power and are, thus, not terribly different from the motives that lead to Luit's demise.) Clearly, however, the idea that this chimp "murder" was politically motivated automatically lends it a patina of sophistication. If Yeroen and Nikkie are viewed as co-conspirators against Luit, then their act of violence must be seen as transcending the level of instinct. Indeed, it becomes a self-consciously planned and premeditated act of violence — the kind that requires a human level of sophistication and intelligence.

2. The key to the development of real intelligence, according to Leakey and Lewin, is social interaction. As they point out, chimps in the wild have little need for the kinds of sophisticated mental processes involved in consciousness. Most chimps find it relatively easy to meet the "cognitive demands" associated with locating ample supplies of food and water in their normal habitats. However, the complexities of chimp social life do require a relatively high level of mental ability. In order to survive in chimp society, an individual chimp must be able to keep track of complex kinship patterns, form alliances with other chimps, and use them creatively to "outwit" others. Thus, the complex patterns of a chimp's social world, not the demands of its natural environment, make it so intelligent. Every social "transaction" a chimp engages in is freighted with meaning, and, as a result, chimps develop amazing levels of "social intelligence" that allow them to use one another as "social tools" to achieve their ends. Female chimps form alliances to help them bear and nurture their offspring; males form alliances as they vie for power and breeding rights. But what adds extra complexity to the social games that chimps play is the fact that these alliances themselves can change unexpectedly over time, just as Yeroen's alliance with Luit shifted in the weeks that preceded Luit's death. In addition to this tale of "murder," Leakey and Lewin offer several other examples of "social intelligence" at work among chimps, including the example of how Cyclops uses Phoebe and Phyllis to defeat the more powerful Triton and the example of the protracted process that Alex and Thalia go through to develop a "friendship." Such alliances are important in primate societies because they "govern" individual interactions and provide the sense of cohesion that holds social groups together.

3. The primary aim of Leakey and Lewin in this selection is to explain the origin of human consciousness — not simply to discuss animal behavior. As they indicate, most humans, like most chimps, live lives that involve little in the way of real cognitive challenge. Thus, the kind of complex consciousness that we enjoy can't be explained in purely adaptive terms. In other words, we didn't evolve the ability to think three or four moves ahead or to deceive one another in response to environmental demands. We developed these "Machiavellian" aptitudes in response to the requirements of the complex social networks in which we live. Perhaps the most telling assumption that Leakey and Lewin make is that human beings, like our primate kin, are primarily motivated by "reproductive success" and that such success is associated with access to power. It might be objected, however, that since humans are generally monogamous, it's difficult to see how the sexual imperatives of the average polygamous chimp apply to human relations. Indeed, it might be observed that the implied comparison that Leakey and Lewin present in this selection between chimp and human minds simply doesn't hold, because chimps and humans are essentially different in many ways. It may be true that we, like chimps, form alliances and play interpersonal games in the quest for social power. But it might also be noted that we've broken the connection between reproductive success and group dominance and created complex institutions to help us mediate interpersonal and group conflicts. In fact, it might even be objected that instead of illuminating the human condition, Leakey and Lewin are simply "naturalizing" violence and male domination by linking these all-too-human phenomena with evolutionary theory and the experiences of other species.

4. The question of whether Yeroen and Nikkie actually murdered Luit crystallizes the problems we face in trying to transcend our historical attitudes toward animal minds. If we accept everything that Leakey and Lewin claim in this selection about

chimp minds and motivations, it's hard to see why we shouldn't view Luit's death as an act of premeditated murder. Of course, murder itself is a human concept and any attempt to apply it to Yeroen and Luit should probably be viewed as a gross example of anthropomorphism. But, then, doesn't this suggest that the way Leakey and Lewin present this entire case is itself grossly anthropomorphic? How can we view these chimps as capable of deception, intrigue, guile, and organized conspiracy and not judge what they do as wrong? Then again, it might also be suggested that although these chimps are capable of such sophisticated behaviors, they don't live in a society of self-imposed laws and thus can't be held accountable to a standard that they themselves cannot possibly be aware of. The killing of an alpha male is completely within the acceptable framework of expectations for chimp society, and thus, it shouldn't be confused with the human concepts of murder, vengeance, or conspiracy.

Further Explorations

1. Chances are that Lame Deer wouldn't be shocked by the idea that animals can act in a premeditated manner and even commit violent acts. He clearly believes that animals in the wild have power and that we've lost the ability to appreciate the kinds of activities of which they're capable. Lame Deer has no doubt that animals can think, plan strategies, and even strike back at those who hunt them. Thus, he warns us that a badger can pull a horse underground if it wants to and that a black-tailed deer can ward off a hunter's bullet and send it back at him. Lame Deer might view animals this way because, unlike the whites, he still sees animals as creatures with their own desires and intentions. He has not, like most of us, been raised to view such ideas as "romantic" or anthropomorphic.

2. The case for naïve anthropomorphism in relation to Leakey and Lewin rests most clearly on their use of the term "murder," as discussed above in ET #4. The idea of murder can exist only within the context of a judicial system with all the institutional structures that such a system entails. Thus, the idea that these chimps committed a real murder is clearly an exaggeration. It's also questionable, then, that chimps do anything even remotely related to forming alliances, coalitions, or nonintervention treaties or that they might understand anything about "political manipulation" or a "balance of power." If students take the time to explore the implications of each of these very human concepts, they shouldn't have too much trouble appreciating why these ideas fall beyond the ken of the average chimp. Thus, it might be safe to say that Leakey and Lewin (and de Waal, as well) do, in fact, indulge in a fairly serious display of highly sophisticated naïve anthropomorphizing in this selection. Despite this, however, their central claim about chimp minds — the notion that primate and even human intelligence has developed in response to the complexities of social interaction rather than as a result of environmental adaptation — might still be seen as essentially sound.

3. It might be argued that we can't possibly see any animal other than a human being as a murderer because we've been so conditioned by Disneyfication or Bambification to view all animals in the wild as essentially "innocent." Certainly, the case of Luit, Yeroen, and Nikkie challenges this comic-book perspective on nature. As de Waal might note, nature is often an exceptionally "nasty" place whose "glory and horror" are largely ignored by the average urban human being. The kind of manipulation and cold-blooded violence that Leakey and Lewin attribute to chimps in this selection simply doesn't square with most contemporary beliefs about how the natural world works. Of course, as suggested above, Leakey and Lewin may also be overdramatizing the motives of their primate subjects. Indeed, as Siebert might point out, the picture of murderous intrigue, falsity, and betrayal that they offer might actually be more appropriate on an afternoon soap opera than in a scientific treatise on the natural world. Leakey and Lewin might themselves be charged with a kind of "reverse Bambification" in that they seem to portray animal minds as more human and more dramatic than they really are. How hard is it, after all, to imagine the scenario they offer as a PBS nature

docudrama like the one that Siebert watches, complete with a spine-tingling voice-over and the plaintive moan of a distant Andean flute?

4. Of course, McNulty's mouse might also be seen as almost as Machiavellian as Yeroen and Nikkie. Mouse is an affectionate type, but only as long as you don't get too close to her beloved food supply. If you're a human, she'll warn you off with a growl. If you're another mouse who's too big for her to dominate, she'll leap into action and thwart you by plugging up her food bank with leftover bedding. Luckily, we never find out what she might do to an opponent who couldn't equal her ounce-for-ounce in size. Luit's experience suggests that it wouldn't be a pretty sight.

5. The contrast between Leaky and Lewin and Garbarino might seem too odd to even bother with, yet it also seems too compelling to pass up. Garbarino equates violent behavior with mental numbness — with the loss of mental function — whereas Leakey and Lewin associate it with the highest expression of mental ability. Violence, for Garbarino, indicates the death of the soul, or the demise of empathy and consciousness. For Leakey and Lewin, the ability to empathize with others and to consciously calculate three or four moves ahead of one's own mental state makes violence possible. Politically progressive thinkers who tend to view violent criminals as victims, as Garbarino does, may well dismiss Leakey and Lewin as simply "normalizing" violent behavior. From such a liberal point of view, Leakey and Lewin might be seen as "naturalizing" violence by presenting it as a normal feature of human relationships and by linking it with the highest level of human mental function. Of course, consciousness is not the result of violence, per se, according to Leakey and Lewin, but the result of the complex social interactions that typify the primate's social world. Such complex behavior patterns might be seen as promoting the ability to deceive and harm others, or they may be seen as promoting the ability to bond with one another and to build complex social institutions that help individuals transcend violent behavior. Indeed, as Garbarino might point out, in order to engage in violence, a human being must first overcome his "natural" tendency to empathize with others — and in many cases this happens only after an individual is so abused or abandoned that he literally gives up on further human contact.

6. In his account of the problems associated with the notion of "animal equality," Shepard condemns all forms of anthropomorphic thinking. To Shepard, the attribution of human concepts like "rights" to animals is a gross distortion of animal reality. Animals exist, in Shepard's view, within ecosystems, not societies. As a result, they cannot engage in any form of "social" activity as we might recognize it. Animals are not "friendly" with one another or even "attached" to each other. They inhabit a universe where concepts like guile, deception, murder, and violence don't exist and thus are completely irrelevant. In "Shepard's view, individual animals don't have any "interests" and therefore can't have any goals or strategies. Instead, they live in food chains and have "natural histories." Yet, it's hard to read Leakey and Lewin and accept Shepard's view, at least in relation to higher primates like chimps. While it may be true that Leakey and Lewin exaggerate the anthropomorphic aspects of the "murder" in the Arnhem colony, the evidence they offer to document the complexity of chimp society does seem plausible. It may be too much to believe that Yeroen and Nikkie "conspired" against Luit, but it does not seem beyond the realm of possibility that chimps do live in systematic social structures with changing patterns of alliances founded on something at least akin to friendship or fear.

Essay Option

The sole assignment associated with this selection invites students to research and report on the controversy surrounding sociobiological analyses of human behavior like Leakey and Lewin's analysis of the origin of consciousness in this selection. You might want to pursue this topic if your students have a special interest in finding out more about sociobiology. Otherwise, you may want to postpone your next paper assignment until after you've completed Patterson and Gordon, so that you can offer students a more balanced view of primate minds as they consider the nature of animal intelligence (see Patterson and Gordon, EO #1).

FRANCINE PATTERSON and WENDY GORDON, *The Case for the Personhood of Gorillas* (p. 592)

This argument for the "personhood" of Koko the signing gorilla offers a necessary balance to Leakey and Lewin's exploration of primate intelligence. Whereas "Murder in a Zoo" cites deception, shifting alliances, and struggles for power as signs of higher mental function among chimpanzees, Patterson and Gordon emphasize Koko's empathetic and creative abilities. As a result, you can use these readings to raise questions about what we mean by "intelligence" and about how we recognize its manifestation in other minds. Together, these two readings prepare students for an academic essay in which they compare and evaluate arguments for primate intelligence. In addition, you can use them to introduce ideas that will loom large in the selections by Singer and Shepard — ideas about animal interests and rights. To begin, ask students to define the idea of "personhood," as suggested by the Before Reading activity. This is a rather odd concept. Being a person might be associated with being independent, having a mind of one's own, being aware of one's self and one's relations with others, having a sense of a future and a past, having certain identifiable goals or interests, and having a coherent and consistent identity. The intriguing question is whether all humans fulfill these criteria. For example, is a week-old fetus, a day-old infant, someone who's in a coma, or someone who has suffered irreversible brain damage a person? Or is it possible that human beings are persons regardless of mental state or ability, simply because we all belong to the same species? You might also want to take ten or fifteen minutes during class at this point to screen of one of several documentaries available on Koko to prepare students for this selection.

Exploring the Text

1. Patterson and Gordon pepper us with evidence of Koko's personhood. They tells us that she deserves to be seen as an "individual" with basic moral rights because she understands spoken English and communicates in sign language, she scores between 85 and 95 on the Stanford-Binet Intelligence Test, she demonstrates self-awareness, she's capable of deception, she anticipates others' reactions to her behavior, she engages in imaginary play, she creates representational works of art, she feels and expresses a wide range of emotions, and she empathizes with the feelings of others. Indeed, this is only the basic list. Patterson and Gordon go on to point out other reasons why we should be impressed by Koko: she teaches what she has learned to other gorillas, she is fiercely independent, she has created new signs and uses them in communication, she has even indulged, at times, in gorilla humor. Most of these behaviors would seem to indicate that Koko does possess the kind of reflective self-consciousness that might be associated with personhood. Yet it might be argued that a genuine "person" must be able to do even more than what Koko appears to be capable of. Koko seems able to communicate and to engage in rudimentary forms of play and imagination games, but does she have the kind of durable, long-term goals that we might associate with being a person? For that matter, is it possible to be a person without being part of a specific social, historical, and cultural context? Is Koko aware of her position in relation to her trainers and the other humans around her? Is she at all aware of the way she differs from other gorillas? Shouldn't we expect a person to be able to speak for herself and to ask for equal consideration on her own behalf? But then, how many of us have ever done that?

2. Perhaps the most sweeping assertion that Patterson and Gordon advance here is the notion that Koko is an "individual" who has "a claim to basic moral rights." They never bother to define what specific rights this might entail, however. We can probably assume that they would grant Koko at least two of the three rights guaranteed all human

individuals under the Declaration of Independence — the rights to life and the pursuit of happiness. Given the fact that they believe Koko to be self-conscious and sentient, we might also assume that they would insist that she not be subjected to deliberate cruelty or physical harm. But as soon as you begin to explore the issue of Koko's potential rights, you run into problems related to issues of equality. If Koko has a right to be safe from harm, would she then enjoy the same protections as any human being? If a human being killed her, would it be considered murder? Might striking her be seen as assault? And, then, if Koko has a right to happiness, shouldn't she be free, legally and intellectually, to determine her own future? It may, in fact, be difficult to extend any special "rights" to Koko that we wouldn't normally grant to almost any common house pet. We wouldn't condone the mistreatment of somebody's Pekingese, nor would we put up with someone abusing Koko. But granting her additional "moral rights" would require a huge leap in logic. If Koko is a person, shouldn't she be free? Shouldn't she — and all of her primate cousins — be repatriated to their natural habitat?

3. Patterson and Gordon stress that Koko and Michael are not "significantly different from other gorillas in their inherent linguistic capacities, self-awareness or other mental abilities." Indeed, they argue that sign language itself is a natural way of communicating for gorillas and that it is not a behavior that they have "imposed" on Koko. It's possible that they stress these ideas in order to counter the suggestion that Koko and Michael are "geniuses" and are thus not really representative of the average gorilla. It's also likely that they want to anticipate the argument that the remarkable behaviors that Koko and Michael manifest are simply "tricks" — imitations of human behavior that have been imposed on them by their handlers. These concerns make it clear that Patterson and Gordon want to do much more in this essay than simply build a case for Koko. They want to suggest that there is actually very little difference between human and animal minds *in general*. Their real aim is to "force us to reexamine the ways we think about animals."

4. The way Patterson and Gordon anticipate the expectations and reactions of their audience is discussed at length in the introduction to this chapter in the text (see *Mind Readings,* p. 509). By postponing identification of Koko, they are asking us to put our anthropocentric biases aside for a moment so we can appreciate the "logic" of their case. They also work hard throughout the essay to anticipate likely counterarguments, as when they note that the reputation for "aloofness," low motivation, and contrariness that's often associated with gorillas is "evidence of intelligence rather than stupidity." They anticipate the concern that they are overinterpreting Koko's responses by explaining how they "discover" the meanings of Koko's signs. They offer counterexplanations of why gorillas in the past have failed the "mirror test" for self-consciousness. They take the time to respond to specific objections to the equal consideration of human and animal interests, as when they pause to rebut Arthur Caplan's claim that primate mothers do not grieve over the loss of an infant. And, as noted above, they attempt at the end of their presentation to counter the objection that Koko possesses unusual intelligence or that her natural behavior has been unduly influenced by the instruction she's received in sign language.

Further Explorations

1. Leakey and Lewin's approach to primate intelligence contrasts sharply with that of Patterson and Gordon. Both of these selections focus on what Leakey and Lewin call "social intelligence." They both stress the kind of mental abilities that are involved in negotiating relationships and interpersonal communication rather than the kind of analytic intelligence that's associated with problem solving and other more abstract mental functions. But whereas Leakey and Lewin tend to emphasize the role that chimp minds play in situations involving competition and conflict, Patterson and Gordon tend to stress the way that Koko's intelligence connects her with others in her environment. Koko does seem to manifest "social intelligence," but she uses it to tease her handlers, to make jokes, to play games with language, to empathize with others, and to reflect on

her own feelings. She does not, by contrast, use it to engage in power struggles or to gain an advantage over other animals. In fact, when we do see Koko and Michael relating to other animals, we see them using her intelligence to connect with other minds. Thus, Michael tries to "teach" other gorillas signs and Koko actively empathizes with Michael when she hears him crying alone in his room. And this doesn't appear to be simply a matter of emphasis. Leakey and Lewin make it clear that intelligence, as they see it, exists to help individuals achieve evolutionary "success." The idea of competition thus underlies not only the way they view intelligence but even their distinctly Darwinian view of the struggle for existence. Patterson and Gordon, by contrast, present intelligence as a way of connecting with others and building relationships.

2. De Waal would likely judge Patterson and Gordon's interpretations of Koko's behavior as involving mature anthropomorphism. It's clear that Patterson and Gordon are well aware that the meanings they see in Koko's use of sign language might be construed as a kind of anthropocentric Bambification. It might be argued, for example, that when asked about the loss of her kitten, Koko's response "Open Trouble Visit Sorry" might be interpreted in a great many possible ways and that it might even be viewed as a random string of words that Patterson and Gordon force to fit the meaning they are predisposed to discover. To counter such suspicions, they emphasize that signing is not an unusual behavior for gorillas. Like the experienced horse trainer that de Waal praises, they make it clear that their interpretations take the animal's natural behaviors and predispositions into account. They also stress that they strive to understand Koko's signs in the context of her own particular Umwelt. When they interpret the signs she uses, they try to understand what she intends to communicate by playing association games and by asking her for "definitions." Thus, when they describe a "joke" that Koko makes, they detail the situation that surrounds the event and offer supporting evidence of Koko's own intention by noting that she "laughed" several times during the exchange.

3. Despite the authors' claims to the contrary, however, it may still be possible to argue that teaching a gorilla human sign language is just another form of Disneyfication. What's the difference between claiming that a gorilla is just like a human because she's been trained to use a number of signs and claiming that a gorilla is just like a human because she has been trained to ride a bicycle or to play baseball? Indeed, the very impulse to demonstrate that other species can do what humans do or think the kinds of thoughts that humans think might itself be seen as a kind of Disneyfication. From this perspective, it might be noted that teaching a gorilla sign language doesn't really tell us anything about the way gorillas actually think or behave in their natural surroundings — it only suggests that, under laboratory conditions, gorillas can be induced to imitate human behaviors. Thus, Patterson and Gordon's work with Koko might be viewed as a kind of desperate attempt to remake a primate in a person's image. And this insight itself might lead to other questions such as why it's necessary for an animal to resemble a human in order to qualify for equal consideration or "basic moral rights."

4. Most likely, these are the kinds of objections that Singer might raise in response to Patterson and Gordon. According to Singer, all sentient animals deserve "equal consideration" simply because of the fact that they are capable of suffering. As he sees it, the issue of intelligence has nothing to do with the essentially ethical question of whether it's right to inflict suffering on another creature. Thus, as Singer might point out, we assume that it would be wrong to make a retarded person or an infant suffer, despite the fact that they might not be able to function at the same cognitive level as an adult human being. In Singer's view, then, whether or not Koko is capable of expressing herself in sign language is beside the point. The very fact that she is aware of pain and seeks to avoid it establishes the fact of her sentience, and this alone is enough to qualify her for equal consideration.

5. If you haven't already done so, you may want to take this opportunity to screen one of several documentary videos available on Francine Patterson's work with Koko. These films, produced with Patterson's cooperation, allow students to see Koko's mind

at work for themselves and thus provide additional information that students can use for either of the Essay Options that follow.

Essay Options

1. This assignment calls for students to synthesize information from Leakey and Lewin and Patterson and Gordon on the topic of primate intelligence. The contrasting views of intelligence in these two readings offer students enough information for their own exploration of primate intelligence. This assignment also allows students to reflect on a number of issues that are raised in discussion questions associated with these readings. If, however, you want to enrich this assignment, you can ask students to supplement the ideas they find in these selections with additional outside research.

2. Essay Option #2 invites students to learn more about animal "languages" and other attempts to communicate directly with animal minds. Most social animals have at least a rudimentary form of communication. Even the pheromone trails of ants and the "dance" of the common honeybee can be see as involving symbolic expression. More complex animals, like porpoises, whales, seals, and elephants, have evolved far more sophisticated systems of communication, complete with vocabularies and grammars. If your students are particularly interested in this topic, or if you want to offer them a traditional research paper assignment, you may want to consider this assignment.

PETER SINGER, *Equality for Animals?* (p. 607)

Singer introduces the last major theme in this chapter — the idea of animal rights or animal liberation. Patterson and Gordon touch on this issue in their argument for the personhood of Koko the gorilla, but Singer places the question in the appropriate ethical context. Singer's philosophical treatment of the issue of animal equality offers a good example of close reasoning at work and demonstrates the role that audience analysis plays in the structuring of logical arguments. It also raises questions that students will enjoy debating in class. If you're running short on time, you can use Singer as the basis for a one-reading assignment leading to a paper on the issue of animal liberation. But if time permits, you'll want to follow up with Shepard's trenchant response to arguments for animal rights. Together, Springer and Shepard set the stage for a major paper on the issue of animal equality and offer a terrific object lesson in the way writers read and respond to each other's assumptions and intentions. If you haven't read Patterson and Gordon, you may want to begin by asking students to discuss what "rights" an animal might possibly be granted in the first place, as suggested in the Before Reading activity. This will help your class begin to tease out some of the difficulties involved in the application of legal concepts like rights to questions of interspecies relationships.

Exploring the Text

1. Singer begins his case for animal rights by asserting that we should extend to animals the same "equal consideration of interests" that we have proffered our fellow humans. His argument is simple: group membership isn't enough to justify the exploitation of an individual, and thus species membership shouldn't be enough to justify our exploitation of animals. As the subheading of this section suggests, Singer equates "racism" with "speciesism" and establishes his case for animal rights on this equation. Just as it is not ethically justifiable to disregard the interests of some people because they are of a different race, a different gender, or a different level of intelligence, so it isn't acceptable to disregard the interests of animals simply because they belong to a different species. This idea might be seen as having some merit, because there do seem to be some clear parallels between specisism and racial and gender prejudice. Like racism and sexism, discrimination against other species seems "natural" until it is challenged and enough people begin to question the flaws in its logic. Speciesism also might be thought of as establishing an arbitrary line between groups that then is used to justify differen-

tial treatment. And, of course, like racism and sexism, speciesism might be seen as an attempt to promote the status and consolidate the power of a dominant group. Still, some students may find fault with Singer's equation of human prejudices and what might be seen as biological "fact." Race, as most biologists today believe, is not a scientific category at all. Race differences are based almost entirely on perceptions and beliefs and not on real biological differences. And although physical differences obviously do exist between the sexes, sex is not linked to significant differences in key high-level mental functions such as consciousness and decision-making. However, it might well be argued that there are obvious psychological and physiological differences between human beings and other species and that, as a result, it is not a matter of simple prejudice when we note and act on them. Of course, some students may also take offense at Singer's wholesale equation of racism, sexism, and speciesism on the grounds that it belittles principles that women and people of color have struggled toward for the past several hundred years.

2. Singer bases much of his reasoning on Jeremy Bentham's notion of animal sentience. According to Bentham, the interests of any creature merit "equal consideration" if that creature is capable of suffering. The capacity for suffering and happiness is the "prerequisite" for having interests at all. Thus, while a stone can't have interests, a child or a dog certainly may, in the sense that both are able to experience both pleasure and pain. Other considerations — the capacity for language or higher mathematics, or the color of one's skin — are not sufficient to define the "boundary of concern for others." Thus, no other clear boundary separates human beings from "non-human animals." The problem, from Singer's perspective, becomes how we can possibly compare suffering across species as we weigh the relative claims of human and animal interests. Singer himself admits that it isn't possible to equate the suffering of a mouse with that of a human being dying of cancer. The "greater awareness" of humans suggests that the average human being will suffer more than will the average mouse. But even this situation becomes more complicated as Singer continues to explore the implications of his topic. He would agree, for example, that the same slap applied to a horse and a baby will occasion different levels of suffering. He suggests, too, that adult humans may suffer more than animals as the result of our highly developed self-consciousness, which can add "terror" to the physical pain we might have to endure in a given situation. Yet he also notes that the superior mental power of adult humans may help us cope with suffering in ways that aren't available to most animals, and, hence, in some situations self-consciousness will result in *less*, not more, suffering. Singer himself begins to anticipate some of the obvious problems with this comparative approach to interspecies ethics. He recognizes that we might reject the principle of "sentience" because of the difficulty involved in comparing mental states across species. He also agrees that it's impossible to make such comparisons in precise terms. Yet he suggests that even if we were to apply the principle of equal interests to nonhuman animals in only the most clear-cut cases, we would have to change our relation to other species in radical ways.

3. Singer presents several arguments against the use of animals as a source of food. He points out that "animal flesh" is neither a necessary nor a particularly healthy source of nourishment, nor is it an efficient way to produce food. It is an expensive "luxury" and a relatively unethical one when we consider the living conditions of animals on the average factory farm. Within the context of modern commercial farming, animals are "machines that convert fodder into flesh" to cater to our palates. Anticipating possible objections to these arguments, Singer notes that although "free-range" animal farming is better than factory farming, it still doesn't address the principle of the equal consideration of animal interests. Furthermore, he asserts that the real issue is whether we can be certain that no suffering occurs as the result of our consumption of animals. If there is even the chance that it does, he suggests that we have an ethical obligation to avoid sacrificing important animal interests for the sake of less important interests of our own. Singer makes similar arguments in relation to the use of animals as experimental subjects. As he notes, in many cases animals are involved in tests of things such as food addi-

tives and cosmetics that are not involved in preventing human suffering. He also suggests that much university research involving animals has no real human application and thus cannot be defended in terms of alleviating human suffering. He critiques "absolutist" arguments for animal experimentation, observing that they often present hypothetical cases. In principle, he agrees that it would be justifiable to sacrifice a few animal lives if thousands of human lives would be saved as a result. But he wonders if, by the same token, we would be willing to sacrifice a few brain-damaged orphans given the same scenario, suggesting that our willingness to swap animal for human suffering is just another lingering trace of speciesism. Students may well wonder about how genuinely "comparative" or relative Singer's ethical approach to suffering actually is at this point. Earlier, he claimed that we would have to weigh the suffering of animals against that of humans in every case of animal use. At this point, however, he seems unwilling to admit that even the use of a few animals in order to save thousands of human lives is justified. Thus, it may be argued that he himself clings to a kind of ethical absolutism despite his assurances to the contrary.

4. Singer concludes this segment of his exploration of animal rights by anticipating and refuting additional counterarguments against his position. He refutes the notion that we can never be sure what another creature is feeling by noting that this is as true for humans as it is for animals and that the similarity between our nervous system and that of most vertebrates suggests that we all respond in roughly the same way. He counters the "Benjamin Franklin Objection" that it's acceptable to eat creatures that eat other creatures by observing that, unlike most carnivores, we don't have to kill in order to live and that we do have the ability to reflect and act on our ethical principles. That killing may come naturally to us does not mean that we have to do it. He also notes that while such reasoning might hold in "primitive cultures," it has no place in a world of mass production and modern farming technologies. He also counters the position that animals are inherently inferior to humans because they are not autonomous and lack self-consciousness. In response to this position, Singer notes that differences of ability and aptitude between animal and human minds do not justify sacrificing animal interests any more than differences in ability or aptitude between humans would justify the exploitation of one group of humans by a more able group. To privilege humans this way over animals seems like sheer prejudice and offers no basis for a real system of ethics. Finally, Singer takes on the "slippery slope" objection that once we start comparing levels of suffering between species, we open the door to the possibility of experimenting on anyone or using any kind of creature for dinner. Singer rejects this idea out of hand because he feels that the principle of equal consideration has the virtue of being honestly drawn and openly debated and thus does not rely on an "arbitrary" criterion such as, we presume, species membership.

Further Explorations

1. Lame Deer obviously believes that animals are sentient and that they can suffer; in fact, he seems to think that animals are conscious in much the same way that humans are. In Lame Deer's world, animals can retaliate against human hunters. The badger can pull a horseman down into his hole and a black-tailed deer can send a bullet right back at the hunter who pursues him. Despite this fact, however, Lame Deer doesn't view killing animals as an ethical problem. Unlike people in the white world who have become afraid of death, Lame Deer still has the "courage" to kill. In fact, Lame Deer seems to feel justified in killing animals for food, because he sees them as his spiritual and intellectual equals. Thus, he notes that when Indians killed a buffalo in the past, they always "apologized" to him and prayed for his life to return. Chances are, then, that Lame Deer would view Singer's portrayal of animals and animal minds as being just another example of the white world's alienation from nature. Singer, unlike Lame Deer, does not see animals as independent equals — as powerful creatures with wills and desires of their own — but as helpless victims that can do little more than suffer as the result of human exploitation.

2. Singer would surely dismiss Patterson and Gordon's claims about Koko's intellectual abilities as irrelevant in relation to the case they make for the equal consideration of her interests. Equal consideration of interests isn't something that has to be "earned," in Singer's view. All creatures merit equal consideration if they reach the threshold of sentience — that is, if they have the ability to feel happiness and pain. If they appear to be capable of such mental states, then they clearly have "interests," and it is our ethical duty to take their interests into account in our relations with them. Koko, thus, would have a claim to "basic moral rights" even if she had never learned a single sign. What's more, it's likely that Singer would see the kind of prolonged experiment that Patterson and Gordon perform "on" Koko as a violation of her natural rights as a sentient creature. Given the fact that gorillas clearly "suffer" as the result of captivity, Singer would probably argue that they should never be kept as experimental subjects or as specimens in zoo exhibits.

3. At first, the kind of chimp-instigated violence that Leakey and Lewin describe would seem to challenge Singer only if you accept the "Benjamin Franklin Objection" that he rebuts toward the end of this selection. From this perspective, it might be wondered why we worry about inflicting suffering on animals that show so little concern themselves for the suffering for members of their own species. But Singer has anticipated this objection. Regardless of what animals do, we humans still have an ethical obligation to take their interests into account, because we are humans, not animals, and thus have the ability to reflect on our own behavior, weigh ethical considerations, and act accordingly. Still, the case of Luit, Yeroen, and Nikkie might be troubling when considered from another perspective. If we, as humans, have the ethical responsibility to reduce animal suffering that results from our own activity, don't we also have the responsibility to stop all instances of animal suffering that we are aware of? Since Singer bases his case for the equal interests of animals on the fact that they are capable of suffering, don't we bear an ethical responsibility to stop such suffering whenever we can? Thus, it's possible that Singer might feel that de Waal should bear direct responsibility for the suffering that Luit experienced at the hands of Yeroen and Nikkie. The principle of equal consideration of animal interests based on the ability to suffer might also suggest that humans have an ethical responsibility not merely to abstain from behavior that harms other sentient species but to *intervene* in all situations that might lead to the injury of animal others. Thus, humans might be seen as bearing an ethical responsibility for intervening on the behalf of animals involved in natural disasters, droughts, or the outbreak of epidemic diseases. Singer might likely agree with this in principle and even be expected to argue that, once we have weighed animal interests against those of humans, we are ethically bound to do what we can to mitigate the suffering of all human *and* nonhuman creatures involved in such situations.

4. This question sends you ahead to Shepard's rebuttal of arguments in favor of animal liberation. Singer takes on what might be seen as a "straw man" version of the case for animal rights. He doesn't directly attempt to refute the idea that all animals should enjoy some legal rights, only the rather extreme idea that we have a responsibility to protect the rights of animals in the wild. Shepard charges that animal ethicists such as Singer have lost touch with the realities of the natural world and that what they really aim at is transforming the earth into a kind of gigantic "barnyard" where suffering and death are "banished forever." The essence of the problem, as Shepard sees it, is that the idea of "rights" is a human construct that has no place and can be of no value in the discussion of natural systems. The idea of having an "ethical" relation to animals is, thus, itself a mistaken imposition of human values on the world of nature. In nature there are no "individuals" and no "rights" — only species in "ecosystems" and "foodchains," and whether we wish to acknowledge it or not, we're included. Indeed, what seems to bother Shepard the most about the case for animal rights is that it seems to deny the reality of nature as well as our own place in the natural world. Shepard's critique might, then, be seen as weakening Singer's claims to the extent that Shepard forces us to carry Singer's logic to its illogical extreme. Of course it's wrong to treat animals like com-

modities on factory farms, Shepard suggests, but it's also absurd to think that we can or should try to prevent animal suffering where and whenever we can.

Essay Options

1. This assignment invites students to do further research on the issue of animal liberation and then use it as the basis for a comprehensive essay on the topic of animal rights. Organizations such as PETA have active chapters on most university campuses, and there are a number of Internet sites devoted to the cause of animal liberation that students may want to consult. Interestingly, not all animal liberationists share Singer's philosophical perspective on the topic of animal rights. Some have moved far beyond "speciesism" and embraced even more radical ideas about the similarity of animal and human minds. For others, the drive to protect animals has more to do with ecological anxieties than it does with issues related to animal suffering.

2. As an alternative, you might want to ask students to explore the issue of the treatment of animals on your own campus, particularly if you teach at a major research or agricultural institution. Essay Option #2 encourages students to examine and evaluate the protocols that govern animal experimentation and research in the science labs at your college. To extend this assignment, you might want to have students locate, read, and report on one or more articles written by scientists in support of the use of animals in pure and practical scientific research.

PAUL SHEPARD, *Rights and Kindness: A Can of Worms*
(p. 624)

Shepard offers a perfect complement to Singer's appeal for animal equality. In Shepard's view, the application of human concepts such as "equality," "rights," "liberation," and "interests" to animals is an absurdity that does little more than show how estranged we've become from other creatures and the natural world. Read against Singer, Shepard prepares students for either a focused academic paper comparing the positions of these two authors or for a more wide-ranging essay on the issue of animal liberation. It can also be used as the point of departure for a research paper exploring a particular form of animal "abuse" such as factory farming, the use of animals in the fashion and cosmetic industries, or their exploitation as forms of entertainment in circuses, rodeos, and films. Shepard also offers you a good example of how a writer can use "mind reading" to probe and critique the motives and assumptions of his opponents. In fact, you might want to use Shepard as an occasion for raising questions about the pitfalls involved in overpersonalizing arguments and debates. You can prepare students for Shepard by asking them to explore the concept of "legal rights" in small groups, as suggested in the Before Reading activity. The Constitution, for example, specifies the legal rights of citizens of the United States, but even these rights are not meant to be extended to all individuals — only to citizens. What, then, makes a right a right? What requirements or responsibilities, if any, do rights involve? Are there, in fact, any universal "human" rights — rights that would be recognized in any country under any conditions?

Exploring the Text

1. Shepard prefaces his rebuttal to arguments for animal rights with a synopsis of the history of human cruelty to animals. He notes that we've been mistreating other species since biblical times and that even the dawn of modern science didn't dissuade us from cutting up animals without a qualm. In modern times, despite concerns about "animal welfare" that "trickled down from bourgeois pet-love," we've continued to abuse chickens, sows, and calves on factory farms. The fact that Shepard spends so much time recounting the horrors of industrial farming may add to his credibility as a critic of the animal rights position. He demonstrates, in advance, that he's well aware of the history of his subject, and he makes it clear that, in general, he doesn't condone how

we treat "animal captives." Then, he shifts the ground of his argument. Shepard begins by agreeing with — or by appearing to agree with — the proponents of animal rights, at least in relation to what he calls "enslaved animals." He hints that he has no argument with the idea that we have a moral responsibility to treat domesticated animals with humanity and to minimize their suffering whenever we can. His argument is with extreme activists who would extend the notion of animal rights to creatures living wild in nature. This might seem like a fairly good strategy, since it would be difficult to argue that we have no particular responsibility to the animals we raise for food or for use in lab experiments. Indeed, it allows Shepard to portray his opponents as wild-eyed idealists off on a seemingly impossible mission to save wild animals from the realities of their own existence. But once we begin to understand that Shepard's critique of "kindness" toward animals may itself extend beyond the limits he initially sets, this approach might seem a bit disingenuous. It might, in fact, be viewed as a "straw man" that allows Shepard to build his case against animal activists without directly confronting some of their most persuasive claims.

2. Shepard addresses and rebuts a number of specific arguments associated with the case for animal rights. He claims that the idea of extending protection to animals in the wild illogically projects human concepts on the natural world. He suggests that this leads to semantic confusion as we try to apply ideas that make sense only in the context of human interactions to nature — "natural rights," "liberation," "individuals," "friend-ship," and "bonding." The notion of natural rights is a "legal fiction," according to Shepard, that can be created and bestowed only within the context of participation in a legal or political system. Since animals can't participate in such systems, they cannot have legal rights. The only "natural right" an animal can have, in Shepard's view, is the right to belong to the ecosystem and foodchain into which it was born. Thus, it makes no sense to debate a predator's right to a square meal versus the prey's right to exist. Nor does it make sense to talk about animal "liberation," because the notion of liberation assumes the possibility of escape from an oppressive situation. In Shepard's view, the only state that wild animals might be liberated into is the barnyard — a world of per-manent captivity and human control. Shepard also notes that it is absurd to differenti-ate between animals the way that animal liberationists do as they sort out which species to save or prefer. The notions of "intrinsic" and "instrumental" value that animal rights activists often appeal to in weighing the conflicting interests of different species is itself freighted with species bias. Why, Shepard wonders, should we assume that more "sen-tient" animals, such as elephants or apes, have more intrinsic value than their less sen-tient brethren? The only possible response is that they seem more like us. From the per-spective of nature, however, all animals have only "instrumental value" — all are embed-ded in "natural systems" and have value only in relation to them. Thus "Wild animals do not have rights; they have a natural history." Grass has no right not to be eaten by a deer, and a deer has no right not to be eaten by a lion, and a lion has no right not to fall prey to a hunter or a lethal strain of bacteria. Shepard also rejects the idea that we must protect animals because we have a deeply felt "bond" with them. In the wild, animals cannot feel "friendship" for humans because the relationships between species are not "social" in any real sense of the word. Humans may invade an animal's habitat and dis-tract it with food, but the "bond" that some animal activists sense between themselves and other species is, according to Shepard, nothing more than another example of "barnyard hypocrisy." It arises because we confuse wild animals with domesticated pets. The bonds we imagine between ourselves and wild creatures imply a kind of mutual commitment and reciprocity that simply do not exist.

3. From the start of this selection, Shepard adopts a particularly caustic and dis-missive tone toward animal liberationists. He condemns them for their "infantile" view of other species and belittles their "hearth rug altruism." As he builds his case against them, he pathologizes their cause and tries to analyze the hidden motives that underlie their "neurotic zeal." And his final diagnosis tells us as much about his own intentions as it does about those of his opponents. In Shepard's view, those who argue for animal

rights are "deeply estranged" from the natural world. They are so steeped in their own human perspective on things that they've lost the ability to comprehend the way that natural systems really work. Beneath their posturing about "animal friends" lies a hidden "guilt" that results, we can only presume, from the fact that we humans are omnivorous predators ourselves. And beneath this guilt lies a wish to deny our own involvement with nature and with what might be seen as the ultimate predator — death. Animal activists behave, in Shepard's view, like people who want to "banish death forever" by turning the world into a "prophylactic zoo." They have adopted what Shepard sees as an "anti-organic stance" toward life — one that expresses their own "dread of the cycle of birth and death." In fact, Shepard suggests that advocates of animal rights are actually "using" animals, just as we have always used them for wool and milk, in order to combat their own fear of death.

4. Those who thus claim to be closest to animals, in Shepard's view, are, in fact, utterly "estranged" from the natural world. Animal activists claim to feel kinship with their animal "friends," yet when it comes to the use of animals for food, they draw the line and assert their moral superiority over other species. According to Shepard, they deny the fact that they are "a participant in a world where life feeds on death" and attempt, instead, to adopt the distanced perspective of the "spectator." They are content to watch and appreciate nature as a pleasant "background" from a comfortable distance, as if it were a movie or a museum exhibit, without having to acknowledge their own inherent involvement in it. This is the source of the "hypocrisy" that most troubles Shepard. In his view, animal liberationists are like the Jains, who appear to love nature but in reality deeply fear the "pollution" it represents. The alternative is to embrace our "true vocation" and to "puzzle out [the] reciprocity" of our ongoing "participation" with other species. We must learn how to accept our own role in the natural history of the planet and to acknowledge our proper place in the "mystery" of our relation to animal others. What this all adds up to isn't particularly clear, but Shepard does offer a few hints at what it might mean in practice. It certainly doesn't mean that we should all stop eating our animal friends and adopt vegetarianism, "a state of beatific mastication" that Shepard mockingly notes we left behind several million years ago. We got our omnivorous tendencies along with the ecological niche we inherited when we were born, and we shouldn't try to deny them. Nor should we necessarily give up hunting and fishing, which "hark back to a positive genetic layer of human being." In fact, it's not really even clear if Shepard thinks we should or can do much to improve the lot of animals on farms or in research laboratories, since he hints that the "ethic" against using monkeys in experiments, raising animals for fur, or using them in fox hunts or movies reveals "the deeply felt absence of the natural in our lives." Indeed, one comes away from Shepard suspecting that, from his point of view, there could be nothing worse than simply being an "enslaved" animal in the first place and that civilization itself is the primary problem, not the way we relate to the animals around us.

Further Explorations

1. This selection brings the chapter full circle. In it, Shepard offers what might be viewed as an intellectualized version of Lame Deer's original critique of white society in relation to the world of nature. Both agree that most animals in today's world are pathetic "enslaved" creatures that have little resemblance to animals in the wild. Both also agree that Western civilization produces "neurotic," "infantile" people as well as "crazy, no-good" animals and that the problem lies in people themselves, in their fear of nature and, ultimately, in their fear of death. According to Lame Deer, the white world is bent on the destruction of everything that's natural, primarily because nature reminds whites that they, like animals and Indians, are part of the processes of birth, life, and death. Shepard sounds exactly the same theme when he declares that animal rights activists want to "banish death" from the world by denying that bad things can happen to innocent animals. Shepard damns animal activists as "hypocrites" because he believes that

they are only using animals to deal with their own cowardly fears in relation to their own mortality. Echoing Lame Deer, he says that animal activists are tying to flee a "world where life lives on death." Both Lame Deer and Shepard also gladly embrace what they see as humanity's position somewhere near the top of the food chain. Thus, Lame Deer blames the white world for not having the "courage" to kill honestly and to confront the real meaning of death. Similarly, Shepard defends the practice of hunting and notes that hunting and fishing "harken back to a positive generic layer of human being." If there is a difference between Lame Deer and Shepard, it might lurk in the fundamental assumptions that underlie their ideas. Shepard seems to view nature as a place of honest cruelty — a world that is beyond the reach of Judeo-Christian morality and Greek ethical philosophy. For Shepard, nature is a place of "systems," "facts," and "history" — a state that we're born into and that we, as individuals, really have no right to question. For Lame Deer, however, nature is more than this. It is a family, a place of spirit and belonging. It is a home of "brothers" — and, thus, precisely the kind of place that Shepard faults animal rights proponents for craving.

2. Shepard and Berger agree that most people today have become estranged from animals and nature. As a result of this estrangement, we take a distanced view of animals. We see them as a matter of spectacle or display and not as real "others" or potential equals with whom we share our lives and experiences. The sheer act of looking at animals transforms them and removes them from the possibility of direct interaction with us. It changes them from "subjects," full of "experience and secrets," into "objects" — empty vessels without any more meaning or significance than simple "innocence." In much the same way, Shepard sees animal liberationists as assuming the "distanced," essentially passive position of the spectator in relation to nature and the world of animals. We want to appreciate nature and animals from a safe distance; we don't want to acknowledge our own relatedness to them and the mortality they represent. In Shepard's view, the position of distanced observer falsifies our real relation to animals by transforming them into cuddly "friends" and us into distanced connoisseurs who appreciate them but have nothing really to do with them. Both agree, then, that animals are becoming "marginalized" in modern society. In their view, animals are moving away from us and becoming literally harder to see.

3. Shepard would probably see the "bond" between McNulty and her pet mouse as just another manifestation of misplaced human sympathies. Just as primates in the wilds of Africa have tolerated the intrusions of humans like Jane Goodall and Dian Fossey, so too does Mouse tolerate the daily intrusions that McNulty visits upon her. Indeed, Mouse would clearly qualify as an example of an "enslaved" animal in Shepard's view. The relationship that McNulty imagines she has with Mouse would simply be a matter of anthropomorphic projection, simple wish fulfillment on her part and, thus, it would have nothing to do with the actual field mouse whose misfortune it is to live in her kitchen. Similarly, we might expect that Shepard would also see Koko as an animal "captive" — a poor natural creature who has been torn from her native environment by a couple of anthropocentric humans determined to "prove" that she's just like them. Indeed, Shepard reserves particular scorn for humans who insist on seeing human attributes in animals or who practice the "barnyard hypocrisy" of arguing for special considerations for certain species based on their resemblance to human beings. Of course, McNulty and Patterson and Gordon would certainly reject these criticisms. They might well point out that, unlike many modern human beings, they do, in fact, live in close proximity to another species and that they have been actively engaged in precisely the kind of relational "reciprocity" that Shepard so admires. McNulty makes it clear that her relationship with Mouse has changed her and even her view of her fellow humans. And there can be little doubt that Patterson and Gordon feel that their lives have been touched and transformed by their relationship with Koko. It might thus be difficult to assert that McNulty's relation with Mouse or Patterson and Gordon's relationship with Koko in any way resemble the kind of distanced, disconnected relationship that Shepard envisions between animal liberationists and the creatures they claim to represent.

4. We might expect Shepard to scoff at the idea that chimps contemplate and carry out acts of murder, as claimed by Leakey and Lewin. The idea of "murder," as Shepard would probably point out, can exist only within the context of a human legal system with a full complement of laws, responsibilities, rights, and clearly delineated penalties. In the world of animals, the idea of murder simply doesn't make sense. Shepard would probably remind us that the behavior of Yeroen and Nikkie isn't a matter of morality but a matter of "natural history." It reflects the way that chimps typically behave in their own natural environment and thus has nothing to do with human judgments of right or wrong. We might, then, expect that Shepard would insist that officials at the Arnhem Zoo not get involved in this completely natural power struggle, since to do so would be to try to impose human standards of behavior on animal others.

5. As described by Siebert, television nature shows tend to portray animals in an "operatic" manner that emphasizes their resemblance to human beings. Thus, the seal pup that he watches on TV is cast as the show's "protagonist," who faces the challenge of finding a surrogate mother. We follow this little "orphan" through a series of adventures above and below sea level, never losing sight of her or of the fact that her emotional world resembles ours. Television nature shows cultivate what Shepard might view as "barnyard hypocrisy" by reinforcing the idea that animals in the wild "feel" things exactly as we do as we watch them on television from the safety of our living rooms. To keep us involved, nature programming on TV remakes the world of nature in our own image and projects it back at us. The animals we see on television thus play out roles that are deeply familiar to us, roles that derive from essentially human stories. As Shepard might note, the very fact that we gather so much of our knowledge about nature from TV might explain why people today are more comfortable taking the "distanced" role of observer or spectator in relation to the natural world. It's not that we self-consciously prefer to see nature as an "amenity" or as a pleasant "background" to our lives: it's just that this is the way many of us have been raised to see nature on TV.

Essay Options

1. The debate between Singer and Shepard is almost too good to pass up. Don't be put off by the obvious contrast between their positions on animal rights. Both of these writers take the issue so seriously and both are so smart that it's not easy to dismiss either of them. This assignment challenges students to tease apart the arguments and counterarguments that they present and to evaluate their strengths and weaknesses. As students examine Singer and Shepard, you should also expect them to clarify where they stand on the issue of animal rights and to offer some support for why they take this position.

2. This assignment offers a broader approach to the issue of animal liberation. Given the interest in this topic and in related ecological issues on many campuses today, you may want to give students the option of doing additional research on the controversies involved in the animal rights movement.

3. Essay Option #3 offers a more focused research project on animal rights. Shepard touches on a number of issues that tend to surface in discussions of animal abuse — the treatment of animals on so-called factory farms, the breeding of animals for the manufacture of fur, leather, and clothing, the use of animals in scientific research, their exploitation as a source of entertainment in zoos, circuses, rodeos, and movies, and their destruction as prey in hunting and fishing. Have students focus on one of these commonplace uses of animals and ask them to research the questions related to animal rights that it raises. Have them explore all the arguments that are made for and against this use of animals and then summarize and discuss their findings in a formal report. Finally, you'll want to be sure that they stake out their own position on this topic and explain, in detail, the reasons that led them to support it.

6

Reading Cyberminds:
The Internet to Artificial Intelligence (p. 640)

Getting Started

I hope you'll have the chance to explore this chapter with your students. It contains some of the most challenging readings in the book, and it carries the notion of mind reading to what might be thought of as its logical extreme. We are born reading the minds of other human beings, and we find it relatively natural to interpret even the thoughts and feelings of animal minds as well. But today we face the challenge of reading minds of our own creation — the minds of machines that are just now beginning to "think" for themselves. This chapter also continues several important themes that have been developing throughout the text: the dehumanizing impact of technology and modern society, the idea of gendered minds, and the emergence of what might be seen as the "imperial" self. It also invites students to think seriously about the future and the problems that we as a species will face as we confront a world increasingly of our own making. So, I hope you'll consider spending some time here and that you won't be discouraged by the idea of artificial intelligence or daunted by the topic of computing. I realize that these are themes that composition instructors may not feel immediately comfortable with, but I assure you that your students, having been raised "online," will have plenty to say about computers, the impact of the Internet, and the idea of smart machines. In fact, it's quite possible that as you approach this chapter, you'll find that you come up against the opposite problem. High technology is already such an integral part of our daily lives that students may actually have trouble appreciating the impact it has on us or imagining what the world was like just a few years ago before the invention of the silicon chip. So, you'll probably want to spend some time in class introducing and contextualizing the idea of "cyber minds" before you begin reading.

The chapter introduction is designed to help with this effort. It appeals to student interest by linking the history of computing to the pop cultural mythology surrounding the idea of creating an artificial human being. As noted in the introduction, the project of creating intelligent machines has long been associated with the dream of creating artificial human life. The fantasy of the robot and the cyborg grew up side by side with the effort to replicate human intelligence in machine form. The introduction offers a quick overview of the development of thinking machines and touches on some of the key figures in the effort, such as Charles Babbage, Ada Lovelace, and Alan Turing. It also highlights some of the most famous imaginative depictions of cyborg malevolence, such as Mary Shelly's *Frankenstein*, Fritz Lang's *Metropolis*, and Stanley Kubrick's *2001*. These dramatizations of human-machine relationships introduce the chapter's primary themes: the impact of electronic technology on human minds in the present and the future of artificial intelligence. They also suggest an interesting way to open your exploration of cyberminds. Before you begin reading, you might want to screen any one of several classic films that focus on the clash between humans and the machines we build for our own convenience. Films such as *Forbidden Planet, Modern Times, Metropolis,* and *2001* all raise questions about the relationship between people and machines, and all are bona fide classics that students should be familiar with. A few minutes of any one of these movies can serve as the basis for an open discussion of human feelings — positive and negative — in relation to machines and machine intelligence. *Metropolis,* for example, offers a good illustration of our ambivalence toward machine minds. Lang's demonic Eva, featured in the chapter's frontispiece (p. 640), allows you to raise some thought-provoking questions about the gender of artificial minds. Why, for example, is Lang's automaton so clearly female? And what does her obvious sexuality imply about our relation to cyborgs and cyborg bodies? The film also underscores the role played by industrialization and capitalism in the genesis of modern cyborg fantasies. If fact, while Lang's dystopic vision of the future bears all the recognizable traces of 1920s socialist thought, it also remains remarkably prescient in linking the rise of artificial intelligence to the displacement of workers and the working class. If you do lead off with a film, you might also want to speculate for a moment or two about why movies are so obsessed with themes related to cyborgs, androids, robots, machine minds, and artificial creatures. Why do technologically enhanced characters crop up in films from decade to decade? One obvious explanation is that movies tend to favor artificial creatures because they're terrific excuses to use lots of special effects. A more insightful response is that film itself is a highly mechanized medium — a form of communications technology that relies on motor-driven mechanical reproduction — and thus has a natural affinity with all things technological and artificial.

The introductory subsection "Cyber Writing" touches on an idea that today's students often tend to take for granted — that writing and the book are themselves forms of high technology. It also offers a brief introduction to the concept of hypertext and the problems associated with Web research. Many of the Essay Options in this chapter offer topics that can be used as the basis for either online hypertext assignments or more traditional paper assignments. Students who already have experience developing Web sites or doing hypertext "reports" may want to pursue these options, but, clearly, you'll need to offer extra guidance to students who have never composed online if you want to have them assemble hypertext projects. If you want more information on hypertext composition, you might consult George P. Landow's *Hypertext 2.0: The Convergence of Contemporary Critical Theory and Technology* (Johns Hopkins University Press, 1999), which offers a general introduction to the art of writing online. Of course, students who aren't up to the requirements of building a Web site can simulate hypertext writing "offline" in a number of creative ways. At the most basic level, they can build a collage mixing text and visuals on topics like the history of "cyberselves" in popular culture or the future of artificial intelligence. At a more ambitious level, they can expand the idea of a multimedia collage into a conceptual "installation" that blends segments of text and photos with audio recordings and videotape. This kind of installation can also be presented as an interactive CD or in the form of an interactive Web site if students have access to the proper computer equipment and the knowledge they'll need to develop multimedia programs. The advice on Internet research offered in the chapter introduction may not be needed by some of your more savvy students. Those who have already done some serious online research probably are well aware of the dangers associated with cruising for information on the Web. For many students, however, the Internet is still a relatively magical place — a source of entertainment and a forum for human contact that's infinitely more attractive than any "old-fashioned" book. Many students also think the Net is a lot faster and easier to use than traditional library resources. As a result, it sometimes helps to offer a word of caution about the unreliability of Internet research and about the need to document and validate Net sources. Chances are your college library has a brochure available on approaches to researching on the Web. You may want to have copies on hand when you discuss this topic in class.

Sequences and Pairings

This chapter gets off to a fast start with Clifford Stoll's "Isolated by the Internet." Despite the recent downturn in the dotcom industry, most students still take a distinctly uncritical view of the Net — a fact that isn't terribly surprising given the drumbeat of pro-technology publicity that dominates popular culture. Stoll challenges students to consider the possible negative influence of the Net, and he does it in near record time. You'll probably want to assign this selection no matter how you approach the rest of the chapter. If you don't have much time left at this point in the term, read Stoll in conjunction with Bill McKibben's "Television and the Twilight of the Senses" and Mark Slouka's "Listening for Silence" (both in Chapter 1) as the basis for a paper on the erosion of solitude in contemporary society. Or, if you do have the leisure for an in-depth investigation of the Internet and its impact on human identity and relationships, read Stoll as an introduction to any of the selections by Ullman, Gómez-Peña, and Turkle. All four selections lead to assignments assessing the culture, impact, or "gender" of the Internet and high technology. As a follow-up, Claudia Springer's "Muscular Circuitry" pairs well with William Gibson's "Johnny Mnemonic" on the topic of cyborgs, gender, and the history of cultural attitudes toward technology. You might assign these two selections as preparation for a multimedia project on the history of the robot (Springer, EO #1), on the role of women in science fiction (Springer, EO #2), or on recent depictions of cyborgs in popular culture (Gibson, EO #2).

Use Hofstadter's "The Turing Test" to segue from earlier assignments on the Internet or cyborg imagery to the last section of the chapter, addressing the nature and implications of artificial intelligence. Hofstadter would be a good bet if your class is more technically inclined — or if you think they'd appreciate some background on the history and theory of AI. Hofstadter can also be used effectively as the basis of a one-reading paper assignment that challenges students to create their own version of the Turing test (Hofstadter, EO #1) or as the set-up for a research paper on the current state of the quest to simulate human intelligence (Hofstadter, EO #2). The last three readings raise social, political, and ethical issues related to the future of AI and machine minds. Maureen Caudill's "Redefining the Measure of Mankind" is the central selection here, because it outlines the case for the inevitability of computer intelligence and it raises both social and ethical issues that make the topic immediately relevant. Caudill also offers assignment options for media-based and traditional research papers. Moravec's chilling scenario of downloading a human mind into a robot body can be paired with Caudill to offer an even more dramatic view of the cyber future. Wertheim's analysis of the essentially religious nature of the quest for machine intelligence introduces the concept of cyberspace into the chapter and provides a challenging ideological analysis of Moravec's robot fantasy and a critique of the entire AI movement. It also raises questions about the ethics of high technology that connect well with Stoll, Ullman, and Turkle.

Recommended Stand-Alone Readings

The personal, social, and ethical impact of the Net	*Isolated by the Internet* (Stoll)
Access to and the culture of the Internet	*The Virtual Barrio* (Gómez-Peña)
The gender of pop cultural cyber imagery	*Muscular Circuitry* (Springer)
Differences between machine and human minds	*The Turing Test* (Hofstadter)
The social and ethical implications of AI	*Redefining the Measure of Mankind* (Caudill)

Recommended Pairings

Dehumanization online	*Isolated by the Internet* (Stoll) and *Out of Time* (Ullman)
The culture of the Internet	*Isolated by the Internet* (Stoll) and *The Virtual Barrio* (Gómez-Peña)
Alienation, identity, and Net fantasy games	*Isolated by the Internet* (Stoll) and *Who Am We?* (Turkle)
The gender of cyber imagery in pop cuture	*Muscular Circuitry* (Springer) and *Johnny Mnemonic* (Gibson)

The future of AI   *Redefining the Measure of Mankind* (Caudill)
                                     and *Grandfather Clause* (Moravec)

Suggested Thematic Clusters

The impact of electronic technology *Isolated by the Internet* (Stoll)
                                      Listening for Silence (Slouka, Ch. 1)
                                      *Television and the Twilight of the
                                      Senses* (McKibben, Ch. 1)
The impact of the Internet   *Isolated by the Internet* (Stoll)
                                      Out of Time (Ullman)
                                      The Virtual Barrio (Gómez-Peña)
                                      Who Am We? (Turkle)
The Internet and identity   *Isolated by the Internet (Stoll)*
                                      The Virtual Barrio (Gómez-Peña)
                                      Who Am We? (Turkle)
                                      The Self and Society (Baumeister, Ch. 3)
                                      Living Backwards (Ludwig, Ch. 3)
Electronic technology and human   *Isolated by the Internet (Stoll)*
    relations   *Out of Time* (Ullman)
                                      Who Am We? (Turkle)
The ethics of high technology   *Isolated by the Internet (Stoll)*
                                      Out of Time (Ullman)
                                      Who Am We? (Turkle)
                                      *Redefining the Measure of
                                      Mankind* (Caudill)
                                      Cyber Soul-Space (Wertheim)
                                      The Narrative Imagination (Nussbaum, Ch. 4)
The gender of computer technology   *Out of Time* (Ullman)
                                      Who Am We? (Turkle)
                                      Muscular Circuitry (Springer)
                                      Heart to Heart (Blum, Ch. 4)
Cyborgs in the popular imagination   *Muscular Circuitry* (Springer)
                                      Johnny Mnemonic (Gibson)
Animal, human, and cyber   *The Turing Test* (Hofstadter)
    intelligence   *The Case for the Personhood of Gorillas*
                                      (Patterson and Gordon, Ch. 5)
                                      Murder in a Zoo (Leakey and Lewin, Ch. 5)
The future of human and machine   *Redefining the Measure of Mankind*
    minds   (Caudill)
                                      Grandfather Clause (Moravec)
                                      Cyber Soul-Space (Wertheim)
Simulation and machine intelligence *Who Am We?* (Turkle)
                                      The Turing Test (Hofstadter)
                                      Grandfather Clause (Moravec)

Essay Options

Isolated by the Internet, Clifford Stoll

Option #1. Respond to Stoll's claim that the Internet "dehumanizes" its users.

Option #2. Discuss the impact of electronic technology on solitude and the self. (Slouka and McKibben)

Out of Time: Reflections on the Programming Life, Ellen Ullman

Option #1. Compose a hypertext, multimedia, or formal essay on what it means to live "close to the machine" (Stoll and Turkle)

Option #2. Examine the "gender" of computer technology. (Turkle and Springer)

The Virtual Barrio @ the Other Frontier, Guillermo Gómez-Peña

Option #1. Research and report on the issue of equal access to the Internet.

Option #2. Compose a hypertext, multimedia, or formal essay on the culture of the Internet.

Who Am We?, Sherry Turkle

Option #1. Assess the impact of electronic media on human relationships. (Stoll and Ullman)

Option #2. Research and analyze the implications of online fantasy games (MUDS).

Muscular Circuitry, Claudia Springer

Option #1. Compose a hypertext, multimedia, or formal essay on the history of the robot.

Option #2. Analyze the changing role of women in recent science fiction films, TV shows, books, and so on.

Johnny Mnemonic, William Gibson

Option #1. Write your own gender analysis of "Johnny Mnemonic."

Option #2. Analyze the gendering of current depictions of machine minds in pop culture.

The Turing Test: A Coffeehouse Conversation, Douglas R. Hofstadter

Option #1. Create and evaluate your own version of the Turing test.

Option #2. Research and report on recent developments in the field of artificial intelligence.

Redefining the Measure of Mankind, Maureen Caudill

Option #1. Research and report on the social costs of automation over the past twenty years.

Option #2. Compose a hypertext, multimedia, or formal essay on the current state of robot development.

Option #3. Analyze images of human-android interactions in films such as *A.I.* and *Blade Runner.*

Grandfather Clause, Hans Moravec

Option #1. Assess how computing is changing our view of human identity. (Stoll, Ullman, Turkle, and Hofstadter)

Option #2. Compose a hypertext, multimedia, or formal essay on the role of simulation in smart machines. (Hofstadter and Turkle)

Cyber Soul-Space, Margaret Wertheim

Option #1. Research the issue of the "crypto-religiosity" of AI enthusiasts.

Option #2. Compose a hypertext, multimedia, or formal essay on the concept of cyberpace.

Option #3. Assess the ethical implications of electronic technology. (Stoll, Ullman, Turkle, and Caudill)

Media Connections

Electronic technology (TV) and the loss of solitude	Stoll, EO # 2
Online fantasy games	Turkle, EO #2
Recent cyborg media images	Springer, FE #1
Fritz Lang's *Metropolis* and early androids	Springer, FE #5
Women in science fiction and film	Springer, EO #2
Johnny Mnemonic film comparison	Gibson, FE #4
Film noir and cyberpunk genre comparison	Gibson, FE #5
Cyberpunk classics (*Blade Runner, ExistenZ,* and so on)	Gibson, FE #6
Fast, Cheap, and Out of Control	Caudill, FE #6
Human-machine relations (*A.I., Blade Runner, Bicentennial Man*)	Caudill, EO #3
Concepts of cyberspace in pop culture	Wertheim, EO #2

CLIFFORD STOLL, *Isolated by the Internet* (p. 648)

No matter what approach you take to Chapter 6, you'll probably want to assign this selection. Stoll's frontal assault on the Internet may not be deathless prose, but it does raise important questions about the Internet, and it raises them with enough edge to provoke strong student response. Stoll damns the Net, but he doesn't bother offering much support for his claims. Still, although this may make for a less than perfect essay, it does give students something to cut their teeth on in class. Students enjoy leaping into the debate that Stoll sets going in these pages. Those who cherish the hours they spend in chat rooms and playing fantasy games will try their best to prove Stoll a Luddite lunatic; those who are more skeptical of the hype about life online will work to fill in the blanks that Stoll leaves in his argument. Students respond well to Stoll, I suspect, because they find his "take-no-prisoners" style so refreshing and because he has them in mind when he registers his complaints. Few students can resist debating the claims he makes about the "epidemic" of shyness that's sweeping American college campuses or the academic "programming" of American family life. Because this selection offers such a wide-ranging critique of the Net, it pairs well with any of the selections by Ullman, Turkle, and Gómez-Peña. If you want to supplement Stoll with a few more "positive" perspectives on the Net, try browsing the archives of the *Wired* magazine Web site (wiredmagazine.com). Among the many pro-Net pieces you'll find there, you may want to consider Michelle Slatella's "Who Can I Turn To?" This piece describes how the spouses of Alzheimer's victims have used the Internet to build a nationwide support group. In "Birth of a Digital Nation," Jon Katz discusses how the Internet is producing what he sees as a new generation of political activists who transcend traditional political labels. The Before Reading exercise asks students to reflect on the claims that have been advanced about how the Internet is supposed to change the world. Since the collapse of the dotcoms, Net hype has cooled rather dramatically, but students are probably still aware that the Internet was originally sold as "silicon snake oil," in Stoll's own words. The Net was going to make it possible for all of us to become independent contractors who'd work flexible hours at home. It was supposed to save us time normally spent on shopping for clothes, groceries, and cars and paying bills. We were supposed to learn online, get all of our news from Web sources, and even "date" via Web matchmaking services. Of course, some students may justifiably wonder why the misanthropic lifestyle promised by the Internet sounded appealing in the first place.

Exploring the Text

1. Although Stoll doesn't defend the assertions he forwards in this selection very vigorously, his claims are wonderfully engaging. The Net, as he sees it, undermines "deep" social relationships, those that depend on sustained cooperation and commitment, and favors instead the development of "weak" social ties based on "information" rather than on "proximity." Because Net relationships are always maintained "at a distance," they never, in Stoll's mind, require the kind of "tangible favors" that cement face-to-face friendships.

2. They also undermine the kind of social skills that Stoll feels are needed to sustain deep relationships, skills like those involved in reading physical gestures and facial features, expressing feelings openly, initiating conversations, knowing when to interrupt, and even telling jokes. These, he believes, develop over years of live interaction and can be lost when kids spend endless hours online. The result, for Stoll, is a generation that is becoming increasingly shy in person, although exactly why Stoll feels that today's college students are more withdrawn than those of earlier generations isn't clear. The stereotypical computer nerd is often depicted as shy and lacking in social graces; your students will probably have a good time correcting — or supporting — Stoll on this point. Urge them to share experiences of their own related to the idea of an "epidemic of shyness" on America's college campuses. What specific experiences have they had that would suggest that Stoll is right? Of course, the crucial distinction he's making is that due to the Internet, students are "less prepared" for social interaction than they were in the past. They may be spending just as much time out in public, but they lack the social poise of their noncomputing predecessors.

3. Stoll also addresses the notion of being "addicted" to the Internet. This claim is at least as old as electronic technology itself. The idea that you could get "hooked" on TV was one of the central preoccupations of media critics during the '50s and '60s. Students will want to address some of the weaknesses in the Net/drug comparison. For example, they might observe that use of the Internet doesn't involve the kind of physical dependency associated with drugs. No matter how thoroughly "hooked" you are on the Web, you don't go into withdrawal when you sign off of AOL. Nor does use of the Internet put you in harm's way on the street the way that drug addiction might. But Internet addiction might be seen as resembling drug dependency in several important respects. Like a drug habit, heavy use of the Internet might be seen as altering your consciousness. It clearly takes a toll on its users in terms of time, money, and even physical fitness. And, like drugs, the Net is associated with its own "alternative" subculture. And then there's the issue of psychological dependency. Clearly, it could be argued that heavy Internet users may have trouble coping with real life because they've become so accustomed to life online. Again, students will want to compare their own experiences on this issue.

4. The values Stoll associates with the Net are those of business. The Internet, in his view, has infected the personal and private world of the home with the goals of the workplace — goals like productivity, profit, efficiency, competition, and speed. Again, you'll want to take the time in class to question whether the experiences of your students confirm Stoll's vision of the home as a place that has been colonized by the values and attitudes of the corporate sector. Chances are that students who have survived the tensions of two-career families and the recent mania with SAT scores and academic achievement will agree that the home is, in fact, becoming more like the Fortune 500 every day.

5. Overall, Stoll paints a bleak picture of the Internet and its impact on heavy users. The Net depresses us, cuts us off from real relationships, erodes essential social skills, makes us uneasy in social situations, undermines our families, and subverts what little real sense of community we have left. Most important, in Stoll's view, the Net isolates us by robbing us of the time we need to build real relationships and real communities. You might want to round off your discussion of Stoll's ideas by exploring the issue of

time with your students. Do they feel under constant pressure today to live their lives at a faster pace? What takes up their time? The Internet? Work? Studies? Friends? What might they do to overcome the isolation that Stoll describes?

Further Explorations

1. Whereas Stoll believes that the Internet isolates us by robbing us of time and our ability to focus on others, Ullman would likely associate alienation online with what she terms the cult of the "boy engineer." The programmers who built the Internet are, in Ullman's view, a surly, unwashed, sociopathic lot whose ideal of human relationship is embodied by e-mail — a form of communication that is unilateral, asynchronous, abstract, and totally divorced from living presence. Programmers love cubicles, long work days, and machines, and these, according to Ullman, are the values they've built into the software they sell us. The culture of computing, in Ullman's experience, propagates the culture of those who live "close to the machine" — the entrepreneurial culture of the 1990s that divides society into winners and losers, into those with secret knowledge and the "idiots" who are forced to use it.

2. Turkle's exploration of the impact of the Internet on devoted MUD users is more complex than Stoll's. For Stoll, those who spend hours every day logged onto Internet fantasy and role-playing games represent the Net's most dramatic casualties. For Turkle, MUD devotees may, in fact, be destructively "addicted" to the games they play, but they may also be using these fantasy games to "try out" different identities in a way that is personally liberating. By wearing different "virtual masks," women may learn online to be assertive, taking chances they would never take in reality. Similarly, men, by acting out female parts, may learn to be more empathetic with women in real life. The games also allow users to experiment with fantasies that might be too dangerous or threatening if played out in reality. Yet even Turkle voices some concerns about the impact of Internet use. Certainly, the ethical questions she raises about gender-swapping and "tiny sex" outside wedlock might be seen as confirming some of Stoll's worst fears about how the Net works against "deep" commitment and enduring human relationships.

3. This question can be used as a pre-writing activity for Essay Option #2. Stoll claims that the Net robs us of time and distances us from others by depriving us of live, face-to-face interpersonal contact. In addition, he suggests that life online infects what was once the realm of private life with the values of the business world. He believes that when we're connected to the Internet, we're buying into entrepreneurial goals such as success and productivity and losing sight of life's more reflective pleasures. As a result, we bring the stress and the technology of the workplace with us even when we're at home or when we venture out into nature. McKibben might see this as an extension of the impact that television has had on us for the past fifty years. In McKibben's view, TV isolates its viewers by reducing their sensory involvement with their immediate natural and social contexts. At the same time, it restricts sensory input, narrowing our perceptions to the rather meager visual and auditory forms of stimulation offered over the tube. Both the Internet and television, then, might be seen as isolating us, robbing us of time, and narrowing the natural "bandwidth" of our senses. They might also be seen as undermining the internal reflective balance we need to appreciate the natural world. Students might agree with McKibben about this in relation to television, particularly since it's such a passive form of technology. But they may want to argue that the Net is, as advertised, a more "interactive" medium that invites relationship and actually expands the options for community building. In fact, it's relatively easy to make the case that while the hours we spend online reduce the richness of our sensory contact with the world, they also multiply our connections with other minds — with people from different backgrounds and walks of life. However, this idea itself might be countered by pointing out that most folks online talk to people who are remarkably like themselves in the first place, thus reinforcing social as well as sensory isolation. In any case, there's ample room here for students to debate issues raised by Stoll and McKibben.

Essay Options

1. This assignment gives students the chance to argue with Stoll — or to fill in the many blanks he's conveniently left for supporting arguments in this selection. You'll want to encourage students to spend some significant time brainstorming and pre-writing this paper so that they have a number of specific experiences or situations they can use to illustrate their points for or against Stoll.

2. This paper takes students in another direction. The Net, Stoll argues, doesn't simply isolate us from others; it isolates us from nature and even from ourselves. Like the hiker Stoll meets who comes to Yosemite equipped with GPS, we all run the risk of living in a world where we are always "in reach." Slouka's "Listening for Silence" (*Mind Readings*, p. 50) and Bill McKibben's "Television and the Twilight of the Senses" (*Mind Readings*, p. 109) expand on the idea that electronic technology deprives us of the kind of solitude we need in order to be fully human. This assignment also challenges students to think about a distinction that's becoming harder to hold on to in the welter of modern society — that between purposeful solitude and meaningless isolation.

ELLEN ULLMAN, *Out of Time: Reflections on the Programming Life* (p. 656)

In this selection, Ullman isn't as interested in the impact that computing has had on contemporary society as she is in exploring the "culture" of computing and the way that it will impact us in the future. Ullman developed her views on the culture of computing in her widely praised memoir, *Close to the Machine: Technophilia and Its Discontents* (1995). In this account of what it was like to live as a highly paid programmer during the early years of the computer revolution, Ullman anatomizes the "cult of the boy engineer" — the cluster of adolescent male attitudes and values that she associates with those who live and work "close to the machine." Although she doesn't identify herself as a feminist in this piece, there's little doubt about where her sympathies lie. Two decades spent supervising cubicles full of programmers have left her with a highly gendered analysis of the world of electronic technology. This selection connects neatly with Clifford Stoll's critique of the Internet and also serves as a bridge between Stoll and Guillermo Gómez-Peña's "The Virtual Barrio" (*Mind Readings*, p. 667), which looks at the notion of Internet culture from the perspectives of access and ethnicity. In addition, Ullman pairs well with Sherry Turkle's exploration of online fantasy games and gender-swapping. The narrative nature of Ullman's memoir also offers a nice change of pace, particularly coming as it does immediately after Stoll's diatribe and before Gómez-Peña's manifesto. However, students might have a little trouble getting into the Before Reading exercise for this selection, because they may not feel confident about what it means to live "close to the machine." With a little prompting, though, most seem to grasp the stereotype that underlies Ullman's catchphrase. The interesting question is whether they see themselves in this light. You'll want to spend some time in class exploring any differences in gender, ethnicity, or economic background that arise in student responses to the question of whether men are still more likely to see themselves as being close to the machine than are women. Is one ethnicity closer to the machine ethic than others? Just what might it mean for an individual to see herself this way? Does it, for example, suggest that she is less emotional? Less interested in things "warm and fuzzy"? Does it mean that she is more machine-like? And what might that mean?

Exploring the Text

1. In Ullman's professional opinion, computers are stupid. Compared to human minds, she feels they're "idiots." Because they must follow absolutely explicit directions, the process of programming them is exceedingly tedious: the programmer has to think through all the complexities of a natural process and then "translate" it into the linear, step-by-step machine instructions used to direct computer actions. As Ullman says, it's

like "taking dictation from your own mind." And, to a certain extent, it's like learning how to write in the sense that the novice writer has to learn how to slow the process of thinking down and make all of the logical moves of thought explicit so that the reader can follow all the creative twists and turns of his mind. The difficulty of putting thoughts into words may help students appreciate the difficulty that Ullman identifies with the task of programming.

2. Living close to the machine for Ullman is, thus, a complicated idea. It implies a host of what might be seen as admirable personal qualities such as absolute dedication and incredible intellectual energy. It's also associated with status. Those at the top of the computer industry — those who, paradoxically, are as "low" as possible — are also the closest to the machine. They're the programmers who "speak" the digital code of the CPU, and, as a result, receive the highest pay and have the nicest offices. They also enjoy the most independence. Being close to the machine means you're free of the social conventions that govern most common workplace relationships. Thus, the most sought-after programmers often live like adolescent boys. Focused exclusively on their work, they neglect themselves, each other, and their families. In fact, for those who are closest to the machine, it's a badge of honor to ignore things like time and cleanliness. After all, "machines don't care how you live."

3. The two extended anecdotes that Ullman offers illustrate what such "closeness" means in practice. The programmers who hit on the idea of genocide as a logical solution for genetically transmitted diseases symbolize the shortsightedness of the ethic of the "boy engineer." These guys are so caught up in the search for solutions to "problems" that they forget about the people lurking behind the problems they seek to solve. They exemplify several of the most negative characteristics of the culture of computing — raw competitive intelligence, a fondness for logical reasoning without consideration of the consequences, and the failure of imagination, empathy, and moral vision. When they turn on Ullman and disparage her criticisms as something a "wife" might say, they add insensitivity and sexism to the list. The story about Paolo demonstrates that the cult of the boy engineer even cuts across cultural lines. Ullman expects Paolo to be a sophisticated European who appreciates the more "human" aspects of existence, but he ends up being a badly behaved child just like his American counterparts. Even the Japanese value this boyish independence and disorder when it comes to hiring programmers.

4. Of course, the unspoken assumption behind Ullman's critique of computing is that the cult of the boy engineer is a distinctly male phenomenon. The programmer, according to Ullman, is self-centered, contemptuous of others, and self-satisfied. He is weirdly independent; in fact, he is misanthropic to the point of being deliberately offensive. He is both foolish and competitive. Ullman identifies these attitudes with the egocentric arrogance of the immature male — the kind of person who can engage in water-balloon fights one minute and seriously contemplate organized mass murder the next. Your class can debate whether such values are, in fact, designed into the attractive, interactive "toy" that the computer represents. Do computers force all users to emulate the values of the boy engineer? Do they turn all of us into "users" at some level — people who are ultimately closer to their machines than they are to each other? How does this square with all the talk about "connection" and community surrounding computers and the Internet?

Further Explorations

1. It's relatively easy to discern the shadowy influence of the boy engineer in the identity games that Sherry Turkle describes in "Who Am We?" Turkle sees Internet fantasy games as an exciting realm that challenges traditional notions of personal identity and gives players the chance to experiment with alternative ways of feeling, thinking, and behaving. But, as Ullman might note, such fantasy games also offer an unprecedented dose of irresponsibility — a prime trait of the adolescent male psyche. Going transgender online still leaves the user completely in control and completely unaccountable. A

male who dresses virtually as a woman gets to inhabit a momentary fantasy — even if it stretches out over several months or years — and then return to the safety of his traditional gender role. How different is this from the water-balloon play that thirty-year-old programmers indulge in before getting back to what they see as the serious work of talking to their machines?

2. Students who grasp this connection will have no difficulty appreciating the relevance of Ullman's gendered reading of computer culture to Claudia Springer's "Muscular Circuitry." Springer argues that cyber imagery in pop culture has always favored adolescent male fantasies of hard bodies and domination, even while she, along with feminist cultural critics such as Donna Haraway, sees the computer itself as a distinctly "female" technology. The apparent agreement between Springer and Ullman might be dismissed as the result of the fact that Hollywood moguls often aim science fiction films at an adolescent male audience, but the connection becomes more interesting when you consider how the notion of indestructibly dominant cyber bodies is infecting popular culture at large. This notion shows up in almost every cultural fad, from tattooing to the new "hard-bodied" heroines who populate videogame culture. Indeed, given the culture of computing and the film industry, it could be argued that male values and identities are quickly displacing those traditionally associated with females.

3. Hans Moravec's serious fantasy of downloading human minds into indestructible cyborg bodies might be seen as a simple extension of this kind of masculine thinking. In a sense, what Moravec does in "Grandfather Clause" is to imagine what it would be like to go "asynchronous" with the entire human race by literally getting as close to the machine as possible. To download your consciousness into the hardbody of a robot might be the ultimate fantasy of any boy engineer. Caudill, by contrast, keeps both feet on the ground of her own humanity and raises questions about what the desire to create artificial minds suggests about us as a species. The dream of creating artificial minds, for Caudill, isn't a pleasurable source of fantasy; it's more of a potential nightmare that echoes age-old human aspirations like the desire to "own" other intelligent beings and to control other minds.

4. The attitudes and values associated with the cult of the boy engineer might also be seen as reflecting the distinctions between male and female minds that Deborah Blum summarizes in "Heart to Heart: Sex Differences in Emotion." Blum would not be surprised to learn that the men who spend their lives programming computers are highly competitive and relatively inexpressive and unempathetic. Indeed, from Blum's perspective, living close to the machine might be seen as compensating for the emotional insecurity that troubles young boys more than girls. The computer, for Blum, might be seen as a form of defense that distances others, reinforces male independence, and compensates for the male's relative inability to form supportive networks of real relationships.

5. Still, the idea of a gendered reading of technology is complicated by the relationship between Scott Russell Sanders and his hammer. It would be difficult to argue that this tool, passed from father to son for generations in Sanders's family, is anything but male. Sanders is himself well aware of this, and he acknowledges it as an essential aspect of his identity. Yet Sanders's hammer isn't something that distances him from others; on the contrary, it connects him to his grandfather and his father and to generations of other men who lived their lives as they built their homes — with the sides plumb and the corners squared. And, interestingly enough, Sanders bothers to note that he has taken it upon himself to pass these same skills and virtues down to his daughter. Sanders's hammer is gendered male like the computer, but it's associated with a distinctly adult rather than with an adolescent understanding of masculinity — a maleness that takes pride in carefulness, connection, and relationship.

Essay Options

1. The response to this assignment can take the form of a hypertext, multimedia, or mixed media presentation, depending on the technical abilities of your students. No

matter how students approach this project, you'll want to encourage them to search widely for materials — particularly for visuals. Films, television shows, ads, and comic books will provide plenty of images on the subject of living close to the machine. Students can write their own text based on readings and additional research and blend it with passages from the essays they cover in class.

2. This assignment calls for a more traditional academic paper on the topic of the gender of computer technology. Before attempting this paper, students should spend some time reviewing ads and stories in popular computer and news magazines to see how high-tech tools are typically represented. This research might be even more interesting if you ask students to look back ten or more years ago to see how the gender of computer images has evolved since the appearance of the first PCs. In addition, students may want to consider the extent to which the gender of computer culture is changing as more women enter the high-tech labor market and are portrayed in the media as computer savvy.

GUILLERMO GÓMEZ-PEÑA, *The Virtual Barrio @ the Other Frontier* (p. 667)

Before you assign this essay, you may want to log onto Web sites that host some of Gómez-Peña's work and browse around a bit to get a sense of what this "techno-pirate" is all about. Gómez-Peña's qualified *corrido* to the Internet offers a refreshing contrast to both Stoll and Ullman. Gómez-Peña may have a bone to pick with the Net about issues of access and the "whiteness" of Web culture, but, ultimately, he likes to go online. For him, the Internet does in fact live up to all the hype that surrounds it. It's a place where you can meet others, create community, and savor all the freedoms of the artistic life. He is, thus, the honorary "spokesperson" in this chapter for the virtues of life online, and I think his essay serves this function particularly well because it not only testifies to the power of the Internet but also highlights some of its most troubling weakness as a form of worldwide communication. If you've just finished Ullman, it shouldn't be too hard to solicit images of the average computer nerd for the Before Reading assignment. As you do this, you'll want to remind your class that this is a cultural stereotype, not a reality. It will help if you follow up by discussing the various sources that contribute to this image. Chances are that most students have bumped up against the computer nerd in at least a couple of films, television shows, or comic books. The point, of course, according to Gómez-Peña, is that this stereotype excludes some just as unfairly as it categorizes others. It may appear to mock the kind of kid who's good with technology, but it does an even better job of discouraging those who don't live up to the image it projects.

Exploring the Text

1. Gómez-Peña describes a number of Latino stereotypes in this essay. Latinos are warm, affectionate, spiritual, imaginative, poetical, sentimental, romantic, and passionate. They are into things such as mythology, revolution, and their "primal selves" — and not into things that involve high or even low technology. Gómez-Peña clearly wants to reject this image, but at the same time much of what he says here about his own personal and family history seems to confirm it. His grandmother was wise enough to avoid using the microwave oven she got as a present, and his family decorated the television as if it were a kind of "postmodern" electronic altar. Indeed, the point is that Latino views of high technology are quite complex. Technology may represent the future for many Latinos, but it also remains connected to the cultural past. High technology isn't a pathway to a new and different life or a new and different self, according to Gómez-Peña's way of thinking; it's a new way of experimenting with and celebrating what it means to be Latino.

2. In general, then, Gómez-Peña sees the Internet as a new, more powerful medium for cultural expression. He is "seduced" by the Net, yet he recognizes its shortcomings. He knows that he is an interloper in the essentially white world of high technology, a

denizen of what he terms the "virtual barrio." The "Cyber-Migra" of the Internet denies access to Latinos, women, and other peoples of color in two ways: by perpetuating stereotypes that discourage broader participation and by maintaining an ethnically homogenized, essentially alien cultural world online. The question here is whether students will agree with the suggestion that there is a conspiracy to deny women and people of color access to the world of high technology, or whether students will view the Net as just another impartial medium, just another color-blind communications tool.

3. Gómez-Peña gives us only a few hints at the sort of things he's done as an artist to "brownify" the Net. Perhaps the most intelligible of these is the segment he offers from his "Naftaztec" television project. Students will have a much clearer sense of what he means by his desire to "infect the lingua franca" if they log onto one of his interactive Internet art presentations, as suggested in Further Exploration #4. It will be interesting to see how they react to this attempt at subverting Net culture. In fact, you may want to reserve time in class to debate whether there actually is a single identifiable culture that dominates the Net. It might well be argued that the chaos of choices and voices that constitutes the Net hasn't the coherence to be categorized as a genuine culture in the first place.

Further Explorations

1. Ullman's programmers probably wouldn't be very gentle in their response to Gómez-Peña's program for subverting the Net. Chances are, the idea of "culture" would strike these condescending "techies" as something remarkably old-fashioned, maybe even as something obscene. Living close to the machine themselves, and thus by definition almost completely estranged from human contact, they wouldn't be disposed to comprehend Gómez-Peña's affection for home, family, and things Latino. In fact, these "boy engineers" are exactly the source of the faceless elitism that Gómez-Peña describes as the "Cyber-Migra." And given the fact that she sees the cult of the boy engineer as something that's literally been programmed into the culture of high technology, it's unlikely that Ullman would be sanguine about Gómez-Peña's chances for subverting the World Wide Web.

2. Unlike Stoll, Gómez-Peña does not see the Net as a destructive force in and of itself. Although he may have logged on rather reluctantly at first, it's clear that he appreciates the freedom he finds online — even if it's only freedom to bait the Internet's dominant culture. Also, unlike Stoll, Gómez-Peña affirms the relatively common view of the Net as a way to maintain existing communities and to build new ones.

3. Although he savors the expressive freedom that the Internet offers, Gómez-Peña might part ways with Sherry Turkle when it comes to the issue of identity-swapping online. Given his identification as a Latino, it would be hard to imagine Gómez-Peña seeing ethnicity as "just another window" or as something you might "try on" just for the fun of it. The kind of endless fantasy games that Turkle describes actually threatens to undermine the concept of authentic ethnic identity that Gómez-Peña so obviously values.

4. Latino cultural imagery and themes dominate Gómez-Peña's web sites, but students will want to debate whether there is anything particularly "revolutionary" about his attempts to "brownify" the Internet. Try his "Temple of Confessions" web site at www.echonyc.com/~confess/ for a start. For additional sites, have your class do a "Google" search under "Gómez-Peña."

Essay Options

1. The issue of access to the Internet, and to computer technology in general, has been widely covered both in the popular press and in scholarly publications during the past few years. Students should be able to find ample information as they research this topic. If you want to focus this assignment more narrowly, you might consider dividing your class into groups specializing in issues of access related to particular geographical regions (Africa, Latin America, and Asia, for example) or particular demographic groups.

2. This assignment offers a possible hypertext/mixed media project that calls for students to explore what might be viewed as "alternative" or subversive Web sites. You'll certainly want to caution students about what they're sure to find as they begin to probe the many "virtual barrios" that constitute the Internet. Pornography, that bastion of e-commerce, should be excluded from the assignment — not only because it's sexist and exploitative, but because it clearly doesn't qualify as a "pocket of resistance" on the Web.

SHERRY TURKLE, *Who Am We?* (p. 675)

This selection brings the first half of the chapter to a close and rounds off the chapter's quartet of selections on the Internet. But while Turkle comes last in this series, she certainly is still worth reading. Turkle is an expert on issues of Net culture and speaks with real authority when it comes to the bizarre world of MUDs ("Multiple User Dungeons") — the Dungeons and Dragons–like role-playing fantasy games that have been enormously popular on the Net since it came into being. Turkle's analysis of the implications of gender-swapping and "Tiny sex" online raises questions about identity that resonate with selections earlier in this and other chapters. Turkle pairs well with Stoll on the theme of isolation and with Ullman on the theme of the Internet and gender relations. Begin by challenging students to imagine what role they might be tempted to assume if they were to enter into the fantastic world of an online MUD. The Before Reading exercise asks students to write a quick profile of the person, animal, or object they might become. Then have them swap these profiles in small groups, preserving the anonymity of their authors, and have students try to match each imaginary figure with its creator. The point of this parlor game, besides engaging students in the topic, lies in the creative capacity of unfettered imagination. Liberated from the restraints of our daily identities, we can, along with Turkle's subjects, become literally anyone — or anything — in the virtual world of the Internet.

Exploring the Text

1. The Internet has ushered in the era of the "postmodern" self, according to Turkle. Before the Internet, the self was seen as a stable, authoritative entity. Coherence and unity were the hallmarks of the traditional self, which was always reassuringly the same and comfortingly predictable. Online, however, the self can divide to become many different "selves." Participants in MUDs can change identities, genders, ages, and ethnicities. They can "try on" personalities that differ dramatically from the personality they live with in their daily life. They can even become animals or objects. Turkle's point is that the self is radically "decentered" online. It becomes a mask — just one more "window" like the multiple screens you see in a video game or fantasy gamesite.

2. Turkle generally finds the decentering of the self online to be a positive phenomenon. Playing roles on the Net "liberates" MUDders. It frees them to experiment with different ways of feeling, being, and behaving. Women who would normally tend to be self-effacing in "RL" (real life) can enter a chat room as a man and see what it's like to indulge in some simple self-assertion. A man can don the "virtual mask" of a woman and find out "first hand" what it's like to be "hit on" or ignored. A pathologically shy graduate student like Stewart can leave his real self behind and become the heroic Achilles in a fantasy world where he "gets the girl" and is quite literally the center of attention. Of course, Turkle acknowledges the dangers in these imagination games. She's wise enough to recognize that the Stewarts who spend upwards of forty hours a week logged on to MUDs may, in fact, be unable to integrate what they experience online with their real personalities. But while MUDs may lead to addiction and perhaps even depression, Turkle still credits them with being a source of valuable self-knowledge.

3. The situation, however, becomes somewhat more complicated when Turkle considers issues such as gender-swapping and Tiny sex. Some people may impersonate the opposite sex online in order to deepen their understanding of what others experience, but many may engage in such gender-swapping out of less savory motives. The question

is, where does healthy experimentation give way to prurient interest and perversion? Although it may initially seem harmless for a man to take on the role of a woman, the picture gets cloudier when Turkle contemplates the scenario of a nineteen-year-old college freshman making cyberlove as a forty-year-old woman to a middle-aged man — or, even more disturbingly, the scenario of a twelve-year-old girl doing the same. The text presents some test cases for your students to weigh for themselves. Of course, you may want to have your students brainstorm other situations involving even more complicated moral dilemmas. Perhaps the most disturbing ethical question that Turkle considers in this essay involves Martin and Beth and their experience with "Tiny adultery." If all acts online are just "simulations" with no grounding in reality, then what could possibly be wrong with Martin's pursuit of electronic sex with other women over the Internet? For centuries, readers have identified with the characters in steamy novels and enjoyed "virtual relationships" in print. Doing the same online can't be all that different, even if it is a little more interactive. Yet isn't fidelity really a matter of intention? If Martin intends to violate Beth's trust — even "virtually" — isn't it pretty much as if he picked someone up in a local bar?

4. All of these ethical questions lead back to the issue of the relationship between reality and accountability. One of the things that distinguishes real life from "windows" and simulations is that the choices you make in life entail actual consequences. Martin's cheating on Beth may take place in the realm of electrons instead of the realm of bodies, but the consequences of his choices in terms of their impact on her feelings may be as real as if he had, in fact, violated her trust.

Further Explorations

1. Turkle's view of the Internet is obviously more optimistic than Stoll's. Whereas Stoll is appalled by folks like Stewart, who spend most of their day online, Turkle holds out hope that MUDers may actually be learning valuable lessons about themselves and others as well as valuable social skills. Yet, she does acknowledge some of the problems that Stoll addresses in his essay. Stewart's inability to integrate what he learns online with his real life and the ethical questions implied in Martin's virtual extramarital affairs do disturb her.

2. The kind of personal identity-swapping that Turkle describes among MUDers grew out of the old "Dungeons and Dragons" fantasy games that have been a fixture of male adolescence for the past thirty years, so it isn't too difficult to see this practice as another expression of the mentality of Ullman's boy engineer. Pretending you're a person of the opposite sex, like pretending you're an oversexed plush animal, is just another form of outrageous play, and Ullman makes it clear that the grown men she associates with love to indulge in forms of play that might seem ridiculous in any other business context. The boy engineer prides himself on his ability to slip out of his adult persona to become a child again at the drop of a hat. Why not become a woman or a four-teen-year-old girl when playing online? What's particularly "boyish" about such games is the fact that they deny the very things that stabilize identity for adults — mutual commitment and accountability.

3. If you've already read Douglas Hofstadter's account of Alan Turing's famous discursive method for judging machine intelligence (*Mind Readings*, p. 719), it might be tempting to think of the gender-bending antics of someone like Turkle's Case as a kind of Turing test. Turing introduces his test by comparing it to a parlor game in which an unseen man tries to convince an interrogator that he's actually a woman through his responses to the interrogator's questions. If a machine can convince a human interrogator that it's a human by virtue of its responses to his questions, then, according to Turing, it has demonstrated the equivalent of human intelligence. Seen in this light, the world of MUDs does resemble a kind of enormous, ongoing Turing test. But whether "passing" such a test means anything is open to debate. Passing for a woman online might suggest that Case does grasp some of what it means to be female, but it also might

be seen as simply suggesting that he has mastered a few stereotypical female "behaviors" that are readily accepted by other men who themselves may or may not be very insightful judges of female character. In other words, the Turing test may be a better measure of the gullibility of the interrogator than it is of the mentality of machine, or man, that seeks to trick him. We know that it's possible for white writers to impersonate black characters in works of fiction, and vice versa, but this doesn't prove that such writers deeply comprehend what it means to be racially other. It only suggests that they have the ability to create a convincing character from a few carefully nuanced cultural stereotypes and to use this illusion to effect a "willing suspension of disbelief" in the reader.

4. Returning to Roy F. Baumeister's survey of changing attitudes toward the self in Chapter 3 gives you the chance to place Turkle's analysis of identity games online in a historical context. At first, it might seem hard to square Baumeister's notion of the modern "sovereign" self with the "postmodern" fragmented and experimental "selves" that Turkle describes here. After all, according to Baumeister, the self has emerged as the only stable source of value and authority in contemporary Western society. How, then, could it be open to the kind of free play that Turkle documents among avid MUDders? Turkle's postmodern view of the self might, thus, be seen as a radical change in Western notions of personal identity. It's clear that she sees it this way herself. But students might wonder if this new, fragmented view of personal identity isn't just a logical extension of Baumeister's imperial view of selfhood. It might require a deeply centralized and ego-bounded self to take the kind of psychological risks involved in assuming a different gender identity, even in play. Indeed, the kind of psychological experimentation that Turkle describes might be seen as a way of strengthening the hidden "inner" self even further. Being able to suspend your personal identity for short periods of time may be possible only in the context of a culture in which the self has become a "project," an artifact that is developed, tended, and cared for by its "owner."

5. Martha C. Nussbaum's analysis of literature, empathy, and civic culture offers yet another approach to the experience of Turkle's MUDders. Nussbaum might well argue that the imagination games of someone like Case actually do stimulate the development of empathy, just as attending a play might help men in the audience comprehend the challenges of being a woman in a sexist society. Still, there are significant differences between the experience of reading great literature and that of improvising imagination games online. Works of literature such as *Antigone* or *The Invisible Man* embody ideas and experiences that challenge us to reconsider culturally dominant values and beliefs. There's no guarantee, however, that the improvised interactions you find in an online fantasy game or in a chat room do more than reproduce stereotypical ideas and attitudes. Indeed, it might even be possible to argue that online fantasies actually reduce our ability to empathize with others in reality because they undermine the concept of reality itself. The young Greek male watching a Sophoclean tragedy unfold before him understands that women face realities that he will never have to suffer himself. Identity, for him, is the same as fate. For Turkel's MUDders, however, identity is just a mask that can be tried out and then discarded. If identity is just a matter of choice, then why empathize with the circumstances that surround another person's life? All they have to do is to "choose" another identity to become.

6. Given the fact that Ludwig's story-based theory of identity construction is itself postmodernist in flavor, he would probably view online identity games as a valuable form of self-experimentation. Such free play gives individuals the chance, as Turkle says, to "try on" new personae, and since Ludwig believes that we each create a self by "adopting" a role to play from the storehouse of roles and scripts our cultures provide us, he would probably view MUDs as a step in the right direction. Better to experiment with a new self online before committing to play the part in reality. That way you can see how well it fits or whether it entails any particularly unpleasant consequences.

Essay Options

1. This assignment offers the chance for a comprehensive academic essay focusing on the issue of the impact that electronic media have had on human relationships. Students should be able to glean plenty of ideas on this topic from their reading of Stoll, Ullman, and Turkle. You'll also want to encourage them to draw on their own experiences as they reflect on the impact of the Internet and other forms of communications technology.

2. This option invites students to test some of Turkle's assertions by exploring the world of online fantasy games. They'll want to investigate a number of actual MUDs, and chances are that some of your students are already familiar with several. They'll also probably have to do some additional library or Internet research. Because MUDs tap into the idea of decentered, postmodern identity, they have attracted the attention of quite a few media critics over the past few years, so students shouldn't have much trouble finding MUD-related information.

CLAUDIA SPRINGER, *Muscular Circuitry* (p. 689)

You'll want to reserve time for this selection, particularly if your class needs some diversion after dealing with issues of identity and human relationships on the Internet. Springer's analysis of the gendered imagery associated with cyborgs could be deadly stuff, but her references to Hollywood cyber-classics like the *Terminator* and *Robocop* film series make this bit of feminist techno-criticism highly appealing for most students. Springer is also useful because she offers a concise historical overview of attitudes toward machines and machine intelligence from ancient Greece to the present. You can read this selection productively in association with the gender issues raised by Ullman and Turkle. It also pairs effectively with Gibson's "Johnny Mnemonic," which offers a test case for Springer's assertions about the world of cyberpunk fiction. If you decided to skip the earlier selections on the Internet and to focus your efforts in this chapter exclusively on the theme of artificial minds, this would be an engaging place to start. It also offers you the chance to work a contemporary film into your syllabus, and it sets the stage for other films that you might consider viewing in relation to selections later in the chapter. The Before Reading activity can be instructive as well as a lot of fun. You can and should expect just about anything from students on this one — from aluminum-can assemblages reminiscent of the Tin Man in the *Wizard of Oz* to sophisticated renderings of humanoid "borgs" that signal their robotic origins only through a little extra mascara or a pair of unduly pointed ears. What's interesting is the way these images encode cultural attitudes about the concept of artificial or mechanical creatures. What's the overall "feeling" of your students' artwork? Are the robot images they create high-tech affairs full of wires and flashing lights echoing notions about computers that have been around since the 1950s? Or are they threateningly anthropomorphic characters that have more in common with 1990s punk rockers than they do with R2D2 and Robbie the Robot? What do these collective renderings suggest about the way we see machine intelligence today? Do they convey the presence of beings that are benign or hostile? Do they embody images you might associate with servants, co-equals, foes, competitors, or predators? What response are they meant to evoke in their viewers? Why do you think so?

Exploring the Text

1. Students should find Springer's thumbnail sketch of the history of machines interesting and useful. As she points out, prior to the industrial revolution, machinery was typically viewed as something mysterious and magical. Before the seventeenth century, machines were often designed in ways that disguised the operations of their moving parts. This was done to enhance the wonder associated with mechanization and to protect the special knowledge of the craftsmen who created them. With the Enlightenment, all this changed and the inner "secrets" of machine processes were

revealed. The image of the machine that emerged from the industrial revolution was that of a powerful, dominating giant. Machines in the nineteenth century were no longer mysteries; they were massive emblems of industrial power and efficiency. In the twentieth century the unlimited power of the machine would endow the robot with fearsome strength. As Springer indicates, the robot arrived on the scene not as a "charming novelty" but as a dangerous threat to humanity. The central paradox that Springer sees in the popular image of the cyborg is that the strictly "mechanical" aspect of the computer is once again hidden in the twentieth century, yet the mechanical nature of the cyborg is most commonly expressed through an external show of metallic "muscle." Cyborgs in comic books, dime novels, and science fiction films are typically distinguished by their massive bulk and shiny metallic surfaces. They thus have more in common with the kind of bulky external mechanics of the industrial revolution than they do with the hidden integrated circuitry that actually does the work in today's intelligent machines.

2. Springer explains this apparent contradiction in terms of the development of dimorphic gender identities in use since the Enlightenment. Prior to that era, according to Springer, the West was dominated by a "one-sex" model of gender within which women were seen as "less perfect than men but not altogether different from them." After the Enlightenment, the genders parted ways owing to the "requirements of the ascendant bourgeoisie," and women came to be seen as the "opposite" of their male counterparts. Whereas men in the "two-sex" model were identified with "solidity and hard physical strength," women were associated with fluidity and internal complexity. Based on this dichotomy, Springer identifies the muscularly aggressive body images of the pop cultural cyborg with stereotypical images of masculinity. Computers, by contrast, with their labyrinthine microcircuitry, are distinctly feminine. Springer reads the fact that machine minds in pop culture tend to be depicted in ultramasculine terms as the expression of a "misogynistic resistance to change." Heavy-metal cyborgs, like the Terminator, deny the fact that the era of phallic dominance is on the wane and that computers are hastening its closure. This denial occurs, Springer suggests, because males fear the dissolution of ego boundaries associated with the "fluidity" of computer technology. Thus, hyper-male cyborgs are always fortifying themselves with tough or metallic exteriors out of "nostalgia" for bygone days when men ruled a world dominated by big machines and heavy industry.

3. Springer's claims may be a lot to swallow for many students. It may even be a challenge for many to grasp the general outline of Springer's argument. But most will be able to appreciate the way this gendered reading of cinematic cyborgs plays itself out on film. You'll want to give students the chance to debate Springer's claims in class. It might be pointed out, for example, that the era of heavy-metal cinematic cyborgs itself has already passed. Since the 1980s, a number of cyber-themed movies have appeared featuring android characters that, although still incredibly violent, are not remarkably "male." Indeed, some borg villains, like those on recent editions of the *Star Trek: Next Generation* television series, are distinctly female. In relation to this development, Springer might observe that recent depictions of threatening female cyborgs still express male fears of the essentially "female" nature of electronic technology. The only difference is that they do so more directly than earlier heavy-metal films by casting women as dangerous predators.

Further Explorations

1. You may want to pause at this juncture to view a classic cyborg movie and see how well it illustrates Springer's reading of machine culture. And you'll probably want to spend some time discussing whether the stereotypes that Springer describes still dominate the science fiction genre. Clearly, there have been a number of sci-fi heroines of late who appear to defy the "two-sex" model.

2. Gibson's "Johnny Mnemonic" offers a chance for students to do their own gendered reading of cyberpunk fiction. Springer touches on the outline of the cyberpunk

genre in passing. The "tough guy" hero and film-noir settings borrowed wholesale from "hardboiled" detective fiction are identified by Springer as reflecting a "boy's sensibility." Yet Gibson's story might be seen as having more going for it than adolescent sexism. A good case could be made that Molly Millions is the story's real cyber hero and that Johnny is only a kind of passive Everyman who's redeemed by her countercultural, crypto-erotic dance routine (see Gibson, ET #1–3). Springer might argue that such passivity is also part of the "boy's sensibility" underlying the cyberpunk worldview, but passivity could be seen as a refreshing departure from the armored aggression of figures like the Terminator.

3. Sherry Turkle's analysis of identity online generally supports Springer's identification of computer technology with the concepts of fluidity and change. The multiple experimental postmodern identities that Turkle sees developing on the Net echo Springer's notion of an essentially female technology that favors open ego boundaries. Thus, it might be reasonable, from Springer's perspective, to say that the many "selves" of a MUDder are, in fact, all essentially feminine in that they subvert the traditional male notion of a dominant, inflexible, and well-defined ego. Of course, it might also be argued that the subversive play of Turkle's MUDders is carrying them beyond all traditional gender categories and that, in fact, they are becoming essentially genderless — like the machines they use to construct their ever-shifting identities.

4. Then again, your students should also have the chance to challenge Springer's own categorization of male and female identities. In his historical overview of changing notions of selfhood, Roy F. Baumeister suggests that women are just as dedicated as men are to the concept of the modern centralized self and the belief that the self is the source of all value and motivation. Thus, Baumeister might be seen as challenging Springer's basic understanding of female identity. The images of the female self discussed by Deborah Blum and Mary Catherine Bateson, by contrast, generally confirm Springer's view. According to Blum, women are generally both more open and empathetic than men, who, from a psychological perspective, are emotionally remote and highly competitive. Approaching the issue cross-culturally, Bateson sees the male self as relatively rigid and insulated by power against the need to accommodate others or to adapt to new circumstances. Dominance, for Bateson, makes men generally Terminator-like.

5. Your class can pursue the psychological and political complexities of gender and technology further by taking the time to screen Fritz Lang's *Metropolis*. Lang's dystopic 1926 vision of the capitalist future in which workers live underground and labor like slaves in grotesque factories provides plenty of techno-imagery — male and female — for students to cut their teeth on. Filmed on the cusp of the electronic age, *Metropolis* harkens back to an earlier industrial era when the factory was a distinctly male universe. Yet women figure heavily in Lang's script. Your students will enjoy deciphering the gender symbolism of Eva, Lang's evil erotic robot mistress, and Maria, her revolutionary human counterpart.

6. If your class is ready for an even more serious intellectual challenge, you may want to segue from Springer into Donna Haraway's "Cyborg Manifesto." Haraway's essay on the gender of cyborgs is widely considered a classic on the subject. But it is so conceptually difficult that you'd probably only want to use it, or excerpts from it, if you plan to devote a considerable segment of your class to the subject of gender and technology.

Essay Options

1. Students enjoy both of the Essay Options associated with Springer. They'll have no trouble locating resources, on- and offline, about the history of the robot, and a hypertext presentation or mixed media report works well with this highly visual theme. Reading Springer also helps prepare students for the task of interpreting the meanings of pop cultural imagery, so they should have a fairly clear idea of how to approach this assignment.

2. Involving another research-based paper, this assignment invites students to explore the general issue of the representation of women in science fiction. Much of the legwork for this assignment can be done by browsing the many Web sites that are devoted to the history of sci-fi books and movies and by screening a few carefully selected recent sci-fi films or TV shows. Both assignments allow students to update Springer's analysis by considering how the imagery associated with robots and women in science fiction has changed since she took up the topic in the mid-1990s. Women have come a long way since Princess Leia picked up a blaster in the first *Star Wars* film. Indeed, the case could easily be made that women are now emerging as the dominant figures in the world of science fiction fantasy.

WILLIAM GIBSON, *Johnny Mnemonic* (p. 703)

This story extends the theme of cyber imagery in popular culture and offers a point of comparison with Springer's gendered analysis of cyborg heroes. It can be paired with Springer as the basis for several possible writing assignments, and it also gives you the chance to program one or more films into your course. As explained in the headnote, William Gibson is widely known as the inventor of the concept of cyberspace and as the creator of the genre of "cyberpunk" fiction. Cyberpunk, as the name suggests, results from a weird combination of cultural tendencies. The world of cyberpunk is a dystopic future that blends elements of film noir moodiness, punk rock anti-establishment rebellion, Hollywood Western heroics, and computer jock technophilia. It's a heady mix, and one that your students may already be intimately familiar with, because it's the official *Weltanschauung* of the contemporary video game. Of course, for those who aren't accustomed to cyberpunk conventions, the going may be a little rough at first. A modern mythmaker, Gibson throws his reader into an alternate universe without bothering to explain himself, so it may take a couple of pages for some students to understand his references to nonexistent corporations and mysterious places such as Chiba City. The glosses provided with the text should help in this regard, as should the discussion of cyberpunk conventions suggested in the Before Reading activity. But once students get acclimated to Gibson's fictive environment, "Johnny Mnemonic" provides a refreshing alternative to the more serious analytic readings they'll encounter elsewhere in the chapter.

Exploring the Text

1. The boundary between humans and machines is obliterated — or simply ignored — in the world of cyberpunk. Gibson's characters have no particular affection for their own humanity; in fact, they often seem to view it as a liability. In a world dominated by intelligent super-machinery, being human means being weak or fallible. Thus, Johnny's one talent lies in his memory implants. His problems, however, are caused by his human frailty. His "meat" mind is too slow to deal with the content of his prosthetic memory, and his body and bad judgment get him into all kinds of trouble. Every character in Gibson's story is, in fact, a true cyborg. Everyone has been modified or augmented in some way, whether through massive plastic surgery or through mechanical implants. Of Gibson's creations, Molly Millions is perhaps the most mechanized. During the course of the story, we learn that she has retractable surgical steel scalpels under her fingernails, visual imaging screens permanently sealed over her eyes, and electronic circuitry boosting the output of her nervous system. She is also clearly the story's central figure and hero. By contrast, her rival, the "little tech" with the deadly mechanized thumb, seems almost ridiculously human in his Hawaiian shirt.

2. Gibson's story is set in the standard "dark" dystopic future of cyberpunk fiction. Inspired by the oppressive cityscapes of film noir, Gibson's future is dirty, seedy, and worn out. Like the gloomy backdrop of the gothic romance, to which it's also related, the cyberpunk future is a world full of lurking menace, nuclear anxieties, and impending doom. It's a world that has lost its soul under the yoke of corporate power, a neo-

Darwinian techno-jungle ruled by violence and intrigue. In this imaginative context, governments are ineffective or negligible and the idea of civilization is, at best, a kind of obscene joke.

3. That's why the story inevitably ends up in "Nighttown" — Gibson's underworld vision of a culture of resistance. Populated by social outcasts and low-level gangsters, Nighttown is an inverted hell — and hence a possible Eden — for those who have opted out of the nightmarish world of Gibson's cybersociety. It's society's sewer, but it's also a place where people can get connected and form tribes — or gangs — that have some meaning. The "Killing Floor" where Molly Millions confronts the little tech and saves Johnny can be read as a symbol of this alternative anti-utopia. Composed of an ever-moving webwork that springs to life in response to heavy metal music, it's a cross between a boxing ring and a dance floor — a place where violence and art combine. Its pulsing web can be read as a cipher for the Net, for tribalism, or for the kind of essentially "female" technology that Claudia Springer discusses in her "Muscular Circuitry" (see FE #1 below). Perhaps representing the "millions" who find themselves outside the inner circle of corporate society, Molly uses "culture shock" to dispose of her rival. She kills him with music, dance, rhythm, and the grungy ambiance of the tribal society that she and her fellow "Lo Teks" embody. Thus, it may be possible to read Gibson's story as an allegory on the competing cultures emerging from the development of high technology. In this way, the little tech might be seen as representing the essentially conservative culture of corporate domination, while Molly and the Lo Teks might symbolize tribal techno countercultures like those found online or associated with artistic adaptations of technology like techno and hip-hop music.

4. Seen as a showdown between different cultural responses to electronic technology, the story of Johnny Mnemonic plays itself out as a tale of personal liberation. Johnny enters the story as a cog in the corporate wheel. He's a mere "technical boy," a passive "receptacle " for information that he has no way of understanding or using himself. By the story's end, however, he's dropped out of corporate/syndicate culture and signed on with Molly and the Lo Teks, and in the process he's learned how to access and take control of his own memory. Johnny empowers himself by dropping out of the dominant culture and by networking, instead, with the alternative culture. He doesn't rebel against technology; he simply rejects its dehumanizing aspects and uses it to reintegrate himself into a more authentic alternative community.

Further Explorations

1. If Claudia Springer were to undertake a gendered reading of Gibson, she'd probably start by interrogating the story's portrayal of Molly Millions. Molly can be interpreted as embodying yet another male fantasy. Seen from this perspective, she's just another iteration of the caretaking mother who fights to protect her ineffectual high-tech "boy." Actually, she might be seen more accurately as a cross between the motherly caretaker and a kind of techno-hooker, particularly given the sadomasochistic implications of her knife prostheses and eye masks. Johnny, by contrast, might not live up to the image of Robohulks like the Terminator, but he does fit the role of the adolescent male antihero so frequently associated with cyberpunk fiction. Read in this way, Gibson's story, like the heavy metal cyborg films Springer analyzes, also expresses male angst — but it does so in a different respect. Instead of communicating anxiety over the loss of the rigidly defined masculine self or over the displacement of males in the industrial hierarchy, "Johnny Mnemonic" expresses the unfocused dread the adolescent male feels when confronted with the task of integrating himself within the system of male dominance — in this case, represented by the phallically fingered little tech and the world of the Yakuza/corporation. Of course, students may also see the possibility of a more positive gender interpretation of Gibson's tale. Sexual symbolism aside, Molly Millions it a powerful figure and clearly the story's hero. She represents the only positive fusion of human and machine characteristics in the story, and she also embodies the notion of

countercultural resistance. Even the way she defeats the little tech and his creepily Freudian super finger suggests that she might be read as a female answer to male power. Fighting the tech on a pulsing webwork high above the city, she might be seen as a matriarchal techno-Amazon, riding the waves of the matrix while dancing her opponent to death. And she is also the story's sole source of human connection. She introduces the distinctly unmasculine Johnny into the world of the Lo Teks and even links Johnny to the drug-abusing "squid," who, although he's completely mechanical, might be seen as a distant echo of the natural world. Thus, Gibson's story might be viewed as a parable of female resistance against the masculine use of technology as a form of dehumanization and domination.

2. Chances are that Guillermo Gómez-Peña would be sympathetic to this overtly revolutionary interpretation. Given his sensitivity to the issue of the culture of the Internet — and his self-identification as a cultural revolutionary — he'd undoubtedly appreciate the notion that Molly kills her adversary "with culture shock." From his perspective as a cultural outsider, he'd see Molly's ultra-amplified dance on the Killing Floor as an assault on the conservative values of the corporate world. In fact, he'd probably see Molly as a kind of performance "martial artist" who attacks the established order with the weaponry of tribal aesthetics.

3. Of course, the real question is, why should we care? What meaning can a story like this have beyond simple entertainment? Martha C. Nussbaum suggests that we read literature in order to appreciate the situations and empathize with the feelings of those who are culturally other. But students might justifiably wonder who — or *what* — we learn to empathize with by reading a story like "Johnny Mnemonic." One possibility is that science fiction stories like this prepare us to deal with social, political, and ethical dilemmas that we'll eventually face. Another possible explanation is that learning to appreciate cyborg values and the cyborg worldview is desperately important because we, in fact, already are cyborgs even if we tend not to recognize it. We are all netted together today by high and low technology; we all rely on literally hundreds of "prostheses" to enhance our natural biological attributes — everything from clothing and makeup to alphabets, books, automobiles, and super computers. In a real sense, we are all "very technical boys" like the namesake of Gibson's story, and we are all, more or less, trying to learn how to cope with the technologies that have been implanted in our heads. Reading Gibson, then, can be seen as an exercise in self-understanding, because it puts us into empathetic contact with the technological cyber-"other" who, whether we want to acknowledge it or not, lives today inside every one of us.

4. The next three questions offer suggestions for working cyberpunk-related films into your course. Longo's stylish if poorly received film, a 1995 adaptation of "Johnny Mnemonic," gives you the opportunity to contrast Gibson's original story with its mass-market retelling.

5. If time permits, you may want to screen a classic example of the film noir genre to assess its influence on cyberpunk writers such as Gibson. This activity offers you the chance to explore the source of the darkness that underlies cyberpunk's dystopic vision of the technological future. As suggested above, the lurking gloom of cyberpunk might be seen as expressing adolescent anxieties about impending adulthood, or they may echo fears about being part of a huge, impersonal, and vaguely threatening system.

6. You may also want to consider screening another exemplary cyberpunk film such as *Blade Runner, Videodrome,* or *ExistenZ,* in order to prepare students for a writing assignment on the genre. *Blade Runner,* for example, touches on several of the themes that dominate "Johnny Mnemonic." It has the same dark tone; its human hero is, like Johnny, part of a system that he himself can only vaguely understand; and its android characters are determined to resist their manipulative human masters. After a bit of focused discussion, students will be able to see other connections as well between these cyberpunk classics.

Essay Options

1. This option challenges students to write their own gendered interpretation of Gibson's story. Although this assignment makes reference to Springer as a source of inspiration and as a possible point of comparison, it calls for a rather straightforward interpretive essay. (For some possible approaches to the story, see ET #1–3 and FE #1 above.)

2. This assignment is more wide-ranging. It offers students the chance to survey cyber hero imagery in a number of different sci-fi genres. Students may want to use this as an opportunity to explore the differences between aggressive cyber types such as the Terminator and their more laid-back cyberpunk counterparts. Do they see "cool" cyberpunk figures such as Johnny Mnemonic as fundamentally different from the rampaging industrial-strength electronic figures of earlier decades? What do they make of the many female figures that have entered the world of cyber fiction? Certainly, films such as David Cronenberg's *ExistenZ* suggest that women have come into their own in the realm of science fiction. As students work on this paper, they should consider whether the female images that have come to populate cyber fictions reflect real-world changes in attitudes toward women and their relationship to the world of high technology — or whether "tough" cyber heroines simply reinforce traditional sex role stereotypes.

DOUGLAS R. HOFSTADTER, *The Turing Test: A Coffeehouse Conversation* (p. 719)

This selection can be worked into your syllabus in a number of ways. You can use it as a gateway reading to introduce the theme of artificial intelligence. Hofstadter covers most of the key AI concepts in this informal "conversation" — everything from the problem of defining intelligence to the issue of simulated as opposed to "real" thinking. By raising questions about the boundary between human and machine thinking, Hofstadter also looks forward to the next three selections, which focus on the personal, social, and ethical implications of android intelligence. Students will be able to draw on ideas they encounter here for paper assignments throughout the rest of the chapter. If you don't plan to cover Caudill, Moravec, and Wertheim, you still may want to consider including Hofstadter as a one-reading unit on AI. His treatment of the fundamental issues is self-contained enough to provide the basis for a solid research assignment exploring current developments in AI research (EO #2). Essay Option #1, involving a dry run of Allan Turing's famous test for artificial intelligence, invites students to participate directly in the AI debate by reflecting critically on fundamental intellectual issues like the nature of thinking and the relationship between thought, language, and behavior. To begin, have students work in groups to think about how they might create a test for human intelligence as suggested in the Before Reading activity. This will help them appreciate the economy of Turing's "discursive" approach, and it will open up some interesting questions about what we mean by intelligence in the first place.

Exploring the Text

1. The Turing test centers on a gender-based "imitation game," a version of a parlor game in which an interrogator puts written questions to a man and a woman in remote rooms in order to distinguish which is which. If the man fools the interrogator into believing he is a woman, then he wins the game. The key question is what this might prove. It clearly does not mean that the man is a woman; it only indicates that the man has insights into feminine behavior that allow him to simulate it through discourse. Of course, to suggest that a machine might have insight into what it means to think like a human represents a much greater leap. Presumably, any machine that could "pass" for a human in the Turing test — that is to say, any machine that could be mistaken for a human — would demonstrate the equivalent of human intelligence. To get past the cultural prejudices that draw a sharp boundary between people and machines, Turing side-

stepped the physical dimension of human presence. In his test, human intelligence doesn't depend on the ability to wear a suit or dance or throw a rock; it depends on the most disembodied things that humans produce: words. Of course, it might be argued that Turing is unnecessarily restrictive in his definition of intelligence. It's not particularly clear why dance or music, for example, conveys evidence of human intelligence any less effectively than speech. Indeed, genuine human intelligence might be defined as involving multiple, even simultaneous, forms of expression. Still, it might also be argued that it's much easier to build a player piano or a dancing robot than it is to construct a machine that carries on a convincing conversation. To the extent that the complexity of thought is best expressed through the medium of language, the ability to engage in discourse does remain a relatively valid way to measure intelligence.

2. We need a "probe" for thought because we don't have direct access to the inner workings of other minds. The minds of other people exist as abstractions for us — a theory of mind — that we build based on the evidence we gather through indirect experience. We tend to assume the existence in others of intentional states, desires, feelings, and so on based on the assumption that their internal mental machinery resembles ours. We also assume that others have minds like ours because we monitor their consciousness — the "organizational structure" of their minds — by probing their mental states. Most commonly, we do this by talking to them about their moods, feelings, needs, observations, and desires. The use of such linguistic probes allows us to assume "the intentional stance" in relation to other minds. Again, however, students might question the wholesale disposal of the body in this approach to reading other minds. The body, just as much as the word, can be seen as a probe for consciousness. People's expressions, gestures, and actions can tell us a great deal about their mental states; in fact, sometimes these physical signs can tell us even more than words.

3. Hofstadter's bias against things physical becomes clearer when we consider the case he makes for the similarity of human and machine thought. He argues that human thinking and identity emerge from the data we collect through the use of probes in much the same way that the picture of a hurricane emerges from the data fed into a computer simulation. For Sandy, human and machine thinking are absolutely parallel: the human mind is an abstraction that emerges from the physical brain as a pattern of activity that follows predictable physical laws. Sandy's argument is essentially Platonist: it asserts that there is no real difference between a physical hurricane, the hurricane simulation on a computer, and the idea of a hurricane that exists only in the mind. All three are simply instances of the pattern that underlies the concept of "hurricaneness." That's why a hurricane can exist in the mind or on a screen in simulated form as effectively as it does over the Gulf of Mexico. It's not the individual atoms that make the storm but the pattern that underlies them. Seen thus as a pattern or an abstract "code," the mind amounts to a kind of "software" program that "plays" on the hardware of the brain, and people, then, are really not terribly different from machines. This is the central assumption of AI: if human intelligence isn't directly connected to the atoms of the body and is, instead, encoded in the patterns of thought, then it should be possible to re-create this pattern as a program that runs on silicon chips. Whether or not students feel ready along with Sandy to acknowledge their own "machinehood" will depend at least in part on how carefully they've followed Sandy's arguments.

4. Students usually find Hofstadter's "conversational" approach a refreshing break from straightforward academic discourse. Hofstadter employs this dialogical strategy in order to lighten an otherwise weighty and abstract topic and to demonstrate the discursive principle that underlies the Turing test. Conveying Turing's view of human and machine minds through a three-way conversation gives Hofstadter the chance to model the skepticism of his audience within the essay itself. As Sandy responds to the objections raised by Pat and Chris from the perspective of the "hard sciences," presumably the reader is carried along by the case that he — or she — makes. It's also clear that Hofstadter is playing his own sort of Turing imitation game here. What better way than

a conversation to demonstrate that discourse is the essential principle in human thought?

Further Explorations

1. The kind of identity swapping that Turkle documents among MUDers offers an exact parallel to the Turing test. In fact, it's possible to view the entire Internet as one vast, ongoing Turing test in which people are able to assume identities and play various sorts of imitation games. When seen from this perspective, the Internet emerges as a place that undermines all the time-honored notions of character that underlie social relationships. In a sense, there really are no "individuals" online — only verbal simulations of individuals. If a man like Case can fool others into believing he's a woman, then perhaps he has shown that he does understand female consciousness at some deep level. Of course, this parallel also suggests one of the Turing test's weaknesses: the test itself is only as good as the thinking of its interrogator. Case may pass easily online for a woman not because he's terrifically empathetic but because the standards of his fellow Web-crawlers are so low. It's possible that for some Netizens even the shallowest attempts at imitating a few female stereotypes might be enough to confirm the gender of their otherwise anonymous correspondents. The same holds true for the Turing test. If a given interrogator's standards of discourse are particularly low, then it may not be difficult for a good laptop to pass as a person. In fact, every year for the past decade, businessman Hugh Loebner has offered a cash prize of $100,000 to any software engineer who can develop a program smart enough to actually fool a panel of judges in a Turing test staged at California State University at San Marcos. According to *Wired* magazine's Charles Platt ("What's It Mean to Be Human Anyway?" *Wired* Archive 3.04: April 1995), the year he participated as one of those interrogated, he received the "most fully human" award because his responses to judges' questions were the most ill-tempered and cranky. Does this suggest that human thinking is inherently combative, or does it simply suggest that Loebner's panel of judges was itself particularly feisty on the day of the test? Rather than offering an absolute measure of thought, then, the Turing test itself might easily be dismissed as involving only a few stereotypical assumptions about what it means to be human.

2. Springer would probably be very sensitive to the gendered imitation game on which Turing models his test. Computers involve what Springer sees as a distinctly "female" form of technology. In comparison with the "muscular," male technologies that dominated the industrial revolution, computers conceal their complexity: they contain labyrinths of networks that function not by breaking things into pieces the way that nineteenth-century machines did but by making connections between bits. Springer also sees computer technology as subverting or "dissolving" the well-defined ego boundaries she associates with male identity. Given this gendered view of computing, Springer would probably find it difficult to think about Turing's gender imitation game without being reminded of Turing's gender identity. Living in an era when gays were often forced to imitate the lifestyles of heterosexuals, Turing was undoubtedly sensitive to the power of simulation and the meaninglessness of overt physical appearances. The imitation game, from Turing's perspective, does more than simply undermine the prejudice that distinguishes man from machine; it also subverts the rigid, socially enforced gender categories that dominate Western culture. Springer would also note that Turing's invention — the programmable computer does, in fact, subvert the notion of fixed identity — an idea she sees as central to traditional sexist thought. As for the gender of Hofstadter's conversationalists, it's obvious that he deliberately chose names that were gender-neutral. He seems, thus, to support the idea that traditional binary notions of gender identity are relatively meaningless if the essence of what it means to be human can be conveyed solely in words.

3. Like the Turing test, the American Sign Language that Francine Patterson teaches Koko might also be seen as a "probe" for consciousness. Signing enriches the data we

have about the inner workings of Koko's mind. It gives us more clues to interpret and to use in taking "the intentional stance" in relation to her mental functions. Patterson and Gordon spend a great deal of time decoding and interpreting the intentions that lie behind Koko's signings. They use these abstract symbols as evidence for the claim that Koko deserves acknowledgment as an individual because of her complex consciousness. Of course, it would be interesting to see if Koko would win the title of "person" if she actually participated in a Turing test against a computer. Most probably, she wouldn't do well based only on verbal output. But chances are that students might still tend to see Koko as more "human" than any computer, based solely on what might be called their "bio-centrism."

4. De Waal would be sure to recognize nascent anthropomorphism in the way we commonly attribute intentions to our thinking machines. He would, however, probably view this trend as a case of naïve rather than mature anthropomorphism. Naïve anthropomorphism involves attributing human intentions to other creatures even if there is no real basis for such attribution. This is like the kind of superficially sympathetic thinking that children engage in with their stuffed animals. Mature anthropomorphism means seeing things from another creature's point of view and requires, according to de Waal, long association with other species. Is it possible to see things from a machine's point of view? Ellen Ullman might think so, at least for those who are "close to the machine" — those who spend their days thinking in machine code. And it might be argued that other types of people may also be able to empathize with the machines they use. Aren't mechanics famous for developing what's commonly known as a "feel" for the cars they repair?

5. This question can be used as a small group activity in class and as preparation for Essay Option #1. It gives students the chance to evaluate how hard it might actually be to pass the Turing test — and the chance to think about what passing such a test might prove. If you don't have easy access to computers in class, you can conduct your own "low-tech" Turing imitation game by using handwritten notes passed from room to room.

Essay Options

1. You'll want to give students plenty of opportunity to pre-write and plan their responses to this assignment. This paper challenges students to think critically about what's involved in the idea of "intelligence," and thus is both harder and more rewarding than it might look at first glance. Ask them to brainstorm and critique lists of possible Turing questions in groups. With a little luck, this will help them move beyond simple queries for exotic information. Ideally, they should hit on a wide range of questions that call for responses with strong affective or experiential foundations. They might, for example, ask their respondent to describe its favorite childhood memory and then to explain what it means. Or they might ask how it would feel if it were identified as a machine and why it would feel that way. The real challenge in this assignment lies in the follow-up analysis of the questions. You'll want to encourage students to probe what their questions suggest about the nature of human thinking.

2. This option can be used as the basis for either a traditional research assignment or a hypertext presentation. The topic of AI is a natural for Web research. Begin by checking sites associated with major institutions such as MIT and Cal Tech. And be sure to explore the "Cyc" (pronounced "Psych") site mentioned in the chapter introduction.

MAUREEN CAUDILL, *Redefining the Measure of Mankind*
(p. 736)

This selection introduces the notion of artificial intelligence not as a matter of fictional speculation but as an inevitable fact. We're used to thinking about robots and cyborgs in relation to works of pure imagination, and we're also used to thinking of high technology as something you use or play games with. Even the recent development of "cyberpets" hasn't challenged us to reconsider this basic orientation to high technology.

Caudill, however, wants us to acknowledge that technology will soon be more than a matter of convenience or a source of fun. Within a few generations, according to Caudill, computer technology will evolve into a radically "other" form of intelligence, a form of mind that we will have to learn how to live with and that will test our fundamental assumptions about what it means to be human — or even what it means to be alive. The best part of this essay is that Caudill never loses sight of our fallibility. Instead of launching into flights of fantasy about the future of machine minds, she stays focused on the key social and ethical issues that will emerge from the development of things that think. Begin by asking students to imagine how electronic technology will change the world over the next century, as suggested in the Before Reading activity. Since the hype associated with high technology is relentlessly upbeat, we often tend to assume that more machine intelligence will inevitably lead to more efficiency and more freedom. Getting such cultural prejudices out on the table will help prepare students for the disconcerting view of the technological future that Caudill offers here.

Exploring the Text

1. Like many AI advocates, Caudill makes predictions about the future that have already been shown to be unrealistically optimistic. In her view, we should see the first glimmers of machine intelligence — and perhaps of machine consciousness — just about any day now. But while her prediction of widespread robot use in the early years of the twenty-first century may seem pretty wide of the mark from our vantage point, most AI experts still agree that it's only a matter of a few decades before mechanical "others" make their presence felt in nearly every walk of life. Caudill bases her optimistic predictions on the breathtaking technological breakthroughs that have occurred in just the past ten years — things such as "heads-up" video displays in cars and advances in genetic engineering. Yet she acknowledges that unexpected obstacles may slow the pace of technological progress. Epidemics, political movements, and other purely social or political factors could conceivably retard the development of machine minds. Students may come up with their own list of obstacles, as well, including things such as war, economic downturns, or even legislation regulating or outlawing certain forms of research.

2. Students usually react strongly to the issue of the social impact of AI. Many students have already worked in the kinds of service-sector and low-skill jobs that robots are likely to fill sometime within the next generation. The question is whether they'll be glad or sad to see them go. According to Caudill, security guards, farm workers, bank tellers, cab drivers, nannies, house-cleaners, cooks, and even teachers may soon be replaced by smart machines. Caudill suggests that replacing large numbers of workers with androids will inevitably lead to widespread social unrest. But students might want to question this conclusion. Robots have already displaced workers in the auto and other manufacturing industries, and they have eliminated many traditional secretarial functions, yet there hasn't been a lot of organized protest from the affected groups. In fact, it could be argued, for example, that the automation of office procedures has actually benefited those who once filled purely secretarial positions.

3. Perhaps even more disturbing than the specter of social disruption due to the emergence of android intelligence is the possibility that "artificial" humans will be engineered by means of genetic manipulation. Caudill believes that it's only a matter of time before we build "biological androids" tailored to carry out specific workforce functions. Students might find that this alternative is even less palatable than the rise of intelligent machines. Certainly, it might seem more ethical to build a robot to serve as an android soldier than it would to grow or clone a biological android for the same purpose. Caudill's point is that our preference for using mechanical rather than "homegrown" androids is simply a matter of our prejudice for things that resemble us. We find the notion of replicating ourselves in metal more acceptable than doing so in the flesh because we're used to using metal for technological purposes, and we don't associate metallurgy with consciousness and emotional states.

4. And prejudice is clearly one of the issues that's troubling Caudill in this selection. Lurking behind every question is her concern about the ethical implications of AI. If machines do, in fact, become genuinely intelligent in the near future, as Caudill claims they must, how will we view them? Will they be seen simply as smart appliances, or will we be forced to acknowledge them as potential equals? Some of Caudill's questions concerning the ethics of AI may strike students as more than a bit bizarre. Maybe it's just too soon — or too ludicrous — to worry about whether you'd consider marrying a machine or having an android officiate at your wedding ceremony. But, then, it might help to remind students that one of the first human functions that software engineers have tried to duplicate is that of the teacher, through programmed instruction and distance learning. In fact, it's quite possible that some of your students may have learned how to type from "Mavis Beacon, Typing Teacher," a popular instructional application. What if Mavis could have held individual conferences with them, cracked jokes, and shared stories from her own prior teaching experiences with them as a form of encouragement? How much trouble would they have had accepting her as a "teacher"? Why would having a computer therapist, minister, or rabbi be any different?

5. Caudill is clearly troubled about what the quest for AI suggests about us humans. As she explores the ethics of AI in this selection, she challenges us to wonder about why we want to "own" and exploit others. Indeed, she seems to imply that AI returns us to the ethical universe of slavery. Isn't the motivation behind AI essentially the same as the motives that fueled the slave trade? We want to possess and control intelligent beings who will carry out our wills and do our work without complaint. Clearly, Caudill is more concerned about what the exploitation of sentient machines might do to upset humanity's moral compass than she is about the fate of future machine minds themselves.

6. Still, students may have trouble pinning down Caudill's tone toward her subject. She worries about the social and ethical implications of machine intelligence, yet she seems almost enthusiastic about the prospects for future AI research. The Woody Allen quotation can be read in at least two ways: either Caudill is mocking the apocalyptic tone of much popular AI criticism or she is signaling her own ironic ambivalence about her subject. Does she feel conflicted about what intelligent machines are doing and will yet do to human beings? Yes. Does she feel excited about the possibility of sharing the earth with creatures as brainy as we are — even if it leads to unforeseen and perhaps tragic consequences? Yes again. Overall, she seems confident about the ability of science to handle this issue but less sure about the ability of the average human to cope with the challenges and temptations of AI. Thus, she offers no solutions to the problems posed by AI research. We will inevitably use the technology we have the ability to create, and just as inevitably we will reap the problems that we sow. If there is a "solution," she seems to suggest that it lies in how we reassess the "measure of mankind" — how, in other words, we as a species understand our motives for creating other equally sentient minds and how we re-evaluate what it means to be human and act "humanely" in an era of machine intelligence.

Further Explorations

1. A computer that passes the Turing test might be viewed as being able to mimic certain aspects of human discourse on certain limited topics, but most of us would probably hesitate to recognize it as an "independent being." The difficulty here lies in what's meant by "independent." A computer program requires computer hardware to run and a programmer to create it. But then, human beings require even more support to become fully functional. It takes a couple of parents and the genetic information they provide, a nurturing environment for a couple of decades, and somewhere between six and sixteen years of education just to "build" a fully functioning modern human. Maybe the issue of independence, then, boils down to independent action. A computer might simulate anger, but it won't walk out from behind the curtain and punch you in the nose if you insult it. An android, however, just might, and that's exactly Caudill's

point. The ultimate test of AI might just be bad behavior. The day computers act up and threaten to treat us like "objects" might be the day we are forced to grant them their individuality.

2. Anxieties related to the idea that our own creation may rebel against us may also help account for the gothic darkness of much recent science fiction. The quest for AI taps into a number of psychologically charged issues — guilt over usurping the power of creation, suspicions about the fallibility of modern technology, the stigma of slavery, the terror of violating the categorical imperative separating man and machine, and so forth. Clearly, the neo-gothic gloom of stories such as Gibson's "Johnny Mnemonic" are related to the prospect of human domination run wild. Gibson's characters live under the constant threat of anonymous yet overwhelming state and corporate interests. Like Johnny with his transistorized brain, they recognize that they are themselves already components of a larger machine that conspires against their individual interests and rights.

3. For guidance on the issue of equal rights, students can turn to the debate in Chapter 5 between Peter Singer and Paul Shepard over animal equality. Although Singer might object to using the standard of intelligence as a means of assigning legal rights, he would probably agree that once machines become sentient and self aware — a distinct possibility, according to Caudill — they would merit the same "consideration of interests" as do humans and animals. We might clone a pig or build a computer brain, but once these creations begin to feel, they develop ethical claims against us.

4. Shepard, by contrast, would be likely to reject this argument by asserting that androids do not have equal rights but only the machine equivalent of a "natural history" — something like their industrial function. Outside of this function, they simply do not make sense. Thus, we might expect Shepard to oppose the idea that machines might ever really become the equals of their human "owners."

5. The conflict between function and freedom also connects AI with the debate about cloning. Kitcher and other proponents argue that cloning does not threaten the autonomy of the individual because individual development involves much more than simple genetic programming. Presumably, a machine that exhibits human-level intelligence would also undergo a process of individuation that would result in the creation of a unique and independent identity. Elshtain, by contrast, would probably see in AI just another technological means for creating whole teams of Michael Jordans. She would likely be repulsed by the idea of defining a sentient being in terms of a function — even if that function is to provide a mother with the child she desires to make her life complete. And like Caudill, Elshtain might also be concerned about what the desire to reproduce ourselves mechanically in a form we can control suggests about us as creatures. Are we so self-involved as a species that our dreams are limited to the reproduction of our own minds? Elshtain's critique of what she sees as the essentially selfish or egotistical motives behind cloning might apply as well to the desire to reproduce human intelligence in mechanical form.

6. For a well-deserved break from the moral implications of AI, you may want to spend a day screening the award-winning documentary film *Fast, Cheap, and Out of Control,* available at most arts-oriented video rental stores. Tracing the obsessions of four men — a lion tamer, a topiary gardener, a hobbyist specializing in the study of mole rats, and MIT robotics professor Rodney Brooks — this film explores the all-too-human quest for control over other creatures and, in the process, it says a good deal about the nature of human intelligence. The portrait of AI specialist Brooks is particularly interesting. Working in his MIT lab with a group of talented, mostly female graduate students, he comes across as a benevolent deity or at least as an oversolicitous parent. He's a "creator" who genuinely loves his creations and wants to grant them the freedom they need to develop to their fullest potential. The film's title was taken from a paper in which Brooks outlined his vision of what robots should be like in the future. In fact, one way to interpret the film is to see it as illustrating evolving attitudes toward human intelli-

gence, dominance, and other forms of life. The lion tamer featured in the movie uses his mind as a weapon to intimidate "wild" animals; the topiary gardener sculpts living creatures to fit his human conception of beauty; the mole rat enthusiast calls on intelligence and empathy to help him grasp what it's like to be a mole rat; the computer scientist uses his mind to envision minds that will someday transcend and perhaps even dominate those of their creators.

Essay Options

1. This assignment brings issues down to earth a bit by inviting students to consider some of the social, economic, and political implications of intelligent machines in the present. The issue of automation has slipped somewhat from public view over the past twenty years — ever since heavy industry began to replace blue-collar workers with robotic assembly lines. But, as Caudill indicates, automation is here to stay. Over the next few decades, many professional tasks, such as those of doctors, lawyers, and teachers, as well as most low-skilled jobs, may be performed by a workforce of increasingly intelligent gadgets. It might behoove students to spend some time exploring the outlook for automation and considering how the coming age of robots will shape their own futures.

2. This option invites students to compose a hypertext or mixed media project on the visually appealing theme of robot development. Students should have no difficulty finding good sources of images and text for this report, although they may have some trouble, given the pace of recent strides in research, making sure that their information is up to date.

3. This option provides a more focused, interpretive assignment if you haven't time for a full-blown research project. As a medium, the cinema has long been obsessed with the theme of artificial life, with new films on the subject coming out almost yearly. You can use a large number of movies as the basis for this analytic essay — anything, really, from *Frankenstein* to Spielberg's *A.I.: Artificial Intelligence*. As an alternative to this assignment, you might consider having your class write a paper on the theme of human intelligence and other minds in *Fast, Cheap, and Out of Control* (FE #6).

HANS MORAVEC, *Grandfather Clause* (p. 752)

This reading isn't meant to stand on its own. Use it with Caudill or Wertheim as part of a suite of selections on the future of artificial intelligence. Caudill offers a good overview of some of the social and ethical questions associated with AI research; Moravec offers a stunning illustration of the spirit of the quest. His vision of downloading human minds into shiny robot bodies will strike some students as madness and others as pure fantasy, but all indications are that he's absolutely serious. In fact, he's published yet another book recently in which he supports his earlier predictions. Then, too, Moravec is also an entertaining read. He doesn't stint on the drama as he invites us to have our heads hollowed out by robot surgeons and our bodies thrown on the junk heap of history. Covering Moravec is a must before Wertheim, who critiques what she calls the "crypto-religious" goals of the entire AI movement and singles out Moravec for his extremism. If you undertake the Before Reading activity, you may want to remind students about the number of body parts that actually are replaceable today. A 2001 *Time* article noted that it's now possible to replace bones, joints, hearts, lungs, kidneys, skin, endocrine glands, and parts of the eye and ear. With the development of stem cell research and genetic engineering, it will soon be possible to "grow" bio-cyber replacements for almost any body part. So where do we draw the line? When do you cease to be you and become something essentially artificial?

Exploring the Text

1. Moravec is a materialist, a mechanist, and a determinist, and, naturally enough, much of this comes across in his view of the future of AI. Given the current pace of tech-

nological development, he's convinced that only a few decades stand between us and the advent of intelligent machines. And although he acknowledges that robots might cause some trouble, he's equally convinced that we can't really do anything to stop technological "progress." The desire for political and economic domination drives the development of technology, in his view, and any nation that opts out of the technological future will simply fall prey to its more aggressive neighbors. In Moravec's rather Hobbesian view of things, we are thus already part of a monstrous worldwide machine that's pushing us forward toward the silicon future, whether we will it or not. This weird blend of what might be seen as technological optimism and political pessimism may strike some students as off-putting. But to keep them honest, those who reject Moravec's techno-determinist views should try to explain why they think it might in fact be possible to halt the inexorable march toward AI.

2. The advantages to "transmigration" for Moravec are many, but they boil down to the chance to live eternally in a shiny new robotic body. According to Moravec, we'll have to become cyborgs just to keep up with the robots next door. Downloading our minds into machines will make it possible for us to speed ourselves up so that we can think more thoughts in a shorter period of time. It will allow us to make multiple copies of ourselves for different environments. It will make it possible for you to "re-engineer" your own personality and to "learn" by simply merging other people's memories and experiences with your own. Ultimately, it will mean attaining the age-old dream of immortality, as you download yourself eon after eon into the latest cyborg physique. Would students consider doing it? A century ago, only a few would have felt comfortable having their image captured on film or flying nonstop from coast to coast. Does anyone really think they'd decline the offer if the technology were available to make transmigration a reality?

3. Transmigration would destroy all of our basic concepts of identity, memory, and communication. As Moravec notes, once the self is liberated from the body as a "program," there's not much reason to hold on to old-fashioned ideas such as personal identity. Once you were "cyborged," you'd be able to create multiple "yous" and dispatch them to different parts of the solar system and then remerge them at a future date. You'd be able to meld your mind with other minds — and even incorporate the memories and experiences of animals. You would, if you chose, be able to take animal form and to experience for yourself what it's like to live as another kind of creature. Even the idea of communicating with others could be replaced by the notion of a "negotiated merger" of minds. As Moravec eventually confesses, transmigration would render the concept of the self an antique curiosity — a throwback that would be discarded once you got over your "sentimental" attachment to the personal past. The central assumption behind Moravec's vision and his understanding of the mind is the central assumption behind most AI research: the mind is a pattern of information that is separable from the "mere jelly" of the material body. He offers the traditional AI argument in support of this assumption. Over the course of a lifetime, every atom that constitutes our physical selves is recycled. Every individual molecule is discarded and replaced. Thus, what makes us "us" isn't any particular amount of material stuff but the pattern of information that underlies the structure of our being. That's also why we maintain a consistent sense of self even as we develop from a mere ten-pound infant to a hundred-plus-pound adult. On the face of it, this is a fairly persuasive argument. It's hard to imagine that we'd cease to exist if we lost too many amino acids or too many body parts. It also taps into the Platonic idealism that underlies much Western religious thinking. When you stop to think of it, there isn't much difference between the ineluctable pattern that Moravec sees as the basis of individual identity and consciousness and the fundamentally religious concept of the immortal soul, or spirit.

Further Explorations

1. Given that they agree on the outline of what we can expect in the technological future, the contrast between Moravec and Caudill is striking and certainly worth explor-

ing. Caudill sees androids as a kind of pathetic subspecies, really as a new group of sentient second-class citizens available for human exploitation. The cyborgs in Moravec's vision of the future, by contrast, are supermen. They are literally transhuman, having rapidly outstripped even the comprehension of their creators. For Moravec, the future is inevitable because it's determined by competition with other cultures. For Caudill, the development of AI is more a matter of national pride and general technical curiosity. In Caudill's opinion, we will build robots to assure ourselves that we remain on the "cutting edge" of civilization and simply because we can.

2. Moravec's view of human selfhood in the age of intelligent machines merely extends Turkle's observations on the impact of the Internet on human identity. According to Turkle, identity online loses touch with the stabilizing influence of the body and thus becomes multiple and variable. And roughly the same thing happens to individual identity in Moravec's cyborg utopia. Once the pattern of consciousness is liberated from the body, it is free to multiply and divide at will. In the context of electronic information technology, the idea of the self seems to be little more than a quaint vestige of the world of "presence."

3. Moravec's surgical transmigration scenario and Turing's imitation test both hinge on the concept of simulation. In a Turing test, the computer "tries" its best to simulate the responses of an actual human being. In Moravec's surgical fantasy, a computer simulates the ever-eroding brain function of his transmigrant. The disturbing implication in this comparison is that simulating consciousness is not necessarily the same thing as experiencing it. As layer after layer of the transmigrant's brain is vaporized by Moravec's robotic surgeon, what happens if the internal experience of consciousness evaporates with it while the external simulation of intelligence appears to be uninterrupted? This counterscenario, first proposed by the philosopher John Searle, builds on the idea that the felt experience of consciousness isn't necessarily the same as its outward manifestation. Thus, while Moravec's surgical scenario might appear to reproduce the mind of the transmigrant, it may in fact only reproduce the outward simulation of this mind, much in the same way that a recording reproduces a simulation of a voice but is not the actual voice itself.

4. Perhaps a more down-to-earth critique of Moravec's transmigration fantasy could be forwarded by John "Fire" Lame Deer. Lame Deer claims that white civilization is founded on a fear of death. This, in his view, is what makes the white world so obsessed with controlling nature, the self, and other human beings. By contrast, death is perceived as a natural state in Native American culture. In fact, Lame Deer brags that almost any day is a good day to die for a true Indian. Moravec clearly would not understand Lame Deer's stoicism in relation to death. To Moravec, death is simply another physical limitation that science will grapple with and eventually overcome. Still, it might also be possible to see the idea of the animal totem as roughly parallel to Moravec's notion of the transmigrant body. According to traditional Native American beliefs, individuals live through their totem animal and share in its knowledge and experiences, both in the past and in the present. Moravec's desire to live on in multiple human and animal forms might thus be seen as a weird echo of this same idea.

5. De Waal, however, would probably not have much patience with Moravec's dream of merging animal and human minds through transmigration. De Waal's concept of mature anthropomorphism is founded on the recognition of the differences between species. A person who exploits mature anthropomorphism tries, through years of experience and close association, to see things from an animal's point of view; he tries to imagine how a particular animal might view the world given his intimate knowledge of the behavior of that species. Moravec, by contrast, seems to suggest that we might someday simply be able to "download" animal experiences and memories into our transmigrant minds wholesale. This would ignore the real differences between animal and human experiences. In other words, this kind of cross-species mind meld would be about as successful as running a Macintosh application on a Windows platform.

6. Eviatar Zerubavel and bell hooks might also point out that, despite Moravec's claims about merging our minds with the memories of others, memories themselves are not decontextualized mental phenomena that exist independent of a specific personal, cultural, and historical context. Every memory exists within a matrix of cultural and personal recollections that gives it value and meaning. What good is a memory of the Holocaust if you don't comprehend the history of World War II and the conflicting cultures of Nazism and Judaism at that precise historical moment? And given the impact of historical memories on the individual, what might happen if you were to download memories from an antagonistic culture into your own mind? The fantasy of mind melding is attractive as long as you forget about the cultural, political, and psychological realities that have kept minds apart since the dawn of human history.

Essay Options

1. This option offers students the chance to synthesize information from Moravec, Ullman, Turkle, and Hofstadter on the topic of information technology and human identity. This can be approached as a major assignment in its own right or as a prelude to a paper based on the ethics of electronic culture (see Wertheim, EO # 3). Electronic technology appears to be subverting traditional concepts of selfhood and identity. Freed from the body online or in the form of a downloaded program, the mind becomes plural and pliant; it plays with multiple selves and wears multiple masks. The value of "free play" cuts across the culture of electronic technology, from the adolescent games of Ullman's "boy engineers," to the identity games of Turkle's MUDers, to the parlor games of Turing's test and the brain-swapping fantasies of Moravec's cyber transmigrants. Students should be able to do a lot with what's here — and you should encourage them to look for examples of this kind of "free play" in relation to identity in contemporary popular culture as well.

2. This assignment is more ambitious. The idea of simulation is central to the entire idea of computing. It underlies Turing's initial theory of the "universal Turing machine" — a simple gadget that could hypothetically simulate any process by following binary instructions printed on a tape. It also underlies every computer program that has been written since. You'll want to advise students to do more reading about Turing and his basic theory of computing before tackling this assignment, if possible, and you'll also want to have them explore all the ways that simulations are currently used in computing. The obvious areas include weather and economic forecasting, the testing of buildings and vehicles, the modeling of dangerous situations such as nuclear explosions, the training of doctors, athletes, police, even the purchasing of automobiles and the planning of vacations. Today, the notion of simulation has penetrated just about every aspect of popular culture. It's there in video games, in rock music extravaganzas, in Las Vegas resorts, in the movies — even in the so-called reality shows that offer us simulations of real-life experiences like being stranded on a desert island or having to share the same dorm room with strangers for months at a time.

MARGARET WERTHEIM, *Cyber Soul-Space* (p. 764)

This selection completes the chapter's final set of readings on artificial intelligence. In it, Wertheim offers an ideological and ethical critique of what she sees as the essentially "religious" assumptions underlying many of the goals and visions of AI as a scientific enterprise. It's a challenging reading for most students. Wertheim's analysis of AI draws on philosophical concepts and ways of thinking that may be new territory for many. It's also studded with historical terms and references that will fall beyond the ken of most — things like "Pythagorian Gnosticism" and "Christian dualism." Yet students often appreciate the insights that Wertheim offers. By the time they have worked their way through Caudill and Moravec, some students are bound to feel uneasy about the tone and direction of the AI enterprise. Wertheim helps them articulate their misgivings by providing an intellectual and ethical context for their own critical intuitions. The trick here is to help students separate Wertheim's argument from the heavy-duty terminology and historical references she uses to explain it. This may seem like a lot to ask of first-year students, but in fact Wertheim is fairly representative of the kind of historically based conceptual discourse that students are likely to encounter in a number of disciplines — even during their first term of college-level work. This selection also links to three important writing assignments, including a major academic essay on the ethics of cyberspace and a more creative mixed media project on the notion of cyberspace itself. Both offer students the chance to reflect on readings they've done throughout the chapter and to reach their own conclusions about the promise of machine minds. The Before Reading activity may seem a bit odd at first. The idea of religious "dualism" is central to Wertheim's critique of AI, and students will need to understand it before they can appreciate her argument. This activity is meant to open up a discussion of how dualistic thinking creates oppositions or dichotomies between things like soul and body, heaven and earth, spirit and substance, mind and matter. Wertheim offers her own thumbnail definitions in the text, and the headnote to the selection should also help clarify the issue, but a little in-class discussion can't hurt before students begin reading on their own.

Exploring the Text

1. Wertheim sees a number of similarities between Christian philosophy and the ideology of cyberspace. First, there's the apocalyptic tone that runs throughout AI. The overheated predictions of AI enthusiasts about how intelligent machines will transform the earth do at times sound more like the millennial predictions of religious visionaries than the measured pronouncements of objective scientists. Among its most radical supporters — including Mark Pesce, Jaron Lanier, and Nicole Stenger — AI is commonly linked with traditional Christian ideas of "worship" and "transcendence." The matrix — another term for cyberspace — is often associated with heaven or even with God. In Wertheim's view, cyberspace itself is the major connection between AI and Christian thinking, because this concrete metaphor for the abstract phenomenon of electronic communication offers the promise of "a new immaterial space," a transphysical domain or "New Jerusalem" where the mind can be liberated from the constraints of bodily existence. Underlying the aspirations of Christians and AI enthusiasts, according to Wertheim, is the dream of immortality: download yourself like a William Gibson hero into "digital eternity," and you've solved the problem of the ages.

2. The paradox in the connection between Christianity and AI, according to Wertheim, is that the "cybernauts," as she calls them, want to have their cake and eat it, too. In traditional Christianity, the spirit jettisons the body at the moment of death; transcendence to a higher plane of existence brings with it a purgation and purification of the flesh. The "cybernautic body," by contrast, offers immortality without the loss of sensual pleasure. In fact, in many AI scenarios, downloading consciousness leads to an increase in sensual gratification as well as the promise of immortality and omniscience. All this is made possible within the framework of AI theory because of one fundamental assumption — the belief that the mind exists as a pattern of information and not as a fixed structure built from material components. We are "data," not the individual atoms that give us our physical form.

3. Thus, as Wertheim notes, AI returns us to what she calls the world of Christian dualism by holding out the promise of "technologically feasible" transcendence. Once we believe that a computer can contain a mind of its own as a complex pattern of information, it requires only a short logical leap to believe that a human mind can exist in a machine. And once that's accepted and the mind is liberated from the flesh, we're back in the realm of medieval Christian theology. In Wertheim's view, AI turns the fundamental assumptions of Western science inside out. By transforming the essence of being human into information, it abandons the materialist basis of modern science and embraces in its stead the possibility of an immortal "cyber-soul." But Wertheim doesn't

necessarily see this as a betrayal of science's intellectual roots. She claims that science has entertained this yearning for transcendence all along — at least since the time of the Pythagorians, who were, in her view, the founders of the modern Western scientific enterprise. For Pythagoras, the soul was a mathematical concept, the result of a system of "ratios" that could be expressed "rationally" by the mind. After death, the immortal spark of the soul would be freed from the body to return to the realm of pure numbers. The idea that we can capture the essence of the mind in the ones and zeros of digital code is, for Wertheim, the ideological link between AI and Pythagorian theology.

4. Other than the fact that this "crypto-religiosity" seems to have been slipped in through the back door of modern science, what really bothers Wertheim is that AI enthusiasts want the perks of immortality and omniscience without paying the price. Most dualist philosophies believe that in order to transcend the body you have to purify the soul through ethical conduct and good works in the material world. Whether it's Hinduism or Pythagorianism, the soul is a "quintessentially moral entity" and one that is bound by the body to communities defined by mutual obligations and responsibilities. The new cyber-dualism, by contrast, seems to promote "cyber-selfishness" because it turns away from real-world communities and seeks immediate gratification for the individual. Whether students will agree with Wertheim's critique is another matter. Several of the earlier selections in this chapter suggest that electronic culture does promote a kind of "selfishness" among its users — selfishness not in terms of greediness or possessiveness, but in terms of ego-centrism and alienation from the broader concerns of society at large. Certainly, Stoll's critique of the Internet suggests that life online makes us more solitary and less open to the kind of face-to-face contact and "deep" relationships that provide the basis for real community. Does computing make people turn inward? Does it reduce or augment our sense of mutual connection and commitment? Most students have already put in enough time online to offer at least a tentative answer to these questions.

Further Explorations

1. Wertheim's critique of AI is clearly aimed at Moravec and other cyber-visionaries like him. From her perspective, Moravec's "transmigration" fantasy is full of holes. What would you do for all eternity even if you could ensconce yourself in robo-flesh? How could you create real memories when many of our recollections are false or only imperfectly recalled to begin with? How would you re-create the unconscious? How could you have access to all knowledge the way a computer does and still retain the quality of human consciousness, since our natural minds are limited to a finite range of thoughts and memories at any one time? Moravec's dream of expanding consciousness beyond mortal limits ignores the fact that the mind is a fundamentally "dynamic phenomenon," in Wertheim's view. The human mind has been sculpted by time; it is, thus, in the nature of consciousness to be fragmented, changing, and incomplete. To transcend time and the body would be to cease to be human in any meaningful way. Of course, Moravec might attempt to rebut any and all of these points. Since false memories and the unconscious are also mapped in the synapses of the brain, they, too, can be scanned and their "code" copied and reproduced, and so forth. But Wertheim's point about the dynamic nature of the mind might be more difficult for Moravec to dispose of. Does he want to liberate humanity from the weaknesses of the flesh, or does he really just want to turn us all into abstract computer programs? Certainly, there's much in Moravec that echoes the "crypto-religiosity" that Wertheim sees at the heart of the AI enterprise: his obsession with omniscience and immortality, his distain for the imperfections of the body, his absolute faith in the future and the promise of human transformation. Yet his tone isn't quite as "feverish" as you might expect from reading Wertheim. Indeed, Moravec seems less like a religious mystic as he presents his modest proposal for the future of humanity than he does like a rather cheerfully upbeat television pitchman. So it might be argued that while his thinking about body and soul is, in fact, eerily reminiscent of Christian dualism, it does not actually represent science's return to the spir-

it of medieval theology. Moravec might argue that his is the least "selfish" possible vision of the future, for what he's proposing is a kind of collective consciousness — a matrix of many minds that takes the idea of community far beyond the boundaries imposed by individual physical existence.

2. Students should also be able to see some connections between the "crypto-religiosity" of cyberspace and the ethic of the boy engineer as described by Ullman. Two of the most enduring values for Ullman's male programmers are asynchronicity and reclusiveness. These are guys who work hard at staying out of contact with others and who clearly enjoy feeling superior. All of these negative characteristics resonate with the "cyber-selfishness" that Wertheim sees at the heart of AI's pseudoreligious culture. Indeed, the story that Ullman tells about a group of programmers at lunch hitting on the idea of genocide as a "solution" for communicable diseases illustrates how divorced these men are from any ethical relation to society. And, naturally, given their obvious contempt for their own bodies, Ullman would have little trouble understanding cyberculture's dismissive attitude toward bodies made of "meat."

3. The ethical issues that Turkle touches on in her exploration of identity-swapping online can also be seen as illustrating the idea of "cyber-selfishness." MUDders have, in a sense, already "transcended" the bounds of the body. Decked out online as women, men, or furry critters, they have been liberated from the constraints of the flesh. They can, when necessary, even "reboot" themselves and claim a kind of eternal existence. And, as Turkle suggests, being freed from the body also loosens the ethical ties that bind them in real social relationships. Thus, married men can have "Tiny sex" with strange women they pick up in cyber bars while their "real" wives cook dinner for them in the kitchen. But MUDders represent only a fraction of the social world online. What about the millions who use the Net to build real electronic communities around important personal and social issues every day? To what extent do these "cyber citizens" challenge Wertheim's interpretation of the essential selfishness of electronic culture?

4. Another apparent contradiction in the ethic of cyberspace seems to crop up when you compare Wertheim with Springer. Springer argues that the cybernautic body in pop culture is often represented as superphysical and that the body looms even larger in cyberfiction than it does in reality. It might be argued that the pop cultural cyber icons that Springer discusses are actually throwbacks to comic book superheroes who originally were meant to embody the bulk and power of industrial machinery. But it might also be claimed that characters like the Terminator actually embody the paradoxical "ambivalence" toward things physical that Wertheim associates with cyber religiosity. Just as AI enthusiasts seem to want to leave the body behind and still savor the sweetness of carnal pleasures, so too do Springer's cyber heroes both transcend and epitomize corporeal existence.

5. This question offers you the chance to challenge the dualistic thinking that seems to underpin most AI fantasies. If the self is just a pattern of information in the brain, then minds might be simulated in machines or downloaded into robot bodies. But if minds, thoughts, and memories are inextricably bound up with the body, then many of the claims for AI may prove to be little more than wishful thinking. Certainly, the personal essays by Lopez, Sanders, and McKibben suggest that the body plays a central role in defining a self and creating a mind. Lopez quite literally reads his identity in the scars on his hands: each physical feature awakens a memory that contributes to his understanding of who he is. The same can be said for Sanders, who is physically linked through a hammer to widening circles of community bound by ethical principles and a strong sense of mutual responsibility. To get back to the real world, and to himself, McKibben clicks off the TV — and, we assume, the computer — and drenches himself in direct sensory experience. He relies on his body and not on an antenna to put him into a relationship and not simply "in touch" with the world he lives in. Kleege feels pretty much the same, even with her defective vision. At the end of her essay, she says she would refuse corrective treatment for her eyes if it were available, because seeing the

world as she does has become part of who she is. This might seem like bizarre obstinacy on her part, or it can be seen as verifying the fact that the mind, body, and self are all inextricably connected. She clearly feels that the quality of her relationship to the world around her — and her commitment to it — result from the special attributes of the eyes she was born with.

Essay Options

1. I'd recommend this option if your students have a particularly strong personal interest in artificial intelligence theory. Otherwise, it's doubtful whether they will be committed enough to explore this topic in the kind of depth that the assignment requires. Books on AI can be tough going, as reading Wertheim herself suggests, so you may want to reserve this paper for students who are particularly interested in the technical aspects of AI research. The names listed represent some of the leaders in the field as of 2002, although relatively accessible books on the subject appear almost monthly.

2. This assignment is far more appealing to most students. This hypertext/mixed media presentation on cyberspace gives your class the chance to blend research with imagery from books, films, and the Internet. As Wertheim notes, cyberspace has captured the modern imagination in much the same way that heaven and hell once did in earlier eras. This assignment asks students to locate and analyze visual and verbal representations of this new transphysical "place" and to speculate about what it all might mean. For an even more challenging assignment, you might consider having students compare depictions of Christian and cyber otherworlds.

3. Essay Option #3 presents a traditional academic essay on the issue of the ethics of cyberspace. This topic connects readings throughout the chapter and so can be viewed as the occasion for a final paper on the issue of machine minds. Use Further Explorations #2 and 3 as pre-writing exercises for this one. They'll help students begin to appreciate some of the ethical issues associated with computers, the Internet, AI, and cyberspace. As students begin to work on this paper, they should address such topics as the way that electronic technology supposedly undermines community and human relationships, the way it dehumanizes us, and the impact of the cult of the boy engineer. They may also want to discuss questions that the quest for artificial intelligence raises about human values, the specter of slavery, and the idea of "cyber selfishness."

Research and Writing Online

Whether you want to investigate ideas behind a thought-provoking essay or conduct in-depth research for a paper, the Web resources for *Mind Readings* can help you find what you need on the Web — and then use it once you find it.

The English Research Room for Navigating the Web

www.bedfordstmartins.com/english_research

The Web brings a flood of information to your screen, but it still takes skill to track down the best sources. Not only does *The English Research Room* point you to some reliable starting places for Web investigations, it also lets you tune up your skills with interactive tutorials.

- Want to improve your skill at searching electronic databases, online catalogs, and the Web? Try the *Interactive Tutorials* for some hands-on practice.

- Need quick access to online search engines, reference sources, and research sites? Explore *Research Links* for some good starting places.

- Have questions on evaluating the sources you find, navigating the Web, or conducting research in general? Consult one of our *Reference Units* for authoritative advice.

Research and Documentation Online for Including Sources in Your Writing

www.bedfordstmartins.com/resdoc

Including sources correctly in a paper is often a challenge, and the Web has made it even more complex. This online version of the popular booklet *Research and Documentation in the Electronic Age,* by Diana Hacker, provides clear advice for the humanities, social sciences, history, and the sciences on —

- Which Web and library sources are relevant to your topic (with links to Web sources)

- How to integrate outside material into your paper

- How to cite sources correctly, using the appropriate documentation style

- What the format for the final paper should be